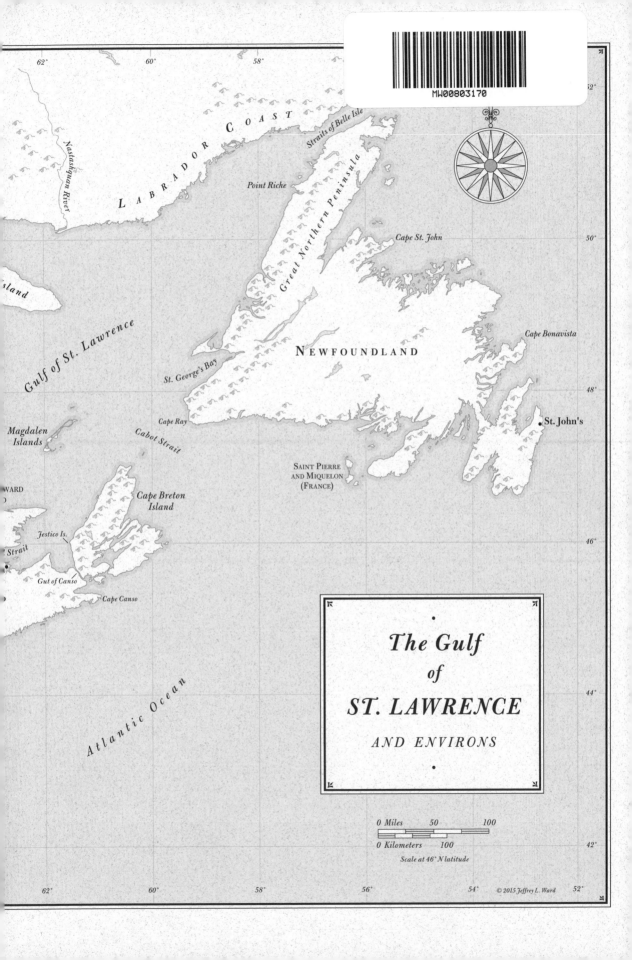

62° 60° 58° 52°

L A B R A D O R   C O A S T

Nastashquan River

Straits of Belle Isle

Point Riche

Great Northern Peninsula

Cape St. John   50°

Gulf of St. Lawrence

NEWFOUNDLAND

Cape Bonavista

St. George's Bay   48°

Magdalen Islands

Cape Ray

Cabot Strait

St. John's

SAINT PIERRE
AND MIQUELON
(FRANCE)

WARD

Jestico Is.

Cape Breton
Island

46°

Strait

Gut of Canso

Cape Canso

Atlantic Ocean

The Gulf
of
ST. LAWRENCE
AND ENVIRONS

44°

0 Miles   50   100

0 Kilometers   100

Scale at 46° N latitude

42°

62°   60°   58°   56°   54°   52°

© 2015 Jeffrey L. Ward

Audubon

Audubon

America's Greatest Naturalist and
His Voyage of Discovery to Labrador

PETER B. LOGAN

ASHBRYN PRESS *San Francisco, 2016*

Publisher's Cataloging-in-Publication Data

Names: Logan, Peter Burton, author.

Title: Audubon : America's greatest naturalist and his voyage
of discovery to Labrador / Peter B. Logan.

Description: Includes index and bibliographical references. |
San Francisco [California] : Ashbryn Press, 2016.

Identifiers: ISBN 978-0-9972282-1-2 | LCCN 2016933302.

Subjects: LCSH Audubon, John James, 1785–1851. | Ornithologists—United States—
Biography. | Naturalists—United States—Biography. | Audubon, John James, 1785–1851—
Travel—North America. | BISAC BIOGRAPHY & AUTOBIOGRAPHY / Historical |
BIOGRAPHY & AUTOBIOGRAPHY / Environmentalists & Naturalists.

Classification: LCC QL31.A9 L64 2016 | DDC 598/.092—dc23

First Edition

10   9   8   7   6   5   4   3   2   1

The paper in this book meets the guidelines for permanence and durability of the Committee on
Production Guidelines for Book Longevity of the Council on Library Resources.

Printed in the United States of America.

For

Christopher, Andrew, Caroline, and Pierce,

who have brought me joy beyond measure.

And for Deborah, my lodestar.

CONTENTS

APPENDIX

MAPS

Preface

Since his death in 1851, John James Audubon has proved a popular subject to art historians and biographers alike. The magnificent prints made from his drawings of North American birds, compiled in four oversized volumes as *The Birds of America*, have become part of our cultural landscape and serve as an enduring milestone of ornithological illustration. But Audubon's personal story, although less familiar, is even more enthralling. He arrived in America from France in 1803 at the age of eighteen, fleeing conscription in Napoleon's army. With little formal art training but bursting with talent, he spent the next three and a half decades capturing images of the avian splendor of his adopted country at the dawn of ornithology, when Ivory-billed Woodpeckers still hammered on dead snags in Southern swamps and flocks of Passenger Pigeons darkened the skies of eastern North America by the billions. And, with his pen, he recorded in shimmering prose his detailed observations of the natural world. His indefatigable will, coupled with the love of an extraordinary woman, enabled him to overcome personal hardships, business failure, rejection, and lengthy absences from his family on the way to becoming the most celebrated American naturalist of all time.

It is small wonder that scores of authors have sought to bring this icon and his art to life. Over the past two decades, we have seen a veritable explosion in Audubon-related works. In 1999, The Library of America issued an extensive anthology of his writings edited by noted Audubon scholar Christoph Irmscher. The next year saw the publication of *John James Audubon in the West: The Last Expedition*, the story behind Audubon's second great work, *The Viviparous Quadrupeds of North America*, with chapters by Ron Tyler, Robert McCracken Peck, and others. Two separate books about the prints of *The Birds of America* were published by Audubon scholars Susanne Low and Bill Steiner in 2002 and 2003, respectively. Also in 2003, John Chalmers, M.D., a retired orthopedic surgeon from Edinburgh, opened a window on Audubon's important time in Scotland in his wonderful monograph *Audubon in Edinburgh*. The following year, Pulitzer Prize–winning author Richard Rhodes published a significant new biography and, in 2006, came out with *The Audubon Reader*, a selection of the naturalist's writings intended to complement The Library of America collection. A pair of other well-received biographies appeared in 2004 from writers on both sides of the Atlantic, William Souder and Duff Hart-Davis, who chronicled Audubon's life and the making of his magnum opus. Souder's work was a finalist for the 2005 Pulitzer Prize in biography. In 2006, *The Double Elephant Folio* by the late Waldemar Fries, often referred to as "the bible of Audubon scholars" and long out of print, was reissued in a second, revised edition by Susanne Low. Two years later, Harvard University Press published a superb volume of Audubon's early drawings, which are housed at the Houghton Library, with commentary by Richard Rhodes and others. More recently, in 2011, a scholarly new transcription of Audubon's most important extant journal from 1826 appeared. This was followed in 2012 by Roberta Olson's *Audubon's Aviary*, a sumptuous coffee table book intended to accompany a three-part, multiyear exhibition of virtually all of Audubon's original drawings in the collection of the New-York Historical Society. In 2013, Joel Oppenheimer, an Audubon print dealer in Chicago, published a beautiful facsimile of the Bien chromolithograph edition of *The Birds of America*. In the same year, the respected English natural-history writer Christine E. Jackson gave us *John James LaForest Audubon: An English Perspective*. Clearly, Audubon makes good copy.

With this amount of attention, it would be easy to believe that there is very little that hasn't already been said. The obvious question is, why yet another book about Audubon, especially one revolving around his journey to a remote part of Canada in the summer of 1833?

The reasons are many, but the simple answer is that Audubon's Labrador expedition occurred during a critical juncture in his life which, up until now, has escaped a comprehensive examination by any of his previous biographers. Most of the conventional biographies provide overviews of the trip but lack the space to provide an in-depth look, although those by Richard Rhodes (Alfred A. Knopf, 2004), Shirley Streshinsky (Villard Books, 1993), Alexander Adams (G. P. Putnam's Sons, 1966), and Francis Hobart Herrick (Appleton-Century, 1938) are worth noting.

Two books ostensibly focus on the expedition but provide limited contributions to Audubon scholarship. *In Audubon's Labrador* (Houghton Mifflin, 1918), by Charles W. Townsend, M.D., includes an opening chapter summarizing the details of the voyage. However, it is principally devoted to recounting the author's four trips to the Labrador coast during the early years of the 20th century as he retraced Audubon's journey. Katherine Govier's *Creation* (The Overlook Press, 2002) is a biographical novel about Audubon and the expedition which is grounded loosely in the historical record but uses the novelist's craft to tell an engaging story. It does not pretend to be an erudite work.[1]

The lack of a definitive account of the Labrador expedition is particularly surprising given the crucial role it played in shaping the remainder of Audubon's life. It was not just another of his excursions into the wilds in search of new species to paint, as many of his biographers believe. In truth, it was a voyage of personal discovery that helped get Audubon back on his feet, both physically and emotionally, after he suffered a frightening neurological attack — what he termed a "spasmodic affection" — in mid-March 1833. He badly needed that push.

By early June, as he and his party prepared to sail north from Eastport, Maine, he was not even halfway toward his goal of publishing the four hundred life-sized prints he had promised his subscribers. There were still countless species missing from his portfolio despite a near lifetime of drawing birds. To maintain his publication schedule, he could not afford to miss the coming season, especially now that he was looking to fill his third volume with images of waterbirds, many of which were said to breed in Labrador.

However, at the rate the prints were being issued in London, it would take another decade before the project would be completed. Audubon was growing old fast, the price of his grueling lifestyle, and he was beginning to doubt that he would live long enough to see the culmination of his life's effort. The awareness he gained during the expedition, of his increasing physical limitations as well as his own mortality, was vitally important in spurring him on to the finish line. The expedition, in a very real sense, was a pivotal moment in Audubon's life, one that altered his priorities and ultimately led to his successful completion of *The Birds of America*.

At the same time, the voyage helped open his eyes to the impact of man's heedless exploitation of the natural world. Audubon sailed to the Labrador coast as one who had long believed that nature's bounty on the American continent was virtually inexhaustible, although he had recently begun to voice concerns about the destruction of its old-growth forests.[2] After seeing the methods used by commercial "eggers" to harvest vast numbers of eggs from northern seabird colonies, he returned as a thoughtful, nascent conservationist. Just as importantly, he was well aware that he was documenting North America's birdlife at a time when great changes driven by civilization were sweeping over the continent. He doubted that the natural world he knew would still be around in a hundred years, and he surely recognized that his publication would serve as a record for future generations.

Further, this period in Audubon's life is unusually well documented from multiple perspectives, which allow us to examine his daily activities and bring us closer to knowing Audubon the man — the colorful and complicated one his friends knew — as opposed to the looming historical figure. There are few other time frames for which we can do this, and none while he was in the middle of his colossal work. However, as will be seen, this book goes beyond the three months Audubon was pursuing birds along the shores of Labrador. For necessary context, which is essential to anyone wishing to understand the importance of the voyage, it places the expedition within the framework of his entire life and, in so doing, seeks to draw a multidimensional image of this fascinating man. This has also afforded me an opportunity to correct the many misstatements and factual errors that have appeared in other recent works. For those who are already familiar with Audubon's story, some of these corrections will come as a surprise.

Finally, serendipity sometimes plays a role in the topic a writer selects. That was certainly true in this case. In December 2006, I had an opportunity to examine two scrapbooks of newspaper clippings and miscellaneous documents about Audubon that had been collected over the years by his spinster granddaughter Maria Rebecca Audubon.[3] Maria apparently kept several such scrapbooks during her life. When she died, she bequeathed one of them to Chicago businessman Ruthven Deane—a founder of the Nuttall Ornithological Club, a fellow of the American Ornithologists' Union, and an Audubon scholar—who had been instrumental in persuading her to publish three of the naturalist's surviving journals along with his brief autobiography under the title *Audubon and His Journals* (Charles Scribner's Sons, 1897).[4] The Deane scrapbook was donated to the Missouri Historical Society (now the Missouri History Museum) in 1960 by his son H. Towner Deane. The route taken by the scrapbooks I examined is less clear. They surfaced at a New England auction in 1998 and are now housed in a private collection.

Among the articles I found was one from a September 1896 issue of *The San Francisco Call*, which provided the reminiscences of the Labrador expedition of Joseph A. Coolidge, at that point a San Francisco octogenarian and one of two surviving members of Audubon's party.[5] It appears that, with the exception of Ruthven Deane, who corresponded with Coolidge prior to the latter's death and whose own Maria scrapbook contained a copy of the *Call* article, Audubon scholars generally have been unaware of or not interested in Coolidge's account of the voyage.[6] As far as I have been able to determine, the article has never been referenced in any Audubon biography, bibliography, or other related work since its appearance in the *Call* over a century ago.[7]

Coolidge's connection to San Francisco, near my home in Northern California, sent me on a genealogical search that ended a few weeks later in a small, tired cemetery in the East Bay community of Livermore, where Coolidge and his wife, Clara, are buried. Along the way, I was drawn to this man, whose fleeting connection to Audubon had, for me, given him new life. As a tribute to him, I felt that his vivid recollections of the voyage should be shared. But the lack of an authoritative history of the expedition persuaded me that something more substantial was needed.

In pulling the threads of this story together, I have relied upon a variety of sources. The backbone of any examination of this period in Audubon's life is, by necessity, his Labrador journal, which was one of those published by Maria in *Audubon and His Journals*. However, Audubon scholars have known for decades that Maria rewrote, condensed, and frequently bowdlerized the texts of these journals, expunging or altering any passage that she thought would tarnish his legacy or simply made her feel uncomfortable.[8] This became clear when a portion of what Maria called the European journal, covering his trip to England and Scotland in 1826 and his search for an engraver, was microfilmed and later transcribed and published in 1967 by Audubon scholar Alice Ford.[9] Fragments of his journal from 1843 during his journey up the Missouri River are also extant.[10] One need only compare these to Maria's heavily edited and rewritten accounts for the same periods to see how strongly her Victorian sensibilities and desire to enhance her grandfather's name affected her editorial pen. While she generally stayed true to the basic facts, much that was lively and fresh about Audubon's writing, including his sometimes bawdy sense of humor and roving eye, was expurgated.

In view of the repressed cultural attitudes that prevailed at the time, it is perhaps not surprising that there were aspects of Audubon's private musings Maria did not wish to share with the public. Audubon used the pages of his journals during separations from his family as a kind of continuing letter to his wife, Lucy. He expected her and presumably his sons, Victor Gifford and John Woodhouse Audubon, to eventually read them, but he almost certainly never anticipated they would be presented to the world in published form.[11] Maria can perhaps be forgiven for honoring her grandfather's unstated wishes, the family's understandable desire to maintain his reputation, and the societal dictates of the day. However, she can never be forgiven for subsequently burning the original journals that she held in her hands.[12] How the surviving journals escaped this fate is unclear.[13] What is relatively certain is that the original Labrador journal was destroyed and is lost forever.

There exists an alternate version of the Labrador journal, which was published in London in 1868 and in the United States the following year as part of a full-scale biography of the naturalist. But it, too, is no substitute for the missing original. Lucy Audubon, looking for a way to cement her husband's legacy while generating some badly needed income after the family's finances suffered a disastrous turn with the death of her two sons and the commencement of the Civil War, put together a lengthy account of her late husband's life with the help of a friend, using Audubon's original journals and his other writings as source materials.[14]

In 1867, she sent the massive manuscript to the London publisher Sampson Low, Son & Marston, which sent it out to be edited by twenty-six-year-old Scottish writer and poet Robert Buchanan. As Buchanan explained in the Editor's Preface to *The Life and Adventures of Audubon the Naturalist*, it was necessary for him "to cut down what was prolix and unnecessary, and to connect the whole into some sort of running narrative,—and the result is a volume equal in bulk to about one-fifth of the original manuscript."[15] Unfortunately, this manuscript material was reportedly never returned to Lucy and presumably no longer exists.[16]

Lucy did not care at all for Buchanan's effort, which listed him as editor and included critical observations of her husband. In 1869, she had the biography republished in New York under her own name.[17] However, despite her complaints, she made only minor changes to the work and even failed to correct the erroneous date given for her wedding. Still, as a revised edition with Lucy's corrections, this stands as the definitive text for purposes of Audubon scholarship.

Given Buchanan's original charge, this abridged version of the Labrador journal tends to be far less detailed and is lacking in many of Audubon's vivid observations of the natural world, the birds, and the people he encountered on the trip. Additionally, several of the early entries in June as well as later entries in July 1833 were misdated by Buchanan and went uncorrected in Lucy's publication.[18] However, there is much to commend here. Audubon's unique voice and word usage appear to be more intact in this edition of the journal than in Maria's. This, too, comes as no surprise. Buchanan was more interested in culling out what he perceived to be unnecessary than in altering Audubon's prose.

Of course, Buchanan started with what he had been provided, and Lucy was no less motivated than her granddaughter in seeking to protect the memory of her husband. But it seems to me, having read reams of Audubon's handwritten letters and manuscripts in the course of my decade-long research, that Lucy remained truer to the original holograph, at least as to Audubon's manner of expression. Maria had multiple agendas guiding her hand. Additionally, in several entries, Lucy's edition provides details that are noticeably absent from Maria's offering. The two, then, must be read side by side to fill the holes left by the other. Still, there can be little doubt that substantial portions of the original are missing or have been changed. It is far from ideal, but it is the best we have.

Another vital source of information is Audubon's *Ornithological Biography*, the five-volume examination of North American birdlife that he wrote to accompany the prints for *The Birds of America*. Beginning with Volume II, first published in Edinburgh in 1834, Audubon sprinkled references to the Labrador expedition throughout his individual species accounts as well as in several of his "Episodes" delineating scenes, both real and imagined, of American life. However, one must approach the particulars given by Audubon in the *Ornithological Biography* with caution, especially with respect to dates. Although he reportedly relied upon his journals as he wrote these volumes, he saw little reason to be factually precise about those sorts of details. He probably never expected that biographers almost two hundred years hence would be mining every word for information about his doings. He was simply writing for a general audience and wanted to make the work entertaining. He was also often pressed for time, dashing off species accounts between social engagements, canvassing for additional subscribers, traveling in search of new birds to paint, and supervising the completion of the remaining prints. As a consequence, he frequently took liberties with the truth or was simply sloppy in recounting the facts.

I have also looked to Audubon's correspondence for additional details about the trip. Audubon was a prodigious letter writer, especially to his wife. Although he wrote relatively few letters during the voyage, what he did write still survives for the most part and provides further backup to the edited versions of the journal. There are also more than a dozen of his letters in existence written from Eastport, where he traveled in early May 1833 to finalize his preparations for the expedition. His letters offer a more reliable account of events inasmuch as they were written contemporaneously and did not go through the filter of an editor. Many of the pertinent letters have been previously published, though in professional journals and limited-edition or out-of-print books that have generally been unavailable outside major research libraries. To the extent it was possible, I have gone back to the original letter manuscripts, housed in various academic institutions and private collections around the country, to examine them anew. I have found the editors of the published versions were not always able to accurately decipher Audubon's handwriting or just simply transcribed them incorrectly. In some cases, the mistakes are glaring.

Several young men accompanied Audubon to Labrador and, with the apparent exception of his son John, all of them left written accounts of the expedition. Joseph Coolidge provided Ruthven Deane with additional memories of the voyage in a letter that he wrote in December 1896. William Ingalls, M.D., who in 1833 was studying medicine with his father, a respected Boston physician, also corresponded with Deane shortly before he died in 1903. Both of these narratives were published by Deane in 1910 in *The Auk*, the journal of the American Ornithologists' Union.[19] Further, Thomas Lincoln, the son of Judge Theodore Lincoln of Dennysville, Maine, kept a journal during the trip. While this journal remains unpublished and may be lost, portions of it appeared in a 1924 article by Charles W. Townsend, M.D., in *The Auk* and in 1969 in a newspaper article in the *Sunday Maine Telegram*.[20]

The last and, for purposes of my research, most important member of the "Young Gentlemen" who made up Audubon's party was George Cheyne Shattuck Jr., the son of a wealthy and esteemed Boston physician who was an original subscriber to *The Birds of America*. Shattuck received the naturalist's invitation to join the expedition while he was finishing up the spring term at the Medical School of Maine at Bowdoin College in Brunswick and met up with the Audubons in Eastport in early May. For the remainder of that month and the early part of June, while they waited for better weather and Audubon's chartered schooner, Shattuck kept a record of his daily activities in a small, leather-bound journal.[21]

This journal, previously overlooked by Audubon scholars, lies in the Harvard Medical Library in the Francis A. Countway Library of Medicine in Boston. The pertinent portions are published for the first time in the Appendix, and I thank the Countway Library of Medicine for granting me permission to do so. Shattuck also wrote several letters to his father both before and during the voyage that are held by the Massachusetts Historical Society. In addition, Bowdoin College has in its archives a letter written by Shattuck to one of his professors shortly after his return to Boston. Some of these letters have been previously published in abridged form by Dr. Townsend in *In Audubon's Labrador.*[22]

I have also scoured old newspapers for contemporary accounts of the voyage. Working with the friendly and capable research librarians at the American Antiquarian Society in Worcester, Massachusetts, I located a lengthy article detailing Audubon's journey from an interview that he gave to the *Boston Daily Advertiser & Patriot* after he returned to Boston on September 4, 1833. At the New-York Historical Society, I found several pertinent articles about Audubon and the expedition that appeared in the pages of the *New-York Gazette & Daily Advertiser.* These articles are republished in full in the Appendix with the permission of these institutions and with my thanks.

Finally, we have the benefit of the published journals of Cmdr. Henry Wolsey Bayfield of the British Royal Navy, who was surveying and mapping the Labrador coast aboard the schooner *Gulnare* during the summer of 1833. Between late June and the end of July, Bayfield and Audubon crossed paths on several occasions, and Bayfield's personal account of their interaction provides still another perspective.

In early August 1833, shortly before he sailed home from Labrador, Audubon wrote to Lucy and remarked that if he wanted to write a novel about the voyage, he would call it *Tales of Labrador.*[23] Audubon never seriously considered the idea of a novel, but he left tens of thousands of words about his adventure. Combined with those of his intrepid companions, they enable us to examine a vital period in the life of a singular American and his unfaltering determination to portray, not only for his time but for all time, the birds of America.

Audubon

[I]n all the world's history of wonderful men,

there is not to my mind one story of life so filled

with beautiful romance as this of J. J. Audubon, . . .

and what a wondrous tale it is!

CHARLES WILKINS WEBBER

Prologue: Boston

MARCH 1833

The Die is cast, I go to the coast of Labrador this season.
JOHN JAMES AUDUBON

Upon meeting him you were immediately struck by the intensity of his eyes—these extraordinarily bright, penetrating hazel eyes. The Boston portrait painter George P. A. Healy, a student of many an illustrious face, called them "the most piercing eyes I ever saw,—real eagle eyes."[1] It was a fitting characterization.

They were the eyes of a man best known for his study and illustration of North American birds. However, he had worn many a label during his peripatetic life: émigré, clerk, storekeeper, husband, father, frontiersman, slave owner, town leader, deadbeat, artist, naturalist, salesman, author, explorer. A dynamic and complicated man, he was as much at home in the primeval forests of America as in the elegant salons of England. And wherever he went, people remembered his flashing eyes. But now, as those eyes darted about the room in his Boston apartment, they were clouded with fear.

John James Audubon lay abed, his heart pounding, his mind awhirl, as he frantically awaited the doctors who had been summoned to Sarah Lekain's stately Pearl Street boardinghouse. With each breath, he struggled to maintain his composure. His beloved wife, Lucy, sat next to him murmuring words of comfort and support. Their marriage had survived nearly twenty-five often difficult and tumultuous years, the last thirteen as he single-mindedly pursued his life's passion. Though she was trying desperately to remain calm, he knew her every look.

She was terrified.

It was Saturday, March 16, 1833.[2] The French-American naturalist and painter had been in the city with his wife and youngest son, John Woodhouse Audubon, since the previous October, working on his ornithological masterpiece, *The Birds of America*. At the age of forty-seven, Audubon was slowly approaching the halfway point in the publication of his stunning, life-sized illustrations of North America's avifauna. Prints of his mixed-media drawings were being engraved, printed, and hand colored in London and then issued serially to subscribers in sets of five—designated as sequential "Numbers"—at the rate of five Numbers per year.

Since 1827, when the first Number appeared, fully 155 images had been published

[3]

in the same size as the originals on enormous double elephant folio paper measuring roughly 26½″× 39½″.[3] Another five prints were currently in production, with an additional twenty drawings ready to be engraved, and Audubon was preparing to send over ten more compositions that he had recently completed.[4] But he still had much to do before his vision could be realized. He projected that the work would ultimately comprise a total of four hundred individual prints in four separate volumes at a subscription price of $800, which today would exceed $23,000.[5] To procure additional specimens for his brush, he was making plans for an expedition that spring to the distant coast of Labrador, where he hoped to find a myriad of different species of waterbirds breeding.[6]

The day had dawned fair, a pleasant enough change from the winter storm that had dropped a layer of fresh, dry snow over the city the day before.[7] During the late morning and early afternoon, the Audubons received visitors in their rooms at No. 3 Pearl Street, as they often did.[8] Audubon and Lucy attended few of the parties to which they were invited, and many of Boston's finest citizens wanted to call upon the distinguished naturalist.[9]

They would have found the Audubon family comfortably ensconced three doors down from Milk Street in the Federal-style mansion constructed in 1812 to serve as the residence of merchant John Prince. Prince eventually moved out to Jamaica Plain, and Mrs. Lekain subsequently converted the home into an urbane boardinghouse.[10]

The Pearl Street address brought a certain cachet to her refined guests. Following the Boston fire of 1794, which swept through and destroyed the area along what was then Hutchinson Street, the thoroughfare was renamed and chosen by a number of prominent Bostonians as the site for their magnificent new dwellings. At one time or another, Pearl Street had been the home of Massachusetts Governor Christopher Gore, Lt. Governor William Phillips Jr., Chief Justice of the Supreme Judicial Court Theophilus Parsons, and former Boston Mayor Josiah Quincy. James Perkins, an immensely wealthy merchant and philanthropist who had made his fortune in the China trade, owned the mansion at No. 13 until 1822, when he donated the building to the Boston Athenaeum. His business partner and equally prosperous brother, Col. Thomas H. Perkins, still had a home at No. 17 near the intersection at High Street.[11]

Among the people who stopped by to see the Audubons on that Saturday was the Reverend William Ellery Channing, a minister at the Federal Street Church and one of the country's leading Unitarian theologians. During Channing's visit, Anna Quincy, the twenty-year-old daughter of now Harvard University President Josiah Quincy, and her close friend Louisa Gore swept into the apartment in their cloaks and fashionable morning dresses to pay their respects.[12]

The young, single women were probably more interested in seeing the devilishly good-looking John Woodhouse, a contemporary who enjoyed making the social rounds and, with his Southern charm, had developed quite a female following.[13] To her diary Anna whispered that he was her *"favorite* Mr. John Audubon." But she could not help marveling at the naturalist's recent artwork, particularly a powerful composition of a female Golden Eagle he had completed earlier in the month. Anna noted that "really the eyes of Mr Channing Mr Audubon, & the Eagle together were worth seeing."[14]

It was later that day when Audubon was stricken, suddenly and without warning.

At first, he thought that his right hand and arm had fallen asleep. He tried to restore the feeling in them, rubbing his fingers and hand and shaking his arm. Lucy could not help seeing what he was doing and asked him what was wrong. Audubon no doubt trivialized it as men are apt to do, assuring her it was nothing. But the paresthesia quickly became weakness and then, to his horror, paralysis. Ashen-faced, he turned to Lucy and, in his accented English, groaned that he could no longer move his arm — the arm and hand he used for drawing. The ghastly numbness then swiftly spread to his mouth and lips, leaving his speech unintelligible.[15]

Pushing aside the panic that threatened to overwhelm her, Lucy immediately sent word to two of Boston's foremost physicians, Dr. John Collins Warren and Dr. George Parkman.[16] Warren was on the faculty of the Massachusetts Medical College of Harvard University and was president of the Massachusetts Medical Society.[17] Parkman, who had a private practice on Cambridge Street, was looked upon by Audubon as a dear and trusted friend.[18]

The wait was interminable. Despite the naturalist's generally positive attitude, it was impossible not to fear the worst. A stroke! He had known of others who became permanently incapacitated or died after suffering a stroke.[19] As much as he tried, he was unable to fight the rising dread that the doctors, no matter how skilled, would be powerless to help.

He surely recognized that the continued production of *The Birds of America* was in jeopardy. Fewer than half of the promised prints had been issued, and scores of additional species remained to be collected and illustrated. There was no one he deemed capable of finishing the task if he were disabled. He had been grooming John to replace him as an artist should something like this occur, but it was too soon. The younger man was still developing his talents and, while beginning to contribute in small ways to the latest drawings, was certainly not yet skilled enough to assume that burden.[20] Audubon's other son, twenty-three-year-old Victor, had sailed for England five months before and was overseeing the production of the prints as well as canvassing for additional subscribers. Audubon thought he might be able to acquire the necessary knowledge and skills to complete the publication, but realistically that would take years.[21]

As Audubon and Lucy listened intently for the knock on the door that would signal the doctors' arrival, they could not help agonizing over how far they had traveled and all they risked losing if his crippling condition prevented the completion of what they called his "Great Work."[22]

———

By the winter of 1833, the publication of *The Birds of America* had brought Audubon a measure of renown and financial stability he scarcely could have imagined only seven years before as he sailed from New Orleans to Liverpool, a virtual unknown, seeking a publisher for his portfolio of bird illustrations. The wealthy and privileged on two continents were subscribers to his work, and he dined with prominent members of society in every city he visited. Even President Andrew Jackson had welcomed him to the White House during a brief visit to Washington City three years before. He had been elected a member of the leading scientific and intellectual organizations in England, Scotland, and the United States, including the august Royal Society of London. He carried with him a personal letter of introduction from the Duke of Sussex, younger brother of William IV, King of England, directing British civilian and military authorities in North America to assist him in his endeavors. The secretary of the U.S. Treasury Department had also recognized the value of his work by authorizing him to use the department's revenue cutters, at government expense, to advance his project during a bird-collecting expedition to the Floridas the year before. Like a modern-day celebrity, his comings and goings were reported in the major daily newspapers.

Yet the fame and approbation had arrived late in life and only after years of hardship, struggle, and disappointment. Audubon was forty-one years old, well into middle age, before his creative genius was truly appreciated. He did not even embark on an artistic career until he was thirty-four, and only then when he could find no gainful work after his business failed in the Panic of 1819. His wife was obliged to take jobs as a governess and teacher to support herself and their two sons during the years he was focused on completing his portfolio. He could not interest a single engraver or publisher in America to print his compositions. His wife's family believed he would never amount to anything. One of them famously wrote: "He neglects his material interests and is forever wasting his time hunting, drawing and stuffing birds, and playing the fiddle. We fear he will never be fit for any practical purpose on the face of the earth."[23]

And, at his core, Audubon carried with him the shameful stigma and insecurity of his origins that he kept hidden from all but his immediate family.[24] Unbeknownst to the world, Audubon was illegitimate. He had been born Jean Rabin on April 26,

1785, in the port city of Les Cayes on the Caribbean island of Saint-Domingue in what is now Haiti.[25] His father, Jean Audubon, was a married French sea captain and merchant from Nantes who owned a sugar plantation on the island and traded in sugar and slaves.[26]

During a voyage from France in 1783 to manage his holdings, the elder Audubon met and later developed an intimate relationship with an unmarried, extraordinarily beautiful twenty-five-year-old French woman named Jeanne Rabine, who was traveling to the French colony to serve as a chambermaid for a nearby family.[27]

Jean Audubon's wife, Anne Moynet, fourteen years his senior and childless, remained in France during his periodic trips abroad.[28] She presumably knew nothing of his liaison with Mademoiselle Rabine or of the existence of a quadroon mistress, Catherine "Sanitte" Bouffard, who lived with him on his island estate, served as his housekeeper, and gave him several illegitimate daughters.[29] Audubon's mother died of a tropical infection just six and a half months after his birth, and he was raised on the Les Cayes plantation by his father's servants.[30]

By 1788, there were growing signs of unrest among the large slave population on Saint-Domingue. Recognizing the dangers an insurrection would pose to the French plantation owners, Jean Audubon sold most of his property on the island and sent the young Jean Rabin to France, where the boy was warmly welcomed by the kind-hearted and indulgent Anne.[31]

The following year, Jean Audubon sailed from Les Cayes for America with a cargo of sugar that he used as a down payment to acquire Mill Grove, a roughly 285-acre estate northwest of Philadelphia along the Perkiomen Creek near Valley Forge.[32] He returned to the island, which had already been wracked with sporadic fighting in areas distant from Les Cayes, to secure whatever profits he could derive from his remaining assets before sailing for France by way of Philadelphia in 1790.[33] When he reached Nantes, he learned that a slave uprising had taken lives in Les Cayes. He was able to prevail upon an acquaintance that was making one last trip to the island in 1791 to return with his and Sanitte's youngest child, a light-skinned four-year-old daughter named Rose.[34] Both children were formally adopted by Jean and Anne Audubon on March 7, 1794.[35]

Growing up at a time when France was rocked by revolutionary turmoil, the young Audubon received only a rudimentary classroom education.[36] But he was privately tutored in the social requisites of a gentleman, including dancing, drawing, shooting, and fencing.[37] He was also instructed in music, for which he had a natural aptitude, and he became skilled at playing the violin, flute, and flageolet.[38]

His real passion, though, was for the natural world, birds in particular. He spent as much time as he could roaming the fields and forests near his parents' homes in Nantes and at La Gerbetière, the Audubon summer residence outside Couëron along the Loire River west of Nantes, often at the expense of his studies. As he grew older and with the encouragement of his father, he began to draw the birds and mammals that he was able to collect with his developing skill as a marksman.[39]

Audubon would later claim that he studied art at the Paris atelier of the famous French Neoclassical painter Jacques-Louis David.[40] However, this was decidedly untrue. It is possible that he took lessons from a student of David's, one of the unnamed "good masters" from whom he reportedly received instruction. But he was never one of David's pupils.[41] It would seem that Audubon initially promoted an association with David after arriving in America to mask his latent insecurities and later to burnish his reputation as an artist. The desire to craft his own persona and exaggerate his accomplishments became a hallmark of the man. He could lie with aplomb and did so readily if he stood to gain and, just as importantly, thought he could get away with it. But, in truth, Audubon was largely self-taught, which makes his ultimate accomplishments even grander.

His father, who had joined the National Guard in 1791 and was subsequently placed in command of vessels for the French Navy, attempted to focus his son's mind and prepare him for a career at sea by enrolling him at the naval training station at Rochefort-sur-Mer in 1796.[42] Audubon spent the next four years receiving nautical instruction, but a seafaring life was not for him. He could not overcome his propensity for seasickness and failed the entrance examination to the School of Mathematics and Hydrography.[43]

The young Audubon returned to Nantes in March 1800, shortly before his father retired from naval service.[44] His stepmother, who thoroughly adored him, was delighted to have him home again. As he later recalled, she "completely spoiled me, hid my faults, boasted to every one of my youthful merits, and, worse than all, said frequently in my presence that I was the handsomest boy in France."[45] He believed every word of it, and a healthy ego along with an oversized touch of vanity would accompany him throughout the course of his life.

1

America, My Country

1803–1826

For a period of nearly twenty years, my life was a succession of vicissitudes.
JOHN JAMES AUDUBON

In the summer of 1803, the eighteen-year-old Audubon was sent by his father to America, ostensibly to help manage his affairs at Mill Grove, where a lead deposit had recently been discovered. A French mineralogist and purported mining expert, Francis Dacosta, had already been dispatched to evaluate the prospects for opening a mine. Although Jean Audubon hoped his son would learn English and gain valuable knowledge about farming and, perhaps, mining, his real purpose was to remove his son from the grasp of Napoleon's burgeoning army.[1]

Audubon arrived in New York by sail in late August and almost immediately exhibited symptoms of what he later recalled as yellow fever.[2] He was nursed back to health by two Quaker women who ran a boardinghouse in nearby Morristown, New Jersey.[3] They began his instruction in Quaker English, and he thereafter customarily used "thee" and "thou" in referring to his intimates.[4]

Audubon reached Mill Grove later that fall. He initially roomed in nearby Norristown, the county seat, before taking up residence on the estate with the family of tenant farmer William Thomas. Within months of his arrival, Audubon met and quickly fell in love with Lucy Green Bakewell, the seventeen-year-old eldest daughter of William and Lucy Bakewell of Derbyshire, England, who had recently moved with their six children from New Haven to a neighboring property called Vaux Hill. Bakewell would rename it Fatland Ford.[5]

Lucy was dark-haired with blue eyes, a slightly turned-up nose, and a slender, attractive figure.[6] Although not a classic beauty, she was intelligent, educated, gentle, and steadfast. She and Audubon shared a love of music, books, and the bucolic life in the country.[7] Audubon found her intensely alluring. When he sat down years later to write an autobiographical essay, he still recalled being captivated at their first meeting in mid-January 1804:[8]

> Well do I recollect the morning, and may it please God that I may never forget it, when, for the first time, I entered the Bakewell household. It happened that

Mr. Bakewell was from home. I was shown into a parlour, where only one young lady was snugly seated at work, with her back turned towards the fire. She rose on my entrance, offered me a seat, and assured me of the gratification her father would feel on his return, which, she added with a smile, would be in a few minutes, as she would send a servant after him. Other ruddy cheeks made their appearance, but like spirits gay, vanished from my sight. Talking and working, the young lady who remained made the time pass pleasantly enough, and to me especially so. It was she, my dear Lucy Bakewell, who afterwards became my wife and the mother of my children.[9]

When William Bakewell returned to the house, he asked Lucy to prepare lunch before the men left to go on a hunt:

Lucy rose from her seat a second time, and her form, to which I had before paid little attention, seemed radiant with beauty, and my heart and eyes followed her every step. The repast being over, guns and dogs were provided, and as we left I was pleased to believe that Lucy looked upon me as a not very strange animal. Bowing to her, I felt, I knew not why, that I was at least not indifferent to her.[10]

The dashingly handsome young Frenchman indeed had no difficulty attracting her attention, as he did many others'. He was not quite five feet nine inches tall, only slightly above average height for his time, with a Gallic nose, thick, wavy, chestnut hair, and, as he recalled, "muscles of steel."[11] He had a spirited, engaging—some might say cocky—personality that he used effectively to mask his lingering self-doubt. His striking good looks, intense hazel eyes, and strong personal magnetism had a powerful effect on women.[12] Martha Pope, the wife of one of his later friends, may have forgotten the color of his eyes when she set down her memoirs years afterward, but her description of the man leaves no doubt about how he was viewed by the opposite sex:

Audubon was one of the handsomest men I ever saw. In person he was tall and slender, his blue eyes were an eagle's in brightness, his teeth were white and even, his hair a beautiful chestnut brown, very glossy and curly. His bearing was courteous and refined, simple, and unassuming. Added to these personal advantages he was a natural sportsman and natural artist.[13]

Men were equally impressed by his athleticism and congeniality. David Pawling, whose forbears had settled the area, recounted seeing the eighteen-year-old Audubon for the first time in January 1804:

Today I saw the swiftest skater I ever beheld; backwards and forwards he went like the wind, even leaping over large air-holes fifteen feet or more across, and continuing to skate without a moment's delay. I was told he was a young Frenchman, and this evening I met him at a ball, where I found his dancing exceeded his skating; all the ladies wished him a partner; moreover, a handsomer man I never saw. His eyes alone command attention; his name, Audubon, is strange to me.[14]

Audubon was also a crack shot, a skill that was highly regarded in early 19th century America, where wild game often made up a portion of the diet. He had learned how to shoot as a boy, but he honed his talent in the bountiful forests surrounding Mill Grove. One winter day in 1804, Lucy's fifteen-year-old brother, Tom, challenged him to shoot Tom's hat in midair from twenty-five feet away while Audubon skated at full speed along the frozen Perkiomen Creek.[15] Audubon accepted:

Off I went like lightening, up and down, as if anxious to boast of my own prowess while on the glittering surface beneath my feet; coming, however, within the agreed distance the signal was given, the trigger pulled, off went the load, and down on the ice came the hat of my future brother-in-law, as completely perforated as if a sieve. He repented, alas! too late, and was afterward severely reprimanded by Mr. Bakewell.[16]

With the arrival of spring in 1804, the woodlands along the river and around Mill Grove became a haven for birds, and Audubon continued his fledgling efforts to illustrate them. He tried a number of different approaches that he hoped would impart a lifelike attitude to the specimens he had collected, but he was repeatedly displeased and frustrated by the results.[17]

Then, early one morning before dawn, Audubon came up with a solution and galloped off to purchase supplies in Norristown, about five miles away.[18] When he returned to Mill Grove, he shot a Belted Kingfisher along the Perkiomen and then used sharpened wires to penetrate the body and fasten it to a wooden mounting board. He went on later to refine this technique by placing gridlines on the board, and a grid of equal size on his drawing paper, so that he could capture the bird's outline while simultaneously dealing with the problem of foreshortening.[19] He found that this enabled him to draw the specimen precisely, at the size of life, and, more importantly, in a way that to him re-created the living bird.[20]

Audubon was compelled to shoot birds for his art, but he also understood the importance of studying them in the wild to learn how they behaved. At Mill Grove he began to develop the keen observational skills that would turn him into a first-rate field naturalist. He discovered a pair of Pewee Flycatchers (now known as Eastern Phoebes) nesting in a cave along the banks of the Perkiomen in the spring of 1804 and spent hours watching them. He later tied silver wire around the legs of the young before they left the nest to determine if they returned the following year to the nesting site.[21] This is the first known instance of bird banding in America.[22]

Lucy would sometimes accompany Audubon in his forays to the cave, and word of their sojourns eventually reached the ears of Lucy's father. A practical man, William Bakewell disapproved of their courtship, convinced that they were not yet old enough to wed. When Audubon approached him toward the end of the summer and asked for Lucy's hand in marriage, Bakewell demurred, insisting that Audubon first obtain his father's approval.[23]

Audubon sailed for France in mid-March 1805 to seek his father's permission to marry and to raise concerns about the motives of the mine overseer, Francis Dacosta, who had already persuaded Jean Audubon to grant him a half interest in Mill Grove in exchange for developing the lead mine.[24] The elder Audubon, whose financial condition had worsened with the loss of his remaining Les Cayes investments, was forced to raise funds by selling half of his remaining interest in the Pennsylvania estate to Claude Rozier, a friend and Nantes merchant.[25] Rozier's son Ferdinand had previously spent several months visiting Audubon at Mill Grove.[26]

The two young men could hardly have been more different. Ferdinand Rozier was stolid, serious, and older than Audubon by eight years. Audubon was exuberant, magnetically charming, and, at the age of twenty, a bit of a dandy. Despite the age disparity and personality contrasts, the young men enjoyed a natural camaraderie. Their fathers arranged a business partnership for them in America with the aim of resolving the dispute with Dacosta and placing them in a position to pursue "some commercial occupation, whether inland or maritime."[27]

Audubon and Rozier left France on false passports and reached New York on May 28, 1806.[28] Audubon brought with him a number of drawings of French birds that he had made during his visit as a present for Lucy, who greeted him excitedly at Fatland Ford a week later.[29]

The young Frenchmen whiled away the summer at Mill Grove, much to the consternation of Lucy's father, who did not approve of their "idleness." Audubon had still not received his father's permission to marry.[30] And, in any event, he lacked a trade or profession that would have persuaded William Bakewell to consent to a union. But Rozier, having concluded that the prospects for the lead mine were questionable, began negotiations with Dacosta over the future ownership of Mill Grove.[31]

On September 15, 1806, Audubon and Rozier sold him their interest in 113½ acres of the estate, including the two-story house, outlying buildings, and the lead mine, with Dacosta quitclaiming his half interest in the remaining farmland to them. The sales agreement called for Dacosta to pay for a portion of the sales price with proceeds from the mine.[32]

In the same month, the two young men separated to gain experience in commerce — Audubon working as a clerk for Lucy's uncle, Benjamin Bakewell, in his New York counting house, and Rozier, who was not conversant in English, employed at an import firm owned by French immigrants in Philadelphia.[33] However, before leaving for his new position, Audubon appeared in Philadelphia and applied to become a naturalized citizen.[34]

By the following summer, the partners had decided to move west and open a general store in Louisville, Kentucky.[35] They viewed the frontier town "as a spot designed by nature to become a place of great importance."[36]

It was an inspired choice. Louisville was a gateway to New Orleans and the recently acquired Louisiana Territory. It was also strategically situated on the southern banks of the Ohio River above the Falls of the Ohio, a series of rapids that forced ship traffic descending the waterway in low water to unload passengers and cargo before navigating them. Below the falls, the smaller settlement of Shippingport had been founded by French merchants who had seen an opportunity to service vessels blocked by the falls from proceeding farther upstream, as well as those that had made it through the falls and needed to reload their cargo and passengers.[37] Louisville considered itself to be more sophisticated than its sister community and had been growing rapidly. Its population, approximately a thousand strong, made it the largest municipality between Cincinnati and New Orleans.[38]

With goods purchased from Benjamin Bakewell, who had agreed to accept a promissory note payable in eight months, and a mortgage on the remaining Mill Grove acreage, Audubon and Rozier left Fatland Ford on August 31, 1807.[39] They traveled by stage across Pennsylvania to Pittsburgh and then down the Ohio by flatboat, reaching Louisville by early October.[40]

They had barely begun to establish themselves when, on December 22, President Thomas Jefferson signed the Embargo Act of 1807, a measure blocking American trade with foreign nations.[41] Jefferson's principal aim was to punish England and France, who were at war and had adopted policies hostile to American merchant shipping. The English had continued to impress American sailors at sea, and France had erected a naval blockade of American vessels in English ports.[42] However, the Act crippled the American economy. Merchants like Benjamin Bakewell, who exported American commodities and imported finished European goods, watched helplessly as their businesses failed.[43]

Audubon and Rozier managed to keep their concern going despite the difficult economic times. However, with the Bakewell firm in receivership and their note coming due on April 7, 1808, the partners traveled east that spring to negotiate an extension, leaving the business in the hands of their nineteen-year-old clerk, Nathaniel Wells Pope.[44] William Bakewell had finally granted Lucy his consent to marry Audubon, and on Tuesday, April 5, the young lovers were wed before friends and family in the parlor of Fatland Ford.[45]

Audubon, Lucy, and Rozier left for Kentucky three days later.[46] When they arrived in Louisville, Audubon and Lucy boarded at the Indian Queen, a hotel and tavern along the river.[47] It was a difficult adjustment for Lucy, who was in a new town with no friends, no house of her own, and a husband who was frequently away.[48]

Audubon was often traveling the surrounding countryside looking for customers as well as birds, while Rozier manned the store. "[B]irds were birds," Audubon later recalled, "then as now, and my thoughts were ever and anon turning toward them as the objects of my greatest delight."[49] The avian richness of the Ohio River valley, part of the Mississippi Flyway for migrating birds, enabled him to add a substantial number of drawings to his growing portfolio.[50] Meanwhile, Lucy had little to occupy her time. Writing to her English cousin on May 27, 1808, she complained of the lack of a library or bookshop, "for I have very few of my own and as Mr Audubon is constantly at the store I should often enjoy a book very much whilst I am alone."[51]

However, as Lucy's education and refinement became known, she became popular among the Louisville gentry, who would invite her to stay with them when Audubon was away canvassing for business or hunting with friends.[52] Lucy's flamboyant and convivial husband was well liked by the men of both Louisville and Shippingport, who viewed him as an amiable companion even if they could not understand his infatuation with birds. In the French community, he grew particularly close to the family of James Berthoud, who had fled France during the Revolution and now headed up a successful shipping business.[53] Audubon and Berthoud's twenty-one-year-old son, Nicholas, became fast friends.[54] Nicholas would go on to marry Lucy's younger sister Eliza in 1816.[55]

Audubon and Lucy continued to make their home at the Indian Queen, and on June 12, 1809, she gave birth there to a son, Victor Gifford Audubon.[56] Later that summer, Audubon rode east to settle the debt owed to Benjamin Bakewell's creditors and to purchase additional goods for the store.[57]

On March 19, 1810, a slight man with black, thinning hair, dark eyes, and a long, thin nose entered Audubon and Rozier's store with two books under his arm and asked for Audubon.[58] His brogue identified him as a Scotsman, and he introduced himself as Alexander Wilson. A former poet and schoolteacher who had immigrated to the United States in 1794, the thirty-three-year-old Wilson was the author of *American Ornithology*, a projected ten-volume compilation describing and illustrating the birds of North America.[59] The first volume had been published in Philadelphia in 1808 and the second only the preceding January, with hand-colored engravings of Wilson's original artwork by Alexander Lawson of Philadelphia, the finest engraver in America.[60]

Now Wilson was traveling through the Midwest looking for subscribers who would order the entire work in advance and pay with each volume. This was a standard approach at the time in issuing expensive or multivolume books to help finance the publication costs. Earlier in the month, Wilson had visited Pittsburgh, where he met Benjamin Bakewell, who had moved there and started a glassworks after the collapse of his importing business.[61] Bakewell had almost certainly given Wilson the name of his niece's bird-obsessed husband to look up when he reached Louisville.[62]

Wilson opened one of the books and began turning the pages, showing Audubon a few of the nine hand-colored plates that appeared in each volume.[63] The illustrations were flat and stiff, depicting the birds in simple profile views with several species per page. But Audubon's interest was piqued. He was just about to sign his name in Wilson's subscription book when Rozier interrupted in French. "My dear Audubon," he said, "what induces you to subscribe to this work? Your drawings are certainly far better, and again, you must know as much of the habits of American birds as this gentleman."[64]

Audubon put down the pen. As he later noted, "Whether Mr. Wilson understood French or not or if the suddenness with which I paused, disappointed him, I cannot tell; but I clearly perceived that he was not pleased. Vanity and the encomiums of my friend prevented me from subscribing."[65] Audubon proceeded to show Wilson the contents of his own portfolio:

> His surprise appeared great, as he told me he never had the most distant idea that any other individual than himself had been engaged in forming such a collection. He asked me if it was my intention to publish, and when I answered in the negative, his surprise seemed to increase.[66]

Audubon agreed to lend Wilson some of his drawings and took him hunting for some of the local birds the Scotsman had never seen — or at least that is Audubon's story.[67] An entry from Wilson's diary, which was published a year after his death in 1813, paints a somewhat different impression of his visit to Louisville.[68] When he departed on March 23, he commented bitterly:

> I bade adieu to Louisville, to which place I had four letters of recommendation, and was taught to expect much of everything there, but neither received one act of civility from those to whom I was recommended, one subscriber, nor one new bird; though I delivered my letters, ransacked the woods repeatedly, and visited all the characters likely to subscribe. Science or literature has not one friend in this place.[69]

The encounter with Alexander Wilson would prove to be a pivotal moment in Audubon's life, although he would not fully recognize it for another decade. In the interim, his young family required his attention, as did his business, which continued to struggle despite Louisville's expanding population.[70] Rozier suggested they move another two hundred miles downriver to Henderson, Kentucky, a sparsely populated settlement where they would face less competition for business.[71] Audubon relented, as he later acknowledged, because he "longed to have a wilder range."[72] Lucy's sentiments are not known, but she could not have been happy about leaving her Louisville friends and moving to a backwater hamlet even closer to the edge of the frontier.[73]

———————

Upon their arrival in Henderson later that spring, the partners took their remaining stock and opened a store in an abandoned log cabin located between two tobacco warehouses a stone's throw from the river.[74] With a population of only 159 people, business was slow. Rozier once again found himself behind the counter, while Audubon and their clerk from Louisville, Nathaniel Pope, spent much of their time furnishing food for the table by hunting in the surrounding forests and fishing in the Ohio River.[75]

Within a matter of months, Rozier began pressing Audubon to move still farther west, to the French community of Ste. Genevieve in what was then Upper Louisiana (now Missouri), located along the western banks of the Mississippi River about 125 miles above its confluence with the Ohio. Rozier had never mastered English as had Audubon and felt uncomfortable around the English-speaking Kentuckians. The partners agreed to hazard a trip by keelboat to Ste. Genevieve in late December 1810, taking whiskey, gunpowder, and dry goods to sell upon their arrival.[76] Lucy was invited to stay with the family of Dr. Adam and Elizabeth Rankin just outside Henderson.[77]

As Audubon and Rozier descended the Ohio River, winter settled in over the Midwest. They found themselves stranded, first at the Cache River just six miles above the Mississippi and then at Tawapatee Bottoms on the Missouri side of the frozen river, waiting for a thaw.[78] The ice did not break up until February, and then their party had to pole the keelboat upstream to Cape Girardeau and finally to Ste. Genevieve.[79]

When they reached their destination, Rozier elected to stay. The partnership was dissolved, and Audubon returned overland to Henderson in early April.[80] In attempting to explain Rozier's decision, Audubon later wrote, "Rozier cared only for money and liked St. Geneviève." Rozier remarked that "Audubon had no taste for commerce, and was continually in the forest."[81]

Without Rozier's steady hand on the tiller of the business, Audubon was adrift. He was still searching for a suitable vocation at midsummer, when he and Lucy rode east with little Victor to visit her family. They stopped in Louisville along the way and boarded at the Indian Queen for several weeks to give Audubon a chance to see what opportunities their former abode might offer. When word reached them that Lucy's twenty-three-year-old brother, Tom, was on his way west with a business proposition, they decided to wait for him instead of continuing on to Fatland Ford.[82]

Tom reached Louisville in September.[83] He had spent the past three years working in New York as a clerk for Arthur and Thomas Kinder of Robert Kinder & Co., which served as a receiver for Benjamin Bakewell's failed business.[84] He was now headed to New Orleans to open his own mercantile house that would trade goods on consignment from a Liverpool firm, and he believed it would be advantageous to have the French-speaking Audubon as a partner.[85] Audubon readily agreed, and the firm of Audubon & Bakewell, Commission Merchants, was born.[86] Over the next year, Audubon would contribute nearly all of his funds to get the business started.[87]

Audubon and Lucy resumed their journey east in early November. Audubon carried with him a request from Tom to William Bakewell for a loan to help set up the new commission house.[88] After twenty-one days on the road, they arrived at the Bakewell homestead on November 30.[89] Audubon stopped by Mill Grove to see whether the lead mine was in operation but found it abandoned.[90] He informed Rozier of this on December 9, adding that "I am very much afraid that we will never get anything out of this bad bargain."[91]

Leaving Lucy and Victor with his in-laws, Audubon set out in mid-December to return to Henderson with the plan of proceeding to New Orleans. In the mountains of Pennsylvania, he met Vincent Nolte, a wealthy and well-connected Continental merchant who was also headed to New Orleans to open a mercantile house.[92] Nolte later described their unforgettable encounter at a small inn near the falls of the Juniata River, where he had stopped for breakfast:

> The landlady showed me into a room, and said, I perhaps would not object to taking my meal at the same table with a strange gentleman, who was already there. As I entered I found the latter personage, who at once struck me as being, what, in common parlance, is called an odd fish. He was sitting at a table, before the fire, with a Madras handkerchief wound around his head, exactly in the style of the French mariners, or laborers, in a seaport town. I stepped up to him, and accosted him politely, with the words, "I hope I don't incommode you, by coming to take my breakfast with you." "Oh no, sir," he replied, with a strong French accent, that made it sound like "No, sare." "Ah," I continued, "you are a Frenchman, sir?" "No, sare," he answered, "hi emm an Heenglishman." "Why," I asked, in return, "how do you make that out? You look like a Frenchman, and you speak like one." "Hi emm an Eenglishman, becas hi got a Heenglish wife," he answered.[93]

The two men decided over breakfast to journey on together to Pittsburgh, and Nolte found Audubon "to be an original throughout."[94] Eventually, Audubon acknowledged that he was "a Frenchman by birth, and a native of La Rochelle."[95] However, extending the fiction about his origins, he told Nolte that "he had come in his early youth to Louisiana, had grown up in the sea service, and had gradually become a thorough American." Nolte was confused. " 'Now,' I asked, 'how does that accord with your quality of Englishman?' Upon this he found it convenient to reply, in the French language, 'When all is said and done, I am somewhat cosmopolitan; I belong to every country.' "[96]

After their arrival in Pittsburgh, Nolte invited Audubon to accompany him down the Ohio River. They left in early January 1812 aboard one of two flatboats Nolte had purchased. They landed in Maysville, then also known as Limestone, Kentucky, and the two men continued on horseback to Lexington, where they went their separate ways.[97] Once more in Henderson, Audubon received word from Tom Bakewell that the growing tension between the United States and England had hampered his efforts to launch their mercantile firm.[98]

In February, Audubon elected to return to Fatland Ford, where he arrived in early March.[99] He took advantage of spring migration to add close to a score of drawings to his expanding collection.[100] He also visited Philadelphia and paid a brief call on Alexander Wilson.[101] The Scotsman greeted him "with civility" and invited him to visit the museum run by Rembrandt Peale. But Wilson was not interested in discussing either birds or drawings, the two topics they had in common. Concluding that his "company was not agreeable," Audubon "parted from him; and after that I never saw him again."[102] Wilson died of dysentery in August of the following year.[103]

April brought welcome news along with Audubon's twenty-seventh birthday. Lucy was expecting their second child.[104] It must have been an idyllic time for Audubon, who spent his days rambling through the verdant Pennsylvania fields and forests searching for birds, which he would collect and take back to his room to draw. On one such excursion in late May with Lucy's twelve-year-old brother, Will, they found a large nest belonging to either a crow or hawk at the top of a tree along the Perkiomen Creek. Will was sent up to retrieve an egg so that Audubon could try to identify the species. When Will reached the nest, he shouted down to Audubon that there was a hawk in the nest which could not fly. Audubon suggested he place a handkerchief over the bird and bring it down along with the eggs. The boy did so, and Audubon returned to Fatland Ford with a female Broad-winged Hawk in hand. He reportedly placed the docile bird on a stick in his studio, and it sat there quietly while he illustrated it. When he was done, he released it through an opened window.[105] Though his story is highly suspect — no healthy, wild raptor would likely remain quiescent in an enclosed room in the presence of a human being—that is the tale he has left us.

On June 1, the conflict that had been brewing between the United States and England for a decade finally came to a head. President James Madison submitted a request to Congress for a declaration of war in retaliation for England's impressment of thousands of American seamen, its illicit seizure and sale of American merchant vessels, and the continuing raids by English-allied Indian tribes along the western frontier. Congress complied on June 18, and the British promptly responded with an embargo of American ports.[106]

Two weeks later, on July 3, Audubon appeared in the U.S. District Court in Philadelphia to complete the process of becoming a naturalized citizen.[107] He would forever after proudly consider himself an American.[108]

With the prospect of war hanging over the nation and Lucy's pregnancy advancing, the Audubons left Fatland Ford a fortnight later to return with Victor to Kentucky.[109] They were safely back in Henderson in August, living again with the Rankin family, when Tom Bakewell arrived on foot from New Orleans and announced that, due to the war, their commission house had failed.[110] Audubon invited Tom to remain in Henderson and join him as a partner in the general store under the Audubon & Bakewell name.[111] Lacking other prospects, Tom agreed, though without any real enthusiasm.[112]

Audubon later wrote that the loss of his investment in the New Orleans venture had greatly reduced his "pecuniary means." He claimed that he returned to drawing birds and "only now and then thought of making any money."[113] But this was written years later, when he was busy fashioning his own mythology for an eager public. In fact, by the early part of 1813, his financial condition had improved sufficiently that he was able to purchase a spacious log house on some acreage adjacent to the Henderson store as an abode for his expanding family.[114] Lucy had given birth to a second son, John Woodhouse Audubon, on November 30, 1812, while they were still enjoying the Rankins' hospitality.[115] Now they could live in a home of their own. Tom, who was single, moved in with them.[116]

Henderson was expanding rapidly. As a consequence of its designation in 1801 as a tobacco-inspection station for dark-leaf tobacco being shipped downriver, the town was becoming a commercial center for the tobacco trade.[117] A second inspection station for other farming products was built a short time later. Between 1810 and 1820, the town's population jumped in size from 159 to 532 persons.[118]

Encouraged by an ambitious partner, Audubon began focusing on his business for the first time in his career.[119] Their store found a ready clientele and prospered. In January 1814, Audubon & Bakewell opened a second branch downriver in Shawneetown, Illinois.[120] With the earnings from the business, Audubon began investing in Henderson property, which he then subdivided and sold for a substantial profit.[121]

The Audubons were enjoying life in Henderson. Lucy had adapted to frontier living and made the most of her rustic surroundings. She transformed their log house into a warm and inviting home, stylishly decorated with dark cherry and walnut furniture, including a pianoforte that had come all the way from Fatland Ford. She nurtured her love of reading by acquiring books for her growing library. Eventually, some 150 volumes would grace the shelves of her bookcases. Evenings would find her at the piano with Audubon on his fiddle, filling the air with music. During the days, they would go riding and, in the summer when the river had warmed, swim to the Indiana shoreline and back.[122]

With his gregarious personality and marked financial success, Audubon had cemented his position as one of the town's leading citizens, both popular and respected.[123] His ebullience enabled him to mix easily with the town's gentry as well as the rougher, hardscrabble elements common in towns along the river. He not only accepted but welcomed the responsibilities that came with his position in the community.

One story told by longtime residents recalled the day the town's deputy sheriff went to arrest a river pirate who had landed his canoe along the Henderson shoreline. Audubon heard about it and insisted on coming along. The pirate took the deputy's measure and concluded he was a coward. But the self-possessed Audubon could not be dismissed so readily, and the pirate pulled "a long, dangerous, murderous-looking knife" and accosted him. Audubon picked up a nearby oar and, when the man refused to heed a warning to stop, dropped him with a single swift blow that fractured the pirate's skull. Dr. Rankin was called to attend to the man, who was treated and then marched off to jail.[124]

Audubon would later rhapsodize about those early years in Henderson: "The pleasures which I have felt at Henderson, and under the roof of that log cabin, can never be effaced from my heart until after death."[125]

It was not to last.

During the spring and summer of 1813, the partners began looking for other business opportunities. Tom, both young and impetuous, advanced the idea of building a steam-powered gristmill and sawmill.[126] There were no mills in Henderson, and Tom convinced his partner that the combination would meet a pressing need as the community grew.[127] However, neither man had the slightest idea how to design and build a steam engine. They would need someone with the necessary mechanical knowledge as well as the additional capital or investors to bring it about.[128]

Tom left Henderson in late August 1813 to return to Fatland Ford to discuss the mill proposal with his father and seek a loan for his share of the construction costs.[129]

Before he departed, word reached Henderson that Lucy's cousin Sarah Pears and her husband, Thomas, who owned a farm near Fatland Ford, were considering moving west because the war had led to a collapse in the market for exported agricultural goods.[130] The Audubons asked Tom to deliver letters to the Pearses, suggesting they visit Henderson and possibly invest in the mill.[131]

Tom returned before year's end with his father's support and a commitment for a loan of between $3,000 and $4,000.[132] And, when Thomas Pears arrived in Henderson in 1814, having sold his farm and moved his family temporarily to Pittsburgh, he also expressed an interest in becoming a partner. The three men ultimately agreed that Pears and Tom would contribute about $4,000 each, with Audubon & Bakewell responsible for the remainder of the $10,000 that they had initially estimated it would cost to erect the structure and build and install the equipment.[133] The cost would eventually climb to about $15,000, with Audubon assuming the responsibility for the excess.[134] The partnership hired David Prentice, a Scottish mechanic living in Philadelphia who had successfully constructed a steam-powered thresher at Fatland Ford, to relocate to Henderson and both design and build the steam engine.[135]

Pears brought his wife and four young children downriver in the spring of 1815.[136] Sarah Pears was not happy about the move. A woman of strong views who was quick to complain, she had opposed her husband's decision to relocate to Kentucky.[137] Her letters to him from Pittsburgh voiced concerns about possible slave uprisings and attacks by warring British troops or hostile Indians.[138] Even news of a negotiated peace with England, which reached American shores in February 1815, did little to alter her thinking.[139]

The Pears family was welcomed into the Audubon home, now fairly bursting with houseguests.[140] Besides Tom Bakewell and the Pearses, the Audubons were hosting Lucy's twenty-four-year-old sister, Eliza, who had fled Fatland Ford because of lingering conflicts with her stepmother. In addition, Lucy's youngest brother, Will, now fourteen, had been sent out by their father to apprentice with Audubon & Bakewell.[141]

The crowded conditions and domestic demands could not have made life easy for Lucy. Even though the Audubons, like many affluent Kentuckians, owned several slaves, Lucy still had to fulfill her duties as hostess, wife, and mother. Moreover, she was once again pregnant.[142] She gave birth later that year to a daughter they named Lucy in honor of her deceased mother. Unfortunately, the baby girl was sickly, which only added to Lucy's burdens.[143]

Meanwhile, Audubon was deeply involved with his partners in developing the plans for the mill. Over the next several years, his business and family obligations occupied most of his time, leaving him little opportunity to study birds. There is not a single extant drawing of his that dates from between 1815 and 1820.[144]

No doubt compounding the strains on the Audubons, Sarah Pears thoroughly detested life in Henderson. She viewed the townspeople as coarse and contemptible.[145] But she also grew to resent her resourceful cousin, whose ability to maintain a lovely home and thrive at the edge of civilization only reinforced Sarah's own inadequacies.[146] In the early part of 1816, Sarah learned that she was pregnant and insisted the family return to Pittsburgh.[147] Thomas Pears eventually relented and demanded a return of his investment.[148] The timing could not have been worse for his partners, who were beginning construction of the mill on the banks of the river and were hard pressed to buy him out.[149] Although they managed to scrape together the funds to do so, Pears's departure saddled them with more of the risks.[150]

The mill venture proved to be a financial disaster. According to Tom, "it cost $5,000 more than it ought to have done owing to going through so many hands & so many different plans begun, & not finished together with the inexperience of the parties in that business." The partners spent money wastefully, purchasing French burr stones for $2,000 when they could have obtained comparable native burr at a tenth the price.[151] Moreover, Prentice had difficulty getting the steam engine to work properly. As Tom would later remark in a letter to his father:

> Mr. Prentice has an excellent head, but no hands—we have a very good Engine put up in a very slovenly imperfect manner which we are remedying by degrees ourselves. He is a capital man to prescribe, but not to administer—his *advice & opinion* in matters of his profession are invaluable, but his execution worthless.[152]

Meanwhile, Tom's attention to business matters was diverted by a romantic interest upriver. Following Eliza's marriage to Nicholas Berthoud on March 16, 1816, Tom had proposed to Elizabeth Rankin Page, the daughter of one of Benjamin Bakewell's partners.[153] They were married in Pittsburgh on July 27, and Tom brought her back to Henderson after the wedding.[154] Like Sarah Pears, Elizabeth despised the backwater town.[155] She soon learned that she was expecting a child and convinced Tom that the Kentucky frontier was no place to raise a family.[156] Tom, who had never felt an affinity for Henderson, used Elizabeth's discontent as an excuse to withdraw from the partnership in December.[157]

Tom would suggest in a letter to his father that Audubon had received the better end of the deal, but Audubon was now burdened with the mill and its continuing mechanical difficulties. He had also reportedly assumed the debts of Audubon & Bakewell and given Tom a promissory note for $5,500 with annual interest at twenty percent as payment for Tom's ownership interest.[158]

Tom agreed to stay on for another six months to help Audubon get the mill up and running as well as retire some of the debts of the partnership.[159] Around July 1, he left for Louisville with his wife, infant son, and brother Will.[160] David Prentice joined him there as a partner in a new steamboat-building enterprise.[161]

After numerous delays, the gristmill was finally completed in 1817. The sawmill followed a year later.[162] However, the mill continued to be plagued by mechanical problems. Audubon referred to it as the "bad establishment" and recalled that it "worked worse and worse every day."[163]

He soon discovered that they had wildly overestimated the profits the mill would generate. There was insufficient grain production in the vicinity to keep the gristmill operating.[164] And, the demand for sawed lumber was substantially less than originally projected.[165] Looking back years later, Audubon acknowledged that the region in which they had constructed the mill was "then as unfit for such a thing as it would be now for me to attempt to settle in the moon."[166]

Audubon began struggling with the crushing debt he had assumed. The general store, which had expanded to include new branches in Vincennes, Indiana, and along the Mississippi River, was also facing hard times.[167] Money was tight and, as Tom had advised his father and stepmother the year before, "we can sell no Goods nor collect any money worth speaking of."[168] Audubon found several local investors willing to purchase small interests in the mill, but he later claimed that he "was gulled by all these men."[169] His brother-in-law Nicholas Berthoud, who was now a successful Shippingport businessman, as well as Benjamin Page, the father of Tom Bakewell's wife, also invested.[170] But Audubon remained the majority partner in the business, with the greatest financial exposure.

Toward the end of 1817, after a steady decline, two-year-old Lucy died of hydrocephalus, a congenital brain disorder.[171] "Alas! The poor, dear little one was unkindly born, she was always ill and suffering," Audubon would later tell his sons.[172] For both Audubon and Lucy, their daughter's death left a sizable hole. "[T]he Loss of My Darling Daughter affected Me Much," he confided in his 1820 journal. Lucy, he added, "apparently had Lost her spirits."[173]

The Audubons' economic situation worsened when, in 1818, the Kentucky banks began to fail.[174] At that time, banks were permitted to print their own paper money, but they were originally required to redeem it in gold and silver upon demand.[175] During the war, the federal government was forced to borrow heavily and suspended this requirement for banks outside New England, which fostered a business environment marked by easy credit, speculation, and inflation.[176]

These trends, which had accounted for much of Audubon's financial success, continued after the war, especially in Kentucky, where the demands of a westward-expanding population increased the value of land and commodities. In January 1818, the Kentucky legislature chartered forty-six independent banks to increase the availability of money and credit.[177]

However, beginning in the fall of 1818, the federal government was obligated to begin paying off the bonds issued to finance the Louisiana Purchase and needed hard currency to do so.[178] That summer, the Second Bank of the United States, established in 1816 to help stabilize the economy with a safe national currency, ordered the state banks to redeem their balances and notes in gold and silver. This led to calls by the state banks for the payment of their outstanding loans, which precipitated a deflationary spiral as debtors scrambled to sell their assets.[179]

At the same time, a sharp drop in the price of American exported cotton resulted in a tightening of the London credit market, which had earlier helped fuel the postwar demand in America for English manufactured goods.[180] As a consequence, the American economy collapsed. Audubon, who had borrowed heavily to purchase goods for the general store and to finance the construction of the mill, began selling his Henderson real estate.[181] It was not nearly enough.

Audubon was engulfed by the Panic of 1819 like countless other Americans who watched helplessly while their businesses and livelihoods failed. As Audubon described it, "a *Revolution* occasionned by a Numberless quantities of Failures, put all to an end."[182] His neighbors no longer looked upon him with admiration. He was now met with the "surly Looks and Cold receptions of those who so Shortly before Were [MS: Where] pleased to Call me Their Friend."[183] He later explained, "I had heavy bills to pay which I could not meet or take up. The moment this became known to the world around me, that moment I was assailed with thousands of invectives; the once wealthy man was now nothing."[184]

Hounded by his creditors, Audubon relinquished the ownership of his stores in June 1819. Still unable to satisfy his debts, Audubon turned to Nicholas Berthoud, who agreed the following month to purchase his remaining assets.[185] Berthoud acquired everything—Audubon's home and its contents, including Lucy's treasured books, wedding silver, family china, and pianoforte; his seven slaves; his majority interest in the mill; even his portfolio of bird drawings, although his brother-in-law had no use for them and apparently returned them as a gift. Nonetheless, the slightly more than $25,000 Audubon received was still less than he owed.[186]

Now destitute and with no means to support his family, Audubon left Henderson on foot and headed for Louisville, where he hoped to find work. Lucy was again expecting and remained in Henderson with the boys. As he trudged toward an uncertain future, Audubon was despondent. The shame of his failure consumed him and was almost more than he could bear. Lucy had tried her best to maintain a brave face, offering him comfort and reassurance, but he wasn't fooled. She had delighted in the life they had built in Henderson, and he knew that she was feeling "the pangs of our misfortunes perhaps more heavily than I."[187] Though he had been ruined by economic forces almost entirely beyond his control, he could not help blaming himself. His soul was shattered, and the birds he saw along the road did nothing to lift his spirits:

> Without a dollar in the world, bereft of all revenues beyond my own personal talents and acquirements, I left my dear log house, my delightful garden and orchards with that heaviest of burdens, a heavy heart, and turned my face toward Louisville. This was the saddest of all journeys,—the only time in my life when the Wild Turkeys that so often crossed my path, and the thousands of lesser birds that enlivened the woods and the prairies, all looked like enemies, and I turned my eyes from them, as if I could have wished that they had never existed.[188]

Louisville offered no refuge from his travails. Audubon was arrested and jailed for debt shortly after he reached the city. Lucy received news of his incarceration and looked in desperation for a way to travel to Louisville to be near him. One of Audubon's old friends, U.S. Senator Isham Talbot, heard about her need and sent a carriage to take her and the children to Shippingport, where Eliza invited them to stay.[189] Meanwhile, another Audubon friend, Judge Fortunatus Cosby, advised him to file a bankruptcy petition under a recently enacted Kentucky law, which won his release although it did not extinguish his debts. He was out of jail by the time Lucy arrived.[190]

Finding employment, however, proved to be a much greater challenge. At first Audubon thought he might be able to use the shipping contacts Tom Bakewell and Nicholas Berthoud had formed in Louisville and Shippingport to obtain a job as a clerk aboard a steamboat. However, they rebuffed him, no doubt fearing he would vanish along the river and abandon his family.[191] Without support from his in-laws, Audubon fell back on the only other ability he had—his artistic skills. He began doing black chalk portraits of the residents of Shippingport and Louisville at five dollars per drawing and soon found that he had as many commissions as he could handle.[192] He supplemented this income with drawing lessons he advertised in the local paper.[193]

That autumn, while the Audubons were still being hosted by the Berthouds, Lucy delivered a daughter of "extreme loveliness." They named her Rose, in honor of Audubon's half sister. Audubon had planned to move his family into a small house he had rented in Louisville, but this was delayed when Lucy and little Rose contracted an autumn fever that swept through the community.[194]

Audubon began again to focus his attention on birds. He later recalled that he would sometimes forgo a commission "the profits of which would have supplied our wants for a week or more, to represent a little citizen of the feathered tribe." Given his family's desperate financial straits, this appears to be hyperbole crafted as part of his later attempt to shape his public image. It is more likely that he found time between portraits to return to his first love. His in-laws could not comprehend or appreciate his passion and considered it at least one of the reasons for the failure of his business.[195]

———————

In early 1820, just as Audubon seemed to have exhausted the local demand for chalk portraits and drawing lessons, he learned of an opportunity upriver in Cincinnati at the Western Museum.[196] The founder, Daniel Drake, M.D., was a prominent physician and naturalist who also served as a trustee of the recently established Cincinnati College. Drake had prevailed upon the college to set aside space for a museum, and he needed a skilled taxidermist and artist to prepare natural-history displays.[197] Audubon applied for the position with letters of recommendation from his illustrious friends, including one from Robert S. Todd of Lexington, whose two-year-old daughter, Mary, would grow up to wed Abraham Lincoln.[198] Audubon was hired at a monthly salary of $125 and prepared to leave Louisville to take his new position. However, his departure was marred by yet another family tragedy when his beloved little Rose died at seven months of age.[199]

During the first part of March, Audubon got settled in Cincinnati, a "flourishing place" of almost ten thousand residents, and then sent for Lucy and the boys.[200] He quickly found that the bleak economic times prevented the museum from honoring its commitment to pay him. Accepting Drake's assurance that he would be paid as soon as the museum had the money, Audubon agreed to continue working. At the same time, he realized that he would need to find another source of income. He returned to drawing chalk portraits and accepted a position as a drawing instructor at a local girls' school.[201] Lucy also began taking in students to help support the family.[202] At the end of June, Audubon was dismissed from his position at the museum and opened up his own art academy.[203]

A series of events that spring convinced Audubon and Lucy that his future lay with his passion. His drawings of America's avifauna were displayed at the Western Museum and received a glowing review in the *Cincinnati Inquisitor Advertiser*: "[W]e believe we hazard nothing in saying, there have been no exhibitions west of the mountains which can compare with them."[204] Then, in June, shortly before Audubon left his employment at the museum, Drake spoke to a gathering at the official opening of the museum and noted that Audubon's collection of bird illustrations now surpassed Alexander Wilson's in the variety of species he had depicted.[205] To Audubon and Lucy, the message was clear.[206]

By August, Audubon had formulated a plan for his future. On the 12th of that month, he wrote to U.S. Congressman Henry Clay of Kentucky, the Speaker of the House of Representatives, to request a letter of introduction for an expedition he intended to take to the territories southwest of the Mississippi River beginning around the middle of September. It was his intention, Audubon explained, to complete his collection of bird illustrations "with a view of Publishing them."[207]

Clay was only too happy to supply the requested letter, but in separate correspondence to Audubon cautioned, "Will it not be well for you before you commit Yourself to any great Expenses in the preparation and publication of your Contemplated Work to ascertain the Success which attended a Similar undertaking of M[r] Wilson?"[208]

Audubon was not deterred. On October 12, 1820, he left Cincinnati aboard a New Orleans-bound flatboat captained by Jacob Aumack, "a good Strong, Young Man, Generously Inclined rather Timorous on the River, Yet Brave, and accustomed to hardships."[209] Aumack's flatboat was lashed to a second flatboat captained by a man named Lovelace.[210]

Lacking the money for passage, Audubon had agreed to pay his way by supplying the party with fresh game. He had packed his chalks, watercolors, and paper along with his two portfolio cases. Audubon expected his hunting excursions on shore would enable him to procure new specimens to draw as the flatboats descended the river.[211] He was accompanied by Joseph Mason, a gifted eighteen-year-old botanical illustrator who was one of his art students.[212] Among the other passengers was Samuel Cumings, a civil engineer who was gathering information on the navigable channels of the Ohio and Mississippi Rivers. He would go on to publish an essential river guide, *The Western Navigator*, in 1822.[213]

The Ohio was running low, and it took the travelers almost two weeks to reach Henderson, which they passed at dawn on November 3. In his journal Audubon wrote, "I Looked on the Mill perhaps for the Last Time, and with thoughts that Made My Blood almost Cold bid it an eternal farewell."[214]

Two weeks later they were swept into the "Muddy Current" of the Mississippi River.[215] On December 10, they pulled out at a cutoff to the Arkansas River, and Audubon, Mason, Aumack, and a crewmember, Anthony Bodley, hiked upstream to the territorial capital known as the Arkansas Post.[216] According to Audubon, the old trading post had "flourished in the time that the Spaniards & French kept it," but now "the decrepid Visages of the Wornout Indian Traders and a few American famillies are all that gives it Life."[217]

The party began their return trek to the boats the next day. Four days later, they pushed off and reached Natchez, Mississippi, on December 26.[218] Audubon remained onboard drawing a Great-footed Hawk (Peregrine Falcon) that Aumack had shot on Christmas.[219] The following day, the artist got washed up before walking from the rough-and-tumble riverfront town where they had tied up, Natchez-under-the-Hill, to the genteel town of Natchez, situated on a bluff overlooking the river. "[T]here to my utmost surprise," he wrote, "I met Nicholas Berthoud, who accosted me kindly, and ask^d me to go down to New Orleans in his Boat." Audubon readily accepted both for himself and for Mason.[220]

They left Natchez on December 31 and were pulled downriver by the steamboat *Columbus*. But to Audubon's utter dismay, his small portfolio, which included fifteen "very Valuable Drawings" and a cherished miniature portrait he had done of Lucy, had been left on the dock by a slave while Berthoud's keelboat was being loaded. Audubon promptly drafted a letter to the proprietor of the Natchez Hotel where he had stayed with his brother-in-law, begging the innkeeper to send someone to hunt for it as well as place an advertisement in the local paper. However, he was under no illusion that it would be returned.[221] To the contrary, he told his journal, "no Hopes can I have of ever seing it, when Lost amongst 150 or 160 flat Boats and Houses filled with the Lowest of Caracters—No doubt My Drawings will serve to ornement their Parlours or will be nailed on Some of the Steering Oars."[222]

After a stop at the village of Bayou Sarah, Louisiana, the keelboat continued on its own power and landed in New Orleans on January 7, 1821. Audubon ran into David Prentice, the former Henderson mechanic, almost as soon as he stepped onto dry land. Prentice directed him to the office of the cotton merchants Gordon, Grant & Company, where he caught up with Berthoud and was introduced to Scottish-born Alexander Gordon, one of the partners. Meanwhile, Mason went off to explore the city, America's fifth largest, with a population of over twenty-seven thousand.[223] Despite its size, the city had yet to pave a single street.[224]

Audubon set about almost immediately to find a way to put some money in his empty pockets. Over the following days, he began making the rounds of the city's best known painters, hoping to enlist their help in procuring some work, if only as an assistant.[225] His lack of skill with oils made this problematic. One of the painters he called on, John Wesley Jarvis, gave his entreaty some consideration before rejecting it, bluntly telling Audubon "he could not believe, that I might help him in the Least." With Audubon's poverty magnifying his insecurities, he took the snub as a personal affront. But Audubon's facility with chalks soon began to attract commissions, for which he charged $25 apiece.[226] By January 29, he was able to send Lucy $270, along with a crate of Queen's ware to replace the family china she had been forced to give up in Henderson.[227]

However, Lucy was beginning to question her decision to let Audubon leave the family for seven or eight months to pursue his dream. Still in Cincinnati, she was finding it difficult to support herself and their growing children without his help.[228] Her earnings from teaching were barely enough for their subsistence.[229] And although she doggedly pursued the Western Museum for Audubon's unpaid salary, Dr. Drake was not immediately forthcoming.[230] She wrote Audubon a letter on the last day of 1820 that, as he confessed in his journal when it reached him in late January, "rufled My Spirits Sadly."[231]

In the early part of 1821, just about the time Audubon began to find his footing, Lucy decided to retreat with the boys to the safety of Shippingport, where Eliza had once again extended them her family's hospitality. It could not have been easy for Lucy to swallow her pride and accept the charity of her younger sister, but she had little choice.[232]

Meanwhile, Audubon had not lost sight of his purpose. He found southern Louisiana a rich source of birds for his portfolio. The New Orleans market, known as the Halles, was stocked each day with a wide variety of dead birds, although they were often either partially plucked or too mangled for him to draw. The earnings he made from his portraiture enabled him to hire a hunter at $25 per month to supply him with intact specimens from the surrounding forests and cypress swamps.[233] By the time Nicholas Berthoud left the city on February 22 to return home, Audubon was able to send Lucy twenty new drawings that he had completed since leaving Cincinnati.[234] These demonstrated a noticeable improvement in his technique over what he had produced during his time in Henderson.[235]

Deprived of accommodations aboard Berthoud's keelboat, Audubon and Mason rented quarters in a small house located at 34 Barracks Street. Audubon's intermittent journal entries over the next few weeks speak of the variety of birds he observed and collected as well as of the information he was able to gather from the city's residents about the local bird distribution.[236]

On March 16, he received a letter from Natchez with the gratifying news that his portfolio had been located. Alexander Gordon, whom Audubon barely knew, promptly wrote to a Natchez friend and asked him "to have it forwarded imediatly and pay whatever Charges there might be."[237] When the portfolio arrived on April 5, Audubon was delighted to find it in the same condition as when he had lost it, save for a single missing drawing.[238] He suggested later that the illustration had probably been taken as a commission by the person who had found the portfolio along the banks of the river.[239]

The recovery of his portfolio was not the only gratifying development in Audubon's life. He was equally enlivened by the prospect of joining a surveying expedition to the Pacific Ocean as part of the treaty whereby Spain ceded its Florida territory to the United States. When he read news on March 21 of the treaty's ratification, Audubon's attention was drawn to a provision in the agreement that required the parties to draw the western boundary line separating the two countries. An expedition for this purpose was to leave Natchitoches, Louisiana, within the course of the year.[240] Audubon had been looking for an opportunity to explore parts of the country where the avifauna had yet to be catalogued, and he threw himself with his typical frenetic fervor into soliciting political support for an appointment as "Draftsman for this So Long wished for Journey."[241]

One of the eminent persons he called upon for a letter of recommendation was John Vanderlyn, a well-known and accomplished portrait and historical painter.[242] The thin-skinned Audubon bristled at what he considered to be Vanderlyn's shabby treatment when he arrived at the artist's studio, but he badly wanted Vanderlyn's endorsement.[243] And, when Vanderlyn finally examined Audubon's drawings, he pronounced them "handsomely done." Vanderlyn was less complimentary about one of Audubon's chalk images.[244] However, the letter Vanderlyn wrote out and handed him praised his compositions, "Which appear to be done with great truth & accuracy of representation as much so, as any I have seen in any Country."[245]

Alexander Gordon, a "truly Kind Gentleman," encouraged Audubon to petition President Madison directly for appointment to the expedition and helped with the language in his correspondence. Louisiana Governor Thomas Robertson, with whom Audubon dined on May 8, also drafted a letter on his behalf.[246]

Audubon's extended family apparently did not share his enthusiasm for a western journey that would allow him to continue to shirk his familial duties. He had written to Nicholas Berthoud shortly after learning of the expedition "to request his Imediate assistance" but was still waiting for a response in early May. In his journal entry of May 6 he expressed surprise "at having Nothing from N. Berthoud."[247] He unleashed a torrent of hard feelings toward his brother-in-law when he drafted a long letter to Lucy over a number of days at the end of the month.[248] Alluding to Berthoud's refusal to help him find work when he had arrived in Louisville the year before and now this, Audubon wrote, "[H]is silence on the second aid I have been fool enough to ask of him since I have *fooled* what I had—Gaggs me."[249]

Lucy had evidently resigned herself to his continued absence. In an April 1 letter, she informed her English cousin Euphemia Gifford that Audubon was "on a tour" looking for birds as part of his prosecution of a "large work on Ornithology" and that he was not expected to return for another year. She mentioned that she was giving some thought to how she could continue to support herself in the interim and suggested she might take up housekeeping work or return to Cincinnati, where the cost of living was lower.[250]

But Lucy's letters to Audubon reflected a growing bitterness about her circumstances. In May she wrote him asking again for money and made it clear that she did not want him to return to Kentucky until his financial condition had improved.[251] It was hard enough for her to be around her sister Eliza's well-to-do husband and to witness the success that her brother Tom had achieved since moving to Louisville, without being further humiliated by her own husband's failures.[252] She also made it plain that she was unwilling to leave the security of her sister's home until he could once again support her and the children.[253]

Audubon, whose anger and hurt spilled out through his pen, suggested in response that she "probably would be better pleased should I never return—and so it may be."[254] The next day, the first of June, his emotional fires had abated, and he added a brief apology before sending the letter off: "I am sorry of the last part I wrote yesterday, but I then felt miserable. I hope thou wilt look on it as a momentary incident. I love thee so dearly, I feel it so powerfully that I cannot bear anything from thee that has the appearance of coolness."[255]

On June 16, Audubon and Mason found themselves heading 125 miles upriver aboard the steamboat *Columbus* to Oakley House, a 3,100-acre cotton plantation owned by James and Lucretia Pirrie in West Feliciana Parish near Bayou Sarah, Louisiana. Audubon had been giving their fifteen-year-old daughter, Eliza, drawing lessons in New Orleans and was hired by Mrs. Pirrie at a monthly salary of $60 to continue her instruction in art, music, and dancing during the family's stay at Oakley during the summer and fall.[256]

The arrangement was an ideal one for Audubon. It committed him to tutoring Eliza for only half of each day, leaving him ample time to devote to supplementing his drawings.[257] After he and Mason reached their destination on the 18th, they quickly discovered that the area was an ornithological oasis abounding with thrushes, flycatchers, orioles, buntings, warblers, and a multitude of other birds.[258] The ensuing months were productive ones as Audubon went on to complete twenty-two images of the area's avifauna, complemented by Mason's exquisite illustrations of trees, plants, and flowers.[259]

He was discharged by Mrs. Pirrie on October 10 after Eliza fell ill and the young physician who attended her recommended she not resume their lessons "untill some Months."[260] It appears that there was more to the story than Audubon recorded in his journal.[261] Nevertheless, Audubon beseeched Mrs. Pirrie to allow them to remain several days "as visitors" so that he could continue working on his drawings and finish compiling the notes of his field observations.[262] She consented, although their stay ended in acrimony when Audubon sought to bill her for ten days that Eliza had been sick.[263] The two itinerant artists left Oakley on October 21, bound again for New Orleans.[264]

Within days of their arrival, Audubon rented a small cottage at 55 Dauphine Street where he hoped to greet his family.[265] He spent the next several weeks dividing his time between giving drawing lessons and portraying the specimens that were being collected by his hired hunters. He urged Lucy to join him and, on November 24, sent her money for steamboat passage to New Orleans. When he received a letter from her on December 1 announcing they would be arriving "in a few days," he was elated. But as each day came and went, Audubon became increasingly anxious. Finally, at noon on December 18, Lucy and the boys stepped off the steamboat *Rocket* and into his arms.[266] "[A]fter 14 Months absence the Meeting of all that renders Life agreable to Me, was gratefully Wellcome and I thanked My Maker for this Mark of Mercy."[267]

The following day, Audubon looked over the drawings that Lucy had brought with her, including those he had sent north the previous February with Nicholas Berthoud. Comparing them to his much improved recent output, he found them wanting.[268] During this period, Audubon was gradually perfecting a multimedia technique in which he used a combination of pencil, pastel, gouache, and transparent watercolor to render not only the images of the birds he was drawing but also the feel of the species' individual physical structures.[269] But, more than that, he was beginning to master the skill of injecting a feeling of vitality and movement into his compositions. He realized that he would have to redraw many of his earlier illustrations.[270] At year's end, as he finished a drawing of a Ferruginous Thrush (Brown Thrasher), he resolved to complete another ninety-nine drawings in as many days.[271]

The first few months of 1822 found Audubon actively engaged at his craft. He continued to offer instruction in drawing and painting, which earned him just enough to support his family and send Victor and John to a local school. However, he could not afford to purchase a new journal for the year until March.[272] And, as he recounted in his journal, "Every moment I had to spare I drew birds for my ornithology, in which my Lucy and myself alone have faith."[273]

In March, Audubon accepted employment upriver in Natchez with a family who wanted him to instruct their teenage daughter in drawing, music, and French.[274] He left New Orleans accompanied by Joseph Mason on March 16. Lucy and the boys stayed behind and moved into the home of William Brand, a prosperous New Orleans architect and builder for whom Lucy had been working both as a governess to his son and as a companion for his pregnant wife, Anne, who was near term.[275]

By mid-May, Audubon was hired as a drawing instructor at Elizabeth Female Academy, a girls' school in Washington, Mississippi, about eight miles distant, and was making the trip from Natchez on foot each day.[276] Victor and John soon joined him and were sent to school at Brevost Academy, a recently established school in Natchez.[277] When Audubon contracted yellow fever in July, a newly minted friend, Dr. William Provan, paid for the boys' tuition while Audubon recovered.[278] His health restored, Audubon was offered a post at Brevost Academy, which he accepted.[279]

On July 23, Audubon said farewell to Joseph Mason, who had decided to return to Cincinnati.[280] The two had grown close over the past two years, and Audubon confided in his journal that "we experienced great pain at parting."[281]

Audubon welcomed Lucy to Natchez in early September.[282] The Brands' infant had died the previous month, and Lucy was eager to be reunited with her family.[283] She initially took a position as a governess with a local family but quit when they could not pay her.[284] In October, a Natchez paper, the *Mississippi State Gazette*, carried advertisements for Lucy's services as a tutor to young women and for Audubon's classes in drawing and singing "at Mr. Davis' Seminary."[285]

That December, Audubon met John Steen, a traveling portrait painter from Pennsylvania who had stopped in Natchez looking for business. In exchange for lessons in pastel, Steen provided Audubon with his first instruction in oil painting.[286]

In early 1823, Lucy moved with ten-year-old John to Beech Woods, a sizable plantation of over two thousand acres near Bayou Sarah, to serve as a teacher for the children of a wealthy, strong-willed widow named Jane Middlemist Percy. It was a stable, well-paid position, and Lucy was anxious to equip her husband with the funds necessary to travel to Europe to develop his skill as an oil painter. In the school she opened for the four Percy offspring, she also offered instruction to the families of neighboring plantation holders.[287]

Audubon, now partnered with Steen, remained in Natchez with thirteen-year-old Victor.[288] In February, the two artists attempted to attract commissions with advertisements in the *Mississippi State Gazette*. Business being slow, they left Natchez in March with plans to travel by a horse-drawn wagon through parts of Mississippi and Louisiana, offering their services to wealthy plantation families.[289]

The partnership did not last, and Audubon and Victor moved into Lucy's cottage at Beech Woods later that spring. At Mrs. Percy's request, Audubon agreed to provide instruction in music and drawing to the schoolchildren. Meanwhile, he continued to try his hand at oils.[290] He painted his sons and completed a brooding self-portrait using the new medium.[291] Seeing these, Mrs. Percy asked him to paint two of her daughters, but he struggled to find the right color mix to match their complexions. Mrs. Percy strongly disapproved of how he had depicted them. Audubon's sensitivities were inflamed, there was an ugly confrontation between the two, and Mrs. Percy demanded he leave the plantation. When he tried to sneak back a few days later to spend the night with Lucy, Mrs. Percy was alerted by a servant. She burst into the cottage and ordered Audubon out of bed and off her property for good.[292]

With Victor in tow, Audubon returned to Natchez, where he obtained a $300 commission to paint an oil landscape of the town. However, he was denied the promised compensation when the woman who had hired him died.[293]

In August, Audubon and Victor contracted yellow fever, and Lucy hastened to their bedsides to care for them. She returned with them in early September to Beech Woods, where Mrs. Percy, anxious to have her governess back, had invited father and son to recuperate. By the end of the month, the two had recovered sufficiently that Audubon made plans to travel to Philadelphia, where he hoped to find a teaching position.[294] But he forwarded his drawings and obviously wanted to see how they were received in the heart of American science and publishing.[295] He intended to take Victor with him to Shippingport, where Nicholas Berthoud had agreed to employ the fourteen-year-old as an apprentice in his counting house.[296]

They left Bayou Sarah on October 3 aboard the *Magnet*, a steamboat constructed by Tom Bakewell's firm.[297] The vessel could not ascend the Ohio River because of low water, so Audubon and Victor traveled the remaining 250 miles to Louisville on foot.[298] As he approached his former home, Audubon felt utterly defeated by life. He had only $13 dollars in his pocket when he reached the city on October 25, and no promise of a brighter future.[299] Asked by a fellow passenger aboard the steamer for a letter of introduction to Ferdinand Rozier in Ste. Genevieve, Audubon opened his soul to his old friend:

> I am yet My Dear Rozier on the Wing & God only knows how Long I may yet remain so — I am now bound to Shippingport to see if I can through my *former Friends* there, bring about some changes in My situation — I am now rather Wearied of the World. I have I believe seen too much of it — [300]

His four-month stay in Shippingport did little to change his mood or his prospects. His in-laws again offered little support, and he spent his time scrounging for odd jobs as a painter, doing everything from landscapes on the walls of newly built steamboats to the lettering on commercial signs.[301]

By early March 1824, Audubon was ready to continue his journey. Climbing aboard a steamboat bound for Pittsburgh, he fastened his eyes and his hopes on Philadelphia. He arrived on April 5 and, after picking up his portfolio and purchasing a new suit, paid a visit to Dr. James Mease. During Audubon's time at Mill Grove, Mease had been a frequent visitor to Fatland Ford, where Audubon first met him in 1804. The fifty-two-year-old physician and author was a leading light among Philadelphia's intellectual class. As a founder of the Philadelphia Athenaeum and curator of the American Philosophical Society, he was particularly well positioned to introduce his old acquaintance to the city's important men of science and the arts.[302]

Mease took Audubon to meet Thomas Sully, only two years older than Audubon but already recognized as among America's preeminent portrait painters. Sully examined Audubon's portfolio and came away impressed. He agreed to instruct the naturalist further in the use of oils in exchange for lessons for his daughter in pastels and watercolors.[303]

On April 10, Mease introduced Audubon to Charles-Lucien Bonaparte, the twenty-year-old nephew of the late French emperor, Napoleon Bonaparte.[304] The young Prince of Canino and Musignano, two Italian principalities, had arrived in America the previous September and quickly distinguished himself as a serious student of ornithology.[305] He had been elected a member of the prestigious Academy of Natural Sciences of Philadelphia and was already working on an update of Alexander Wilson's *American Ornithology*, with a revised taxonomy and illustrations of new species discovered over the last decade.[306]

Told that Audubon had put together a portfolio of bird illustrations, Bonaparte probably expected to see images similar to those that marked Wilson's work—birds shown at a reduced scale and drawn stiffly in profile against a plain background. What he discovered as Audubon opened the thick cover of the portfolio and began to slowly turn the pages must have astonished him. Here were life-sized birds as they existed in nature—swooping, soaring, feeding, fighting, living.[307]

Bonaparte was eager to give Audubon's drawings a wider audience and invited him to show them before a meeting of the Academy of Natural Sciences of Philadelphia on the evening of Tuesday, April 13.[308] In view of the warm reception Audubon had received during his first week in the city, he undoubtedly thought that the members of the academy would similarly applaud his efforts and bestow the recognition he craved after years of sacrifice and want.

However, Audubon did not fully comprehend the makeup of this learned group of men. He brashly declared the superiority of his drawings to those of Wilson, utterly failing to appreciate the degree to which Wilson was revered in Philadelphia for his pioneering work. The Scotsman still had many friends who had no wish to see his legacy supplanted by an uneducated backwoodsman with a brush.[309] Some also had a vested interest in maintaining Wilson's primacy. Chief among these was the caustic, arrogant vice president of the academy, George Ord, a well-to-do Englishman who had served as Wilson's executor and had posthumously published the last two volumes of *American Ornithology*.[310] Ord was in the process of bringing out a new edition of Wilson's work.[311] Not surprisingly, he took an immediate dislike to Audubon and openly criticized the quality and accuracy of the drawings.[312]

So too did Alexander Lawson, one of Philadelphia's finest engravers. Lawson was a close friend of Wilson's and had engraved his birds for publication. He was now working on the illustrations being done for Bonaparte's work by Titian Ramsey Peale and Alexander Rider. Bonaparte brought Audubon to Lawson's home on the morning of April 14 to show the engraver his drawings.[313] Lawson acknowledged that they were "very extraordinary" for one who was untaught but told his patron that he would not engrave them.[314] According to Audubon's journal, the engraver found the pastels to be "too soft, too much like oil paintings."[315] Lawson later provided his recollections of their initial encounter to William Dunlap, a chronicler of the arts in America, during an interview in 1833:[316]

> Lawson told me that he spoke freely of the pictures, and said that they were ill drawn, not true to nature, and anatomically incorrect. Audubon said nothing. Bonaparte defended them, and said he would buy them, and Lawson should engrave them. "You may buy them," said the Scotchman, "but I will not engrave them." "Why not?" "Because ornithology requires truth in forms, and correctness in the lines. Here are neither." In short, he refused to be employed as the engraver, and Audubon departed with the admirer who had brought him. During this visit Lawson said that Audubon did not once speak to him.[317]

Lawson, like Ord, came to believe that Audubon was "a liar & imposter."[318] This was due, at least in part, to a falling-out that Audubon had with his erstwhile student and companion, Joseph Mason. Now living in Philadelphia and working as an artist at the Botanic Garden, Mason came to see Audubon on May 30.[319] Audubon recorded the meeting in his journal and described it as "a delightful visit."[320] But Mason determined that Audubon no longer intended to abide by an earlier promise to share the credit for the drawings they had done together.[321] No doubt hurt and embittered, Mason let it be known around town that he had drawn many of the botanical images that Audubon was now claiming as his own.[322] Ord was also not shy about brandishing Wilson's 1810 journal, which he now held, and pointing out to his colleagues that the entries did not substantiate Audubon's claim to having assisted Wilson during his visit to Louisville.[323]

The criticism leveled at Audubon had no immediate impact on Bonaparte. He remained among Audubon's strongest advocates, although the extent to which this was dictated by self-interest is not entirely clear. Bonaparte obviously hoped to benefit from the rich contents of Audubon's portfolio as well as his intimate knowledge of bird behavior. He even proposed a joint publication, with Audubon supplying the illustrations while he contributed the ornithological text.[324] This idea went nowhere.[325] However, Audubon did agree to provide him with some notes of his observations, and he sold Bonaparte a drawing of a pair of Great Crow Blackbirds (Boat-tailed Grackles) for use in his update of Wilson's publication.[326]

Others in the Philadelphia scientific community also embraced the obviously talented French-American. Richard Harlan, M.D., a young Quaker physician and naturalist, became a lifelong friend and supporter.[327] Audubon called him "one of the best men I have met with in the city, and the very best among the naturalists."[328] Charles-Alexandre Lesueur, Reuben Haines, and Isaiah Lukens jointly nominated him to become a member of the Academy of Natural Sciences of Philadelphia on

July 27.[329] However, with a unanimous vote required and the academy divided on the merits of his accomplishments as a result of Ord's whisper campaign, Audubon was denied membership.[330]

In July, Audubon met and developed what became an enduring friendship with Edward Harris, a wealthy twenty-four-year-old farmer and amateur naturalist from Moorestown, New Jersey.[331] On July 19, Harris agreed to purchase all the early draw-ings that Audubon had failed to sell during an exhibition of his work.[332] Audubon was delighted. "I would have kissed him, but that it is not the custom in this icy city," he exclaimed in his journal.[333] Harris turned down an offer to acquire Audubon's painting of the Falls of the Ohio at a reduced price but pressed a hundred-dollar note into the naturalist's hand, saying, "Mr. Audubon, accept this from me; men like you ought not to want for money."[334] In gratitude, Audubon gave Harris the draw-ings he made for Lucy during his visit to France from 1805 to 1806.[335]

By July 31, Audubon was ready to leave Philadelphia for New York City. His hopes for scientific acceptance, if not acclaim, had been crushed. As he noted in an earlier journal entry, "Those interested in Wilson's book on the American birds advised me not to publish, and not only cold water, but ice, was poured upon my undertaking." But he also received encouragement from men who greatly ad-mired his work and urged him to take his drawings abroad to be published. The Philadelphia engraver Gideon Fairman recommended he "go to England, to have them engraved in a superior manner."[336] So did naturalist and conchologist Henry McMurtrie, M.D.[337] Bonaparte and the French consul both advised him to consider publishing in France.[338]

Audubon arrived in New York by stage on August 1.[339] Word of the charges made by Joseph Mason, perhaps spread by George Ord, had preceded him, and he found no interest among New York publishers.[340] But Samuel L. Mitchill, M.D., an old friend from his clerking days who had since founded the Lyceum of Natural His-tory of New-York, helped open the doors of that institution to membership and an exhibition of his drawings.[341]

Audubon left on August 15 on a steamer heading up the Hudson River, bound for Albany. Over the next six days, he made his way across upstate New York via canal boat on the Erie Canal to Rochester and reached Buffalo on August 24, where he stopped to witness the grandeur of Niagara Falls. From there he took a schooner across Lake Erie to Erie, Pennsylvania, and, after a stop in Meadville, Pennsylvania, reached Pittsburgh on foot on September 7. He announced to his journal that he "was more politely received than on former occasions," a likely reference to his wel-come by Benjamin Bakewell's family, which had apparently heard favorable reports of his visit to Philadelphia.[342]

He remained in Pittsburgh for seven weeks, waiting for the water to rise in the

Ohio River. During this time, he gave drawing lessons and painted an occasional portrait while also "scouring the country for birds."[343] Among the images he produced during his stay was a pair of the now extinct Passenger Pigeon.[344]

Audubon resumed his journey on October 24, heading downriver to Cincinnati.[345] He visited "many old friends," but there is no record that he paid a call on Tom Bakewell, who had moved to Cincinnati earlier that year and started a new foundry in partnership with Alexander Gordon, the New Orleans merchant.[346] Gordon was now part of the extended Bakewell family, having married Lucy's youngest sister, Ann, in Louisville on May 3, 1823.[347] Gordon had since cooled to his former acquaintance and evidently decided that his penniless in-law was a ne'er-do-well.[348]

Again short on cash, Audubon managed to borrow $15 from a local merchant who knew him. He used a portion of the funds to pay for deck passage to Louisville, where he arrived on November 20. He checked on Victor in Shippingport and then boarded a steamboat for New Orleans, arriving at Bayou Sarah near midnight toward month's end. Eager to be reunited with Lucy and John, he borrowed a horse and made his way through the dark woods, losing his way but arriving at Beech Woods after dawn.[349] "It was early," he wrote, "but I found my beloved wife up and engaged in giving lessons to her pupils, and, holding and kissing her, I was once more happy, and all my toils and trials were forgotten."[350]

Audubon and Lucy now understood that his only chance to realize his dream was to take his drawings abroad to Europe. He spent the ensuing seventeen months at Beech Woods focused on adding new drawings to his collection.[351] On many of his forays into the Louisiana forests and swamps in search of specimens, he was accompanied by Nathaniel Wells Pope, M.D., his former Kentucky clerk, who had married the daughter of a West Feliciana Parish planter in 1823 and opened up a medical practice in St. Francisville, near Bayou Sarah.[352]

Audubon was now at the height of his artistic powers. Some of his compositions, including the Wild Turkey cock and the Mockingbird, are among his very best. In addition to expanding his portfolio, he provided instruction in drawing, French, and music at Beech Woods.[353] He also raised funds for his planned trip by giving lessons in dancing, both at Beech Woods and in nearby Woodville, Mississippi.[354]

By April 1826, Audubon had completed his preparations. He left Beech Woods and the embrace of Lucy and thirteen-year-old John on April 25.[355] He was carrying almost $1,900, the equivalent of roughly $46,500 in 2016 dollars, which he and Lucy had managed to set aside.[356] The following day, his forty-first birthday, he hopped aboard a steamboat at Bayou Sarah with his luggage and two portfolios and headed downriver to New Orleans.[357]

Arriving on April 27, he booked passage aboard the *Delos*, a ship out of Kennebunk, Maine, that was bound for Liverpool with a cargo of cotton bales.[358] He soon learned the vessel would not sail for several days, so he returned to Beech Woods for a two-day visit to say his final goodbyes and receive a last dose of encouragement from Lucy.[359]

Once back in New Orleans, he obtained letters of introduction from Louisiana governor Henry S. Johnson and his old friend, the cotton merchant Vincent Nolte, among others.[360] Nolte's letter to Richard Rathbone, a partner in Rathbone Brothers & Co., a major Liverpool cotton firm, praised Audubon's "Collection of upwards of 400 Drawings, which far surpass any thing of the kind I have yet seen."[361]

The *Delos* pulled away from the New Orleans docks as the sun was setting on the evening of May 17.[362] She was towed downriver by the *Hercules*, a steamboat built in Cincinnati by Tom Bakewell's company and jointly owned by Bakewell, Nicholas Berthoud, and Alexander Gordon's mercantile concern, Gordon, Forstall & Co. Ten hours later, the *Delos* reached the Gulf of Mexico.[363] Over the next nine weeks, the vessel made her way slowly through the summer doldrums of the gulf, past Cuba, and then, with sails full, northeast to the Grand Banks off Newfoundland and across the Atlantic.[364]

With little to do during the voyage, Audubon developed an affection for spirits. One of the passengers had brought along some American porter and eleven gallons of whiskey, which they sampled along the way.[365] The *Delos* finally reached Liverpool on the night of Thursday, July 20, and anchored in the Mersey River. From the deck, Audubon could look across the water and see the city's gas lamps holding back the gloom.[366] He could only hope that he would be able to find an equally well-lit path to achieve his audacious goal.

2

The Birds of America

1826–1833

[I]t is the most magnificent monument which has yet been made to ornithology.
BARON GEORGES CUVIER

Filled with a mixture of apprehension and excitement, Audubon stepped foot on English soil on Friday morning, July 21. He left the commotion of the docks behind and made his way through a steady rain and the dirty Liverpool air, thick with coal smoke, to the Exchange Building, where Gordon, Forstall & Co. had its offices.[1] He was carrying letters to Alexander Gordon from a New Orleans merchant, Charles Briggs, and was anxious to put them in his brother-in-law's hands. Gordon was not expecting him and seemingly had no idea who he was at first. With a face tanned and hair grown long from weeks at sea, dressed in the clothes and baggy trousers of a provincial, Audubon was almost unrecognizable. However, it is unlikely he would have been granted access to his brother-in-law's offices without giving his name. Rather, the staid businessman apparently pretended not to know him in the hope he might depart. Audubon made no move to leave and, as he was just about to speak, Gordon finally acknowledged him. But it was a very cold reception.[2]

Like the rest of the Bakewell clan, who were contemptuous of Audubon's grandiose scheme and felt that he had unfairly placed the burden of supporting his family on Lucy's slender shoulders, Gordon wanted nothing to do with him.[3] He pointedly withheld an invitation for Audubon to pay a visit to his residence to see Lucy's sister Ann by not giving the naturalist his calling card.[4] Moreover, as Audubon took his leave, Gordon told him curtly not to call on him again.[5] Back that night at the Commercial Inn on Dale Street where he had taken a room, Audubon acknowledged in the journal he was keeping for Lucy that he had been mistreated, "but it must be endured, and yet what have I done–Ah, that is no riddle, my Friend, I have grown poor."[6]

Indignant but brimming with determination, Audubon retraced his steps to Gordon's offices on Saturday morning to seek their assistance with customs in retrieving his portfolios. Gordon's demeanor had not changed, but he did offer Audubon his card, albeit grudgingly, and directed an assistant to accompany his brother-in-law to the Custom House.[7]

Audubon's reception by Richard Rathbone was considerably warmer. Rathbone

had been unavailable when Audubon had dropped by his firm with Vincent Nolte's introductory letter on Friday.[8] However, on Saturday morning, a message from the prominent Quaker businessman was delivered to Audubon's hotel with an invitation to join him and William Roscoe, one of Liverpool's most eminent figures, for dinner on Wednesday evening.[9] Audubon was too eager to wait. On Monday morning, he called first at Rathbone's home and, when informed that the gentleman had already left for work, hastened to his counting house at the Salt Dock.[10] The thirty-seven-year-old cotton merchant treated him *"as a Brother ought to do"* and asked him to dine that afternoon with his family.[11]

The next day, July 25, Audubon was invited to accompany Rathbone and his wife to Greenbank, the country estate of Rathbone's widowed mother, Mrs. William Rathbone IV, whom Audubon soon dubbed the "Queen Bee."[12] Surrounded by several guests and a younger member of the family, likely Rathbone's attractive, un-married sister, Hannah Mary, Audubon felt awkward and shy as he generally did with strangers.[13] But he had been asked to show his portfolio, and after nervously unbuckling the ties and opening the thick covers to display the contents for the first time to an English audience, he was greeted with enthusiastic praise.[14] On Wednes-day, July 26, Rathbone introduced Audubon to his older brother, William, the man-aging partner of the family concern, who extended an invitation to dinner on Friday night and just as quickly took the naturalist to his bosom.[15]

The Rathbone family was respected, prosperous, and extremely well connected. They agreed to place their formidable name and reputation behind him, introducing him to their wide circle of influential friends in Liverpool and throughout England as a means of soliciting support for his ambitious project.[16] As the month of July came to an end, a mere ten days after his arrival, Audubon was being lionized by Liverpool society and had opened an exhibition of his drawings to fawning crowds at the Liverpool Royal Institution.[17] Witnessing these remarkable events, even the Gordons softened, and he was welcomed into their home on Norton Street.[18]

The exhibition, which was open but a week and was free to the public, drew a sizable crowd each day.[19] It was so popular that people traveled from as far away as Manchester to see it.[20] Several members of the institution, including William Roscoe and its president, Dr. Thomas Stewart Traill, urged Audubon to charge admission.[21] He was ambivalent, desirous of the income but preferring to be known as a naturalist instead of as a showman.[22] Roscoe's counsel eventually prevailed, and at his behest a committee of the institution passed a resolution asking Audubon to reopen the ex-hibit with a cover charge of a shilling.[23] When the paid show closed in early Septem-ber after a four-week run, Audubon had made a badly needed £100.[24]

The timing of Audubon's visit to England was unexpectedly propitious. There was a renewed interest among the country's well-to-do in the subject of natural history.[25] Moreover, James Fenimore Cooper had just published *The Last of the Mohicans* in London, and the British public was absorbed by his tales of life on the American frontier.[26] With Audubon's shoulder-length hair slicked back with bear grease, an intimate knowledge of woodcraft acquired from years of hunting in the wilds, and an unassuming manner that Richard Rathbone aptly described as "*simple Intelligent*," this American import had seemingly stepped out of the pages of Cooper's novel.[27]

At social gatherings, he would entertain guests with bird calls and Indian war cries.[28] He began to style himself the "American Woodsman" and shrewdly declined to cut his locks or replace his unfashionable clothing despite the urging of Ann Gordon.[29] Walking briskly through the streets of the city, Audubon attracted attention everywhere he went, as a young admirer and frequent guest at Greenbank, Henry Fothergill Chorley, recalled decades later:

> The man also was not a man to be seen and forgotten, or passed on the pavement without glances of surprise and scrutiny. The tall and somewhat stooping form, the clothes not made by a West-end but by a Far West tailor, the steady, rapid, springing step, the long hair, the aquiline features, and the glowing angry eyes, — the expression of a handsome man conscious of ceasing to be young, and an air and manner which told you that whoever you might be he was John Audubon, will never be forgotten by anyone who knew or saw him.[30]

Despite the near-celebrity status he enjoyed in Liverpool, Audubon was plagued by self-doubt. The trials and disappointments that marked his adult life had robbed him of the cocky swagger of his youth. Now, he questioned his good fortune and silently feared he would be labeled an "impostor" as he had been in Philadelphia.[31] He confided these truths to Lucy in the pages of his journal, but he had not heard a word from his beloved since his arrival.[32] The constant anxiety of not knowing if she and their sons were still in good health wore on his soul and, on some nights, brought him to tears.[33] He found solace at Greenbank, where the warm and lively Rathbone family welcomed him and made him feel at ease.[34]

When September came, Audubon decided it was time to take the next step toward his avowed goal of publication. He had been advised by those whose opinions he respected that he should tour the major cities of England and Scotland, exhibiting his drawings as he went, so that he could make himself known and best determine where they could be published.[35] On September 10, he clambered aboard a coach for the thirty-eight-mile trip to the industrial city of Manchester, where he hoped to repeat his auspicious reception in Liverpool.[36] A pocketbook given to him by the wife of William Rathbone held a thick packet of letters designed by his many Liverpool friends to open the doors of the privileged and learned across England and Scotland.[37]

However, Audubon found that, overall, Manchester had little interest in his portfolio. A two-week exhibition of 240 of his drawings at the Exchange Building did not attract large enough crowds to even cover his expenses.[38] He looked to reduce his costs by moving the exhibit to free quarters offered by the Manchester Natural History Society.[39] But he also decided to retreat to Liverpool for a brief visit to seek the counsel of the Rathbones and William Roscoe about advancing his project.[40] Regardless, his stay in Manchester had its bright spots. He formed some fast friendships, as he invariably did, and finally received two letters from Lucy, dated May 28 and June 3, which confirmed she was well.[41]

Audubon boarded the coach for Liverpool on September 28 and received a genial welcome that evening at Greenbank.[42] The next day, Dr. Traill introduced him to Henry G. Bohn, a successful London bookseller who recommended that Audubon go immediately to London, as well as to Paris, to identify which city would be best suited to publish his work.[43] Then he advised Audubon to issue a prospectus and come out with a Number, consisting of the first several of his engraved drawings, to show prospective subscribers a sample. Although Bohn was not familiar with Audubon's illustrations, which were still on display in Manchester, he thought the naturalist would "succeed and do well."[44]

However, the bookman cautioned that the English market would not reward Audubon if he insisted on publishing them at life size, as he had long desired, because the volumes would be overwhelming "and bring shame on other works, or encumber the table" on which they sat.[45] At most, Bohn indicated, they should be twice the size of Alexander Wilson's work, which was imperial quarto ($10\frac{3}{8}'' \times 13\frac{3}{4}''$). Then, Bohn confidently predicted, they would sell a thousand copies.[46] Audubon's friends concurred, and Audubon resolved to "follow this Plan and no other untill I find it impossible to succeed."[47]

After a full week in Liverpool, Audubon set off on October 6 for Manchester in one of the Rathbones' carriages.[48] He was accompanied by the Queen Bee and her daughter, Hannah Mary, who intended to visit friends and relatives in the nearby city.[49] In the previous two months, Audubon had formed a particularly close attachment to the beguiling thirty-five-year-old Hannah Mary.[50] He relished their moments together, bestowed on her his attention, and spoke to his journal of her "Dazzling" dark eyes.[51] He had always been flirtatious with attractive women, another way he tried to feed his insatiable ego. Reading between the lines of his journal, there can be little doubt that he was smitten. However, their relationship was evidently never more than platonic, although there are strong hints that he wished otherwise.[52] As a proper English lady, she would never allow it, and Audubon must have known he could not risk a scandal.[53]

On their arrival later that day, Audubon went to the Natural History Society and was chagrined to find the doorman at his exhibition had consumed "too much Irish Whiskey to Look with care on American Birds."[54] The man was promptly terminated.[55] On October 10, Henry Bohn stopped by the show and, after viewing Audubon's drawings for the first time, had a change of heart.[56] He advised the naturalist "to publish them the full Size of Life" and thought they would prove a success.[57]

A fortnight later, following a brief tour with the Rathbone women and some of their relatives of the Derbyshire countryside where Lucy had grown up, Audubon boarded an early-morning stage for Edinburgh, Scotland.[58] He had decided to defer an immediate assault on London, as Bohn had suggested, in favor of a two-week visit to the heart of Scottish science and learning. His confidence had been shaken by the weak reception his drawings had received in Manchester. A visit to Edinburgh would give him an opportunity to replenish his courage while postponing, however briefly, the sizable challenges he knew were waiting for him in the giant metropolis to the south.[59]

Riding through the changing English landscape on a "Clear & beautifull" day, he lamented the fact he was leaving Manchester poorer than when he had arrived.[60] But he had expanded his circle of friends still further and collected an additional sheath of letters to introduce him to those who might support his efforts.[61]

The stage reached the "Splendid City," as Audubon nicknamed Edinburgh, at 11:00 p.m. on Wednesday, October 25, and clattered through the gaslit streets to the terminus at the Black Bull Inn.[62] Over the next two days, Audubon walked around the picturesque city above the Firth of Forth, delivering his letters of introduction to such luminaries as Robert Jameson, who was the Regius Professor of Natural History at the University of Edinburgh and founder and president of the Wernerian Natural History Society; and Patrick Neill, the society's secretary, whose printing business was located in Fish Market Close in the city's Old Town section.[63]

When few of the recipients had returned his call by October 30, the impatient naturalist strode off to Neill's office to complain about the lack of interest shown by the city's scientific establishment.[64] Neill offered reassurances, but when the two men went to visit "one of the most scientific men" in the city and found him indifferent, Neill decided to take Audubon to see Scotland's finest engraver, William Home Lizars.[65]

The thirty-eight-year-old Lizars, who had begun his career as an artist, was then in the midst of publishing a major illustrated work on British birds by the Northumberland naturalist Prideaux John Selby.[66] Lizars somewhat reluctantly agreed to return with Audubon to his rooms at No. 2 George Street in the city's New Town section to examine his drawings.[67] Sharing an umbrella with Audubon along the way, the engraver could not stop talking about Selby's work.[68] However, when Audubon opened his portfolio and turned up the first image, Lizars was transfixed, declaring, "My God, I never saw any thing like this before."[69]

Lizars immediately wrote letters to Selby and his collaborator, Sir William Jardine, urging them to come to see Audubon's illustrations.[70] The following day, Lizars came back with Prof. Jameson, who joined the engraver in extolling Audubon's birds and, a day later at breakfast, promised his "Powerfull assisstance."[71]

On November 2, Audubon treated Lizars to a showing of his largest drawings — the two Mockingbird pairs battling a rattlesnake that had reached one of their nests; the elegant male Wild Turkey striding through a Louisiana canebreak; the female of the species on a separate sheet being followed by her inquisitive poults; a covey of Virginia Partridges (Bobwhites) scattering in terror before a diving immature Red-shouldered Hawk; and a Whooping Crane bowing gracefully to the ground to dine on newly hatched alligators.[72] All were, in the engraver's view, "Wonderfull productions."[73] At first he spoke of engraving the composition of the partridges. But when he saw a pair of Great-footed Hawks (Peregrine Falcons), fierce-eyed and proud as they stood hunched over their partially devoured prey, he stood silent for a moment and then proclaimed, "*This* I will Engrave and Publish."[74]

Audubon returned to his rooms that evening elated, his emotions borne aloft on triumphant wings and likely some Scotch spirits, as reflected in the pages of his journal:

> Then, Fame, extend [MS: expend] thy unwearied Pinions, and far, far, and high, high soar away!, yet smoothly Circle about me wherever [MS: whe eve] I go and call out with musical mellowness the name of this Child of Nature, her humble but true Admirer. Call out, call out, Call out—Loud, *Loud, Loud, Audubon*!!!!—[75]

The next few weeks were a blur of activity as word of Audubon's remarkable compositions spread through the city. His sitting room was crowded with visitors each day, and in the evening he made the rounds of dinners and social gatherings where he "was every where kindly received."[76] Through the "astonishing perseverance of some unknown Friends," the Edinburgh Royal Institution on Princes Street offered him a "splendid Room" gratis to display his drawings to the public.[77] The exhibition of "139 land and 70 water birds" opened on Tuesday, November 14, and drew large crowds until it closed on Saturday, December 23.[78]

More importantly, by November 10, Audubon had worked out an arrangement with Lizars to engrave, print, and color the first fascicle, or "Number," of five prints of *The Birds of America*.[79] The prints would each be engraved at life size, the same as the original drawings, on a sheet of copper and then printed on fine Whatman cotton rag paper.[80] Audubon was sensitive to the fact that publishing the images life-sized would make his "Enormously Gigantic Work" "rather Bulky."[81] But, as he confided in a letter to William Rathbone announcing the project, "my heart was always bent on it, and I cannot refrain from attempting it so."[82]

To accommodate even the largest species, Lizars intended to use double elephant folio sheets for each print. The engraver employed a staff of colorists in his shop who would each apply a single shade of transparent watercolor to the black-and-white print as it was passed around the room, using a sample proof impression that Audubon had endorsed as a guide.[83]

Audubon had earlier recognized that his illustrations were, by "[c]hance and

PLATE 1. *Mill Grove, a 285-acre estate along the Schuylkill River near Valley Forge, Pennsylvania, was acquired as an investment property by Audubon's father in 1789 and became the naturalist's first home in America when he arrived from France in 1803.*

PLATE II. *Known as the "father of American ornithology," the Scottish immigrant Alexander Wilson (1766–1813) self-published a multivolume work on the birdlife of the early U.S. beginning in 1808. He met Audubon in Louisville in 1810 while canvassing for subscribers, and his example inspired Audubon a decade late to undertake* The Birds of America.

PLATE III. *The bombastic George Ord (1781–1866), a close friend of Alexander Wilson's and executor of his estate, quickly recognized the threat that Audubon posed to Wilson's legacy and blackballed Audubon's 1824 nomination for membership in the prestigious Academy of Natural Sciences of Philadelphia.*

PLATE IV. *Hannah Mary Rathbone I (1761–1839) was the "Queen Bee" of Greenbank and mother of William and Richard Rathbone, the Liverpool cotton merchants who were instrumental in mustering support for Audubon's publication after he arrived in England.*

PLATE V. *With the encouragement of George Ord, the arrogant English naturalist Charles Waterton (1782–1865) launched a series of vitriolic attacks on Audubon in England's foremost natural history journal beginning in 1832.*

PLATE VI. *Rev. John Bachman (1790–1874), a Lutheran minister and avid naturalist, met Audubon in Charleston, South Carolina, in 1831 and quickly became Audubon's closest friend. This portrait was painted by John W. Audubon in 1837.*

PLATE VII. *An early 1840s view of Boston from Dorchester Heights, drawn and engraved by Robert Havell Jr. after he immigrated to America.*

PLATE VIII. *Dr. George C. Shattuck Sr. (1783–1854), a distinguished and very wealthy Boston physician, was one of Audubon's strongest supporters in the city the naturalist called "the Athens of our Western World." This portrait by Gilbert Stuart was painted in 1827.*

PLATE IX. *An 1830s view of Passamaquoddy Bay with Eastport in the distance, as seen from the town of Lubec, Maine.*

chance alone," of three different sizes.[84] His largest images, like those that had persuaded Lizars to undertake the project, filled virtually an entire sheet of the mammoth 26½″× 39½″ paper.[85] Midsized birds, comprising such groups as ducks, hawks, and many seabirds, filled an area on the paper ranging from 20″× 25″ to 21″× 30″.[86] Small birds, like songbirds, created a third-sized image that took up an area of approximately 12″× 20″, with some waterbirds in this category requiring an image up to 15″× 21″.[87] In light of the predominance of smaller birds in the wild and in his portfolio, Audubon determined that each Number would consist of one large, one medium, and three small images.[88]

When Audubon opened his journal on November 19 after a twelve-day absence, he reported that the first two drawings were already in the process of being engraved.[89] Lizars showed him the first proof impression of one of the prints on November 28.[90] Six days later, on December 4, the naturalist and Lizars determined that the first plate of *The Birds of America* should be the Wild Turkey cock "to prove the necessity of the size of the Work."[91] The remaining plates in the first fascicle consisted of the Yellow-billed Cuckoo, Prothonotary Warbler, Purple Finch, and Bonaparte's Flycatcher (Canada Warbler).

Audubon intended to bring out the first Number at his "own Expense and risk."[92] Then, as Alexander Wilson had done, he would set out with a copy to solicit subscribers whose payments would enable him to finance the continuation of the project.[93] He priced each Number at two guineas, or £2.2s (two pounds, two shillings)(roughly $230 in 2016 dollars).[94] Given the manpower required to produce the prints, he projected that only five Numbers would be printed per year.[95] With an anticipated four hundred prints issued as eighty Numbers, the naturalist was embarking on a path projected to consume the next sixteen years of his life.[96]

The realization of his ambition after so many years of hard work left Audubon feeling sanguine about his prospects. On December 9, he penned a long letter to Lucy to revel in the success he had achieved in Edinburgh and to raise the possibility of her joining him.[97] He missed her terribly and longed to have their family together again. He envisioned Victor, who was now seventeen, traveling on his behalf to locate new subscribers and collect payments. John, recently turned fourteen, could obtain an education far superior to that available in America and refine his budding artistic talent under Audubon's watchful eye.[98]

"I am now better aware of the advantages of a familly in Unisson than ever," he wrote, "and I am *quite* satisfied that by acting conjointly and by my advise we can realize a handsome fortune for each of us—it needs but Industry and perseverance."[99] At the same time, he was ever mindful of Lucy's sentiments that he first be able to provide for them monetarily. He well knew that she would never leave the comfort of her teaching position at Beech Woods for a vague promise of future wealth and stability.[100] Nevertheless, he asked her to "set and Consider well" and write him "thy own kind Heart entire!"[101]

It was a bold request in view of the fact that his publication had barely commenced and that there was absolutely no assurance it would find an audience. Indeed, some of his staunchest supporters, including William Rathbone and Dr. Thomas Stewart Traill, had their doubts.[102] But the arrival the following day of two of Lucy's letters, dated August 9 and 27, the first he had received since Manchester, buoyed his spirits and provided reassurance.[103] Her correspondence indicated that she too had grown weary of their separation, saying that she would probably join him the following summer.[104]

However, despite Audubon's conviction that his efforts would eventually prevail, he remained uncertain that he could currently meet Lucy's need for financial security. In a letter to her on December 22, he included another copy of his December 9 missive under a date of December 21 and then issued a partial retraction of his earlier appeal, cautioning that "we must not hurry too much. I wish to sound all well, and be perfectly assured of the general ultimate success of my work."[105]

Meanwhile Audubon's letters announcing his triumphs in Liverpool and Edinburgh were slowly making their way to Bayou Sarah.[106] As Lucy learned of his ascending star, she became less confident about the enduring strength of their relationship and Audubon's desire to have her with him. Their situation was certainly not helped by the lengthy delays associated with transatlantic communication, which increased the potential for misunderstandings.[107] Over the next two and a half years, an ocean apart, they would each come to question the depth of the other's love and commitment.

⸻

Audubon remained the toast of Edinburgh until April 5, 1827, when he boarded a coach to begin a circuitous trip south through Scotland and England to his ultimate destination—London.[108] He planned to stop in each of the sizable cities through which he passed—Newcastle upon Tyne, York, Leeds, Manchester, and Liverpool—to canvass subscriptions for *The Birds of America*.[109] Along with a box holding 250 of his drawings, he took with him copies of a printed prospectus for the work and a fully colored copy of the first Number, which Lizars had completed by early February.[110] The copies for subscribers were issued around March 1.[111] In a matter of weeks, production would begin on the second fascicle, comprising the female Wild Turkey and her poults, Purple Grakle (Common Grackle), White-throated Sparrow, Selby's Flycatcher (Hooded Warbler), and Brown Lark (American Pipit).[112]

Audubon also carried the satisfaction of knowing that his prospectus had been enhanced by a list of Edinburgh's distinguished societies that had elected him a member, including the Wernerian Natural History Society, the Edinburgh Society of Arts, and most importantly, the Royal Society of Edinburgh.[113]

To open the path to membership in the Wernerian Society, the naturalist had been called upon to write and present several scientific papers on American natural history based upon his years of observations in the wild.[114] One that he had cobbled together on the rattlesnake was wildly inaccurate, a sloppy if not fraudulent piece of scholarship that would provide ample fodder for his critics.[115] Another on the olfactory sense of the Turkey Buzzard (Turkey Vulture), though scientifically more sound, would prove to be almost as controversial.[116]

By the time Audubon arrived in London on Monday, May 21, he had added forty-nine subscriptions to the nineteen or so he had collected over the course of his stay in Edinburgh. However, he was quick to inflate the number when he wrote home to Lucy, claiming that he had already reached the century mark.[117]

Though it may seem odd that he would lie to his devoted wife, the one person in the world whom he could completely trust, this was certainly not the first time he had done so. He had lied to her years before about having studied under Jacques-Louis David. His purpose now was to have her and, just as importantly, the members of her family view him as a success. He craved this as much as he desired anything in life. The failure of his businesses in Henderson had robbed him of more than material wealth. He had lost respect and a feeling of self-worth. With each new subscriber, he was slowly regaining a measure of what he once had. And he doubtless justified the falsehood to himself, believing that he would rapidly achieve that milestone just as soon as the worthies of England's grand metropolis were given an opportunity to see his publication.

Audubon did not care at all for London, a smoky, "overgrown City" of over a million people that he described to Lucy as "a Vortex indeed." He likened it to "the mouth of an immense monster, guarded by millions of sharp-edged teeth, from which if I escape unhurt must be called a miracle." However, he located comfortable rooms at 55 Great Russell Street and began making the rounds "on foot and in Hackney Coaches" to deliver his letters of introduction.[118]

One of the recipients was John G. Children, a zoologist and curator with the British Museum who also served as secretary of the illustrious Royal Society of London. Children invited Audubon to a meeting of the Linnean Society on May 23, where the naturalist was permitted to display his prints from the first Number.[119] "All those present pronounced my work *unrivalled*, and warmly wished me success," he told his journal.[120] He received similar praise at meetings of the Royal Society, the Royal Institution, the Zoological Society of London, and the Athenaeum Club.[121] However, Audubon quickly discovered that many of the prominent persons to whom the letters of introduction were addressed had already left the city for their summer estates in the country.[122]

As May morphed into June, Audubon was growing increasingly concerned about delays plaguing Lizars's shop. He had begun to hear grumbling from some of his Manchester subscribers who were unhappy they had still not received their copy of the first Number. He evidently attempted to control the damage when he penned a letter on June 2 to one of his Manchester friends, Walter H. Bentley. "I am sory about the Gentlemen of Manchester," he wrote, "who are so impatient, they little know the vexations I experience daily about my publication—I *am* doing my utmost to please them and *they* apparently damn me for it—that is hard indeed—*I have here* 25 Men employed in Colouring and Mͬ Lizars is also doing his best."[123]

There was utterly no truth to Audubon's claim that he had hired colorists in London to supplement the work that Lizars was doing. But he was hoping to buy some time while he worked with the Scottish engraver to resolve the problems engulfing the project.

Then, in mid-June, Audubon received an unnerving letter from Lizars, who reported that his colorists had laid down their brushes and gone on strike for better pay, bringing the already protracted publication of the second fascicle to a complete standstill.[124] Although the engraver was hopeful the matter would be resolved, he recommended that Audubon look for someone in London who could undertake that portion of the work.[125] Audubon was eventually referred to Robert Havell Sr., a highly regarded printer and colorist located at 79 Newman Street.[126]

A distant Havell descendant, writing almost ninety years later, related that Audubon approached Havell about completely replacing Lizars, but the fifty-eight-year-old printer declined.[127] Havell reportedly concluded that the demands and duration of the enterprise would be too much for him to undertake at his age. However, as an accommodation to the disheartened naturalist, he agreed to look for an engraver whom he could hire and supervise on the project. Havell discussed his needs with a colleague, who showed him the work of a young engraver in his employ.[128] "That's just the man for me!" Havell declared. His colleague reportedly replied, "Then send for your own son."[129]

Under this telling, the senior Havell had been estranged from his thirty-three-year-old son and namesake, Robert Havell Jr., since 1825.[130] The younger man had left London and the family business after his father had refused to sanction his pursuit of a career in the arts.[131] Audubon's pressing need and the opportunity and challenge presented by the naturalist's venture led to the reconciliation of father and son.[132] Together, the Havells embarked on the publication of *The Birds of America* and, in the process, made history.

It is a dramatic and uplifting tale, which has been invariably repeated by many of

Audubon's biographers.[133] It is also almost certainly a myth.[134] Robert Havell Jr. had been in business with his father under the name Robert Havell & Son as early as 1818.[135] In 1824, the Post-Office London Directory of the city's businesses still listed them as Robert Havell & Son, Engravers at 3 Chapel Street.[136] During this time, the junior Havell was actively engaged in engraving many of the prints of James Baillie Fraser's *Views of Calcutta*, published in eight parts between 1824 and 1826.[137] The directory for 1826, the year after their putative estrangement and a full year before Audubon arrived in London, had them pursuing separate trades in the same shop at 79 Newman Street. Robert Havell & Co. was operating as "Letter-press-printers," while Robert Havell Jr. was listed as an "Engraver."[138] The same listing appears in the succeeding directories through 1829 without substantive change.[139]

Although such sources are not always completely reliable, the alterations made to the listings over the years establish that the compilers made at least some effort to verify the data annually. And if that isn't proof enough, it seems rather unlikely that the younger Havell, having returned to London, could have been working as an engraver in the publishing industry—for a friend of his father, no less—without his father's having heard about it.

Based upon the edited fragments that were ultimately published from Audubon's journal, it would seem that when the naturalist first walked through the door at 79 Newman Street he was only looking for a colorist to take on the coloring of Lizars's engravings.[140] The senior Havell examined the first fascicle, and by June 21, he had apparently struck a deal with Audubon to color the prints for even less than Lizars was charging.[141] However, that day brought a further letter from Edinburgh. From its contents Audubon concluded that, notwithstanding their friendship, Lizars simply did not wish to continue with the project.[142] The naturalist did not have to look far for an engraver.

Robert Havell Jr. was the ideal man to assume the challenge of reproducing Audubon's work. He was a skilled practitioner of the art of aquatinting—a technique Lizars did not employ—which enabled him to add degrees of shading and depth to his engravings by dipping the copper plates in successive baths of nitric acid (*aqua fortis*). But, equally important, he was also a gifted artist whose talent would enhance the translation of Audubon's drawings into the finished prints for *The Birds of America*.[143]

Over the next year, the Havells would take on the project together under the banner Robert Havell & Son, with the junior Havell working his magic on copper and his father overseeing the printing and coloration of the prints.[144] In 1828, the Havells dissolved their formal business relationship but independently continued the work under their separate purviews. Robert Havell Sr. would step away from the project with the completion of No. 15 (Plates 71–75) in 1829.[145] He retired the following year and died in November 1832.[146] Robert Havell Jr. took over exclusive management of the enormous enterprise and, in 1831, moved the business to 77 Oxford Street.[147]

Audubon was decidedly pleased with the arrangement when he composed a letter to Lucy on August 6. He noted that, in addition to the improved quality of the colored prints, he was saving about £25 pounds per Number, almost a quarter of what he had been charged by Lizars.[148]

Later that month, he had even more reasons to celebrate. He had added the subscriptions of King George IV and the Duchess of Clarence, later Queen Adelaide, wife of George's eldest son and successor, William IV.[149] In addition to this royal pair, his list boasted the distinguished names of Charles-Lucien Bonaparte; John G. Children; and Lord Stanley, who was president of the Zoological Society and had met Audubon and admired his drawings a year before in Liverpool.[150] On September 16, when Audubon left London on a canvassing trip north to collect amounts due from his subscribers and to deliver copies of the Havell-produced third Number, his subscriptions had reached the hundred mark.[151]

His travels took him back through Manchester, Leeds, York, Newcastle, Alnwick, and Edinburgh.[152] Along the way he added nineteen new subscribers.[153] A visit to Glasgow raised the total by one, with the subscription of the university.[154] However, at the same time that he was attracting new subscribers, he was losing others. On October 31, he recorded in his journal that six of his original subscribers in Edinburgh had canceled their subscriptions.[155]

Given the high cost of the work and the length of time it was projected to take, Audubon would find that the loss of subscribers was an ongoing problem. Death, disinterest, and occasional dissatisfaction with the quality of the prints resulted in the termination of scores of subscriptions as the years passed.[156] As a consequence, he was compelled to focus almost constantly on wooing possible new subscribers.[157] Still, on November 25, when he sat down during a lengthy stay in Liverpool and took up his pen, he could report to Lucy that his list now stood at 114.[158] Liverpool added three more subscribers to whom he delivered a full set of prints, including the just completed fifth Number, when they arrived from London on December 28.[159]

For months Audubon had been telling Lucy that when January came he hoped his financial situation would be such that he could write and ask her to join him.[160] In a letter from Liverpool on December 26, he provided an accounting of his current assets and assured her that they could live together in England "much more comfortable than any time since my failure at Henderson."[161] He could not help thinking that "all this will make thee wish to come to me" and declared that when he returned to London, "I may and probably will write for thee to come." However, when the calendar turned and it was time for him to make a commitment, now back in London at 95 Great Russell Street, he held back, fearing that she would expect a more lavish lifestyle than he was capable of affording.[162] He insisted that he was thinking only of her comfort, but the years of privation they had faced following the collapse of his Henderson businesses had left deep and lasting scars on them both.[163] He could not bring himself to ask her to cross the ocean only to see her disappointed again.

Hoping to supplement his income, Audubon attempted to find employment with a public institution or a wealthy nobleman while continuing the publication of his work.[164] But when a position failed to materialize, he resolved to augment his subscription list and thereby swell his annual profits. In early March 1828, he visited Cambridge, where he added five new subscribers.[165] A trip to Oxford later in the month, however, was a disappointment, as only one of the colleges signed on.[166] By early August, he informed Lucy that the eighth Number was being delivered to 125 subscribers and that the remaining two fascicles for the year were on schedule.[167] He had just moved his lodgings to rooms in the home of Robert Havell Jr., above the shop at 79 Newman Street.[168]

At the beginning of September, Audubon left London and journeyed to Paris with a small coterie of friends and a copy of his work to continue his marketing efforts.[169] Among his companions was William Swainson, a thirty-eight-year-old writer and naturalist from Tittenhanger (now Tyttenhanger) Green near St. Albans, who had written a blushing review of his "magnificent undertaking" for the inaugural May issue of *The Magazine of Natural History*, published by John C. Loudon.[170] Their friendship deepened over a several-day visit that Audubon made to the Swainson home at the end of May.[171] In mid-August, Swainson had offered the naturalist solace and a respite in the country when Audubon was wracked by a bout of depression, the "blue devils" as he called it and from which he periodically suffered, after he received a letter from Lucy declaring that she had "positively abandoned her coming to England for some indefinite time."[172]

The naturalist found France sadly diminished as an economic power and remarked to his journal that, had he chosen to take his portfolio first to the land of his fathers as some had advised, his ambitious project "would have perished like a flower in October."[173] The visit also reopened the painful stigma of his birth. He spent several sleepless nights gripped with the fear that the secret of his origins would be revealed by someone from Nantes who knew the truth, destroying his reputation and access to members of polite society who were the very source of his success.[174] His secret held, and when he returned to London at the end of October, his list of subscribers was richer by fourteen names, including those of King Charles X and Louis Philippe, the Duc d'Orléans, who succeeded to the throne after the Revolution of 1830.[175] Writing to Lucy on November 2 to apprise her of the results of his travels, he tallied his subscribers and counted a total of 144.[176]

In early January 1829, Audubon received a letter from his "dearest friend," dated

November 8, in which Lucy reiterated her doubts that his situation would ever reach a point where he would ask her to join him. He brooded over it for a fortnight, thinking about the proper course of action to take. On January 20, he penned a reply and announced his intention to sail for America on April 1. He recognized that his departure could lead his subscribers to believe he had abandoned the project, but he felt the trip was necessary to persuade her, once and for all, to return with him to England.[177] At the same time, he wanted to use the opportunity to procure additional bird species to finish his portfolio and perhaps redraw some of his earliest compositions.[178] The boys, both of whom were now in Louisville where Victor was working with Nicholas Berthoud and John was attending college at Bardwell Academy, wished to remain in America.[179] When Audubon wrote to Lucy again on February 1, he informed her that John G. Children, the British Museum librarian, had offered to supervise the work during his absence.[180]

Meanwhile, based upon some frustrated and angry comments Audubon had made in his November correspondence, Lucy had independently concluded that if she did not make the decision to give up her teaching position and travel to England, Audubon would continue to temporize and she would likely lose him forever.[181] She had not yet received the letter announcing his plans to sail to her, but she resolved to terminate her employment at year's end, collect what she was owed, and cross the ocean to be with him.[182] In early February, she let him know her desires but asked him to write and confirm his own.[183]

Unaware of Lucy's plans to join him, Audubon left Portsmouth on the first of April aboard the packet ship *Columbia* bound for New York.[184] He arrived on May 5 and promptly wrote to her to let her know of his safe passage.[185] In a follow-up letter of May 10, he explained that he intended to "remain as stationary as possible" in those sections of the country where he could maximize his output of additional drawings, by which he meant east of the Appalachian Mountains. He asked her to journey upriver to meet him in Louisville or Wheeling, Virginia (now West Virginia) or, alternatively, sail directly for New York or Philadelphia. But he stressed he could not come to her in Louisiana and risk loss of "*regular news*" from his agents in London. Meanwhile, he spent several days visiting the city's eminent scientists and was invited to exhibit a copy of his work at the Lyceum of Natural History of New-York.[186]

Audubon left New York on May 14 for Philadelphia, where he remained three days before moving across the Delaware River to a boardinghouse in Camden, New Jersey, to chase spring migrants for the next three weeks.[187] June took him to Great Egg Harbor along the coast in search of waterbirds.[188] Although Lucy was unhappy that he had not immediately set out to see her after landing in America, his excursions proved remarkably productive. Back in Philadelphia in July, he could report to Victor that he had already completed twenty new drawings.[189] Audubon spent the month of August and the early part of September in the Great Pine Swamp along the Lehigh River near Mauch Chunk (now Jim Thorpe), Pennsylvania. By October, back in Philedelphia, he had increased his output to forty-two compositions.[190] He was being assisted by a Swiss-German landscape painter, George Lehman, whom he had first met in 1824 on his way to Pittsburgh and who had agreed to add botanical backgrounds to the illustrations.[191]

Having heard from Lucy that she could not leave Louisiana until after the first of the year and wanted Audubon or one of the boys to bring her north, the naturalist finally left Philadelphia in early November, stopped for "a few days" in Louisville to see his sons, and reached Bayou Sarah by steamboat on November 17. It was early morning as he made his way to Beech Grove, the plantation of William Garrett Johnson where Lucy was now teaching.[192] He came upon her suddenly, and they threw themselves into each other's arms. He told his journal, "we were both overcome with emotion, which found relief in tears."[193]

United once more in their hearts and purpose, Audubon and Lucy left Beech Grove on the first day of January 1830 and proceeded to New Orleans with their three remaining slaves, who were left with the Brand family. On January 7, the couple boarded the "splendid steamer *Philadelphia*" for the trip upriver to Louisville, but it took them fourteen days to reach their destination due to engine trouble. Over the next six weeks, they visited with the families of Will Bakewell in Louisville and Nicholas Berthoud in Shippingport and prepared to say goodbye to their sons.[194] On March 7, they resumed their journey and passed through Washington City on their way to New York.[195] Audubon succeeded in obtaining the subscription of the Library of Congress, one of five he procured during his visit to America, and met with President Andrew Jackson, who received him at the White House "with great kindness."[196]

The Audubons departed New York on April 1 as passengers aboard the packet *Pacific* and arrived in Liverpool without incident on April 27.[197] The previous day, the naturalist had turned forty-five. Lucy was now forty-three.

Two days later, Audubon was off to Manchester, where he planned to open an exhibit of his newest compositions before returning to "Smoaky London."[198] Lucy remained behind to care for her sister Ann, who was gravely ill from a pelvic infection.[199] Early May saw Audubon back in London, and on the 6th of the month he was seated as a Fellow of the Royal Society of London, an honor accorded him through the auspices of Lord Stanley and John G. Children.[200] Although he was justifiably proud of his 1828 elections to membership in London's Zoological Society and Linnean Society, both distinguished learned organizations, the Royal Society of

London was considered to be the most prestigious body of scientists and scholars in the world.[201] Thereafter, when listing his numerous honorary titles, Audubon would append the initials F.R.S. or F.R.S.L. to his name before any others.

Audubon's absence from England for over a year had indeed resulted in the loss of a number of subscribers as he had feared. Some believed he had forsaken the project.[202] Others, including several from Manchester, complained of inconsistent coloring by Havell's staff. Audubon excoriated the engraver by letter when he returned to Liverpool in early June after spending a week in Manchester, where he heard the criticism and personally saw two sets "that I scarcely could believe had been sent from your House."[203] In Birmingham at month's end, he received similar complaints and took up his pen again to warn Havell that if this continued, "I must candidly tell you that I will abandon the Publication and return to my Own Woods untill I leave this World for a better one."[204] Havell was surprised and hurt by the attack, but he redoubled his efforts to ensure a consistent quality of the prints.[205] Audubon was delighted by the results when he saw the proofs of the first few prints of Number 19, calling it "the best of your productions."[206]

With Ann Gordon finally recovering, Lucy was able to leave Liverpool in July.[207] The Audubons traveled to London for a brief visit and then spent the remainder of the summer and early fall traveling across the English countryside, reassuring existing subscribers and canvassing for new ones.[208] After stops in Birmingham, Manchester, Leeds, York, Hull, Scarborough, Whitby, Newcastle on Tyne, and at Prideaux John Selby's home near Belford, they reached Edinburgh on October 13 and found rooms in the naturalist's former boardinghouse at No. 2 George Street.[209]

Audubon intended to spend the winter months in his favorite city working on his *Ornithological Biography*, a letterpress of individual species accounts that he had long planned to publish as a separate work for his subscribers.[210] With Havell about to issue the twentieth Number, completing the first volume of one hundred prints, Audubon envisioned an accompanying text containing a description of each illustrated bird, along with its habitat, range, and behavior, based upon his extensive field observations. He also planned to intersperse the biographies with a series of separate "Episodes" through which he could introduce the reader to America, share anecdotes of its inhabitants and their customs, and offer some of his own often embellished adventures on the frontier.

He had approached William Swainson back in August about collaborating on the work, believing he needed a trained ornithologist to add the necessary scientific detail to each account.[211] Swainson was more than willing to lend a hand, but Audubon took umbrage at Swainson's suggested contract terms, which included dual authorship on the title page.[212] The naturalist, both headstrong and egotistical, had no wish to share his growing fame — even with a friend — and summarily rejected

Swainson's proposal.[213] The prideful Swainson took offense, and their friendship never fully recovered.[214]

In Edinburgh, Audubon was referred to William MacGillivray, the former curator of the natural history museum established by Prof. Robert Jameson at the University of Edinburgh. MacGillivray proved to be an ideal choice. He was evidently unemployed at the time, having resigned his position toward the end of the previous year. More importantly, the thirty-four-year-old was both a capable ornithologist and an adroit editor, able to lightly smooth the rough edges of Audubon's sometimes inelegant prose without silencing the naturalist's original voice. He also supplemented each account with a scientific description of the species and, in many cases, offered details about the accompanying plant that Audubon had illustrated. Critically, his professional ego did not demand a share of the authorial credit.[215]

Working tirelessly "from morning to night every day as hard as we can do," Audubon and MacGillivray, with help from Lucy, finished the manuscript in three months.[216] Seven hundred fifty copies of the first volume of the *Ornithological Biography* were published in Edinburgh in March 1831, with an American edition of five-hundred copies appearing in Philadelphia at about the same time.[217]

During his stay, Audubon reached an agreement with Joseph Bartholomew Kidd, a young, talented Edinburgh artist, to copy the first one hundred prints of *The Birds of America* in oils.[218] Kidd had tutored the naturalist in oil painting during Audubon's previous visit to the city and had even served as Audubon's agent in Edinburgh for about a year.[219] Audubon planned the completed paintings "to stand to time immemorial" and serve as the basis for a permanent natural-history gallery that would provide him with another revenue stream.[220]

On April 15, Audubon and Lucy left Edinburgh to return to London, visiting subscribers along the way to deliver copies of the *Ornithological Biography* as well as the twenty-first Number.[221] From Liverpool, they took the newly opened railway and arrived in London on the 27th.[222] Their stay, however, was short. Audubon had mapped out plans for the two of them for a monthlong trip to France in May to collect past-due accounts, to be followed by an August journey once more across the ocean "to beat the bushes" for yet more birds to fill Havell's coppers.[223]

On July 31, Audubon boarded the packet *Columbia* off Portsmouth Harbor, this time with Lucy by his side.[224] He anticipated that they could be away for as long as two years, during which time he hoped to see the issuance of twelve Numbers, having exhorted Havell to increase the production rate from five fascicles to six per year. Traveling with the Audubons was a young taxidermist from London named Henry Ward, who would assist in the collection of specimens and the preparation of birdskins.[225]

The following morning, the *Columbia* lifted anchor, the rigging snapped tight as the canvas caught the air, and Audubon's hopes turned again to the winged wonders of his adopted land. However, he realized that success on this visit would require more than simply finding new birds in parts of the country that had yet to be explored. He also needed to mine a new cohort of potential subscribers who had an interest in natural history and the wealth to afford his monumental work. Edward Harris, the well-to-do gentleman farmer from Moorestown, New Jersey, who had befriended him in Philadelphia in 1824, had called upon him in London only days before and subscribed.[226] Still, Audubon's list was down to 130 subscribers, and while the project was still making money, he needed America to help turn it into a financial triumph.

The Audubons arrived in New York on September 3 and stayed a week "in great Comfort" with the Berthouds, who had since relocated from Shippingport. Nicholas was now a partner in Forstall Brothers & Berthoud at 108 Front Street.[227] Audubon and Lucy then proceeded to Philadelphia, where the naturalist added four names to his subscribers' list. These included that of his friend Richard Harlan, M.D., as well as the Academy of Natural Sciences of Philadelphia, which had rejected him as a member only seven years before.[228] Audubon trumpeted in a letter to Havell that "[m]y Enemies are going down hill very fast and fine reviews of the Work coming forth." Victor soon arrived from Kentucky to accompany Lucy to Louisville. She planned to stay with her younger brother Will and her two sons while Audubon headed to the Floridas. He was intent on following the migrating flocks to their winter homes "as fast as Steam Boats or Coaches will allow."[229]

Before going their separate ways, the Audubon party, now complemented by the Swiss landscape painter George Lehman, traveled together to Baltimore.[230] Audubon and Victor paid a side visit to Washington City, where Audubon successfully petitioned the Treasury Department and the Navy Department to provide him with credentials to the officers of their respective vessels for assistance in prosecuting his scientific explorations around the Floridas.[231]

On October 7, having said farewell to Lucy and Victor, Audubon joined Ward and Lehman as passengers aboard a steamer bound for Norfolk.[232] The party passed through Richmond and Fayetteville before reaching Charleston, South Carolina, on October 16.[233] There, Audubon met the Reverend John Bachman, a blue-eyed forty-one-year-old Lutheran minister who shared the naturalist's passion for birds. Bachman invited Audubon and his companions to stay with his large family at their three-story home on Pinckney Street and eventually became Audubon's closest friend and confidant.[234]

In early November, Audubon was delighted to send Lucy the news that the Academy of Natural Sciences of Philadelphia had finally elected him a member, "the Papers say *Unanimously*."[235] By the middle of the month, having thoroughly scoured the marshes and back country around Charleston for birds to fill his drawing paper, he left the city with his assistants aboard the packet schooner *Agnes* and reached St. Augustine five days later.[236] The first several weeks spent in east Florida were busy and productive ones as Audubon drew seventeen species, including one that he believed represented a new genus for the United States, the Brasilian Caracara Eagle (Crested Caracara).[237] He was in his element and thoroughly energized, telling Lucy that "I feel as young as ever and I now can undertake and bear as much hardship as I have ever done in my life."[238]

By December 5, the area around St. Augustine had been exhausted and the naturalist was looking for new vistas to explore.[239] He paid a ten-day visit before Christmas to the plantation of Gen. José Mariano Hernández along the Matanzas River and then departed with his party for Bulowville, where he stayed with wealthy young plantation owner John J. Bulow.[240]

Writing to Lucy on January 4, 1832, Audubon reported that he now had a total of twenty-nine new drawings, eleven of which had been completed, along with 550 skins.[241] He returned with his party to St. Augustine on January 14, hoping to make use of a letter he had just received from Treasury Secretary Louis McLane directing the officers of the Revenue Cutter Service between Charleston and Mobile to convey him within their established cruising limits. A division of the Treasury Department, the Revenue Cutter Service had been formed in 1790 by an act of Congress and operated under the direction of the local customs collectors. Using fast-sailing schooners known as revenue cutters, the service was assigned the task of patrolling the vast Atlantic coastline to deter smuggling and enforce the customs laws of the United States.[242]

With no revenue cutter to transport him, Audubon's party gained passage in early February aboard a navy war schooner, the USS *Spark*, as it ascended the St. John's River.[243] However, the voyage was aborted when one of the sailors was injured, at which point the naturalist decided to leave the vessel to return overland to St. Augustine.[244]

Audubon concluded it would be easier to find a revenue cutter to do his bidding in Charleston, where one was stationed.[245] So, on March 5, he and his companions boarded the *Agnes* for the return trip.[246] A gale off the coast forced an unexpected stop in Savannah.[247] Audubon used the time to sign up three new subscribers, including William Gaston, a local merchant and Bachman contact.[248] Gaston agreed to serve as the naturalist's local agent and, within days, procured two more subscribers. Audubon reached Charleston by mail coach on the 10th, while his companions remained aboard the *Agnes* and arrived three days later. Once again at the Bachman home, he wrote to Lucy on March 13 to announce that his list of American subscribers now stood at twenty-three, sixteen of whom had been added since their September arrival.[249]

The customs collector in Charleston, James R. Pringle, approved Audubon's request to use the revenue cutter *Marion* for an excursion to the Florida Keys, and on April 18 Audubon's party sailed again for the Floridas with Lt. Robert Day and his crew.[250] They explored Indian Key and Key West, traveled down to the Dry Tortugas and back up to Cape Sable at the tip of the Everglades, collecting and drawing as they went.[251] Dr. Benjamin B. Strobel, a Bachman in-law, published a revealing account of the just-turned-forty-seven-year-old naturalist in the *Key West Gazette*:[252]

> Mr. Audubon is a most extraordinary man;—possessed of an ardent and enthusiastic mind and entirely devoted to his pursuits, danger cannot daunt, and difficulties vanish before him. During his stay here his hour of rising was three o'clock in the morning; from that time until noon, and sometimes even until night he was engaged in hunting among the Mangrove Keys—despite of heat, sandflies and musquitoes. On his return from these expeditions, his time was principally employed in making sketches of such plants and birds as he may have procured: This was not an extraordinary effort for a day—it was continued for weeks; in short, it appeared to constitute his chief aim, as it is his happiness. . . . The private character of Mr. Audubon corresponds with the nature of his mind and pursuits—he is frank, free, and generous, always willing to impart information, and to render himself agreeable. The favorable impressions which he has produced upon our mind will not soon be effaced.[253]

Audubon returned with his party to Charleston in early June.[254] He enjoyed the hospitality of the Bachman clan until later that month when he left for Philadelphia, where he expected to rendezvous with his family.[255] While he awaited their arrival, delayed by low water in the Ohio River, he worked on several compositions of specimens collected during excursions from his boardinghouse in Camden, New Jersey.[256]

He also brooded over an embarrassing article that had appeared in the April issue of Loudon's natural-history magazine, attacking his five-year-old paper in which he maintained that the Turkey Vulture used its eyesight rather than its olfactory sense to locate food.[257] The author, Charles Waterton, was a well-to-do forty-nine-year-old English naturalist who had met Audubon briefly in Philadelphia in 1824 and shared George Ord's vehement dislike of him. By generating controversy, with Ord's wholehearted approval, the combative Englishman hoped to discredit Audubon's growing reputation.[258]

Lucy, Victor, and John finally reached Philadelphia in July, bringing the family together again for the first time in over two years.[259] At month's end they traveled to cholera-ravaged New York to see the Berthouds as well as Lucy's sisters Ann and Sarah, who were visiting. But fear of the epidemic limited their stay to only a day.[260] They left the city on July 31, traveling by steamboat to New London and then by stage to Boston, arriving the evening of August 1.[261]

With a population of over sixty-one thousand residents, Boston was the fourth largest city in America behind New York, Baltimore, and Philadelphia. It was situated on a peninsula bordered on its western side by the Charles River and to the east by Boston Harbor and Massachusetts Bay. Prince Maximilian of Wied, Germany, who had visited the city the month before, described it as "very nice looking, spread out, and large. It has nice long streets, often rather broad but occasionally somewhat narrow, provided with very good sidewalks. There are very pleasing houses, most constructed of brick, some also made of square stone, and, in the oldest sections, also wooden houses . . . covered for the most part with slate or wooden shingles."[262]

In the center of the city was a public promenade called the Commons. "From a slight elevation of the city, a large, wide area covered with grass descends toward the water, and it is bordered by avenues of tall, very shady elms along the row of houses." Boston boasted a "significant number of very fine and diverse shops." As a result of its robust trade with the West Indies, merchants could be found selling a broad selection of tropical fruit, including oranges, coconuts, and Brazilian bananas.[263]

Audubon forever appreciated the warmth of the greeting he and his family received during their visit to "the Athens of our Western World":

> Never, I fear, shall I have it in my power to return a tithe of the hospitality which was there shewn towards us, or of the benevolence and generosity which we experienced, and which evidently came from the heart, without the slightest mixture of ostentation. Indeed, I must acknowledge that although I have been happy in forming many valuable friendships in various parts of the world, all dearly cherished by me, the outpouring of kindness which I experienced at Boston far exceeded all that I have ever met with.[264]

No doubt Audubon's affection for the Bostonians was influenced, in large part, by the ardent support they gave his publication. By August 13 he was able to report to Havell that he had collected seven new subscriptions, including those of Col. Thomas H. Perkins, who was the president of the Boston Athenaeum and one of the city's wealthiest men, and George Cheyne Shattuck, M.D., a prominent physician.[265] He was also busy hunting for new birds on the city's outskirts and, on August 14, happily informed his friend Edward Harris that he had found three rare species with the help of Harvard naturalist Thomas Nuttall.[266]

The following day, the Audubons sailed for Portland and spent the next seven weeks on a working vacation, exploring the coast of Maine and its birds up to the small town of Eastport on Passamaquoddy Bay at the northeastern tip of the state, and then into New Brunswick, Canada.[267] During a stop in the provincial capital of Fredericton, they met Lt. Edward Coke of the British Army's 45th Regiment, who was spending his furlough traveling throughout the eastern United States and Canada. The following year, Coke would publish a two-volume narrative of his journey which included a description of their encounter:

> During my ten days' residence at Fredericton I had the pleasure of meeting Mr. Audubon, the celebrated ornithologist, who, with his sons, was searching for additions to his laborious undertaking. He had only been fortunate enough to meet with one rather rare bird in the province; and I am afraid he would not add many subscribers to his valuable but expensive work. His original drawings were certainly much more beautiful and spirited than the English coloured engravings. His time appeared entirely given up to the performance of what he had undertaken, and in the pursuit of which he has expended a considerable fortune. His manners are very mild, and he has a prepossessing and benevolent countenance, with a sharp eagle eye and prominent features.[268]

The Audubons returned to Boston in early October. The naturalist planned to spend the remainder of the fall and coming winter in the city working on his publication with the assistance of John and Lucy. As part of Audubon's grand design to make this truly a family business, Victor traveled to New York and sailed for England on October 16 to oversee Havell's work and continue soliciting subscriptions abroad.[269] Victor believed that the quality of the prints was inconsistent and, on site in Havell's shop, he planned to do something about it. However, he lacked his father's deft touch in dealing with the engraver's sensitive ego. Within six months of his arrival, the conflict between the two men would come to a head and threaten the future of *The Birds of America*.

Audubon had decided to devote the third volume of the publication to the waterbirds, which had yet to be represented in any of the published prints. While he had already immortalized many aquatic species with his brush, the naturalist knew there were many more to be had. In February, he began planning a spring trip to Labrador, the region of the Province of Lower Canada (now Quebec) along the north coast of the Gulf of St. Lawrence where multitudes of these birds were said to breed.[270] This would also afford him an opportunity to learn more about their life histories, an essential part of writing their biographical accounts.

He was under no illusion that this would be an easy task. "The Land Bird flits from bush to bush, runs before you, and seldom extends its flight beyond the range of your vision," he informed his readers. "It is very different with the Water Bird, which sweeps afar over the wide ocean, hovers above the surges, or betakes itself for refuge to the inaccessible rocks on the shore."[271] On February 19, 1833, he wrote to Bachman saying that he might travel as far inland as Hudson Bay and return via Quebec. He expected he would be under way by the middle of March.[272]

However, what had been a surprisingly mild winter turned bitterly cold and harsh in February.[273] The weather, along with a temporary shortage of funds caused by the unexpected delay of the vessel *Charlotte*, which was carrying additional copies of *The Birds of America* from London, forced Audubon to delay his trip until later in the spring.[274]

In the meantime, he continued to draw specimens "as chance" and a wide circle of friends, acquaintances, and hired gunners brought him birds.[275] When there were no birds to be had, he worked on the second volume of the *Ornithological Biography*.[276] At the same time, he and Lucy enjoyed their enhanced social status, mixing with Boston's most distinguished citizens.[277] The fame he had achieved in England and Scotland from the publication of his work had swept across the Atlantic, and his presence was honored in the finest homes in the city and across the Charles River in Cambridge.

In early February, Audubon's Philadelphia friend and agent, Richard Harlan, M.D., arrived with his new wife for a surprise visit.[278] The couple remained in Boston until the 23rd of the month. Two days later, Audubon paid what was evidently a sales call on Ethan Allen Greenwood, the proprietor of the New England Museum on Court Street, and saw what he considered to be "the finest Golden Eagle alive."[279] The magnificent raptor, uncommon in eastern North America, had been inadvertently caught in a fox trap in the White Mountains of New Hampshire.[280] Audubon had yet to illustrate the species and asked if Greenwood would consider selling the bird. Greenwood agreed and even allowed Audubon to set the price.[281] When the naturalist wrote to Victor later that day, he could not believe his good fortune. "I paid $14.75 a pretty good price but not 100$ as the rascal in Philadelphia [MS: Phil^a] wished to obtain from me for a far less handsome specimen."[282]

After a day of observing the noble creature, he decided to kill it so that he could preserve its image on paper.[283] He worked feverishly on the drawing over the next several days. On March 5, he wrote Victor: "I am just now quite fatigued by the drawing of a Golden Eagle which although it will make a splendid plate has cost me sixty hours of the severest labor I have experienced since I drew the Wild Turkey."[284]

Ultimately, it took the naturalist thirteen days to complete the drawing. One of his most visually powerful and arresting compositions, it depicts a mature female with a Northern Hare (Snowshoe Hare) in her talons, exultant, her wings in midstroke as she struggles to gain altitude above a snow-capped mountain range.[285] It is also the only rendering in which he playfully included a self-portrait—a small figure in the background dressed in buckskins and shinnying along a log lying over a chasm, a dead eagle draped over his back.[286]

Despite Audubon's exhaustion from the prolonged effort of portraying the raptor, he pressed forward relentlessly with his work. Lucy announced in a letter to Victor on March 13 that Audubon had completed a drawing of four Crossbills (Red Crossbills) as well as one of the Great Cinereous Shrikes (Northern Shrikes).[287]

Three days later, Audubon was abruptly seized by a paralytic stroke.[288] He had spent a lifetime overcoming enormous obstacles and adversity on his tortuous path toward greatness. His publication had brought him honor and recognition on two continents. It had also managed to restore the self-respect that he had lost after the collapse of his Henderson businesses. Even the members of Lucy's extended family, who had long mocked and derided him, were impressed by what he had accomplished.

Now everything was in doubt. Audubon fully understood that, as much as his sons might wish to help, he was the inexorable force behind the family enterprise. In his condition, unable to lift a brush or even converse, it would doubtless fail, robbing his family of their only means of support. The recent watercolors he had shown his callers earlier in the day stood mute. Somewhere deep in his soul, the American Woodsman could not help thinking they might be the last drawings he would ever do.

3

New York and Boston

SPRING 1833

Mr. Audubon. —*This gentleman, who has acquired the respect
and esteem of those to whom he has become known during a winter's
residence in the city, has now left Boston with the view of preparing
an excursion to the North.*

BOSTON DAILY ADVERTISER & PATRIOT

In England, Audubon's reputation was under assault. The March issue of *The Magazine of Natural History* had printed another denunciation of his six-year-old Turkey Vulture paper by Charles Waterton, the acerbic English naturalist and rabid Audubon hater. This was merely the latest in a string of published attacks that the squire of Walton Hall had launched over the last year to belittle the American naturalist. Encouraged by the Philadelphian George Ord and armed with a vitriolic pen, Waterton had originally taken to the pages of John C. Loudon's respected bimonthly journal in April 1832 to impugn Audubon's assertion that the Turkey Vulture has a poor sense of smell and relies upon its keen eyesight to locate carrion. Waterton described his own experience with these birds during his travels in South America, from which he had concluded that the species uses both senses in searching for food.[1]

Over the months that followed, the Englishman blasted Audubon whenever he had the opportunity. Writing in the June 1832 issue, he questioned the claim by Audubon and others that birds apply oil from a gland at the base of the tail to lubricate their feathers.[2] Ornithologists today are still debating the function of this gland, which is present in most though not all bird species.[3] However, Waterton mocked the American naturalist's observations, saying that he would "earnestly recommend more practice in ornithology to the writer."[4]

In the November issue, Waterton refused to accept Audubon's statement that he had seen a Chuck-Will's Widow, a ground-nesting nightjar of the southern United States, remove the eggs from its nest after the nest was disturbed. In the *Ornithological Biography*, Audubon indicated that both the male and the female left the nest with an egg in their large mouths. Harking back to Audubon's notorious rattlesnake paper, Waterton thought the claim "ought to be received with no common degree of caution; because the eye which could fancy that it saw a rattlesnake swallow a large

[65]

squirrel, tail foremost, might equally fancy that it could discern, at sixteen or eighteen yards distant, the Carolina goatsucker stowing away its eggs in its mouth, and then flying off with them to another part."[5]

The January 1833 journal included a reply to Waterton's months'-old missive on the Turkey Vulture by an Audubon defender from Oxford, who prevailed upon Loudon to publish excerpts from Audubon's original Wernerian Society paper describing the experiments he had conducted to verify his hypothesis. Waterton pounced on this, and when the March issue appeared, it contained the Englishman's withering critique lambasting Audubon's investigation and his interpretation of the results.[6]

Audubon had no formal scientific training, and his study of this matter during his Louisiana years provided the squire with a ready target. In his first experiment, Audubon had placed a deerskin stuffed with dried grass out in an open field and waited nearby to observe what happened. A vulture spotted the faux deer within minutes and then approached it, first pecking at its hard clay eyes. Finding nothing edible, the bird moved to the deer's hindquarters and tore into its straw-filled abdominal cavity. To Waterton, the principal fallacy of Audubon's experiment was his presumption that the stuffed deer carried no odor:

> No lapse of time could have completely subdued the smell which would arise from the ears, the hoofs, the lips, and the very skin itself of the deer. This smell must have been the thing that instigated the bird to look narrowly into the skin, and detained him so long at the place. I have a better opinion of the vulture's sagacity, than to suppose that he would have spent so much of his precious time upon the rudely stuffed mockery of an animal, unless his nose had given him information that some nutriment existed in that which his keen and piercing eye would soon have told him was an absolute cheat.[7]

Audubon's second experiment involved placing a dead hog in a deep, briar-filled ravine over which cane stalks had been bound to prevent it from being seen from the air. However, after a couple of days in the summer sun, the carcass became putrid and attracted several dogs, although the vultures soaring overhead ignored it completely. Waterton scoffed at the very notion that this could have happened as Audubon said:

> Pray, when the dogs were at dinner on the carcass, and the vultures at the same time were flying over the ravine where the hog lay, what prevented these keen-eyed birds from seeing the hog? The author positively says that none discovered the carcass. Could, then, several dogs devour the hams of swine, and riot on pig's liver, in such amazing secrecy and silence as not to be observed in the act

by the lynx-eyed vultures above? Were there no squabbles amongst the dogs for possession of the pig's cheeks? no snarling for the flitch? no pulling the body this way, or that way? no displacing the materials with which the negroes had covered the hog? In a word, was there no movement on the part of the dogs, by which the passing vultures might receive a hint that there was something in the ravine below "calculated for their voracious appetite?" Fear, certainly, could not have kept them away; because the author tells us, in another part of his account, that he has seen vultures feeding at one extremity of a carcass, and dogs at another.[8]

Moreover, by Audubon's own admission, the stench had prevented him from approaching within thirty yards of the rotting corpse. Waterton posited that Audubon had simply failed to observe that both the dogs and the vultures were by then feasting on the remains.[9]

This was a stinging indictment of Audubon's methods in a forum where his professional colleagues and many of his subscribers were certain to see it. However, the prideful naturalist had decided years before to ignore such attacks and let his published work speak for itself. On one level, he had surely come to appreciate his failures in writing these early papers for a scientific audience. But on another, he recognized that any response on his part would simply draw more attention to the criticism.

Whether his twenty-three-year-old son would be able to adopt a similar measure of forbearance was yet unclear. Victor had spent the last two months traveling through England and Scotland canvassing for new subscriptions and meeting with Audubon's agents to collect amounts owed by the current subscribers.[10] He was now in Sheffield on his way back to London, where he was bound to hear from Audubon's many supporters who were troubled by Waterton's malicious remarks.[11] Victor knew full well that his father would want him to hold his tongue. But he could not help bristling at the cheap shots Waterton had taken while Audubon was abroad.

———

In Boston, Audubon and Lucy were struggling with matters of far greater import. But remarkably, about an hour after being paralyzed, the naturalist began to regain feeling and movement in his arm and face. His symptoms soon dissipated, and with them the tension that had filled the room on Pearl Street. Dr. John Collins Warren, the Harvard professor, and Dr. George Parkman, Audubon's "*worthy Friend*," had arrived and were greatly relieved by his improvement. With little else to offer in the way of treatment, the physicians administered a purgative, believing it was vital to cleanse Audubon's system.[12]

The ordeal left the naturalist feeling generally weak, and he remained bedridden for several days. He later wrote that through the care of his two doctors, as well as Dr. George C. Shattuck, who also stopped by to monitor his recovery, "I was soon restored to health, and enabled to pursue my labours." He blamed the attack on the intensity of his recent work habits, coupled with lack of exercise, and described it as a "spasmodic affection" to the readers of the *Ornithological Biography*.[13] Lucy was of a different view. She preferred to think he had simply wolfed down his food too quickly after several days of fasting.[14] Neurologists today would diagnose it as a transient ischemic attack, commonly referred to as a ministroke, which occurs when a blockage in an artery leading to the brain causes temporary neurological symptoms generally lasting less than twenty-four hours. However, in about a third of patients, such an attack is a harbinger of a future stroke.[15]

Audubon had glimpsed his own mortality, and it struck him to the core. But, ever resilient, he insisted on downplaying the episode in a letter written to Victor the following Tuesday, March 19. "[I]t was only about one hour duration," he emphasized, "and at the axception of a general temporary weakness I am again *Myself*!" He thought a "change of avocations" would do him well. He was already aching to get back to work, and with his planned trip to Labrador on the horizon, he had no time to waste.[16]

Looking over the drawings he had completed in the past sixteen months, he assembled two additional Numbers of land birds that he intended to ship to London before his departure for Labrador. They included his Golden Eagle and a composition of three Pinnated Grous (Greater Prairie Chickens) for the large images, Boat-tailed Grackles and Ground Doves for the two medium-sized plates, and six smaller bird species for the remaining prints.[17]

The following day, Audubon wrote to his Philadelphia friend Richard Harlan, M.D., describing the transitory affliction and insisting that he was on the mend. "Now much debility is all that ails me—moderate exercise and a *cessation of Work* will remove this and I hope soon to be myself again." He also took a moment to express to Harlan how much their friendship meant to him. The incident had provided the naturalist with a new perspective and offered an opportunity to reflect on what was important in life:

> Friendship my Dear Harlan is a Jewel which I hold not only sacred, but one which being hereditary (for I received the principles Thereof from my Father) I never can part with. — Through Friendship and the love of Nature's Works all my happiness on this Earth has been derived — I never redraw it when I have once found it accepted by any one worthy of Such deposit, Ergo, You are my Friend and I am Yours to the end of my days.[18]

The enduring strength of Audubon's loyalty to those who had extended him their hand in friendship was one of his most distinguishing qualities, and a reason his circle included men of great aptitude and accomplishment.

However, Harlan was not comforted. His response, dated Saturday, March 23, called to mind other famous men who had been similarly affected and in some cases permanently paralyzed before their inevitable demise. He urged Audubon to visit him in Philadelphia, where he would prescribe the proper course to a full recovery:[19]

> Your favour of the 20th is written in high spirits considering the melancholy
> and fearful attack from which you had escaped.—God grant you may never
> experience another such—yet I think that M[rs] A. has not been unnecessarily
> alarmed—and I do *know* that whilst you continue exposed to similar causes
> (which I observed when in Boston) it is much to be feared that the destiny of
> a Lord Liverpool—Sir W. Scott, Dugald Stewart and our late friend [MS: fri[d]]
> Z. Collins may also be reserved for you—Depend upon it my friend [MS: fri[d]] a
> total change in diet, habits, &[c] is indispensable to your future health—the cause
> of science, the good of humanity, and the glory of the works of nature—lose no
> time in visiting Phil[a]—there is no one so well acquainted with you as I am—
> and from me alone you will obtain such advice as will secure your future health
> (if followed) and place "The Birds of America" out of danger from a similar
> cause.[20]

Harlan forwarded the letter to Nicholas Berthoud, knowing that Audubon and Lucy would soon be leaving Boston for New York. Lucy's postscript to her husband's letter indicated that she had been expecting their move to take place every day for a fortnight.[21] Audubon's fatigue from painting the eagle, followed only days later by the stroke, had detained them, but the naturalist preferred to look on the bright side. The delay, as he informed Harlan in his March 20 letter, had earned them "five valuable names" for *The Birds of America*.[22] By Saturday, March 23, when Audubon sat down to write to Victor, his subscription list had grown by yet another name, bringing the total number in Boston to thirteen, with another four spread around New England.[23]

The Audubons spent that weekend making the rounds of their many Boston friends to take leave, the customary manner at the time of saying goodbye. They were invited to dine with Dr. Parkman and his family on Saturday. During a stop at the grand home of Dr. Shattuck, Audubon asked if Shattuck's son (and namesake) might be interested in joining him the coming summer on his planned journey to Labrador. The nineteen-year-old was away in Brunswick, Maine, attending classes at the Medical School of Maine at Bowdoin College. Shattuck Sr. mentioned the invitation in a letter to his son on Sunday. But he suggested that the young man would have to forgo the opportunity because Audubon expected to be in Eastport, Maine, by May 1 and would leave from there for Labrador. For young Shattuck the spring term would still be in session.[24]

On Monday, March 25, the Audubons crossed over to Cambridge to take leave of the family of Josiah Quincy, the president of Harvard University. Quincy's youngest daughter, Anna, was disappointed to return home that day to learn she had missed them. However, when she opened her picture book, she found to her delight that Audubon had left his bold signature with its customary flourish, and she told her diary it "will ever be most valuable to me."[25]

Two days later, George C. Shattuck Jr. sat down at his desk at Bowdoin College to reply to his father's letter. He expressed a strong wish to accompany Audubon on the voyage, if only for the adventure, but stressed the trip would also provide instruction in natural history and in observing Audubon's "method of investigation." Still, the dutiful son agreed to spend the season pursuing whatever course his father deemed best.[26]

On the same date, almost a thousand miles away, John Bachman took up a pen to write the naturalist, whom he had affectionately nicknamed "Old Jostle" in reference to Audubon's complaints of being jostled about while riding over the South's badly rutted roads.[27] He filled the paper with a string of ornithological details and then announced, as "a secret to tell you in your ear, softly my friend," that he had procured the male of a new, as yet undescribed species of warbler.[28]

The previous summer, Bachman had collected a female and tried to persuade Audubon that it represented a new species.[29] Audubon did not think so, but the male provided the proof. Bachman had prepared the skin and was sending it along with a drawing of the bird done by Maria Martin, his artistically gifted sister-in-law who, still unmarried, made her home with the Bachman family.[30] Since meeting Audubon during his stay in Charleston in 1831, she had been drawing botanical compositions for his use as backgrounds.[31]

In the next month, Audubon would use Maria's illustration of the male warbler, along with one she had done earlier of the female, to prepare his own drawing of the birds perched on a *Franklinia* bush Maria had painted. He gave them the name Bachman's Warbler in honor of their discoverer.[32] Sadly, the species is now believed to be extinct.[33]

————

The Audubons arrived in New York on Friday, March 29.[34] They moved into the Berthouds' fashionable townhouse at 69 Fourth Street on the southern side of Washington Square. The three-story brick structure was built in the Greek Revival style, with a front stoop bordered on either side by wrought-iron railings. Beneath the stoop was the entrance to the basement where the household staff were stationed. Lucy had been invited to stay with Eliza's family during the ensuing months as Audubon and John made their way to Labrador. Although consideration had been given to having her remain in Boston, Audubon and Lucy agreed it would be better if she could respond to any letters from London as soon as they came off the packet ships.[35]

In short order, Audubon was presenting letters of introduction to Philip Hone, the former Mayor of New York, at his magnificent residence at 235 Broadway across from City Hall Park. Hone had made a fortune in the auction business as a young man before retiring in 1820, at the age of forty, to devote his life to civic and social affairs.[36] His prominence brought virtually every visiting notable to his door, and he described his memorable encounter with the naturalist in the diary he had begun keeping in 1828 and would continue writing until shortly before his death in 1851:

> Monday, April 1. — Mr. Audubon, the celebrated ornithologist, called upon me a day or two since with letters of introduction from Mr. Quincy, president of Harvard College, and Col. Perkins of Boston. He is about setting out on one of his enterprising excursions to the coast of Labrador, in pursuit of information to illustrate his favorite science, to which he is devoted with the ardor of a lover to his mistress. He is an interesting man of about 55 years of age, modest in his deportment, possessing general intelligence, an acute mind, and great enthusiasm. His work on the birds of North America, in which he is now engaged, is probably the most splendid book ever published. I have seen several of the numbers in the Library of Congress; it will require nine years to complete it, and will cost $800; all the drawings are executed by himself or under his special superintendence. Wilson's book on the same subject is deservedly celebrated, — beautiful, no doubt, but comparing with Audubon's as the Falls of Trenton to those of Niagara.[37]

While Hone was adding this entry to his journal, Audubon was writing Victor with instructions for getting bound copies of the first volume to some of the New England subscribers, now numbering a total of eighteen. In addition to many distinguished Bostonians, the list included the names of the library of Harvard College, the Boston Society of Natural History, the library of the state legislature known as the General Court of Massachusetts, and the Providence Athenaeum. The naturalist was optimistic that a subscription proposal making its way through the New York State Legislature would also prove successful.[38]

That evening, Audubon dined with an illustrious group that included Mayor Gideon Lee, Philip Hone, Washington Irving, British envoy Sir Charles Vaughan, and Capt. George Back, a British Arctic explorer recently arrived from Liverpool.

Back was on his way to Montreal to head a polar expedition in search of Capt. John Ross, a fellow countryman who had vanished with his party during a quest for the Northwest Passage.[39]

Meanwhile, far to the south in Charleston, Bachman had finally received word of Audubon's illness and scratched out a letter to his dear friend to recommend that he "abandon for a time your sedentary pursuits."[40] He need not have worried. Audubon was reenergized by his new surroundings.

The following day, April 2, the naturalist exhibited his work to a group of invited guests in the rooms of the president of Columbia College, William A. Duer. Philip Hone was in attendance and described the drawings as "truly splendid."[41] Audubon also received a visit from Francis Lieber, a German-American political philosopher and editor of the thirteen-volume *Encyclopædia Americana*.[42] Audubon and Lieber had become acquainted the previous August in Boston as fellow boarders at Mrs. Lekain's and had swum together at Lieber's swimming school, the nation's first, which Lieber had opened along the banks of the Charles River, just north of the Mill Dam, shortly after his arrival from England in 1827.[43] Told of Audubon's forthcoming trip, Lieber was almost inclined to join the expedition and "uncivilize myself, which I would gladly do." But the press of business, including his English translation of Alexis de Tocqueville and Gustave de Beaumont's landmark report on the American prison system, forced him to pass.[44]

Always a tireless promoter, Audubon accepted the invitation of the Trustees of Columbia College to use their Library Room for a public exhibition of his original drawings and engravings from the first folio. During the week of April 8, he could be found there each day from 1:00 p.m. to 3:30 p.m. greeting the large crowds who had read or heard about his "magnificent work."[45]

The local papers stoked an interest in this "native American," who had "devoted nearly forty years to the illustration of the history and habits of the birds of America."[46] It was actually only thirty, but no matter. They hailed his genius and called upon the residents of the city to match the support Boston had given his publication. On April 3, the *New-York American* ran an article that was picked up and republished two days later by the *New-York Gazette & General Advertiser*, proposing the formation of syndicates to acquire copies for the city's leading public institutions:

> *Boston* afforded Mr. Audubon *eighteen subscribers—New-York*, as yet, *not one*. The work is indeed too costly, generally speaking, for individuals, though our city can and should furnish many exceptions to this remark—but a plan quite within the reach of even moderate means, is this—that several individuals, as many or as few as may be requisite, should associate together and present copies

to different public institutions. Columbia College, the University, the City Library, the Historical Library, the Athenæum, the Library of the New-York Hospital, the Lyceum, all should possess this admirable national work.[47]

Audubon received particularly favorable coverage from the *New-York Gazette*, which should have come as no surprise. Edward Harris, whom Audubon considered one of his closest friends, had recently moved to the city from his farm in Moorestown, New Jersey, and taken on an editorial position at the paper. John Lang, the father of Harris's deceased wife, Mary, was the owner and publisher.[48] In its April 5 issue, the paper declared:

> It is to us astonishing and unaccountable, that among the wealthy inhabitants of this city, that so few are to be found, who patronize the enterprize [*sic*] and skill of men of the first order of talent. The work of Mr Audubon is unequalled, and, being a native American, must 'ere long, be amply rewarded.[49]

The New Yorkers responded. Over the next several weeks, Audubon succeeded in augmenting his list with twelve new names, including the State of New York; the library at Columbia College (now Columbia University); P. J. Stuyvesant, M.D., of New York; and Gen. Stephen Van Rensselaer of Albany.[50] In addition, he received a letter from the librarian of the State Library of Maryland asking to be added as a subscriber.[51] While the *New-York Gazette* would later credit New York State with fourteen new subscribers for the month and the *Boston Daily Advertiser* would boost that number by two more, perhaps with a wink and a nod from the naturalist, Lucy informed Victor that the list had increased by only thirteen during their stay.[52]

On April 17, Audubon traveled to Philadelphia with some of his recent drawings and spent a couple of days visiting friends.[53] He saw Dr. Richard Harlan the day after he arrived, and almost certainly received a forceful lecture about the necessity of changing his work habits and diet to minimize the risk of a future attack. Harlan also gave him a copy of *Fauna Americana*, a volume on North American mammals that Harlan had published in 1825.[54]

The naturalist was back in New York by April 19, when he dashed off a quick note to James Curtiss, the Eastport postmaster, to say that he expected to reach the northern Maine town by May 1.[55] The two men had met the previous summer during the Audubon family's excursion, and the twenty-seven-year-old Curtiss had since become one of Audubon's correspondents..[56]

Back on January 25, Audubon had written to his Eastport friend, beseeching Curtiss to collect any owls or hawks that he could find, especially "an *Owl* of a *light grey colour, very large* with yellow eyes and a *long Tail* ^without tufts on its head^ for which I would willingly pay any extra price, you might offer for Such or Several of the same." The naturalist was looking for a specimen of what was known as the Hawk Owl (Northern Hawk Owl), a diurnal hunter of the northern boreal forests. Curtiss was evidently unable to satisfy the request. However, in February he was out hunting on Passamaquoddy Bay and collected another bird Audubon needed, a Large-Billed Guillemot (Thick-billed Murre). The bird, along with several others, was promptly packed in ice and shipped to Boston, where Audubon painted it.[57] Curtiss had agreed to arrange accommodations for the Audubons during their upcoming visit to Eastport.[58]

The following day, the naturalist spent considerably more time on a letter to Havell. He was pleased to report that the number of his American subscribers had reached fifty-five. But he stressed that Americans were *"excellent Judges* of Work particularly of Such as are drawn from their Country's Soil" and urged the engraver to focus his attention on the coloration of the plates. He also raised the possibility of stepping up the rate of publication to seven or eight Numbers per annum once Havell began issuing the prints for the third volume the following year.[59] This was doubtless another consequence of Audubon's neurological spell. Audubon recognized, as never before, the urgency of his task, not only in completing the drawings necessary to fill the promised four volumes but in advancing the culmination of the work.

With an eye to the former, Audubon advised Havell of his plans for the coming months: "My Youngest Son and I are going on a long & tedious Journey this Spring & Summer.—I intend to Visit the Whole coast of Labrador into Hudson's Bay and reach Quebec by returning over Land—No White Man has ever tramped the Country I am about to Visit, and I hope the result will prove profitable to all concerned." He reminded Havell that since there would be *"no Post offices in the Wilderness before us,"* Victor, his "Right Arm and hand," should be consulted on any matters that might arise regarding the publication.[60]

If Audubon had picked up a copy of that day's issue of *The New-York Mirror*, a weekly paper dedicated to literature and the fine arts, he would have been gratified to see an article extolling the virtues of his work and urging every public institution to subscribe:

> Mr. Audubon.—This distinguished ornithologist has been the object of a general interest among the most intelligent classes of society, during his visit to this city. His pictures of the different kinds of wild-fowl are greatly admired. They are full of spirit and animation, and seem startling with the sudden alarms and impulses of actual life. Mr Audubon well merits the respectful attention which every where welcomes his approach, for his eager devotion to the branch of natural history which he has so ably and beautifully illustrated. His exhibitions

of paintings have been thronged with beauty and fashion, and we learn that in the extension of his subscription list he has received substantial tokens of regard. Every public institution should possess itself of his costly and superb work, with a view to testify their interest in the subject of ornithology, and their admiration of the art, as well as their admiration of the man. A more prolific theme could scarcely be selected for the painter and the historian, if not the poet, than the birds of America. They are beings, indeed, of almost incredible beauty, some of them arrayed with a splendour of attire which only nature could bestow, and moving with a grace and celerity, to furnish any idea of which on paper requires the hand of a master. In examining the collection of drawings made by this intelligent and eminent traveller, the dullest observer must be surprised and delighted, and more deeply impressed with the wonders of creation.[61]

During the course of his New York stay, Audubon found time to sit for a portrait by Henry Inman, a Baltimore painter. It was completed by April 28, when the naturalist began a long letter to Victor. The naturalist was pleased with Inman's work, telling his son the painting was a truer likeness than a miniature that had been done two years earlier in London. It shows him in a Byronesque pose, gazing off into the distance with his lips pursed, an open but resolute expression on his face, and his long, wavy hair wrapped around his ears and hanging down to a set of broad shoulders. Often reproduced, it depicts Audubon just as he was about to celebrate his forty-eighth birthday, middle-aged but still vital and strong. To the casual observer, this may well have been how he appeared. The physical symptoms of his stroke had mostly resolved. However, the emotional impact lingered yet.[62]

Continuing his letter to Victor, Audubon enumerated the drawings he was sending, which were to be issued as "Two very beautiful Numbers" — No. 37 (Plates 181–185) and No. 38 (Plates 186–190). He anticipated that a London packet ship would be leaving New York on May 1 and had carefully packaged the drawings in a large tin box, soldered the top, and insured the contents for $2,000.

However, when Audubon traveled down to "the bustle of the Lower part of the City" on April 30, he learned that the next packet would not be leaving until May 10. He returned to the Berthouds' and updated his letter to Victor, saying that the ten drawings would be forwarded to London at that time. He had wanted to include two additional Numbers in the shipment, the final prints of Volume II, but lacked the large drawings for them. He hoped to find something new along the shores of Labrador that would meet the need.[63]

Spring was in the air. The weather in New York was "extremely Warm," almost 72°F that afternoon. During his trip to lower Manhattan, Audubon had seen Purple

Martins darting high above him through the skies. The seasonal migration was under way. Tomorrow, like the birds, he planned to "fly toward the Coast of Labrador."[64]

Before he left, the naturalist took some time to compose a written apology to Charles-Lucien Bonaparte.[65] Audubon had attended a meeting of the Lyceum of Natural History of New-York on April 29 and learned from William Cooper, a founder of the organization and a Bonaparte confidant, that the French ornithologist was upset about a passage in the introduction to the first volume of the *Ornithological Biography*.[66] Audubon had criticized the lengths to which some ornithologists would go for the privilege of describing and naming a new species and, perhaps without meaning to, implied that Bonaparte fell among this group:

> Since I became acquainted with MR ALEXANDER WILSON, the celebrated author of the well-known and duly appreciated work on American Birds, and subsequently with my excellent friend CHARLES LUCIAN BONAPARTE, I have been aware of the keenness with which every student of Natural History presses forward to describe an object of his own discovery, or that may have occurred to travellers in distant countries. There seems to be a pride, a glory in doing this, that thrusts aside every other consideration; and I really believe that the ties of friendship itself would not prevent some naturalists from even robbing an old acquaintance of the merit of first describing a previously unknown object. Although I have certainly felt very great pleasure, when, on picking up a bird, I discovered it to be new to me, yet I have never known the desire above alluded to.[67]

Audubon would never admit it to his readers, but he was just as eager to find an unknown species as his contemporaries, which doubtless only magnified the prince's pique.[68] At the time, scientific reputations and lasting fame were to be won by those who discovered new birds and were first to publish their findings. It was a competitive if not ruthless environment, as the naturalist discovered when he visited Philadelphia with his portfolio in 1824. Along with bragging rights, a discoverer was given the customary right to name the species.[69] This honor afforded Audubon a way of recognizing individuals who had assisted him in his endeavors and simultaneously enhanced the overall reputation of his work. It was for this reason that he planned to send his recently completed drawing of the Bachman's Warbler to Victor with instructions to publish it as part of No. 37.[70]

Whether or not the naturalist had actually intended the perceived slight in reference to Bonaparte, he was quick to deny it in his letter. He insisted that he had never held "even a thought of disparagement" toward the prince and had sung his praises "to all persons who ever have spoken of you." Audubon characterized himself as a "plain sailing man" without a classical education who told the truth as he saw it. But he pointed out that he would be unworthy of the good wishes of anyone, let alone of Bonaparte, if he had sought to criticize the prince in one section of the introduction while simultaneously commending him as the "celebrated CHARLES LUCIAN BONA-PARTE" in another.[71]

The relationship of these two men was a complicated and changing one.[72] It is evident from Bonaparte's surviving correspondence that he thought highly of Audubon's artistic skill but held a generally low opinion of him as a student of the scientific discipline of ornithology.[73] Audubon was admittedly less interested in the detailed, scientific study of birds. He proudly boasted that he was not a "closet naturalist" as were men like Bonaparte and Swainson, who spent most of their time poring over dried birdskins kept in dusty, arsenic-filled cabinets. His labors took him to the open fields, forests, and swamps of his adopted country, where he observed birds in their natural environment and focused on their behavior. Both approaches had substantial value, but the two men did not necessarily see it that way. Audubon, however, had no wish to impair his standing with Bonaparte, whom he viewed as both a current subscriber and longtime supporter. He therefore went to substantial lengths to smooth over any misunderstanding that his publication may have caused.

At 5:00 p.m. on May 1, Audubon and his son John, now twenty years of age, left New York for Providence aboard the steamer *Benjamin Franklin*.[74] The two-engine vessel, constructed in 1828, was 144 feet long. She was also ship-rigged with three masts. Her design and appointments made for a pleasant trip across Long Island Sound:[75]

> She bore, by way of ornament, an excellent bust of the philosopher from whom she was named. On the left of the bust was a figure of Fame in the act of crowning the sage with an olive wreath; while on the right was the Muse of History with her scroll to record the deeds and the lessons of wisdom which fall from his lips. Reaching the deck, one looked in vain for the ponderous machinery, and the numerous little cabins and offices usually to be seen. With the exception of a small enclosure around the head of the stairs leading to the ladies' cabin, the deck was open and unencumbered from stem to stern. On each side of this open saloon was what appeared to be a long range of rooms furnished like the fronts of summer houses. Within the seemingly beautiful rooms, however, were the boilers, baggage rooms, offices, kitchen, etc.
>
> The boat was finished, as the veracious chronicler hath it, "with an eye to neatness, plainness, comfort, and convenience." The ladies cabin had a rich Brussels carpet, damask curtains and furniture to correspond. The panel work was finished in imitation of satin-wood and bird's-eye maple. The dining room

was 75 feet long, 24 feet wide, and arranged for two rows of tables. The bar was in the forward cabin. So were generally the male passengers. The Franklin was considered the crack boat on the Sound.[76]

Audubon had hoped Edward Harris would see them off but, more importantly, throw in his lot and accompany them to Labrador. However, the gentleman farmer and newspaper editor was nowhere to be seen as the steamer left the pier at the foot of Cortlandt Street on the western side of lower Manhattan.[77] The following morning, an article that undoubtedly expressed Harris's sentiments appeared in the pages of the *New-York Gazette*:

> Mr. A. carries with him the good wishes of many warm friends in this city. May a kind Providence guard him, as hitherto, and preserve him through every difficulty and danger, and restore him to his beloved family and friends. We feel proud that New York has not been backward in doing justice to the merits of this extraordinary man, (as all the world will pronounce him when his history shall be better known.) Fourteen names are now on his list of subscribers from this State, and his work is only beginning to be known among us.[78]

For Lucy, the loss of her two men left her feeling anxious and alone. She was deeply concerned about Audubon's health, telling Victor that he "is not so strong as he was."[79] But she, like Audubon, knew that he had no choice but to make the trip. In order to keep his publication on track, he was under constant pressure to find and paint additional species, especially the waterbirds that would fill the next volume of his work. He also had to gather information about the life histories of these birds—their habitats, behaviors, and geographic ranges—in order to pen the accompanying species accounts.

However, that was only part of it. Audubon now defined himself by the success of his enormous project. It had renewed his dignity, and he was driven to complete it. For this reason alone, Lucy was willing to give him up to Labrador, which beckoned with its avian riches.

Though there were risks to such a journey, she took some comfort from the fact that John was accompanying him, and she knew that the restorative power of an adventure into the wilds was precisely what Audubon needed after his recent stroke.[80] Indeed, within weeks she would inform Victor that Audubon's letters exhibited "the same enthusiasm as if he was just going to enter into possession of Paradise."[81]

Still, she was dreading the months of silence that would face her once Audubon and John sailed north. At the same time, she was uncomfortable living at the Berthouds'. While she got along well enough with her sister Eliza, Lucy had always been afraid of Nicholas, for whom, she confided to Victor, "age has not added the milk of human kindness in the least."[82]

Moreover, Audubon's success had given rise to new demands by his brother-in-law for payment of the remainder of the old Kentucky debts, which had not been extinguished by the naturalist's 1819 bankruptcy petition.[83] Lucy took to calling Nicholas "Mr. Graspall" when writing to Victor.[84] For his part, Audubon had resisted Nicholas's requests during his visit. But before he left for Boston, he sought to mollify the merchant and forestall future efforts to collect on these sums by presenting Nicholas with a gift of a bound copy of the first volume of *The Birds of America*. At the same time, the naturalist's largess served a second, unstated purpose. Nicholas was now serving as Audubon's New York agent, and this would enable potential subscribers to view the work.[85]

———

In London, the May issue of *The Magazine of Natural History* appeared on the first of the month, and Victor could not have been happy when he opened it. Charles Waterton had returned again to the journal's pages with another polemic maligning Audubon's good name. He wondered that this man, "[w]ithout leaving behind him in America any public reputation as a naturalist," arrived in England and was "immediately pointed out to us as an ornithological luminary of the first magnitude." Waterton discounted Audubon's drawings as the reason because they were "solely a work of art." And, in his view, Audubon's esteem could not possibly derive from the infamous Turkey Vulture paper as "that production is lamentably faulty at almost every point." Instead, Waterton suggested that the naturalist's high regard must have been attributable to his *Ornithological Biography*, ignoring the obvious fact that this work was published five years after Audubon was first celebrated in England. In comparing the *Ornithological Biography* to the Turkey Vulture paper, Waterton concluded that "these two productions could not have been written by the same person, though they both have the name of Audubon attached to them. The first is that of a finished scholar; the second that of a very moderately educated man."[86]

Waterton believed he had found the answer in the book's introduction, where Audubon freely admitted to having received assistance from a friend in "completing the scientific details, and in smoothing down the asperities of his ornithological biographies." But Waterton questioned whether this was all that was done. He had "undeniable proof," he told Loudon's readers, that Audubon initially approached an unnamed English gentleman — obviously William Swainson — to write the book. "The gentleman," according to Waterton, "at first consented to write it; but the agreement subsequently fell to the ground, on account of Mr. Audubon insisting that *his own name* should be given to the world as the *author of the work*." The fact that Audubon had thought it necessary to solicit another author demonstrated he was not capable of writing the book himself. Moreover, the entire work, in Waterton's view, bore "evident and undeniable marks of being the produce of one pen," and that pen was clearly not Audubon's.[87]

Victor must have read the Englishman's disparaging attack in anger and disbelief. It was entirely fallacious, filled with erroneous assumptions and patent untruths. The question was, how should he handle it? His parents would not be able to offer any guidance. As far as Victor knew, his father was either on his way to Labrador or soon to depart, and it would take almost two months to obtain an answer to any letter sent home to his mother. The next issue of Loudon's magazine would appear on July 1 and go to press even earlier. If there was to be a response, Victor realized that it would have to come from him. He was not alone in thinking that Waterton's baseless charges could not go unanswered.

Audubon and John reached Providence on the morning of Thursday, May 2, and took the stage to Boston, where they arrived at around 3:30 p.m., just twenty-two and a half hours after leaving New York.[88] They were evidently invited to stay with Boston merchant Joshua Davis and his wife in their apartment at Mrs. Lekain's boardinghouse on Pearl Street.[89] The naturalist spent part of Friday with Dr. Parkman, "as ever the most remarkable good Man I know," and delivered copies of the first volume of *The Birds of America* to recent subscribers, including the Commonwealth of Massachusetts.[90] He collected a total of $1,221, $691 of which he immediately sent to his brother-in-law in New York with instructions to forward £100 to Victor.[91]

Boston's *Daily Evening Transcript*, picking up a blurb from the *Philadelphia Gazette*, reported on Audubon's forthcoming voyage in its Friday edition:

> MR AUDUBON has left us, and is now on his way to Labrador. He will return rejoicing, bringing his birds with him. Among his recent drawings which we have had the pleasure of examining, is one large and splendid sheet, representing the Golden Eagle. The picture seems instinct with life, and one can almost see the tremor of the bird and hear the rustling of his wings. The scenery, with which the back ground of Audubon's drawings are always clothed, is of the most faithful character, and shows his botanical as well as ornithological skill and knowledge.[92]

That evening, Audubon paid a call on Dr. Shattuck at his elegant home on the corner of Staniford and Cambridge streets.[93] One of Boston's most highly regarded physicians, the forty-nine-year-old Shattuck was an 1803 graduate of Dartmouth College. He had gone on to study medicine at Dartmouth Medical School under its founder, Nathan Smith, M.D., who also played a role in establishing the medical schools at Yale, Bowdoin, and the University of Vermont.[94] Shattuck received a Bachelor of Medicine degree from Dartmouth in 1806 and an M.D. degree from the University of Pennsylvania the following year. Dartmouth bestowed an honorary M.D. degree on him in 1812. The young doctor demonstrated brilliance early in his career, winning the prestigious Boylston Prize from Harvard University once in 1806, and twice in 1807, for the best dissertations submitted on medical questions posed by a committee of esteemed physicians.[95]

Shattuck's skill as a physician earned him prominence and success. His marriage to Eliza Cheever Davis in 1811 brought him substantial wealth. She was the daughter of Caleb Davis, a well-to-do Boston merchant and the first Speaker of the Massachusetts House of Representatives under the commonwealth's Constitution of 1780. Eliza's forebears on the Cheever side were even more prosperous. Elizabeth Cheever Derby, her aunt, was among the wealthiest women in Boston.[96]

The Shattucks had seven children, but only three of them survived to school age. In addition to their son, George, they had two younger daughters: Eleanor, or Ellen, as she was commonly known, born in 1819; and Lucy, who was born four years later.[97]

A portrait of Dr. Shattuck painted by Gilbert Stuart in 1827, the year before Eliza's untimely death, shows the blue-eyed physician with a benign, round, almost cherubic face framed by wavy locks of reddish-brown hair tumbling haphazardly over his forehead and encroaching upon his ears. His was an open, approachable mien, and patients from every social class turned to him for treatment along with his sage counsel. He was known to ask needy patients if they would mind carrying a sealed note to his Congress Street tailor while they waited for their prescription to be filled by the apothecary on Washington Street. Invariably, the note to the tailor read, "Please give this man a coat, or vest, or pair of pantaloons, or greatcoat, cloak, or a suit of clothes suited to his condition."[98]

Each year, Shattuck would serve as an adjunct instructor to several of the medical students who were attending the lectures at the Massachusetts Medical College of Harvard University, providing them with a real-life learning environment in his medical office, and a space over a nearby stable to dissect animals. A colleague who studied under him recalled that "there was such an affectionate kindness of manner, so much gravity and wisdom in his conversation, such a rare sincerity of speech, and he manifested so much interest in the persons with whom he had intercourse, that he won the strong attachment of those who put themselves under his care." The same could be said for those whom he had befriended, like the noted naturalist who stopped by on this evening for a visit.[99]

After an exchange of pleasantries, Audubon renewed his invitation for Shattuck's son to join him on the expedition.[100] The naturalist had almost certainly given this some thought. He knew that he was likely to need some youthful energy to search for birds once his party reached Labrador. He would be busy painting and would not have the time to procure specimens. He also could not ignore the fact that he was still regaining his strength and stamina following the stroke. But, just as importantly, he hoped that by recruiting the sons of well-to-do families he might be able to persuade them to defray some of the substantial costs of the trip.

Shattuck Jr. was still at medical school in Maine, where the term was coming to an end.[101] The senior Shattuck assured the naturalist that he would convey the invitation but indicated he would leave the decision to his son. As he explained in a letter written and posted to Brunswick the following day, "I told him I should submit it to your option, that if you had an ardent desire to go, I would not repress it, and if you had no special desire to go, I would not urge it." If the young man elected to join the expedition, his father advised him to "settle up at Brunswick all your accounts, and start for Eastport," where Audubon was heading and planned to stay about ten days before sailing for Labrador. Shattuck asked his son to write to him with his answer by the next mail.[102]

Also on Friday evening, Audubon saw Col. Thomas H. Perkins, one of his subscribers and the immediate past president of the Boston Athenaeum. The wealthy merchant invited him to pay a call the following morning.[103] There was much talk in the city about the fair that had been held over the past three days at Faneuil Hall to raise money for the newly established Perkins Institution for the Blind. Perkins had agreed to donate his palatial mansion on Pearl Street to house the institute, and a group of society women came up with the idea of holding a fair to raise money for the building fund.[104] The acclaimed young British actress Frances "Fanny" Kemble, who was in Boston as part of an American acting tour with her thespian father, Charles Kemble, captured the spirit of the fair in her journal. "The whole thing was crowd, crush, and confusion, to my bewildered eyes," she observed. "I thought the prices enormous, but the money is well spent in itself, or rather, on its ultimate object, and the immediate return is of no import."[105]

Audubon booked passage for himself and John aboard the *Edward Preble*, a coastal packet schooner of 133 tons burden that ferried passengers and cargo between Boston and Eastport.[106] Built by the master shipbuilders of Eastport in 1825, the vessel was named after Edward Preble, the captain of the USS *Constitution* during the first Barbary War in 1803.[107] Audubon noted in a letter to Lucy on Saturday morning that there were twenty-six passengers making the trip and that "we will have to Pig together on the floor of the cabin." He was expecting the schooner to sail at around 3:00 p.m. on Saturday afternoon.[108]

At noon he picked up his pen to continue the letter after he had stopped by to see

Col. Perkins. He told Lucy that Perkins had invited him to dinner that evening with the Kembles, but the expected departure of the *Edward Preble* at 4:00 p.m., "Wind ahead or not," had forced him to decline.[109]

Audubon was in New York when the Kembles arrived in Boston, and he was seemingly unaware of the excitement their presence in the city had generated. Throngs of admirers gathered in front of the Tremont Theater, the most popular theater in Boston, waiting for tickets. Ticket scalpers, whom Fannie described as "men of low order," had come up with an "ingenious" way to force an opening to the front of the crowds. "[T]hese worthies smear their clothes with molasses, and sugar, &c., in order to prevent any person of more decent appearance, or whose clothes are worth a cent, from coming near the box office."[110]

Audubon, however, did not even know how to spell the Kembles' surname. In his letter to Lucy, he twice misspelled it phonetically as "Campbell" before he went back and corrected it.[111] But he took the opportunity to pay a call on them on Saturday morning and presented Fannie with a copy of the first volume of the *Ornithological Biography*.[112] Fannie, he told Lucy, was "not handsome I guess, but appears quite amiable & without humbug."[113] He was more impressed by her father, who "looks *like a Gentleman*." Their reactions to him were measured, and Audubon came away with the sense that they looked at him "as an Original bear, but I care not for that." Fannie, who kept a diary of her activities and the people she met, did not mention Audubon's visit when she published her journal two years later, although some Audubon biographers have mistakenly thought otherwise.[114]

The Saturday edition of the *Boston Daily Advertiser & Patriot* notified its readership of Audubon's imminent departure from the city:

MR AUDUBON arrived in this city on Thursday, and leaves it to-day on his excursion towards the North. We understand that sixteen subscriptions to his great work have been recently received in New-York. Every one must wish him abundant success in his important and interesting labors.[115]

On the same day, one of the Philadelphia papers, the *National Gazette and Literary Register*, ran a similar piece:

The departure of John A. [*sic*] Audubon, Esq., the celebrated naturalist, on an expedition to Labrador by Boston, Maine, Newfoundland, &c. has been announced. He has already, with indefatigable zeal, visited every state and territory of our immense country, in pursuit of his favorite objects of science. He now goes to complete his present plan of enquiry and toil in those more Northern regions where alone some of our birds develope [*sic*] their peculiar characteristics. We wish him a degree of success and prolongation of vigor equal to his great merits: indeed, for the past at least, success is fully assured. His work on Ornithology is a lasting monument of genius and zeal, of which Cuvier, the first of natural philosophers, did not say too much, when he declared that it "surpasses all others in magnificence."[116]

The *Edward Preble* could not sail that afternoon as planned, when the vessel became caught in the mud at low tide, "hard & fast," as Audubon related to Lucy in a letter he sat down to write at 7:30 p.m.[117] Capt. Bowman, the master of the schooner, was sure that they would be ready to leave at around nine o'clock with the high tide.[118] However, the heavens were clouding up, and Audubon was not sure if they would leave even then. If not, he did not expect they would leave on Sunday, in which case, he told Lucy, "I am a Christian I will go to Church & pray for thy health & Happiness in this World and all other Worlds."[119]

In view of the delay, Audubon regretted that he had been unable to join the Kembles and Col. Perkins for dinner.[120] He had seen Josiah Quincy and his "beautiful Daughter" Maria Sophia Quincy, who had come into Boston that afternoon from their home in Cambridge. Both had sent their remembrances to Lucy, which Audubon dutifully relayed.[121]

When John returned from the harbor with word from Capt. Bowman that the vessel would "undoubtedly go at 9 o'clock," Audubon hastily closed the letter to his wife. He urged her to sit for a companion portrait by Henry Inman, which he felt sure would be "good & true."[122]

Audubon and John headed down to the docks and boarded the packet, which was crowded with passengers. The schooner, once again afloat and its canvas sails unfurled, pulled away from the wharf at 10:45 p.m. and glided into the dark, cloud-filled night.[123]

In Brunswick the next day, Sunday, May 5, George C. Shattuck Jr. received his father's letter of the day before and broke the seal. He "pondered over the invitation of Mr Audubon with a great desire to accept it" but did not feel capable of making the decision by himself.[124]

The bookish young man had grown up in a family of great privilege, but the early deaths of three younger brothers had left him his father's only surviving son. George C. Shattuck Sr. was a controlling, autocratic parent, in marked contrast to the warmth and humanity he showed his patients. From the outset, he had taken a firm hand in the boy's education, dictating the path he expected his son to follow. Shattuck Jr.'s early years were spent at the Boston Latin School. Then, as an eleven-year-old in 1824, he was sent away to attend the recently founded Round Hill School in Northampton, Massachusetts, a two-day ride from Boston in the western part of the state. His mother, Eliza, who was in frail health, longed for the boy to continue his education closer to home, where she could see him more often. But his father would not hear of it. The young Shattuck was in Northampton when his mother died in June 1828. The following year he entered Harvard as a junior, graduating at the age of eighteen as a member of the Class of 1831.[125]

Reading Shattuck's response to his father, carefully composed later that day, it is apparent that he desperately wished to join the expedition. But to obtain his father's sanction, which had been missing from Shattuck Sr.'s letter, the young man recognized he would need the support of men his father knew and respected.[126] He turned to two of his instructors, Dr. Reuben D. Mussey and Dr. William Sweetser.[127]

Mussey and Shattuck had been classmates and friends at Dartmouth and studied medicine together at Dartmouth Medical College.[128] Sweetser had taught for several years at the medical school at the University of Vermont, where Shattuck's erstwhile student and protégé, Benjamin Lincoln, M.D., was the professor of anatomy and surgery.[129] And, indeed, both men were enthusiastic about the prospect of their student sailing with Audubon to Labrador:

Dr Mussey not being at home, I called first on Dr. Sweetser, stated to him the invitation, my own views and requested his advice. He thought were he in my situation he would certainly go. I found Dr. Mussey on my return, and talked over the affair with him and he used the same expression were he in my situation he should go. I interpreted your letter also, as expressing an opinion that it would be well for me to go, and therefore I have made up my mind to go.[130]

If the counsel of his professors was not enough, the young man offered his father additional reasons favoring the decision:

Could such a tour be deferred for one year I should then be able to improve more from it, but the question is not shall I go now or next year, but; shall I go at all. With such a man as Mr Audubon under what great advantages shall I prosecute the study of natural history, of comparative anatomy. And are not these worth acquiring of themselves, are they not worth acquiring as bearing upon the profession I am to pursue. Can I ever study them under so great advantages. Then I expect great benefit to my bodily health, from the bodily exertions I shall be compelled to make, and from the exposure to the open air. You see then the objects which I expect to gain. I have also reflected on the probable acquirements I should make did I stay at home, and am convinced I should do more in the course I am determined on.[131]

The senior Shattuck had wanted his son to practice law following his graduation from Harvard, evidently fearing the strains a medical career would place on the

young man's weak constitution. To placate him, Shattuck Jr. had attended a semes-
ter at Harvard's law school before asserting his independence and insisting on following his eminent father into the practice of medicine.[132] Shattuck Jr.'s letter, laying out a persuasive case for accompanying Audubon, undoubtedly reinforced Dr.
Shattuck's belief that his son could have enjoyed a successful career before the bar.

In finishing the letter to his father, Shattuck provided a list of several books from
their extensive library in Boston which he wished to have shipped to Eastport so
that he could learn more about natural history, comparative anatomy, botany, and
mineralogy.[133]

Shattuck also wrote to Dr. Lincoln in Burlington for advice as to what areas of
natural history he should attempt to study during the trip and which volumes he
should take along. The young man acknowledged that up to this point in his life his
learning had come almost entirely from books. "[N]ow my senses are to be put to their
full task in the study of nature's page."[134] Shattuck hoped Dr. Lincoln could find a
few moments to write to him at Eastport. He then began making plans for his departure.

That evening, Shattuck returned to his writing table to tell his father that he had
met with Prof. Parker Cleaveland, one of the country's foremost geologists, to discuss the geology and mineralogy of the Labrador coast.[135] In addition, he had spoken
once more with Dr. Mussey, who had invited him to come to Dartmouth to resume
his medical studies when he returned from the voyage. Shattuck told his father that
he intended to continue with a vegetarian diet, which he had adopted weeks earlier
at Mussey's suggestion:

> I have promised him to adhere to my vegetable diet, as long as I can, and I shall
> do it most strictly, where I can find sufficiency of any one vegetable article. I can
> be very well satisfied on dry bread and water. For this last week I have cut off
> butter cheese and apple sauce from my bill of fare for I found that the pimples
> on my face still lingered while I continued to use them. I must say that I never
> remember feeling so perfectly well and clear about every part of me as at the
> present moment, and for the last weeks![136]

Monday morning arrived in Brunswick, bright and beautiful. Shattuck stopped
by the bank when it first opened, hoping to obtain an advance of funds for the trip.
However, when the bank declined despite his use of Dr. Mussey's name, Mussey
agreed to lend him $250. Shattuck informed his father about this in a quick note he
added to his letter of the night before.[137] At 10:00 a.m., the young man shook hands
with Dr. Mussey and boarded a mail stage bound for Augusta, the state capital, on
his way to Eastport and the grand adventure of a lifetime.[138]

4

Eastport

MAY 1833

We are safely landed at this shockingly cold place of Eastport.

JOHN JAMES AUDUBON

Passamaquoddy Bay lies off the Bay of Fundy at the mouth of the St. Croix River and sits astride the border between the northeastern corner of Maine and the Canadian province of New Brunswick. Dotted with fir- and spruce-covered islands and bounded by rocky shores, it is an often fog-enshrouded place of treacherous currents and extreme, twenty-five-foot tidal swings. It is also the home of Eastport, Maine, a small community nestled on Moose Island, the largest of the islands on the American side of the border. This irregular-shaped land area, roughly four miles in length and two miles across at its widest point, boasts one of the finest harbors on the Atlantic coast.[1]

Over the years, Eastport's proximity to Canada has shaped its history in ways both large and small. It was settled toward the end of the Revolutionary War by fishermen from Massachusetts when Maine was a district of that state. In 1798, it was incorporated as a town.[2] It became a haven for smugglers of Canadian gypsum during the Embargo Act of 1807 despite the presence of the Passamaquoddy Customs District, formed by Congress in 1790 to collect duties from foreign imports.[3] The innumerable inlets of the islands in Passamaquoddy Bay made smuggling a relatively safe venture.[4]

In 1812, with the declaration of war between the United States and England, a committee of Eastport citizens adopted a resolution declaring their desire to avoid conflicts with their neighbors across the water in New Brunswick.[5] But two years later a British fleet sailed into Passamaquoddy Bay and seized the city.[6] Eastport remained under British control until 1818, when it was returned to the United States as a result of negotiations associated with the Treaty of Ghent.[7] Due to the failure of Massachusetts to defend the Maine district during the war, a movement to create a separate state took root and ultimately resulted in Maine's joining the United States in 1820 as part of the Missouri Compromise.[8]

The town had grown substantially since its early days when only a handful of families occupied the island. A total of 2,450 residents were counted in the 1830

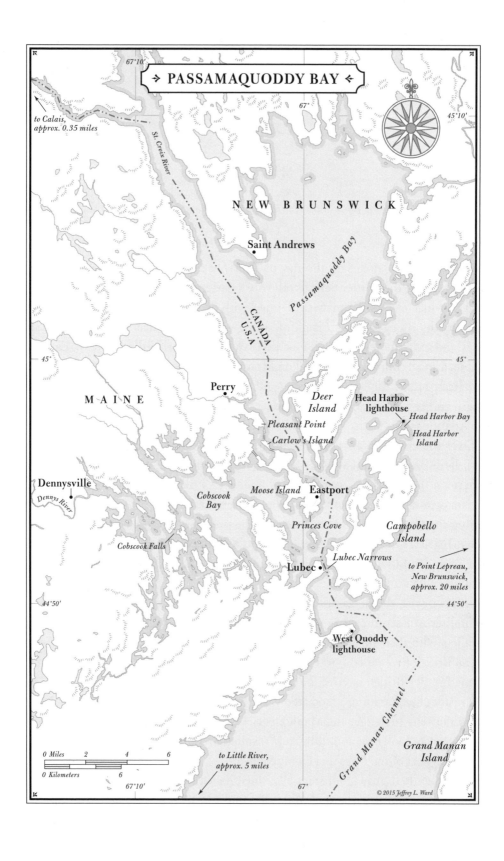

↠ PASSAMAQUODDY BAY ↞

67°10'

67°

45°10'

to Calais,
approx. 0.35 miles

St. Croix River

N E W   B R U N S W I C K

Saint Andrews

Passamaquoddy Bay

CANADA
U.S.A.

45°

45°

M · A · I · N · E

Perry

*Deer
Island*

**Head Harbor
lighthouse**

Head Harbor Bay

*Head Harbor
Island*

Pleasant Point

Carlow's Island

Dennysville

Dennys River

*Cobscook
Bay*

Moose Island **Eastport**

*Campobello
Island*

Princes Cove

to Point Lepreau,
New Brunswick,
approx. 20 miles

Cobscook Falls

Lubec Narrows

44°50'

Lubec

44°50'

**West Quoddy
lighthouse**

Grand Manan Channel

0 Miles   2   4   6

0 Kilometers   6

to Little River,
approx. 5 miles

*Grand Manan
Island*

67°10'

67°

© 2015 Jeffrey L. Ward

U.S. Census. An accounting for the state in the same year identified "209 dwelling-houses, 72 barns, 34 stores and shops, 11 warehouses, 2 brick-yards, 1 ship-yard, [and] 117,530 superficial feet of wharf."[9]

By 1833, Eastport was one of the busiest shipping ports on the Eastern seaboard. During the course of that year, 1,820 vessels from the Canadian provinces, Liverpool, the West Indies, and American ports docked at Eastport carrying goods subject to inspection by the customs collector.[10] Only New York received more ships from foreign lands. But Eastport's contact with the outside world was not limited to seagoing crafts. On the opposite side of the island, two wooden bridges spanned the water to the mainland—the first having been built in 1820 to connect the town to the community of Perry, Maine, and a second at Pleasant Point by way of Carlow's Island in 1832.[11]

The streets of Eastport were "regularly laid out as per compass and rule," and, as in most New England communities, the homes were painted "white as the driven snow."[12] On a hill on the northern side of town sat Fort Sullivan, where Company A of the 3rd Artillery Regiment of the U.S. Army was garrisoned. Fort Sullivan had been built in 1808 as part of the "second system" of coastal defense for the young country.[13] It had a clear view of the surrounding bay waters and could fire upon any hostile vessels approaching the island.[14] A large, twenty-four-star American flag the size of a topsail flapped above the red roofs and white walls of the fort's several buildings. A contemporary visitor to Eastport noted that the flag was "[t]he first object, which is supereminently apparent from the deck of a vessel" approaching the town.[15]

It was on the afternoon of Tuesday, May 7, following three nights and three days at sea, that the *Edward Preble* sailed into Passamaquoddy Bay and approached one of the many weathered wharves along the Eastport waterfront. During her first day out of Boston, the wind had died and, according to Audubon, the vessel "stood almost still." The naturalist, who almost always suffered from seasickness, felt fine throughout the voyage, but John was ill until the morning of their arrival.[16]

Standing on the schooner's deck as the vessel made her way along the ship channel into Passamaquoddy Bay, Audubon could see no evidence that spring had made its presence felt here along the northern Maine coast. There was "[n]ot a sign of vegetation."[17] Snow could still be seen on the ground in the woods, ice hung from the rocky cliffs, and large mounds of snow and ice several feet high were massed along the shoreline.[18] It was "shockingly cold," and the thin coats and outer coats he and his son were wearing offered little warmth.[19]

Ever watchful for birds, Audubon observed Surf Ducks (Surf Scoters) migrating eastward over the bay.[20] Flocks of black-hooded Bonapartian Gulls (Bonaparte's Gulls) soared above the water and flew around the vessel.[21] Barn Swallows and

Cliff Swallows, recently arrived from warmer climes, wheeled through the frigid air searching for insects.[22]

After disembarking, the Audubons were greeted by James Curtiss, the Eastport postmaster and past editor of *The Northern Light*, a weekly newspaper with Jacksonian Democratic leanings.[23] In response to a question from the naturalist about the amount of snow they had seen coming into the bay, the postmaster remarked that it had been deeper that winter than for many years past.[24]

Curtiss had arranged for the Audubons to stay at the home of Jonathan D. Weston, a fifty-one-year-old Eastport attorney who also served as deputy revenue collector and town clerk.[25] Although the two families had never met, Weston was only too happy to offer them accommodations. With Weston's wife, Jane, away in Boston, his raven-haired daughter Lucy, twenty-six and still unmarried, would be their hostess.[26]

The Weston house, located at the southeast corner of Boynton and Middle streets, was a two-story Federal-style clapboard structure with a hipped roof which had been built in 1810.[27] The Audubons were given a large upstairs bedroom that looked out over Passamaquoddy Bay. When the naturalist sat down to write his wife just two hours after landing, he assured her that they were "very agreably situated."[28]

Another prominent Eastport attorney, Maj. Ichabod Rollins Chadbourne, also paid his respects shortly after the Audubons' arrival.[29] Two years junior to the naturalist, Chadbourne was, in the words of a local historian, "a man of commanding presence, a marked figure in our streets, an effective public speaker, and was often heard at town meetings and on other occasions."[30] In his letter to Lucy, Audubon referred to him phonetically as "Major Shatburn," the title an allusion to Chadbourne's previous service as division inspector for the 10th Division of the Maine Militia commanded by Gen. Jedediah Herrick.[31]

Chadbourne's thirty-two-year-old wife, Hannah, was the eldest daughter of Judge Theodore Lincoln of Dennysville, Maine, a small inland community on the Dennys River about eighteen miles west of Eastport.[32] Judge Lincoln had arrived in northern Maine in 1786, fresh out of Harvard and seeking adventure as the leader of a group of settlers from Hingham, Massachusetts. They carved the town out of a wilderness tract acquired by a group of Boston land speculators that included Lincoln's father, Maj. Gen. Benjamin Lincoln, a Revolutionary War hero who accepted the surrender of British Gen. Lord Cornwallis at Yorktown. The first frame house to be constructed in Dennysville was built for Lincoln in a style similar to the family home in Hingham. In 1799, he married Hannah Mayhew, a young woman from Machias. She had originally been hired to serve as his housekeeper but quickly captured his attention and his heart. Lincoln fathered nine children, became a local leader, and was appointed judge of the Court of Common Pleas and Sessions for Washington County.[33]

According to George F. Talbot, who served as U.S. attorney for the State of Maine and later as solicitor of the U.S. Treasury Department, the judge was both personable and down-to-earth:

> He was familiar and friendly with all. He loved anecdotes and told them well. He had a keen sense of the ludicrous. He liked nicknames and used them freely. He called his acquaintances by their Christian names, and shortened William into Bill. He had a word for everybody, and always a cheering word. His thinking was of practical things, his interests in the world of nature, in the crops and the cattle, the freshets, the cedar swamps, the rockweed, the head of water, the dry hard wood, the meadow hay. His activity was irrepressible.[34]

Lincoln was just the sort of man Audubon would gravitate to. And he did. The Lincolns had hosted the Audubon family for a few weeks during their visit to northern Maine the previous summer, a stay that the naturalist described as "exceedingly agreeable."[35] Audubon grew particularly fond of the judge's youngest son, Tom, who was nine months older than John and shared an interest in birds and the natural world. Tom took Audubon, John, and Victor on a search through the woods around Dennysville for the elusive Canada Grous (Spruce Grouse). After returning to Boston, the naturalist invited Tom to visit and stay with his family for the winter, an invitation the young man appreciated but found impossible to accept.[36]

Chadbourne told Audubon that his brother-in-law had recently collected a rare bird and was very eager that the naturalist see it. Audubon was skeptical. "Tomorrow," he wrote Lucy, "we go in a Gig to Dennis-ville to see a Bird which has been kept in the Ice these 3 weeks by Thoˢ Lincoln and one which is described to us a[s] a great wonder, but which I fear will prove like many others nothing either new or even very Strange."[37] As the most famous birdman of his day, the naturalist undoubtedly received frequent invitations of this sort from people who had spotted or procured what to them was an unusual bird, and thought sure it would interest him. However, there were few birds he was unfamiliar with, and it would appear he had grown accustomed to being disappointed.

Audubon had observed relatively little birdlife as the *Edward Preble* approached Eastport, but he was looking forward to taking a trip to Point Lepreau, New Brunswick, about thirty miles northeast along the coast on the Bay of Fundy, the day after he returned from Dennysville. Curtiss had planted the seed in a letter he had written to the naturalist back in January and now reassured him an "aboundance of Birds are to be found" there.[38]

Audubon expected to receive the cooperation of the Revenue Cutter Service in transporting him to Point Lepreau.[39] He carried the December 1831 letter written by Treasury Secretary Louis McLane, authorizing him to make use of the department's revenue cutters stationed from Charleston to Mobile to advance his scientific explorations. He evidently viewed this as a license to request accommodations and transit on any of the service's vessels. In the Passamaquoddy Customs District, there were two schooners plying the coastline from the Eastport wharves on behalf of the service—the 110-ton cutter *Swiftsure* and her smaller tender, the *Fancy*.[40] Audubon wrote Lucy that "the Revenue Cutter," by which he meant the *Swiftsure*, was at sea "but is expected in a day or 2 when we will institute ourselves Passengers in Chief."[41]

Audubon had not given up hope that Edward Harris would join him and accompany the expedition to Labrador. In his letter to Lucy, he asked her to let Harris know that there was still time for him to reach Eastport before the expedition departed. "Tell Friend Harris that the weather is too cold to proceed eastwards at present and that we will remain *here* and *about here* for a fortnight to come and that he may expect a letter from me a few days after this—and should like amazingly to see him forthcoming."[42]

Audubon mentioned that he had briefly seen the commander of the garrison at Fort Sullivan, Capt. Thomas Childs, an 1814 graduate of West Point and veteran of the War of 1812. He knew Lucy would be interested. Both Childs and his pregnant wife, Ann, who was due almost any day, had befriended the naturalist and his family the previous summer.[43]

Audubon hastily closed the letter in order to get it in the mail, reminding Lucy that it would have to be transported three miles across the bay to the smaller village of Lubec, Maine, which was situated on the mainland near the entrance to the Bay of Fundy. He still needed to write in his journal "ere I go to bed, and I feel the want of a good night's rest very much."[44]

———

That evening, Lucy was sitting at a writing table in her sister's home in New York looking over a letter she had just received from Victor. Her son related that the mother of Henry Ward, the English taxidermist who had been employed by Audubon during his 1832 southern excursions, was making noises in London about the birdskins she claimed Ward had been promised by the naturalist but never received.[45] At the time, English collectors would pay high prices for natural-history specimens from America. Indeed, Havell would soon be expanding his shop on Oxford Street to capture a portion of this market.[46] Mrs. Ward was also demanding that Audubon abide by his agreement to pay for her son's return passage to England. Lucy recalled that a written agreement had been drawn up between Audubon and Ward in London before they all embarked for America, but she did not remember the details. Audubon's copy was sitting in a trunk of papers at Dr. Parkman's home in Boston and could not be readily retrieved.[47]

Victor's letter unsettled her, and she took pen to paper to write to John Bachman asking for his counsel. She knew that Bachman would soon be arriving in New York by steamer from Charleston, but she was hoping that before his departure he could speak to Ward, who was working as a taxidermist at the museum of the Literary and Philosophical Society of South Carolina, now the Charleston Museum. Perhaps, she suggested, the pastor might obtain a certificate from Ward verifying that Audubon had fully satisfied the terms of their agreement.[48] After finishing the letter to Bachman, she started one to her husband. She was uncertain that a letter posted to Eastport would reach him before he departed for Labrador, but she began it anyway.[49] She then turned to crafting an answer to Victor.[50]

––––––

The next day, Wednesday, May 8, Audubon met with the customs collector, Gen. James Wheelock Ripley, to arrange for his assistance in placing a vessel at the naturalist's disposal. A year younger than Audubon, Ripley was a former attorney from Fryeburg, Maine, who had been an officer in the Maine volunteers during the War of 1812 and then served as a Maine representative in the Massachusetts legislature from 1814 to 1819. In 1826, he was elected as a Jacksonian Democrat from Maine to the 19th U.S. Congress to fill the unexpired term of Enoch Lincoln, who had resigned. On the same date, Ripley was elected to the 20th Congress and was subsequently reelected to the 21st Congress. He served his district on Capitol Hill from 1825 to 1830, when poor health forced him to resign. He returned to Fryeburg to practice law but was appointed collector of customs for the Passamaquoddy Customs District on December 17, 1830.[51] Ripley assented to Audubon's request, but the *Swiftsure* had still not returned to port. In her place he offered the *Fancy*, which could be ready to sail the following day. Audubon eagerly accepted.

Audubon also traveled that day to Dennysville to pay his planned call on the Lincoln family.[52] The Lincoln home was a spacious two-story Georgian-style structure set on a grass-covered knoll above the Dennys River.[53] Under the eaves of an adjacent barn, the remnants of the gourd-shaped mud nests built by Cliff Swallows the previous year awaited possible repair and reuse with the commencement of the breeding season.[54] Swallows just back from South America were making aerial flights across the surrounding fields in search of food and swooping in to inspect possible nesting sites for the coming months, chattering as they did so.

Judge Lincoln, gray-haired but still hale and hearty at sixty-nine, and his wife, Hannah, a tall, willowy woman who would celebrate her fifty-eighth birthday in two days, welcomed their distinguished guest, as did their son Tom.[55] As it turned out, Audubon's hunch about the supposedly rare bird that Tom had discovered was right. Although no record survives to identify it, the bird was apparently not unique, because it was not one of the species Audubon illustrated during his stay in Eastport. However, the trip proved to be productive in another way. The naturalist told Tom about his forthcoming trip to Point Lepreau and recruited the young man as a member of the party.[56]

In Boston, Dr. Shattuck received the two letters his son had posted just before leaving Brunswick. He sat down and crafted an immediate reply, which read in part:

> Both of your letters of the 5th and 6th instant [MS: inst.] have come to hand. the books as found will be sent by the packet to sail on Saturday for East Port directed to the care of Mr. Chadbourne. I have also sent you letter paper said to be made of linen rags, both for your journal and for the letters you may have occasion to write. I beg you to make a daily record of what you may see, and to write to me as opportunity may offer. Let your journal be written in a *legible* hand writing.[57]

Dr. Shattuck suggested that the young man call on Mr. Chadbourne, whom the Shattucks knew through the Lincoln family, as well as on Dr. Isaac Ray, a Harvard- and Bowdoin-trained physician who had studied medicine in Dr. Shattuck's office and recently established a practice in Eastport, "both of whom may possibly be courteous to you for your father's sake."[58] He thought a side trip to visit the Lincolns in Dennysville might also be in order.

Before sealing the letter and posting it the next day, Dr. Shattuck wrote out a brief note to Audubon to accompany the correspondence to his son:

> My Dear Sir,
> My son, you now perceive, accepts your polite invitation to accompany him to the Labrador Coast. I commit & commend him to your fatherly care. Should his wants transcend his supplies, I beg you to supply him, or should your own preparation require addition, I beg you to draw on me at sight, and your draft shall be honored.
> Tender my love to your son, and accept a prayer for your safety from,
> My Dear Sir,
> Geo. C. Shattuck
> Boston May 9 1833.[59]

That Thursday afternoon, May 9, Audubon and John prepared to sail aboard the *Fancy* to Point Lepreau.[60] According to Audubon, the schooner was set to sail around 3:00 p.m. with the turn of the tide, "without which nothing can be accomplished in this wonderful bay of Fundy."[61] The Audubons would be joined by James Curtiss, the Eastport postmaster, in addition to Tom Lincoln.[62]

From the Weston house, Audubon, John, and Tom walked the short distance downhill on Boynton Street and turned right onto Water Street, the center of Eastport's commercial district, heading first for Maj. Chadbourne's law office. Water Street was a narrow, dirt-covered thoroughfare bordered on either side by "ordinary" wood-framed structures of two or three stories, with storefront businesses on the ground floors.[63]

At the corner of Boynton and Water streets, they passed Byram's Medicine Store, the local apothecary, which stocked "a good assortment of Confectionary." Over at No. 25, opposite the Brick Store, E. Y. Sabine had a store offering "[a]n extensive assortment of Ladies', Gentlemen's and Children's Boots and Shoes," along with a "Large Assortment of Crockery and Glass Ware of the newest patterns all of which will be sold at the Boston retail prices for cash." H. S. Favor's Bookstore, with a broad selection of titles, was located on the street level of the Green Building. Upstairs was the office of the *Eastern Democrat*, one of Eastport's two weekly newspapers. Samuel Witherell's millinery shop, showcasing the latest fashions in caps and hats, was at No. 19. The Washington Hotel was situated across from George W. Folsom's dry-goods store, which was at No. 3.[64]

Wharves extending out into Passamaquoddy Bay could be accessed from walkways between the buildings on the eastern side of the street. The attorney's office was located about halfway down the block at the head of Union Wharf.[65] There, much to Audubon's surprise and satisfaction, he was greeted by George C. Shattuck Jr.

The medical student had only just arrived in Eastport after taking the stage from Columbia to Lubec, followed by a short ferry ride across the bay. As he stood in the middle of Water Street waiting for another passenger to accompany him to a nearby tavern, he was spotted by Maj. Chadbourne. The barrister was understandably amazed to see him and asked what in the world he was doing in Eastport. Shattuck announced that he had come to join Audubon's expedition. Chadbourne suggested that they walk over to his office, where the naturalist was expected shortly. They reached the office just moments before Audubon walked through the door.[66]

The serious young man who shook hands with the naturalist was pale complexioned with blue eyes, and brown hair atop a high forehead. At five feet, eight inches tall, he was just slightly shorter than Audubon.[67] However, his focus in recent years on his college and medical studies had left him little time for physical activity, and he was out of shape. Audubon recognized that he would need to be in far better condition before they embarked on their journey to the north. The difficult, rocky terrain of the Labrador coast was unforgiving.

With an eye toward getting him started or simply because it was in Audubon's gregarious nature to surround himself with people whose company he enjoyed, the naturalist invited Shattuck to join him on the trip to Point Lepreau. However, Chadbourne suggested it would be better if the young man remained in Eastport and got settled.[68]

After a discussion of Audubon's plans for the Labrador expedition and an exchange of farewells, the naturalist and his companions headed for the wharf where the *Fancy* was tied up. Audubon made sure that a letter he had just written to Edward Harris, the second of the day, was posted before he left.[69] In the letter he announced his decision to charter a schooner of about sixty tons burden which would enable him to travel wherever he wished to go.[70] Chadbourne thought a suitable vessel could be procured for around $250 per month and agreed to make the arrangements. Audubon still held out hope that Harris would "make haste" and reach them before they sailed fifteen days hence for the Sable Islands off the coast of Nova Scotia, where Audubon planned on spending two weeks before circumnavigating Newfoundland:

> The near I approach to the desired object of this Voyage the more boyant my Spirits and the greater my Hopes that when I return I will bring a Cargo (not of Cod Fish) but of most valuable *Stuff* in the way of Information. — Make up your Mind, pack up your effects, Shoulder your firelock and away to the Fields where [MS: were] Science awaits us with ample Stores the contents of which are the rarest Materials ever employed by Nature —[71]

Back in Chadbourne's office, Shattuck was at work on a letter to his father. He had promised Audubon that he would write immediately to request some essential items for the trip. He surely also wanted to let his father know that he had arrived safely and been invited to stay with the Chadbournes at their large Federal-style home on Shackford Street, a quick walk from the Westons'.[72] Although the lawyer and his wife had six young children, two of them were presently visiting their grandparents in Dennysville.[73] The family would make room for their guest. Shattuck advised his father that Audubon felt he would need a double-barreled gun, along with eight or ten pounds of powder and four or five thousand percussion caps:

> He also insists much on a large journal in which he will make me write every night an account of the day's work, and then read it to him. I shall have to work like a horse as he says. He is going to charter a vessel for himself, which is to move entirely as he directs. He has written to a friend in Philadelphia to come on and join us, and Tom Lincoln will probably go too. The advantages will be great, and I can not be too grateful to you for the permission and means to go. He will probably sail in about a fortnight, and will be absent two and a half or three months. In the mean time I shall be in training, under the direction of Mr. Chadbourne. The prospect before me is delightful, and I am rejoiced I came on.

I have seen young Audubon also, and everything looks favorable, for a season of interest and instruction.[74]

The letter completed, Chadbourne and Shattuck stopped in at the Eastport Athenaeum, known locally as the "Club." Founded around 1821 by a handful of young men, the Athenaeum now had about forty members and held close to nine hundred books comprising "standard works of literature and taste" along with the "best periodical publications of the day." Shattuck noted in his journal that he found "many interesting works" on the shelves. Chadbourne arranged for Shattuck to have access to the "Club Room" and granted his young guest leave to use any of the select volumes in his own library.[75]

Out on the open waters of Passamaquoddy Bay, Audubon and his party were now bouncing over the waves aboard the *Fancy*, "a charming name for so beautiful a craft," commanded by thirty-one-year-old Capt. Joseph H. Claridge, one of several customs inspectors working under Gen. Ripley.[76] According to the naturalist, "[t]he cackling of the 'old wives' [Long-tailed Ducks] that covered the bay filled me with delight, and thousands of Gulls and Cormorants seemed as if anxious to pilot us into Head Harbour Bay, where we anchored for the night."[77]

Head Harbor Bay is located at the northern tip of Campobello Island, a long landmass running north–south that lies between Passamaquoddy Bay and the Bay of Fundy on the New Brunswick side of the border.[78] To aid navigation into the main ship channel used by commercial vessels approaching Eastport, a lighthouse was constructed on a rocky outcropping at the head of the harbor in 1829.[79] Locals know it today as the East Quoddy Light. At high tide the promontory on which it sits is surrounded by water. When Audubon and his party arrived, they rowed to the island, and Audubon paid a visit to the lighthouse keeper, Mr. Snelling, "a good and honest Englishman from Devonshire." Audubon described Snelling's three daughters as "wild looking lasses, beautiful, like the most finished productions of nature."[80]

Back in Eastport, Dr. Isaac Ray had heard of Shattuck's arrival and invited him to take a tour of the town that evening.[81] The twenty-six-year-old physician was born in Beverly, Massachusetts, and entered Bowdoin College in 1822 as a member of the Class of 1826. Among his classmates were Benjamin Lincoln, one of Judge Lincoln's five sons, of the Class of 1823; future U.S. President Franklin Pierce, of the Class of 1824; and Henry Wadsworth Longfellow and Nathaniel Hawthorne, both of the Class of 1825. Poor health had compelled Ray to drop out after just two years. However, he began to study medicine the following year, first at Harvard, where he got to know the Shattuck family, and then later back at Bowdoin at the Medical School of Maine, which awarded him a degree in 1827. He had practiced in Portland, Maine, until 1829, when he moved to Eastport. In 1831, he married Abigail Frothingham, a young Portland woman. Their first child, a daughter, was born the following year and given her mother's first name.[82]

When the two young men returned to the Chadbournes', Ray stopped in for a chat. He was interested in discussing the work that had been done in the last few decades on the anatomy of the brain by the German phrenologists Franz Gall, M.D., and his disciple, Johann Gaspar Spurzheim, M.D.[83]

Gall hypothesized that the brain did not function as a whole, as some believed, but was composed of separate, localized regions or "organs" that controlled different functions. He and Spurzheim, who had traveled throughout Europe as Gall's assistant and began lecturing on the subject after receiving his M.D. degree in Vienna in 1813, also maintained that an individual's "aptitudes and tendencies," i.e., physical talents and dispositions, were controlled by specific, independent areas of the brain and were manifested in corresponding bumps and contours in the person's skull.[84] Their theories had gained many adherents in both Europe and America, one of whom was Dr. Ray.

Shattuck was intrigued but not yet convinced. He had hoped to hear Spurzheim speak the previous fall when the phrenologist was in Boston giving a series of lectures. At the time, Shattuck was away at the University of Vermont Medical School studying under Dr. Benjamin Lincoln. He considered returning to Boston, but, unfortunately, Spurzheim contracted typhoid fever and died on November 10 at Mrs. Lekain's boardinghouse on Pearl Street, where he had been a guest along with the Audubons.[85] The naturalist called it a "melancholy death."[86]

Although phrenology would eventually be discarded as a scientific discipline, Ray's interest in the human brain would lead him to become a pioneer in the field of forensic psychiatry. In 1838, while still an Eastport practitioner, he published *A Treatise on the Medical Jurisprudence of Insanity*, a landmark work in the field. Three years later, he was appointed superintendent of the Maine Insane Hospital in Augusta. In 1845, he accepted the position of superintendent of Butler Hospital, a newly established private asylum in Providence, Rhode Island. He left Butler in 1867 for health reasons and moved to Philadelphia, where he died in 1881. He is remembered today as the "father of American forensic psychiatry."[87]

———

Audubon awoke the next day before dawn "to see fair Nature open her graceful eyelids." From the deck of the *Fancy* he could hear the high musical trill of a Winter Wren and the cheery caroling of a male Robin coming from the nearby forest. A Red Squirrel announced its presence with a rattling call. In a still-barren maple, a Rose-breasted Grosbeak moved slowly through the branches nibbling the tender, green buds. Overhead, several pairs of Loons (Common Loons) could be seen beating their way north with quick, powerful wingstrokes.[88]

At the appointed hour, the schooner sailed up the bay, picking up her pilot, who had been fishing for Atlantic Cod (*Gadus morhua*). Part of his catch, cooked over embers on a plank onboard, served as a tasty breakfast for Audubon's party. A light breeze carried the *Fancy* to Point Lepreau Harbor, where she arrived after noon, and everyone dispersed "in search of curiosity and provender."[89] Audubon watched as waves swept in and crashed against the rocky shoreline. American Crows, Ravens (Common Ravens), and White-headed Eagles (Bald Eagles) dined on mussels and sea eggs revealed by the retreating tide. Above the rocks, a line of "melancholy firs" with broken branches bore witness to the brutal storms that battered this remote, rugged coast.[90]

Audubon told the readers of the *Ornithological Biography* that his party spent "three pleasant days" exploring the area around Point Lepreau. However, the truth was decidedly different. The winds turned to the east on Saturday, bringing steady rain and fog that lasted through the remainder of the trip. Audubon admitted to Lucy that it was "extremely disagreable to us."[91] Nevertheless, he "obtained most valuable information, and 4 Rare Birds," one of which was evidently the Buffel-headed Duck (Bufflehead).[92]

It was still raining and "shockingly cold" when the *Fancy* left Point Lepreau to return to Eastport on Tuesday, May 14. As the schooner made her way south, the wind picked up and the seas became rough. Capt. Claridge ordered the crew to reef the sails to reduce the amount of canvas exposed to the wind. Along the way, they passed a smaller "heavily laden" schooner that Audubon noted was "gallantly running across our course with undiminished sail." The other vessel was almost out of sight of the *Fancy* when it capsized, throwing the three men aboard into the frigid waters.[93]

Capt. Claridge barked a command to the helmsman to bring the *Fancy* about, and the crew sprang into action. John and Lincoln ran to assist on the lines and the sails.[94] When they reached the vessel, surrounded by floating staves and spars, they found the three desperate seamen atop the keel. A local fisherman had also seen the schooner overturn and had rowed in to lend a hand, his small craft rising and falling on the heavy seas as he approached the scene. The waterlogged sailors were brought onboard the government vessel, and the *Fancy* towed the stricken schooner into the harbor of a nearby "Small Rocky Island."[95]

Audubon was most impressed by the nautical skill of the crew. "[D]epend upon it," he told Lucy when he sat down with a pen later that day in Eastport, "the Yankees are the Lads for the Ocean—they are firm, cool, considerate, humane &

generous when ever these qualities are called for." An addendum to the letter from John echoed his father's appraisal. He assured his mother she "would be pleased to see the style in which these Yankees manage a vessel and feel confidence in all that they undertake."[96] Both of them no doubt wanted to ease her mind about their upcoming voyage.

In the same letter, Audubon answered Lucy's May 7 correspondence, which had been waiting for him upon his return. He insisted Victor should not concern himself about the threats from Henry Ward's mother. The contract he had with the taxidermist contained no language about birdskins. While Audubon had admittedly promised Ward "*some* if he should behave well, these would amount to about 50 or 60, and no more, and if his Dear Mother wishes to make any fuss about it let her!" He expressed delight that Henry Inman had started to paint Lucy's portrait.[97]

Audubon went on to report Shattuck's arrival and noted that Tom Lincoln had decided just that afternoon to join the expedition. He thought the young men would probably pay a portion of the cost. Still looking for Edward Harris to come on, he asked Lucy to tell his friend that this could be accomplished provided Harris arrived in Eastport by the end of the month. Audubon felt that they "ought & must sail on the 1ᵗ day of June."[98]

He also revealed his plans to charter a schooner for the voyage, explaining that it would "save money & add wonderfully to our Comfort."[99] Initially, he had considered traveling to Labrador aboard one of the many fishing vessels that made the trip every summer, but he recognized that this would severely restrict his range and ability to explore the country. Alternatively, he thought that he might charter one of these vessels but decided against it because the small size, cramped accommodations, and distinctive fish odor would have been unpleasant on so long a trip.[100] A chartered schooner sailing at his direction would best suit his needs. He expected the details to be arranged within a day or two and promised a letter with the particulars. While recognizing the trip would be costly, he believed that "[i]f God grants us success & a safe return" it would pay dividends in the "knowledge of the Birds of our Country" that he would derive.[101] He added that he had written to Dr. Parkman in Boston and asked him to procure their provisions. Although he did not explain his reasons for doing so, Audubon apparently did not have sufficient funds with him to cover both the cost of the vessel and the supplies. He knew that the wealthy Parkman would gladly advance the funds, and he evidently instructed his friend to draw on Nicholas Berthoud for the expense.[102]

Above all, Audubon wanted Lucy to know that they would be careful. This trip was viewed by the locals as a "very common Voyage, and the Cold is all we need to fear." But, as a consequence, they would need to outfit themselves with new clothes, their existing wardrobes being too thin for the colder conditions they expected to meet. He also let her know that he was feeling "much better in health" and was avoiding the consumption of spirits, one of his weaknesses. He had not had a drink since departing for Point Lapreau and assured her that he would continue to abstain *"whilst on Duty."*[103]

After finishing the letter to Lucy, Audubon passed it to John and then pulled out another piece of paper to write to Edward Harris. Harris had written to him on May 6 and, based upon Audubon's response, suggested that his other commitments might preclude him from joining the expedition. Although the naturalist understood completely, he would not relent in his desire to share his friend's company on the adventure. "Should you not Join us I Shall feel Sorry, yes very sorry and yet not blame you, for I know that *the World* bends us to obligations which are at times undeniable—but if you can come with a Will—do so pray and act promptly."[104]

Audubon planned to sail for Bay Chaleur in the Gulf of St. Lawrence on June 1. He was anxious to depart. During the excursion to Point Lapreau, he had seen relatively few waterbirds. They had already moved farther north to their breeding grounds. He felt that he needed to arrive there soon if it was to be a productive trip. With all the demands attached to his publication, he could not "afford to lose another Season."[105]

Over at the Chadbournes', Shattuck was giving Tom Lincoln an account of his past several days.[106] He had spent his first full day in Eastport with Dr. Ray, who took him over to the Army garrison and showed him "the beauties of the island."[107] On Saturday and Sunday, as a heavy rain pounded the area, the two spent the time together indoors at Dr. Ray's home studying shells.[108] Ray had a serious interest in the subject and had prevailed upon Audubon when they met the previous summer to use his contacts in England to procure a number of shells from that country.[109] Monday brought the arrival of the coastal packet *Splendid*, a 147-ton schooner built in Eastport in 1829.[110] With strong winds along the coastal route from Boston, the vessel reached the Eastport wharf in a mere twenty-six hours. It carried Dr. Shattuck's May 8 letter to his son, along with notes to Audubon from both Dr. Shattuck and Dr. Parkman. In addition, Dr. Shattuck had shipped a box containing books, rag letter paper, and some clothing for his son. That afternoon, the young man wrote a letter back asking for a thermometer, suggesting that perhaps he could borrow the family's combination barometer-thermometer that hung in their back entry so that he could keep track of the weather during the trip. He also hoped he could use his father's horse pistols.[111]

On Tuesday morning, Dr. Ray had joined Shattuck on a visit to the saltworks, which had been established in 1828 at Prince's Cove on the southern end of the island and was producing over a thousand bushels of salt each day.[112] Shattuck then accompanied Dr. Ray on his medical rounds, including a stop at Fort Sullivan, which could be reached from the town by a wooden staircase that scaled the face of the steep bluff on which the garrison sat. The post had no army surgeon on staff, so Dr. Ray had been appointed to serve their medical needs. He was asked to see a soldier who was complaining of back pain. Capt. Childs thought the man's complaints a sham.[113]

The two medical men next paid a call on 1st Lt. George S. Greene at his spacious apartment in the officer's quarters, situated next door to the home of Capt. Childs on the western side of the parade grounds.[114] The darkly handsome Rhode Island native, whose second cousin was Maj. Gen. Nathaneal Greene of Revolutionary War fame, had been graduated second in his class at West Point in 1823. He so impressed his superiors that he was invited to remain there to teach mathematics and engineering over the course of the next three years. He had been posted at Fort Sullivan since 1831, the second time he had served at this garrison.[115]

Greene's apartment seemed to Shattuck to be the abode of a student or an unmarried man, the contents confused "yet very comfortable."[116] It was not until Shattuck and Dr. Ray had left the lieutenant's company that the physician told him the painful truth. Only a year before, Greene had been blessed with a beautiful and growing family. His wife Elizabeth, "lovely and sweet in person and disposition," had given him two children—a daughter named Mary who would be celebrating her third birthday in July and a toddler son of almost seventeen months named George, after his father. A third child was due toward the end of the summer. In the nine months that followed, the family was devastated by one tragedy after another. Young Mary died of croup in early June 1832. The family's grief was eased somewhat when Elizabeth gave birth in August to a second son, Francis Vinton Greene. But in early October, little George died. His death may have been too much for Elizabeth to bear. She took ill and died of rapid consumption the day after Christmas. Their lastborn died less than two months later, in February 1833.[117] Even during an era when medical care was primitive by today's standards and sudden, unexpected death was not uncommon, a loss of this magnitude touched the entire community. At least one Eastport resident, Sarah Connell Ayer, the pious wife of an Eastport physician, was deeply concerned about Greene's soul.[118]

Lincoln and Shattuck's discussion soon turned to more pleasant topics, and the young men found themselves engaged in "quite an interesting conversation" about the medical profession.[119] Lincoln believed that it took more time and commitment for one to become a good physician than a good lawyer or minister. He knew what he was talking about. For a time, he had considered pursuing a career in medicine like his brother Benjamin and, in 1830, moved to Brunswick to attend the Medical School of Maine. But he had dropped out and returned home to Dennysville.[120]

Shattuck, still actively engaged in his medical studies, would probably not have disagreed.

Lincoln also spoke of the amazing directional skills of the Native Americans. The Passamaquoddy Indians lived in the area, and Lincoln had hunted with them over the years. He told Shattuck that an Indian could track a deer through the woods all day and still know in which direction the compass points lay and where every nearby river and stream was located. White men, even those raised in the woods, were simply not their equals.[121]

———

That same day, Victor Audubon put the final touches on a long letter to his parents. The news from London could not have been much worse. To begin with, Charles Waterton's venomous attacks presented a serious problem, raising doubts among Audubon's subscribers about his competence and expertise. However, having discussed the matter with Audubon's friend John G. Children of the British Museum, Victor had come to the conclusion that he should pay them no mind.[122] Anything he could say would only inflame the controversy.

More alarming and likely ruinous, his relationship with Havell, never a particularly good one, had suddenly reached its breaking point. The engraver was ready to quit. The day before, Havell had exploded and ordered Victor out of the shop, the result of months of the younger man's heavy-handed oversight of the engraver's work. In his letter Victor sought to deflect any blame for these developments, pointing to Havell as the cause:

> He seems to have had an almost absolute dislike to me, and to have supposed me desirous to take the work from him, and also to have thought Mr Children his enemy. I told him all this was quite ridiculous and that I entertained very different feelings, I added that I had not told either Mr Children or anyone else here anything of his (Havells) conduct of late, and after telling him further that as long as I remain your agent and representative here I must be treated by him with respect, he requested me to leave him to finish the engraving of the large & middle plate of No 34 before I saw him again or went into the work room.[123]

Victor seems to have been completely oblivious to his own role in all of this. In part, Havell was upset that Victor never praised the work as Audubon regularly did. The engraver took enormous pride in the quality of the prints being produced by his shop, and his ego was easily bruised. Victor seemed to delight in finding things to complain about. "I have been as strict with Havell about all these things as I thought necessary," he had written his parents on May 6, "and have never failed to find fault when I saw it, at the time."[124] While Havell could barely tolerate Audubon's input, the two had succeeded in building an effective working partnership. Havell found it impossible to accept criticism from Victor, someone he considered a crass young upstart.

Havell also could not have been happy when, in late March, Victor began to dictate how the copper engravings were to be aquatinted. Audubon had urged the engraver many times to scale back on the acidic "Black Biting of the plates," which was used by Havell to create shading on the black-and-white prints, greatly simplifying the coloring process. The colorists could then apply a single wash of watercolor to the print rather than a series of washes to achieve a three-dimensional effect. That was the entire purpose of aquatinting, of which Havell was a recognized master. However, Audubon believed that it was "very injurious" to the copper plates because "not above 200 or 300 impressions can be taken from such plates fit for colouring & delivery." In his defense, Audubon was interested in controlling his costs. The number of subscribers was still below two hundred, but the naturalist fully expected his list would continue to grow. He had no desire to see the copper sheets wear out, which would require the preparation of costly replacements. Moreover, Audubon no doubt believed the plates might have a future should he or his family ever wish to republish the Double Elephant Folio.[125]

Havell considered himself a gifted artist and largely ignored the naturalist's wishes. Victor, however, refused to be put off. He had been standing over the engravers, supervising the amount of aquatinting that was used. Victor's object was "to have the plates only tinted by the acid" and the proper effect achieved by using engraved lines in the copper. Havell objected strenuously, insisting that without the proper biting the images were "feeble" and completely lacked any "force."[126]

As if this was not enough, Havell was no longer satisfied with the financial terms of his contract. He had approached Victor on May 4 "with a great deal of nervous agitation" and declared that he was losing money on the project and would be ruined. After six years of employment, he "found he had saved nothing, found he had lost money by No. 31, lost by the colorers &c." Whether there was any truth to this is unclear. Regardless, Victor anticipated the engraver would be seeking higher fees.[127] Sure enough, within days Havell was demanding £10 more for producing the large prints and an additional £8 for the smaller ones.[128]

Raising Havell's rates would be disastrous. It would place pressure on Audubon to pass the increase along to his subscribers in order to maintain his profit margin, which had made the family comfortable but by no means well-to-do. Not only would he face the possible exodus of some who were unwilling to pay more, but a higher price for the set would make it difficult to replace them, let alone augment their number. It was a relatively small group of individuals and institutions that were wealthy enough to subscribe to such an expensive work, and, of those, even fewer that shared an interest in birds. Most of the obvious candidates in both England and America had already been approached. Additionally, with the project nearly halfway to completion, a new subscriber would be immediately called upon to pay for all of the prints that had been issued to date, a sizable sum that was apt to discourage anyone who might otherwise be inclined.[129]

As a consequence, Victor was already thinking it might be necessary to move the publication to another printer. He had his eye on an engraver in Havell's shop, a young man named Blake, who had been quietly critical of Havell's work and was positioning himself to replace him. However, this would pose yet another dilemma. A change in printers at this stage would likely lead to a slowdown in the regular publication schedule and, even worse, cancellations by subscribers who were tiring of the seemingly endless enterprise. Havell's "tantrum," as Victor called it, threatened the very future of *The Birds of America*.[130]

Until he could get some direction from his parents, Victor sought to placate Havell, telling him that it was doubtful Audubon would be able to increase his prices, but agreeing to send a letter to America for a response. Victor also suggested that his father would probably want to leave the work with the engraver, hoping that this would keep him working on it in the meantime. But it was clear that Havell was prepared to quit if the terms of his engagement were not altered. He informed Victor that he would make "the No. 34 a farewell plate too good to be equalled hereafter."[131]

Faced with this turmoil, Victor urged his parents to sail for England just as soon as Audubon and John returned from Labrador. A few days later, Victor met with William Rathbone, the Liverpool cotton merchant, who had come down to London to deal with some matters before Parliament. As an astute businessman, Rathbone would have understood the threat Havell's ultimatum posed for the project. He also could not have been unaware of the damage Waterton was doing to the naturalist's reputation. He agreed that Audubon needed to hurry back to England and promised to write him with that recommendation.[132]

———

Blissfully unaware of these developments, Audubon awoke early on Wednesday morning, May 15, and began the day, as he routinely did, with his correspondence. He maintained a steady stream of outgoing letters to his large and always expanding circle of friends, acquaintances, and others who might prove of assistance to him. He had mentioned to Lucy the night before that he owed letters to Nicholas Berthoud; William Oakes, a subscriber from Ipswich, Massachusetts; and Ethan Allan Greenwood, the proprietor of the New England Museum in Boston.[133]

At 4:30 a.m., before sealing his letter of the night before to Lucy, he added a line on the first page, crosswise to the original content, commenting on the weather—it was raining, with fog "thick as ever"—and saying that he had already written to both

Berthoud and Edward Harris.[134] He was still at work with his pen when Lincoln and Shattuck came over to see him later in the morning. James Curtiss was also visiting, having stopped by earlier to pay a call. Shattuck had not yet warmed to the Eastport postmaster. He commented in his journal that Curtiss was considered "something of a sportsman," but that others viewed him as "a very low fellow."[135]

The naturalist greeted his young friends, made "the usual inquiries," and then had Shattuck sit down and write to his father to request a gun for Tom Lincoln, along with other items for the expedition. It was important for Shattuck to get the letter to his father as quickly as possible, so he carried it down to the packet, which was set to sail that afternoon, and gave instructions to the steward to see that it be delivered immediately upon their arrival in Boston.[136]

Maj. Chadbourne had been working with his brother-in-law Spencer Tinkham on arrangements for a chartered schooner to transport Audubon and his party to Labrador. Tinkham, who was married to Judge Lincoln's twenty-five-year-old daughter, Sarah, owned a suitable vessel with his partner, Jonathan Buck.[137] The *Ripley* was a 106-ton two-masted schooner that had been constructed by Eastport shipwrights only the previous year and launched at the end of the summer bearing the surname of the local customs collector.[138]

When Audubon wrote again to Lucy on Thursday, an agreement had been struck. It called on Audubon to pay $350 per month for the "fine" vessel beginning June 1, with the naturalist expecting the cruise to last through the end of August. The owners of the vessel agreed to assume responsibility for feeding the crew, but Audubon would be expected to supply the food for his party at his own cost. The *Ripley*'s captain, according to Audubon, was "a Man of Information and I am glad to say a Gentleman besides." The pilot, he had been assured, was "well acquainted with the Coast," a critical necessity because the Labrador waters had yet to be properly surveyed, and a navigational misstep could lead a craft to founder upon a hidden shoal.[139]

Audubon had been told that birds bred in Labrador by the millions, and he was anticipating a season of success. He informed Lucy that it was likely they would collect so many specimens that he might only have time during the voyage to finish the outlines of the birds, along with "Coloured bills, eyes & feet." The colors of the birds' soft parts faded quickly, so Audubon's practice was to capture them first. He would complete the drawings upon his return, just as he had done with the Florida birds he had collected during his expedition the year before.[140]

Audubon also tried once more to assure Lucy that he would be cautious and not try to do too much. "I . . . will act with all the prudence & care in my possession not derogatory from My present purpose of doing all in my power during this Voyage," he wrote.[141] He was well aware of Lucy's fears about his health.

John, like his father, had been up at daybreak.[142] He was still getting used to these early mornings. During the years he had lived in Louisiana with his mother, he had developed an indolence common to many young Southern white men who grew up surrounded by slaves and saw little need to apply themselves.[143] Lucy had expressed her concern about this in a letter to Victor the previous November while the family was staying in Boston.[144] However, Audubon, once again asserting his paternal authority, would have none of it. He expected John to follow the same daily regimen that he did. The young man, described by his father as "in good Spirits," left the Weston house at 4:30 a.m. for an early morning shooting excursion with Shattuck and Lincoln, although they reportedly did not see any birds.[145]

When the young men returned tired and famished at around noon, they dined at the Chadbournes' with Audubon, Maj. Chadbourne, Dr. Ray, and Jonathan Weston. Between bites, Dr. Ray asked the naturalist whether he thought natural history flourished more in England or in France. Audubon replied that while France had some notables like Baron Cuvier, who "belong to the world," England clearly held that distinction. In his view, "numerous country gentlemen" developed a familiarity with the subject "beginning with objects of natural history in their own farms and towns" and were more knowledgeable than "many who publish works on these subjects." Indeed, he asserted that many recently published works on ornithology suffered from errors because they had been written by men who did not get outdoors and explore the natural world. Shattuck recorded Audubon's views later in his journal: "If a person would study natural history, continued Mr A., let him not go into museums containing stuffed specimens but let him go out into the woods, and till natural history is thus studied, we can expect no decided progress in this science."[146]

After dinner, Tom Lincoln returned home to Dennysville by steamboat, while John and Shattuck headed to the waterfront to go fishing with James Curtiss on Passamaquoddy Bay. They had to wait some time until Curtiss arrived. Once they were all in the boat, Curtiss concluded that the conditions were not safe, and the idea was abandoned. Shattuck and John then walked over to the saltworks, talking about the expedition to Labrador. When they got back to town, they joined Audubon at the Curtiss residence for tea, although the naturalist did not drink any and had not done so for years. They sat around socializing for a time with Curtiss, his wife Mary, and one of her cousins, a Miss Estabrook from Brunswick. However, Shattuck was shocked when Curtiss launched into a "tirade against the aristocracy of the place, and went on with an argument against union doctrines, revealing plainly what manner of person he was."[147] Coming from a privileged Unitarian background, Shattuck obviously took offense at the postmaster's comments.

The next day, Friday, May 17, Audubon finally got around to answering a letter dating back to March 29 from Ethan Allen Greenwood. The entrepreneur, skilled portraitist, and state legislator from Hubbardston, Massachusetts, had paid a call on the Audubons' Pearl Street boardinghouse shortly after the family left for New York. Mrs. Lekain informed Greenwood that they would be returning in a few days, so he directed the letter to Audubon at the Pearl Street address. However, Audubon failed to retrieve it during his brief return to Boston, so Greenwood forwarded it to Eastport on May 6. When the naturalist opened it, he found to his delight that Greenwood was anxious to devise a way that he might subscribe to *The Birds of America*.[148] Always eager to add to his list of subscribers, Audubon evidently provided a response that led Greenwood to commit to the publication, allowing the patrons of the New England Museum to enjoy the naturalist's magnificent prints.[149]

Later in the morning, the Audubon men and Shattuck made an excursion across the bay in Capt. Childs's "beautiful Barge" to see the West Quoddy lighthouse, which was located on a coastal bluff a little over three and a half miles southeast of the village of Lubec and about six miles from Eastport.[150] The lighthouse had been constructed in 1808 by the U.S. government on West Quoddy Head, a promontory at the opening of the western approach to Passamaquoddy Bay and the treacherous Lubec Narrows between the mainland and the southern shores of Campobello Island. West Quoddy Head also had the distinction of being the most eastern point of land in the continental United States. The decision to build the lighthouse was grounded not only on navigational concerns. The United States wanted to reinforce its claim to this area of Maine, where there had been a long-running dispute with the British over the location of the border between the two countries. The original wood structure had rotted in the salt air and heavy fogs of the Bay of Fundy, so it was replaced in 1831 by a tower built of rubble masonry. With a fixed light standing ninety feet above sea level, the beacon was visible in clear weather from a distance of seven leagues.[151]

The barge was rowed by six soldiers and commanded by 2nd Lt. Napoleon Bonaparte Buford.[152] Audubon described the twenty-six-year-old West Point graduate as a "fine fellow & agreable companion."[153] Shattuck agreed, calling him a "very pleasant fellow."[154] Buford had been assigned to Fort Sullivan in 1830.[155] The following year he received permission from the War Department to attend classes at Harvard's law school, but he left the same year and never received a degree.[156] During his time in Boston he became acquainted with Shattuck's father, who had occasion to see him as a patient.[157]

Audubon's party landed on a beach at what was known locally as "the carrying place," a narrow neck connecting the promontory to the rest of the mainland.[158] The Native Americans of the region used the neck as a shortcut to the waters of the Atlantic, carrying their boats across rather than paddling around the headland.

Audubon's party spent the better part of the day exploring the area's beaches, forests, and rocky shoreline.[159]

The weather was still "extremely cold & uncomfortable" along the coast. The party saw few birds, although Audubon succeeded in collecting a Cliff Swallow and two plovers. At a stop in Lubec before returning to Eastport, the naturalist was shown a Yellow-rumped Warbler that a resident had captured and placed in a cage. Knowing that the songbird would never survive in captivity, he advised the owner to release it. The trip back across the bay took only about twenty minutes. As the barge approached the town around 3:00 p.m., Audubon and his party saw that the revenue cutter *Swiftsure* had finally returned to port. Audubon anticipated sailing aboard her on Monday for the island of Grand Manan and two other islands in the Bay of Fundy known as the Wolves and the Seal Islands.[160]

After their return, Audubon, John, and Shattuck paid a call on Lt. Buford at Fort Sullivan.[161] Word was still circulating about Capt. Childs's wife, Ann, who had given birth the day before to a daughter they named Mary Virginia.[162] Buford had a "beautifully furnished" parlor in the officers' quarters, which was decorated with framed lithographs of scenes from "Mazeppa," Lord Byron's popular 1818 poem in which horses play a central theme.[163] According to Shattuck, "Audubon remarked that on the same bench with himself under David, sat the man who painted those horses, and who paints horses better than any man now living, and another as distinguished in fishes."[164]

Shattuck did not identify the equine artist to whom Audubon was referring. Several famous French painters had tried their hand at depicting scenes from "Mazeppa" and published lithographs of their work, including Horace Vernet, Théodore Géricault, Eugène Delacroix, and Louis Boulanger. Of these, only Vernet was a living contemporary of Audubon's and could possibly have studied with him under the great French Neoclassical painter.[165] However, Vernet was never a student of David's.[166] Nor, clearly, was Audubon, despite claiming for almost thirty years that he had honed his artistic skills at David's atelier in Paris.[167]

Throughout his life, Audubon never allowed the facts to get in the way of a better story, especially one that placed him in a positive light. His oversized ego demanded it. The David falsehood had originally given him standing as an artist at a time when his own abilities fell far short of the mark. However, his raw talent and perseverance through the years had enabled him to develop into a fine and frequently inspired painter. He no longer needed to wrap himself in an association with David. His body of work, admired by both European and American artists of the first order, could at last stand on its own. Yet he could never seem to master his deep-seated insecurities or feel comfortable in his own, entirely self-generated success. Trapped by his previous fabrications, he continued to deem it necessary to tell people that the Neo-classical master had been his guide.

Back in Boston, Dr. Shattuck sat down with pen and paper to inform his son that he was shipping to Eastport via the packet *Boundary*, as requested, "[a] double bar-reled gun with percussion locks, custom work and proved, & 10 lbs. of powder & fifty pounds of shot & five thousand caps."[168] A carrying case made by John Allen of Boston included "wads & ball, and another pound of Mr. Ware's best powder."[169]

The younger Shattuck's thoughts also turned to the members of his family that Friday. He evidently began a letter to his younger sister Ellen "explaining our situa-tion and our prospects." He told her of the Chadbournes' hospitality and described Maj. Chadbourne as a "very well informed and courteous gentleman" and his wife Hannah as "a very superior woman." The four of the Chadbourne's six young chil-dren who were at home included two boys and two girls ranging in age from ten months to ten years. All were as healthy as any children he had ever seen, which Shattuck attributed to their bread and milk diet, together with the country air. "You will never have occasion to regret the time you have passed in the country," he ad-vised his sister, "for the more I see of those brought up in the country, the more am I impressed that those have the finest constitutions whose youth has been passed in the country."[170]

Early Saturday morning, Audubon dashed off a quick letter to Lucy. Prelimi-narily, he lamented the lack of any word from her over the past three days. This was a frequent complaint on his part. When they were separated, he eagerly awaited the mail each day, hoping for a letter. He was deeply disappointed when one failed to arrive, and he let her know it. He went on to describe his party's ramble to the light-house the day before and their planned excursion to Grand Manan on Monday. He did not believe they would be away more than three days. On Tuesday, he said, he was expecting their provisions from Boston to arrive. He was eager to commence the voyage to Labrador, "for I am as anxious as I ever was in my Life to be *at Work* either with the Pen or with the Pencil."[171]

The recent physical exertion agreed with him. "My health has much improved I am fast recovering my habitual activity, and strange as it would appear a hard Life is the one best suited to my Constitution.—No snuff—no Grog.—and plenty of exercise."[172]

Although Audubon had originally intended to draw all day, his plans took a dif-ferent direction as the day progressed.[173] He went off with Shattuck for a five- mile walk in the morning. The thick fog that hung over the island as they started had begun to clear, and they had a "very pleasant" time.[174] Tree Sparrows (American Tree Sparrows) were common, and it was not unusual to see a flock of twenty or more perched in the branches of a tree along with one or two White-throated Fin-

1. *A well-to-do merchant, Audubon's brother-in-law Nicholas Berthoud (1786–1849) held a generally low opinion of the naturalist's publishing venture until Audubon's international success could no longer be ignored.*

2. *Lucy's brother Thomas W. Bakewell (1788–1874) was Audubon's partner in Henderson for several years but withdrew from the business before it failed during the Panic of 1819, leaving Audubon bankrupt and penniless. Audubon sketched his portrait in Louisville in 1820.*

3. Dr. Richard Harlan (1796–1843), a Quaker physician and naturalist, became an ardent Audubon supporter after meeting him in Philadelphia in 1824.

4. William Rathbone V (1787–1868), the managing partner of Rathbone Brothers & Co., joined his younger brother in opening the doors to Liverpool society for Audubon.

5. Richard Rathbone (1788–1860), a partner in Rathbone Brothers & Co., a major Liverpool cotton firm, welcomed Audubon upon his arrival in Liverpool and solicited support for his publication among Liverpool's leading lights.

*6. An 1816 view of Greenbank, the country estate of Hannah Mary Rathbone I (1761–1839),
the "Queen Bee" of the well-to-do and influential Rathbone family.*

*7. Young Henry Fothergill Chorley (1808–
1872), a frequent guest at Greenbank, met
and became friends with Audubon during
the naturalist's 1826 visit to Liverpool.*

8. *Audubon drew this self-portrait in Liverpool in September 1826 as a parting gift
for Hannah Mary Rathbone III (1791–1865), the younger sister of William and
Richard Rathbone, on whom he had developed a serious crush.*

9. *William Home Lizars (1788–1859) in a self-portrait. Lizars was considered the finest engraver in Scotland when he undertook the production of* The Birds of America *in November 1826. He engraved and printed the first ten prints before his colorists went on strike for better pay, forcing Audubon to move the publication to London.*

10. *Robert Havell Jr. (1793–1878), perhaps the finest aquatint engraver in England, agreed to continue the production of* The Birds of America *in partnership with his father, Robert Havell Sr. This drawing was done by his daughter in 1845.*

11. The ever-patient but steel-willed Lucy Bakewell Audubon (1787–1874) sat for this miniature portrait while living with Audubon in London around 1831. She wore "sham curls" to hide her gray hair but abandoned the practice three years later, which Audubon felt made her look "all the better."

12. Audubon's eldest son, Victor Gifford Audubon (1809–1860), assumed responsibility for supervising the production of The Birds of America in London from late 1832 to mid-1834, while Audubon was in America. However, Victor's demands and unvarnished criticism antagonized Robert Havell Jr. to such an extent that the engraver was ready to quit. This miniature was painted in 1836.

13. *John Woodhouse Audubon (1812–1862), Audubon's youngest son, inherited much of his father's artistic talent but could never escape the naturalist's enormous shadow. This miniature was painted in 1836.*

14. *Bowdoin College Professor Parker Cleaveland (1780–1858), the "father of American mineralogy," instructed George C. Shattuck Jr. on the minerals of the Labrador region before the young man left the Medical School of Maine to join Audubon in Eastport.*

15. *Water Street was the center of Eastport's commercial district.*
This view, looking north toward Fort Sullivan, was photographed in the 1870s.

16. *James Curtiss (1806–1859) was the U.S.*
postmaster in Eastport in 1833. A member of
Audubon's circle, Curtiss joined the naturalist
on his excursions to Point Lepreau and
Grand Manan, New Brunswick. A year later,
Curtiss was removed from office, prompting a
relocation with his family to Chicago, where he
became active in local politics and eventually
served two terms as the city's mayor.

17. *Theodore Lincoln (1763–1852), a Harvard graduate and founder of the town of Dennysville, Maine, hosted Audubon and his family during their 1832 visit to northern Maine. A contemporary noted that Lincoln "had a word for everybody, and always a cheering word." He was photographed toward the end of his life.*

18. *Tom Lincoln (1812–1883), the youngest son of Judge Theodore Lincoln of Dennysville, Maine, had a lifelong interest in the natural world. Recognizing a kindred spirit, Audubon recruited him for the Labrador expedition.*

19. The Lincoln house still stands on a knoll overlooking the Dennys River in Dennysville, Maine. This view is from an early 20th century photograph.

20. George C. Shattuck Jr. (1813–1893) had obtained a medical degree from Harvard and was practicing in Boston with his father when this photograph was taken around 1846.

21. *Dr. Isaac Ray (1807–1881), a Harvard and Bowdoin trained physician, was practicing medicine in Eastport in 1833. Five years later, Ray published a landmark treatise on the medical jurisprudence of insanity. He is known today as the "father of American forensic psychiatry." This photograph was taken in later life.*

22. *George S. Greene (1801–1899) was serving as the 1st lieutenant at Fort Sullivan when he met Audubon in 1833. This image was painted in 1836, a year after Greene had resigned his commission. However, he reenlisted and served as a colonel and later as a brigadier general for the Union Army during the Civil War. During the battle of Gettysburg, his troops successfully defended Culp's Hill against repeated assaults by a much larger Confederate force.*

23. *Napoleon B. Buford (1807–1883) was the 2nd lieutenant at Fort Sullivan during Audubon's 1833 visit. He resigned his commission in 1835 but reenlisted during the Civil War, serving first as a colonel and later as a brigadier general in the Union Army.*

24. *Dr. William Ingalls (1813–1903) served as a Union Army surgeon in the Civil War. He was the oldest enlisted medical officer from Massachusetts.*

25. *Joseph A. Coolidge (1815–1901) was a successful businessman living in San Francisco when this photograph was taken.*

26. *Capt. William Willcomb (1797–1852) met Audubon's party at Bras d'Or, Labrador, in August 1833. Willcomb had brought the schooner* Wizard *from Boston to fill her hold with cod for the Mediterranean market. This image is from a miniature portrait painted in 1835.*

27. *The* Wizard *was a topsail schooner of 105 tons burden, approximately the same size as the* Ripley. *She was painted in 1833 entering the harbor of Smyrna, Asia Minor, now Izmir, Turkey.*

28. Edward Harris (1799–1863), one of Audubon's closest friends, helped keep the naturalist in the public eye during the Labrador expedition through reports published in the New-York Gazette & General Advertiser, *a daily newspaper owned by Harris's father-in-law, John Lang.*

29. Isaac Sprague drew this image of a clean-shaven Audubon at the beginning of the naturalist's last collecting expedition to the upper Missouri River in 1843.

30. *Victor Gifford Audubon (1809–1860), in a photograph taken in 1853.*

32. *Lucy Bakewell Audubon (1787–1874), from a photograph taken in 1854.*

31. *John Woodhouse Audubon (1812–1862), from a photograph taken in 1853.*

33. *Tom Lincoln (1812–1883) lived in Dennysville the rest of his life, overseeing his family's multiple businesses and large land holdings. This photograph was taken in his later years.*

34. *After the Civil War, Dr. William Ingalls (1813–1903) had a distinguished medical career in Boston. In addition to a successful private practice, he was a founder of Boston Children's Hospital and served for many years as a visiting surgeon at Boston City Hospital. He was photographed in 1882.*

ches (White-throated Sparrows), all filling the spring air with their songs. To Audubon, the latter were "like leaders of an orchestra," with their "still clearer notes" that "seemed to mark time for the woodland choristers."[175] American birders know the song of the White-throated Sparrow sounds like "Old Sam Peabody, Peabody, Peabody." Canadians prefer to think of it as "O sweet Canada, Canada, Canada."[176]

That afternoon, Audubon, John, Shattuck, and ten-year-old Lincoln Chadbourne, the Chadbournes' eldest child, boarded Capt. Childs's barge for a voyage to Pleasant Point along the St. Croix River, where the local tribe of Passamaquoddy Indians made their home.[177] They were accompanied by a crew of soldiers headed by both Lt. Greene and Lt. Buford.[178]

Lt. Greene had given the naturalist something to ponder several days before when he stopped by the Weston home with a specimen of a Black-capped Titmouse (Black-capped Chickadee) that he had shot just that morning.[179] At the time, Audubon believed that there was only one species of this small, vocal sprite of the Eastern woodlands. The specimen that Greene showed him, however, was significantly larger than the similar-appearing bird that he knew from the South. The naturalist began to wonder if these were actually separate species, a question he would answer affirmatively when he reached Charleston in the autumn and had a chance to compare notes and skins with Bachman. Bachman was instrumental in convincing the naturalist that the new species was the one that bred in the South, which Audubon named the Lesser Black-headed Titmouse (Carolina Chickadee).[180]

Today, birders would find their confusion difficult to understand because the songs and calls of the two species are noticeably different. But in the early 19th century, similar-appearing species were differentiated from one another by subtle distinctions in physical morphology, not vocal clues. Bachman was one of the few naturalists who believed that bird vocalizations could be used to identify birds at the species level.[181]

Audubon's party arrived at Pleasant Point, where they were met by Maj. Chadbourne and Dr. Ray. While the barge had been carefully navigating the waters to avoid the currents caused by the tides, Chadbourne and Ray had taken the land route across the bridge from Moose Island to the smaller Carlow's Island and then over a second bridge to Pleasant Point. Shattuck described the Passamaquoddy village in his journal, noting that the Indians lived "mostly in rude huts constructed of board and bark with a hole at the top—as a passage for the smoke. There are a few framed houses."[182]

The visitors spent some time in one of the latter, speaking to the tribe's chief, a wizened old man now confined to bed who could recall fighting alongside the French in the French and Indian War and watching as Gen. Louis-Joseph de Montcalm fell at the Battle of Quebec in 1759. Shattuck and his companions later entertained themselves by putting up pennies for the youngsters to shoot at with their arrows. "The moment the money was placed for them twenty arrows flew in that direction," Shattuck wrote, "and it almost always fell, nor was there any doubt as to the successful marksman." However, the Bostonian came away with a poor impression of the Native Americans, expressing an all-too-common 19th century opinion: "They are a lazy set," he told his journal, "supporting themselves by gaming, fishing, basket making, neglecting tillage, and keeping no domestic animals but dogs."[183]

In London, it was a beautiful Sunday morning as Victor left his apartment on Great Portland Street. He had just completed a letter to his parents and was now heading for the New England Coffee House on Threadneedle Street, where he could drop the letter into a mail bag for the New York packet *Philadelphia*, due to leave Portsmouth the following day. He wanted them to know that Havell's attitude toward the publication had improved since their confrontation several days before. Victor was "pleased *now* with his attention to it, and the manner in which he has finished No. 33, which is now nearly ready for delivery." The engraving on No. 34 was already under way, and Havell had just requested that Victor supply him with the drawings for the two Numbers to follow, an indication that he did not intend to end his involvement with the project—at least not yet.[184]

Consequently, Victor no longer felt the urgent need for his parents to return upon conclusion of the Labrador expedition. However, he still recommended an autumn departure and suggested they "write to Havell saying you cannot raise his prices, at all events until you return to England, but that, should the work go on well under his hand until then, you may be willing to give the extra price on the Water birds." He would leave to them the decision as to whether this was the proper course.[185]

The residents of Eastport awoke on Sunday to find that a wave of migrating songbirds had landed on the island, the result of an adverse change in the weather.[186] The winds had shifted to the east, and there was thick fog and rain.[187] Most passerines migrate at night and are forced to land when there is inclement weather.[188]

Shattuck spent the morning indoors on a lengthy letter to his father, relating in fine detail the course of his travels from Brunswick to Eastport and an account of some of his recent activities.[189] He then finished the letter he had started two days before to his sister Ellen. He provided her with a more cursory summary of his trip from Brunswick and then told her of their plans to sail on June 1 for Labrador. He was hoping to return to Boston by the middle of September.[190]

Audubon was out and about in the morning and located a Red-bellied Nuthatch (Red-breasted Nuthatch) in the process of building a nest.[191] He also observed a Canada Jay (Gray Jay) steal a recently laid egg from the nest of an American Crow, something that it had done for several days in succession. The jay waited until the female crow left the nest unattended before swooping in and flying away with the prize.[192]

At about this time, Dr. Shattuck had occasion to visit a senior colleague, Dr. William Ingalls, at his home at 2 Hamilton Place in Boston.[193] The subject of their discussion evidently turned to the summer pursuits of Dr. Shattuck's son. Ingalls's twenty-year-old son and namesake was six months older than the younger Shattuck.[194] He had also decided upon a career in medicine, although he had abandoned an undergraduate education at Harvard after finishing his freshman year in 1832 and was now receiving instruction from his father.[195] The young man was then in bed with what he recalled many years later as a "trifling ailment" when the two physicians came into his room:[196]

> Dr. Shattuck looked at me a moment and both men turned away to the window; presently Dr. Shattuck said to me, "William, my son George is going to Labrador with Mr. Audubon, would you like to go with him?" I did not spring out of bed but I grasped his hands with both of mine. How George and I got to Eastport I have not the faintest idea, but I presume we took a run on the Mall and then leaped from Boston to Eastport and if you do not believe this you have no imagination.[197]

In the afternoon, back in Eastport, Audubon was joined by John and Shattuck on a two-and-a-half-mile walk. As they spoke of Audubon's study of natural history, they saw countless birds, including American Redstarts and other brightly plumaged warblers, Robins (American Robins), and a few Brown Creepers. Audubon believed "that a great number of birds must have arrived on the island that very day."[198]

A letter from Lucy written just a week before arrived and brightened the naturalist's spirits. That evening, he took some time to reply. Audubon noted that he had been "fretting" over her recent silence and that when he was idle, as he had been of late, he found "the days and *the Nights* more particularly sadly too Long without thy Company." Although he had been in Eastport for twelve days, he had found only one new bird to draw, a Black Guillemot.[199]

No doubt he hoped to find some valuable specimens on his excursion to Grand Manan and the nearby islands in the Bay of Fundy, set to begin the following day. However, it was raining as his pen filled the page, and he knew the revenue cutter would not sail unless the weather improved. If the rain kept him in Eastport, he planned to draw some Winter Wrens for his portfolio. "[T]hese sweet little creatures are now singing from the top of every prostrate moss covered log in the Wood of this very Island," he told his wife.[200]

He reported that his chartered schooner, the *Ripley*, was returning from a run to

Baltimore and was expected to arrive by the end of the coming week. The owners had advised him that it would take only two days to unload the vessel and install the ballast for the cruise to Labrador, but Audubon still expected to delay his departure until June 1 due to the continuing cold weather. He had spoken to the pilot hired to navigate the schooner's passage, a Nova Scotia man named Godwin, who had worked for five straight years as a commercial "egger" collecting seabird eggs from breeding colonies along the Labrador coast to sell in the markets of St. John's, Newfoundland, and Halifax, Nova Scotia. Godwin knew the territory and assured the naturalist that, even with a departure at the beginning of June, they would still arrive at the start of the nesting season.[201] The schooner, Audubon added, had been described as a "a fine sailor," and the commander, a Mr. Emery, was "a School mate of Thoˢ Lincoln and a man represented to be a gentleman of some education and a first rate Seaman."[202]

Finally, Audubon told Lucy that he now doubted that Edward Harris would join them for the voyage. He had heard nothing from his friend since returning from the trip to Point Lepreau. But he was pleased to report that his health was "quite restored." He had "taken a great deal of hard exercise and it agrees well with me."[203]

It was still raining and cold when Audubon awoke early on Monday morning. He added a note to the outside of his letter to Lucy that they would wait for better weather before setting out on their voyage.[204] It would appear that Audubon then began a lengthy letter to Victor with instructions for handling the publication during his absence. He postdated the letter May 31, anticipating that the expedition would depart for Labrador on June 1. The content, however, indicates that he wrote it at about this time.[205]

In it, Audubon asked Victor to have twenty bound volumes of the work waiting for him in New York upon his return so that he could then make a major push to sign up additional subscribers. He also stressed, in stark but practical terms, that he expected Victor to complete *The Birds of America* for Lucy's benefit and long-term support should the expedition end in tragedy. He would never hint at such a possibility to her, knowing that she was already anxious about the voyage. But with Victor he could be candid and ensure that his eldest son understood his final wishes. He believed the young man was capable of taking his place as artist and author and bringing the grand project to a close. Like John, Victor had shown talent with a brush. Audubon suggested that several months of practice would provide him with the necessary skills "to finish in that way all that my Portfolio might call for":[206]

Study my Drawings, chuse positions in imitation of them, read works on Ornithology and finish the Work!— Your own observations would soon enable you to acquire all *necessary* facts to serve you in the letter press — a good Journey through the United States would suffice and the advice and friendly assistance of our worthy friend John Bachman of Charleston would be sufficient — You might also be assisted by W*am* McGillivray. The completion of that Work will be a fortune to you & your Dear Mother; our Country will appreciate its intrinsic merits more & more every day and *I have no doubt* that in time and perhaps indeed before its completion *several hundred patrons* will be found in the *Union alone* — You have and your Mother has a good number of most valuable Friends in our Country and abroad — Boston alone would enable you to keep up the Publication as soon as it was there understood that Pecuniary assistance was required. — *I have faith in the Bostonians!* — when once the *publication* is finished, almost every copy sold will be nearly clear profit — & by searching a few years for purchasers you would amass enough to render you and your dear & excellent Mother quite comfortable to say the least.[207]

John and Shattuck took a rain-soaked walk to the Custom House after breakfast and called on the commander of the *Swiftsure*, Capt. Uriah Coolidge. Shattuck described him as "a singular looking genius."[208] In his early fifties, Coolidge had been born in Massachusetts and lived for many years in Portland, Maine, where he started a family.[209] In 1819 he was commissioned as a first mate in the Revenue Cutter Service and assigned to the Passamaquoddy Customs District.[210] He had taken command of the *Swiftsure* the previous June after being promoted to captain, succeeding Capt. William A. Howard.[211] His eldest son, Uriah Coolidge Jr., who lost an arm in a gun-related accident in 1824, had served during the past year as the warrant officer aboard the *Swiftsure* but had since left the service.[212] A younger son, eighteen-year-old Joseph, known as Joe, was still at home.[213] The Coolidges had lived across the bay in Lubec since moving to northern Maine, but later that year the captain would purchase a four-year-old Cape-style home on Washington Street in Eastport that had been built by Capt. Henry Hunter.[214]

Like Audubon, Coolidge had previously suffered a paralytic stroke that affected half of his body and for a time left him incapable of speech. But he was now fully recovered. He confirmed that the coastal waters appeared bereft of birds, saying that "he saw not one fowl this year where he saw a hundred last year." John acknowledged that this seemed to be the case up and down the coast. The young men then went hunting for birds, and John sat and drew a landscape view, while Shattuck shot a warbler sporting a yellow breast.[215]

After the shooting excursion, Shattuck stopped in at the Club Room and met Dr. Ray. They dined together at Ray's home and dissected a clam. Later, the two medical men visited Audubon at the Westons', where Dr. Ray and the naturalist discussed the relative differences between the rabbit and the hare. Although Audubon noted that the behavior of the two species differed, he doubted there were structural variations to explain it. John and Shattuck headed out again, Shattuck in search of small game and John in search of a subject for his pencil and paper. After tea at the Westons', they cleaned their guns. Shattuck was back at the Chadbournes' by nine o'clock.[216]

The readers of the *New-York Gazette* opened the paper on Tuesday, May 21, to find a brief account of Audubon's activities, compiled from his recent letters to both Lucy and Edward Harris:

> We learn by a letter from Mr. AUDUBON, to one of the editors of the Gazette, dated Eastport, May 9, that he has chartered a schooner of about sixty tons, in which he intends to make his expedition. On the 14th, he writes that he has just returned from an excursion up the Bay of Fundy, where he had derived much useful information; that he should sail on the first of June from Eastport to Halifax, thence to Sable Island, to New Foundland and to the coast of Labrador. After the breeding season of the birds is over, he will pass through the province of New Brunswick, towards Quebec, and return to the United States by way of Niagara.[217]

In Eastport, the winds were still due east and northeast, and a heavy rain continued to fall. Shattuck stopped in to visit Audubon, and together they compiled a list of needed articles for the expedition to Labrador. Audubon mentioned that Capt. Coolidge had told him they would find gulls nesting in trees during their visit to the islands of the Grand Manan archipelago. Since gulls ordinarily are ground-nesters, Audubon knew that this type of unexpected behavior would be greeted skeptically by other naturalists. He told Shattuck that they would "signify their distrust of it by a note wonderful if true, or by some other similar expressions."[218]

Shattuck returned to the Chadbournes' home and accompanied the major to his office. He stopped in at the tailor's shop to pick up the warm clothes that he had ordered for the trip and visited other establishments to purchase the extra items he had discussed with Audubon.[219] The young man kept a precise record of every dime he spent so that he could provide an accounting to his father. According to his correspondence home, Shattuck paid $18.99 for the cloth for a pea jacket and pantaloons, $3.50 for flannel, and $9.25 for the tailor's bill. A shot bag cost $0.75, an oiled suit for the rain $3.50, and a sailor's chest $3.50. He also picked up a copy of the first volume of the *Ornithological Biography* from H. S. Favor's bookstore for $4.25.[220] This was the second American printing, published in Philadelphia the year before. He would ask Audubon to inscribe it to his father, which the naturalist happily did on the front free endpaper: "With J. J. Audubon's respectful compliments to George C. Shattuck, M.D."[221]

Audubon awoke on Wednesday morning to find no improvement in the weather. The rain continued to fall, and the dense fog prevented him from seeing across the street. In a letter to Lucy that he penned before breakfast, he adopted a local expression, saying that the fog was so thick "one may drive a nail in it & hang his hat upon it."[222]

The winds were blowing due east, as they had been for the past few days. Audubon noted that with these headwinds neither the *Ripley* nor the Boston packet carrying the supplies that Dr. Parkman had procured would be able to make the approach around the northern end of Campobello Island into Passamaquoddy Bay. To reach the ship's channel that ran along the island's western shoreline, a sailing vessel would have to sail into the wind. The only other route was via the Lubec Narrows, and few masters were comfortable taking their ships through that difficult passage.[223]

Since Audubon's latest correspondence, he had spoken to the owners of his chartered schooner and altered the arrangements for the party's provisions. He had decided that it would be less costly and simpler to have the owners supply each passenger with food during the voyage for $3 a week as opposed to supplying it himself and having a member of his party deal with the cook at each meal, which Audubon feared would allow the cook to cheat and rob him. Messrs. Buck and Tinkham had accordingly agreed to pay for the stores that were due to arrive on the packet.[224]

The clothes that Audubon and John had ordered from the tailor were ready, and Audubon described their strange new attire for his wife:

> We will be comfortably fix as to clothes &c a strange figure indeed do we cut in our dresses I promise thee—Fishermen Boots, the Sowls of which are all nailed to enable us to Stand erect on the Sea weeds—Pantaloons of Fearnought so coarse that our legs look more like bears legs than any thing else; Oil Jackets & overtrowsers for Rainy weather and Round White wool Hats with a piece of oil cloth dangling on our shoulders to prevent the wet running down our necks.— a course bag strapped on the shoulder to carry provisions during inland excursions, hunting Knifes at our sides and Guns on the back—add to these the full grown beard which thy Friend will have on his return and form an Idea of his Looks next Autumn.[225]

In speaking to some of the men who made the trip to Labrador every summer to fish for cod, Audubon had heard some incredible tales of the region. The fish were said to be abundant, crowding together so thickly in shallow waters that two fishermen sleeping only three hours could load their vessel with as many as 3,600 cod a day. The weather was reportedly "so pure, clear and regular without fogs that they all return home in better condition than that in which they depart from it." He had been told that they would find the "Exquimaux" to be "good & *trusty* Guides at a cheap rate — a little chewing Tobacco will make them give up a fine skin, or take you to places where rare birds or quadrupeds may be procured &c." Both John and the "Young Gentlemen" of his party were "almost wild with anxiety" about the prospects and envisioned returning home with eiderdown beds for their mothers, bear and wolf skins, and other curiosities of a thousand types "as if they had these already in their possession." Audubon was more circumspect and would await their visit before declaring these things to be so. Regardless, he anticipated he would acquire valuable information about the birds of the area and planned to "work like a Horse every moment that Sleep will not Stop me."[226]

Having seen a list of passengers in a New York paper, Audubon was aware that Bachman had landed safely in New York on May 11. He told Lucy to convey his best wishes. As for Edward Harris, the naturalist had received no word about his plans. Consequently, Audubon had *"almost* abandoned the Idea of Seing" him, but he evidently still held out some hope for his friend's arrival. With breakfast being made downstairs, Audubon closed the letter to ensure that it could be posted with the mail leaving Eastport at 8:00 a.m.[227]

After breakfast, Audubon joined Shattuck for a long walk in the rain.[228] They located the nest of a Canada Flycatcher (Canada Warbler) in a small bush growing over a rivulet and, upon flushing the female, found five eggs.[229] When Shattuck returned to the Chadbournes', he picked up a pen to write to his father. The weather was beginning to clear, and the young man thought they might sail that afternoon aboard the revenue cutter. He described their recent excursions on Capt. Childs's barge to West Quoddy Head and Pleasant Point. He thought that the regular daily exercise had been good for him. He had never felt better. He told his father that Audubon had completed the arrangements for the 106-ton schooner that would transport them to Labrador, with each member of the party expected to pay for his food at $3 weekly. He anticipated they would "live like princes" with meals benefiting from the beef, pork, rice, flour, beans, potatoes, butter, and cheese to be placed onboard. At the end of the voyage, Audubon said he was planning on making a side trip to Quebec before returning to Boston, and Shattuck sought instructions as to whether he should accompany the naturalist or return home directly. If the former, Shattuck did not think they would be back in Boston until the beginning of October.[230]

By noon, the skies over Passamaquoddy Bay had cleared at last, and Audubon and his party were notified that the *Swiftsure*, anchored in the harbor, would be ready to sail with the tide that night.[231] Audubon, accompanied by John, Shattuck, and James Curtiss, boarded the schooner in the evening and were taken on a tour by Capt. Coolidge.[232] The captain was sharply dressed in a navy-blue double-breasted jacket, with nine brass buttons on each lapel displaying the insignia of the Treasury Department and a half-inch strap of gold lace on each shoulder, and blue trousers.[233]

At 110 tons burden, the *Swiftsure* was smaller than most of the other cutters in the Revenue Cutter Service, but Coolidge said he preferred her.[234] She was a staunch craft in bad weather, a worthy trait in this part of the country where, as Shattuck noted in his journal, the fogs "are very thick, and continue a long while, and are pronounced by all a decided bore." Coolidge had helped design the vessel when she was being built in New York in 1825, although he did not like the fact that the two cabins, one aft for the captain and the other forward for his lieutenants, projected two feet above the level of the deck. There were two berths in each cabin, and the crew had their own space beneath the berth deck. In the captain's quarters, Coolidge showed his guests "several specimens of his handy work, many of which were in conveniences about his cabbin."[235]

Audubon's party was given use of the lieutenants' cabin. John and Shattuck were asked to share a single berth, and they turned in at their "proper bed time."[236] While the young men slept crammed next to each other, the crew was alive topsides readying the *Swiftsure* for departure.

5

Grand Manan

*The Appearance of the Island of Grand Manan is sublime and terrific
as you approach its stupendous bold & rugged rocky Shores.*
JOHN JAMES AUDUBON

At 3:00 a.m. on the morning of Thursday, May 23, the officers of the *Swiftsure* were notified that the preparations for the voyage had been completed. In addition to Capt. Coolidge, the revenue cutter was commanded by 1st Lt. John Whitcomb and 2nd Lt. Thomas Stoddard.[1] The thirty-nine-year-old Whitcomb had been born in North Yarmouth, Maine, and was commissioned as a second lieutenant in 1819. He had served in that capacity alongside Coolidge for many years. With Coolidge's promotion to captain, Whitcomb had been elevated to the rank of first lieutenant the prior December.[2] Stoddard was forty-six and hailed from Cohasset, Massachusetts, where he had gone to sea at the age of seventeen and ultimately captained a series of commercial vessels. He joined the Revenue Cutter Service as a warrant officer in 1831. He initially served under a Shattuck relation, Capt. Richard Derby, aboard the Boston cutter *Hamilton* before being promoted to second lieutenant and taking his place aboard the *Swiftsure* earlier that year.[3] Whitcomb and Stoddard wore uniforms similar to that of the captain, except that the first lieutenant had a single gold lace strap on the right shoulder, while the second lieutenant wore one on the left.[4]

A boat was ordered to shore to pick up Jonathan D. Weston, who had expressed an interest in joining Audubon's party, but the deputy revenue collector had changed his mind about coming. However, for this excursion with its celebrated passenger, Capt. Joseph H. Claridge of the *Fancy* had been welcomed onboard. The anchor was weighed, and, with a "delightful breeze" filling her canvas, the schooner turned toward the rising sun and sailed for the British-owned island of Grand Manan.[5]

Grand Manan is situated southeast of Campobello Island approximately fifteen miles from Eastport at the entrance to the Bay of Fundy. Stretching just about fifteen miles in length north to south and six miles across at its widest point, it juts out of the ocean depths like a massive fist. The western face of the island is marked by sheer basalt cliffs and precipices rising to heights of up to 350 feet, "offering a very rough reception to any vessel driven upon it by storm." The opposite side of the island is

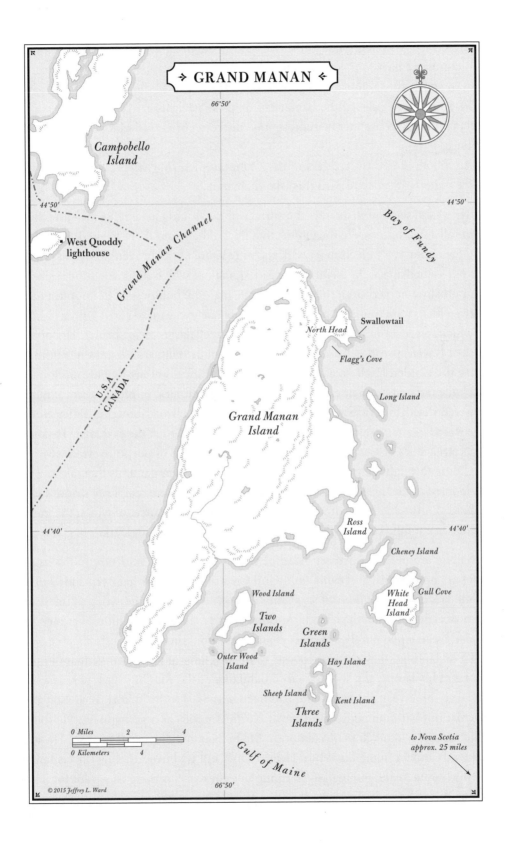

⟶ GRAND MANAN ⟵

66°50'

Campobello
Island

44°50'   44°50'

West Quoddy
lighthouse

Bay of Fundy

Grand Manan Channel

U.S.A.
CANADA

North Head   Swallowtail

Flagg's Cove

Long Island

Grand Manan
Island

44°40'   Ross   44°40'
                                          Island

                                                    Cheney Island

                                          White   Gull Cove
                                          Head
Wood Island   Island

            Two
            Islands   Green
                         Islands
Outer Wood
Island   Hay Island

Sheep Island   Kent Island
        Three
        Islands

0 Miles   2   4

0 Kilometers   4

to Nova Scotia
approx. 25 miles

Gulf of Maine

66°50'

© 2015 Jeffrey L. Ward

gently sloped with fields and forests that terminate in an irregular-shaped coastline of picturesque bays and coves.⁶ A necklace of smaller islands runs down along the eastern shore, the largest of which is White Head Island. The thick fogs, changing tides, and vicious gales of the Bay of Fundy make navigation in the area hazardous, and many a vessel has met her end against the rocks of Grand Manan and its lesser siblings.

Audubon offered the readers of the *Ornithological Biography* a vibrant account of the cutter's advance toward this island chain:

> The vessel seemed to fly over the surface of the liquid element, as the sun rose in full splendour, while the clouds that floated here and there formed, with their glowing hues, a rich contrast with the pure azure of the heavens above us. We approached apace the island of Grand Manan, of which the stupendous cliffs gradually emerged from the deep with the majestic boldness of her noblest native chief. Soon our bark passed beneath its craggy head, covered with trees, which, on account of the height, seemed scarcely larger than shrubs. The prudent Raven spread her pinions, launched from the cliff, and flew away before us; the Golden Eagle soaring aloft, moved majestically along in wide circles; the Guillemots sat on their eggs upon the shelvy precipices, or plunging into the water, dived, and rose again at a great distance; the Broad-breasted Eider Duck covered her eggs among the grassy tufts; on a naked rock the seal lazily basked, its sleek sides glistening in the sunshine; while shoals of porpoises were swiftly gliding through the waters around us, shewing by their gambols that, although doomed to the deep, their life was not devoid of pleasure. Far away stood the bold shores of Nova Scotia, gradually fading in the distance, of which the grey tints beautifully relieved the wing-like sails of many a fishing bark.⁷

Sailing around the northern head of Grand Manan, the *Swiftsure* followed the compass point south and came to in Gull Cove along the northeastern shoreline of White Head Island at around 8:30 a.m.⁸ It was a beautiful, sunny day as the shore party of eight rowed to the island.⁹ Audubon and his three companions were accompanied by an equal number of officers and crew from the *Swiftsure*.¹⁰

Upon landing, they made their way to the dwelling of Governor William Frankland and his family, the sole human inhabitants of the roughly 1,525-acre island.¹¹ The sixty-nine-year-old Frankland had been born in Whitby in Yorkshire, England, in 1764, but had immigrated to British North America as a young man. He found a life partner in Ann Ross of Falmouth, Maine, whom he married in 1789. He subsequently built a home on White Head Island and had lived there with his family for thirty-four years, culling hay, farming potatoes, and serving as a pilot for ships sailing through the archipelago.¹²

Although Frankland was not in when Audubon's party called at the house, they met him out on the island a short time later. Shattuck noted that the governor still retained a trace of his Yorkshire accent and "was very polite." The naturalist described him as "a worthy Englishman." Frankland was delighted to see them. He granted them "leave to ransack his domains, and invited us to remain as long as we pleased." Audubon was particularly interested in confirming Capt. Coolidge's claim that gulls could be found nesting in trees, so he and his companions headed toward the thick pine woods that covered a section of the island. Their path took them through an "elevated marsh of great extent," and the party found themselves sinking in mud and ooze past their ankles. Shattuck was grateful he had donned a new pair of long fisherman's boots that morning.[13]

As they approached the trees, a multitude of Herring Gulls filled the air, wheeling on bended wings high above the treetops. Others, situated in their nests on the boughs of the firs, took wing and cried out in alarm. Audubon was "greatly surprised" to find these ground-nesting birds building their nests at various heights in the trees:[14]

> It is true I had been informed of this by our captain, but I had almost believed that, on arriving at the spot, I should find the birds not to be gulls. My doubts, however, were now dispelled, and I was delighted to see how strangely Nature had provided them with the means of securing their eggs and young from their arch-enemy man.[15]

For the most part, the birds flew beyond the range of the party's guns, but twelve dipped too close and were felled. John, an excellent shot like his father, was particularly adept at bringing them down and killed more than anyone else.[16] He was using a fowling piece that had been made by Conway of Manchester, England, and, according to Audubon, was the "best Gun" they ever produced. The naturalist had ordered it the year before, originally intending to give it as a present to his brother-in-law Will Bakewell. But a blowup between Lucy and her younger brother while she was staying with his family in Louisville during Audubon's Florida excursion had led to mutual embitterment that had yet to heal. When the naturalist mentioned the coming gift in a letter the previous September, Will refused to accept it. "[U]nder other circumstances," he replied, "it would afford me great pleasure to receive it from One whose greatest fault has been generosity and hospitality to those who were ungrateful or insincere but altho I can charge myself with neither ingratitude, insincerity or anything but an undeviating solicitude for your welfare as well as that of your Family, I must decline receiving any presents from you until we meet." Will Bakewell's loss was John's gain. He was overjoyed with the firearm, gushing to his mother that it was "the finest gun I ever saw."[17]

Another gull, "flying at a great height," had been winged by one of the blasts and could no longer fly, the tip of its wing broken. It was caught, and as the party proceeded along on their ramble, the gull ran before them. Claridge helped the bird get over any difficult spots along the path, although Audubon noted that it "bit severely." The party searched for gull eggs, but it was still early in the nesting season, and they found only a couple. They also collected a White-crowned Bunting (White-crowned Sparrow). Very few flowers were yet in bloom, but they did see some wild blackberries, strawberries, and raspberries.[18]

The party returned to the *Swiftsure* at 3:30 p.m. and eagerly attacked the dinner prepared for them. Audubon then instructed his son and Shattuck to skin the birds that the shore party had collected. He handed Shattuck his annotated copy of Bonaparte's *The Genera of North American Birds, and a Synopsis of the Species Found within the Territory of the United States*, published in New York in 1828, and told the medical student to use it to identify the various species.[19] Audubon certainly did not need the information. He would have known these common birds on sight. But he obviously hoped to begin training Shattuck in the methodology of identifying a bird by using the physical descriptions that appeared in Bonaparte's work, which would accompany them to Labrador. The *Synopsis*, however, was by no means easy to use, having been written for ornithologists and lacking images to assist in species identification. The description of the Herring Gull, *Larus argentatus*, was representative and illustrates the difficulty Shattuck would have faced in separating this species from other similar-appearing gulls:

> Mantle bluish-gray; quills black at the point, tipped with white, reaching much beyond the tail; shafts black ; first primary only, with a white spot besides the narrow tip;* tarsus nearly three inches; nostrils linear. Length two feet.
>
> Summer plumage, head and neck pure white; winter, head and neck with brown lines.
>
> Young blackish cinereous, mottled with yellowish rusty.[20]

John and Shattuck headed down to the lieutenant's cabin to begin the process of preparing the skins. Claridge offered to assist them. John, who had been skinning birds since boyhood, completed ten of the skins, while Shattuck was able to finish only two. Shattuck admitted that he was still not "very expert at the business."[21]

Meanwhile, Audubon had returned to the island with Capt. Coolidge and James Curtiss to pay a call on Governor Frankland. Over tea, the naturalist questioned the old farmer about the nesting adaptation he had observed among the island's Herring Gulls. Audubon was pleased to hear that the birds had developed this habit within recent memory, and he repeated Frankland's account in the *Ornithological Biography*:[22]

[W]hen I first came here, many years ago, they all built their nests on the moss and in open ground; but as my sons and the fishermen collected most of their eggs for winter use, and sadly annoyed the poor things, the old ones gradually began to put their nests on trees in the thickest parts of the woods. The youngest birds, however, still have some on the ground, and the whole are becoming less wild since I have forbidden strangers to rob their nests; for, gentlemen, you are the only persons out of my family that have fired a gun on White Head Island for several years past, and I daresay you will not commit any greater havock among them than is necessary, and to that you are welcome.[23]

At around 8:00 p.m., having completed their work aboard the vessel, John and Shattuck proceeded ashore to join their companions. It was a lovely evening with the silver light of a waxing crescent moon glinting off the water. They found their friends at a table in Frankland's home conversing. Shattuck noted derisively in his journal that Curtiss was "talking politics as usual." Shattuck may not have appreciated Curtiss's abiding interest in politics, but to the young postmaster it was a passion. Within two years, he would be resettled with his family in Chicago, a small but rapidly growing community on the banks of Lake Michigan, where he would become a rising political star in the Democratic Party and ultimately serve two separate one-year terms as mayor.[24]

The discussion soon turned to Audubon's planned trip to Labrador. The men assured Shattuck he would abandon his vegetarian diet and return to Eastport "eating meat stoutly."[25] Audubon and his young companions wished they were already on their way, and the naturalist expressed regret he had not sought approval from the government to sail north aboard the *Swiftsure*.[26] Coolidge and his officers concurred, saying they would have welcomed it.[27]

The group rowed back to the schooner sometime after 9:00 p.m. Two of Frankland's sons accompanied them, having been sent by their father to act as guides to the two sets of smaller islands that Audubon hoped to explore in the morning. Before turning in at half past ten, Shattuck sat down with his journal to record the day's events. Audubon then read his own journalized account of the day to Shattuck and John before they all fell asleep.[28]

Audubon, always an early riser, awoke the young men at 5:00 a.m. The sun by then had been up for more than an hour. Shattuck came above deck and was surprised to find the *Swiftsure* anchored in a new harbor. At around 11:30 p.m., the crew had raised anchor and sailed five or six miles west of White Head Island to the Green Islands, where they had anchored for the night.[29] Breakfast was served at 6:00 a.m. under a cloudless blue sky. Audubon's party then divided into two groups and left in separate boats piloted by the cutter's officers and crew to explore the outer islands. Audubon, Shattuck, Claridge, and one of Frankland's two sons were in one boat that headed south to the island cluster known as the Three Islands — Hay Island, Sheep Island, and Kent Island. The other group, which included John, Curtiss, and the other Frankland son, proceeded west to the Two Islands — Wood Island and Outer Wood Island.[30]

At the outset of their excursion, a member of Audubon's party shot a pair of Harlequin Ducks, which the locals referred to as "lords and ladies." The male of this species is beautifully patterned with white markings on a slate-blue head and back bordered with cinnamon-colored sides. The female, as in many ducks, is drab colored, an evolutionary adaptation that serves to camouflage her while nesting. The distinctive difference in appearance between males and females is an example of what ornithologists term "sexual dimorphism."[31]

Having collected their prizes, the party then approached and landed on an islet situated near the Three Islands, where they observed numerous Black Guillemots, known locally as "sea pigeons," and Puffins (Atlantic Puffins), which were called "sea parrots." A search for nests was unsuccessful, but the men added two guille-mots to their specimen bags. Continuing on, Audubon and his companions landed at Hay Island and explored the seventy-five-acre land area before making their way on foot across the mudflats that separate it at low tide from Kent Island.[32]

The largest of the Three Islands, two-hundred-acre Kent Island was named after Capt. John Kent, a British subject who settled there with his family in 1799. Kent died in 1828, but his wife, Susanna, continued to make the island her home. The house that Kent built had since been improved by one Mr. China, who greeted the party when they arrived. He offered them the use of his hunting dog, described by Shattuck as "so well trained, that he would creep with the shooter." With the dog by their side, Audubon's party tramped around the island, a mixture of open mead-ows and "swampy woods" of white spruce. But they evidently were not successful in collecting any specimens. China told them that the "lords and ladies," which could be found off the island in the spring, had moved on for the most part, and that the gulls had yet to begin nesting.[33]

The party continued its search of the surrounding waters, allowing their boat to drift in hopes of shooting some ducks in passing flocks. However, the rocking of the boat made it impossible to hit any.[34] A pair of Red-necked Grebes, diving for food, also avoided their guns as Audubon related in the *Ornithological Biography*:

> On the Bay of Fundy, and among the islands at its entrance, I saw these Grebes already in their spring plumage, it being then the beginning of May. On one occasion our boat was rowed over an eddy in which a pair had dived in search of food. On emerging they were only a few yards distant; but, although several

guns were fired at them, they escaped unhurt, for they instantly dived again, passed under the boat at the depth of about a yard, and did not rise until at a safe distance. None of us could conceive how they had managed to elude us, for as they were so near, the shot threw up the water in its course, and I had expected to find them completely mangled.[35]

Audubon then observed a new species of phalarope, known locally as a "sea goose" but formally called a Hyperborean Phalarope (Red-necked Phalarope). He desperately wanted to collect it, but the party was unable to do so. The only other bird they obtained "after some difficulty" was a Ruddy Turnstone, a not uncommon species.[36]

When they returned to the revenue cutter around 2:30 p.m., Audubon's group found that the other party had similarly enjoyed only marginal success, procuring several Eider Ducks (Common Eiders), some "sea pigeons" (Black Guillemots), and an unidentified "old duck."[37] The consensus was that the seabirds had largely left these waters for their breeding grounds to the north.[38]

The *Swiftsure* made her way back to White Head Island, where Frankland's sons were restored to their family, and Capt. Coolidge, joined by Audubon and his associates, came ashore to bid the governor farewell. Frankland presented Audubon with thirty gull eggs that had been gathered that morning, a portion of which were later blown out by John and Shattuck, while the remainder were cooked. Coolidge and Shattuck spent some time beachcombing, and they both returned to the vessel with some interesting shells and stones. According to Shattuck, Coolidge was "a connoisseur in these articles."[39] As the *Swiftsure* prepared to depart, the governor and his sons stood on the shore and shouted out "three hearty cheers," which the crew and passengers returned in kind.[40] The revenue cutter then ran northwest and came to in Flagg's Cove, a sheltered bay along the northeastern coast of Grand Manan in the crook of a peninsula called North Head, where they spent the night.[41]

Saturday, May 25, proved to be another beautiful day on the Bay of Fundy. Audubon and his companions were up at 5:00 a.m. After breakfast, they split up into three groups and departed in separate crafts to explore the area. One of the parties rowed east to a peninsula called the Swallowtail, where they shot some Black Guillemots nesting among the rocks. John and Shattuck were taken ashore in another boat and spent several hours on a ramble through the fields and thick forests of North Head. The third party, with Capt. Coolidge aboard, went to a spot that had a vein of clay, some of which Coolidge extracted and brought back to the vessel. All of the boats were back by noon. With a "very fair breeze," the *Swiftsure* began her return trip to Eastport at upwards of ten knots.[42]

As the cutter cruised along the rugged Grand Manan coast, Audubon expressed a desire to stop in order to capture some young Ravens (Common Ravens) from a large nest built into a cleft on the side of a steep rock. The good-natured captain acquiesced. A boat was launched, and a sailor from Mount Desert Island accomplished the task by tying a rope to a tree at the top of the rock and climbing down forty feet to the nest "the way they are caught in the Orkneys." The rock face jutted out considerably above the entrance to the shelf on which the nest was located, so he was forced to push off the rock and swing in to reach the nestlings. He returned with four of the still-flightless birds, which Audubon estimated had hatched only three weeks before. Shattuck described them as "the ugliest birds without exception that I ever saw." Audubon hoped to teach one of them to talk and have it accompany them to Labrador.[43]

The revenue cutter resumed her journey, ran through the Lubec Narrows, and reached Eastport at 5:00 p.m. On landing, Shattuck found that the packet *Boundary* from Boston had arrived during their absence carrying the fowling piece and ammunition his father had sent.[44] Audubon was pleased to learn that the provisions procured by Dr. Parkman had also come. But he had been hoping to find several letters from Lucy and others upon his return and was "cruelly disapointed" to discover not a single one waiting for him.[45] He knew that with his party's anticipated departure for Labrador but a week away there was little time remaining to hear from those to whom he had written. However, some question yet remained as to precisely when they would commence their journey. His chartered schooner, the *Ripley*, was still at sea.

6

Departure

[O]ur Vessel is in excellent trim, my Youthfull Party all spirit and hopefull expectation.
JOHN JAMES AUDUBON

Audubon was out of bed by 4:00 a.m. on Sunday morning, the 26th of May. With pen in hand, he sat down to provide Lucy with an account of their short excursion to Grand Manan. However, he could not let the silence of those in his circle pass without comment, and he bemoaned the lack of correspondence from her, Edward Harris, Nicholas Berthoud, and John Bachman—but especially from her. "I cannot conceive the reason why," he wondered.[1] In fact, Lucy had been seriously ill with a liver ailment from May 13 to 19 and had been unable to write.[2] Still, he could never understand why her letters and those from his friends were not delivered to him almost daily. The truth was that no one was as devoted a letter writer as he. He was inevitably bound to be disappointed.

Turning his pen to the trip, he expressed overall satisfaction at their success. He had "derived much information and procured Some Valuable rare Birds, some Shells and Some plants which I had never met with before—The Capⁿ Officers & Crew made our time extremely agreable and our Jaunt has been altogether a pleasing and a fruitfull one." He was particularly "delighted with Young Shattuck and John, they worked well, walked well, Skinned Many Birds well and Shewed a great willingness at turning out early of a Morning."[3]

He went on to say that he intended to spend the day drawing the Harlequin Ducks they had collected on their voyage, and John would be preparing the skins of about twenty birds. He was also looking for the arrival of the *Ripley*, which he expected to dock at Eastport that day. Shattuck, he added, was planning to travel on foot to Dennysville to visit the Lincolns and would return the next day. Audubon noted that this would be "more than he ever Walk^d in his life." Finally, he insisted they were "*perfectly* Well and in a Month More hope to be all as tough as pine knots."[4]

John added a postscript to report that he had received a "first-Rate pointer dog" from Lt. Buford. The young man called it "Dash" and planned to train it during the trip to Labrador.[5]

That letter completed, Audubon began another to Dr. Harlan in Philadelphia. He summarized their activities over the previous three days and added, as a measure of reassurance about his health, that "we have had rare sport & plenty of it and I am Audubon again!" He was still expecting to sail for Labrador on June 1. "God granting us a safe return we must do well if not Wonders in accumulating knowledge for the *Great Book* and something for our Friends." They would be taking along "plenty of N.E. [New England] Rum" in which to store the natural-history articles they collected.[6] He followed this letter with one to Dr. Parkman, presumably thanking him for shipping the provisions and instructing him again to draw on Nicholas Berthoud for the amount.[7]

Over at the home of Maj. Chadbourne, Shattuck spent the morning on a long, richly detailed letter to his father, describing the voyage to Grand Manan. He promised to write again before the party's departure, which he believed could be as early as Thursday, May 30, or Friday, May 31, depending on when the *Ripley* reached port. He hoped to have a letter from home recounting all that had happened during his absence when he arrived back in Eastport at summer's end.[8]

Although Shattuck had then intended to walk the eighteen miles to Dennysville, his recent diet aboard the *Swiftsure*, which included hard pilot bread, had left him costive, and he was forced to his bed with debilitating gastrointestinal pain. Dr. Ray was consulted and recommended the administration of castor oil. Along with some phosphate of soda, the laxative senna, and the tender care of the Chadbournes, Shattuck was returned to health by the following afternoon.[9] Audubon was convinced that the young man's vegetarian diet was at fault, and he was intent on getting Shattuck to change it. Relaying his concerns to Lucy, he noted that Shattuck "has for the last month or so eat nothing but bread & potatoes, and drank Water only— With the exercise which he now takes he would dwindle away into a drum stick."[10]

On Sunday evening, Audubon received a letter from Lucy dated May 19, just one week earlier, the first she had written after recovering from her illness. He was greatly relieved to hear from her and put the letter aside to write a response in the morning.[11]

Shattuck also received two pieces of mail on Sunday, a letter from Eliza Prentiss, a family friend, and the other from his father.[12] The latter contained the news that young William Ingalls would be heading to Eastport to join the expedition.[13] Indeed, Ingalls had boarded the *Edward Preble* in Boston only the day before and was in transit.[14] Still confined to bed, Shattuck passed the news on to Audubon, who was no doubt thrilled to recruit another scion of a prominent family that could help defray the costs of the expedition. As he later told Lucy, "I shall make these Young Men pay a proportion of our general expenses and make them work hard besides."[15]

Monday dawned fair with winds blowing to the northeast. Audubon's day began at his writing table with Lucy in his thoughts. He was concerned about her recent illness and, in his letter, urged her to exercise more. He also suggested that she drink "a little wine every day and particularly before thy going to bed as thou did in Boston when I never saw thee in better health for many Years." He wanted her "to accept of Harlan's invitation and go to Phil^a for a Month or so it will do Thee good." He referenced her portrait by Henry Inman, evidently unsure if she had received it given her latest infirmity. If not, he wanted her to contact the artist in Baltimore. The change in the winds, he told her, would prevent the *Ripley*, as well as the Boston packet carrying William Ingalls, from entering Passamaquoddy Bay because both vessels would have to sail into the wind to get around Campobello Island.[16]

Meanwhile they were "most comfortable" at the Westons'. The house must have been busy and lively, not to mention crowded. In addition to the Audubons, the Westons had been hosting Congregational minister Aaron B. Church and his wife from Calais, Maine. Lucy Weston also had a cousin visiting. With Mrs. Weston still away in Boston, Audubon indicated that the two young women were both "extremely kind to us." John thought Lucy Weston "quite an agreeable young Lady very gay and *very* very obliging." From time to time, John would accompany her on the piano with his violin.[17]

Lucy Weston certainly did not mind accommodating the Audubons. She remarked in correspondence to her mother that they were "very pleasant and unpretending, plain kind of folks, appear like Judge Lincoln's family."[18]

Before closing the letter to his own dearest Lucy, Audubon added some thoughts about their son. John was waking with him at 4:00 a.m. and they were having "famous long days of it." The lassitude that had characterized the young man and given rise to the concerns Lucy had expressed when writing to Victor only months before appeared to be a thing of the past. Audubon now thought he "will be industrious on our return."[19]

The naturalist resumed his work on his drawing of the Harlequin Ducks that Monday.[20] John was invited out onto Passamaquoddy Bay in one of the *Swiftsure's* boats, the revenue cutter having been hauled into Hobb's Wharf off Water Street for caulking and other repairs.[21] To the delight of the naturalist, John returned from his time on the water with three Hyperborean Phalaropes (Red-necked Phalaropes), the same species that had eluded Audubon's party just days before near the Three Islands.[22]

That afternoon, Shattuck was once again on his feet and feeling well enough to travel to Dennysville by water. He took passage in a vessel operated between March and January by Capt. Bela R. Reynolds, who plied the route across Passamaquoddy Bay into Cobscook Bay, through the rocks and shoals of the Cobscook Falls, and up the Dennys River.[23] With the incoming tide, which raised the river's water level by fifteen feet, it was the fastest way to travel.[24]

Shattuck was greeted by Tom Lincoln and his parents and welcomed to their home looking out over the river. Judge Lincoln and his wife, Hannah, both impressed him as being exceptional individuals:

> Judge Lincoln must certainly be a remarkable man, and coming down here so early as he did, there being now such fruits of his labor, shows that he must be a man of practical wisdom, great enterprise and hardihood. Though now in his seventieth year, his step is firm, his limbs unbowed by age, and from his appearance you would hardly pronounce him over fifty. Mrs L. also must be a very superior woman, having a well educated mind, and at the same time well versed in all the accomplishments of the farmer's wife. . . . We should not forget what a noble set of children, the sons all high minded, enterprising active men, the daughters amiable and notable housewives.[25]

According to Shattuck, the Lincolns had "quite an extensive farm," where they grew wheat, Indian corn, and hay.[26] They also harvested fruit, including apples from an apple orchard that had been planted near the house. But grapes and peaches could not withstand the brutal cold of the northern Maine winters.[27] In the fields, Shattuck counted "fourteen cows, ten oxen, [and] a large number of sheep."[28]

In the evening, Tom showed his guest the town of Dennysville, a small community with a population of about three hundred. He also pointed out the Lincoln family's saw-, grist-, and fulling mills, which had been built along the edge of the river and used the flowing water to run their machinery.[29]

The following morning, Tuesday, May 28, Tom took Shattuck out to see his older brother Belah, who was supervising a crew of men constructing a road through the woods to Charlotte, Maine.[30] Shattuck described the twenty-seven-year-old Belah in a subsequent letter to his father, saying that a "smarter more enterprising man I have seldom seen. He worked as if he were to be stopped by no obstacles, and as if his cunning in contrivance was equal to his force of execution." Shattuck wished he could have extended his stay, but word reached him that the *Ripley* had finally made port. Although the news would prove to be erroneous, he acted on it and made plans to return the following day.[31]

In Boston, Dr. Shattuck took time away from his medical practice to acknowledge receipt of his son's letter of May 22, written before the young man sailed for Grand Manan. The senior Shattuck wanted his son to know that the items the latter had recently requested, including the gun for Tom Lincoln, the barometer, and the books, were aboard the *Edward Preble* with William Ingalls. He asked his son to acknowledge their receipt and, in response to his son's query about the expedition, granted him permission to accompany Audubon to Quebec if he wished to do so.[32]

Back in Eastport, the naturalist received a letter from Lucy, this one dated May

21. He was gratified to hear that she was improving in health, "if not quite restored at least out of Danger." In his response, he noted that John was working on a "beautifull Drawing" of one of the rare phalaropes he had killed the day before. Audubon was impressed by how well the young man was doing: "[H]is improvement at Drawing certainly surpasses all I had anticipated and I hope to see him *compleat* Many a fine drawing for our Familly Work."[33]

Audubon thought the *Ripley* would finally arrive that night. If so, he wrote, they would plan to sail on June 1. He longed for yet another letter from her before they left, and promised to write again prior to boarding. He urged her to speak "very freely" to John Bachman, who was visiting New York. "[T]hou cannot help but admiring him as much as I do—he is the *only parson on Earth* for Me!" he exclaimed. Audubon added that a letter from Edward Harris had arrived "in which he gives up the Idea of Joining our party and I regret it most truly."[34]

Wednesday morning began cold and foggy, with rain developing during the day. The wind was blowing due east. Audubon added a brief postscript to the letter he had written to Lucy the day before to let her know that no vessels had landed overnight. And until there was a change in the winds, that would probably remain the case.[35]

Audubon expected that they would complete the drawing of three phalaropes that day. John was already at work on the drawing but complained about how cold it was in their room. With his Southern blood, Audubon did not care for the low temperature, noting that "this is a part of the World where I could not easily be induced to reside I promise thee." He asked her to send letters during his absence to the customs collector, who might be able to forward them via one of the fishing vessels leaving Eastport for Labrador. "Merely Mention thy good health and that all was well when Writing, it will be a great source of pleasure to us." Perhaps most importantly, he wanted her to know just how much he missed her. "I would give much to see & kiss thee at this moment," he declared.[36]

———

Lucy's thoughts that morning mirrored her husband's as she looked over his letter of May 22 and sat down to draft a reply. At the outset, she expressed surprise that he had not received more of her letters, as she had been a faithful correspondent, this being her seventh letter since May 8. She wanted him to know that she approved of his decision to alter the arrangements for the provision of food aboard the Labrador schooner. She had copied a portion of his last two letters for Edward Harris to enable him to keep Audubon in the public eye through the *New-York Gazette*. Harris had also written a notice for publication aimed at correcting an erroneous statement in the *Louisville Journal* that Audubon claimed to be a native Kentuckian. She passed along some family news and reminded her husband that Eliza was hoping he would return from Labrador with Gray Fox or Brown Bear skins for her to have a muff and tippet made for the coming winter. Nicholas was interested in receiving birds' eggs. Lucy then closed the letter with heavenly blessings and a prayer that her men would return safely from their travels.[37]

Despite the inclement weather, Audubon took a walk and observed some Chimney Swifts flying overhead, the first he had seen since his arrival. These charcoal-gray aerial acrobats are swift flyers, darting through the air on narrow wings in pursuit of insects while chattering incessantly. Before Europeans arrived in North America, they nested communally in hollow tree trunks. They quickly found chimneys a suitable alternative, gluing their stick nests to the masonry with their saliva. Audubon indicated in the *Ornithological Biography* that a few pairs nested in the vicinity of Eastport during the breeding season.[38]

When Shattuck finally arrived back in Eastport, his excitement at their anticipated departure turned to disappointment upon discovering that the *Ripley* had still not landed. He began a letter home to his father to relate the details of his recent illness and recovery, along with a description of his trip to Dennysville. The *Ripley*, he said, had "been expected every moment for some days" but had not arrived due to the headwinds. "The owners of the Ripley say, that in fourty eight hours after her arrival she will be ready to speed again, and you may depend upon it that we shall not stop one moment longer than is absolutely necessary."[39]

Around this time, Audubon was invited to dine at the Coolidge home across the water in Lubec. During the meal, the naturalist spoke about his forthcoming trip to Labrador and asked the Coolidges' eighteen-year-old son, Joe, if he knew how to sail. Like his father and older brother, Joe was born to the sea and replied readily that he did.[40] Audubon knew that the *Ripley* would be carrying a small sailing craft known as a Hampton boat for use on their daily excursions and thought Joe would make a welcome addition to the group of "Young Gentlemen" who had signed on for the voyage.[41] With his usual flair and likely promise of adventure, he extended an invitation to the young man to join them. The Coolidges doubtless said they would consider Audubon's offer and provide a prompt answer. It evidently did not take much discussion. As Coolidge recalled years later, "readily did I consent to go with him when he invited me, and when my parents expressed their willingness that I should go."[42]

The rain that had begun on Wednesday continued to fall on the morning of Thursday, May 30. Although Eastport was covered in a heavy fog, John joined Lt. Greene on a hunting foray for phalaropes on the bay in Capt. Childs's barge. The visibility was so poor they could barely see twenty feet, and they were soon lost even with a compass. Fortunately, they were eventually able to find their way back to shore. However, the steamer *Henrietta*, bound for Eastport from Saint John, New Brunswick, lost her way and became trapped against a rock just below Dog Island, a small offshore island a little more than a mile northwest of town. The passengers and crew were rescued, and every item aboard was salvaged except the engine. An effort to remove the vessel could not begin until the tide turned. When it did, the boat filled with water, and a pair of schooners were unable to pull her off. It would take a second attempt the following day to be successful. The accident had an immediate impact on a current guest of the Weston family, Miss Farley, a wealthy middle-aged "Lady Merchant" from Saint John whose departure would be delayed as a consequence. She knew many of Audubon's friends and subscribers in Liverpool, Manchester, and Leeds and offered the naturalist her hospitality should his travels take him through Saint John on his way to Quebec.[43]

In the afternoon, Audubon and Shattuck paid a visit to the home of Dr. Ray. Audubon freely admitted that he thought both Gall and Spurzheim were "quacks," although he remained "ready to learn, and took every occasion to study phrenology whether it be true." He pointed out that, notwithstanding their claims, even the leading practitioners of the science could not consistently identify a man's talents from the location of bumps on the skull.[44]

During Audubon's stay in Edinburgh in 1826, he had dined on several occasions with George Combe, an attorney and dedicated follower of Gall's, and permitted his head to be examined by Combe and other phrenologists.[45] As Shattuck related in his journal, "Combe thought he had the bumps for drawing," but another phrenologist "said he would make a great general." When the naturalist met Spurzheim in Boston in 1832, "Spurzheim said his case was one in a thousand, and that he had none of these bumps." Audubon also believed that phrenology would ultimately harm society. "Education is everything," he explained, "and phrenology would do mischief, for people would no longer educate all their children equally, and many mistakes would thus be made, and the poor neglected child would say, my father says I'm a rascal, so I may as well be one."[46]

Audubon's skepticism of phrenology would eventually be validated. Some of his other scientific views did not hold up as well. According to the young Bostonian, "[h]e thought our knowledge could be increased only to a certain extent, and at these limits men should contentedly stop." In addition, Audubon "intimated that he was not quite convinced that the brain was the seat of the mind."[47]

Dr. Ray was intrigued by Audubon's comments and said he was unaware of certain supposed truths the naturalist presented, such as the claim that a bird's singing ability could be determined from the appearance of the trachea, just as the lungs in humans born without a voice had been found by anatomists to be smaller in volume than in those who could speak.[48]

Friday morning brought a welcome change in the weather. The skies cleared and the wind began blowing due west for the first time in days. By 4:00 a.m., Audubon was up and sitting at his writing table with pen in hand to reply to Lucy's May 24 letter that had arrived the day before.[49] She reported seeing Edward Harris, who had confirmed he would not be able to join the expedition, although he was interested in meeting up with Audubon either in Eastport or somewhere in Canada on the party's way home. She also provided instructions to John "to *press all*" the plants he came across. Most importantly, she said that her health had returned, and she promised to write frequently in care of the Eastport postmaster. "Now farewell," she added in closing, "a long farewell but time will roll on and many a happy day I hope is yet in Store for us."[50]

In his response, Audubon expressed his gratitude for her letter and the news that she was once again feeling well. He noted the improvement in the weather and thought their schooner would reach port in a matter of hours. Within two days they would be underway, his party now grown to six with the addition of Joe Coolidge, whom he described as "a Sturdy, active Youth of 21."[51] Whether Audubon knew that Coolidge was actually three years younger is unknown. He was often imprecise on matters of this sort.

After reporting on the accident involving the *Henrietta*, Audubon told Lucy that Dr. Harlan would be leaving for Europe the following day and had requested letters of introduction to Audubon's friends in Paris, London, and Edinburgh. Audubon intended to send them to Lucy so that they could be forwarded. He had no advice to give to Harris as to the timing of their return, writing "that My wishes now are that we may be *here* by the first of Octr or before, but that I cannot well say because when once at Labrador I wish to do all I can and stay there as long as the Season will admit of with safety." He still thought they might spend the month of October traveling from Eastport to Quebec by way of the Saint John River, although he would make that decision based upon the content of her letters waiting for him when he returned to Eastport. They had tried to use their time in Eastport productively. "We draw, write, Hunt and Make Music, according with the weather. John is now gone Shooting and will return before breakfast, I Make [him] get up at ½ past 4 every Morning and that good Habit is now growing upon him."[52]

Everyone in the Weston household had come down for breakfast, so Audubon brought the letter to a close. However, before he sealed it there was a knock at the front door. William Ingalls, fresh off a six-day journey aboard the *Edward Preble*, walked into the house and introduced himself. Audubon added a short postscript to the letter, describing Ingalls as "a very *handsome*, round open Countenanced Gentlemanly Youth."[53] The young man presented him with a brief letter of introduction from Dr. Parkman, dated May 25:

> Dear Sir
> Through the unceasing & active good-will of our Friend, Dr. Shattuck,
> I present to you Mr. Ingalls, son of Dr. Ingalls, one of our senior physicians,
> & an experienced ^public^ teacher of Anat^y & Surg^y —
> — The son is the father's pupil; & we have reason to expect that he will prove a satisfactory disciple to you.
> The enclosed I claim for you the right to read, & for myself to repossess, when we meet again.
> respectfully
> G. Parkman.[54]

From his spacious second-floor bedroom, Audubon could look out over Passamaquoddy Bay and see the sails of many ships, long delayed by the winds, approaching the Eastport waterfront.[55] It was his fervent hope that the *Ripley* had finally come. However, he was to be disheartened when it was not among the vessels to dock that day.

In the afternoon, Shattuck, no doubt accompanied by Ingalls and John, walked out to Point Pleasant. When the young men returned from their ramble that evening, they found Maj. Chadbourne visiting Audubon. The two men had laid a wager on whether the *Ripley* would arrive by 10:00 a.m. the following morning. Which side of the bet Audubon took is not recorded. A bottle of wine was promised the winner.[56]

———

Meanwhile, Victor Audubon was getting ready to leave London on a tour of the Continent in search of new subscribers. He had originally planned to visit only Paris in order to deliver the recent Numbers and collect what was owed from Audubon's agent. However, he decided to add Austria, the German states, and Prussia to the itinerary after hearing that John Gould, the talented British ornithological illustrator, would be traveling there within six weeks on a similar mission. Like Audubon, Gould was publishing his *Birds of Europe* in serial form and by subscription and would be seeking out the same potential customers. Victor wanted to make sure that he was first on the scene to maximize the chance that potential subscribers would subscribe to *The Birds of America*.[57]

Victor assured his parents in a letter dated May 31 that all would be well with the publication during the two months he anticipated being gone. Since his blowup with Havell, the engraver had "become more careful and attentive to the work," and

promised Victor that he would carry on "as fast and well" as he could while awaiting word from America. Victor believed him but was not taking any chances. He
intended to obtain a commitment from Blake, the engraver working under Havell
who hoped to replace him, to send word if Victor needed at any point to cut short
his trip.[58]

Though Victor did not mention it in his correspondence, he was also reconsid-
ering his earlier decision to ignore Waterton. A few days earlier, he had dined with
Robert Bakewell, the prominent Hampstead geologist and cousin of Lucy's deceased father.[59] In 1813, Bakewell published his best-known book, *An Introduction
to Geology*, which went through multiple editions and, in 1829, was published in
America.[60]

Bakewell strongly believed that in Audubon's absence someone had to answer
Waterton's recent attacks. He had already composed a response and fired it off to
Loudon's magazine. While Victor had not seen a copy, he thought it unlikely it
would be printed. Bakewell did not wish his name to be used, doubtless because it
would reveal his familial bias. But he probably feared becoming another of Waterton's targets just as much. Loudon, however, had indicated that he would not publish it anonymously and wanted to see some other changes to the text.[61] Thus, unless
Victor stepped forward on his father's behalf, it was likely that Waterton's malicious
falsehoods would remain unchallenged, giving them even greater credence.

Moreover, Waterton's conjecture about the authorship of the *Ornithological Biography* had since been picked up and published in the May 18 issue of *Mechanics'
Magazine*, a London weekly devoted to matters of science and engineering.[62] This
was just the latest in an ongoing exchange between the magazine's editor, a measured but still unabashed Audubon critic, and some of Audubon's friends, dating
back more than a year.

It had all started with the magazine's issue of March 10, 1832, which reprinted a
scathing critique of Audubon's rattlesnake paper from an 1828 issue of *The Franklin
Journal and American Mechanics' Magazine*, edited by Thomas P. Jones, M.D., the
then superintendent of the U.S. Patent Office.[63] Jones had published Audubon's
paper from the *Edinburgh New Philosophical Journal*, where it originally appeared,
without first reading it. In a subsequent issue, he apologized to his readers for doing
so. He admitted that this had been a mistake and quoted from an unnamed "scientific friend"—George Ord, most likely—whose views of Audubon's paper he now
fully embraced:

> It is a tissue of the grossest falsehoods ever attempted to be palmed upon the
> credulity of mankind; and it is a pity that any thing like countenance should be
> given to it, by republishing it in a respectable Journal. The romances of Audu-

bon, rival those of Munchausen, Mandeville, or even Mendez de Pinto, in the total want of truth, however short they may fall of them in the amusement they afford.[64]

After reissuing this derisive blast, the editor of the London *Mechanics' Magazine* had continued to raise legitimate questions about Audubon's credibility even as the naturalist's supporters both in Liverpool and America rose to his defense.[65] Audubon's tale of watching a rattlesnake pursue a Gray Squirrel through the trees generated the most ink. But corroborating evidence that rattlesnakes had been found in trees soon came from multiple American observers, as recounted by Col. John J. Abert of the U.S. Topographical Engineers.[66]

Still, Audubon's claim to having witnessed a caged rattlesnake survive for three years without consuming "a morsel" was, in the view of the editor, absurd. "Why should rattlesnakes be such hunters after squirrels, and other living things," he queried, "if they can thus subsist, and be well and hearty on nothing?" Similarly dubious was Audubon's contention that rattlesnakes reproduced in the spring in large groups when they would gather and "roll and entwine their bodies together, until twenty or thirty or more may be twisted into one mass, their heads being all turned out and in every direction, with their mouths open, hissing and rattling furiously, while, in the mean time, the secret function is performed." To this the editor asked pointedly, "[D]oes any person believe it?" He certainly did not and refused to accept Audubon as an honest observer. "We *may* be mistaken," he wrote. "[W]e sincerely hope we *are*; but at present the evidence, and the impressions resting upon it, lean all the other way."[67]

The most recent issue of Loudon's magazine had given *Mechanics' Magazine* yet another opportunity to denounce the American naturalist. Before quoting directly from Waterton's piece, the editor observed disparagingly:

When we some time ago presumed to call in question the truth of the stories related to the American bird-catcher, Audubon — only echoing in this, however, the opinions of his own countrymen — our British naturalists were in general very wroth with us for going out of our way (as they said) to cast dirt on a man whom it had delighted them — "much better judges of his merits than we could pretend to be" — to honour above all ornithologists, living or dead. We begin now, however, to meet with proofs that even among naturalists themselves Mr. Audubon's reputation is very much on the wane. In the last Number of the *Magazine of Natural History* there is a very smart paper by Mr. Charles Waterton, the eminent naturalist and traveller, in which he speaks thus freely of Audubon's pretensions, both scientific and moral:[68]

Over the past few months, Victor had been willing to watch quietly from the sidelines as his father was castigated mercilessly in print. But this was finally more than he could tolerate. He could not help feeling that Robert Bakewell was right. Since Audubon could not defend his reputation, those who knew him would have to do so. And no one in England knew the naturalist better or cared more about him than his eldest son.

————

As if on cue, the *Ripley* finally reached Eastport at 10:00 a.m. on Saturday morning, June 1, following a prolonged fourteen-day passage from Baltimore. The process of unloading her cargo of "seven hundred barrels of flour and thirteen hundred bushels of corn" began immediately. It would take the remainder of that day and all day Monday to empty the hold.[69]

Upon hearing of the vessel's arrival, Audubon and his companions hurried down to the docks to look her over. They were pleased by what they saw.[70] The two-masted topsail schooner was approximately seventy-one feet from bow to stern and eighteen feet broad at her widest point.[71] She was reputed to be a "fast sailor" and, without the added weight of a cargo, would be in fine sailing trim.[72] To accommodate Audubon's party, the owners planned to expand the small cabin beneath the deck by creating an entrance into the hold and flooring the space, which was eight feet deep, so that it could be used as a dining room, parlor, and living area.[73]

Audubon described Capt. Henry T. Emery, the schooner's twenty-four-year-old master, as "a fine looking small Yankee."[74] To John, the mariner seemed "as fine a little fellow as could be wished."[75] Shattuck considered him "a good seaman, and an intelligent well informed man."[76] Born in Sanford, Maine, on November 10, 1808, Emery had lived in Eastport for much of his life.[77] He married Rebecca McKinney in 1830, with Maj. Chadbourne presiding at the ceremony. Three years later, the couple were still waiting for their first child.[78] Some Audubon scholars have confused Emery with his father, Henry Tilton Emery, erroneously believing that the senior Emery was the *Ripley*'s captain; the schooner was in fact commanded by his eldest son.[79]

Audubon spoke to the captain about the expedition and learned that he "was delighted with the contemplated Voyage."[80] The party came away feeling that they were in good hands. In addition to Emery, the *Ripley* would carry a crew of six: a pilot, who would serve as first mate and had made the trip several times before; four sailors; and a cook.[81] Audubon began to consider adding some additional crewmen to assist in their exploratory efforts once they reached Labrador.[82]

The "Young Gentlemen" spent Saturday afternoon on a cruise to Dog Island to look for shells. Shattuck complained that he grew tired from the rowing. At midmorning on Sunday, it began to rain again. Shattuck and Ingalls visited Dr. Ray at his home, where Ingalls dissected a calf's brain "a la Spurzheim."[83] Shattuck devoted part of the day to writing a letter to his father which included an accounting of all of his expenses to date and a separate letter directed to both his younger sister Lucy and a family friend Eliza Prentiss.[84] In the latter, he described the bountiful wildlife they anticipated meeting in the untrodden country that lay before them:

> We expect to find birds in abundance, deer, beaver, seals, bears, wolves, and fish of the best quality. Eggs we may see by the bushels. However we can not place much reliance on the stories told us, for the country has been visited only by fishermen, never by naturalists, so that we have an unknown field to explore.[85]

Audubon remained at the Westons' and worked on a drawing of two Winter Wrens that he placed on a background of "fine mossy ground," while John continued his efforts on the phalaropes.[86]

On Monday morning, June 3, the air was thick with fog as the members of Audubon's party made their way into downtown Eastport to make last-minute purchases for the journey, before going over to Dr. Ray's home to dine.[87] While they "feasted very sumptuously," Audubon and Dr. Ray resumed their debate over the merits of phrenology. Later that afternoon, Tom Lincoln arrived from Dennysville anticipating an immediate departure. When he was informed that the *Ripley* would likely not be ready to depart until Wednesday, he elected to return home. Shattuck decided to join him, and they hopped aboard Mr. Reynolds's vessel for the trip to Dennysville.[88] Meanwhile, Audubon returned to his art and completed the drawing of the wrens, while John finished the drawing of the three phalaropes. Their four-week stay in Eastport had given the naturalist a total of only four new compositions for *The Birds of America*—Winter Wren, Hyperborean Phalarope (Red-necked Phalarope), Harlequin Duck, and Black Guillemot.[89] He would need more—many more—from the wilds of Labrador for this trip to be a success.

The following day, the *Ripley* received her ballast, and by noon the ship carpenters began to lay flooring over it in the hold. Audubon took some time to reply to a letter Lucy had written on May 27. He told her that he was already counting the days until they were together again. He thought the preparations for their vessel might be completed that day and, if so, they would embark "pretty comfortably" on Wednesday. The rain had stopped the day before, and the wind was now from the northwest. He urged Lucy to send some letters to him by way of Dr. Parkman, who could put them aboard vessels bound from Boston in early August for the Straits of Belle Isle, situated between Labrador and the western coast of Newfoundland. According to the Passamaquoddy customs collector, these ships made the trip to fill their holds with fish before embarking for the Mediterranean. Audubon said he would be leaving his completed drawings along with his journal at the Westons'. He would be starting a new journal with their departure. He also intended to leave behind his paper money, although he would be taking along $300 ($8,800 in 2016 dollars) in hard currency—$200 in silver and $100 in gold. His companions were each planning on bringing money of their own to acquire "natural objects of Curiosity, Furrs and Eiderdown." Audubon reported that the "Young Gentlemen" were all "great Friends at present and I intend they shall remain so." He promised another letter before they left Eastport.[90]

On a morning ramble, Audubon observed several Black-throated Blue Warblers, both males and what he thought were females. This led him to believe that the birds bred in the vicinity since other warblers were actively nesting.[91] However, like many early ornithologists, Audubon was confused by the sexual dimorphism of this and other warbler species.[92]

The male Black-throated Blue is easily identified by its slate-blue head and back, black throat and flanks, and white underparts. However, Audubon and his contemporaries believed, erroneously, that male Black-throated Blues with paler coloration, what birders now recognize as first-year males, were the females. Female Black-throated Blues, which are a drab olive to a brownish olive on their upperparts, with a pale-yellow belly, were understood to be a completely different species called the Pine Swamp Warbler, a name bestowed by Alexander Wilson.[93] Not surprisingly, given Audubon's observation of several male Black-throated Blues during his excursion, he found that Pine Swamp Warblers were also "exceedingly abundant near Eastport."[94] Eventually, he realized his mistake and corrected the error in the final volume of the *Ornithological Biography*.[95]

At the time, errors of this type were not uncommon. The science of ornithology was still in its infancy, and early ornithologists like Wilson and Audubon were blazing the trail as they endeavored to discover, identify, and classify the incredibly varied avifauna of the North American continent.[96] It was inevitable that they would make blunders along the way and that it would take time to sort them out.

Continuing on his ramble, Audubon discovered the nest of a pair of American Crows high in a tree and decided to investigate. As he pulled himself into the lower branches and started his ascent, the parents began cawing in alarm and seemingly attracted all of the crows in the neighborhood.[97] Ornithologists refer to this as "mobbing," a form of cooperative behavior among corvids. The alarm calls are designed to warn nearby crows of a predator, usually a hawk or an owl. Acting collectively, the crows harass the predator and seek to drive it away. Smaller woodland birds like warblers, chickadees, and titmice will similarly join together to mob predators perched in their midst.[98] Audubon estimated that "fifty pairs" of crows "had joined in their vociferations" within a fifteen-minute period. Upon reaching the nest, he counted five small nestlings before he quickly retreated to the ground.[99]

Shattuck and Lincoln began their morning in Dennysville trying out their new guns. After an hour, they headed for the woods to inspect three traps that had been set for bears, but all were empty. According to Lincoln, four or five of the creatures were caught each year. Shattuck was bitten "most abominably" by black flies (family *Simuliidae*), the small, notorious biting insects of the North Woods. When the young men returned to the Lincolns' house, Shattuck was told to apply soft soap to help reduce the painful itching and swelling. The two then took a "very pleasant walk up the river" and came back for supper "lazy and hungry as bears."[100]

That afternoon, Audubon visited Fort Sullivan to dine with Capt. Childs. He remarked in his journal that they "had a pleasant dinner, but I am impatient to be under weigh for Labrador."[101]

Wednesday, June 5, dawned fair. The work aboard the *Ripley* was finished, and she would be ready to sail with the high tide at midnight, weather permitting. At noon, Audubon sat down to write what he anticipated would be his last letter to Lucy. He had received another letter from his beloved just the day before, this one from May 29. It put his mind at ease with the news that she was once again feeling completely well.[102] However, his heart ached with the prospect of their months-long separation:

> I cannot refrain Shedding tears at the thought of leaving my own dear Country and My Dearest, best beloved Friend, my own love and true consoler in every adversity & moment to Phisical illness behind — Oh My Dearest Lucy this appears to me one of the most agonising day I ever felt — May our God grant us the privilege and Happiness to Meet again![103]

Audubon acknowledged to Lucy that he and his company would be "Phisically Speaking pretty comfortable" aboard their vessel, but he was already looking forward to "the moment when next I fold thee to my arms!" In closing, he asked for God's blessing and hoped it would be "his will to grant us peaceful & Happy old days *altogether!*" He added a brief postscript noting that the steward sailing with them to Labrador had worked for eleven years as a body servant to Vincent Nolte, who had been so instrumental in opening the doors to the naturalist's early success in Liverpool.[104]

Shattuck, now back in Eastport, finished off the letter he had written to his father on June 2 with a short postscript about his trip to Dennysville. He and Lincoln had left Dennysville at 2:00 a.m. that morning, but the full moon had brought "12 oclock tides" and they had had to row back most of the way. As a result, they did not reach Moose Island until 6:00 a.m.[105]

With their departure at hand, Shattuck and his companions spent the morning packing their things and making sure everything was loaded aboard the schooner. At the Coolidge home across the water in Lubec, Mary Coolidge packed her son's trunk and carefully placed a bottle of brandy and a tin of snuff among his clothing — the former for possible medicinal use in the wilderness and the latter as a token gift for Audubon.[106]

In the afternoon, Audubon met with Jonathan Buck, the *Ripley*'s thirty-seven-year-old co-owner, to prepare and sign the formal charter-party agreement for the vessel. The two men were joined by Jonathan Weston, Buck's brother-in-law, who was present as an attorney to witness and formally seal the document.[107] Audubon understood from their previous discussions that he would be required to pay $350 per month for the use of the schooner, fully manned and fed, as well as $18 per week for feeding the six members of his party.[108] But he had since decided to hire on, at his own expense, "two extra sailors, and a [cabin] boy, to be a sort of major-domo, to clean our guns, hunt for nests and birds, and assist in skinning them, etc."[109] Consequently, the charter agreement called on him to pay $10 per month in wages and $2 per week for food for each of the additional crewmembers.[110]

Audubon complained to his journal that an unspecified "difficulty arose between myself and Mr. Buck" during the course of the meeting. It must have been over an amount he was being asked to pay, and it almost killed the deal. But the naturalist, swallowing hard, relented. "Pressed, however, as I was, by the lateness of the season," he noted with evident bitterness, "I gave way and suffered myself to be imposed upon as usual, with a full knowledge that I was so."[111]

Buck wrote the terms out on a preprinted legal form, filling in the spaces in his small hand, and then signed it at the bottom on behalf of Buck & Tinkham. Audubon added his signature beneath Buck's, followed by the initials F.R.S.L. — Fellow, Royal Society of London. To the left of these signatures, Jonathan Weston placed his own, sealing the document. The original of the document, bearing the added interlineations, was given to Audubon, who placed it in an envelope he intended to leave at the Westons'.[112]

According to John, there was a delay in the *Ripley*'s scheduled departure "[o]wing to some little things not being ready."[113] A possible if not likely explanation is that the Hampton boat, a small but essential two-oared sailing craft that had been promised by Buck & Tinkham, had not yet arrived.[114] As a consequence, Audubon and his party planned to sail with the high tide the following morning at 11:00 a.m.[115]

After John awoke on Thursday, June 6, he added a note to his mother on Audu-

THIS CHARTER-PARTY OF AFFREIGHTMENT,

indented made and fully concluded upon this *fifth* day of *June*
in the year of our Lord one thousand eight hundred and *forty three* between
Buck & Finckleton of Eastport in the County of Washington and State of Maine

Owner of the good *Schooner Ripley* of the burthen of *one hundred*
tons, or thereabouts, now lying in the harbour of *Eastport*
whereof *Henry T. Emery* is at present master, on the one part, and

J. J. Audubon &c

on the other part.

WITNESSETH, That the said *Buck and Finckleton*
for the consideration hereafter mentioned, ha*th* letten to freight the aforesaid
Schooner with the appurtenances to her belonging, for a voyage to be made by the said

Schooner along the Labrador Coast and elsewhere and back to Eastport —

where she is to be discharged (the danger
of the seas excepted).....And the said *Buck & Finckleton*
do*th* by these presents covenant and agree with the said *J. J. Audubon*
in manner following, THAT IS TO SAY, That the said *Schooner*
in and during the voyage aforesaid, shall be tight, staunch, and strong, and sufficiently tackled and
apparelled with all things necessary for such a vessel and voyage; and that it shall and may be
lawful for the said *J. J. Audubon his*
agents or factors as well at *as at*
to load and put on board the said *Schooner —*
loading of such goods and merchandize as they shall think proper, contraband goods excepted.

IN CONSIDERATION WHEREOF, The said *J. J. Audubon*
do*th* by these presents, agree with the said *Buck & Finckleton*
well and truly to pay, or cause to be paid, unto *them* in full for the freight or hire of said
Schooner and appurtenances, in manner following, THAT IS TO SAY, *Three hundred
and fifty dollars for month Eastern three mens wages two
e fifteen & one & ten dollars for month and two dollars for
week for victualing each of them Three dollars for week
for victualing each of the Passengers that are of
on mainland — and in case of the said Schooner being
be continued on the on & fifteen as the said Schooner shall
remain those & free hundred — last to pay on those time*
And the said *Buck & Finckleton* do*th*
agree to pay the charge of victualling and manning *Schooner —* and
port charges and pilotage during said voyage, *excepting
when she go into Hallifax or any other Port
excepting on the Labrador Coast shall are to be paid
by said Audubon —*

And to the true and faithful performance of all and singular the covenants, payments and agreements aforementioned, each of the parties aforenamed binds and obliges himself, his executors and
administrators, in the penal sum of *one thousand Dolars*
firmly by these presents..........IN WITNESS WHEREOF, the parties aforesaid have hereunto
interchangeably set their hands and seals the day and year aforewritten.

Signed, Sealed, and Delivered }
in Presence of us, }

J W Eaton

Buck & Finckleton

*John J Audubon
F.R.S.*

Charter-Party of Affreightment for the *Ripley*
Courtesy Beinecke Rare Book & Manuscript Library, Yale University

bon's letter of the day before. He told her that he was decidedly pleased with the young men who were accompanying them. He had found "Shattuck a very fine young man and a most agreeable companion and Thos Lincoln also but indeed all the party seem to be very good tempered and obliging and I have no doubt we shall enjoy ourselves after we are on the coast, very much." He was delighted with his gun and thought his pointer would prove to be "first rate."[116]

Audubon followed his son's note to Lucy with a quick one of his own. It was 6:00 a.m. as he touched the paper with his pen like a farewell kiss. He noted that the weather was beautiful with light winds. He sent Lucy his blessings and hoped she would be "Happy & Well."[117]

After breakfast, Audubon and his companions took a long morning walk and saw some warblers flitting among the trees. On their return, Shattuck went to see Dr. Ray to express his thanks for the attention he had been shown and to say goodbye. The good physician loaned him Combe's 1828 book on phrenology, entitled *The Constitution of Man Considered in Relation to External Objects*. They spoke again about Spurzheim's visit to Boston, and Shattuck concluded that Dr. Ray was firmly persuaded by Spurzheim's views "even independent of bumps."[118]

Shattuck impressed many, Isaac Ray among them. Later that summer, the Eastport practitioner would offer a flattering assessment of the young man to Dr. Benjamin Lincoln, Tom's older brother at the University of Vermont:

> Young Shattuck was with us several weeks & scarcely ever, have I seen the young man who has left so favourable an impression on my mind, as he had. Indeed I became so attached to him, I felt quite lonesome when he had gone. His search for knowledge seems to be unwearied, & there is a modesty in his manner & an elevated tone of principle that are rather remarkable. But above all there was one trait in him which I was peculiarly glad to see i.e. an entire freedom from any undue notions of the value of money, or the least idea that money is to be relied upon for the attainment of any worthy object, any more by him than by others.[119]

As the hour of departure approached, a throng of well-wishers crowded the wharf to speed the *Ripley* on her way.[120] It seemed to Audubon as if every man in Eastport had shown up "just as if no schooner of the size of the 'Ripley' had ever gone from this mighty port to Labrador."[121] Friends and family were welcomed onboard to inspect the accommodations.[122] In the hold, an "extravagantly long deal table" had been nailed to the flooring in the center of the room, a portion directly beneath one of the deck hatches to admit the light Audubon would need while he was working. In addition to serving as a drawing table, it would be used for skinning specimens and for dining. In the cabin, there was a smaller table and a stove. For sleeping,

Audubon's party would use straw beds in the cabin's side berths. The crew picked out spots in the hold, some men tying up hammocks while others preferred the floor.[123]

At around noon, an announcement was made that the vessel was ready to sail. With handshakes, hugs, and hearty farewells, the vessel was left to the crew and passengers. The thick ropes were cast off, and as the *Ripley* was pushed away from the wharf and the American flag made its way to the masthead, a booming salute of four cannons came from the garrison at Fort Sullivan. This was followed by another four-cannon report from the *Swiftsure*, still tied up at Hobb's Wharf.[124]

One of Eastport's weekly newspapers, reporting on the expedition's departure, called Audubon "truly a wonderful man" and described the scope of his unparalleled work:

> The fruits of his untiring efforts to enlarge the boundaries of science will be a rich legacy to future generations. He has already been engaged thirty-five years in his great work on ornithology, and we understand he intends to spend nine years more in its completion. During this period of forty four years he will have travelled over almost every portion of the American Continent. He is to return to this place in three months. May health, happiness, and abundant success attend him.[125]

Capt. Coolidge came aboard to pilot the schooner through the Lubec Narrows.[126] After he had said his goodbyes and departed in a small craft, Audubon ordered all the liquor aboard the vessel to be brought to him on deck. The schooner was passing the West Quoddy Light when the naturalist took a long swig from one of the bottles that had been gathered and announced, "Boys, no more drink for me." He then tossed the bottles into the water, leaving onboard some bottles of wine and a single large barrel of rum, which had been salted with arsenic to preserve the natural-history specimens they would collect. Audubon next stuck his hand into a pocket and dug out his box of snuff. He took a pinch and declared, "No more snuff" before the box followed the liquor over the side.[127]

As darkness descended on the first day of the party's long-awaited journey, the *Ripley* was cutting through the waters of the Bay of Fundy. With a light wind blowing ahead, the schooner beat her way southwest along the ironbound Maine coast, her advance aided by the powerful, relentless sweep of the outgoing tide.[128]

7

Magdalen Islands and Gannet Rocks

JUNE 1833

They were indeed birds, and such a mass of birds, and of such a size as I never saw before.
JOHN JAMES AUDUBON

The wind faltered during the night, and Audubon awoke on Friday to find the *Ripley* anchored "near some ugly looking rocks" at the entrance to Little River, about twenty-five miles down the coast from Eastport near the small village of Cutler, Maine.[1] The crew spent the morning in an unsuccessful attempt to tow the vessel into the harbor.[2] Audubon's party made a brief trip to shore, where they saw and collected a Hermit Thrush. However, further exploration was put off when "the wind sprang up" around noon and they were compelled to return to the schooner.[3] Capt. Emery had a difficult time fighting the current, which carried them dangerously toward some rocks. But a better wind arrived and he succeeded in putting out to sea.[4]

By midafternoon they were enveloped by a dense fog that limited visibility and left them to face the night "in direful apprehension of some impending evil."[5] A squall began around midnight. By the following morning, Saturday, June 8, the schooner had a north wind and was "crossing that worst of all dreadful bays, the Bay of Fundy."[6] Buffeted by the rough water, Audubon's party was "all shockingly sea sick," and "scarcely one of us was able to eat or drink this day."[7]

Mariners of the day relied upon Edmund M. Blunt's *American Coast Pilot*, a navigational guide to assist them through unfamiliar waters along the Atlantic seaboard. As its subtitle reflected, Blunt had packed into a single thick, leather-covered volume the "Courses and Distances between the Principal Harbours, Capes, and Headlands, on the Coast of North and South America: with Directions for Sailing into the Same; Describing the Soundings, Bearings of the Light-Houses and Beacons from the Rocks, Shoals, Ledges &c. with the Prevailing Winds, Setting of the Currents, &c. and the Latitudes and Longitudes of the Principal Harbours and Capes. Together with a Tide Table."[8]

The guide was intended by its author not only "to enable the mariner to recognize the coast at a distance, but to direct him into a port when pilots cannot be obtained."[9] While the *Ripley* was being piloted by a Nova Scotia man who had sailed on multiple occasions to Labrador, Capt. Emery undoubtedly had with him the most recent edition, published in New York in 1827, as well as Blunt's annual *Nautical Almanac*, which included important navigational tables.

The path around Cape Sable at the southern tip of Nova Scotia was fraught with danger, as the crews of many a vessel had discovered. Blunt underscored the hazards to the unwary sailor:

> An inspection of the S.W. coast of Nova Scotia, and a consideration of the relative situation of that coast, as exposed to the ocean, with the consequent and variable set of tides about it . . . will naturally lead the mariner to consider that its navigation, involving extraordinary difficulties, requires extraordinary attention. Previous events, the great number of ships lost hereabout, even *within a few years*, will justify the supposition. It is, indeed, a coast beset with peril; but the peril may be avoided, in a great degree, by the exercise of skill and prudence. To the want of both is to be attributed many of the losses which have occurred here.[10]

To the west of Cape Sable was a group of islands through which Capt. Emery took the *Ripley*. Seal Island, running north and south more than two miles, was the southernmost in the chain. The Mud Islands comprised "five low rugged islands" to the north-northeast. There was a navigable path between them, but it was important for a vessel to stay toward the northern tip of Seal Island to avoid the shoals running off its nearby neighbor.[11]

As they passed Seal Island, Audubon observed thousands of Herring Gulls perched on the scrubby trees. He had been told that they nested on the island as did Fulmar Petrels (Northern Fulmars). On the Mud Islands, he understood that enormous numbers of Wilson's Petrels dug nesting burrows in the sand, of two to two and a half feet in length, where they laid their eggs.[12] Even Edmund Blunt would mention their presence in the next edition of his guide, to be published the following month. However, he did not identify the species, referring to them only as "petrels, or Mother Cary's chickens."[13] The latter appellation, also written as "Mother Carey's Chickens," was a name bestowed by sailors to storm petrels generally out of the superstitious belief that they embodied the souls of brutal skippers or sailors lost at sea.[14] However, Audubon never set foot on the islands, and the source of his information was mistaken. The species that actually nested there was the related Forked-tailed Petrel (Leach's Storm-Petrel), the only petrel to breed off the Atlantic coast of North America.[15]

The *Ripley* completed its passage around Cape Sable on Saturday afternoon. Shattuck said that they rejoiced now that they "were clear of the bay of Fundy with its confounded tides."[16] Along the shore they saw a shipwreck, a reminder of the very real dangers they faced.[17] Indeed, the farther north they were to journey, the magnitude of the risk would increase as they entered waters that were still largely uncharted. Although Blunt's guide provided information about some of the principal harbors and bays of Labrador, much remained to be discovered about that treacherous coastline.

With his spyglass in hand, Audubon was more interested in the birds. Foolish Guillemots (Common Murres) and several Common Gannets (Northern Gannets) were on the wing near Cape Sable.[18] Toward sunset, he observed large numbers of Wandering Shearwaters (Greater Shearwaters) "flying from the rocky shores, which induced [him] to think that they bred there." Razor-billed Auks (Razorbills) were abundant, hurtling through the air "a few yards from the water, in a rather undulating manner, with a constant beat of the wings."[19]

That night, the *Ripley*'s occupants made audible contact with or, in the nautical parlance of the time, "spoke" the *Caledonia*, a schooner from Boston also making her way to Labrador. Her captain wished to accompany the *Ripley*, and the two vessels stayed within close proximity throughout the night and into the following day. That Sunday, June 9, saw the schooners proceeding up along the eastern coast of Nova Scotia, passing Halifax at a distance of thirty miles. Audubon said that they "now had a splendid breeze, but a horrid sea, and were scarce able to keep our feet, or sleep." When the winds began blowing a gale, both vessels reefed their sails, but the *Ripley* proved to be the faster sailor and quickly outdistanced her companion.[20]

On Monday morning, the winds had placed them within thirty miles of Cape Canso, the "easternmost point of St. Andrew's Island" along the northeastern coast of Nova Scotia and also a landmark used by mariners sailing for the passage separating Nova Scotia from Cape Breton Island known as the Gut of Canso.[21] Describing this shortcut to the Gulf of St. Lawrence in his next edition, Blunt wrote: "Its length is about 5 leagues, and breadth more than three quarters of a mile. The east side is low, with beaches, but the west shore is for the most part high and rocky."[22]

Audubon noted in his journal that the word *Canseau*, as it was also spelled, was Spanish in origin and adopted in reference to the multitudes of Canada Geese that long ago supposedly frequented its waters.[23] His information came from *An Historical and Statistical Account of Nova-Scotia*, a two-volume work published by Thomas Haliburton in 1829, which was among the several books Shattuck had brought along on the voyage. According to the author, the name was derived from the Spanish word for goose, *ganso*.[24] In actuality, it appears that the name originated from *kamsōck*, a word used by the local Mi'kmaq Indians to mean "the place beyond the cliffs."[25]

With a favorable wind, Capt. Emery wished to proceed on their current heading

and sail around Cape Breton Island via the Cabot Strait into the Gulf of St. Lawrence. He sought direction from Audubon, who preferred to explore the Gut of
Canso, "anxious as I am not to suffer any opportunity to escape of doing all I can
to fulfill my engagements."[26] This was also the recommended approach to the gulf,
as mariners bound for Labrador well knew. Blunt would confirm this in the forthcoming edition: "When off *Cape Canso* and bound for the *Gulf of St. Lawrence*, the
best passage is through the *Gut of Canso*, being shorter and having the advantage of
several anchoring places out of the strength of the tide, in case of contrary winds or
bad weather."[27]

The *Ripley* ran into Canso Harbor under gray skies at around 3:00 p.m. and
"found twenty vessels, all bound to Labrador, and, of course, all fishermen." The
wind was ahead, so Capt. Emery located a suitable anchorage to wait for it to shift.
Audubon watched the crew drop anchor and looked up to see that it had begun to
snow. The weather would remain unsettled for the rest of the day, with intermittent
snow, rain, and even hail.[28] Nevertheless, the naturalist and his party set off in one of
the boats to explore the area, as he recounted that evening in his journal:

> Going on shore we found not a tree in blossom, though the low plants near
> the ground were all in bloom; I saw azaleas, white and blue violets, etc., and in
> some situations the grass really looked well. The Robins were in full song; one
> nest of that bird was found; the White-throated Sparrow and Savannah Finch
> [Savannah Sparrow] were also in full song. The *Fringilla nivalis* [Snow Bunt-
> ing] was seen, and we were told that *Tetrao Canadensis* [Spruce Grouse] was
> very abundant, but saw none. About a dozen houses form this settlement; there
> was no Custom House officer, and not an individual who could give an answer
> of any value to our many questions.[29]

According to Shattuck, one of the inhabitants was willing to part with "some milk
and eggs, which savored very well, especially as we bad adieu to the latter when we
pushed off from Eastport." They were now fully recovered from their seasickness,
and their appetites "had returned most wonderfully sharpened." When they got
back to the schooner, they had a supper of "fine codfish." Shattuck was now eating
regular food again, having abandoned his vegetarian diet after his recent bout of mal
de mer had soured him on potatoes.[30]

Audubon's party used the remaining light to catch lobsters in the shallows from a
rowboat. The water was crystal clear, and Ingalls recalled tickling "their backs with
oars which they grasped with their great mandibles and held on till they were let
into the boat." Audubon wrote in his journal that "[t]hey were secured simply by
striking them in shallow water with a gaff hook." In either case, the men returned to

the schooner with forty of the dark-brown crustaceans, which would make a savory meal the following day. As Audubon and his companions prepared to retire for the night, the sound of frogs "piping in the pools on the shore" could be heard clearly across the water.[31]

Early Tuesday morning, June 11, was clear and cold, with the thermometer reading a brisk 46°F. Audubon, full of unbridled energy and enthusiasm, was out of bed and on deck by 4:00 a.m.[32] The "Young Gentlemen" undoubtedly soon followed. There would be no late risers among this group. He expected them all to keep up with his frenetic pace.

The *Ripley* was already underway at the rear of a small flotilla of fishing vessels, all headed north with a fair wind and smooth water toward the Gut of Canso, twenty-one miles distant. The schooner gradually overtook and passed each of the fishing boats in turn before reaching the narrow passage.[33] Shattuck described their trip through the Gut of Canso as "a most delightful sail."[34] Audubon used the pages of his journal to paint the surrounding landscape:

> The land on each side now rose in the form of an amphitheatre, and on the
> Nova Scotia side to a considerable height; dwellings appeared here and there,
> but the country is too poor for comfort; the timber is small, and the land too
> stony; a small patch of ploughed land planted, or ready for potatoes, was all the
> cultivation we saw. Near one house we saw a few apple trees, which were not yet
> in bloom. The general appearance of this passage reminded me of some parts
> of the Hudson River, and, accompanied as we were by thirty sail of vessels, the
> time passed agreeably. Vegetation appeared about as forward as at Eastport: saw
> a few chimney swallows and heard a few blue jays.[35]

The hours aboard ship with little to do provided an opportunity for Audubon's party to get better acquainted. Ingalls, one of the newest members of the group, had already begun to form impressions of his companions:

> Mr. Audubon was known by many and I think there is no exception to the fact
> that those who have spoken of him have testified to his great amiability and
> manliness, his humanity and it has always seemed to me he was one of those
> men who on meeting, one would at once say, "Bless you, dear man."
>   Tom Lincoln, quiet, reserved, sensible, practical and reliable. George C.
> Shattuck, a quiet man, but if you had thought him a goose you would soon have
> discovered your mistake. Joe Coolidge, unselfish, with a lot of sea and other
> practical knowledge and a right good fellow. John W. Audubon, always good
> natured, he and his papa the best of (boyish) friends, cheering us sometimes
> with his violin.[36]

The taciturn Lincoln had his own opinion of their leader. Asked years later to describe the naturalist, he responded, "He was a nice man but Frenchy as thunder."[37]

As is not uncommon among a close-knit group of men, some received nicknames. Only two are known today. Audubon was given the sobriquet "Dad," which no doubt stemmed from the paternal direction he gave his younger companions.[38] His son called him "Papa."[39] The naturalist, for reasons now lost to time, decided to call Ingalls "Sangrido," a nickname he bestowed the day they first met.[40]

The group's free hours were also spent on other pursuits. Shattuck, for one, pulled out the leather-bound journal he had carried with him from Brunswick and used the time to record the details of the remainder of his Eastport stay.[41] When he was done, he closed the book and put it away in his sailor's chest for the remainder of the voyage, turning to the rag paper his father had sent him to tell the tale of the Labrador expedition.[42]

Near Cape Porcupine, "a high rounding hill" with an elevation of 562 feet on the western shore, Audubon spied a party of Native Americans on the water in their birch bark canoes. Farther on, the vessel left the Gut of Canso and entered a wide expanse of water known as St. George's Bay. In the distance, off the port side, they could see Cape St. George, a bold promontory on the Nova Scotia coastline that marked the entrance to the Gulf of St. Lawrence.[43]

Slicing through the azure waters of St. George's Bay, the schooner ran north-northwest along the western shores of Cape Breton Island, a land of "large undulating hills" that "were covered with many hamlets, and patches of cultivated land."[44] As the vessel approached Jestico (now Henry) Island, which lies about three and a half miles off the coastal village of Port Hood near the entrance to the gulf, Audubon insisted on going ashore with his party. The winds had calmed and the "weather was pleasant" with bright sunshine. They found the island alive with birds, including Robins (American Robins), Savannah Finches (Savannah Sparrows), Song Sparrows, Tawny Thrushes (Veeries), and American Redstarts.

In the course of their ramble, the party disturbed several nests of Spotted Sandpipers hidden in the "tall slender grass that covered the southern part of the island." Audubon watched as the adults used a distraction display, flying "slowly with the common tremor of their wings, uttering their 'wheet-wheet-wheet' note, to invite me to follow them."[45] This behavior is intended to divert the attention of a predator that has come too close to the nest.[46] The shore party also located a nest of Ravens (Common Ravens), the young birds grown sufficiently that one was already out of the natal home and perched nearby. The naturalist noted that Foolish Guillemots (Common Murres) and Black Guillemots were breeding among the island's rocks. John counted several pairs of Great Blue Herons on the wing, and the group saw a pair of Red-breasted Mergansers struggle to fly after gorging themselves on fish. A rising breeze necessitated a return to the schooner, and, as they were being rowed back by the crew, a seal popped up by the boat. John and the sailors tried but failed to kill it with the oars.[47]

Before darkness fell, the *Ripley* made its way into the Gulf of St. Lawrence. This vast body of water of more than ninety-two thousand square miles was first explored by French explorer Jacques Cartier in 1534. It extends from the mouth of the St. Lawrence River northeast to the Straits of Belle Isle, which separates the Labrador coast from the western shores of Newfoundland, and south to Nova Scotia and Cape Breton Island. Fresh water from the Great Lakes basin flows into the gulf through the St. Lawrence River, forming one of the largest estuaries in the world.[48]

During the night, the schooner sailed through the Northumberland Strait between Prince Edward Island and Cape Breton Island. She had left both islands behind and was headed north out into the gulf when Audubon awoke at 4:00 a.m. on Wednesday morning. From the *Ripley*'s deck, looking past the bow, he could just make out the outline of the Magdalen Islands on the distant horizon, twenty miles away.[49] This forty-eight-mile-long chain of islands, discovered by Cartier during his 1534 voyage, was sparsely settled by French-speaking Acadians who fished the neighboring waters.[50]

With the wind ahead, Audubon did not believe they would reach the islands that day and uncharacteristically went back to his berth.[51] He returned to the deck after breakfast, by which time a fog bank on the horizon had hidden the islands from view.[52] The *Ripley* maintained her heading throughout the day and slowly advanced across the waters of the gulf toward her target. In the opposite direction, Audubon's party saw a number of vessels "beating their way to the Atlantic" with timber from Miramichi Bay.[53]

The schooner reached the Magdalen Islands that evening and anchored in what Audubon called Entrée Bay around 9:00 p.m.[54] This body of water, actually then known as Pleasant Bay, is situated on the eastern side of the islands and offers a safe harbor for larger vessels, sheltered as it is by Amherst Island (Île du Havre Aubert) and Grindstone Island (Île du Cap aux Meules), the southernmost landmasses in the archipelago.[55] Mr. Godwin, the *Ripley*'s pilot, explained that with the exception of Entry Island (Île d'Entrée) to the east, the major islands in the chain were connected to one another by "dry sand-bars."[56]

The sun had already set before the *Ripley* dropped anchor, but Audubon had gotten a good look at their surroundings in the waning light as the *Ripley* threaded her way through the channel between Entry Island and the Sandy Hook spit extending northeast from Amherst Island.[57] To starboard on the red sandstone cliffs of Entry Island, he had seen Black Guillemots with their jet-black bodies and white wings "seated upright along the projected shelvings in regular order, resembling so

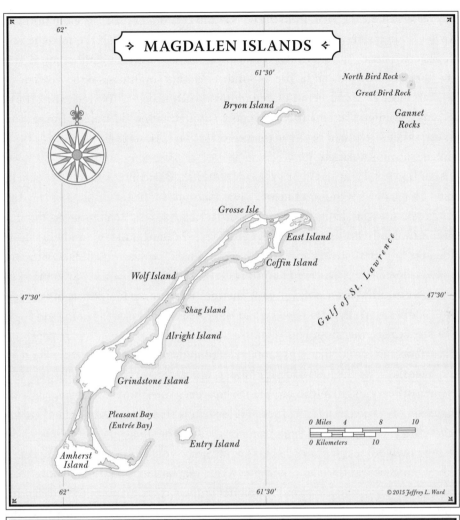

↣ MAGDALEN ISLANDS ↢

61°30'

62°

North Bird Rock

Great Bird Rock

Bryon Island

Gannet
Rocks

Grosse Isle

East Island

Coffin Island

Wolf Island

47°30'   47°30'

Shag Island

Alright Island

Gulf of St. Lawrence

Grindstone Island

Pleasant Bay
(Entrée Bay)

Entry Island

0 Miles   4   8   10

0 Kilometers   10

Amherst
Island

62°   61°30'   © 2015 Jeffrey L. Ward

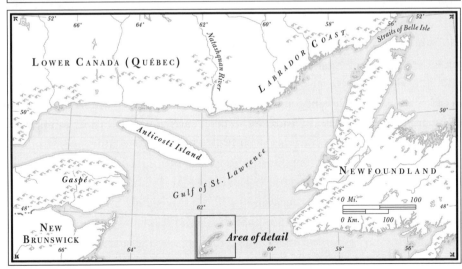

52°   66°   64°   62°   60°   58°   56°   52°

LOWER CANADA (QUÉBEC)

Natashquan River

LABRADOR COAST

Straits of Belle Isle

50°   50°

Anticosti Island

NEWFOUNDLAND

Gaspé

Gulf of St. Lawrence

0 Mi.   100

0 Km.   100

48°   48°

NEW
BRUNSWICK

66°   64°   62°   60°   58°   56°

Area of detail

many sentinels on the look-out."[58] He also identified a number of Common Gannets (Northern Gannets) "on the extreme points of the island."[59] Across the water on Amherst Island, the homes of the inhabitants stood out in stark relief. A small church was also visible and, at the top of the island, a large cross. Several vessels lay at anchor close to shore. It was a cold night as Audubon's party turned in.[60] They had brought warm blankets and comforters for just such conditions.[61] In the morning, they would row ashore and set out to investigate the islands.[62]

Breakfast on Thursday, June 13, was served at 4:00 a.m. and eaten at the great table in the hold.[63] The "good Thermometer & Barometer" that Shattuck had brought with him recorded the cabin temperature as a chilly 44°F.[64] On the deck, it felt "like mid-winter," in Audubon's words.[65] Mugs of hot coffee helped to warm bodies and hands stiff from the cold.[66] The party headed for shore in the boats and landed on Amherst Island between "two large bluffs" on which Audubon identified Black Guillemots and Ravens (Common Ravens).[67] Everyone then broke into two groups, with Audubon, Coolidge, and Shattuck taking a narrow path that wound its way upward toward the inhabited portions of the island. John, Lincoln, and Ingalls agreed to explore the shoreline.[68]

Audubon and his companions soon encountered "one of God's best-finished jewels, a woman."[69] In his journal that evening, the naturalist would wax poetic about the extraordinary traits of women, writing that they "are always keenest in sight and perception, in patience and fortitude and love, in faith and sorrow, and, as I believe, in everything else which adorns our race."[70] The woman on the path, "dressed in coarse French homespun" and "a close white cotton nightcap," was rushing back to her home with a scantily clad infant pressed to her bosom.[71] Audubon spoke to her in French, but she responded in "an unintelligible jargon, about one third of which I understood, which enabled me to make out that she was the wife of a fisherman who lived there."[72]

Continuing along toward the church, they met the local priest, Père François X. Brunet, who was on his way to an early-morning mass to celebrate the festival of La Petite Fête de Dieu with his Roman Catholic congregation.[73] Audubon described the "shrewd-looking" twenty-nine-year-old as "a handsome, youthful, vigorous, black-haired and black-bearded fellow, covered with a long garment as black as a raven, and a heart as light as a young lark's." It seemed to the naturalist, "if I do not mistake his character," that there was "a good deal of the devil in him."[74]

Brunet was from Quebec and had been on the island since 1830. His conventional French enabled Audubon to question him about the islands, their people, and the animals that lived there. Brunet indicated that about 160 families made their homes on the island chain and subsisted by fishing for cod, herring, and mackerel. The land was too poor for cultivation, he said. They also harvested seals, but the last season had not been as profitable as those in the past. Brunet evidently knew little of the natural fauna, claiming that there were no reptiles anywhere, which turned out to be erroneous when John and his party discovered a snake. As for birds, all Brunet could tell the naturalist was that there were none "to be found larger than a Robin." The priest extended an invitation to Audubon and his troupe to join him later at his boardinghouse for "a glass of good French wine."[75]

Audubon paid a brief visit to the church, noting the lighted candles that filled the chapel, and the parishioners who had made the early morning trek from their homes to occupy the pews.[76] He also observed that a pair of Barn Swallows had begun to build their nest of mud and dried grass in the cupola of the church.[77]

Audubon, Shattuck, and Coolidge continued on, meeting other islanders along the way. Invariably, the naturalist would engage them to the extent the local dialect allowed. After a while, Coolidge became frustrated at their slow advance:

Now, every man he met there he stopped and entered into conversation with him. He was as affable as he could be; he had an attractive personality; you had only to meet him to love him, and when you had conversed with him a moment you looked upon him as an old friend rather than as a stranger. Well, I accompanied him on one of his journeys through a French settlement, and he stopped to talk so many times that I grew quite weary at our lack of progress on foot. Finally I could not refrain from asking him, 'Dad (for we called him by that fatherly name), why is it that you have to stop and talk to every person you see?'

"My boy," replied the naturalist, smiling and patting me on the back, "in all my years I have never met a person from whom I could not get at least a little information of value."[78]

They eventually turned their attention to the hunt for birds and discovered the island was a haven for migrating passerines. The woods were composed largely of "small, scrubby evergreens, almost impenetrable and swampy beneath," but they were filled with songbirds.[79]

Robins were plentiful. Hermit Thrushes, Tawny Thrushes (Veeries), and Wrens (Winter Wrens) were also abundant. Audubon found Fox-colored Sparrows (Fox Sparrows) and Siskins (Pine Siskins) already nesting. There was a multitude of colorful warblers, including Black-capped Warblers (Blackpoll Warblers), Black-and-Yellow Warblers (Magnolia Warblers), and Yellow-rumped Warblers.[80] There were also Blackburnian Warblers, each emblazoned "in all the brilliancy of its spring plumage."[81] The male of this species has a throat of blazing orange that stands out against its black back and whitish underparts like a bonfire in the night.[82] Its song is high pitched and distinctive, and Audubon "had the pleasure of hearing its sweet song while it was engaged in pursuing its insect prey among the branches of a fir tree, moving along somewhat in the manner of the American Redstart."[83] Audubon also saw flocks of Tree Sparrows (American Tree Sparrows) with their gray faces, rufous caps, and solitary dark chest spots.[84] These birds used the islands as a way station to rest and refuel before continuing their migration flight to breeding grounds near the Arctic tundra.[85]

When Audubon's party returned to the shore, they worked their way to the end of the sand spit that stretched toward neighboring Entry Island.[86] Great Terns (Common Terns), the black-capped, long-tailed birds whose graceful flight, piercing "kee-ar-r-r" calls, and steep dives into the ocean are familiar to summer residents along the Atlantic seaboard, were beginning to nest in small depressions scooped out of the sand.[87] Loading their guns with mustard-seed shot, Audubon, Shattuck, and Coolidge quickly had four specimens at their feet.[88]

Audubon also saw his first Arctic Terns, a closely related species distinguished by its slimmer build, longer tail, and uniformly gray primary wing feathers that lack the dark wedge generally found in the upper wing of its chunkier cousin.[89] As the Arctic Tern was a "life bird" for the naturalist and one that he needed for his publication, he "felt agitated with a desire to possess it." Again his party took aim and fired away, and "one after another you might have seen the gentle birds come whirling down upon the waters."[90] Audubon did not take their lives without feeling some degree of remorse, although it did not stay his hand:

> Alas, poor things! how well do I remember the pain it gave me, to be thus obliged to pass and execute sentence upon them. At that very moment I thought of those long-past times, when individuals of my own species were similarly treated; but I excused myself with the plea of necessity, as I recharged my double gun.[91]

Having collected a sufficient number for his purpose, Audubon quietly observed the behavior of those that had escaped destruction, "among whom confusion and dismay prevailed, as they dashed close over our heads, and vociferated their maledictions."[92] As his description of the chaotic scene suggests, Audubon had a tendency to anthropomorphize the feathered tribe, and he has been chastised by ornithologists for imbuing some of his graphite creations with personality and emotion.[93]

However, Audubon also considered himself a man of science. He had carefully observed the terns react to the deaths among them and wanted to conduct an experiment that, deprived of scientific justification, would seem heartless and cruel. One of the birds they had killed was a female, whose lifeless body had landed in the water. Audubon initially watched as "[h]er mate, whom I was unwilling to destroy, alighted upon her, and attempted to caress her, as if she had been alive." The carcass was retrieved, and then Audubon tossed it back on the water three separate times to see what would happen. On each occasion, the male returned and repeated the same behavioral response.[94] It would be difficult for anyone watching that scene not to attribute feelings to the bereft male.

Along the sandy ridge, Audubon also found nesting Piping Plovers.[95] These small, compact shorebirds have a back and head the color of the sandy beaches where they make their home. During the breeding season, they sport a partial or complete black breast-band that wraps around the neck.[96] The species is endangered today because its nesting habitat conflicts with human recreation and oceanfront development.[97] In Audubon's day, the bird was more common. Audubon had yet to illustrate it for *The Birds of America* and returned to the *Ripley* carrying two males and a female. He almost certainly could have collected more. However, as he explained to his journal, "so plaintive is the note of this interesting species that I feel great aversion to killing them."[98]

In the afternoon, Audubon returned to the island, having heard of traders in Black Fox skins. The Messieurs Muncey were "keen fellows" and wanted £5 per skin. They agreed to part with the more common Red Fox skins for only $1.50, but Audubon thought the asking prices of both were too high. He doubtless anticipated he would find such skins at a better price when he reached Labrador.[99]

Still later that day, Capt. Emery was joined by John, Lincoln, and Coolidge for an excursion to Entry Island to explore its rugged red cliffs for the eggs of nesting Black Guillemots.[100] Audubon watched their efforts with trepidation from the deck of the *Ripley*, as he later recounted for the readers of the *Ornithological Biography*:

> It was a frightful thing to see my good Captain, HENRY EMERY, swinging on a long rope upon the face of a rocky and crumbling eminence, at a height of several hundred feet from the water, in search of the eggs of the Black Guillemot, with four or five sailors holding the rope above, and walking along the edge of the precipice. I stood watching the motions of the adventurous sailor. When the friction of the rope by which he was suspended loosened a block, which with awful crash [*sic*] came tumbling down from above him, he, with a promptness and dexterity that appeared to me quite marvellous, would, by a sudden jerk, throw himself aside to the right or left, and escape the danger. Now he would run his arm into a fissure, which, if he found it too deep, he would probe with a boat-hook. Whenever he chanced to touch a bird, it would come whirring like a shot in his face; while others came flying from afar toward their beloved retreats with so much impetuosity as almost to alarm the bold rocksman. After much toil and trouble he procured only a few eggs, it not being then the height of the breeding season. You may imagine, good Reader, how relieved I felt when I saw

Mr EMERY drawn up, and once more standing on the bold eminence waving his hat as a signal of success.[101]

When everyone was safely back aboard the schooner, Audubon mapped out his plans for the following day. He intended to take the boats to East Island (Grosse-Île), the last island in the chain, to investigate reports he had received of breeding Geese (Canada Geese), Brants, Mergansers (Red-breasted Mergansers) and other water-birds on freshwater ponds.[102] The evening temperature was 44°F.[103]

The following morning, Friday, June 14, Audubon's party was awakened at 2:00 a.m.[104] The naturalist wanted to get an early start because of the distance they would need to travel to reach the outer islands. However, just as they were preparing to launch the boats, a favorable wind arrived that allowed them to resume their voyage to Labrador.[105] Since this was "the ultimatum of our present desires," Audubon elected to abandon his plans and weigh anchor.[106]

The course set by Mr. Godwin, the *Ripley*'s pilot, was toward the Bird Rocks, or, as Audubon termed them, the Gannet Rocks, a pair of rocky islets located about fifty-two miles northeast of the schooner's anchorage. The rocks were used as a major breeding site by Common Gannets (Northern Gannets) and, to a lesser extent, by Foolish Guillemots (Common Murres) and Kittiwake Gulls (Black-legged Kittiwakes).[107]

The number of gannets had been growing steadily with each passing day, and Audubon was anxious to see where these large white seabirds with their long bills and distinctive black primaries nested.[108] As the morning progressed, the birds could be seen on either side of the schooner in "long and numerous files, all flying in the direction of the rocks. Their flight now was low above the water, forming easy undulations, flapping thirty or forty times, and sailing about the same distance; these were all returning from fishing, and were gorged with food for their mates or young."[109]

The naturalist had already begun gathering information about the species. The day before, John had shot one in flight and brought it back to the vessel. Audubon had it skinned and asked the cook to prepare some of the flesh so that he could sample it. He often did this as part of his ornithological studies and included many of his gastronomic assessments in the *Ornithological Biography*. In this case, he found the flesh "black and unpleasant."[110]

Godwin told Audubon that the rocks were visited annually by cod fishermen who killed thousands of the birds for their flesh, which was cut up into chunks and used over the course of two to three weeks as bait. For ten years running, the pilot had been part of this destruction and had witnessed six men with clubs slaughter 540 birds in an hour. He estimated that as many as forty vessels sailing from the vicinity of Bryon Island (Île Brion) at the northern end of the Magdalen Islands satisfied the fishermen's need for bait in this way.[111]

Audubon's first look at this rookery came at around 10:00 a.m., when the rocks were just barely visible as a "white speck" on the horizon. Within an hour, a stiff breeze had brought the *Ripley* near enough for Audubon to make out distinctly the top of the larger islet, Great Bird Rock, about 140 feet above the water.[112] To the keen-eyed Audubon there still appeared to be several feet of snow at the summit. The naturalist made a remark to Godwin about his observation. With a smile, Godwin replied knowingly that what appeared to be snow was, rather, the colony of breeding gannets.[113]

Audubon pulled out his telescope and looked again.[114] He could not believe his eyes. "They were indeed birds, and such a mass of birds, and of such a size as I never saw before."[115] His young companions were equally amazed.[116] To a man, they agreed "that it was worth a voyage across the Bay of Fundy and the Gulf of St. Lawrence to see such a sight."[117] But their wonder only increased as the schooner advanced and the islets of red sandstone and conglomerate grew in size off the vessel's bow.[118] There were, as Audubon told his journal, an "enormous number of these birds, all calmly seated on their eggs, and their heads turned to the windward towards us."[119] Moreover, "[t]he air for a hundred yards above, and for a long distance around, was filled with gannets on the wing, which from our position made the air look as if it was filled with falling snowflakes, and caused a thick, foggy-like atmosphere all around the rock."[120]

The wind was blowing stoutly, and Godwin warned that they would be unable to land a boat. But the young men in Audubon's party would not be denied. They were too excited by the prospect and undeterred by the risks. John and Lincoln, armed with their guns and clubs, clambered into a whaleboat along with Godwin and two sailors just as a "fearful storm" sprang up.[121] Not so long before, Audubon would have been the first to have jumped aboard. Now, feeling every one of his forty-eight years, he stood on the deck in a downpour and watched the whaleboat disappear to the lee side of the island, steered by his adventurous son and propelled by the strong arms and sturdy hearts of the men at the oars:[122]

For nearly an hour it became hidden from my sight; but now and then the report of a gun brought intimation that all was as yet safe; and at length I had the great pleasure of seeing it advancing towards the Ripley, which stood off and on, shivering as it were under the heavy blast. My eye fixed to the telescope, watched every movement of the boat, as with fear I saw it tossed from billow to billow, this moment a glimpse of her keel appearing over the edge of a wave, the next a foot of her stem only seeming to float on the waters. "Pull steadily on, my good lads," at last came on my ear, when, by a heavy surge, the floating shell was driven back some twenty yards, as I thought, and the wave, foaming with wrath, broke over her. Breathless and exhausted, the crew at length came within reach of a line, as the boat was dangerously plunging, when by good luck the rope was thrown across her, and in a few moments she lay snug under our lee.[123]

The men climbed aboard covered with "the nauseous excrements of hundreds of gannets and other birds." Audubon told the readers of the *Ornithological Biography* that the sailors were issued "a double allowance of grog," a mixture of rum and water, to help restore them.[124] However, given Audubon's weakness for liquor and his promises to Lucy, it is unlikely he permitted it onboard.

As Godwin had predicted, the shore party had been unable to land their craft in the furious surf that exploded against the rocks. Nevertheless, they had managed to collect a number of birds that tumbled into the sea after being shot, as well as eggs that rolled out of the nests and dropped into the water by the hundreds as the birds scrambled to escape the carnage.[125]

The whaleboat was stowed, and then the helmsman of the *Ripley* once more swung her bow around to the north. With reefed sails, she fought her way through rough seas and a pounding rain and made for the coast of Labrador.[126]

8

American Harbor, Labrador

*And now we are positively at Labrador, lat. 50°, and farther north than
I ever was before on this continent. But what a country!*
JOHN JAMES AUDUBON

The tempest raged throughout the night and into Saturday, June 15. Capt. Emery
decided to lay to, turning the schooner into the gale to stay her advance and control
her movement. It was bitterly cold. The temperature was 43°F, but the wind chill on
deck made it feel like winter, which gave rise to much grumbling among the crew.
Below deck, the members of Audubon's party—all but Coolidge—were "deadly"
seasick. The naturalist was only able to find some relief when he moved from his
berth in the wall of the cabin to an empty hammock in the hold.[1]

At daybreak, Anticosti Island off the Labrador coast made a brief appearance in
the distance, but it soon disappeared as the schooner was enveloped in a heavy fog.
The rain continued to fall until early afternoon. Around 2:00 p.m., the sun finally
broke free of the clouds. The wind was dead ahead as the *Ripley* resumed her journey under a single sail.[2]

By the following day the wind had died.[3] The *Ripley* sat rocking gently on the
open waters of the gulf under a clear, cerulean sky, still miles away from her destination. Audubon and his companions took the boats out and whiled away the hours
fishing for cod. Of the many they caught, the largest was a twenty-one pounder measuring just over three and a half feet.[4] Fulmars (Northern Fulmars) and Wandering
Shearwaters (Greater Shearwaters), both fish-eating seabirds, landed on the water
in close proximity. Two of the shearwaters were inadvertently snagged by hooks and
brought onboard the schooner.[5] Audubon provided an account of their brief visit in
the pages of the *Ornithological Biography*:

Two that had been caught with hooks, walked as well as Ducks, and made no
pretense of sitting on their rumps, as some writers have said they do. On being
approached, they opened their bills, raised their feathers, and squirted an oily
substance through their nostrils, which they continued to do when held in the
hand, at the same time scratching with their sharp claws and bills. They refused

all sorts of food; and as they were unpleasant pets, they were set at liberty. To my great surprise, instead of flying directly off, as I expected, they launched toward the water, dived several yards obliquely, and on coming to the surface, splashed and washed themselves for several minutes before they took to wing, when they flew away with their usual ease and grace.[6]

The naturalist may have released these birds, but he evidently took the opportunity to collect others that ventured too close to the party's guns. In his annals he would describe the "fishes, portions of crabs, sea-weeds, and oily substances" that he found in their stomachs.[7]

Skeins of Surf Ducks (Surf Scoters)—the males with brightly colored bills and coal-black plumage highlighted by white foreheads and necks; the females a drab brown with facial patches of white—passed the vessel, heading north toward Labrador.[8] Audubon also saw Sanderlings—those small shorebirds that appear to play tag with incoming waves at the beach—migrating in small groups over the water.[9] A mixed flock of White-winged Crossbills and Mealy Redpolls (Hoary Redpolls) landed briefly on the schooner's topsail yards. Before anyone could grab a fowling piece from below deck, the birds flew onward "as if intent on pointing out to us the place to which we were bound."[10]

On Monday, June 17, the *Ripley* was underway once more when Audubon climbed on deck at 3:00 a.m.[11] The wakening light of a new dawn revealed the sea "literally covered with foolish guillemots [Common Murres] playing in the very spray under our bow, plunging as if in fun under it, and rising like spirits close under our rudder."[12] Puffins (Atlantic Puffins), with their clownish-looking faces and multihued bills, also filled the surrounding sea, forming large rafts of "half an acre or more."[13]

The schooner was hauling for the coast with a "favorable" wind and "fairly skipped over the water." From a perch atop the mast, land could be seen in the distance. Audubon's party, excitedly anticipating their long-planned arrival, feasted on fresh cod for breakfast. At last, Labrador, a realm of promise and hopeful reward, came into view at around 5:00 a.m. as the crew's cry of "Land!" brought joy to Audubon's heart.[14]

Still miles off the coast, the naturalist and his companions could make out the white sails of hundreds of fishing vessels plying the shoreline.[15] A closer approach, however, showed these to be mighty banks "of drifting snow and ice, which filled every nook and cove of the rugged shores."[16] Birds were everywhere, in the air and on the waters of the gulf in enormous numbers. Velvet Ducks (White-winged Scoters) congregated in "dense flocks" so great that Audubon's party "could not help imagining that all the Velvet Ducks in the world were passing before us."[17] Razor-billed Auks (Razorbills) and Foolish Guillemots (Common Murres) were also abundant,

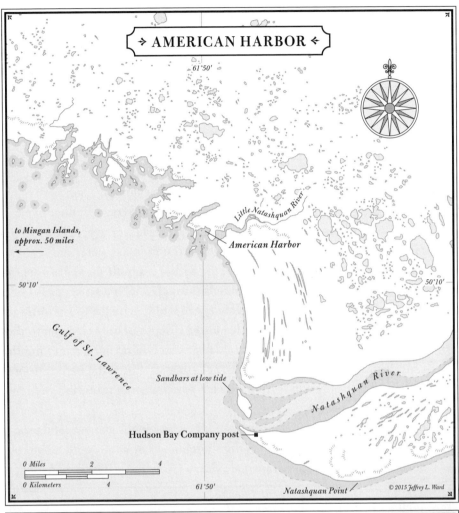

✣ AMERICAN HARBOR ✣

61°50'

Little Natashquan River

American Harbor

to Mingan Islands,
approx. 50 miles

50°10'   50°10'

Gulf of St. Lawrence

Sandbars at low tide

Natashquan River

Hudson Bay Company post

0 Miles   2   4
0 Kilometers   4

61°50'

Natashquan Point

© 2015 Jeffrey L. Ward

52°   66°   64°   62°   60°   58°   56°   52°

LOWER CANADA (QUÉBEC)

Natashquan River

L A B R A D O R   C O A S T

Straits of Belle Isle

50°   50°

Area of detail

Anticosti Island

NEWFOUNDLAND

Gaspé

Gulf of St. Lawrence

0 Mi.   100
0 Km.   100

48°   48°

**NEW
BRUNSWICK**
66°   64°   62°   60°   58°   56°

"flying in long files a few yards above the water, with rather undulating motions, and passing within good gunshot of the vessel, and now and then rounding to us, as if about to light on the very deck."[18]

Capt. Emery headed for a schooner sitting at anchor off the wide mouth of the Natashquan River and found, closer to shore, a flotilla of thirty or so smaller boats fishing for cod.[19] To Audubon's pleasure, they were hailed from the bow of the schooner by Capt. William Billings, a thirty-nine-year-old seaman from Eastport who had accompanied his five fishing schooners to this coast and was taking in cod "by the thousands."[20] The American vessels were barred from entering the river by the Hudson Bay Company, which had a trading post along the southern bank.[21] Consequently, the *Ripley* continued her journey along the coast another five or so miles farther north to American, or Little Natashquan, Harbor, where at 12:20 p.m. she "came to anchor in a beautiful bay, wholly secure from any winds."[22]

A "reef of rocks" located in the center of the harbor's mouth, as well as islets and rocks near both shores, created two channels through which a vessel could safely enter. Neither entrance exceeded ninety fathoms in width, with the western entrance being the wider of the two. The harbor itself had a depth of only eighteen to thirty feet, which effectively limited its usage to smaller vessels of no more than a hundred tons. By virtue of the configuration of the rocks that separated the harbor from the waters of the gulf, the only winds from which a vessel was not protected were those blowing from the southwest.[23]

The *Ripley*'s boats were launched, and Audubon was soon again on solid ground. As he trudged with his company along the shoreline, he spotted his first land bird. It was, of all things, a very pedestrian male Robin (American Robin), heralding the day in song.[24]

Beyond the beach, Labrador was a land of vast granite outcrops of the Canadian Shield. Among the oldest rocks in North America, dating back to the Precambrian period, they were interspersed with thick, cushiony mosses of various species which gave way underfoot, sinking the explorers almost to their knees.[25] The naturalist and his companions found the going difficult as they scrambled over the rough terrain, still covered in spots by snow. Audubon described it as "a poor, rugged, and miserable country; the trees are wiry and scraggy dwarfs; and when the land is not rocky it is boggy to a man's waist."[26] He was not the first visitor to complain about this desolate landscape. After exploring the Labrador coastline in 1534, Cartier remarked that he was "rather inclined to believe that this is the land that God gave to Cain."[27]

There were birds, but not in the variety or numbers Audubon had expected to find. After hours of searching, the party returned to the boats, having collected only a Pigeon Hawk (Merlin), a Tell-tale Godwit (Greater Yellowlegs), and a Razor-billed Auk (Razorbill). However, they had seen many others, including Wild Geese

(Canada Geese), Loons (Common Loons), Eider Ducks (Common Eiders), Dusky Ducks (Black Ducks), American Scoter Ducks (Black Scoters), Red-breasted Mergansers, and Yellow-rumped Warblers. They had also located the nest of a Spotted Sandpiper with four eggs hidden in the grass.[28]

Above them, mighty Great Black-backed Gulls floated on outstretched wings of almost five and a half feet, while Great Terns (Common Terns) were "plunging after shrimps in every pool."[29] Audubon also claimed to have seen large numbers of Least Terns, a smaller cousin with a yellowish bill tipped with black, a black cap, and a white forehead, although the species no longer breeds in that vicinity.[30]

Coolidge long remembered an incident that occurred during the voyage involving Audubon and the pilot, Mr. Godwin. Although there is no indication as to when it occurred, it must have happened in the early days of the expedition before the naturalist's remarkable skill with a shotgun became known to the crew:

> Audubon was a good shot. In killing birds the instructions were to use as few shot as possible, in order that the skin of the birds might not be damaged any more than was absolutely necessary. One day our pilot went ashore with him, and saw him shoot at a bird at seemingly easy distance and miss it. The pilot laughed out loud.
>
> "If I'd throw up my hat," he declared, "you couldn't hit it."
>
> Audubon put another load in his gun. "Throw it up and I'll try," said he.
>
> The pilot had but one hat, and it would be a long time before he could get one to replace it. He threw it in to the air, and Audubon blazed away and blew it all to pieces.
>
> "I always thought I was a darned fool," sadly murmured the pilot as he tied knots in the corners of the handkerchief, so as to make a headcovering.[31]

Once more aboard the *Ripley*, the naturalist sat down with his party and the ship's crew to lay out the schedule he expected them to follow during the days to come, as he later delineated for the readers of the *Ornithological Biography*:

> Every morning the cook was called before three o'clock. At half-past three, breakfast was on the table, and every body equipt. The guns, ammunition, botanical boxes, and baskets for eggs or minerals, were all in readiness. Our breakfast consisted of coffee, bread, and various other materials. At four, all except the cook and one seaman, went off in different directions, not forgetting to carry with them a store of cooked provisions. Some betook themselves to the islands, others to the deep bays; the latter on landing wandered over the country, until noon, when laying themselves down on the rich moss, or sitting on the granite rock, they would rest for an hour, eat their dinner, and talk of their successes

or disappointments. I often regret that I did not take sketches of the curious groups formed by my young friends on such occasions, and when, after returning at night, all were engaged in measuring, weighing, comparing and dissecting the birds we had procured, operations which were carried on with the aid of a number of candles thrust into the necks of bottles. Here one examined the flowers and leaves of a plant, there another explored the recesses of a diver's gullet, while a third skinned a gull or a grous. Nor was our journal forgotten. Arrangements were made for the morrow, and at twelve we left matters to the management of the cook, and retired to our roosts.[32]

The next day, Tuesday, June 18, the naturalist turned his attention to drawing the specimens that had been collected as the *Ripley* crossed the Gulf of St. Lawrence. The rest of the company divided into groups to explore the nearby islands.[33] Audubon indicated that, as a general rule, "[t]he physical powers of the young men were considered in making our arrangements." Ordinarily, John and Lincoln, "being the strongest and most determined hunters," paired up. Shattuck and Ingalls, who shared similar backgrounds and a future vocation, made up the second party. And Coolidge generally joined Capt. Emery "as they were fond of each other," both being down-easters.[34] All were charged with the task of collecting birds, eggs, nests, and plants as well as with making notes of their observations of bird behavior to relay to Audubon upon their return.[35]

It seems likely that Audubon's directive to the "Young Gentlemen" was to shoot any bird that came within range of their fowling pieces. Other than John, none of them had any significant experience in identifying birds. Moreover, they were not equipped with field glasses or binoculars, which were still decades away from being developed. While the naturalist sometimes used a handheld telescope to visualize distant objects, there is no evidence the members of his party did likewise. So, the best advice he could have given them was that, except when they were exploring the offshore rookeries filled with thousands of individuals of the same species, if they saw a bird they should try to collect it.

Once the shore parties had shoved off in their smaller craft, Audubon made his way through the cabin to the hold, where he set up his mounting board on the great table under an open hatch that bathed the table in natural light.[36] He was still employing the same basic technique of capturing images on paper that he had developed almost thirty years before at Mill Grove. First he would use "long thin pins" to secure the specimen on a pine board that contained a previously drawn grid, placing the bird in the attitude in which he intended to illustrate it. His goal was not only to inject the subject with energy and movement but to illustrate the critical field marks — the "*necessary characteristics*," as he put it — for the ornithologist.[37] At times this dual purpose resulted in a figure contorted in a way that would never be seen in the wild. But his method constituted a breakthrough in scientific illustration which made his birds seem to fly off the paper.

Having decided on the specimen's positioning, Audubon would outline the bird in pencil on a piece of Whatman cotton rag paper on which he had very lightly penciled a grid of identical size.[38] Interestingly, a careful inspection of his original drawings shows no evidence of a penciled grid on any of them, and some Audubon scholars believe that he had grown so proficient at drawing birds that he no longer needed to use a grid on his paper.[39] However, this appears unlikely. A decade later, he was still using squares in drawing his compositions.[40] And the fact that even his earliest published drawings dating back to his Henderson days reveal no signs of a grid, when we know that he was relying on this technique, suggests instead that the graphite in the pencils he used was so soft or the lines were drawn so lightly that they could be easily erased without leaving telltale marks.

With the board placed upright before him, Audubon could rapidly transfer the exterior lines of the figure to the paper by noting where the specimen intersected the lines of the grid. In doing so, he was able to foreshorten those elements of his composition that required the necessary depth perspective.[41] He would then carefully measure the length of the feathers and the distance between given features using a compass or caliper. The result was a precise two-dimensional copy of the bird tacked to the board before him. Finally, he would bring the illustration to life using a mixture of watercolors, pastels, gouache, chalks, oil paints, black ink, and graphite.[42]

Audubon's journal does not record which species stared back at him that day from the mounting board.[43] He always worked, whenever possible, from recently killed birds.[44] "I have ascertained," he wrote a colleague during his Florida excursion, "that *feathers* lose their brilliancy almost as rapidly as flesh or skin itself, and am of opinion that a bird alive is 75 per cent more rich in colours than twenty-four hours after its death; we therefore skin those first which have been first killed, and the same evening."[45] During the Labrador voyage, it appears that Audubon and his companions followed the same routine. In this instance he may very well have tried his hand at drawing the Piping Plovers they had collected on Amherst Island five days before. These were among the oldest of the specimens onboard, and he was anxious to portray them. His composition pictures a male and a female on an eroded beach, a stone's throw from the water's edge.[46]

While Audubon was working on his drawing, his companions were exploring the low, rocky islands eight to ten miles to the west of their anchorage. Lincoln identified them as the Esquimaux Islands. It would appear that he was referring to the coastal islands in the vicinity of today's hamlet of Île-Michon, just outside the Mingan Archipelago National Park Reserve. The shore parties landed on a group of three small islands, two of which supported "considerable numbers" of Great Terns (Common Terns) nesting in the grass. According to Lincoln, "they keep up a great outcry when disturbed, flying over our heads above the reach of our guns."[47]

Elsewhere, Audubon's companions found the nests of Eider Ducks (Common Eiders) hidden beneath the overhanging boughs of stunted fir trees, which could grow no taller than several feet due to the lack of nutrient-rich soil. The species was also found nesting on islands covered with grass. In both habitats, the female would lay her eggs on a bed of down that she had plucked from her breast.[48]

One group of rocks John visited was the breeding ground of Great Black-backed Gulls, the largest of the North American gulls, which took to the air when the boats approached. The explorers collected eggs and some of the young to bring back to the schooner. Nearby, they saw a rock where large numbers of a similar-sized, whitish gull congregated but were not nesting.[49] Hearing this, Audubon thought these were likely Herring Gulls, which he considered to be the immature form of the Great Black-backed Gulls because he could not conceive that the Great Black-backs, with their "tyrannical disposition," would tolerate an unrelated species in such close proximity.[50] However, John noted that the Herring Gulls never landed on the island where the Great Black-backed Gulls made their nests.[51] Audubon would realize the error of his thinking before he wrote the biographies of these two species for his letterpress.[52]

The shore parties returned to the *Ripley* with around a dozen Razor-billed Auks (Razorbills), Foolish Guillemots (Common Murres), a female Eider Duck (Common Eider), and a male Surf Duck (Surf Scoter). They also shot a small sandpiper that Audubon had trouble identifying.[53] He consulted Bonaparte's *Synopsis* but found the ornithologist's description of this group of birds hopelessly confusing. Bonaparte had included in his discussion similar birds of purely Old World distribution, which complicated Audubon's effort.[54] Eventually, the naturalist concluded that what he held in his hand was a Little Sandpiper (Least Sandpiper), an abundant breeder along the Labrador coast.[55]

Audubon was told that many of the islands visited by the shore parties had been raided recently by commercial eggers from Halifax, who had destroyed virtually every egg in sight in order to force the females to lay a second clutch that could then be gathered and shipped to market.[56] This was Audubon's first introduction to the ugly business, and he quickly grew alarmed and disgusted at the wholesale devastation being wreaked on the nesting seabirds. "Much had been said to me respecting these destructive pirates before I visited the coast of Labrador, but I could not entirely credit all their cruelties until I had actually witnessed their proceedings, which were such as to inspire no small degree of horror." He would later spin the lurid tale for his readers, describing the arrival of a small band of eggers on an island "for a century past the breeding ground of myriads of Guillemots":[57]

> At the approach of the vile thieves, clouds of birds rise from the rock and fill the air around, wheeling and screaming over their enemies. Yet thousands remain in an erect posture, each covering its single egg, the hope of both parents. The reports of several muskets loaded with heavy shot are now heard, while several dead and wounded birds fall heavily on the rock or into the water. Instantly all the sitting birds rise and fly off affrighted to their companions above, and hover in dismay over their assassins, who walk forward exultingly, and with their shouts mingling oaths and execrations. Look at them! See how they crush the chick within its shell, how they trample on every egg in their way with their huge and clumsy boots. Onward they go, and when they leave the isle, not an egg that they can find is left entire.[58]

Audubon came to learn that the previous spring a single vessel carrying four eggers from Halifax made off with close to forty thousand eggs.[59] There were about twenty vessels involved in the trade that year, "and by this one may form some idea of the number of birds annually destroyed in this way."[60]

The naturalist decried the dreadful practice, knowing full well that without some form of restrictions it would inevitably lead to the extirpation of these enormous rookeries.[61] The populations might recover from a single act of destruction, but there was no limit to the number of times the eggers could descend on an island to smash the eggs of the nesting adults. At some point the birds would simply give up and forsake their nests:

> So constant and persevering are their depredations, that these species, which, according to the accounts of the few settlers I saw in the country, were exceedingly abundant twenty years ago, have abandoned their ancient breeding places, and removed much farther north in search of peaceful security. Scarcely, in fact, could I procure a young Guillemot before the Eggers had left the coast, nor was it until late in July that I succeeded, after the birds had laid three or four eggs each, instead of one, and when nature having been exhausted, and the season nearly spent, thousands of these birds left the country without having accomplished the purpose for which they had visited it. This war of extermination cannot last many years more.[62]

Audubon has often been criticized by bird lovers for what they consider to be his own mindless destruction of birds. Indeed, during his expedition to the Floridas only eighteen months before, he wrote to a colleague and said that he considered "birds few, when I shoot less than one hundred per day."[63] Audubon justified his own sometimes rampant killing because it was in pursuit of what he perceived to be a scientific purpose.[64] However, it is hard to ignore that he and his assistants frequently took far more birds than were required, bagging large numbers of the same species.[65] Certainly he did not need that many specimens to complete a single drawing for *The Birds of America*. The simple truth is that he enjoyed hunting and the birds seemed limitless. Moreover, there was now a flourishing market for objects of natural history in England, and he could sell his extra skins or give them away to his benefactors or to friendly ornithologists in exchange for their support and assistance.

By the environmental ethos of today, Audubon's apparently insatiable bloodlust is difficult to fathom or countenance. However, he was a creature of his time. Like those of his generation who came of age in an America blessed with seemingly infinite resources, Audubon had long looked upon the multitude of birds and wondered how their numbers could ever be impacted by man. But he was not obtuse. He was a keen observer of the natural world, and in recent years his thinking had slowly changed as he witnessed the leveling of America's great primeval forests. He recognized that with the relentless advance of civilization across the continent, the pristine wilderness he loved would soon be gone forever, and with it the plentiful native wildlife that relied upon this habitat to survive.

In his 1826 journal, Audubon had sounded an alarm while making a silent plea to Sir Walter Scott to travel to America so that the great Scottish novelist could record for posterity its natural splendor:

> Oh, Walter Scot, where art thou? Wilt thou not come to my Country? Wrestle with Mankind and stop their Increasing ravages on Nature & describe her Now for the sake of Future Ages — Neither this Little stream — this swamp, this Grand sheet of Flowing Watter, nor these Mountains will be seen in a Century hence, as I see them now. Nature will have been robbed [MS: rob^d] of her brilliant charms — The currents will be tormented and turned astray from their primitive courses — The Hills will be levelled with the swamp and probably this very swamp have become a mound covered with a Fortress of a thousand Guns — Scarce a Magnolia will Louisiana possess — The Timid Deer will exist no more — Fishes will no longer bask on the surface, the Eagle scarce ever alight, and those millions of songsters will be drove away by Man — Oh, Walter Scott, come, Come to America![66]

The wanton destruction of seabird colonies along the dreary coast of Labrador convinced the naturalist that something had to be done to preserve this bounty. The eggers' unhindered exploitation could not be allowed to continue unchecked. In

Audubon's mind, the British government had to act to stop the plunder.[67] At that moment, long before it became fashionable, a nascent conservation ethic began to shape Audubon's views, which he would advocate with fervor in writing his Episode describing "The Eggers of Labrador" for the *Ornithological Biography*.[68]

It would emerge more fully formed half a century later from the passionate pen of a well-to-do New Yorker named George Bird Grinnell. Schooled as a boy by an aging Lucy Audubon, Grinnell grew up to become the editor of *Forest and Stream* magazine. In 1886 he founded the first Audubon Society, to stop the indiscriminate slaughter of wild birds, many killed simply for a few feathers to adorn ladies' hats. Grinnell was appalled not only by what he observed happening all over the country but by an awareness of what had been lost — an awareness that came from the pages of Audubon's work. Though the organization was short lived — discontinued less than three years later because Grinnell lacked the administrative resources to keep it going — it led to the formation of similar groups around the country. In 1905 they banded together as the National Association of Audubon Societies for the Protection of Wild Birds and Animals, the forerunner of today's National Audubon Society.[69]

Doubtless, Audubon would have enjoyed the irony associated with the use of his name. But in a very real way he was responsible for inspiring the conservation movement. The images he created with his pencil and brush opened the eyes of America to its incredibly rich wildlife heritage and gave people both a deep appreciation for and a fervent desire to protect it.

Aboard the *Ripley*, Audubon took some time away from his drawing table on Tuesday afternoon to join the "Young Gentlemen" on an excursion to shore to set up a bear trap after a bear had been observed in the vicinity. The naturalist also spotted some large terns with "a large orange bill" that were similar in size and appearance to the Cayenne Tern (Royal Tern) of the Floridas. His colleagues had located a nest of these birds during the morning and provided him with a detailed description of the nest and eggs.[70] He would include this information in his biography of the species and indicate, as he frequently did in recounting the observations of the members of his party, that he had personally witnessed what he described.[71] However, he was mistaken in his identification.[72] What he actually saw were Caspian Terns, whose substantially thicker bill, lack of a deeply forked tail, and dark primaries visible on the underwing in flight distinguish them from the Cayenne Tern.[73]

The following morning, Wednesday, June 19, Audubon awoke his companions at 3:00 a.m. Within an hour, the young men were in the boats and headed for some breeding sites of the Great Black-backed Gulls, while Capt. Emery and another group ascended the Little Natashquan River, a small stream flowing into the gulf to the east of their harbor. Audubon remained onboard to continue drawing. The wind was blowing smartly from the southwest, which caused a "disagreeable motion of the vessel" and made it difficult for him to work.[74] Again the available records are silent on the subject of his attention, but we know that he drew a Wandering Shearwater (Greater Shearwater) that was likely done around this time.[75]

The boats returned later in the day after the shore parties had visited some islands where Razor-billed Auks (Razorbills), Great Black-backed Gulls, Herring Gulls, and Arctic Terns nested. The men had also seen Wild Geese (Canada Geese), Red-breasted Mergansers, and an unidentified species of cormorant. John's party collected eight Razor-billed Auks (Razorbills) and some of their eggs, along with the eggs of Arctic Terns. He also brought a sample of "a fine male of the Scoter Duck [Black Scoter], which is scarce here." However, the group found collecting specimens along this part of the coast a challenge, the birds on the whole being very "shy and wary."[76]

Of more immediate interest, the explorers had captured five recently hatched Great Black-backed Gulls and brought them back alive to the *Ripley*. According to Audubon, the chicks were "small and beautifully spotted yet over the head and back, somewhat like a Leopard; they walked well about the deck, and managed to pick up the food given them." They would often fight over the scraps of cod. "[W]hen one was about to swallow a piece of flesh, a brother or sister would jump at it, tug, and finally deprive its relative of the morsel in an instant."[77]

Audubon spent the afternoon with Capt. Emery, hiking up the Little Natashquan, which he described as "small, its water dark and irony, and its shores impenetrable woods, except here and there a small interval overgrown with a wiry grass, unfit for cattle, and of no use if it were, for there are no cattle here."[78] Audubon hypothesized that the "rusty color" of the water came from the "decomposing mosses" that comprised the soil in this land of seemingly endless granite.[79] They turned around after reaching a set of "falls or rapids" four miles upstream, and arrived back at the *Ripley* by evening. In an attempt to find an anchorage in the harbor which offered more protection from the southwest winds, Capt. Emery had earlier moved the schooner to within a hundred yards of the shore. The tide was so low when Audubon got back that he and his young companions were able to cross the harbor to an island a mile and a half away by wading through "a few inches of water." The crew dragged a boat behind them so that they would not be left without a means of return when the tide came back in.[80]

Thursday, June 20, was "[c]alm and beautiful." Audubon was awake at 2:00 a.m., there being "scarcely any darkness now." He started work on a drawing of two Foolish Guillemots (Common Murres), one a female of the "bridled" form, with a white eye ring and a thin white line extending from the back of the eye, and the second a young bird that lacked the marking.[81] While he drew, he could hear the "sonorous"

PLATE X. *Audubon sat for a portrait by Henry Inman in April 1833, shortly before leaving New York City for his planned expedition to Labrador. This copy is by Nicola Marschall.*

PLATE XI. *Audubon drew this magnificent composition of the Golden Eagle over a thirteen-day period in late February and early March 1833, while he was residing in Boston.*

PLATE XII. *The adult Black Guillemot, shown swimming, was painted by Audubon in May 1833 from a specimen collected during his stay in Eastport, Maine. The other figures were added at a later time.*

PLATE XIII. *During an excursion to the Grand Manan archipelago in the Bay of Fundy in May 1833, Audubon's party collected a pair of Harlequin Ducks. The naturalist painted the adult male, upper right, and female, lower right, before sailing for Labrador. They were later cut out and pasted to a drawing of a lone male.*

PLATE XIV. These Hyperborean Phalaropes (Red-necked Phalaropes) were drawn by Audubon, with help from his son John, in late May and early June 1833 while in Eastport, Maine.

PLATE XV. *Audubon drew the Winter Wrens at lower left and upper right in Eastport in early June 1833, shortly before sailing for Labrador. The images were later cut out and pasted to a background composition, as was his earlier drawing of the species, lower right. The larger bird is a Rock Wren, a western species collected by Thomas Nuttall and John Kirk Townsend.*

PLATE XVI. *Audubon collected several Arctic Terns at the Magdalen Islands and drew this one in late June 1833 after reaching American Harbor, Labrador.*

PLATE XVII. *Audubon collected these Piping Plovers during a stop in the Magdalen Islands in the Gulf of St. Lawrence and illustrated them shortly after he reached Labrador on June 17, 1833.*

PLATE XVIII. *Audubon's party collected several Gannets (Northern Gannets) during their stop at the Bird Rocks in the Gulf of St. Lawrence. He illustrated the white-plumaged adult and dark immature bird upon reaching American Harbor, Labrador, in June 1833.*

Cineraceus Petrel
Cineraceus Petrel, Male.
Puffinus cinereus, Cuv.

N° 57. Plate 285. —

Cineraceus Petrel, Lath.

PLATE XIX. *This Wandering Shearwater (Greater Shearwater) was drawn by Audubon in June 1833 at American Harbor, Labrador, from a specimen evidently collected during the* Ripley's *voyage across the Gulf of St. Lawrence.*

PLATE XX. *Foolish Guillemots* (Common Murres) *were abundant breeders on offshore islands in Labrador. Audubon drew these birds during his stay at American Harbor, Labrador, in the latter half of June 1833.*

PLATE XXI. *These Razor-billed Auks (Razorbills), common breeders in Labrador, were drawn by Audubon in late June 1833 while at American Harbor, Labrador.*

PLATE XXII. *This pair of adult Surf Ducks (Surf Scoters) — the male, left, and female, right — were illustrated by Audubon at American Harbor, Labrador, in late June 1833.*

PLATE XXIII. *Audubon named the Lincoln's Finch* (Lincoln's Sparrow) *after Tom Lincoln of Dennysville, Maine, who collected the first specimen during an excursion in the vicinity of American Harbor, Labrador, on June 27, 1833.*

PLATE XXIV. *These active little birds are male Ruby-crowned Wrens* (Ruby-crowned Kinglets),
drawn by Audubon at Wapitiguan Harbor, Labrador, at the end of June 1833.

PLATE XXV. *Audubon illustrated these White-winged Crossbills from specimens collected at Wapitiguan Harbor and Bras d'Or, Labrador, in July 1833.*

song of a Fox-colored Sparrow (Fox Sparrow) from the shore a quarter mile distant.[82]

At 4:00 a.m., a sailor from Capt. Billings's schooner, which was anchored nearby, came over to the *Ripley* to join an excursion party Capt. Emery was leading to Partridge Bay about forty miles to the west. Another group, led by John, took a boat to shore and hiked inland three or four miles to explore some large ponds of several miles in length. When the younger Audubon and his companions returned at around 4:00 p.m., they had little to show for themselves—a single male Scoter Duck (Black Scoter). They had found the ponds destitute of fish, which Audubon attributed to the fact that the shallow waters were likely frozen solid during the long winters. A variety of birds were seen, including "about twenty Wild Geese" (Canada Geese), a pair of Red-necked Divers (Red-throated Loons), a Velvet Duck (White-winged Scoter), a Three-toed Woodpecker (Black-backed Woodpecker), and some Tell-tale Godwits (Greater Yellowlegs). Audubon recorded his son's description of the terrain, saying it was a country of "barren rock as far as the eye extended; mosses more than a foot deep on the average, of different varieties but principally the white kind, hard and crisp."[83]

Audubon worked throughout the day on his drawing, completing the images of both birds. But, after seventeen and a half hours of toil, he complained that "my poor head aches badly enough." The evening saw Capt. Billings and one of his mates arrive for a visit. Audubon was rightfully impressed by the Eastport man's industry, which he termed "extraordinary." He was also grateful for the captain's offer "to change our whale-boat for a large one, and his pilot boat for ours." Always one to seek out information from people he met, Audubon spoke to the mate and obtained a description of the habits of the Forked-tailed Petrels (Leach's Storm-Petrels) that nested in the vicinity of Mount Desert Island off the coast of Maine.[84]

Audubon devoted the following day, Friday, June 21, to drawing an adult Common Gannett (Northern Gannet) that had been collected a week before during their stop at the Bird Rocks. He wrote that "it was still in good order," which suggests that it had been either skinned or stored in the barrel of rum and arsenic.[85]

John and Coolidge teamed up to visit some islands where Arctic Terns were breeding. These birds, like all those they had met with over the past several days, were extremely wary and rose en masse as the boat approached, soaring "high overhead, screaming and scolding all the time the young men were on the land." Audubon knew from his experience on the Magdalen Islands that the trick to collecting these birds was to shoot one. Others would "plunge toward it, and can then be easily shot." He believed this was also an effective strategy for procuring Great Black-backed Gulls. The young men gathered a substantial number of tern eggs to take back to the schooner.[86]

Capt. Emery and his party returned from their excursion to Partridge Bay with "about a dozen female Eider Ducks [Common Eiders], a great number of their eggs, and a bag of down; also a fine Wild Goose [Canada Goose], but nothing new for the pencil." According to Audubon, the eider eggs made "excellent eating," but most of the eggs on the islands the men visited had already hatched. The naturalist had been informed that as the schooner proceeded north his party would find the species at an earlier stage in the breeding process. The men complained about the mosquitoes and black flies, which Audubon described as "bad enough."[87] Ingalls recalled years later that the black flies in Labrador were "beastly" and could "easily draw one on to suicide."[88]

When the naturalist sat down to record the day's events, he invariably added some details of the bird behavior that had been observed, whether by him or by members of his party, so that he would eventually be able to use it when writing the species accounts for his *Ornithological Biography*. That night, he described the Wild Goose (Canada Goose) as "an excellent diver" and praised its use of "many beautiful stratagems to save its brood and elude the hunter":[89]

> They will dive and lead their young under the surface of the water, and always in a contrary direction to the one expected; thus if you row a boat after one it will dive under it, and now and then remain under it several minutes, when the hunter with outstretched neck, is looking, all in vain, in the distance for the *stupid Goose*! Every time I read or hear of a stupid animal in a wild state, I cannot help wishing that the stupid animal who speaks thus, was half as wise as the brute he despises, so that he might be able to thank his Maker for what knowledge he may possess.[90]

Saturday, June 22, dawned under a bleak, rainy sky. The high temperature of the day was only 54°F. Audubon and Capt. Emery left the *Ripley* after breakfast to visit the Hudson Bay Company trading post at the mouth of the Natashquan River, five miles away. Audubon donned his oilskin clothing to keep dry, and presumably every other man on the excursion followed his example.[91]

As the crew rowed the whaleboat out of the harbor at around 7:30 a.m., they observed "a black man-of-war-like looking vessel entering it, bearing the English flag."[92] Shattuck, standing on the deck of the *Ripley*, also saw the two-masted British schooner coming into the harbor and thought her crew might agree to accept a letter for posting to his father at their next port.[93] Retrieving some paper from his sailor's chest, he sat down to provide an account of the expedition since the company's departure from Eastport. He described the first ten days of their voyage and then turned his pen to their experience thus far in the wilds of Labrador:

We passed Anticosti and arrived at this place last Monday [June 17], having had a very comfortable passage. We have been shooting away here but have not come to the parts where birds are most abundant. There are five vessels in the harbor from Eastport, fishing for cod, and they average about a thousand a man. Most American vessels go farther north, but we have one here from Newbury-port, and one from Halifax Nova Scotia. The fishermen are up every morning at half past two work eighteen hours in the day, and sleep four. The fishing is done in boats off from the shore, the fish are brought to the vessels, where they are opened by one man, their heads cut off and guts removed by another, whilst a third cuts out the back bones, and throws them in the hold, where two men are employed salting and packing them away. Afterwards they take the fish out and dry them. A Captain Billings from Eastport owns these five vessels and is here with them. He is going north, and expects in August to keep two vessels for the mackerel fishery. They throw out pieces of mackerel to toll the fish, put on bait to their hook which lasts all day, and throw the fish on the deck without touching hands to them. One man can catch fourty in a minute. The fishing on this coast is said to be better than off Newfoundland. The country is very rough sterile covered with moss and a few scraggy fir trees for forrests. You can not conceive more fatiguing walking than over this moss, and can be compared to wading through snow drifts. Our excursions will be made mostly in boats. We start hence with the fair wind which first blows.[94]

Shattuck advised his father that he had never felt better and that his companions were also in "excellent health and spirits."[95]

The whaleboat carrying Audubon and Capt. Emery continued southeast along a coastline of sandy beaches.[96] Seals would poke their heads out of the water at the vessel's approach, "snuff the air, and you also, and sink back to avoid any further ac-quaintance with man." Great Black-backed Gulls and Kittiwake Gulls (Black-legged Kittiwakes) were congregated in large numbers near the tips of sandbars at the open-ings of several streams pouring their rusty-colored water into the gulf.[97]

The name *Natashquan* is believed to be a Montagnais Indian word meaning either "where the seals land" or "where we hunt bears." When Audubon's party reached the Natashquan River, they could see that the river mouth, more than a mile wide, was largely taken up by a low sandy island that extended nearly three quarters of a mile out into the gulf. A heavy surf was breaking along the island's steep seaward shore. On either side of the island, narrow channels provided access upriver. The northern channel, running along spruce-covered cliffs of sand, had too little water at times to be navigable. The southern channel offered a deeper anchorage that could accommodate small schooners, and there, half a mile from the waters of the gulf, sat the houses of the Hudson Bay Company trading post.[98]

When the men reached the post, they beached the boat and climbed up the steep, sandy embankment to one of the wood-framed houses. They found it "a tolerably good cabin, floored, containing a good stove, a chimney, and an oven at the bottom of this, like the ovens of the French peasants, three beds, and a table whereon the breakfast of the family was served."[99]

The inhabitants, consisting of two French-Canadian couples, one with a baby, and their three Labrador dogs, were welcoming. The men were employed as agents for the Hudson Bay Company, fishing for salmon with nets stretched across sections of the river and, in winter, hunting Foxes, Martens, Sables, and Black Bears for their furs. They had no skins to show Audubon, having shipped them all to Quebec when the ice melted in the spring. Although they did have freshly caught salmon, some of which was being fried for breakfast, they declined to sell a single one, saying the company strictly prohibited it. If they were caught doing so, they risked losing their home as well as their livelihood. The company provided them with food, clothes, and an annual salary of around $80. This, together with about an acre of potatoes grown in the sand, a cow, and an ox, enabled them to subsist in the harsh environment where seven feet of snow in winter was the norm.[100]

However, their future was clouded. They told Audubon that the salmon fishery was being depleted, producing only a hundred barrels a year in comparison to the three hundred they had caught a decade before. The naturalist was not surprised, for the fish were being taken as they ascended the river to spawn as well as on their descent to the gulf.[101]

A party of about twenty Montagnais Indians (now known as Innu) — men, women, and children — had also arrived at the post in two large boats, with smaller canoes for seal hunting "lashed to the sides."[102] Audubon described the men as "stout and good-looking" with skin "redder and clearer than any other Indians I have ever seen. The women also appeared cleaner than usual, their hair was braided, and dangled over their shoulders, like so many short ropes."[103] Their clothes were European in style, but their feet were covered with "coarse moccasins made of seal skin."[104]

Audubon was able to communicate with the Montagnais in French and quickly struck a bargain with them to supply him with specimens of the Willow Grouse (Willow Ptarmigan). This species was missing from his portfolio, but he had been told by the Hudson Bay Company agents that it could be found locally.[105]

In due course, Audubon and his companions made their way back to the *Ripley*. The naturalist learned that the British schooner, which had anchored in the harbor a cable length, approximately six hundred feet, away, was the *Gulnare* of the

Royal Navy.[106] He had his card, along with a written note, delivered to her captain and received an invitation to come aboard in two hours. Audubon first enjoyed a "very good" dinner of hashed Eider with his shipmates on the *Ripley*. He then took a razor to the frost-colored beard he had grown since leaving Eastport and dressed in "clean linen."[107]

In his pocket Audubon carried a letter of introduction he had obtained two years earlier from the Duke of Sussex, who was president of the Royal Society and younger brother of King William IV. Directed to "The Civil & Military Authorities in British America," the letter referenced Audubon's "splendid work" and "earnestly" recommended him "to the kindness and assistance of every officer of His Britannic Majesty, bearing Authority, whether Civil or Military, in any part of British America, which Mr. Audubon may chance to visit—well knowing His Majesty's gracious desire to patronice [*sic*] Science, and favor the efforts of all those persons, who seek to promote its interests, in every part of his Dominions."[108]

Under threatening skies, Audubon climbed up onto the deck of the *Gulnare* and was "received politely" by the captain, Cdr. Henry Wolsey Bayfield, and his two officers and assistants, Midshipman Augustus Frederick James Bowen, who served as first lieutenant, and Midshipman William Barrie.[109]

Bayfield was thirty-eight years old and had spent most of his life in the Royal Navy, having volunteered for service as a lad of ten. In 1816, after a decade of serving aboard British warships on both sides of the Atlantic, he was assigned to Capt. William Fitzwilliam Owen, who was charged with surveying the Great Lakes as part of Britain's strategic planning for the defense of its North American territory following the War of 1812. Bayfield quickly earned the respect of Capt. Owen for his intelligence and skill as a surveyor during their survey of Lake Ontario. When Owen was unexpectedly called back to England in 1817, the twenty-two-year-old Lt. Bayfield was assigned the task of continuing Owen's work with a survey of Lake Erie. Between 1817 and 1825, he and his assistants would complete surveys of Lake Erie, Lake Huron, and Lake Superior. The next two years saw Bayfield at the Hydrographic Office of the Admiralty in London working on completing the associated navigational charts.[110]

Bayfield was promoted to commander, one rank below that of captain, prior to returning to Canada in 1827. That year the admiralty approved his request to continue his work with surveys of the St. Lawrence River and the Gulf of St. Lawrence. The following year, he assumed command of the *Gulnare*, a 140-ton schooner constructed to his specifications by a private Quebec contractor who entered into an agreement with the admiralty for its seasonal use. The vessel was copper bottomed and copper fastened and carried several smaller craft to facilitate her work. At the time Audubon boarded her, she was equipped with two gigs, a launch, and a six-oared surveying cutter called the *Owen*. She also had two four-pound cannon "for the purpose of making Signals, for a Pilot, or of distress . . . , to recall her Boats, and measure Bases by Sound." At her prow she featured the carved bust of a woman.[111]

In addition to the officers and a ship's surgeon, the *Gulnare* was manned by a crew of thirty-one: "a master, quarter-master, boatswain's mate, carpenter's mate, seven able seamen, seventeen Canadian boatmen, a steward, a cook, and a boy."[112] They would be resuming a survey of the rugged Labrador coastline that summer and expected to follow the *Ripley*'s course over the weeks to follow.[113]

Audubon and his hosts conversed for a while on deck before repairing to the cabin, where the naturalist met Dr. William Kelley, the ship's medical officer.[114] Kelley "seemed a man of ability" and, according to Audubon, was "a student of botany and conchology."[115] Audubon learned that Bowen, the first lieutenant, was "a student of ornithology, and [was] making collections."[116] "Thus," the naturalist later acknowledged to his journal, "the lovers of nature meet everywhere, but surely I did not expect to meet a naturalist on the Labrador station."[117]

At an opportune moment, Audubon pulled out the Duke of Sussex's letter from his pocket and presented it to Bayfield.[118] Bayfield was probably aware that the duke was Bowen's godfather.[119] Regardless, the British officer displayed no reaction as he scanned its contents and handed the paper back to Audubon. However, as Audubon prepared to depart in a pouring rain, the captain told the naturalist that he would "do anything for me in his power."[120]

Bayfield sat down later that evening to recount the day's events in the pages of his journal and described his meeting with Audubon:

> Found 6 American Schooners belonging to East Port in the State of Main all belonging to one person who is here with them. — We also found another American Schooner here the *Ripley* of Eastport employed in a very different [MS: diff^t] way having Mr Audubon onboard the Naturalist with several young men ^two of them^ medical students of Boston. these take the departments of Botany &c &c in short they collect everything. — But Mr Audubon has come principally for the purpose of studying the habits of the water Fowl with which the Coast of Labrador abounds and to make drawings of them for his splendid work upon the Birds of America. — He sent his Card onboard [MS: onb^d] with a polite note & I received him onboard and we found him a very superior person indeed. — It is probable we shall meet often as he proceeds along the coast which we are going to Survey.[121]

In the left-hand margin of the journal, next to his entry, Bayfield listed the members of Audubon's party:

Capt. Henry Wolsey Bayfield Journal
Courtesy Library and Archives Canada

Mr. J. J. Audubon Senior
—J. W Audubon junior his Son
—Thoˢ Lincoln Maine
—Joshʰ Cooledge — Mate of the Ripley
Geoᵉ G. Shattuck Boston Medical Student
Willᵐ Ingall — Do ----------------Do
—Emery Master of the *Ripley*[122]

When the sun rose on Sunday, June 23, American Harbor was shrouded with fog. The winds were light but dead ahead, which postponed the *Ripley*'s planned departure for another anchorage fifty miles to the east.[123] Audubon remained onboard during the morning to add a background to his gannet composition, now depicting both an adult and an immature, with a distant view of the Gannet Rocks under dark storm clouds.[124]

Meanwhile, the "Young Gentlemen" continued to scour the area for interesting specimens, although they found nothing new. John and his group collected six guillemots and gathered "ten or twelve dozen eggs" from a colony six miles away.[125] Coolidge's party was successful in shooting some Arctic Terns and capturing a pair of three-week-old Great Black-backed Gulls, which they brought back to the schooner and released on deck. Audubon noted that the young birds "ran about the deck, and fed themselves with pieces of fish thrown to them." When they grew tired, they sat down on their legs, "with their feet extended before them in a very awkward-looking position, but one which to them is no doubt comfortable."[126]

The fog burned away before noon and "the sun shone pleasantly." Audubon left the *Ripley* to take a walk "over the dreary hills" with Shattuck. When they returned, Capt. Bayfield and Dr. Kelley rowed over to extend an invitation to Audubon to join them for dinner the following day. The naturalist showed them his recent work, which found in them an appreciative audience. Bayfield was, as his journal later recorded, most "delighted with [Audubon's] drawings, the Birds being represented of the same size as when alive, and most beautifully painted."[127]

That evening, Audubon's party took the boats and paid a visit to the Montagnais Indians, who had set up their summer encampment just half a mile away on the coast and were busy harvesting seals. The men of the tribe greeted the naturalist and his companions when they landed and, to Audubon's surprise and evident pleasure, immediately offered them "some excellent rum."[128] The chief was "a fine-looking fellow, about forty years old" who was "well informed" and could communicate in French "so as to be understood."[129] He entertained them inside a tent in which two boiling kettles sat over a "cheerful fire" that sent its smoke through a hole in the roof.[130]

Audubon was eager to know more about the surrounding country and queried the chief and his brother about what he might find. The picture they painted was of a bleak land increasingly impoverished by the avarice of the Hudson Bay Company. Back aboard the *Ripley*, Audubon recorded the sobering details in the pages of his journal, even as the joyful song of a Robin (American Robin) floated across the waters of the harbor:

The country from this place to the nearest settlement of the Hudson Bay Company is as barren and rocky as this about us. Very large lakes of water abound two hundred miles inland from the sea; these lakes contain carp, trout, white fish, and many mussels unfit to eat; the latter are described as black outside and purple within, and are no doubt "unios." Not a bush is to be met with; and the Indians who now and then cross that region carry their tent-poles with them, and also their canoes, and burn moss for fuel. So tedious is the travelling said to be, that not more than ten miles a day can be accomplished, and when the journey is made in two months, it is considered a good one. Wolves and black bears abound, but no deer and caraboos are seen, and not a bird of any kind except wild geese and brants about the lakes, where they breed. When the journey is undertaken in winter, they go on snow shoes, without canoes. Fur animals are scarce, but a few beavers and otters, martins and sables, are caught, and some foxes and lynxes, while their numbers yearly diminish. Thus the Fur Company may be called the exterminating medium of these wild and almost uninhabitable regions, which cupidity or the love of money alone would induce man to venture into.[131]

Labrador, it was now clear, was not the untamed wilderness it had been portrayed during Audubon's time in Eastport. He sensed that the world he knew was vanishing. In the past three decades he had witnessed enormous changes sweep across America. An ever-expanding population had felled the native forests, built towns and cities, brought steam power to vessels plying the coasts and mighty rivers, and constructed the first railroads. Labrador had been described as a land yet untouched by man, where the abundance of birds and wildlife rivaled what Audubon had found when he first moved to the Kentucky frontier. No doubt his eagerness to journey here had not just been about the search for waterbirds to be added to his publication. This was as much a quest for physical and spiritual renewal. He had effectively recovered from his neurological attack, but it pained him to see that even here, in this remote region, the assaults of man had taken their toll. "Where can I now go," he asked wistfully, "and find nature undisturbed?"[132] It was to be a question that loomed over him as the journey continued.

The winds continued to blow lightly from the southwest on Monday, June 24, again delaying the *Ripley*'s departure from American Harbor. Fog and clouds obscured the sun until the afternoon.[133] Audubon worked all day on a drawing of a species that he failed to identify in his journal.[134] However, given the number of Razor-billed Auks (Razorbills) that had been collected since their arrival, it is quite possible this was the one he was illustrating. He pictured two of the large black-and-white-plumaged seabirds floating in the water against a background of high, gray-hued mountains.[135] The shore parties returned in the afternoon with some plant specimens but without any birds, although Coolidge had shot a male White-crowned Sparrow that was carrying nesting materials in its beak, evidence the birds bred in the vicinity.[136]

Audubon arrived onboard the *Gulnare* at 5:00 p.m. after having shaved and dressed. This extra grooming, he complained to his journal, was "quite a bore." However, he greatly enjoyed his dinner with Capt. Bayfield, Dr. Kelley, and the officers and master of the British vessel.[137] The meal consisted of fish and roasted mutton along with a good wine. Audubon was offered "some excellent snuff" and could not resist taking "a pinch or two."[138] Over dinner, a lively discussion ensued on a variety of topics, including "Botany, politics, and the Established Church of England, and ranged as far as hatching eggs by steam."[139] Audubon informed his hosts about the eggers who were filling their boats with plunder from the breeding bird colonies.[140] The Englishmen had never before heard of the sordid business. Audubon was shown some of the maps on which Bayfield's assistants were working. He was particularly impressed by the one of American Harbor, which demonstrated "great accuracy."[141]

It was 10:00 p.m. when the naturalist made his way back to the *Ripley*. He was "longing to be farther north," but the winds were blowing "so contrary it would be a loss to attempt it now." The mosquitoes were getting more active as the temperature warmed, and he declared them to be "abundant and hungry."[142]

The following day was clear and beautiful. The winds were from the south-southwest, so the *Ripley* again remained trapped in her anchorage. The several fishing schooners also riding in the harbor were smaller and more maneuverable. Consequently, they were able to beat their way out into the gulf and resumed fishing off Natashquan Point about a mile southeast of the mouth of the Natashquan River. Capt. Bayfield supposed the *Ripley* had made no effort to follow them because she was "of 106 Tons & drawing between 9 & 10 feet."[143]

Audubon began yet another drawing, this one depicting an Arctic Tern in flight.[144] Years later, Ingalls still remembered the events that provided a backdrop to the composition:

> One day Mr. Audubon and all of us went upon a not very large island well covered with nests of Guillemots and other seabirds, there was much shooting. Eggers go upon these rocks and smash every egg they can find. Next day they find plenty of fresh laid eggs. Now, I was standing watching the actions of the birds, Mr. Audubon being a little ways from me; presently a Tern, *Sterna arctica*, flew towards me swiftly, falling very near my feet seeming to be in consternation or fright; with flashing swiftness another Tern descended and in his dart came within a very few inches of the terror stricken bird. The next day on our return towards night from our excursion, I darkened a little table at which Mr.

Audubon sat. He looked up and saluted me with "Hollo, Sangrido (he gave me this name the first day), "he is here, he is scared, afrighted, he is looking up at you, you cannot help him." Now, the dear man had his chalks upon the table and upright in front of him was a pine board upon which was secured in position by means of long thin pins, the bird whose likeness he was transferring to the cardboard before him. When you look at this picture you will see with wonder *expression*, even after reading this lame description.[145]

Meanwhile, the naturalist's young companions, "who are always ready for sport," went fishing for cod. In half an hour, they succeeded in pulling up a hundred fish and "*somewhere* secured three fine salmon." Audubon was not about to inquire where they had managed to find or, more likely, steal the salmon from one of the Hudson Bay Company's weirs. They shared their catch, including a salmon, with the crew of the *Gulnare*.[146]

Writing in his journal, Audubon noted the duplicity of the agents of the Hudson Bay Company, "who evade all questions respecting the interior of the country, and indeed tell the most absurd things, to shock you, and cut short inquiries."[147] The naturalist suspected that this stratagem was designed to dissuade "strangers from settling here, or interfering with their monopoly."[148]

Turning his attention to birds, Audubon noted that he had seen some Bank Swallows that evening, although he had no idea where "these delicate pilgrims" were headed. He also heard the oft-repeated song of the Black-capped Warbler (Blackpoll Warbler), an abundant bird locally and one of the few warbler species he had met with in Labrador. According to Audubon, its song, "if the noise it makes can be called a song," sounded like "the clicking of small pebbles together five or six times, and is renewed every few minutes."[149]

Rain began to fall during the night and continued through most of the next day, Wednesday, June 26.[150] Audubon joined the "Young Gentlemen" on a visit to shore, but they were "beaten back by the rain and the mosquitoes." However, John managed to collect a female White-crowned Sparrow that appeared identical in coloration to the male. Audubon was excited by the find, believing this was atypical of the species.[151] Here again the naturalist was confused by the intermediate plumages of a bird he thought he knew.

As an immature, this sparrow sports a buff-colored head bordered by darker, rust-brown stripes.[152] By the following spring, both sexes have acquired the distinctive white-and-black-striped head pattern that gives the bird its name. The adult birds keep this plumage year-round.[153] However, Audubon was initially of a mind that the adult female was the color of the immatures, which explains his excitement at the specimen his son found.[154] Further contact with the breeding birds in Labrador evidently changed his thinking, because he later told his readers that "[d]uring spring and summer the male and the female are of equal beauty, the former being only a little larger than the latter." Still, he remained "convinced that these birds lose the white stripes on the head in the winter season, when they might be supposed to be of a different species," a point on which he was mistaken.[155]

In keeping with his views, his illustration for *The Birds of America*, done in Henderson in October 1814, shows an adult male with its black-and-white crown and, poking its head from behind a leaf of the summer grape, an immature bird that he erroneously identified on the finished plate and in the *Ornithological Biography* as an adult female.[156]

Once back aboard the *Ripley*, the naturalist likely resumed work on his drawings or possibly began a new one. He did not, however, mention it in his journal.[157] Shattuck took a moment during the day to add an update to the letter he had begun to his father after first spotting the sails of the *Gulnare*. He explained that the letter he had hoped to send had not left his hands because the British vessel was surveying the Labrador coast, a task its crew had begun the previous summer and anticipated spending another three or four summers to complete. Among them was a physician, Shattuck related, "who is a good deal of a botanist; conchologist; something of an ornithologist." This was not something anyone in Audubon's party had expected. "Thus," Shattuck added, "this coast has been much more explored than we thought for, and the field we expected to find unexplored has been pretty well beaten." He noted that they were presently "doing nothing waiting for a west wind these last five days, for we have explored the country very thoroughly, and find almost nothing of interest."[158] That would change the following day.

When Thursday, June 27, dawned, the *Ripley* was wrapped in yet another thick fog. A hard rain pelted the deck, accompanied by winds from the south-southeast, marking yet another day when the schooner would remain harborbound. Capt. Bayfield aboard the *Gulnare* was also anxious to weigh anchor, but his topsail vessel was similarly limited in its ability to sail into the wind from the confines of this anchorage. With the rising sun the weather cleared, and Audubon joined his young friends as they rowed out to the Esquimaux Islands for an excursion after breakfast.[159]

Their ramble took them through forests of stunted evergreens, which Audubon referred to as "the brushwoods." Swarms of mosquitoes and black flies looking for a meal rose to meet them. The party came upon an adult and fledgling Canada Jay (Gray Jay) and collected the birds while the juvenile was being fed. Audubon gauged the age of the young bird at around three weeks and calculated that the temperature must have been below freezing when its egg was laid around May 10.[160]

The juvenile's coloration was dramatically different from that of the adults. It had "no white about the head; the whole plumage was of a very deep slate colour approaching to black, excepting the ends of the tail feathers, which were of a sullied white, the lower mandible almost white." When he had first seen it, Audubon considered it a possible new species and told the members of his party to collect as many specimens as they could find. But once he saw the adult swoop in to feed its young, he recognized them to be Canada Jays.[161]

Farther along, Audubon heard a cascade of high, thin musical notes from an unfamiliar bird he believed to be a new kind of warbler. With a quickened pulse, he looked around and located the small, olive-green songbird atop one of the tallest firs. "We all followed its quick movements, as it flew from tree to tree backwards and forwards without quitting the spot, to which it seemed attached." John felled it with a single blast from his shotgun, but it dropped into the undergrowth, and the six members of the party could not locate it. Disappointed, they finally gave up and proceeded on.[162]

Audubon was likely still thinking about the lost bird when they "chanced to enter one of those singular small valleys here and there to be seen," and he heard the "loud and sonorous" song of a sparrow that was new to him:[163]

> I immediately shouted to my companions, who were not far distant. They came, and we all followed the songster as it flitted from one bush to another to evade our pursuit. No sooner would it alight than it renewed its song; but we found more wildness in this species than in any other inhabiting the same country, and it was with difficulty that we at last procured it. Chance placed my young companion, THOMAS LINCOLN, in a situation where he saw it alight within shot, and with his usually unerring aim, he cut short its career. On seizing it, I found it to be a species which I had not previously seen; and supposing it to be new, I named it *Tom's Finch*, in honour of our friend LINCOLN, who was a great favourite among us.[164]

Lincoln received three hearty cheers for his feat. Audubon gave the newly discovered bird the Latin name *Fringilla lincolnii* and, when he published his biography of the bird, changed the name to Lincoln's Finch (Lincoln's Sparrow). He noted that it was similar to the Swamp Sparrow "in general appearance, but is considerably smaller, and may be known at once from all others thus far described, by the light buff streak which runs from the base of the lower mandible, until it melts into the duller buff of the breast, and by the bright ash-streak over the eye." The members of the party soon located and collected two others, but one was again lost in the brush.[165]

On their way back to the *Ripley* in the afternoon, they were passing through the area where the unidentified warbler had fallen.[166] Audubon thought another attempt should be made to find it, and his five young companions waded across a "deep, narrow creek" separating them from the woods and continued their search in the under-growth. John succeeded in discovering the small bird "among the moss near the tree from which it was fallen," but presented it to his father "greatly disappointed." Audubon took one look at the tiny bundle of feathers and understood why. This was not a new species of warbler at all, but rather a Ruby-crowned Wren (Ruby-crowned Kinglet), a common bird he had long known though never illustrated. The naturalist was nonetheless thrilled with the discovery, for he had never before heard its song in all its glorious splendor.[167]

Audubon awoke at daylight on Friday, June 28, and immediately sat down to begin drawing one of the two Lincoln's Finches that had been collected. The weather above deck was "shocking—rainy, foggy, dark and cold." He completed the drawing and then pinned the second specimen to the board and began to add its outline to the paper.[168] However, he could not continue when a squall blew in around noon with strong winds from the west-northwest, bringing with it a swell that rolled the schooner and made it impossible for him to work.[169] He joined his companions for dinner while Capt. Emery and the crew made ready to sail.[170] At around 2:00 p.m., the *Ripley* weighed anchor. As she beat her way toward the harbor's eastern entrance, the wind swung around by degrees to southwestward of west, and the schooner barely managed to clear the shoals and sail into the gulf.[171]

The *Gulnare*, less than five minutes behind the Americans, was met with a wind dead ahead as she reached the eastern point. Capt. Bayfield ordered the helmsman to tack, but there was insufficient room for the *Gulnare* to beat through the passage. Bayfield swung her around and she "ran back hauling, close as we dared" past the rocks in the center of the harbor entrance to make an attempt through the wider western channel. However, the vessel soon encountered a hidden shoal that Lt. Bowen had failed to discover during his survey. The water was "dead low" and the English schooner was aground not "more than a minute or two," but the commander had had enough. When she was once again afloat, Bayfield ran her back inside the harbor, where she dropped anchor near her old mooring at around 4:30 p.m.[172]

Out on the waters of the gulf, the *Ripley* was being tossed about by high seas from the storm as she followed the coastline eastward toward a new harbor. Audubon and his companions were soon seasick and retired early to their berths, hoping for an end to their misery and wondering what the following day would bring.[173]

9

Wapitiguan Harbor, Labrador

JUNE–JULY 1833

The appearance of the country round is quite different from that near American Harbor;
nothing in view here as far as eye can reach, but bare, high, rugged rocks, grand indeed,
but not a shrub a foot above the ground.

JOHN JAMES AUDUBON

By the following morning, the churning seas had calmed, as had Audubon's stomach. The naturalist was feeling himself again when he climbed on deck at 3:00 a.m. to greet the day. With a favorable wind, the *Ripley* had advanced about fifty miles from her anchorage in American Harbor. However, the pilot, Mr. Godwin, was unfamiliar with this part of the coastline and, without reliable charts, had elected to take the vessel some fifteen miles offshore, where she was now slicing through the waves under a light breeze.[1]

The *Ripley* was bound for Wapitiguan Harbor, but Godwin could not identify the coastal landmarks and was of little help in finding the entrance. So, Capt. Emery became involved in the search.[2] There was said to be a distinguishing rock known as Mistassini, or "the great stone," resembling "a large cannon" that was situated "on the top of a high sharp pinnacle" at the harbor's edge. According to Ingalls, the harbor was named for this "whopping great gun."[3] In truth, the name *wapitiguan* was actually a Montagnais word for cormorant, a large seabird that nested in great numbers on islands in the vicinity.[4]

Cruising along the coast, the schooner's captain honored Audubon's request to visit a Foolish Guillemot (Common Murre) rookery on a low, rocky island, where the naturalist hoped to collect some eggs.[5] Audubon and his companions managed to land their boat "through a great surf" and met two eggers already at work.[6] Audubon questioned the men and learned that they had thus far collected eight hundred dozen eggs from this and other islands nearby and were looking to sail for Halifax with two thousand dozen in the hold. With the breakage of eggs by these two-legged human marauders as well as by hundreds of Great Black-backed gulls that fed on the eggs "by thousands," an unbearable stench filled the air. Audubon's group gathered close to a hundred eggs for the *Ripley*'s stores before retreating to the schooner.[7]

A mile farther east, the *Ripley* came to again, and Audubon's group launched a boat to explore a small, grass-covered island of a few acres where Puffins (Atlantic Puffins) were breeding in horizontal burrows of three to six feet in length, dug in the "light black loam formed of decayed moss":[8]

> The shores were exceedingly rugged, the sea ran high, and it required all the good management of our captain to effect a safe landing, which, however, was at length accomplished at a propitious moment, when, borne on the summit of a great wave, we reached the first rocks, leaped out in an instant, and held our boat, while the angry waters rolled back and left it on the land. After securing the boat, we reached with a few steps the green sward, and directly before us found an abundance of Puffins. Some already alarmed flew past us with the speed of an arrow, others stood erect at the entrance of their burrows, while some more timid withdrew within their holds as we advanced towards them. In the course of half an hour we obtained a good number. The poor things seemed not at all aware of the effect of guns, for they would fly straight towards us as often as in any other direction; but after a while they became more knowing, and avoided us with more care. We procured some eggs, and as no young ones were yet to be found, we went off satisfied.[9]

Along with the eggs, Audubon took three of the adult Puffins back to the schooner and clipped their wings so that the birds could be added to the vessel's growing outdoor aviary. He noted that "[t]hose caught at the holes bit most furiously and scratched shockingly with the inner claw, making a mournful noise all the time."[10]

Audubon had been told that these birds were ignored by the eggers, who were "indifferent" to their eggs.[11] Never one to accept another man's opinion when he had the means to form his own, Audubon asked the cook to boil them up. However, other than the captain, none aboard the schooner had stomachs adventurous enough to sample them. The naturalist took a bite out of one of the cooked eggs, the white of which had been turned a "livid-blue" by the scalding water, and pronounced it "very bad."[12]

Farther east, the *Ripley* passed an island black with cormorants, whose "effluvia could be perceived more than a mile off." The vessel did not tarry there, and from his position aboard the schooner, Audubon was unable to identify the species.[13] He would determine later that they were Double-crested Cormorants, a seabird widespread along the Labrador coast.[14]

By early afternoon, the "curious beacon" of Wapitiguan Harbor came into view. However, Godwin would not bring the *Ripley* in, whether "from fear or want of knowledge." Audubon had decided the Nova Scotia man was an "ignorant ass" of a pilot when they twice passed over rocks that were visible beneath the water's surface. Capt. Emery took the matter in hand and set out in one of the smaller boats to see if he could find a navigable passage into the harbor.[15] The image of the stalwart seaman as he left the schooner remained with Ingalls for the rest of his life, as he related in a letter to Audubon scholar Ruthven Deane almost seven decades later:

> This is a good place for me to tell of the sagacity of our Captain upon getting into the harbor, his manner of doing it and the feeling of responsibility he mani-fested. The boat launched and manned, Captain with lead-line in hand, and *eating* tobacco, standing aft, eyes everywhere, excited yet weary, slow, easy, pull hearty, accomplished. He was very alert, always willing and ready.[16]

Audubon picked up the tale there and related it to his readers in the pages of the *Ornithological Biography*:

> He was absent more than an hour. The Ripley stood off and on, the yards were manned on the look-out, the sea was smooth and its waters as clear as crystal, but the swell rose to a prodigious height as it passed sluggishly over the great rocks that seemed to line the shallows over which we floated. We were under no apprehension of personal danger, however, for we had several boats and a very efficient crew; and besides, the shores were within cannon shot; but the idea of losing our gallant bark and all our materials on so dismal a coast haunted my mind, and at times those of my companions. From the tops our sailors called out "Quite shallow here, Sir." Up went the helm, and round swung the Ripley like a duck taken by surprise. Then suddenly near another shoal we passed, and were careful to keep a sharp look-out until our commander came up.
>
> Springing upon the deck, and turning his quid [i.e., chewing tobacco] rapidly from side to side, he called out, "All hands square the yards," and whis-pered to me, "All's safe, my good Sir." The schooner advanced towards the hue barrier, merrily as a fair maiden to meet her beloved; now she doubles a sharp cape, forces her way through a narrow pass; and lo! before you opens the noble harbour of Whapati Guan.[17]

Wapitiguan Harbor is actually a sheltered channel situated between Wapitiguan Island (Île de Ouapitagone) and a group of outer islands to its east. These overlap-ping adjacent rocks of bare granite, with elevations ranging up to seventy or eighty feet, serve as a virtually complete barrier to the sometimes turbulent waters of the gulf. From a distance, they would seem to form one long landmass. However, there are two narrow passages into the harbor that can be navigated safely. The East Pas-sage, which is the one the *Ripley* evidently took, is situated about three-quarters of a mile to the east of Mistassini, the large block of granite resembling a mortar sitting atop one of the outer islands. Two miles west of Mistassini lies the West Passage.[18]

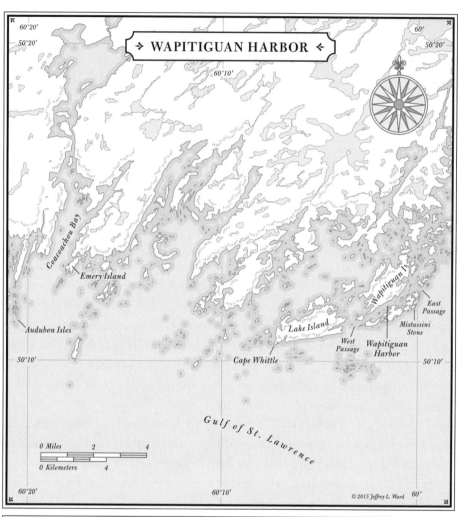

⟷ WAPITIGUAN HARBOR ⟷

60°20'
50°20'
60°

50°20'

60°10'

Coacoachou Bay

Emery Island

Audubon Isles

Wapitiguan Is.

East
Passage

Mistassini
Stone

West
Passage

Wapitiguan
Harbor

Lake Island

Cape Whittle

50°10'

50°10'

Gulf of St. Lawrence

0 Miles   2   4

0 Kilometers   4

60°20'

60°10'

60°

© 2015 Jeffrey L. Ward

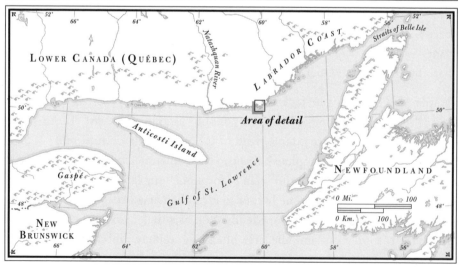

52°   66°   64°   62°   60°   58°   56°   52°

LOWER CANADA (QUÉBEC)

Natashquan River

LABRADOR COAST

Straits of Belle Isle

50°

Area of detail

50°

Anticosti Island

NEWFOUNDLAND

Gaspé

48°

Gulf of St. Lawrence

0 Mi.   100

0 Km.   100

48°

NEW
BRUNSWICK

66°   64°   62°   60°   58°   56°

Once inside the harbor, a vessel is "separated from the rolling swell of the Gulf of St. Lawrence by an immense wall of rock."[19]

The *Ripley* dropped anchor at around 4:00 p.m., and Audubon and his party were soon in the boats and being rowed to shore. Looking around their anchorage, the naturalist marked a change in the landscape. "The moss is shorter and more compact, the flowers are fewer, and every plant more diminutive. No matter which way you glance, the prospect is cold and forbidding" with "deep banks of snow" appearing in spots.[20]

Still, there were birds, which is all that really mattered to Audubon. At the base of a rock, he located a neatly woven nest of "fine grass" that held five eggs of a Brown Lark (American Pipit). Shore Larks (Horned Larks) were dressed in their "beautiful summer plumages." The party collected a White-crowned Sparrow, two Savannah Finches (Savannah Sparrows), and a Red-bellied Nuthatch (Red-breasted Nuthatch) that Audubon was sure had been blown off course because there was "not a bush" for this active little bird of the northern boreal forests "to alight upon." John found a cormorant nest and returned with a live nestling, but Audubon needed an adult in order to identify it by species. John planned to return to the nest the next day to see if he could procure one.[21]

That evening, the hold of the *Ripley* was alive with the boisterous voices and laughter of Audubon's party as they stood around the deal table bathed in candlelight, skinning the Puffins (Atlantic Puffins) that had been shot earlier in the day. A schooner passed by the opening to the harbor at dusk and was mistaken for the *Gulnare*. In fact, the British surveying vessel had managed to escape American Harbor only that evening and was just rounding Natashquan Point at around 7:00 p.m.[22]

The next day, Sunday, June 30, was a productive one for the naturalist. It was a clear day with brisk temperatures that never reached above 50°F.[23] Audubon began drawing at 8:00 a.m. and, before the light faded, he had completed drawings of the second of two Lincoln's Finches (Lincoln's Sparrows) to adorn his paper; a male Ruby-crowned Wren (Ruby-crowned Kinglet); and a male White-winged Crossbill that one of his companions had collected on a small coastal island earlier in the day.[24] The shore parties were also successful. They discovered the nest of a Savannah Finch (Savannah Sparrow) hidden in the moss. It was woven out of thin strands of grass and contained two eggs. Several molting Great Black-backed Gulls were shot, as were six adult Common Cormorants (Great Cormorants), distinguished from Double-crested Cormorants by their larger size and white throat.[25]

The weather turned colder on Monday, with a recorded high temperature of only 48°F. Aboard the *Ripley*, Audubon was at work most of the day at his drawing table, although he complained to his journal that it was "so cold that it has been painful for me to draw."[26] He added a second image of the male White-winged Crossbill to his earlier composition and began a drawing of Puffins (Atlantic Puffins) with the first of two birds that he would depict in their grassy island home. His attention was diverted from time to time by the antics of the captive Puffins, which had been given free rein to move about the schooner. "[I]t is amazing to see them running about the cabin and the hold with a surprising quickness, watching our motions and particularly our eyes," he wrote.[27] One look would send the birds scurrying for safety. They also "ran about incessantly during the night, when each footstep could be counted."[28]

Meanwhile, the members of Audubon's party were combing the surrounding countryside for new or interesting birds. They located the nest of a Pigeon Hawk (Merlin), a small, dark falcon, "on the top of a fir-tree about ten feet high, made of sticks and lined with moss, and as large as a Crow's nest."[29] Two of the five eggs had just hatched, with the remaining three soon to follow. The young birds were "pure white, soft and downy" and were brought back to the vessel, although they did not survive.[30]

Along the edges of a small lake bordered by short grass, the party also discovered two adult and three young American Ring Plovers (Semipalmated Plovers).[31] Closely related to the beach-nesting Piping Plovers that Audubon had collected on the Magdalen Islands, the adult of this species has white underparts, a single dark breast band, and a chocolate-colored back that enables it to blend into the background on the mudflats where it is commonly found.[32] Like many ground-nesting birds, this species gives birth to "precocial" young that are able to follow their parents away from the nest and feed on their own within hours of hatching, thus reducing the risk of predation. In comparison, the "altricial" young born to tree-nesting songbirds, among others, are born naked, with their eyes closed, and are helpless for days. The Pigeon Hawk (Merlin) is an example of a bird that has "semi-altricial" nestlings, which hatch with a thick coat of down but are still dependent upon their parents for food and protection.[33]

In addition to birds, the shore parties found evidence of mammals in the areas they visited, including either hares or rabbits and on one island some shallow burrows made by an unknown species of rat. But the furred creatures were elusive, and none of them were actually seen.[34]

That evening, the *Gulnare* sailed into the waters beyond Wapitiguan Harbor. Capt. Bayfield had sent Mr. Bowen ahead in the *Owen* the day before to scout out the harbor entrance, but the small surveying cutter had arrived only a short time earlier, and Bowen had no opportunity to identify a navigable route. However, Capt. Emery rowed out, fulfilling a promise he had made back in American Harbor to pilot the British schooner through the narrow passage if he arrived there first. The *Gulnare* dropped anchor in Wapitiguan Harbor at around 7:00 p.m. A short time later, the crews of the two vessels were treated to a partial lunar eclipse as the full moon, already obscured, rose into the chill night air.[35]

———————

In London, the first day of the month marked the publication of the July issue of *The Magazine of Natural History*. This time around, Charles Waterton could not have been pleased by its contents. Victor was now in Paris, but before leaving London he had contacted William Swainson and obtained the ammunition he needed to demolish Waterton's ridiculous assertion that Audubon was not the author of the *Ornithological Biography*. That should have been sufficient, but Victor wanted to make it sting. So he coupled his response with a heavy dose of sarcasm:

> I have the authority of the gentleman Mr. Waterton refers to, in stating that "Mr. Audubon's proposal to him was to obtain his assistance in the scientific details, and in no other part of the work whatsoever;" and further, I have the authority of this gentleman, for stating his "firm conviction, arising from personal intercourse and the perusal of the original manuscripts, that Mr. Audubon, and no other person, is the boná fide author of the *Ornithological Biography*.
>
> I shall not notice Mr. Waterton further, except to express my thanks for his generous conduct, in withholding his attacks on Mr. Audubon for two years after the book in question was published, and during the time the author was in England, and bringing these charges forward when my father has returned to the forests of America, and is unable to answer for himself.
>
> Should my father hereafter think it worth his while to notice Mr. Waterton, he will be quite able, on his return to England, to prove the correctness of all that he has said on the natural history of America.[36]

Further, John Loudon had agreed to publish Robert Bakewell's supportive remarks under his initials rather than his name. The Hampstead geologist began his defense of Audubon by pointing out that the attacks against the American naturalist were not unexpected:

> The biography of men who have devoted their lives to the acquisition of knowledge, led on by a lofty enthusiasm in pursuit of a favourite science, regardless of danger, and foregoing the pleasures and comforts of civilised life, — I say, the biography of such men is particularly instructive; but it frequently presents us with facts not very creditable to human nature. Numerous are the instances of the unjust treatment which they have received from their contemporaries. While occupied in distant countries with their favourite pursuits, they have sometimes found on their return that envy and jealousy have been busily employed in detracting from their merits, and endeavouring to blight their fair fame,

and deprive them of the just reward of their labours. Such is now the fate of a man whom posterity will regard as the most distinguished ornithologist of the present age; I mean, Mr. Audubon.[37]

Bakewell noted that Waterton had ridiculed the naturalist's research on Turkey Buzzards (Turkey Vultures) with "a series of quizzing interrogatories" but had presented "no facts or arguments whatever to invalidate the descriptions of Mr. Audubon." As to Waterton's contention that Audubon had not written the *Ornithological Biography*, Bakewell reminded the readers of Loudon's magazine that Audubon was of French parentage and had not spoken a word of English for the first seventeen years of his life. It was therefore not at all surprising that "when he had a valuable work to publish in English, he should wish to receive the assistance and correction of a native." Moreover, even Waterton could not "pretend to deny that the facts on which the value of the work solely rests were ascertained and furnished by Mr. Audubon."

As to the claim that Audubon had approached an unnamed "gentleman" to write the book, Bakewell thought there were few "*gentlemen* who would expect Mr. Audubon to be so unmindful of what was due to his own reputation as to suffer a hired writer to arrogate to himself the honour of his, Mr. Audubon's, labours or discoveries."[38] Finally, by drawing a contrast between the disparate approaches these two men had taken to the study of nature, Bakewell skewered the English naturalist on a personal level:

> Mr. Waterton travelled from his own rich plantations in Demerara, surrounded with his slaves and attendants. Mr. Audubon was a solitary wanderer in the forests of America, often dependent on his gun for support. While Mr. Audubon is exposed to dangers and privations, and looks forward to the patronage of the public for his sole support and reward, Mr. Waterton is tranquilly seated in a magnificent English mansion, surrounded by paternal acres, and endeavouring to deprive the solitary wanderer of that patronage, the expectation of which is the only hope that can cheer his labours.[39]

Bakewell expressed "much reluctance" in issuing his response, but he felt that he could not stand by and "see what appeared to me great injustice done to a highly meritorious character, without endeavouring to repel it."[40] In tone, it was all very dignified—very British. However, substantively, Bakewell's remarks were as sound a thrashing in print as anyone had given Waterton to date. Sweet as that may have been to Audubon's many friends, no one who knew the caustic English naturalist believed he would ever allow this to be the last word.

On Tuesday morning in New York, Lucy devoted time before breakfast to respond to Victor's two letters from mid-May, which Nicholas had brought home the afternoon before. She was gratified that they had been delivered together, as the distressing news of Havell's demand for a rate increase for the prints, and his threatened resignation, had been softened by her son's subsequent letter indicating that Havell seemed once again to be attending to the work as Victor desired. She believed that Victor had done an admirable job of handling a difficult situation:

> I cannot help being pleased to see how *far* you saw into his feelings and motives and how they coincide with mine. I do think a little praise, even flattery works well upon him, and I always perceived a disposition to quarrel with any other interference than your Fathers and his solely, and many a thing passed by when Father was engaged or absent that ought not to have done.[41]

If it became necessary to replace Havell, Lucy did not view Blake, the young engraver in Havell's shop, as a suitable alternative. "I am of opinion that Blake never can be able to undertake such a work as ours," she wrote. Rather, she suspected her husband would "prefer removing the work to France."[42]

However, these decisions would have to wait until Audubon was back from his voyage. And, in any event, Lucy did not think that the two of them would be in a position to return to England until the following spring. Audubon's charter for the *Ripley*, she knew, would be up at the end of August. But then he planned on traveling to Quebec in search of subscribers and more birds. "[S]uppose your Father returned from Labrador the middle of october it would be November before we could sail and I know he wants to spend a month or two in the Floridas before he again leaves America; and also to procure about another fifty of names to the *list*."[43]

Lucy recognized that it was critical to keep the publication on schedule, which meant keeping Havell mollified. She agreed to write the engraver as Victor had suggested and tell him that he would have to wait until Audubon returned from the expedition before they would be able to address Havell's demands.[44]

As an aside, Lucy approved of Victor's decision to ignore Waterton's attacks. "You are quite right," she told her son, "to leave Wharton [*sic*] alone, silence in this case is most magnanimous and politic, your Father will rise above it all."[45] She was unaware that Victor had already decided to take a different course. Copies of Loudon's magazine containing Victor's response were still weeks away from arriving on American shores.

Almost 950 miles northeast of New York, it was, in Audubon's words, "[a] beautiful day for Labrador."[46] He spent the morning adding a second Puffin to his drawing and then took advantage of the fine weather to take a break from his work and further explore his surroundings:[47]

> The country is so grandly wild and desolate, that I am charmed by its wonderful dreariness. Its mossy grey-clad rocks, heaped and thrown together in huge masses, hanging on smaller ones, as if about to roll down from their insecure resting places into the sea below them. Bays without end, sprinkled with rocky [islets] of all sizes, shapes, and appearances [where in every fissure a Guillemot, a Cormorant, or some other wild bird retreats to secure its egg, and raise its young, or save itself from the hunter's pursuit.] Besides this there was a peculiar cast of the uncertain sky, butterflies flitting over snow-banks, and probing unfolding dwarf flowerets of many hues pushing out their tender stems through the thick beds of moss which everywhere cross granite rock. Then there is the morass, wherein you plunge up to your knees, or the walking over the stubborn, dwarfish shrubbery, whereby one treads down the forests of Labrador."[48]

On the summits of some of the "greatly elevated islands" were freshwater lakes teeming with fish, where Red-necked Divers (Red-throated Loons) and Black-necked Divers (Pacific Loons) "swim as proudly as swans do in other latitudes."[49] A family of American Ring Plovers (Semipalmated Plovers) caught his eye, and he watched as the parents engaged in a distraction display to protect their young. Both of the adults lay "on the rocks as if shot, quivering their wings and dragging their bodies as if quite disabled."[50] He collected several of the young, "apparently about a week old; they ran briskly to avoid us, and concealed themselves so closely by squatting, that it was very difficult to discover them even when only a few feet distant."[51] Overhead, Great Black-backed Gulls rode the soft breezes on their long pinions.[52] Audubon noted that with no eagles and few hawks at this northern latitude, these gulls were the chief avian predators, "forever harassing every other bird, sucking their eggs, and devouring their young."[53]

The weather turned sour on Wednesday, with "a stiff easterly wind all day, rainy, and the water so rough" that Audubon was unable to send someone to shore to collect plants for his drawings.[54] By the afternoon the storm had blown through, and Audubon headed to the top of one of the outer islands at the harbor's entrance.[55] Looking out over the roiling waters of the gulf, he watched as the savage surf exploded against the rocks below, tossing water and foam high into the air. He was thankful that the *Ripley* was safely moored in the harbor. A colony of Common Cormorants (Great Cormorants) had constructed their nests of matted sticks and seaweed on the ledges of the steep granite cliff beneath him, and he crawled over to get a better look:[56]

I lie flat on the edge of the precipice some hundred feet above the turbulent waters, and now crawling along with all care, I find myself only a few yards above the spot on which the parent bird and her young are fondling each other, quite unconscious of my being near. How delighted I am to witness their affectionate gratulations, hear their lisping notes, mark the tremulous motions of their expanded throats, and the curious vacillations of their heads and necks! The kind mother gently caresses each alternately with her bill; the little ones draw nearer to her, and, as if anxious to evince their gratitude, rub their heads against hers. How pleasing all this is to me! But at this moment the mother accidentally looks upward, her keen eye has met mine, she utters a croak, spreads her sable wings, and in terror launches into the air, leaving her brood at my mercy. Far and near, above and beneath me, the anxious parent passes and repasses; her flight is now unnatural, and she seems crippled, for she would fain perform those actions in the air, which other birds perform on the ground or on the water, in such distressing moments of anxiety for the fate of their beloved young. Her many neighbors, all as suspicious as herself, well understood the meaning of her mode of flight, and one after another take to wing, so that the air is in a manner blackened with them. Some fly far over the waters, others glide along the face of the bold rock, but none that have observed me realight, and how many of those there are I am pretty certain, as the greater number follow in the track of the one most concerned. Meanwhile the little ones, in their great alarm, have crawled into a recess, and there they are huddled together. I have witnessed their pleasures and their terrors, and now, crawling backwards, I leave them to resume their ordinary state of peaceful security.[57]

The only other birds to find these rocky cliffs a suitable place to raise their young were Ravens and Peregrine Falcons, some of which had built their nests surprisingly near those of the cormorants.[58] The falcon nests were littered with the "remains of Ducks, Willow Grous, and young Gulls."[59]

Thursday, July 4, dawned under gray, cloudy skies.[60] Audubon was eager to finish his drawing of the two Lincoln's Finches (Lincoln's Sparrows) and at 4:00 a.m. asked Tom Lincoln to go ashore to collect four different plants for the background. Lincoln was joined on the early-morning excursion by John and Coolidge. In addition to finding the plants, the party returned to the spot where Audubon had spent the previous afternoon watching the nesting Common Cormorants (Great Cormorants), having been asked by him to retrieve a nest he needed for his drawing of that species. They had to scrape the fifteen-pound mass off, as it was "literally pasted to the rock's edge, so thick was the decomposed, putrid matter below it." The young men also caught several young birds and brought them back to the schooner, where "[t]hey crawled sluggishly about, aiding themselves in their progress with their bills, and at times looked extremely clumsy."[61]

Of the plants Lincoln gathered, Audubon added three to his composition—a Dwarf Cornel (*Cornus suecica*), Cloudberry (*Rubus chamaemorus*), and Bog Laurel (*Kalmia polifolia*).[62] He spent the better part of the day completing the drawing and thought it "very fitting" that Lincoln had contributed the plants to the illustration of the species that bore his name.[63]

While Audubon worked at his drawing table, the rest of the company "divided as usual" into three groups. John and Lincoln joined forces to search for loons, returning later in the day with a Red-necked Diver (Red-throated Loon). Coolidge, Shattuck, and Ingalls collected a pair of molting Dusky Ducks (Black Ducks) on the mainland.[64] They also brought back the nest and two eggs of a Loon (Common Loon) that they came upon about a mile inland at the edge of a "considerable pond of limpid water" apparently formed out of snowmelt.[65] Capt. Emery led a third party of four crewmen to go fishing with a seine in a nearby pond.[66]

Once back onboard, everyone dined on fresh fish along with a quarter of mutton that Capt. Bayfield had sent over in commemoration of American Independence Day.[67] Audubon was touched by the gesture, noting that the meat was "a rarity on this coast of Labrador, even on this day."[68]

Following their celebratory meal, Audubon and his son set off in a "heavy rain & thick fog" to terminate a scientific study he had commenced shortly after arriving at Wapitiguan Harbor.[69] Five days earlier, as he had initially explored their new anchorage, Audubon blocked the opening to a fissure where a Black Guillemot was nesting, to test the limits of its endurance without food.[70] However, he had recently begun to have second thoughts about the experiment and had decided to give the bird its freedom. The obstruction was removed, the hole was poked with a stick, and the "sadly weak" bird came running out and flew off toward the sea. Audubon expected the bird to "soon recover from this trial of ours."[71] However, he later admitted that this was one experiment "on which I have never since been able to think, without some feeling of remorse."[72]

The weather on Friday was marked by strong winds blowing in from the west.[73] Audubon went to his drawing table at 4:00 a.m. to begin putting the figure of an adult male Red-necked Diver (Red-throated Loon) on paper. Meanwhile, his young companions took to the boats and began another day of exploration. Coolidge, Shattuck, and Ingalls returned later in the day with a family of Willow Grous (Willow Ptarmigan), the species that had eluded Audubon at American Harbor despite his seeking the help of the Montagnais Indians in obtaining specimens. Shattuck received credit for shooting the parents, but it probably required the rest of the party to round up the seven small, precocial young that Audubon believed had hatched only the day before.[74]

At around 3:00 p.m., Audubon completed his image of the Red-necked Diver (Red-throated Loon) and took a boat ashore for some much-needed exercise.[75] Capt. Emery and a few crewmen accompanied him to a "rugged island" located about four-miles northeast of their anchorage. There they collected Razor-billed Auks (Razorbills) by introducing long poles with hooks into the fissures where the birds nested and then pulling out both the brooding bird and its single egg.[76] "[O]n a tremendous cliff," they located the nest of a Peregrine Falcon with a single, week-old nestling.[77] The parents, who are fierce defenders of their young, flew at the eyes of the intruders in an attempt to drive them away. At a freshwater pond, the men startled a family of Red-necked Divers (Red-throated Loons). The parents flew off, but the captain was able to collect their young, "not having yet learned from experience the danger of the proximity of man."[78]

During their jaunt, Audubon experienced firsthand the difficulty of rambling over the moss-covered terrain and grumbled about it in his journal that evening:

> [W]alking on this spongy moss of Labrador is a task no one can imagine without trying it; at every step the foot sinks in a deep moss cushion, which closes over it, and requires considerable exertion to draw it up. When the moss is over a marshy tract, then you sink a couple of feet deep every step you take, and to reach a bare rock is delightful, and quite a relief.[79]

Ingalls echoed these comments, although he was quick to point out that Audubon had far less reason to complain than the younger members of his party, who were faced with the arduous task of traversing the rugged country every day:

> Mr. Audubon being almost all the time aboard at work did not have so good a knowledge of the *moss* of which he speaks, as we boys did, for we were sent out to different distances from the ship to explore, to gather information, to hunt and to bring ourselves and *new species of birds*, home at night.
>
> You must fancy the surface over which we toiled, a rich, thick, beautiful, spongy moss, in lumps as though baskets with rounding bottoms the size of a peck, up to two bushels, turned bottom upwards and laid together, joined, the rounding elevation being five to ten inches. Do you get it from my clumsy description? Now, walk. No, proceed for a mile over this carpet and you will experience the fatigue of a walk from Cambridge to Boston and return. It was different from walking through snow six to ten inches deep; 'twas lovely moss to look upon.[80]

John and Lincoln did not get back to the vessel until sunset.[81] In their bags they carried another Red-necked Diver (Red-throated Loon), along with one of its eggs, an Arctic Tern, and "some curious Eels."[82] They reported seeing signs of Caribou, White-tailed Deer, and the North American River Otter. They also saw a number of Loons (Common Loons) on the lakes they had visited and had used a technique called "tolling" to bring the birds within twenty yards of them. Audubon described for his readers this "curious and wonderful" method of luring these wary birds to within shooting range:[83]

> On seeing a Loon on the water, at whatever distance, the sportsman immediately places himself under the nearest cover on the shore, and remains there as carefully concealed as possible. A few minutes are allowed to pass, to give the wary and sharp-sighted bird all due confidence; during which time the gun, charged with large shot, is laid in a convenient position. The gunner then takes his cap or pocket handkerchief, which if brightly coloured is so much the better, and raising it in one hand, waves it three of four times, and then suddenly conceals it. The bird commonly detects the signal at once, and, probably imagining the object thus exhibited to be one of its own species, gradually advances, emitting its love-notes, which resemble a coarse laugh, as it proceeds. The sportsman imitates these notes, making them loud and yet somewhat mellow, waving his cap or kerchief at the same time, and this he continues to do at intervals. The Loon, in order to arrive more quickly, dives, perhaps rises within fifty yards of him, and calling less loudly, advances with considerable caution. He shews the signal less frequently, imitates the notes of the bird more faintly, and carefully keeps himself concealed, until the Loon, having approached within twenty or even ten paces, dives and on emerging raises itself up to shake its wings, when off goes the shot, and the deluded bird floats dead on the water.[84]

If John and Lincoln got off a shot at any of the Loons they attracted, their efforts were not successful. The two young men also located the nests of Black Guillemots under boulders on the ground rather than in the fissures where these nests were normally found.[85] This led Lincoln to hypothesize that the birds were not of the same species, but John thought otherwise.

When Audubon retired for the night "much fatigued," he was pleased that he now had his "hands full of work."[86] The next day, he would begin a drawing of the grouse family.

Saturday morning, July 6, came early for the naturalist, who awoke at 3:00 a.m. and was soon seated at his drawing table.[87] He started out working on his drawing of the Red-necked Diver (Red-throated Loon), adding the figure of an adult female in profile to highlight the distinctive thin streaks of white plumage running down the back of the bird's neck.[88] This complemented perfectly the first image he had drawn of the male bird, with its body facing the viewer and its head turned to the right where it had been impossible for Audubon to illustrate that field mark. With the two birds he could now show the entirety of the bird's plumage, creating a valuable reference for the ornithologist while simultaneously producing an aesthetically pleasing image for the art lover. He finished the drawing with the image of one of the young birds Capt. Emery had obtained the day before. Later, he would add an immature bird in winter plumage and a Pitcher Plant (*Sarracenia purpurea*) to the left of these birds to complete the composition.[89]

Pulling out a large piece of Whatman paper, Audubon then began to sketch a female Willow Grous (Willow Ptarmigan) from the specimen that Shattuck had procured.[90] The naturalist had decided this would be a large print for his publication, so he positioned the bird to the right of center, intending to place the male of the species on the other side of the sheet.[91] He had almost completed the image by 5:30 p.m., when he had to stop because "my fingers could no longer hold my pencil."[92] He hopped into a boat to "go on shore for exercise" and spent some time watching a male Brown Lark (American Pipit) singing "both on the wing and whilst sitting on the ground."[93] But he was troubled by his inability to work at his drawings as long as he wished, and that night, as he opened his journal, he could not deny the truth of what was happening to his body. "The fact is that I am growing old too fast; alas! I feel it — and yet work I will, and may God grant me life to see the last plate of my mammoth work finished."[94]

Coolidge's party succeeded in collecting two Oyster Catchers (American Oyster-catchers), a large black-headed, dark-backed shorebird with a white belly and a long red bill it uses for prying open mollusks and crabs.[95] Audubon noted that these birds were "becoming plentiful." John returned with the nest and eggs of a White-crowned Bunting (White-crowned Sparrow) that he had discovered while "creeping through some low bushes after a Red-necked Diver," inadvertently flushing out the brooding female. Audubon described the nest as being "formed of beautiful moss outwardly, dried, fine grass next inside, and exquisitely lined with fibrous roots of a rich yellow color; the eggs are light greenish, slightly sprinkled with reddish-brown, in size about the same as eggs of the Song Sparrow." The explorers had seen many of this species, and Audubon indicated that the bird was the most abundant of the sparrows locally. By comparison, only two Swamp Sparrows had been observed.[96]

Lt. Bowen rowed over from the *Gulnare* to present the naturalist with a Peregrine Falcon he had collected along with two recent hatchlings of the Razor-billed Auk (Razorbill).[97] The surveyor had just returned from a four-day excursion to Coacoa-chou Bay to the west "to sketch & Survey from where he left off last year up to the Vessel's anchorage."[98] In drafting a map of this area, Capt. Bayfield would honor

Audubon by bestowing his name on a set of islets situated at the southwestern edge of the opening to the bay. Capt. Emery received a similar tribute when an island on the opposite side of the bay's entrance was given his name.[99]

Audubon was grateful for Bowen's gift of the specimens. He recorded in his journal that his own group had already located two Peregrine nests "placed high on rocky declivities," but that these were the first young auks anyone had found.[100]

At around this time, Audubon released the three Puffins that had spent the last week, day and night, running about the schooner. He thought them "agreeable pets" but decided it was time for them to go. Donning a glove to avoid being scratched by their inner claw, he tossed them over the side. The birds "plunged through the air, entered the water, and swam off, assisting themselves by their wings to the distance of from fifty to an hundred yards. On coming up, they washed their plumage for a long time, and then dived in search of food."[101]

The following morning, Sunday, July 7, brought "a little rain" with haze and a light breeze.[102] Audubon returned to his drawing table and continued working on his Willow Grous (Willow Ptarmigan) composition. In another long day spent hunched over his work, he was able to complete the figure of the female, add five of her young, and prepare her mate for drawing.[103]

That morning, the *Gulnare* was alive with activity as Capt. Bayfield and Lt. Bowen pushed off in separate craft to begin a three-week surveying expedition along the coast to Great Mecattina, situated northeast of their anchorage.[104] Midshipman Barrie and eight crewmen accompanied the commander in the launch, while Bowen took a crew of seven along in his small surveying vessel, the *Owen*. Audubon noted in his journal that the two parties went "with tents and more comforts than I have ever enjoyed in hunting excursions."[105] Mr. Hall, the master of the British schooner, remained onboard with command of the vessel. Dr. Kelley was given responsibility for the chronometers, the highly accurate and essential timepieces that were used for determining the ship's longitude.[106]

The afternoon saw John, Lincoln, and Capt. Emery leave the *Ripley* in one of the boats for a distant bay some ten miles off, where they planned to camp overnight. Not too long after they left, a series of thunderstorms swept through the area, which likely forced the adventurers off the water to seek shelter.[107]

Late in the day, after Audubon had grown "fatigued with drawing," he joined Dr. Kelley for a ramble onshore, where they "saw many pretty flowers, amongst them a flowering Sweet-pea, quite rich in color."[108] The air was as thick with mosquitoes as in the Louisiana swamps. A mile inland, the men came upon a small pond, bordered by a carpet of deep moss, where two female Eider Ducks (Common Eiders) and their young broods were swimming. Audubon took aim and fired at the birds without any shot in his gun, in order to test their reaction. The birds dived in unison but soon reappeared, "the mothers quacking and murmuring." The young birds then disappeared below the surface, not to be seen again. The parent birds took off and beat their way toward the waters of the open gulf. Audubon was perplexed by what he had witnessed, not knowing how the still-flightless young would follow their mothers. However, he determined that the female birds would return to their broods once the threat posed by their human onlookers had ended.[109]

The next day, Audubon awoke to a morning soured by "[r]ainy, dirty weather," the winds blowing from the east and the temperature a chilly 48°F.[110] He sat down with his drawing of the Willow Grous (Willow Ptarmigan) at 3:30 a.m. and spent the better part of the day completing images of the male bird and adding two more young birds grouped with their siblings in various poses around their mother — one sheltered behind a wing, another looking up at her from beneath her breast, others still close but tentatively beginning to explore their new world.[111]

Audubon considered it "a handsome large plate," but the harsh weather made painting it a "disagreeable" experience.[112] "The fog collects and falls in large drops from the rigging on my table, and now and then I am obliged to close the skylight, and work almost in darkness."[113] He also was not happy with the white paint that he used to illustrate the outer primary feather on the male. It was bad and showed up as a dirty rather than pure white.[114]

John and his bedraggled company returned from their camping trip "cold, wet, and hungry." They had nothing to show for their day abroad other than reports of a wolf howling nearby and an island where they had seen "thousands" of breeding Puffins (Common Puffins).[115]

Audubon opened his journal that evening and said he planned to "draw the beautiful *Colymbus glacialis* [Common Loon] in most perfect plumage" in the morning.[116] Although he did not say who had procured the specimen, Coolidge may have provided a clue in his reminiscences more than six decades later. If so, Coolidge had since forgotten which species he had actually collected:

Our custom while there was to anchor our vessel in some harbor and cruise in two boats (east and west) commanded by John Audubon and myself. Of course there was some rivalry as to who should be the most successful, not in number of birds, but in the quality of specimens. Our orders were to kill them with as few shot as possible, so as not to disfigure them. On one occasion I returned to the vessel late at night and found those aboard in ecstasies over a very fine bird which John W. Audubon procured. I examined it and pronounced it the finest specimen of the cruise, but that I could procure a better one and would wager the wine for the company upon it. I then brought my bird and all examined it and finding no shot mark upon it said I must have found it, but I convinced them that I did shoot it by exhibiting the shot mark near the neck. I had killed it flying with only one fine shot; it dropped dead without a struggle, showing a slight stain on the feathers, which I pulled out. A copy of this specimen (I think) may be seen in the plate representing the Red-throated Diver. I do not mention this to assert my superiority as a marksman over Audubon's son, but consider it merely a chance shot.[117]

True to his word, the following day — a wet and foggy one — Audubon embarked on his drawing of the Loon or Great Northern Diver (Common Loon) as it was also known, "a most difficult bird to imitate."[118] Its head and long neck are a dark greenish-black with a partial collar of narrow white stripes. Its black back and wings are broken up by a pattern of white-checkered markings.[119] This is a bird most at home in the water, with a torpedo-shaped body powered by large webbed feet placed toward its tail to propel it underwater in pursuit of the fish that make up a good portion of its diet. However, the naturalist chose to illustrate the specimen on land, standing upright with its beak open and its tongue visible as it calls to another loon somewhere in the distance.[120]

That evening, he went to shore with Capt. Emery for a walk.[121] Clouds of mosquitoes followed them as they trekked over the ground where plants were now "blooming by millions, and at every step you tread on flowers such as would be looked on in more temperate climates with pleasure."[122] Audubon bemoaned his lack of knowledge of botany and appreciated receiving a list of the plants Dr. Kelley had identified along this section of the Labrador coast.[123] The naturalist observed flocks of female Eiders (Common Eiders) that were molting into their "basic" or winter plumage, and whose flightless condition kept them bound to the waters near the shoreline. He speculated that these birds were sterile because those with nests or young broods had yet to show signs of beginning their molt. The men also startled a female Eider that was sitting on its nest on a "broad flat rock" without nearby vegetation to hide it from predators. The bird flew off and circled around them until they withdrew, "when we had the pleasure to see her alight, walk to her nest, and compose herself upon it."[124]

The wet weather continued into Wednesday, July 10. In the pages of his journal, Audubon reflected on the northeastern storms that periodically drenched the dreary Labrador landscape:

> Could I describe one of these dismal gales which blow ever and anon over this desolate country, it would in all probability be of interest to one unacquainted with the inclemency of the climate. Nowhere else is the power of the northeast gale, which blows every week on the coast of Labrador, so keenly felt as here. I cannot describe it; all I can say is that whilst we are in as fine and safe a harbor

as could be wished for, and completely land-locked all round, so strong does the wind blow, and so great its influence on our vessel, that her motion will not allow me to draw, and indeed once this day forced me to my berth, as well as some others of our party. One would imagine all the powers of Boreas had been put to work to give us a true idea of what his energies can produce, even in so snug a harbor. What is felt outside I cannot imagine, but greatly fear that few vessels could ride safely before these horrid blasts, that now and then seem strong enough to rend the very rocks asunder. The rain is driven in sheets which seem scarcely to fall on sea or land; I can hardly call it rain, it is rather a mass of water, so thick that all objects at any distance from us are lost to sight every three or four minutes, and the waters comb up and beat about us in our rock-bound harbor as a newly caged bird does against its imprisoning walls.[125]

Audubon tried to work on his Loon composition, but water dripping from the open hatch made this difficult. "I covered my paper to protect it from the rain, with the exception only of the few inches where I wished to work, and yet that small space was not spared by the drops that fell from the rigging on my table; there is no window, and the only light is admitted through hatches."[126]

By midnight the storm had moved on, and at daybreak the rising sun turned the horizon a "fiery red." Audubon had hoped to depart for another harbor farther north, but the winds were contrary and he was left to his drawings for another day. John and Lincoln were dispatched before 3:00 a.m. to procure an adult Common Cormorant (Great Cormorant) and two young birds for Audubon's next illustration, which he began soon after the young men's successful return.[127] He depicted the female bird at her nest on a rocky shelf high above the waters of the gulf, with her two downy nestlings, nearly half grown, looking up at her, their beaks open, begging for food.[128] "Look at the birds before you," he would instruct his readers, "and mark the affectionate glance of the mother, as she stands besides her beloved younglings!"[129] To an ornithologist, these birds were simply following an eons-old script dictated by biological imperatives. To Audubon, the familial affection they displayed to one another had human parallels, and he could not help injecting a subtle anthropomorphic feel to the lifelike images he drew with his hand.

The shore parties returned from their excursions with "nothing new." Although someone found a tail feather from an immature Red-tailed Hawk, Audubon thought it curious they had seen neither hawks nor owls about, because there were signs of large avian predators that had devoured "hundreds of sea birds," leaving only their wings behind.[130]

The fair weather did not last. By midday on Friday, July 12, another gale had blown in from the east bringing rain and strong winds.[131] Having started work early,

Audubon was able to complete his drawing of the Common Cormorant (Great Cormorant) family despite the storm-induced motion of the *Ripley*.[132] He took to the schooner's deck at one point and watched as a Great Black-backed Gull plunged into the water near shore and seized a large crab the size of the naturalist's two fists, which it tore apart and ate before flying to its nest to likely regurgitate the food for its young. The pet Great Black-backed Gulls onboard the schooner were "now half fledged" and behaved like vultures, ripping apart any dead duck or gull tossed in their direction, "drinking the blood and swallowing the flesh, each constantly trying to rob the other of the piece of flesh which he has torn from the carcass."[133]

It was another day of scanty production by the shore parties. The only item Audubon felt worth recording in his journal was a Red-breasted Merganser nest with ten "dirty yellow" eggs, which his son and Lincoln retrieved "near the edge of a very small fresh-water pond, under the creeping branches of one of this country's fir-trees, the top of which would be about a foot above ground."[134]

Audubon was up and about by 3:30 a.m. on Saturday, a "cloudy and dull" morning.[135] He had agreed to join Dr. Kelley for the day aboard the *Gulnare*, where he hoped to finish the background of his composition of the Willow Grous (Willow Ptarmigan).[136] However, his plans changed when the winds shifted from the northeast to the west around 7:00 a.m. and Capt. Emery ordered the crew of the *Ripley* to prepare to depart. An hour later, the schooner weighed anchor, sailed past the *Gulnare* to exchange mutual farewells, and made its way through the "narrow passage" between the outer islands to reach the gulf.[137]

Their destination was Little Mecattina (Île du Petit Mécatina), northeast about forty-three miles, which the naturalist had hoped to reach by day's end. However, the winds died at noon. The "Young Gentlemen" took the opportunity to cast their fishing lines into the depths, catching a number of cod. A Pomarine Jaeger, a large oceanic predator that resembles a heavyset dark-brown gull with longer middle-tail feathers, landed on the water nearby to eat a cod's liver thrown from the deck. But the bird remained out of range of the fowling pieces, much to Audubon's dismay, as he needed a specimen to illustrate the species for his publication. The naturalist's party also could not get a shot at "[s]everal small petrels," likely Forked-tailed Petrels (Leach's Storm-Petrels), that were similarly attracted to the offal.[138]

When the wind picked up again in the afternoon, it came from the east and brought with it intermittent rain. The rolling waters of the gulf sent Audubon and his companions once more to their berths to quiet the commotion in their stomachs.[139] For Capt. Emery and his sturdy Yankee crew, the inclement weather and angry seas were of no consequence. They had their heading. The *Ripley* beat her way northeastward as the light faded and, under a clearing sky, followed the wakening stars into the brief Labrador night.[140]

10

Little Mecattina Cove, Labrador

JULY 1833

*Our harbor represents the bottom of a large bowl, in the centre of which
our vessel is anchored, surrounded by rocks full a thousand feet high, and the wildest
looking place I was ever in.*

JOHN JAMES AUDUBON

The following morning, Sunday, July 14, dawned cold and clear. A brisk wind, now blowing from the northeast, had brought the *Ripley* to within twenty miles of the tall, rugged island of Little Mecattina (Petit Mécatina).[1] Approximately seven and a half miles long and roughly three miles wide, this was "the highest land" the expedition had yet encountered. The vessel was bound for a small, deep anchorage along the island's eastern side, known to mariners as Little Mecattina Cove (Anse du Petit Mécatina).[2] Audubon referred to it as the "harbor of Little Macatine."[3] The wind and "heavy sea beating against the vessel's bows" slowed the schooner's advance, and Capt. Emery was compelled to "tack and tack against the wind."[4] When the breeze vanished around noon, there were doubts they would reach their destination that day.[5] But a favorable wind rose as the afternoon advanced, and by 4:00 p.m. they were only a mile and a half away from the island. Eager for exploration and discovery, Audubon and his companions jumped into a boat and rowed for shore:

> As we came near it, the rocks appeared stupendously high and rough, and frowned down on our little boat, as we moved along and doubled the little cape which made one side of the entrance of Macatine's Harbour, but it looked so small to me, that I doubted if it were the place; and the shores were horribly wild, fearfully high and rough, and nothing but the croaking of a pair of ravens was heard mingling with the dismal sound of the surge which dashed on the rocky ledges, and sent the foaming water into the air.[6]

With sails full from a freshened wind, the *Ripley* soon followed and came to anchor in the center of the harbor. Audubon's party returned to the vessel and downed "a hasty supper."[7] From the deck, the naturalist took in a view of the surrounding topography and provided the readers of the *Ornithological Biography* with a word sketch:

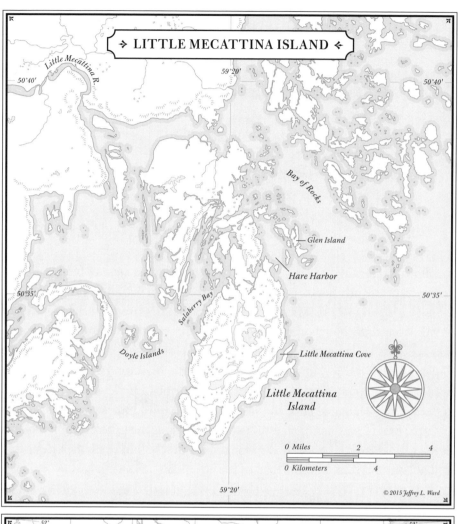

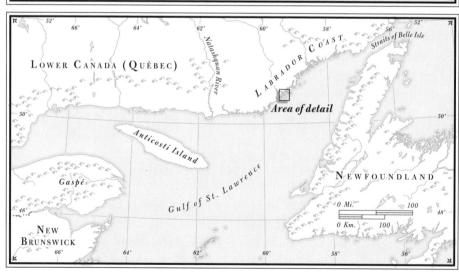

It was the middle of July, the weather was mild and pleasant, our vessel made her way under a smart breeze through a very narrow passage, beyond which we found ourselves in a small circular basin of water, having an extent of seven or eight acres. It was so surrounded by high, abrupt, and rugged rocks, that, as I glanced around, I could find no apter comparison for our situation than that of a nut-shell in the bottom of a basin. The dark shadows that overspread the waters, and the mournful silence of the surrounding desert, sombred our other-wise glad feelings into a state of awe. The scenery was grand and melancholy. On one side, hung over our heads, in stupendous masses, a rock several hun-dred feet high, the fissures of which might to some have looked like the mouths of some huge undefined monster. Here and there a few dwarf-pines were stuck as if by magic to this enormous mass of granite; in a gap of the cliff the brood of a pair of grim Ravens shrunk from our sight, and the Gulls, one after another, began to wend their way overhead towards the middle of the quiet pool, as the furling of the sails was accompanied by the glad cries of the sailors. The remark-able land-beacons erected in that country to guide vessels into the harbour, looked like so many figures of gigantic stature formed from the large blocks that lay on every hill around. A low valley, in which meandered a rivulet, opened at a distance to the view. The remains of a deserted camp of seal-catchers was easily traced from our deck, and as easily could we perceive the innate tendency of man to mischief, in the charred and crumbling ruins of the dwarf-pine forests. But the harbour was so safe and commodious, that, before we left it to find shel-ter in another, we had cause to be thankful for its friendly protection.[8]

Audubon's party and the crew broke into separate groups and "all scampered ashore again, and climbed the nearest hills."[9] Capt. Emery joined the "more active" party that aimed to scale "the most difficult heights."[10] Audubon, John, and Shat-tuck took an easier path. They rowed to the head of the harbor, where they beached the craft, and made their way "to the top of a mountain (for I cannot call it a hill)," as Audubon related that night to his journal. From there they "went down a steep in-cline, up another hill, and so on till we reached the crest of the island, and surveyed all beneath us. Nothing but rocks–barren rocks–wild as the wildest of the Apen-nines everywhere."[11] The naturalist estimated the height of Little Mecattina Island at a thousand feet, but he was off by almost half.[12] Capt. Bayfield's surveyors would measure the highest peak at 560 feet.[13]

From their perch they could see wisps of fog forming out over the cold, gray waters of the gulf and decided to return to the schooner, knowing from experience how quickly the fog could overtake them and make negotiating the rough terrain a daunting task.[14] During their ascent, Audubon and his companions had found the ground covered with moss but "a few inches deep, and the soil beneath it so moist, that whenever the declivities were much inclined, the whole slipped from under us like an avalanche, and down we would slide for feet, and sometimes yards."[15] Now, on their descent, they slid for "forty or fifty feet, and brought up in a little valley or pit filled with moss and mire."[16]

Dwarf alders and spruces filled the ravines between the hills.[17] In the midst of one such thicket, John flushed a female Black-capped Warbler (Blackpoll Warbler) from her diminutive nest in a fir tree. The naturalist was elated. "Reader, just fancy how this raised my spirits. I felt as if the enormous expense of our voyage had been refunded. 'There,' said I, 'we are the first white men who have seen such a nest.'"[18] For the pioneering ornithologists of the 19th century, being the first to discover the nest and eggs of a species was almost as exciting and scientifically important as finding a bird unknown to science.

Monday morning began with an early breakfast at 3:00 a.m. as the company excitedly anticipated a full day of exploration. However, the skies were cloudy, and an east wind portended a day of rain. The "Young Gentlemen" took to the boats, with John and Lincoln, "the strongest and most active, as well as the most experienced shots," headed off in one direction. Coolidge, Shattuck, and Ingalls rowed off in another. Audubon noted in his journal that while Shattuck and Ingalls were perhaps less adept with a shotgun than his son and Lincoln, they were "not far behind them in this."[19]

Audubon returned to his drawing table in the hold and worked for several hours adding a moss-and-lichen-covered ground to his composition of the family of Willow Grous (Willow Ptarmigan). However, by 9:00 a.m. it was raining so hard that he could no longer keep his paper dry from the hatch overhead. Unwilling to quit, he picked up his paper and watercolors and moved to the cabin, where he continued his labor.[20]

On deck, Capt. Emery was learning that the Common American Gulls (Ring-billed Gulls), which frequented this harbor in numbers Audubon had never seen before, seemed "to know gunshot distance with wonderful precision, and it is seldom that one comes near enough to be secured." The able seaman's efforts succeeded in adding only a single specimen to the naturalist's collection.[21]

John's party was back onboard the *Ripley* at 10:00 a.m., having collected a Red-necked Diver (Red-throated Loon) and an egg from its nest, which Audubon was told had been built adjacent to a small, ten-square-yard pond. Coolidge's party returned later carrying three White-crowned Buntings (White-crowned Sparrows), along with a nest of the species and two American Ring Plovers (Semipalmated Plovers). Their excursion also took them to an island littered with "old and abandoned nests" of the Double-crested Cormorant where they saw but a single egg.[22] Audubon did not say whether this was the inevitable outcome of the scourge of the eggers' visits, though it seems likely.

The nest of the White-crowned Buntings (White-crowned Sparrows) had eggs in it, and Audubon took some time that day to illustrate one of them.[23] He had been making life-sized drawings of the eggs that his companions had collected over the past several weeks as part of a plan, described in his original prospectus, to provide his subscribers with illustrations of the eggs of many of the species depicted in his plates.[24] However, as the project progressed and the years passed, he realized there would simply not be room for them.[25]

On a rocky shelf on the steep side of Little Mecattina Island, a Raven (Common Raven) nestling that was almost fledged had sought to escape from one of the explorers and tumbled into the water. It was retrieved and brought onboard the *Ripley*, where Audubon clipped the primary feathers of one wing to prevent it from flying away. He then released it on deck to join the other birds in the vessel's open aviary. However, high above the schooner, the bird's mother circled on broad wings and "called most loudly" to her offspring in her hoarse, croaking voice. As Audubon told the tale, the nestling "walked carefully to the end of the bowsprit, opened its wings, and tried to fly, but being unable, fell into the water and was drowned" before anyone could save it. Audubon learned from members of the crew who had worked along this coast in seasons past that a pair of Ravens had nested here for the previous eight or nine years. The rest of the clutch fledged within days and, according to the naturalist, both parents and young were not seen again.[26]

Tuesday, July 16, was "[a]nother day of dirty weather" that prevented the young men from heading to shore in the morning. Audubon returned to the drawing of his Willow Grous (Willow Ptarmigan) and added three plants. The "wild peas," which he illustrated at the bottom left-hand corner of the composition, are Beach Peas (*Lathyrus japonicus*), a perennial herb that can be found growing on sand and gravel beaches throughout the temperate coastal areas of North America, South America, Europe, and Asia. Its global reach is a function of the seeds' ability to survive in salt water for up to five years. The naturalist placed Roseroot (*Rhodioloa rosea*), a plant he did not know, adjacent to the ptarmigan cock. Named for the odor generated by its roots, this perennial herb is distributed throughout northern North America and Eurasia. Labrador Tea (*Rhododendron groenlandicum*), pictured between the two adult birds, is commonly found in northern bogs in the United States and Canada. The leaves were used by Native Americans to brew a tea concoction.[27]

By afternoon the weather had improved sufficiently that the boats could be launched. Audubon's companions returned with three White-crowned Buntings (White-crowned Sparrows) and a female Black-capped Warbler (Blackpoll Warbler). Capt. Emery and some of his crew had taken a third boat out to go fishing and, in under an hour, caught "thirty fine codfish" that made an excellent evening meal. He also presented the naturalist with a different species that Emery referred to as the Esquimaux Codfish. Audubon did not know if it had ever been described to science and had it placed in their cask of rum. By then a thick fog had made its way in from the gulf, enveloping the harbor and completely obscuring the upper reaches of the adjacent hills.[28]

That night, the mosquitoes were voracious, driving Audubon from his berth to the deck where, though "the fog was as thick as fine rain, the air was filled with these insects."[29] He tried his bunk again but found no respite until morning "when I had a roaring fire made and got rid of them."[30] Female mosquitoes, the only ones that bite, have chemoreceptors that draw them to carbon dioxide and certain chemical compounds emitted by the skin of human beings, and smoke can evidently disrupt their ability to sense the source of their next meal.[31]

The shore parties left the schooner, making their way through the fog and rain, while Audubon went back to work on his drawings.[32] He completed the Willow Grous composition, as least for the time being, by penciling in a distant background of one of the hills surrounding the *Ripley*'s anchorage. Havell's print would show only a portion of it. Audubon also worked on the drawings of "several birds," although he failed to identify in his journal which species they were. The young men returned with "several specimens, but nothing new." Coolidge had used his gun rod to capture two immature Red-necked Divers (Red-throated Loons) while they were swimming underwater in a small pond. In the afternoon, Audubon took a break from his drawing table and accompanied Capt. Emery to a large Double-crested Cormorant rookery on a nearby island. The naturalist noted that there were "thousands of young of all sizes, from just hatched to nearly full-grown, all opening their bills and squawking most vociferously; the noise was shocking and the stench intolerable." Back aboard the *Ripley*, Audubon transplanted "[a] beautiful species of violet," which had been discovered by a member of his party, in the hope that it might last long enough for him to bring home to Lucy.[33]

When Audubon awoke on Thursday, July 18, a thick fog blanketed the harbor. "[T]he wind promised fair weather" for the day, although the temperature would ultimately not exceed 55°F.[34] Breakfast was served at 3:00 a.m., and then everyone but the cook piled into the three boats and headed for the mainland five miles away to begin another day of discovery.[35]

The parties separated, and Audubon and the captain set off through an extensive marsh, "the first we have seen in this country; the soil was wet, our feet sank in it, and walking was tiresome."[36] As they moved with caution over the oozing muck, Audubon flushed a female Surf Duck (Surf Scoter) from her cover. His shotgun leapt to his shoulder and, an instant later, the bird tumbled to the ground. Audubon marked the spot where she had exploded into the air, and located a nest, one he had longed for weeks to find. "It was entirely composed of withered and rotten weeds, the former being circularly arranged over the latter, producing a well-rounded cavity, six inches in diameter, by two and a half in depth. The borders of this inner cup were lined with the down of the bird, in the same manner as the Eider Duck's nest, and in it lay five eggs, the smallest number I have ever found in any duck's nest."[37] He retrieved the downed bird and placed the eggs carefully in his specimen bag.

Upon reaching dry land, the two men came to a scrubby wood and divided up to search for birds. Within minutes, Audubon heard the roar of a shotgun, followed by the captain's excited shout. After "much tugging and tearing" through the "stubborn tangled trees," the naturalist reached him and heard the agitated call of a Canada Titmouse (Boreal Chickadee).[38] The captain had collected its mate and discovered their nest after watching the two birds enter a hole "in a dead and rotten stump, about five feet from the ground."[39] The surviving parent—the male—continued to flit around its home, angrily scolding the two men, and flew so close to the naturalist that he was almost able to grab it. But eventually Audubon felled it with a blast of fine shot from his fowling piece. He captured the four young birds and retrieved the nest, which had been built within a cavity inside the decaying wood. "It was entirely composed of the finest fur of different quadrupeds, but principally of the great northern hare, so thickly and ingeniously matted throughout, that it looked as if it had been felted by the hand of man."[40] Audubon knew he would be the first ever to illustrate this species, a relative of the Black-headed Titmouse (Black-capped Chickadee), and he was eager to begin drawing the family of birds the following day.[41]

As Audubon and Capt. Emery left the woods, a female Canada Grous (Spruce Grouse) with her young crossed their path and, in a protective display, "ruffled her feathers like a barnyard hen and rounded within a few feet of us to defend her brood." Audubon considered sparing her, "but the enthusiastic desire to study nature prompted me to destroy her, and she was shot, and her brood secured in a few moments; the young very pretty and able to fly."[42] This was not, however, how he chose to describe his actions when it came time to write the species biography for his letterpress. Knowing full well how callous the truth would sound, he elected to give his readers a more palatable outcome:

> The affrighted mother on seeing us, ruffled up all her feathers like a common hen, and advanced close to us as if determined to defend her offspring. Her distressed condition claimed our forbearance, and we allowed her to remain in safety. The moment we retired, she smoothed down her plumage, and uttered a tender maternal chuck, when the little ones took to their wings, although they

were, I can venture to assert, not more than *one week old*, with so much ease and delight, that I felt highly pleased at having allowed them to escape.[43]

Audubon noted that the coloration of the adult bird differed from those he had collected a year before when he was visiting the Lincoln family in Dennysville, this one being grayer. Although this might have led some ornithologists to conclude the two were distinct species, he realized the color differences were a factor of geography.[44] Some species of birds have different color forms or "morphs" that prevail in certain parts of the country, a fact he had witnessed in his many wanderings.[45]

From the scrub forest, Audubon and the captain proceeded over a great expanse of savanna:

> Its mosses were so wet and spongy, that I never in my life before experienced so much difficulty in travelling. In many places the soil appeared to wave and bend under us like old ice in the spring of the year, and we expected at each step to break through the surface, and sink into the mire below. In the middle of this quagmire we met with a fine small grove of good-sized white birch trees, and a few pines full forty feet high, quite a novelty in this locality.[46]

Capt. Emery flushed a Fox-colored Sparrow (Fox Sparrow) from her nest, but "she fluttered off with drooping wings, and led him away from the spot, which could not again be found." The song of the male of this species filled the Labrador air. So, too, did the musical notes of the Ruby-crowned Wren (Ruby-crowned Kinglet). Audubon thought of this little olive-green sprite as a *"northern Humming-Bird"* and desperately wished he could discover its nest.[47]

The other parties had mixed success. One of the crew had shot a beautifully plumaged Pigeon Hawk (Merlin). Audubon had never seen a finer specimen. In addition, two Willow Grous (Willow Ptarmigan) were procured when they flew straight at the hunters in a futile attempt to protect their young.[48] John's party had landed on "a low rocky island at the bottom of a bay ten miles from the open sea, opposite the harbour of Little Macatina." This was a nesting place for close to two hundred pairs of the Common American Gull (Ring-billed Gull). However, none of their eggs, laid in a mass of seaweed on the rocks, had yet hatched. The party also saw a nesting pair of the Cayenne Tern (Caspian Tern), but they could not get close enough to collect a specimen.[49]

The competition among the members of the shore parties to return with the greatest prize was always intense and gave rise to occasional shenanigans, as Audubon later told his readers:

> Among our crew was a sailor, who was somewhat of a wag. He was a 'man-of-war's-man,' and had seen a good deal of service in our navy, an expert sailor,

perhaps the best diver I have seen, always willing to work hard, and always full of fun. This sailor and another had the rowing of our gig on an excursion after Grous and other wild birds. THOMAS LINCOLN and my son JOHN, managed the boat. The gig having landed on the main, the sailors, who had guns, went one way, and the young travelers another. They all returned, as was previously agreed upon, at the same hour, and produced the birds which they had procured. The sailor had none, and was laughed at. While rowing towards the Ripley, we heard cries of birds as if in the air; the rowing ceased, but nothing could be seen, and we proceeded. Again the sounds of birds were distinctly heard, but again none could be seen, and what seemed strange was, that they were heard only at each pull of the oars. The young men taxed the tar with producing the noises, as they saw him as if employed in doing so with his mouth; however, the thing still remained a mystery. Sometime after we had got on board, the provision basket was called for, and was produced by Master BILL, who, grinning from ear to ear, drew out of it two fine old Grous, and a whole covey of young ones, in all the exultation of one who had outwitted what he called his betters.[50]

When all of the men were back aboard the schooner, "wet, shivering with cold, tired, and very hungry," they sat down to dine on fresh lobsters the cook had managed to catch. Audubon noted that a full day of hunting by fourteen armed men had given them a mere nineteen birds. Everyone agreed that it would not be easy for anyone to live off the meager game found in this desolate land.[51]

Audubon's initial sense of wonder about Labrador had soured over the past month. During his ramble, he had gazed upon the surrounding terrain from one of the hills and pronounced it "the most extensive and dreary wilderness I ever beheld. It chilled the heart to gaze on these barrens of Labrador. Indeed I now dread every change of harbor, so horridly rugged and dangerous is the whole coast and country to the eye, and to the experienced man either of the sea or the land."[52]

On Friday, July 19, Edward Harris left New York with two friends, bound for Eastport, where he hoped to do some fishing and meet up with the naturalist upon the expedition's return.[53] In his satchel he carried a July 14 letter from Lucy, which she had composed as soon as she heard of Harris's travel plans from Nicholas Berthoud. She wanted her husband to have the latest, albeit troubling, news from London regarding Havell's demand for an increase in the cost of the prints. She had written to the engraver and told him that he would have to wait until Audubon's return before instituting these changes, and she understood from Victor that he had agreed to "go on as usual until then." But it was clear to her, as she told her husband, that Havell "does not seem to like anyone but yourself about the work." Victor was convinced they would have to find another printer to keep the costs for the next volume flat.[54]

In other news, Lucy reported that Nicholas was doing nothing to expand the number of New York subscribers. "[T]here are not many Dr Parkmans," she noted pointedly. The portrait of Audubon that Henry Inman had done was now hanging in the parlor. But Lucy had heard nothing further from the Baltimore painter, and her own portrait remained undone. Mostly, she told Audubon, she was just "counting the weeks till your probable and expected return."[55]

————

Audubon's plan to spend Friday at his drawing table was thwarted when rain and cold blasts sent waves into the harbor tossing the schooner "very disagreeably." The young men stayed onboard while Audubon struggled against the pitching of the vessel and began his illustration of the first two figures of the Canada Titmouse.[56] By evening he was ready for some exercise, and the weather had improved sufficiently that he and Capt. Emery, bundled up and wearing mittens against the cold, rowed to shore for a ramble:[57]

> We climbed over one rocky precipice and fissure after another, holding on to the moss with both hands and feet, for about a mile, when we came to the deserted hut of a Labrador seal-catcher. It looked snug outside, and we walked in; it was floored with short slabs, all very well greased with seal oil. A fire-oven without a pipe, a salt-box hung to a wooden peg, a three-legged stool for a table, and wooden box for a bedstead, were all its furniture. An old flour-barrel, containing some hundreds of seine floats, and an old seal seine, comprised the assets of goods and chattels. Three small windows, with four panes of glass each, were still in wooden hinges, for which I will be bound the maker had asked for no patent. The cabin was made of hewn logs, brought from the mainland, about twelve feet square, and well put together. It was roofed with birch bark and spruce, well thatched with moss a foot thick; every chink was crammed with moss, and every aperture rendered air-tight with oakum. But it was deserted and abandoned. The seals are all caught, and the sealers have nothing to do now-a-days. We found a pile of good hard wood close to the cabin, and this we hope to appropriate to-morrow. I found out that the place had been inhabited by two Canadians, by the chalk marks on the walls, and their almanac on one of the logs ran thus: L 24, M 25, M 26, I [J] 27, V 28, S 29, D 30, giving the first letter of the day of the week.[58]

The handwritten calendar referenced the days of the week in French: *lundi* (Monday), *mardi* (Tuesday), *mercredi* (Wednesday), *jeudi* (Thursday), *vendredi* (Friday), *samedi* (Saturday), and *dimanche* (Sunday). Based upon the corresponding numbers, which represented the days of the month, it would appear that the calendar was created in either September or December 1832.

As they carefully retraced their steps, high above the rolling waves below, Audubon watched in wonder as forty- to fifty-foot swells crashed furiously against the rocks beneath them. He turned to the captain and wondered aloud how a vessel would fare in these waters and was assured that none "could stand the sea we gazed upon at that moment."[59] Audubon thought "how dreadful it would be for any one to be wrecked on this inhospitable shore."[60]

Safely back aboard the *Ripley*, the naturalist sat and listened as John entertained the company with the sweet strains of his violin.[61] As the music drifted into the cold night air, Audubon's mind wandered, as it often did, to Lucy, fervently hoping she was happy and in good health.

Coolidge well recalled the evenings spent with the naturalist on the voyage. Decades later, one in particular stood out in memory:

> Audubon was always busily engaged at night measuring and drawing birds. He would work oftentimes until completely worn out. One night he turned to me from his labor and said, "I do not know what I would not give for a glass of good brandy!"
>
> "I think I can get you a little," I responded.
>
> "What!" exclaimed he in surprise. "You know where there is brandy?"
>
> When I left home my mother packed my chest with care. She left nothing out that she deemed useful or necessary. She did not even neglect to put in a bottle of brandy, which might serve as a medicine in the northern wilderness. I brought it out and Audubon sipped of it.
>
> "Don't touch this, any one of you!" he commanded. "It is for me only," and gradually he emptied the bottle.
>
> When I went aboard the schooner at Eastport I had taken along with me a box of snuff to present to the old gentleman, with whom I wanted to be on pleasant terms. When he threw that snuffbox of his overboard I did not feel like presenting the gift. Here in the solitude, however, it was different.
>
> "Now, how would you like a pinch of snuff?" I laughed.
>
> "As mortals seldom obtain all they wish," replied he, "they should study to be contented with what they can get."
>
> "But I can find you some snuff."
>
> "If you can you will be quite an angel." And when I brought the snuff to him he was as happy as a child on Christmas morning with a wealth of gifts in its lap.[62]

The weather improved markedly overnight, and Saturday, July 20, dawned clear and warm.[63] "The country of Labrador deserves credit for *one* fine day," Audubon wrote.[64] He compared the day to one that might be seen "in the Middle States about the middle of May."[65] At 3:30 a.m., as the young men headed out in the boats, he was already at his table[66] He drew steadily until 10:00 a.m., when he took advantage of the nice weather and left the schooner with Capt. Emery to visit the island next to their anchorage. Their bird observations proved somewhat of a disappointment. They saw only a Brown Lark (American Pipit), "some Gulls," and a couple of White-crowned Buntings (White-crowned Sparrows).

But Audubon discovered a nest of the Little Sandpiper (Least Sandpiper) and was as thrilled as he had been just days before on finding that of the Black-capped Warbler (Blackpoll Warbler). He had observed the adults fly from the vicinity of the nest and located it after treading carefully back and forth over the moss. He told his readers that his "pleasure would have been greatly augmented had any of my young companions been near; but the sailors who had rowed me to the foot of the rocks exhibited little more delight than they would have done on finding that their grog had been stopped."[67]

Evidently, more than a month in close proximity to America's greatest naturalist had yet to give the members of the crew an appreciation for ornithology. Audubon reported that the parent birds were noticeably distressed, "flew from the top of one crag to another in quick succession, and emitted notes resembling the syllables *peep*, *peet*, which were by no means agreeable to my feelings, for I was truly sorry to rob them of their eggs, although impelled to do so by the love of science, which affords a convenient excuse for even worse acts."[68] He clearly was not oblivious to the destruction he had often wreaked in pursuit of his grand mission.

Returning to the schooner, Audubon and Capt. Emery rowed past some small bays, and the naturalist pondered the source of "vast quantities" of stones that had been seemingly "thrown up by the sea" on the shoreline to a depth of ten to a hundred feet. He had observed these "immense beds of round stones of all sizes, some of very large dimensions rolled side-by-side and piled one upon another many deep" and "cast hundreds of yards on shore" in bays and inlets all along the coast. He now thought it most likely they had been deposited by icebergs from the Arctic which were driven onshore during winter storms.[69] These are actually raised beaches—ancient beaches that were raised above sea level as the land, compressed by the Laurentide Ice Sheet that covered this portion of eastern Canada during the Ice Age, gradually rebounded during the postglacial period through a process known as isostatic uplift.[70]

In the afternoon, Audubon was back onboard the *Ripley* and resumed working on his drawing of the Canada Titmice (Boreal Chickadees). He added another bird to the composition and placed the two adults and one juvenile on a branch of the Black Chokeberry (*Photinia melanocarpa*) with a trailing vine of what might be False Buckwheat (*Fallopia* sp.).[71] In the lower-right margin he inscribed the completion date and location: "Labrador July 20th 1833 Opposite Island by Macatine."[72] Meanwhile, Capt. Emery had gone fishing for cod and in under an hour had pulled in thirty-seven of the tasty fish.[73]

The young men were late returning to the vessel, and Audubon began to worry with the approach of evening, especially as the wind had picked up and the waters were angry. "Coolidge is an excellent sailor," he assured himself, as was John. But his son was "very venturesome; and Lincoln equally so," and he wondered why they were so long delayed. His anxiety grew by the minute until the boats came into view near 9:00 p.m. The explorers were exhausted and hungry, and Ingalls's mud-caked clothing cried out for the tale. Audubon commented later in his journal that, "tired as they are, they have yet energy to eat tremendously."[74] And, as they did so, Ingalls and his companions related the remarkable events of their excursion. Almost seventy years later, Ingalls would revisit that day in a letter to Audubon scholar Ruthven Deane:

Earlier than usual we set off for a long row to [the] mainland. We hauled the boat up high and men and boys scattered, but not so very far apart as to be out of reach in an emergency. A pretty extensive plain we had to cross to arrive at the foot of rather abrupt ledges in which a little way in, there were trees of a stunted growth. As to game, I think all our bags were empty as we found on assembling at the hour agreed upon at the foot of the hill. To cross the plain from where the most of us were there was one pretty large, damp looking area, with sparse grass and other growth upon it. This spot was not especially avoided by us, some were one side and some another. I happened to be the one who while going directly across found myself over my ankles; suddenly a step or two more and my knees were wet, in about two more I was down to my waist. Now, I said to George Shattuck, "This seems to be serious, the flat of my gun laid down does not help me and I am getting deeper." By this time Shattuck, Lincoln, Coolidge, and John Audubon were looking around for something to afford me a purchase. Fortunately, Tom found a bit of wood, some part of a ship, and by this I was helped out of the quag-mire, a sort of boggy mud sticking all over me and I was cold, but thankful. The jolly tars launched the boat and as there was a breeze, set the sail. In ten minutes the breeze became a wind, in ten minutes more the wind became a tempest; William Ingalls shivering and wet. Down came the sails, out the oars, I rowed but it did not warm me and I returned to [the] aft part of the boat. It blew harder and the waves were higher; again it blew great guns and the waves were higher yet. It seemed to me that more than a third of the keel was out of water at every recovery from a plunge. Stout four rowers; we came abreast of a little island and near enough, so that some one suggested camping there for the night. I noticed we did not gain a foot for as much as twenty minutes while trying to get by the island. At last we did move and got under the lee of some high land and then went ahead until we gained the ship. I think every one of us who were in the boat were conscious of being in great peril; there was a subdued expression prevailing, if I may say so, and when we struck the lee [of the *Ripley*] there were long drawn sighs; no word was spoken unconsciously. I verily believe there was a spirit of thanksgiving even by the roughest, careless, sailor boy, — and why not?[75]

The young men did not in fact return empty-handed, though the results of their daylong adventure were, according to the naturalist, "poor" as usual. Besides two Canada Grous (Spruce Grouse) in the process of molting, they brought back some White-throated Sparrows, Yellow-rumped Warblers, and a Green Black-capped Flycatcher (Wilson's Warbler). Of significantly more interest, they had collected a specimen of what Audubon called "the small Wood Peewee," a possible new species in the genus *Muscicapa*. However, he could not, as yet, be certain.[76] He had observed this bird during his own excursions, but the *Muscicapa* comprised a group of similar-appearing flycatchers that were difficult to separate in the field.[77] He would have to find others and compare them side by side to the species he knew before he would feel comfortable making that declaration.

In New York, Lucy had spent some time in the morning filling up the pages of a letter to Victor with the latest news. She intended to see it safely onboard the London packet set to sail that day. She regretted not providing her son with a list of the American subscribers as he had asked but anticipated that she would mail it on August 1. She explained that she had been "a good deal engaged with my needle." In any case, there was no reason to rush. "No *new* names need be looked for here unless your Papa was on the spot," she remarked, an allusion to Nicholas's wholesale indifference to promoting the sale of Audubon's work.[78]

Lucy's sister and brother-in-law Ann and Alexander Gordon were expected to arrive any day for a visit. Lucy had been asked to vacate her room for them and move to a higher floor, which served to reinforce her doubts about the degree to which she was really welcome there. Notwithstanding Eliza's continuing efforts to make her feel comfortable, "a preference to M^r & M^rs G is very manifest in the whole family from various motives," leading Lucy to think "they may desire my *room* rather than *myself*."[79]

She had been invited to travel to Niagara Falls and Saratoga Springs with her Boston friends Joshua Davis and his wife, "but as it would have cost me several hundred dollars more than I have to spare I did not join them at their request, otherwise it would have been a delightful trip to me." She could not help feeling constrained by her circumstances and anxious beyond words to have her husband back. But Lucy was not a woman to dwell on the negatives. Hardheaded and sensible, she was deeply thankful for the blessings she had. "I often pause when I am at work alone to reflect upon how many good things I have, and the best of all my *good children*, for that is a comfort beyond all others, and my good husband, and our rising from depressions and difficulty by our own efforts, all with the divine will and favour."[80] She could not help praying for that "divine will and favour" to protect Audubon and John as they made their way through the bleak and forbidding Labrador wilderness.

11

Portage Bay, Labrador

JULY 1833

*I write now from a harbor which has no name, for we have mistaken it for the one
we were looking for, which lies two miles east of this. But it matters little, for the coast
of Labrador is all alike, comfortless, cold and foggy.*

JOHN JAMES AUDUBON

The wind began blowing stoutly from the southwest, and the crew of the *Ripley*
made preparations to sail just after dawn on Sunday, July 21. By 5:00 a.m., the
schooner was underway, her destination the harbor of Great Mecattina, also known
as Mecattina Harbor (Havre du Mécatina), about twenty miles distant.[1] Blunt had
termed this "a safe, but small" anchorage formed by Mecattina Island and the mainland. It was situated approximately two and a half miles north-northeast of Cape
Mecattina (Cap du Gros Mécatina), the landmark toward which Capt. Bayfield and
his company had been working since leaving Wapitiguan Harbor two weeks before.
They had arrived at Cape Mecattina Point only that morning to begin their survey of
the area, and the British commander watched from one of the islands off the point
as the American schooner approached.[2]

However, once again, the *Ripley*'s pilot was as unfamiliar with this stretch of the
coastline as he had been of any other, and he took the vessel into Portage Bay (now
Mutton Bay), fully two miles short of her goal.[3] At the entrance to this harbor, named
for a portage long used by the Native Americans, stands "an island of moderate
height" that creates a broad and relatively deep channel to the west for vessels of any
size and a smaller eastern passage for vessels of lesser burden.[4] Whether or not Capt.
Emery knew of the pilot's error, the *Ripley* found a suitable mooring place within
the confines of the protected cove at around 10:00 a.m. and dropped her anchor.[5]

They were soon enveloped by fog, which had blown in with a southwest gale.
Nevertheless, the boats were launched, and Audubon joined his companions on an
excursion to the inner portion of the sheltered bay. They scattered a hundred or so
Eider Ducks (Common Eiders) and Red-breasted Mergansers, both females and
young, which had been floating together in large rafts near shore. The men beached
the boats and spent a couple hours searching for birds. Although there was nothing

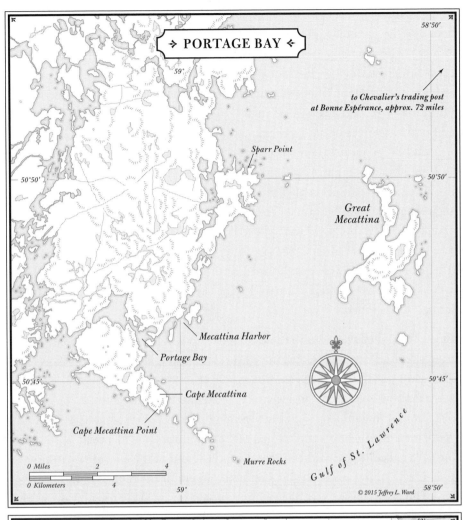

⟶ PORTAGE BAY ⟵

58°50'

*to Chevalier's trading post
at Bonne Espérance, approx. 72 miles*

59°

Sparr Point

50°50'   50°50'

*Great
Mecattina*

Mecattina Harbor

Portage Bay

50°45'   50°45'

Cape Mecattina

Cape Mecattina Point

Murre Rocks

Gulf of St. Lawrence

0 Miles   2   4
0 Kilometers   4

59°   58°50'

© 2015 Jeffrey L. Ward

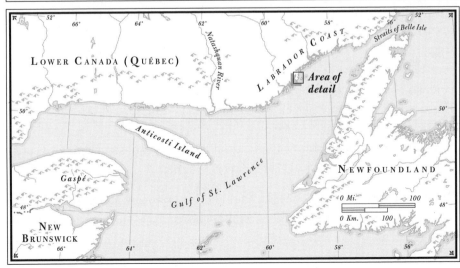

52°   66°   64°   62°   60°   58°   56°   52°

Natashquan River

LOWER CANADA (QUÉBEC)

LABRADOR COAST

Straits of Belle Isle

**Area of
detail**

50°   50°

Anticosti Island

NEWFOUNDLAND

Gaspé

Gulf of St. Lawrence

48°   48°

**NEW
BRUNSWICK**

0 Mi.   100
0 Km.   100

66°   64°   62°   60°   58°   56°

new, the naturalist observed a recently fledged small Wood Pewee, leading him to
believe that the parents might raise two broods in a season.[6]

When the shore party got back to the schooner, Audubon was pleased to find
the two British surveying craft alongside and Capt. Bayfield with his assistants onboard waiting for them. The naturalist invited them to stay and dine. According to
Bayfield, they "passed a very pleasant afternoon with him & his party." During the
course of their conversation, Bayfield mentioned that their provisions were running
low. Audubon graciously agreed to help. The appreciative commander purchased
from Capt. Emery "a barrel of ship-bread, and seventy pounds of beef," enough
to last three days. Audubon also insisted the naval officer accept a ham as a token
of their friendship and goodwill. In like fashion, Capt. Emery had some potatoes
added to the stores. Bayfield was relieved, telling his journal that this "set me quite
at ease on the score of provisions."[7]

That evening, Audubon and his men returned the visit onshore, where the surveyors had established their camp and were "living in great comfort," as Audubon
described in his journal:[8]

> [T]he tea-things were yet on the iron bedstead which served as a table, the
> trunks formed their seats, and the clothes-bags their cushions and pillows.
> Their tent was made of tarred cloth, which admitted neither wind nor rain. It
> was a comfortable camp, and we were pleased to find ourselves on the coast
> of Labrador in company with intelligent officers of the royal navy of England,
> gentlemen of education and refined manners; it was indeed a treat, a precious
> one. We talked of the wild country around us, and of the enormous destruc-
> tion of everything which is going on here, except of the rocks; of the aborigi-
> nes, who are melting away before the encroachments of a stronger race, as the
> wild animals are disappearing before them. Some one said, it is rum which is
> destroying the poor Indians. I replied, I think not, they are disappearing here
> from insufficiency of food and physical comforts, and the loss of all hope, as he
> loses sight of all that was abundant before the white man came, intruded on his
> land, and his herds of wild animals, and deprived him of the furs with which he
> clothed himself. Nature herself is perishing. Labrador must shortly be depopu-
> lated, not only of her aboriginal men, but of every thing and animal which has
> life, and attracts the cupidity of men. When her fish, and game, and birds are
> gone, she will be left alone like an old worn-out field.[9]

The following morning, Capt. Bayfield and his company struck camp to begin
their return journey to the *Gulnare*, still anchored back in Wapitiguan Harbor.
They planned to continue their survey work along the way, including a stop at Little

Mecattina Cove. It was a beautiful day, with a soft breeze blowing from the west, as Bayfield's company stopped by the *Ripley* at 6:00 a.m. to bid farewell to the Americans and to thank them again for their courtesies. They then made their way out to the storm-tossed waters of the gulf, which was agitated even yet by the force of the previous day's gale. The swells were so high that when the boats dipped between the walls of water, the men could see neither their companions in the other surveying craft nor the tops of the mountains on the mainland.[10]

Audubon and his party jumped into the *Ripley*'s three boats and followed a similar path out of the harbor but took a northeastern course toward Mecattina Harbor.[11] There the crew of a fifty-five-ton whaling schooner out of Cape Gaspé, New Brunswick, was at work boiling the blubber of a North Atlantic Right Whale (*Eubalaena glacialis*) to produce whale oil.[12]

Whalers called this species the "right" whale because for them it was the ideal cetacean to hunt. It traveled slowly through the cold northern waters and could be more easily pursued by an oar-powered whaleboat than could other types of whales. It also carried a thicker layer of blubber per unit weight than other species and had hundreds of baleen plates that could be turned into a variety of whalebone products. And, critically, it usually floated after it was killed.[13] Right whales, which frequented the Labrador coast only during the summer months, had been hunted there by Europeans for centuries.[14]

Audubon's group found the shore littered with chunks of blubber of various sizes which had been flensed from the carcass and were being tossed into the boiler, described by the naturalist as "a large iron vessel like a sugar-boiler."[15] The captain seemed "to be a good sensible man of his class."[16] He obliged Audubon's curiosity about the large barnacles growing on the throat of the whale by carving off some strips of skin from that area and offering them to the naturalist for closer inspection.[17]

Nearby, in a lush little valley, Audubon's group visited the humble cabin of Pierre Jean Baptiste Michaux, a French-Canadian trapper and sealer who had come to this bleak shore after deserting a French fishing boat ten or so years before.[18] A man "of moderate stature, firmly framed, and as active as a wild cat," Michaux told his guests that the land was free for the taking by anyone who wished to live there. He and a partner had constructed their single-room dwelling out of "stones plastered with mud to a considerable thickness" and had covered the low structure with a thatched roof of "weeds and moss." They slept on piles of deer skins and cooked on a Dutch stove that took up almost half of the living space.[19]

Outside, Michaux and his colleague had eight "Esquimaux dogs" that "were extremely gentle" and romped with the strangers as if they "were old acquaintances."

The two men used the dogs in the winter when hunting for seals along the ice packs. Harnessed to sledges, the dogs were trained to return to camp on their own with the dead seals, to push the seals off with their snouts, and then to return to the hunters—or so Michaux claimed. Audubon was skeptical. The sealer indicated he could sell the seal oil in Quebec for $0.50 per gallon.[20]

The two men also spent the winter trapping Black Foxes, Silver Foxes, Otters, Martens, and Sables, although the latter two were uncommon and becoming rarer with each passing year. Black Bears and Gray Wolves were also abundant at that season but were shot rather than trapped. Michaux described the wolves as "very ferocious and daring," and indicated they had killed his dogs on occasion, right on his doorstep. The animal skins found a ready market in Quebec, where the sealer's partner had taken them some weeks ago. He was expected to return shortly with their supplies for the coming winter.[21]

Audubon discovered that the valley where Michaux had made his spartan home was an ideal spot for birds. Situated on the southwestern side of the harbor and sheltered by the nearby island and the high hills of the mainland, which Bayfield estimated were not less than 750 feet above sea level, it was warmer and more luxuriant than the surrounding area.[22] The vegetation was flourishing, with "leaves twelve inches broad, and grasses three feet high."[23] There the naturalist saw his first Winter Wren since arriving in Labrador. He also encountered White-crowned Buntings (White-crowned Sparrows) "singing melodiously from every bush;" several Lincoln's Finches (Lincoln's Sparrows); a White-throated Finch (White-throated Sparrow); a Black-capped Warbler (Blackpoll Warbler); a Fox-colored Sparrow (Fox Sparrow); nesting Shore Larks (Horned Larks), although Audubon's party was unable to locate the nest; and even a Peregrine Falcon.[24]

By the afternoon, the shore parties were back aboard the *Ripley* when "a tremendous gale" blew in from the northwest with such force that the schooner's anchors dragged along the bottom of the harbor despite sixty fathoms—360 feet—of chain. However, the weather was not too rough for the hardy whalers, six of whom rowed over to visit and inspect Audubon's drawings. They promised to return the favor by letting Audubon see an entire whale should they kill one before he left.[25]

Although this day marked Shattuck's twentieth birthday, Audubon made no mention of it in his journal. The young Bostonian probably let the day pass without disclosing its significance, not wishing to draw undue attention to himself. Almost certainly, no one aboard the schooner knew that Shattuck was but a year away from inheriting a sizable estate through a bequest from his great-aunt Elizabeth Cheever Derby, who had been among the richest women in Boston when she died in 1831.[26]

The next day, Tuesday, July 23, Audubon accompanied his colleagues to Sparr Point, near what is now La Tabatière, located about seven and a half miles northeast of Portage Bay, to pay a call on a prosperous sealer and trader named Samuel Robertson.[27]

The forty-year-old Scotsman had been born in Stromness in the Orkney Islands in 1793 and arrived in Canada as a young man in the early 1800s. He went to work for the Labrador New Concern, a company that had acquired the principal seal- and salmon-fishing establishments along this part of the coast in 1808. When the company went into bankruptcy in 1820, Robertson raised £500 to purchase the post at Sparr Point and a second one farther up the coast at Bras d'Or, also known as Bradore Bay.[28]

According to Audubon, Robertson had lived and worked there for two decades. His first wife, Irene Boulay, died soon after they married. In approximately 1820, Robertson wed eighteen-year-old Mary Anne ("Anne") Chevalier, whose father, Louis Chevalier, owned the fishing station and trading post along the western side of the Esquimaux River, now St. Paul's River (Rivière Saint-Paul), up the coast at Bonne Espérance. Robertson subsequently sold the Bradore Bay station to his brother-in-law Capt. William Randall Jones, who was married to a second Chevalier daughter, Mary Sophia ("Sophia") Chevalier.[29]

On their approach to Sparr Point, Audubon observed "[s]everal neat-looking houses" situated across from the trading post where a schooner was docked at the wharf. In the bay lay "several small schooners at anchor." Audubon's party landed and was welcomed by the owner of the establishment, who quickly proved by both his manners and dress to be "a man of the world":[30]

> A handsome fur cap covered his dark brow, his clothes were similar to our own, and his demeanour was that of a gentleman. On my giving my name to him, he shook me heartily by the hand, and on introducing each of my companions to him, he extended the like courtesy to them also. Then, to my astonishment, he addressed me as follows: — "My dear Sir, I have been expecting you these three weeks, having read *in the papers* your intention to visit Labrador, and some fishermen told me of your arrival at Little Natasguan. Gentlemen, walk in."[31]

Robertson led the Americans to his home, a "neat and comfortable mansion" with an adjacent small vegetable garden. Audubon described Robertson's wife as an attractive woman and, though Labrador born and raised, she was "sufficiently accomplished to make an excellent companion to a gentleman." Their six children were "all robust and rosy."[32] The visitors sat down with their host to a fine luncheon of "bread, cheese, and a good port wine," apparently served by the Robertsons' twelve-year-old daughter Marie Anne ("Anne"), whom Audubon described as "a smart girl."[33] Robertson offered Audubon and his colleagues newspapers from the United States, and others from Quebec, as recent as June 25, which reported on

President Andrew Jackson's visit to Boston and the summer cholera epidemic then plaguing the southern and western states. The trader also showed them his "small but choice" library and took them on a tour of the grounds.[34]

Characteristically, Audubon peppered Robertson with questions. In particular, the naturalist wondered how this man of "liberal education" had come to turn his back on the world and make this remote and desolate land his home:[35]

> "The country around," said he, "is all my own, much farther than you can see. No fees, no lawyers, no taxes are *here*. I do pretty much as I choose. My means are ample, through my own industry. These vessels come here for seal-skins, seal-oil, and salmon, and give me in return all the necessaries, and indeed comforts, of the life I love to follow; and what else could *the world* afford me!" I spoke of the education of his children. "My wife and I teach them all that is *useful* for them to know, and is not that enough? My girls will marry their countrymen, my sons the daughters of my *neighbours*, and I hope all of them will live and die in the country!"[36]

Robertson employed only men who were white, and refused to trade with the Montagnais Indians, twenty of whom nonetheless hung around the post.[37] His business had netted £600 the previous year, a not insubstantial sum and comparable to what Audubon had been earning as a profit in the early days of his publication.[38] Even now, the schooner *Angelica* was at Robertson's wharf taking on a cargo of seal oil for Quebec, and more vessels would unquestionably follow in the waning days of summer. However, Audubon was convinced his host was ever relieved to see the last of these "hardy navigators" as the weather turned cold.[39]

Robertson's Esquimaux dogs, of which he had more than forty, would then provide the only means of transportation across the vast, frozen expanses of snow and ice. The sturdy Scot thought nothing of loading his large family on a sledge to travel to Esquimaux River for a visit with his wife's father, or even farther north to Bras d'Or near the Straits of Belle Isle, where his brother-in-law and his wife's sister lived. It was during this season, he said, that birds were most common. Willow Grous (Willow Ptarmigans) and Ivory Gulls were hunted and taken in substantial numbers.[40]

Robertson told Audubon that he had no love for the eggers and cared even less for the American fishermen, whom he accused of mistreating not only the local Indians and the white settlers, but the eggers as well. This had periodically led to violent altercations between these groups. The fishermen also received his ire for the way they destroyed nesting guillemots, killing the birds by the thousands merely for their feathers.[41]

Before leaving Sparr Point, the naturalist stopped and conversed with the captain of the *Angelica*, securing a promise from him to post a letter upon the vessel's arrival at Quebec. When he reached the *Ripley* later that day, Audubon picked up his pen while the young men of his party were off "Scrambling on the Mountains."[42]

In what appears to have been the first letter he had written to Lucy since leaving Eastport, Audubon offered only a brief account of their voyage to Labrador, saying it "was as prosperous a one as we could possibly have wished for." He told her of their arrival at American Harbor after eleven days at sea and of their chance meeting there with the "Men of Science" aboard the *Gulnare*, who were "not only polite but truly kind to us." This country was beyond his abilities to describe, or so he said, but he could not help giving Lucy a sense of what it was like to be here:[43]

> Scarcely Not a day that have We been without a constant fire—We see Snow in all our Walks—Musquitoes and Caraboo flies in thousands at every Step— a growth of Vegetation that would astound any European Gardner and yet not a *Cubic foot of Soil*!—Granit—Granit—Granit—Moss—Moss—Moss—and nothing but Granit Rock and Moss of thousands of Species.[44]

The mosses, he explained, were "Soft as Velvet, and as rich in Colour" but "at every Step you take You sink in up to Your Knees."[45]

He complained that they had not found the numbers of birds he had been told to expect. On this score they had been "deceived." Indeed, he continued, "Birds are rarer here than even on the St John's River of the Floridas at the exception of those of a few Species of which thousands may be seen on the outer Sea Islands." Nevertheless, he had discovered two new species, "one a *Fringilla* [Lincoln's Finch (Lincoln's Sparrow)] and the other *a Parus* [Canada Titmouse (Boreal Chickadee)]," drawn a total of seventeen compositions, and gathered information about the birds of this land that was "unprecedented," making him "feel well satisfied." Too, he expected to be able to write Episodes for the *Ornithological Biography* depicting the people he had met, "A Labrador Squater—the Cod Fisherman—the Eggers—the Sealers &c &c."[46]

Importantly, everyone in his party was well in health and disposition, and he declared that he was satisfied with both their vessel and the captain: "Our Vessel proves a fine sailor and a staunch one—Our Captain a first rate Man, Active, Industrious and pleasing in his Manners—Our Young Gentleman agree delightfully together and thus far I am pleas[ed] with the charge I have of them."[47]

The expedition would be leaving for Bras d'Or, approximately a hundred miles up the coast, "as soon as the wind will admit." The cod fishermen congregated there, and it was hoped one of them would have a letter for him from home. He was deeply anxious to hear from Lucy. He missed her terribly, a fact he was sure she knew. "[T]o tell thee how I long to see thee again would be superfluous," he noted.[48]

Audubon asked Lucy to copy his letter for his good friends John Bachman and Dr. Parkman, and to show it to Edward Harris and Nicholas Berthoud. He would be returning with eggshells for Nicholas, but, sadly, he had not yet obtained any fine animal furs for Eliza, the asking prices being too high.[49] Just that morning he had purchased the skin of a Cross Fox from Samuel Robertson for $3, but apparently he did not believe this would be suitable for Eliza's rich tastes.[50]

When the "Young Gentlemen" returned to the schooner, they were covered with the bites of caribou flies, which had become a scourge of late. These were either a species of horsefly (genus *Tabanus*), which are close to three-quarters of an inch in length, or deerfly (genus *Chrysops*), a little under half an inch long. Nasty and aggressive, the females of these species need a blood meal in order to produce their eggs. Lincoln, who was particularly susceptible to their attacks, "was actually covered with blood, and looked as if he had had a gouging fight with some rough Kentuckians."[51]

The mosquitoes were almost equally bad and bothered everyone, even aboard the vessel, causing Audubon to inadvertently sprinkle ink droplets on the pages of his journal that night as he tried to shoo them away.[52]

Shattuck took out the letter he had started to his father back in American Harbor on June 22 and added a brief update so that it could finally be mailed when the *Angelica* reached port. He assured his father of his "continued health and happiness" and said the company would be sailing "by the first fair wind" to Bonne Espérance, where he was expecting to find some Boston vessels carrying letters.[53] He too complained about the mosquitoes, adding in a postscript that they were "so troublesome that I can scarcely write."

Wednesday, July 24, was a "beautiful day" with a favorable wind, but the *Ripley* could not sail when its anchor became caught on a rock on the harbor bottom and could not be dislodged. With another day before them, Audubon's party divided up as usual and headed in different directions. Audubon joined his son and Lincoln on an excursion to one of the nearby islands in pursuit of two bears the naturalist had heard. However, the animals fled by swimming across the water to the mainland. Accordingly, Audubon turned his attention to the birds. While rambling over the moss-covered side of a high hill, he observed a female American Ring Plover (Semipalmated Plover) performing a distraction display, "trailing her wings and spreading her tail" to lure him away from her nest. This of course convinced him that her nest was near, but he could not locate it. He also watched Shore Larks (Horned Larks) running "as nimbly as can be imagined" over the moss. He was equally sure that their nest was hidden in the vicinity, but again he was unable to discover their secret.[54]

Meanwhile, Coolidge, Shattuck, and Ingalls had left with some crewmen for the Murre Rocks, "several low islands, destitute of vegetation, and not rising high above the waters" a few miles southeast of Cape Mecattina Point.[55] The islands were covered with thousands upon thousands of Foolish Guillemots (Common Murres), each caring for a single chick or egg:

> As you approach these islands, the air becomes darkened with the multitudes of birds that fly about; every square foot of the ground seems to be occupied by a Guillemot planted erect as it were on the granite rock, but carefully warming its cherished egg. All look toward the south, and if you are fronting them, the snowy white of their bodies produces a very remarkable effect, for the birds at some distance look as if they were destitute of head, so much does that part assimilate with the dark hue of the rocks on which they stand. On the other hand, if you approach them in the rear, the isle appears as if covered with a black pall.[56]

With orders to retrieve a few dozen eggs, the crewmen went off in one direction and the young men went in another.[57] The guillemots panicked as the intruders made their way over the island, and "scrambled off in such a hurried, confused, and frightened manner" that they "could scarcely take to wing." The smell of rotting eggs, bird excrement, and decomposing feathers was so vile that Coolidge and Ingalls were soon "quite sick." Coolidge managed to shoot a female White-winged Crossbill, and Shattuck wounded two Common Gannets (Northern Gannets) before ending their misery with a stick.[58] When the young men returned to the boat with their prizes, they could only stop and stare. The craft was filled almost to the gunwales with eggs, close to 1,500 in all.[59]

Coolidge and his companions positioned themselves gingerly in the few remaining spaces, and the crew rowed back to the schooner. Those onboard had a good laugh when they saw the enormous number of eggs that had been collected. The only excuse the embarrassed tars could muster was that they had forgotten their instructions. Many of the eggs were addled, which was determined by placing them in a tub of water and waiting for a minute or two to see which floated even a little and which sank to the bottom.[60] The former were discarded over the side, while the latter, still fresh, would be cooked and eaten.

With the anchor finally freed from the rocky bottom, everything was now ripe for departure. But a cold fog had moved in from the gulf and ended any hope the *Ripley* would sail that day.[61] Audubon, anxious to see a different horizon, would have to wait for yet another dawn.

12

Bras d'Or, Labrador

JULY–AUGUST 1833

This Bras d'Or is the grand rendezvous of almost all the fishermen,
that resort to this coast for codfish.
JOHN JAMES AUDUBON

When Audubon climbed up on deck on the morning of Thursday, July 25, the *Ripley*'s crew was already making preparations to bid farewell to Portage Bay.[1] Before 5:00 a.m., they were again headed out into the gulf with a favorable wind, their destination Chevalier's settlement at Esquimaux River, now St. Paul's River (Rivière-Saint-Paul). Audubon recorded in his journal that it was only forty-seven miles up the coast, but it was actually closer to seventy. They managed to sail only about thirty of that before the wind died.[2]

Common Gannets (Northern Gannets), soaring aloft on black-tipped pinions high above the sea, would fold their wings and plunge into the water after schools of Capelin (*Mallotus villosus*) near the surface. Audubon decided to release three of the Foolish Guillemots (Common Murres) onboard so that he could see how they behaved. "Two fluttered on top of the water for twenty yards or so, then dove, and did not rise again for fully a hundred yards from the vessel. The third went in head-foremost, like a man diving, and swam *under the surface* so smoothly and so rapidly that it looked like a fish with wings."[3]

Later in the day, the adventurers found themselves beset with "severe squalls" and "a tremendous sea" that "threatened to shake our masts out."[4] Audubon would give his readers a taste of what it was like to sail into such a tempest:

Stay on the deck of the Ripley by my side this clear and cold morning. See how swiftly scuds our gallant bark, as she cuts her way through the foaming billows, now inclining to the right and again to the left. Far to the east, dark banks of low clouds indicate foul weather to the wary mariner, who watches the approach of a northern storm with anxiety. Suddenly the wind changes; but for this he has prepared; the topsails are snugged to their yards, and the rest are securely reefed. A thick fog obscures all around us. The waters, suddenly checked in their former course, furiously war against those which now strike them in front.

The uproar increases, the bark is tossed on every side; now a sweeping wave rushes against the bows, the vessel quivers, while along her deck violently pour the waters, rolling from side to side, seeking for a place by which they may escape.[5]

That evening, at around 8:00 p.m., the *Ripley* was being pitched about in the waters off the harbor of Bonne Espérance, near Chevalier's fishing station, but Mr. Godwin had neither the knowledge nor the confidence to pilot her in. With the roiling seas crashing against the nearby rocks, Capt. Emery proposed they continue onward to Bras d'Or. Audubon relented, the specter of shipwreck an ever-present fear. "The coast here," he later explained, "like all that we have seen before, was dotted with rocky islands of all sizes and forms, and against which the raging waves dashed in a frightful manner, making us shudder at the thought of the fate of the wretched mariners who might be thrown on them."[6]

The following morning, Audubon awoke to find the schooner anchored in an expansive bay off the entrance to the harbor of Bras d'Or, situated between a large, low-lying granite mass called Ledges Island and the mainland to the east.[7] A fine mist floating just off the water obscured the shoreline and the many vessels already safely anchored nearby.[8] To the northeast, the three hump-backed Bradore Hills could be seen several miles inland. The tallest of these would be measured by Capt. Bayfield's surveyors at an elevation of 1,264 feet.[9] Across the Straits of Belle Isle the western coast of Newfoundland rose up to summits high above the clouds.[10]

Once again Godwin was helpless to guide them despite his years of fishing these waters, so Capt. Emery ordered the vessel's ensign raised to seek the assistance of a capable pilot. To Audubon's great pleasure, a Hampton boat soon approached with Capt. William Billings of Eastport at the helm.[11] Billings piloted the *Ripley* into the broad harbor, which was covered with "a flotilla of about one hundred and fifty sail, principally fore-and-aft schooners, a few pickaxes, etc., mostly from Halifax and the eastern portions of the United States."[12] Cod fishermen had congregated there in large numbers beginning in mid-July when, with warming days, the last vestiges of ice that had earlier filled the harbor finally disappeared.[13] The fish had moved along the coast from Natashquan toward the straits as the summer progressed, and the boats had followed them there.[14] This would be the last opportunity for the fishermen to fill their holds with cod, caught by the thousands using seines or Capelin-baited hooks and then cleaned, salted, and dried onshore before the vessels would return heavily laden to port.[15] According to Capt. Bayfield, the average haul per vessel amounted to fifteen hundred quintals, the equivalent of 168,000 pounds.[16]

To the voyagers on the *Ripley*, who had grown accustomed to the emptiness and solitude of the barren Labrador coastline, the harbor of Bras d'Or presented a kalei-

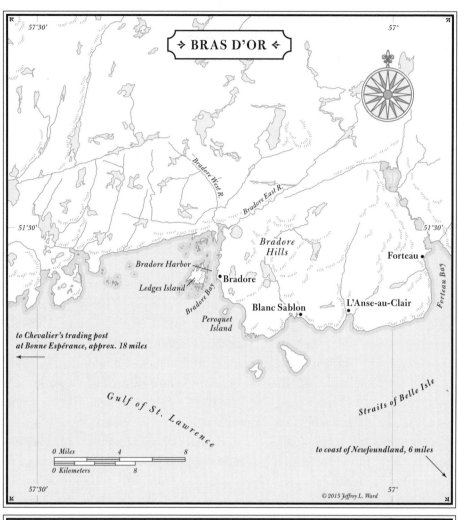

⟶ BRAS D'OR ⟵

57°30'   57°

—Bradore West R.

Bradore East R.

51°30'   51°30'

Bradore
Hills

Forteau •

Bradore Harbor ⟶

• **Bradore**

Forteau Bay

Ledges Island

Bradore Bay

Blanc Sablon

L'Anse-au-Clair

•

Peroquet
Island

to Chevalier's trading post
at Bonne Espérance, approx. 18 miles

⟵

Gulf of St. Lawrence

Straits of Belle Isle

to coast of Newfoundland, 6 miles

⟶

0 Miles   4   8

0 Kilometers   8

57°30'   57°

© 2015 Jeffrey L. Ward

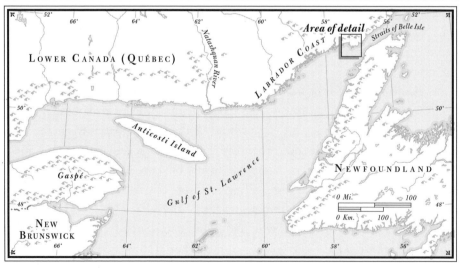

52°   66°   64°   62°   60°   58°   56°   52°

Area of detail

Straits of Belle Isle

LOWER CANADA (QUÉBEC)

Natashquan River

LABRADOR COAST

50°   50°

Anticosti Island

NEWFOUNDLAND

Gaspé

Gulf of St. Lawrence

48°   48°

0 Mi.   100

0 Km.   100

NEW
BRUNSWICK

66°   64°   62°   60°   58°   56°

doscope of bustle and noise.[17] Hampton boats filled to the gunwales moved between the fishing grounds a mile away and the schooners anchored in the harbor. As soon as the catch was tossed onboard, the boats would return for yet another load. The voices of the fishermen and their "Billingsgate slang, and stories, and songs" filled the crisp, salt-tinged air.[18] So too did the revolting odor of a pile of 1,500 rotting seal carcasses piled in heaps on the shore.[19]

As was his wont, Audubon eagerly scanned the skies and water to see what birds might be found about this new mooring. He had observed a small species of gull, as yet unidentified, as they entered the harbor, as well as two species of jaegers of different sizes. Although he was eager to jump into one of the boats with his colleagues to begin exploring the area, he chose to stay onboard and add the images of two female White-winged Crossbills to the drawing he had earlier done of two males.[20]

The "Young Gentlemen" rowed to shore after breakfast to introduce themselves to the proprietor of the sealing station, Capt. William Randall Jones, "a rough, brown" Nova Scotian of forty-one years of age who was "the lord of this portion of Labrador."[21] Jones greeted them politely and, like his brother-in-law Samuel Robertson, knew of the expedition and had been anticipating their arrival. He sat down and patiently answered their questions about the local birdlife, of which he was quite knowledgeable. He indicated that numerous species bred inland along the margins of the widespread lakes and ponds, and near the "swampy deserts at the head waters of the rivers." These included four to five species of grouse, the Velvet Duck (White-winged Scoter), Old Squaw (Long-tailed Duck), Harlequin Duck, and Wild Goose (Canada Goose), among others.[22]

The young men banded together for their initial foray into the surrounding terrain, a landscape as bleak and bare as elsewhere along the coast but still covered here and there with patches of snow.[23]

They succeeded in collecting eight Lesser Red-polls (Common Redpolls), both adults and immatures, which congregated in the low bushes that bordered the ponds and brooks. In addition, they returned to the vessel with several Savannah Finches (Savannah Sparrows) and White-crowned Sparrows. A female Canada Grous (Spruce Grouse) with her young, all capable of flight, were flushed and "alighted on trees and bushes" nearby, but "they were so trusting" that John forbade his colleagues to shoot them. The party could not get a shot at a solitary Willow Grous that took flight upon seeing them at a distance and then flew off "with a loud, cackling note, but no whirr of the wings" when the men came into view a second time.[24]

They also observed an enormous brown-plumaged eagle about three hundred yards off that had a wingspan so great they concluded it must be a female Washington Eagle.[25] First described by Audubon, who named it in honor of George Washington, the "Bird of Washington" was reputedly larger than either the Bald Eagle or the Golden Eagle, the only two eagles endemic to North America today. Audubon procured and drew a male Washington Eagle near Henderson sometime around 1819 and claimed that it weighed fourteen and a half pounds and had a wingspan of ten feet, two inches.[26] Birds of prey are reverse sexually dimorphic, which means that the females exceed the males in size and weight—in this group by as much as twenty-five percent. Thus, a female Washington Eagle would have been proportionately larger than the male that Audubon collected. By comparison, the Bald Eagle—the largest of the North American eagles and the only sea eagle like the Washington Eagle—has a maximum wing span of only eight feet.[27]

However, this species is one of several Audubon painted for his publication which ornithologists have questioned for well over a century.[28] No independent evidence of a third North American eagle has ever been found, and ornithologists are convinced that Audubon simply confused a brown-plumaged, immature northern Bald Eagle for this supposed new species.[29]

Certainly, Audubon and his contemporaries faced considerable challenges in the first half of the 19th century in linking immature birds to adults of the same species, due to the birds' often disparate plumages. In the case of the Bald Eagle, the birds do not acquire their distinctive white heads and tails until their fourth or fifth year. Considering that immature Bald Eagles are somewhat larger than their parents, with northern migrants from the Arctic region surpassing the size of their southern counterparts, it is easy to see how Audubon could have been misled.[30] But there are a number of problems with this explanation. For one, it simply does not square with the measurements the naturalist allegedly recorded at the time he obtained the specimen, or with the size of the image he drew.[31] Further, many of the features of the Washington Eagle are wholly inconsistent with those of an immature Bald Eagle.[32]

Audubon's credibility as a scientist has suffered over the years due to his marked tendency to embellish the truth, particularly when it came to himself. However, it is important to separate the two. He was serious-minded about his craft, especially after he committed himself to his "Great Work" in 1820, and his field notes remain a valuable source of information to ornithologists today. No less an authority than Robert Cushman Murphy, the former Lamont Curator of Birds at the American Museum of Natural History in New York, knowingly remarked: "Many ornithologists have had the experience of making some new discovery in bird behavior, which has proved unknown likewise to their most erudite colleagues, only to find that keen-eyed old Audubon had minutely described the same phenomenon a hundred years before!"[33]

As an ornithological illustrator, Audubon had no equal during his lifetime. He took great pride in the exactitude of his drawings. Ever since developing his double-grid system of capturing the images of birds on paper, he had always drawn his sub-

PLATE XXVI. *Double-crested Cormorants were widespread breeders on offshore islands along the Labrador coast. Audubon evidently illustrated this adult while the* Ripley *was anchored at Wapitiguan Harbor, Labrador, in July 1833.*

PLATE XXVII. *This pair of nesting Puffins (Atlantic Puffins) was drawn by Audubon at Wapitiguan Harbor, Labrador, in early July 1833.*

PLATE XXVIII. *The summer-plumaged Red-necked Divers (Red-throated Loons), swimming, and the chick to their left were illustrated by Audubon from specimens collected during the Ripley's stay at Wapitiguan Harbor, Labrador, in July 1833. The winter-plumaged bird, far left, was added later.*

PLATE XXIX. *This family of Willow Grous (Willow Ptarmigan) was drawn by Audubon in July 1833 at Wapitiguan Harbor, Labrador.*

PLATE XXX. *Audubon illustrated the summer-plumaged Great Northern Diver, or Loon (Common Loon), right, from a specimen collected by his party near Wapitiguan Harbor, Labrador, in July 1833. The bird to the left is a winter bird, illustrated later.*

PLATE XXXI. *The female Common Cormorant (Great Cormorant), left, and her two young were drawn by Audubon in July 1833 at Wapitiguan Harbor, Labrador. He added the male, right, at a later date.*

PLATE XXXII. *Audubon originally planned for The Birds of America to include his illustrations of the eggs of many of the birds shown in the work. This drawing, prepared by Audubon during the Labrador expedition, depicts the eggs, from left, of the Black-capped Warbler (Blackpoll Warbler), Brown Lark (American Pipit), Savannah Finch (Savannah Sparrow), and White-crowned Bunting (White-crowned Sparrow).*

PLATE XXXIII. *Audubon and Capt. Henry Emery collected the specimens
of the Canada Titmouse* (Boreal Chickadee) *during an inland excursion near
Little Mecattina Island, Labrador, in July 1833.*

PLATE XXXIV. *Ornithologists maintain that Audubon's Washington Eagle, drawn from a specimen he collected in Kentucky in 1819 and named for George Washington, was merely an immature Bald Eagle. However, the illustrated bird is much larger and has other distinguishing features.*

PLATE XXXV. *These Lesser Red-polls* (Common Redpolls) *were drawn by Audubon at Bras d'Or, Labrador, in July 1833.*

PLATE XXXVI. *Audubon drew this family of Shore Larks (Horned Larks) during the Ripley's stay at Bras d'Or, Labrador, in July 1833.*

PLATE XXXVII. *This female Pomarine Jager (Pomarine Jaeger) was collected by John W. Audubon's party during an excursion to Blanc Sablon, Labrador, in late July 1833. Audubon illustrated the bird aboard the Ripley a few days later.*

PLATE XXXVIII. *The Esquimaux Curlews (Eskimo Curlews) that once fattened themselves on the Crowberries growing along the Labrador coast before beginning their long migratory journey to South America, are now believed to be extinct. Audubon illustrated this pair in early August 1833 at Bras d'Or, Labrador.*

PLATE XXXIX. *Audubon believed that these Labrador Falcons* (Gyrfalcons), *which he illustrated in August 1833 at Bras d'Or, Labrador, represented a new species. Rather, they are examples of the bird's brown, or dark, color phase.*

PLATE XL. *In August 1833, Audubon's party collected Pine Grosbeaks during their visit to St. George's Bay, Newfoundland, and Audubon may have illustrated them during the journey home.*

PLATE XLI. *Audubon had difficulty classifying one of the flycatchers that he found in Labrador and Newfoundland and apparently relied upon William Swainson's earlier illustration, left, in drawing this image of the Short-legged Pewee (Western Wood-Pewee), right.*

jects life sized. The "Bird of Washington" that he illustrated for *The Birds of America* was far too large to be an immature Bald Eagle.[34] Also, except in their earliest natal plumage, young Bald Eagles invariably show some evidence of white feathering in their tails and beneath their wings, a feature that is wholly absent in Audubon's written description and illustration of this bird.[35] Further, Bald Eagles, regardless of age, do not show the uniform scaling of the tarsus—the portion of the lower leg between the ankle and the talons—that Audubon illustrated on the Washington Eagle. Finally, the Washington Eagle's cere—the fleshy growth over the nostrils on the beak—is different from that of the other North American eagles.[36]

Moreover, Audubon knew the Bald Eagle, including its immature plumage phase, especially well. In his day, the species was much more common than it is today. He was also familiar, though to a lesser extent, with the Golden Eagle.[37] He firmly believed this newly discovered bird to be a completely separate species. His own experience with the Washington Eagle was limited, which alone suggests it was unique.[38] Audubon first observed the bird near Grand Tower while he ascended the Mississippi River in February 1811.[39] A few years later he discovered a breeding pair that had built their nest on a cliff near the mouth of the Green River in Kentucky, but he was then unable to collect either the adults or their young. He had to wait another two years, until 1819, before he shot the bird near Henderson.[40] Audubon supposedly took careful measurements of its features before drawing it in pastels for his portfolio.[41] A few months later, in January 1820, he saw a pair flying in the vicinity of the Falls of the Ohio.[42] He saw another on November 15, 1820, as he was descending the Ohio River by flatboat on his way to New Orleans.[43] Had this been merely an immature Bald Eagle from the north, one would expect that Audubon would have seen a great number of them among the large congregation of Bald Eagles, including northern birds, that wintered along the Ohio and Mississippi rivers.[44]

Is it possible then that Audubon discovered a remnant species, a holdover of the megafauna that once dominated Ice Age North America, just as the species was about to vanish into extinction? Or, rather, is there a more mundane explanation tied to his duplication of an earlier drawing?

Audubon's drawing of the "Bird of Washington" appears in *The Birds of America* as Plate 11, the first image printed by the Havells after Audubon transferred the publication to London in 1827.[45] Perhaps significantly, the image Robert Havell Jr. engraved in copper was not taken from Audubon's 1819 drawing but from a mixed-media copy the naturalist drew during his stay in New Orleans in 1822.[46] By that time, Audubon had improved his technique considerably, and sought to redo many of his earlier pastel drawings that he now found wanting. It would be hard to imagine that in copying his previous composition Audubon would have magnified the bird's scale—unless he no longer had the drawing he had originally made and was attempting to redraw the bird from memory. There is no evidence of this in his writings, but it would explain much.

In judging the legitimacy of Audubon's claim, it is worth noting that specimens of the Washington Eagle were being displayed at the time in museums in Philadelphia and Boston. However, Harvard naturalist Thomas Nuttall, a friend of Audubon's who acknowledged the existence of the species and noted that individual birds had been seen during the winter around Cambridge, Massachusetts, refused to accept Audubon's size measurements.[47] In Nuttall's 1832 publication, *A Manual of the Ornithology of the United States and of Canada*, he wrote:

> The quantity of food consumed by this enormous bird is very great, according to the account of those who have had them in confinement. Indeed they appear almost always plump and fat. Mr. Audubon's male bird weighed 14½ pounds avoirdupois. One in a small museum in Philadelphia (according to the account of my friend Mr. C. Pickering), also a male, weighed much more, by which difference it would appear that they are capable of becoming exceedingly fat; for the length of this bird was about the same as that of Audubon, 3 feet 6 or 7 inches. The width, however, was only about 7 feet, agreeing pretty nearly with a specimen now in the New England Museum; so that I must necessarily believe that the measure, given by Mr. Audubon, of 10 feet 2 inches is a typographical error, and should be probably 7 feet 2 inches.[48]

If these large eagles identified at the time as Washington Eagles indeed sported wingspans of just over seven feet, then they would fall well within the range recorded for the Bald Eagle. Of course, this would still not explain the various differences in plumage and physical characteristics between the Washington Eagle and the Bald Eagle which Audubon had noted. Ultimately, one is left with uncertainty and a lack of proof for the existence of a race of giant North American sea eagles. The discovery of any new species requires concrete evidence of its existence, and here there simply is not enough to validate Audubon's assertion that his Washington Eagle was distinct from a juvenile Bald Eagle. Audubon's drawing, even buttressed by his supposed measurements, is certainly intriguing. But, absent a preserved skin or a stuffed specimen, neither of which exists, it is not scientifically conclusive.

The Washington Eagle observed by the "Young Gentlemen" disappeared over the Labrador hills, and Audubon was unable to confirm their sighting when he made his way to shore later that day with some of his colleagues.[49] He was told by those to whom he spoke that eagles were rarely seen in the vicinity. Apparently no one was familiar with the Bald Eagle, although today it is known to breed along the Labrador coast.[50]

The naturalist made his way to the home of Capt. Jones to pay his respects but learned that both the gentleman and his wife, Sophia, age thirty-three, were out for a stroll.[51] They returned shortly and invited the party in for a visit. Capt. Jones evidently did not stay long, being obliged to return to the harbor, where he was busy caulking a schooner.[52]

The house, which had been built from materials shipped from Quebec, was receiving an exterior coat of whitewash and was still unfinished inside. A large Dutch stove "formed a principal feature of the interior." At first the usually personable naturalist did not warm to his hostess. He felt that she was putting on airs, something he genuinely disliked. Aware of his background, she pretended to know something of the fine arts, pointing to several cheap framed prints on her walls that she believed to be "*elegant* Italian pictures" although she had purchased them for a shilling apiece from an Italian peddler who had a trunkload. Audubon considered them "vile."[53]

However, his impression of the woman abruptly changed when she rescued a Siskin (Pine Siskin) that one of her children had captured and was tormenting. "[S]he rose from her seat, took the little fluttering thing from the boy, kissed it, and gently launched it into the air."[54]

Over fresh milk "poured out in clean glasses," Sophia proceeded to describe her interest in music and her family's skill at playing an instrument of theirs that was currently away in Europe to be repaired. Everyone in the family "could use it with ease," she said, and when they grew tired of playing it one of their servants would take over:[55]

> Rather surprised at the extraordinary powers of this family of musicians, I asked what sort of an instrument it was, when she described it as follows: —
> "Gentlemen, my instrument is large, longer than broad, and stands on four legs, like a table. At one end is a crooked handle, by turning which round, either fast or slow, I do assure you we make most excellent music." The lips of my young friends and companions instantly curled, but a glance from me as instantly recomposed their features. Telling the fair one that it must be a hand-organ she used, she laughingly said, "Ah, that is it; it is a hand-organ, but I had forgot the name, and for the life of me could not recollect it."[56]

After a pleasant stay, Audubon and his group thanked Sophia for her hospitality and said their goodbyes. They returned to the field to see what new birds might be discovered. Hiking through the "high table lands" of sandstone located inland from their anchorage, an area Audubon described as "arid, poor, and rocky," the naturalist came upon the nest of a Shore Lark (Horned Lark). This was a treasure he had sought in vain for the past several weeks, and he was thrilled by the discovery. "[I]t was embedded in moss, so exactly the colour of the bird, that when the mother sat on it, it was impossible to distinguish her." The land they crossed was marked by small streams bordered by a luxuriant growth of grasses and weeds. In one he found some "fine trout."[57]

A "tremendous gale" roared in during the night and blew all day on Saturday, July 27.[58] With several specimens of the Lesser Red-poll (Common Redpoll) to draw, Audubon was content. He transferred the image of the birds from his mounting board to the paper before him while John was busy nearby skinning fourteen small birds the shore parties had collected. Other members of the company spent the morning in search of one of the pet Great Black-backed Gulls that had fallen over the side during the night as the schooner "rolled heavily" in the tempest. They found it on shore "shivering by the lee of a rock."[59] When it was restored to its brethren, the birds exchanged "mutual congratulations, which were extremely animated." Audubon had formed an attachment to the birds and was no doubt pleased at their reunion. John's pointer probably had a different view. An animal "of a gentle and kindly disposition," Dash was tormented by the gulls, which "would tease him, bite him, and drive him fairly from the deck into the cabin."[60]

Around midday, Capt. Jones came onboard the *Ripley* to join the naturalist and his companions for dinner. Audubon thought him "an excellent fellow":[61]

> Like his brother-in-law, he had seen much of the world, having sailed nearly round it; and, although no scholar, like him, too, he was disgusted with it. He held his land on the same footing as his neighbours, caught seals without number, lived comfortably and happily, visited his father-in-law and the scholar, by the aid of his dogs, of which he kept a great pack, bartered or sold his commodities, as his relations did, and cared about nothing else in the world. Whenever the weather was fair, he walked with his dame over the moss-covered rocks of the neighbourhood; and during winter, killed ptarmigans and karaboos, while his eldest son attended to the traps, and skinned the animals caught in them. He had the only horse that was to be found in that part of the country, as well as several cows; but, above all, he was kind to every one, and every one spoke well of him.[62]

Audubon was particularly intrigued by the captain's reports of the winter ptarmigans. Jones said that at this season large numbers of Rock Grous (Rock Ptarmigan) could be found in the hills surrounding Bras d'Or. These birds, which Audubon had never seen before, mingled with enormous flocks of Willow Grous (Willow Ptarmigan). The birds were so abundant that "a hundred or more could be shot in a day." Salted and stored, the birds made up a part of the family's summer fare.[63]

As they ate, Jones also described the method of winter travel by Esquimaux dog.[64] A team was made up of an odd number of seven or more animals, depending on the distance or load. Each dog was capable of pulling two hundred pounds and could travel as fast as five or six miles per hour. "The leader, which is always a well-broken dog, is placed ahead of the pack, with a draft line of from six to ten fathoms in length, and the rest with successively shorter ones, until they come to within eight feet of the sledge. They are not coupled, however, as they are usually represented in engravings, but are attached each loose from all others, so that when they are in motion, travelling, they appear like a flock of partridges all flying loosely, and yet all the same course."[65]

The dogs knew the paths they commonly traveled to other homes in the area and, with an unerring sense of direction, could be counted upon to stay the course even during the fiercest blizzards. Men who had ignored their dogs' superior instincts had been known to perish in the frozen wastes.[66] Indeed, according to Audubon, Jones's fourteen-year-old son had died only a few years before when a servant with whom he was traveling by sled turned the dogs from their path in a snowstorm. By the time the man realized his mistake, it was too late to save the boy, who died of hypothermia.[67]

It is a heart-wrenching tale, but one for which independent evidence is lacking. The family genealogy includes only one son, Louis Lloyd Jones, who reached the age of fourteen prior to Audubon's 1833 visit. Louis was the eldest child, born on April 1, 1817, the same year his parents wed. However, Louis lived to a respectable age of seventy, dying in Lewis Cove, Quebec, in 1887. A younger son, Alfred Randal Jones, died in 1844 at the age of fourteen, but this was more than a decade after Audubon heard the story.[68]

It seems inconceivable that Capt. Jones would have told Audubon a tall tale about a nonexistent child for the purpose of emphasizing a point, especially when the naturalist might then have expressed his condolences to Jones's wife. At the same time, Audubon had utterly no motivation to concoct such a story between the covers of his journal. There are a number of possible explanations for the confusion. Perhaps Audubon misunderstood Jones, who was speaking of a godson or of another family's child. Or perhaps Jones had another son who was born prior to his marriage to Sophia who is missing from the family genealogy. This is all speculation, so the mystery remains.

With dinner completed, Capt. Jones returned to shore while Capt. Emery led the "Young Gentlemen" across country on a four-mile, rain-soaked ramble to Blanc Sablon, a settlement near the entrance to the Straits of Belle Isle named for its white, sandy beaches. According to Audubon, the English-speaking fishermen at Bras d'Or referred to the area as "Nancy Belong."[69] The young men found a number of empty nests built on the top of "low tangled fir-bushes" along the way. At the fishing station at Blanc Sablon, John spoke to the English clerk and learned that these nests were those of the Pied Duck (Labrador Duck).[70]

Audubon had illustrated a male and female of this species of sea duck during his stay in Boston the previous fall from a pair that had been sent to him by U.S. Senator Daniel Webster, who had shot them on "the Vineyard Islands," presumably Martha's Vineyard.[71] The male was particularly striking in appearance, with a contrasting black body and white head, chest, and wings.[72] The naturalist was fortunate to have obtained the specimens since these birds were becoming increasingly uncommon. Audubon did not spot a single one during the expedition.[73] Over the next forty years, the population dwindled for reasons that remain unclear. The last confirmed record of the Labrador Duck was in 1875, when a hunter killed a specimen off the coast of Long Island, and, either then or within a short period of time, the species slipped quietly into the eternal void of extinction.[74]

By evening, Capt. Emery's band of adventurers had made their way back to the *Ripley*. The rain and wind had blown through, but a high sea from the storm continued to toss the schooner about at her mooring. Audubon's stomach, heavy from supper, was uneasy. After almost two months at sea, he still was uncomfortable on rough water.[75]

Sunday, July 28, dawned with fine weather.[76] Audubon ate breakfast with his young companions and then joined them on an excursion to shore.[77] With their footwear now in tatters, Shattuck and Lincoln sought to acquire some Esquimaux moccasins, along with some robes, from the Montagnais Indians encamped at the Jones trading post, but they were rebuffed.[78] The naturalist also attempted to hire a native guide to lead a smaller group thirty to forty miles into the interior. The chief suggested that it was possible his son, who was twenty-three and, according to Audubon, "looked more like a brute than a Christian man," might be willing.[79] But it would be necessary for the young Montagnais to obtain his mother's consent because she "was always fearing some accident to her darling"; she summarily refused.[80]

Consequently, Audubon's party spent the day exploring several bodies of water located in the tablelands inland from the coast. Three juvenile Shore Larks (Horned Larks), "about a week old" and still flightless, had left their nest in the moss and were hopping around "pretty briskly" on the ground.[81] Pleased at the discovery, Audubon stopped to collect them for the composition he had been planning for some time. "I am glad that I shall now have it in my power to make a figure of these birds in summer, winter, and young plumage," he wrote.[82]

Farther along, they came to a small pond where they found the nest of a Harlequin Duck placed among "some low bushes."[83] The female, however, was too wary to fall to their guns. The nest of a Velvet Duck (White-winged Scoter), known to the locals as a White-winged Coot, was located at another pond, where "it was placed on the moss, among the grass, close to the edge of the water, and contained feathers, but no down, as others do."[84] The six young birds—"black and hairy (not downy)," about a week old, and already on the water with their mother—were described by Audubon as swift, beautiful swimmers. The men hoped to capture them alive by driving them toward shore, but the young birds were not so easily caught. They reversed course while still in their element, dived, and swam away to the middle of the pond. With no other option, one member of Audubon's party took four of the birds with a single shotgun blast. A fifth bird was also collected. The remaining youngster sought refuge in the grass on shore, where Lincoln found it. The anxious mother remained on the pond, making "a short squeaking note by no means unpleasant." Audubon, who evidently decided they had taken enough of her offspring, "begged for its life, and we left it in the care of its mother and of the Maker!"[85]

Capt. Jones later informed the naturalist that a female Velvet Duck had used this pond as a nesting site for the past six to seven years. This year, the breeding pair had arrived "nearly a month later than usual," which explained why the young were still so small this late in the season. According to Audubon, this "good-hearted and benevolent man" was "fond of observing nature." Indeed, the naturalist described him as "the first person I met with who could give me any rational account of the ducks which bred in his vicinity."[86]

Another lake about two miles inland was the home of eleven families of the Long-tailed Duck. The large number of broods on the water led Audubon to hunt for their nests. After finding the first hidden beneath an alder bush about eight or nine feet away from the shore, he succeeded in locating another six in the course of an hour or so. Audubon captured several of the young birds and shot one of the adult females. Back aboard the *Ripley*, he placed the down-covered ducklings in a tub and left soaked biscuits for them to eat, but all were dead by morning.[87] He would later add images of the female and the young birds to a drawing of two males he had evidently begun during his stay in Boston.[88]

––––––––––

In New York, Lucy had been busy copying Victor's recent letters from London to send them on to Eastport so that Audubon would be in a position upon his arrival "at that place to see how all things are all round" and could act accordingly. She was convinced that her letter to Havell would "not only pacify him but make him *think* and as he says in his letter to me he will go on doing all his best till he hears [MS: hars] from you on your return from Labrador, I think you may be easy about him till you have time to write fully to him." She added that "when he has time to cool he will see his error." As for her life with the Berthouds, Lucy was "more and more convinced of the covetousness" of those around her and had no doubt that if Audubon had "presented 10 vols [of the Double Elephant Folio] instead of one they had been all accepted." Ann and Alexander Gordon had arrived the night before after touring Niagara Falls. They were "quite well," Lucy reported, and did not intend to return to England for the remainder of the year.[89]

The Labrador weather turned foul again that night. It had been calm when Audubon retired to the cabin to write in his journal, but before he finished he noted that "now it blows a hurricane, rains hard, and the sea is as high as ever." The miserable weather continued throughout the night and most of the next day. Audubon groused that it was "[a]nother horrid, stormy day." So much so that even the usually tolerant fishermen were complaining.[90]

All of the "Young Gentlemen" but Coolidge left the schooner in the morning for an eighteen-mile excursion to Forteau — referred to by the naturalist as "Port Eau" — where they hoped to obtain some Esquimaux moccasins and other attire. It would be a long journey and they would not return until the following day, a fact the naturalist lamented in his journal: "I feel quite lonesome on account of their absence, for when all are on board we have lively times, with music, and stories, and jokes, and journalizing."[91] Audubon was also growing increasingly uneasy whenever his companions were out of his sight. He told his journal that he was relieved when the boat ferrying them to shore had returned, because he knew then that they were on solid ground.[92] With the end of the expedition approaching, he was now more focused on their well-being. He doubtless wanted to ensure that all his young charges would be safely restored to their families.

The naturalist spent part of the day working on a drawing of three of the young Shore Larks (Horned Larks) he had procured the day before. He was still waiting for a perfect specimen of the adult male to illustrate. In the afternoon, he went off for a ramble with Capt. Emery and John's pointer, Dash.[93] Along the rocks near the water's edge, where the cod were being dried, they observed recently fledged Spotted Sandpipers.[94] Farther along they found a pair of Hyperborean Phalaropes (Red-necked Phalaropes) swimming in a freshwater pond.[95] Audubon was fairly certain that the birds had a nest nearby in light of their anxious response to his presence. Hoping that he might eventually be able to discover it, he elected to forgo collecting them. However, he admitted that it would be a challenge to find their nest, "for the whole country looks alike."[96]

That evening, it was "calm for a wonder but as cold as vengeance." The stove in the *Ripley*'s cabin was well stoked, and Audubon sat nestled nearby with his journal, "writing that which is scarcely worth recording, with a horridly bad patent pen," a reference to one of a number of steel pens with patented designs which had recently been introduced to the market and were becoming increasingly popular.[97] Despite his complaints, the moments he spent at the end of each day journalizing, as he called it, brought him closer to Lucy. He spoke to her in these pages, and his thoughts and longings drifted back to her with each pen stroke.

The icy air was able to enter the cabin via the stairway that led to the deck, so Audubon groused that he was "roasting on one side and freezing on the other." Coolidge, meanwhile, was in the hold engaged in skinning a bird, while Capt. Emery was busy topsides. Audubon remarked that the smell of codfish was now everywhere, and the surrounding waters glistened with a sheen of codfish oil from the offal that had been tossed into the water by the fishermen and now littered the harbor bottom.[98]

Everyone at Bras d'Or was talking about the migrating curlews. "The Curlews are coming" was the favorite expression, though the naturalist did not yet know the species of curlew to which this referred. He had heard tales of these birds from the fishermen that "border[ed] on the miraculous" and called to mind the massive flocks of Passenger Pigeons that once filled the skies of Kentucky. The fishermen considered them "great delicacies," and everyone had been anticipating the birds' arrival for more than a week. One of the sailors in John's excursion party, unable to continue with the group, had returned to the vessel and brought word that he had seen some of the curlews on his way back. Audubon refused to leap to any conclusions based on hearsay. He knew enough from the wild stories the Eastport fishermen had related of Labrador that he would have to witness the spectacle for himself.[99]

Tuesday morning, July 30, was marked by beautiful weather. Audubon could not help noting that such a morning "in this mournful country amounts almost to an unnatural phenomenon."[100] Coolidge left the vessel with a party of sailors to hunt for more birds, while Audubon, accompanied by Capt. Emery, rowed to a nearby island in search of a male Shore Lark (Horned Lark) for his drawing. Among the many adult and immature members of this species they saw, "both equally wild," the naturalist finally succeeded in collecting a "beautiful male in full summer dress."[101] Audubon spent the rest of the morning at his deal table onboard the *Ripley* adding the bird, along with a mossy background, to his composition. He aimed to complete it later with the images of two winter-plumaged birds.

In the afternoon, he and the captain rowed to shore to pay a visit to the Jones family. Sophia was at home and invited them in. Audubon described her on this occasion as a "good motherly woman, who talked well."[102] She offered them some milk and promised to send along some freshly made butter, and apparently did so daily from that point on. Audubon greatly appreciated the gesture and made sure to reference it when he wrote his account of their meeting for the *Ornithological Biography*.[103]

As expected, John and his group returned from their journey to Forteau that afternoon, "fatigued, and as usual, hungry." The young men had found a general store at this large fishing station, which was operated by fishermen from the Isle of Jersey, but had been unable to acquire any Esquimaux footwear. Audubon remarked that both Lincoln and Shattuck were "now barefooted." The party had some success in procuring specimens along the way, having collected a female Pomarine Jager (Pomarine Jaeger), which Audubon looked forward to drawing, along with an immature Raven and several Pine Finches (Pine Siskins). They also returned with the tale of seeing an enormous iceberg in the waters off the coast. But their account of the journey was peppered with complaints "of the country, the climate, and the scarcity of birds and plants."[104]

Coolidge and his party were considerably more successful, although they had little to show that was new. From their specimen bags they pulled out several Lesser Red-polls (Common Redpolls), Swamp Sparrows, three Black-capped Green Fly-catchers (Wilson's Warblers), some adult and immature Black-capped Warblers (Blackpoll Warblers), a Lincoln's Finch (Lincoln's Sparrow), and a Pine Grosbeak.[105]

By nightfall, a falling barometer portended another change in the weather.[106] Audubon sat belowdecks with his journal as a "young hurricane" began to blow outside the vessel. He had heard a cannon blast in the distance and thought it might be the *Gulnare* seeking a pilot to bring her into the sanctuary of Bras d'Or Harbor. He wished "she was at our side and snugly moored as we are."[107]

A strong easterly gale with heavy rain struck early the following morning, July 31, and continued throughout the day. With the waters kicked up by the storm, Audubon was unable to return to his drawing table. He and his young companions, also hampered by the weather, spent the day cooped up aboard the schooner.[108]

Regrettably, Audubon's hoped-for reunion with the officers of the *Gulnare* went unrealized. The British vessel had left Mecattina Harbor only the day before and had sailed on a northeastern course in the direction of Bras d'Or. But, unable to find an anchorage as the light fell, she was forced to spend the night in open water between Labrador and the western shores of Newfoundland. As the gale bore down on them that morning, Capt. Bayfield sought refuge in Forteau Bay near two brigs from the Isle of Jersey and a group of seven schooners, most of which were flying American flags.[109]

———

That same day, in New York, Lucy sat down to write a letter to Victor that she planned to send via one of the London packets due to sail from the city the following day. She was still upset by Havell's demand for higher pay, but she was equally distressed over the "malicious" attacks on Audubon that had appeared in *Mechanics' Magazine*. It seemed to her that the magazine's editor wrote "out of sheer ill nature and spite," and she wondered who the instigators, "Dr Jones of Washington and his Scientific friend," were. She could "not help thinking the parties are *using their utmost endeavours* to draw your Father into a paper war, which I hope and pray he will steer clear of, and continue to preserve towards them a magnanimous silence." Victor had sent her a copy of his letter to Loudon with his response to Waterton, which she thought "spirited and just and genteel." She passed it along to Dr. Parkman, knowing that he would see it anyway when copies of the magazine reached Boston. But she urged caution: "I hope you will not go further into these matters than is *absolutely* necessary, at the same time you must deal most candidly and fully to us on how can we shape our course for the mutual benefit of *all*."[110]

Life at the Berthouds' was still tense. "No one *here* now cares for us further than their own interest," she observed. She was determined never to stay with her siblings again. If she could not live with her immediate family, she would board elsewhere.[111]

Henry Ward, the English taxidermist whose mother had been making demands of Victor in London, was now in New York, having recently lost his position at the museum of the Literary and Philosophical Society as a result of behavior that Audubon later described as "of the darkest cast." Ward had paid a visit to Lucy and seemed "quite anxious to be on good terms" with Audubon. She convinced him to store his "fine collection" of birdskins, along with a number of nests and eggs, with Nicholas Berthoud, no doubt thinking this might give Audubon a better chance to examine them when he returned from his voyage. Ward also had with him two live Pigeon Hawks (Merlins) that she thought her husband would want, but Ward evidently had no interest in selling them.[112]

Finally, Lucy asked Victor to write quickly if he still felt that they should return to England that fall. She continued to hope they could delay their departure until the following spring so that Audubon could spend the winter gathering additional specimens in America. She closed the letter saying that she intended to make the long walk downtown the following day to make sure it sailed with the packet ship.[113]

––––––––

Audubon was hard at work again the next morning, the first day of August, drawing the Pomarine Jager (Pomarine Jaeger) that John's party had procured during their excursion to Forteau Bay.[114] The specimen pinned to his pine board was an example of the "light morph" of the species, one of its three color phases. In this phase, the bird's plumage is distinguished by a dark-brown facial helmet along with a lightish, barred breast and underbelly.[115] The naturalist figured the heavy-bodied, gull-like bird on his paper slightly left of center and provided a simple profile view of it walking on the ground, a large, empty clamshell positioned to one side.[116] It was not an inspired or informed composition by any means. These are birds more commonly seen simply sitting on the ocean surface or in midair chasing after gulls, kittiwakes, and shearwaters to steal their food.[117] However, the naturalist knew little of the habits of the species, and the conditions under which he worked were less than ideal. A strong gale without rain was blowing from the southwest throughout the day. The added motion of the schooner made it difficult for Audubon to draw, but he nevertheless managed to complete the illustration.[118]

At the entrance to the bay, an iceberg that had drifted with the wind and currents from the Arctic down through the Straits of Belle Isle had become grounded, pushed shoreward by the easterly winds of the previous day.[119] The naturalist described it as looking "like a large man-of-war dressed in light greenish muslin, instead of canvas; and when the sun shines on it[,] it glitters most brilliantly. When these transient monuments of the sea happen to tumble or roll over, the fall is tremendous, and the sound produced resembles that of loud distant thunder."[120]

Capt. Bayfield and his crew apparently observed the same iceberg off the coastal settlement of L'Anse-au-Clair, a little over four miles east of Blanc Sablon, as they made for Forteau Bay the day before. According to Bayfield, "it looked like a ruined castle having one immense tower left standing at the West end, t'was about 100 feet high."[121] In an appropriate touch, Havell would add an image of an iceberg to the background of the Pomarine Jager print.[122]

Audubon had decided to conduct a "last thorough ransack" of this part of the Labrador coast before sailing for home.[123] He wanted to make sure they had not missed anything in their rambles, but he was anxious to be back in the arms of his beloved. "[B]lessed will the day be when I land on those dear shores where all I long for in this world exists and lives, I hope," he declared to his journal.[124] It had been almost two months since he had last received a letter from Lucy. He had no way of knowing the state of her health, and all he could do was pray she was well. Later in the day, he and his companions went ashore to get some exercise. The fierce winds had not abated, and after an hour the party was "glad to return" to the *Ripley*.[125]

Friday, August 2, was yet another brisk, rain-soaked day, the noontime temperature a cool but tolerable 58°F. As Audubon's party was about to dine that afternoon, the *Wizard*, a "handsome schooner" nine days out of Boston, sailed into the harbor and anchored nearby.[126] The 105-ton vessel, launched only a year before from a shipyard in Essex, Massachusetts, measured seventy-four feet in length and almost nineteen feet in breadth, roughly the same size as the *Ripley*.[127]

The schooner was under the command of thirty-five-year-old Capt. William Willcomb of Ipswich, Massachusetts. He was the eldest son of a prominent Ipswich seafarer who had died when Willcomb was only twelve. The boy had followed the path set by his father and grown into a man at sea. Back in Ipswich, Willcomb's pregnant wife, Sarah, and son of five years, William Augustus, looked for his return to the family home, a two-story First Period structure built around 1668 that still stands today on High Street.[128] The captain was acquainted with William Oakes, one of Audubon's subscribers, and had seen the Ipswich botanist a couple of days before sailing.[129]

The *Wizard*'s crew also included a pair of young Italians serving jointly in the role of supercargo. Raised in the warmth of the Mediterranean, they did not care at all for Labrador. On their visit that afternoon to the *Ripley*, they "complained bitterly of the cold and the general appearance of the country." They had come for one purpose only—to purchase cod for the *Wizard*'s hold.[130]

Audubon expected to find the newly arrived schooner carrying letters addressed to him and his companions, along with some recent newspapers.[131] He was deeply disappointed to learn she had neither. Still, he was able to confirm that the nation's "great cities" had experienced "a healthy season," which gave him some degree of solace.[132] New York, it seemed, had escaped another cholera epidemic, increasing the likelihood that Lucy was safe.

Before retiring for the night, Audubon sat down in the cabin with his journal to record the day's events. Outside, the squall continued to rage.[133] He wrote that he had begun to see signs of autumn migration, "more especially that of the lesser species."[134] He had observed numerous immature Black-and-Yellow Warblers (Magnolia Warblers) with their parents during his trips to shore and believed they were already beginning their autumnal trek.[135] Eider Ducks (Common Eiders) had virtually disappeared from the coast. "The young were then able to fly, the old birds had nearly completed their molt, and all were moving southward."[136]

At around 1:00 a.m., as the *Ripley* slept, the *Wizard*'s stern chain, attached to a rear anchor, snapped from the force of the gale, and the schooner swung around and smashed into one of the *Ripley*'s boats hanging over her side. The sudden jolt startled everyone awake. Capt. Emery leapt out of his bunk and was topsides in an instant to survey the damage. Fortunately, the *Ripley* was still intact. Not so the "beautiful and most comfortable gig," whose bow had been crushed. As this was John's craft, he could not hide his dismay. But there was nothing that could be done. The two schooners were soon separated and, as Audubon noted, "tranquility was restored."[137]

First light brought no improvement in the weather. The pounding rain and high winds were unrelenting. A morning excursion ashore by an adventurous Lincoln procured several birds, but none that were new.[138] Twenty to thirty Jagers (Pomarine Jaegers) blown in from the sea by the gale gave Audubon an opportunity to increase his knowledge of their behavior. "They flew wildly about, yet with much grace, moving rapidly to and fro, now struggling against the blast, now bearing off and drifting to a considerable distance." The large birds were wary and would not approach within gunshot, but they could be seen chasing the smaller gulls in the harbor, principally the Kittiwakes (Black-legged Kittiwakes) and Common American Gulls (Ring-billed Gulls). They knew enough to leave the mighty Great Black-backed Gulls alone. Normally, pursuit by the Jagers would cause the smaller birds to disgorge whatever fish or other food they had recently consumed, leaving the Jagers with an easy meal. However, the recent storm had kicked up the waters and left the gulls unable to fish. Instead, both they and the Jagers turned to feeding on fish that had been tossed onshore by the fishermen.[139]

In the afternoon, Audubon led his colleagues "through a high and frightful sea which drenched us to the skin" and then inland to the tablelands, where he confirmed that the species of curlew now gathering in large flocks was the Esquimaux Curlew (Eskimo Curlew). He was already familiar with the bird, having previously received three specimens from William Oakes.[140]

The smallest of the four North American members of the genus *Numenius*, Esquimaux Curlews bred in the high Arctic. Beginning in late July and early August, they congregated in vast numbers along the Labrador coast, fattening themselves on Crowberries (*Empetrum nigrum*), known locally as curlew berries, in preparation for their twenty-five hundred- to three thousand-mile flight over the Atlantic Ocean to South America, where they wintered in the pampas of Argentina.[141] That evening, Audubon put to work his descriptive powers as he recorded his observations of the species, which reminded him of the Passenger Pigeon:

> I have seen many hundreds this afternoon, and shot seven. They fly in compact bodies, with beautiful evolutions, overlooking a great extent of country ere they make choice of a spot on which to alight; this is done wherever a certain berry, called here "Curlew berry," proves to be abundant. Here they balance themselves, call, whistle, and of common accord come to the ground, as the top of the country here must be called. They devour every berry, and if pursued squat in the manner of Partridges. A single shot starts the whole flock; off they fly, ramble overhead for a great distance ere they again alight. This rambling is caused by the scarcity of berries.[142]

The following day, Sunday, August 4, was a cold one with a daytime temperature of only 49°F.[143] It was still raining, though the winds had died. The naturalist focused his attention on drawing a pair of curlews and found "them difficult birds to represent."[144] Ultimately, he settled on depicting one walking in the background, its head and back to the viewer. The other was shown dead, on its side in the foreground with its light-cinnamon-colored breast displayed.[145]

It was a curious choice. He had depicted birds that had been killed as the prey of a raptor, as in the drawings of the Great Footed Hawk (Peregrine Falcon), Rough-legged Falcon (Rough-legged Hawk), and Marsh Hawk (Northern Harrier).[146] He twice resorted to showing birds that had been shot, including the Great Black-backed Gull and Golden-Eye Duck (Common Goldeneye).[147] But this was the only drawing in his entire publication that illustrated the principal subject in a lifeless state.

The hallmark of Audubon's innovative approach to bird illustration, which repudiated the static style preferred by 19th-century ornithologists, was the way in which he injected life into his images. Depicting a bird that was dead was the very antithesis of this. Even so, Audubon made the image work by positioning the bird in a posture that would effectively show the underside and wing linings of its plumage, essential field marks for the species.

As unprecedented as Audubon's decision was to draw the bird in this fashion, it was also, in a sense, almost prescient. The population of the Eskimo Curlew, like that of the Passenger Pigeon, dropped precipitously in the second half of the 19th century. Uncontrolled market hunting played a critical role in the curlews' decline, especially as the birds' spring migration route took them over the American Midwest. Widespread land-use changes in that region, with native prairies giving way to tilled agriculture, coupled with the extinction of the Rocky Mountain Grasshopper (*Melanoplus spretus*) that the birds fed upon as they flew north, were evidently also contributing factors.[148] By the latter half of the 20th century, the bird was critically endangered.[149] The last confirmed sighting in North America occurred on Galveston Island, Texas, in 1962.[150]

Still, every year or so into the mid-1980s, unconfirmed reports of an individual or two being spotted during migration would surface. In 1981, a flock of twenty-three curlews was purportedly sighted on Atkinson Island in Galveston Bay, offering hope of a viable breeding population.[151] However, annual searches conducted of the species' historical nesting areas in the Northwest Territories by the Canadian Wildlife Service from the early 1970s through the mid-1980s failed to locate a single bird.[152] More-recent searches, in the 1990s, of known breeding grounds as well as of wintering habitat have been equally unsuccessful.[153] If the species yet exists, it is but a breath away from joining the Passenger Pigeon and Labrador Duck as a withered memory of a once richer, more vital America.[154]

While Audubon toiled away at his drawing, the "Young Gentlemen" made their way once again to the tablelands, where they managed to shoot another four curlews. The cold weather did little to impede the mosquitoes, which Audubon described as "shockingly bad." The men all reported observing a certain defensive behavior of the curlews which Audubon had seen in a number of sandpipers as well as some plovers. When pursued, the birds would freeze and squat with their tail facing their pursuer and their head lying flat on the ground, minimizing their profile. The men also must have procured some immature Shore Larks (Horned Larks) because

Audubon noted that the inner wing feathers, known as "secondaries," as well as the "small wing coverts" had appeared in these young birds and had assumed here and there the "beautiful rosy tints" seen in the adults.[155]

Along the shoreline, small flocks of Little Sandpipers (Least Sandpipers) and Purple Sandpipers were everywhere.[156] The former, some of which bred locally, were already on their way south, where they would winter across a broad swath of the southern United States.[157] As to the latter, these stocky shorebirds were recent arrivals. Audubon had seen no evidence of them nesting in Labrador.[158] The species breeds in the Arctic and migrates in late summer to the Atlantic seaboard, where it winters from Newfoundland to as far south as South Carolina.[159] The men collected a number of adult and fully grown immature birds of both species before returning to the vessel.[160]

Everywhere he looked, Audubon saw early signs of the fall migration. The initial rustlings of what would soon become a thunderous passage of birds from the northern latitudes filled Audubon with awe as he considered the spectacle of this remarkable annual phenomenon:

> That the Creator should have ordered that millions of diminutive, tender creatures, should cross spaces of country, in all appearance a thousand times more congenial for all their purposes, to reach this poor, desolate, and deserted land, to people it, as it were, for a time, and to cause it to be enlivened with the songs of the sweetest of the feathered musicians, for only two months at most, and then, by the same extraordinary instinct, should cause them all to suddenly abandon the country, is as wonderful as it is beautiful and grand.
>
> Six weeks ago this whole country was one sheet of ice; the land was covered with snow, the air was filled with frost, and subject to incessant storms, and the whole country a mere mass of apparently useless matter. Now the grass is abundant, and of rich growth, the flowers are met with at every step, insects fill the air, and the fruits are ripe. The sun shines, and its influence is as remarkable as it is beautiful; the snow-banks appear as if about to melt, and here and there is something of a summerish look. But in thirty days all is over; the dark northern clouds will come down on the mountains; the rivulets and pools, and the bays themselves, will begin to freeze; weeks of snow-storms will follow, and change the whole covering of these shores and country, and Nature will assume not only a sleeping state, but one of desolation and death. Wonderful! wonderful![161]

Word reached Audubon that the *Gulnare* was now at Bonne Espérance, about twenty miles southwest of Bras d'Or.[162] He missed the camaraderie he had developed with her officers and told his journal he hoped they would meet again. Had he known that the British vessel was actually still anchored in Forteau Bay, he might well have made an overland trip to pay a visit.[163]

The clouds finally cleared, and Monday, August 5, was a rare day of fine weather. Audubon continued to work on his composition of the Esquimaux Curlews. He was able to finish the images of the two birds but still had to complete the background. His young companions spent the day ashore and returned with some more curlew specimens, as well as a Black-breasted Plover (Black-bellied Plover). A juvenile Shore Lark (Horned Lark) collected by John appeared to have almost fully molted, which led Audubon to conclude that birds from the northern climes reached maturity more rapidly than those to the south.[164]

One of the vessels in the harbor, commanded by one Capt. Williams of Portsmouth, New Hampshire, was due to sail the following day for Mount Desert Island off the coast of Maine.[165] Seeing an opportunity to send letters to their loved ones, both Audubon and Shattuck sat down and began to write.

Audubon started out his correspondence to Lucy with the expressed hope that it would find her "well and Happy." He wanted to assure her that he and everyone in the party were "quite well thank God." Now that the birds were commencing their southerly migration, he knew that his visit to Labrador was rapidly drawing to a close. He expected the *Ripley* to depart for Newfoundland on the following Sunday, August 11, "provided the Wind may be fair and no *new bird* comes to hand which alas is scarcely to be hoped for." He was a little disappointed at the number of drawings he had produced over the past seven weeks—"21 Drawings is all I have made although I have laboured hard and all hands have ransacked this Wonderful rocky & Mossy desart," he reported. They also had collected fewer than two hundred skins. However, on the positive side, he had obtained "a good deal of most valuable information" about the avian tribes of this region that would serve him well in writing the species accounts for the *Ornithological Biography*.[166]

Outlining the course of the expedition's future travels, Audubon indicated they would stop at "one or two Harbours of New Found Land," pay another visit to the Magdalen Islands and the "wonderful" Gannet Rocks, and then stop at Pictou, Nova Scotia. He thought it possible they might cross that province to Halifax and visit Saint John, New Brunswick, before again returning to Eastport while the *Ripley* proceeded there by sea. The bonds among the company, he assured Lucy, remained strong. "We have all lived in the greatest Harmony and as belonging to one well regulated family &ᶜ." He asked her to write Dr. Parkman and John Bachman with the news and to "remember me kindly" to the Berthoud family and Edward Harris, who he was "truly sorry has not seen this most wonderful Country." He bade her farewell with the hope that in a month or so they would be together again.[167]

In a letter to his father, Shattuck confirmed that he was "well, and in good condition." The expedition had been at Bradore, he wrote, using the place's English spelling, since "Friday, July 24"—actually Friday, July 26—after a day and night at sea from their previous anchorage, from which he had forwarded his last letter. He noted that they would soon sail for home "with the first fair wind which may blow next week." After stops in Newfoundland and at Pictou, he expected to arrive in Eastport the first week of September. In six weeks he would be back in Boston. "How much I have improved by my opportunities, must be left to your judgment, when we meet," he added. He was pleased to have come along on the voyage, although he admitted Labrador had not lived up to its original promise:[168]

> We have not found Labrador, the country that the fishermen would have us believe. I expected to have obtained many curious specimens in comparative anatomy, but we have seen no quadruped larger than a rat. We have found no new plants, though we have looked closely over all the ground. Birds are much less plenty than we had been taught to expect them. Mr Audubon has obtained much valuable information, and we all are glad that we have seen this country, for no description can convey a just idea of it. Labrador was not made for white men, and it is to be wished that it had been left in the possession of those whom God placed there. We have travelled over the country very thoroughly, and can bid adieu to Labrador without regret. If I was to come here again, I should wish to spend here the winter and the spring, as the quadrupeds of the country, such as rein deer, bears, foxes, hares, are to be seen only in this season. In the summer they retire into the interior, no one knows where. We have heard one bear, but could not obtain a sight of him, though we sought his acquaintance eagerly. Mosquitoes, and gnats are in greater abundance than any thing else.[169]

Shattuck would save the details of all he had seen until his return, when he planned to read his father the journal he had been keeping since sailing from Eastport.[170]

The following day, John, Lincoln, and Coolidge headed to shore with the intent of exploring the largest river shown on their chart, now known as the Brador West River, which was located at the head of Bradore Bay about four miles from their anchorage. According to Lincoln, it turned out to be "a mere rocky brook," but they nevertheless came upon "a beautiful little waterfall of about thirty feet." They could not resist the urge to leave some sign of their visit. Lincoln wrote in his journal that "[l]ike true Yankees we cut our names in the rock that if perchance some luckless fellow should wander so far away from the habitable part of the earth he should find that he was not the first outcast."[171]

A few miles farther upstream, the party found the brook "banked by stupendous rocks" rising to a height of over 150 feet. Suddenly, the young men were "startled by a loud and piercing shriek, which issued from the precipices above them." John looked up to see "a large, dark colored hawk plunging over and above him." Bringing his shotgun up to his shoulder, he tracked the path of the bird and fired. The hawk, hit by the blast, tumbled to the ground, a lump of misshapen feathers. A second bird swooped from the sky "as if determined to rescue it." Another blast from the fowling piece brought it down as well.[172]

Over a hundred feet above the young men, two birds wearing what appeared to be the same plumage launched themselves from the nest where they had been sitting and flew into the distance. John and his companions went to investigate, making their way "by a circuitous and dangerous route" to the top of the rocks, where they were able to see the empty nest fifty feet below. "It was comprised of sticks, seaweeds, and mosses, about two feet in diameter, and almost flat. About its edges were strewed the remains of their food, and beneath, on the margin of the stream, lay a quantity of wings of the *Uria Troile* [Common Murre], *Mormon arcticus* [Atlantic Puffin], and *Tetrao Saliceti* [Willow Ptarmigan], together with large pellets composed of fur, bones, and various substances."[173]

Audubon was overjoyed when the shore party returned to the vessel that evening and presented him with what he believed to be a new species.[174] His excitement was still palpable when he wrote the biographical account for what he called the Labrador Falcon:

> The two hawks which they had brought with them, I knew at once to be of a species which I had not before seen, at least in America. Think not that I laid them down at once—No, reader, I attentively examined every part of them. Their eyes, which had been carefully closed by the young hunters, I opened, to observe their size and colour. I drew out their powerful wings, distended their clenched talons, looked into their mouths, and admired the sharp tooth-like process of their upper mandible. I then weighed them in my hand, and at length concluded that no Hawk that I had ever before handled, looked more like a great Peregrine Falcon.[175]

Audubon determined from a dissection of the two birds that one was a male. The other was a mature female showing evidence of having recently laid eggs. Taken together with the birds' described behavior, he was convinced these were adults, while the two that had flown off had been juveniles.[176]

Reinvigorated by this splendid discovery, Audubon stayed up past midnight hunched over the deal table with a pencil, carefully outlining the first bird by candlelight as members of the crew slept around him. He wanted to complete the pencilwork that night so that he could use the daylight hours to wield his watercolors.[177]

The images of these enormous, chocolate-colored falcons would ultimately fill the entirety of the double elephant folio sheet with one bird on a branch looking up, its mate positioned at the top of the paper looking down.[178] The composition was more scientific illustration than art. In this drawing, unlike many others he had done, the naturalist made no effort to mimic a scene in the wild. But as in virtually all of his work at this stage of his career, Audubon was able to inject his two-dimensional picture with the life force of the three-dimensional creatures that only hours before had ruled the northern skies.

By the time Audubon wrote the species' description for his letterpress, he was able to examine museum skins in England and reached the conclusion that the Labrador Falcon was in fact the immature of the white-plumaged Iceland, or Jer, Falcon (Gyrfalcon). "I have seen several specimens," he told his readers, "which, though not altogether similar in the tints of the plumage, agree in most other respects with them, in so far as I can judge from the comparison of skins shrunk or distended beyond measure, such as we often see in museums." However, since his birds had nested and produced young, he found it necessary to explain that this was "not a singular phenomenon" and could be seen in other species.[179] Audubon was correct about the identification, but he erred as to the relative age of the birds. They were indeed adults as he initially suspected. He was simply unaware that the Gyrfalcon has three separate color morphs—white, gray, and brown (or dark). The Labrador Falcon, an example of the brown phase of the species, would never molt into a different-colored plumage.[180]

The next morning, Wednesday, August 7, Audubon resumed his place at the drawing table in the hold and picked up his brush. It was raining yet again, and he complained that this "was one of the severest tasks which I ever performed, and was done under the most disagreeable circumstances" as "the water fell on my paper and colours all the while from the rigging of the Ripley."[181]

To help clear his mind, Audubon joined a company that included Shattuck, Ingalls, and Capt. Emery on a visit to Peroquet (or, as Audubon spelled it, "Perroket") Island, located about a mile and three-quarters from their anchorage.[182] Named for the Puffins (Atlantic Puffins) that bred there in multitudes and were known by the fishermen as peroquets or sea parrots, the island was described by Audubon as "of considerable extent," although Bayfield indicated that its diameter was under half a mile. It was shaped "in the form of an amphitheatre to the height of about seventy feet, the greatest length being from north to south, and its southern extremity fronting" the Straits of Belle Isle.[183]

Thousands of Puffins covered the water and skittered away as the company's two boats approached. An even greater number filled the air, their wings beating rapidly as they flew about in search of sand eels, also known as sand lances, a slender four-to five-inch fish "with a beautiful silvery hue," for the birds' hungry offspring. Audubon described the number of birds as being so great that "one might have imagined half the Puffins in the world had assembled there."[184]

Audubon had come along to procure some of the young birds for his drawing of the species. As it turned out, they "were all too small to draw with effect." However, he had brought along two shotguns for some sport. Assisted by a pair of crewmen who made sure he didn't have to pause to reload, he was able to take twenty-seven birds on the wing without missing a single one.[185] Twenty-seven shots—twenty-seven dead Puffins. His companions joked that "the birds were so thick no one could miss if he tried," but the naturalist's skill with a fowling piece was unmatched, and everyone knew it.[186]

Audubon's killing spree on this occasion is difficult to square with his abhorrence of the depredations attributed to the eggers. He admitted that his group that day had killed more Puffins than they wanted.[187] The distinction in his mind was likely a subtle one. For him, there was joy in hunting, and he saw no reason to apologize for taking a few dozen birds from a population too numerous to count. The eggers, on the other hand, were pursuing a course that he was convinced would systematically lead to the wholesale destruction of entire seabird colonies. Audubon apparently failed to recognize that the only difference between him and the eggers was a matter of degree. If enough individual hunters visited the Puffin rookery with the same self-oriented myopia he exhibited, the colony would quickly be extirpated. Notwithstanding Audubon's slowly developing conservation ethic, he still lacked the self-awareness to recognize his contribution to the annihilation of the continent's native wildlife.

During the jaunt to Peroquet Island, Audubon observed that there were now very few gulls about. These birds, including the Great Black-backed Gulls, appeared to have already moved south.[188] It was yet another sign of the advancing season and a harbinger of the deadly-cold winter that lay ahead.

Meanwhile, at Audubon's direction, John, Lincoln, and Coolidge returned to the falcons' nesting site in hopes of collecting the young birds. They were successful in wounding one of the two, but "it flew off to a great distance, fell among the deep moss, and was never found." The young men climbed up to the aerie, thinking that the other bird might have returned to its natal home. The nest, however, was empty, and Audubon concluded that the bird probably had abandoned the area for good.[189] The young men spent a portion of their day fishing in a small brook located near their anchorage. According to Lincoln, they "caught a mess of the finest trouts we ever saw but paid dearly for our sport being nearly destroyed by the black flies and musquitos."[190]

Over the next several days, the naturalist spent virtually all his time at his drawing table, working on his composition both of the Labrador Falcons and evidently of a second, unnamed species that had been collected.[191] He found himself so weary at night that he was incapable of taking even a few moments to record the day's events in his journal. He would collapse into his bunk for a few hours of badly needed sleep before resuming his work at dawn. When he finally caught his breath and, days later, opened the covers of the journal, he sought to explain the pause:

> I now sit down to post my poor book, while a heavy gale is raging furiously around our vessel. My reason for not writing at night is that I have been drawing so constantly, often seventeen hours a day, that the weariness of my body at night has been unprecedented, by such work at least. At times I felt as if my physical powers would abandon me; my neck, my shoulders, and more than all, my fingers, were almost useless through actual fatigue at drawing. Who would believe this? — yet nothing is more true. When at the return of dawn my spirits called me out of my berth, my body seemed to beg my mind to suffer it to rest a while longer; and as dark forced me to lay aside my brushes I immediately went to rest as if I had walked sixty-five miles that day, as I have done *a few times* in my stronger days. Yesternight, when I rose from my little seat to contemplate my work and to judge of the effect of it compared with the nature which I had been attempting to copy, it was the affair of a moment; and instead of waiting, as I always like to do, until that hazy darkness which is to me the best time to judge of the strength of light and shade, I went at once to rest as if delivered from the heaviest task I ever performed. The young men think my fatigue is added to by the fact that I often work in wet clothes, but I have done that all my life with no ill effects. No! no! it is that I am no longer young. But I thank God that I did accomplish my task; my drawings are finished to the best of my ability, the skins well prepared by John.[192]

Audubon was bone-tired, no doubt. He had maintained a punishing pace since leaving Eastport, and the long hours and arduous conditions had finally caught up with him. As with many middle-aged men, in his mind he still believed he could do the things that had come so easily two decades before. But his body, pushed beyond endurance over the years, knew better. The dawning realization that he was getting older reinforced his sense that time was working against him.

There was still so much to be done before Audubon could lay aside the burden of his massive publication. After almost seven years, less than half of the promised prints had been delivered. There was a sizable number of birds yet to be found and illustrated. Alongside the drawings, each species would have to be described for the *Ornithological Biography*. And, as always, he would have to continue the search for new subscribers to replace those who had for any number of reasons dropped out.

Victor had tried to replicate his father's marketing success since arriving in England, but he was not the showman his father was.[193] Audubon's magnetic personality and charm were infectious, and prospective subscribers were much more apt to commit when called upon by the famous birdman. With all the work ahead of him, it was no wonder he was beginning to question whether he would have the strength and stamina to see it all to completion.

As Audubon brought his journal up to date, the pounding rain and ferocious winds of the storm made it "impossible to stand in the bow of our vessel." The *Ripley*'s anchors had been "dragged forty or fifty yards, but by letting out still more chain we are now safe." That evening, the two Italians from the *Wizard* came onboard and added their sonorous voices to the melodious strains of John's violin.[194] Audubon's party was greatly amused to hear that, due to low food stores, the Italians had resorted to eating Puffin meat, since virtually none of the Americans could abide the tough, fishy-tasting flesh.[195]

By the following morning, Sunday, August 11, the storm had moved on. A favorable wind was now blowing, and, in accordance with Audubon's previous plan, Capt. Emery and the crew of the *Ripley* made ready to sail. Fresh water was brought aboard, while John and Coolidge made a quick excursion to shore to seek out a few more curlews.[196] These birds, fattened by a steady diet of Crowberries, could be seen proceeding south whenever the weather improved, flying at a great height over the harbor.[197]

In a parting gesture, Capt. Willcomb sent his crew aboard the schooner to help raise the anchors. He and the two Italians also rowed over to say their final goodbyes. Everything was in order and ready for departure by late morning. At 11:00 a.m., the *Ripley* sailed out of Bras d'Or's harbor and, with her canvas trimmed, turned her bow for home.[198]

13

Newfoundland

AUGUST 1833

Now we are sailing before the wind in full sight of the [north]-west coast of Newfoundland, the mountains of which are high, spotted with drifted snow-banks, and cut horizontally with floating strata of fogs extending along the land as far as the eye can reach.

JOHN JAMES AUDUBON

From the deck of the *Ripley*, Audubon gazed back at Labrador, with its "high and rugged hills, partly immersed in large banks of fog, that usually hang over them," and contemplated the success of the voyage.[1] He was returning with twenty-three drawings, two more than just a week before, in various stages of completion.[2] Some were ready for the engraver, while others still needed images of the birds in alternate plumages or the addition of an obligatory background. However, it had not been as profitable a season as he had originally hoped. The number of different species that made this land their summer home had proved to be far fewer than he had expected. Apart from the vast colonies of seabirds, there were actually relatively few birds, and it had been a daily struggle to find and collect each one. There were only 173 skins in the hold despite the best efforts of Audubon's party and the crew.[3] Summing up his feelings about Labrador, the naturalist was unequivocal. "Seldom in my life have I left a country with as little regret as I do this," he told his journal. The mosquito-infested swamps along the St. John's River of East Florida ranked a close second.[4]

Lincoln, who had worn through his footwear in barely six weeks of trudging over the rough terrain, echoed the naturalist's disillusionment in the pages of his own journal:

> We bid adieu to Labrador without much regret probably never to see that wretched country again. We had been disappointed in every thing concerning it. Indeed we had never the truth told us concerning any one thing and it was only the outrageously exaggerated accounts and in many cases stories wholly without foundation that induced us to come hither. We were told that the sea birds of nearly all kinds that live on the coast of Maine were so abundant at Labrador in the breeding season that we should have no difficulty at any time of getting any numbers we might want. The Esquimaux were represented to us as in-

numerable, and it was constantly reported that Chevalier [at Esquimaux River] had more than two hundred constantly in his employ. The Moravian settlement which makes such a figure in the accounts of Labrador and which is reported to have made such an improvement in the condition of the Esquimaux, and to be of such magnitude and importance in the country was equally magnified in our eyes before learning the true state of the case. But instead of all this the birds excepting two or three species were *exceedingly* rare, so scarce that with all our exertions we failed in getting one fifth as many as we intended. As to the Esquimaux, we did not see *one* and there was not one within a thousand miles of us. The hopeful "Moravian Settlement" consists of five miserable wretches who being clothed and fed by those who know no better are content to lay torpid like toads in their holes; they cannot do the Esquimaux much harm for there is not one within two hundred leagues of them. As for the latter it is no wonder that there is none on this part of the coast; it is impossible for them to exist. For the Hudson's bay Company have destroyed every living thing on the land. . . . When the fish are destroyed as according to present appearances they soon will be and the birds too, what will then be in Labrador. The destruction of fish by the cod fishers, of the birds by the *eggers* and men employed in getting feathers is too *wicked*.[5]

Still, Audubon was in large measure content.[6] He had discovered several species he believed were new to science and had acquired a great deal of information about the life histories of the northern birds. Moreover, everyone in his company had survived the journey without injury or illness. And, in the days ahead, there would be an opportunity to add to his drawings and his store of knowledge. Whether the rest of the voyage would "prove as fruitful" remained to be seen.[7] For now, he was looking forward to their next anchorage along the western coast of Newfoundland and, even more so, anticipating his long-desired reunion with his dearest Lucy.

By 7:00 p.m., the *Ripley* had advanced a distance of fifty miles through the waters of the gulf. Audubon sat on deck "scribbling" in his journal while John played his violin with Lincoln accompanying him on the flute.[8] The naturalist noted that "[t]he sea is quite smooth, or else I have become a better sailor by this rough voyage."[9]

The breeze remained fair throughout that night and into the following day. According to the naturalist, the *Ripley* remained in visual range of the northwestern shores of Newfoundland, which presented "the highest lands we have yet seen. In some places the views were highly picturesque and agreeable to the eye, although the appearance of vegetation was but little better than at Labrador."[10] As the light dwindled, the wind slowly swung around by degrees until it was ahead, making for a "boisterous" and "uncomfortable" night for Audubon's party.[11]

The following morning, Tuesday, August 13, the *Ripley* rounded the bold red cliffs of Cape St. George on the northern side of St. George's Bay.[12] This sizable gulf, the largest on the western coast of Newfoundland, is almost forty miles wide at its mouth and extends in a northeasterly direction for roughly thirty-five miles.[13] It took the better part of the day for the vessel to make its ascent toward the head of the bay. Audubon was impressed by the sheer magnitude of this body of water, saying that "a more beautiful and ample basin cannot easily be found; there is not a single obstruction within it. The northeast shores are high and rocky, but the southern are sandy, low, and flattish."[14]

As the schooner proceeded, woodlands began to replace the rough, barren terrain Audubon's company had grown so accustomed to in Labrador. The air also warmed, and they "found it agreeable lolling on deck."[15] Audubon, with his Southern blood, was particularly pleased by the change and noted that the thermometer had climbed twenty-two degrees over the past two days. Capt. Emery took aboard two local men from a small boat on the water to serve as pilots. The pair had a half barrel of recently caught salmon in their craft, and Audubon quickly negotiated a deal to buy the fish for $10.[16]

At 5:00 p.m., the schooner finally dropped anchor in St. George's Harbor, a broad harbor just off the village of Sandy Point near the head of St. George's Bay. With a seasonal population in excess of a hundred, Sandy Point was the largest settlement the party had yet encountered.[17] The community was "built on an elongated point of sand or sea wall" that extended out into the waters of the bay.[18] This natural barrier provided protection for vessels riding at anchor on the inland side of the sand spit except for when the winds blew from the northeast. Several fishing vessels were moored nearby, and on shore lay the rotting remains of the *Charles Tennison*, which had come aground four years earlier while returning home to Hull, England, from Quebec. The opposite shore of the harbor was dotted with the huts of the local Mi'kmaq Indians and showed "[s]ome signs of cultivation."[19]

The young men launched the boats to pay a visit to Sandy Point in the hope they could purchase some fresh supplies for the *Ripley*'s stores, but two bottles of milk were all they had to show for their efforts.[20] They had also made some inquiries about the local birds and received conflicting reports. "Some persons say birds are plenty, others say there are none hereabouts," Audubon wrote.[21] He planned to join his companions the following day to determine what was true.

When Wednesday dawned, it was "[a]ll ashore in search of birds, plants, and the usual et ceteras belonging to our vocations."[22] According to Audubon, the community of forty or so homes appeared to be made up mostly of poor fishermen.[23] "Some of the buildings looked like miserable hovels," he noted, "others more like habitable houses."[24] Still, Sandy Point was a remarkably cosmopolitan community made up of

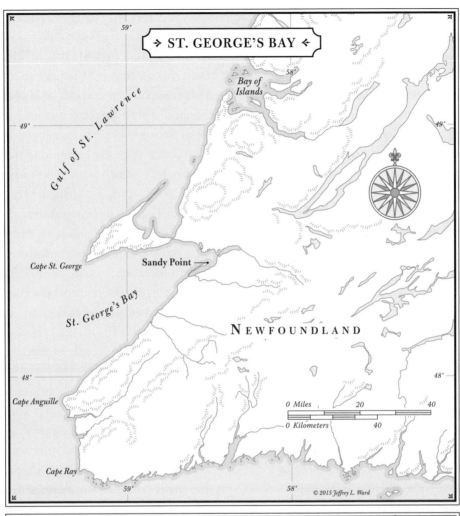

→ ST. GEORGE'S BAY ←

Gulf of St. Lawrence

Bay of Islands

59°

58°

49°

49°

Cape St. George

Sandy Point →

St. George's Bay

N E W F O U N D L A N D

48°

48°

Cape Anguille

0 Miles   20   40

0 Kilometers   40

Cape Ray

59°

58°

© 2015 Jeffrey L. Ward

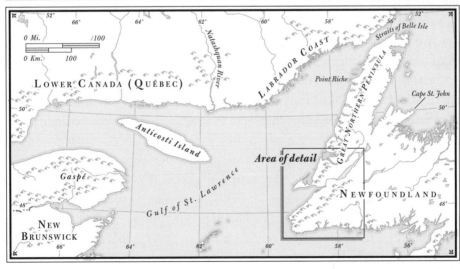

52°

66°

64°

62°

60°

58°

56°

52°

0 Mi.   100

0 Km.   100

Natashquan River

LABRADOR COAST

Straits of Belle Isle

L O W E R C A N A D A (Q U É B E C)

Point Riche

GREAT NORTHERN PENINSULA

Cape St. John

50°

50°

Anticosti Island

Area of detail

Gaspé

Gulf of St. Lawrence

N E W F O U N D L A N D

48°

48°

N E W B R U N S W I C K

66°

64°

62°

60°

58°

56°

settlers from France, England, Ireland, and the Isle of Jersey who had been attracted by the abundant salmon, cod, and herring fisheries in St. George's Bay.[25]

The existence of such a multicultural population in this part of British North America was unusual, and stemmed, at least in part, from a series of treaties between France and England dating back to the early 18th century. In the Treaty of Utrecht in 1713, France ceded its sovereignty over Newfoundland to England but retained fishing rights along a section of the northern coast between Cape Bonavista on the eastern shore and Point Riche on the northwestern coast opposite Labrador. Originally, St. George's Bay was not included in this territory, which became known as the French, or Treaty, Shore. However, that changed in 1763 with the Treaty of Paris, which brought an end to the Seven Years' War (known in North America as the French and Indian War). Under the treaty's terms, the two countries shifted the French Shore to the west, running from Cape St. John, on the north shore, up and around the Great Northern Peninsula and down the western coast to Cape Ray in the south, and thereby encompassed both St. George's Bay and Sandy Point. Technically, neither French nor English settlers were permitted to reside along the French Shore, but they did so anyway.[26] The opportunities afforded by the local fisheries made this inevitable. By the time of the *Ripley*'s visit, the mix of disparate nationalities at Sandy Point were living and working in relative harmony.

That feeling of amity, however, did not necessarily extend to outsiders. Audubon's party was not warmly received, especially by the women of the village. Those females who ventured outside, he wrote, wore "cotton caps covering their ears" and "flew before us as if we were wild beasts." One woman, "who had a pail of water, at sight of us dropped it, and ran to hide herself; another who was looking for a cow, on seeing us coming, ran into the woods, and afterwards crossed a stream waist deep to get home to her hut without passing us."[27]

The locals' response to the strangers was completely understandable, however. After two months of hard living, the members of Audubon's party undoubtedly looked rough and dangerous. Audubon, for one, never shaved when he was out in the wilds, and he had evidently stopped using a razor after his early meetings with Capt. Bayfield in American Harbor. With his hair grown long and his face covered with a thick beard, he must have appeared to be quite a vagabond. Collectively, the group could not help causing a stir as they walked through the quiet community with shotguns nestled in the crooks of their arms or draped over their shoulders.[28]

The group made another attempt to supplement the *Ripley*'s provisions but were again largely rebuffed. They received offers of some milk, herring at $0.10 a dozen, and "a tolerable calf" for $8. They had hoped to purchase some chickens, but these "were too scarce to be obtained." Audubon was also on the lookout for some Newfoundland dogs, which he had promised friends back in Boston. But all he could see were mongrels.²⁹ According to Ingalls, one was "very large, tawney [*sic*] and so fierce that they kept him chained."³⁰

The naturalist tried to find a guide among the Mi'kmaq Indians who could take a party inland, where he had been told the "Small or True Ptarmigan," also known as the Rock Grous (Rock Ptarmigan), could be found in large numbers. This was a species he eagerly wished to find, having never encountered one before. However, the natives were not interested, supposedly being "too lazy even to earn money."³¹

The shore party's excursion did not last long. They were soon forced to return to the vessel "on account of a storm of wind and rain, showing that Newfoundland is cousin to Labrador in this respect."³² However, there were also distinct differences between the two. Newfoundland was considerably richer in plant growth than the group's former stomping grounds. "[A]ll the vegetable productions are large and more abundant," the naturalist observed.³³ The birds were also abundant, with flocks of numerous species moving southward in anticipation of the approaching change of seasons. Barn Swallows, which had only recently nested under the eaves of the buildings in the village, were now darting through the air as they winged their way to the southwest.³⁴ Despite the weather, it was a good day for birding, and Audubon itemized the additional species he had seen when he sat down later in the day with his journal:

> I saw here the Blue yellow-eyed Warbler [probably the Blue-eyed Yellow Warbler (Yellow Warbler)], the Fish-Hawk [Osprey], several species of Sparrows, among them the Lincoln's Finch [Lincoln's Sparrow], the Canada Titmouse [Boreal Chickadee], Black-headed ditto [Black-capped Chickadee], White-winged Crossbill, Pine Grosbeak, Maryland Yellow-throat [Common Yellow-throat], Pigeon Hawk [Merlin], Hairy Woodpecker, Bank Swallow, Tell-tale Godwit [Greater Yellowlegs], Golden-eyed Duck [Common Goldeneye], Red-breasted Merganser, three Loons [Common Loons],—of which two were young and almost able to fly; the Spotted Sandpiper, and a flock of Tringas [a genus comprised of sandpipers], the species of which could not be ascertained.³⁵

The storm kicked up the waters in the harbor. As the crew rowed the party back to the vessel, with the indomitable Capt. Emery at the helm, the waves crashed over the boat, and everyone was thoroughly soaked by the time they made it on deck. Audubon could not recall having spent a rougher time in a small boat on the water.³⁶

The wind and waves prevented the naturalist from working on any of his drawings, but by the time he sat down to add the day's events to his journal, the wind had died away. He planned to spend the following day incorporating into a few of his illustrations some of the plants the company had discovered during their recent excursion. Earlier that evening, a more enterprising group of Mi'kmaq Indians, who had apparently heard of the naturalist's offer, paddled out to the schooner for a visit and agreed to go hunting in the morning for hares, an animal Audubon was interested in obtaining.[37] While on deck, he observed a "very clamorous" flock of twenty or thirty migrating Little Terns (Least Terns) as they passed the vessel, beating their way south "against the gale most beautifully."[38]

Thursday, August 15, dawned fair and beautiful. True to their word, the Mi'kmaqs stopped by the vessel in the morning with half a freshly killed Caribou and a "remarkably large" species of hare, with black eartips and a coat of "a fine pearl-grey colour above, and white beneath," which Audubon did not recognize and thought might represent a new species.[39] He would later identify it as a Polar Hare (Arctic Hare).[40] The Indians and the Americans proceeded to haggle over the price for the game. Audubon noted that "[t]he Indians showed much cleverness in striking the bargain."[41] Eventually a deal was reached, and the Mi'kmaqs paddled off with twenty-one pounds of pork and thirty-three pounds of ship-biscuit. Audubon threw a quarter into the deal to get the hare, which was later skinned and cooked. He described the meat as "white, tender, and excellent eating."[42]

The naturalist resumed work on his drawing of the Red-necked Diver (Red-throated Loon), adding a Pitcher Plant (*Sarracenia purpurea*) to the illustration. This unusual plant shares the distinction of being among a small number of plants in North America that are carnivorous. Found primarily in wet, boggy areas and swamps with nutrient-poor soil, the Pitcher Plant has leaves that are individually shaped in the form of a tubular-shaped "pitcher" that attracts insects and other small prey via a patch of light at its opening. Once inside, the insects are drawn downward by a trail of nectar secreted by glands in the leaf, until they reach a slick patch that slides them into a small pool of rainwater that has accumulated at the bottom of the tube. There they drown and are digested by enzymes and bacteria, with the resulting nitrogen and phosphorous being absorbed by the plant.[43] It does not appear that Audubon had any understanding of how this plant survives, as he made no mention of it in the *Ornithological Biography*, which contains occasional references to other plants he depicted in his drawings.[44]

Later in the day, Audubon crossed the bay with his colleagues to visit the Mi'kmaq encampment.[45] The Mi'kmaqs had made St. George's Bay their home for decades, but they were not indigenous to Newfoundland. When Europeans began arriving in growing numbers in the early 16th century, led by fishermen from France, Portugal, and Spain, the island was peopled by the Beothuk, who came to be known as "Red Indians" because they used red ochre mixed with grease to paint their bodies and many of their other possessions during an annual rite of spring.[46] Disease and violent clashes with European fishermen and colonists had decimated their relatively sparse population over the ensuing centuries.[47] The Beothuk also suffered periodically at the hands of Mi'kmaqs from Cape Breton Island, who since the late 16th century, if not earlier, had made seasonal visits to Newfoundland to fish and hunt.[48] By the latter half of the 18th century, Mi'kmaqs had established permanent settlements in St. George's Bay and elsewhere along the Newfoundland coast with the approval of the British authorities.[49] A census performed in 1830 counted sixty-six Mi'kmaqs residing in St. George's Bay.[50]

According to an English naval officer who visited the Mi'kmaq village near Sandy Point in 1813, the Indians were "robust and tall; with amazing course features, very high cheek bones, flattened noses, wide nostrils, small eyes widely separated from each other, and thick black hair hanging perpendicularly from either temple. They are dressed, for the most part, in apparel which they procure from the *Europeans* at *Sandy Point*, in exchange for *fish*, *oil*, and *furs*: however, they still preserve a few originalities in their costume, such as *deer-skin* sandals, embroidered red caps, and red cloth greaves in lieu of stockings." He described them as "naturally good-natured, and exceedingly civil toward strangers." Their villages were dotted with conical wigwams covered with birch bark. In the Mi'kmaq culture, the women did much of the work in camp, leaving the men with hours free for idle pleasures, which gave white visitors the impression that they were lazy and shiftless.[51]

Audubon was singularly unimpressed by the natives he met. "We found them, as I expected, all lying down pell-mell in their wigwams, and a strong mixture of blood was perceptible in their skins, shape and deportment: some were almost white, and sorry I am to say, that the nearer they were to our noble race the filthier and lazier they were. The women and children were particularly disgusting in this respect."[52] Still, the camp was buzzing with activity, belying the naturalist's contemptuous description of its inhabitants. He noted that the women were hard at work, either weaving "rough baskets" or harvesting the wild-growing, amber-colored fruit of the Cloudberry (*Rubus chamaemorus*), which was commonly known as "baked apple" because of its flavor when lightly roasted. Audubon had illustrated the ground-hugging shrub in its flowering stage in his drawing of the Lincoln's Finch (Lincoln's Sparrow).[53]

Out in the shallow waters of the bay, the children of the village were busy wading through the eelgrass in search of eels and lobsters. The Mi'kmaqs ate the lobsters plain, "without any salt or any other *etceteras*," after roasting them in a brushwood fire.[54] Audubon tried them and declared the flavor to be far superior to that of boiled lobster.[55] The crustaceans were prevalent here, whereas they had been uncommon along the shores of Labrador. The crew of the *Ripley* was able to catch ninety-nine in the bay, making for a welcome change in the shipboard diet.[56]

Audubon remained eager to enlist some Mi'kmaq guides who could take his young companions inland to hunt for hares and Caribou, as well as Rock Grous, and any other avian rarities they might find. He ultimately managed, "[a]fter much parley," to hire two of the men for $1 each per day. They would all start in the morning.[57]

The naturalist, always inquiring about the local natural history, noted that the Caribou meat was not well regarded there. "[I]t tastes like indifferent, poor, but very tender venison."[58] The animals generally ranged in the interior except during late winter, when the lack of forage brought them to the coast by the hundreds. There they found nourishment in the kelp and other seaweed brought ashore by the ice and waves.[59]

The weather continued to favor the fall migration. Audubon had seen several pairs of Cayenne Terns (Caspian Terns) as well as large numbers of Great Terns (Common Terns) moving south. The former "flew high, and were very noisy." The latter, on a fair day like this, also preferred flying at high altitudes and were "more at leisure" than in inclement weather when they tended to hug the water. Tell-tale Godwits (Greater Yellowlegs) were now, according to the naturalist, "extremely fat, extremely tender, and extremely good," an endorsement of their gastronomical value. Audubon also observed substantial numbers of Pine Grosbeaks "in a shocking state of moult" and Canada Titmice (Boreal Chickadees).[60]

That evening, Audubon was finishing up his journal entry for the day when a group of Sandy Point residents rowed out to the *Ripley* to invite him and his party to a community dance due to start at 10:00 p.m.[61] It would appear that this was a Sandy Point tradition. Two decades before, the officers of a visiting English navy vessel, the HMS *Rosamond*, received an invitation to a similar "rustic ball."[62] Moreover, by this time Audubon's name and purpose must have become known to the village elders, who doubtless wished to extend a suitable welcome to the famous naturalist. His young companions jumped at the opportunity. Audubon agreed to go along as well, but more "out of curiosity" than for a desire to dance.[63]

The Americans were punctual. The crew rowed them to shore and beached the boat at ten o'clock. Audubon and the "Young Gentlemen" made their way to the home of a fisherman, where the dance would be held, their path lit by paper lanterns set at intervals along the route. The naturalist brought along his flageolet, and John and Lincoln their instruments, having been asked to do so by their hosts, who had evidently heard music emanating from the schooner on its first evening in the bay.[64]

The house was a framed structure with a single story and a makeshift loft. The ground floor had been opened up for dancing by pushing the furniture against the walls, leaving an open area in the middle for the festivities. Audubon was introduced to the man's wife, who curtseyed politely and then resumed her last-minute preparations to make the house ready for her guests:[65]

In one hand she held a bunch of candles, in the other a lighted torch, and distributing the former at proper intervals along the walls, she applied the latter to them in succession. This done, she emptied the contents of a large tin vessel into a number of glasses which were placed in a tea-tray on the only table in the room. The chimney, black and capacious, was embellished with coffee-pots, milk-jugs, cups and saucers, knives and forks, and all the paraphernalia necessary on so important an occasion. A set of primitive wooden stools and benches was placed around, for the reception of the belles of the village, some of whom now dropped in, flourishing in all the rosy fatness produced by an invigorating northern climate, and in decoration vying with the noblest Indian queen of the west. Their stays seemed ready to burst open, and their shoes were equally pressed, so full of sap were the arctic beauties. Around their necks, brilliant beads, mingled with ebony tresses, and their naked arms might have inspired apprehension had they not been constantly employed in arranging flowing ribbons, gaudy flowers, and muslin flounces.[66]

Coolidge recalled that the women and girls, who were mostly of French extraction, came dressed in styles that were "half a century out of date." To him "[i]t seemed like a bit of the France that existed before the Revolution transplanted on American shores, and the old fashions had never changed."[67] Ingalls remembered that some of the girls "were pretty and all were jolly and good."[68]

The men began drifting in. They were nicely dressed, but the hostess's son, just off his fishing boat, headed to the loft, composed of loose boards overhead, to change into more suitable attire. Soon enough, there was a call for music, and John stepped forward with his violin. He opened the evening by playing "Hail Columbia, Happy Land," which at the time served as the unofficial national anthem of the United States. He followed this up with the French national anthem, "La Marseillaise," for those residents who originally hailed from France, and "God Save the King" for those of English blood. Audubon retreated to a corner to watch the evening unfold. In his younger days he would have enjoyed standing with his instrument in the center of the room, the object of everyone's attention. Now there was nothing for him to prove, and he was just as content sitting on the sidelines, watching as his son took the spotlight. He struck up a conversation with "an old European gentleman, whom [he] found an agreeable and well-informed companion":[69]

The dancers stood in array, little time having been spent in choosing partners, and a Canadian accompanying my son on his Cremona, mirth and joy soon abounded. Dancing is certainly one of the most healthful and innocent amusements. I have loved it a vast deal more than watching for the nibble of a trout, and I have sometimes thought enjoying it with an agreeable female softened my

nature as much as the pale pure light of the moon softens and beautifies a winter night. A maiden lady, who sat at my side, and who was the only daughter of
my talkative companion, relished my remarks on the subject so much, that the
next set saw her gracing the floor with her tutored feet.[70]

According to Ingalls, they all danced "reels and country dances—no minuet"
and had "a good jolly time."[71] When the musicians tired and took a break, the assemblage turned to the refreshments. The hostess and her son made sure that everyone had a glass, and Audubon was "not a little surprised to see all the ladies, maids
and matrons, swallow, like their sweethearts and husbands, a full glass of pure rum,
with evident pleasure." The naturalist did not fully approve until he considered that
"in cold climates, a dose of ardent spirits is not productive of the same effects as in
burning latitudes, and that refinement had not yet induced these healthy and robust
dames to affect a delicacy foreign to their nature."[72]

Audubon departed early, well aware that he had much to do when the sun came
up in a few hours. He wandered back to the beach and woke the crew, who had
fallen asleep in the boat. By 11:00 p.m., he was back aboard the *Ripley*. He retired
to his berth in the cabin but was awakened shortly after 2:30 a.m., when his companions called from shore for a boat to retrieve them. Back at the ball, some of the
young revelers were having too good a time to turn in. They continued dancing until
after the Americans had finished their early-morning breakfasts.[73]

Lucy would have appreciated knowing that her men were safe. The day before, as
Audubon was seated in the hold of the *Ripley* working on his image of the Pitcher
Plant, she was responding to a letter from Victor sent from Paris on June 22.[74] She
was grateful for his news, reading it "with the most heartfelt pleasure." She needed
the periodic cheer his letters brought. It had been a difficult summer for her. She
had recently recovered from yet another bilious attack, her third that season. And
with each passing day without word from her husband, she could not help feeling
increasingly anxious about the fate of the expedition, fearing "that some flaw of
wind or some Iceberg in that dreadful region should prove fatal to the Ripley and
her Crew."[75] She would not allow her fears to overwhelm her, of course. She was too
strong and self-possessed a woman for that.

Victor had sent her two fashionable ladies' caps from Paris as she had requested.
Although she had originally planned to give one to Eliza, her thinking had since
changed "for what with the Vol[ume of *The Birds of America*], the presents I have
made and my attention to the Children, all is amply paid." She continued to feel out
of place with her sister's family. Had she to do it all over again, she related, she never
would have left Boston.[76]

In his letter, Victor had continued to press his parents to return to England that autumn.[77] Lucy again asked him to write and explain the urgency. She knew her husband wanted to head to the Floridas come winter and complete as much work as possible on this side of the Atlantic before sailing again for London. If they did return, she wrote, they would have to turn around almost immediately so that Audubon could resume his activities in America the next spring. It seemed to her "labour time and money lost" to embark on such a course. But she was expecting to hear from, if not see, her beloved husband within two weeks or so, and she promised Victor they would soon send word of their plans.[78]

———

For his part, Audubon was back at his drawing table on Friday morning, August 16, adding a branch of the Sheep Laurel (*Kalmia angustifolia*) to his composition of the Ruby-crowned Wren (Ruby-crowned Kinglet).[79] Though this plant flowers in early summer, the naturalist found one that still had some reddish-pink blossoms, which nicely complemented the scarlet-red crown patches of the two birds.[80]

The "Young Gentlemen" departed for the interior of the country, guided by the Mi'kmaq Indians that Audubon had hired. They were back by evening, having retreated in the face of hordes of nasty mosquitoes and flies. Lincoln had been bitten ferociously and, according to Audubon, was "really in great pain."[81] The party had collected an adult and immature Willow Grous (Willow Ptarmigan) and seen a variety of birds, including "Canada Jays [Gray Jays], Crossbills [Red Crossbills], Pine Grosbeaks, Robins [American Robins], one Golden-winged Woodpecker [Northern Flicker], many Canadian Titmice [Boreal Chickadees], a Martin Swallow [Purple Martin], [and] a Kingfisher [Belted Kingfisher] (none in Labrador)."[82]" John evidently procured a number of adult and immature specimens of the Pine Grosbeak. The adults were molting, and both sexes had sores on their feet that Audubon attributed to the sap on the branches of the pine trees where they fed.[83] The young men reported that the terrain was hilly, requiring them to go "'up and down the whole way.'" The moss was not quite as thick as in Labrador, and there was "no tall wood, and no hard wood."[84] By the time they got back to the schooner, they were exhausted, and were asleep before the naturalist sat down with his journal.

Audubon had hoped the new day would bring a fair wind that would allow them to resume their journey, but it was blowing dead ahead, and they remained anchored off of Sandy Point. "The truth is," he wrote, "we have determined not to leave this harbor without a fair prospect of a good run, and then we shall trust to Providence after that."[85]

With another day before him, the naturalist returned to his drawings. The composition he had made of the White-winged Crossbills lacked foliage, a situation he remedied by adding "a curious species of alder" on which he perched the two pairs of birds.[86] This was the Green Alder, also known variously as the American Green Alder or the Mountain Alder (*Alnus viridis crispa*).[87] Audubon also may have begun illustrating the Pine Grosbeaks that his son had collected the day before, although it is not mentioned in his journal.[88]

During the day, Audubon played host to Henry Essex Forrest, his wife, Julia, and his thirty-six-year-old spinster daughter, Ann, who had all rowed out to the schooner to pay a call.[89] Forrest was the "old European gentleman" the naturalist had met at the community ball.[90] Now seventy years old, Forrest had been born in Ireland in 1763 and immigrated to the British West Indies as a young man in 1784. He arrived in Canada in the late 1790s after spending time in New York, where Ann was born in 1797. He subsequently worked for many years as a merchant in Montreal. His first wife, Mary, the mother of Ann and his three other surviving children, died in 1810. Forrest remarried in 1819 and eventually moved to Sandy Point, where he established a successful mercantile business. He was evidently very well-to-do and lived in the nicest home in the community.[91]

Mrs. Forrest had made a fresh salad for the Americans and also gave them some fresh butter. Over a glass of wine and raisins from the *Ripley*'s stores, Audubon learned that the Forrests were related to the current Lord Chancellor of Ireland, William Conyngham Plunket. They also knew Edward Harris and his family, presumably from their New York stay. According to Audubon, "[t]he old lady and gentleman talked well," although Mr. Forrest grumbled about his situation. "[H]e complained of the poverty of the country and the disadvantages *he* experienced from the privileges granted to the French on this coast." In view of their relationship to Lord Plunket, Audubon thought they might be interested in seeing his letter from the Duke of Sussex. They asked if they might borrow it to make a copy, and he graciously agreed. He also gave Mr. Forrest his calling card before the family returned to shore.[92]

Another visitor to the vessel that day was an old Frenchman who had come to Newfoundland fifty years before. Audubon was eager to hear about the Red Indians. The Frenchman said that they had been gone for decades. "[T]he last he had heard of were seen twenty-two years ago," the naturalist reported.[93] In fact, there were Beothuk still living in small, impoverished groups deep in the interior of the island barely fifteen years before. Over the decade that followed, a piteous remnant of the tribe lingered in the form of a few individuals taken as captives by white settlers. The last of these, a young woman named Shanawdithit, died of consumption, the popular name for tuberculosis, in St. John's in 1829.[94]

The Frenchman described the Red Indians as fierce warriors who gave no quarter. They would behead their fallen foes and let the wild animals dispose of the remains.[95] Their behavior, however, paled in comparison to the dreadful treatment they received at the hands of the European colonists, who forced them from their land and brutally attacked them whenever they retaliated.[96] The English merchant and adventurer George Cartwright, who observed the interaction of the settlers and the natives far more objectively than most Europeans, described his brethren as "much greater savages than the Indians themselves, for they seldom fail to shoot the poor creatures whenever they can."[97]

Audubon found some time during the day to go ashore, where he managed to purchase seven Newfoundland dogs—a two-year-old male, two females, and four puppies—for $17. Given his promise to procure such dogs for his friends in Boston, he was relieved that he would not be returning empty-handed.[98]

It would have been interesting to see how these new additions were received by the *Ripley*'s resident Great Black-backed Gulls, which had terrorized poor Dash. The birds, now fully grown and able to fly, had fattened themselves over the summer on scraps thrown to them by the cook and some of the sailors. They sometimes flew into the water to bathe but needed help getting back onboard. Audubon indicated that they were eating two codlings of eight to ten inches each day.[99]

Audubon continued to observe the passage of birds on migration. He noted in his journal that he had seen a number of flocks of Golden-winged Plovers (American Golden-Plovers) winging their way south that morning. Thousands of Great Terns (Common Terns) were also making the flight, as were small flocks of Canada Geese. He had also seen two Jagers (Pomarine Jaegers) about the harbor. His colleagues had been out hunting and had returned with an immature Golden-crested Wren (Golden-crowned Kinglet) and a *Muscicapa* flycatcher that he thought was "probably new." He anticipated that he would be able to procure some additional specimens of the flycatcher the next day so that he could confirm that it had never previously been described for science. But he had been struggling with the identification of these individual birds since the *Ripley*'s stay at Little Mecattina Cove.[100]

The physical similarities between many of the small, olive-green songbirds in this avian family made separating them exceedingly difficult.[101] However, Audubon's close observation of the flycatcher in its natural habitat had pretty much convinced him that it was a distinct species. In both appearance and behavior the "small wood Pewee," as he called it, differed from the other flycatchers he knew.[102] His analysis was correct, but he ultimately stumbled in presenting his identification to the public.

When Audubon returned to civilization, he consulted the *Fauna Boreali-Americana*, a partially illustrated work on the birds of the northern regions of British America, which had been published in 1831 by his once-close friend William Swainson and the arctic explorer Dr. John Richardson. Audubon concluded that his Labrador bird was a Short-legged Pewit (*Tyrannula richardsonii*) (Western Wood-Pewee), a species Richardson had collected in eastern Saskatchewan. How

Audubon arrived at this decision is a mystery. He originally described the Labrador birds as smaller than three other flycatchers with which he was familiar—the Wood Pewee (Eastern Wood-Pewee), Traill's Flycatcher (Willow Flycatcher), and the Small Green-crested Flycatcher (Acadian Flycatcher). Yet, according to Swainson, the *Tyrannula richardsonii* was larger than any of them.[103]

A few years later, Audubon received a number of skins of western birds from John Kirk Townsend, a young Philadelphia ornithologist who had traveled overland to the Pacific Ocean in 1834 with Harvard naturalist Thomas Nuttall, one of Audubon acquaintances. Among the specimens was a *Tyrannula richardsonii*, which Audubon evidently used to illustrate the bird for his publication, although his drawing bears a close resemblance to Swainson's illustration in the *Fauna Boreali-Americana*.[104] Audubon called it the Short-legged Pewee and relied upon his notes of the birds he had observed on the Labrador expedition in writing his biography of the species in the final volume of the *Ornithological Biography*.[105] Later ornithologists were baffled by the naturalist's identification because the Western Wood-Pewee is not found in eastern North America.[106]

Audubon was not alone in his confusion. Based upon his description of the bird, it is believed that what he discovered was an Alder Flycatcher, one of the hard-to-differentiate flycatchers included in today's *Empidonax* genus.[107] This is a bird that even modern-day ornithologists failed to identify as a separate species until the 1970s. For over a century, the Alder Flycatcher was lumped with a very closely related sister species that Audubon had collected along the Arkansas River and named Traill's Flycatcher in honor of Dr. Thomas Stewart Traill, the president of the Liverpool Royal Institution.[108] Ornithologists were long aware of the behavioral distinctions between the two birds, including their completely different songs and nest construction.[109] However, the scientists considered them separate races of the same species because of the birds' virtually identical physical appearance. The American Ornithologists' Union, the final arbiter on matters of speciation, finally split Traill's Flycatcher into two species in 1973 and renamed them the Alder Flycatcher and the Willow Flycatcher.[110] Audubon may have erred, but give him his due. He was on the right path during the Labrador expedition and came closer to determining the truth than generations of ornithologists who followed him.

14

Nova Scotia

AUGUST 1833

We were now, thank God, positively on the main shore of our native land.
JOHN JAMES AUDUBON

When Audubon awoke at dawn on the morning of Sunday, August 18, the winds were again fair. However, the skies were cloudy, and the flight of the birds about the harbor told him that harsh weather lay ahead. Capt. Emery, who was anxious to resume the journey, discounted the naturalist's forecast and ordered the crew to prepare to sail.[1]

By 5:00 a.m., the *Ripley* was once more underway, retracing her route through St. George's Bay toward the waters of the gulf. With the approach of evening, the skies darkened, and a tremendous gale set in from the southwest. The schooner dropped its sails and laid to for the night as it was pounded by the storm. The weather remained equally bad throughout the following day. The schooner was pitched about on its anchor, leaving the naturalist and his party thoroughly seasick. While Audubon was below deck, a wave swept one of the two remaining pet Great Black-backed Gulls over the side. The bird made a valiant attempt to return to the schooner, but the wind and the waves were too strong. The sailors last saw it swimming toward the not-too-distant shore, where Audubon presumed it arrived safely.[2]

The storm finally dissipated on Tuesday, August 20. The schooner was now north of the Magdalen Islands. Audubon had hoped to revisit the Gannett Rocks, but the winds remained contrary to such a course. No one "could bear the idea of returning to Labrador," so Capt. Emery turned the vessel back toward Newfoundland, although the winds would not allow them to make port. The weather improved that night, and when daylight greeted the company, the good captain changed their heading to sail for the Gut of Canso. However, the winds died before they could reach the passage.[3]

As they sat aboard the becalmed vessel, Audubon suggested that they make for Pictou, Nova Scotia, where he proposed to disembark with his companions and travel overland through the province while the schooner made its way back to Eastport. This was an itinerary he had already mapped out during his time at Bras d'Or. As the naturalist explained to his journal, "The great desire we all have to see Pic-

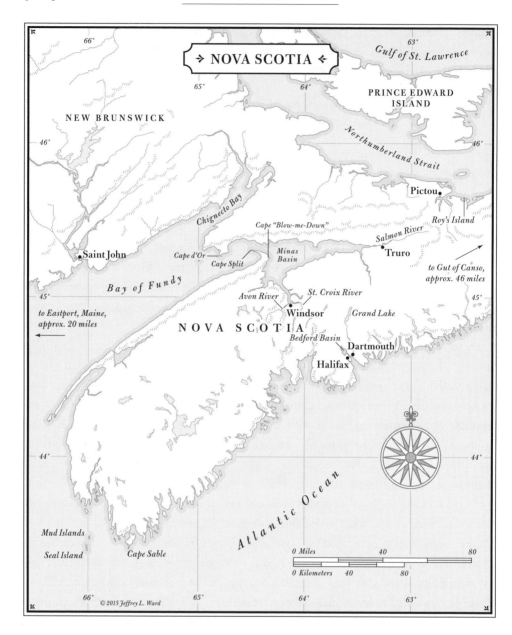

tou, Halifax, and the country between there and Eastport is our inducement." Capt. Emery ordered the new heading, and when the winds finally returned, the *Ripley* began beating her way south.[4]

The schooner reached the waters beyond the port of Pictou on Thursday, August 22, but the winds would not permit her further advance. With their destination so close at hand, Audubon decided after dinner that they would take a boat to shore and make their way to Pictou on foot.[5] The contrary winds may not have been the only factor influencing his decision. Under the terms of the charter-party agreement, he was personally responsible for paying the port or pilotage charges as well as the costs of feeding the crew should the schooner enter any port other than those along the Labrador coast.[6]

The crew loaded one of the boats with their things as Capt. Emery and Audubon's party "drank a parting glass to our wives and friends." Then, the "excellent little captain" piloted his esteemed passengers to Roy's Island, a small island located east of the entrance to Pictou Harbor.[7]

A group of men were at work in the fields making hay when the boat landed. Audubon quickly hired a couple of them to transport the baggage and two of his company to the town after dropping the rest of them off on the mainland, all for a mere $2. The trunks were quickly moved to the other boat. The naturalist and the members of his party said goodbye to the crewmembers who had brought them ashore and shook hands with the captain, "towards whom we all now feel much real attachment, and after mutual adieus, and good wishes for the completion of our respective journeys, we parted giving each other three most hearty cheers." Capt. Emery and his men returned to the schooner, which stood just offshore with her sails raised. Both the wind and the tide promised a speedy voyage back to the Gut of Canso.[8]

Audubon was grateful to be once more on solid ground, especially after the trials of the past several days at sea:

> [A]fter four days' confinement in our berths, and sea-sickness, and the sea and vessel, and all their smells and discomforts, we were so refreshed, that the thought of walking nine miles seemed nothing more than figuring through a single quadrille. The air felt uncommonly warm, and the country, compared with those we had so lately left, appeared perfectly beautiful, and we inhaled the fragrance of the new-mown grass, as if nothing sweeter ever existed. Even the music of crickets was delightful to my ears, for no such insect is to be found either at Labrador or Newfoundland. The voice of a blue jay sounded melody to me, and the sight of a humming-bird quite filled my mind with delight.[9]

The short trip to the mainland took almost no time, and Audubon, John, Lincoln, and Shattuck were soon on the road to Pictou, while Coolidge and Ingalls stayed with the baggage. The naturalist's portfolio containing his Labrador drawings was among their things, of course. He would not risk losing his last two months' work should something untoward happen to the *Ripley* as she sailed for home.[10]

Striding along the road as it wandered through woods of "tall timber," the naturalist and his companions felt like "boys just released from school." They found reminders of home in every plant and enjoyed the fresh aroma that filled the air. "Now and then as we crossed a hill, and cast our eyes back on the sea, we saw our beautiful vessel sailing freely before the wind, and as she diminished towards the horizon, she at last appeared like a white speck, or an eagle floating in the air, and we wished our captain a most safe voyage to Quoddy."[11]

The nine-mile trek took two and a half hours and brought Audubon's party to the shore across the harbor from Pictou. The boat carrying their friends had not yet arrived, so they whiled away the time relaxing on the grass and surveying the town. Pictou was situated "at the bottom of a fine bay on the northwest side" of the harbor. Although it appeared small, it had approximately two thousand residents. Three churches were in evidence, standing taller than the surrounding structures, some of which were built of wood, others of stone. Down along the water's edge, a number of vessels sat in stocks. And, out in the harbor, several American vessels were taking on coal from mines in the vicinity.[12]

The boat with the baggage finally picked up the group and transported them all across the harbor to the town. They found rooms at the Royal Oak, the finest establishment in Pictou. Audubon relished the feel of carpeting once more beneath his feet. He and his party sat down to an "excellent supper" and then made their way out on the Old Road to the home of Prof. Thomas McCulloch. McCulloch was the head of the local college, Pictou Academy, which boasted a fine natural-history museum that almost certainly was the object of Audubon's interest. The McCulloch house, located on a knoll overlooking the harbor a quarter mile from town, was a modest one-and-a-half-story brick structure built in the Scottish tradition, with a peaked roof and freestone facings around the doors and windows. According to Audubon, it resembled "a small English villa." The McCulloch clan called it "Sherbrooke Cottage."[13]

The Scottish-born McCulloch, now fifty-seven years of age, had attended the University of Glasgow and subsequently received theological instruction at the Secession Divinity Hall at Whitburn. In 1799, he was ordained in the Secession Church, an offshoot of the Church of Scotland. He arrived in Pictou with his wife and three young children in November 1803 while on his way to Prince Edward Island, where he was to take over a congregation. With the crossing of the ice-filled Northumberland Strait fraught with danger so late in the season, two of the town's leaders persuaded McCulloch to spend the winter in Pictou. Their motives, however, may not have been entirely altruistic. The story goes that they instantly recognized the value a man of his background and intelligence would bring to their growing community. By spring, McCulloch and his family had decided to remain in Pictou for good.[14]

He became the local Presbyterian minister and within a few years started a grammar school, initially in his home and later in a separate building on his property, which attracted students not only from Nova Scotia but from as far away as the West

Indies. His dream, though, was to establish an institution of higher learning. With financial support from the residents of Pictou and an 1816 charter granted by the Nova Scotia legislature, Pictou Academy opened in May 1818. It was nonsectarian in keeping with McCulloch's liberal view that a college education should be available to young men regardless of their religious beliefs. At the time, the only other college in the province was King's College in Windsor, which effectively limited its instruction to Anglican students. However, unlike King's College, Pictou Academy was not authorized by its charter to award college-level degrees.[15]

Nevertheless, within two years, the academy had an enrollment of thirty-four students, a newly constructed two-story wooden building with a short, rounded cupola on Church Street, and a curriculum that included the subject of natural history. McCulloch had by then begun to lay the foundation for a museum to be devoted to the natural world in one of the academy's four rooms.[16] Writing to a colleague in Scotland, he remarked, "I am become a mighty hunter of flies."[17] The ornithological collection would take off after McCulloch returned from a visit to Scotland in 1825 that lasted a little over a year. During the trip, he witnessed the public's interest in the subject, which Audubon had been able to capitalize upon when he first arrived in Liverpool and later reached Edinburgh.[18]

In 1828, McCulloch provided a report on his budding museum to a Scottish colleague who was looking for New World specimens:

> Hitherto, for the sake of the Academy, we have been obliged to provide only for ourselves, and when I tell you that within these ten months my family have filled with birds and beasts the side of a room thirty feet long and ten feet high, made and painted the stands for them, etc, you will see that we have not been idle. It is the first thing of the kind in the Provinces, and will add greatly to the popularity of our Institution."[19]

Audubon had heard of the museum, presumably from the pages of *An Historical and Statistical Account of Nova-Scotia* by Thomas C. Haliburton, which Shattuck had carried along on the voyage. Of Pictou Academy, Haliburton said:

> It contains a library, not very extensive but valuable, and also a museum of the Natural History of Nova-Scotia. It is the most extensive collection of the Zoology of the Country, which has yet been made. The birds in particular are finely preserved and make a beautiful appearance. This branch is nearly completed, and exhibits in one group almost every variety in the Province.[20]

In the past several years, the museum had continued to grow with the active participation of McCulloch's children, especially his fourth son and namesake. Thomas Jr., now twenty-four, had demonstrated not only a knack for finding birds but for skinning and mounting them as well. According to a biography of the educator written by his son William, "[a]t every spare moment some of the family were off to the woods with the guns, which were generally kept loaded in case of a stray visitor to the trees around the house. Soon the collection came to be the talk of the countryside, and many a rare bird found its way to the house."[21] Is it any wonder that Audubon found his way there as well?

The dark-haired McCulloch greeted the Americans "in the most cordial manner" and invited them in for a glass of wine. He then returned with them to town to show them the museum, a large room fitted with glass display cases on the second floor of the academy building. Audubon noted that there was an impressive "collection of well-preserved birds and other things." William McCulloch recalled that the naturalist "spoke very warmly of the truth to nature of the form and attitude of the birds and animals." But it was getting late, so the professor invited them to return to his home at 8:00 a.m. the next morning for breakfast, after which he would give them more time to peruse the collection.[22]

The following day, Friday, August 23, McCulloch was joined by his wife, Isabella, her sister, four of his five sons, and one of his daughters in hosting Audubon's party for what the naturalist termed "an excellent Scotch breakfast."[23] During the meal, McCulloch impressed Audubon with his intellect. "The more I saw and talked with the professor, the more I was pleased with him," the naturalist wrote.[24] Audubon had brought along his portfolio and, following the meal, pulled it out to show several of his recent drawings to the McCulloch family.[25] Finding a kindred spirit in Thomas Jr., Audubon naturally gravitated to the young man and predictably solicited his future help in obtaining rare specimens for *The Birds of America.*[26]

McCulloch accompanied his guests to the academy building, where they once more roamed among the glass cases in the museum and "examined his fine collection" of birds, mammals, insects, fresh-water shells, and minerals endemic to the province.[27] Audubon recalled that there were "several beautiful specimens" of the Snowy Owl as well as "about a dozen well mounted specimens of both sexes [of Goshawks], and of different ages."[28] One case featured the nests and eggs of various birds.[29] The naturalist walked around the room and counted half a dozen species that he needed for his work. Never shy about expressing his desires when it mattered, Audubon told his host that he had been looking in vain for these birds and was anxious to include them in his publication.[30] Without a second thought, McCulloch had the cases opened and presented the birds to Audubon "with so much apparent good will, that I took them and thanked him."[31]

Among the specimens were two beautifully plumaged adult Hudsonian Godwits.[32] John had illustrated an immature bird during the Audubons' stay in Boston, and with the adults now in hand, Audubon would finally be able to complete the drawing.[33] McCulloch told Audubon he was free to take anything else he liked. In addition to a "few specimens of iron and copper," the naturalist looked enviously at the nest of a Yellow-rumped Warbler, containing four eggs, as well as the nest and three eggs of the Blackburnian Warbler. These were also quickly bestowed.[34]

McCulloch asked for Audubon's opinion as to the value of the collection. The naturalist may not have been aware of it, but the academy was facing a doubtful future. For years McCulloch had been contending with a committed opposition to his liberal approach to education among the more conservative Anglican members of the provincial legislature in Halifax. He struggled each year to obtain financial support from the government, while King's College was the beneficiary of a permanent annual grant of £500 buttressed by an additional £1,250 yearly from the British authorities. By comparison, from 1820 to 1823 Pictou Academy had limped along with a mere £325 in annual aid.[35]

Efforts begun in 1823 to pass a bill authorizing a permanent grant to the school found support in the popularly elected House of Assembly but inevitably failed in the twelve-member Legislative Council, which was dominated by Anglican members appointed by the lieutenant-governor. Over the next seven years, through 1830, the Council repeatedly blocked bills awarding Pictou Academy a permanent grant. The college obtained annual awards of £400 from 1824 to 1827, but changes in the makeup of the Council, especially the 1825 appointment of Anglican Bishop John Inglis, made it disinclined to support the institution. From 1828 to 1831, assembly bills for the academy's annual support died in the Council. McCulloch and the trustees had only managed to keep the college going with the largess of supporters in Pictou and Scotland. Then, in 1832, with pressure from the colonial secretary in London, a compromise was struck in the legislature which threatened to destroy all that McCulloch had built. The final bill provided an annual grant of £400 for ten years but gave McCulloch's opponents a toehold on the board of trustees and called for a significant shift in the college's purpose by requiring it to take on grammar-school students as well.[36]

McCulloch knew that, with the changes imposed by the legislature, the academy would have to do without the museum, especially as it took up one of the building's four rooms. Moreover, its sale would result in an infusion of needed cash. However, an offer to sell the museum to the province for £500 had been declined. Audubon was surprised there had been no interest. Given the scope and quality of the collection, he believed it was worth twice that. He offered his appraisal in writing, making sure the honorific F.R.S. followed his signature to reflect his fellowship in the Royal Society of London, with all the authority that might convey. As he handed it to the professor, the naturalist expressed his hope to McCulloch that "it might prove useful to him."[37]

When Audubon and his companions returned to the Royal Oak, U.S. Vice Consul Jotham Blanchard was waiting for them. The thirty-three-year-old Blanchard had lived most of his life in Nova Scotia but was an American by birth. His family moved from Peterborough, New Hampshire, where he was born, to Truro when he was still an infant. In 1813, his parents relocated to West River in Pictou County and later to the town of Pictou. He had been a member of the first class of sixteen students at Pictou Academy and, following his graduation, studied law. In 1822 he was admitted to the bar. A man of strong, progressive views like his former professor, Blanchard became the editor of the *Colonial Patriot*, a liberal weekly newspaper that began publishing in Pictou in 1827 as a counterbalance to the conservative Halifax press. Three years later he was elected to the provincial assembly.[38]

Blanchard had learned of Audubon's arrival in Pictou and wanted to offer assistance as the local U.S. representative. However, the naturalist had already booked passage for his group on the Eastern Mail Coach to Truro, which was being readied for departure. With the specimens from the museum carefully packed and the hotel bill paid, Audubon had a little extra time and agreed to walk with the younger man ahead of the stage. It would have been a leisurely ramble, as Blanchard had a crooked leg from a serious knee injury suffered in a boyhood fall on the ice. Their conversation quickly turned to England, which Blanchard had visited in 1831 to meet with the colonial secretary on behalf of Pictou Academy. Over a distance of a mile or so, Audubon learned that they had mutual friends in Newcastle upon Tyne. The naturalist thought Blanchard "an agreeable man."[39]

With the arrival of the stage, Audubon bade Blanchard goodbye and joined his companions in the coach. The road was a good one, having been macadamized using the state-of-the-art road building techniques pioneered in England by Scottish-born John Loudon McAdam. By compacting layers of small, broken stones on top of an elevated, cambered roadbed of native soil, rainwater would be diverted to the edges, and the roadway would provide a firm surface for traveling. It promised Audubon's party a smooth ride to Truro, which was situated thirty-nine miles away near the head of the Bay of Fundy. During the early part of the journey, it began to rain, with winds from the east, a propitious wind for the *Ripley*.[40] The "well wooded, well cultivated" country through which they passed was a pleasant change from the "desolate regions, snow, and tempestuous storms" that had marked their days in Labrador.[41]

By the time they stopped at a roadhouse around 4:00 p.m. to fill their aching bellies, the clouds had opened and it was pouring. A gentleman, his wife, and another lady were already inside, having traveled through the rain in an open cart driven by a man and his Irish wife. Audubon offered the strangers seats in the stage so that they could stay dry. It was a gallant gesture and one the trio gratefully accepted, although they inexplicably failed to express their gratitude. Regardless, when dinner was over, Audubon, Shattuck, and Ingalls wrapped themselves in their respective cloaks and climbed into the open wagon, the naturalist seated by the "so-so Irish dame." The rest of his party and the three new passengers squeezed into the crowded stage and set off. Audubon's cart was pulled by a strong horse and traveled at a fast clip. To the naturalist's delight, the rain soon stopped, and he was treated to a better view of the countryside than the coach would have afforded. As they made their way along the roadway, a horse pulled up to them carrying Prof. McCulloch. He indicated he was heading to Truro and would see them there.[42]

Audubon and his party arrived at the "pretty, loosely-built village" as the sun was setting.[43] From the Jersey cart, the naturalist had a good view of the place and filled part of his journal with a description of it later that evening:

> It is situated in the centre of a most beautiful valley of great extent, and under complete cultivation; looking westerly a broad sheet of water is seen, forming the head of the beautiful Bay of Fundy, and several brooks run through the valley emptying into it. The buildings, although principally of wood, are good-looking, and as cleanly as any of our pretty New England villages, well painted, and green blinds. The general appearance of the people quite took me by surprise, being extremely genteel.[44]

Truro was another step closer to New York and Lucy. For Audubon, the anticipation of his homecoming was beginning to build. He knew that in a matter of days he would be in the arms of his beloved, and the mere thought of their reunion brought joy to his heart.[45]

The cart and the stage came to a stop in front of an inn. Audubon and his companions headed inside to see if they could get a bite to eat. The place was noisy and crowded, and they were told that only three of them could be seated for supper. They located another establishment across the street which could feed them all. While they were dining, Prof. McCulloch found them and, seeing several members of the Assembly at nearby tables, proceeded to make the introductions. McCulloch also cemented his relationship with Audubon by offering him some snuff. In his journal the naturalist remarked excitedly that the professor "*loves it.*"[46] He was doubtless very appreciative of the tobacco after weeks of going without.

Audubon did not wish to linger in Truro. His plans called for the company to continue on to Halifax, although he hoped to hire someone to drive them in the morning so that they could avoid having to make the sixty-four-mile journey in the overnight mail stage. However, he could find no volunteers. Since the coach was not scheduled to depart until 11:00 p.m., the naturalist had some time to kill. Prof. McCulloch suggested they pay a call on the speaker of the House of Assembly,

Samuel G. W. Archibald, who lived in Halifax most of the year but spent several weeks during the summer in Truro at his magnificent country estate along the banks of the Salmon River.[47]

Archibald had been born in Truro in 1777, the grandson of one of the town's founders, David Archibald. He was raised by his grandfather following his father's untimely death and his mother's subsequent remarriage. At the age of fifteen, his older sister took an interest in his education, and he was sent to Massachusetts, where he attended Haverhill Academy and later Andover Academy. He returned to the province in 1796 with plans to enter the Presbyterian ministry. However, he gravitated to the law after serving as a prothonotary of the Supreme Court and a clerk of the peace for the District of Colchester. He married into a politically connected family, became an attorney and barrister in 1805, and followed his father and grandfather into provincial politics, running successfully for a seat in the Assembly in 1806. As one of its more liberal members, he became a vigorous supporter of Pictou Academy, served on its board of trustees, and advocated forcefully in the legislature for a permanent annual grant to the institution. He assumed the position of speaker in 1824 and, since 1830, had served concurrently as attorney general.[48]

A later historian described Archibald as "a more than ordinarily handsome man, of great suavity of manner, with a melodious voice, fascinating address, and a thorough knowledge of human nature."[49] He was one of the most powerful and influential men in the province—precisely the type of person the naturalist would wish to meet.

Audubon and McCulloch found Archibald at home along with his second wife, Joanna, and his seven-year-old "handsome young daughter" by his deceased wife. The naturalist had brought along his portfolio and, following the formal introductions, showed the Archibalds some of his recent work. Archibald was sufficiently impressed to supply him with a letter of introduction to Chief Justice Brenton Halliburton, the president of the council, who made his home in the provincial capital. Though Audubon did not mention it, the speaker evidently also gave him a letter for Bishop John Inglis, another Halifax resident. When Audubon rejoined his friends back at the inn, there was still some time to visit his journal before the stage arrived.[50] Finally, with the coachman calling for the naturalist's luggage and the "the cover of my trunk . . . gaping to receive this poor book," Audubon tossed the journal in and climbed aboard.[51]

According to Audubon, it was a "beautiful" night. A brilliant moon just past the first quarter hung in the heavens, but the passengers could see little of the hilly countryside through which they were passing. The horses, characterized by the naturalist as "lazy," were swapped for a fresh team after the first twenty miles. However, a broken linchpin brought the stage to a halt after only another mile and a half.

The driver took a lit candle and went back to search the roadway for the missing pin while Ingalls agreed to hold the horses. Audubon and Coolidge kept him company as John, Lincoln, and Shattuck napped in the coach. The silence of the night was broken periodically by the hooting of owls secreted in the nearby woods. Ingalls amused himself by trying to answer them. As the wait became longer, the three travelers began feeling "wolfish" and added a chorus of howls to the cool night air. The driver eventually gave up his search and returned to the stage to connect the separated pieces using a length of rope. He was just finishing up as dawn broke on Saturday, August 24, and brought the first touch of daylight to a lovely late-summer morning.[52]

Hoping to get the blood moving in his body after standing about on a chilly night, Audubon jogged a mile up the road and waited for the coach to catch up. When it did, he climbed up next to the driver and, as was his wont, began asking questions about the poor-looking country through which they were traveling. The stomachs of Audubon's party began to growl with the rising sun, and the naturalist queried the driver about the options for breakfast. The man replied that the tavern where his passengers normally ate was twenty-five miles from the spot where the stage had broken down, still some distance away. Audubon prevailed upon him to stop at a residence along the way to see if they could get some coffee and something to eat. However, its owner took one look at the motley group and refused to serve them.[53]

The travelers finally reached the breakfast tavern on the shores of Grand Lake later that morning. Audubon noted that the lake was reportedly a great spot for fishing and thought it would make a "pleasant residence" during the summer.[54] It was also the centerpiece of an ambitious engineering project by the Shubenacadie Canal Company, a private enterprise formed to construct a canal across the province, connecting the Atlantic Ocean at Halifax to the Minas Basin, the eastern arm of the Bay of Fundy. But the project had been halted when the company failed in 1831 after expending £90,000. With the provincial government refusing to step in and provide financing, the naturalist doubted the canal would ever be completed.[55]

Following breakfast, the Americans reboarded the stage for the final seventeen miles of the trip. The road was "level and good, though rather narrow, and a very fine drive for private carriages."[56] As they approached their destination, still two miles away, they could see the British flag flying from the large military garrison on Citadel Hill above the city. Around 10:00 a.m., the stage pulled up to a wharf in the smaller community of Dartmouth, situated across the harbor from Halifax, and came to a stop.[57] There the passengers would disembark and, along with the stage, continue the journey across the water via a "small steam-ferry boat."[58] But the gate to the wharf was closed, and they had to wait an hour before someone came to open it.[59]

From the deck of the ferry they could see the city from the best possible vantage point. According to author Thomas C. Haliburton, "[f]ew places present so pleasing an aspect as Halifax, when viewed from the harbour. Its streets are laid out with regularity, its spires have a picturesque and even magnificent effect, and the trees which are scattered throughout it, give it an appearance softened and refreshing."[60] Audubon's attention was also drawn to a sixty-four-gun flagship of the Royal Navy that was sitting anchored in the harbor.[61] The naturalist observed a Fork-tailed Gull (Sabine's Gull), a small, Arctic-nesting gull distinguished by its slate-colored head and dark primaries, flying above the harbor among a group of Common American Gulls (Ring-billed Gulls).[62]

The steamer landed at Halifax around noon.[63] The coach took them to a boardinghouse, operated by one Mr. Paul, which was reputed to be the finest in town. Audubon and his party had a difficult time getting a room and ultimately had to accept one with only four beds. The naturalist was not at all impressed with the accommodations. In a city with eighteen thousand civilians and another two thousand military personnel, he had expected something better.[64] "Halifax has not one good hotel, and only two very indifferent boarding-houses, where the attendance is miserable, and the table by no means good," he groused.[65]

Having deposited their trunks in their room, the travelers set out to explore the city. Audubon was shocked at the number of poor, "beggarly-looking blacks" on the streets.[66] During the War of 1812, the British had offered sanctuary for runaway slaves aboard its naval vessels in Chesapeake Bay and had subsequently shipped them off to Halifax to be resettled. Some of the newcomers were successful in finding positions as domestic servants among the city's well-to-do. Others established communities outside the city at Preston and Hammond's Plains, where the provincial authorities made land available for tillage. But many, finding themselves ill equipped to live off the land in such a hostile climate, returned to Halifax to eke out an impoverished existence on the streets.[67] Audubon thought Mrs. Frances Trollope, the Englishwoman who had published a vituperative account of the American people in her 1832 book *Domestic Manners of the Americans*, should have visited Halifax and seen these sad souls. It would have certainly "furnished materials for her descriptive pen," he said.[68]

As Audubon and his companions rambled about, they discovered that two months of struggling over "the soft, deep mosses of Labrador" had ill prepared them for the hard pavement of city streets. Their feet and legs were all sore in no time, and they soon retreated to the boardinghouse to rest.[69] While they were sitting around, a card was delivered from an Italian gentleman who ran a nearby bathhouse with "fine baths of all sorts." Eager to wash off the grime of their journey, the Americans headed over to his establishment. Here again they were disappointed. The rooms had a single tin bathtub, along with "a hole underground, into which the sea-water filters, about the size of a hogshead." Audubon was not deterred. He stripped off his clothes and climbed down into the hole. He was quickly joined by Shattuck and Ingalls. When they were done, they dried themselves "with curious towels." For only $0.06 apiece, it was worth it.[70]

That evening, Audubon's party was entertained by the nightly procession of the drum-and-fife corps of the British Army. At 8:00 p.m., the corps assembled in front of the town clock on Barrack Street and marched to either the seat of local government known as Province House or the residence of the commanding general before returning to the garrison. Back at their room, Audubon sat down to bring his journal up to date. Then, having heard that the aide-de-camp to the governor of Newfoundland made his home in the boardinghouse, the naturalist had his calling card delivered.[71]

On Sunday morning, Audubon was awake by 4:00 a.m. and was soon seated at a writing table, where he first penned a letter to Lucy to let her know that he and his party had arrived safely in Halifax and they would soon be on their way to Eastport. He then dashed off a note to advise his dutiful Boston friend Dr. George Parkman that he was running short of cash and might need the good physician's short-term financial support:[72]

> We are all safely landed here and more than that we are all well and as Happy as Men can be who have run out of Money (nearly). We left our vessel in Pictou Bay on Thursday last. She is now on her passage towards Eastport and so far has had a fair wind.
>
> We landed with the purpose of seeing as much as possible during this interesting voyage and tour of ours. We leave this on Tuesday morning next for Windsor; by steam to St. John's, New Brunswick and down the Bay of Fundy to Quoddy. We hope to reach Boston in about 10 days from this date Should we give up the Journey by land to Quebec which I most likely will abandon for want of Cash—indeed I will have to ask of you to accept and pay a Draft to assist me in the fitting of our Chartered Schooner. I must acknowledge to you that I may take this liberty in preference to Drawing on my Brother at Law of New York.[73]

Shattuck was anxious to let his father know of their safe passage as well as the anticipated timing of his arrival in Boston should Audubon decide not to continue on to Quebec:

> We arrived in this place, dear Father, yesterday noon, and are safely thus far on our way home. We left our vessel on Thursday last at Roys island when we walked nine miles westward to Pictou. We stopped here only long enough to

see the collections of birds, and then started in the mail stage for this place. We found the country interesting, the roads good, and our travelling accommodations much better than could have been expected. We shall stay in this place no longer than is necessary, and shall push on for Eastport with all possible speed. Should Mr Audubon return to Boston directly I shall hope to see you by the last of next week, and it is with no little pleasure, I can assure you, that I anticipate a return home after so long an absence. Our party are all in fine health and spirits and we can only hope that we shall find our friends as well and as prosperous as ourselves.[74]

With their letters in hand, Audubon and Shattuck headed down to the water to find a vessel to carry them to Boston.[75] As it was Sunday, the docks were deserted. Locked gates greeted them at every wharf, with army "sentinels standing guard everywhere."[76] Nevertheless, they eventually found someone from an English schooner who would take them. Audubon then sought a barber to remove his beard but had a hard time finding one. The stores and businesses were all closed for the Sabbath. However, when the naturalist claimed to be unfamiliar with the local blue laws and pleaded for a shave, he finally succeeded in locating a man who was willing to bend the rules.[77]

Once again whisker free, Audubon and three of his compatriots attended services at the Anglican church, St. Paul's, where they heard Bishop John Inglis preach. A portion of the congregation was made up of uniformed soldiers. The naturalist was informed that each of the local churches received a similar complement of troops from the garrison every Sunday.[78]

In the afternoon, Audubon and the "Young Gentlemen" attended a military funeral, which the naturalist called "a grand sight."[79] "[T]he soldiers walked far apart, guns inverted, to the sound of the finest anthem, and wonderfully well executed by an excellent band."[80] At some point in the day, he met one "Mr. Tremaine" and gave the man letters of introduction from Boston. This was likely Richard Tremain, a fifty-nine-year-old magistrate and the former president of the Chamber of Commerce. Until 1831, Tremain had operated a flour mill and bakehouse across the harbor in Dartmouth. He sold the business to the Shubenacadie Canal Company and retired from a successful mercantile career. Audubon described him as "an amiable gentleman."[81]

On Monday, Audubon spent much of the day at his writing table. He drafted a second piece of correspondence to Lucy before preparing letters to Nicholas Berthoud and John Bachman.[82] To Edward Harris he finished a lengthy dispatch that he had evidently begun the day before with details of the expedition, no doubt hoping to see it published in the pages of the *New-York Gazette*. He was not aware that Harris had left New York more than a month before to rendezvous with him at Eastport. The letter, which ultimately appeared in the paper's September 10 issue, made no effort to romanticize the expedition's difficult days along the Labrador coast:

> To ramble through the rich shady forests of our country has ever been a plea-
> sure to me, and every one who now formed our party; to wade through deep
> swamps under a scorching sun, I have even thought very bearable; but, to raise
> the feet from such matted beds of mosses as we had now to move through, and
> clothed so as to defend our bodies from the piercing air of that region, proved
> a most severe undertaking to all of us; we tugged and plunged, and managed
> slowly to move onwards; saw a very few birds, a few small flowrets [*sic*], and
> scarcely any thing that with us could be called a tree. Every day was nearly alike;
> we never were without a good fire in our camp or cabin, and for the distance of
> about three hundred miles, such was the country of Labrador.[83]

At the same time, Audubon assured his good friend that the trip had been well worth the effort. They had "collected some curious information" and discovered six new species of birds: "two species of falcons, one uncommonly large and beautiful; one species of grouse; one titmouse, and a sparrow" as well as "a fly catcher of rich plumage."[84]

The reference to finding a second unknown falcon species is puzzling because the naturalist never mentioned it in what was ultimately published from his jour-nal. Nor did he allude to it in any of his bird biographies. He eventually must have concluded that he was mistaken. Most likely, his confusion arose regarding a Pigeon Hawk (Merlin), a small, compact falcon that is sexually dimorphic and shows some plumage variations among the eastern-breeding "Boreal" subspecies, *Falco colum-barius columbarius*.[85] He had already confused the immature birds of this species for adults. In addition, Charles-Lucien Bonaparte had recently informed him that an adult male he had considered a unique species and had named Le Petit Capo-ral after Bonaparte's illustrious uncle was in fact the mature form of the species.[86] Audubon had seen Pigeon Hawks during the voyage, and at least one remarkably beautiful specimen had been collected. But it would be entirely understandable that he was still experiencing difficulties in sorting out the variants.

Shattuck was also busy writing another note to his father, this one offering a less than admiring picture of the provincial capital:

> We have been in Halifax two days and are heartily tired of it. It is very dull,
> and you hear none of of [*sic*] those business noises which almost stun one in
> an American city. The harbor is certainly excellent and the country very fine,
> but the inhabitants do lack enterprise. We have walked over the town and been

to see the public buildings, of which there are some very beautiful. The province house and Dalhousie college may be mentioned amongst these. The private
houses are generally built of wood, but the streets are wide regular and macadamized. Three regiments of soldiers are now stationed here, and you see the red
coats every where in the street. Sentinels are stationed in all the streets, and we
are fairly tired of the sight and name of soldiers.[87]

Audubon placed the letters onboard the packet *Cordelia*, which was bound for
Boston that Wednesday.[88] Vessels sailing between the two ports usually completed
the journey in three to six days, making it likely the letters would precede the arrival
of their senders.[89]

The naturalist then visited the homes of Chief Justice Halliburton and Bishop
Inglis to deliver his letters of introduction. Neither man was in, or at least so Audubon was told.[90] For some reason he did not believe this was true of the bishop, and
the snub rankled. "Audubon was a very sensitive man," as Coolidge recalled.[91] Since
his final days in Henderson, the naturalist had many times faced the indignity of
being slighted by those who considered him their inferior. However, with his international fame, he almost certainly did not expect such a cold reception now. It must
have served as a painful reminder of the years he had struggled to regain respect.

In his journal, Audubon mentioned that John and Ingalls had "spent their evening very agreeably with Commissary Hewitson."[92] William Hewitson was a deputy
commissary general in the Commissariat of the British Army, the civilian department responsible for seeing that the garrison was supplied with food stores.[93] How
the two young men met the forty-six-year-old Hewitson and what the three of them
did over the course of the evening the naturalist did not say.

The following morning, Tuesday, August 27, Audubon received a note indicating
that the bishop would be returning his call that evening. However, the naturalist's
plans called for his party to leave for Windsor on the morning stage. Although this
itinerary had been established for some time, Coolidge could not help thinking that
Audubon rather enjoyed not being able to receive His Lordship. "He chose to be
'out' when the Bishop came," the down-easter recalled years later.[94]

It was raining when Audubon and his companions boarded the Royal Western
Mail Coach at 9:00 a.m. There were only seats enough for five of them inside the
coach, so one of their group had to face the elements on top. The roadway, like the
others they had traveled on in the province, was macadamized. With the solid pavement under their wheels and a pair of good horses in front, they were able to make
six and a half miles an hour as they wound their way "through undulating hills and
valleys" toward their destination off the Bay of Fundy, forty-five miles away. For

over an hour, the passengers had a "pleasant" view of the Bedford Basin, the broad body of water at the head of Halifax Harbor. They also saw a number of "tolerably, good-looking summer-houses" that had been built "here and there" along the way.[95]

Their route took them past Rockingham, the former manor of Prince Edward, the fourth son of King George III. The prince had come to Halifax in 1794 to serve as commander of the British garrison. He had resided here in comfort for several years before returning to England, first in 1798 after injuring his leg in a riding accident and then for good in 1800. The estate, built at a cost of around £1 million, had long since been abandoned and now lay in ruins. However, the prince's name lived on in British North America. In 1799, it was bestowed on the island in the Gulf of St. Lawrence formerly known as the Island of St. John. Today Prince Edward is perhaps best remembered as the father of Queen Victoria.[96]

From the harbor, the road ran for a time along the Salmon River, "a small rivulet of swift water, which abounds with salmon, trout, elwines [alewives], etc."[97] The countryside was dotted with trout-filled lakes and cultivated fields, though the rocky soil was poor. The travelers saw a gradual shift in the makeup of the woodlands as they progressed, with fir, spruce, and dwarf beech giving way to beech, hemlock, elm, and maple about twenty miles from the capital.[98] The stage made a stop at a roadside inn, where Audubon and his comrades had dinner. The naturalist engaged the innkeeper in conversation and learned that the rooms there went for only $5 per week during the summer season and that the hunting and fishing in the vicinity were excellent.[99]

Thirty miles from Halifax, the coach passed the large, well-appointed Georgian summer home of acting Lieutenant-Governor Thomas Nickleson Jeffery, an estate known as Lakelands. The name derived from the fact that the grounds of the stately residence were bordered by "two handsome fresh-water lakes."[100] Audubon identified Jeffery as president of the Assembly, but he actually served on His Majesty's Council. As the senior member who was not a sitting judge, he took over the administrative duties of Lieutenant-Governor Sir Peregrine Maitland and assumed the title of president when Maitland left the province to return to England in October 1832.[101]

Once the stage crossed the headwaters of the St. Croix River, "which rolls its waters impetuously into the Bay of Fundy," Audubon's party observed a marked improvement in the state of cultivation. The fields were now diked, and grain as well as a variety of fruit—peaches, pears, plums, quinces, and grapes—were being grown in the rich soil.[102] The travelers continued on past King's College and its affiliated secondary school, located on one hundred acres of land about a mile outside Windsor. Audubon described both facilities as "looking well, and built of fine freestone."[103] The preparatory school was built of stone, but the college, set atop a hill with panoramic views of the surrounding area, comprised a long edifice of five adjoining three-story buildings constructed of wood, under a single flat roof.[104]

It was late afternoon when the stage finally pulled up to the "best private boarding-house" in Windsor.[105] As elsewhere in the province, the town did not boast a hotel. No rooms were available, so Audubon's party had to obtain accommodations at another boardinghouse nearby. Although everyone was hungry, they were forced to wait a couple of hours for supper. In the interim, they walked around the town. Audubon described Windsor as "a small and rather neat village."[106] It was situated on the eastern side of the Avon River near the point where the watercourse flows into the Southern Bight, an inlet of the Minas Basin. In addition to agriculture and shipbuilding, the town was known for its vast supplies of gypsum plaster, commonly known as plaster of paris. The material was mined in quarries and from the banks of the St. Croix River and then shipped to the United States via Eastport. Farmers used it for treating their soil.[107]

The extraordinary tidal flows for which this region is known made the setting, for Audubon, "as novel to me as the coast of Labrador."[108] The tide was now at its ebb, and for nearly ten miles, as far he could see, the bed of the river and the bay was bare. A reddish mud covered the embankments on either side of the river for a distance of a hundred yards. Sticking out from the shoreline into empty space were wooden wharves, to which vessels being loaded with gypsum were tied. As the fre-netic Fundy waters had receded, the boats had come to rest on the banks far above the river's gravel-strewn bed. Occasionally, the naturalist was told, a vessel would break its lines and slide all the way to the bottom, sixty-five feet below the wharf. When the tidal flow was reversed, the basin would fill at a rate of four knots per hour, a sight Audubon eagerly anticipated witnessing the following day.[109]

Back at the boardinghouse, Audubon's party was finally served their supper. The food that arrived proved not to be worth the wait. The naturalist described it as an "indifferent" meal.[110]

In the morning, Audubon and his young friends walked down to the river to ob-serve the remarkable tidal phenomenon of the Bay of Fundy.[111] The tides there, as in most spots around the globe, are semidiurnal, occurring twice a day a little over six hours apart. However, the differential between high and low tides, or tidal range, is among the greatest in the world.

The wharves were now empty, the vessels from the day before having sailed with the tide during the night. To help gauge the speed of the waters' rise, Audubon's group placed several markers in a vertical line down the side of the river bank. Each marker extended from the ground three feet and was positioned so that the top of one marker was at the same elevation as the base of the one above it. The men took a seat on one of the wharves and waited.[112] According to Audubon, the water rose "with a rapidity I cannot describe."[113] When the tide was halfway up the bank, it was rising three feet every ten minutes. By the time it reached its high point, it had filled the river with sixty-five feet of water, by the naturalist's estimate. Then, within minutes, the waters began to recede even more rapidly than they had advanced, "and in a few hours the whole bed of the river is again emptied."[114]

In the afternoon, Audubon's party roamed the countryside with their guns in search of birds. The open fields and meadows were prime hunting habitat for Marsh Hawks (Northern Harriers), and the men saw a significant number of females and immature birds of the species but not a single adult male.[115] These large, sexually dimorphic raptors are typically seen soaring low over open ground, their long wings held in a slight dihedral as they search for prey like mice, birds, and frogs. The adult males are gray above and whitish below, with dark wing tips, while the females are brown, with brown streaks on their white breasts. The immatures of both sexes are similar to the adult female but have breasts of solid cinnamon. From a distance, the species can be distinguished by its mode of flight and the white rump patch that is visible in all plumages.[116]

John was able to collect a female and an immature male. Audubon immediately noticed that the birds were significantly darker in color than the birds he was familiar with from the Midwest and the South. "Indeed," he declared, "it may be said that the farther north I have been, the deeper in tint have I found the birds."[117]

Later in the day, a steamer called the *Maid of the Mist* arrived in Windsor from Saint John, New Brunswick.[118] Built for James Whitney, the owner of the *Henrietta*, which ran aground off Eastport back in May, the *Maid of the Mist* had made her inaugural voyage in June.[119] She was now running twice weekly between Passamaquoddy Bay and Windsor by way of Saint John, Parrsboro, and Horton Bluff.[120] Since she was scheduled to leave in the morning for her return trip to Saint John, Audubon sent the "Young Gentlemen" aboard to reserve their space. He also wished to know if she was carrying any letters for him. He was disappointed to hear she was not.[121]

Before their departure, Audubon had hoped to call upon Thomas C. Haliburton, the judge and former member of the Nova Scotia Assembly who wrote the highly regarded two-volume work on the history and geography of the province. However, Haliburton was in Boston, and the desired meeting never occurred.[122]

The following morning, Thursday, August 29, the naturalist and his companions packed up their belongings and boarded the steamboat. She pulled away from the dock at 11:45 a.m. and, with a thick cloud trailing behind her, steamed down the

Avon River and into the Southern Bight of the Bay of Fundy.[123] Saint John was about
143 miles away, and the steamer could make the journey in roughly fourteen hours
provided there were no delays from the tides or the often capricious weather.[124]

Their route took them past Cape Blow-Me-Down (now Cape Blomidon), a bold
and soaring prominence towering above the Minas Basin, its forested heights dropping off into steep cliffs of weathered red sandstone. The name for this landmark
comes from the strong winds that frequently blow off its point. The headlands terminate to the northwest at Cape Split, its perpendicular face of dark volcanic basalt
rising two hundred feet or more above the basin waters. Farther along, as the steamer
chugged her way southwest, Audubon could see Cape d'Or on the north shore of
Nova Scotia, where the Bay of Fundy divides into the Minas Basin and Chignecto
Bay.[125]

It was a comfortable journey. Only a small number of passengers were making the
trip, and Audubon's party had the compartment largely to themselves. The *Maid
of the Mist* reached Saint John at 2:00 a.m. under a moonlit sky. New Brunswick's
largest municipality, of roughly twelve thousand souls, was quiet as the naturalist
and his companions disembarked and walked the empty streets. When the sun rose,
the city stirred and slowly came to life. Audubon stepped into a clothing shop when
it opened and "purchased two suits of excellent stuff for shooting garments." The
Maid of the Mist was due to leave for Eastport at 7:00 a.m., and he and his group
made their way back to the steamer. After getting settled, to Audubon's utter astonishment and delight, Edward Harris boarded the vessel for the fifty-five-mile run
down to Passamaquoddy Bay and found them there.[126]

It must have been a case of pure serendipity. Harris and his friends had arrived in
Eastport in mid-August and had spent several days exploring the area. When word
got around that one of Audubon's colleagues was in town, Harris was quickly befriended by the officers of the garrison at Fort Sullivan. On August 20 they invited
him out on Passamaquoddy Bay to go fishing with the garrison's physician, presumably Dr. Ray, for what Harris described as a chowder party. The group rowed about
four miles from Eastport, dropped anchor, and caught enough fish for a meal. On
their return, they beached the boat on Deer Island on the British side of the border,
and the doctor cooked up "one of the finest chowders" Harris had ever tasted. Two
days later, one of the officers took Harris and his companions out to Pleasant Point
to show them the Passamaquoddy Indians.[127]

Harris had been in Saint John for almost a week, likely on a fishing or hunting
excursion.[128] He could not have known Audubon's overland itinerary since it had
taken shape only that month. Even Lucy had no idea where or when her husband
was likely to land. The naturalist's August 5 letter from Bras d'Or, suggesting the
possibility of stops in Nova Scotia and Saint John, had yet to reach her. Indeed, it

had not even been posted. Capt. Williams, in whose hands the letter had been entrusted at Bras d'Or, would finally send it from Portsmouth, New Hampshire, the following day, August 31.[129]

Based on what Harris had been told by the people of Eastport, he was not expecting Audubon to return to Eastport until mid-September. He was equally "surprised and gratified" to find the naturalist and his party "in excellent health, and well pleased with the excursion," although he noted in a letter back to New York that "they have experienced a very boisterous season, and visited a most inhospitable region."[130]

Harris wanted to hear all about the trip. However, for the past six weeks he had been carrying the letter Lucy had written to her husband back on July 14, and he knew that Audubon would want to read it first.[131] The naturalist broke the seal and scanned its contents with a combination of both relief and concern. Knowing that his beloved had been in good health just six weeks before eased his mind considerably. But her news that Havell was demanding higher rates for producing the prints in each Number came as a blow. An increase in Havell's compensation would either reduce Audubon's profits or force him to raise the price of his publication. Neither choice was appealing. *The Birds of America* was generating only a modest profit as it was, and the naturalist had no desire to lessen his income. However, passing along the costs to his subscribers would almost certainly lead to defections and make it nearly impossible to replace them. This was not good news—not good at all. As the steamer made her way south along the rugged, rocky coast, the naturalist began contemplating how he should respond.[132]

15

Home

I have returned nearly to the day appointed for this—we are all quite well thank God.
JOHN JAMES AUDUBON

The *Maid of the Mist* reached Eastport just before noon on Friday, August 30.[1] Audubon's party was required to report to the customs inspector, but the official did not open their trunks, and Audubon did not have to pay a duty on the clothing he had just purchased. Their return was anticipated, the *Ripley* having docked two days earlier. It seems likely that the directive had been passed down from the customs collector, Gen. James Ripley, to speed their passage through customs—a nod, no doubt, to Audubon's celebrity. The naturalist thought "this ought to be the case with poor students of nature all over the world."[2]

In the Custom House book of arriving passengers, the officer dutifully recorded the name of each member of the party along with his respective age, gender, country of origin, and country to which he intended to return. For a few he listed an occupation. It was not a model of exactitude. Although Audubon was correctly described as an "Ornithologist" who hailed from the United States, he was stated to be forty-nine years old, a year older than he actually was. Many of the particulars as to the "Young Gentlemen" were similarly off the mark. John was identified as James W. Audubon. All of them were listed as twenty years of age, when in truth they ranged from eighteen to twenty-one. Harris's age, thirty-three, was correctly given, but he was listed as a merchant from New Brunswick, when he had been born and raised an American.[3]

Word of the company's arrival spread quickly, and they were soon being greeted by their many friends and admirers. According to Audubon, they "had the whole town to Shake hands with for all welcomed our return." Gen. Ripley and James Curtiss, the Eastport postmaster, personally delivered the letters they were holding, including another five addressed to the naturalist from Lucy.[4]

Audubon was happy to be once more on American soil, and even happier to be able to restore Coolidge and Lincoln to their families. The responsibility for their safe return had weighed on him heavily throughout the voyage, as he later told his readers:

I had left Eastport with four young gentlemen under my care, some of whom were strangers to me, and I felt the responsibility of my charge, being now and then filled with terror lest any accident should befall them, for they were as adventurous as they were young and active. But thanks to the Almighty, who granted us his protection, I had the satisfaction of restoring them in safety to their friends. And so excellent was the disposition of my young companions, that not a single instance of misunderstanding occurred on the journey to cloud our enjoyment, but the most perfect cordiality was manifested by each towards all the rest. It was a happy moment to me when I delivered them to their parents.[5]

Audubon was relieved that he could stop worrying, at least about these two young men. And, within a few days, when Shattuck and Ingalls were both safely back in Boston, he would be able to relinquish the burden for good.[6]

Audubon and John "took up quarters with good Mr. Weston" and started packing.[7] Shattuck and Ingalls were doubtless offered the Chadbournes' hospitality and did likewise. The Boston mail packet was scheduled to sail on Monday, and the naturalist planned to be on it.[8] He had abandoned his original plans to make a side excursion to Quebec. If his current lack of funds had not sealed that decision, the letter from Lucy with the alarming news from London had.[9] It was now paramount that he address the situation with Havell—and quickly—so that there would be no disruption of the publication schedule. Audubon wanted the engraver to increase his output over the next several years, and that goal would likely never be achieved if he and Havell could not reach an understanding.

On Saturday morning, the naturalist was awake before anyone else in the Weston household and promptly picked up his pen to write to Lucy. Without any paper at hand, he reached over to his journal and carefully tore out an empty page from the back of the book. On the other side of the sheet, the names of two *Tringa* sandpipers had been scribbled lengthwise in the margin, but he still had plenty of room for his ink.[10]

Audubon started out by announcing their arrival and assured Lucy that everyone had made it through the voyage without incident. He briefly recounted their travels since reaching Pictou and then turned to what was foremost on his mind—Havell's demands:

> Havel must have become either a knave or a fool or crazed Man which is about
> Synonimous—I Shall never raise his prices and there can be no dificulty in pro-
> curing an Engraver as competent—I think at present that Some Rascal such as
> Watterton for Instance may have had the impudence to put him up to Such a
> thought—I am delighted with Victor's letters in which I observe Industry, care

and prudence of thought. — I hope his visit to Austria and Prussia &c may prove worth his while but I doubt it — my Hopes for Subscribers are now almost turned on our Country — Havell's letter is as thou sayest quite a Humbug — but I think I will cool him very Soon.[11]

This self-important rant was quintessential Audubon. Since the early years of the project, he had been quick to threaten to cut Havell loose and take his business elsewhere whenever he was unhappy about how the publication was proceeding. But by this point, with *The Birds of America* nearly halfway to completion, both he and the London engraver had formed a synergistic relationship that would be difficult to end. Havell had assembled a trained staff of engravers and colorists for issuing the prints on a schedule that met Audubon's needs. And in the coming months, Havell would be prepared to ratchet up the production schedule to complete the work even sooner, in keeping with the naturalist's fervent desire to bring it to a close while he was still alive. Audubon needed his partner now more than ever, and at some level must have understood that.

Unbeknownst to Audubon, the situation in London had improved greatly since the explosive clash between Havell and Victor back in May. Victor had just returned from his European tour that Wednesday. Although he had obtained only one new subscription as reward for all his effort, he was pleased to find that Havell had made real progress in addressing the quality issues that had been the source of the young man's complaints since first arriving in England. Victor declared the prints in No. 34 (Plates 166–170) to be "very good." And the first rendering in No. 35, depicting a pair of Barn Owls perched at night high above a distant river bottom, was in the process of being printed. In Victor's opinion, this was going to "make a capital plate."[12]

While Audubon's vessel was steaming toward Eastport on Friday, Victor had been sitting in his rooms on Great Portland Street, pen in hand, writing to his parents to give them the particulars. He noted that Havell's shop was presently "all in confusion" because a party wall was being removed to expand the shop for a new business Havell was starting in the sale of birdskins. Victor thought the remodel would "make the shop very handsome, and I think will do us no harm."[13]

Addressing Lucy's repeated requests for an explanation as to why he wanted his parents to return to England that autumn, Victor offered his reasoning: To begin with, he thought the subscribers would "be freshened in their desire to have the work & you will have no falling off to think about." In addition, his father's presence would enable them to procure new subscribers and "create new enthusiasm for the work." Finally, he felt strongly that "Havell would do the work a little better" in the naturalist's presence.[14]

However, Victor emphasized that his parents should only consider returning now if Audubon's work was sufficiently completed that he would have no reason to sail back to America next year. If it was necessary for his parents to extend their stay to accomplish this, Victor was confident he could prevent Havell and his team in the interim "from going back in the execution, by Care & watchfulness." He hoped to be able to persuade Havell to finish all of the remaining land birds for the second volume in accordance with the present terms and leave Audubon to address the engraver's demand for higher rates when the naturalist finally reached London. As partial inducement, Victor planned to advance the idea that his father would likely permit Havell to sell some of his birdskins and shells, which were much in demand in England.[15]

Although optimistic that the issue of compensation could be resolved, Victor continued to contemplate other options. He was decidedly against shipping the work over to France as Lucy had suggested, asserting that his father "would lose ¾ of your English friends." Blake, the young engraver in Havell's shop, remained a possible alternative. Victor would be sending his parents an engraving that Blake had recently completed of Audubon's drawing of White-crowned Sparrows as an example of Blake's skill. Victor thought the family "would lose little by a change" in printers, although there was one particular reason for caution: "Havell is not perhaps honourable enough to keep secrets which he might know about our affairs," Victor wrote. William Swainson's willingness to reveal the arrangement that Audubon had originally proposed for writing the scientific descriptions of his letterpress made this a factor they could not ignore.[16]

"Waterton & the other scribblers" were, of course, their other worry. Victor felt that his reply to the British naturalist was "enough for the present." He had heard that the squire was traveling in Europe and believed it unlikely Waterton would issue a response, although the Englishman had evidently not been convinced by Victor's rebuttal. Several weeks before, Waterton had dropped by Havell's shop and had continued to insist that someone other than Audubon had written the *Ornithological Biography*. As for *Mechanics' Magazine*, Victor had no intention of answering anything that appeared in its pages, calling the publication "a dirty thing that could do no harm to anyone." He could shed no light on who Dr. Jones and his "scientific friend" were. Regardless, Victor would "not notice them at all, they are only mosquitoes."[17]

Lucy already had some sense about the positive change in Havell's attitude. Just that past Tuesday morning, as Audubon's party was rattling by stage across the Nova Scotia countryside to Windsor, she had opened a letter from Havell dated July 9 in which the engraver reported that he and Victor were getting along well and were in agreement about the course of the work. Lucy wanted her husband to know of this development and wrote him immediately with a copy of Havell's letter. However, her correspondence would not reach Eastport until Audubon was already on his way home, and it was returned by James Curtiss to New York.[18]

———

Of course, the naturalist knew nothing of these events as he hurried about Eastport that Saturday to wrap up his business. He stopped in to see Messrs. Buck and Tinkham to formally return possession of the schooner and to finalize the details for payment under the terms of the charter agreement. The balance due was $862, and the only question Audubon had was whether to draw on Dr. Parkman or on Dr. Shattuck for the payment.[19] He also had to take charge of the live cargo. The remaining juvenile Great Black-backed Gull had returned with the vessel, and the naturalist had to decide what to do with it. In addition, he had to arrange to transport the Newfoundland dogs to Boston. Dash, John's pointer, was now considered part of the family and would be accompanying them to New York.[20]

Audubon, John, Shattuck, and Ingalls said farewell to Eastport on Monday, September 2, and boarded the packet sailing for Boston.[21] Harris planned to stay in Eastport for several days before embarking on a hunting and fishing trip through the backwoods of Maine and New Brunswick.[22] Audubon made sure to ask him to keep an eye out for any interesting birds along the way.

Whether to aid Harris in his identification skills or as a token of affection, Audubon presented the younger man with his personal copy of Bonaparte's *Synopsis*. He inscribed the back of the title page, "John. J. Audubon to his good Friend Ed^d Harriss Es^q, Eastport, Sepr 1^t 1833." Harris would treasure the gift for the remainder of his life.[23]

As a favor, Harris agreed to assume responsibility for the Newfoundland dogs and see them safely shipped to Boston before he left town.[24] Audubon had found a good home for their gull at the garrison at Fort Sullivan, where Lt. George Greene agreed to adopt it. The bird became a popular pet among the soldiers, and the lieutenant wrote the naturalist the following winter to say it was doing well but had yet to undergo a molt of its feathers.[25] This species is known to birders as a "four-year gull," acquiring its distinctive adult plumage in its fourth year through a series of molts that occur along the way.[26]

The packet docked in Boston on Wednesday, September 4.[27] Audubon and John were invited to stay at the ample Shattuck home on Staniford Street.[28] The naturalist's arrival was of interest to many in the city, and he agreed to accommodate the *Boston Daily Advertiser & Patriot* when it requested an interview.

In a conversation that must have lasted well over an hour, the newspaper's reporter was regaled by Audubon's expressive account of the trip. An article in excess of 2,200 words appeared in the paper's Saturday-morning edition. The editors were pleased to report on Audubon's safe return and believed there was "no one who will not be gratified to learn the progress of his arduous and unremitted labors in a branch of science, which he has made peculiarly his own." Their only regret in publishing the story was "that we are unable to present it in his own rich and animated language, and to invest it with the attractions which it would derive from his own descriptive power."[29]

With the clarity of perspective that time affords, the Labrador expedition looms large in Audubon's life. It helped get him back on his feet after his stroke and enabled him to achieve his immediate purpose of completing additional drawings, including those of many waterbirds, for *The Birds of America*. Since leaving Bras d'Or, he had supplemented his portfolio and now had twenty-five fresh compositions for future Numbers.[30] When he combined those with the four that he had illustrated during his month's stay in Eastport, he could not help but feel that it was a productive season indeed. Moreover, several of the species his party had collected were, in his opinion, new to science, which would bring even greater esteem to his publication. Further, his journals contained notes of previously undescribed bird behavior that would enrich the remaining volumes of the *Ornithological Biography*.

At the same time, Audubon was returning home with a broader understanding of just how far the footprints of civilization now extended. He had asked his journal after arriving at American Harbor, "Where can I now go and find nature undisturbed?" Certainly not in Labrador, though he and his party had been led to believe otherwise. The wholesale destruction of seabird colonies by the eggers, overhunting of fur-bearing mammals by the Hudson Bay Company, and overfishing both of salmon by the Hudson Bay Company and of cod by English, Canadian, and American fishermen pointed inexorably to a natural world that, without government intervention, would soon be thoroughly impoverished, a hollow echo of the wild America he once knew.

On a personal level, the trip had awakened in him a realization, perhaps for the first time, that he was no longer a young man. The unlimited energy that for so long had allowed him to work seventeen or eighteen hours a day was gone. Given how much remained to be done before his "Great Work" could be completed, he was anxious beyond words that he might fail to live long enough to see the final print. This provided him with even greater incentive—as if he needed it—to make every minute count.

With so many benefits accruing from the expedition, Audubon's investment of both time and treasure was amply repaid. However, there was one sore point that rankled—that he had been forced to bear almost the entire cost of the voyage. Audubon had originally informed Lucy that he anticipated Shattuck, Ingalls, and Lincoln would help defray some of the "general expenses."[31] This expectation was formed before Coolidge was recruited, so the naturalist's expectations as to the final member of the party are unknown. What Audubon meant by "general expenses" is also unclear. The $3 per week that Shattuck said he had been asked to pay for food would have netted the naturalist a mere $36 per man for the roughly twelve-week trip, a trifling sum in the face of the overall cost of $2,000 ($58,700 in 2016 dollars) and hardly enough to have triggered his sentiments.[32]

But if Audubon was looking for a more substantial contribution from these families, his expectations were wildly unrealistic. He had worked the "Young Gentlemen" from dawn to dark under miserable conditions for almost three months, for which they had received little more than regular meals and an uncomfortable place to sleep. They, as well as their families, must have felt that Audubon had reaped the benefit of their participation, and that he alone should be responsible for the attendant costs. However, that was not the way the often self-absorbed naturalist saw it. Between the covers of his journal where he was able to speak his mind, he admitted that "I was not very well pleased that nearly the whole burden of the Labrador voyage was put on my shoulders, or rather taken out of my poor purse; but I was silent, and no one knew my thoughts on that subject."[33] Though he may have grumbled about it privately, Audubon was ever a pragmatist. These were all families of influence, and he never lost sight of the fact that they might be of assistance to him in the future.

Audubon was impatient to reach New York and remained in Boston but a single day.[34] Before his departure that Friday morning, he called upon his dear friend and agent, Dr. George Parkman. Parkman had reimbursed the senior Shattuck a total of $430 for drafts that Audubon had evidently written while in Eastport, drawing on Shattuck to cover a portion of the expedition expenses. Audubon made sure the amount was fully paid, most likely by issuing a draft on his brother-in-law in New York, who was holding most of his remaining cash.[35]

With their business completed, Audubon and John set out eagerly on the final phase of their journey. The naturalist's journal provides no account of the trip, but they would have taken the 5:00 a.m. stage along the broad, well-tended turnpike to Providence, where they could take a steamer for New York, the fastest, most convenient mode of travel between the two cities. The *Benjamin Franklin*, under the command of Capt. Elihu S. Bunker, left the Fox Point wharf at noon on Friday, September 6, bound for the waters of Long Island Sound, and the two adventurers with their hunting dog were aboard.[36]

Word of the Audubons' safe return to Boston had already reached New York. When Lucy began a letter to Victor on Friday evening, she relayed the good news to him and indicated that she was anticipating their arrival the following day. She had originally planned to travel downtown on Saturday to see Capt. Joseph C. Delano, the master of the New York–Liverpool packet *Roscoe*. She wanted Victor to have the last three letters from the naturalist, and Delano, an Audubon friend, had periodically served as her personal courier. However, with Audubon and John so soon to dock, Lucy was now uncertain whether she would make the trip. She decided to write a few quick lines in case she did not go. Nicholas was headed to his office the next morning and would see her parcel placed aboard the packet before the vessel sailed on Sunday. She really had nothing else to say that hadn't already been included in the letter she had sent with the London packet on the first of the month.[37]

On Saturday, September 7, the morning sun rose into a fair sky over Manhattan.[38] Lucy returned to her writing table before breakfast to finish her note to Victor, reiterating that she was still looking for Audubon and John's homecoming that day. If not, with the last steamer of the week leaving Providence in a matter of hours, she was quite sure they would reach her on Sunday. She assured her son that he would receive another letter with all of the details by way of the London packet of September 10.[39]

———

In London, Victor had reason once more to pick up his pen. The September issue of Loudon's magazine was out, and Waterton had struck again, with blistering replies to both Victor and Robert Bakewell.[40]

The squire's opening salvo was directed at Victor's defense of his father's authorship of the *Ornithological Biography*. Waterton quoted from a July 20, 1831, letter from George Ord, "the elegant biographer of Wilson," in which the Philadelphian declared that William Swainson had personally informed him that Swainson had declined to write the work because Audubon "insisted upon his own name being given to the world as author!" Waterton went on to note that it was "somewhat singular that Mr. Audubon, jun., should complain . . . of what he calls my 'attacks' on his father, when he has taken no notice of the momentous charge which Dr. Jones brought against his father in the *Franklin Journal*; a full account of which is to be found in the *Mechanics' Magazine* for March, 1832." Waterton challenged Victor to "either refute my arguments, or send over an express to his father to come back from America without loss of time, and mount guard over his own *Biography of Birds*; which shall feel the weight of my arm in earnest, if the son returns me sarcastic thanks a second time."[41]

As for the remarks of "the person who signs himself R.B.," Waterton wondered, had the writer not questioned why Audubon had been denied honors in Philadelphia? "Is R.B. so rash," he continued, "as to trumpet Mr. Audubon's 'high credit' as a naturalist, while there is his name attached to an account of a rattlesnake swallowing a large American squirrel *tail foremost*?" Addressing the authorship issue, Waterton pointed to conflicts in what "R.B." (Robert Bakewell) had said about

Audubon's wife serving as his editor and Victor's claim that Swainson had vouched for "Mr. Audubon and no other" being "the *bonâ fide* author of the *Ornithological Biography*." Finally, Waterton sought to correct the record, insisting that he had never owned slaves or a plantation as "R.B." charged. He had only "administered to the estates of an uncle, and others" in South America at various times between 1807 and 1812.[42]

Victor had somewhat naively hoped that his volley back in July would silence Waterton for good, and he was now sorry that Bakewell, "altho' well meant," had taken up the naturalist's cause. It was clear that Victor would have no choice but to respond. He was already planning to prepare a "temperate and Inclusive statement of the facts" as well as to solicit Swainson to answer Ord's specious claims. Victor wanted his father to "rest with confidence in my discretion & ability to settle this in one good paper, and be assured that I shall not do or say anything to embarras [*sic*] your future statements."[43]

Victor also had some positive news to relay. Havell had decided to complete the work on the second volume based upon the existing pricing. This would give Audubon an opportunity to negotiate the terms of a new contract once he was back in England. However, Victor thought it likely the engraver would probably continue the publication "on the same or nearly the same terms, rather than lose the work."[44] Havell was evidently eyeing the profits he might make in selling some of Audubon's birdskins and shells and wanted to maintain his relationship with the naturalist.

The past several months had tested the mettle and judgment of this young man. While he lacked many of his father's strengths, Victor had demonstrated that he was more than capable of meeting the challenge.

———

At the Berthoud residence, breakfast was over and Nicholas had already left for the office when a hackney carriage pulled up outside.[45] The carriage doors opened, and Audubon and John bounded up the front stairs, Dash at their heels. There was excitement and commotion as the American Woodsman and his son strode into the house. Lucy, looking her finest, flew into Audubon's arms.[46] The anxiety and longing that had filled each day over the past several months vanished in their embrace. There would be separations and joyful reunions yet to come, but for now they were together. And for these two, whose timeless love and abiding friendship had forged an immutable bond, their hearts were content.

16

A Monument to Natural History

1833–1839

[T]here is something within me that tells me that Should I
be so fortunate as to see the close of my present publication, my name will be
honourably handed to Posterity.

JOHN JAMES AUDUBON

Audubon settled in for a brief stay at the Berthouds' and immediately began devising his future plans. He made sure that the London packet that sailed on September 10 carried correspondence to both Havell and Victor. He hoped the missive to Havell would "restore him to his proper senses." He thought it likely that his son's "diligence at overseeing the Work was a great source of discontent" on the engraver's part. However, the naturalist read Havell's latest letter, from July, as suggesting the latter had a "good disposition to continue the work on the same terms he has heretofore done it." This may have been wishful thinking, but Audubon was counting on Havell to recognize the prestige and intrinsic value in being the publisher of *The Birds of America*. As he told Victor, Havell "does not lose *by our Work*, whatever he does in other speculations, and *I think* that should we remove it from his hands into any other persons that his name would soon suffer as well as his business." Consequently, Audubon was almost insulted by Havell's demand for additional compensation, thinking him "very ungrateful to have even mentioned such an intention."[1]

The way Victor had managed the family's affairs received his father's highest praise. Audubon told him that he was "indeed proud to have such a son," adding, "I look on your prudence, your improvements and your Industry as unparalleled [MS: unparralled] in a young man of your age, in a Word I look upon you as on a true friend and a most competent partner in the completion of the arduous undertaking before us." Indeed, when Audubon finally had a chance to examine the most recent Numbers, Nos. 32 and 33, he wrote again to say they were "the best I ever saw."[2]

Victor's response to "that crazed man" Waterton also did not go unmentioned. Audubon considered it "good" but thought the better approach was to remain silent, which he believed was "the best way of punishing both the writers and publishers."[3]

Despite Victor's numerous entreaties for his parents to return to England, Audubon wished to remain in America one more year. He was willing to consider an earlier return if Victor insisted, but the naturalist felt the extra time would allow him to finish collecting specimens for the publication as well as information for his letterpress. He could then return "full headed and full handed" and would not have to contemplate yet another trip to America before Havell issued the final print. Audubon recognized that he was slowing down, and it would not do to postpone his remaining collection efforts. "I am growing old," he told his son, "and will have to abandon the severe manner in which I have been obliged to travel in search of Birds and knowledge of their Habits, in a few more years."[4]

Audubon's current plans called for him to leave New York with Lucy later that month and travel overland to Charleston, where the family had previously been invited to spend the winter with the Bachmans. In a remarkable display of hubris, the naturalist hoped to rustle up another fifty subscribers during stops along the way. John would stay behind and take a steamship to Charleston on October 5. Over the ensuing months, Audubon intended to complete the species accounts for the second volume of the *Ornithological Biography* and, in the spring, sail to the Floridas and possibly tour the Gulf of Mexico as far west as Tampico, Mexico. He would petition the Treasury Department for permission to use the Charleston revenue cutter when he and Lucy stopped in Washington City on their journey south.[5]

In the meantime, Audubon found some space to work in the Berthouds' full house, now overcrowded with eighteen people. With John's assistance, he completed several of the landbird compositions from the Labrador expedition and shipped them off with a complement of others aboard the London packet of September 20. He directed Victor to issue them as part of Nos. 39 and 40, the final two fascicles of the second volume. When subscribers eventually received the prints, they were treated to the naturalist's dynamic and colorful images of the Willow Grous (Willow Ptarmigan), Lincoln's Finch (Lincoln's Sparrow), Canada Titmouse (Boreal Chickadee), Ruby-crowned Wren (Ruby-crowned Kinglet), Labrador Falcon (Gyrfalcon), and Shore Lark (Horned Lark).[6]

Audubon could now focus his attention on volume three. He organized the first twenty-five drawings for Nos. 41 to 45 and planned to send Victor those that were not already in London. He also began outlining preliminary plans for the publication of a smaller, less expensive edition of his work to follow *The Birds of America*. He envisioned combining uncolored images of the prints alongside his text in the manner of Alexander Wilson and others. It was an idea that had been gestating for several years, and Audubon thought the lower price would place it within reach of "almost every person."[7]

In Charleston, John Bachman rejoiced when he finally received news of the naturalist's return to civilization. Audubon's letter from Halifax was delivered on September 14, and, thoroughly delighted, Bachman read it to his family over dinner. Later, from his desk, the pastor's elation poured out through his pen:

Hail! my old Friend, all hail! Health, success and happiness, attend you — the winds, the waves, the heavens and fortune, have all smiled on you. Welcome, thrice welcome, to the homes and hearts of your friends! Long may you be spared to be the honored instrument of giving to the world the figures and the biography of that beautiful feathered race, that seem to acknowledge you alone as worthy of commemorating their forms and their histories. Your letter from Halifax has made me quite happy. I am like a boy that has just heard of a month's holiday.[8]

Bachman simply could not wait to see the naturalist and hear all about his journey. Unaware that the Audubons had already decided to accept his earlier invitation, he again beseeched his friend to visit. "You must pay me a visit this autumn; you must just pay me a visit. Bring, if you can, the wife and son; you shall all be welcome — doubly so; but *you*, I must see."[9]

Audubon and Lucy left New York under fair skies on the morning of September 25 and arrived that afternoon in Philadelphia, where they found accommodations at Mrs. Newlin's boardinghouse at 112 Walnut Street. After making the rounds, the naturalist concluded that new subscribers were not to be had.[10] Still, he was presented with a new species of bunting by John Kirk Townsend, an eager, young ornithologist and a member of the Academy of Natural Sciences of Philadelphia who would join Thomas Nuttall on a cross-country scientific expedition to the Columbia River the following year.[11]

Audubon was also presented with an arrest warrant, for a prior debt stemming from the Henderson mill, that was delivered by the sheriff just as Lucy and he were preparing to leave for Baltimore. Audubon would have been jailed but for the timely intervention of an old friend, James Norris, who agreed to serve as his bail. The court subsequently transferred the claim to Charleston and, in 1835, Audubon was ordered to pay an adverse judgment of $630. He was by then abroad, but he grudgingly directed Bachman to pay the amount with sums collected from local subscribers.[12]

In contrast to his time in Philadelphia, Baltimore lifted the naturalist's spirits with four new names for his list. A brief side trip to Washington City also proved productive. After an unsuccessful meeting with Secretary of War Lewis Cass, who was cool to the idea of naming him to a future Rocky Mountain expedition, Audubon ran into Washington Irving. Irving had spent time in England as a State Department employee, knew his way around the capital, and agreed to help. He accompanied

Audubon to the office of acting Treasury Secretary Roger B. Taney, who was also serving in the cabinet as attorney general. Taney had only just assumed the Treasury Department position on September 23 as a recess appointment after his predecessor, William J. Duane, was dismissed for refusing to comply with President Jackson's directive to withdraw federal deposits from the Second Bank of the United States.[13]

Taney's willingness to implement the Democratic president's policy, without making a specific finding that the deposits were unsafe as required by federal law, did not endear him to the opposition Whig majority in the U.S. Senate. It ultimately refused to confirm him to the post as well as to a subsequent opening on the U.S. Supreme Court. Jackson, however, did not forget the service Taney had performed. When Chief Justice John Marshall died in 1835, Jackson nominated Taney to replace him. After a protracted debate in the Senate, now under Democratic control, Taney was confirmed as the nation's fifth chief justice in March 1836. His majority opinion in the *Dred Scott* case in 1857, ruling that African-Americans were not citizens under the Constitution and had no standing to sue in federal court, would forever stain Taney's legacy as well as the Supreme Court's. Audubon's meeting with Taney left him feeling gratified, as the secretary evidently promised a letter authorizing the naturalist to use the department's revenue cutters situated south of Delaware Bay, precisely what Audubon would need for his planned excursion.[14]

From Baltimore, the Audubons passed through Richmond, Petersburg, Halifax, Raleigh, Fayetteville, and Columbia before reaching Charleston on October 24. John had arrived by steamer on October 11 and had already charmed every member of the Bachman clan, including the pastor's two oldest daughters, sixteen-year-old Maria Rebecca, known to her family as "Ria," and her vibrant fourteen-year-old younger sister, Mary Eliza, whom everyone called "Eliza."[15]

Over the next several months, the Audubon family worked in tandem on the drawings and bird biographies for *The Birds of America*. Audubon was assisted by John, who was drawing "sufficiently well for publication now," and by Bachman's able sister-in-law Maria Martin, as he strived to complete all of the waterbird compositions needed for the third volume. Lucy busied herself compiling her husband's field notes from the Florida and Labrador expeditions so that he would have easier access to the information as he resumed writing the second volume of the *Ornithological Biography*.[16]

Audubon was drained by the effort. By late November, he admitted to Victor that he had not completed as many of the biographies as he wished, "for when evening comes and I draw the whole of the day, I feel weakened and fatigued and frequently am found to retire to bed when my duty calls me to set up & write." He was "getting old *rather* fast, and more anxious about the Work than ever." He appealed to both Victor and Havell to accelerate the production of the Numbers for the third volume from the previous five, to eight or ten annually. That would bring the project to a close in a little over four years as opposed to nine. He desperately wanted to see the project through to completion. "So much travelling exposure and fatigue do I undergo," he wrote Havell, "that the Machine me thinks is wearing out; and it would indeed be a pleasure for me to see the last plate of the present Publication." Within days of writing these words, the naturalist took to his room and was bedridden for ten days with an incapacitating bout of piles, today commonly known as hemorrhoids.[17]

However, being around Bachman afforded Audubon a measure of spiritual refreshment that he sorely needed. Their common passion for natural history had, in only two years' time, nourished the growth of an intimate friendship. They enjoyed each other's company immensely, bantering and teasing as close friends often do. At the Bachman home, the naturalist could be utterly himself, although the pastor could not ignore some of his friend's less than admirable qualities. Audubon would seldom admit he was mistaken, especially when it came to birds. He enjoyed his drink, often and embarrassingly to excess. He hated to lose, whether at shooting or evening backgammon games, and he could be petulant when he did. Indeed, he had been known to storm off to bed in a huff after Bachman handed him a defeat at the backgammon board. Audubon also had grown fond of Bachman's lively sister-in-law, and he sometimes went overboard in talking about her as his "sweetheart." But Bachman's deep affection and respect for Audubon—whom he referred to as "Old Jostle"—invariably smoothed over any unpleasantness. Aside from the Audubon family, Bachman was the naturalist's most stalwart supporter, sharing his detailed knowledge of Southern birds and offering his unflagging encouragement. He was also prepared to enter the fight against Audubon's harshest critic.[18]

During the second half of December, Audubon and Bachman conducted a series of further experiments to investigate whether Turkey Vultures eat fresh meat and locate their food strictly by sight. Audubon was well aware of Waterton's censorious commentary and was anxious to put the squire in his place. "[T]he moment is at hand," he wrote Victor, "when these Scoundrels will be glad to find some hiding place to resort to, and to wait for time to obliterate their obvious Jealousy and falsehoods." Distinguished members of the local scientific community, including the president of South Carolina College and professors at the Medical College of South Carolina, were invited to participate and to serve as witnesses. The experiments completely validated Audubon's earlier findings.[19]

In keeping with the naturalist's desire to remain above the fray, Bachman agreed to author a scientific paper detailing the results. The pastor's reputation was unimpeachable, but as he was not well known in England he had six of the observers certify the conclusions with their names. Bachman also planned to use the opportunity to address questions Waterton had raised regarding Audubon's rattlesnake paper as well as the authorship of the *Ornithological Biography*.[20]

By January 1, Bachman's manuscript was finished, and Audubon conveyed a copy to Victor. "It is a plain paper," he told his son, "no nonsense, no fudge; but so simple & full of truth that I greatly fear that even the *Armour* of Waterton will fall to the Earth, and leave the man, a poor worthless Carcass fit (if fresh) for the very Buzards which he has so deeply abused." Audubon instructed Victor to print up two hundred copies to distribute to each of the subscribers along with the next Number. He also asked him to submit it to John C. Loudon for inclusion in the March issue of *The Magazine of Natural History*. Although the naturalist did not realize it, the timing could not have been better. Waterton had filled several pages of the January issue with criticism of Audubon's biography of the Turkey Vulture, among other species, and belittled Victor and Swainson for insisting that Audubon and no other had written the *Ornithological Biography*.[21]

Since his visit to Washington City, Audubon had been waiting to receive the promised letter from the Treasury Department. When it failed to materialize, he wrote to the secretary in early December. Taney's response, dated December 16, indicated that he could not, after all, accede to the naturalist's request. "The laws having designed the Revenue Cutters to be employed exclusively for the protection and security of the Revenue and enjoined on the officers in charge of them the performance of specific duties, I do not feel myself authorized to withdraw the vessels from their appropriate stations or extend the order already given for your accommodation so as to interfere with their legitimate operations."[22]

Audubon had been counting on the government to subsidize his travels to the Gulf of Mexico. With Taney's refusal to approve his petition, it became apparent that the trip, which he had figured to be his last, would not transpire. The naturalist simply did not have the funds available to finance another expedition. At the same time, Victor's letters from London were seeking Audubon's return "as early in the Spring as possible," although they offered no explanation for the rush. Audubon guessed that his son might be facing a cash shortage. In any case, when the naturalist sat down to write him on January 14, 1834, he had decided to honor Victor's wishes and sail for England in late spring when the Atlantic's stormy winter weather would have subsided. Lucy's health was increasingly delicate, and she did not travel well by sea. He expected the family to be reunited once more by July 4.[23]

On March 1, the Audubons said farewell to the Bachman family and left Charleston for Baltimore. They were all sorry to go, but no one more so than John, who had fallen in love with the Bachmans' eldest daughter, Maria. A week later, the Audubons reached Baltimore, where they remained for several weeks. The naturalist had hoped to add some names to his subscription list, and some drawings of ducks to his portfolio. However, the specimens he needed were hard to come by, and the country was now mired in an economic recession, triggered when the powerful Second Bank of the United States contracted credit in retaliation for President Jackson's bank policy. Audubon lost one of his Baltimore subscribers, the president of the now failed Bank of Maryland. Fortunately, the naturalist was able to replace the subscription with one from a local gentleman of independent means. Audubon was also pleased to hear from Victor that Havell would be hiring an additional engraver, which would allow future Numbers to be issued at up to ten per year.[24]

The Audubons were back in New York by early April.[25] Before their scheduled departure at midmonth, Audubon and John were delighted to receive a visit from two of their former Labrador compatriots, George Shattuck and William Ingalls.[26]

———————

On April 16, the Audubons sailed for Liverpool aboard the 650-ton packet *North America*.[27] In a letter sent the day before, Audubon exhorted Victor to "*continue the Publication of the Birds of America to the best of your Abilities*" should the sea claim their lives.[28] The passage, however, was both uneventful and relatively swift, and in nineteen days the vessel docked in Liverpool. Lucy, who frowned on drinking, withstood the rigors of the voyage with the help of a shot of brandy—morning, noon, and night. It was not something of which she was particularly proud, but she was willing to do just about anything to alleviate her seasickness. The Audubons arrived in London on May 12 and shortly moved into rooms at 73 Margaret Street near Cavendish Square, within close proximity to Havell's shop.[29]

The naturalist was probably not surprised to hear that Waterton had appeared once more in the pages of that month's issue of *The Magazine of Natural History*, this time to do battle with Bachman. The squire had relished the challenge, as he related to George Ord after seeing the pastor's article in print. "Audubon's gulled friends and supporters in London are in the highest spirits," he noted in correspondence on March 4, "and feel sure that I cannot answer the Charleston letter. By the first of May next their crowing will cease."[30]

However, his response was largely a rehash of the same tired points he had made before. He insisted that the deductions drawn by the "American philosophers" from their experiments were fallacious and that the odor of the rotting carrion, which he claimed was lighter than air, had indeed attracted the vultures.[31] He attempted to counter Bachman's corroboration of Audubon's authorship of the *Ornithological Biography* by pointing out the niggling conflicts in statements made by Audubon's other supporters on the subject.[32] He took issue with Audubon's description of his 1810 meeting with Alexander Wilson and with the factual details of the naturalist's biographical account of the Passenger Pigeon.[33] But, overall, it was a strained effort. Loudon's readers had grown weary of the debate in any event, and with no one from

Audubon's camp inclined to issue a reply, Waterton had nothing more to say. At Walton Hall, the pen he used as a rapier found a moment to rest, at least for a time.[34]

Audubon's immediate concern was reaching an accommodation with Havell, which was soon achieved. The pricing for each of the Numbers and for the complete work did not change, which suggests that Havell agreed to continue working at his old rates.[35]

Backed by three assistants—Messrs. Blake, Stewart, and Edington—and an army of almost fifty colorists, Havell was able to complete the remaining three Numbers of the second volume and publish the first seven fascicles of the third volume—No. 38 (Plates 186-190) through No. 47 (Plates 221-235)—over the course of 1834.[36] The following year saw the issuance of another ten Numbers—No. 48 (Plates 236-240) to No. 57 (Plates 281-285). With all the work coming out of Havell's shop, Audubon's production costs jumped to £100 per week, the equivalent of about $450 ($12,500 in 2016 dollars).[37] This added immeasurably to the pressure the naturalist felt to collect promptly from his subscribers.

Meanwhile, Audubon spent the summer of 1834 continuing his work on the *Ornithological Biography*. He had once again engaged William MacGillivray to edit his drafts and prepare the scientific descriptions. Although the Scotsman was now employed as the conservator of the museum at the College of Surgeons in Edinburgh, he felt he could handle the assignment in his spare time. Audubon forwarded a batch of twenty-five biographies by post, and by July 18 MacGillivray had completed the first eighteen. MacGillivray thought "[t]his volume will certainly be much richer and more interesting" than the last.[38]

As of August, Audubon had finished all one hundred species accounts and thirteen of the twenty Episodes for the second volume. Several of the Episodes were built around tales of his days in Labrador. But the concentrated two-month effort had cost him. He was once again laid up for ten days with piles. On August 25, now recovered and preparing to leave London on a canvassing trip that would ultimately land him in Edinburgh, Audubon took a moment to write to Bachman. He could not help chastising his friend. "I have been in England—Four months, have written to you God knows how often, and yet the *only* letter I have received from you reached us 15 minutes ago.—Now when I receive letters I write in Answer at once you see; and If I receive none, I keep hammering at My Friends doors like a Woodpecker on the bark of Some Tough Tree, the inside of which It longs to see."[39]

Audubon reported that Victor and John were busy daily "studying music and other matters." John had been working on black-chalk portraits, which were now "pretty good." Victor was better with oils and could make a "pretty Landscape." Lucy was also doing well, but she had decided to "cast off her purchased Sham

Curls" and "wears her own dear grey locks," which the naturalist felt made her look "all the better."[40]

During the month of September, Audubon made his way north but had very little success as he called on prospective subscribers in Manchester, Liverpool, Leeds, Halifax, York, and New Castle before arriving in Edinburgh in early October. He found rooms at 5 Lothian Street, where he welcomed Lucy later that month. Victor and John remained in London, "hard at Work."[41]

With MacGillivray and Lucy by his side, Audubon was closeted from morning to night "revising, correcting, and sending fourth for 'Press' each Successive Sheets [*sic*] of the 2^d Vol. of my 'delightfull' Biographies of birds," as he informed Bachman on November 5. By December 10, a total of 750 copies of Volume II had been printed by the Edinburgh publishers Charles and Adam Black. An American edition of equal size would appear the following year in Boston, overseen by Dr. George Parkman, Audubon's Boston agent.[42]

The Audubons returned to London in December, and the naturalist immediately began scratching out biographies for the third volume. He was driven by an overwhelming sense of urgency. "I am almost mad with the desire of publishing my 3d Vol this year," he declared to Bachman in mid-January 1835.[43] One consideration was no doubt the rapid pace at which Havell and his staff were producing the associated prints of waterbirds. Additionally, Audubon was planning a return trip to America with John in April of the following year to make one final expedition along the Gulf Coast. He wanted this next volume completed before his departure. But most of all, he was pushing himself relentlessly "at a double quick time" to finish the production while he still lived, not only for the self-satisfaction it would bring but for what he anticipated would be a lasting legacy:[44]

> I am quite Sure I never have been half So anxious as I am at this moment to do all in my power to *compleat* my Vast enterprise, and Sorrowful indeed would be my dying moments if this Work of mine was not finished ere my eyes are for ever closed. — Nay my Dear Friend there is *something* within me that tells me that Should I be so fortunate as to see the close of my present publication, my name will be honourably handed to Posterity and the Comforts of my Sons and their Families much augmented through this means.[45]

Audubon quickly recognized that he lacked some of the essential information he would need in order to write the life histories of certain species. A surfeit of his letters began making their way across the Atlantic, imploring friends and acquaintances — even some he knew would never respond — to assist him by procuring specimens, nests, eggs, and further details of the habits of these birds. Bachman and Harris no doubt received the bulk of the requests. Audubon did not care how his two closest friends procured whatever it was he needed, just so long as they got it and weren't too slow in sending it to him. Only half in jest, he instructed the good pastor to "buy, borrow, nay *pocket* if you *dare* all you can for the sake of science." He also begged Bachman for stories — "any sorts of things" — that he could turn into Episodes.[46]

In only one month of concentrated writing, Audubon was able to finish a quarter of the biographies for the third volume. But his health once again suffered. He reported to Bachman that the intensity of the work "rendered me *puffy* I could Scarcely breath — my appetite was gone — My digestion bad." He obtained some relief from his dyspepsia by picking up a paintbrush. Capt. James Clark Ross and Dr. John Richardson generously agreed to share some of the birds they had collected during their visits to arctic and subarctic Canada. The Zoological Society of London, also, opened up its collection of skins. Working with these specimens, the naturalist was able to complete illustrations of thirty-three additional North American birds. He anticipated that more than half of the birds in the third volume of his work would be species that had never been described by Alexander Wilson.[47]

Audubon and Lucy remained in London until early June and then traveled once more to Edinburgh, where they took up residence at 5 India Street. Over the ensuing months of summer and fall, MacGillivray again assisted the naturalist in preparing the waterbird biographies for publication. Victor and John, who had joined their parents after a walking tour of Wales, continued their training as artists under the watchful and increasingly proud eyes of their father. By December 1, as Volume III of the *Ornithological Biography* made its publishing debut in Edinburgh, Audubon boasted to Bachman that his sons were "Improving in their different ways of painting at a surprising rate." Victor was doing well with painting fine "Landscapes, Battles, and other subjects." John was also working in oils, and had obtained commissions for upwards of fifty portraits. Audubon made a point of saying that John could now support himself and a wife "very decently in Edinburgh through his painting."[48]

It was now settled that John and Maria would wed, their union forever linking the Audubon and Bachman families. A steady stream of correspondence between the couple had kept their young love fresh throughout the many months of their separation. By mid-September 1835, Audubon counted fifty-two letters from his future daughter-in-law. Writing to Bachman, the naturalist was quick to compare that total to the seven letters his friend had managed to send during the same period. "[O]nly think of the disparity between Lovers of the one Sort and those who call themselves Lovers of *Science*," he remarked drolly.[49]

Audubon and Lucy left Edinburgh by coach on December 21 to return to London, with stops along the way to settle the accounts with his agents. The boys had taken a steamer from Leith two days before and had settled into a house Audubon had rented at 4 Wimpole Street, Cavendish Square. It became a popular destination for many of the naturalist's large circle of friends, including Lord Stanley and British ornithologist John Gould. Henry Fothergill Chorley and his brother John, young friends of Audubon's from his days at Greenbank, had gotten to know Victor and John and were frequent visitors. Even Lt. Bowen of the *Gulnare* stopped by to pay his respects. Bowen's godfather, the Duke of Sussex, thought Audubon's original drawings should be housed in the British Museum and was pressing Parliament to appropriate funds to purchase them.[50]

At his estate in Yorkshire, Waterton had found it impossible to stay silent. He had resumed his sniping in the April issue of Loudon's journal, where he pointed to the conflicting statements that had appeared in print, by both Audubon and Swainson, as to the number of years it had taken Audubon to complete his illustrations.[51] In the December issue, the squire once again mocked Audubon's rattlesnake paper as well as Audubon's depiction of a rattlesnake with recurved fangs in his Mocking-bird print. A rattlesnake's fangs, Waterton insisted, were shaped like a scythe, "with their points *downwards*."[52] Although this is true in some species, Audubon correctly depicted the recurvature present in the species of rattlesnake he used for his drawing.[53] The naturalist ignored the attacks, and Waterton eventually moved on to other targets.

By January 22, 1836, Havell had begun to engrave the drawings for No. 61 (Plates 301–305), the first of a projected twenty Numbers illustrating 125 separate species that would appear in the fourth and final volume of *The Birds of America*. Havell believed that he could complete the project in another twenty-two months so long as Audubon did not slow him down. Writing to Bachman, the naturalist was ecstatic. "[H]ow delicious is the Idea, and how comfortable should I feel at this moment were I able fully to say to Havell *you shall not be detained a Moment!*" But he was ever mindful that there remained so much yet to be done, including his planned trip to America "to ransack the Wildest portions of our Southern Country." He beseeched Bachman to throw himself into the effort at once, stressing that when the work was finally completed all subsequent "exertions will be useless and as it were quite dead and for ever gone by." Consequently, there was not a moment to lose:[54]

> Then take to your Gun at all your *leisure hours*, go the Woods [*sic*], and go to the Shores, or if you cannot at all, send Some worthy one on whom you can and I also can depend—Note down every *Insignificant* Incident brought forth to your Eye, and to your Minds eye, for of Course any Incident of Consequence, will count [ms: compt] one and these I am Sure you will not forget to *Write*

down! Measure, the depths, the diametrical width, of every Nest you Meet with this *Coming Spring*—Mark the Substance of their outward and Inner formation.—See to the period of the first Deposits of the Eggs, ennumerate them—Nay Measure them as the Nest themselves, save the Shells if you Can, but at all events describe them in *Writing* and on *the Spot!* What ever Yunglings you meet with do describe, or put them in plain Whiskey or Common Rum, the Cheapest will answer for that as if the very best.—And now when ever you secure an adult, down with it in Spirits also with a Memorandum of the Date of your procuring the Same.—*Look not to the expense* in any portion of this for God granting me life I shall pay for all, except for your own trouble, and that must ever remain an unsettled account, which *Science* may *perhaps* some days balance with you—[55]

MacGillivray had persuaded Audubon that the most effective way to differentiate groups of birds for purposes of scientific classification was by examination of their internal anatomy. In the remainder of his letterpress, the naturalist was "extremely desirous to give such anatomical descriptions of each Species, as may hereafter lead to the formation of a *positively natural system* [of classification] Without a Word of humbug or *theory!*" He urged Bachman to obtain a pair of every species of bird to be found around Charleston and to store the birds in spirits to await his examination. He exhorted the pastor to enlist all of their mutual friends, to place advertisements in the local papers, to solicit the help of the revenue-cutter commanders, and to rouse the South Carolinians to the task. "In this manner you will procure in a fortnight of exertions all that South Carolina can afford."[56]

Audubon had originally intended to sail for America at the beginning of April. However, the Great New York Fire back in mid-December had consumed a good portion of lower Manhattan, including the Berthoud warehouse where the naturalist's guns, books, and other possessions had been stored. Audubon would need to order new fowling pieces for his forthcoming expedition, and the guns would not be ready until mid-May at the earliest. Although it pained him to postpone John and Maria's reunion, he now planned to sail with John on August 1. He would put the additional time to good use writing species accounts for the fourth volume of the *Ornithological Biography* and working on an autobiographical sketch of his life that he had begun while in Edinburgh. John and Victor left London in March to travel through France and Italy over the next three and a half months.[57]

Meanwhile, Havell continued to turn out prints "at a grand rate." By July 30, as Audubon and John left London for Portsmouth, the engraver had already issued nine Numbers in 1836—Nos. 58 (Plates 286–290) to 66 (Plates 326–330). In addition, the remaining copper engravings for the first half of the final volume of *The Birds of America* were nearing completion.[58]

———————

Audubon and John set sail on August 2 aboard the *Gladiator*, a "Superb and fine ship" that required thirty-three days to make the crossing to New York. When the crew finally dropped anchor off the entrance to New York Harbor on the evening of September 3, Audubon's eyes were filled with tears, so grateful was he for their successful voyage. Both he and John celebrated their safe arrival, raising glasses of the captain's whiskey punch with the other passengers until 2:00 a.m. On the following morning, the Audubon men landed in New York. Although the naturalist's reputation continued to soar—he learned that a "beautiful Brig" carried his name—he had aged appreciably since his last visit just under two and a half years before. At fifty-one, his dangling locks were now gray, and he had lost most of his teeth.[59]

The Audubons were invited to stay at the Berthouds', where the naturalist found a lengthy letter from Charleston recommending that he wait until mid-October before heading south. Bachman was recovering slowly from an attack of rheumatism, and there were growing fears that the Southern city would be struck by a cholera epidemic. A second letter from Dr. Harlan reported that the Academy of Natural Sciences of Philadelphia had just received a shipment from Nuttall and Townsend of "about 100 New Species of Birds from the Pacific Side of the Rocky Mountains." Audubon could barely contain his excitement. Eager to see the skins as soon as possible, he took the 10:00 a.m. steamer from New York on September 13 and was greeted by Dr. Harlan at the wharf in Philadelphia that evening.[60]

The naturalist doubted whether the academy, which had helped bankroll Townsend's expenses and was jealously guarding the skins, would ever permit him to study, let alone illustrate, these new birds, especially if George Ord had any say in the matter. However, the next morning, Dr. Charles Pickering, a friend and supporter at the academy, granted him access to the collection. For Audubon, who had long dreamed of traveling across the Rockies, handling these strange and beautiful new birds was a thrill beyond imagining. But he was not permitted to do anything more than examine them without Townsend or Nuttall's explicit approval. Unfortunately, Townsend was at Fort Vancouver on the Columbia River and Nuttall was en route to Boston by sea. Hearing of the academy's intransigence, Harris stepped forward and was prepared to give Audubon $500 to purchase the entire collection, but to no avail.[61]

Audubon had business in Boston and left New York on September 18 aboard the steamer *Massachusetts*, bound for Providence. He reached Boston the following afternoon after taking the new rail line running between the two cities. Dr. Shattuck opened up his home to the naturalist and offered the same comfortable accommodations Audubon and John had shared after their Labrador trip. Unfortunately, Shattuck Jr. was then abroad studying medicine in Paris, but Audubon had seen the young man earlier that spring when Shattuck stopped in London on his way to France.[62]

Quite fortuitously, Nuttall arrived in Boston on September 20. The two naturalists met the following day, and Nuttall agreed that Audubon could have any duplicates from the shipment of birds that he and Townsend had forwarded to the academy. Nuttall also had the skins of six new species with him and gladly turned them over as well. Although Nuttall was a capable ornithologist and had authored separate volumes on the land and water birds of North America, his primary interest lay in botany. He doubtless felt that he had more than enough botanical specimens from the trip to occupy his time and that Audubon could put the birdskins to better use.[63]

Audubon succeeded in obtaining four new subscribers during his stay, including U.S. Senator Daniel Webster. He added two more on a brief visit to nearby Salem. Dr. Shattuck also honored him by agreeing to pay the last portion of the subscription price for the Double Elephant Folio ordered by the Boston Society of Natural History during the winter of 1833. The good doctor had previously made a personal commitment to fund one-tenth of the cost. He now put his wife down for the same percentage, and his son for one-twentieth, which in the aggregate amounted to fully one-quarter of the total. "Without the assistance of this generous man," Audubon told his journal, "it is more than probable that the society never would have had a copy of the 'Birds of America.'"[64]

The naturalist returned to New York on October 2.[65] He was gratified to report to MacGillivray on October 8 that New York now accounted for six of the twelve new subscribers on his list.[66] He also was pleased to learn that William Cooper, a founder of the New-York Lyceum and never a particularly strong supporter, was now willing to share some of the rare birds in his personal collection.[67]

Audubon remained in New York until October 15, when he and John left for Philadelphia.[68] Eight days later, his list had grown to fifteen. But, more importantly, he had managed to purchase ninety-three of Townsend's birdskins from the academy with the understanding that "the specific names agreed upon by Mr. Nuttall and myself were published in Dr. Townsend's name." The skins were "Cheap as Dirt too," and he couldn't help boasting about the news when he wrote to Bachman on October 23. "Such beauties! such rarities! Such Novelties! Ah my Worthy Friend how we will laugh and talk over them!" His good fortune did not end there. Artist and naturalist Titian Ramsay Peale had presented him with a new species of rail, known today as the Black Rail.[69]

Everything now seemed to be going Audubon's way, and he was willing to hazard a guess as to why. "Simply because I have laboured like a cart Horse for the last thirty years on a Single Work, have been successful almost to a miracle in its publication thus far, and now am thought a—a—a—(I dislike to write it but no matter here goes) a Great Naturalist!!!"[70]

From Philadelphia the Audubons moved on to Baltimore, where they arrived on November 4. They left for Washington City three days later. Audubon carried several letters of introduction from Washington Irving and other men of influence, and spent the next two days meeting with various government officials to advance his agenda. Treasury Secretary Levi Woodbury approved the naturalist's request to use a revenue cutter for the planned excursion to the Gulf of Mexico. The secretary also arranged to subscribe to a set of *The Birds of America* on behalf of the Treasury Department and the Departments of State, War, and the Navy.[71]

President Jackson extended an invitation to Audubon and John to dine with him before they departed for Charleston. The naturalist enjoyed the president's company as they "spoke about olden times, and touched slightly on politics, and I found him very averse to the cause of the Texans." But Audubon was by no means blind to the impact of some of Jackson's policies, such as the forced relocation of the Native American tribes from their ancestral homes in the southern United States along the "Trail of Tears" to Oklahoma. Audubon ended his journal entry of November 9, "bidding adieu to a man who has done much good and much evil to our country."[72]

The two travelers, "hungry, thirsty, and dusty as ever two men could be," reached Charleston on November 16. "[W]e found our dear friends all well, tears of joy ran from their eyes, and we embraced the whole of them as if born from one mother."[73] Over the next month, Audubon worked steadily to depict the birds from Townsend's collection, completing "31 in 20 days."[74] Given the number of new western birds and faced with the original promise to his subscribers that *The Birds of America* would consist of only four hundred prints, he took to making composite illustrations that presented several different species in a single drawing. As ever, he was aided by Bachman's unmarried sister-in-law, Maria Martin, who added the backgrounds, and by John, who continued to improve as an artist.[75]

On February 17, 1837, Audubon and John, joined by Edward Harris and Dash, left Charleston bound for Mobile, Alabama, where they hoped to arrange passage along the Gulf Coast aboard a revenue cutter.[76] The Florida War with the Seminoles was coming to an end, but many of the revenue cutters Audubon was looking to use were still stationed about the Floridas, and it was unclear when they would return to their home ports.[77] As Audubon's party traveled through Alabama, they witnessed the anguish of thousands of Creek Indians "under an escort of Rangers, and militia mounted Men, destined for distant lands, unknown to them, and where alas, their future and latter days must be spent in the deepest of Sorrows, afliction and perhaps even phisical want." For the naturalist, who had long before hunted with and enjoyed the company of Native Americans, it was heartbreaking to see the wretched misery of these poor, dispossessed souls. He hoped never to see such a sight again.[78]

After several weeks' delay, Audubon and his colleagues sailed from New Orleans on April 1 aboard the *Campbell*, a revenue cutter under the command of Capt. Napoleon L. Coste. Audubon already knew Coste, who had served as a lieutenant and pilot aboard the *Marion* during the naturalist's tour of the Florida Keys five years before.[79] When the cutter reached the waters of the gulf, the travelers met up with the *Crusader*, a small revenue schooner commanded by Capt. W. G. B. Taylor. Taylor had been ordered by the customs collector in New Orleans to help pilot the *Campbell* to Galveston Bay. His vessel, "a somewhat curious craft, small, snug withal, and considerably roguish looking," with a black hull and sails of "pure white cotton," was towed behind the cutter. With her shallower draft, the *Crusader* was better able to ply the bayous and keys than the *Campbell*, and Audubon's party would use her for "ransacking the shores of this Coast" in search of birds. But they also had their eyes out for mammals. Bachman was developing a reputation as a serious mammalogist, and he was eager to obtain new specimens for his research. His was a field of study that Dr. Harlan was also pursuing, and professional conflicts between the two had already begun to surface.[80]

The *Campbell* reached Galveston Bay on the afternoon of April 24, two days before the naturalist's fifty-second birthday. Audubon and his companions explored Galveston Island and the surrounding area over the next two weeks and then sailed for Houston on May 8. A week later they reached the Texas capital, situated along the banks of the Buffalo Bayou, and met with President Sam Houston. According to Audubon, "He was dressed in a fancy velvet coat, and trowsers trimmed with broad gold lace; around his neck was tied a cravat somewhat in the style of seventy-six. He received us kindly, was desirous of retaining us for awhile, and offered us every facility within his power."[81]

The following day, the company began their return journey to Galveston and arrived back in New Orleans on the evening of May 25.[82] They had no new species of birds to show for their efforts, but to Audubon "the mass of observations that we have gathered connected with the ornithology of our country, has, I think, never been surpassed."[83] The trip had not been an easy one for the aging naturalist. He was physically exhausted and had found the shipboard rations difficult to eat without a mouthful of teeth. He reached the Crescent City weighing twelve pounds less than he did at the start of the journey.[84]

Audubon and John left New Orleans on May 31 and retraced their route to Charleston, where the Bachman clan greeted them on June 10.[85] Harris made a trip up the Mississippi River to obtain "a collection of preserved Reptiles and other objects" for Audubon before joining everyone back in Charleston.[86] Dash was given a new home with Lucy's youngest brother, Will Bakewell of Louisville, who had been visiting New Orleans with his wife.[87]

With Audubon desirous of an early return to England, the Bachman household was bustling as the final preparations were made for John and Maria's wedding. On June 21, the two were finally married, the proud but wistful father of the bride presiding at the ceremony.[88] Two days later, the newlyweds said their tearful good-byes and headed north with Audubon and Harris by steamer, stopping first in Norfolk and then Washington City, where the naturalist paid a call on recently inaugurated President Martin Van Buren. The group then traveled through Baltimore and reached Philadelphia at the end of the month. John and Maria left for New York on July 1 and continued on to Niagara Falls for their honeymoon; Audubon repaired to Harris's farm in Moorestown to rest, "*gradually* recovering both my health and my former good spirits."[89]

On July 3, Audubon arrived in New York City, where he waited for his son and daughter-in-law to join him. He purchased three tickets for passage to Liverpool aboard the *England*, a 733-ton packet due to depart on July 17. Relatively few passengers would be accompanying them.[90] The nation was in the grip of yet another economic panic, one that had seen businesses collapse across the land, including the Cincinnati business of Lucy's brother Tom. Even Nicholas Berthoud's mercantile house, Forstall, Gordon & Berthoud, was struggling and had suspended payments to its creditors.[91] "There is scarcely a Dollar of silver in Circulation," Audubon wrote to his Charleston friends.[92] In a letter to Lucy he explained that there was no reason to delay their departure. "There is no money, no Credit, and I assure you no likelyhood of New Subscribers."[93] The economic situation in England was not much better.[94]

Despite the trying times, Audubon would be sailing with £1,106 ($125,000 in 2016 dollars) in hand, enough "to finish our Work with the usual annual collections we make in England." Another $8,000 ($200,000 in 2016 dollars) was in the hands of his brother-in-law, who had come to recognize for perhaps the first time the true extent of Audubon's personal achievement, calling him "one of the Happiest of Men—Free of debts, and having *available funds* and *Talents!*"[95]

———

On August 4, following a "*fine passage*" of eighteen days, the *England* docked in Liverpool.[96] Audubon, John, and Maria reached London three days later. Lucy had not been well, and their "arrival produced a great revolution of her nervous system, but after a while all was gayety and Happiness at our House in Wimpole Street."[97]

During the twelve months Audubon was abroad, Havell had issued ten fascicles— No. 67 (Plates 331 to 335) to No. 76 (Plates 376 to 380). The engraver anticipated completion of the work by January 1, 1838.[98] This presumed that the publication would consist of a total of eighty Numbers, with four hundred prints, as Audubon had originally declared in his prospectus.[99] However, the naturalist continued to add western species from Townsend's collection, including a second group of western birds Townsend had brought back to Philadelphia in 1837, which would ultimately raise the number of fascicles to eighty-seven for a total of 435 prints.[100]

In a formal announcement penned on November 1, 1837, and published early the following year in a New York paper and in the London literary magazine *The Athenaeum*, the naturalist urged anyone who had been thinking of subscribing to do so promptly. Preparing a copy of all of the prints would be a time-consuming and expensive proposition, and Audubon did not think that more than another ten or fifteen sets could be produced. Moreover, Havell was planning to close his establishment at 77 Oxford Street when the project was concluded and move to America with his family. Therefore, no additional subscriptions would be accepted after April 30, 1838. Audubon calculated that not more than 190 complete sets were in existence, of which around eighty were in the hands of his American subscribers.[101]

With the end of his Great Work now in sight, the naturalist drove himself mercilessly to finish the remaining illustrations. He told Bachman in April that he had "never laboured harder than I have done within the last Two Months," during which time he had "drawn One hundred Birds."[102] He also continued to work on the bird biographies for the fourth volume of the *Ornithological Biography*.[103]

The final print of *The Birds of America* came off the press at Havell's shop on June 16, 1838. By that time, only about 161 active subscribers were still on Audubon's list and stood to enjoy his illustration of a pair of Water Ouzels (American Dippers), pictured in their typical habitat on the edge of a tumbling mountain stream. Nine days later, Audubon picked up a pen to announce the milestone to his friends in Philadelphia. He was now back in Edinburgh, residing at 7 Archibald Street near the museum of the College of Surgeons and working once more with MacGillivray on his letterpress while the rest of the family remained in London. Writing to Dr. Samuel G. Morton, the corresponding secretary of the Academy of Natural Sciences of Philadelphia, Audubon noted that the completion of the work was "[a]n immense weight from my shoulders and a great relief to my ever fidgety anxious mind respecting the Immense undertaking."[104]

It had indeed been a monumental effort. From late November 1826, when Lizars began engraving the first copperplate, the project had consumed over eleven and a half years of Audubon's life. He had traveled thousands of miles by every conceivable mode of transportation in his endless search for specimens. He had drawn and painted 1,065 separate life-sized images of birds.[105] By his count, a total of 497 species were depicted.[106] With changes in nomenclature and scientific classification since 1838, the number of species accepted today stands at 449.[107] Adding the handful of birds Audubon illustrated but which ornithologists have never been able to confirm—his so-called "mystery birds"—the number rises to 454.[108]

The costs associated with self-publishing his Great Work and his letterpress ran to £28,910, a sum that did not include any of Audubon's personal expenses between 1826 and 1839.[109] In a memorandum in which he tallied the numbers, the naturalist converted this sum to dollars using an exchange rate of $4.00 to the pound for a total of $115,640 (roughly $3.13 million in 2016 dollars), and this is the figure generally referenced by Audubon scholars.[110] However, over the many years it took Audubon to realize his dream, the exchange rate was both variable and significantly higher, ranging from $4.44 to $4.80 per pound.[111] Using an average exchange rate of $4.50, the total comes to a more precise $130,095 (approximately $3.5 million in 2016 dollars).[112]

When one considers that Audubon had to finance the entire cost of publication himself, largely through individual subscriptions—the vast majority of which he solicited through interminable sales calls in virtually every city he visited—while simultaneously producing the drawings, writing the biographies, and overseeing Havell's printing operation, one gains a deep appreciation not only for the naturalist's unrelenting zeal but for his impressive business acumen.[113] There is some debate among Audubon's biographers as to whether or not he was a good businessman during his earlier years in Louisville and Henderson.[114] Regardless, there can be no question that, once he found his calling, he proved as capable an entrepreneur as any graduate of today's Harvard Business School.

On July 5, Bachman arrived in London for a visit. His health over the past year had deteriorated dramatically. He was suffering from chronic fatigue and had developed both weakness and numbness in the extremities on his left side. Although his congregation had made arrangements to relieve him of many of his pastoral duties, his condition showed little improvement. News that John and Maria were expecting their first child, and the hope that a trip abroad might prove salutary, persuaded Bachman to sail for Liverpool on June 7.[115] He was accompanied by a fourteen-year-old traveling companion, Christopher Happoldt of Charleston.[116] Audubon was not at Wimpole Street to welcome his friend when Bachman knocked on the door, but the pastor was overjoyed to meet his new granddaughter, Lucy Green Audubon, who was born on June 30 and promptly nicknamed "Lulu" by her still-beaming father.[117] Bachman remained in London for only two days, taking an evening steamer with Victor on July 7, bound for Edinburgh.[118]

The printing of the sheets for the next volume of the *Ornithological Biography* was already under way, and Victor was given the task of correcting the galleys.[119] Bachman found lodgings nearby and, feeling refreshed, offered his assistance to his old friend, who was working on the appendix to the letterpress.[120] When the pastor left about two and a half weeks later to return to London for Lulu's christening and to make use of his proximity to the British Museum to study its collection of North American mammals, Audubon was sorry indeed to see him go.[121] "The days which we enjoyed together were few, but delightful," he told his readers, "and when at the end of a fortnight my friend left us, I felt as if almost alone, and in the wilderness."[122]

Victor followed Bachman to London, arriving two days later on July 30.[123] John had expressed a strong desire to return at once to America with Maria and Lulu, and Victor conveyed Audubon's wishes that they remain until the following year, when the work would be done, at which point the family could travel back together.[124] John deferred to his father, perhaps after hearing the gentle counsel of his father-in-law. Lucy and the rest of the family packed up their belongings and left Wimpole Street on August 8 to relocate to an "extremely comfortable" situation at 6 Alva Street in Edinburgh.[125]

Bachman remained in London and spent long hours at the British Museum before taking a steamer for Germany on August 14. His travels would take him through Germany and Switzerland to Freyburg, where he spoke at a natural-history conference in September; and then on to Belgium and finally Paris, where he suffered a relapse. He returned to London on October 20 and spent several weeks recuperating while continuing his studies at the museum.[126] Audubon had hoped to see him again in Edinburgh, but the pastor could not find the time. On November 11, Bachman and his young companion sailed from Liverpool to Charleston aboard the barque *America* and arrived home on December 28.[127] His family was shocked by his appearance. He was now seventeen pounds lighter and in no better health. His physicians prescribed complete rest for the next several months.[128]

Audubon had spent August laboring on the *Ornithological Biography*. His toil was eased the following month by a week's vacation with the entire family to the Scottish Highlands with MacGillivray as their guide. Then it was back to work on the bird biographies.[129] The naturalist quickly realized that he had depicted so many separate species in the final folio of prints that it would be impossible to publish in a single volume all of their life histories as well as corrections to errors he had made in previous species accounts. He decided to devote Volume IV of his letterpress to descriptions of the next one hundred species, which would cover those through Plate 387. The remaining biographies, along with the appendix supplementing earlier histories, would make up a fifth and final volume.[130] With the additional space required for the anatomical descriptions by MacGillivray of the many birds that had made their way to Edinburgh in casks of rum or whiskey, there was no room for more of Audubon's diversionary Episodes.[131] He had struggled to find entertaining anecdotes to relate in any event.

The fourth volume appeared in early November.[132] Audubon then turned to completing Volume V, which was published in Edinburgh in May 1839.[133] This was quickly followed by *A Synopsis of the Birds of North America*, a single work in a small edition of five hundred that provided an index of all the known birds in North America arranged in phylogenic order, with a brief description of the physical appearance and geographical distribution of each species, coupled with citations to their appearance in both the Double Elephant Folio and the letterpress. The final sheets left the printer at the end of June, and the bound books came out in early July.[134]

After packing up and making arrangements with Havell to ship to New York the original drawings, the copperplates, and an additional fifteen bound and several unbound folio sets that had been produced for later sale, Audubon and Lucy left England for the last time on July 25 aboard the *George Washington*.[135] Victor had sailed the previous January and had already paid a visit to Charleston, where he fell in love with and became engaged to Eliza Bachman, Maria's twenty-year-old spritely younger sister.[136] John and Maria traveled to France with Lulu in May and, with Maria once again pregnant and the baby due in October, sailed directly to America. They arrived in New York in mid-July.[137] Within the month, John had opened up a portrait studio at 300 Broadway.[138]

The naturalist's departure did not escape the notice of his many English admirers. Henry Fothergill Chorley, the literary critic for *The Athenæum* in London and later a close friend of Charles Dickens, paid tribute to the American Woodsman upon completion of the *Ornithological Biography*:[139]

> It seems but yesterday that we were walking about with a transatlantic stranger, picturesque enough, in his appearance and garb, to arrest the eye of every passing gazer; a tall, stalwart man, with hair sufficiently long to qualify him to serve as a model to Gray's "Bard," and trousers ample almost as petticoats, of "good Harmony cloth," so absorbed in the enthusiastic prosecution of his gigantic plan—a life's labour—as to be heedless of the singularity of those meteoric locks, and those liberal nether garments. Some dozen of years, however, have elapsed since that day; the American Woodsman's hair—long since cut short—has grown white; his magnificent undertaking is completed, and he is now on the point of quitting England, to settle himself for the remainder of his days—whether by the side of a bayou, in some forest clearing, or as an inhabitant of one of the American cities which have learned to know his value, report saith not. This fifth volume, in short, brings Mr. Audubon's work to a close. It will be readily understood, why, as a closing volume, though indispensable to the completeness of the publication, it furnishes little matter extractable for the

amusement of the general reader. We, however, avail ourselves of its publication, to shake hands with its author, tendering him our hearty congratulations
on the completion of a task almost as arduous as has ever been proposed to a
literary man, and expressing our earnest hopes, that, in his approaching retirement, he will keep the promise made in his preface, and continue to use the pen
and the pencil, not only for the edification of the scientific, but for the delight of
the wider circle of general readers. The confidential simplicity of Mr. Audubon's
own prefaces would make yet more personal leave-takings and farewells, on the
critic's part, natural and graceful, — but it must suffice us to say, that few have
quitted England, carrying with them a larger portion of honest regard and sincere good wishes.[140]

Audubon left England with far more than the warm wishes of his friends. The
fifty-four-year-old naturalist was now internationally famous. The Double Elephant
Folio, an incomparable achievement in the annals of natural history, had assured
him a place in the pantheon of great Americans. But let it be said that Audubon
would never have attained his success had he remained in America, the source of his
inspiration. It was his legion of supporters and many subscribers in Britain, the first
to truly appreciate the magnitude of his genius, that were willing to back his daring
plan and ultimately enabled him to realize his dream.

17

America's Greatest Naturalist

1839–1851

*[W]e recognise in Mr. Audubon a man who has happily lived to fulfill
his destiny as an explorer of the great field of American Zoology, while the splendid
volumes which are the fruit of his labors, will diffuse the knowledge and love
of science to the latest generations.*

ACADEMY OF NATURAL SCIENCES OF PHILADELPHIA

The Audubons arrived in New York on September 2, 1839, and moved with the family into a leased house at 86 White Street.[1] Although the naturalist was now a bona-fide celebrity, his name known in every corner of the country, he had not earned sufficient sums from *The Birds of America* to be able to set aside his brush and pen. He was preparing to undertake two new projects—the small, royal octavo edition of *The Birds of America* and a work on the continent's mammals, or, as it would ultimately be titled, *The Viviparous Quadrupeds of North America*.[2]

The octavo *Birds* was by far the easier of the two to launch, especially as Audubon had already laid the groundwork for it and been considering the basic idea for a number of years.[3] It would combine a revised text of Audubon's letterpress, with hand-colored, lithographed images of individual species, reduced in size from the plates of the Double Elephant Folio by both Audubon and John using a camera lucida. Like its predecessor, it would be sold serially and by subscription. Each Number would consist of the images and associated text for five species and sell for $1, with a total of one hundred fascicles eventually completing the work in 1844.[4]

Audubon hired J. B. Chevalier, who had offices in both New York and Philadelphia, to serve as copublisher and business manager, and E. G. Dorsey of Philadelphia to print the text. For the all-important lithographic work, Audubon turned to John T. Bowen of Philadelphia, an Englishman who was in the midst of producing the beautiful hand-colored prints of Native American chieftains for Thomas L. McKenney and James Hall's *History of the Indian Tribes of North America*.[5]

The *Quadrupeds* was another matter entirely. Audubon and Bachman had previously discussed in broad terms a joint collaboration on the subject, with Audubon and John doing the illustrations while Bachman authored the text. But the pastor was taken aback to learn that, within days of reaching New York, Audubon had already begun to publicize the work although almost nothing had yet been done.[6] Unlike the naturalist, who knew little about mammals, Bachman was fully aware of the enormous commitment the publication would demand. "These creatures—the majority of them nocturnal & living in concealment are not so easily obtained as birds," he noted in a letter later that year.[7] Moreover, there was a paucity of information about the habits and distribution of many of the species. Bachman insisted that the text be both "original & credible—no compilation & no humbug," and this would necessitate field research that he expected Audubon and his sons to pursue.[8]

In mid-November, as production of the first fascicle of the *Birds* was under way and Audubon was making plans for a canvassing trip to New England, word reached White Street that Eliza had begun to cough up bright-red blood, a hallmark of an active tuberculosis infection, or, as it was known at the time, consumption. Bachman had contracted the disease as a teenager decades before, but he had recovered from it. In a case such as his, the bacterial infection lies dormant, encased by granulomas in the lungs which are formed by the body's immune response. The means by which the disease is transmitted was poorly understood at the time, and Bachman probably could not have imagined that he might have passed the infection on to his daughter; he suggested to Audubon that she had something else entirely, a twenty-four-hour bug he called "breakbone fever." Taking no chances, Victor hurried south aboard a packet, and he and Eliza were married by Bachman in a hastily arranged ceremony on December 4.[9] Although Eliza's symptoms quickly eased, leading the Bachmans to hope it was not consumption at all, both families well knew the prognosis if it were. There was no treatment or cure, and unless the disease became inactive, it was invariably fatal.[10]

The Bachmans wanted the newlyweds to remain in Charleston, where they felt the milder winter would be better suited to Eliza's condition. Audubon was quick to inform Victor by letter on November 24 that, with the press of the family's business, that would never do. "Now such an event would prove far from pleasant to me, as I will in all probability be necessitated to travel during the greater part of this Winter, leaving Mamma and Maria under the Sole charge of John, who with his present work, and the appearance of more in Store for him could scarcely manage our other affairs besides."[11] With this as an impetus, Victor and Eliza returned to New York shortly after the wedding.[12] Audubon could not have been happier to see the families united for a second time, sending Bachman a congratulatory note from Boston.[13] Bachman, who felt "a very great loss" in parting with his beloved daughters, was unable to share his friend's joy and refused to pretend otherwise.[14]

As the calendar turned to reflect the start of a new decade, Audubon was back in New York following a successful three-week tour of New England. He had added ninety-six names to the list of subscribers for the *Birds*, including those of Thomas H.

Perkins, John Collins Warren, M.D., and industrialist Abbott Lawrence, bringing the total number to upwards of 160.[15] Fifteen subscribers had already agreed to purchase the *Quadrupeds* sight unseen and with, as yet, no set price. Audubon was confident that within the next two years he could complete the drawings for the mammals and, with Bachman putting his "able and broad shoulders to the Wheel," the life histories could be written and printed a year after that. He knew he was "growing old," as he told his Charleston friend, "but what of this? My Spirits are as enthusiastical as ever, my legs fully able to carry my body for some Ten Years to come."[16]

Bachman was ready and willing, but he thought the naturalist unduly optimistic. "Dont flatter yourself that this Book is childs play," he cautioned in a letter on January 13. "[T]he birds are a mere trifle compared to this." Despite the anticipated labor, Bachman was expecting no remuneration for his efforts. He wanted his share of any profits to benefit "John & Victor, which alas in addition to the treasures they have already"—a reference to his daughters—"is all I can do for them whilst my head is warm."[17]

The pastor was anxious to sit down and talk about the project and hoped to see Audubon in Charleston before the spring. Bachman wanted Maria to accompany him, having heard that his daughter was ailing. She had developed a cough, persistent oral ulcers that interfered with eating, and generalized weakness that raised concerns on White Street.[18] "This lovely climate is a cure for sore mouths & sore hearts," Bachman pointed out.[19] No one was yet prepared to acknowledge a dreadful possibility—that Maria, too, had been stricken by tuberculosis.

John, Maria, and little Lulu headed south during the second week of February. Victor and Eliza, who was still under the care of her New York doctors, remained behind with Lucy and Maria's infant daughter, Harriet ("Hattie") Bachman Audubon, born on October 30 and named in honor of Maria's mother.[20] Audubon was taking a different route south on another canvassing trip and visited Philadelphia for a few days before meeting up with John's family in Baltimore on February 14. John, Maria, and Lulu left for Charleston two days later. The naturalist planned to stay in Baltimore for a week to continue his hunt for subscribers, which now exceeded three hundred. He was hoping to knock on the Bachmans' door within a matter of weeks after stopping in Washington City, Richmond, Petersburg, Lynchburg, "and all other Burghs" along the road to Charleston.[21]

However, Audubon was delayed when his visit to Baltimore proved wildly successful. A very complimentary unsigned review of the work, evidently from Bachman's pen, had been printed in John D. Legare's *Southern Cabinet*, a Charleston paper, and was picked up by all of the papers in Baltimore. Audubon reported that it had "produced a capital effect."[22] Several of the city's prominent citizens, including members of the respected Brune family, whom he had met through the Shattucks, escorted him around town and personally introduced him to potential subscribers. With their imprimatur he was able to add 171 names to his subscription list in the course of three weeks.[23] He picked up another eight subscriptions during a brief visit to Annapolis.[24] When he wrote to John on March 9, he noted that he had managed to double the number of his subscribers over the past thirty days and now had in excess of 520.[25]

Audubon did not have enough copies of the first several fascicles to distribute to the new subscribers, so he returned to New York while more were being printed. On his way back through Philadelphia, he picked up as many sets as Chevalier had available. He then delivered those to his Baltimore agent; added three more names to the list; and moved on to Washington City on March 29.[26] Nine days in the capital netted fifty-three subscribers, a tally that was disappointing only when compared to Baltimore's.[27] An eleven-day visit to Richmond brought another twenty-nine, with an additional ten or fifteen expected.[28] Audubon decided to forgo the remainder of his overland itinerary because of the terrible state of the Southern roads. He left Richmond on April 18 for Wilmington, North Carolina, where he boarded a steamer for Charleston.[29] He arrived on April 21 and by May 4 could report that the total number of subscribers now stood at 650.[30]

John and Maria were away, having traveled inland to Aiken, South Carolina, on the recommendation of her doctors, who hoped the pure air might foster a recovery. John's letters back to Charleston had been full of promising reports of Maria's improving health, and Audubon was thinking about leaving on May 8 for a canvassing trip to Savannah. However, his plans changed when Bachman brought Maria home.[31] As she was being carried into the Bachman house, Audubon could see that her condition had worsened considerably since Baltimore. She was "now extremely feeble and so emaciated" that it was painful for Audubon to look at her.[32] She was dying, and everyone but John, who refused to accept the truth, knew it.[33]

With not nearly enough to do to occupy his time and overwhelmed with a feeling of helplessness as he watched Maria grow steadily weaker, Audubon began drinking early in the day, sometimes before the midday meal was served. The whiskey made him, as Bachman put it, "garrulous — dictatorial & profane," which was upsetting to the entire Bachman family. The pastor did not have the heart to tell him to leave and implored John to intercede. The naturalist ignored John's suggestion to return to New York, convinced that it was his duty to remain to provide emotional support to his son and daughter-in-law.[34]

However, the conflict eventually came to a head in an argument between the two old friends at the dinner table in early June. Audubon was intoxicated and took umbrage at Bachman's observation that Audubon had been unduly pessimistic in describing Maria's condition in a letter to Lucy. Their exchange grew heated, Bachman finally snapped, and Audubon left the table, announcing his departure a short time later. His behavior over the last few days of his stay became highly formalized and proper, just as it had nearly twenty years before when he was ordered to leave Oakley Plantation. He said his goodbyes on June 6, boarded a steamer to Wilmington, and was back in New York six days later.[35]

Victor could tell from his father's subdued behavior that something had happened in Charleston, but he could not get him to talk about it. A letter to Bachman was met with a detailed reply laying out the offenses that had led to Audubon's departure. The pastor hastened to add that he would welcome his friend again provided he drank only in moderation. This was a harsh stand, Bachman admitted, but he felt it necessary if his friend was to be saved from degradation.[36] The rift in the friendship would heal, assisted by their mutual affection, familial ties, and joint involvement on the *Quadrupeds* project. But Audubon, despite being invited, would never again find a reason to visit Charleston.[37] Nor would he ever completely abandon his taste for spirits, although he was evidently able to control his drinking so long as he was able to keep himself occupied.

Audubon's mood had improved sufficiently by July that he returned to the road, touring New England once more for subscribers.[38] He was in Boston on September 22, staying at the home of Dr. Shattuck, when he stopped by the post office and picked up a letter from Victor, the black seal a sign of grave tidings. With trepidation, he opened the letter and learned with deep sorrow that Maria had passed away in Charleston a week before. She was only twenty-three.[39] Victor added that he was now anxious about Eliza's worsening health and requested his father's advice about whether they should winter in Cuba, where many consumptives sought a miracle cure in the tropical climate. The naturalist left Boston that afternoon to return to New York to be with his family.[40]

On October 20, Victor and Eliza took a steamer south, bound for New Orleans, where they waited almost a month for a cholera epidemic in Cuba to dissipate. They were accompanied by Maria Martin, who had traveled with John and Lulu to New York and was serving as Eliza's nurse.[41] During their stay in the Crescent City, Victor attempted to peddle the *Birds* and managed to sign up twenty-three new subscribers before his little party sailed for Havana.[42] Audubon received news of Victor's efforts on December 3.[43] He was then in Boston in the midst of yet another canvassing tour of New England after having made a similar trip to Philadelphia, Baltimore, and Washington City in early November.[44] Looking at his subscription list, the naturalist calculated that he now had a total of 977 names.[45] He would add another seventy-nine before he arrived back in New York on December 19.[46] The next fascicle, No. 24, was issued in early January 1841 in a first printing of 1,250 copies.[47]

For Eliza, several months in San Pedro on the southeastern coast of Cuba brought no improvement to her condition. With encouragement from Audubon and Lucy, Victor and Eliza determined to return to New York, stopping in Charleston along the way. The doctors there could offer no hope, and the Bachman family was distraught when they had to say their final farewells as the couple prepared to sail on May 8. Eliza, who had brightened the lives of her loved ones with her songs, poetry, and playful personality, passed away at the age of twenty-two in the house on White Street at 2:00 a.m. on May 25.[48] A heartbroken Audubon, looking for some relief from his anguish, picked up a brush and spent the day illustrating a young hare for the *Quadrupeds*. "I drew this Hare," he noted on the back of the painting, "during one of the days of deepest sorrow I have felt in my life, and my only solace was derived from my Labour."[49]

Audubon had been working intermittently over the past two years on illustrations for the *Quadrupeds*, and he now threw himself into the task. On August 15, he informed Long Island naturalist W. O. Ayres that he had "already drawn about one hundred figures of these, including thirty-six species."[50] But this was just a fraction of the roughly 190 full species that Bachman indicated had been scientifically described, and the pastor believed that more remained to be discovered.[51]

Audubon urged friends and acquaintances alike to send him representative specimens. From Ayres he sought "Bats, Wood Rats and Wood Mice, Shrews, Shrew Moles," Cat Squirrels, and Woodchucks.[52] An eighteen-year-old correspondent from Carlisle, Pennsylvania, by the name of Spencer Fullerton Baird, who would grow up to become the first curator and, later, secretary of the Smithsonian Institution, received a similar list.[53] Dr. Parkman in Boston was asked to supply a "live Hare in the Summer dress" that could be found in the northern reaches of Massachusetts.[54]

Bachman had likewise enlisted his contacts to provide Audubon with specimens, and he occasionally ventured into the field to do his own collecting. As his duties to his church and congregation allowed, he busied himself researching and writing the manuscripts describing each species.[55] His close study of the subject over the past several years had made him the preeminent expert in the field. "I know more of our quadrupeds than anyone else," he casually declared to Audubon in a November letter.[56] However, he struggled to make sense of the confusing taxonomy for this class of animals, a task made more difficult by Charleston's lack of many of the published resources on the subject.[57]

On the first of October, Audubon purchased a secluded, heavily forested fourteen-acre parcel along the eastern banks of the Hudson River, nine miles north of the heart of the city in what is now Washington Heights. Three additional parcels acquired in July 1843 would increase the size of the property to just shy of twenty-four acres between today's 155th and 158th Streets. For more than twenty years the

PLATE XLII. *Jonathan D. Weston (1782–1834), a highly respected Eastport attorney who served as both town clerk and deputy revenue collector of the Passamaquoddy Customs District, hosted the Audubons during their 1833 visit.*

PLATE XLIII. *Capt. Joseph H. Claridge (1801–1874) was a customs inspector with the Passamaquoddy Customs District. He also commanded the schooner* Fancy, *which transported Audubon's party from Eastport to Point Lepreau, New Brunswick, for a five-day excursion in May 1833.*

PLATE XLIV. *Henry Wolsey Bayfield (1795–1885) was a commander in the Royal Navy and captain of the 140-ton surveying schooner* Gulnare *when Audubon first met him on June 22, 1833, at American Harbor, Labrador. Bayfield and his hydrographic crew were conducting a survey of the Labrador coastline and planned to follow the* Ripley's *path as she proceeded north to the Straits of Belle Isle. This portrait was done around 1840.*

PLATE XLV. *Thomas McCulloch (1776–1843), a Presbyterian minister and liberal thinker, founded Pictou Academy, the first nonsectarian college in Nova Scotia. The academy boasted a natural history museum, which Audubon was eager to explore during his return from Labrador.*

PLATE XLVI. *Audubon sat for this portrait by George P. A. Healy in London in the first half of 1838. It was painted by gaslight in the evenings, Audubon being too busy during daylight hours with his work on the final compositions for* The Birds of America *and the fourth volume of the* Ornithological Biography.

PLATE XLVII. *This was the Audubon family home at Minnie's Land, the estate Audubon acquired in 1841 along the shores of the Hudson River in upper Manhattan with proceeds from the sale of the octavo edition of* The Birds of America. *The view is toward the back of the house, which faced the river.*

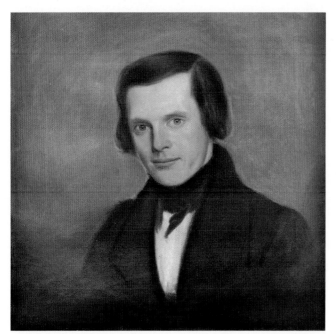

PLATE XLVIII. *Isaac Sprague (1811–1895), a natural-history artist from Hingham, Massachusetts, was recruited to assist Audubon in illustrating specimens during the naturalist's final collecting expedition to the upper reaches of the Missouri River in 1843. This is a self-portrait.*

PLATE XLIX. *Fort Union on the upper Missouri River, drawn by Isaac Sprague in July 1843, was operated by Pierre Chouteau Jr. and Company, commonly known as the American Fur Company.*

PLATE L. *This 1843 portrait of Audubon was painted by his son John upon the naturalist's return from the Missouri River expedition. John's wife noted that he arrived at Minnie's Land in this dress and "made a fine and striking appearance."*

PLATE LI. *Dr. George C. Shattuck Jr. (1813–1893) practiced medicine for many years in Boston with his eminent father and later served as a professor and dean of the faculty at Harvard Medical School. He was also active for most of his adult life in the Episcopal Church and founded St. Paul's School, an elite private boarding school in Concord, New Hampshire. This portrait was painted in 1889.*

family had been without a home of their own. Now, with the robust sales of the octavo *Birds*, Audubon finally had the means to remedy that. He recorded the deed in Lucy's name to place the property beyond the reach of his Kentucky creditors. As a tribute to her, the family called it Minnie's Land, having adopted the old Scottish endearment for "mother" during their days in Edinburgh.[58]

Almost immediately, John began construction of a two-story clapboard-sided mansion having both an attic and basement. It was situated in a vale near the river and surrounded by mature oaks, pines, and chestnuts. A veranda at the front of the house welcomed guests, and one at the back had a view of the water through the trees, with a stairway to a path leading to a beach in the cove that ran along the edge of the river. By the following April, the house was completed and the entire Audubon family had moved in along with a menagerie of animals.[59]

John was now remarried. The previous October he had wed Caroline Hall, a twenty-nine-year-old English-born woman whose family had immigrated to Brooklyn.[60] Victor, who was still in mourning, would marry one of Caroline's friends, Georgianna Richards Mallory, in March 1843.[61] They would eventually have six children.[62] John and Caroline would have another seven.[63]

John took charge of developing the upper portion of the property into a working farm with peach and apple orchards, fields of corn, and livestock, using hired help from the small village of Carmansville just to the south.[64] Later that year, the writer Parke Godwin paid a visit to the Audubon home on a bright, beautiful Sunday and marveled at the splendor of the estate:

> After wandering for some hours, I turned into a rustic road which led directly down towards the river. A noble forest was planted on the one side of it, and on the other vast grainfields lay laughing in the sun, or listening to the complacent murmur of a brook that stole along in the midst of clumps of bushes and wild briers. About the half-worn path groups of cattle loitered, some cropping the young grass, and others looking contemplatively towards the distant shine of the stream, which flashed through the vista of trees in molten bands of silver. It was such a scene as Cuyp or Paul Potter would have loved to paint, if the native country of those artists had ever furnished them with so lovely and glorious a subject.
>
> But my walk soon brought a secluded country house into view,—a house not entirely adapted to the nature of the scenery, yet simple and unpretending in its architecture, and beautifully embowered amid elms and oaks. Several graceful fawns, and a noble elk, were stalking in the shade of the trees, apparently unconscious of the presence of a few dogs, and not caring for the numerous turkeys, geese, and other domestic animals that gabbled and screamed around

them. Nor did my own approach startle the wild beautiful creatures that seemed as docile as any of their tame companions.[65]

Another caller who interviewed the naturalist at Minnie's Land was struck by the character of the man as well as by the evident love and intimacy that marked his relationship with Lucy:

In my interview with the naturalist, there were several things that stamped themselves indelibly upon my mind. The wonderful simplicity of the man was perhaps the most remarkable. His enthusiasm for facts made him unconscious of himself. To make him happy, you had only to give him a new fact in natural history, or introduce him to a rare bird. His self-forgetfulness was very impressive. I felt that I had found a man who asked homage for God and Nature, and not for himself.

The unconscious greatness of the man seemed only equalled by his child-like tenderness. The sweet unity between his wife and himself, as they turned over the original drawings of his birds, and recalled the circumstances of the drawings, some of which had been made when she was with him; her quickness of perception, and their mutual enthusiasm regarding these works of his heart and hand, and the tenderness with which they unconsciously treated each other, all was impressed upon my memory. Ever since, I have been convinced that Audubon owed more to his wife than the world knew, or ever would know. That she was always a reliance, often a help, and ever a sympathising sister-soul to her noble husband, was fully apparent to me.[66]

On July 11, 1842, Audubon set off for Philadelphia on the first leg of a canvassing trip for the *Quadrupeds*. He had hired John Bowen, the lithographer of the *Birds*, to print and hand color the images of the mammals on imperial folio sheets measuring approximately 28"× 22" in size. There would be five prints in each fascicle, which would cost $10, just like the Double Elephant Folio, and be issued bimonthly.[67]

Bowen had completed four of the five prints that would comprise the first Number, and, as Audubon made his sales calls, he showed prospective subscribers the plates of Richardson's Columbian Squirrel (Richardson's Ground Squirrel), the Woodchuck, the Florida Rat (Southeastern Pocket Gopher), and Townsend's Rocky Mountain Hare (White-tailed Jackrabbit). From Philadelphia the naturalist proceeded to Baltimore, Washington City, and Richmond. The Library of Congress agreed to take two copies of the work. U.S. Senator Benjamin Tappan from Ohio also added his name to the list, but subscriptions were otherwise slow in coming.[68]

After a brief stay at Minnie's Land, Audubon packed up his *Quadrupeds* portfolio again and left for New England on August 8. He made stops in Hartford, Springfield, Worcester, Boston, New Bedford, and Providence, showing off his new work and collecting amounts owed by his *Birds* subscribers. President John Tyler had just vetoed a tariff bill critical to the protection of New England's manufacturing interests, and several of the naturalist's friends, including Dr. Parkman, told Audubon "that this was not the time to procure subscribers." Ever confident in his ability to charm, he could not be dissuaded. By the time he returned to New York on August 26, he had obtained another twelve names. Not surprisingly, one of the prominent ones on the list was that of his friend Dr. Shattuck.[69]

During Audubon's visit to Springfield, he stayed at the U.S. Hotel, "undoubtedly the best Public House I ever was at in America," he told his journal. Henry Giles, a Unitarian minister, writer, and popular lecturer who was also a guest, was unaware that the "elderly man of very marked appearance," with whom he had spoken in the hotel sitting parlor and then joined for supper, was Audubon. "His face was oval, of beautiful contour;" Giles wrote, "his white hair combed back from a forehead of noble height, his eye benignant, but piercing. His conversation—for we had conversation—was calm, intelligent, singularly correct, and elegant in phraseology. I am not given to the superstition, that you may know a remarkable man by his forehead or his nose; and yet I was impressed by this man. I had, one way or the other, an idea that he was somebody."[70]

It was not until Audubon had eaten "very slightly" and left the table that another diner informed Giles of his supper companion's identity. Giles was delighted, replying: "There is no man in the United States, whom I am more pleased to see than Mr. Audubon." He joined the naturalist again in the parlor, where Audubon "gratified us by showing some magnificent prints of a grand new work he is about to publish, on the Quadrupeds of America."[71]

The admiring Giles described the naturalist as "one of the most distinctive instances of the union of enthusiasm with patience, of genius with labor. His devotion to his favorite pursuit has been as unremitting as it has been fervid; through travel, fatigue, danger, he has still preserved the glow of his soul and the tenor of his way."[72]

The following month brought yet another sales trip, this time to Canada, which Victor viewed as an important and still untapped market for both the *Birds* and the *Quadrupeds*. On September 12, Audubon traveled by steamer up the Hudson River and asked the captain to have the vessel hug the shoreline as she passed Minnie's Land on the way to Albany. The naturalist's family waved their handkerchiefs from the beach, while John and Victor took to the water in a small sailboat to say their goodbyes. As their sail receded in the distance and then disappeared from Audubon's view, the already-homesick naturalist broke down and wept.[73] It would be a full month before he could turn around and begin his journey back to those he loved.[74]

Audubon's itinerary took him north across Lake Champlain via steamer, where he picked up a subscription to the *Quadrupeds* from a New York passenger and received an indication from the state's lieutenant governor, who was also onboard, that the state would take a copy.[75]

The naturalist visited the cities of Quebec, Montreal, and the capital city of Kingston, netting him another fourteen subscribers, among which were the Legislative Council of Canada Library, the Legislative Assembly, and Charles Bagot, the governor general. He also added several names to his list for the octavo *Birds*, which was now well over halfway to completion with the issuance of fascicle No. 62. But he was particularly pleased to place two of the remaining copies of the Double Elephant Folio with the Canadian Parliament and a third with Lord Caledon, the third Earl of Caledon in Northern Ireland, who served as a captain of the Coldstream Guards in Quebec.[76] The naturalist was not as happy to overhear a Quebec physician on whom he had just called remark that he would never live to see the *Quadrupeds* completed.[77] He was old beyond his fifty-seven years and needed no reminder.

Audubon arrived home in mid-October and began making arrangements for what he knew would be his last expedition, one to the western United States. For more than twenty years he had longed to explore the wilderness of the Rocky Mountains and beyond. Moreover, he realized that the *Quadrupeds* could not be completed to his or Bachman's satisfaction without extending their collections into that territory. In anticipation of such a trip, he had obtained letters of introduction from President John Tyler, Secretary of State Daniel Webster, Secretary of War John C. Spencer, and Gen. Winfield Scott of the U.S. Army, among others, during his July visit to Washington City.[78] He had also discussed the idea with Pierre Chouteau Jr., a New York businessman who headed an eponymous concern that was more commonly known as the American Fur Company. Chouteau was staying at the same Washington hotel and offered the naturalist free transportation on one of the company's steamers from St. Louis up the Missouri River into fur country in the spring.[79]

Looking to put together a small party to accompany him, Audubon wrote to now nineteen-year-old Spencer Fullerton Baird on November 29 with an invitation and a description of his alternate plans:

> It is now determined that I shall go towards the Rocky Mountains at least to the Yellowstone River, and up the latter Stream four hundred of miles, and *perhaps* go across the Rocky Mountains. I have it in my power to proceed to the Yellowstone by Steamer from St. Louis on the 1st day of April next; or to go to the *"Mountains of the Wind"* in the very heart and bosom of the Rocky Mountains in the company of Sir William Drommond Stewart, Baronet who will leave on the 1st of May next also from St. Louis.[80]

Baird suffered from heart palpitations, and the fears of his mother for his health and safety could not be allayed. In his stead, Audubon recruited Lewis M. Squires, a young man from Carmansville, who would serve as the naturalist's assistant and secretary. Audubon described Squires as "a tough, active, and very willing person," though, unlike Baird, he was "no naturalist." The other members of the party included Audubon's old friend Edward Harris, who would share a portion of the expenses; Isaac Sprague, a thirty-one-year-old natural-history artist from Hingham, Massachusetts, whose paintings of birds had first caught Audubon's attention during his 1840 sales trip to New England; and John G. Bell, age thirty, a highly regarded New York taxidermist who had been hired at Bachman's urging.[81] Bachman had also been invited, and briefly considered joining the company, but he could not leave his congregation.[82]

On Saturday, March 11, 1843, Audubon, Victor, Sprague, Bell, and Squires took a train to Philadelphia, where they met up with Harris and Harris's pointer, Brag, at Sanderson's Hotel.[83] Bell traveled ahead to Baltimore on Sunday while Audubon and Victor met with John Bowen to discuss business matters. The following day, Victor returned to New York as Audubon and the remainder of the company headed for Baltimore by rail.[84] From there the group journeyed by train to Cumberland, Maryland, and then by stagecoach through the Allegheny Mountains in a snowstorm, arriving on March 16 in Wheeling, Virginia (now West Virginia), as the snow continued to fall.[85]

The steamer *Eveline* transported the travelers down the Ohio River to Cincinnati, where they hopped aboard the mail steamer *Pike*. They docked in Louisville at 11:00 p.m. on March 18. The city, blanketed with snow, had "grown beyond all calculations" to Audubon's eyes.[86] He stayed with his in-laws, Will and Alicia Bakewell, while his companions boarded at the Scott House.[87] Will was "in good spirits" despite having been forced into bankruptcy the year before as a consequence of his brother Tom's defaulting on $125,000 in notes that Will had agreed to cosign.[88]

Over the next four and a half days, the naturalist made the rounds, saw many of the people he had known decades before, and on two occasions even danced late into the night.[89] Three of the Berthouds' seven children—James, Annie, and Gordon—were in Louisville waiting for their mother to return from Pittsburgh, where she had gone to enroll her youngest daughter, fourteen-year-old Elizabeth, in school.[90]

Eliza and these three would soon be following Audubon to St. Louis. Nicholas had moved there recently to start a general commission business that showed promise, "having already received considerable consignments."[91] The naturalist learned that Alexander Gordon had just formed a new mercantile partnership in New Orleans. Gordon and his two partners, Alexander H. Wylie and Juan Ygnacio de

Egaña, would be operating under the name A. Gordon, Wylie & Co.[92] Gordon and Wylie were both subscribers to the octavo *Birds*.[93]

Audubon and his colleagues left for St. Louis on the morning of March 23 aboard the steamer *Gallant*, "the very filthiest of all filthy old rat-traps I ever traveled in," the naturalist groused in a letter to James Hall, Caroline's brother. He was no more impressed by the passengers she carried. "Our *compagnons de voyage*, about one hundred and fifty, were composed of Buckeyes, Wolverines, Suckers, Hoosiers, and gamblers, with drunkards of each and every denomination, their ladies and babies of the same nature, and specifically the dirtiest of the dirty."[94] Hampered by low water and ice floes along the way, they reached the Mississippi River two days later and landed in St. Louis on March 28.[95]

Audubon's party found lodging at the Glasgow House, a newly opened, sixty-room hotel in the bustling city of twenty thousand. Visiting the local office of Pierre Chouteau Jr. and Company, Audubon and Harris learned that it would be several weeks before they could leave for the fur country. The Missouri River, which they planned to ascend to Fort Union near the mouth of the Yellowstone River in the Unorganized Territory, was still icebound. Moreover, the company's side-wheel steamer on which they would receive free passage, the *Omega*, was sitting in dry dock and would not be ready to depart until the third week of April.[96]

Audubon was very impressed with the *Omega's* captain, Joseph Sire, whom he described as "one of the finest-looking men I have seen for many a day, and the accounts I hear of him correspond with his noble face and general appearance."[97]

On April 4, Harris, Bell, Sprague, and Squires crossed the river and spent the next two and a half weeks hunting and collecting specimens around Edwardsville and then Bunker Hill, Illinois. Game was plentiful, and the accommodations were vastly cheaper than the $9.50-a-week rooms at the Glasgow House.[98]

Audubon remained in St. Louis, having been invited by Nicholas Berthoud to stay at the home he was renting "in such a friendly manner that I could not but accept." He basked in the attention showered upon him as a visiting celebrity but was vexed that not a single person was interested in subscribing to his work.[99]

Audubon was called on to give interviews to the local papers and did so willingly, always conscious of the need to keep his name before the public.[100] One writer provided a revealing description of the aging naturalist as he approached his fifty-eighth birthday:

> Mr. Audubon is a man of about the middle statute [*sic*, i.e. stature]; his hair is white with age, and somewhat thin; he combs it back from an ample forehead, his face being sharp at the chin; has grey whiskers, an aquiline nose, and a hazle [*sic*] eye, small, keen and indicative of great tranquility, and sweetness of tem-

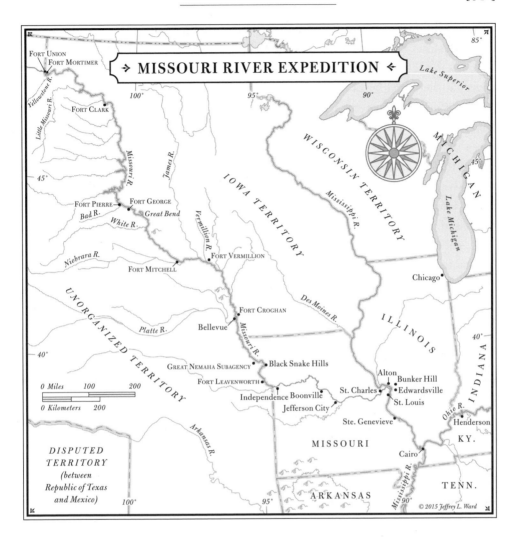

per, cheerfulness and genius. He is a man of robust constitution though not of stout frame. He told me he had not taken a particle of medicine for twenty years. He is capable of any fatigue; can walk thirty-five miles a day with ease, for months; can sleep any-where in the open air; endure all climates; his principal food being soaked sea biscuit and molasses. He cannot well masticate meat on account of having lost his teeth, from which he suffers, and is obliged to boil his meat to rags.[101]

Clearly, Audubon's penchant for self-promotion remained as strong as ever. Although he had indeed lost his last remaining tooth that April, the claims about his stamina, as those close to him knew, were grossly exaggerated.[102] However, he had prospered over the years by spinning tales about himself and his exploits, and he was not about to stop now. His fame was one of the things that helped him market his works, and he wanted the public to believe he was still the tireless, intrepid explorer—the iconic American Woodsman—about to embark on a mission of discovery at the very edge of the frontier.

Harris's company returned to St. Louis on April 21 and moved onboard the *Omega* with Audubon three days later. Each of the explorers was given "a fine state room" in the ladies' cabin, which was "finer and better furnished" than in most vessels of this type. In a letter home to Minnie's Land, the naturalist boasted that his room was 8' × 10' in size, with a double bed and a stove. However, within days, he would have both items removed when he found the bed occupied by bed bugs. He then used the space to store his things and slept with his colleagues in the cabin on India-rubber beds they had brought with them. The *Omega* would have "everything agreeable & necessary for our comfort.—Only think that our worthy Cap^n has 500 Dozens of Eggs for the trip upward! We have 15 dozen of Claret, some Brandy and Whiskey." Audubon also mentioned that the local Superintendent of Indian Affairs, Maj. David D. Mitchell, had presented him with an original journal from the Lewis & Clark expedition, written by Capt. William Clark in the final few months of 1805. Audubon's party would be following the same path up the Missouri River that the Corps of Discovery had taken nearly forty years before. Audubon rightly considered the gift "a gem" and left it with Nicholas for safekeeping, along with the skins his companions had collected so far.[103]

At around 11:30 a.m. on April 25, the *Omega* left St. Louis and steamed slowly up the Mississippi toward the mouth of the Missouri River.[104] In addition to Audubon's party, the flat-bottomed steamboat carried 101 fur trappers, or engagés as they were also known—"mostly French Creoles and Canadians," who were bound for the various posts and forts operated by the American Fur Company along the way. When these "rough-hewn" men came onboard, Audubon noticed "[s]ome drunk, some half so, and a very few sober. They are spoken to as if slaves and treated much as if such, but the more so, the better they seem to like their employers." The trappers stood on the upper deck as the vessel pulled away from the wharf and "fired different scattering salutes and were somewhat uproarious" for the next hour as the busy St. Louis waterfront dwindled astern. After dinner, the sober ones were "all singing on the top Deck, and Hallowing as if Mad Indians.—The Drunken ones are all below sound asleep."[105]

A small group of seven or eight Native Americans—Sacs, Iowas, and Foxes— were also onboard, returning to their villages upriver. Audubon was asked to show his *Quadrupeds* prints to them, "and the effect was beyond belief surprising.—One of the women actually ran off at the sight of the Wood Chuck exclaiming that they were alive &c.—The chiefs all knew of the animals except the Little Squirrels from the Oregon. Their signs were most significant, and the Interpreter told us of their delight and amusement."[106]

The Missouri River was running high and swift, which slowed the *Omega's* early advance to a crawl. For the first several days, she was able to operate both day and night, passing small settlements on both sides of the roiling watercourse. The land was rich and covered with stands of enormous timber that Audubon said "astonished my young companions not a little." When the banks gave way from the rising water, whole trees with their dirt-clogged roots would tumble into the river. As the steamboat moved farther upstream, fighting the powerful current, the dangers of navigating the twisting channel with its uncharted snags and shifting sandbars forced Capt. Sire to tie up to shore in the evenings. Other stops were occasioned by the periodic need to cut firewood for the boilers, as well as by high winds that made it difficult to steer the vessel.[107]

Whenever possible, Audubon's party used these opportunities to go ashore and hunt for birds and mammals, although the naturalist quickly concluded that it was difficult for him to keep up with his younger companions.[108] On one such excursion on May 4 between Fort Leavenworth and the Black Snake Hills (now St. Joseph, Missouri), Harris managed to collect a *"fine large and handsome"* pink-billed sparrow with a black crown, face, and bib which Audubon felt certain was new. In tribute to his friend, he gave it the name Harris's Finch (Harris's Sparrow). The bird had actually been found by Thomas Nuttall near Independence, Missouri, during his 1834 trek with Townsend, but Audubon's given name has been attached to the bird since its appearance in the octavo *Birds*. Two days after Harris's discovery, Bell returned to the boat with a new species of vireo for which he was similarly honored. Bell also had a hand in collecting two other species on their ascent which Audubon later determined were new—the Missouri Meadow-lark (Western Meadowlark) and LeConte's Sharp-tailed Bunting (LeConte's Sparrow).[109]

Audubon's companions had far less success in collecting quadrupeds, just as Bachman had warned. The high water had flooded the bottomlands, and in places mud as deep as twenty inches had been deposited, making game "not only Scarce but dificult to be got at."[110]

As the *Omega* left the political borders of the United States and made her way into Indian country, the topography began to change. The large timber gave way to belts of smaller trees on the hills, surrounded by broad prairie.[111] By May 9, when they reached Bellevue, just south of what is now Omaha, Nebraska, Audubon noted that the hills were now "nearly bare of timber and have no underwood or brushwood; the shores along these Hills look wilder the further we proceed, and from their tops we see nothing but miserable and interminable Prairies, which we are told reach all the way to the Rocky Mountains." Much of the prairie was still under water.[112]

The party saw relatively few Indians.[113] Those with whom they came into contact were, by and large, viewed contemptuously by the aging naturalist.[114] When the Indians the steamboat had been ferrying were dropped off at the Great Nemaha Subagency on May 6, Audubon was "heartily glad" to be rid of them. One had evidently stolen "a good knife" from Audubon's party. "They are cunning beyond conception," he grumbled in a letter to his family, "and we will have to be on the alert when any of them 'call' on a visit." Audubon also thought it odd that the eighty or so Indians who met their tribesmen at the agency were more interested in eating the food that the arrivals had brought from St. Louis than in welcoming their return.[115]

At Bellevue, the naturalist recorded that "[w]e had a famous pack of rascally Indians awaiting our landing—filthy and half-starved."[116] On May 22, a Santee war party fired on the steamer after their signal for the vessel to land was ignored. One of the rifle balls came within inches of hitting a trapper sleeping below deck.[117] Even a small party of four "fine-looking" Sioux the party met toward the end of the month turned out to be "a poor set of beggars after all."[118]

On June 7, the *Omega* arrived at Fort Clark, which was situated near a once-thriving Mandan village. Audubon noted that as the steamboat approached the shore, "every article that could conveniently be carried off was placed under lock and key, and our division door was made fast, as well as those of our own rooms." Along the shoreline, the Indians—identified by the naturalist as mostly Riccarees (Arikaras)—"stood in the pelting rain and keen wind, covered with Buffalo robes, red blankets, and the like, some partially and most curiously besmeared with mud; and as they came on board, and we shook hands with each of them, I felt a clamminess that rendered the ceremony most repulsive. . . . They all looked very poor; and our captain says they are the *ne plus ultra* of thieves."[119]

These were certainly not the noble savages described and illustrated by Philadelphia painter George Catlin in his two-volume *Letters and Notes on the Manners, Customs, and Condition of the North American Indians*, a work published in 1841 and included among the items Audubon had brought along on the trip.[120] Catlin had traveled to St. Louis in 1830 and spent the next six years using his skills to record the members of the Missouri River tribes and their ways of life.[121] In 1837, an American Fur Company trader came upriver carrying smallpox. The disease swept through the Native American villages, killing tens of thousands.[122] Prince Maximilian of Wied, who had visited these tribes with Swiss painter Karl Bodmer in 1833, tracked reports from the Missouri River trading posts of the terrible epidemic:

> The disease first broke out about the 15th of June, 1837, in the village of the Mandans, from which it spread in all directions with unexampled fury. . . . Among the remotest tribes of the Assiniboins from fifty to one hundred died daily. . . .

The ravages of the disorder were most frightful among the Mandans. That once powerful tribe was exterminated, with the exception of thirty persons. Their neighbors, the Gros Ventres and the Riccarees, were out on a hunting excursion at the time the disorder broke out, so that it did not reach them till a month later; yet half the tribe were destroyed by October 1. Very few of those who were attacked recovered. . . . Many put an end to their lives with knives or muskets, or by precipitating themselves from the summit of the rock near the settlement. The prairie all around is a vast field of death, covered with unburied corpses. . . . No language can picture the scene of desolation which the country presents. . . . According to the most recent accounts, the number of Indians who have been swept away by the small-pox, on the Western frontier of the United States, amounts to more than 60,000.[123]

In less than a decade, these once fiercely proud native people had been reduced, in Audubon's judgment, to "squalid and miserable Devils" willing to feed upon the dead, bloated Buffaloes (Bison) often found floating in the river.[124] The naturalist had lost any degree of respect or sympathy for them, characterizing the ones he met as "stupid, and very superstitious." "Ah! Mr. Catlin," he told his journal wistfully, "I am now sorry to see and to read your accounts of the Indians *you* saw—how very different they must have been from any that I have seen!"[125] Harris noted that Catlin was widely derided in this part of the country, "and if we are able to believe all we hear of him there is not a word of truth nor a faithful illustration in the whole of his book."[126]

At about 7:00 p.m. on the evening of June 12, the *Omega* finally reached her destination at Fort Union, about six and a half river miles above the confluence of the Yellowstone and Missouri rivers.[127] Despite a number of delays from being caught on sandbars, repairing a broken rudder, and replacing a burned-out plate on one of the boilers, the steamboat had completed the almost 1,800-mile journey in under forty-eight and a half days, weeks faster than any vessel had made the trip before. A cannon salute was fired from the fort as the *Omega* made her approach. Audubon wrote that "we fired guns in return, six in number."[128]

Alexander Culbertson, the thirty-four-year-old bourgeois, or superintendent, of the fort, who was also a partner in Chouteau's firm, rode out at the head of "quite a cavalcade" to greet them. Audubon and his party followed their new hosts back to the fort for conversation and "some first-rate port wine."[129] While they moved most of their things to the fort the following day, they slept aboard the steamboat until she departed for St. Louis on June 14.[130] The room they were given in the fort's main building was the same one that Prince Maximilian had used during his visit a decade before. However, according to Audubon, it was "small, dark, and dirty, and crammed with our effects."[131] Culbertson quickly recognized that the accommodation was totally unsuited for a party the size of Audubon's, so he arranged for them to move to a "larger, quieter, and better one" upstairs.[132]

According to Harris, Fort Union was "superior to any Fort we have seen on the river."[133] It had been built on the northern banks of the Missouri over a four-year period, beginning in 1829. Its rectangular palisade was constructed of large, stout cottonwood pickets twenty feet high set into a stone foundation running 220 feet along the front and rear and 240 feet on the sides. An interior walkway of sawed planks, placed five feet below the top of the pickets, offered a panoramic view of the surrounding prairie and the bluffs to the north, as well as provided a place to mount a defense of the fort. Stone bastions measuring twenty-four feet square and standing over thirty feet tall, with three-foot-thick walls, were situated on the southwest and northeast corners. Each was stocked with armaments to repel any surprise attack by the Indians. Multiple buildings to house and serve the inhabitants were constructed against the interior walls, leaving a spacious, open parade yard, at the center of which was a sixty-three-foot flagpole displaying a large American flag. The fort had two entrances, front and back, with the front gates on the river side opening into a reception area enclosed by pickets and leading to a second set of gates. In this way, trading could be conducted with the Indians in the intermediate area without allowing them access to the fort itself.[134]

Over the next two months, Harris, Bell, and Squires scoured the area for wildlife, while Audubon and Sprague busied themselves with their pencils and paintbrushes.[135] To assist with the hunting, Audubon hired Étienne Provost, a skilled hunter and trapper, at $50 a month. Provost had been responsible for managing the engagés during the *Omega's* upstream voyage and was famous for having discovered the southern pass through the Rockies that was used by most settlers bound for California and Oregon.[136] Audubon hired other hunters at the fort as well, in addition to some of those at Fort Mortimer, located downriver across from the mouth of the Yellowstone River and built the year before by the rival fur business of C. Bolton, Fox, Livingstone and Company.[137]

For the most part, Audubon's colleagues were relegated to hunting within several miles of Fort Union. The naturalist had originally hoped to extend the party's explorations farther up the Missouri River into Blackfoot country, but one of the American Fur Company clerks had killed a tribal chief that spring, making such travel too dangerous.[138] However, beginning in mid-July, Audubon and his party were able to make several excursions as much as twenty or so miles out into the plains between the Yellowstone and Missouri rivers, accompanied by Culbertson and a small group of his men.[139]

Much of what they managed to collect during their stay was large game. Gray Wolves roamed the prairie and made regular forays in the vicinity of the fort to scrounge for garbage, allowing them to be picked off from the ramparts or run down and shot from the back of a horse.[140] White-tailed Deer, Black-tailed Deer (Mule Deer), Antelopes (Pronghorns), Bighorn Sheep, and Elk were present in small numbers.[141] But no quadruped generated as much excitement among Audubon's party as the Buffalo (Bison). After their first hunt in mid-July, they quickly grew to enjoy the adrenaline rush that came from chasing the fleet-footed creatures while riding horseback.[142] The naturalist, feeling every bit his age and cognizant of the dangers, left the Buffalo hunting to his companions.[143] However, he was disturbed that the animals were often killed for no useful purpose, the hunters simply cutting out their tongues and taking their tails as a trophy.[144] Even Harris, a sportsman who relished the thrill of the hunt, was touched with remorse at the utter waste:

> We now regretted having destroyed these noble beasts for no earthly reason but to gratify a sanguinary disposition which appears to be inherent in our natures. We had no means of carrying home the meat and after cutting out the tongues we wended our way back to camp, completely disgusted with ourselves and with the conduct of all white men who come to this country. In this way year after year thousands of these animals are slaughtered for mere sport and the carcasses left for the wolves.[145]

The smaller mammals were much harder to find. For weeks, the party tried to procure a decent specimen of a variety of small hare that Bell had killed near the fort on June 21. Bell's rifle blast had so mangled the pelt that he returned with only the head and feet, but these were sufficient to convince Audubon that it was a new species. Despite being relatively common, the hares were timid and remained hidden during the day. Subsequent efforts by the party to find another, even with the help of Harris's dog, Brag, proved unsuccessful.[146]

As always, Audubon's party was on the lookout for birds. They collected several specimens the naturalist considered new to science, including a pipit that Harris and Bell found a week after their arrival. In honor of Sprague, Audubon named it Sprague's Missouri Lark (Sprague's Pipit).[147] Audubon also bestowed the names of friends on two other birds: Brewer's Blackbird after Thomas M. Brewer, M.D., of Boston, and Baird's Bunting (Baird's Sparrow) for young Spencer Fullerton Baird.[148] Yet another bird, Shattuck's Bunting (Clay-colored Sparrow), was named for George C. Shattuck Jr. However, it would prove to be an already discovered sparrow that Swainson had previously described.[149]

Audubon's companions also collected several hybrids, or intergrades, as ornithologists call them, of what is known today as the Northern Flicker. This species of woodpecker has two forms, the "Yellow-shafted Flicker" found in eastern North America and the "Red-shafted Flicker" of the west. In the upper plains, where their geographic ranges overlap, they frequently interbreed, giving rise to offspring with field marks from each form. Audubon believed that these intergrades represented a new species, which he named the Missouri Red-moustached Woodpecker.[150]

In keeping with the naturalist's original plans for a mid-August departure, the expedition left Fort Union at noon on August 16 and headed downstream aboard a forty-foot-long mackinaw boat that Culbertson's men had constructed.[151] Audubon christened it the *Union*, "in consequence of the united exertions of my companions to do all that could be done, on this costly expedition."[152] The explorers were joined on their descent by Culbertson, his Blackfoot wife, Natawista, and their infant son; Étienne Provost; a clerk at the fort named Jean Baptiste Moncrévier; and four Canadian boatmen, who would occasionally break into lusty song as they rowed.[153] In addition to the skins, minerals, and souvenirs the expedition had collected, Audubon was returning with cages holding a juvenile Badger and a young Rocky Mountain Deer (Mule Deer). When they reached Fort Clark, Audubon would add a young Swift Fox that had been captured and kept for him since his visit in early June.[154]

The group camped at night and during high winds, using the time ashore to hunt for fresh meat and, where possible, add to Audubon's collections. On September 7, Bell shot a nightjar that looked like a smaller version of the Whip-poor-will (Eastern Whip-poor-will) of the eastern United States. Audubon had "no doubt" that this was the species Nuttall had seen but was unable to collect on his trek through the Rocky Mountains.[155] Based on Nuttall's report, Audubon had listed it in the final volume of the *Ornithological Biography*, among the species that had been observed within the limits of the United States but had yet to be described for science. Audubon called it Nuttall's Whip-poor-will (Common Poor-will) after his Boston friend.[156] However, that honor belonged instead to the person who first published a formal description of the bird in the scientific literature. With a specimen now in hand, Audubon was able to do so in the penultimate Number of the octavo *Birds*. He officially named the bird after Nuttall, "whose worth as a man and a scientific naturalist, are both so well known."[157] It would be Audubon's final contribution to the discovery of North America's avifauna.[158]

The following day, the *Union* arrived at Fort Pierre, a major American Fur Company post about two and a half miles north of the confluence of the Missouri and Bad rivers in what is now South Dakota. Culbertson was compelled to disembark with his family after receiving orders to travel to the American Fur Company's post on the Platte River. Audubon very much regretted seeing him go.[159]

The naturalist enjoyed Culbertson's company and appreciated the hospitality the superintendent had shown to the members of the expedition over the course of the summer. With some help from Sprague, Audubon had painted portraits both of Culbertson and of his wife and son in the first few weeks of the party's stay.[160]

And, on August 11, as he was packing up to leave Fort Union, he presented Culbertson with a proof copy of one of the imperial-sized *Quadrupeds* prints that he had brought along on the trip.[161] Culbertson returned the kindness before leaving Fort Pierre, giving the naturalist a Sioux painting on Buffalo hide, known as a parflèche, which illustrated a victorious Sioux battle against a rival tribe, the Gros Ventres.[162] Two years later, Culbertson would send Audubon, through Bell, the skin of a never-before-identified species of weasel that Bachman named the Black-footed Ferret.[163]

This member of the genus *Mustella* was widespread but seldom seen in Audubon's time. Today, it is considered among the most critically endangered creatures in North America, its population driven to near extinction in the 20th century by expanding agricultural production; campaigns by farmers and ranchers to eradicate the Prairie Dogs on which it preys; and the spread of sylvatic plague and canine distemper into its range. In 1987, the population of Black-footed Ferrets had dwindled to only eighteen individuals, found in a single population in Wyoming. The entire group was live-trapped and placed into a captive-breeding program overseen by the U.S. Fish and Wildlife Service. Since 1991, ferrets have been reintroduced at multiple sites throughout their historic range, with their numbers in the wild hovering around a thousand.[164]

Audubon's party pushed off from Fort Pierre on September 14 aboard a larger mackinaw boat they had exchanged for the *Union*.[165] The remainder of the trip would take another five weeks, the expedition finally landing in St. Louis around 3:00 p.m. on October 19. After seeing his collection unloaded and placed in temporary storage at Nicholas Berthoud's warehouse, the naturalist sat down and wrote home to his family to announce his safe return.[166]

The *Daily Evening Gazette* for October 20 celebrated his arrival: "Mr. Audubon with his party, arrived in the city, last evening, in good health and spirits, and brings with him a rich harvest of his labor and industry."[167] In fact, the expedition had largely failed to accomplish its principal purpose—collecting a wide array of western mammals and information about their life habits for inclusion in the *Quadrupeds*. Of the 350 skins that Harris itemized in his diary, less than fourteen percent, forty-eight in total, comprised mammals, and many of these were duplicates.[168]

On October 22, Audubon, Bell, Sprague, and Squires boarded the steamer *Nautilus* bound for Cincinnati. They would continue up the Ohio aboard a second steamer to Pittsburgh and then cross the Allegheny Mountains by way of the Pennsylvania Canal on their way to Philadelphia.[169]

When a fellow passenger on the canal boat, twenty-four-year-old Charles W. Webber, learned that Audubon might have to sleep on the floor because of the crowded conditions, he readily relinquished his berth. The young man, a longtime admirer and budding naturalist, would never forget his first sight of Audubon after months on the frontier. "A patriarchal beard fell, white and wavy, down his breast; a pair of hawk-like eyes gleamed sharply out from the fuzzy shroud of cap and collar." Despite his age, Audubon's "physical energies seemed entirely unimpaired." When the two men sometimes left the boat to get some exercise by walking ahead along the towpath, Webber was astonished to see "this old man leave me, panting to the leeward." Audubon also still enjoyed remarkably keen vision, "an Indian's eye" as he called it, and was able to spot and identify wildlife at a distance of several hundred yards. However, Webber noted that Audubon "was not very talkative," and that when he did speak, "[h]is conversation was impulsive and fragmentary."[170]

Harris remained in St. Louis until October 30 and then took passage for Cincinnati on the *Belle Air*. During a stop in Louisville, he suffered a serious asthma attack and decided to head south to New Orleans to recuperate.[171]

Audubon reached New York City on Sunday, November 6, and took the train to Harlem, where he hired a carriage to drive him with his things out to Minnie's Land. His family had gathered outside, as Victor's wife recalled, eager to greet him:

> It was a bright day, and the whole family, with his old friend Captain Cummings, were on the piazza waiting for the carriage to come from Harlem. There were two roads, and hearing wheels, some ran one way and some another, each hoping to be the first to see him; but he had left the carriage at the top of the hill, and came on foot straight down the steepest part, so that those who remained on the piazza had his first kiss. He kissed his sons as well as the ladies of the party. He had on a green blanket coat with a fur collar and cuffs; his hair and beard were very long, and he made a fine and striking appearance. In this dress his son John painted his portrait.[172]

Bachman was anxiously anticipating the return of his old friend and penned a letter on November 1 imploring him to travel at once to Charleston with the quadruped skins they had collected. "Tell me of all your new discoveries. You must have things rare and new. O, how I long to tumble over the specimens," the pastor rhapsodized. The shipment of the expedition's cargo from St. Louis was still making its way east, but Audubon had no interest in leaving his family and hopping aboard another boat after so long a journey. He preferred to have Bachman come to New York. However, as in the past, Bachman could not leave his pulpit.[173]

So, over the months that followed, letters steamed back and forth between the two cities. Bachman begged Audubon to provide his journal, skins, and other materials from the expedition, while the naturalist for the most part temporized. Audubon needed these items for his own work on the project. At the same time, he surely knew that he had failed to meet Bachman's perhaps unrealistic expectations and had relatively little to show for his nine months away.[174] In a letter dated November 12,

1843, the naturalist tried to dampen Bachman's hopes, cautioning him that "[t]he variety of Quadrupeds is small in the Country we visited, and I fear that I have not more than 3 or 4 New ones." He felt better about the job they had done in procuring new birds, reporting that they had discovered "no less than 14 New Species of Birds, perhaps a few more."[175]

Audubon spent the next few months completing the drawings and species accounts for the remaining Numbers of the octavo *Birds*. On May 29, 1844, Bowen published 1,050 copies of the final fascicle, No. 100, which was delivered to subscribers the following month.[176] The work had proved to be an overwhelming success, generating a profit for the family of about $35,980 (roughly $1,075,000 in 2016 dollars).[177] It would be enough to support the Audubon clan in relative comfort for several years to come.[178]

The Audubons could now focus their attention on the *Quadrupeds*. Audubon and John, who was now almost as talented as his father in depicting wildlife, worked on the drawings. The naturalist's finest work came in illustrating live animals, including those he had observed in the wild. However, even the best of his mammal renditions could not compete with the illustrations found in the *Birds*. In addition to the drawings, he worked on manuscripts for the letterpress that Bachman was preparing. Victor contributed backgrounds to the compositions while continuing to manage the business side of the venture.[179]

As with the *Birds*, Audubon remained the primary salesman, taking full advantage of his engaging persona and celebrity status to attract new subscribers. Dr. Shattuck referred to this as "the talismanic influence of your presence."[180] But the naturalist hated the travel and was nearly always homesick.[181] On May 5, 1844, he left Minnie's Land for New England, where he managed to add thirty-three names to his growing list. This was followed by a summer tour of cities in western New York—Auburn, Geneva, Rochester, Canandaigua, Buffalo, Utica, and Schenectady. In September, he headed once again to New England.[182] His efforts raised the total number of subscribers to almost two hundred, and Victor thought it prudent for Bowen to print three hundred of each plate in order to fill future orders.[183] It was an astute decision, as that figure was surpassed by the following spring when Audubon and Victor made a sales trip to Philadelphia and Baltimore.[184]

The individual Numbers, with five prints each, were now appearing at regular intervals approximately every other month.[185] Bowen had issued the tenth Number in late January 1845, bringing the total number of prints to fifty and completing the first of three projected volumes of equal length.[186]

The Audubons hoped the accompanying letterpress would soon follow. However, Bachman was struggling with the species accounts and growing increasingly frustrated as his requests for essential information from Minnie's Land went unanswered. Audubon withheld his Missouri River journal, even during a visit Bachman made to Minnie's Land in the fall of 1845 after attending a meeting of the General Synod of the Lutheran Church. Moreover, for the past several years, the pastor had asked the Audubons to provide him with published sources that were unavailable in Charleston. "Sometimes I have to set aside a species, for the lack of specimens and books," he explained in an 1844 letter to Victor. "The books are to be found in New York and Philadelphia, but are expensive. I would not have you buy them; but could you not copy for me such articles as we need?" Despite Victor's "solemn promise" to attend to his father-in-law's requests, nothing changed.[187]

Bachman had finally had enough. He was prepared to abandon the project when he sat down with paper and pen on Christmas Eve 1845 to ask Harris for his help:

> I find the Audubons are not aware of what is wanted in the publication of
> the Quadrupeds. All they care about is to get out a No. of engravings in two
> months. They have not sent me one single book out of a list of 100 I gave them
> and only 6 lines copied from a book after having written for them for four years.
> . . . Now he is clamorous for the letter press — on many of the Quadrupeds
> he has not sent me one line & on others he has omitted even the geographical
> range — I know nothing of what he did in the West having never received his
> journal & not twenty lines on the subject. I am to write a book without the in-
> formation he promised to give — without books of reference & above all what is
> a sine qua non to me without specimens. In the meantime my name is attached
> to the book, and the public look to us to settle our American species, and alas I
> have not the materials to do so.[188]

Bachman knew that as soon as the first volume of text was completed, which he expected to be shortly, the Audubons would "be clamorous for the second volume." At the rate Bowen was turning out prints, the second set of fifty prints would be in the hands of subscribers by March 1846.[189] Bachman had been forced to work with "scanty materials" thus far and was not willing to proceed further unless his conditions were met. "Now I do not like to make any threats," he told Harris, "but if my reasonable requests are not complied with I have made up my mind not to write another line at the end of the first volume. I have not made up my mind hastily. It is the result of four years remonstrance, mortification, and disappointment."[190]

After receiving Bachman's letter, Harris almost certainly raised the issue with both Audubon and Victor. John was then in Texas, having traveled there in the fall on a several-month field expedition to obtain specimens of southwestern mammals. He would return to New York in April only to turn around and leave for England with his family in June. Over the next year, John pored over the collections of the British Museum and other museums in Europe, as Audubon related, in order to illustrate "figures of those arctic animals, of which accessible specimens exist only in the museums of that quarter of the globe."[191]

Meanwhile, Audubon and Victor sought to make amends with Bachman. Even before Harris spoke to them about Bachman's concerns, Audubon and Victor had put together a lengthy letter detailing the measurements of twenty-four species and the distribution ranges of all of the species illustrated in the first volume.[192]

Beginning in January 1846, as the pastor was endeavoring to finish the text for the initial volume of the letterpress, a shipment of skins made its way to Charleston, followed a month later by a copy of the long-secreted Missouri River journal.[193] While Bachman found the narratives "particularly spirited—often amusing & instructive," the contents largely confirmed what he had feared. "I cannot find that you ever set a trap or looked at the smaller rodentia—this was a terrible error. . . . I am afraid the broad shadows of the Elk Buffaloe & big horn hid all the little Marmot squirrels, Jumping mice rats & Shrews," he grumbled in a letter back to Minnie's Land.[194]

Audubon was understandably defensive when he replied on March 12:

> You speak of our not having Sat Traps to catch small animals but there you are Sadly mistaken. Not a day or night without our having Some dozens, but could catch nothing in them, and true, however, we never thought of putting up a fence, and wire Snares.—You will have found by now that the Hare I brought, though Sadly mutilated will prove a new Species—You appear to forget that we waited 2 Months at St. Louis for the River to open. As to digging for Foxes; It would have taken 12 Men a week under the masses of Rocks under which they burrow. [195]

Working almost nonstop, Bachman was finally able to send off the first half of the manuscript to Victor in February, and followed with the other half on March 22.[196] Victor had it typeset and returned the galleys to Bachman for correction. The pastor welcomed the diversion from his grief following the death of his wife, Harriet, on July 15. She had been chronically ill for years and suffered from a painful neurological condition of the face known as tic douloureux. The published book, which listed Audubon and Bachman as coauthors, appeared in a printing of a thousand copies in December 1846.[197]

Bachman had hoped to begin writing the next volume after Christmas and to have it to the printer by the end of 1847, but he needed additional information about the many species of which he had no knowledge, and Victor was once again ignoring his requests to copy the relevant texts. The pastor would have been hard pressed to tackle the writing, in any event, having faced a series of personal trials over the course of the year, including the illness and death of his daughter Julia, who died of consumption in September 1847.[198]

By that time it had become clear to everyone at Minnie's Land that Audubon had slipped into senile dementia, what today would likely be diagnosed as Alzheimer's disease. There had been previous hints, such as a diminished interest in the publication, although he had been able to continue working with a pencil and brush until the early months of 1846, when his aging eyesight robbed him of the ability to focus, even with glasses, at the middle distances so essential for drawing.[199] John would shoulder the burden of completing the remaining illustrations for the imperial folio, eventually painting almost half of the compositions.[200]

Audubon had also been able to keep up with his correspondence into early 1847, including a forceful letter of recommendation on behalf of Spencer Fullerton Baird, who was seeking the post of curator of the recently founded Smithsonian Institution. But by the second half of that year, with John's family back from England and the entire Audubon clan once again in residence at Minnie's Land, the signs of Audubon's mental decay could not be ignored. When Baird, who had received the coveted appointment, stopped by in July to pay his respects, he found the naturalist "much changed."[201]

Fearful that the truth about Audubon's deteriorating state might get out and undermine their continued promotion of the *Quadrupeds*, the family maintained a carefully orchestrated silence.[202] Bachman had no idea of the extent of the naturalist's decline until he paid a visit in May 1848, prior to a meeting of the Synod.[203] In a letter home to his sister-in-law Maria Martin, the pastor described his old friend with sorrow: "His is indeed a most sad and melancholy case," he wrote. "I have often sat down sad & gloomy in witnessing a ruin, that I had seen in other years in order & neatness, but the ruins of a mind once bright & full of imagination is still more melancholy to the observer. The outlines of his countenance & his general robust form are there, but the mind is all in ruins."[204]

Without their father's assistance, John and Victor had no choice but to continue on with the publication. This remained the family's principal business even though both men had developed independent careers as painters. Victor exhibited his landscapes multiple times during the 1840s at the National Academy of Design, the Apollo Association, and the American Art-Union. In 1846, he was elected by his peers as a full member of the National Academy of Design. The following year, the academy elected John as an associate member in recognition of his portrait paintings, which had been exhibited at both the academy and the Apollo Association.[205] However, as Victor conceded in an 1846 letter to his uncle Will Bakewell, "it is *very difficult* in America to make a *comfortable and respectable* living by Painting."[206]

The third and final volume of imperial folio prints was completed in 1848. The following year, Victor began issuing a royal octavo edition in a format similar to that of the octavo *Birds*. It united Bachman's text with hand-colored lithographs of the first fifty illustrations and was sold serially in ten individual parts at a cost of $1 each. Nagel & Weingaertner of New York produced the prints for the first several Numbers and was then replaced by John Bowen. The remaining two octavo volumes would have to wait until the pastor completed his work on the letterpress. That would take another three years, even with the capable assistance of Maria Martin, whom Bachman married in December 1848.[207]

John, now thirty-six and interested in building financial security for a family all too dependent on the hit-or-miss sale of books, signed on in early 1849 as second-in-command to Col. H. L. Webb, who was leading an overland expedition to the California goldfields. John also hoped to use the trip to procure additional undescribed birds and quadrupeds for his brush. With $27,000 raised from investors to cover expenses, a sum to be repaid with interest and a hoped-for profit by the earnings of each member over the next year, the company of some eighty men left New York on February 8 bound for New Orleans via the Ohio and Mississippi rivers.[208] They would be joined by a smaller group from Philadelphia as well as a few others, including Col. Webb, who met them en route, bringing their total complement to ninety-eight.[209]

Will Bakewell, who dined with John during a quick stop in Louisville, was also headed to New Orleans and accompanied his nephew down the Mississippi aboard the steamer *General Scott* from Cairo, Illinois. His companionship made John's trip "as agreeable as it could be, where all my associations were of a melancholy nature. I thought of past joys and friends dead and scattered since the days when I knew this country so well." Like Audubon in his earlier years, his younger son suffered from periodic bouts of depression, and John's brief journal entry suggests that he may have been depressed during this portion of the journey. When the company reached the Crescent City on February 18, John helped them find lodgings but stayed at the home of his aunt, Ann Gordon.[210] Alexander Gordon had passed away the previous May in Louisville.[211]

From New Orleans, where the men purchased supplies, the company proceeded by steamer to Brazos Island, just north of the mouth of the Rio Grande. The southern route that Col. Webb had mapped out, which would take them across Texas and northern Mexico and through what is now southwestern Arizona to San Diego, led instead to calamity.[212] Cholera swept through their camp in the Rio Grande Valley, sickening John and many others and taking ten lives. Thieves made off with their remaining stake, about $14,500, although John was successful in recovering all but $7,000. Twenty men decided to turn back, and Col. Webb, weakened by cholera, chose to do likewise, taking another ten or twelve with him, along with $2,000 of the investment money.[213]

At the urging of his companions, John agreed to assume command. He led the remaining forty-eight men of the company, as well as several others who had joined them, across the hard, rough trail through the mountains and desert to San Diego, where they arrived in early November. Eleven remained there to convalesce and travel north by boat, while about forty continued on to Los Angeles. From there a majority sailed for San Francisco. John led a party of ten others, with the mules, through the San Joaquin Valley to Stockton. They reunited with the rest of the company in San Francisco on December 22. After a tour of the goldfields, John decided not to stay and sailed for home via Panama in July 1850, arriving in New York with little more than some landscape drawings and a journal to show for his efforts.[214]

John's investors expected repayment, and the Audubons had to scramble to pull together the necessary funds. Victor took to the road in December in an effort to sell additional subscriptions to the *Quadrupeds* but found little interest in New England, which had always been fertile ground for his father. In correspondence home to John, he suggested that if Harris declined to make them a loan, perhaps Caroline Hall's father would. Meanwhile, John was arranging to be appointed Audubon's legal guardian.[215]

As 1850 passed into history and the promise of a new year beckoned, the sixty-five-year-old patriarch of the Audubon clan began to fade. He stopped eating during the third week of January and was confined to bed.[216] On Wednesday, January 22, he suffered a mild stroke that resulted in his partial paralysis. John waited until the following day to telegram his brother, who was in Philadelphia. By the time Victor arrived at Minnie's Land, Audubon had developed a fever and was suffering. His condition was compounded on Friday night by an erysipelas rash about his head, a symptom usually caused by a streptococcal infection. By Sunday, the rash was a source of intense pain. At 2:30 a.m. on Monday, January 27, Audubon's rapid decline brought the family to his bedside in the ground-floor room he had once used as an artist's studio, a visible reminder of his past glory.[217]

In the hours that followed, the naturalist was quiet and sleeping with his eyes partially closed.[218] Perhaps somewhere in the swirling mists of his broken mind he dreamed of hunting ducks again near Henderson with a young Will Bakewell, a memory still so crisp that it had awakened him from a long-silent reverie during a visit by his brother-in-law the year before. "Yes, yes, Billy!" he had exclaimed, his eyes sparkling once more with excitement. "You go down that side of Long Pond, and I'll go this side, and we'll get the ducks!"[219] Those were his last recorded words and an appropriate metaphor for his extraordinary life.

Later that Monday morning, the American Woodsman stirred and opened his eyes, turning his head and gazing upon his beloved Lucy and dutiful sons one last time before drifting off to sleep. With a final, serene breath at 10:15 a.m., his quest had come to an end, and the dazzling luminescence of those remarkable eagle eyes was extinguished forever.[220]

Epilogue

It had not been easy for Lucy to see her husband's colorful personality disappear into the shadows. But steel-willed and resolute, she had prepared herself for his death. She told a friend that the impact was softened as she had watched him grow increasingly feeble over the past few months, coupled with the "melancholy state" in which he had long been. "I trust his spirit is now amongst the blessed," she added, "and I have only to reflect that soon I shall be called away to join him."[1]

News of Audubon's death began to appear in the New York papers on Wednesday, January 29, just as final preparations were being made for a 3:00 p.m. funeral service at the nearby Church of the Intercession, to be followed by interment just south of Minnie's Land at Trinity Church Cemetery.[2]

Horace Greeley's *New-York Daily Tribune* was one of the first to publish, carrying a glowing tribute in its Wednesday-morning edition:

> This distinguished son of America is numbered with the dead. At an age beyond the period usually allotted to man, he has departed from among us, and another name has been stricken from the roll of living illustrious men.
>
> The character and career of Mr. Audubon were alike remarkable. Possessed of an indomitable spirit, an energy of purpose almost unequaled, a masterly intellect and physical powers rarely to be found, for upwards of forty years he devoted himself to his favorite pursuit — the study of Ornithology.
>
> The allurements of home, the blandishments of society, the domestic ties, which none more fully appreciated than himself, (for he was beautiful indeed in his conjugal and parental affections,) could not swerve him from his object. He was truly a wanderer in the wilderness. From Labrador to the banks of the Rio Grande, from the Atlantic to the base of the Rocky Mountains, every stream has witnessed his presence, and every hill and valley awakened to the echoes of his voice. Wherever the winged denizens of the air were to be found, he tracked them to their nests, followed them in their flight, studied their habits[,] analysed their species, and from the mighty "Bird of Washington" — fit name for this monarch of birds — to the tiny humming-bird which lives on perfume — all are portrayed in that immortal record of his fame, "The Birds of America." In the branch of science to which he devoted himself, he stands like Franklin and

Fulton towering above all American compeers and the savans of Europe have not hesitated to yield their undissembled homage to his worth.

In the private relations of life he was an ardent friend, an affectionate husband and father, and emphatically a kind and benevolent man; and among his associates and admirers none will feel more keenly his loss than he who was among his earliest friends, the veteran Statesman of Kentucky.

After a painful affliction of over two years, the struggle has ended, and we know him now but as

> "One of the few, the immortal names,
> That was not born to die."[3]

Newspapers in other parts of the country followed suit as word was relayed by telegraph, the new communication device that its inventor, Samuel F. B. Morse, had tested a few years earlier with a wire strung from the laundry room at Minnie's Land, across the river to New Jersey.[4] In Boston, Audubon's friend Dr. Thomas M. Brewer, an editor at the *Boston Daily Atlas*, offered his sentiments in the paper's February 3 issue:

> He who has done so much alike for his own fame, and that of his country — so much to illustrate the natural history of his country, and by his great example to arouse among his countrymen an interest in the study of the natural sciences, has departed. Another great name must be stricken from our roll of living fame, to be placed in that of the imperishable dead. This event, although not unexpected to the friends of the departed, involves a public loss which should not be permitted to be passed over in silence. His life has been too remarkable, his fame too extended, his example too important, his claims upon our admiration are too prominent, for the cold grave to be suffered to close over the mortal remains that enclosed his gifted spirit, without our publicly expressing our deep sense of the great loss we sustain when so great a light goes out amongst us.[5]

The March issue of *Harper's New Monthly Magazine* carried an obituary offering similar praise and ended with this recognition:

> His was a happy life. He had found his vocation, and pursued it for long years, earnestly, faithfully, and triumphantly. The forms of beauty which won his early love, and drew him into the broad forests, he brought back to cheer us who can not follow his footsteps. He has linked himself with the undying loveliness of Nature; and, therefore, his works are a possession to all men forevermore.[6]

Even Audubon's harshest critics had come to develop a grudging respect for his artistic achievements, although they could never bring themselves to acknowledge his contribution to the scientific study of ornithology.[7] In a letter to George Ord on

July 27, 1849, exactly eighteen months before Audubon's death, Charles Waterton responded to news that the naturalist was ailing. "Poor fellow!" he wrote. "Had he merely stuck to the painting of birds he might have jogged on pretty fairly. But when he borrowed the character of an ornithologist, it bore him too high up, and then let him fall, to rise no more."[8]

Ord and Waterton both predicted that future generations would judge the naturalist poorly.[9] "If the fidelity of his narrative had corresponded with his perseverance, his fame would repose on a basis which time would not diminish," Ord admitted, "but what will be the decision of posterity on the merits of one who has wantonly violated the dignity of truths by rendering her subordinate to fiction!"[10]

Audubon had his failings, to be sure. He was insecure, vain, and egotistical. He could be petty and mercurial at times. He was not averse to lying when he had something to gain. One of his boldest lies, about having studied under Jacques-Louis David, was repeated not only to prospective subscribers but to his own family. He was often impulsive. Prone to alcoholism, he needed to keep himself occupied to avoid the bottle. He was never able to give up his fondness for snuff.

At the same time, Audubon was also dynamic and indefatigable in pursuit of his dream. A charismatic individual, he made friends easily, and as a friend he was intensely loyal. He inundated those he cared about with letters and despaired when they failed to respond in kind.

He was truly a study in contrasts. Although he was born illegitimate, he grew up to rub elbows with the bluebloods of English and American society. He was mostly self-taught as an artist, but he created a lasting tribute to ornithological illustration which has never been equaled. He could be painfully shy with people, especially those he considered his superiors. Yet he succeeded in marketing, usually face to face with the wealthy, one of the largest and most expensive books the world has ever known. He was only an average businessman into his midthirties, but he went on to single-handedly finance and supervise what today would be a multi-million-dollar publishing venture. With little formal education, he became one of a select group of Americans to be elected a member of the Royal Society of London, the most prestigious learned organization in the world.

To this day, Audubon remains America's best-known and most-admired naturalist. His bold, bright images, particularly of North America's avifauna, have become a part of our cultural heritage. There have certainly been better wildlife artists since Audubon, including Louis Agassiz Fuertes, J. Fenwick Lansdowne, Guy Coheleach, Robert Verity Clem, and Robert Bateman, among others. But no one has managed to capture the public's imagination or delight the senses as Audubon did. He was a larger-than-life personality in his day, and his shadow, if anything, has only grown as the years have passed. He could not have wished for a finer epitaph.

Victor and John did their best to carry on their father's legacy, although both were at times incapacitated—John with depression and Victor from intemperance.[11] Volume II of the letterpress for the *Quadrupeds* was published in 1851, several months after Audubon's death. Bachman completed the manuscript of the third and final volume in March 1852 after Victor traveled to Charleston to personally lend a hand; it appeared in print two years later. Subscribers to the imperial folio who wished to have the complete work could purchase six additional hand-colored octavo prints to be bound up with the corresponding text of the third volume. Since two of the earlier folio images had since been determined to be of the same species, a total of 155 separate species were represented in the finished folio publication. The same number appeared in the octavo edition, with the second and third volumes being published on the heels of the letterpress in 1851 and 1854, respectively.[12]

Victor was now spending much of his time canvassing for subscribers, and while not the compelling personality his father was, proved adept at marketing the work. Overall, neither the illustrations nor the text of the octavo *Quadrupeds* could compare to the small edition of the *Birds*. Audubon knew his birds much better than his mammals, and it shows in how they are depicted. His bird biographies, while perhaps not as scientifically rigorous as the text written by Bachman, were far more interesting and entertaining. And yet the *Quadrupeds* proved to be an even better seller, with just over two thousand subscribers, although many of the sales were undoubtedly driven by its substantially lower cost.[13]

John hoped to extend the family's publishing success by serializing the journal of his trip to California. In 1852 he published the first of a projected ten-part account of his overland travels which included four prints of his landscape drawings, either colored or uncolored. However, his plans ended after lackluster sales of the first Number.[14]

By that time, Minnie's Land had begun to take on a decidedly different look from the estate Audubon knew and loved. Passengers traveling between New York and Peekskill on the trains of the Hudson River Railroad Company now passed his home using a right-of-way that ran along the edge of the river, acquired from the Audubons in 1847. New houses also dotted the property. A series of poor financial decisions by Victor and John in the early 1850s, including speculative investments in Brooklyn real estate and a metalworks foundry, had forced the family to begin selling off portions of Minnie's Land to well-to-do New Yorkers around the time of Audubon's death.[15]

In addition, both Victor and John had constructed large, three-story homes on separate riverfront parcels immediately north of Lucy's house. Victor's house next door had a footprint of 2,142 square feet and boasted ten rooms in addition to the kitchen and basement. Lucy had moved into Victor's home less than two months after Audubon's funeral, leasing her house to John's brother-in-law James Hall while John built a rental home for Hall at the northern edge of the property. She would continue to lease out her house, and planned to divide her time between her sons' families, living with each of them for half the year.[16]

The Audubons also built other rental homes on the property, generating a steady stream of income. The once proud and private Audubon homestead began to be referred to as Audubon Park, a tony address for those of the New York gentry who were eager to flee the congestion of city living and could meet Lucy's class-conscious standards. By the time the New York State Census was taken in 1855, there were nine households on the property, with twenty-three adults, thirty-one children, and twenty-nine servants.[17]

Lucy's grandchildren needed an education, and she began operating a school for them in Victor's home as early as 1853. For a fee, she welcomed neighborhood children as well. She had lost none of her dedication. "If I can hold the mind of a child to a subject for five minutes, he will never forget what I teach him," she asserted.[18]

In 1856, Victor published a second edition of the octavo *Birds*, along with a further printing, generally considered the third edition, of the octavo *Quadrupeds*.[19] The most noticeable difference between these editions and those that came earlier can be seen in the *Birds*, where Bowen incorporated a bluish-green tinted background on the plates that lacked a landscaped background. Evidently because of wear to the lithographic stones used to print the bird plates, several images had to be redrawn, and new title legends were added.[20]

At some point around this time, Victor injured his back in a fall. The official account was that he had fallen while getting off a railcar.[21] Like many fabrications, there was a modicum of truth to the story. He had suffered a leg injury in this way several years before.[22] However, family members admitted quietly that the accident occurred when Victor stumbled into a basement window well of his house during one of his frequent bouts of intoxication.[23]

Initially, the injury was not thought to be serious. However, Victor's condition worsened, and he was left an invalid, drowning his pain and self-pity in alcohol.[24] During moments of sobriety, he was able to continue with some of his correspondence as late as 1859.[25] But his injury effectively saddled John with the responsibility for managing the family's business interests. John was not by nature a businessman, and lacked his older brother's temperament and years of experience. Moreover, it was a terrible time to assume this burden, as the country was mired in yet another economic panic. But John had no choice.[26]

Looking for another source of revenue, John began making plans in 1858 to reissue the Double Elephant Folio using a recently developed printing process known as chromolithography. This enabled a printer to print in color by using multiple lithographic stones, each of which applied a separate color to the printed plate. It was vastly more complex than simple lithography because the printer not only had to select the appropriate mix of inks to match the various colors in the original artwork, but he had to determine the sequence for printing each color as well. Still, the process was less expensive than hand-colored lithography, which made it an attractive alternative.[27]

Working in association with the New York publishing house of Roe Lockwood & Son, John hired Julius Bien, a thirty-two-year-old German lithographer and map engraver who had immigrated to America in 1849 and was pioneering the art of chromolithography from his printing shop at 180 Broadway. An advertisement for the work appeared on the front page of the *New-York Daily Tribune* on January 31, 1859, and ran for three consecutive days. It declared: "This edition, in softness, finish, and correctness of coloring, will be superior to the first; every plate being colored from the original drawings still in the possession of the family." The completed work, sold only by subscription, would consist of forty-five Numbers—forty-four with prints and one with the text of the octavo *Birds*—at $10 per Number, just over half the original cost of the Havell edition. Each of the print Numbers would include ten images on seven double elephant folio sheets measuring 27"× 40", with two large and two medium-sized images on individual sheets, and six small images, two per sheet, on the remainder.[28]

Bien had begun issuing the prints beginning in 1858, and John was actively engaged in marketing the new work. On May 3, 1859, he informed Edward Harris that he had already obtained sixty subscribers and had done particularly well in the South. By 1860, the first fifteen Numbers had appeared, showcasing 150 species on 105 separate sheets. *The New-York Times* gushed that the birds were "drawn with a fidelity only equaled by the faithfulness of color which their plumage is rendered" and claimed the work rivaled "anything of the kind ever before undertaken in this country."[29] In truth, while the prints represented a groundbreaking use of this new printing technology, they paled in comparison to the richness and depth of Havell's finest work. The paper was also decidedly inferior to the Whatman rag paper used by Havell. The text for the Bien edition was issued in seven volumes in 1861, along with No. 15. There is no record of the total number of subscribers who signed up, but it is believed there were fewer than had subscribed to the Havell edition.[30]

Meanwhile, in 1859, John partnered with Roe Lockwood & Son to print a third edition of the octavo *Birds*. John again turned to Bowen & Company to provide the hand-colored prints. Bowen had died in 1856, but his firm was still in business and now being run by John Cassin, a Philadelphia ornithologist. Cassin already knew the Audubons, having approached them in 1851 with a proposal to revise and correct Audubon's text with updated scientific nomenclature. He also wanted to supplement the work with three additional volumes covering the newly discovered birds of the western United States. Victor felt the family needed to remain focused on marketing the octavo *Quadrupeds*, and the parties could never agree upon terms.[31]

Cassin was subsequently hired by Bowen's widow to help manage the printing business and, by 1858, owned half the company and was serving as its president. Whether or not Cassin suggested changes to the third edition of the *Birds*, several of the prints underwent stylistic improvements with more-detailed backgrounds and, in some cases, repositioning of the figures.[32] The third edition was followed in quick succession by a fourth edition in 1860 and a fifth in 1861, both published by Roe Lockwood & Son.[33]

Since his accident, Victor's health had steadily declined. When the enumerator for the 1860 U.S. Census stopped by Victor's home on August 10, 1860, he listed Audubon's eldest son as intemperate and insane. Victor died a week later, on Friday, August 17, at the age of fifty-one. His funeral took place at 3:00 p.m. the following Sunday, and he was interred alongside his father in the family vault at Trinity Church Cemetery.[34]

John's teenage daughter Maria Rebecca Audubon, born in 1843, watched the toll these years of stress took on her father. "Never a 'business man,' saddened by his brother's condition, and utterly unable to manage at the same time a fairly large estate, the publication of two illustrated works, every plate of which he felt he must personally examine, the securing of subscribers and the financial condition of everything—what wonder that he rapidly aged, what wonder that the burden was overwhelming! After my uncle's death matters became still more difficult to handle."[35]

In April 1861, the Civil War erupted with a barrage of Confederate artillery fire on Fort Sumter in Charleston Harbor. The reverberations shook the foundation of the Union and were felt across the continent. For the Audubons, the impact was economically devastating. The startup costs of producing the Bien edition were substantial, and a sizable number of subscriptions for it had come from the South. John was unable to collect on volumes that had been ordered or find buyers for the unsold stock. Heavily in debt, principally to Roe Lockwood & Son, he was forced into bankruptcy. Lucy had cosigned some of the notes and was sucked into John's financial morass. As part of the settlement, the publishing house walked away with the copyrights and lithographic stones to Audubon's works.[36]

Bibliographic evidence suggests that a sixth edition of the octavo *Birds* was issued in 1863, although no copy has ever been found. A seventh edition under the names of both J. W. Audubon and Roe Lockwood & Son appeared in 1865. Subsequent editions in 1870–1871 and 1889 were published by Roe Lockwood's son, George R. Lockwood. A second edition of the imperial folio *Quadrupeds* appeared in 1865, followed by the fourth edition of the octavo *Quadrupeds* in 1870.[37]

Forced by creditors to begin liquidating her assets, Lucy put pen to paper in November 1861 and wrote to George Henry Moore, the librarian of the New-York Historical Society on Second Avenue, with an offer to sell her husband's original watercolor drawings, including those used for *The Birds of America*, at a price of $5,000, or about $10.64 each (roughly $295 apiece in 2016 dollars). She noted that "[i]t was always the wish of Mr. Audubon that his forty years of labour should remain in his country." While interested, the society lacked the funds and appointed a special committee to consider the matter.[38]

On November 5, 1861, John wrote to John Taylor Johnston, the president of the Central Railroad of New Jersey and later founder and president of the Metropolitan Museum of Art, to inquire as to whether he would be interested in purchasing some of the valuable works in the family's library, including their specially printed copy of *The Birds of America*. This was one of a handful of sets for which Havell had been asked to print thirteen extra composite plates in order to bring together the images of the birds that Audubon had originally identified and published as separate species. In addition, the prints were bound with the birds presented in phylogenic order rather than the order in which the prints had been issued. A deal was struck, and on December 7 Johnston acquired the Double Elephant Folio for $600 and the imperial folio of the *Quadrupeds* for another $200, a substantial discount from their subscription prices.[39]

Two and a half months later, John was dead. "Worn out in body and spirit," his daughter Maria wrote, "overburdened with anxieties, saddened by the condition of his country, it is no matter of surprise that my father could not throw off a heavy cold which attacked him early in 1862."[40] The cold evidently developed into pneumonia, and he succumbed on the evening of Friday, February 21, at the age of forty-nine.[41] The notice of his death in *The New-York Times* reported that his funeral would take place from his home in Audubon Park at 3:30 p.m. on Sunday. In addition to his family and friends, the academicians and associates of the National Academy of Design were invited to attend.[42]

Maria paid homage to her father years later in a brief biography she wrote to accompany the publication of his journal from the ill-fated California expedition:

His forty-nine years of life had been very full ones, he had touched the extremes of joy and sorrow, he had known failure and success; like his father he had never done anything indifferently. His enthusiasm carried him over many difficulties, his sympathy and generosity endeared him to every one and, when the end of the busy life came, there was left a vacant place, never to be filled, in the hearts of those who knew and loved him.[43]

Lucy soldiered on, surviving her youngest son by twelve years. They were not easy ones. Following John's death, she moved out of Audubon Park, where she had been renting a room in Georgianna's house, and took a room in a boardinghouse on 152nd Street run by a Mrs. Price. She lived there with John's second daughter, Hattie, who had moved with her and was working as a music teacher. The two women were devoted to one another. Since the death of Hattie's mother in 1840, when Lucy stepped in and raised little Hattie and her older sister, Lulu, as her own, these two had been Lucy's obvious favorites among her many grandchildren.[44]

Later that year, Lucy sold the rental home that had been built for James Hall at the northern end of Audubon Park almost a decade before, receiving $13,000 to go toward her debts. She also resumed her efforts to sell Audubon's original drawings. She informed the New-York Historical Society that she had other interested buyers, including some friends in Philadelphia, and she was not above playing prospects off one another to get a sale. The special committee of the society undertook a subscription drive, and in June 1863 it succeed in purchasing 470 of Audubon's drawings, including 434 of those engraved by Havell for *The Birds of America*, for a total price of $4,000.[45]

Despite her best efforts, Lucy could not interest anyone in the purchase of the copperplates and eventually sold them for scrap. Fortunately, the teenage son of the foreman of the Ansonia Brass and Copper Company of Ansonia, Connecticut, where they had been sent to be melted, recognized the images as Audubon's and was successful in saving many from destruction. As of 1973, Audubon scholar Waldemar Fries was able to locate seventy-eight in private and institutional collections.[46]

In 1864, the mortgages that Lucy and Caroline Audubon had on their homes in Audubon Park went into foreclosure, and the two women were forced to sell their properties. Lucy continued to live with her granddaughter at Mrs. Price's for a time despite an offer from Georgianna to rent a room in her house at $16 a week. Lucy declined, whether out of pride or because of a conflict with her daughter-in-law, saying that she would not pay that sum "for a cold room and many very disagreeables besides."[47]

Lucy could not help feeling bitter about her circumstances. In an 1865 letter to the daughter of Capt. Samuel Cumings, she wrote, "It does seem to me . . . as if we were a doomed family for all of us are in pecuniary difficulty more or less. As to myself I find it hard to look back patiently upon my great ignorance of business and the want of a wise adviser who I now find could have saved me half the property I have under errour and ignorance sacrificed and have just enough left to keep us but not enjoy life by travelling about in this beautiful World."[48]

In 1866, Lucy began collaborating with a friend, the Reverend Charles Coffin

Adams, on a biography of her husband. Adams was the rector of St. Mary's Church in nearby Manhattanville and had opened up his home to Lucy and Hattie. Other biographies of the naturalist's life had begun to appear, and Lucy doubtless wanted to shape her husband's legacy. She also must have hoped that she would be able to generate some income in the process.[49]

Over several months, Lucy and Adams used Audubon's journals and his published materials, particularly the Episodes, to put together a lengthy manuscript, which they finished in the summer of 1867. A short time later, she had it shipped off to the London publishing firm of Sampson Low, Son, & Marston, which had expressed an interest in publishing it. Adams evidently believed that his contribution to the effort entitled him to be listed as a coauthor. Lucy was unwilling to share the credit or, presumably, the royalties, and there was a falling out between the two that resulted in her and Hattie's moving out.[50]

The task of editing the manuscript fell to Robert Buchanan, a twenty-six-year-old Scottish writer and poet hired by the publisher. Concluding that the text was far too long, he proceeded to eliminate any portion he considered prolix and chopped it down to a fifth of its original size. Buchanan freely admitted that he had virtually no knowledge of ornithology and was in no position to judge the merits of Audubon's work.[51] However, he succeeded in capturing the essence of the relationship between the man and his remarkable wife:

> Audubon was a man of genius, with the courage of a lion and the simplicity of a child. One scarcely knows which to admire most—the mighty determination which enabled him to carry out his great work in the face of difficulties so huge, or the gentle and guileless sweetness with which he throughout shared his thoughts and aspirations with his wife and children. He was more like a child at the mother's knee, than a husband at the hearth—so free was the prattle, so thorough the confidence. Mrs. Audubon appears to have been a wife in every respect worthy of such a man; willing to sacrifice her personal comfort at any moment for the furtherance of his great schemes; ever ready to kiss and counsel when such were most needed; never failing in her faith that Audubon was to be one of the great workers of the earth.[52]

The volume appeared in England in 1868 under Buchanan's name as editor. Lucy was incensed, particularly as to several critical though largely valid observations Buchanan had made about her husband's character, including his vanity and selfishness. The following year, she arranged to have an American edition published in New York by G. P. Putnam & Son with her name as editor, along with some minor additions and corrections and the deletion of Buchanan's objectionable passages.[53]

Lucy was ever intent on protecting the Audubon family name. In 1868, *The New-York Times* reprinted a Charleston paper's claims that the family was destitute and seeking public assistance. A letter to the editor from an unidentified member of the family, most likely the ever-prideful matriarch, quickly appeared to correct the record:

> Two notices have lately appeared in your paper, to the effect that the family of JOHN J. AUDUBON, the naturalist, has made application for public assistance, and also that they reside in Charleston. You would confer a favor by publishing a statement contradicting the above assertions, which contradiction we wish to be copied by the Charleston *Mercury*. All the branches of the family reside in or near New-York, and no application for assistance has ever been required or made. The works of Mr. AUDUBON, to which allusion has been made, are published by the Messrs. LOCKWOOD, of New York.[54]

Partially blind and almost penniless, Lucy lived another six years, moving west with Hattie in 1870 to spend the remainder of her days with Will Bakewell's family in Kentucky. She and Hattie visited New York briefly in the late summer of 1873 as guests of Lucy's longtime friends George and Valeria Burgess. But Lucy was injured in a fall at the Burgess home in early September and returned to Louisville as soon as she recovered. On Thursday, June 18, 1874, she died of pneumonia at the home of Bakewell's widowed second wife, Maria, in Shelbyville. She was eighty-seven.[55]

Maria Bakewell and Hattie brought Lucy's remains back to New York, arriving on Monday, June 22.[56] A funeral service was held the following morning at the Church of the Intercession. The rector of the church was in Europe, so the Reverend Dr. Thomas McClure Peters of St. Michael's Church at 99th Street and Amsterdam officiated. He was assisted by the Reverend Dr. Richard M. Abercrombie of the Diocese of New Jersey, who had presided at Audubon's funeral. Among the distinguished pallbearers were George Blake Grinnell, one of Lucy's neighbors from Audubon Park, and Frederic De Peyster, the president of the New-York Historical Society, who had helped facilitate the society's purchase of the naturalist's original watercolor drawings. Following the service, Audubon's dearest friend was taken by a horse-drawn hearse to Trinity Church Cemetery. There, amidst the towering oaks, sycamores, maples, and elms standing like sentinels above the river, she was reunited at last with the husband and sons she had loved so well.[57]

In the wake of the Labrador expedition, TOM LINCOLN returned to Dennysville, where he lived out his days in the family home above the Dennys River. Along with his older brothers Theodore Jr. and Edmund, he became responsible for overseeing the family's extensive farming, lumbering, and milling operations. The business included a carding mill, a lath-and-shingle mill, a gristmill, a fulling mill, a tan house, and a double sawmill.[58]

Lincoln was a bachelor until he was forty. On November 20, 1852, several months after the death of his father, he wed thirty-year-old Emma Johnson. She bore him two children: Edith, on June 24, 1855, and Arthur Talbot, on September 16, 1856. Less than two years later, on May 6, 1858, Emma died. Lincoln waited more than a decade before remarrying. His second wife was Mary E. Eastman of Dennysville, who was thirty-six when they wed on April 10, 1869. Together they had a son, Edmund, born on January 31, 1870.[59]

According to a contemporary of Lincoln's, "[t]he years of his life passed away quietly and, in the main, uneventfully. The wellbeing of his little family, the care of his large farm occupying largely his time and attention. He was a studious, retiring, but very companionable man. His large intellectual powers were well improved, and his agreeable and useful conversation pleased and profited his numerous friends. Thoughtful, kind, conscientious and liberal, he endeared himself to the poor. In his earlier days he was politically an abolitionist, but connected himself with the Republican party at the time of its organization. He loved his country, but never filled any political office. He loved his native town, but never accepted any municipal place, excepting that of school committeeman."[60]

George F. Talbot, a lawyer who served as Solicitor for the U.S. Treasury Department, knew Lincoln as did few others:

> Perhaps the hasty judgment of some of his friends may have been that he did not achieve either in reputation or influence that position which his talents and education seemed to make easily attainable. His mind of great originality and comprehensiveness had been furnished and enlarged by an appreciative reading of the best books, and as he grew older his taste in reading became more discriminating and severe. There was nothing in philosophic discussion, or metaphysical speculation or poetic inspiration, too deep or subtle for his understanding and sympathy, and he liked best the few great authors, who discover new truths or who give new directions to the world's thoughts. The tendency of his mind seemed in early life toward the natural sciences, and stimulated and encouraged by his elder brother, Dr. Benjamin Lincoln, he seemed likely to devote himself to the service of the community where he lived, in the profession of a physician. But his health was always delicate; he was unambitious of wealth or of reputation, and he shrank with instinctive delicacy from the competitions and antagonisms in which all the honors of a professional career must be won.[61]

Lincoln's brief study of medicine at the Medical School of Maine in 1830 led his neighbors to call on him from time to time for medical care. Fred L. Gardner, looking back from his midfifties in 1916, recalled Lincoln removing one of his teeth when he was young. "It was one Sunday in late fall. I had been suffering from an unsound tooth so after church, my father took me down to Mr. Lincoln's to have the troublesome tooth extracted. I was a very small boy but I well remember being taken to a back room and seated in a high chair while Mr. Lincoln got his forceps and performed the deed. Afterwards he gave me some nice apples raised on the farm to keep me feeling right."[62]

To the residents of Dennysville, Lincoln's life was a model of Christian virtue. His concern for the needs of the less fortunate was widely known. "When sending his crops to market, it was his custom to keep back a portion, that when the next sowing time came he might be able to help those who, through misfortune or neglect, were in need." As he aged, he "allowed new cares to be laid upon him. At a time of life when most persons think less and less of others and more of themselves, he thought more of others' burdens and less of himself; his sympathies widened; his charities increased."[63]

Though outwardly religious and in regular attendance at the local Congregational Church, Lincoln was a reticent man when it came to discussing his personal religious views. "His most intimate friends," wrote George Talbot, "did not know to what extent, if at all, his speculative opinions upon matters of faith differed from those of the friends in whose worship he decorously joined. How profoundly religious his character was, every one noted, who recognized the high standard of integrity, by which he regulated his own thinking and living, the magnanimous patience with which he had borne the several sorrows, and the rounded symmetry into which he had wrought a perfected manhood."[64]

Lincoln remained in contact with the Audubons, although only intermittently. There was an exchange of correspondence between Lincoln and Audubon soon after their return from Labrador. On October 22, 1833, the young man wrote to let the naturalist know that he had seen Canada Titmice (Boreal Chickadees) in the vicinity of Dennysville. Audubon appreciated the news and made sure to include it when writing the species account for the *Ornithological Biography*.[65]

In a response to Lincoln's letter, dated November 7, Audubon asked for "a few good skins of that bird" and "as many of the Pine Gros beak [Pine Grosbeak], White winged and common Cross beaks [White-winged Crossbills and Red Crossbills] and Canada Jays [Gray Jays] as you can or will spare me." In addition, he was seeking examples of "Northern Owls and Hawks" along with some skins of the Black Headed Titmouse (Black-capped Chickadee). After conferring with Bachman, the naturalist was looking to confirm that there were actually two separate but similar-appearing species of Black Headed Titmice in America. He needed measurements and specimens of the northern birds to compare to those found in the South.[66]

John also sent Lincoln a letter in January 1834 on Bachman's behalf, asking him to supply the pastor with specimens of small mammals from Maine and offering some hints on how to better skin both mammals and birds.[67] Six years later, John wrote to Lincoln from Charleston but never received a reply.[68]

In 1845, as the Audubon family was in the midst of their work on the *Quadrupeds*, John wrote to Lincoln again from Minnie's Land, seeking information about the mammals of northern Maine and Canada, as well as specimens, particularly of Caribou, Black Foxes, White Foxes, Black Bears, and Polar Bears. "You will greatly oblige us," he explained, "by giving us as full histories of the animals you have about you as you can get or know already also the mode of hunting or procuring them, the number taken etc in short every thing you think of interest to those desirous of information of any natural history subject."[69] The Audubons considered Lincoln to be one of the most knowledgeable men in America on the topic and felt that his contribution to the project would be invaluable.[70] Lincoln replied in a lengthy missive that evidently never reached his former colleague.[71]

Not having heard anything from Dennysville, Audubon wrote again in early 1846 with a similar entreaty. Lincoln received the letter in March, but, for a variety of reasons—including the press of other matters, the hope that he would acquire more of the information Audubon wanted in the interim, and simple procrastination—he did not sit down to reply until November 17 of that year. He then filled page after page with intimate details of the knowledge he had acquired in his many years of exploring the wilds. On a solemn note, Lincoln reported that Capt. Henry Emery, who had guided Audubon and his party so ably on their northern expedition, died six years earlier of yellow fever while in the West Indies. Sadly, the *Ripley* had been lost in Bay Chaleur, New Brunswick, off the Gulf of St. Lawrence.[72]

Lincoln's love for the natural world never waned. He enjoyed illustrating shells and birds with watercolors, although he was "extremely modest" about his skill and destroyed many of his paintings. A keen observer of virtually every facet of nature, he was consulted in 1872 by Spencer Fullerton Baird, recently appointed Commissioner of Fish and Fisheries for the United States Fish Commission, about the presence of Atlantic Salmon along the Dennys River. Lincoln loved to hunt, and it was only in later life that he put away his guns and his traps for good.[73]

Lincoln died on his seventy-first birthday, March 27, 1883, following a brief illness. A Dennysville friend wrote in tribute: "Mr. Lincoln will be chiefly missed in the old home in which he has always lived. He was a man of such quiet, retiring spirit that he was fully known only by his immediate family and a few other friends.

And yet it is remarkable that a man so modest and unobtrusive should be so widely known and esteemed and loved. When the word spread through the community that he was dangerously ill, it was the universal feeling that we could not spare him yet. We could not believe that we were to be so greatly bereaved. It seemed to us that Heaven was rich enough without him."[74]

GEORGE CHEYNE SHATTUCK JR. resumed his medical studies in Boston, enrolling at the Massachusetts Medical College of Harvard University for the winter term of lectures that began in mid-October. Among his classmates was William Ingalls. Although attendance at the lectures was a degree requirement, Shattuck believed that he gained more from reading on his own and performing dissections in his father's office. However, at the same time, he admitted in a letter to Benjamin Lincoln, M.D., Tom's older brother, who was still teaching anatomy and surgery at the Vermont Medical School, that at home he found "it more difficult to sit down to study, and I am more liable to interruptions." Among the activities that stole time from his academic work was assisting in the education of his fourteen-year-old sister, Ellen.[75]

The term ended in February. Shattuck traveled to Brunswick the following month and met with Dr. Reuben Mussey at Bowdoin College. Shattuck was already thinking about pursuing postgraduate studies in Paris. At the time, the French capital was widely considered to be at the center of advancements in medicine, and a number of young physicians from Boston, including Drs. Henry Bowditch and Oliver Wendell Holmes, had made the trip in an effort to expand their knowledge and improve their skills. Mussey took a dim view of the idea, cautioning his erstwhile student that Paris had a corrupting influence on those who lingered there.[76]

In April, Shattuck visited Dr. Lincoln in Burlington. He was accompanied by Francis Boot, a friend and former Harvard classmate. The three had originally planned to explore the mineralogy of western New York and nearby Canada over the summer. But Dr. Lincoln's health, which had long been problematic, was now materially worse. The gifted educator soon decided to give up his teaching position and return to Dennysville, where he died in February of the following year, four and a half months after his thirty-second birthday.[77]

With Shattuck's father still very much involved in directing his activities, the young man spent the early part of the summer back in Brunswick studying mineralogy with Bowdoin professor Parker Cleaveland before returning to Boston to celebrate his twenty-first birthday on July 22, and with it the financial independence his great-aunt's bequest provided. The following month, he received a Master of Arts degree from Harvard, bestowed without examination three years after he received his Bachelor's degree. Fred Brune, Shattuck's best friend from his early days at the Round Hill School and then at Harvard, traveled from his home in Baltimore to re-

ceive his own degree. He was accompanied by one of his older sisters, Anne Henrietta ("Nancy") Brune. In September, Shattuck was in Hanover, New Hampshire,
attending lectures at the New Hampshire Medical School at Dartmouth, where Dr.
Mussey had returned to teach.[78]

Then, at the beginning of December, Shattuck embarked on a lengthy tour of
the United States, which was intended "for the improvement of mind and manners." Armed with letters of introduction from his father and his father's influential
friends, he journeyed from Boston to New York and then south through Philadelphia to Baltimore, where he spent the Christmas holidays with the close-knit and
spirited Brune clan. From Baltimore he made the short trip to Washington City
and met with many of the nation's leaders, including Daniel Webster, Henry Clay,
John C. Calhoun, Chief Justice John Marshall, and President Andrew Jackson. An
excursion into the Virginia countryside to visit Mount Vernon gave him his first real
opportunity to learn about the evils of slavery from one of George Washington's
former slaves, who was freed under a provision in Washington's will. But the bitter
taste from this experience would ease as Shattuck's travels progressed and he heard
from impassioned white Southerners who took a very different and more beneficent
view of the practice.[79]

Shattuck's itinerary took him from the nation's capital to the Montpelier plantation of James and Dolley Madison and then on to Richmond, Raleigh, Charlotte,
and Charleston, where he paid a call on John Bachman and "was very much gratified with the opportunity of seeing him & his family."[80]

Stops in Savannah, Pensacola, Mobile, and New Orleans followed. By early April,
Shattuck was in Louisville, having ascended the Mississippi River by steamboat to
Memphis, where he boarded a stage and visited Nashville and nearby Mammoth
Cave en route. From Louisville he descended the Ohio by steamboat on his way to
St. Louis. The vessel docked at Henderson, and Shattuck went ashore to see Audu-
bon's former abode. After reaching St. Louis, he headed upriver to Alton and then
decided to return home rather than continuing on to Chicago and the Great Lakes.
He passed through Louisville, Cincinnati, Pittsburgh, Philadelphia, and New York
before reaching Boston on May 17, 1835. Maj. Chadbourne was in town visiting
Shattuck's father, which must have been a pleasant surprise.[81]

On August 26, Shattuck received his medical diploma at Harvard's annual commencement. He had completed the final requirements for the degree after returning
from his grand tour. These included the submission of a written dissertation on a
subject related to the field of medicine. Shattuck then had to undergo an oral examination conducted in private by members of the faculty to test him on his knowledge
of anatomy, physiology, chemistry, materia medica, pharmacy, midwifery, surgery,
and the theory and practice of medicine. This was followed, within a week, by a cere-

monial public event at which Shattuck was required to read and defend his dissertation. The sole questioner at the public examination was John Collins Warren, M.D., the Hersey Professor of Anatomy and Surgery who had treated Audubon following his 1833 stroke.[82]

Degree in hand, Shattuck began assisting his father. Shattuck Sr. had just remarried after seven years as a widower, and his honeymoon gave Shattuck an opportunity to assume responsibility for the busy medical practice. But the young physician had made up his mind to continue his medical education in Paris, notwithstanding the cautionary warning he had received from Dr. Mussey. The ensuing months were spent reading and preparing for this next phase of his life and, sadly, coping with the death of his twelve-year-old sister, Lucy, in December.[83]

In the early part of 1836, Dr. George Parkman showed Shattuck a letter he had received from Audubon in London asking about his "young friend Wm Shattuck." Recognizing that the aging naturalist had misremembered his name, Shattuck replied on February 13. It had been almost two years since they had last seen each other, and Shattuck provided a recap of his recent travels. He noted that he had not had an opportunity to do anything of an ornithological nature of late, although he had "shot & skinned several birds" the summer after they returned from Labrador. He also had "just purchased a live hyena" and planned to present its skeleton to the Boston Society of Natural History.[84]

On April 8, 1836, Shattuck boarded the steamer *Independence* in New York Harbor, bound for Liverpool. He was joined by his close friends Fred Brune, who was heading to Germany to study law, and Francis Boot. The vessel docked in Liverpool on April 23, and the trio made their way through Manchester and Oxford to London. During his stay in London, Shattuck paid a call on the Audubons and accompanied the naturalist on a pleasant visit to the Zoological Gardens. Not so pleasant was his news that a Boston fire had destroyed the bulk of the 750 copies of the second volume of the American edition of the *Ornithological Biography* that had been printed the year before.[85]

Shattuck arrived in Paris on May 17. Over the course of the next three years, he would intern under Dr. Pierre-Charles-Alexandre Louis at La Pitié Hospital. Louis was in the vanguard of a revolution in medical diagnostics, which relied upon clinical observations and a patient's symptomatology to deduce the nature and etiology of the person's malady. Louis had attracted an eager and devoted following, especially among the American physician émigrés. Those interns who demonstrated a commitment to and mastery of his methods were invited to join a select group that called itself the Society of Observation. Composed of upwards of twenty young men, the society met every Saturday evening to listen to detailed case reports presented by two or three of the members, who would then be questioned and critiqued by their colleagues. Admission required the presentation of "three perfect cases" and the expiration of a six-month probationary period. Eager to participate despite the extra work it entailed, Shattuck joined the group in March 1837.[86]

That summer, Shattuck interrupted his internship to visit England, Scotland, and Ireland with Fred Brune, who had completed his studies in Germany and would be returning to New York. Louis had approved of the trip and suggested that Shattuck use some of his time to visit the fever hospitals in London and Dublin to collect case histories involving typhus fever so that Shattuck could compare the disease to typhoid fever and possibly publish his conclusions in the society's annals. Shattuck also met with prominent British physicians along the way to better understand their approach to the practice of medicine. Three months later he was back in Paris. In November, Shattuck was admitted to full membership in the Society of Observation. He wrote to his father with the news, remarking with some pride that he was "the only American in Paris" who belonged.[87]

The following March, Shattuck traveled to Italy with some friends to tour the country, visit remnants of its golden past, and, on a professional level, compare its hospitals to those in Paris. During his stay in Rome he attended religious services at St. Peter's Basilica. He had been raised a Unitarian but had been willing to explore other faiths. While studying in Burlington, he made it a point to attend services at several different churches. He had never cared for Roman Catholicism, but in this magnificent edifice his eyes were opened to the soaring pageantry and emotional power of the church's liturgy.

Perhaps more significantly, Shattuck's heart was opened by a young American woman, Anna Barker, who was traveling through Italy with mutual friends and whose beauty, grace, and enthusiasm for life captured the attention if not the hearts of a number of men, including Ralph Waldo Emerson. Shattuck's relationship with her was fleeting, but it convinced him that he would one day be ready to marry.[88]

By the time Shattuck returned to Paris in the fall, he had determined to complete his studies with Louis and return to America at the beginning of the following year. He left Paris on January 25, 1839, bound for London, where he spent the next two months gathering additional case reports for his continuing research on typhus fever. He would publish the results of his research in consecutive issues of the weekly *Medical Examiner* in 1840. He also visited London bookstores and purchased several hundred books, mostly medical texts, for the Shattuck family library. Among the books he acquired was the fourth volume of Audubon's *Ornithological Biography*, which had been published the previous November in Edinburgh. Before shipping it home with the other books, he carefully wrote his surname on the title page, the only occasion he did so in the set.[89]

Shattuck left Bristol for New York on March 23 aboard the *Great Western*, the first wooden-paddle passenger steamship to make regular runs across the Atlantic. He arrived in Boston in mid-April, a little over three years after his departure. With his formal medical education at an end, he set about practicing medicine in his father's office. He also found an outlet for exchanging medical knowledge with other young physicians, the Boston Society of Medical Improvement, a group he had joined in 1836 that included some of Louis's disciples.[90]

With his life assuming a more domestic tone, Shattuck was now open to the idea of marriage. The focus of his attention was Fred Brune's older sister Nancy, to whom he had evidently begun writing during his time in Europe. In October, he traveled to Baltimore with his sister Ellen, his only remaining sibling, intent on seeing if Nancy shared his feelings. It was a bold move. Neither the Shattuck family nor the Brunes were aware of the depth of his affection for her, and Nancy was naturally hesitant, particularly because of their four-year age difference. She had known Shattuck for years, but as her brother's best friend rather than as a suitor. Not surprisingly, she rebuffed his proposal, and Shattuck was despondent when he and Ellen returned to Boston three weeks later. However, she soon reconsidered, and by mid-December their engagement was official. They were married in Baltimore at St. Paul's Episcopal Church on April 9, 1840.[91]

The newlyweds settled into the house at 15 Cambridge Street, next door to the Shattuck family residence on the western corner of Staniford and Cambridge streets. An enclosed walkway was built between the second floors to connect the two dwellings. The couple's early months together acquired a golden hue as Nancy learned she was pregnant. When Audubon visited Boston in September while on an early canvassing trip to sell the octavo *Birds*, he dined with the two of them. But that autumn, Nancy miscarried. Her normally irrepressible spirits were dampened by the loss and by her overwhelming homesickness. Looking for a way to help brighten her mood, Shattuck took her back to Baltimore the following March for an extended visit with her family. Within months of her April return to Boston, she was once again expecting. Nancy's mother, and then her older sister Ellen, responded to Shattuck's entreaties and traveled north to help Nancy through the pregnancy.[92]

In early January 1842, the Shattuck household suddenly found itself in mourning after twenty-two-year-old Ellen died unexpectedly from an infected ovarian cyst. Her father and her brother, as well-trained and experienced as any physicians in Boston, were unable to save her. Shattuck was more than devastated. He was guilt-ridden, and took her death especially hard. The two siblings had grown particularly close over the years, having each found solace and support in the other as the children of a detached and often overbearing father.[93]

Shattuck turned to his faith for comfort. Since his marriage, he had worshipped as an Episcopalian with his wife at Trinity Church in Boston. He now fully embraced his new religion to the wonderment of some of his medical colleagues, who viewed it as incompatible with the principles of reason and science that had marked his medical training. For Shattuck, his commitment to the Episcopal Church would form a central pillar of his life and continue for the rest of his days.[94]

Shattuck became active in the church's affairs and was a forceful advocate for restoring beauty and pageantry to the liturgy, a practice growing out of what was known as the Oxford Movement in England. The movement had its adherents in other American cities, including New York and Baltimore, but found scant support with the Bishop of Boston. Eager to see these practices adopted, Shattuck was instrumental in founding the Church of the Advent, a new Episcopal church in the city's West End, in 1844. But his views injected him into ecclesiastical politics and brought him into conflict with the church hierarchy.[95]

Meanwhile, the Shattuck clan was growing. On April 9, 1842, the Shattucks celebrated not only their second wedding anniversary but also the birth of a daughter they named Eleanor Anne ("Ellen") Brune Shattuck. Over the next five years, they would add two boys: George Brune Shattuck, on August 18, 1845, and Frederick Cheever Shattuck, on November 1, 1847.[96] Both would follow their father into the field of medicine.

As Shattuck's family expanded, so too did his medical practice. The elder Shattuck's advancing age saw him cutting back on his case load and taking extended vacations with his wife. Shattuck was compelled to assume the additional burden. However, his constitution was not always up to the task. He suffered from periodic and disabling gastrointestinal discomfort, along with depression, and at times was unable to carry out his professional duties. Looking for a solution, he turned to Dr. William Coale, a fellow Episcopalian and a Baltimore friend of Fred Brune's who had been courting Ellen Shattuck at the time of her death. Shattuck offered Coale a yearly stipend for six years to help Coale establish a private practice in Boston in exchange for Coale's periodic assistance.[97]

Ultimately, the myriad demands on Shattuck became too much for him to handle. By the summer of 1847 he was talking to Nancy about retiring from medicine and relocating from Boston to the country. The following May, he moved with his family to Millville, outside Concord, New Hampshire, and took up residence on a farm purchased from his father for a token $1. The elder Shattuck felt partially responsible for his son's condition and hoped his son would forever remain a country squire. Shattuck viewed the relocation more as an interlude that would enable him to restore his physical and spiritual energy so that he could return to a more active future.[98]

One of the options Shattuck began considering was entering academia. He applied for a position at the medical school at the University of Maryland but withdrew from consideration when it became apparent the post would not materialize.

However, with the support of some of his father's friends who sat on the board of trustees of Massachusetts General Hospital, he was able to secure an appointment to the visiting staff in early 1850. He assumed his new responsibilities in September after he and Nancy returned from a trip to the Caribbean and then Europe, where he renewed his contacts with many of the leading medical figures he had met almost fifteen years before. He also spent time touring English cathedrals and meeting with followers of the Oxford Movement.[99]

As a member of the visiting staff, Shattuck was required to spend his mornings at the hospital for only four months out of the year, leaving him a substantial amount of time to pursue other interests. He agreed to give a series of lectures at the College of St. James near Baltimore in 1851 and 1853 and accepted a position as a Professor of Anatomy at Trinity College in Hartford from 1852 to 1854.[100]

On March 18, 1854, Shattuck's father passed away, leaving an estate that had placed him in the upper echelon of New England's wealthy. He had been an imperious figure in his son's life, both demanding and inflexible. He had opened doors and created opportunities for the younger man which sometimes led Shattuck to question his own self-worth. Still, the elder Shattuck had always sought the best for his son, and his material generosity was boundless. Although Shattuck had originally found it difficult to develop a close relationship with his father, that had changed in recent years. Shattuck and Nancy were by his father's bedside when he took his last breath.[101]

Within months of his father's death, Shattuck had decided to turn his beloved pastoral retreat at Millville into an Episcopal school for boys. He had been looking for an ecclesiastical mission he could fund with some of his fortune. At the same time, he had been considering the best way to have his sons educated. The two interests coalesced in St. Paul's School, which was incorporated on June 29, 1855.[102]

Shattuck was convinced that students who "live with, and are constantly under the supervision of, the teachers, and in the country" would be better educated, both morally and physically. His experience at the Round Hill School, as well as his trip to Labrador, had also taught him that learning was not limited to the classroom. "Green fields and trees, streams and ponds, beautiful scenery, flowers and minerals are educators," he noted. "The things which are seen are very valuable, and may be used to teach of Him Who made them, and thus of the things unseen."[103] From its early beginnings when the only students were the Shattuck boys and one of their cousins, St. Paul's grew rapidly, and quickly became one of the elite private boarding schools in New England, a status it continues to enjoy today.[104]

In December 1854, Shattuck was invited to become the Professor of Clinical Medicine at the Harvard Medical School. He was honored, and happily accepted. The series of lectures he was called upon to give in 1855 still allowed him to maintain his relationship with both Trinity College and St. James College. The following year, Shattuck and Nancy left for Europe with fourteen-year-old Ellen. They remained abroad for fifteen months, returning to Boston in the summer of 1857. A short while later they moved across the river to live in Cambridge. They lived there for a year before leasing and then purchasing a home at 15 Pemberton Square in Boston.[105]

In January 1859, Shattuck was named to the much-coveted post of Hersey Professor of Theory and Practice of Physick at Harvard. Five years later, he assumed the additional role of dean of the faculty. Though the position was largely administrative and carried little authority, it provided a vehicle for him to speak in favor of expanding the length of Harvard's two-year course of instruction, which merely required attendance at lectures given during the four-month winter term. He was not alone in believing that the ever-growing volume of medical knowledge demanded a longer period of instruction. The American Medical Association, founded in 1847, was proposing three years of medical education, with terms lasting nine months. However, the idea found little support among members of the Harvard faculty, who were concerned it would discourage applicants and thereby threaten the livelihoods the professors derived from the lecture fees each student paid. Shattuck had no such worries and was clearly ahead of his peers on the issue. But he was by no means a progressive thinker; he was a traditionalist by nature. When several women sought admission to the medical school, he remained steadfast in his opposition, declaring that the difference between the sexes had been preordained by God.[106]

During the Civil War, the Shattucks were buffeted by the scorching winds of the conflict. Nancy and her family, like most Baltimore natives, were strongly supportive of the Southern cause. Her brother-in-law, George Brown, the mayor of Baltimore from 1860 to 1861, was arrested and imprisoned after President Lincoln sent federal troops to occupy the city in order to ensure safe passage for Northern regiments making their way to Washington. Shattuck did not share his wife's closely held views, which would have made her a pariah in a city that was a hotbed of abolitionist sentiment. At the same time, he did not favor the abolitionist cause, fearing what emancipation of the slaves might do to the country. He preferred to view the war as God's will, designed to punish those in both the North and the South for their sins.[107]

Shattuck remained deeply involved in the affairs of the Episcopal Church. For many years he was a fixture at the conventions of the Massachusetts diocese. In 1862, he began attending the triennial General Conventions of all the dioceses throughout the country. He also continued to find ways to provide financial support to the church and its missions. In the early 1860s, he donated property with rich coal reserves in Galena, Illinois, to the Bishop of Minnesota, who used the sales proceeds to help construct buildings at a secondary school and divinity college he had founded in the small community of Faribault outside of Minneapolis. Today, Shattuck St. Mary's School and Seabury Divinity School remain a testament to Shattuck's ample generosity toward the church.[108]

The Shattucks moved again in 1867, purchasing a home in Boston's Back Bay at 6 Newbury Street. Two years later, Shattuck relinquished his duties as dean of the medical-school faculty. He continued to hold the position of Hersey Professor of the Theory and Practice of Physick until August 31, 1874, when he resigned. By this time, Harvard University president Charles Eliot had revamped the medical school program and adopted many of the changes Shattuck had earlier advocated. That year also saw the end to Shattuck's two-year term of service as president of the Massachusetts Medical Society. In 1877, he received the honor of being elected as a fellow of the American Academy of Arts and Sciences. Nine years later, at the age of seventy-two, he was forced to resign from his position as a visiting physician at the Massachusetts General Hospital.[109]

Shattuck's health declined after he suffered a heart attack in 1890. He died at his home in Boston on March 22, 1893. Three days later, following a service at the Church of the Advent, he was laid to rest in the family mausoleum at Mt. Auburn Cemetery in Cambridge.[110] *The Boston Medical and Surgical Journal*, now edited by his son George Brune Shattuck, M.D., published an obituary in early April that described him best:

> Dr. Shattuck was a man of excellent judgment and discrimination, of a very liberal training, of wide acquaintance with the world and with human nature, of a firm purpose but a tender heart, of a rare unselfishness, a constant courtesy and thoughtfulness for others. Of deeply religious instincts and beliefs, he still had an invariable charity for all men and all differences of opinion and belief. He had, moreover, a keen sense of humor, and was a delightful companion whether at home or abroad. In a word, he combined many characteristics not often united in one person. He had a genius for friendship, and the old friends for him were always the same. He was a man who looked at this world and beyond it to the next in a truly broad and catholic spirit. He was not too good for this world or the work of this world; but if he was not good enough for a better one, there will be few who find [a] place in such.[111]

JOSEPH APPLEBY COOLIDGE remained in Eastport and became a merchant. On March 5, 1837, at the age of twenty-two, he married Clarissa ("Clara") Goold, a young woman of seventeen who had been born on Indian Island, New Brunswick, one of the British-controlled West Isles situated in Passamaquoddy Bay. Their first child, Ada Josephine, arrived in Eastport on December 4, 1844. A second daughter, Mary Vose, was born sixteen months later but died within the year.[112]

Coolidge's business in Eastport evidently struggled. He was a party to a number of lawsuits, both as a plaintiff and as a defendant.[113] In November 1846, Tom Lincoln informed Audubon that Coolidge was "doing little I believe in the way of trade."[114]

In 1848, when Coolidge was thirty-three, news that gold had been discovered in California reached Eastport. Like thousands of other young men on the Atlantic seaboard, Coolidge left his family the following year to seek his fortune 3,500 miles away. He stopped in New York en route and traveled up to Minnie's Land:

> When I visited New York in 1849, on my way to California, I intended to pay
> my respects to the aged naturalist, but I was informed by his son that the old
> man's mind was failing; that he would hardly recall me, and that it would not
> be a pleasure for me to meet him in that melancholy decline. Thus, I chose
> to remember him as of old, and I came West, and to this day I can see him—
> a magnificent, gray-haired man, childlike in his simplicity, kind-hearted,
> noble-souled, lover of nature and lover of youth, father and brother, friend
> of humanity, and one whose religion was the golden rule.[115]

Coolidge evidently arrived in San Francisco toward the end of 1849 or the early part of 1850. There is no indication that he saw John Audubon before John returned to New York. Coolidge initially took a job at the Custom House, situated at the corner of California and Montgomery streets. He was instrumental in preparing copies of its records, which were stored offsite and thereby avoided destruction when the building burned in 1851. What is unclear is why Coolidge didn't head off to the goldfields to make his fortune like most of the men who arrived in San Francisco in those early days.[116] That was certainly Clara's expectation. When the enumerator of the 1850 U.S. Census stopped by her home in Eastport on August 20, Clara identified her husband's occupation as "Gold Digger."[117]

Coolidge celebrated his first San Francisco Thanksgiving on November 30, 1850, an event he still vividly recalled years later:

> There was nothing very remarkable about it, but of course we had to celebrate
> by eating turkey. I bought one, a small one, and paid $16 for it. But it was young
> and alive. I bought it several days before and gave it in charge of a French cook
> to fatten. He stuffed it alive until it was as plump as a partridge. It made my
> mouth water to look at it. The day before Thanksgiving he picked it alive and al-
> lowed it to run around without any feathers. But when that turkey was served I
> tell you it was fit for Luculius. I don't know where it came from, but I was sat-

isfied with it. I think that by the time I paid the cook for preparing that turkey and the extras that were necessary to go with it, together with a few other things requisite for the dinner, it must have cost at least $50. But it was worth it, and I didn't leave much.[118]

Coolidge's name does not appear in the 1852 edition of the San Francisco City Directory. But by the time the 1852–1853 directory was published, he was engaged in the lumber business at 57 Pine Street.[119] In a rapidly growing city where wood-framed construction was the norm, Coolidge had positioned himself in a business with enormous potential growth.

In 1855, having established himself in his adopted city, Coolidge returned to Maine to bring Clara and Ada westward. They reached Panama in January 1856 and left on January 30 aboard the SS *Golden Gate*, commanded by Capt. A. V. H. Leroy, bound for San Francisco. The ship's records identify "Coolidge, J. A., lady and child" as passengers. After making stops in Acapulco and San Diego, the *Golden Gate* arrived in San Francisco at 10:30 a.m. on February 14.[120]

According to an advertisement in the *Daily Evening Bulletin* for July 29, 1857, Coolidge was serving as an agent of Pope's Warehouse, located at the corner of Pine and Battery streets and offering lime made from Suisun marble to plasterers. "Quantities delivered at any of the accessible points on the Bay or rivers at San Francisco Prices," it declared.[121]

By 1859, Coolidge was in partnership with G. M. Burnham, doing business under the name Burnham & Coolidge, with a lumber yard on Stewart Street.[122] His business was thriving. The following year, in the 1860 U.S. Census, he listed real estate assets valued at $20,000 and personal property worth $15,000 (collectively approaching $1.3 million in 2016 dollars).[123] The 1863 San Francisco Directory lists Coolidge singly as a lumber dealer at Pier 13 on Stewart Street.[124]

Coolidge rapidly assumed a role as a civic leader. In October 1863, he was elected a justice of the peace for the Fifth Township, comprising the Ninth and Tenth districts, with offices at 613 Market Street. At that time, San Francisco had only six justices of the peace, who served two-year terms.[125]

In 1865, Coolidge joined a group of the city's most prominent businessmen in founding the San Francisco Merchants' Exchange Association. Created to track and publicize the arrival of ships from around the world, the exchange soon became a center for the city's business class to gather and socialize at its lavish building at the corner of California and Leidesdorff streets. Coolidge was named secretary and manager of the association, a title he held until 1882.[126]

In 1868, Ada married Charles Evans Kilbourne, a 2nd lieutenant who was stationed at the nearby U.S. Army base at the Presidio. The Kilbournes' first child, Lincoln F. Kilbourne, was born the following year.[127] When the 1870 U.S. Census was taken, Ada was living off the base, nearby with her parents.[128]

At a time when there was rampant racism toward Chinese immigrants in the city, Coolidge spoke up forcefully in their favor. A Joint Committee of the U.S. Congress appointed to investigate Chinese immigration held hearings in San Francisco in November 1876. Although its members included California's two U.S. senators, who were proud members of the city's Anti-Coolie Union, Coolidge offered a clear-headed perspective of Chinese character, countering the negative stereotypes promoted by others. Coolidge described the Chinese as "intelligent, shrewd, courteous, and gentlemanly, honorable in their business transactions." He had been "informed by merchants who have had extensive business transactions with them that the usual contracts in writing were unnecessary, their word being a sufficient guarantee for their fulfillment, and in a term of years, in which business to the extent of millions of dollars was transacted, not one cent has been lost by bad faith on their part." He also attested to their personal hygiene. "In cleanliness of person they are remarkable," he said. "I have observed them closely in their various occupations, and on the streets, and cannot call to mind an instance of dirty face, or hands, or of soiled garments."[129]

In July 1880, Coolidge was appointed pilot commissioner of the ports of San Francisco, Benicia, and Mare Island by Governor George C. Parkins. The appointment, which required legislative approval, sailed through the California Senate on a vote of 34-1. Coolidge served in this capacity until the expiration of his term in 1882.[130]

Toward the end of his life, Coolidge went to work as a storekeeper, and later as a clerk, for the Spring Valley Water Works, a private water supplier in San Francisco. Clara passed away on April 12, 1894, at the age of seventy-four and was buried across the bay in the Masonic (now Roselawn) Cemetery in Livermore, California. Her older brother, Gardner, who had come to the Bay Area and farmed in Contra Costa County, lay nearby.[131]

On Sunday, September 6, 1896, *The San Francisco Call* ran an article entitled "A Californian's Recollection of Naturalist Audubon." The reporter noted:

> There is probably not another man in the world to-day who can look back to personal association with the famous ornithologist and ornithological painter, John James Audubon, with the vividness that characterizes the recollections of Joseph A. Coolidge, who for more than two score years has been a prominent citizen of San Francisco, and who is hale and hearty now at the advanced age of 81 years.[132]

Coolidge recounted the rich memories of his time with the naturalist during their months together in Labrador. Maria Audubon saw a reprinted copy of the article and, from her home in Salem, New York, wrote to Coolidge on September 24, 1896. Coolidge replied on October 5, expressing his pleasure at receiving her letter since he had not heard from anyone associated with Audubon since his visit to Minnie's Land forty-seven years before. "The feeling of high regard which I have always entertained for your dear Grandfather naturally inspires an interest in all connection with him," he noted. As far as Coolidge knew, he was the last surviving member of the expedition.[133]

Maria subsequently sent Coolidge a copy of a portrait her father had painted of Audubon.[134] Coolidge thanked her in a letter dated November 18. "You can hardly imagine the pleasure the reception of the copied likeness of your dear grand father has given me. I have it framed and hung where I can look upon it whenever I enter my room. The likeness is a good one, as I remember him, the co[s]tume, position and surrounding excellent, and I value it above price, the more so as the work of your dear father."[135]

Maria apparently informed Audubon scholar Ruthven Deane of her correspondence with Coolidge. Deane himself wrote to Coolidge and, in 1910, published Coolidge's December 31, 1896, reply in *The Auk*, the journal of the American Ornithologists' Union, in which Coolidge offered some additional memories of the expedition.[136]

Coolidge lived another five years, passing away from complications of asthma and old age on July 30, 1901, in San Francisco.[137] He joined his beloved Clara in the Masonic Cemetery in Livermore, where they rest together beneath a single four-sided obelisk. The inscription gives no hint of his reflected fame from the Labrador expedition, stating simply:

Joseph A. Coolidge

DIED

July 30, 1901

AGED

86 Years

———

WILLIAM INGALLS returned to Boston, where he enrolled in the medical school at Harvard. His medical education included training in his father's medical office in Boston, as well as with his brother-in-law, Dr. Charles H. Stedman, at the Chelsea Marine Hospital. He completed the course of study and was awarded an M.D. degree in 1836. Following his graduation, Ingalls began practicing in Boston.[138]

On December 3, 1840, he married Julia A. M. Davis of Roxbury, Massachusetts. The twenty-five-year-old Julia was the daughter of Ezra Davis, a successful Boston merchant.[139]

Soon after their marriage, the couple moved to Laurel Hill in West Feliciana Parish, Louisiana, not too far from Bayou Sarah. Ingalls took over a large general practice, traveling up to forty miles on horseback to visit his patients, one of whom was Gen. Zachary Taylor.[140] Ingalls's first son and namesake was born on January 20, 1843. A second son, Ezra Davis Ingalls, followed a little over four years later, on February 14, 1847.[141]

After six years in Louisiana, Ingalls returned with his family to Boston. The Ingalls's moved in with Ingalls's father at 17 Bedford Street, and it appears that Ingalls assumed his elderly father's practice. In 1848, Ingalls was appointed physician and surgeon at the Chelsea Marine Hospital. He was described several years later as being "skillful, attentive and humane."[142]

During their residence in Boston, the Ingallses lost six-year-old William, who died on February 8, 1849. A daughter, Mary Elizabeth, was born three years later, on January 7, 1852, in Chelsea.[143]

The family subsequently moved to a home in the Boston suburb of Winchester, where Ingalls opened up a general practice with an emphasis in obstetrics. It was in Winchester that Ezra drowned on July 18, 1856, at the age of nine.[144]

With the outbreak of the Civil War, Ingalls answered President Lincoln's August 1862 call for three hundred thousand men to serve nine months. He enlisted as a surgeon on September 20 and received a commission in Company S, 5th Infantry Regiment Massachusetts, on October 8. The official records reflect that he was forty-five years old at the time of his enlistment. He was in fact forty-nine, the oldest medical officer to enlist from the Commonwealth of Massachusetts.[145]

The regiment left Massachusetts on October 22 aboard transport vessels bound for North Carolina. Over the ensuing months, the regiment was involved in battles against the Confederate army in Kinston, Whitehall, and Goldsboro, North Carolina.[146] The regiment returned to Boston on June 26, 1863, and proceeded to Camp Lander in Wenham. Enthusiastic crowds lined the route of their march, giving them a warm reception. On July 2, the men were mustered out.[147]

Ingalls was promoted to major and full surgeon on October 13 and reenlisted in Company S, 59th Infantry Regiment Massachusetts, four days later. He was placed in charge of the post hospital in Readville, Massachusetts, from March 10 to June 1864. His regiment left for Washington on April 26, 1864, and had already been engaged in some of the fiercest fighting of the war in the battles of the Wilderness, Spotsylvania, North Anna, and Cold Harbor before he rejoined them on June 23 at Petersburg, Virginia. This was the site of numerous battles as the Army of the Potomac sought to break the Confederate supply lines. Over the ensuing months, the 59th Infantry saw action at the battles of Weldon Railroad, Poplar Spring Church, Hatcher's Run, and Fort Stedman.[148]

During these engagements, Ingalls preferred to have the surgical tents set up as close to the front lines as possible:

It is said that in times of battle it was his custom to be as near the firing line as his duties would permit, and that his interpretation of the limits of his sphere of duty, so far as they related to the front, was liberal. In consequence of this tendency of his, he barely escaped the fate which overtook so many of the soldiers of the Northern army when the mine exploded at Petersburg. In answer to a question he said, in his gentle voice, the tone of which seemed to contradict the thought that the joy of battle could ever have dwelt in him: "Well, perhaps we were rather far forward now and then, but I do not think improperly. Derby and I could never see any harm in it, and sometimes we thought that the boys rather liked to have us there, and perhaps found some comfort in our being near at hand."[149]

He also apparently displayed remarkable powers of concentration and endurance during long hours of treating the wounded:

On one occasion he worked, with the exception of six hours' sleep, taken at odd moments, continuously for five consecutive days and nights, during which the only food he had was one glass of milk in the first twenty-four hours, and for the rest of the time a small bit of hard tack or bacon at long intervals. He was on his feet, and either operating or dressing wounds almost the entire time.

"And," he said, when speaking of it, "I was not tired at the end of it." "In fact," he remarked on another occasion, "I never knew what men meant when they said they were tired out, until after I was seventy years old."[150]

By the end of the war, Ingalls had been promoted to brigade-surgeon and was serving with the artillery company of Gen. John Caldwell Tidball. Ingalls mustered out of the Army on June 12, 1865, "with the honorable record of having performed every duty demanded of him, invariably, promptly, thoroughly, courageously, and of having displayed marked ability in every post of responsibility that he held."[151]

After the war, Ingalls resumed his medical practice in Boston. His office was initially located at 2 Dover Street, where he lived with his wife and their adult daughter. The family later moved to 556 Tremont Street. Ingalls was a member of the Massachusetts Medical Society, the Boston Society of Medical Observation, the Obstetrical Society of Boston, and the Suffolk District Medical Society. He was also the medical director of the 2nd Brigade of the Massachusetts Militia.[152]

In 1869, Ingalls joined several other Boston physicians and a like-minded group of civic leaders in founding the Boston Children's Hospital, a twenty-bed pediatric facility housed in a townhouse at 9 Rutland Street in the city's south end. Serving mostly children of poor Irish immigrants, the hospital quickly outgrew its quarters.

The following year, the hospital was moved down the street to a larger building at the corner of Rutland and Washington streets. Ingalls served as a physician on the small staff until 1872 and thereafter provided surgical consultations.[153]

In 1870, at the age of fifty-seven, Ingalls became a visiting surgeon at Boston City Hospital, a public hospital for the poor which had been founded in 1864. He served in this capacity until 1883 and subsequently became a member of the Consulting Board.[154] Writing a history of the first forty years of the hospital, one of his colleagues said of Ingalls: "Professional spirit was with him a religion. A calm advisor, a gentle friend, precise, punctilious, careful, he gave a conscientious service to the Hospital."[155]

Ingalls was described by another colleague as a skilled surgeon with a "deliberate and well balanced" judgment. "As an operator, he was neither bold nor brilliant, but accurate, careful, thorough, effective and very neat. No one surpassed him in the after-care of the patient. He was nearly, if not actually, the first American surgeon to do a nephrolithotomy, extracting a very large calculus from the kidney, the patient living for many years afterward."[156]

Throughout his career, Ingalls had the reputation of being a skilled obstetrician. At a time when physicians were only beginning to understand the role of bacteria in causing infection and often worked without following an aseptic regimen, he delivered two thousand infants consecutively without experiencing a single case of puerperal sepsis, a common cause of postpartum maternal death. He was an active member of the Obstetrical Society of Boston and, in February 1877, read a paper to the society in which he discussed the obstetrical cases "of special interest or importance" that he had encountered during the first forty-two years of his private practice. The paper was later published in *The Boston Medical and Surgical Journal*. A colleague from the society remembered that Ingalls "had a most attractive personality. We can all recall with love and pleasure the kind refined face, the soft voice, the gentle manner, and the carriage of a well-bred gentleman. He never ceased to win affection; and many of those most devoted to him were among the younger and more brilliant men in the profession."[157]

In 1891, Ingalls retired from active medical practice and moved to Roxbury, just south of Boston, where he lived out his retirement years with his wife and daughter. However, he continued to be interested in medical advances and periodically attended medical-society meetings.[158]

On July 12, 1896, the *Boston Daily Globe* ran an article in which Ingalls offered his advice to those seeking to live a long life:

> Every man's life, in at least his own estimation, is so peculiar in its experience
> that he feels very unwilling to draw from it lessons for the guidance of other

lives. It is very difficult to express briefly a man's ideas of the causes of long life, if he cares to avoid the beaten path of the moralist, who has always at ready command a few general maxims.

Each man seems to me to be a law unto himself in the broad field of physical living, and I don't believe that anybody can point out with exactitude a special line of habit for some one else to follow. For example, a young man is cautioned usually to be regular, and yet physicians, among whom many attain to long life, are the most irregular of men.

Exercise and moderation are two good words for men to consider in the consideration of the causes of happiness and longevity, but obviously they cannot take the place of a strong constitution.

The general subject is one which it is not easy to discuss with satisfaction except at much length and after great thought, but if I am urged to give a man a rule to follow in the pursuit of long life and happiness, I should say:

Don't fret. Worry I believe to be one of the chief causes of disease and disintegration.[159]

In 1902, Ruthven Deane learned that Ingalls was still living, and corresponded with him about the Labrador expedition. Ingalls's response, dated October 30, 1902, was published by Deane in the January 1910 issue of *The Auk* and offered a series of vibrant memories of the expedition and the men who made the voyage. Eight months later, in July 1903, Deane visited the venerable physician at his Roxbury home. Ingalls's memory, according to Deane, "was very clear as to many of the experiences of his Labrador trip of seventy years before."[160]

The last surviving member of the Labrador expedition died at Boston City Hospital less than six months later, on December 1, 1903, at the age of ninety. He remained vigorous, displaying "an erect carriage, firm step, bright pink color to the cheeks, and an unclouded intellect until the end."[161] *The Boston Medical and Surgical Journal* published an obituary that ended with this simple tribute: "A noble, useful and unostentatious life, ending quietly and peacefully."[162]

And so passed from living memory the exploits of John James Audubon and his adventurous band of "Young Gentlemen" as they sought new discoveries along the bleak and far-flung Labrador coast. Yet the magnificent compositions of North American birds that Audubon completed during that memorable summer of 1833, overcoming perilous seas, grueling living conditions, and miserable weather, will forever inspire those who love the natural world and ensure that the efforts of the men of the Labrador expedition are never forgotten.

Appendix

Letter of Introduction from the Duke of Sussex

JULY 21, 1831

John James Audubon Esqᵘ F.R.S. and author of "*The Birds of America*," now in course of publication; being about to return to that Country for the purpose of once more exploring it, in order that no native Bird, from the Floridas to Canada, may be omitted in his splendid work—I, Augustus Frederick, Duke of Sussex, President of The Royal Society of London, earnestly recommend Him to the kindness and assistance of every officer of His Britannic Majesty, bearing Authority, whether Civil or Military, in any part of British America, which Mr. Audubon may chance to visit—well knowing His Majesty's gracious desire to patronice [*sic*] Science, and favor the efforts of all those persons, who seek to promote its interests, in every part of his Dominions—

Augustus Frederick, President of the Royal Society

Kensington Palace
July 21ˢᵗ 1831

To The Civil & Military Authorities in British America

(Morris Tyler Family Collection of John James Audubon, General Collection, Beinecke Rare Book and Manuscript Library, Yale University, Box 18, p. 94)

Eastern Democrat Eastport, Maine

John James Audubon, Esq. — This distinguished American Ornithologist, with his lady and two sons, arrived in this town on Tuesday evening last, with the intention, as we understand, of prosecuting his scientific researches in our section. Mr. Audubon is a native of Louisiana. While very young he visited Paris, where he studied drawing under the celebrated painter, David. At the age of seventeen he returned to this country, and commenced a collection of drawings, under the title of Birds of America, since which time he has been devoted to what appears to be the ruling passion of his life — to the studious observation of nature in the ways of her winged children. To use his own language "to nature he went, and tried to imitate her." So well has he succeeded in his imitation that an eminent European artist expressed the opinion that *"not more than three Painters ever lived who could draw a bird."* Of these, the lamented Barrabaud, of whom France may be justly proud, was the chief. He has long since passed away, but his mantle has, at length, been recovered in the forests of America, by John James Audubon. In his researches, Mr. Audubon has visited nearly every section of our country. He has ransacked the forests, the prairies, the lakes, the rivers, the brooks, and the shores of the wide Atlantic. A few years since he visited England, with his drawings, where he was received with that respect and attention which were due to his genius and his exertions. Blackwood's Magazine uses the strongest language in speaking of the excellence of his drawings and their truth in nature, and the magical effect of his exhibition of them in Edinborough. The editor describes the birds as being of "the size of life, from the wren and the humming bird, to the wild turkey and the bird of Washington" — their colors — their attributes and postures — the trees on which they sported, were all true to nature. And all — the atmosphere — the skies — "the ground flowers, the weeds, and the very grass — all *American*." It was to them "a wild and poetical vision of the heart of the new world."

"That all this wonderful creation, (he says,) should have been the unassisted work of one man — in his own country almost unknown, and by his own country wholly unbefriended, was a thought that awoke towards "the American woodsman" feelings of more than admiration, of the deepest personal interest; and the hearts of all warmed towards Audubon, who were capable of conceiving the difficulties, and dangers, and sacrifices, that must have been encountered, endured, and overcome, before genius had thus embodied these, the glory of its innumerable triumphs."

We could extend our notice of this distinguished "self-tutored" "American woodsman," if our limits would permit. But we have said enough to express our satisfaction in welcoming him to this section of our country, and to bespeak for him every aid and facility in the prosecution of his researches, which it may be in the power of our friends and fellow citizens to afford. We wish him every success, and are gratified to learn that our Revenue officers and the Commandant of Fort Sullivan have offered him any aid which it may be consistent with their duties to afford. — [*Com.*

(*Eastern Democrat*, Vol. 1, No. 14, p. 2, cols. 2–3 (Friday Morning, August 24, 1832)

Letters Between John J. Audubon and Richard Harlan, M.D.

MARCH 1833

John J. Audubon to Richard Harlan, M.D., at Philadelphia

Boston 20ᵗʰ March 1833 —

My Dear Friend —
The hand which now drives my pen was *Paralised* on Saturday last for about one hour — the attack seized on my Mouth & particularly my lips — So much so that I neither could articulate or hold any thing. — My good Dear Wife was terribly frightened and yet acted so promptly with prudence & knowledge that I was relieved as I have already Said in about one hour. — Docʳ Warren came in with our ever *worthy Friend* Parkman and administered me a dose which kept me "a going" for 24 hours — Now much debility is all that ails me — moderate exercise and a *cessation of Work* will remove this and I hope soon to be myself again —

Friendship my Dear Harlan is a Jewel which I hold not only sacred, but one which being hereditary (for I received the principles thereof from my Father) I never can part with. — through Friendship and the love of Nature's Works all my happiness on this Earth has been derived — I never redraw it when I have once found it accepted by any one worthy of Such deposit, Ergo, You are my Friend and I am Yours to the end of my days. —

Money — the curse of Man Kind — never contributes to ameliorate our dispositions unless when it is delt through benevolence's hand — I Shall be proud to have been poor as much as I am proud to receive Money through generous benevolence. — Money is wanted Money must be had and money Shall be had as long as my fingers will not be *Palsied* — Sometimes (and that is pretty frequently too) I feel myself as if about to be cast on a Lee Shore it is true, — but I Shake myself on all such occasion, make a Drawing and away with it to the nearest market — it brings something always, and *Sometimes* more than its intrinsic value. — I have an extraordinary degree of confidence in Providence, and thank God *that Power* has never failed towards me!

Docʳ Chalmer himself could scarce have delivered a better lecture on the subject of money & Friendship than I have accomplished and thus Ends the Subject —

Your Well come Bill for one hundred & fifty Dollars is now snug in the care of my better half — I wish you were as well in health as that bit of paper is in safety. —

I regret however that you Should have been *pushed* for it. — Your Wife would not have been *your Friend* had She nursed you any otherway than kindly — What do you think of *the Balm* which ever and anon circulates through a Man's veins on such occasions? The blessings of a happy marriage is the finest emblem of God's powers in behalf of the beings which *he* has created to "go forth and multiply!" — God bless her and protect you both!! —

My old Friend [i.e. Lucy] says She will write to you as well as to her as soon as we reach New York, where we expected to have been more than a week since — but to Shew you that all is for the best — we by having been unexpectedly detained here have augmented our list of Subscribers with *Five* valuable names — and more over we have received 7 Volumes *handsomely* coloured to supply those and receive "The Ready"[1] — See thou how Strangely our Bark is tossed — poor as Job Yesterday — rich as Cressus Tomorrow! — and who would not wish to live to enjoy this Life of plea-surable anxiety? Not I believe me. —

Two days after you left us I received a Splendid Specimen of the Golden Eagle. — 6 hours of confinement under a blanket ^in a tight closet^ with a Pot of Coal (Lighted) So as to be carbonnic Gass had no effect. — ¼ of a pound of the best powdered Sulfur was added — we were all drove off but Mrs Eagle *paid no attention* to our doings. — a fine Tale this to relate to Monsieur G. Ord of Phil^a! — It [took] me 13 days to draw it and depend upon it; I ha[ve the] drawing! — *the Bird did not cost me 100$* — it was a female, caught in a fox trap and brought in per[fect] order.═I had a great desire to try ellectricity but cou[ld] not obtain a Battery suficiently powerful to be trusted for a Single Stroke. — tell all this to your Society and assure them in my name that the experiments were made with care by an F.R.S. of *Some* merit! —

The Numbers up to 31 of Birds of America are now in New York. — that work enters the U.S. Free of Duty. the Numbers for your fair City will be there as soon as possible after I reach New York. —

Now My good Friend Adieu, get well quickly — remember us all kindly to your Dear Wife & Family and Friends. — & believe me ever Yours —

John J. Audubon
To Richd Harlan
&^c &^c &^c —

My Dear Sir —
I am sorry to hear of your having been ill, tell Mrs Harlan that for a fortnight I have been expecting every day to move, and have put off writing till then partly to

---

1. This is Audubon's shorthand expression for "ready money," i.e., cash.

say something new, and partly because I have really for three weeks past hardly had a moment to call my own. With sincere good wishes to you both I am Sir in great haste your friend LA [Lucy Audubon]——

(Filson Historical Society, Louisville, Kentucky)

Richard Harlan, M.D., to John J. Audubon at New York

Phil^a March 23^d 1833

My dear A—

Your favour of the 20th is written in high spirits considering the melancholy and fearful attack from which you had just escaped. — God grant you may never experience another such — yet I think that Mrs A. has not been unnecessarily alarmed — and I do *know* that whilst you continue exposed to similar causes (which I observed when in Boston) it is much to be feared that the destiny of a Lord Liverpool — Sir W. Scott, Dugald Stewart and our late friend [MS: fri^d] Z. Collins may also be reserved for you — Depend upon it my friend [MS: fri^d] a total change in diet, habits, &^c is indispensable to your future health — the cause of science, the good of humanity, and the glory of the works of nature — lose no time in visiting Phil^a — there is no one so well acquainted with you as I am — and from me alone you will obtain such advice as will secure your future health (if followed) and place "The Birds of America" out of danger from a similar cause —

Be sure and come, and bring *Madame* along with you — I desire much also to see the drawing of the Golden Eagle — it might have cost more than 100 times a hundred dols — had its completion cost you the use of a right arm —

I have a pretty ornithological anecdote for you, of a battle between a pair of blue birds and an old Hen, both defending their young — the action lasted 4 hours — and the hen died of her wounds and fatigue during the same night!

As I expect to see you here very soon, I need only add

Yours ever

R Harlan

(Morris Tyler Family Collection of John James Audubon, Gen MSS 85, Box 4,Folder 173, Beinecke Rare Book and Manuscript Library, Yale University)

Journal of George C. Shattuck Jr.

MAY 7 TO JUNE 13, 1833

May 7. 1833.

Little did I think when I last wrote in that I should take up my pen for the next time for that purpose in the hotel at Bangor but so it is, and I must now briefly describe the scenes I have passed through. At ten oclock Monday morning I took a seat in the Augusta mail having received from Dr Mussey his parting blessing and a farewell present of two scalpels, and a handsome pocket knife. The day was beautiful, warm for the season, and wind enough to blow the dust from us. The first part of our route through Topsham was very sandy, but the soil improved as we advanced till we came opposite the merry meeting bay, and then the prospect! This bay is where the Androscoggin flows into the kennebec, there being found in it several little islands. By some of these the channel of the kennebec is almost closed just before the Androscoggin joins it, and we could see a fishing smack, threading her way between these islands. Cathance is the name of the next town partly built on a side hill, a dirty looking place kept alive by ship building, which is done on the banks of the Cathance river, a narrow but deep stream flowing into merry meeting bay. Gardiner six miles from Augusta was the next town worth noticing, for here we again saw the kennebec. We approached this hill from the hills, and at some distance saw the Episcopal church a beautiful Gothic edifice of Granite, and near it, the building for the Gardiner Lyceum constructed of similar material. We descended into the main street of the town which runs along the bank of the river. We saw some six or eight sail at the wharfs, and we noticed that many of the stores were of brick. This is quite a considerable place, kept alive by the Lumber trade. Two miles more, we came to Hallowell, as I should judge a larger town than Gardiner built very much in a similar manner. Only two miles more and we rode into Augusta, past the new state house, and stopped a little farther on at Steven's, said to be the best hotel in the state. I immediately proceeded to survey the state house. It was begun two years since, and though finished and surrounded with iron rails set in Granite, the grounds are not yet ornamented. The state keeps a superintendant there to show it. The stone of which it is constructed is beautifully hammered, and very white. On the outside it presents a centre building surmounted by a dome and lantern, and two wings. The first story is occupied in the first story by a large entry, where are great wooden pillars. On each side are offices. In the centre is th second story is the chamber of the representatives, a room very much like the rep's chamber in Boston, smaller and more handsomely finished. The speaker's chair is at the ~~east~~ west end. ~~At the~~ In the north wing second story is the senate chamber, the governor and councillors occupying the ~~sp~~ corresponding space in the other wing. The former at any rate, resembles that at Boston, and adjoining to the latter is an anti room and a room for the messenger. I ascended to the lantern which commands an extensive prospect, yet not very interesting for you can see the kennebec for but a short distance on account of the steepness of it's banks, and its windings. ~~D~~ Almost directly opposite on the other side of the river are the United States arsenals, four or more stone buildings, of which one is much larger than the others. The state house cost 130,000 dollars. I then hastened to survey the place. On the upper street were several fine dwelling houses, streets at short intervals running down to the main streets in which, the stores in the eastern side looked directly upon the river. In one of these my hair was cut but by a lady of color. There were a few vessels at the wharfs. I continued down the street, to get a peep at the river. The banks are quite steep and wooded, and from a hill at a short distance I had a fine view of the town. The business part is very much lower than the other, and the streets running up are quite steep. The surrounding country is well diversified. The next morning at half past four we started off again crossed the bridge, which is high above the river in piers at the upper part of the town. We kept along the kennebec for ten miles through Vassalboro a very large town and breakfasted at China, where a pond was most worthy of note, it appearing to be a small farming place. We accomplished this distance five minutes short of three hours. We kept on through Unity and Dixmont, a very hilly country, land pretty good, many sheep, also bees. We struck the river six miles from Bangor, where we arrived about three oclock. Bangor is built on the sides of the river, and through the middle of it runs a stream, tolerably wide near it's mouth. The road as you come in from the south is at some little distance from the river; being curved, streets run from it to the river. The stream is crossed by a bridge, and on its ~~left~~ North bank is a block of sixteen brick stores, on the South, there being several. On the south side of this stream the land rises rather more abruptly, streets running up on both sides. The course of this stream also is curved. The hotel is situate [*sic*] on the first street running east after you have passed this small stream. On this same street towards the West is a meetinghouse and other buildings. The ~~first west~~ street west before crossing the stream runs up steep. half way up, is the court house, a ~~ha~~ tolerably handsome brick building, and at the top of the hill is a white three story square house, the seat of the Bangor theological seminary. Behind the court house, a steep ~~hill~~ bank rises at the summit of which is the powder house. I ascended this to survey the country. But a more extensive prospect, is to be had from the grounds on which is situate [*sic*] the aforesaid seminary, from which the prospect must be very extensive on a clear day, but as it was smoky I could not judge at all. I noticed some fine houses north on the high grounds above the river. I next crossed the river by a bridge built upon three piers at the north part of the town, and ascended the bank of the river which at that place was very steep. I could see all the vessels and the town principally on the west bank of river, though one meeting house was on the east bank.

Friday May 10. 1833.

Wednesday at a quarter after six AM. we started in a waggon [*sic*] to which four good horses were attached for Ellsworth. The road had been made only three years, had been travelled by stage only one, and as it was cut through woods was very rough. We stopped to change horses and to breakfast at No eight, where we found a small one story house made by rudely nailing the boards to a frame. Our breakfast consisted of apple sauce, bread, butter, cheese, and was quickly dispatched. The remaining thirteen miles was through a similar country and we arrived at Ellsworth at half past ten. I should have mentioned a settlement we saw on a swell of land, by people from Wrentham mass, where the land appeared good, and, the farmers four handed. Ellsworth is a tolerably large place, on the union river, and the inhabitants are engaged in the lumber business. We now were placed in a waggon for four, there being so many passengers, the driver taking his seat on the mail bags, but presently another was added. Our road the first part of the way was better than it had been, and the country was more settled. ~~Presentl~~ About ten miles and we came to a ferry, which we were some time in crossing, having to go as the tide was. Thus we passed from Hancock to Sullivan ~~to~~ and here we dined. The tavern commands a fine water view: as a bay comes up on which we observed several vessels, and at a little distance could discern Mt dessert. We passed through Steubens, Cherryfield, two quite pretty villages, the latter on cherryfield river which we crossed by ferry, as the bridge had lately been swept away. In the afternoon we had showers and a rain bow. The road now was very bad but we kept on, and arrived at Columbia at half past eight. We passed several miles of land where the fire had prevailed, and dead trees with blackened stumps were left—a most dreary view. In a few such places we saw new trees going up, but I am told that generally little regard is paid to sitting out or preserving young trees. Lee the owner of the stage, a brother of the mayor of N. York was at Columbia and an officer who had attached his horses. We started next morning a little before four, and rode on to Machias sixteen miles before breakfast. The roads were very dreary, as mostly through burned lands, but as far as Jonesboro we had a gentleman from Plymouth county, Mass. quite a pleasant fellow. He had given up tea, and was none the worse for it. Machias is quite a flourishing place containing three villages and almost five thousand inhabitants. Lumber is the article of trade, and many saw mills were going in both villages through which we passed. The country was rough, the houses chiefly built of logs, except in the villages, and the roads far from smooth. The land was rocky, but in some parts, quite good. But little was cultivated. We arrived at Lubec at a little before one, and almost immediately went down to the ferry boat. This is quite a village, and situated on a point or cape of the main land. As the wind was not very favorable, we made many tacks, and occupied some time in crossing to Eastport. We landed at the salt works with the mail, whilst the boats went round with the baggage. A Mr Lane a fellow passenger walked up with me to the tavern. as I waited for him whilst he went up to the printing office, Mr Chadbourne came up, could not conceive how I should be standing there, and on an explanation of circumstances I went up into his office where in a few moments came Mr Audubon.[1] He appeared very much pleased to see a recruit, said he had just written to my father for me, and gave me instructions on what to send, telling me to write immediately, which I promised and did. Himself went off an excursion to point le prow, whislt Mr C. told him he would look out for me, and invited me to stay at his house, to feel at home there, and he should consider me so, certainly one of the kindest invitations I had ever received. He introduced me to the club room, where I found many interesting works, and offered me the use of his own library, which is very select. In the evening Dr Ray called, and took a walk ~~to~~ with me.[2] He told me that the island had been settled within a little more than twenty years it previously having been resorted to for the purpose of curing fish. It was taken possession of by the British and retained till 1819, and since then the growth has been steady, and such as it can bear. On an island opposite which he pointed out ~~an offi-cer~~ fellow of Cambridge lived many years, but at length died, and was sent home in a hogs head of rum two years since. ~~He stop~~ We met an Indian, and heard him talk of a proposal to cut through his lands, where he was very eloquent. A tribe of them are in the neighbourhood, and with the Penobscots and a tribe in Canada, are subject to a common chief. Dr R. stopped in we talked of Spurzheim, how much he and Gall had done for the anatomy of the brain, other distinguished men contested every step of it, and finally gave in.[3] Spurzheim's work on education too much considered, and the language a little vague, in consequence of imperfectly understanding the language. The next morning we were to meet, and we have been through the Garrison

1. Ichabod Rollins Chadbourne (1787–1855), a prominent Eastport attorney and friend of the Shattuck family.

2. Dr. Isaac Ray (1807–1881), an Eastport practitioner who studied medicine in Boston under George C. Shattuck Sr., M.D. In 1838, Ray would publish a landmark work on the medical jurisprudence of insanity. He is known today as the "father of American forensic psychiatry."

3. Franz Gall, M.D. (1758–1828), and his disciple, Johann Gaspar Spurzheim, M.D. (1776–1832), leading proponents of phrenology.

with lieutenant Greene, a very intelligent gentleman.[4] It is situated on an eminence commanding the town, there are buildings for officers on the side opposite, and adjoining are barracks for soldiers.

Tuesday May 21.

The wind has been east and N East since Sunday [May 19], and the rain has poured in torrents this morning. On the Saturday after my arrival [May 11] the east wind began to blow, and the storm continued till Thursday [May 16]. I passed that Saturday, and Sunday studying shells with Dr Ray. There are five societies for public worship in this place: unitarian; calvinist; Baptist; free will baptist; roman catholic. Most of the ministers are now out of town, the Unitarian minister being allowed absence during six Sundays each year. The Unitarian minister from Calais preached here, but we were not aware of the fact at Dr Rays till after evening service. This gentleman called at Mr Chadbourne's in the evening, and spoke rather more freely of Judge Lincoln than he would have done, had he known Mrs Chadbourne's relationship to that gentleman.[5] Tuesday forenoon [May 14] we visited the salt works. The mineral salt is brought from Liverpool, is thrown into large troughs or vats into which water is pumped from the sea by a steam engine. When the water has dissolved, all the salt that it will, it is drawn off into larger boilers and there evaporated. The salt is then dried, and improves in quality by age. This salt is now the best in the market, though formerly in bad repute in consequence of being exposed to sale before it was dry. Several thousand bushels of salt are manufactured every week. The same company own other works where fresh water is used, and table salt prepared. They also own iron works. The capital is nominally owned in this town, perhaps really in England. With Dr Ray I saw a case of rheumatic affection of the scalp. The patient had had severe head ache for the day and night previous; his general health was little affected. He was treated with cupping on the upper part of the neck, and a blister ordered to be applied to the same spot the next night but one. Dr R. mentioned a singular case of spinal irritation connected with amenorrhea. The patient lost entirely the use of her lower limbs, there being some difficulty in moving them for some days previous. She was treated with emenagogues, and irritations over the spine, but one remedy seemed to counteract the other. However she now can creep. We saw at the Garrison a soldier who complained of pain about the dorsal vertebra. He was treated in the same manner but refused to allow the application of the blis-

4. First Lt. George Sears Greene (1801–1899), stationed at Fort Sullivan.

5. Hannah Lincoln Chadbourne (1801–1882), the eldest daughter of Judge Theodore Lincoln (1763–1852) of Dennysville, Maine.

ter. Report was made to Captain Childs who seemed to consider the application of the blister unnecessary, as the man complained of no pain at the time.[6] The captain thought the sickness a sham. We called at Mr Green's room and found him furnished with a large apartment, in which all things looked confused as belonging to a student, and an unmarried man, but yet very comfortable. This gentleman had the misfortune to lose his wife and three children within nine months. On ~~Wednesday~~ Tuesday [May 14] Mr A. returned from point Le prou, having had bad weather the whole time they were there. Thomas Lincoln returned also, and we had quite an interesting conversation together on the medical profession: the Indians. He thinks more required to be a good physician, than to become a good lawyer, or a good devine. He says of the Indians, that it is remarkable how much at home they are in the woods. An Indian may chase a deer all day double his track several times, and yet he will point without hesitation to the four points of compass, and will say in what direction any remarkable river or brook lies. A white man can never acquire this, though brought up in the woods, and it is very difficult for the white hunters to keep up with these Indians. Thomas L. went out last winter with a mixed party of Whites and Indians, to hunt the Cariboo. ~~Thursday morni~~ Wednesday [May 15] we went to call on Mr A. He was writing, and after greeting and the usual inquiries he had me set down and write home for such articles as I might want, and for a gun for Thomas Lincoln. I saw Curtis there the postmaster of the place, something of a sportsmen, but according to some a very low fellow.[7] We wrote again to Boston by the packet which was to sail that afternoon, and delivered the letter to the steward, charging him to attend to its' delivery in Boston immediately after the arrival of the vessel. Thursday morning [May 16] we took a cruise in the woods but saw no birds and returned by twelve oclock. Mr A. dined with Mr C. as did Dr Ray, and Mr Weston, who were late, but for whom we did not wait.[8] In reply to a question of Dr Ray, where natural history flourished most in England or in France, the answer was in the former, for there numerous country gentlemen, beginning with objects of natural history in their own farms and towns, knew much more, than many who publish works on these subjects Cuvier and such distinguished men born in France, belong to the world. He thought numerous works on ornithology lately published, being so incorrect, would not promote the general study of this science. If a person would study natural history, continued Mr A., let him not go into museums containing stuffed specimens but let him go out into the woods, and till natural history is thus

---

6. Capt. Thomas Childs (1796–1853), the commander of the U.S. Army garrison at Fort Sullivan.

7. James Curtiss (1806–1859), the U.S. postmaster of Eastport.

8. Jonathan D. Weston (1782–1834), a highly regarded Eastport attorney presently serving as deputy collector of customs and town clerk. Weston and his family were hosting Audubon and his son.

studied, we can expect no decided progress in this science. After dinner T.L. went up in the boat to Dennysville, and John and myself endeavorerd to go fishing but after waiting some time for Curtis, and getting him into the boat, he concluded the voyage was not safe, and we abandoned it. We then took a walk as far as the salt works, and back, conversing about our intended expedition. I left John at the club room to go to Mr Curtis, but I was soon sent after, and went accordingly. We were introduced to Mrs Curtis, and to Miss Estabrook from Brunswick, a cousin of Mrs C.[9] Curtis commenced a tirade against the aristocracy of the place, and went on with an argument against union doctrines, revealing plainly of what manner of person he was was. Mr A. left soon, after tea, taking no tea, ~~but I~~ which he has not drank for years. He never ate meat till his wedding day when he was twenty one years of age. On Friday [May 17] we went in the Captain's barge accompanied by Lieutenant Buford and rowed by six soldiers, to the carrying place about six miles from Eastport.[10] Where a promontory goes out into the sea, the Indians instead of circumnavigating it will carry their boats across. We wandered along the beach seeing no birds, and then cut across the woods, which were almost impervious, and clambering back over the rocks. We had a delightful prospect, and Mr Buford shot a brown thrush. We saw the excrement of deer. We walked to Lubec, and Mr A. shot some swallows, and two plover. Mr A. though [*sic*] it very singular that we saw no birds, and remarked that they must have gone north to their breeding places. At Lubec we saw a yellow rumped warbler which Mr A. advised them to set at liberty, as he could not live in a cage. We were little more than twenty minutes returning. We took the birds killed, and some others and placed them in a lane above Mr Chadbourne's, under the fence on the right hand side. The revenue cutter came in to day and Mr A. concluded to start on Monday. We called at Mr Buford's and were admitted to his parlor which was beautifully furnished. The pictures of Mazeppa were there, and Mr A. remarked that on the same bench with himself under David, sat the man who painted those horses, and who paints horses better than any man now living, and another as distinguished in fishes. We then proceeded to a barn where the swallows built their nests last year, but they had not yet arrived, though Mr A. thought that if the weather continued warming we might expect them in a few days. All who lived there last year, and all the young would return. Saturday morning [May 18] I walked two and a half miles and back with Mr A. The fog which had been very thick, was clearing away, and our walk was very pleasant. In the afternoon we went in the Captain's barge to pleasant point. Our party consisted of Mr A. and son, Mr ~~R~~ Green and ~~R~~

9. Mary Curtiss *née* Kimball (b. 1809), the wife of postmaster James Curtiss.

10. Second Lt. Napoleon Bonaparte Buford (1807–1883), posted to Fort Sullivan.

Buford, and Lincoln Chadbourne.[11] We noticed the currents caused by the tides and were obliged to steer our course accordingly. Mr Chadbourne met us there. Pleasant point is situated directly on the river. The Indians live mostly in rude huts constructed of boards and bark with a hole at the top—as a passage for the smoke. There are a few framed houses. In one of these we found the governor reclining on a bed, being unable to walk about. He was very childish, laughed at every thing said to him, and spoke English very imperfectly. He is over eighty years of age, and was with Montcalm when he fell. This was the last time their tribe went to war. An old squaw was washing the floor of the governor's room. He was lying on an old ticking wrapped up in blankets, and appeared destitute of the comforts of life. I could see a few kettles, and household articles of furniture round the room. A cradle formed of some blankets, was suspended by two ropes so as to rock. In another hut which we entered a fire was in the middle, the smoke ᵍ escaping through the hole at top. An old Indian was seated on the floor, one side of the fire smoking his pipe. One or two grand children were on the other side. In answer to our inquiries as to his age, he replied that he could not tell exactly, was over eighty, yet younger than the governor. Going out of this hut, we amused ourselves setting up pieces of money for the Indian boys to shoot at. The moment the money was placed for them twenty arrows flew in that direction and it almost always fell, nor was there any doubt as to the successful marksman. The general impression left in the mind of one who has visited these Indians is unfavourable. They are a lazy set, supporting themselves by gaming, fishing, basket making, neglecting tillage, and keeping no domestic animals but dogs. These dogs have a very foxy appearance, and pains are taken, it is said, to keep the breed unmixed. The Indians are very proud of White blood, one took occasion to boast of it whilst we were present, and a child was pointed to us as the son of a young man of Eastport. A road is now making leading through their lands. Two bridges have been built, one from Eastport to a small island, and the other from this island to the main land. I walked home with Dr Ray. He told me the Indians were Catholics, and a priest visited them every six months. In the mean time they worship at Eastport. The tribe is evidently diminishing and will soon disappear. We went down to the beach and found some of the niza, and the common muscle. These latter differ in general shape, having only one muscle and a less prominent cardinal tooth. We noticed some men fishing with nets by the bridge, pulling up eels, catfish. I took tea with Dr Ray, and sat a little while. Mrs Tinkham came in, but it being dark and we unable to see her distinctly. I passed the next day [Sunday, May 19] writing a letter of two sheets to father in which I gave an account of my journey from Brunswick, and another to Ellen. In the afternoon we took a walk of about two miles and a half.

11. Lincoln Chadbourne (1822–1846), the eldest child of Ichabod and Hannah Chadbourne.

We saw many birds, warblers, American redstarts, robbins [*sic*]. We also saw some of the creepers. We talked about nat. hist, the manner in which the study of it had been pursued by Mr Audubon. Returning Mr A. told us that a great number of birds must have arrived on the island that very day. Monday morning [May 20] John and myself went to the custom house to see the captain of the rev. cutter. He told us he saw not one fowl this year where he saw a hundred last year. John said this thing was said all along the coast. The Captain told us of a paralytic stroke he had, in consequence of which he was unable to speak, one half of his body being affected. He attributed it to violent exertion. He has totally recovered from it. This fellow is a singular looking genius. He thought we had better wait for fair weather. We then went shooting small birds, John taking a landscape view. I shot a yellow breasted warbler. Returning to the clubroom I met Dr Ray, and going home with him we dissected a clam. We made out several nerves, the stomach, saw a tube, which I knew not if a blood vessel or an intestine. The cloak [i.e., mantle] was to be seen very distinctly. We concluded that a larger specimen was necessary. I dined there and after dinner we went to see Mr Audubon. He talked with Dr Ray about he [*sic*] hare and rabbit, their differences. Their shape is different, the rabbit moves in a zigzag line, the hare straight; the hare has fur on bottom of paws, the rabbit none. The rabbit burrows, the hare build breeds in forms. We have no rabbit. Gidman has omitted two species in his work one a water hare, the other found in Louisiana called a fox hare. Mr A. thought we could find no differences of structure accounting why one should burrow, the other form. John again went to draw, and I in quest of small game. I brought home a bob a links, a swamp sparrow, black throated warblers. I took tea at Mr Weston's, and after tea we cleaned our guns. We then discussed some points of physiology, and I was at home by nine oclock. I went to Mr A. this morning [Tuesday, May 21] and we made a list of articles we might need. Speaking of a fact told him by Coolidge, that gulls within the past seven years breed on trees, Mr A. said naturalists will signify their distrust of it by a note wonderful if true, or by some other similar expressions. I then went to Mr C's office with him, procured my clothes from the tailors, and bought some necessary articles. Then I took hold of this journal with a determination that henceforth I will allow no day to pass without writing.

Swiftsure off Grand Manan Thursday evening May 23. 1833

We came on board this vessel last evening, it having cleared off towards noon. At proper bed time we turned in John and myself in one birth. At three oclock, the officers were called, a boat sent on shore for Mr Weston who declined coming, anchor weighed and we were off. Our Captain is named Coolidge a very ingenious fellow.[12]

---

12. Capt. Uriah Coolidge (c. 1781–1838), commander of the U.S. Revenue Cutter *Swiftsure*.

He showed us several specimens of his handy work, many of which were in conveniences about his cabbin [*sic*]. The vessel is very convenient, has two cabbins, two births in each, and a very convenient place for his men under the birth deck. She was partly modelled by the Captain, but the cabbins rise two feet above the deck which he does not like. He says she is a fine vessel in bad weather, built for use entirely, and though one of the smallest cutters belonging to the country, he prefers her. He says Maine has more harbors than all the other states of the union, over three thousand. The fogs here are very thick, and continue a long while, and are pronounced by all a decided bore. Mr Whitcomb is the first lieutenant, Mr Stoddard the second.[13] We had a most delightful breeze immediately on getting out of the harbor, and were conveyed very rapidly to Grand Manan, the sun shining, and the atmosphere clear. We came to anchorage about half past eight, and went on shore. We first went to White head a small island, and called on the governor whom we afterwards met, and had some talk about the colors, for it seems a foreign vessel raises her colors, and is saluted with the cross of St George in return. This governor came from Yorkshire, about fourty years ago, and has visited England, seven years ago.[14] He has a little the Yorkshire brogue was very polite, and we proceeded. The road was little more than a swamp, sinking over ankles frequently. We penetrated into the woods, and the return was accomplished only by dint of the sturdy boots which I put on this morning for the first time on my first visit to his majesty's dominions. We found a pond near ~~the~~ a beautiful beach emptying into the sea. The banks were covered with reeds, and we concluded that ducks must have their nests there. Two young ones were seen by Claridge.[15] The gulls were shy flying very high, and ~~unless~~ not near enough for our shot. They were all of one species the argentata, the young ones being grey, they measured about two feet in length, intestines four feet long. They measured nearly five feet from tip to tip. Mr A. tells me that gulls of a species generally associate together. A white crown sparrow was shot, a not of a peculiar species. We saw very few flowers. The gulls shot were in numbers twelve, John A. shooting more than any other one. We returned at half past three and partook of our dinner with great relish. Afterwards we set about skinning, and I accomplished only two, serving them all up. Claridge assisted us, operations being carried on in the lieutenants cabin. We finally finished about eight and then went on shore, to breathe the

13. First Lt. John Whitcomb (1793–1861), commissioned August 23, 1819. The 2nd lieutenant was Thomas Stoddard (1787–1854), commissioned on March 21, 1831.

14. William Frankland (1764–1840), whose family resided on 1,525-acre White Head Island.

15. Capt. Joseph H. Claridge (1801–1874), the commander of the *Fancy*, a schooner used as a revenue tender by the Passamaquoddy Customs District.

fresh air. Half of the moon was visible and a lovelier evening I have seldom seen. We visited Mr Frankland, and there found our party, sitting round a table Curtiss talking politics as usual. An old man was there who had lived fourty on the island. He said the sea ducks bred there, not the lords and ladies, many of whom passed the winter there. The black ducks are more frightened at the peculiar note emitted by the gull when frightened than at the sight of a man. The governor has been very kind to our party, and Mr A. is much peased with him. All tell me I shall return from Labrador eating meat stoutly. I have an idea what our our [*sic*] labors will be at Labrador. Immediately after dinner Mr A. sent me with the synopsis to ascertain the species of the birds we had killed. We all wished we were now bound for Labrador, and the Capt. and mates were very desirous to go. Mr A. almost regretted that he did not apply to government for a cutter. We certainly have had a delightful time so far. We found some gulls nest in the trees, but we were too early by a fortnight. I should have mentioned the steep shores of Grand Manan, the rocky walls rising perpendicular. Lead and copper is said to be found on the island. The rock is trap. This trap rock is said by our Captain to extend fourty miles south where the granite rock commences. One of our gulls was wounded and it was amusing to see her keeping the path, being assisted by Mr Claridge over the rough spots, and when she manifested a desire to leave the path. These gulls are said to assume the white plumage at three years of age; in one grey female we found no eggs. White head island contains about two hundred acres. Grass is the principal produce, sheep are fed upon it. Mr Frankland with his family are all the inhabitants. The blackberry, strawberry, raspberry grow there.

Friday May 24.
We tumbled in last night, about half past ten, when Mr Audubon read me his journal. I soon dropped asleep. We awoke at five, Mr A. coming to call us, and we learnt with astonishment that we had moved five or six miles, starting at half past eleven, and so strong was our sleep, that we did not hear the grating of the chain as we weighed anchor. The rocking of the vessel was the last thing of which I was conscious. We breakfasted at six, and immediately proceeded in boats, to the three islands, one party; another to the two islands. The sun was beautiful, there being no clouds to be seen. Our party was composed of Mr A., Mr C. and Young Frankland. We landed on a small island around which sea pigeons and sea parrots were very abundant, in hopes to find nests, but none were seen. We then steered for the three islands, explored one and passed over to another it being low tide. We went to the house, the island belonging to a Mr Kent, now improved by a Mr China. He tells us sea ducks, lords and ladies stop there in the spring, and may then be shot, but now they have mostly left. The gulls have not commenced laying. The sea pigeon

has a white plumage in the winter. We took with us a fine dog belonging to this man, so well trained, that he would creep with the shooter. We walked on over rocks and through swampy woods, and falling in with the boat. We rowed between two islands and then suffered the boat to drift, hoping to take some ducks. One or two flocks flew by us, but our party was unable to hit them owing to the motion of the vessel. We saw a bird called the sea goose, very rare, and which Mr A. was very anxious to get. It was not very shy for we passed it thinking a chip, but when we discovered our mistake it was too late. We also saw two birds, one of which we succeeded in obtaining after some difficulty, and it proved a turnstone, by no means a rare bird. In the first of the morning a lord and lady were shot, and as we stopped a little while at the small island, we obtained two sea pigeons. The other party obtained three or four eider ducks, mostly drakes, an old duck weighing four pounds and three quarters. We returned at half past two hungry enough. We then weighed anchor and pushed off to White head, and going ashore there found thirty speckled gull's eggs which had been found by the boys that morning. The gull argentata never lays but three eggs at a time. We bid good bye to the governor and returning to the vessel weighed anchor again, and were off at first ten knots the hours. I found a few shells on the beach, some stones, as did the Captain, a connoisseur in these articles. We blowed a dozen of our own eggs, and the rest are to be cooked. A nest was brought at the same time. These gull's eggs are very large, as I am told are those of the sea pigeon. We stopped for the night at long ~~har~~ island harbor, and after tea went ashore hoping to find shells, yet we saw but few.

Saturday May 25 1833.

We rose at five and having breakfasted we pushed for shore in three parties. John and myself pushed off into the woods which were about quarter of a mile from the shore. There were three of four houses in sight, and much cleared land. Two small fishing vessels were in the harbor. The trees were beginning to leave. We found a beautiful stream on which were some falls. The woods were very thick, and as the sun shone bright, every thing appeared in their best colors. Several sea pigeon were killed by the party which went to the swallows tail, and the Captain procured some clay from a vein which is readily worked with a knife, but soon acquires great hardness. We had a fine breeze to waft us on our return which was accomplished at the rate of eight or ten knots the hour. We stopped however and sent out our boat to a clift whence we procured four young ravens. The nest, quite large, was on the rocks, and a man from Mount dessert who descended to it was obliged to fasten a rope to a tree above and climbing down to swing in. On my return, a [sic] five PM. I found that my gun was here but that the Ripley had not arrived.

Sunday June 22. [June 2]

A week to day [Sunday, May 26] I was laid up with an attack of the colic, which finally yielded to cast. oil; injections senna; phosphate of sodaz. Mr A. attributes it to my vegetable diet, but I am inclined to think that a previous free use of meat would not have saved me, though the hard pilot bread is undoubtedly binding. On Monday [May 27] I was very weak and sore, without appetite, without energy. I think I can never remember suffering so much pain in one day as I did on Sunday, nor can I remember feeling so compleatly unmanned. Monday afternoon I went to Dennysville in about three hours in Mr Reynold's boat, as fine a sailing boat as one often sees. He runs from March to January. Last year the bay was frozen, a very un-usual thing. That evening we took a walk through the town, looked at the mills. The Dennysville river extends up into the country about thirty miles, but already, the best of the timber has been cut down. Dennysville contains about three hundred inhabitants. Judge Lincoln undertook to construct a road to Charlotte through the woods, of which he had to pay more than half. His son Belah superintended it and with ten or twelve hands camped on the spot. We visited him the next forenoon and dined there. He slept on duck stretched over poles so as to be quite comfortable, the cooking was done in the open air, and they took their meals under some trees, which afforded a very good shade. We had for dinner boiled beef, potatoes, beets, rice, good bread and buter. The road is perfectly straight and is wide with ditches on each side. This year is the fourth or fifth, during which they have been construct-ing new roads. Returning I was much interested observing the hovering of the fish hawk over the river, and finally his diving after his prey. An eagle was near but did not happen to see him. Judge L tells me that the blue bird, ~~nor~~ and the red winged blackbird are not found so far north, and that they have no snakes except the little adder. He has quite an extensive farm—fourteen cows, ten oxen, a large number of sheep. His family is generally large, and food for his men costs him a dollar a week each. With Mrs L. also I was very much pleased, for she must have a very cultivated mind, and her sons and daughters show what a mother they had to take care of them. Thursday it rained all day, and in the morning the fog was very thick. The steam boat Henrietta run upon a rock just below dog island and lay all that day, it being very much feared that she would be destroyed. She was got off the next day. Friday morning [May 31] the Preble arrived after a six days passage, it being a beautiful day with a strong west wind. The afternoon before [Thursday, May 30] I called with Mr Audubon on Dr Ray, when commenced a discussion on phrenology. Mr A. said he considered Gall & Spurzheim quacks, still he was ready to learn, and took every occasion to study phrenology whether it be true. He thought our knowledge could ~~on~~ be increased only to a certain extent, and at these limits men should contentedly stop. If he wished to know if a bird sing he would look at the trachea, by a sight of which Cuvier and James Wilson could tell every singing bird. Cuvier specifies a difference of the trachea in singing birds, accounting why they should sing. So anatomists say that the lungs of the dumb are much less capacious. Originally all individuals of the same species are in every respect equal but men had introduced vices into the breed, and the same equality no longer prevailed. Education is everything, and phrenology would do mischief, for people would no longer educate the all their children equally, and many mistakes would thus be made, and the poor neglected child would say, my father says I'm a rascal, so I may as well be one. As for himself, Combe had delivered lectures on his head, he was a member of the phrenological society of Edinburgh. One said he would make a great general, Combe thought he had the bumps for drawing, but Spurzheim said his case was one in a thousand, and that he had none of these bumps. Phrenology in England was at a very low ebb, and had never been tolerated in France. He intimtated that he was not quite convinced that the brain was the seat of the mind. Dr Ray was compleatly astounded, he never learnt there existed any peculiarity in the tracheas of singing birds, accounting why they should sing, nor did he know the lungs of the dumb were much compressed and their air cells fewer in number, and smaller in volume. He thought in a Finch the bump of tune was very much developed. Friday afternoon [May 31] we took a walk to point pleasant it being a beautiful day. In the evening we arrived and met Mr C. with Mr. A. they having bet a bottle of wine, that the Ripley would arrive before ten the next day. After all our expectation the Ripley came in on Saturday [June 1] after a passage of fourteen days, bringing seven hundred barrels of flour and thirteen hundred bushels of corn. They commenced discharging her instanter. In the afternoon we cruised for shells to dog island, and the oar tired me very much. This morning at Dr Ray's we had a calf's brain, which Ingalls dissected a la Spurzheim. We saw the decussation of the anterior pyramids, the fibres under the pons, the fibres of the corpus callosum, those of the corpora striata running into the hemispheres. It has rained hard since ten. Mr & Mrs C. being at Calais.

Tuesday June 11. 1833

It is high time that I should give an account of the manner in which I passed the last few days at Eastport. Monday [June 3] we ran about to the stores all morning, and dined with Dr Ray. We feasted very sumptuously and had some very interesting conversation on phrenology. Mr Audubon disbelieved the science entirely, thought that the practical application of it would be injurious. T.L. came down in the afternoon and as the Ripley was not to sail for two days, he went up again and I jumped into the boat. We went as far as the falls at in 42 minutes but thence the breeze was not so favourable. I laid down under the tarpaulin on some bags of wool and thus kept comfortable. We reached Dennysville by half past ten, found all a bed, but sufficient fire in the kitchen, and sitting till twelve talking, we turned in. The next morning [Tuesday, June 4] for an hour we tried our fowling pieces with bullets, and then took a stroll into the woods to look at the bear traps. They sometimes catch in these traps four bears a year, more in the steel traps than in the log traps. They told me that a bear would climb up a tree very expeditiously, with seventy pound weight attached to one ~~claw~~ fore paw. We found nothing in the trap to day but I was singled out as a victim of the black flies who bit me most abominably. I was advised on my return to apply soft soap, and thus prevented many of the usual ill consequences of these bites. We had a very pleasant walk up the river, found the bunch berry very abundant, the trillium, the rhodora canadensis, saw some birds and killed a blue throated warbler. We returned lazy and hungry as bears. After supper T. brought down his snow shoes, and showed me how they go on the grass. He says it is surprising how quick and how far the Indians travel on them. An Indian has an instinct of penetrating the woods never found in the white man, and on snowshoes they altogether beat the white hunters. We went down to the boat at two next morning [Wednesday, June 5], the full of the moon bringing there twelve oclock tides, and were obliged to row down thus arriving about six oclock. That day was passed in running about, and packing up, seeing that all things were put on board. The next morning [Thursday, June 6] we took a long walk to the carrying place, seeing a few warblers. I then called on Dr Ray, and he lent me Combe on the natural powers of man, and talked about Spurzheim and his visit to the schools of Boston, especially to Mr Fowles'. Dr R. evidently was much pleased with Spurzheim's philosophy, even independent of bumps.

Thursday June 13.1833.

Mr A. told me he was present at the dinner at which Sir W. Scott confessed himself the author of Waverly. It was the anniversary of the Scotch royal society of which Sir W. was president. The writers to the cygnet were also present, invitations were given out, and two guineas were paid by each. The toast was given by Combe the vice president of the society, and Sir W. replied in quite a short speech. Mr A. had a very good toast at the dinner. Mr A. saw Sir W. every day for nine months when he was writing the history of Napolean. He wrote a page, handed it to his daughter who corrected it, put it aside for Sir Walter's inspection the next day, and then looking it over ~~for~~ herself it was ready for the printer. Sir W. told Mr A. he considered that history as a sort of romance. He used to visit Mr A. and occasionally would suggest that such a word would sound better but Mr A. replied he was writing no novel. Sir W. said he pitied the poor naturalists who were obliged to stick to facts. Mr A. said Sir W. was very interesting when talking about events in Scottish history, or Scottich scenery, but was very dull when talking about subjects in which he took no interest.

He described every thing in exaggerated terms, and yet so that you would recognize ~~no~~ every object. His son is a major with a sword and whiskers, his daughter Anna is ugly but the superior of the family in intellect. She asks many questions for information, and says she never found a man nor a woman, who could not tell her something new. Sir Walter's son in law the editor of the London quarterly is a very superior man. ~~He~~ Sir W. writes a very small and illegible hand, and the printer of the biography of Napolen assured Mr A. that he was obliged to send back the manuscript several times, for an interpretation. His daughter told him that she often found it impossible to read the manuscript.

(Papers of George Cheyne Shattuck Jr., 1832–1872 (GA 80.25, Vol. 1), Harvard Medical Library in the Francis A. Countway Library of Medicine)

Captain's Log: U.S. Revenue Cutter *Swiftsure*

MAY 23–25, 1833 / JUNE 6, 1833

[THURSDAY, MAY 23, 1833]
Thursday 23,, at 4 AM took on Board Mr Audubon the American Ornithologist
Sailed for Grand Mannan [*sic*] at 9 came too in Gull cove officers & crew
accompanyed [*sic*] Mr Audubon on shore at 3 PM they returned wighed anchor &
run to Green Island came too

[FRIDAY, MAY 24, 1833]
Friday 24,, at anchor in Green Island officers & crew accompanyed (sic) Mr
Audubon in the Boats out among the outer Islands at 2 PM they returned wighed
anchor Run to Gull cove then to flaggs Cove came too

[SATURDAY, MAY 25, 1833]
Saturday 25,, at anchor in flaggs Cove officers & crew accompanyed by Mr
Audubon with the Boats cruising among the outer Islands Noon Boats returned
wighed anchor Run for West Quoddy through Lubec Narrows came to off
Eastport

[THURSDAY, JUNE 6, 1833]
Thursday 6,, at Hobbs wharf employed in painting spars &c M Audubon sailed
for the Labrador fired salute of four Guns

(Transcript of the U.S. Revenue Cutter *Swiftsure*'s Journal, National Archives, Washington, D.C.)

Charter-Party of Affreightment for the Ripley

THIS CHARTER-PARTY OF AFFREIGHTMENT, indented made and fully concluded upon this *fifth* day of *June* in the year of our Lord one thousand eight hundred *thirty three* between *Buck & Tinkham of Eastport in the County of Washington and State of Maine,—*

Owners of the good *Schooner Ripley* of the burthen of *one hundred* tons, or thereabouts, now lying in the harbour of *Eastport* whereof *Henry T. Emery* is at present master, on the one part, and *J J Audubon Esqr* on the other part.

WITNESSETH, That the said *Buck and Tinkham* for the consideration hereafter mentioned, ha*th* letten to freight   the aforesaid *Schooner* with the appurtenances to her belonging, for a voyage to be made by the said *Schooner along the Labrador Coast and Elsewhere and back to Eastport—*

where she is to be discharged (the dangers of the seas excepted).....And the said *Buck & Tinkham* doth by these presents covenant and agree with the said *J.J. Audubon* in manner following, THAT IS TO SAY, That the said *Schooner* in and during the voyage aforesaid, shall be tight, staunch, and strong, and sufficiently tackled and appareled with all things necessary for such a vessel and voyage; and that it shall and may be lawful for the said *J.J. Audubon his* agents or factors ~~as well at~~   as ~~at~~   to load and put on board the said *Schooner* loading of such goods and merchandize as they shall think proper, contraband goods excepted.

IN CONSIDERATION WHEREOF, The said *J J Audubon* doth by these presents, agree with the said *Buck & Tinkham* well and truly to pay, or cause to be paid, unto *them* in full for the freight or hire of said *Schooner* and appurtenances, in manner following, THAT IS TO SAY, *Three hundred and fifty dollars per month charter, three mens wages, two @ sixteen & due @ ten dollars per month, and two dollars per week for victualling each of them. Three dollars per week for victualling each of the Passengers which are six in number—and so in proportion for a less time, as the said Schooner shall be continued in the aforesaid service—And in case the said vessell should be lost to pay them three months charter &c as above agreed upon.*

And the said *Buck & Tinkham* do*th* agree to pay the charge of victualling and manning s^d *[i.e. said] Schooner* and port charges and pilotage during said voyage, *excepting she should go into Halifax or any other Port excepting on the Labrador coast, which are to be paid by said Audubon—*

And to the true and faithful performance of all and singular the covenants, payments and agreements aforementioned, each of the parties aforenamed binds and obliges himself, his executors and administrators, in the penal sum of *one thousand dollars* firmly by these presents . . . . IN WITNESS WHEREOF, the parties aforesaid have hereunto interchangeably set their hands and seals the day and year aforewritten.

Signed, Sealed, and Delivered   *Buck & Tinkham*
      in Presence of us,
        JD Weston   *John J. Audubon*
                                  F.R.S.L.

(Morris Tyler Family Collection of John James Audubon, General Collection, Beinecke Rare Book and Manuscript Library, Yale University, Box 16, Folder 719)

New-York Gazette & General Advertiser

Saturday Morning, March 30, 1833
(Vol. 45, No. 16,827, Pg. 2, Col. 4)

We take great pleasure in transferring to our columns the annexed paragraph from the [New-York] American of last evening.

Mr. AUDUBON, whose unequalled work on the Birds and Plants—for it truly embraces the history of both—of the United States, is now in this City. He has with him many of his original drawings from which the engravings for the book are made, and will, we hope, afford and [*sic*] opportunity to the public of seeing them, and thus effectively awaken their interest in a truly national work. No State, or College or other public Library should be without it; and every individual who can afford the substantial and enduring luxury of a well chosen private library, should possess this publication—costly though it be—yet more valuable than costly.

Friday Morning, April 5, 1833
(Vol. 45, No. 16,832, Pg. 2, Col. 1)

Being in possession of the invaluable work spoken of by the [New-York] American in the following remarks, we copy them with much pleasure:—

THE BIRDS OF AMERICA.—Mr. *Audubon*, whose arrival here we announced a few days ago, yesterday exhibited to a number of our citizens at the Presidents's rooms, in Columbia College, a series of the original drawings for his great work, and the plates of the only volume yet completed. The gratification was universal. Each plate and drawing presented a picture of itself, by showing the bird in some characteristic attitude or action, and in the midst of scenery habitual to it.

This magnificent work of Mr. Audubon, unequalled by any other, possibly, in existence on any subject, is complete, *so far as the original drawings are concerned*, Mr. A. having finished them all. But it will require several years for the execution of the engravings from these drawings. One volume, containing 100 plates, of the largest folio size, and where each bird, even to the wild turkey, is represented in his natural proportions, is now finished. Three more are to follow. The subscription price for the whole is $800, payable on the delivery of each volume, so as to make it $200 for the volume now ready, and the same sum every second or third year, till the four volumes are completed. We are thus particular in specifying the terms, because, being most desirous that the liberality and good taste of this city should be stirred up to the encouragement of so magnificent a work, we wish to show how conveniently it may be accomplished.

Boston afforded Mr. Audubon *eighteen subscribers*—New-York, as yet, *not one.* The work is indeed too costly, generally speaking, for individuals, though our city can and should furnish many exceptions to this remark—but a plan quite within the reach of even moderate means, is this—that several individuals, as many or as few as may be requisite, should associate together and present copies to different public institutions. Columbia College, the University, the City Library, the Historical Library, the Athenæum, the Library of the New-York Hospital, the Lyceum, all should possess this admirable national work.

Mr. Audubon is a native American, and he has now devoted nearly forty years to the illustration of the history and habits of the birds of America. The actual cost of publishing the first volume was $25,000, independent of the time, talents, labors, and exposure of the ornothologist [*sic*] himself.

As many persons will doubtless desire to see this work and the drawings, Mr. Audubon is making arrangements for gratifying this desire in the course of a few days. When these are completed, due notice will be given.

The American of last evening, observes: "It gives us pleasure to state that a copy of this magnificent work has been subscribed for, to be presented to the library of the Columbia College, by a number of gentlemen interested in that institution.

"The State of Maryland, as we learn, has also ordered a copy. We trust, and presume, indeed, that the resolution offered by Mr. Sudam in the Senate of this State—to procure a copy for the State Library at Albany—will be adopted.

"The Library room of Columbia College having been assigned by the Trustees for the use of Mr. Audubon, that gentleman will attend there next week *every day*, from 1½ to 3½ o'clock, for the purpose of displaying to all who will do him the favour of calling, the plates and original drawings of his work. This will be an opportunity eagerly embraced we are sure by many."

[It is to us astonishing and unaccountable, that among the wealthy inhabitants of this city, that so few are to be found, who patronize the enterprize [*sic*] and skill of men of the first order of talent. The work of Mr Audubon is unequalled, and, being a native American, must 'ere long, be amply rewarded.]

Thursday Morning, April 11, 1833
(Vol. 45, No. 16,837, Pg. 2, Col. 1)

AUDUBON'S AMERICAN ORNITHOLOGY.—Our countryman AUDUBON, whose work upon American Birds is so justly the admiration of the learned and curious in both hemispheres, is now exhibiting his drawings and engravings at Columbia College daily from one to half-past three o'clock. We are pleased to learn that he has already received a number of individual subscriptions besides several from our public institutions, and we indulge a hope that our Legislature and Corporation will soon be among the number of patrons for this really magnificent undertaking.

The drawings now exhibited, attracted the attention of an immense number of ladies and gentlemen on Monday and Tuesday, and we are sure that they cannot devote an hour or two, in any manner from which so much amusement and instruction may be derived. — *Cour.*

Monday Morning, April 29, 1833
(Vol. 45, No. 16,852, Pg. 2, Col. 3)

From the Philadelphia Gazette.
Mr. AUDUBON has left us, and is now on his way to Labrador. He will return rejoicing, bringing his birds with him. Among his recent drawings which we have had the pleasure of examining, is one large and splendid sheet, representing the golden Eagle. The picture seems instinct with life, and one can almost see the tremor of the bird and hear the rustling of his wings. The *scenery*, with which the back ground of Audubon's drawings are always clothed, is of the most faithful character, and shows his botanical as well as ornithological skill and knowledge.

[Mr. A. leaves New York tomorrow for Labrador. He has our best wishes.]

Thursday Morning, May 2, 1833
(Vol. 45, No. 16,855, Pg. 2, Col. 1)

Mr. AUDUBON, accompanied by his second son, Mr. John Audubon, took his departure from our city yesterday afternoon in the steamboat Benjamin Franklin, on his long contemplated excursion to the Coast of Labrador. His object is to study the habits of the numerous water birds which visit us *en passant* to and from those almost uninhabitable regions, where they retire during the breeding season. This is a field which naturalists have but partially explored, and none have contributed so largely as Mr. A. to this interesting subject, as will be proved when his charming biography of birds shall be completed.

Mr. A. carries with him the good wishes of many warm friends in this city. May a kind Providence guard him, as hitherto, and preserve him through every difficulty and danger, and restore him to his beloved family and friends. We feel proud that New York has not been backward in doing justice to the merits of this extraordinary man, (as all the world will pronounce him when his history shall be better known.)

Fourteen names are now on his list of subscribers from this State, and his work is only beginning to be known among us. The liberality of the American and British authorities in affording every facility to Mr. A. in the prosecution of his arduous undertaking, is spoken of by him in the warmest terms. His friends will have an opportunity of seeing at the next exhibition of the Academy, his portrait by Inman, which will do credit to the talents of that excellent artist. We will not, however, anticipate public opinion, but we intend to give our own when the exhibition opens.

Monday Morning, May 6, 1833
(Vol. 45, No. 16,858, Pg. 2, Col. 1)

The Boston Daily Advertiser of Saturday says — "Mr. Audubon arrived in this city on Thursday, and leaves it to-day on his excursion towards the North. — Every one must wish him abundant success in his important and interesting labors."

Tuesday Morning, May 21, 1833
(Vol. 45, No. 16,871, Pg. 2, Col. 2)

We learn by a letter from Mr. AUDUBON, to one of the editors of the Gazette, dated Eastport, May 9, that he has chartered a schooner of about sixty tons, in which he intends to make his expedition. On the 14th, he writes that he has just returned from an excursion up the Bay of Fundy, where he had derived much useful information; that he should sail on the first of June from Eastport to Halifax, thence to Sable Island, to New Foundland and to the coast of Labrador. After the breeding season of the birds is over, he will pass through the province of New Brunswick, towards Quebec, and return to the United States by way of Niagara.

Wednesday, May 29, 1833
(Vol. 45, No. 16,878, Pg. 2, Col. 2)

MR. AUDUBON. — "Our friends of the Lexington Observer think us mistaken in saying, that Kentucky is the native State of Mr. Audubon. Perhaps we are; but, if so, we have been misled by Mr. Audubon himself [*sic*] In introducing to the public his first great work on Ornithology, he announced it as the production of "*a native of Kentucky.*" Possibly he was misinformed on the subject of his own nativity."

It appears, from the above paragraph, which is copied from the Louisville Journal & Focus, of April 30, that the Lexington Observer and the Journal are at variance in regard to the birth place of our distinguished naturalist. We think a more careful perusal of Mr. Audubon's Ornithological Biography will satisfy Mr. Prentice that he has no where in that work "announced it as the production of *a native of Ken-*

tucky." Mr. A. it is true almost speaks of himself as a Kentuckian, when he says, in the chapter describing the sports of Kentucky: "*We* have individuals in Kentucky, &c. &c." and in other parts of the work he calls himself a *backwoodsman.* These expressions, taken in connection with his long residence at Louisville and Henderson, and the fact that his two sons are natives of the State, may have left an impression on the mind of Mr. P. that Mr. A. had positively asserted that he was a native of the State. After a most rigid perusal of the Biography, we have not been able to discover any stronger evidence within it than we have quoted above, whereon the paragraph could have been based, but it furnishes, in the following quotation from page 15, in his description of the Wild Turkey, much stronger evidence on the other side of the question. He says "*At the time when I removed to Kentucky more than a fourth of a century ago.*" From our first acquaintance with Mr. Audubon in 1824, we have invariably heard him speak of himself as a native of Louisiana, and since the above paragraph met our eye our impression has been confirmed by a reference to Mrs. Audubon, who is now in this city, where she will probably remain during Mr. A.'s expedition to the Coast of Labrador. A copy of Mr. Prentice's reply to the above would be acceptable to the Editors of the Gazette.

———————

Extract of a letter from Mr. Audubon, dated EASTPORT, May 20th.

"After scouring the country all round, but one subject for my pencil have I found, and that drawing have we made. Should it rain to-morrow, I shall make another drawing of the "Winter Wrens." These sweet creatures are singing from the top of every prostrate moss-covered log in the Woods. The name of our vessel is the Ripley, our commander's Emery, a person who has been in the *Egg** business for the markets of Halifax and St. Johns for five years in succession. On the first of June, we sail for Labrador, wind and weather permitting."

*It is not perhaps generally known, that the Eggs of the water fowl, which frequent certain spots on the Coast of Labrador and the Islands of those Seas, are to be procured in such immen[s]e quantities, that the vessels are loaded with them for the above markets, and that they are even brought to Boston—[*Eds. Gaz.*]

Thursday Morning, June 13, 1833
(Vol. 45, No. 16,891, Pg. 2, Col. 2)

Mr. Audubon.—It is with pleasure that we lay before our readers, the following interesting extracts of letters from our friend AUDUBON. Letters received on Monday announce his departure from Eastport on the morning of the 6th inst. for the coast of Labrador.

Eastport, May 26th.

We returned last night from an excursion to Grand Manan and other Islands; we were absent three days and have obtained much information, procured some valuable rare birds, some shells, and some plants, which I never had met with before. The appearance of the Island of Manan is sublime and terrific as you approach its stupendous, bold and rugged rocky shores on the north side of it. Not a spot can you find where to land, or if put ashore, where one can climb to its summit without being the possessor of extraordinary activity and strength. We sailed within a few hundred yards of these bold walls, in great depth of water and in full security, the wind being quite fair and the sea smooth. The croaking of the Ravens, which build their tenements and raise their broods amongst the fissures of these rocks, was the only sound that reached our ears, and the minds of landsmen at least, becomes chilled at the relation and recollection of lost vessels and their crews as one passes, one after another, hundreds of these sharp capes, all ready to crush the unfortunate or unwary ship in an instant. The southern aspect of this Island (20 miles in length) is entirely different; its shores rise gradually in the form of an immense amphitheatre, displaying a great portion of its contents, houses, cleared spots of land, and its forests, mixed with *hard* timber and firs; all of which look of a tough and dwarfish nature. We landed and found the soil indifferent, being extremely rocky and full of *peat*. The woods filled with mosses a foot deep, under which one sinks up to the knees in mire at every step. I found there growing wild, the common currant, gooseberry, strawberry, raspberry, and various species of whortleberry; all these, we were assured, were found here by the first settlers. *Not a wild quadruped*, except a species of *wood rat*, which I never saw before, and which I procured. Attempts have been made to introduce the moose deer [*sic*], but they did not live long. The islanders have some very indifferent cattle, a few horses and sheep. They grow little or no grain, and it appears as if potatoes and fish was their main support. The bays are swarming with cod and other fishes, and even now abundance of water fowl. The eider duck and a few other species breed on all the rocky islets that seem to stud the neighbouring sea. — The black guillemot, and razor bill, also breed here, and a species of large gull by millions, that are protected by the inhabitants, who feed on their eggs, and rob all these birds of their valuable feathers. I have had the best opportunities of studying them and their habits. My son found an eider duck's nests [*sic*] with three eggs in it, but it is too early for these birds yet. We here caught four *ravens*, by letting a sailor down forty feet from the top of the rocks by means of a rope. I mean to take them with me to Labrador as *compagnons de voyage*. I have procured one of the best water dogs I ever saw, equal to man in intellect, tho' he does not *speak the dead languages*. On *White Island*, Mr. Frankland (the owner) received us kindly, and sent his sons to assist us in our researches. He entertained us hospitably, and gave us a round of cheers as our little vessel departed from the shore. We landed on six other Islands in quest of birds; and as we sailed on, we could plainly see the land in Nova Scotia, though more than 40 miles distant.

Within three days, nature seems to have made a Spring towards perfection, for we found trees open, upon which scarce a bud was visible, when we left Eastport.

EASTPORT, May 29.

We have been busily engaged in drawing and saving our skins since my last, I have made a drawing of two very rare ducks, and my son has completed a drawing of three Phalaropes, which he had the good fortune to shoot; a bird which I scarcely ever could find any where else that I have been. Our vessel is about 100 tons, the whole of it so arranged as to enable us to pursue our employments in rainy weather within. Our party now consists of six persons besides our crew. The son of Dr. Shattuck, Dr. Ingalls, and Mr. Jos. Coolidge, from Boston, Mr. Thomas Lincoln, son of the Judge, from this neighborhood, and ourselves. Our party possess every thing that will be useful, necessary, or indeed comfortable; our drawing table is firmly fixed under the main *hatch*, so that we have a pretty good light. Since we have been here, we have completed four valuable drawings, added much to our journal, and objects of Natural History, and we have made three pretty views from this region.

Friday Morning, June 14, 1833
(Vol. 45, No. 16,892, Pg. 2, Col. 2)

EASTPORT, June 7.—Yesterday, Mr. J.J. Audubon sailed in the schr. Ripley, from this place, bound to Labrador. He is accompanied on his voyage by his son, Messrs. Shattuck and Ingalls, of Boston, Mr. Lincoln, of Dennysville, and Mr. Coolidge, of Lubec. Mr. Audubon is truly a wonderful man. The fruits of his untiring efforts to enlarge the boundaries of science will be a rich legacy to future generations. He has already been engaged thirty-five years in his great work on ornithology, and we understand he intends to spend nine years more in its completion. During this period of forty four years he will have travelled over almost every portion of the American Continent. He is to return to this place in three months. May health, happiness, and abundant success attend him.

Monday Morning, September 9, 1833
(Vol. 45, No. 16,965, Pg. 2, Cols. 1–2)

MR. JOHN J. AUDUBON.—This distinguished gentleman returned to this city on Saturday morning, and we are happy to say, in perfect health. By the Eastern

Mail, the editors of the New-York Gazette received a letter from Mr. A. dated at Halifax. As it is highly interesting, and as it is on a subject connected with Mr. A.'s great work, we intend to publish it. In the interim our readers will be highly interested with the following statement, which we find in the Boston Patriot.

[See Appendix H]

Tuesday Morning, September 10, 1833
(Vol. 45, No. 16,966, Pg. 2, Col. 1)

Agreeably to our promise yesterday, we now presen[t] to our readers the following extract of a letter from Mr AUDUBON, to the Editors of the New York Gazette dated

HALIFAX, N.S. Aug 25, 1833.

My Dear Friends—Myself and party arrived here last evening by land from Pictou, in this Province, near which place we landed three days ago. Our chartered vessel was ordered by us, to proceed to Eastport, Me. and we had the pleasure of seeing her under full sail with a fair breeze. We shall leave this, on Tuesday next, for Windsor on the Bay of Fundy, and make our way to Eastport, through St. John, New Brunswick, &c. We are all well, and now I will give you a sketch of our voyage, to Labrador, &c.

Favored with a good wind, we reached the Straits of Canso, on the third evening after we left Eastport; came to anchor and paid a visit to the shores. Nothing of any import to be seen, poor country, &c. Sailed the next day up the Bay and through the Straits; and I must say that this passage was extremely agreeable to us all—this Strait indeed resembles somewhat the North River, and as the weather was fair, the wind favorable, and we recovered from sea-sickness, we enjoyed it much. Nearly 50 vessels were in view at once all bound to the fisheries of Labrador. On entering the Gulph of St. Lawrence our course was bent towards the Magdalene Islands, at which we arrived the next day in the evening; anchored and spent a day and a night amongst them. To persons who had lately left the fertile shores of our country, these Isles appeared barren, if not desolate. No birds for us, no plants, and only a few fishermen to whom we could put questions, but who proved unable to answer them. We sailed towards the famous *Gannet Rocks*, which came in sight at an early hour. Many files of Ganets [*sic*] were constantly passing us on the wing, moving to, or from, this, their breeding place; but as soon as near enough to distinguish the bold summit of this stupendous Rock, we saw through the glass, that it was covered with what we supposed was a deep bed of snow; nay the atmosphere above the rock exhibited a heavy fall of snow. We sailed on and approached it; imagine our astonishment when we found that instead of snow covering the summit of the rock, the white bed consisted of Gannets seated on their nests, in close parallel lines, fronting the southern aspect! Millions in number, and the grey haze above, was produced by millions more hovering, alighting, arriving or departing! The pure whiteness of their bodies, mingling as they passed, crossing each other on the wing, and melowing the contrast observable in their jetty black-tipped pinions. The approach of our vessel did not alarm them, and we sailed as near the rock as prudence would allow—we wished to land there and ascend the rugged sides of this huge Aviary— a boat was launched and proceeded towards it: but all at once the wind freshened, the clouds thickened, the waves rose and rolled furiously; the base of the rock was now covered with foam. The boat however, proceeded, under the lea, a few guns were fired, thousands of eggs were seen to roll into the sea, as the birds took wing, affrighted by the report, and still the rock and every projecting shelf, was thickly covered and remained so. After vainly attempting to make a landing, the party was forced to return to the vessel; and well it was that our boat was one such as whalers use, or it would have proved a hard matter to row it in such a wind as now blew, and such waves as now heaved in fearful commotion. Ask me not to estimate the number of these birds, for it would be a difficult task, and yet how much more difficult to enumerate the quantities of fishes which this congregation of Gannets destroy each day. When we meet, and I hope it will be shortly, I will show a rough sketch of this place. The gale increasing we bore away towards the Island of Anticosti; famed from the many lives lost on its shores from the vessels wrecked on them almost annually; our sails were reefed, and after a while we scudded before the tempest, but so rough was the weather, we the next morning, when in sight of the Island, were obliged to go before the wind to Labrador. Labrador! who can describe the sensations at the first view of it while yet in the distance. Where millions and millions of water fowls which are only seen on our coast during severe winters, are here observed passing on whistling pinions, and constantly where deep beds of snow fill every rough valley at mid-summer: where fogs are so thick at times as almost to obscure the iron bound shores, and which are ever lashed angrily by the waves. When all that is seen of the country proves to be sterile, miserably sterile, scarcely inhabitable, and (when worse than all) you can only approach it in the fiairest [*sic*] of weather, or run the risk of being wrecked. —We landed, guided by the fishermen into what is called a harbour, by those daring adventurers, in latitude about 50 north, longitude 61 53, off Greenwich, and filled with that enthusiasm without which no student of nature can prosper, proceeded at once to investigate the country.

To ramble through the rich shady forests of our country, has ever been a pleasure to me, and every one who now formed our party; to wade through deep swamps under a scorching sun, I have even thought very bearable; but, to raise the feet from such matted beds of mosses as we had now to move through, and clothed so as to defend our bodies from the piercing air of that region, proved a most severe undertaking to all of us; we tugged and plunged, and managed slowly to move onwards; saw a very few birds, a few small flowrets [*sic*], and scarcely any thing that with us could be called a tree. Every day was nearly alike; we never were without a good fire in our camp or cabin, and for the distance of about three hundred miles, such was the country of Labrador. Yet Labrador offered us pleasures; we have collected some curious information, and among the rare species of Birds five new ones, as follws [*sic*]—two species of falcons, one uncommonly large and beautiful; one species of grouse; one titmouse, and a sparrow.—I have found the nest, eggs and young of many species hitherto not known, or undescribed, &c. and I am content.—I wish you, my dear good friends, had been of the party; we had an amiable and excellent man in Mr. Henry Emery, our Captain, who contributed much to our comfort and safety. The young gentlemen whose names you know were all congenial spirits, and during the three months of our absence from Eastport, we have lived in the most perfect harmony and respectful familiarity. On our return we visited St. George's Bay, New-Foundland, where we procured what I think a new species of hare; also, a bat and perhaps a new shell. As soon as we reach Eastport, I will write to say if, or not, we go to Quebec. This will depend on the news I receive from England, respecting the publication of my work.

Believe me,

Your ever attached friend,

J.J. AUDUBON.

P.S. I had almost forgot to say it was our good fortune, whilst on the coast of Labrador, to meet H.B. [*sic*] Majesty's Surveying schooner, the "Gulnare," commanded by Capt. Bayfield, R.N. who, as well as his officers and physician, we found extremely kind; all highly scientific men, the latter a Botanist. We parted company with the "Gulnare," at a harbor called *Wapaty-guan*, and from Capt. Bayfield, Lieut. Brown [*sic*], Midshipman Barry, out on a surveying expedition in an open boat, at another harbor called "*Great Macatina*;" all well on the 21st July last. We expected to have seen again the "Gulnare" in the harbor of Bras d'Or, but she had not reached that place when we left it on the 11th of August.—I have also to mention to you a sixth new bird, a fly catcher of rich plumage.

J.J. AUDUBON

"Mr. Audubon" *Boston Daily Advertiser & Patriot*

Mr. Audubon. — This distinguished naturalist returned from his Northeastern excursion to Boston on Wednesday last. — We believe that there is no one, who will not be gratified to learn the progress of his arduous and unremitted labors in a branch of science, which he has made peculiarly his own; and he has kindly favored us with information on the subject of his recent tour, which we are glad to lay before our readers; regretting only, that we are unable to present it in his own rich and animated language, and to invest it with the attractions which it would derive from his own descriptive power.

Mr. Audubon, in company with a few friends, left Eastport on the 6th of June, in a vessel hired for the purpose. His course was first directed to the Straits of Canso, and thence to the Madalene Island; a poor and barren spot, inhabited by a few persons, who are principally French Canadians. — From these islands, he sailed towards the Gannet rock, which derives its appellation from the birds of the same name that resort to it in multitudes large enough to wring the heart of Mr. Malthus. The rock is four hundred feet in height, and several acres in extent; when it was visited by Mr. Audubon, it was covered with innumerable birds upon their nests, which gave it the appearance of a huge mass of snow, while the countless numbers of those hovering above it presented a perfect image of a snow storm. The report of muskets did not appear in the slightest degree to alarm them. A severe gale prevented the party from attempting to explore the extraordinary colony and the rock is in fact regarded by the fishermen as inaccessible. The same gale carried them rapidly by the southern extremity of Anticosti, in the mouth of the St. Lawrence, to the coast, of Labrador, which they reached in the 51st degree of latitude. The shore of this iron country is extremely bold, and presented a most desolate appearance: the land was covered with heavy fogs, and diversified, even at this summer season, with numerous deep drifts of snow. Mr. Audubon spent a fortnight in the harbor called Little Nitasguan, employing his time in making excursions in the country, and along the coast, to the distance of about forty miles. The whole appears to be a solid rock, covered with mosses of uncommon depth and beauty; the vegetation in the valleys, which lie open to the sun, is remarkable for it luxuriance, and variegated with beds of rich plants, which were entirely new to every member of the party; the only forests are composed of thin and scattered dwarf trees, principally firs. Here, Mr. Audubon was enabled to ascertain the habits of many of the birds, which resort to our coast during the winter, and discovered two new species, a *Fringilla* and a *Parus*. In the harbor of Nitasguan, he met with a British surveying schooner, the Gulnare, under the command of Capt. Bayfield, from whom, together with his officers, Lt. Bowen and Dr. Kelly, the party experienced a very friendly and kind reception.

On leaving this place, Mr. Audubon proceeded eastwardly to the fine harbor of Wapatiguan, where he was a few days afterward followed by the Gulnare. Here he procured specimens of the willow grouse, old and young, ascertained the habits of many land and water birds, examined the country and neighboring islands, gathered a few new plants and shells, and departed for the port of Little Macatine. The shores of this coast were more bold and rugged than any he had yet visited; the aspect of the country became more sterile, and a corresponding change was observable in the climate. The excursions of the party in this quarter were numerous and fatiguing, and it was with difficulty that any of their number could walk for a greater distance than ten miles a day. On ascending the highest hills, the prospect in every direction was of an uniform and very cheerless character: the same thick mosses were spread over the table land, the plants were nearly the same, and lakes, formed by the melting of the snows of winter, were every where spread out around them. In this solitary spot, a Scottish settler had fixed his abode for more than twenty years, and seemed quite contented with the beauties of the scene. His sole occupation was that of taking seal and salmon, which were tolerably abundant in their respective seasons, and which he exchanged for requisite supplies, with vessels from Quebec and Newfoundland. He had a wife and six children, by whom the travelers were received with hospitality and kindness. All of them appeared contented with their situation, and had contracted a strong attachment to their wild and dreary residence. Mr. Audubon here found the wild goose in its breeding season, and was favored with an opportunity of observing the habits of several rare species of water birds.

Brador was the next stage in the progress of the travelers; on their way to this port, they explored several of the intermediate islands, where many species of birds were found breeding in abundance. These islands are resorted to by people from Nova Scotia, for the purpose of procuring eggs; they commence their operations by trampling on all which they find on the islands, and on the following day being to collect those which are newly laid; and, so successful are they in their search, that Mr. Audubon fell in with a party of three persons, who, in the course of six weeks, had found thirty-two thousand dozen, of the estimated value of four hundred pounds. There is no limit to the havoc made by these people: not content with carrying away the eggs merely, they kill the birds by thousands, in order to pluck a few feathers from the breast, and then throw them into the sea, or leave them on the rocks; and if this wanton destruction should be pursued a few years longer, it is obvious that they must exhaust the sources of their profit, by driving the birds from their accustomed haunts. In the port of Brador,* where they found excellent anchorage, the party met with sixty or seventy fishing vessels, the crews of all of which were actively employed. The fish were very abundant, and all expected to obtain what they denominate a fare. Mr. Audubon was, however, convinced, that a due regard to the season, and the proper application of their labor, might render the fishery far more productive than it is; and we hope hereafter to have it in our power to offer the result of his inquiries to our readers.

The cold at this place was much more severe than was to have been expected in July. The party found it necessary to make larger fires, than on the other portions of the coast; and even then the cold was so intense that Mr. Audubon's pencil occasionally dropped from his fingers, while engaged in drawing by the fireside. Icebergs were here for the first time seen. In fact, as the party advanced along the coast, they found that a distance of only a hundred miles produced a very remarkable difference in the progress of vegetation. Here also they encountered a brother-in-law of the anchorite of Little Macatine, occupying an equally independent situation, his nearest neighbors residing at a very serious distance. This personage had maintained his post for more than thirty years, and was decidedly of the opinion, that the country was the finest he had ever seen. He cultivated a small garden, in which were growing a few indifferent vegetables, and was the owner of the only horse, which was seen by the travelers in the country; but for the purpose of visiting those whom he called his neighbors, he was accustomed to employ Esquimaux dogs, of which about forty were attached to his establishment. These were fed upon the seals which he catches in the Spring, and which are piled in a huge mass in the vicinity of his front door, where they remain, until his neighbors have reason to rejoice at their remoteness from his villa. At this place, Mr. Audubon had the fortune to procure the male and female of a very large and beautiful new species of Falco, with several smaller birds. Some of the party visited a settlement, thirty miles distant, while the rest traversed this wild region in different directions, whenever the weather would permit.

On their departure from Brador, they crossed the Straits of Belle Isle, and sailed along the coast of Newfoundland, until they reached St. George's Bay, which they describe as the finest that they ever saw. The coast of Newfoundland was more elevated and broken, and even more sterile, than that of Labrador. At St. George's Bay, they found a village, consisting of forty houses and two hundred inhabitants, all of whom were fishermen. These people enjoy none of the luxuries, and few of the comforts of life; in the winter season, the want of fuel, and the apprehension of exposure to the violent gales, compel them to invert the order of fashionable usage, and to retire to small camps or cabins erected in the interior. When the party left this anchorage, they were driven by a severe storm to some distance north of the Madalene Islands, and for two days and nights were tossed in the sea of the Gulph, which

Mr. Audubon emphatically describes as the vilest of seas. As soon as the weather permitted, he sailed in the direction of Pictou, in Nova Scotia, where he discharged his vessel, in order to visit a portion of the British provinces. Pictou is a pleasant village on the margin of a beautiful bay, in which twenty or thirty vessels were at anchor, waiting for supplies of coal. The country in its vicinity is more fertile than is usual with those which abound in minerals. At Pictou, Mr. Audubon received many attentions from the Consul, Mr. Blanchard, and Professor Maculloch of the University, who has a rich collection of well preserved birds, and presented him with several valuable specimens. The road from this place to Truro is macadamized, and resembles the finest roads of that description in Europe; and the country is rich and diversified, both in its aspect and natural productions. Truro is situated in the centre of a luxuriant valley, adorned with neat farm-houses and villas; it was there, that the party caught a first view of the head waters of the bay of Fundy. Professor Maculloch was there, having gone thither for the purpose of introducing them to some gentlemen of the Provincial Assembly, in whose company they passed several agreeable hours. From this place to Halifax, the appearance of the country becomes less and less attractive.

The appearance of Halifax is pleasing at a distance, but a residence of a few days did not incline the travelers to feel much regret at the period of their departure; they were so unfortunate as not to see any of the gentlemen to whom the letters of introduction, which they received at Truro, were addressed. From this place to Windsor, which is situated on the river of the same name, eight or ten miles above its confluence with the Bay of Fundy, the aspect of the country is not very inviting; though on the road which winds along the bay immediately after leaving Halifax, there are many fine seats, with ornamented grounds around them. At Windsor, the tide was observed to rise more than sixty feet, and, when at half-flow, it rose three feet perpendicularly in the space of ten minutes. At low water, the bed of the river is almost dry; the vessels which were scattered along the bank to be laden with gypsum, the great commodity of the place, appeared to have been stationed there by some magic power. Mr. Audubon embarked at Windsor on board the steamboat Maid of the Mist, a most appropriate name for the latitude in which she plies, and after touching at St. Johns, returned at length to Eastport, and thence to Boston; where he arrived in good health, and without having met with any disastrous accident in the whole course of his tour.

In this excursion, it was not the expectation of Mr. Audubon to make many new discoveries; the coast of Labrador is not one, which judicious birds would be likely to select for any other than summer residence. He has, however, in ascertaining the habits of those already known, procured information, which must materially enhance the value of his great work; and the drawings, executed during his absence, particularly of the three birds which have been mentioned as discovered by him, are exquisitely beautiful.

*The schr. Wizard, of Boston, arrived at Brador while Mr. Audubon was there, and remained at his departure on the 12ᵗʰ of August. It was the intention of the Captain to leave in about a month for the Mediterranean. He was then waiting to dry his fish, for which the weather had been unfavorable, being cold and wet. While Mr. A. was in the harbor, a severe gale passed over in which many vessels were lost. It was ascertained that thirteen, of which two were American, were wrecked upon Prince Edward's Island.

(*Boston Daily Advertiser & Patriot*, Vol. XLII, No. 11,166, Pg. 2, Cols. 4–5)

"A Californian's Recollection of Naturalist Audubon"

The San Francisco Call

SUNDAY, SEPTEMBER 6, 1896

There is probably not another man in the world to-day who can look back to personal association with the famous ornithologist and ornithological painter, John James Audubon, with the vividness that characterizes the recollections of Joseph A. Coolidge, who for more than twoscore years has been a prominent citizen of San Francisco, and who is hale and hearty now at the advanced age of 81 years. Audubon's lifework is more appreciated to-day than it was fifty years ago, when he was at the summit of his celebrity, and his studies of birds and animals in the original editions are valued as among the rarest treasures. Audubon was born on his father's plantation, near New Orleans, May 4, 1780, and breathed his last at his home on the Hudson January 27, 1851. As a child, lying among the flowers of the sunny southland, sheltered by the orange trees and watching the movements of the mockingbird, "the king of song," dear to him in after life, the career of the naturalist was opened out to him unconsciously. His father gave him a thorough education, but the old man who was a commodore in the French navy, designed John to be a follower of Napoleon in the Grand Army. The boy, too, longed to be a soldier at one time during his youth, but his nest-hunting propensities led him away from that notion. While being educated in France, he made frequent excursions into the rural regions, supplied with haversack and provisions, and usually returned loaded with objects of natural history, birds' nests, birds' eggs, specimens of moss, curious stones, and other objects attractive to the eye. Warfare, he found, was not his bent, and he came to America again, after finishing his schooling, to superintend his father's lands.

In 1833, when Mr. Coolidge, then a lad of 18, first met the great ornithologist, Audubon's locks were gray, and he looked quite venerable, although his age was only three years over the half-century mark. At that time he was distinguished the world over. He was the possessor of letters from the British Government which would place at his service in the interest of his studies any man-of-war belonging to the crown and not under orders and anchored on a coast along which he was desirous of cruising. Young Coolidge accompanied him on the trip to Labrador during the summer of that year.

"My father had charge of a revenue-cutter, and had taken Audubon around to various islands on the Maine coast in quest of rare birds," said Mr. Coolidge, yesterday, in a reminiscent mood. "Audubon dined at our house in Eastport, Maine, and there he informed us that he had chartered a schooner for a cruise on the Labrador coast and was nearly ready to start. His party consisted of two young physicians from Boston – Drs. Ingalls and Shattuck – Thomas Lincoln of Bangor[1] and John Audubon, Jr. Audubon asked me if I knew how to sail a boat and I readily replied in the affirmative. As readily did I consent to go with him when he invited me, and when my parents expressed their willingness that I should go. Well, he gave me charge of a sailboat and we were shortly cutting the waves on our voyage from Eastport.

"And now let me tell you an incident. Audubon was what you may term a free drinker, and, furthermore, he was a great snuff taker. He took on the schooner only a barrel of rum to be used in preserving birds. What other liquors there were the old man collected, and as we were passing the Eastport Lighthouse he took a last drink and said to us, 'Boys, no more drink for me.' With that he threw the liquors into the waves. Then he fished out his snuffbox, and after taking a pinch, exclaimed, 'No more snuff,' and flung the box and its contents after the liquors into the tide.

"First we skirted the Magdalene islands, and then struck the coast of Labrador. The people of the Magdalenes were all French. I should tell you right here that Audubon was a great talker. Now, every man he met there he stopped and entered into conversation with him. He was as affable as he could be; he had an attractive personality; you had only to meet him to love him, and when you had conversed with him a moment you looked upon him as an old friend rather than as a stranger. Well, I accompanied him on one of his journeys through a French settlement, and he stopped to talk so many times that I grew quite weary at our lack of progress on foot. Finally I could not refrain from asking him, 'Dad (for we called him by that fatherly name), why is it that you have to stop and talk to every person you see?'

" 'My boy,' replied the naturalist, smiling and patting me on the back, 'in all my years I have never met a person from whom I could not get at least a little information of value.'

"Reaching Nathasguan, a Hudson Bay station on the coast of Labrador, on the 3d of July[2] we sent to buy some salmon in order that we might celebrate the Fourth with a fresh-fish dinner. So strict were the rules of the Hudson Bay Company that we were unable to purchase fish or any kind of provisions at all. The people positively refused to sell us anything. But we did not yield so easily to fate, and when

1. Coolidge made a point of correcting this error in a letter to Maria Audubon dated October 5, 1896, in which he stated, "The Lincoln's residence should be *Dennysville* not Bangor."

2. Coolidge's recollection on this point was faulty. Audubon's party had already left Natashguan/American Harbor and reached Wapitiguan Harbor by July 3. However, Audubon's journal does confirm that on July 4 Capt. Henry Wolsey Bayfield of the Royal Navy schooner *Gulnare*, which was anchored nearby, sent the Americans a quarter of mutton.

night came down we secretly lowered our nets and drew up four splendid salmon. At the station in question we met a British surveying schooner, and the party on board was our only company there. Well, Audubon had us take two of our salmon to the surveyors, and so delighted were they with the kind consideration, as well as the present, that they sent us in return a quarter of fresh mutton, so that we feasted on both flesh and fish that Independence day.

"We went on cruising, going into bays and inlets, and now and then taking trips inland, examining the country as carefully as our limited time would permit.

Our object was to get birds and to learn as much as possible about their habits; studying them as far as we could before killing them. Strange birds we would shoot when chance offered; bring them aboard the schooner in the night, and there have them skinned, stuffed, and hung up.

"One of the islands on the west coast of Labrador discovered to us a most peculiar situation, politically speaking. It was occupied at that time by a Frenchman and his family, and he was in reality monarch of all he surveyed. His island had not been included in the terms of the treaty ceding Canada to Great Britain, and he paid no tax to any nation, and was, as it were, the king of the island. This particular Frenchman had been to Quebec for provisions, and had there learned of Audubon's contemplated voyage to the Labrador coast. The naturalist visited the owner of the island, and was astonished to hear the man greet him by name.

"Audubon was always busily engaged at night measuring and drawing birds. He would work oftentimes until completely worn out. One night he turned to me from his labor and said, 'I do not know what I would not give for a glass of good brandy!'

" 'I think I can get you a little,' I responded.

" 'What!' exclaimed he in surprise. 'You know where there is brandy?'

"When I left home my mother packed my chest with care. She left nothing out that she deemed useful or necessary. She did not even neglect to put in a bottle of brandy, which might serve as a medicine in the northern wilderness. I brought it out and Audubon sipped of it.

" 'Don't touch this, any one of you!' he commanded. 'It is for me only,' and gradually he emptied the bottle.

"When I went aboard the schooner at Eastport I had taken along with me a box of snuff to present to the old gentleman, with whom I wanted to be on pleasant terms. When he threw that snuffbox of his overboard I did not feel like presenting the gift. Here in the solitude, however, it was different.

" 'Now, how would you like a pinch of snuff?' I laughed.

" 'As mortals seldom obtain all they wish,' replied he, 'they should study to be contented with what they can get.'

" 'But I can find you some snuff.'

" 'If you can you will be quite an angel.' And when I brought the snuff to him he was as happy as a child on Christmas morning with a wealth of gifts in its lap.

"At St. Georges Bay we found a French settlement, the people of which were all educated and of most refined appearance. They had been there many years. They tendered our party a grand ball. The dresses worn on that occasion were all of a pattern half a century out of date. It seemed like a bit of the France that existed before the Revolution transplanted on American shores, and the old fashions had never changed. We spent a week enjoyably there. Thence we returned by way of Pictou, Nova Scotia, where the museum of Professor McCullough was thrown open to us and every courtesy shown to us. The overland stage brought us to Halifax. Here Audubon made a call upon the Bishop. He had good reason to believe that his Excellency was at home, but he was told upon sending in his name that the Bishop was away. Audubon was a very sensitive man. The next day he received word that the Bishop would call on him on the following evening. Before that time arrived, however, Audubon had packed up his traps and left with his party. He chose to be 'out' when the Bishop came.

"Audubon was a good shot. In killing birds the instructions were to use as few shot as possible, in order that the skin of the birds might not be damaged any more than was absolutely necessary. One day our pilot went ashore with him, and saw him shoot at a bird at seemingly easy distance and miss it. The pilot laughed out loud.

" 'If I'd throw up my hat,' he declared, 'you couldn't hit it.'

"Audubon put another load in his gun. 'Throw it up and I'll try,' said he.

"The pilot had but one hat, and it would be a long time before he could get one to replace it. He threw it in to the air, and Audubon blazed away and blew it all to pieces.

" 'I always thought I was a darned fool,' sadly murmured the pilot as he tied knots in the corners of the handkerchief, so as to make a headcovering.

"In his drawings, Audubon was particular in the extreme. All his drawings are life-sized, and his desire to be perfectly accurate was such that he would measure the features to get the actual size, and take particular note of the over-lapping features.[3]

"When I visited New York in 1849, on my way to California, I intended to pay my respects to the aged naturalist, but I was informed by his son that the old man's mind was failing; that he would hardly recall me, and that it would not be a plea-

---

3. In his October 5, 1896 letter to Maria Audubon, Coolidge also corrected this error in the published article. "The other (probably typographical [*sic*]) is in the paragraph next the last, features instead of feathers." As revised, the sentence should read: "All his drawings are life-sized, and his desire to be perfectly accurate was such that he would measure the features to get the actual size, and take particular note of the over-lapping feathers."

sure for me to meet him in that melancholy decline. Thus, I chose to remember him as of old, and I came West, and to this day I can see him – a magnificent, gray-haired man, childlike in his simplicity, kind-hearted, noble-souled, lover of nature and lover of youth, father and brother, friend of humanity, and one whose religion was the golden rule."

(*The San Francisco Call*, Vol. LXXX, No. 98, p. 25, col. 1–7)

NOTES

TO THE READER: Most biographers use endnotes solely to reference the source material from which they derived the statements in their text. Any significant information is generally included in the narrative, so there is rarely any reason for a reader to refer to the notes unless they have an interest in going back to the original or secondary sources. My approach in writing this book was to follow the main current of the story without traveling up side tributaries. However, my research uncovered a great deal of information about Audubon and those in his circle that seemed to have no ready place in the story or would interrupt the narrative flow. I have incorporated this material in the endnotes, sometimes extensively, because I found it interesting and think many readers will as well.

I have also pointed out where I believe previous biographers erred in their research, misstated facts, or reached unsound conclusions in their interpretation of the evidence. History is often written based upon the research performed by others. Therefore, it is critically important to correct mistakes in the published record so they do not find their way into future works. Since the most recent biographies are those to which readers and scholars are apt to turn for reliable information, I have given them a closer look. These include those by Alice Ford (Abbeville Press, 1988), Shirley Streshinsky (Villard Books, 1993), Dr. John Chalmers (NMS, 2003), Duff Hart-Davis (Henry Holt and Company, 2004), William Souder (North Point Press, 2004), and Richard Rhodes (Alfred A. Knopf, 2004).

For those unfamiliar with these authors or their works, Alice Ford (1906–1997) was an art historian and Audubon's principal biographer during the latter half of the 20th century. Beginning in 1951, with the publication of *Audubon's Animals* (Studio Books), Ford published eight well-received volumes on Audubon, including a groundbreaking biography in 1964 (University of Oklahoma Press). In 1988, she updated this work in a second edition (Abbeville Press). Among a multitude of scholarly discoveries, Ford determined that Audubon's natural mother, Jeanne Rabine, had grown up in a village outside Nantes in France and had met Audubon's father, Jean Audubon, aboard a ship bound for the West Indies in 1783. Ford also located the records reflecting that Jean Audubon had sent his young son to France in 1788, while he remained in Saint Domingue. She sifted through the records of the famous French Neoclassical painter Jacques-Louis David in Paris to finally lay to rest Audubon's oft-repeated but unsubstantiated claim that he had studied art at David's atelier. In addition to her seminal biography, Ford was also responsible for originally transcribing and publishing Audubon's 1826 journal, his most important extant journal written when he sailed from America to England to find a publisher for *The Birds of America* (University of Oklahoma Press, 1967; Abbeville Press, 1987). Though more recent scholarship has raised questions about the quality of this transcription, her contributions to Audubon scholarship are legion and rightfully place her at the pinnacle of Audubon's biographers.

Shirley Streshinsky (1934–) is a California novelist, biographer, and travel writer. Her 1993 book, *Audubon: Life and Art in the American Wilderness* (Villard Books), was published to coincide with the opening of a major touring exhibition of Audubon's original watercolors, which are in the collection of the New-York Historical Society. By her own admission, she was not trying to break new ground but merely sought to recount the Audubon story in a new way. She relied heavily on Ford's biography, but she also performed her own research of original sources, visiting many of the major Audubon archives in the United States and England. In the course of her research, she located an important Audubon letter at the Filson Historical Society Library in Louisville, KY, which had been overlooked by previous scholars and that I relied upon in the opening pages of this book. Her volume is a highly readable account of Audubon's life.

Dr. John Chalmers (1927–) is a retired orthopedic surgeon from Edinburgh. In 2003, he published *Audubon in Edinburgh* (NMS), a splendid monograph that covers the crucial time Audubon spent in his favorite city and details how Edinburgh's scientific community helped make *The Birds of America* a success. Thoroughly researched and beautifully illustrated, this is an important addition to the Audubon canon.

Duff Hart-Davis (1936–) is a London-based writer whose biography, *Audubon's Elephant: America's Greatest Naturalist and the Making of* The Birds of America (Henry Holt and Company), appeared in 2004. It covers the great expanse of Audubon's life with particular emphasis on the years Audubon was working on the publication of *The Birds of America*.

William Souder (1949–) came out in 2004 with another Audubon biography, *Under a Wild Sky* (North Point Press). Unlike Audubon's other chroniclers, Souder weaves together the stories of the lives of both Audubon and Alexander Wilson, the "father of American ornithology," before concentrating on Audubon's struggle to bring *The Birds of America* to life. Souder has a breezy style that humanizes his subject and makes his story a pleasure to read. His endnotes are often informative and well worth exploring. Notably, this work was a finalist in 2005 for the Pulitzer Prize in biography.

Richard Rhodes (1937–), a Pulitzer Prize winner for *The Making of the Atomic Bomb* (1986), was the author of yet a third Audubon biography in 2004, *John James Audubon: The Making of an American* (Alfred A. Knopf). More comprehensive than its peers, this book combines Rhodes' exhaustive research and literary writing style to take a fresh look at Audubon's evolution as an artist, naturalist, and writer against the backdrop of early 19th century America. It is a worthy successor to Ford's landmark biography.

My critical review of these fine works does not lessen my great respect and admiration for their authors as well as all of the serious scholars whose contributions to the Audubon canon provided a foundation for this book. And, I recognize that my efforts here will invite scrutiny by those who follow, as they should. In those instances where I have identified errata in another author's work, I have cited the sources I relied upon so that anyone with the inclination can confirm my conclusions. Where I merely disagree with the deductions drawn by other scholars based on the available evidence, I have presented the details of my reasoning.

ABBREVIATIONS

AAS: American Antiquarian Society, Worcester, Massachusetts.

AHJ: *Audubon and His Journals*, edited by Maria R. Audubon and Elliott Coues, 2 vols. (New York: Charles Scribner's Sons, 1897).

APS: John James Audubon Papers 1821–1845 (Mss.B.Au25), American Philosophical Society, Philadelphia, Pennsylvania.

Audubon Museum: John James Audubon Museum, John James Audubon State Park, Henderson, Kentucky.

BOA: The Birds of America, published by John James Audubon in Edinburgh and London, 1827–1838.

Bowdoin: George J. Mitchell Department of Special Collections & Archives, Bowdoin College, Brunswick, Maine.

College of Physicians: College of Physicians, Philadelphia, Pennsylvania.

Columbia: Rare Book & Manuscript Library, Columbia University, New York, New York.

Countway: Papers of George Cheyne Shattuck Jr., 1832–1872 (GA 80.25, Vol. 1), Harvard Medical Library in the Francis A. Countway Library of Medicine, Boston, Massachusetts.

Dartmouth: Rauner Special Collections Library, Dartmouth College, Hanover, New Hampshire.

Filson: Filson Historical Society, Louisville, Kentucky.

GCSJr: George Cheyne Shattuck Jr., M.D. (1813–1893).

GCS: George Cheyne Shattuck Sr., M.D. (1783–1854).

Harris Papers: Edward Harris Papers (LPR98), Alabama Department of Archives and History, Montgomery, Alabama.

Harvard: John James Audubon Papers (MS Am 1482), Houghton Library, Harvard University, Cambridge, Massachusetts.

Harvard (Letters): John James Audubon Letters and Drawings (MS Am 21), Houghton Library, Harvard University, Cambridge, Massachusetts.

Howland: Howland Collection, Buffalo Museum of Science Research Library, Buffalo, New York.

JJA: John James Audubon (1785–1851).

JWA: John Woodhouse Audubon (1812–1862).

LBA: Lucy Bakewell Audubon (1787–1874).

Letters: Howard Corning, ed., *Letters of John James Audubon, 1826–1840*, 2 vols. (Cambridge: Club of Odd Volumes, 1930).

Linnean Society: Correspondence between John J.

Audubon and William Swainson, Linnean Society of London, London, England.

LOC: Chronicling America: Historic American Newspapers, Library of Congress, Washington, D.C. (http://chroniclingamerica.loc.gov/).

MHS: George Cheyne Shattuck Papers (Ms. N-909), Massachusetts Historical Society, Boston, Massachusetts.

MHM: John James Audubon Collection, Missouri History Museum Archives, St. Louis, Missouri.

Mill Grove: John James Audubon Center at Mill Grove, County of Montgomery, Department of Parks and Heritage Services, Audubon, Pennsylvania.

Newberry: Newberry Library, Chicago, Illinois.

NYHS: New-York Historical Society, New York, New York.

OB: John James Audubon's *Ornithological Biography*, published in Edinburgh in five volumes: Vol. I (1831); Vol. II (1834); Vol. III (1835); Vol. IV (1838); Vol. V (1839).

Princeton: John James Audubon Collection, Department of Rare Books and Special Collections, Princeton University Library, Princeton, New Jersey.

Rosenberg Library: Lucy P. Shaw Papers (MSS #24-0043).24), Rosenberg Library, Galveston, Texas.

Shaffer Collection: Audubon-Bakewell-Shaffer Family Papers, John James Audubon Center at Mill Grove, County of Montgomery, Department of Parks and Heritage Services, Audubon, Pennsylvania.

VGA: Victor Gifford Audubon (1809–1860).

Yale (Coe): John James Audubon Collection, General Collection (GEN MSS 829), Beinecke Rare Book and Manuscript Library, Yale University, New Haven, Connecticut.

Yale: Morris Tyler Family Collection of John James Audubon, General Collection (GEN MSS 85), Beinecke Rare Book and Manuscript Library, Yale University, New Haven, Connecticut.

PREFACE

1. As a fictionalized account of the Labrador expedition, Katherine Govier's *Creation* (Overlook Press, 2002) does not attempt to meet the rigid standards of scholarship expected in a biography.

For example, her description of Audubon's arrival in Eastport, ME, in early May 1833 is riddled with errors, as Chapter 4 in this book demonstrates.

Beyond that, some of Govier's ornithological references are uninformed. If Audubon listened for birds after reaching Eastport, as Govier imagines, he certainly did not hear "the Cardinal's whistle" or the "low warble of the Snow Bunting." Govier (2002), p. 1. In Audubon's day, the Northern Cardinal, as it is now known, was a bird of the southern and mid-Atlantic U.S. Audubon noted in the *OB* that "some are also seen in the State of New York, and now and then a straggler proceeds into Massachusetts; but farther eastward this species has never been observed." *OB* II, p. 336. It has only been within the last century that Cardinals have extended their range into northern Maine and southern Canada. Kaufman (1996), p. 564.

Nor is there any likelihood he would have heard a Snow Bunting (*Plectrophenax nivalis*). These birds are migratory, spending their summers in the arctic and only wintering in New England. According to Audubon, "The Snow Birds enter the eastern portions of the Union sometimes early in November, and remain in such parts as suit them best until the month of March." *OB* II, p. 515. Ora Willis Knight, who authored an early book on Maine birds, noted that the species was "locally and sporadically common until late March, a few exceptionally remaining until even April twelfth." Knight (1908), pp. 395–396. By early May, they would have long since departed the coast of Maine for their nesting grounds in the north.

2. Rhodes (2004), p. 331; Ford (1987), p. 388; *OB* I, pp. 54–55.

3. Maria Rebecca Audubon (1843–1925) was the daughter of Audubon's youngest son, John Woodhouse Audubon (1812–1862), and his second wife, Caroline Hall (1811–1899). She was named after John's deceased first wife, Maria Rebecca Bachman (1817–1840), the eldest daughter of Audubon's close friend and collaborator, the Reverend John Bachman of Charleston, SC. Sanders & Ripley (1986), p. 49.

4. Osgood (1935), pp. 8–9; *AHJ* I, p. vii. The presentation copy of *AHJ* given by Maria Rebecca Audubon to Ruthven Deane is now housed in the Edward D. Graff Collection of Western Americana

at the Newberry Library in Chicago. Storm (1968), p. 21.

5. "A Californian's Recollection of Naturalist Audubon," *The San Francisco Call*, Vol. LXXX, No. 98, p. 25, cols. 1–7 (Sunday, 6 Sept. 1896)(LOC). The full article containing Joseph A. Coolidge's vibrant memories of the Labrador expedition is published for the first time in over a century in Appendix I. The other survivor of the expedition at that point was Dr. William Ingalls (1813–1903) of Roxbury, MA.

6. While the copy of Maria Audubon's scrapbook bequeathed to Ruthven Deane also contains a copy of the *Call* article, it seems likely that Deane was already aware of Coolidge's account long before the scrapbook came to him in 1925. Shortly after the publication of the article in 1896, Maria apparently informed Deane that Coolidge was still alive and living in San Francisco, and Deane subsequently began a correspondence with him. Deane (1910). But Deane never referenced the *Call* piece in any of his many published articles about Audubon.

7. Maria Audubon did quote a paragraph from the *Call* article in the biographical sketch of her grandfather that she wrote for *AHJ*, but she deliberately misrepresented its source. She claimed that Coolidge had written her on October 9, 1896, and recalled the American Woodsman fondly: "You had only to meet him to love him; and when you had conversed with him for a moment, you looked upon him as an old friend rather than a stranger. . . . To this day I can see him, a magnificent gray-haired man, child-like in his simplicity, kind-hearted, noble souled, lover of nature and lover of youth, friend of humanity, and one whose religion was the golden rule." *AHJ* I, p. 68.

However, the original letter from Coolidge is tipped into her Scrapbook No. 2, which is now in private hands. It is dated October 5, not October 9, and is a response to a letter Coolidge had received from Maria after she had evidently spotted a reprinted copy of the *Call* article in another newspaper. While Coolidge's letter references this paragraph from the article, it was clearly not the source of the description that Maria published. For reasons that are unclear, Maria elected to take Coolidge's quote virtually wholesale from the *Call* and attribute it to a non-existent letter rather than the original

source. A possible, if not likely, explanation is that she did not want to draw attention to the article and Coolidge's description of her grandfather as a "free drinker."

8. Harwood & Durant (1985), pp. 89, 92.

9. Ibid., pp. 86–89. The 1826 journal was owned for many years by the famed American bibliophile H. Bradley Martin (1906–1988), who permitted Audubon scholar Alice Ford to transcribe and publish it in 1967. Ford (1967). In 1987, she published a second edition, supplemented with a new drawing and the missing final page of the journal, which had surfaced in the interim. Ford (1987), p. 10. She claimed that her transcription was "scrupulously faithful to the original manuscript, except of course where failure to transpose a phrase, or add and bracket a word, would mean certain confusion for the reader." Ibid., p. 11.

In June 1989, following Martin's death, the journal was sold at Sotheby's in New York. Sotheby's (6 Jun. 1989), Lot 20. A decade later, in December 1999, it was given by Charles W. Palmer and his family to the Field Museum in Chicago. Field Museum (2000), p. 117.

At about the same time, The Library of America published an abridgement of the 1826 journal, consisting of sporadic entries between July 9 and December 1826. Audubon (1999), pp. 159–192. Transcribing it from a microfilm copy of the original at the New-York Historical Society, editor and Audubon scholar Christoph Irmscher, now Provost Professor and George F. Getz Jr. Professor in the Wells Scholars Program in the Department of English at Indiana University, discovered that Ford had made widespread revisions to the journal, which he mentioned in his notes. By contrast, his production was faithful to the original holograph, adopting Audubon's idiosyncratic use of capital letters and misspellings. Ibid., p. 871.

Daniel Patterson, a Professor of English at Central Michigan University, followed up on Irmscher's discovery of the problems with Ford's transcription and, with the assistance of Patricio J. Serrano, Director of the Applied Linguistic Career at Escuela Politécnica del Ejército in Quito, Ecuador, meticulously transcribed and, in 2011, published a vastly superior edition of the journal. Audubon (2011). The editorial policies they adopted resulted in minor variations from the text, as might be expected. Ibid., pp. lv-lix.

The Field Museum plans to publish online the original journal in facsimile along with a transcription by Prof. Irmscher. Olson (2012), p. 437; Field Museum (2000), p. 117.

10. The Newberry Library in Chicago holds a copy of a fragment of the latter portion of the Missouri River journal, spanning the period from August 16, when he left Fort Union, to October 19, 1843, when he arrived in St. Louis, followed by a final note "Reached Home on Sunday afternoon at 3 o'clock P.M. 6th Novr and thank God found all my family quite well." Storm (1968), p. 20. The Beinecke Rare Book and Manuscript Library at Yale also has a copy of a fragment of the journal that runs between August 5 and August 13, 1843. (Yale, Box 8, Folder 446).

In the mid-1980s, when Michael Harwood was conducting research for an article on the expedition for *Audubon* magazine, an unnamed Audubon descendant permitted him to examine a portion of the original journal that was still in the family's possession. Harwood & Durant (1985), p. 116. This reportedly contained entries for two months of the trip, although Harwood does not say what period it covered.

Using three extant fragments of the journal that he was able to locate, Daniel Patterson has published *The Missouri River Journals of John James Audubon* (University of Nebraska Press, 2016), which offers a new and more authentic version of the Missouri River journal.

11. There is no evidence to support the view of Audubon biographer Shirley Streshinsky that Audubon "probably thought they [his journals] would one day be published." Streshinsky (1993), p. xiii. Audubon's unedited journals contain too many expressions of his most intimate thoughts and feelings, such as his physical longing for his wife Lucy, for one to reasonably conclude that he ever intended to share them, at least unabridged, with the public.

12. Harwood & Durant (1985), pp. 89, 92. Maria admitted burning at least one of Audubon's journals, that covering the period 1822 to 1824, in a letter she wrote to Ruthven Deane on July 4, 1904: "I was quite truthful as to the destruction of the journals by *fire* so far as this one goes for *I burned it my-*

self, in 1895. I had copied from it all I ever meant to give the public, & if you will go back to that bitter year, *you* will perfectly understand why mother, the other members of my family & Dr. [Elliott] Coues who read it *all*, thought that in view of the existing circumstances, fire was our only suriety [*sic*] that many family details should be put beyond the reach of vandal hands." Maria Audubon, Salem, NY to Ruthven Deane, 4 Jul. 1904, tipped into a presentation copy of *AHJ*. *AHJ* I, pp. 48 and 49 (Edward D. Graff Collection of Western Americana (VAULT Graff 112), Newberry). See also, *AHJ* I, p. 51 (referencing "the worn, brown volume, the journal of 1822-24, with its faded entries").

13. In addition to the 1826 journal and a portion of the Missouri River journal of 1843, there is an extant journal from 1820-1821, known as the Mississippi River journal, as well as Audubon's journal during the period 1840-1843, when he was canvassing the eastern United States looking for subscribers to the octavo *BOA* and folio *Quadrupeds*. Audubon (1999); Corning (1929a); Corning (1929b).

We know that the Mississippi River journal did not find its way into Maria Audubon's hands until after she had published *AHJ*. Deane (1904), p. 334 ("This [journal] would have been included in 'Audubon and his Journals' but unfortunately it did not fall into the hands of the author until more than a year after this work had been completed and published."). Joseph M. Wade, the editor of *Familiar Science and Fancier's Journal* and a noted collector of Auduboniana, subsequently acquired the journal from a member of the Audubon family. Harwood & Durant (1985), p. 92. Francis H. Herrick, Audubon's first legitimate biographer, reportedly theorized in a letter to Howard Corning, the editor of the journal for the Club of Odd Volumes in Boston, that Wade had borrowed the journal and never returned it. Alice Ford (Personal communication). Wade's collection was later purchased by Col. John E. Thayer of Lancaster, MA, who, in 1913, donated the Mississippi River journal along with the 1840-1843 journal to the Museum of Comparative Zoology at Harvard University. Corning (1929a), pp. vii-ix.

The 1826 journal was held by the Audubon family until at least 1946. In September of that year, the owner, Victor Morris Tyler, permitted the New-

York Historical Society to microfilm the journal. Four years later, in approximately 1950, the journal was acquired by H. Bradley Martin, a noted American bibliophile, from a Beverly Hills dealer. Sotheby's (June 6, 1989), Lot 20; Alice Ford (Personal communication).

The Missouri River journal fragment at the Newberry Library was hand-copied by Audubon, contrary to Daniel Patterson's conclusion. It may have been intended for John Bachman of Charleston, SC, who was collaborating on Audubon's natural history of North American mammals, and was later acquired by Edward D. Graff, who donated it.

14. Harwood & Durant (1985), p. 78.

15. Buchanan (1868), p. v.

16. Herrick (1938) I, pp. 18–19; L. Audubon (1869), p. iii.

17. Harwood & Durant (1985), p. 80.

18. Both the Buchanan and Lucy Audubon versions of the Labrador journal are misdated by a day or two beginning with Audubon's entry of June 12, 1833. This error is established by comparing Maria Audubon's transcribed Labrador journal with other independent evidence, such as the journal of Cmdr. Henry Wolsey Bayfield of the British Royal Navy surveying schooner *Gulnare*, who recorded his first meeting with Audubon on June 22, 1833. Bayfield's journal squares with Maria's transcription at this point, suggesting that her earlier dating, with one exception (June 22, which is repeated twice), is correct. The Buchanan/Lucy journal returns to the correct dating on June 26. There are also dating errors with the Buchanan/Lucy entries of July 26 to July 28.

19. Deane (1910, pp. 42–48. Early issues of *The Auk* are now accessible via the Searchable Ornithological Research Archive (SORA) portal on the internet, http://sora.unm.edu/.

20. Spiker (1969); Townsend (1924), pp. 237–242.

21. George C. Shattuck Jr.'s 1833 journal provides a periodic record of his activities beginning on February 20, 1833, when he left Boston to attend the spring term of the Medical School of Maine in Brunswick. He references his social doings, lectures, and the medical cases in which he participated, among other things. He continued to use the journal to record his activities from the time

he left Brunswick on May 6 to his arrival in Eastport on May 9, as well as during the remainder of that month when he was in Eastport waiting for the expedition to depart for Labrador. Once they were finally underway in early June, he added several entries to the journal regarding the tail end of his stay in Eastport. GCSJr Journal (Countway).

Shattuck kept a separate journal of the expedition itself, but it apparently has been lost. According to Charles W. Townsend, M.D., the author of *In Audubon's Labrador* (Houghton Mifflin Company, 1918), Shattuck's son Frederick C. Shattuck, M.D., had no knowledge of it. Townsend (1918), p. 335, note 1; GCSJr, Bradore, Labrador, to GCS, Boston, 5 Aug. 1833 (MHS, Vol. 11, 1–8 Aug. 1833).

22. Townsend (1918), pp. 319–337.

23. JJA, Bras d'Or, Labrador, to LBA, New York, 5 Aug. 1833 (Princeton, Box 2, Folder 24), *Letters* I, pp. 239–240.

PROLOGUE: BOSTON

1. Healy (1894), p. 204. The striking quality of Audubon's eyes was noted by numerous observers. See, e.g., Bakewell (1911), p. 40; Coke (1833) II, p. 100; North (1831), p. 11.

2. JJA, Boston to Richard Harlan, M.D., Philadelphia, 20 Mar. 1833 (Filson), Audubon (2006), p. 372.

3. Low (2002), p. 10; VGA, London to JJA, New York, 23 Apr. 1833 (Yale, Box 2, Folder 37); VGA, London to JJA, New York, 29 Mar. 1833 (Yale, Box 15, Folder 693); VGA, Liverpool to JJA, New York, 15 Jan. 1833 (Yale, Box 15, Folder 693); VGA, London to JJA, New York, 6 Jan. 1833 (Yale, Box 2, Folder 37). For the first six years of the project, five Numbers were issued per year. Fries (1973), pp. 399–400. According to the cited letters written by Audubon's eldest son, Victor, who was in London attending to the publication while the rest of the family was in Boston, No. 31 (Plates 151 to 155) was in the process of being published as of early to mid-January 1833. No. 32 (Plates 156 to 160) was not ready for delivery until the end of April. Thus, as of mid-March, a total of 155 prints had actually been issued. See also, Chapter 2, note 225, *infra*.

4. On March 19, 1833, Audubon informed Victor that he had "finished some beautiful Drawings" and was preparing to send him "Two Numbers of Land

Birds." JJA, Boston to VGA, London, 19 Mar. 1833 (APS). These paintings, intended for No. 37 (Plates 181–185) and No. 38 (Plates 186–190), were shipped to Victor by Audubon's brother-in-law Nicholas Berthoud on May 10, 1833. JJA, Eastport to VGA, London, 31 May 1833, *Letters* I, p. 232; JJA, New York to VGA, London, 28 Apr. 1833, Grinnell (1916), pp. 120–123.

5. Audubon *Prospectus* (1831), p. 4. The original cost of *BOA* in America was $1,000 or $12.50 per Number of five prints. Hart-Davis (2004), p. 111; Ford (1988), p. 490; Ford (1987), p. 430. However, in 1832, Congress passed a law that allowed the prints of *BOA* to come into the country free of duty. JJA, Boston to Richard Harlan, M.D., Philadelphia, 20 Mar. 1833 (Filson), Audubon (2006), p. 373. As a consequence, Audubon was able to reduce the price to his American subscribers. In 1833, the cost in America of an unbound set of *BOA* was $800, based on a cost of $2.00 per print or $10.00 per Number. Fries (1973), p. 198; Tuckerman (1889) I, p. 73. See also, GCSJr, Boston to Parker Cleaveland, Brunswick, ME, 12 Sept. 1833 (Bowdoin). Shipping from New York was charged to the subscriber. Subscribers could have each volume of prints bound at an extra cost. With a half binding, the cost was $220 per volume. A full binding was $250 per volume. Fries (1973), p. 197; JJA, New York to Parker Cleaveland, Brunswick, ME, 17 Sept. 1833 (Ayer Collection, Newberry); JJA, Boston to LBA, New York, 4 May 1833 (Princeton, Box 2, Folder 14), *Letters* I, p. 214; GCS, Boston to GCSJr, Brunswick, ME, 24 Mar. 1833 (MHS, Vol. 11, Mar. 14–31, 1833). See also, Hart-Davis (2004), p. 198 (noting the reduced pricing schedule). The inflation conversion factor used to calculate the approximate cost of a subscription to *BOA* in estimated 2016 dollars is based upon Sahr (2015).

6. JJA, Boston to VGA, London, 24 Feb. 1833 (APS), *Letters* I, p. 200; JJA, Boston to John Bachman, Charleston, 19 Feb. 1833 (Harvard (53));

7. Quincy (2003), p. 35; Dane Papers, Massachusetts Historical Society (Ms. N-1090, Vol. 5).

8. LBA, Boston to VGA, London, 13 Mar. 1833 (Yale, Box 1, Folder 5); Stimpson (1833), p. 221. See also, Colonial Society of Massachusetts (1907), pp. 77–78, note 3.

9. LBA, Boston to Mrs. Robert Havell Jr., Lon-

don, 15 Feb. 1833 (Harvard (Letters), b (119)); LBA, Boston to VGA, London, 13 Mar. 1833 (Yale, Box 1, Folder 5).

10. Colonial Society of Massachusetts (1907), pp. 77–78, note 3; Drake (1873), p. 275. Alice Ford's statement that the Audubons resided at Joshua Davis's boardinghouse during their stay in Boston is misleading. Ford (1988), p. 302; Ford (1964), p. 298. Davis was a Boston merchant with a business on Broad Street who lived at the Pearl Street address. Stimpson (1833), p. 132. However, contemporary sources clearly establish that Mrs. Lekain operated the establishment. See, e.g., Ethan Allen Greenwood, Boston to JJA, "Mrs Le Cain's Pearl Street," 29 Mar. 1833 (MHM); Richard C. Derby, Boston to JJA, "Miss Le Kane," 3 May 1833 (MHM).

11. Frederic C. Detwiller Consulting Services Group (1980); Quincy (1851), pp. 68–71.

12. Quincy (2003), pp. 25, 35. Anna Cabot Lowell Quincy, the youngest daughter of Harvard University President Josiah Quincy, was born on June 27, 1812, and died on October 14, 1899, at the age of eighty-seven. Public Family Trees, www.ancestry.com (accessed 17 Jan. 2014); Perkins Institution (1901), p. 37.

13. JWA addendum to LBA, Boston to VGA, London, 28 Jan. 1833 (Yale Box 1, Folder 5).

14. Quincy (2003), pp. 35, 38. See also, note 1, *supra*. The names of birds in this book are those that Audubon used in either *BOA* and/or in *OB*. Where the 19th century species name differs from that in use today, the current name, as reflected in the American Ornithologists' Union (AOU) *Check-list of North American Birds* (7th ed., 1998), through the Fifty-fourth Supplement in 2013, is given in parenthesis. Bird names are capitalized using the format in the AOU check-list and modern field guides. See, e.g., Sibley (2014).

In this regard, I have elected not to follow the *Chicago Manual of Style*, which recommends capitalizing only proper nouns and adjectives that are part of an animal or plant's species name (e.g., Cooper's hawk, named for the 19th-century naturalist William Cooper). Many bird names are descriptive (e.g., Yellow-rumped Warbler, Ruby-crowned Kinglet), and a reader unfamiliar with birds might be confused in thinking that a "yellow-rumped warbler" is merely a warbler with a yellow rump, not a specific species. The names of non-avian species are treated similarly for consistency sake. Whenever animals or plants are referred to by a common or generic name as opposed to a species name, e.g., cod vs. Atlantic Cod or rattlesnake vs. Timber Rattlesnake, the common name is not capitalized unless it begins a sentence.

15. Richard Harlan, M.D., Philadelphia to JJA, New York, 23 Mar. 1833 (Yale, Box 4, Folder 173); JJA, Boston to Richard Harlan, M.D., Philadelphia, 20 Mar. 1833 (Filson), Audubon (2006), p. 372. Several of Audubon's biographers assert that he was ambidextrous. Hart-Davis (2004), p. 55; Ford (1988), p. 38; Murphy (1956), p. 318. Cf. Arthur (1937), p. 20 (claiming Audubon was left handed). It is true that Audubon had some degree of skill with his left hand and sometimes showed it off as a parlor trick. Audubon (2011), pp. 108, 231; Ford (1987), pp. 139, 262. However, his many letters were written exclusively with his right hand. And his good friend Dr. Richard Harlan of Philadelphia confirmed in the cited letter that he relied upon his right hand to draw and paint.

16. JJA, Boston to Richard Harlan, M.D., Philadelphia, 20 Mar. 1833 (Filson), Audubon (2006), p. 372.

17. Dr. John Collins Warren (1778–1856) was born in Boston on August 1, 1778, to John Warren, M.D., one of the founders of Harvard Medical College. The young Warren graduated from Harvard College in 1797. He studied medicine for a year under his father, who was the Professor of Anatomy and Surgery at Harvard. He then continued his medical studies in Europe. He returned to Boston in 1802 and began practicing medicine with his father. Within a decade, he had been named an Adjunct Professor of Anatomy and Surgery at Harvard. He joined several other distinguished Boston physicians in 1811 to create the *New England Journal of Medicine and Surgery*, a publication that joined another in 1828 to become *The Boston Medical and Surgical Journal*. This was the predecessor to *The New England Journal of Medicine*, widely considered to be the most prestigious American medical journal today. In 1815, following his father's death, Warren succeeded his father as the Hersey Professor of Anatomy and Surgery at Harvard and held

this position until his retirement in 1847 at the age of seventy. In 1820, he was instrumental in founding Massachusetts General Hospital. He served as president of the Massachusetts Medical Society from 1832–1836. He was fascinated by the natural sciences and, in 1834, became a member of the Boston Society of Natural History, serving as its president from 1847 until his death, at the age of seventy-seven, on May 4, 1856. Warren is perhaps best remembered for the first use of ether as an anesthetic during surgery in 1846 at Massachusetts General Hospital. Creed (1930), p. 19; Burrage (1923), pp. 108–109, 462; Muzzey (1883), pp. 233–235; Arnold (1882), p. 19; Warren (1860); "The Late Dr. John C. Warren," *New-York Daily Times*, Vol. V, No. 1445, p. 1, col. 6 (May 6, 1856); Loring (1832), p. 155. Rhodes erroneously refers to him as Joseph C. Warren. Rhodes (2004), p. 379.

Warren lived across from the Public Common at 2 Park Street in Boston. Stimpson (1833), p. 331. His sister Harriet was married to Capt. John Prince, who had originally built the house at 3 Pearl Street, where the Audubons were staying. Drake (1873), p. 275; Warren (1860) I, p. 364; *Massachusetts, Town and Vital Records, 1620–1988, Interments by Undertakers of Boston*, 25 Dec. 1859, www.ancestry.com (accessed 22 Sept. 2013).

18. *OB* II, p. xviii; Stimpson (1833), p. 32, 260. Dr. George Parkman (1791–1849) was born into a well-to-do Boston mercantile family. He graduated from Harvard in 1809 and was a member of the Hasty Pudding Club. He went on to receive his Master of Arts degree from Harvard in 1812 and his medical degree from Aberdeen University the following year. Harvard (1895), pp. 120; Hasty-Pudding (1841), p. 7. Through inheritance and marriage, he became one of the wealthiest men in Boston, eventually abandoning his medical practice in favor of overseeing his significant investments in land and commercial property around the city. Patton (2000), pp. 42–43; Schama (1990), pp. 17, 23. However, as of 1833, he still maintained a private practice at 2 Cambridge Street, next door to his home at 1 Cambridge Street. Stimpson (1833), p. 32, 260. Audubon scholar Waldemar Fries claims that Parkman taught at Harvard's medical school. Not so. Cf. Fries (1973), p. 68; Harvard (1895), pp.

29–32. However, in 1845, Parkman donated land on North Grove Street across from Massachusetts General Hospital for Harvard to construct a new building for what was then known as the Massachusetts Medical College. Patton (2000), p. 42; Traux (1968), p. 204.

Audubon first met Parkman in 1832 when his family arrived in Boston. In his Introduction to Vol. II of the *OB*, Audubon wrote of the warm welcome he had received and the many "estimable friends whose society afforded me so much pleasure in that beautiful city. . . . But besides these honourable individuals whom I have taken the liberty of mentioning, many others I could speak of with delight, and one I would point out in particular, as he to whom my deepest gratitude is due, one whom I cannot omit mentioning, because, of all the good and estimable, he it is whose remembrance is most dear to me—that generous friend is GEORGE PARKMAN." *OB* II, pp. xvii–xviii. Parkman eventually became Audubon's agent in Boston for *BOA*, although the timing of this arrangement is not entirely clear. See, e.g., JJA, Boston to VGA, London, 1 Apr. 1833 (APS), *Letters* I, p. 204; JJA, Boston to John Bachman, Charleston, 19 Feb. 1833 (Harvard (53)), *Letters* I, p. 197.

On November 23, 1849, Parkman was murdered over an outstanding debt owed by John White Webster, the Erving Professor of Chemistry and Mineralogy at Harvard. Parkman's dismembered body was discovered by a suspicious janitor beneath the floor of Webster's lab. Webster was tried in what was then considered "the trial of the century" and, despite professing his innocence, was convicted. He was sentenced to death and confessed as part of an appeal. His appeal was denied, and he was hanged on August 30, 1850. Patton (2000), pp. 40–47; Harvard (1895), p. 28.

19. Richard Harlan, M.D., Philadelphia to JJA, New York, 23 Mar. 1833 (Yale, Box 4, Folder 173).

20. Ford (1988), p. 303; JJA, New York to Robert Havell Jr., London, 20 Apr. 1833 (Harvard (54)), *Letters* I, p. 213; LGA, Boston to VGA, London, 4 Feb. 1833 (Yale, Box 1, Folder 18). According to Lucy's letter of February 4, 1833, cited here, it was felt that John would be skilled enough in perhaps a year to assume the responsibility for complet-ing the work if something happened to Audubon. He clearly was not in a position to do so yet.

21. JJA, Eastport to VGA, London, 31 May 1833, *Letters* I, pp. 232–233.

22. JJA, Eastport to LBA, New York, 19 May 1833 (Princeton, Box 2, Folder 18), *Letters* I, p. 225.

23. Bakewell (1911), p. 36. See also, Harwood & Durant (1985), p. 63; Durant & Harwood (1980), p. 295. This quote about Audubon from one of his in-laws appears without attribution in an address given to the Louisiana Historical Society in 1910 by Audubon's nephew the Reverend Alexander Gordon Bakewell (1822–1920). Bakewell was the fourth child of Lucy Audubon's younger brother Thomas W. Bakewell, suggesting that the comment may have originated with the pastor's father. Bakewell (1896), p. 39. Rev. Bakewell, whose earliest recollections of his famous uncle were from his childhood, told the audience that "It was the common talk of the family that James—that is, Audubon—had no business capacity, no practicability about him, unsuccessful in all his undertakings, always in pecuniary want, and his family often in dire distress for the necessities of life." Bakewell (1911), p. 36. However, by the time Bakewell was ten years old, Audubon was being celebrated on both sides of the Atlantic, so what he had heard about his uncle's financial difficulties was probably after the fact.

24. In a brief autobiography penned for his sons during a trip down the Mississippi River by flatboat in the fall of 1820, Audubon wrote two lines that were subsequently obliterated with ink by a descendant and are believed to have acknowledged his illegitimacy. Arthur (1937), pp. 118–119. In the early 1940s, an examination of this passage with infra-red photography by the Harvard Museum of Comparative Zoology, the institutional holder of the journal, failed to recover the lost lines. Christy (1942), pp. 450–451. It remains to be seen if more modern forensic technology might prove successful.

25. The discovery of the timing and circumstances of Audubon's nativity was made by his first serious biographer, Francis Hobart Herrick, a Professor of Biology at Western Reserve University, now Case Western Reserve University, in Cleveland. Prior to the publication of Herrick's *Audubon the Naturalist* in 1917, the Audubon family had

sought to hide his illegitimacy by suggesting various birth dates for him and insisting he had been born in Louisiana. See, e.g., *AHJ* I, p. 6 ("he may have been born anywhere between 1772 and 1783, and in the face of this uncertainty the date usually given, May 5, 1780, may be accepted, though the true one is no doubt earlier"); L. Audubon (1869), p. 14 ("The naturalist was born on his father's plantation, near New Orleans, Louisiana, May 4th 1780."). Herrick located records of Audubon's father in France, which included copies of documents from Les Cayes that definitively established the date and place of the naturalist's birth. Herrick (1917) I, pp. vii-x.

As an illegitimate child, Audubon was not permitted to take his father's surname, so he was given the name of his mother. Alice Ford concludes from her research of genealogical records located in France that the surname of Audubon's mother was actually Rabine. Ford (1988), pp. 466–467. Ford and some later Audubon scholars follow the convention of using this spelling in reference to Audubon's birth name. However, the multiple wills of his adoptive parents all refer to him as Jean Rabin or Rabain. Herrick (1938) I, p. 62 and II, Appendix I, Document Nos. 13–18, pp. 360–368; Ford (1988), pp. 482–484. Moreover, Audubon referred to himself as "Jean Rabin" in a power-of-attorney issued to his brother-in-law, Gabriel Loyen du Puigaudeau, on July 26, 1817. Herrick (1938) I, p. 64, note 16. Thus, the evidence is compelling that Audubon and his family considered his surname at birth to be Rabin, and this is how he is referred to in the text, although his mother retains her proper name.

26. Streshinsky (1993), pp. 8–9.

27. Ford (1988), pp. 21–22. Audubon's mother, Jeanne Rabine, was born on March 15, 1758, in Les Mazures, France. Rhodes (2004), p. 439, note 4; Ford (1988), p. 466. The description of her as an "Extraordinary beautifull Woman" comes from Audubon's earliest surviving autobiography, written for his sons in his journal on November 28, 1820. He indicated that he had been told this, presumably by his father. Audubon (1999), p. 30; Corning (1929a), p. 44. See also, Arthur (1937), p. 118.

28. Ford (1964), pp. 4–5. In the second edition of her biography, Ford states that there was only a twelve year discrepancy in the ages of Jean Audubon and his wife, Anne Moynet. Ford (1988), pp.

15–16. However, in the Appendix to that edition, she provides a transcription of the Act of Marriage recorded on August 24, 1772, in the Parish Register, Paimboeuf, which reflects that Jean was twenty-eight and Anne forty-two when they exchanged their vows. Ibid., pp. 480–481.

29. Ford (1988), p. 18.

30. Jeanne Rabine was twenty-seven when she gave birth to Audubon, not twenty-five as suggested by Hart-Davis. Hart-Davis (2004), p. 21. She died on November 10, 1785, and was buried the following day at the Church of Notre-Dame de l'Assomption in Les Cayes. Ford (1988), pp. 22–23, 466.

31. Ford (1988), pp. 23–24.

32. Ford (1988), pp. 23, 26–27. Herrick indicates that the Mill Grove property consisted of 284½ acres. Herrick (1938) I, p. 105. Ford's review of the property records in Norristown, PA, led her to conclude the property comprised 285¼ acres. Ford (1988), p. 473.

Hart-Davis incorrectly describes the estate as consisting of only 200 acres and states that Jean Audubon bought it "sight unseen." Hart-Davis (2004), p. 22. This appears to have been derived from a statement by Ford in her biography: "The potential of wealth [from a vein of lead] beneath the 200 or more acres of Vaux Hill attracted Audubon, sight unseen, far more than its arable soil." Ford (1988), pp. 26–27. However, a careful reading of Ford makes it clear that Jean Audubon was in the Philadelphia area looking for property and subsequently visited Mill Grove.

33. Ford (1988), pp. 478–479.

34. Audubon's early biographers believed that John James and his half-sister Rose (or Rosa) traveled together with their father to the U.S. and then France in 1789. See, e.g., Herrick (1938) I, p. 57; Arthur (1937), p. 21. However, Ford burrowed into the official vessel passenger lists in the Archives Nationales in Paris and uncovered documents that establish the two children left Saint-Domingue three years apart—John James in 1788 and Rose in 1791—and neither child was accompanied across the Atlantic by Jean Audubon. Ford (1988), pp. 24–30, 477–478. This was a marked revision of the conclusion she had reached in the first edition of her Audubon biography, published in 1964, where she speculated that the two children arrived

together in 1791. Ford (1964), p. 22–23. More recent biographers have overlooked or confused Ford's important research on this issue. Rhodes follows Ford's earlier chronology in his biography and notes that no documentary evidence of Audubon's departure from Saint-Domingue has been found. Rhodes (2004), p. 6 and note, p. 440. Streshinsky relies on Ford's later research for her discussion of the younger Audubon's arrival in France yet incorrectly states that Rose followed him to France in 1789. Streshinsky (1993), pp. xvii, 13.

35. Ford (1988), pp. 35–36, 459. As an illegitimate child, the young Audubon was unable to assume his father's surname or inherit property. That changed when he was formally adopted in 1794. At that time, Audubon received the given name Fougère, which means "fern," apparently to appease Republican officials who had banned the Catholic Church and took a dim view of naming children after the saints. Ibid. See also, Rhodes (2004), pp. 4–5. The Act of Adoption, which can be found in Herrick (1938) I, pp. 59–60 and II, Appendix I, Document No. 2, pp. 328–329, establishes that the adoption occurred on March 7, 1794. Rhodes erroneously places the adoption in 1793. Rhodes (2004), p. 4. See also, Audubon (2008), p. xv. The chronology of Audubon's life provided by Blaugrund and Stebbins is similarly mistaken in placing the adoption in 1789. Blaugrund & Stebbins (1993), p. 69.

Doubtless, at the time of his adoption the boy was already known as Jean Jacques to his father and stepmother. Indeed, when he was ultimately baptized on October 23, 1800, the church records identify him as "Jean Jacques-Fougère, adopted son of Jean Audubon and Anne Moynet, his spouse." Ford (1988), p. 39.

36. Harwood & Durant (1985), p. 62. As Audubon described it in his autobiographical essay *Myself*, "The school I went to was none of the best; my private teachers were the only means through which I acquired the least benefit." *AHJ* I, p. 12.

37. Ford (1988), p. 32; Harwood & Durant (1985), p. 62; *AHJ* I, p. 12.

38. Rhodes (2004), p. 5; Harwood & Durant (1985), p. 62. See also, *AHJ* I, p. 51.

39. *AHJ* I, pp. 12, 15.

40. Jacques-Louis David (1748–1825) was the leader of the French Neoclassical movement, court

painter to Louis XVI, a Republican supporter of the French Revolution, and, later, court painter to Napoleon. Audubon made the claim that he studied under David repeatedly after his arrival in America in 1803, both to members of his family and to the public. Ford (1988), p. 51; Sheehan (1979), pp. 87–88. Audubon's wife, Lucy, was obviously aware of the David claim and evidently believed it, as reflected in a letter she wrote from Louisville to her English cousin Euphemia Gifford on April 1, 1821: "The various losses and misfortunes of my husbands affairs you have probably heard of and for the last year he [h]as supported us by his tallent [*sic*] in drawing and painting which he learnt from David as a recreation in better times." LBA, Louisville to Euphemia Gifford, Duffield Bank near Derby, England, 1 Apr. 1821 (Princeton, Box 1, Folder 10). When he was in Manchester, England, in September 1826, Audubon wrote in his journal of a visit with some friends: "Now, Lucy, I am advising about Drawing and I am quite sure that my old master David never [had] an Easier Task." Audubon (2011), p. 196. Cf. Ford (1987), p. 227. While visiting Paris in the fall of 1828, he recorded in his journal: "To-day I was told that Gerard, the great Gerard, the pupil of my old master David, wished to see me and my works." L. Audubon (1869), p. 174. Audubon also made the claim to the public in the *OB*. *OB* I, p. viii. See also, L. Audubon (1869), p. 26. If this claim was false, which now is indisputable, it speaks volumes about Audubon's character and the extent to which he kept certain secrets hidden even from his family.

41. Audubon (1999), p. 753; Audubon (1979), p. 21. The facts and arguments on both sides of the claim that Audubon received instruction from Jacques-Louis David are laid out neatly by Gloria K. Fiero in Dormon (1990), pp. 41–45. However, the weight of the evidence indicates that Audubon was never professionally trained by David. Additional evidence, uncovered during the research for this book, lays to rest any possibility that Audubon was telling the truth. See Chapter 4, notes 164–167, *infra*.

42. Ford (1988), pp. 28, 33–34, 36–38. In his autobiographical essay *Myself*, Audubon suggested that his involvement with the French Navy occurred when he returned to France from America between 1805 and 1806, years after it actually did. Audubon

(1999), pp. 780–781; *AHJ* I, p. 24. Compare this chronology to Audubon's autobiographical sketch in his November 28, 1820, journal entry where he stated that he entered the navy at the age of fourteen, which would have been 1799 or 1800. Audubon (1999), p. 30; Corning (1929a), p. 44. The extant records in Les Archives de la Marine at Rochefort-sur-Mer demonstrate that Audubon's recollection was faulty on both counts. Audubon entered naval service in August 1796. Ford (1988), pp. 38–39, 459; Ford (1987), p. 247, note 8.

43. Ford (1988), pp. 36–39; Ford (1987), p. 247, note 8. Herrick mistakenly indicates that Audubon only stayed at Rochefort for a year. Herrick (1938) I, p. 96. Rhodes reaches the same conclusion, relying largely on Audubon's autobiographical sketch in his 1820 journal. Rhodes (2004), p. 30; Audubon (1999), p. 30; Corning (1929a), p. 44. However, neither Herrick nor Rhodes evidently examined the official historical records in Les Archives de la Marine at Rochefort-sur-Mer as Ford did. And, contrary to Rhodes's assertion that Audubon returned to Nantes with his father in January 1801, when Jean Audubon retired from active naval duty, the young Audubon had left the navy and arrived back home in Nantes by March 1800. He underwent a baptismal in Nantes on October 23, 1800. Ford (1988), pp. 39–40, 459.

44. Ford (1988), pp. 38–39; Ford (1987), p. 247, note 8.

45. Audubon (1999), p. 768; *AHJ* I, p. 11.

CHAPTER 1: AMERICA, MY COUNTRY

1. Ford (1988), p. 42.

2. Ford (1988), p. 42; *AHJ* I, p. 15. In recounting Audubon's voyage across the Atlantic from France in 1803, Rhodes writes that when the vessel reached the Grand Banks off the coast of Newfoundland, Audubon "scattered ship's biscuit on the deck" and drew "migrating brown titlarks (American Pipits) down from the heavens to feed." Rhodes (2004), p. 3. Rhodes misreads Audubon's description of this incident, which the naturalist described in the *OB*. What actually occurred is that the birds, fatigued by their migratory exertions and far out to sea, landed aboard the ship to rest and only then were attracted to Audubon's offerings. As Audubon

explained, "They came on board wearied, and so hungry that the crumbs of biscuit thrown to them were picked up with the greatest activity." *OB* I, p. 50. The phenomenon of migrating birds landing aboard vessels off the coast is well known to sailors. Able (1999), p. 41.

3. *AHJ* I, pp. 15–16. In his autobiographical sketch *Myself*, written around 1835 and later published by his granddaughter Maria Rebecca Audubon, Audubon indicated that the boardinghouse where Capt. Smith took him to recover from yellow fever was situated in Morristown, NJ. Audubon (1999), p. 772; *AHJ* I, pp. 15–16. Lucy Audubon, who evidently used the original manuscript for *Myself* as a source in compiling a biography of her husband after his death, also referred to Morristown. L. Audubon (1869), p. 17.

The first biographer to question the Morristown reference was Alice Ford, who flatly declares without a source citation that the boardinghouse was actually situated in Norristown, PA, about five miles from Mill Grove. Ford (1988), p. 45 and note 1, p. 434; Ford (1964), p. 41, note 1. Subsequent biographers have followed Ford's lead. See, e.g., Rhodes (2004), p. 6; Streshinsky (1993), p. 6. Cf. Souder (2004), p. 65; Adams (1966), p. 34 (sidestepping the issue by stating that Capt. Smith simply took him by carriage out of the city without commenting on where he was taken).

For a number of reasons, I take issue with Ford on this point. Audubon stated in *Myself* that Capt. Smith "took particular charge of me, removed me to Morristown, N.J., and placed me under the care" of the Quaker women who nursed him back to health. *AHJ* I, pp. 15–16. The implication is that Smith handled this responsibility himself. If true, it seems unlikely that Smith would have taken the time to leave his vessel docked in Manhattan to travel with the sick young man almost to Philadelphia, a hundred miles and more than a day away, when Morristown was just across the Hudson River. More critically, Smith was no doubt eager to place his ill charge in capable hands as expeditiously as possible. "Local Newspapers in 1800," *The New York Times*, Vol. XLIX, No. 15,599, p. 8, col. 3 (Sunday, 7 Jan. 1900)(In 1800, "[i]t took two and a half to three days to reach Philadelphia.").

Another autobiographical essay authored by

Audubon, which appears in his Mississippi River journal on November 28, 1820, also fails to support Ford's thesis. Audubon wrote that "I Landed in *New York*, took the Yellow Fever and did Not reach Philadelphia for Three Months." Audubon (1999), p. 30. Cf. Corning (1929a), p. 45. Unlike *Myself*, the holographic manuscript for the Mississippi River journal still exists and is in the Ernst Mayer Library of the Museum of Comparative Zoology at Harvard. This statement clearly demonstrates that he was not taken there immediately as Ford asserts.

Additionally, Lucy, who knew Audubon's personal history as well as anyone and presumably knew precisely where he had stayed, who lived near Norristown for several years prior to her marriage and would not have confused the two, and who could certainly decipher her husband's handwriting in *Myself*, used "Morristown," not "Norristown," in her biography.

It is true that Lucy's biography contains multiple errors. Even the date of her marriage is misstated. But it is noteworthy that when Lucy took it upon herself to republish the biography in the U.S. the year after the appearance of the 1868 English edition, edited by Robert Buchanan, she corrected Buchanan's erroneous statement that Mill Grove was situated on the road to "Morristown" by changing it to "Norristown." Yet she retained the reference to Morristown only two pages earlier in connection with the location of the Quaker boardinghouse. Cf. L. Audubon (1869), pp. 17, 19; Buchanan (1868), pp. 6, 8.

4. Rhodes (2004), p. 6.

5. Rhodes (2004), pp. 9–10; Audubon (1999), p. 30; Ford (1988), pp. 46–49, 51; Corning (1929a), p. 45. Lucy was born on January 18, 1787. Delatte (1982), p. 2; Bakewell (1896), p. 28. Thus, when she met Audubon for the first time on January 16, 1804, she was two days shy of her seventeenth birthday. Rhodes (2004), p. 9. Ford erroneously states that "In two days she would be eighteen." Ford (1988), p. 49. Souder, relying on Ford, also adds a year to her age. Souder (2004), p. 68 and note, p. 297.

The Bakewell family's six children were: Lucy Green Bakewell (1787–1874); Thomas Woodhouse Bakewell (1788–1874); Eliza Bakewell (1790–1853); Sarah Bakewell (1792–1842); Ann Bakewell (1795–1870); and William Gifford Bakewell (1799–1871).

Tom and Audubon shared the same birthday, April 26. Bakewell (1896), pp. 27–28. See also, Palmer (2004), pp. 194–195.

6. Audubon (2011), p. 119; Ford (1988), p. 49; Ford (1987), p. 150; Durant & Harwood (1980), p. 242. Virtually all of Audubon's biographers erroneously assert that Lucy had gray eyes, evidently based on the comments of a contemporary, Martha Pope, who met Lucy around 1824 and years later remarked in a memoir: "Mrs. Audubon was not handsome. Her face was spoiled by her nose, which was short and turned up. She had fine dark gray eyes shaded by long dark lashes. Expression was her chief attraction. She was very gentle and intelligent. Her whole appearance impressed me with respect and admiration." Arthur (1937), p. 298. See also, Rhodes (2004), p. 9; Ford (1988), p. 49; Delatte (1982), p. 15.

However, Audubon indicated that her eyes were blue. In a passage in his 1826 journal, which he wrote as a continuing letter to Lucy during his visit to England and Scotland to find an engraver for his portfolio, he described Mrs. Richard Rathbone, the wife of one of his new-found Liverpool friends, as having "an Eye just as blue as thine." Audubon (2011), p. 119. Cf. Ford (1987), p. 150. It should be noted that Martha Pope's memory was not infallible. She also recalled that Audubon's eyes were blue when there is overwhelming evidence they were hazel. Arthur (1937), p. 298. See also, note 12, *infra*.

Lucy's principal biographer, Carolyn Delatte, describes Lucy's nose as "a bit too long and low bridged," which together with her thin lips gave her a "rather severe look" as she aged. Delatte (1982), p. 14. The earliest extant image of Lucy is a silhouette rendered by Thomas Edwards in 1825. Rhodes (2004), p. 9; Delatte (1982), p. 150. It evidences the slightly turned-up nose that Martha Pope recalled. The earliest existing portrait of Lucy is a miniature painted by Frederick Cruickshank in London in 1831, when she would have been forty-four years old. In this image, her nose appears long and wide in relation to her face.

7. Rhodes (2004), pp. 9–10; Streshinsky (1993), p. 28; Ford (1988), p. 49; Delatte (1982), p. 14; Durant & Harwood (1980), p. 242.

8. Ford (1988), p. 49. Ford states that the first meeting of Audubon and Lucy Bakewell occurred

on January 16, 1804. She does not identify the
source of this date, but it appears to have come
from the journal of William Bakewell, Lucy's father,
which Ford consulted as part of her research. In
the second edition of her biography, published in
1988, Ford indicated that the journal was part of the
Estate of Susan Lewis Shaffer of Cincinnati. Ford
(1988), p. 435, Ch. II, note 5; Ch. III, note 2. Shaffer
was the granddaughter of Lucy's youngest brother,
William G. Bakewell. Bakewell (1896), p. 44.

9. L. Audubon (1869), p. 18.

10. Ibid., p. 19. An altered version of this passage
describing Audubon's first meeting with Lucy Bakewell appears in *Myself*, the Audubon autobiography
that was edited and likely rewritten by Maria Audubon before she published it in *Scribner's Magazine*
and later *AHJ*. *AHJ* I, p. 18; M. Audubon (1893),
p. 278.

11. *AHJ*, p. 11 Audubon's approximate height is
derived from U.S. State Department records in the
National Archives, which reflect that his 1830 passport, issued on March 19, 1830, when he was forty-
four, listed his height as 5'8½". Dallett (1960) p. 93.
See also, Ford (1988), p. 486. Although Audubon
was often prone to exaggeration when he wrote
about himself for the public, he was generally truthful in statements he made in official government or
legal documents. The height given in this record is
also consistent with the size of clothing he wore during his Missouri River expedition of 1843, now in
the collection of the American Museum of Natural
History in New York. Ford (1988), p. 486.

As a younger man, Audubon could have been
marginally taller given the propensity of humans to
lose height as they age. However, he almost certainly was never as tall as 5'10" or 5'10½", which
he claimed in separate autobiographical sketches.
In *Myself*, he stated, "In personal appearance my
father and I were of the same height and stature, say
about five feet ten inches, erect, and with muscles of
steel;" *AHJ* I, p. 11. The Robert Buchanan and Lucy
Audubon biographies quote from a different Audubon manuscript in which he described his height
and appearance: "I measured five feet ten and a half
inches, was of a fair mien, and quite a handsome
figure; large, dark, and rather sunken eyes, light-
coloured eyebrows, aquiline nose, and a fine set of
teeth; hair, fine texture and luxuriant, divided and

passing down behind each ear in luxuriant ringlets
as far as the shoulders." L. Audubon (1869), pp.
28–29; Buchanan (1868), p. 18. See also, Streshinsky (1993), p. 45; Arthur (1937), p. 36. Here, speaking of his height, Audubon embellished the truth.

12. The color of Audubon's eyes, which are described variously by different observers, was hazel,
as reflected in his 1830 U.S. passport. Dallett (1960),
p. 93. See also, Sage (1917), pp. 239–240. His extant
portraits, including those by his son John W. Audubon, also reflect that he had hazel eyes.

13. Arthur (1937), p. 298. See also, Durant &
Harwood (1980), p. 238.

14. *AHJ* I, p. 75. See also, Arthur (1937), p. 37.
In *AHJ*, Maria Audubon wrote that David Pawling
made the quoted statement about Audubon's skating and dancing in January 1805. I have been unable
to locate the original holograph of the letter or journal in which Pawling's vivid description appears.
Regardless, there is substantial reason to question
the validity of the given date. Audubon moved to
Mill Grove in November 1803, and it is likely he
electrified his neighbors with his amazing skill on
ice during his first winter there. This would point
to Pawling's remark having actually been made in
early 1804. Similarly, it is incomprehensible that
Pawling, presumably a descendant of the brothers
Henry and John Pawling, who acquired large tracts
of land along Perkiomen Creek where they settled
in the early 18th century, would have neither seen
nor heard of Audubon for more than a year after the
young Frenchman had taken up residence at Mill
Grove. Leach (1918), pp. 9–25. Further, in the early
part of December 1804, Audubon became seriously
ill and was bedridden well into January 1805 at Fatland Ford, the home of his future wife, Lucy Bakewell. Rhodes (2004), pp. 18–19; Ford (1988), p. 57.
Alice Ford, whose biography benefits from the contents of a manuscript journal kept by Lucy's father,
William Bakewell, writes that Audubon was unable
to get back on a horse until February 6, 1805. Ford
(1988), p. 58 and note 2, p. 435. It is highly doubtful that he had recovered sufficiently to have been
back on the ice and dancing up a storm the month
before. Ford apparently agrees. Ford (1988), p. 52.
Cf. Rhodes (2004), pp. 22–23 (accepting the January 1805 date).

The dubious date ascribed to the Pawling quotation raises additional questions about its origins. To begin with, I have not located a David Pawling in the 1800 U.S. census for Montgomery County, PA, where Mill Grove was situated and where descendants of the Pawling brothers continued to reside. The census at that time listed only the names of the heads of households, which would indicate that if David Pawling lived in the area he did not lead a household. However, none of the published genealogies for this line of the Pawling family that I consulted identify a David Pawling in this time frame. Leach (1918); Pawling (1905); Kitts (1903). I find this troubling, although it is perhaps not determinative given the difficulty and vagaries of genealogical research.

More critically, if Pawling was indeed a scion of one of the original Pawling brothers and lived nearby, it is hard to accept that he had never before heard the name Audubon. Jean Audubon acquired the Mill Grove property in 1789 and owned the estate for fifteen years before Pawling purportedly made his comment. This region was not densely populated, and the established families must have known the details of every land transaction in their vicinity, especially of a significant parcel the size of Mill Grove. Given Maria Audubon's documented history of doctoring her grandfather's letters and journals, it is certainly not unreasonable to question whether she invented the quotation. The only alternate explanation that comes to mind is that David Pawling did not live in the area and was simply visiting a relative when he first met the young Audubon. Further research on this point is certainly merited.

If Pawling's observations were made in January 1804, Audubon would have been eighteen at the time as reflected in the text. Harwood and Durant reference the Pawling quote and state that Audubon was twenty years old in January 1805 when Maria claimed it was made. Harwood & Durant (1985), p. 62. Even if the date given by Maria was accurate, Audubon would then have been only nineteen. He would celebrate his twentieth birthday in April of that year.

Notwithstanding the lingering questions about the Pawling quote, his putative comment about the striking quality of Audubon's eyes rings true. This was an opinion shared by numerous observers. See Prologue, note 1, *supra*.

15. Audubon (1999) p. 777; *AHJ* I, p. 20. Audubon does not provide a date he shot Tom's hat out of the air while skating on Perkiomen Creek, but I believe that it likely took place in the winter of 1804 for the reasons discussed in note 14, *supra*. Ford is of the same opinion. Ford (1988), p. 52.

16. Audubon (1999) p. 777; *AHJ* I, p. 20.

17. Rhodes (2004), pp. 13–14; Audubon (1999), p. 760; Audubon (1979), p. 16.

18. Rhodes (2004), p. 14; Audubon (1999), pp. 760–761; Audubon (1979), pp. 16–17.

19. Souder (2004), pp. 71–72; Audubon (1999), pp. 760–761; Audubon (1979), pp. 16–17. There is no way to know precisely when Audubon developed his use of a specimen board on which to pin the birds he intended to draw. However, from his account of riding out to Norristown early one morning and swimming in the Schuylkill River while he waited for the stores to open, it appears that this must have occurred sometime in the very late spring, summer or early fall of 1804, when the river would have been warm enough for a swim. By the spring of 1805, Audubon was in France, and he did not return to Mill Grove until June 1806.

20. Audubon (1999), p. 754; Audubon (1979), p. 22.

21. *OB* II, pp. 122–129. Audubon claimed that he found the silver threads on the legs of the Pewees (Eastern Phoebes) the following spring of 1805, and Audubon's biographers have generally accepted this story without question. Rhodes (2004), p. 37; Herrick (1938) I, pp. 107–108. Cf. Adams (1966), p. 490. However, Audubon's chronology does not square with the facts of avian migration. The Eastern Phoebe is a migratory species in the mid-Atlantic region and reaches Pennsylvania in the middle of March. Sutton (1928), p. 88. Audubon left Mill Grove for New York on February 28, 1805, and sailed for France about two weeks later. Ford (1988), pp. 58–59, 459. Thus, Audubon was not at Mill Grove when the banded birds would have returned to their breeding grounds in 1805, the season after they were banded. He did not return to America until May 28, 1806, and did not see Mill Grove again until June 4, 1806. Ibid., pp. 65, 459. Therefore, Audubon's narrative includes a nesting season in 1805—the one where he claimed that "in the very same nest, two broods were raised"—that

he did not, in fact, witness. This is not to question Audubon's statement that he banded Phoebe nestlings. He could have done so in 1804 and observed the banded birds when he returned to Mill Grove in the late spring of 1806. Adams (1966), p. 490. But his account in the *OB* takes substantial liberty with the truth.

Even among those Audubon's biographers who have recognized the problems with his chronology, there has been confusion about his bird banding experiment. Ford and Streshinsky assert that he banded the adults and found the adult male with a silver thread when he returned to the cave in 1806 following his trip to France. Streshinsky (1993), p. 46; Ford (1988), p. 66. In fact, Audubon only banded the nestlings. *OB* II, p. 126. Rhodes also misreads Audubon with respect to the two banded birds he purportedly found the spring after he attached the silver wires to their legs. Rhodes writes: "The following spring, shortly before he left for France, Audubon found two recent arrivals that still carried silver threads nesting in a Mill Grove grain shed." Rhodes (2004) at p. 37. However, Audubon made it clear that the banded birds were found among multiple nearby nesting pairs, and he did not specify the location of their nests as Rhodes declares. *OB* II, pp. 126-127.

22. Leahy (2004), p. 38; Herrick (1938) I, p. 107.

23. Rhodes (2004), pp. 13, 15-16; Ford (1988) p. 53.

24. Rhodes (2004), p. 24; Ford (1988), pp. 54, 58-59, 473. Audubon left New York aboard the *Hope* on March 12, 1805.

25. Ford (1988), pp. 63, 473. Rhodes states that Jean Audubon sold Claude Rozier half of his "doubtful remaining share of his Les Cayes plantation." Rhodes (2004), p. 28. The sale was actually of one half of Jean Audubon's remaining half of Mill Grove, the other half having been earlier committed to Francis Dacosta. Streshinsky (1993), p. 40; Ford (1988), pp. 63, 473; Herrick (1938) I, p. 115. See also, Power of Attorney issued by Jean Audubon, Anne Moinet Audubon, and Claude Francis Rozier to Jean Audubon and Ferdinand Rozier, dated April 4, 1806. Herrick (1938) II, p. 351 (empowering Audubon and Rozier to "govern, conduct, and administer the half, belonging to the grantors, of the farm of Mill Grove in Pennsylvania"). Duff

Hart-Davis also misstates the facts, asserting that "To raise some money, Jean Audubon sold his share in the Mill Grove plantation to a friend, Claude Rozier." Hart-Davis (2004), p. 29.

26. Ford (1988), pp. 54-55.

27. Ford (1988), p. 63; Herrick (1938) II, p. 347.

28. Herrick (1938) I, pp. 133-134; Ford (1988), pp. 63, 65; Rhodes (2004), p. 31. Audubon's passport identified his birthplace as Louisiana, a falsehood that he would later adopt to shield his illegitimacy. See, e.g., *AHJ* I, p. 7. The voyage from Nantes was aboard the *Polly*, commanded by Capt. S. Sammis. Streshinsky spells the name "Samis," although Herrick's biography contains a copy of the holographic receipt from Rozier's papers signed "Sammis." Cf. Streshinksy (1993), pp. 43-45; Herrick (1938) I, p. 134.

Audubon's biographers have been unable to agree on when the *Polly* arrived in New York in May 1806. Herrick, Ford, and Hart-Davis state that the ship reached port on Tuesday, May 28, 1806. Hart-Davis (2004), p. 30; Ford (1988), pp. 65, 486; Herrick (1938) I, p. 134. Rhodes claims it arrived a day earlier, on Monday, May 27. Rhodes (2004), p. 32. Arthur declares that the ship landed on Sunday, May 26. Arthur (1937), p. 47. And Adams asserts the partners landed in "the first week of May, 1806," seemingly unaware that an extant letter from Lucy's uncle, Benjamin Bakewell, to his English cousin Euphemia Gifford announcing Audubon's arrival had been misdated May 6 when it should have been June 6. Cf. Rhodes (2004), pp. 32-33 and note, p. 442; Adams (1966), p. 71.

The evidence is not definitive. Ferdinand Rozier's diary states that they "arrived at New York on Tuesday, the 27th of May." Herrick (1938) I, p. 187, note 2. The day and date are inconsistent, so it is impossible to determine if he meant Monday the 27th or Tuesday the 28th. Herrick's biography contains a copy of the holographic receipt for payment of the cost of their passage written and signed by Capt. Sammis, which Rozier saved. At the bottom of the receipt in a hand other than Sammis's is the notation "New York May 28, 1806." It seems logical to presume this was written by Rozier, although Herrick was uncertain of that. Herrick (1938) I, p. 135, note 9. It would not appear that the receipt was issued by Capt. Sammis on that date because there is an endorsement on the back of the receipt by Rozier reflecting that the young men had made their payment on April 11, 1806, the day before they sailed. Ibid. Presumably, the receipt was issued upon payment. To further confuse matters, more than a year later, Audubon filed a declaration in the U.S. District Court in Philadelphia that expressed his intention to become a naturalized citizen and stated that he had recently returned from France "on or about the twenty Seventh Day of May" 1807. Dallett (1960), pp. 89–90. However, Audubon had a poor memory for dates, and in the same document he asserted he had first arrived in the United States in 1802 rather than 1803. See note 34, *infra*.

Based on the notation on the receipt, it seems most likely that the *Polly* reached New York on Tuesday, May 28, 1806, and this date is used in the text.

29. Ford (1988), p. 65; Rhodes (2004), p. 27. Several of the drawings Audubon prepared during his visit to France in 1805–1806 were later sold by Audubon in 1824 to Edward Harris, a well-to-do farmer from Moorestown, NJ, who became a close friend and benefactor. The drawings are now in the collection at Harvard University and are the subject of a superb book published by Harvard University Press. Audubon (2008).

30. Ford (1988), pp. 65–66; JJA, New York to Jean Audubon, Nantes, 24 Apr. 1807, Herrick (1938) I, p. 160.

31. Rhodes (2004), p. 37.

32. Ford (1988), pp. 65–68, 473; Montgomery County Deed Book, No. 22, p. 377. Ford writes that Dacosta agreed to pay a total of $9,640.30 for the 113½ acre parcel of Mill Grove. The roughly 171 acres of arable land on the other side of the Perkiomen Creek were to be retained by the senior Audubon and Rozier, through their agents. Dacosta's down payment of $4,580 was covered by a bond rather than cash. Dacosta also purportedly agreed to pay an additional $5,000 in proceeds from the lead mine and half of the mine's future grosses. Ford (1988), p. 68.

Herrick's biography contains a transcription of a letter written by Rozier to his father on September 12, 1806, shortly before the real estate transaction was finalized, in which he recounted signifi-

cantly different terms as to the sales price. He stated that Dacosta was to pay $800 to Jean Audubon, with interest, in three years from the date of sale. In addition, Dacosta was to pay $4,000 from the first products of the lead mine. Herrick (1938) I, pp. 149–150. In a footnote, Herrick indicates that Audubon and Rozier sold the remaining half interest in the Mill Grove property to Dacosta & Company for $9,640.33. Ibid., p. 149, note 3. According to Ford, the sale actually was made to Dacosta, not Dacosta & Company, and was for $9,640.30. Ford (1988), pp. 474–476.

33. Rhodes (2004), p. 14; Ford (1988), p. 68.

34. Dallett (1960), pp. 89–90. In his declaration of intention to become a naturalized citizen, submitted in 1806, Audubon admitted that he had been born "at Aux Cayes in the island of St Domingo" but stated that he had been born in 1783 rather than 1785. He also erred in stating the date he originally arrived in New York, claiming it was "on or about the twenty Seventh Day of August one thousand Eight hundred and two" rather than 1803.

35. Ford (1988), p. 71.

36. *AHJ* I, p. 28.

37. Rhodes (2004), pp. 52, 54; Ford (1988), p. 73; Durant & Harwood (1980), pp. 17–18.

38. Streshinsky (1993), p. 55; Herrick (1938) I, p. 196. Some Audubon scholars differ with Herrick and Streshinsky as to how many people inhabited Louisville when Audubon and Rozier arrived. Ford states that the town numbered "1,300 souls." Ford (1988), p. 72. Keating repeats this claim. Keating (1976), p. 12. Souder concurs, stating that there were "about thirteen hundred citizens." Souder (2004), p. 77. On the other hand, Rhodes asserts there were "about one thousand families" in the settlement, which would place the actual population in the several thousands. Rhodes (2004), p. 42. Other than Souder, who relies on Yater (1979), none of these authors cite a source for their respective statements.

In 1800, there were approximately six hundred people living in Louisville. Herrick (1938) I, p. 196, note 9. In 1805, a visitor to the town indicated that there were "about 200 dwelling houses chiefly wooden . . . some large elegant buildings . . . of brick and stone." Book (1971), p. 186, quoting from Josiah Espy, *Memorandums of a Tour Made by Josiah Espy in the States of Ohio, Kentucky and Indi-*

ana Territory in 1805, p. 15 (Cincinnati, 1870). By the time of the U.S. Census in 1810, the population had increased to 1,357. Of this number, 484 were slaves. U.S. Bureau of the Census (1810), Census Place: *Louisville, Jefferson Co., KY*; Roll: 7, Page: *29*; Image: *00036*. See also, Melish (1818), p. 377. Cf. Book (1971), p. 187 (citing Commissioners Tax Records for 1807, Jefferson County, Kentucky indicating that Louisville had 948 white males of over sixteen years of age and 2,283 blacks). Since Louisville was continuing to grow throughout this decade, it is highly unlikely that the population of the town did not increase between 1807 and 1810. The population was more likely around a thousand when Audubon and Rozier moved there and opened their general store, as Herrick and Streshinsky state.

By comparison, Pittsburgh's population in 1800 was 1,565. Herrick (1938) I, p. 191, note 4. By 1810, it had more than tripled to 4,768 persons. Campbell (1998), Table 4. Cincinnati had 2,540 residents in 1810. Ibid. New Orleans had approximately eight thousand residents in 1803. Allen (1994), p. 53. Seven years later, the U.S. Census recorded a population of 17,242. Campbell (1998), Table 4.

39. Ford (1988), pp. 71–72; Herrick (1938) I, pp. 186–187. The date the partners left Fatland Ford—August 31, 1807—comes from a transcript of Rozier's diary, which was provided to Herrick by Welton A. Rozier, one of Rozier's great-grandsons. Rozier informed Herrick that "the original French notes have been mislaid or lost, but that they were closely followed in this translation, whenever complete. Though numerous verbal changes have been made in the present draft, these have not altered the meaning in any respect." Herrick (1938) I, p. 187, note 2.

However, in their more recent history of the Rozier clan, Mary Rozier Sharp and Louis J. Sharp III published the original transcription of the diary by Rozier's daughter, Felicite Rozier Flamm, not the revised and polished version Herrick apparently received. Sharp (1981), pp. 25–31. Although the Sharps recognize that there are numerous discrepancies in the dates, they propose that Felicite may have been confused by her father's handwriting and use of dates in the French style. The Sharps submit that Audubon and Rozier actually left Philadelphia

a month later, on October 1, 1807, notwithstanding the transcription's opening line: "Left Phil. August 31 1807 for Kentucky with Mr. Audubon." The Sharps explain that problems with finalizing the sale of a portion of Mill Grove had purportedly delayed their departure. Ibid., pp. 24–25. However, for the reasons discussed in note 40, *infra*, I believe the August 31 departure date is correct.

The Benjamin Bakewell account book for this time period, which appears in an Appendix to Herrick's biography, indicates that Audubon & Rozier purchased 'Sundry Merchd^ize'''' valued at $2,482.35 on August 1, 1807. On August 4, Bakewell credited their account with $3,647.29 by their promissory note. The note was due and payable in 8 months, on April 7, 1808. On September 29, 1807, an order for "Powder Horns shot bags &c" was recorded on the Audubon & Rozier account. Herrick (1938) II, pp. 354–355.

On March 19, 1810, William Bakewell, acting as an agent for Audubon and Rozier, sold their 171¾ acres of farmland across the Perkiomen Creek from Mill Grove. Ford (1988), p. 473. Bakewell remitted the proceeds ($7,998.50), less his commission ($160.00), to "Messrs Kinder's," a reference to Robert Kinder & Co., which was one of Benjamin Bakewell's assignees, to pay off money owed on the Audubon & Rozier account. Palmer (2004), p. 19; William Bakewell to Messrs. Audubon & Rozier, Louisville, 10 Apr. 1810, Herrick (1938) I, pp. 199–200. See also, Rhodes (2004), p. 69; Palmer (2004), p. 19; Ford (1988), p. 86.

Ford states that when Audubon visited Fatland Ford in December 1811, William Bakewell made it clear to his son-in-law that "no matter how well the proceeds of the property sale might serve his needs for the new firm [of Audubon & Bakewell, formed earlier that fall by Audubon and his brother-in-law Thomas W. Bakewell], it was to go to the Kinders of New York to pay off the mortgage on the land." Ford (1988), p. 86. This implies that Bakewell had not already forwarded the payment to New York, which flies in the face of the letter he wrote to Audubon and Rozier on April 10, 1810, almost twenty months before. Herrick (1938) I, p. 199.

40. There is no record of the date Audubon and Rozier arrived in Louisville. The transcription of the

Rozier diary by his daughter, Felicite Rozier Flamm, is missing the relevant pages. Sharp (1981), p. 32. However, the most reasonable interpretation of the available evidence would indicate they arrived in Louisville sometime in early October 1807.

There is, to be sure, confusion in the existing record, not only over the date the partners left Philadelphia, as reflected in note 39, *supra*, but as to when they reached Pittsburgh and, ultimately, Limestone (Maysville), KY, where Felicite's transcription ends. The principal problem in piecing this trip together is that the original Rozier diary has been lost. His daughter apparently attempted to transcribe the entries, but she clearly had difficulty interpreting her father's references to the dates in the journal. She has the partners leaving Philadelphia for Kentucky on August 31, 1807. The following entry is accompanied by a date of September 1. Two days later, the entry is dated November 3. Sharp (1981), pp. 25–26. However, this would indicate that Audubon and Rozier were delayed on the road to Pittsburgh for two months, an unlikely scenario. It makes no more sense that they started out around October 1, as Mary Rozier Sharp and Louis J. Sharp III claim, and then spent four weeks in some small Pennsylvania hamlet before resuming their travels on November 3.

Rozier's great-grandson Welton A. Rozier presumably recognized the inherent problems in Felicite's transcription and attempted to clean it up before submitting it to Herrick for publication. Herrick (1938) I, pp. 187–192. Other than stating that the partners left Mill Grove on August 31, this revised version does not offer the specific dates the men arrived at or left the towns they visited along the way. However, both versions track each other as to Audubon and Rozier's journey to Pittsburgh, with one exception, which throws the Herrick itinerary off by one day. Herrick has them spending a night at a tavern owned by B. Mastin whereas Felicite's transcription indicates they merely stopped there for breakfast.

Notwithstanding the confused and conflicting journal references, it would appear that it took Audubon and Rozier eight or nine days to reach Pittsburgh. There is no reason to believe they encountered any lengthy delays during this portion of the trip. Rozier's diary includes no such reference. Additionally, the journey was made by stage, which ran pursuant to regular schedules and clearly would have allowed them to arrive in Pittsburgh in this time frame.

Upon their arrival, which Felicite says occurred on November 7, both versions of the diary agree that the partners stayed at the Jefferson Hotel. Felicite writes that they "remained in this city till Nov 11th." Later, she states they left Pittsburgh by flatboat on November 19th at 3 p.m. Sharp (1981), p. 30. The Herrick version says simply that they "remained in Pittsburgh several days." Herrick (1938) I, p. 191. Souder evidently relies on the November 19th departure date for his conclusion that the men stayed in the city for twelve days. Souder (2004), p. 76.

In Felicite's transcription, Rozier later records their arrival in Limestone, KY, on "the 27th Nov 1807 Sunday at 1 A M. after 15 days route extremely disagreeable by many obstacles having several times touched Islands, obliging us at night to get in water, very cold, having no bed and only my rough 'cloak' for covering." Sharp (1981), p. 31. Coupled with the previous entries and assuming a fifteen day trip, this would suggest that Audubon and Rozier left Pittsburgh by flatboat on the 11th, not the 19th as Souder believes.

More importantly, this entry provides helpful clues as to the actual time frame of the journey. Rozier states that their arrival in Limestone was on Sunday the 27th. Felicite reads her father's journal as reflecting that it was in November. However, November 27 was in fact a Friday in 1807. The only month in the fall of that year where the 27th fell on a Sunday was September. In view of the date Felicite recorded Audubon and Rozier's departure from Philadelphia, August 31, 1807, it would appear the partners spent the month of September on their trip to Louisville. The November dates that Felicite gives were, in truth, in September.

The Sharps' assertion that the partners could not leave for Louisville in September because of delays "due to the completion of the final settlement on the Mill Grove property" is not supported by the historical record. Sharp (1981), p. 24. Alice Ford, who thoroughly researched the Mill Grove land records in the Montgomery County Courthouse in Norris-

town, states that the sale of the property to Francis
Dacosta occurred on September 15, 1806. There
were no land transactions in 1807 that would have
prevented Audubon and Rozier's departure for
Kentucky at the end of August. Ford (1988), p. 473.

Thus, clearing out the brush created by Felicite's
confused reading of her father's diary gives us the
following likely chronology for the trip. Cf. Sharp
(1981), pp. 25–31; Herrick (1938) I, pp. 187–192.

August 31
    Audubon and Rozier leave Mill Grove for
    Philadelphia.
September 1
    The partners leave Philadelphia by stage,
    reaching Lancaster at 4 p.m., where they
    dine. They continue on to Big Chickers,
    where they spend the night.
September 2
    Departing from Lancaster at 8:00 a.m., they
    travel through Elizabethtown, Middletown,
    Harrisburg, and Carlisle before reaching
    Walnut Bottom, where they stay the night at
    a tavern.
September 3
    They reach Shipensburg for breakfast and
    continue on to Chambersburg. They ascend
    and descend the mountain on foot and arrive
    in McConnelsburg for the night.
September 4
    Starting out at 5 a.m., they continue their
    journey through the mountains, traveling
    32 miles. They breakfast at a tavern run by
    B. Mastin, cross the Juniata River in a flat
    boat, and at last arrive in Bedford "worn out
    with fatigue from the terrible jarring of the
    Mail [stage]." Sharp (1981), p. 29.
September 5
    They leave at 4:30 a.m. on the stage with
    6 horses. "The roads were better, the
    mountains less painful, the weather was fine
    and we made 38 miles on that day." Sharp
    (1981), p. 29.
September 6
    They start out at 4:00 a.m. under a heavy
    fog, but the day turns fine as they ascend
    the Alleghany Mountains. They stop in
    Greensburg for the night.

September 7
    They leave at 4:30 a.m., travel through Turtle
    Creek, and arrive in Pittsburgh at 2:00 p.m.
    They find rooms at the Jefferson Hotel,
    where they stay until September 11.
September 11
    Audubon and Rozier depart from Pittsburgh
    at 3:00 p.m. aboard a flatboat down the Ohio
    River. They pay $15 to transport themselves
    and their merchandise.
September 27
    After a little over fifteen days on the river,
    they arrive at 1:00 a.m. in a hamlet known
    variously as Limestone and Maysville, KY.
    Rozier specifically notes that their landing
    occurred on a Sunday.

According to the Sharps, Felicite's notes for the
remainder of the trip are missing. Ibid., p. 32. The
Herrick version of Rozier's diary reflects that the
partners completed the trip aboard the flatboat.
Herrick (1938) I, p. 191 (quoting Rozier as stating
that from Pittsburgh, "The remainder of our journey was by way of the Ohio, and we made it entirely
in an open flatboat."). This version adds that they
passed Cincinnati, which sits on the Ohio shore
between Maysville and Louisville. Herrick (1938)
I, p. 192. ("Among some of the places which we
passed *en route*, I remember the following: Wheeling, Marietta, Market Slough, famous for the con-
spiracy of Colonel Burr, Belleville, Litards Falls,
Point Pleasant, Manchester, Maysville, Cincinnati,
and finally our journey's end, Louisville."). Whether
this additional description of the itinerary was still
part of Felicite's notes at the point that Weldon
Rozier reworked them is unknown, but it seems a
reasonable inference.

If the journey to Louisville was completed by
flatboat, the roughly 194-mile distance between
Maysville and Louisville would have taken another
week, assuming they realized the same twenty-seven
miles per day that they had made in their first fifteen days on the river. Jones (1920), pp. 75, 101. This
would put their arrival in Louisville in the first week
of October, around October 3, which is the basis for
the statement in the text. Souder's conclusion that
the partners did not reach Louisville until "probably sometime before Christmas" would appear to

be erroneous. Souder (2004), p. 77. Even if there are questions about the proper reading of the Rozier diary notations, Souder's estimate for their arrival is wholly inconsistent with the ledger for the business, which reflects that the partners had made $319.35 in profits from their sales of goods on the frontier as of December 31, 1807. Book (1971), p. 188; Herrick (1938) II, p. 355. Clearly, Audubon and Rozier had arrived in Louisville much earlier than Souder states. The original ledger is in the collection of the New-York Historical Society.

Several Audubon scholars, however, insist that the partners left the flatboat after reaching Maysville and scouted out possible inland locations for a general store at Frankfort, Paris, Danville, and Lexington before reaching Louisville, which they chose as the site for their business. Streshinsky (1993), p. 55; Adams (1966), p. 89; Arthur (1937), p. 53. Stanley Clisby Arthur, who originated this tale in his 1937 biography, provides no source citations for his work, so it is not possible to determine where he obtained the information. If Audubon kept a journal during the trip to Louisville, it is no longer extant. Arthur's storyline is obviously inconsistent with Weldon Rozier's translation of his great-grandfather's diary. Additionally, it is puzzling that the partners would have purchased merchandise at a cost of $2,482.35 (approximately $52,000 in 2016 dollars) and trekked almost nine hundred miles without a certain destination in mind. Sahr (2015); Rhodes (2004), p. 49; Herrick (1938) I, pp. 186, 192. Absent the evidence Arthur relied upon, his alternate itinerary for the concluding leg of the journey cannot be verified.

41. Rhodes (2004), p. 43; Book (1971), p. 187. The Reverend J. David Book points out that there is no evidence Audubon & Rozier actually opened a store when they first arrived in Louisville in 1807. He posits that they may have peddled their merchandise from a wagon or on horseback as they traveled around the Louisville area.

42. Rhodes (2004), p. 43.

43. Rhodes (2004), p. 44; Streshinsky (1993), p. 58. After the passage of the Embargo Act, Benjamin Bakewell's firm defaulted on close to $200,000 and was forced into bankruptcy. In order to avoid a distress sale of his remaining property, Bakewell assigned the assets to his attorney and two

of his merchant friends, Thomas Kinder of Robert Kinder & Co. and Benjamin Page. Palmer (2004), p. 19.

44. Rhodes (2004), pp. 44, 53. The assignees of Benjamin Bakewell's firm agreed to continue the date for repayment of the note, as reflected on the company's books. Herrick (1938) II, pp. 354–355. See also, Palmer (2004), p. 19. The Reverend J. David Book, an authority on Audubon's time in Louisville, asserts that Audubon and Rozier paid off the note when the partners stopped in Philadelphia on April 7 on their return trip to Louisville after Audubon and Lucy were wed. Book (1971), p. 188. However, the Bakewell ledger for April 7 reflects their note for $3,647.29, "due this day," as a debit, not as a credit, which would indicate the term of the note was extended as Rhodes correctly concludes. Herrick (1938) II, pp. 354.

Audubon and Rozier's clerk, Nathaniel Wells Pope (1789–1836), was born in Shelbyville, KY, on January 23, 1789. He studied medicine at Transylvania University in Lexington and, in the 1820s, began practicing medicine in Feliciana Parish, LA, where he renewed his acquaintance with Audubon. He married Martha Johnson, the youngest daughter of Isaac Johnson and Mary Routh of Troy Plantation in the Felicianas, on February 18, 1823. Pope and his wife had eight children, seven of whom survived him. He died on July 2, 1836, in East Baton Rouge Parish, LA. Arthur (1931), pp. 173–175.

45. Ford (1988), p. 75. The date of Audubon and Lucy's wedding is erroneously given as April 8, 1808, in Audubon's autobiographical essay *Myself*, and this date is repeated in both the Buchanan and Lucy Audubon edited biographies. *AHJ* I, p. 28; L. Audubon (1869), p. 29; Buchanan (1868), p. 19. However, in his brief autobiography in his 1820 journal, Audubon accurately identified the date of their nuptials as April 5, 1808. Audubon (1999). p. 31; Corning (1929a) I, p. 46. That this was the correct date is established by a letter from Lucy's father to his English cousin Euphemia Gifford on April 17. William Bakewell, Fatland Ford to Euphemia Gifford, Duffield, Derbyshire, 17 Apr. 1808 (Princeton, Box 1, Folder 17), Audubon (2006), p. 12. Ford also found a notice of the wedding that appeared in the April 6 edition of the Norristown *Weekly Register*. Ford (1988), p. 75 and note 1, p. 437.

Audubon was twenty-two years old on the day of his wedding, not twenty-three as stated by some of his biographers. Blaugrund (2000), p. 14; Blaugrund & Stebbins (1993), p. 69. He would not turn twenty-three until April 26, 1808.

46. William Bakewell, Fatland Ford to Euphemia Gifford, Duffield, Derbyshire, 17 Apr. 1808 (Princeton, Box 1, Folder 17), Audubon (2006), p. 12. See also, Rhodes (2004), p. 45; Ford (1988), p. 75; Streshinksy (1993), p. 60. In *Myself*, Audubon indicated that he and Lucy left Fatland Ford the day after the wedding rather than three days later as Lucy's father recounted in the cited letter to his cousin Euphemia Gifford. *AHJ* I, p. 28. However, many of the factual assertions in this autobiographical account of his life are erroneous.

During the trip over the mountains to Pittsburgh, Lucy suffered minor injuries when the stagecoach in which she was riding on the rutted and rock-filled road tipped over and was dragged some distance by the team of horses. Rhodes (2004), p. 47.

47. Rhodes (2004), p. 53.

48. Streshinsky (1993), p. 61.

49. *AHJ* I, p. 28.

50. Rhodes (2004), p. 55.

51. LBA, Louisville to Euphemia Gifford, Duffield near Derby, England, 27 May 1808 (Princeton, Box 1, Folder 10). See also, Rhodes (2004), p. 53.

52. Rhodes (2004), p. 53.

53. Delatte (1982), p. 50. At the time of her death, Alice Ford had completed a manuscript for a new book with the preliminary title *The Audubons*, in which she planned to present her research thoroughly debunking the claim by some of Audubon's biographers that James Berthoud and his wife Marie-Anne-Julia were members of the French nobility. Alice Ford (Personal communication). Cf. Rhodes (2004), p. 54; Delatte (1982), p. 50; Herrick (1938) I, p. 326, note 24; Arthur (1937), p. 54. Ford's manuscript, which remains unpublished, can be found in the Alice Ford Papers at the John James Audubon Center at Mill Grove.

54. Streshinsky (1993), p. 57. Nicholas Augustus Berthoud (1786–1849) was born on July 19, 1786, in Paris, France. Ties That Bind Us Family Tree, Ancestry.com, http://trees.ancestry.com/tree/70068667/person/44210525784 (accessed 9 May 2015); Bakewell (1896), p. 41. He left with his parents during the French Revolution, sailing from Germany for Philadelphia on August 25, 1794. His father settled in Kentucky shortly before Audubon and Rozier arrived and established a successful business with Louis Tarascon constructing barges in Shippingport. Ford (1988), pp. 73–74, 437, note 14. There is no record of when Audubon first met Nicholas. However, given Audubon's outgoing personality, he likely introduced himself to the French families living in Shippingport shortly after his arrival in the autumn of 1807. At that point, Audubon was twenty-two, and Nicholas would have been twenty-one, as Streshinksy notes in her biography. Streshinsky (1993), p. 57. Rhodes adds a year to each of their ages, although his only citation is to Streshinsky's work. Rhodes (2004), p. 54. Absent documentation as to when the two young men first became acquainted, it is impossible to determine their respective ages, although Streshinsky is probably closer to the mark.

55. Rhodes (2004), pp. 54, 121, 125–126. Eliza Bakewell, born on June 28, 1790, in Burton-on-Trent, England, was the third of William Bakewell's five children. Bakewell (1896), p. 41. About three and a half years younger than Lucy, Eliza was considered the beauty of the Bakewell family. Ford (1988), p. 50, 91. She married Nicholas Berthoud on March 6, 1816, and had seven children. She died of yellow fever in St. Louis in 1853. Bakewell (1896), p. 41. Nicholas died on November 18, 1849, in St. Louis after a brief illness. *Daily Missouri Republican* (Tuesday, 20 Nov. 1849).

56. Rhodes (2004), p. 61; Souder (2004), p. 93; Streshinsky (1993), p. 61; Ford (1988), p. 76.

57. JJA, Fatland Ford to Ferdinand Rozier, Louisville, 10 Aug. 1809, Christy (1938), p. 169.

58. Rhodes (2004), p. 66. Audubon describes his meeting with Alexander Wilson in an Episode from the first volume of the *OB* entitled "Louisville in Kentucky." *OB* I, pp. 437–440. Audubon wrote that the meeting occurred in March 1810. Ibid., p. 438. The precise date is derived from Wilson's journal entries, which were published in 1828 in a biographical sketch of Wilson by George Ord, the editor of a revised edition of Wilson's *American Ornithology* and, by then, a vocal critic of Audubon and his work. Hunter (1983), pp. 93–96, 370; Herrick (1938) I, p. 224.

59. Herrick (1938) I, pp. 208–210, 217.

60. Rhodes (2004), p. 64; Hunter (1983), pp. 83, 91. The exact publication date of the second volume of *American Ornithology* is unknown, but Wilson dated the preface January 1, 1810, suggesting the book appeared early that year. Hunter (1983), p. 91. Audubon indicated that Wilson arrived at the store carrying "two volumes under his arm," so it would seem that the second volume was published before Wilson made his trip to Louisville.

61. Rhodes (2004), p. 62; Alexander Wilson, Pittsburgh to Alexander Lawson, Philadelphia, 22 Feb. 1810, Hunter (1983), pp. 320–325. Benjamin Bakewell's glass factory in Pittsburgh became known as one of the finest flint glass producers in America. It continued in business under various names until 1882. Palmer (2004), pp. 86–87.

62. Rhodes (2004), p. 65.

63. Hunter (1983), pp. 83, 90; *OB* I, p. 438.

64. *OB* I, p. 438.

65. Ibid., pp. 438–439. Rhodes points to Audubon's "self-restraint" in declining to subscribe to Wilson's work as support for his thesis that Audubon "was not the irresponsible businessman his detractors have painted him to be." Rhodes (2004), p. 67. Rhodes suggests that Rozier's admonition to Audubon was likely due to their "precarious" financial situation, and it was a recognition of this that led Audubon to lay down his pen. Of course, this is pure conjecture on Rhodes's part. Moreover, even if true, it would have been Rozier's clear-headed business judgment that influenced Audubon not to subscribe. It is hard to accept the notion that Audubon would have reached the same decision had Rozier not been present in the store that day. Rhodes may be right that Audubon has been unfairly maligned by his biographers for his poor business acumen, but this incident provides scant support for his position.

Audubon eventually acquired eight of the nine volumes of *American Ornithology* after he had accumulated some wealth during his Henderson days. Souder (2004), p. 189 and note, p. 326. The volumes now sit in the collection of the Audubon Museum in Henderson, KY. The first six volumes were apparently acquired by Audubon in 1816 during a trip to Louisiana as they are inscribed "1816 Louisiana." Ibid. Audubon filled the margins of the volumes with his annotations, some of which are dated in

the late 1820s. Partridge (1996), p. 274, note 16. This would suggest that Audubon did not part with these books in 1819 when he was forced to liquidate his assets through a sale to his brother-in-law Nicholas Berthoud. Audubon also owned a second, unannotated set of Wilson's *American Ornithology*, which is housed at the Henry E. Huntington Library in San Marino, CA. Ibid., p. 273.

66. *OB* I, p. 439.

67. *OB* V, p. 292; *OB* I, p. 439.

68. Hunter (1983), p. 93. This quotation from Wilson's journal, remarking on the poor hospitality he encountered during his visit to Louisville, was included in a posthumous biographical sketch of Wilson added by his friend and executor, George Ord, to the ninth and final volume of *American Ornithology* published in 1814, a year after Wilson's death. Ibid. Wilson's journal disappeared while it was in Ord's hands and was not in the Ord estate when he died in 1866. Ibid., p. 94; Herrick (1938) I, p. 224, note 15.

69. Hunter (1983), p. 93. In his Episode "Louisville in Kentucky," Audubon claimed to have been astonished when, in reading the final volume of Wilson's *American Ornithology*, he came across the quoted paragraph condemning the inhabitants of the river town. *OB* I, p. 440. The original manuscript for this Episode contains a passage that did not make it into print but that reveals the extent to which Audubon was stung by Wilson's criticism.

> Never, Reader, should I have mentioned these meetings, or these circumstances relating to Mr Wilson Louisville and myself, had I not felt grieved as much grieved at the unwarrantable picture he has given of Hospitable Louisville for to have procured no Subscriber at that place, was not in my opinion a sufficient reason, for undervaluing the talents of every one of its Citizens; and to have said that Science or literature had not one friend there is incorrect, as to affirm that not one act of civility was shewn to him at Louisville is ungracious and unjust.

Sotheby's (6 Jun. 1989), Lot 14. In a later edition of *American Ornithology*, Ord published the other entries of Wilson's journal during his visit to Louisville, which suggest there was a genuine basis for Audubon's feelings.

March 19. Rambling round town with my gun. Examined Mr. —'s drawings in crayon—very good. Saw two new birds he had, both Motacillæ.

* * *

March 21. Went out shooting this afternoon with Mr. A. Saw a number of Sandhill Cranes. Pigeons numerous.

Herrick (1938) I, pp. 224–225. See also, Burtt & Davis (2013), p. 334; Hunter (1983), p. 94. It should be noted that Wilson's March 23 journal entry particularly denigrated "those to whom I was recommended." "I had four letters of recommendation, and was taught to expect much of everything there, but neither received one act of civility from those to whom I was recommended, one subscriber, *nor one new bird.*" Herrick (1938) I, p. 225. See also, Burtt & Davis (2013), p. 336. It is unclear if Audubon was one of those individuals, although one can reasonably deduce that Benjamin Bakewell had given Audubon's name to Wilson when Wilson stopped in Pittsburgh. If so, Wilson's disparagement of the people of Louisville is belied by the fact that Audubon had taken him out into the surrounding countryside to look for birds and shown him his drawings, which included two new warblers (genus *Motacillæ*). It is likely that Wilson's diary entry merely reflected his disappointment at leaving Louisville without adding a single subscriber and should be considered in that light. Burtt & Davis (2013), p. 337; Herrick (1938) I, p. 231.

The rancor between the Wilson and Audubon camps first arose during Audubon's 1824 visit to Philadelphia, when he was looking for support for the publication of his portfolio. It would escalate once Audubon began publishing *BOA* in England, with charges and countercharges flying back and forth across the Atlantic.

The lengths to which Audubon would later go to surpass Wilson are suggested by his dating of an early illustration of the Ruffed Grouse "June, 1805" to establish that he had painted it prior to Wilson. However, Audubon was in France at that time and would not have had access to a fresh specimen of this species. Moreover, the watermark on the paper he used for his painting was "1810," establishing that he lied about it. Pick (2004), pp. 144–145. See

also, Audubon (2008), No. 51. This image was apparently painted by Audubon during his trip to Ste. Genevieve in the winter of 1810–1811 and left in Ste. Genevieve with Ferdinand Rozier, who returned it to Audubon in December 1821 when the two men met in New Orleans. Ford (1988), p. 137. See also, Audubon (1999), pp. 131, 148; Corning (1929a). pp. 201, 225. The drawing is now in the collection of the Museum of Comparative Zoology at Harvard University and is illustrated in Audubon (2008), No. 51.

Regardless, the meeting of Wilson and Audubon in 1810 was a critical turning point in Audubon's life. Ten years later, after his business had failed and he was looking for a means to support his family, it ultimately inspired him to complete his portfolio and seek a publisher of his own.

70. Rhodes (2004), p. 69. In *Myself*, Audubon wrote, "Louisville did not give us up, but we gave up Louisville. I could not bear to give the attention required by my business, and which, indeed, every business calls for, and, therefore, my business abandoned me. Indeed, I never thought of it beyond the ever-engaging journeys which I was in the habit of taking to Philadelphia or New York to purchase goods; these journeys I greatly enjoyed, as they afforded me ample means to study birds and their habits as I travelled through the beautiful, the darling forests of Ohio, Kentucky, and Pennsylvania." Audubon (1999), p. 786; *AHJ* I, pp. 29–30.

71. Souder (2004), p. 121; Ford (1988) p. 78; *OB* I, p. 31. Audubon scholars have given disparate figures for the distance between Louisville and Henderson. Ford, evidently relying upon Audubon's autobiography, *Myself*, states that Henderson, or Red Banks as it was once known, is located approximately 125 miles "down the Ohio" from Louisville. Ford (1988), p. 78; *AHJ* I, p. 30. Rhodes asserts that the communities are "125 river miles" apart. Rhodes (2004), p. 69. Souder places Henderson at "more than 200 miles downriver." Souder (2004), p. 121.

There is some validity to both figures, depending on whether one measures the distance by river or over land. According to the U.S. Army Corps of Engineers, the two communities are just under 200 river miles apart. Jones (1920), pp. 101, 125 (196.4 river miles measured between the Louisville public landing and the Henderson wharf). Audubon was certainly aware of the distance along the river, writing in his Episode in the *OB* entitled "The Ohio" that Henderson was "by water about two hundred miles" from Shippingport, the community adjacent to Louisville. *OB* I, p. 31. By land, the distance is approximately 125 miles.

72. *AHJ* I, p. 30.

73. Souder (2004), p. 124; Streshinsky, (1993), p. 64; Delatte (1982), p. 59.

74. Ford (1988) p. 78. The Audubons had relocated to Henderson by early June 1810, as evidenced by the June 4–5 date he recorded on a drawing he did of a Gray Catbird. Audubon (2008), No. 15. He wrote that Henderson was then "quite small" and "consisted of six or eight houses." *OB* III, p. 122. The town was small, but not that small. According to the 1810 U.S. Census, there were 159 people residing there, forty-seven of whom were slaves. Audubon was identified as the head of a household that consisted of one free White male under ten years of age—his infant son, Victor; two free White males between the ages of seventeen and twenty-six—Audubon and Pope; one free White male between the ages of twenty-seven and forty-five—Rozier; and a free white female between the ages of seventeen and twenty-six—Lucy. U.S. Bureau of the Census (1810), Census Place: *Henderson, Henderson Co., KY*; Roll: *6*; Page: *345*, Image: *00367*. Audubon would have been twenty-five that year, suggesting that he knew he had been born in 1785 and not years earlier as he sometimes hinted.

75. Rhodes (2004) p. 70; *OB* III, pp. 122–123.

76. Rhodes (2004), p. 76; Ford (1988), p. 79; Audubon (1828), p. 104. There are conflicting references in Audubon's own writings as to whether they made the journey to Ste. Genevieve aboard a flatboat or a keelboat. In *Myself*, Audubon wrote that "having arranged our goods on board a large flatboat, my partner and I left Henderson in the month of December, 1810, in a heavy snow-storm." Audubon (1999), p. 787; *AHJ* I, p. 30. Rhodes relies upon this statement in his biography. Rhodes (2004), p. 76 and note, p. 446.

However, in Lucy's biography, she quoted her husband as follows: "Putting our goods, which consisted of three hundred barrels of whisky, sundry dry goods, and powder, on board a keel-boat, my partner, my clerk, and self departed in a severe snow

storm." L. Audubon (1869), p. 35. Audubon stated that it was a keelboat in his article "Journey up the Mississippi," published in *The Winter's Wreath* for 1829, as well as in his Episode in the *OB* entitled "Breaking Up of the Ice." *OB* III, p. 408; Audubon (1828), p. 104. Finally, he described the vessel as "a Large Keel Boat" in his 1820 journal. Audubon (1999), p. 20; Corning (1929a), p. 30. The boats were not synonymous. A flatboat, being rectangular-shaped with a flat bottom, made it useful for down-river trips but not for trips upriver. A keelboat had a keel and a tapered bow that enabled the vessel to be more easily poled or pulled against the current. The weight of the evidence would indicate the trip was made via keelboat.

77. Rhodes (2004), p. 76. While Audubon was away on his trip to Ste. Genevieve, Lucy stayed at Meadow Brook, the farm of Dr. Adam and Elizabeth Rankin, and served as a governess and tutor to the Rankins' large family. Ibid.

78. Rhodes (2004), pp. 77, 84; Audubon (1828), p. 105. In Lucy's biography, she stated that Audubon and Rozier were accompanied by Nathaniel Pope on their trip to Ste. Genevieve. L. Audubon (1869), p. 35. Audubon made no mention of this in any of his writings. Audubon (1999), pp. 20, 31; Corning (1929a), pp. 30, 46; *OB* III, pp. 408–410; Audubon (1828), pp. 104–127. If Pope had, indeed, been a member of their company, he likely would have returned with Audubon to Henderson. Since Audubon does not indicate he had a companion on the way back, I am unwilling to accept Lucy's statement as authoritative.

79. Rhodes (2004), pp. 85–86. Audubon's party remained in winter quarters at Tawapatee Bottom on the Missouri side of the Mississippi River for six weeks before the ice broke up and allowed them to proceed farther upriver. Audubon (1828), pp. 113–115. When they reached Grand Tower above Cape Girardeau, they used a cordell rope to pull the craft against the current. Ibid., pp. 122–123.

80. Rhodes (2004), pp. 86–87.

81. *AHJ* I, p. 44.

82. Rhodes (2004), p. 89; LBA, Louisville to Euphemia Gifford, Duffield near Derby, England, 5 Jan. 1812 (Princeton, Box 1, Folder 10).

83. Rhodes claims that the meeting between Audubon and Tom Bakewell took place in Louis-

ville in September 1811. Rhodes (2004), p. 90. He does not cite a source for this date, and other Audubon biographers disagree as to where and when their meeting took place.

Ford, relying on Tom Bakewell's posthumously published autobiography, asserts that he stopped in Henderson on his way to New Orleans in the late summer of 1811 and made his business proposal to Audubon at Meadow Brook, the farm of Dr. Adam and Elizabeth Rankin outside Henderson, where the Audubons were temporarily living. Ford (1988), p. 84-85; Sinclair (1966), pp. 243-244; Bakewell (1935), p. 36. Lucy had stayed at Meadow Brook with her son and served as a governess for the Rankin children during Audubon's winter trip to Ste. Genevieve. See note 77, *supra*. Upon his return, the Rankins invited the entire Audubon family to live with them until Audubon's new business in Henderson became profitable. Ford (1988), pp. 79, 84.

However, a contemporaneous letter from Lucy Audubon to her English cousin Euphemia Gifford establishes that the Audubons met Tom in Louisville, where they had stopped while on their way with Victor to visit Fatland Ford. LBA, Fatland Ford to Euphemia Gifford, Duffield near Derby, England, 5 Jan. 1812 (Princeton Box 1, Folder 10) ("when we got as far as Louisville we heard of my Brother Tom being on his way to New Orleans and as it was necessary for Mr A to see my Brother we determined to wait there for him, that we might not miss each other"). Clearly, as to the location of the meeting between Audubon and his brother-in-law, Ford is mistaken.

Souder declares that Lucy's brother did not reach Louisville until November 1811. Souder (2004), p. 129. He cites as his source Lucy's letter to Euphemia Gifford, referenced above. However, as a careful reading of the letter will attest, Lucy did not specifically state when Tom reached Louisville. She merely wrote that while traveling to Louisville, Tom was detained by business "longer than he expected and it was not till the fourth of last November that Mr Audubon my Son & myself set out on our long journey" to Fatland Ford. Souder obviously presumes that Tom arrived in Louisville in close proximity to the date the Audubons resumed their journey. However, based upon a letter in the

collection of the Missouri History Museum Library and Research Center from Audubon to William Clark, dated October 19, 1811, which enclosed a broadside for the new firm, it is evident that Audubon & Bakewell had been formed prior to that date. Ford (1988), p. 437, note 2. In addition, Audubon's November 2 letter to his former partner, Ferdinand Rozier, would indicate that Tom was by then in New Orleans. Herrick (1938) I, p. 243.

84. Rhodes (2004), p. 90; Palmer (2004), p. 19; Ford (1988), p. 84-85; Sinclair (1966), p. 243; Bakewell (1935), p. 36.

85. Rhodes (2004), p. 90; Ford (1988), p. 85; Sinclair (1966), p. 243. In an autobiographical sketch written as an old man, Thomas W. Bakewell explained his motivation for inviting his brother-in-law to join him in a business partnership: "The French qualities of Mr. A. in language & nationality, it was thought would [MS: w*d*] be an advantage in so Frenchified place as New Orleans, & concluded that Mr. A. should [MS: sh*d*] join me there." Bakewell (1935), p. 36. See also, Sinclair (1966), p. 244. Bakewell's manuscript can be found in the Reuben T. Durrett Collection on Kentucky and the Ohio River Valley at the University of Chicago Library.

86. Rhodes (2004), p. 90; Ford (1988), p. 85. In her January 5, 1812, letter to her cousin, Lucy remarked, "Mr A and Brother Tom have entered into partnership in the Commission business we mean to reside in New Orleans." LBA, Fatland Ford to Euphemia Gifford, Duffield near Derby, England, 5 Jan. 1812 (Princeton, Box 1, Folder 10).

87. *AHJ* I, p. 32.

88. Rhodes (2004), pp. 91-94; Souder (2004), p. 130; Ford (1988), p. 86. There was apparently a delay between the time Audubon & Bakewell was formed and the date Audubon, Lucy, and Victor left Louisville. Rhodes explains that Audubon made another trip to Ste. Genevieve after agreeing to Tom's proposal in order to try to collect the sums Rozier still owed from the breakup of the partnership, presumably to help finance the new business. Rhodes (2004), pp. 90-91. In this telling, Audubon collected what he could and returned to Louisville in late October. Rhodes is silent as to the evidence supporting this chronology, although he does cite to Audubon's November 2 letter to Rozier, writ-

ten from Louisville, in which Audubon remarked, "I reached here on the 31st of last month a little fatigued, as you can well imagine." Herrick (1938) I, p. 243. The implication is that Audubon had just returned from seeing Rozier in Ste. Genevieve.

89. JJA, Fatland Ford to Ferdinand Rozier, Ste. Genevieve, Upper Louisiana, 9 Dec. 1811, Christy (1938), p. 169.

90. Rhodes (2004), p. 94. The lead mining operation having failed, Francis Dacosta would go on to sell Mill Grove the following year. Ford (1988), p. 473. However, note that Audubon informed Rozier in a letter dated December 9, 1811, that "Mr. Dacosta had sold Mill Grove nearly two years ago, and that nobody here knew anything about it. A Mr. Robert E. Hobard of Pottsgrove, fifteen miles from here, has possession." Christy (1938), p. 169. In a follow-up letter of December 30, 1811, Audubon reiterated that the property had been sold to "a Mr. Robert Hobard of Pottsgrove." Ibid., p. 171. Ford's examination of the Mortager Index in the Montgomery County Courthouse in Norristown, Pennsylvania did not locate a record of this transaction. But the records do reflect a sale of the property by Dacosta and his associates to F. Beates on December 31, 1812. Ford (1988), p. 473. Eventually, in 1951, Mill Grove was sold to Montgomery County, which dedicated it as a park. Ibid. It is now known as the John James Audubon Center at Mill Grove and is open to the public.

91. JJA, Fatland Ford to Ferdinand Rozier at Ste. Genevieve, Upper Louisiana, 9 Dec. 1811, Christy (1938), p. 171.

92. Rhodes (2004), p. 94; Nolte (1854), p. 174. Irmscher gives the date of Audubon's first meeting with Nolte as 1817, an obvious typographical error. Audubon (1999), p. 890.

93. Ibid. In the *OB*, Audubon told a different tale of his first meeting with Vincent Nolte. That account appears in an Episode entitled "A Wild Horse," in which Audubon described his exceptional horse Barro.

On my way homewards I met at the crossings of the Juniata River a gentleman from New Orelans [*sic*] whose name is VINCENT NOLTE. He was mounted on a superb horse, for which he had paid three hundred dollars, and a servant on horseback led another as a change. I was then an utter stranger to him, and as I approached and praised his horse, he not very courteously observed that he wished I had as good a one. Finding that he was going to Bedford to spend the night, I asked him at what hour he would get there. "Just soon enough to have some trouts ready for our supper, provided you will join when you get there." I almost imagined Barro understood our conversation; he pricked up his ears, and lengthened his pace, on which Mr NOLTE caracolled his horse, and then put him to a quick trot, but all in vain, for I reached the hotel nearly a quarter of an hour before him, ordered the trouts, saw to the putting away of my good horse, and stood at the door ready to welcome my companion.

OB III, p. 273. Nolte, in his autobiography, politely called this a "circumstantial account" of their first encounter. Nolte (1854), p. 177, note. As in other instances surrounding Audubon's early days, it is impossible to square the contradictory stories told by the participants. Audubon's frequent use of literary license in recounting the Episodes of the *OB* makes his version of the meeting somewhat suspect. For instance, Nolte's autobiography indicates that he was not accompanied by a servant when he met Audubon. At the same time, it is clear that at least some of the details Nolte recalled through the dim haze of his decades' old memory were fallacious. For example, it is highly improbable that Audubon told Nolte that his father-in-law, William Bakewell, was "formerly of Philadelphia, but then residing and owning mills at Shippingport, at the Falls of the Ohio, and in the neighborhood of Lexington." Ibid., p. 178. William Bakewell was still living at Fatland Ford outside Philadelphia, where Audubon had just left Lucy and Victor.

94. Nolte (1854), p. 177.

95. Ibid. Audubon, of course, was not a Frenchman by birth. As one born in a French colony, he was considered a creole, a term used to refer to those of French blood born outside the mother country. Rhodes (2004), p. 131; Harwood & Durant (1985), p. 97.

96. Nolte (1854), p. 177.

97. Ibid., p. 178; Ford (1988), p. 87. Rhodes

asserts that Audubon and Nolte disembarked at Cincinnati rather than Maysville (also called Limestone), KY. Rhodes (2004), pp. 95–96. He cites no authority for this claim, and it is directly contradicted by Nolte's account. Maysville is approximately 60 river miles above Cincinnati on the Ohio River. Jones (1920), pp. 75, 83 (60.7 river miles measured by Army Corps of Engineers between the Maysville public landing and the public landing in Cincinnati). Audubon does not mention sharing a flatboat with Nolte down the Ohio, merely indicating that he rode with Vincent Nolte "as far as Shippingport," which itself is inconsistent with Nolte's recollection. *OB* III, p. 273.

98. Ford (1988), pp. 87, 89; Delatte (1982), p. 68.

99. Ford (1988), p. 87. Rhodes, following the footsteps of earlier biographers, contends that Audubon traveled to Ste. Genevieve in February 1812 to try to collect the monies still owed to him by Ferdinand Rozier. Rhodes (2004), p. 100; Adams (1966), p. 146; Herrick (1938) I, p. 249, note 3; Arthur (1937), pp. 72–73. We know that on January 29, 1812, Audubon had written to Rozier during his stop in Louisville on his way back to Henderson: "I wish to know if you will pay at New Orleans the bill of 1,000 dollars which I have on you, or if I shall have to go to St. Genevieve to get them." Christy (1938), p. 173. But there is substantial reason to doubt that Audubon followed this up with a journey to see Rozier the following month.

The original source of this tale is Audubon's granddaughter Maria, who reportedly had access to Audubon's now lost or destroyed 1812 journal. She states that he made the trip out to Ste. Genevieve with a party of Osage Indians "in February or March 1812." *AHJ* I, p. 44. Maria then purportedly quotes Audubon's lengthy account of his return trip, dated "April 1812," which has him crossing the flooded Illinois prairie, swimming the Muddy River, spending consecutive nights with a squatter family and with an Osage party, passing through Shawnee-town, IL, ferrying from Illinois to Kentucky, and "as night came I found myself with my wife beside me, my child on my knee." Ibid., pp. 44–46. However, we know independently that both Lucy and Victor were at Fatland Ford, not in Kentucky, during the winter and spring of 1812. More-

over, Audubon had rejoined them by early March, as notations on his extant drawings demonstrate. See note 100, *infra*. Thus, he was nowhere near Ste. Genevieve in April 1812.

This raises the question whether Maria lifted Audubon's account from his 1811 journal, when he in fact did leave Ste. Genevieve in early April and trudged across the Illinois prairie to return to Lucy and Victor in Henderson, and gave it a new date. Or, possibly the 1812 date is simply a typographical error. In either case, Rhodes evidently believes that the account given in this journal entry refers to Audubon's return from Ste. Genevieve in the spring of 1811 because he quotes it at length in the context of that time frame. Rhodes (2004), p. 87–88. Rhodes's conclusion is sound and squares with the facts, although he makes no mention of the erroneous 1812 date given by Maria. But if Maria is wrong about the date, where is the evidence of a second trip in the early months of 1812, as Rhodes and the other Audubon biographers believe?

It appears that Audubon himself is the source. His autobiographical sketch *Myself* would suggest that his second trip to Ste. Genevieve indeed occurred in the early months of 1812 as Maria claimed. He indicated that, following the breakup of his partnership with Rozier in 1811, he traveled to Ste. Genevieve a second time.

> I must not forget to tell you that I crossed those prairies on foot at another time, for the purpose of collecting the money due to me from Rozier, and that I walked one hundred and sixty-five miles in a little over three days, much of the time nearly ankle deep in mud and water, from which I suffered much afterward by swollen feet. I reached Henderson in early March, and a few weeks later the lower portions of Kentucky and the shores of the Mississippi suffered severely by earthquakes.

AHJ, pp. 31–32. Audubon's latter reference is to the New Madrid earthquake of December 16, 1811, and its numerous aftershocks, which lasted into March 1812. Rhodes (2004), pp. 96–97. However, Audubon's memory of the timing of this trip is clearly faulty since it has him in Henderson in "early March" when he was actually at Fatland Ford.

The most likely scenario, if one can find a path through the evidentiary thicket, is that Audubon's second trip to Ste. Genevieve actually occurred in October 1811. This is consistent with a contemporaneous letter from Audubon to Rozier, dated November 2, 1811, in which Audubon reported that he had reached Louisville on October 31 after a tiring journey. "I reached here on the 31st of last month a little fatigued, as you can well imagine." Herrick (1938) I, p. 243. Rozier could only appreciate his friend's weariness if he knew of Audubon's recent travels, which would imply that Audubon had recently seen him. This chronology would also fit Audubon's memory that the earthquakes had struck "a few weeks" after his return from Ste. Genevieve, as they did in mid-December.

Moreover, it makes sense that Audubon would have trekked out in October to try to collect the sums that Rozier still owed him, before he left Louisville for Fatland Ford. As reflected in note 83, *supra*, Audubon and Tom Bakewell had just agreed to establish a mercantile house in New Orleans, and Audubon needed to raise capital to finance his share of the venture. Rhodes agrees. Rhodes (2004), p. 90. With a substantial figure waiting to be paid to him in Ste. Genevieve, Audubon would have initially looked there to raise funds. However, if Audubon visited Ste. Genevieve in October 1811, he evidently was not successful in collecting the debt in full as his January 1812 letter indicates.

Thus, the evidence points to Audubon making the trip in October 1811, notwithstanding the contrary claims of both Audubon and his granddaughter. But if this is correct and there were, indeed, only two trips, then there was no journey across the Illinois prairie in February or March 1812. All of the references suggesting the trip occurred in 1812 actually refer to the earlier trip in the fall. While these deductions are entirely plausible, they are, to be sure, conjectural absent other confirming evidence. What can be said with certainty is that Maria Audubon's account of Audubon returning to Lucy and Victor in Kentucky in April 1812 is directly contradicted by the known facts.

100. Rhodes (2004), pp. 101–104; Arthur (1937), p. 73. Among the drawings Audubon completed during his productive visit to Fatland Ford in the spring of 1812 were the following:

Swamp [Song] Sparrow
March 12 (Audubon (2008), No. 4)
Fox Coulor'd Sparrow
March 26 (Audubon (2008), No. 3)
Vigor's Warbler
April 21 (Audubon (1966) I, Plate 23; Havell Plate 30; *OB* I, p. 153)
Spotted Sand Piper
April 22 (Audubon (2008), No. 43)
Yellow rump Warbler
April 22 (Audubon (1966) I, Plate 127; Havell Plate 153)
Le Petit Caporal
April 23 (Audubon (1966) I, Plate 156; Havell Plate 75)
White-throated Sparrow
April 27 (Audubon (2008), No. 5)
Towhee Bunting
May 6 (Arthur (1937), p. 73, ill. facing p. 160)
Whippoorwill
May 7 (Audubon (2008), No. 35)
Nighthawk
May 8 (Audubon (2008), No. 37)
Bay Breasted Warbler
May 12 (Audubon (1966) I, Plate 103; Havell Plate 69)
Blackburnian Warbler
May 12 (Audubon (1966) II, Plate 404; Havell Plate 135)
Yellow-winged Sparrow
May 12 (Arthur (1937), p. 73)
Chestnut-sided Warbler
May 17 (Audubon (1966) II, Plate 369; Havell Plate 59)
Broad-winged Hawk
May 27 (Audubon (1966) II, Plate 259; Havell Plate 91; *OB* I, p. 461)
Cuvier's Wren
June 8 (Audubon (1966) I, Plate 207; Havell Plate 55; *OB* I, p. 288)
House Wren
1812 (Low (2002), p. 77)
Song Sparrow
1812 (Audubon (1966) II, Plate 256; Havell Plate No. 25)

Rhodes asserts that Audubon shot a Merlin on April 25, which he illustrated and later named Le

Petit Caporal in tribute to Napoleon Bonaparte. Rhodes (2004), p. 101. However, the original drawing in pencil and pastel is inscribed "April 23, 1812." Audubon (1966) I, Plate 156.

Edward Dwight, a noted Audubon art critic, believes that Audubon redrew the painting of the pair of Bay Breasted Warblers that is in the collection of the NYHS and was used by Robert Havell Jr. for Plate 69. Audubon (1966) I, Plate 103.

There is some question whether Audubon's drawing of the Broad-winged Hawk, engraved by Havell for Plate 91, included the image of the female that he illustrated in May 1812. According to his account in the *OB*, that was the case. *OB* I, p. 461–462. However, Dwight believes that the entire composition dates to 1829, and the superior technique Audubon used in showing the female's open wing and turned head would attest to that. Audubon had simply not achieved that level of skill by 1812. Audubon (1966) II, Plate 259.

Harvard has a drawing of a wren labeled "House Wren," which is undated and is of a style similar to others drawn by Audubon in the spring of 1812 when he drew a male House Wren that he had lured into his drawing room at Fatland Ford. Audubon (2008), No. 18; *OB* I, pp. 428–429. In the *OB*, Audubon wrote that his 1812 drawing of the male bird "is it which you see placed on the hat" in Havell Plate 83. Dwight believes the drawing used in the plate was made much later, possibly in 1824, but that Audubon used his earlier drawing from Fatland Ford as the basis for his Havell composition. Audubon (1966) I, Plate 4. In either case, it would appear the 1812 drawing is not at Harvard. Scott V. Edwards, Professor of Organismic and Evolutionary Biology and Curator of Ornithology at the Museum of Comparative Zoology at Harvard University, who provides the scientific commentary to the early Audubon drawings in *Audubon: Early Drawings*, identifies the wren illustrated in the Harvard drawing as a Winter Wren based on its shorter tail. Audubon (2008), No. 18. If so, it was not the model for the House Wren in the Havell plate. This would suggest that the drawing Audubon made at Fatland Ford has been lost.

Rhodes claims that the Song Sparrow was drawn on April 27, citing Low (2002), p. 43. Rhodes (2004), p. 101 and note, p. 449. Low does

not substantiate this dating, and the inscription on the drawing states simply "Montgomery County, Pennsylvania, 1812." Low (2002), p. 43; Audubon (1966) II, Plate 256. It should be noted that the drawing of this species, which was used as a basis for Havell Plate 25, was likely made later even though it is inscribed with the 1812 date. Dwight aptly states, "The work has a finesse not found in Audubon's earlier drawings." Audubon (1966) II, Plate 256. Moreover, the handwritten notations appearing on Audubon's drawings are not always definitive. For example, when he redrew his image of the adult Bald Eagle in London in 1828, he recorded the location where he had originally illustrated the species eight years earlier. Burroughs (2001), pp. 58, 61.

101. Ford (1988), p. 88. Unlike Ford, who believes the last meeting between Audubon and Alexander Wilson occurred in the spring of 1812, Rhodes posits that Audubon visited him in December 1811, shortly after the Audubons arrived at Fatland Ford. Rhodes (2004), p. 93. Neither Ford nor Rhodes have any concrete basis for choosing one over the other, as the only evidence of the meeting is a reference by Audubon in the *OB*, which does not provide a date. *OB* I, p. 440. Souder, whose Audubon biography focuses on the Wilson story to a greater extent than any other recent work, takes no position on the timing of this second meeting, saying merely that the men met again two years after their introduction in Louisville. Souder (2004), p. 111. Burtt & Davis erroneously state in their recent biography of Wilson that Audubon and Wilson did not see each other again after Louisville. Burtt & Davis (2013), p. 336.

102. *OB* I, p. 440.

103. Alexander Wilson died in Philadelphia on August 23, 1813. He is buried at Gloria Dei (Old Swedes') Church, the oldest church in Pennsylvania, which is located at 916 S. Swanson Street in Philadelphia. He is known today as the "father of American ornithology." Hunter (1983) pp. 112–113. See also, http://www.colonialswedes.org/Churches/GloDei.html (accessed 19 Oct. 2008).

104. Souder (2004), p. 131; Ford (1988), p. 87.

105. *OB* I, pp. 461–462. Audubon did not know that the bird he and Will Bakewell had captured was a Broad-winged Hawk, describing it as "new to

me." In his account of the species in the *OB*, Audubon stated that his drawing was dated May 27, 1812, which would indicate the bird was likely caught the same day. Audubon also averred that the drawing was completed in 1829 when he added the image of the male. Low (2002), p. 81. However, Audubon art critic Edward Dwight believes the pair was actually painted together in 1829. Audubon (1966) II, Plate 259. See also, note 100, *supra*. The illustration of the birds, sitting in a Pig-nut Hickory tree, was later issued by Havell as Plate 91.

106. Rhodes (2004), p. 104.

107. Dallett (1960), pp. 91-93. The naturalization petition filed on Audubon's behalf, supported by two witnesses, acknowledged that Audubon was "a native of the Island of St Domingo" but stated that he was "about Twenty Six years" of age. As reflected in the text, he had turned twenty-seven in April.

108. Streshinsky, p. 76. Audubon eventually acquired a signet ring with an image of the Turkey Cock, the first plate of *BOA*, with the words, "America My Country," a gift from Hannah Mary Rathbone I of Greenbank, outside Liverpool. Audubon (2011), pp. 209-210, 302.

109. Rhodes (2004), p. 105; Ford (1988), p. 88. Ford and Souder state that Will Bakewell, Lucy's twelve-year-old brother, returned with the Audubons to Kentucky. Souder (2004), p. 132; Ford (1988), p. 88. Ford provides no source for this claim, and Souder cites Audubon's Episode "The Ohio," which makes no mention of it. Souder (2004), p. 132 and note, p. 321. To the contrary, Audubon indicated in that piece that only he, his wife, and their infant son traveled back to Kentucky at that time. *OB* I, p. 29.

This claim is also asserted in the genealogical history of the Bakewell family, but that work is unreliable, misstating the year the Audubons returned to Fatland Ford. Bakewell (1896), p. 43. It appears from contemporary correspondence that Will did not join his sister in Henderson for another two years when, at the age of fourteen, he accepted an apprenticeship with Audubon & Bakewell. Rhodes (2004), pp. 114, 120; Delatte (1982), p. 86.

Streshinsky indicates the Audubons did not leave Fatland Ford until August 1812, but a letter Audubon wrote to Ferdinand Rozier from Shippingport, KY, on August 10, 1812, proves she

is mistaken. Cf. Streshinksy (1993), p. 77; JJA, Henderson to Ferdinand Rozier, Ste. Geneviève, MO, 10 Aug. 1812, Herrick (1938) I, pp. 243-244.

It is worth noting that in later years, as Audubon was marketing subscriptions to *BOA*, he claimed to have returned to Henderson after a months' long business trip to Philadelphia to find that virtually his entire collection of two hundred drawings, illustrating nearly a thousand birds, had been destroyed by a pair of nesting Norway rats that found their way into the wooden box in which the drawings had been stored. *OB* I, pp. xiii-xiv. See also, Rhodes (2004), p. 116. Unlike Audubon's other biographers, I am highly skeptical.

In judging the veracity of Audubon's story, it is first necessary to determine when the incident supposedly occurred. His only trip to Philadelphia after he moved to Henderson that lasted "several months" was evidently the one he took in the late winter of 1812. *OB* I, p. xiii. Audubon did make periodic trips back East to order supplies for his dry goods store. However, if there was an earlier or later trip of similar duration it is not recorded, and there are no extant drawings of birds that reflect such a trip as surely there would have been. So, the evidence would suggest that the trip to which he was alluding took place in 1812. Blaugrund & Stebbins (1993), p. 69.

However, this chronology does not fit with Audubon's description of the events. Audubon maintained that he had left the box of drawings with a relative in Henderson. But as of the first half of 1812, Audubon did not have any relatives living in Henderson other than Lucy, and, as reflected in the text, she had accompanied him to Philadelphia in November of the previous year. His brother-in-law Tom Bakewell would not move to Henderson until after Audubon and Lucy returned in August.

Another aspect of the claim that does not ring true is his assertion that the two hundred lost drawings "represented nearly a thousand inhabitants of the air." *OB* I, p. xiii. During his early years of ornithological illustration, Audubon generally placed one or at most two birds on a page. Audubon (2008). Never did he combine as many as five, which is what his claim would require for each and every drawing.

Finally, if nearly all of his drawings were destroyed at this time, how does one explain the existence of a substantial number, over one hundred, of his early works that were done prior to 1812? These include a portion of the drawings he had made for Lucy during his trip to France from 1805 to 1806 and a series of compositions dating between 1807 and 1811 while he was living in New York, Louisville, and Henderson. These drawings, now in the collections at Harvard, Princeton, and the Smithsonian Institution, show no evidence of having been part of a rat's nest. Audubon (2008); Rice (1960), pp. 23; 27; Arthur (1937), illus. facing p. 160. Even if some of his drawings were damaged or destroyed by rats at one time, many obviously remained intact, belying his claim to the contrary.

Nor was the survival of these early drawings due to the fact he had propitiously sent about thirty to Lucy's English cousin Euphemia Gifford before he and Lucy moved from Louisville to Henderson in 1810, as he later hinted. *OB* V, p. 291. The drawings at Harvard, for example, were owned by Audubon's friend Edward Harris and are separate and distinct from the Gifford drawings.

Admittedly, there are not nearly as many early drawings extant as one would expect from someone who claimed to have been actively engaged in this avocation prior to 1820. But he explained that he would periodically destroy older drawings as he continued to add better drawings of the same birds to his collection. And, it appears his focus on business matters from 1816 to 1819 seriously limited his output. Not a single drawing from this period has been found. Of those he completed prior to 1816, some may have been sold or given away beyond the ones that are now in institutional or private collections.

Audubon apparently wove this fiction as part of a calculated effort to shape his own mythology during the time he was trying to attract subscribers for his monumental publication. Everything in the story was designed to emphasize the almost insurmountable obstacles he was forced to overcome in order to realize his dream. That it was manifestly untrue merely demonstrates his chronic tendency to wrap himself in minor falsehoods when it suited his purpose.

110. Rhodes (2004), pp. 105–106; Ford (1988), p. 89. In his brief autobiography, Tom Bakewell re-

called the failure of Audubon & Bakewell's operations in New Orleans: "The war with G. Britain was declared June 1812, 6 months after my opening the N. Orleans house, & cutting off all hopes of pursuing the contemplated business. Therefore in August 1812, travelled by land to the North, through the Choctaw Cherokee & Chickasaw nations to Nashville & Henderson, the Audubons still remaining there." Bakewell (1935), pp. 36–37. See also, Sinclair (1966), p. 244. Rhodes states that Audubon & Bakewell's establishment in New Orleans "never opened its doors." Rhodes (2004), p. 106. Delatte apparently concurs. Delatte (1982), p. 68. Tom Bakewell's autobiography indicates otherwise.

111. Ford (1988), p. 89; Delatte (1982), pp. 70–71; Sinclair (1966), p. 244; Bakewell (1935), p. 37.

112. Delatte (1982), p. 70. Tom's less than enthusiastic reaction to continuing a mercantile career in Henderson is suggested by his autobiography, where he wrote: "Defeated in the brilliant prospects at N Orleans by the war, continued the business connection with Audubon on the smaller scale of Store Keeping at Henderson." Bakewell (1935), p. 37. See also, Sinclair (1966), p. 244.

113. Audubon (1999), p. 788; *AHJ* I, p. 32.

114. Rhodes (2004), p. 107; Ford (1988), p. 89. Ford claims that the Audubon house was on four acres. Rhodes, without citation, states that it sat on only an acre. The four acre reference comes from Audubon, who wrote in *Myself*: "I now purchased a ground lot of four acres, and a meadow of four more at the back of the first. On the latter stood several buildings, an excellent orchard, etc., lately the property of an English doctor, who had died on the premises, and left the whole to a servant woman as a gift, from whom it came to me as a freehold." *AHJ* I, p. 33. Herrick points out that Henderson was originally laid out in plots of one acre. Herrick (1938) I, pp. 251–252. Indeed, the town was designed in a grid pattern with "two hundred and sixty four Lots, of one acre each, lying in squares of four lots; each lot fronting two streets." Delatte (1982), p. 73.

115. Audubon (1999), p. 788; *AHJ* I, p. 32. Audubon described his second son, John Woodhouse, as "an extremely delicate boy till about a twelve-month old, when he suddenly acquired strength and grew to be a lusty child."

116. Rhodes (2004), p. 108.

117. Delatte (1982), pp. 73–74. Rhodes states that the tobacco inspection station was only in the planning stages when the Audubons returned to Henderson in 1812. Rhodes (2004), p. 107. However, Henderson was named a tobacco inspection site in 1801, and, four years later, a second inspection house was established to inspect flour, pork, beef, and hemp prior to shipment. Kleber (1992), p. 424. The town gradually became a major market for tobacco leaf in the state.

118. Delatte (1982), p. 73.

119. Souder (2004), p. 134.

120. Rhodes (2004), p. 113; Delatte (1982), p. 75. Rhodes states that Shawneetown was "sixty miles downriver" from Henderson. Delatte gives the distance as "thirty miles downriver." Both are incorrect. The Army Corps of Engineers measures the distance at 50.9 miles. Jones (1920), pp. 125, 133 (the Henderson wharf sits at mile 798.0 below Pittsburgh, Shawneetown at mile 848.9).

121. Delatte (1982), p. 74. Audubon acquired four one acre lots in Henderson in 1813 and another five the following year. According to Delatte's analysis of the town's deed books, Audubon realized a profit of approximately $22,500 on property he had acquired for about $4,500. In 2016 dollars, the profit would amount to approximately $384,000. Sahr (2015).

122. Audubon (2006), pp. 93–94; Rhodes (2004), p. 114; Delatte (1982), pp. 76, 78.

123. Streshinsky (1993), pp. 83, 91.

124. Rhodes (2004), pp. 114–115, referencing one of the tales William Alves collected from longtime Henderson residents. The Alves papers are in the collection of the Audubon Museum in Henderson.

125. Audubon (1999), p. 789; *AHJ* I, p. 33.

126. Rhodes (2004), pp. 110–111; Delatte (1982), pp. 74–75. Audubon's biographers generally attribute the original idea for the Henderson mill to Tom Bakewell. Rhodes (2004), pp. 110–111; Streshinsky (1993), p. 80; Ford (1988), pp. 90–91. Souder suggests that the partners arrived at the idea jointly. However, he cites Ford, who clearly states that it was Tom who persuaded Audubon to pursue the project. Cf. Ford (1988), pp. 90–91; Souder (2004), p. 161. Delatte, whose biography of Lucy Audubon offers perhaps the best researched and most comprehensive discussion of this period in

Audubon and Lucy's life, merely says that this was "a scheme that they thought would enhance the profits of their partnership." Delatte (1982), p. 74.

Tom's primary role as the instigator appears to come from Audubon, who refers to the mill in his autobiographical piece *Myself*, where he wrote, "We prospered at a round rate for a while, but unfortunately for me, he took it into his brain to persuade me to erect a steam-mill at Henderson." Audubon (1999), p. 789; *AHJ* I, p. 33. Tom indicated in his autobiography only that "A Steam Grist & Saw Mill was concluded on & built" without discussing whose idea it originally was. Bakewell (1935), p. 37. See also, Sinclair (1966), p. 244.

127. Rhodes (2004), pp. 110–111.

128. Delatte (1982), pp. 74–75.

129. Ibid.

130. Rhodes (2004), p. 111; Delatte (1982), p. 75; Bakewell (1896), pp. 46–47.

131. Delatte (1982), p. 75.

132. Rhodes (2004), p. 113; Delatte (1982), p. 75; Bakewell (1935), p. 37. In his brief autobiography, Tom Bakewell wrote, "Mr. Pears having some capital say 3 or 4000 dolls & my father furnishing me with about like moderate amount, which with what the firm A&B could [MS: *cd*] spare, A Steam Grist & Saw Mill was concluded on." Bakewell (1935), p. 37. See also, Sinclair (1966), p. 244. Rhodes indicates without attribution that Tom Bakewell obtained a $4,000 loan from his father. Rhodes (2004), p. 113. Ford states that Pears agreed to invest $4,000 if Tom would match it, without indicating where Tom obtained the funds. Ford (1988), p. 91.

133. Delatte (1982), pp. 83–84.

134. Keating (1976), p. 62; Herrick (1938) I, p. 255, note 11; Bakewell (1935), p. 37. The terms of the mill partnership obviously did not favor Audubon. Nor did Audubon exercise good business judgment in failing to ascertain what sort of demand there would be in Henderson and the surrounding community for a gristmill and sawmill before he agreed to invest in the venture. See note 164, *infra*.

135. Delatte (1982), pp. 84, 87.

136. Ibid., p. 87. Ford states that Thomas Pears left Henderson in August 1814 to collect his family in Pittsburgh. Ford (1988), p. 91. However, it is clear he did not head downriver with them until the following spring, as Sarah Pears continued to write

letters from Pittsburgh until March 1815. Delatte (1982), p. 87, note 39. In the interim, Pears journeyed east to Philadelphia to discuss employment terms with David Prentice, the Scottish mechanic, and to say goodbye to the senior William Bakewell at Fatland Ford. Ford (1988), p. 91.

137. Delatte (1982), p. 88.

138. Rhodes (2004), p. 119; Ford (1988), p. 91; Delatte (1982), p. 88.

139. Rhodes (2004), pp. 121–123.

140. Delatte (1982), p. 87.

141. Rhodes (2004), p. 120; Delatte (1982), pp. 84–87. The mechanic David Prentice and his wife, Margaret, had also arrived in Henderson and moved into a nearby log house that Tom Bakewell had built but did not occupy. They ate their meals at the Audubon table, which doubtless added to the chaos and congestion in the Audubon home. Delatte (1982), pp. 77, 87.

142. Rhodes (2004), pp. 115, 121.

143. Delatte (1982), p. 87. The record is unclear as to the precise date of little Lucy Audubon's birth. Audubon's biographers cannot even agree as to the year she was born. Delatte and Souder assert she was born in 1815. Souder (2004), pp. 161–162; Delatte (1982), p. 87. Ford gives the year as 1815 in her chronology of Audubon's life in her Appendix but a few pages later, in a genealogical chart of the Audubon family, states that she was born in 1814. Ford (1988), pp. 460, 466. Rhodes asserts, without a reference, that she was born in December 1814. Rhodes (2004), p. 122. The Bakewell genealogy provides no date for her birth. Bakewell (1896), p. 32.

144. Rhodes (2004), p. 116. While there are no extant bird drawings done by Audubon between 1815 and 1820, we do know that he would at least occasionally draw and paint a specimen. For example, in 1819, he painted a large brown eagle that he collected near Henderson, which he called the Washington Eagle. *OB* I, pp. 60–61. See also, Chapter 12, note 26, *infra*.

145. Delatte (1982), pp. 88–89.

146. Rhodes (2004), p. 125; Delatte (1982), pp. 88–89.

147. Delatte (1982), p. 89. Although Delatte does not say when Sally Pears first became aware she was expecting, we know that the family had returned to Pittsburgh by mid-May 1816 when Sally resumed her correspondence from that city. Ibid., p. 87, note 39. This timing, combined with Sally's strident personality, strongly suggests that Sally had learned she was pregnant earlier in the year.

148. Delatte (1982), p. 89. Thomas Pears returned to Pittsburgh in 1816 and accepted employment with Benjamin Bakewell at his flint glassworks. Palmer (2004), p. 37.

149. Delatte (1982), p. 89. On March 16, 1816, Audubon and Tom Bakewell entered into a ninety-nine year lease with the town of Henderson for the riverfront parcel on which they constructed the mill. Rhodes (2004), p. 126. The mill was built predominantly with slave labor. Nathan Brooke, Hendersonville to Susan Brooke c/o William Bakewell, Fatland Ford, 1 Aug. 1815 (Private collection). A Pennsylvania millwright, Brooke evidently came to Kentucky along with David Prentice to help build the mill. He indicated in his letter to his wife that he saw "very few white people from one weeks end to the other." Ibid.

150. Delatte (1982), p. 89.

151. Thomas W. Bakewell, Henderson to William Bakewell, Norristown, PA, 1 Dec. 1816, Bakewell (1935), pp. 39–40.

152. Ibid.

153. Delatte (1982), p. 90; Bakewell (1896), p. 41. See also, Palmer (2004), p. 14.

154. Delatte (1982), p. 90. Streshinsky's biography asserts that Sarah Pears was still living with the Audubons in Henderson when Tom returned with his new bride in the summer of 1816. Streshinsky (1993), p. 89. However, the Pearses were back in Pittsburgh by this time. Delatte (1982), p. 87, note 39.

155. Thomas W. Bakewell, Henderson to William Bakewell, Norristown, PA, 1 Dec. 1816, Bakewell (1935), p. 39. See also, Delatte (1982), p. 90.

156. Ford (1988), p. 93; Delatte (1982), p. 90.

157. Thomas W. Bakewell, Henderson to William Bakewell, Norristown, PA, 1 Dec. 1816, Bakewell (1935), p. 39. See also, Ford (1988), p. 93. Yale's Beinecke Library has two deeds reflecting the sale of lots owned by Tom and Elizabeth Bakewell to Audubon, dated December 31, 1816. They were examined by A. Barbour on February 12, 1817, before the indentures were accepted for recording. (Yale, Box 10, Folder 543).

158. Thomas W. Bakewell, Henderson to William Bakewell, Norristown, PA, 1 Dec. 1816, Bakewell (1935), p. 39. In his letter of December 1, 1816, Tom Bakewell wrote his father that "my great desire to leave Henderson, & to live at Pittsburgh [MS: Pitt*g*] was the motive by which I acted," in reference to the dissolution of Audubon & Bakewell. However, Tom and his family subsequently moved to Louisville.

159. Ibid.

160. Rhodes (2004), p. 131; Ford (1988), p. 94; Thomas W. Bakewell, Henderson to William Bakewell, Norristown, PA, 1 Dec. 1816, Bakewell (1935), p. 39. Tom informed his father that, inasmuch as he was still jointly responsible for the debts of Audubon & Bakewell, "I have agreed to remain here & give my assistance to M*r*. A till 1*st* July next."

According to the published Bakewell genealogy, Tom and Elizabeth celebrated the birth of their first child, William Woodhouse Bakewell, on April 29, 1817, in Henderson. Bakewell (1896), p. 36. Streshinsky and Delatte, however, assert that Elizabeth left Henderson ahead of Tom to give birth to her son in Louisville. Streshinsky (1993), p. 92; Delatte (1982), p. 90. Neither biographer cites a source for this putative fact. Lacking other definitive evidence, the text relies upon the published family genealogy as Rhodes and Ford apparently do.

161. Delatte (1982), p. 94.

162. Rhodes (2004), p. 130; Delatte (1982), p. 92.

163. Audubon (1999), p. 791; *AHJ* I, p. 35.

164. Ford (1988), p. 92; Delatte (1982), p. 92. See also, Rhodes (2004), p. 127. To further buttress his contention that Audubon has been unfairly maligned by his biographers for being a poor businessman, Rhodes evidently believes that Audubon is blameless for the Henderson mill fiasco. He asserts that it was Tom Bakewell who proposed building the mill "without even determining if the region's grain production could support it." Rhodes (2004), p. 127. However, as Tom's partner, Audubon bore just as much responsibility, if not more so, for failing to accurately assess the market for a gristmill and sawmill in Henderson.

The principal reason that Audubon's biographers have formed a negative opinion of his business skills at this stage in his life is that his success had more to do with him being in the right place at the right time than because of his business acumen.

His early years of prosperity in Henderson occurred during a period when the town was growing rapidly, credit was readily available, and the economy was in an inflationary cycle. Like many people along the frontier, he was able to borrow funds easily, which made it possible for him to purchase and subdivide property and to expand his general store. While he did extremely well for several years, the contraction of credit beginning in 1818 and the resulting Panic of 1819 put Audubon in a position where he was unable to satisfy his debts. There is no question that the cost of constructing the mill was a compounding factor in the ultimate demise of his businesses. Clearly, Audubon's failure to analyze the demand for a mill in that location is testament to his business naiveté. Although Rhodes's point is well taken when one considers Audubon's successful management of *BOA*, one cannot seriously contend that Audubon was a shrewd or capable businessman during his Henderson years.

165. Ford (1988), p. 92; Delatte (1982), p. 92.

166. Audubon (1999), p. 789; *AHJ*, Vol. I, p. 33. Audubon scholar Michael Harwood believes that Audubon exaggerated the lack of demand for the mill's services. He points out that Nicholas Berthoud, "an established and successful businessman," put some money into the mill and eventually acquired Audubon's majority interest. As Harwood puts it, "These people weren't stupid. The West was going to grow, everyone knew that. Men who owned land and businesses in the towns along the Ohio stood to do very well for themselves. A mill was a basic business. It could have turned out to be an excellent investment." Durant & Harwood (1980), pp. 107–108. Of course, this begs the question as to whether, in the time period 1817–1819, the demand for grist- and sawmilling was strong enough in the region to make the mill a successful enterprise. And, based on Audubon's later assessment, coupled with the economic collapse that swept Kentucky beginning in 1818, the answer is that it was not.

167. Rhodes (2004), p. 130.

168. Thomas W. Bakewell, Henderson to William Bakewell, Norristown, PA, 1 Dec. 1816, Bakewell (1935), p. 39.

169. Audubon (1999), p. 790; *AHJ* I, p. 33.

170. Ford (1988), p. 94.

171. Delatte (1982), pp. 92–93. According to

Lucy's sister Ann, the Audubons' daughter, Lucy, was born with "dropsy of the head," the medical term for which is hydrocephalus. Rhodes (2004), p. 122. Hydrocephalus is a congenital disorder caused by a buildup of cerebrospinal fluid in the brain. Ibid. Although surgical treatment is available for the condition today, there was no means to cure it in the 19th century, although various remedies were believed to have positive benefits. Cheyne (1808), pp. 91–107. Lucy was "buried in the family graveyard of Gen. Samuel Hopkins's plantation— 'only the birds know just where little Lucy lies.'" Work Projects Administration (1941), p. 75.

172. Audubon (1999), p. 793; *AHJ* I, p. 37.

173. Audubon (1999), p. 31; Corning (1929a), p. 47.

174. Souder (2004), p. 164. The Kentucky Insurance Company was the first to fail in 1818.

175. Rhodes (2004), p. 124. For an excellent discussion of the genesis of the Panic of 1819, see Rothbard (2007).

176. Rothbard (2007), p. 4; Rhodes (2004), p. 124; Connelley (1922) II, p. 593.

177. Souder (2004), p. 164; Connelley (1922) II, p. 596. Cf. Rothbard (2007), p. 11 (stating that Kentucky chartered forty banks in the 1817–1818 legislative session). The banks chartered by the Kentucky legislature in 1818 soon became known as the "Forty Thieves." Souder (2004), p. 164.

178. Rothbard (2007), p. 17; Rhodes (2004), p. 132.

179. Rhodes (2004), p. 132; Howe (2007), pp. 142–143; Connelley (1922) II, p. 595.

180. Howe (2007), pp. 142–143.

181. Rhodes (2004), pp. 132–133; Delatte (1982), p. 93. Audubon sold twelve parcels of land in 1818 for approximately $7,000. The deeds of sale are recorded in Deed Book C and Deed Book D in the Court of the Chancery, Henderson, KY. Delatte (1982), p. 93 and note 54.

182. Audubon (1820–1821); Cf. Audubon (1999), p. 31; Corning (1929a), p. 47.

183. Audubon (1999), pp. 31–32; Corning (1929a), p. 47.

184. Audubon (1999), p. 791; *AHJ* I, p. 35.

185. Audubon (2006), pp. 93–94; Rhodes (2004), p. 141. The indenture by which Audubon sold all of his assets to Nicholas Berthoud, executed on July 13, 1819, is in the collection of the Audubon Museum in Henderson, KY.

186. Audubon (2006), pp. 93–94; Rhodes (2004), pp. 141–142; Delatte (1982), p. 98; Keating (1976), p. 81.

187. Delatte (1982), pp. 98–99; AHJ I, p. 35. Ford asserts that Audubon left Henderson on July 19, 1819, the same day his good friend James Berthoud passed away during a visit to the Audubon home. Ford (1988), pp. 105–106. According to the Berthoud family genealogy, it appears that Berthoud actually died on July 14. Ties That Bind Us Family Tree, Ancestry.com, http://trees.ancestry.com/tree /70068667/person/44210525962?ssrc= (accessed 9 May 2015). It makes more sense that Audubon would have remained in Henderson for Berthoud's funeral as opposed to leaving for Louisville the day he died, as Ford has it.

188. *AHJ* I, p. 47.

189. Rhodes (2004), p. 142; Ford (1988), p. 106; Delatte (1982), p. 100.

190. Rhodes (2004), p. 142; Souder (2004), p. 167; Streshinsky (1993), p. 101; Ford (1988), p. 106; Delatte (1982), p. 101. Since 1792, Kentucky law permitted the release of a debtor after twenty days of imprisonment if he took the oath of insolvency and provided a complete schedule of his assets to his creditors. In 1819, as a result of the enormous increase in the number of bankruptcies, the state enacted a law that allowed the debtor to take the insolvent oath upon being arrested. Mittlebeeler (1975), pp. 174–175. This was obviously the provision that Judge Cosby brought to Audubon's attention after he was jailed in Louisville. However, unlike current bankruptcy laws, the insolvency laws of early 19th century Kentucky did not discharge the debtor's debts. The debtor remained liable for the debts until they were paid. Ibid., pp. 174, 182. As a consequence, Audubon was careful to shield his assets in later life. Rhodes's suggestion that the debts were extinguished is incorrect. Rhodes (2004), p. 387.

191. Rhodes (2004), p. 143.

192. Ibid., pp. 143–145; Audubon (1999), pp. 792; Delatte (1982), p. 101; *AHJ*, pp. 36, 47. One of the first chalk portraits Audubon ever made was of

his friend James Berthoud, the wealthy Shipping-port merchant whose son, Nicholas, had married Lucy's sister Eliza. Rhodes (2004), p. 143. There is some question among Audubon scholars as to precisely when Audubon made this drawing. Some biographers believe the drawing was made posthumously in August 1819, after Audubon arrived in Louisville. Streshinsky (1993), p. 102; Dwight (1965), p. 22. Indeed, Berthoud had died on July 14 while visiting the Audubon family in Henderson and was buried there. Ties That Bind Us Family Tree, Ancestry.com, http://trees.ancestry.com/tree/70068667/person/44210525962?ssrc= (accessed 9 May 2015). Cf. Streshinsky (1993), p. 97 (Berthoud's date of death given as July 18, 1819); Ford (1988), p. 105 (stating that Berthoud died on July 19, 1819); Dwight (1965), p. 22.

Rhodes agrees that the drawing dates to August 1819, although he does not believe it was completed posthumously. Rhodes submits that if it had been, "JJA would have said so, as he did of other instances." Rhodes (2004), pp. 143–144 and note, p. 453. There are two problems with Rhodes's argument. First, and most obviously, Berthoud died in July 1819. Rhodes apparently disputes this as well, although he offers no supporting evidence. He also provides no explanation as to why Berthoud was buried in Henderson. He just baldly asserts that "Sometime that summer after Audubon drew his portrait, James Berthoud died." Ibid., p. 144.

Second, Audubon's own account, although ambiguous, suggests that the drawing was done following Berthoud's death to provide solace to Berthoud's widow as well as to his son: "in Attempting the Likeness of James Berthoud Es^qr—a Particularly good Man and I believe the Only *Sincere* Friend of Myself and Wife We ever had—, to please his Son & Lady I discovered such Talents that I was engaged to proceed and succeeded in a Few Weeks and beyond My Expectations." Audubon (1999), p. 32; Corning (1929a), p. 47.

Ford sidesteps this debate entirely, stating that the Berthoud image, along with a matching image of his wife, was drawn at some earlier time, "in better days." Ford (1988), pp. 106–107. Souder concurs, writing that the drawings were done "years earlier when he lived in Louisville." Souder (2004), p. 167.

It should be noted, however, that Audubon's description of the circumstances surrounding his effort to capture James Berthoud's image, quoted above, was in the context of his successful portrait endeavors in Louisville in 1819, suggesting that it was done around that time, not previously. Also, the drawing of Mrs. Berthoud is inscribed on the back in Audubon's hand, "Audubon fecit August 1819" ("Audubon made August 1819"). Dwight (1965), p. 22. At least as to the timing of Mrs. Berthoud's drawing, Ford and Souder are clearly mistaken. The original Audubon drawings of James Berthoud, his wife, and Nicholas are in the collection of the J.B. Speed Art Museum in Louisville. Dwight (1965), pp. 22–23.

193. Delatte (1982), p. 101. In a 19th century history of Louisville, the author notes that Audubon was advertising drawing lessons in a local newspaper in February 1819, even before he moved there from Henderson. "We find by an advertisement in the Courier of February 12th, in this year, that J.J. Audubon, the world renowned ornithologist, was at that time endeavoring to procure a class in drawing, and was offering to paint portraits here, which his advertisement promises shall be 'strong likenesses.'" Casseday (1852), p. 155. It is unclear if this advertisement actually appeared in 1819. A more likely scenario is that he was offering classes in February 1820, before he left Louisville for Cincinnati.

194. Rhodes (2004), p. 142; Streshinsky (1993), p. 101; Delatte (1982), pp. 101–102; *AHJ* I, p. 35.

195. Audubon (1999), p. 792; Delatte (1982), p. 102; *AHJ* I, p. 36.

196. Streshinsky (1993), p. 103; Ford (1988), pp. 108–109; Delatte (1982), p. 103.

197. Rhodes (2004), pp. 146–147; Ford (1988), p. 111. Cincinnati College is now the University of Cincinnati.

198. Robert Todd, Lexington, KY to Gen. William Lytle, Cincinnati, 12 Feb. 1820 (William Lytle Papers, Box XII, No. 203.1, Cincinnati Historical Society). See also, Rhodes (2004), p. 146.

199. Rhodes (2004), p. 147; Ford (1988), p. 112. In *Myself*, Audubon suggested that Rose died in Cincinnati. Speaking of his new job with the Western Museum, he wrote, "My salary was large, and I at once sent for your mother to come to me, and

bring you. Your dearly beloved sister Rosa died shortly afterward." *AHJ* I, p. 37. Ford notes that this reference is erroneous and that Rose died and was buried in Louisville. Ford (1988), p. 112 and note, p. 439.

200. Rhodes (2004), p. 147; Delatte (1982), p. 103; Sheehan (1979), p. 88; Adams (1966), p. 190; *AHJ* I, p. 36. The precise date of Audubon's arrival in Cincinnati is not known, but Sheehan notes that the Cincinnati papers began carrying advertisements for Audubon's drawing classes as early as March 14, 1820. Sheehan (1979), p. 88 and note 9. The 1820 U.S. Census counted a population in Cincinnati of 9,642. Gibson (1998), Table 5.

201. Rhodes (2004), p. 148. Audubon wrote, "I found, sadly too late, that the members of the College museum were splendid promisers and very bad paymasters." Audubon (1999), p. 793; *AHJ* I, p. 37.

202. Ford (1988), p. 112.

203. Rhodes (2004), p. 151. Ford and Delatte claim that Audubon was dismissed by the museum in April. Ford (1988), p. 113; Delatte (1982), p. 104–105. The evidence would suggest he did not leave until the end of June. See note 230, *infra*.

204. Audubon (1966), p. xix. See also, Rhodes (2004), p. 148.

205. Rhodes (2004), pp. 150–151; Ford (1988), pp. 113–114; Delatte (1982), pp. 105–106.

206. Relying upon *Myself*, Rhodes asserts that the expedition of Maj. Stephen Long, heading west on the steamboat *Western Engineer* to explore the upper Missouri River, stopped in Cincinnati in early May 1820 and visited the Western Museum. There, they were purportedly invited to view Audubon's portfolio. Years later, Audubon recalled how Maj. Long and two members of his scientific staff, Thomas Say and Titian Ramsey Peale, "stared at my drawings of birds at that time." Rhodes (2004), pp. 148–149; *AHJ* I, p. 37. Streshinsky claims, instead, that Audubon met the members of the Long expedition when it "stopped at Cincinnati on its return from the upper reaches of the Mississippi." Streshinsky (1993), p. 105. Both are in error. The Long expedition left Pittsburgh and reached Cincinnati on May 9, 1819, approximately nine months before Audubon moved there. Evans (1997), pp. 25, 31. The expedition broke up at Cape Girardeau, MO, in October 1820, and Long took an overland route

to Washington City, while Say and Peale traveled by steamboat to New Orleans and then Philadelphia. Ibid., pp. 213–217. Notwithstanding Audubon's assertion, he could not have shown these three men his drawings. This is evidently yet another example of his tendency to misrepresent the truth to craft his own mythology.

207. Audubon (1999), pp. 154–155; Corning (1929a), pp. 226–227. See also, Rhodes (2004), p. 151; Adams (1966), pp. 195–196. Rhodes and Adams incorrectly state that Audubon's letter to U.S. Congressman Henry Clay was written six weeks after Daniel Drake delivered his complementary views about Audubon's drawings at the ceremony marking the opening of the Western Museum. Both authors agree that Drake's remarks were given on June 10, 1820. Audubon's letter to Clay is dated August 12, 1820, which would make it exactly nine weeks later. Rhodes (2004), pp. 150–151 and note, p. 454; Adams (1966), pp. 193, 195–196.

208. Audubon (1999), p. 43; Corning (1929a), p. 65.

209. Rhodes (2004), p. 153; Souder (2004), p. 169; Ford (1988), p. 115. Audubon's description of the flatboat captain, Jacob Aumack, appears in his journal entry of Sunday, November 5, 1820. Audubon (1999), p. 11; Corning (1929a), p. 16.

210. Audubon (1999), pp. 5–6, 66. In his 1820 journal, Audubon described Lovelace, the captain of the other flatboat, as "a good Natured, rough fellow, brought up to Work without pride, rather Anxious to Make Money—Playfull & found of Jokes & Woman—" Ibid., p. 11; Corning (1929a), p. 16.

211. Rhodes (2004), pp. 152–153; Audubon (1999), p. 3; Corning (1929a), p. 3.

212. Rhodes (2004), p. 152; Adams (1966), p. 197. In his 1820 journal, Audubon described Joseph Mason as "a Young Man of about 18 Years of age." Audubon (1999), p. 3; Corning (1929a), p. 3. However, due to some faulty genealogical research by early Audubon scholars, his biographers have virtually all ignored this statement, asserting that Mason was actually much younger. Herrick claims that Mason was only eleven. Herrick (1938) I, p. 307. Arthur states that Mason was born on July 24, 1807, which would have made him thirteen. Arthur (1937), p. 98. Ford agrees that Mason was only thirteen when he joined Audubon on this trip, but gives

his birth year as 1808, which would have made him twelve. Ford (1988), p. 112. See also, Audubon (1999), p. 883. Delatte, Streshinsky, and Souder all repeat the conventional wisdom that Mason was thirteen. Souder (2004), p. 168; Streshinsky (1993), p. 108; Delatte (1982), p. 107. Of the principal modern biographers, only Adams and Rhodes have accepted the validity of Audubon's statement. Rhodes (2004), p. 152; Adams (1966), p. 197.

As it turns out, Audubon knew what he was talking about. For confirmation of Mason's age, we can thank Douglas Lewis, Ph.D., the former Curator of Sculpture and Decorative Arts at the National Gallery of Art in Washington, D.C., who determined from his research of the Cincinnati census records and location of Mason's grave that Audubon's assistant was indeed eighteen. Another Joseph Mason in Cincinnati, who was younger, was mistaken for Audubon's companion. Rhodes (2004), p. 152 and note, p. 454. Rhodes is the first Audubon biographer to bring Dr. Lewis's important research to light.

213. Rhodes (2004), p. 153; Ford (1988), p. 115; Audubon (1999), p. 3; Corning (1929a), p. 4. Samuel Cumings published *The Western Navigator* in Philadelphia in 1822. Three years later, the volume was updated and reissued as *The Western Pilot*. It went through multiple revised editions. Wied (2008) I, p. 213, note M13.

214. Audubon (1999), p. 9. Corning (1929a), p. 12.

215. Audubon (1999), p. 21; Corning (1929a), p. 30.

216. Rhodes (2004), p. 165; Audubon (1999), pp. 45–46; Corning (1929a), pp. 67–68. The Arkansas Post was situated only about ten miles upriver, but the roundabout route Audubon's party was forced to take due to the topography and thick undergrowth led them to hike what Audubon estimated to be thirty-two miles.

217. Audubon (1999), p. 47. Cf. Corning (1929a), pp. 70–71.

218. Audubon (1999). pp. 47–48, 51, 58; Corning (1929a), pp. 71–72, 77–78.

219. Rhodes (2004), p. 167; Audubon (1999), pp. 57–59; Corning (1929a), pp. 86–88.

220. Rhodes (2004), p. 167; Audubon (1999), p. 59. Cf. Corning (1929a), p. 89. In an Episode

entitled "Natchez in 1820," Audubon wrote that Nicholas Berthoud was carrying letters from Lucy and his sons. Bumping into Berthoud and being handed the first letters he had received from his family since leaving Cincinnati "put me in high spirits, and we proceeded towards the best hotel in the place, that of Mr GARNIER." *OB* III, p. 540. Rhodes quotes this passage in his biography and gives it the imprimatur of truth. Rhodes (2004), p. 167. However, this appears to be an example of Audubon's not infrequent use of literary license in recounting the episodic tales in the *OB*. In his 1820 journal, which was written contemporaneously and is certainly more reliable, Audubon indicated that on the day he arrived in Natchez, December 26, he received "Two Letters from my Beloved Wife, dated 7th & 14th of Novr." He did not meet his brother-in-law and, indeed, did not know Berthoud was in Natchez until the following day. So, even if Berthoud had some additional letters from Lucy, they would not have been the first ones Audubon received. Audubon (1999), pp. 58–59; Corning (1929a), pp. 88–89.

On a separate point, Ford asserts that Audubon returned to the flatboat after meeting Berthoud on December 27 and spent the night "shivering beneath a buffalo robe in the bitter cold of the choppy river." In Ford's telling, Berthoud, who was staying in one of Natchez's finest hotels, supposedly felt guilty about his brother-in-law's living conditions. The following day, he found Audubon and asked him to share his room. Ford (1988), p. 118. Rhodes and Streshinsky believe, as do I, that Berthoud extended the invitation the day he ran into Audubon. Rhodes (2004), p. 168; Streshinsky (1988), p. 114. In his journal, Audubon wrote that he ate dinner at Berthoud's hotel the night they met. His entry for the following day states: "Nicholas having invited me to stay at his Lodgings I Breakfasted at the Hotel of Mr Garnier." Audubon (1999), pp. 62–63; Corning (1929a), p. 96. Clearly, he spent the night in Berthoud's room and ate breakfast there the following morning. Ford has misread Audubon's journal on this point.

221. Audubon (1999). p. 64; Corning (1929a), pp. 97–98. Audubon described the Natchez Hotel as "a good House built on the spanish plan i.e. with Large Piazas and Many Doors and windows — Well

Kept by Mr John Garnier and is the rendez vous of all Gentill Travellers and Boarders." Audubon (1999), p. 60. Cf. Corning (1929a), p. 91.

222. Audubon (1999), p. 64. Cf. Corning (1929a), p. 98. Audubon also discussed the circumstances surrounding the loss of his small portfolio in an Episode in the *OB* aptly entitled, "The Lost Portfolio." *OB* III, pp. 564–567.

223. Audubon (1999), pp. 65, 72–73; Corning (1929a), pp. 99, 111; Bakewell (1896), p. 27. Rhodes states that New Orleans had forty thousand residents when Audubon arrived in early January 1821, but he does not cite a source for this figure. Rhodes (2004), p. 173. According to the U.S. Census of 1820, the population of New Orleans that year was 27,176. Gibson (1998), Table 5.

224. Vincent Nolte indicated that none of the New Orleans' streets were paved in 1821: "Through the city ran four feet wide side-walks, which were called *banquettes*, and which ran along close to the houses. They were made of brick set loosely in the sand, and in wet weather became almost utterly useless, since nearly every step of the pedestrian produced a spirit of liquid mud from between the loose bricks. The streets themselves were nothing but mud holes, with occasional projecting bits of dried clod." Nolte (1854), p. 298.

225. Rhodes (2004), pp. 174–176; Audubon (1999), pp. 74–76; Corning (1929a), pp. 114–117.

226. Audubon (1999), pp. 76–78; Corning (1929a), pp. 116–118. Around the third week of February 1821, Audubon was approached by a young, beautiful French-speaking woman he referred to as Mrs. André, who asked him to draw her nude figure in black chalk. He openly recounted the details in a letter written to Lucy dated May 24, 1821, which apparently copied entries from his journal. This letter, in the collection of the American Philosophical Society, is quoted in full in Audubon (1999), pp. 886–889. See also, Irmscher (1999), pp. 65–76; Arthur (1937), pp. 159–167. In payment, she asked him to locate a "good quality" gun as a souvenir, for which she gave him $5 to use as a down payment. He "hunted through the stores and found a good one" that cost $120. When he had finished the composition, she gave him another $125. Audubon (1999), pp. 888–889.

Ford errs in her reference to the cost of the gun, which she describes as "his $125-selection." Ford (1988), p. 121. Audubon is clear in saying that he "was asked One hundred and Twenty Dollars" for the gun. Audubon (1999), p. 888.

227. Audubon (1999), p. 79; Corning (1929a), p. 121. See also, Rhodes (2004), p. 178. Ford claims that the Queensware that Audubon purchased was for his sister-in-law Eliza Berthoud. Ford (1988), p. 120. Audubon's journal entry for January 29, 1821, indicates otherwise: "Collected My Earnings, purchased a Crate of queens Ware for My Beloved Wife." Audubon (1999), p. 79; Corning (1929a), p. 121.

228. Audubon (1999), p. 32; Delatte (1982), pp. 108–109; Corning (1929a), p. 48.

229. Ford (1988), p. 114; Delatte (1982), pp. 107–108. Rhodes suggests that Lucy did not teach during her stay in Cincinnati: "With two young boys she was not yet in a position to take up teaching, as she told her cousin 'My two children occupy nearly the whole of my time, for I educate them myself.'" Rhodes (2004), p. 152, citing LBA, Shippingport to Euphemia Gifford, Duffield Bank near Derby, England, 1 Apr. 1821 (Princeton, Box 1, Folder 10). However, the letter Rhodes relies upon for this assertion was authored by Lucy after she had returned to Shippingport and was living with her sister Eliza's family. It is unclear to what degree Lucy was receiving her wealthy sister's largess, but she evidently was not required to work given the quotation from the letter. However, one cannot fairly extrapolate from this letter what Lucy was doing when she was still in Cincinnati. Audubon's other biographers agree that Lucy supplemented her meager savings in Cincinnati by teaching both before and after Audubon left the city. Ford (1988), pp. 112–114; Delatte (1982), p. 107–108; Arthur (1937), pp. 100 (before).

230. Ford (1988), pp. 114, 117; Delatte (1982), pp. 107–108; *AHJ* I, p. 49, note 1. In *AHJ*, Maria Audubon claimed that Audubon was owed $1,200 for his work at the Western Museum. *AHJ* I, p. 49, note 1. Both Rhodes and Adams repeat this patently erroneous statement. Rhodes (2004), p. 152; Adams (1966), p. 192. At a salary of $125 a month, Audubon would have had to have been employed for upwards of ten months to have earned such a sum. The evi-

dence simply does not support this. Audubon apparently moved to Cincinnati to accept the position toward the end of February or early March 1820. The letter of recommendation written by Robert Todd is dated February 12, which suggests that an offer of employment could not have reached Audubon until the third week of February at the earliest. See Rhodes (2004), p. 146. By March 25, Audubon was in Cincinnati and must have been working at the museum long enough to have determined that its lack of ready funds prevented him from being paid, forcing him to look elsewhere for income. On that date, a local paper, the *Cincinnati Western Spy*, carried an advertisement for Miss Deeds's school offering drawing and painting lessons by Mr. Audubon. Ibid., p. 148.

The duration of his employment by the museum is not entirely clear, but it apparently did not exceed four months. Ford asserts that he remained on the museum payroll only until the end of April 1820. Ford (1988), p. 113. See also, Delatte (1982), pp. 104–105. Rhodes states that he remained employed until June. Rhodes (2004), p. 151. The president of Cincinnati College, the Reverend Elijah Slack, provided a letter of introduction to Audubon on October 10, 1820, in which he stated that Audubon had been engaged by the museum "for 3 or 4 Months." Audubon (1999), pp. 42–43.

It should be noted that when Maria made this claim in *AHJ*, she did not have access to the Mississippi River journal, which contains a transcribed copy of the Slack letter. Deane (1904), p. 334. Thus, she apparently did not know how long Audubon had been employed and evidently speculated that he was working there during most of 1820 prior to his departure for New Orleans. Assuming Audubon started work at the beginning of March and left the museum's employ after four months, he would have been due $500. Eventually, Lucy succeeded in getting paid $400. *AHJ* I, p. 49, note 1. Since we do not know if Audubon actually worked for a full four months, this may well have represented the entirety of his earnings.

231. Audubon (1999), p. 78; Corning (1929a), p. 120.

232. Delatte (1982), p. 109. According to Delatte, there is no indication as to precisely when Lucy left Cincinnati. However, she asserts that by late January or early February 1821, Lucy and the boys had returned to Shippingport. Douglas Lewis states in his chronology of Audubon's travels through the South from 1819 to 1837 that Lucy and her sons moved back to Louisville on February 15, 1821. Lewis (1991), p. 64. Lucy continued to write Daniel Drake from Shippingport to request payment of Audubon's unpaid wages. In 2007, Sotheby's auctioned off such a letter, dated March 16, 1821. Sotheby's (2007), Lot 1, p. 16.

233. Audubon (1999), pp. 73–74, 78–79; Corning (1929a), pp. 113, 120–121. See also, Rhodes (1999), p. 173. Audubon's journal entry of February 2, 1821, reflects that the hunter whom he hired to procure specimens of birds for him to draw was named Smith.

234. Audubon (1999), pp. 81, 83; Corning (1929a), pp. 124–125, 127.

235. Rhodes (2004), p. 178; Blaugrund (1993), p. 12.

236. Rhodes (2004), p. 183; Audubon (1999), pp. 83–88; Corning (1929a), pp. 127–135.

237. Audubon (1999), p. 87. Cf. Corning (1929a), p. 133. The letter to Audubon reporting the discovery of his small portfolio was dated March 8, 1821, and was sent by Anthony P. Bodley, one of the men who had served as a crewmember aboard Jacob Aumack's flatboat. Audubon (1999), pp. 12, 87; Arthur (1937), p. 170. He informed Audubon that it had been placed in the hands of the local Natchez newspaper, the *Mississippi Republican*, and could be obtained by writing them. Audubon wondered "how the Book had escaped the researches of Mʳ Garnier," the proprietor of the Natchez hotel whom Audubon had written to find it. Audubon (1999), p. 87. Garnier ultimately was the one who forwarded it to New Orleans by way of his son. In Audubon's journal, he expressed his thanks to whoever was responsible for saving his work from destruction: "I have to thank Mʳ Garnier but More *he* that found it on the River Bank and took Such very remarkable good Care of it." Ibid., p. 95; Corning (1929a), p. 146.

238. Audubon (1999), p. 95; Corning (1929a), p. 146..

239. *OB* III, p. 567.

240. Audubon (1999), p. 89; Corning (1929a), p. 137.

241. Rhodes (2004), pp. 184–185; Audubon (1999), p. 89–91; Corning (1929a), pp. 137–140.

242. Rhodes (2004), pp. 186–187.

243. Audubon (1999), pp. 93–94; Corning (1929a), pp. 143–144. In his discussion of Audubon's meeting with the painter John Vanderlyn on March 31, 1821, biographer Stanley Clisby Arthur transcribes Audubon's journal entry as follows: "When I arrived at M^r V's Room, he spoke to me as if I had been an abject slave, and told Me in Walking Away to Lay my Drawings down *there, the Dirty* - - - - - - - - - - [Audubon scratched out the epithet, or someone else did it for him in later years and with different ink] and that he would return presently and Look them over." Arthur (1937), p. 176 (omitting the vulgarism "son of a bitch"). See also, Rhodes (2004), p. 186 (quoting Arthur's transcription but incorporating the vulgarism).

The Library of America edition of the journal, edited by Audubon scholar Christoph Irmscher, reflects that the journal actually says: "When I arrived at Mr V.'s Room, he spoke to me as if I had been an abject slave, and told Me in Walking away to Lay my Drawings down *there the Dirty Entry* that he would return *presently* and Look them over." Audubon (1999), p. 93. Cf. Corning (1929a), p. 143.

My examination of a copy of the original journal at the Ernst Mayr Library at Harvard validates Irmscher's transcription. There is no scratching out of any words. Moreover, it appears to me that Audubon was being literal when he referred to "the Dirty Entry." This was not a euphemism for "son of a bitch." He said that he "felt so vexed that My first Intention Was to *Pack* off, but the Expedition Was in View." So he "stood patiently *although* not Laying My Drawings *Down there*." Audubon (1999), p. 93; Corning (1929a), pp. 143–144. By "*Down there*," I believe Audubon was referring to the dirty floor of the foyer of Vanderlyn's studio.

244. Audubon (1999), pp. 93–94; Corning (1929a), pp. 143–144. Vanderlyn's tempered opinion of Audubon's chalk portraits was recorded by Audubon in his journal: "of my Likenesses he spoke very diferently, the one I had Was, he said, hard, and without Effect, although he acknowledged it

Must have been a Strong one." Audubon (1999), p. 94. Cf. Corning (1929a), p. 144.

245. Audubon (1999), p. 95. Cf. Corning (1929a), p. 146

246. Audubon, pp. 90, 101; Corning (1929a), pp. 138, 155.

247. Audubon, pp. 90, 100; Corning (1929a), pp. 153.

248. Rhodes (2004), p. 191; Delatte (1982), p. 110, note 26; p. 113.

249. Delatte (1982), p. 113, quoting from JJA, New Orleans to LBA, Shippingport, KY, 24 May-1 Jun. 1821 (APS). See also, Rhodes (2004), p. 193.

250. LBA, Shippingport, KY to Euphemia Gifford, Duffield Bank near Derby, England, 1 Apr. 1821 (Princeton, Box 1, Folder 10).

251. Delatte (1982), pp. 110, 112. See also, Rhodes (2004), p. 194.

252. Delatte (1982), pp. 110, 112. Tom Bakewell had enjoyed almost immediate success in the construction of steam engines upon opening his Louisville foundry with David Prentice in 1817. Within two years, the foundry was employing sixty workers and generating annual gross revenues of $100,000 ($1,900,000 in 2016 dollars). Prentice & Bakewell also owned a steam sawmill they had constructed next to the foundry. However, by 1820, the demand for steam engines had collapsed with the Panic of 1819, and the firm's revenues dropped to $20,000. Sinclair (1966), pp. 236–237. Still, in comparison to the Audubons, Tom's family was still relatively well-off.

253. Delatte (1982), p. 112.

254. Ibid., pp. 113–114, quoting from JJA, New Orleans to LBA, Shippingport, KY, 24 May-1 Jun. 1821 (APS).

255. Rhodes (2004), p. 195, quoting from JJA, New Orleans to LBA, Shippingport, KY, 24 May-1 Jun. 1821 (APS). See also, Delatte (1982), p. 114.

256. Rhodes (2004), pp. 195–197; Audubon (1999), p. 103. Rhodes mistakenly asserts that Eliza Pirrie was sixteen years of age when Audubon agreed to serve as her tutor during the summer and fall of 1821. Rhodes (2004), p. 195. Audubon indicated in his journal that she was only fifteen. Audubon (1999), p. 125. Audubon's other biographers concur. Heitman (2008), p. 2; Souder (2004), p. 187; Streshinsky (1993), p. 129; Durant & Har-

wood (1980), p. 222; Adams (1966), p. 239. Danny Heitman, who published a comprehensive examination of Audubon's four months at Oakley, states that Eliza was born on October 5, 1805, which would have made her fifteen. Heitman (2008), p. 51.

257. Rhodes (2004), p. 195; Audubon (1999), p. 103.

258. Rhodes (2004), pp. 198–199.

259. Heitman (2008), p. 59. Among the drawings for *BOA* believed to have been produced during Audubon's stay at Oakley, listed in the order of completion, are:

*Mississippi Kite
   Inscribed "Drawn from Nature by John J. Audubon./Louisianna parish of Felicianna James Pirrie's Esqr Plantation/June 28th 1821" (Audubon (1966) II, Plate 384; Havell Plate 117).

*Selby's Flycatcher
   Inscribed "Drawn from Nature by John J. Audubon./James Pirrie's Esqr Plantation Louisiana July 1: 1821" (Audubon (1966) II, Plate 391; Havell Plate 9).

*Pine Creeping Warbler
   Inscribed "Drawn from Nature by John. J. Audubon/James Pirrie's Plantations Louisianna July 10th 1821" (Audubon (1966) I, Plate 211; Havell Plate 140).

*Yellow-throated Vireo
   Inscribed "Drawn from Nature by John. J. Audubon/James Pirries' Plantation Louisianna July 11th 1821" (Audubon (1966) I, Plate 83; Havell Plate 119).

*Red-cockaded Woodpecker
   Inscribed "Drawn from Nature by J.J. Audubon Louisiana July 29th 1821." Only the middle bird in the plate was drawn at Oakley. (Audubon (1966) II, Plate 402; Havell Plate 389).

*Indigo Bird
   Inscribed "Louisianna/July./J.J.A" (Audubon (1966) II, Plate 316; Havell Plate 74).

*Children's Warbler
   Inscribed "Drawn from Nature by John J. Audubon/James Pirrie's Esqr Plantation August 4th 1821" (Audubon (1966) II, Plate 263; Havell Plate 35).

Hooded Flycatcher
   Inscribed "Drawn from Nature by John. J. Audubon/Louisianna August 11th 1821" (Audubon (1966) II, Plate 403; Havell Plate 110).

*Blue-green Warbler
   Inscribed "Drawn from Nature by John. J. Audubon/Louisiana August 12th 1821" (Audubon (1966) II, Plate 233; Havell Plate 49).

*American Redstart
   Inscribed "Drawn from Nature by John. J. Audubon/Louisianna August 13th 1821" (Audubon (1966) II, Plate 365; Havell Plate 49).

*Summer Red Bird
   Inscribed "Drawn from Nature by John. J. Audubon/Bayou Sarah Louisianna August 27th 1821" (Audubon (1966) II, Plate 269; Havell Plate 44).

*Yellow-throat Warbler
   Inscribed "Drawn from Nature by John. J. Audubon/Louisiana Augt 1821." (Audubon (1966) I, Plate 14; Havell Plate 85).

*Spotted Sandpiper
   Inscribed "Louisiana—/August—" (Audubon (1966) II, Plate 347; Havell Plate 310).

*Prairie Warbler
   Inscribed "Drawn from Nature by John. J. Audubon/Bayou Sarah Louisianna Sepr 5th 1821" (Audubon (1966) II, Plate 260; Havell Plate 14).

*Louisiana Waterthrush
   Inscribed "Drawn from Nature by J.J. Audubon/Bayou Sarah Louisiana Sepr 27th, 1821" (Audubon (1966) I, Plate 200; Havell Plate 19).

*Roscoe's Yellow-throat
   Inscribed "Drawn from Nature by John J. Audubon/Bayou Sarah Louisianna Sepr 29th 1821.")(Audubon (1966) II, Plate 294; Havell Plate 24).

*White Ibis
   No inscription, but Audubon wrote in the *OB* that he captured a brown plumaged juvenile bird "at the end of summer" in a swamp near Bayou Sarah. He kept it

alive and likely drew the bird at that time.
(Audubon (1966) II, Plate 283; Havell Plate
222).

*Bonaparte's Flycatcher
  Inscribed "Drawn from Nature by John.
  J. Audubon/Bayou Sarah Octr 5th 1821."
  (Audubon (1966) I, Plate 6; Havell Plate 5).

*Tennessee Warbler
  Inscribed "Drawn from Nature by John.
  J. Audubon/James Pirrie's Plantation
  Louisiana Octr 17th 1821")(Audubon (1966) I,
  Plate 80; Havell Plate 154).

*Bewick's Long-tailed Wren
  Inscribed "Drawn from Nature by John.
  J. Audubon/Bayou Sarah Louisanna Octr 19th
  1821." (Audubon (1966) II, Plate 240; Havell
  Plate 18).

*Black & Yellow Warbler
  Faintly inscribed "Octr 20th 1821 Louisia"
  (Audubon (1966) II, Plate 421; Havell Plate
  50).

*Swallow-tailed Hawk
  No inscription as to location or date.
  (Audubon (1966) I, Plate 45; Havell Plate
  72).

Heitman (2008), unnumbered pp. 75–98 (designated by asterisks above); Low (2002); Audubon
(1966). Heitman attributes twenty-three paintings to
Audubon's time at Oakley based upon an analysis
done by Dennis J. Dufrene, an interpretive ranger at
the Audubon State Historic Site at Oakley, of those
drawings he started or completed during his stay.
Heitman (2008), p. 59. Two are debatable and are
not included on the above list. The first is the Pied
Oyster-catcher (American Oystercatcher) (Havell
Plate 223), which is strictly a coastal species. Kaufman (1996), p. 185. In the *OB*, Audubon wrote: "It
is never found inland, nor even far up our largest
rivers, but is fond of remaining at all times on the
sandy beaches and rocky shores of our salt-water
bays or marshes." *OB* III, p. 181. Oakley is located
well inland and approximately 125 miles upriver
from New Orleans. Thus, it is highly unlikely that
Audubon would have found the species during his
summer at Oakley. Dwight and Low both state that
the drawing was completed in Louisiana in June
1821. Low (2002), p. 130; Audubon (1966) II, Plate

242. If Audubon in fact drew the species at that
time, it must have been before he arrived at Oakley.
Heitman suggests that Audubon may have brought a
skin of an oystercatcher he had collected earlier and
worked at it during his stay. Possibly, but where is
the evidence supporting this claim? Audubon makes
no mention of it in his journal or in his biography of
the species.

Another composition on Dufrene's list is the
Mockingbird (Havell Plate 21). The reasoning appears to be that Audubon painted a rattlesnake at
Oakley on August 25, which was later used in this
iconic drawing showing two pairs of Mockingbirds
attacking a rattlesnake in the act of raiding one
of their nests. However, Edward Dwight believes
that the drawing dates from around 1825, when the
naturalist was at the peak of his artistic powers. In
Dwight's opinion, Audubon "probably copied"
the snake from his earlier drawing. The snake's tail
was not added until after Audubon had drawn the
Yellow Jasmine in which the nest was built, so this
is certainly plausible. Low (2002), p. 41; Audubon (1966) I, Plate 44. Thus, it would seem that
the rattlesnake drawn at Oakley was at most a preliminary drawing, and it is unclear what elements
Audubon incorporated into his final composition.
Depending on how loosely one wishes to define the
start of a drawing, this image might or might not
qualify for the list.

One illustration that evidently is not included
on Dufrene's Oakley list is the pair of Hooded Flycatchers (Hooded Warblers)(Havell Plate 110), the
female of which Audubon drew on August 11, 1821,
as indicated by an inscription that appears on the
original drawing. Audubon (1966) II, Plate 403.

260. Audubon (1999), p. 126; Corning (1929a),
p. 193. There are conflicting references in Audubon's 1821 journal as to when he was actually dismissed by Mrs. Pirrie. In his October 20 (misdated,
should be October 21) journal entry summarizing
the events leading up to his and Mason's departure
from Oakley, Audubon wrote that "Mrs P. on the
10th of Octr Dismissed me." Audubon (1999), p. 126;
Corning (1929a), p. 193. Audubon's biographers
generally accept this statement at face value and believe that this is when his services were terminated.
Streshinsky (1993), p. 132; Durant & Harwood
(1980), p. 223; Adams (1966), pp. 241–242; Arthur

(1937), pp. 219–220. However, Rhodes submits that Audubon was actually fired on October 5 based upon another cryptic note in the journal that reads: "Ended My Tuition/at James Pirrie's Es^q/5th of Octr 1820/3. Months & 20 days." Rhodes (2004), p. 203 and note, p. 458. See also, Arthur (1937), p. 206 (facsimile copy).

However, there are several problems with Rhodes's interpretation. To begin with, it flies in the face of Audubon's direct statement that he was dismissed on October 10. Audubon (1999), p. 126; Corning (1929a), p. 193. There is, to be sure, an apparent inconsistency between the two entries, but a close reading of the journal suggests that October 5 was the date on which Audubon believed his professional instruction came to an end, even though he was not formally dismissed for another five days. He noted in his journal that Eliza had taken ill "about a Month before We left," which would put the date around September 20, but stated that he saw her "during this Illness at appointed hours" and charged the family "for 10 days" of the time she was sick. Corning (1929a), pp. 192–194. Cf. Audubon (1999), pp. 126–127 ("15 days"). See also, note 263, *infra*.

Several other statements in the journal reinforce this view. For example, Audubon indicated in his journal that after he was dismissed by Mrs. Pirrie on the 10th, "I begged of her that We Should remain 8 or 10 Days Longer if the familly Would please to Consider us as Visitors," to which she agreed. Audubon (1999), p. 126; Corning (1929a), p. 193. Mrs. Pirrie apparently expected Audubon to leave Oakley on Saturday, October 20, which was ten days after Audubon said he was terminated. Audubon (1999), p. 127; Corning (1929a), p. 195. If he had actually been dismissed on October 5, as Rhodes insists, it is highly doubtful that Mrs. Pirrie would have permitted him to tarry until the 20th, especially when he had only asked to stay on for another ten days.

Also, Audubon stated in his journal that he waited until just before his departure on Saturday morning to submit a final bill for his services to Mrs. Pirrie. "Saturday Came and a Settlement of Money Matter Was Necessary." Audubon (1999), p. 127; Corning (1929a), p. 194. Audubon's total of $204 included charges for ten days that Eliza had been

ill, which sent Mrs. Pirrie into "a perfect Rage fit." Corning (1929a), p. 194. Cf. Audubon (1999), p. 127 ("15 days"). She "told Me that I Cheated her out of 20$." Audubon (1999), p. 127. Cf. Corning (1929a), p. 194. Rhodes submits that this exchange happened around October 5 when he believes Audubon was fired. Rhodes (2004), p. 203 and note, p. 458. If Rhodes is to be believed, Mrs. Pirrie agreed to allow Audubon to stay in her home as a guest for up to fifteen days after she had just accused him of trying to cheat her. Even by the gracious standards of Southern hospitality, this would seem to be an unlikely scenario.

Finally, when Mrs. Pirrie refused to pay him, Audubon "figurd the Bill" and had it delivered to her husband James, who was then "Labouring under one of his unfortunate fits of Antoxication." Audubon (1999), p. 127. Cf. Corning (1929a), p. 194. Later, in a presumably sober state, James Pirrie came to see Audubon, directed his son-in-law to pay him, and asked him to stay until the following morning, which would have been Sunday, October 21. Audubon hints that this was to the likely consternation of Mrs. Pirrie and her female houseguests, who had left Oakley early Saturday morning to go into nearby St. Francisville with the expectation that Audubon and Mason would be gone by the time they returned. Rhodes would move these events back by two weeks, which the plain reading of Audubon's journal simply does not allow.

What remains to be explained is where Audubon obtained the $100 that he indicated in his October 10 journal entry he had sent to Lucy. Rhodes posits, again based upon his conclusion that Audubon was dismissed on October 5, that this was a note for $100 that he had received from James Pirrie as payment for his services. Rhodes (2004), p. 203 and note, p. 458. However, later references in Audubon's journal would suggest that the naturalist returned to New Orleans with Pirrie's note. See note 263, *infra*.

261. Every Audubon scholar has an opinion as to what occurred in the final month of Audubon's stay at Oakley and what led to his dismissal. Heitman (2008), pp. 51–53; Rhodes (2004), pp. 203; Souder (2004), p. 187; Streshinsky (1993), pp. 131–133; Ford (1988), p. 134; Durant & Harwood (1980), pp. 223–226; Adams (1966), p. 241–242.

I am inclined to accept Michael Harwood's reading of the events of that autumn, which plays off Alice Ford's theory that Audubon became closer to his student than was considered appropriate. Ford (1988), p. 134. As Harwood explains, Audubon was naturally flirtatious, free with his kisses, and likely turned the head of his fifteen-year-old student, although it was most likely unintentional. When Eliza became ill in mid-September 1821, her mother as well as her physician thought it wise to limit her contact with Audubon, to which he apparently took umbrage. Audubon (1999), p. 126; Corning (1929a), pp. 192-193. It was presumably the way he reacted to being restricted in his dealings with Eliza or, as Harwood suggests, his protestations of innocence, that led Mrs. Pirrie and the women who were visiting to develop "a remarkable Coolness" towards him, a fact he noted in his journal without explaining exactly why this was the case. Audubon (1999), pp. 126-127; Corning (1929a), p. 194.

Heitman calls this "[o]ne of the more colorful— and perhaps least supportable—theories concerning Audubon's dismissal." Heitman (2008), p. 53. However, Audubon's journal gives several hints that lend some degree of credence to the theory. Audubon described Eliza as having "a good form of *body*," although she was "not Handsome of face." Audubon (1999), p. 125; Corning (1929a), p. 192. Audubon always had an eye for the ladies, and the emphasis he placed on Eliza's figure suggests he was not blind to her shapely attributes. He claimed that she was not a beauty, and she may not have been. But contemporary portraits of her, including a chalk portrait Audubon made, depict a young woman who was decidedly not plain or unattractive. Heitman (2008), p. 3; Durant & Harwood (1980), p. 225. While Audubon almost certainly had no romantic interest in her, a teenage girl like Eliza could well have developed a crush on her flamboyant, handsome instructor. If his looks and manners were not enough, Audubon acknowledged that he fed Eliza's ego with his praise. "God Knows how hard I tried to Please her in Vain." He swore that he would never try so hard again for any pupil. Audubon (1999), p. 125; Corning (1929a), p. 192.

When Eliza sickened, Audubon wrote that "her Phisician the *Man She Loved*, Would not permit her

reassuming her Avavocations near Me." Corning (1929a), p. 193. Cf., Audubon (1999), p. 126 ("Avocations"). Audubon's journal fairly blushes with resentment in the way he takes aim at Eliza's doctor in this passage.

Finally, on the eve of his departure, Audubon visited Mrs. Pirrie, Eliza, her older sister, and some female houseguests to say goodbye. He wrote that "My Pupil Raised from the Sopha and Expected a kiss from Me—but None Were to be disposed off, I pressed her Hand and With a general Salute to the Whole Made My Retreat" Audubon (1999), p. 128. Cf. Corning (1929a), p. 196. Eliza would have expected to receive a kiss from Audubon only if he had dispensed them liberally during his stay.

There is no way we can truly know what happened over the course of the four months Audubon was at Oakley, but there is ample reason to believe that Audubon's journal offers less than a full and honest account.

262. Rhodes (2004), pp. 203-204.

263. Corning (1929a), p. 194. ("I charged for 10 days of Miss E. Ill time"). See also, Adams (1966), p. 242; Arthur (1937), p. 223. The Library of America edition of the journal reads differently: "I Charged for 15 days of Miss E. Ill time." Audubon (1999), p. 127. However, this is in error. The journal, which is housed in the Ernst Mayer Library at the Museum of Comparative Zoology at Harvard University, is admittedly ambiguous as to the second digit of the number Audubon wrote. Audubon sometimes wrote his zeroes with an outward loop that, in this case, approximates the top line in the number "5." The number itself looks almost to be a straight line rather than an oval, and with the top loop it is not surprising that editor Christoph Irmscher concluded it was a "5," although an earlier scholar, Howard Corning, read it as a "0" There is, however, other reliable evidence that Audubon only sought to charge for ten of Eliza's sick days.

Audubon noted in his journal that Mrs. Pirrie accused him of overcharging her by $20. Audubon (1999), p. 127. At a monthly salary of $60, the $20 extra would equate to only ten days. And, indeed, this is what Audubon's final statement and receipt in the archives of the Audubon State Historic Site at Oakley House shows. It reads:

James Pirrie's Esq[r]
To
John J. Audubon

3 Months & 10 days Tuition to Miss Pirrie	
of Drawing &[c]——@ 60$ per Month	$200:00
1 doze Black Lead Pencils 3$.	
1 Stick Ink. 1$.	4.00
	$204:00

Rec[d] on a/c by Draft on Mess[rs]
Gordon Grant & C[o] payable at New Orleans

by you--------------------------------------	$100:00
by Sundries Paper Postage &[c]	13.31¼
	$113.31¼
Balance———	$90.68

Heitman (2008), p. 3. This document also demonstrates that Rhodes's assertion that Audubon presented Mrs. Pirrie "with a bill for three months and twenty days of teaching" is in error. Rhodes (2004), p. 203.

The record is not entirely clear as to when Audubon received payment for his services at Oakley. William Souder, for one, does not believe that Audubon was ever paid in full. Souder (2004), p. 187. We know from Audubon's journal entry of October 20 [21] that Mrs. Pirrie refused to honor his bill after he demanded payment for part of the time Eliza was sick. Audubon then turned to her husband James, who "apologized in the kindest Manner for his Lady's Conduct; ordered his Son in Law M[r] Smith to pay Me, and shewed me all the politeness he his possessed of." Audubon (1999), p. 127. Cf. Corning (1929a), p. 195.

The statement above in the Oakley House collection reflects that a portion of the payment was in the form of a note endorsed by James Pirrie and payable through the firm of Audubon's friend Alexander Gordon, the New Orleans cotton merchant. However, Audubon's later journal entries reflect that he had a difficult time collecting on this note. On October 26, Audubon penned the following: "Wrote a few Lines to *James Pirrie* Es[qr] to Inform him that Mess[rs] D. & G. Flower had not Paid the House of Gordon & C[o] One hundred Dollars according to Promess." Corning (1929a), p. 199. Cf., Audubon (1999), p. 130.

The account had still not been settled by November 4, when Audubon noted dejectedly, "Steam Boat Ramapo arrived Without *James Pirrie* Es[qr] Much Disapointed on a/c of the 100$ that he was to Pay Mess[rs] Gordon Grant & C[o] on the 20th ultimo." Corning (1929a), p. 205. Cf., Audubon (1999), p. 134. It is worth emphasizing that this entry proves that the note endorsed by Pirrie was given to Audubon on October 20 as part of the final settlement of his bill, in contrast to Rhodes's claim that Audubon received the note on October 10 and sent it to Lucy. Rhodes (2004), p. 204.

Audubon's 1821 journal does not mention the unpaid Pirrie note again. There is a November 22 entry in which he states that he had "received 100$ from M[r] Forestal as M[r] Gordon had Not Paid any Money to My Wife at Louisville." Corning (1929a), p. 214. Cf., Audubon (1999), p. 140. Rhodes maintains that this was from a different note dating to the prior winter that had not been paid. Rhodes (2004), p. 207. More likely, this was repayment of the $100 that Audubon had given Forestal on November 5, presumably for transfer to Lucy. "Paid Mr Forestal 100$." Audubon (1999), p. 134; Corning (1929a), p. 206. But the source of this $100 is not clear. Audubon certainly had not earned enough from drawing lessons in the short time he had been back in New Orleans to have had such a sum available to send to Lucy. As of October 27, Audubon told his journal that he only had $42. It would be a reasonable deduction that the $100 Audubon submitted to Forestal for transfer to Lucy was the $100 he was owed and had finally received from James Pirrie.

Moreover, there is ample reason to believe that the balance of the Oakley bill—$90.68 as shown on the statement and receipt—was paid, most likely in cash, before Audubon left Oakley. Certainly, he returned to New Orleans with money in his pockets. When he arrived in the city, he "Rented an Chambre garnie in Rue S[t] Anne N[o] 29 for 16$ per Month" and then spent the next three days "Looking over the City for a Suitable House for My Little familly." Audubon (1999), p. 129. Cf. Corning (1929a), p. 198. He stated under his journal entry of October 25 (apparently again misdated, as the context of the journal indicates it was actually Friday, October 26) that he rented a house on Dauphine Street for $17 a month. Audubon (1999), p. 129; Corning (1929a), p. 199. Presumably, he paid the first month's rent in advance.

At about the same time, Audubon spent $40 on a new set of tailored clothes and a haircut. "Dressed all new, Hair Cut, my appearance altered beyond My expectations. . . . Good God that 40 Dollars Should thus be *enough* to Make a *Gentleman*." After these expenses, he still had $42, which indicates that he left Oakley with almost $100. Audubon (1999), pp. 130–131. Cf. Corning (1929a), p. 200. The fact he does not mention that any amount was owed by James Pirrie other than the $100 note suggests as well that he was paid the remainder.

264. Rhodes (2004), p. 204. Rhodes consulted an 1821 calendar in correctly identifying the date of Audubon's departure from Oakley. It would appear that Audubon lost track of the calendar date when he sat down with his journal to recount the details of the end of his stay. He dated the entry on the day he left "Octr 20th 1821" and stated, "This Morning about 6 o'clock We Left Mr *Pirrie's* Plantation for New Orleans, Which Place we Reach^d on Monday the 21st." Audubon (1999), p. 124. Cf. Corning (1929a), p. 190. He later made it clear they left Oakley "Day Light of Sunday," which the 1821 calendar reflects was October 21. Audubon (1999), p. 128; Corning (1929a), p. 196. Monday was the 22nd. Most Audubon biographers and scholars have overlooked his calendar errors. Heitman (2008), pp. 56, 59; Streshinsky (1993), p. 131; Durant (1980) p. 222; Adams (1966), p. 243; Arthur (1937), p. 220.

265. Audubon (1999), p. 129; Corning (1929a), p. 199. Audubon's journal indicates under the date October 25th that he "Rented a House in *Dauphine* Street for 17$ per Month." Audubon (1999), p. 129. Cf. Corning (1929a), p. 199. However, in the prior day's entry, he described his activities during the evening of the 25th, which suggests he actually misdated the following day's entry as October 25 when it should have been October 26. This is borne out by his misdating of the following Sunday's entry October 27 when, in fact, it was the 28th.

266. Rhodes (2004), pp. 205–208; Audubon (1999), p. 140; Corning (1929a), p. 223; Arthur (1937), p. 228.

267. Audubon (1999), pp. 146–147. Cf. Corning (1929a), p. 224.

268. Audubon (1999), p. 147; Corning (1929a), p. 224.

269. Blaugrund (1993), p. 12.

270. Rhodes (2004), pp. 208–209; Audubon (1966), p. xxi; *AHJ* I, p. 51.

271. Audubon (1999), p. 148; Corning (1929a), p. 226. Ford mistakenly asserts that Audubon's goal was to complete drawings of only ninety-five birds over the next ninety-five days. Ford (1988), p. 137. Audubon's 1821 journal entry for Sunday, December 30, clearly reflects that he was aiming for ninety-nine. Audubon (1999), p. 148; Corning (1929a), p. 226. In addition, Ford wrongly states that Audubon was assisted in this effort by "his hunter, Gilbert." Ford (1988), p. 137. Audubon's note of December 30 states that he had contracted with "*Robert* the Hunter" to supply him with "one hundred Specimen of Diferent kinds," in which case he agreed to pay Robert one dollar per bird. If the hunter failed to supply the requisite number and variety, his compensation would only be fifty cents per specimen. Audubon (1999), p. 148; Corning (1929a), p. 226. Robert and Gilbert were two different hunters that Audubon used to help him collect specimens during his stay in New Orleans. Audubon referred to his "Hunter *Gilbert*" in his misdated journal entry of Sunday, October 27 [28], 1821. Audubon (1999), p. 131; Corning (1929a), p. 201.

272. *AHJ* I, p. 51. During the early portion of 1822, it appears that the Audubons barely scraped by. Audubon did not have sufficient funds until March to purchase a journal to record the events of each day. *AHJ* I, pp. 50–51; L. Audubon (1869), p. 88.

273. *AHJ* I, p. 51.

274. L. Audubon (1869), p. 91. See also, Rhodes (2004), p. 211.

275. Rhodes (2004), pp. 205, 211, 212; Audubon (1999), p. 891; Ford (1988), pp. 137–138.

276. Rhodes (2004), p. 212; Lewis (1991), p. 71; Ford (1988), p. 138; Delatte (1982), p. 126. Audubon scholars offer varying estimates of the distance between Natchez and the Elizabeth Female Academy in nearby Washington, MS, where Audubon was teaching. Rhodes and Delatte give the distance as seven miles. Rhodes (2004), p. 212; Delatte (1982), p. 126. Streshinsky states it was situated "some three miles outside Natchez." Streshinsky (1993), p. 142.

Lewis asserts it was on the Natchez Trace eight miles from Natchez. Lewis (1991), p. 71. Lewis's familiarity with this part of Mississippi lends credence to his estimate, and this is the one used in the text.

277. Rhodes (2004), p. 212; Streshinsky (1993), p. 142; Delatte (1982), p. 125; Arthur (1937), p. 252. There is some question about where Victor and John were originally enrolled in school upon their arrival in Natchez. Lucy's biography states that the boys were sent to school in Washington, MS, where Audubon was teaching at the Elizabeth Female Academy. L. Audubon (1869), p. 91. See also, Arthur (1937), p. 252. Maria Audubon makes the same assertion in *AHJ*. *AHJ* I, p. 52. See also, Lewis (1991), p. 71.

However, Audubon's journal entries for this period indicate that he was walking from Natchez to Washington every day, a round trip of approximately sixteen miles. Lewis (1991), p. 71; L. Audubon (1869), p. 91. It seems unlikely that he would have had his sons make this trek. It is just as improbable that Audubon would have continued to live in Natchez if both he and his sons were occupied in Washington. More likely, as Audubon biographer Stanley Clisby Arthur first concluded, the boys were being schooled in Natchez, where Audubon was living. Arthur (1937), p. 252.

278. Rhodes (2004), p. 212–213; Delatte (1982), p. 126. Ford states that Victor and John were sent to Natchez "as soon as Audubon recovered under the care of his young friend, Dr. William Provan." Ford (1988), p. 138. She is mistaken. Audubon's journal for this time period, which comes to us only through the secondhand transcription appearing in the Buchanan/Lucy Audubon biographies, reflects that the boys were already attending school when Audubon contracted yellow fever. This is also borne out by his entry of July 8, where Audubon wrote: "Constant exposure in the tropical climate, and the fatigue of my journeys to and from Washington, brought on fever and a renewal of a certain kind doctor's attendance, who not only would accept of no remuneration, but actually insisted on my taking his purse to pay for the expenses connected with the education of my sons." L. Audubon (1869), p. 91.

279. L. Audubon (1869), p. 91.

280. Rhodes (2004), p. 213; Ford (1988), p. 138.

281. L. Audubon (1869), p. 92.

282. Ibid., p. 92.

283. Rhodes (2004), p. 213; Ford (1988), p. 139; Delatte (1982), p. 126; L. Audubon (1869), p. 92.

284. Rhodes (2004), p. 213; Delatte (1982), p. 128.

285. Lewis (1991), p. 72.

286. *AHJ* I, p. 52; L. Audubon (1869), p. 93. See also, Rhodes (2004), p. 214; Ford (1988), p. 139. Secondary sources alternately refer to the itinerant painter's surname as Steen or Stein.

287. Rhodes (2004), pp. 214–215; Lewis (1991), p. 73; Ford (1988), p. 140; Delatte (1982), pp. 128–129, 136; *AHJ* I, p. 52; L. Audubon (1869), p. 93. Delatte's review of the succession records of Robert Percy, Jane Percy's deceased husband, reveals that Beech Woods comprised three thousand arpents of land. Delatte (1982), p. 136. An arpent was a French and Spanish measurement originally used in this portion of colonial America and roughly equated to .85 acre, although the historical evidence indicates that the measurement varied from place to place. Holmes (1983), pp. 315–317. Thus, Beech Woods would appear to have been approximately 2,550 acres in size. Delatte's and Streshinsky's description of the plantation as 2,220 acres may be an undercount. Streshinsky (1993), p. 144; Delatte (1982), p. 135.

288. Rhodes (2004), p. 214; Lewis (1991), p. 73–74; Herrick (1938) I, p. 324; *AHJ* I, p. 52. Audubon's biographers do not agree on whether Victor stayed with Audubon in Natchez when Lucy moved to Beech Woods. Maria Audubon asserts that he did, and Herrick, Lewis, and Rhodes have followed suit. However, Stanley Clisby Arthur, whose biography focuses on Audubon's time in Louisiana and Mississippi and provides details missing from other works, asserts that Victor moved with his mother to Beech Woods and was then picked up by Audubon and John Steen at the beginning of their traveling portrait tour. Arthur (1937), p. 260. Ford and Delatte concur. Ford (1988), p. 140; Delatte (1982), p. 129. The segments of Audubon's 1823 journal published in the Buchanan/Lucy Audubon biographies do not address this issue, and none of these scholars have cited documentary evidence supporting their respective views.

289. Rhodes (2004), pp. 214–215.

290. Rhodes (2004), pp. 215–216; Lewis (1991), p. 74; L. Audubon (1869), p. 94. Although Audubon would develop some degree of skill with oils and turned out oil paintings to sell and give away to patrons once he reached England in 1826, he never felt he had mastered the technique. Rhodes (2004), p. 214. In a letter to Lucy from Liverpool on November 25, 1827, he wrote:

> I have painted several pieces in oil, of course *attempts*, but my hand does not manage the oil brush properly — neither the composition nor the effect are good, and disgusted myself, I care not about finishing any of them, although I am perfectly confident that the delineations are correct to perfection and the habits of the individuals quite at my disposal, through a long course of experience. — The pictures I sell are only purchased by my friends, and my heart & natural pride revolt at this, therefore I am very likely to abandon this style for ever; — yet it is with a considerable degree of regret, if it does not amount to sorrow. *Man* and *particularly thy husband*, cannot easily bear to be outdone, and I will think frequently how hard it is for me not to have another life to spend, to acquire a talent that needs a whole life to reach to any moderate degree of perfection.

JJA, Liverpool to LBA, Bayou Sarah, 25 Nov. 1827 (APS), *Letters* I, pp. 49–50.

291. Rhodes (2004), p. 216; Arthur (1937), p. 262. Contrary to the views of Arthur and Rhodes, noted Audubon scholar John Francis McDermott believes that Audubon's self-portrait was not painted until 1825 or 1826, based on the degree of skill that it evidences. He points out that a comparison of this portrait with those that he did of his sons in 1823 "shows such an advance in skill that it could not have been done at this early date." McDermott (1958), p. 435.

292. Rhodes (2004), pp. 216–217; Streshinsky (1993), p. 145; Ford (1988), p. 142; Delatte (1982), pp. 140–141; Arthur (1937), pp. 262–263; L. Audubon (1869), p. 94. Rhodes, Ford, and Delatte all contend that Audubon's return to Beech Woods occurred three days after his blowup with Mrs. Percy. Arthur asserts that Audubon returned to see Lucy "[t]wo or three days later." Arthur (1937), p. 263. There is

no specific reference to this humiliating incident in Audubon's 1823 journal, as recounted in Lucy's biography. All he says is that "On account of some misunderstanding, I left the Percy's." L. Audubon (1869), p. 94. However, in a letter to Lucy from England in 1827, Audubon responded to news that she had left Beech Woods to take a new teaching position nearby, saying, "if I wanted to go to bed to thee there I would not be sent back 15 miles on foot to Bayou Sarah instead!!!" JJA, Leeds to LBA, Bayou Sarah, 1 May 1827 (APS), *Letters* I, p. 21.

Delatte states that Mrs. Percy's "chief objection was finding her children's teacher in bed with a man — even her husband." Delatte (1982), p. 141. However, Audubon had spent some time at Beech Woods, and it is hard to accept that he had not been allowed to stay in the same cottage with his wife. Rather, it seems that Mrs. Percy's ire was over Audubon returning to the plantation when she had ordered him off the property.

293. Rhodes (2004), p. 217; Streshinsky (1993), p. 145; Lewis (1991), p. 75; Ford (1988), p. 142; Peattie (1940), pp. 152–153; Arthur (1937), pp. 264–265. After the death of Mrs. Griffith, who had commissioned Audubon to paint a landscape painting of Natchez, her heirs refused to pay him, and he could not find another buyer. So, he gave it to Emile Profilet, a local storeowner, to hang in his store to sell. Profilet eventually sent it to France to show his relatives where he had made his home in America and found it there when he visited in 1855. He returned the painting to Natchez. It was ultimately purchased by Dr. Stephen Kelly, who took it to Melrose Plantation in Natchez, where it hung for many years. Ford (1988), p. 142; Arthur (1937), p. 265. It is now in a private collection. Jessica L. Coffman, Park Guide, Natchez National Historical Park (Personal communication, 16 May 2009).

294. Rhodes (2004), p. 217; Streshinsky (1993), pp. 145–146; Ford (1988), p. 142; Delatte (1982), pp. 142–143; L. Audubon (1869), p. 94. Many scholars, including Rhodes, Streshinsky, and Delatte, believe that Mrs. Percy was willing to suffer Audubon's return to Beech Woods in order to get Lucy back into the classroom. They are undoubtedly right.

295. Audubon's biographers differ as to Audubon's purpose in traveling to Philadelphia. Ford asserts that Audubon intended to "search for an

American publisher." Ford (1988), pp. 142–143. This is the conventional view. Souder (2004), pp. 5, 189; Streshinsky (1993), p. 146; Delatte (1982), p. 143; Adams (1966), p. 257; and Arthur (1937), p. 266.

Rhodes believes otherwise. He calls the idea that Audubon visited Philadelphia to find an engraver "a myth." Audubon (2008), p. xxiii, n. 18. In his opinion, Audubon's visit had a dual purpose, neither of which was directed at finding a publisher for his work. Rhodes asserts that Audubon hoped to take lessons in oil painting to improve his technique as well as to "show his portfolio of drawings in the preeminent city of science and art in America and perhaps find support for publishing them." Rhodes (2004), pp. 217, 223. Further, Rhodes contends that Audubon was well aware that he would have to go to Europe to find an engraver skilled enough to transfer his life-sized bird images to copper so that they could be printed. Indeed, he quotes from a letter Lucy had written to her English cousin in April 1821 stating that Audubon intended to go first to England to have his work published. Rhodes also points out that the copper sheets required for Audubon's illustrations were not available in the United States. Ibid., pp. 152–153, 223.

However, the historical record is clear that once Audubon reached Philadelphia, he used his contacts to make inquiry of the finest engravers in the city to see if they would have any interest in his project. L. Audubon (1869), pp. 101; Dunlap (1834), pp. 404–404. It is difficult to accept that Audubon did not have this in the back of his mind when he made the decision to travel north.

With respect to the shipment of his portfolio, Douglas Lewis posits that Audubon sent his portfolio to Philadelphia from New Orleans. Lewis (1991), p. 75. According to Audubon's journal, he boarded a New Orleans bound steamer on September 30, 1823, and returned to Bayou Sarah three days later. L. Audubon (1869), p. 94. However, Audubon's reference to shipping his drawings to Philadelphia appears under his journal passage dated September 8, several weeks before he traveled to New Orleans: "September 8. I was asked to go and recruit my health at the Percy's, and I went to Bayou Sara. I sent on my drawings to Philadelphia, and resolved to visit that city and obtain employment as a teacher." L. Audubon (1869), p. 94.

Lewis's supposition may be a reasonable one, but it is not directly supported by the portion of Audubon's journal that Lucy published. Given the heavy editing that is evident in this work, it seems likely that the Philadelphia reference was combined with an earlier passage, leaving the given date a wholly unreliable benchmark. Souder ignores the September passage from Audubon's journal and maintains that Audubon brought the portfolio with him from Louisville. Souder (2004), p. 7. He does not cite evidence to support this conclusion. Herrick takes a different view of the New Orleans trip. He suggests that the naturalist's hasty visit to the Crescent City was not for the purpose of shipping his drawings but to obtain written introductions from his New Orleans friends to eminent residents of Philadelphia. Herrick (1938) I, p. 325.

296. Rhodes (2004), p. 218; Ford (1988), p. 143.

297. Ford (1988), p. 143. The *Magnet* was a 150-ton vessel built in 1822 by Tom Bakewell's foundry in Louisville. Sinclair (1966), p. 248, note 27. Arthur states that Audubon and Victor both took passage from Bayou Sarah to New Orleans in order to board a northern-bound steamboat. Arthur (1937), p. 266. However, a fair reading of Audubon's journal suggests that while Audubon probably picked up the vessel in New Orleans, Victor joined him when the steamboat stopped at Bayou Sarah: "October 3. Left New Orleans for Kentucky, where I intended to leave my son Victor with my wife's relations, and proceed on my travels. I left Bayou Sara with my son Victor on board the steamer Magnet, bound for the Ohio, and was kindly treated by Captain McKnight, the commander." L. Audubon (1869), pp. 94–95.

298. *OB* III, p. 371. The tale of Audubon and Victor's trek from Trinity, IL, a small community on the Ohio River just below the mouth of the Cache River, is told in an Episode entitled, "A Tough Walk for a Youth." Ibid. See also, Callary (2009), p. 351; McDermott (1965), p. 33, note 22.

299. L. Audubon (1869), p. 96.

300. JJA, Trinity, IL, to Ferdinand Rozier, Ste. Genevieve, MO, 14 Oct. 1823 (Yale (Coe), Box 1, Folder 6).

301. Rhodes (2004), p. 218; Ford (1988), p. 144; Arthur (1937), pp. 266–267.

302. Rhodes (2004), p. 219; Souder (2004),

p. 7; Ford (1988), pp. 145–146; L. Audubon (1869), p. 100. Dr. James Mease (1771–1846) was a prominent physician, author, and scientific thinker. In 1811, he published a guide to Philadelphia entitled *The Picture of Philadelphia, Giving an Account of its Origin, Increase and Improvements in Arts, Sciences, Manufactures, Commerce and Revenue* (Philadelphia: B. & T. Kite, 1811). Many Audubon scholars have mistakenly referred to him as "Dr. William Mease." Streshinsky (1993), p. 148; Adams (1966), p. 261; Herrick (1938) I, p. 327; Arthur (1937), p. 269. Audubon described Mease as an "old friend." L. Audubon (1869), p. 100. See also, Streshinsky (1993), p. 148; Herrick (1938) I, p. 327. In fact, Mease was only an acquaintance, having visited Fatland Ford many times for purposes of seeing Lucy's father, William Bakewell, and observing Bakewell's "agricultural experiments." Ford (1988), p. 145. See also, Souder (2004), pp. 7–8.

303. Rhodes (2004), pp. 219–220; Streshinsky (1993), p. 148; Ford (1988), p. 146; L. Audubon (1869), p. 100. Thomas Sully (1783–1872) recalled that when he first met Audubon in Philadelphia in 1824, Audubon told him that his goal was to become a portrait painter. Sully provided him with instruction, "but [Audubon] was soon discouraged and gave up the pursuit." Dunlap (1834) II, p. 405.

304. Mearns (1992), pp. 94–100; L. Audubon (1869), p. 101. Charles-Lucien Jules Laurent Bonaparte (1803–1857), the eldest son of Napoleon Bonaparte's brother Lucien, was born in Paris on May 24, 1803. Mearns (1992), p. 96. Thus, at the time he met Audubon in Philadelphia in April 1824, he was but twenty years of age as Rhodes states. Rhodes (2004), p. 220. Ford inexplicably refers to him as being twenty-three when she has provided his correct date of birth in the previous sentence of her biography. Ford (1988), p. 146. Souder's and Streshinsky's assertions that he was twenty-one are similarly in error. Souder (2004), p. 8; Streshinsky (1993), p. 148.

305. During his voyage across the Atlantic to America in 1823, Bonaparte had collected some storm petrels, a small seabird in the family Hydrobatidae. He subsequently determined that they were a previously unidentified species found along the North American coast that he named after Alexander Wilson. His paper on the subject was read at a meeting of the Academy of Natural Sciences of Philadelphia on January 13, 1824. Stroud (2000), p. 48.

306. Rhodes (2004), p. 220; Souder (2004), p. 9. Bonaparte was elected a member of the Academy of Natural Sciences of Philadelphia on February 24, 1824. Souder (2004), p. 9; Stroud (2000), p. 48.

307. Souder (2004), pp. 9–10.

308. *AHJ* I, p. 56; L. Audubon (1869), p. 101; Academy of Natural Sciences of Philadelphia, Minutes (1824), pp. 32–33. While Maria Audubon destroyed the original 1824 journal after publishing what she was willing to share with the public in *AHJ*, the date Charles-Lucien Bonaparte introduced Audubon to the members of the Academy of Natural Sciences of Philadelphia can be deduced by comparing the references in the published fragments of the journal to the extant minutes of the academy.

In Lucy's biography, there is a journal entry of April 12, 1824, in which Audubon referred to being invited by Bonaparte to a meeting of the academy: "The Prince of Canino introduced me to the Academy of Arts and Sciences, and pronounced my birds superb, and worthy of a pupil of David. I formed the acquaintance of Le Sueur, the zoologist and artist, who was greatly delighted with my drawings." L. Audubon (1869), p. 101. The next entry in this version of the journal is April 14, which would point to the meeting taking place on either April 12 or 13.

Maria quoted from the journal under the putative date of April 10, 1824: "I was introduced to the son of Lucien Bonaparte, nephew of Napoleon, a great ornithologist, I was told. He remained two hours, went out, and returned with two Italian gentlemen, and their comments made me very contented." *AHJ* I, p. 56. Maria then continues the tale in her own words: "That evening he was taken to the Philosophical Academy where the drawings were greatly admired." She goes on to state that "At this meeting Mr. George Ord met Audubon and objected strongly to the birds and plants being drawn together, 'but spoke well of them otherwise.'" Ibid.

Thus, the dates in the journal fragments would suggest the academy meeting was held between April 10 and April 13. According to the actual minutes, a regular meeting of the academy membership was held on Tuesday, April 13, which is evidently the date Audubon accompanied Bonaparte to the academy's headquarters in Gilliams Court on Arch Street. Phillips (1953), p. 269; Academy of Natural Sciences of Philadelphia, Minutes (1824), p. 32. There is admittedly no reference to Audubon's presence in the minutes of the April 13 meeting or, for that matter, at any of the meetings during that year. Presumably, he was introduced by Bonaparte prior to the commencement of the meeting but was not permitted to stay because he was not yet a member. However, in addition to the circumstantial evidence provided by Audubon's edited journal, support for the April 13 date can be garnered from the list of members who were present on that date. The journal states that, in addition to Bonaparte, George Ord and Charles-Alexandre Lesueur were in attendance. L. Audubon (1869), p. 101. The minutes confirm that all three attended the April 13 meeting. Academy of Natural Sciences of Philadelphia, Minutes (1824), p. 32.

Souder maintains that the date of Audubon's visit to the academy is "unclear." Souder (2004), p. 10. He reviewed the academy's minutes in researching his biography, as did I. However, he asserts that the meeting occurred either on May 11, June 29, or July 20 based upon his assumption that the three men who nominated Audubon for corresponding membership at the meeting of July 27—Charles-Alexandre Lesueur, Reuben Haines, and Isaiah Lukens—were also present when Audubon first came to the academy. Souder (2004), p. 10 and note, p. 299. However, it does not necessarily follow that the academy members who nominated Audubon must have met him at this initial meeting. Setting that aside, both Lesueur and Haines were present at the meeting of April 13. Academy of Natural Sciences of Philadelphia, Minutes (1824), p. 32. Lukens may have met Audubon at another time or merely been asked by Lesueur or Haines to join them in placing the nomination.

A determination of the actual date for the meeting is of more than passing interest. It was at this meeting of the academy that Audubon first encountered George Ord (1781–1866), the academy vice president, and friend and supporter of the late Alexander Wilson. Ord recognized almost immediately that Audubon's art posed a threat to Wilson's repu-

tation and, by extension, his own. He had edited the eighth volume of Wilson's work and, following Wilson's death in 1813, completed the ninth and final volume. Ord developed a passionate dislike of Audubon, whom he viewed as an uneducated blowhard, and was instrumental in blocking him from gaining membership in the academy. In later years, Ord would be among a handful of vociferous critics of *BOA* and Audubon's accompanying letterpress, the *OB*. He also would play a behind-the-scenes role in urging a bombastic English naturalist, Charles Waterton (1782–1865), to attack Audubon in print.

Souder also misstates the day of the week the academy met. He claims that "Meetings now took place every Saturday evening in the academy's own building." Souder (2004), p. 9. Burtt and Davis, in their recent biography of Alexander Wilson, make the same assertion. Burtt & Davis (2013), p. 338. In fact, the meetings occurred on Tuesday evenings, as a comparison of the dates in the minutes (e.g., April 6, 13, 20, 27), as well as those mentioned by Souder (May 11, June 29, July 20), to an 1824 calendar will attest. See also, JJA, Philadelphia to John Bachman, Charleston, 1 Jul. 1832 (Harvard (50)), *Letters* I, pp. 195–196 (referencing a Tuesday meeting of the academy).

309. Ford (1988), p. 147.

310. Souder (2004), p. 13.

311. Ford (1988), p. 147.

312. Souder (2004), p. 13. According to Maria Audubon, who quotes from Audubon's 1824 journal in *AHJ*, Ord's principle objection to Audubon's drawings was that Audubon had combined birds and plants on the same drawing. Audubon supposedly wrote that Ord "spoke well of them otherwise." *AHJ* I, p. 56. Even if this were true, Ord recognized almost at once that Audubon was a threat to Wilson's continuing dominance of American ornithology. He did everything he could do from that point forward to weaken Audubon's credibility and prevent his accomplishments from receiving the approval of the Philadelphia scientific establishment.

313. L. Audubon (1869), p. 101. William Dunlap interviewed the Philadelphia engraver Alexander Lawson in 1833 and reported on Lawson's 1824 meeting with Bonaparte and Audubon: "One morning, very early, Bonaparte rouzed him from bed— he was accompanied by a rough fellow, bearing a

port-folio. They were admitted and the port-folio opened, in which was a number of paintings of birds, executed with crayons, or pastils, which were displayed as the work of an untaught wild man from the woods, by Bonaparte, and as such, the engraver thought them very extraordinary. Bonaparte admired them exceedingly, and expatiated upon their merit as originals from nature, painted by a self-taught genius." Dunlap (1834) II, p. 403.

314. Dunlap (1834) II, pp. 403–404.

315. L. Audubon (1869), p. 101.

316. Dunlap (1834) II, pp. 403–404. William Dunlap (1766–1839) was a painter, theater manager, and writer who was collecting stories for his book on the American arts when he sat down with the famous Philadelphia engraver Alexander Lawson on June 24, 1833, to discuss Lawson's relationships with Audubon and Alexander Wilson. Dunlap (1930) III, p. 705.

317. Dunlap (1834) II, pp. 403–404. Another eventual critic whom Audubon met during his 1824 visit to Philadelphia was Charles Waterton, a naturalist from Britain who had spent several years in South America and authored a book about his adventures abroad. In a letter to Lucy, dated June 6, 1824, Audubon wrote: "I spent yesterday morning with Dr. Meaze in company with Mr Vaughn and others, one an Englishman called Waterton who presented much in my department of science, particularly in ornithology, but too great an admirer of himself to suffer any one else to speak much. *He* was about going to the Roanoke river to procure an alligator of *only* 30 ft. in length, *he* had seen some 28 — and had rode on a live one and conquered it with much difficulty. Mr Waterton visited me today in company with Dr. Meaze, and found so many faults of composition and perspective about my birds, that I wished him in Guinea taking alligators again." JJA, Philadelphia to LBA, 6 Jun. 1824, transcribed by Ruthven Deane and tipped into his presentation copy of *AHJ* Vol. I, between pp. 56 and 57 (Newberry).

318. Dunlap (1930) III, p. 706.

319. Rhodes (2004), p. 224; L. Audubon (1869), p. 102.

320. L. Audubon (1869), p. 102.

321. Streshinsky (1993), p. 151; Arthur (1937), pp. 273–274. Joseph Mason made the claim that

Audubon had promised him credit for his botanical illustrations, painted when they were working together between 1820 and 1822. Arthur (1937), p. 274; Richards (1934), p. 131. Both Audubon and Mason's names had been penciled under many of these compositions, and Mason apparently saw during his meeting with Audubon on May 30, 1824, that Audubon had replaced his own penciled name with ink, while Mason's name, in some cases, had been erased. Richards (1934), pp. 129–130.

322. Souder (2004), p. 13; Adams (1966), p. 264; Arthur (1937), pp. 274–275.

323. Ford (1988), p. 284.

324. Rhodes (2004), p. 223. Five years after Audubon showed his portfolio off in Philadelphia, Charles-Lucien Bonaparte would tell William Swainson, a British naturalist, that he had originally decided to avoid a collaboration with Audubon because the artist had failed to retain his birdskins, making it difficult for Bonaparte to provide the ornithological details of the species and respond to queries from other scientists. Ford (1988), p. 260 and note, p. 448.

325. Rhodes (2004), p. 223. Years later, Bonaparte referenced their joint venture discussions in a letter to Audubon, noting that "I should have been very happy to join you or have you to join me." Stroud (2000), p. 106. The failure of the discussions to publish jointly was no doubt due to several factors. Audubon had reached the point where he was not particularly inclined to share the fruits of his years'-long labor with others. As a field naturalist, he also had acquired a wealth of knowledge of birdlife and behavior that Bonaparte lacked. Bonaparte indicated in his later correspondence that Audubon's failure to keep the birdskins from which he had drawn his illustrations also retarded any effort for them to work together, as Bonaparte needed these in order to properly describe the species. But underlying all of this was the concerted effort of George Ord and his circle to undercut Audubon and prevent him from eclipsing Alexander Wilson. Bonaparte, who had been accepted by Ord and the Philadelphia scientific establishment, also had to navigate the political rapids posed by his dual loyalty.

It appears that Bonaparte did hire Audubon briefly to supervise the drawings that were being done by the artists Titian Ramsey Peale and Alexander Rider for Bonaparte's revision of Wilson's *American Ornithology*, but this arrangement did not last long due to the sum Audubon sought for his services. As Audubon related in his journal on April 15, 1824, Bonaparte "engaged me to superintend his drawings intended for publication, but my terms being much dearer that Alexander Wilson's, I was asked to discontinue this work." L. Audubon (1869), pp. 101–102.

326. Rhodes (2004), p. 223; Ford (1988), pp. 159–160. Although it appeared that Audubon's drawing of the Great Crow Blackbird (Boat-tailed Grackle) would be his first published drawing, it did not work out that way. According to the account given by Philadelphia engraver Alexander Lawson to William Dunlap, Lawson initially informed Bonaparte that he would not engrave the drawing unless Audubon reduced it in size:

> Soon after, Audubon came to the engraver with the same picture, and said, 'I understand that you object to engraving this.' 'Yes, it is too large for the book.' 'And you object to my drawing?' 'Yes.' 'Why so?' 'This leg does not join the body as in nature. This bill is, in the crow, straight, sharp, wedge-like. You have made it crooked and waving. These feathers are too large.' 'I have seen them twice as large.' 'Then it is a species of crow I have never seen. I think your painting very extraordinary for one who is self-taught—but we in Philadelphia are accustomed to seeing very correct drawing.' 'Sir, I have been instructed seven years by the greatest masters in France.' 'Then you have made dom [damn] bad use of your time,' said the Scotchman.
>
> 'Sir,' said Lawson, to the writer, 'he measured me with his eye, and but that he found me a big fellow, I thought he might have knocked me down.'

Dunlap (1834) II, p. 404. Ultimately, Bonaparte bowed to Lawson's demands and asked Alexander Rider to completely redraw the composition. Audubon was very unhappy about it when he eventually saw Bonaparte's publication even though he had been given partial credit for the drawing. Ford (1988), pp. 162–168.

327. *AHJ* I, p. 57; L. Audubon (1869), p. 103.

Dr. Richard Harlan (1796–1843) was born in Philadelphia on September 19, 1796, and went on to obtain his medical degree in 1818 at the University of Pennsylvania. In 1825, the year after he met Audubon, he published *Fauna Americana; being a Description of the Mammiferous Animals Inhabiting North America* (Philadelphia: J. Harding for Anthony Finley, 1825). He became a loyal friend to Audubon and later served as his agent in Philadelphia for *BOA*. He died on September 30, 1843, in New Orleans. Sotheby's (1993), Lot 61; Mearns (1992), p. 560.

328. L. Audubon (1869), p. 103.

329. Souder (2004), p. 10 and note, p. 299; p. 14; Ford (1988), p. 148; Herrick (1938), p. 334. In 1824, when Audubon was nominated for membership in the Academy of Natural Sciences of Philadelphia, Reuben Haines was the corresponding secretary and Charles-Alexandre Lesueur was a Curator. Journal of the Academy of Natural Sciences of Philadelphia (1824), Part I, p. 1.

330. Souder (2004), p. 15. See also, Phillips & Phillips (1967), p. 10. The vote on Audubon's prospective membership occurred at the academy meeting on August 31, after Audubon had left Philadelphia for New York City. His nomination was the only one rejected by the membership in 1824. Souder (2004), p. 15 and note, p. 300. Two years after the vote, Audubon was still smarting. In his journal entry of December 13, 1826, he described the British ornithologist Prideaux John Selby by comparing him to George Ord, who was principally responsible for blocking Audubon's nomination for academy membership:

> Mꭆ Selby is a Gentleman Naturalist—not in the least resembling the Venomous Tallow Chandler of Philadelphia [George Ord], the possessor of 3 Greek words, 7 of Latin, none belonging to his [*sic*] what ought to be his usual Language, and the Describer of Objects unknown yet to the Almighty. Mꭆ Selby is not a man that would say at a large meeting of the Wernerian Society that *he* would be damned rather than give me a favorable vote of Election—He is not a man who would say that I knew nothing about Drawing, nor the habits of Birds. No, my Lucy, Mꭆ Selby is not an Hipocritical Fool, I assure thee =

Audubon (2011), pp. 349–350. Cf. Ford (1987), p. 390.

331. Edward Harris (1799–1863) was the eldest of three children born to Edward Harris (1754–1822), an Englishman who came to America in 1796 to serve as the American representative of his Leicester hosiery manufacturing company, and his wife, Jane Ustick, the daughter of a Baptist minister in Philadelphia. In 1822, the younger Harris inherited his father's sizable estate, which included a large farm in Moorestown, NJ. Mearns (1992), p. 218; Read (1979), pp. 1–2; Brannon (1947), p. 11.

332. Rhodes (2004), pp. 224–225; *AHJ* I, p. 57; L. Audubon (1869), p. 103.

333. *AHJ* I, p. 57.

334. L. Audubon (1869), p. 103.

335. Audubon (2008), p. ix; L. Audubon (1869), pp. 103–104.

336. L. Audubon (1869), pp. 101–102, 105.

337. L. Audubon (1869), p. 102. See also, Rhodes (2004), p. 224. Dr. Henry McMurtrie (1793–1865) was born in Philadelphia and obtained an M.D. degree from the University of Pennsylvania in 1814. He married Ann Newnham on May 26, 1814, and a few years later moved with her to Louisville. Thomas & Conner (1969), pp. 312–313. In 1819, he published *Sketches of Louisville and its Environs* (Louisville: S. Penn, Jun., 1819), which apparently led Rhodes to conclude, erroneously, that McMurtrie was "originally from Louisville." Rhodes (2004), p. 224. McMurtrie returned to Philadelphia at around the time the book appeared, apparently as a result of large debts he had incurred in bringing the book to print. Thomas & Conner (1969), pp. 317–318. He remained in his natal city working on other published works, including a translation of French scientist Baron Georges Cuvier's *Le Règne Animal* (Paris: Deterville, 1817). In 1831, he was approached by Audubon for assistance in publishing the American edition of his *OB*. In 1839, McMurtrie was appointed Professor of Anatomy, Physiology, and Natural History at Philadelphia's Central High School. He retired in 1861 and died on May 26, 1865. Thomas & Conner (1969), pp. 318–321, 323. In Audubon's 1824 journal, he noted that McMurtrie had earned his fame from his scientific studies in conchology. L. Audubon (1869), p. 102.

338. L. Audubon (1869), p. 102.

339. L. Audubon (1869), pp. 105–106. See also, Rhodes (2004), p. 227.

340. L. Audubon (1869), pp. 106–107. In his August 9, 1824, journal passage, Audubon wrote, "I have been making inquiries regarding the publication of my drawings in New York; but find that there is little prospect of the undertaking being favorably received. I have reason to suspect that unfriendly communications have been sent to the publishers from Philadelphia, by parties interested in Wilson's volume, and who have represented that my drawings have not been wholly done by myself. Full of despair, I look to Europe as my only hope." Ibid.

341. L. Audubon (1869), p. 106. Dr. Samuel Latham Mitchell (1764–1831) was a distinguished educator, politician, and naturalist from New York. He obtained a medical degree from the University of Edinburgh in 1786, served in the New York legislature in 1791 and 1798, the U.S. Congress from 1801 to 1804, the U.S. Senate from 1804 to 1809, and the U.S. Congress again from 1810 to 1813. He taught at Columbia College from 1792 to 1801 and at the New York College of Physicians and Surgeons from 1808 to 1826. A naturalist of wide ranging interests, he founded the Lyceum of Natural History of New-York in 1817. Biographical Directory of the U.S. Congress, http://bioguide.congress.gov/scripts /biodisplay.pl?index=m000831 (accessed 27 Jan. 2014). The Lyceum of Natural History of New-York is today the New York Academy of Sciences. Mearns (1992), p. 151. Audubon's first published scientific papers detailing his observations of Republican Swallows (Cliff Swallows) in Kentucky and White-bellied Swallows (Tree Swallows) in Louisiana appeared in the Annals of the Lyceum in 1824. Audubon (1824a) and Audubon (1824b).

342. L. Audubon (1869), pp. 107–113.

343. Ibid., p. 113. During his stay in Pittsburgh, Audubon gave drawing lessons to Harriet Basham, the sixteen-year-old daughter of Mrs. Charles Basham, who ran "The School," a female academy located at "the corner of Fourth and Wood Streets." The Basham family befriended the itinerant artist and invited him into their social circle. When he took leave of the city on October 24, 1824, he gave Harriet a fifteen-page sketchbook filled largely with images of a variety of insects. Ford (1952), pp. 14–15. Alice Ford presented the story of Audubon's sketch-

book in her 1952 book, *Audubon's Butterflies, Moths, and Other Studies.* Ford (1952). In later years, Ford changed her views about the sketchbook and acknowledged her "innocent assumption" that it came from Audubon's brush. She ultimately concluded that Joseph Mason was the source of the drawings. Alice Ford (Personal communication, 16 Feb. 1994). See also, Sotheby's (1988), Lot 54.

Most Audubon biographers believe that Audubon left Pittsburgh for a couple of weeks in September or October 1824 to tour Lake Ontario and Lake Champlain and take advantage of fall migration. Rhodes (2004), p. 230; Streshinsky (1993), p. 153; Ford (1988), p. 156; Herrick (1938) I, p. 344. The sole evidentiary basis for their view is a letter Audubon wrote to his new friend Edward Harris on January 31, 1825, after returning to Bayou Sarah. In it, Audubon mentioned that "when on the Lakes, Both Ontario and Champlain I wrote to You—again from Pittsburgh, all without any answer." Audubon added that he had been "delighted with that Tour but will for ever regret that Your Sister's Indisposition could not allow you time to augment my Pleasure by your Company." JJA, Beech Woods near Bayou Sarah, LA to Edward Harris, Moorestown, NJ, 31 Jan. 1825 (Harvard (Letters), pf (110)). Cf. Herrick (1938) I, p. 344.

There is no mention in the edited passages in the Buchanan/Lucy Audubon biographies or in the isolated quotations by Maria Audubon in *Myself*, all that remain of the contents of Audubon's 1824 journal, that he ever took such a trip after reaching Pittsburgh. At that point, he was low on cash and likely did not have the financial resources to retrace his steps to the Great Lakes. The fact that Maria destroyed the original journal precludes a definitive answer.

Nevertheless, it should be noted that his letter to Edward Harris can be read just as easily another way. In referring to the "tour," it appears that he was alluding to his original trip across New York State and along the Great Lakes following his departure from New York City in late August. Audubon spent some time in Rochester, where he presumably had time to explore Lake Ontario, and continued to Buffalo, which is situated on Lake Erie. It is highly doubtful, given the route he was taking and amount of time he recorded for his trip, that he visited Lake

Champlain on the border between New York and Vermont. But he could well have confused Lake Erie for Lake Champlain when writing the letter. Certainly, his statement to Harris that he had written him "when on the Lakes" and then "again from Pittsburgh" would imply that he wrote one letter during his approach to Pittsburgh and a second after he arrived.

344. Audubon (1966) I, Plate 36; Ford (1951), p. 16. When Europeans first arrived in North America, the Passenger Pigeon is believed to have been the most abundant species on the continent, numbering in the billions. The birds nested in communal roosts and congregated in vast flocks of millions of birds that flew over the countryside searching for food. As such, they became a ready target for market hunters and a staple for frontier families. By the latter half of the 19th century, the population of Passenger Pigeons had collapsed, most likely due to loss of habitat and overhunting. The last member of the species, a female named Martha, died at the Cincinnati Zoo in 1914. Blockstein (2002), pp. 1-2, 17-20. Audubon's simple but elegant composition of a female feeding its mate as part of a courtship display known as "billing" is, as a result, one of his most poignant and heartrending. *OB* I, p. 325.

345. L. Audubon (1869), p. 113. See also, Rhodes (2004), p. 230; Ford (1988), p. 156.

346. Ford (1988), p. 157; L. Audubon (1869), pp. 113-114. See also, Sinclair (1966), p. 237; Bakewell (1896), p. 35.

347. Bakewell (1896), p. 27.

348. Streshinsky (1993), p. 157; Ford (1988), p. 157.

349. L. Audubon (1869), pp. 114-116.

350. L. Audubon (1869), p. 116. Maria Audubon apparently re-wrote this passage from Audubon's 1824 journal and dropped it into her imagined recreation of his 1829 reunion with Lucy after their three-year separation while he was in England. Streshinsky (1993), p. xiv; *AHJ* I, pp. 62-63.

As a side note, Streshinsky states in her discussion of Maria's wholesale rewriting of her grandfather's journals that the 1824 quotation in the text comes from Audubon biographer Stanley Clisby Arthur, "who somehow managed to get access to some of the journals before they were destroyed." Streshinsky (1993), p. xiv. Arthur may have had access to manuscript material that had not been seen or used by Herrick for his 1917 biography, as Michael Harwood and Mary Durant indicate, but he actually obtained the quoted section of the 1824 journal from Lucy's 1869 biography. Harwood & Durant (1985), p. 100; L. Audubon (1869), p. 116. Maria had destroyed the 1822–1824 journal in 1895 as she indicated in a letter dated July 4, 1904, to Audubon scholar Ruthven Deane. See Preface, note 12, *supra*.

351. Arthur (1937), p. 290.

352. Rhodes (2004), p. 232; Arthur (1937), pp. 290–291. See also, note 44, *supra*. Not much is known about the medical education of Nathaniel Wells Pope (1789–1836). Arthur asserts that he was receiving medical instruction under Dr. Benjamin W. Dudley (1785–1870) at the time he was hired in 1807 by Audubon & Rozier as a part time clerk. Arthur (1937), p. 53; Peter (1905), pp. 15, 18. J. David Book states that Pope's medical training had been with Dr. Dudley at Transylvania University in Lexington. Book (1971), p. 192. What can be said is that if Pope received a portion of his medical education under the watchful eye of Dr. Dudley at Kentucky's first college, it was not until 1809 and did not last long. Dudley obtained his M.D. degree from the University of Pennsylvania in 1806 and began practicing in Lexington. Peter (1905), p. 16. However, he did not become attached to the medical department at Transylvania University until 1809 and left to further his medical education in Europe the following year. Ibid., pp. 16, 166. Pope moved from Louisville to Henderson with Audubon and Rozier in 1810.

353. Arthur (1937), p. 292.

354. Rhodes (2004), p. 232; Arthur (1937), pp. 292–293; L. Audubon (1869), p. 117.

355. Sahr (2015); Audubon (2011), p. 3; Rhodes (2004), p. 237; Ford (1987), p. 15; Herrick (1938) I, pp. 348–349. Although Audubon recorded in his 1826 journal that he left Beech Woods on "Tuesday afternoon the 26th April," a careful reading of the journal and reference to an 1826 calendar establish that his departure must have been on Tuesday, April 25, as Rhodes indicates. Audubon spoke of spending the night with the Popes in St. Francisville and leaving aboard the *Red River*, a Mississippi steamboat, on "Wednesday 4 o'clock P.M." Audubon

(2011), p. 3; Ford (1987), p. 15; Herrick (1938) I, pp. 348–349. Wednesday was April 26, his forty-first birthday. He arrived in New Orleans on "Thursday 27th." Audubon (2011), p. 3; Herrick (1938) I, pp. 348–349. Obviously, if Thursday was the 27th, Tuesday was the 25th, which the calendar for that year confirms. Ford's statement that he departed the Percy plantation for Bayou Sarah on April 26 is a misreading of the journal. Ford (1988), p. 172. Hart-Davis, Delatte, and Arthur also err on this point. Hart-Davis (2004), p. 54; Delatte (1982), p. 160; Arthur (1937), p. 311.

The primary citations given here from Audubon's 1826 journal are from the excellent 2011 edition prepared by Daniel Patterson and his colleague Patricio J. Serrano. Audubon (2011). This is a superior edition in almost every way to Alice Ford's 1967 and 1987 editions. Patterson's introductory comments reveal that Ford made numerous and sometimes significant departures from the holograph, evidently to polish Audubon's image, much as the naturalist's granddaughter Maria had done. Audubon (2011), pp. xliii-liii. Nevertheless, citations to Ford's 1987 edition are provided as a convenience to the reader who may not have access to this improved text.

356. The estimate of the amount of money Audubon had with him when he embarked on his trip to England comes from two sources. First, in his 1826 journal, he provided a breakdown of his expenses from the moment he left Beech Woods on April 25 until he departed New Orleans on May 17, amounting to a total of $195.25. Audubon (2011), p. 390; Ford (1987), pp. 427–428.

Second, we know from Audubon's letter to Lucy on December 26, 1827, that he left Louisiana with £340. JJA, Liverpool to LBA, Bayou Sarah, 26 Dec. 1827 (APS), *Letters* I, p. 54. Audubon's biographers generally convert this sum into dollars in stating how much he took with him to England. However, there is a wide range of opinion as to what the rate of exchange was in 1826. Rhodes calculates the sum as being worth $1,500. Rhodes (2004), p. 238. Ford and Souter state he had $1,600 with him as he headed for Liverpool. Souder (2004), p. 193; Ford (1988), p. 172. Streshinsky and Arthur declare that it amounted to $1,700. Streshinksy (1993), p. 157; Arthur (1937), p. 311.

The nominal par value of a pound sterling during this time was $4.44.44. Elliot (1845), p. 1047; Blunt (1832), p. 50; JJA, London to LBA, Bayou Sarah, 2 Nov. 1828 (Princeton, Box 2, Folder 10), Audubon (1999), p. 813; Blunt (1822), p. 50. If this figure is used, £340 would equate to roughly $1,500, as Rhodes asserts. However, it is important to understand that Audubon did not actually carry dollars or British currency with him to England. He purchased bills of exchange in New Orleans to present for payment in pounds sterling once he landed in Liverpool. Audubon (2011), p. 53; Rhodes (2004), p. 250; Hart-Davis (2004), p. 12; Ford (1987), p. 82. A bill of exchange required the payment of a premium or advance to the drawer, i.e., the person issuing the bill, which was a percentage of the principal sum. Haven (1827), p. 126.

At the time Audubon departed for England in May 1826, the exchange rate in New York was $4.84.4 to the pound. Elliot (1845), p. 1078. In New Orleans, the rate could have been slightly higher because the rate was a factor, in part, of the cost of moving specie from one location to another. Lawrence H. Officer, a Professor of Economics at the University of Illinois at Chicago, who has done significant historical research in this area, indicates that the exchange rate in that year was $4.92. Officer (2014b). This figure is an average of quarterly data from 1826 based upon actual transactions as opposed to advertised exchange rates. Officer (2007). While we cannot know precisely what exchange rate Audubon was quoted or paid, these figures provide the approximate amount that Audubon would have had to pay in dollars in New Orleans for a "sight" or "demand" bill of exchange to receive one pound sterling upon presentation in England. Ibid.

Based on an average of the data, Audubon would have remitted approximately $488.20 in order to obtain a bill of exchange for £100 sterling. This means that the total cost of a bill of exchange for £340 was roughly $1,659.88. Adding in his expenses of $195.25 leading up to his departure, he must have had at least $1,855 in his purse when he left Beech Woods. Thus, while we cannot be certain exactly how much money Audubon carried as he said goodbye to Lucy, it seems likely it amounted to around $1,900 as stated in the text. The conversion to 2016 dollars is based on Sahr (2015).

357. Audubon (2011), p. 3; Rhodes (2004), p. 237; Ford (1987), p. 15.

358. Audubon (2011), p. 3; Ford (1987), p. 15. Passage aboard the *Delos* cost Audubon $100.00. Audubon (2011), p. 390; Ford (1987), p. 427.

359. Audubon (2011), p. 4; Ford (1987), p. 16.

360. Audubon (2011), Appendix B, pp. 398, 401-403; Ford (1987), pp. 16-19.

361. Audubon (2011), Appendix B, p. 398. Cf. Ford (1987), p. 18.

362. Audubon (2011), pp. 4-5. Cf. Ford (1987), p. 20. In her biography, Ford gives the wrong date for Audubon's departure from New Orleans, stating it was on May 27 rather than May 17, 1826. Ford (1988), p. 173.

363. Audubon (2011), p. 5. Cf. Ford (1987), p. 20. Built by Tom Bakewell's company in Cincinnati, the steamboat *Hercules* arrived in New Orleans in April 1826. She was lost along the Mississippi River in December 1828. Berthoud brought suit in Louisiana against Gordon, Forstall & Co. for the loss of his $5,000 interest in the vessel, claiming that the firm, which had an office in New Orleans, had been obligated to obtain insurance covering his interest. The case was decided in his favor by the District Court, and that ruling was subsequently affirmed by the Louisiana Supreme Court. *Berthoud v. Gordon, Forstall & Co.*, 6 Louisiana Reports 579 (1834).

364. Audubon (2011), pp. 5-51; Rhodes (2004), pp. 240-245; Ford (1987), pp. 20-80. It took the *Delos* over five weeks, until June 23, to make its way through the Gulf of Mexico to reach the Atlantic Ocean off the eastern coast of Florida. The ship was becalmed for days at a time by the summer doldrums. At other times, the trade winds were blowing dead ahead, severely retarding the ship's advance. Audubon (2011), pp. 14, 31-32; Ford (1987), pp. 30, 55. Once in the Atlantic, the winds became favorable, and she reached the Grand Banks off the coast of Newfoundland on July 4. Audubon (2011), p. 23; Ford (1987), p. 45. The crossing to Liverpool took just another sixteen days. Audubon (2011), p. 51; Ford (1987), p. 80.

Souder writes that the ship's voyage across the North Atlantic was similar to its slow passage through the Gulf, "only cold instead of hot. The *Delos* moved imperceptibly to the east, spending long days rolling on a glassy ocean with no wind."

Souder (2004), p. 195. Souder does not provide a citation for this assertion, but he notes that Ford's transcription of the 1826 journal was the "principle [*sic*] source" for the chapter where this quote appears. Ibid., note, p. 328. The journal, however, provides no indication that the vessel encountered the lack of wind in the Atlantic that had delayed its progress to the south. On July 9, Audubon indicated that they had had "fair winds" for eighteen days. Audubon (2011), p. 32; Ford (1987), p. 58. He also recorded the number of miles it had covered each day. From July 4, when the vessel was situated in the Grand Banks near Newfoundland, until the *Delos* reached Liverpool on July 20, the ship exceeded 125 miles a day on all but two days, July 16 and 17, when it covered 61 and 66 miles, respectively. Audubon (2011), pp. 34–35; Ford (1987), pp. 55–56. The journal simply provides no support for Souder's statement.

Hart-Davis states erroneously that the voyage of the *Delos* from New Orleans was only of seven weeks' duration. Hart-Davis (2004), p. 9. In fact, it was just over nine.

Other biographers refer to the number of days as opposed to weeks Audubon was at sea, and here too, there is disagreement. Rhodes refers to the "interminable sixty-four day crossing." Rhodes (2004), p. 245. Herrick and Arthur assert the voyage took sixty-five days. Herrick (1938) I, p. 350; Arthur (1937), p. 315. Souder speaks of the "brutal sixty-six days at sea." Souder (2004), p. 195.

From the *Delos*'s departure at New Orleans on May 17 to its anchorage in the Mersey River off the Liverpool docks on July 20, a total of sixty-four days elapsed. If one prefers to extend the voyage to July 21 when Audubon actually stepped ashore, then it was sixty-five. That was the number of days Audubon told Lucy the voyage took when he wrote her on August 7, 1826. Audubon (2011), p. 97; Ford (1987). p. 130. However, Audubon indicated in his journal that they considered the commencement of their voyage to be at noon on May 18, 1826, when they made their first navigational observation in the Gulf of Mexico. Audubon (2011), p. 5; Ford (1987), p. 20. From that date it was precisely sixty-three days—nine weeks—until the *Delos* reached Liverpool as stated in the text.

365. Audubon (2011), pp. 36, 46; Ford (1987),

pp. 61, 76. Audubon apparently drank little, if at all, during his early years. Hart-Davis (2004), p. 56. He claimed to have had his first glass of wine on his wedding day. Audubon (1999), p. 783; *AHJ* I, p. 27. Martha Pope, the wife of Audubon's friend Dr. Nathaniel Wells Pope, recalled that while Audubon was living at Beech Woods from November 1824 to 1826, he "always drank a glass of weak whiskey and water, which he called grog, for his breakfast." Arthur (1937), p. 302. However, after his voyage to England in 1826, Audubon became a regular consumer of spirits. His 1826 journal is replete with wine- or porter-soaked entries written after he had returned to his room following a night of drinking at a social gathering and was "in his cups." Durant & Harwood (1980), p. 291.

366. Audubon (2011), p. 51; Ford (1987), p. 80.

CHAPTER 2: *THE BIRDS OF AMERICA*

1. Audubon (2011), pp. 51, 53, 93–94; Ford (1987), pp. 80–81, 123.

2. Audubon (2011), pp. 3, 53; Rhodes (2004), p. 249; Ford (1988), p. 177; Ford (1987), p. 81. The description in Ford's biography of Audubon's initial meeting with Alexander Gordon is both imprecise and factually inaccurate. She writes: "At first Gordon, taken aback, pretended not to recognize his caller. Then, almost grudgingly, he went with him to the Customs to help clear the portfolios. Not until the artist put down tuppence on each drawing did Gordon so much as offer his card with a home address." Ford (1988), p. 177. Ford has compressed Audubon's two separate visits to Gordon's office on separate days (July 21 and 22) into what would appear to be one. Audubon (2011), pp. 53, 55; Ford (1987), p. 81, 84. See also, note 7, *infra*.

3. Audubon (2011), p. 53. Clearly, Alexander Gordon's attitude toward Audubon had changed markedly since they first became acquainted in New Orleans in early 1821. Gordon's altered view, no doubt, had been shaped in part by the poor opinion all of Lucy's siblings and their spouses now held of Audubon as an irresponsible husband and father. Ford also posits that Gordon and his wife, Ann, were sensitive to the fact that the wife of George Keats, brother to deceased English poet John Keats, was visiting Liverpool at the same time. The Gor-

dons knew that the Keatses were still angry about a failed business deal they had entered into with Audubon while they were living in Henderson. Ford (1987), p. 79, note 17. See also, Gigante (2011), pp. 303–304; Streshinsky (1993), pp. 96–98.

4. Rhodes (2004), p. 249.

5. Audubon (2011), p. 53; Ford (1987), p. 81. Streshinsky reads Audubon's journal entry differently, stating that Alexander Gordon suggested Audubon "call at his office again" in lieu of giving his brother-in-law leave to call at his home. Streshinsky (1993), p. 163. The journal, however, makes it clear that she is in error. Gordon pointedly directed Audubon, as he took his leave, "If I Should not call again!!!!" Audubon (2011), p. 53. Ford reworded this as "if I would not call there again!!!!" Ford (1987), p. 81. That Gordon did not want to see Audubon at his office again is evident from Audubon's later remark that he would have to endure such mistreatment. See note 6, *infra*.

6. Audubon (2011), p. 53. Cf. Ford (1987), p. 82.

7. Audubon (2011), pp. 54–55; Ford (1987), p. 84. It is clear from Audubon's 1826 journal, cited here, that Gordon did not accompany Audubon to the Custom House to retrieve his portfolios on July 22 as Ford claims. Cf. Ford (1988), p. 177. He directed a subordinate to handle that task. Further, contrary to Ford's assertion, Gordon relented and handed Audubon his calling card at the end of their second meeting as the artist left his offices on the way to the Custom House.

8. Audubon (2011), p. 54; Ford (1967), p. 82. Audubon did not record in his journal whether he left Vincent Nolte's letter for Richard Rathbone when he called at Rathbone's counting house on Friday, July 21. However, given the promptness with which Rathbone responded with a dinner invitation, he must have. Ford, in her biography, takes the position that Audubon did not deliver the letter until the following Monday. Ford (1988), p. 178. This fails to explain why Rathbone sent an invitation over to Audubon's hotel on Saturday asking him to dinner the following week.

Nolte was well known to the Rathbones, having been a significant player in the New Orleans cotton market for fourteen years. Consequently, they had every reason to extend their hospitality to one whom Nolte had praised so lavishly in his letter of intro-

duction. Audubon (2011), Appendix B, p. 398; Ford (1987), p. 18; Nolte (1854), p. 328–329.

Ford asserts that Nolte had also earned the Rathbones' gratitude by helping them "head off a wildcat cotton market." Ford (1987), p. 82, note 1. See also, Audubon (2011), p. 75, note 30. To the contrary, Nolte claimed in his biography that the Rathbones, among other leading Liverpool cotton firms, were complicit in fueling a speculative fever in the market after the price for cotton increased sharply in the early months of 1825. Nolte recognized what was happening and tried to avoid being caught up in the frenzy. However, the failure of a reputable Liverpool firm, for which Nolte had agreed to purchase a large quantity of cotton at the height of the market, forced Nolte's firm into bankruptcy. Nolte (1854), pp. 314–318, 325–329.

9. Audubon (2011), p. 55; Ford (1987), p. 85. See also, Rhodes (2004), p. 251; Streshinsky (1993), pp. 164–165; Bland (1977), p. 4.

10. Audubon (2011), pp. 60–61; Ford (1987), p. 89.

11. Audubon (2011), p. 61. Cf. Ford (1987), p. 89. Richard Rathbone (1788–1860), the second son of William Rathbone IV (1757–1809) and his wife, Hannah Mary *née* Reynolds (1761–1839), was born on December 2, 1788. Hart-Davis (2004), p. 18; Greg (1905), pp. 51, 122; Burke (1847) II, p. 1099. Rhodes's assertion that Rathbone was "a decade younger than Audubon" is incorrect. Rhodes (2004), p. 251. In July 1826 when they met, Audubon was forty-one, while Rathbone was then thirty-seven.

Rathbone was married to Hannah Mary *née* Reynolds (1798–1878), referred to by genealogists as Hannah Mary II to distinguish her from her mother-in-law of the same name, called Hannah Mary I. Hart-Davis (2004), p. 18; Burke (1847) II, p. 1099. The Rathbones resided at 87 Duke Street in Liverpool and had a country home outside the city known as Woodcroft. Ford (1987), pp. 89, 173; Greg (1905), p. 10.

12. Audubon (2011), p. 64–65; Ford (1987), pp. 93–94. In her biography, Ford suggests that Audubon's introduction to the matriarch of the Rathbone clan and the presentation of his drawings took place at the Bedford Street home of her eldest son, William Rathbone V (1787–1868). Ford (1988), pp.

179–180; Rathbone (1905), p. 55–56. The 1826 journal establishes beyond question that this momentous event took place at Greenbank, the Rathbone family country estate, which was situated on twenty-four acres approximately three miles east of the city. Hart-Davis (2004), pp. 16–17.

Audubon wrote in his July 25 journal entry of taking a carriage with Richard Rathbone and his family along with a gentleman named James Pyke to see Rathbone's mother, and described how "The country open^d to our View gradually," a clear indication they were outside the city. Audubon (2011), p. 64; Audubon (1999), p. 166. Cf. Ford (1987), p. 93. That evening, at the conclusion of his visit, Audubon and his hosts took a carriage "and moved threw the avenue by the same way to Liverpool again," another sign he had been in the country. Audubon (2011), p. 65; Audubon (1999), p. 166. Cf. Ford (1987), p. 94. Later journal entries also make it plain that his earlier visit was to Greenbank. On August 4, he spoke of walking out to Greenbank, where he "passed again under the avenüe of Trees" leading to the English Gothic mansion, a reference to his description of "a Cool arbor [MS: Harbour] of English Trees" on his first visit. Audubon (2011), pp. 64, 87. Cf. Ford (1987), pp. 93, 117. On September 6, Audubon reminded Lucy of "The very first day that I visited Green Bank, Thou recollects that I was brought here by Mr R^d Rathbone & Lady & Mr Pyke in company [MS: comp*g*]." Audubon (2011), p. 141. Cf. Ford (1987), p. 174. There is simply no doubt that on July 25 the artist visited Greenbank.

Other Audubon biographers concur. Rhodes (2004), p. 251; Souder (2004), p. 198; Hart-Davis (2004), p. 16. Rhodes, however, erroneously suggests that the visit to Greenbank occurred on Wednesday, July 26. Rhodes (2004), pp. 251–252. It actually was on Tuesday, July 25, as reflected in the text. Audubon (2011), pp. 63–65; Ford (1987), pp. 92–95.

Greenbank was a warm and inviting place as Audubon found. He equated it in his journal to the "Heavenly Gardens." Audubon (2011), p. 65; Ford (1987), p. 94. In large part, this was due to the warm and gentle influence of Hannah Mary I, whom Audubon affectionately referenced in his journal as the "Queen Bee." Henry Fothergill Chorley (1808–1872), who first stayed at Greenbank as boy and later became a regular visitor, recorded for posterity his memories of this remarkable woman and her singularly hospitable home:.

Hannah Mary Rathbone was a noble and fascinating woman; the most faithful of wives, the most devoted of mothers, the most beneficent of friends. In 1819, when I stayed at Green Bank, she was in the last ripeness of her maturity, looking older than her years, but as beautiful as any picture which can be offered by freshest youth. Though she was nominally a member of the Society of Friends, she never conformed to its uniform. Her profuse white hair, which had been white from an early age, was cut straight like a man's, to lie simply on her forehead. Above this was her spotless cap of white net, rescued from meagreness by a quilled border and a sort of scarf of the same material round it—a headdress as picturesque, without being queer, as if its wearer had studied for years how to arrange it. Her gown was always a dark silk, with a quantity of delicate muslin to swathe the throat, and a shawl, which covered the stoop of her short figure—the shawl never gay, though mostly rich. But the face was simply one of the most beautiful faces (without regularity) that I have ever seen; beautiful in spite of its being slightly underhung; the eyes were so deep, brilliant, and tender; the tint was so fresh, the expression was so noble and so affectionate; and the voice matched the face—so low it was, so kind, so cordial and (to come back to my point) as I fancied, so irresistibly intimate, which means appreciating. The welcome of that elderly woman to the awkward, scared, nervous child who entered her house, is to me one of the recollections which mark a life, as having decided its aims, by encouraging its sympathies.

She had been throughout her life the admired friend and counsellor of many distinguished men, all belonging to the liberal school of ideas and philosophies, which were wakened, especially in the world of Dissenters, by the first French Revolution. One of so fearless a brain, and so tenderly religious a heart, and so pure a moral sense as she I have never known. Her moral courage was indomitable; her manners shy, gentle, and caressing.

Since that time, I have been in many luxurious houses; but anything like the delicious and elegant comfort of Green Bank during her reign I have never known—plenty without coarseness; exquisiteness without that super-delicacy which oppresses by its extravagance. It was a house to which the sick went to be nursed, and the benevolent to have their plans carried out. It was anything but a hide-bound or Puritanical house; for the library was copious, and novels and poems were read aloud in the parlors, and such men as William Roscoe, Robert Owen, Sylvester of Derby, Combe of Edinburgh, came and went. There was a capital garden; there was a double verandah—and if I live to see all the glories of sun, moon, and seven stars, I shall never see that verandah equalled; there was a pianoforte—not like my mother's pianoforte at Green End (which Dickens must have known, else he could never have described Miss Tox's instrument, with the wreath of sweat peas round its maker's name, in 'Dombey')—kept under lock and key. There were water and a boat;—but more, there was a touch of the true fire from Heaven in the owner of all these delights which spoke to me in a way hardly to be described, never to be forgotten. In the case of some people, even from childhood upwards, one judges; with others, one hopes; with others, one believes; with others, one learns; with a few, *one knows*; and those few, as I have said, decide one's life.

How that great, and good, and gentle woman ruled her family—having been left a widow at middle age—how *toned* them to a standard such as few even try to reach, many, very many, living know as well as I. Few have influenced so many by their affections, by their reason, by their understanding, so honorably as that retiring, delicate woman; and it is a pleasure (not without tears in it) to me to think that when we are all no more, some one, untouched by family partiality or tradition, shall say this much by way of laying a leaf on a modest, but a very holy, grave.

Jones (1874), pp. 23–25. See also, Greg (1905), pp. 6–8 (with slight variations). Chorley's description of the Queen Bee's appearance makes it clear that by 1826, when Audubon met her, her hair was pure white, not auburn as Rhodes declares. Rhodes (2004), p. 257. Rhodes has confused the Queen Bee (Mrs. William Rathbone IV) with Elizabeth Rathbone *née* Greg (1790–1882), the wife of her eldest son, William Rathbone V. Audubon (2011), pp. 86, 90–91, 128; Nottingham (1992), Appendix Three, p. 109; Ford (1987), pp. 116–117, 120, 159.

Rhodes's quotation from Audubon's journal entry of August 4 of her "dark eyes sparkling" is also misdirected. Rhodes (2004), p. 257. This reference is again to Elizabeth Rathbone, not to the Queen Bee, whom Audubon refers to in the same passage as "the Mother Rathbone." Audubon (2011), pp. 86–87, 90–91; Ford (1987), pp. 116–117, 120. Audubon would begin to allude to the elder Mrs. William Rathbone as the "Queen Bee" in his journal on August 15. Audubon (2011), p. 121; Ford (1987), p. 152.

13. Audubon (2011), p. 65, 346; Ford (1987), pp. 94, 388. Hannah Mary Rathbone (1791–1865) (referred to as Hannah Mary III), the younger and only sister of William V and Richard Rathbone, was thirty-four, attractive, and unmarried when Audubon arrived at Greenbank in late July 1826. She would celebrate her thirty-fifth birthday on August 3. In January 1831, at the age of thirty-nine, she married a twenty-seven-year-old cousin, Dr. William Reynolds (1803–1877). She was known within the family as "Annie." Hart-Davis (2004), p. 18, note 3; Streshinsky (1993), p. 171; Greg (1905), pp. 5, 10, 84, 93, and Appendix VI, pp. 204–205; Burke (1863), p. 1252.

14. Audubon (2011), p. 65; Ford (1987), p. 94.

15. Audubon (2011), p. 66; Hart-Davis (2004), p. 18; Ford (1987), p. 96. William Rathbone V (1787–1868) was two years Audubon's junior, having been born on June 17, 1787. Hart-Davis (2004), p. 18; Greg (1905), p. 49. William was married in 1812 to Elizabeth Greg (1790–1882), the daughter of industrialist Samuel Greg of Quarry Bank outside Manchester. Pedersen (2004), pp. xv, 10; Nottingham (1992), Appendix Three, p. 109; Ford (1987), p. 82, note 1; Greg (1905), p. 93 and Appendix VII, p. 205. William V lived with his family on Bedford Street on the southwest corner of Abercromby Square in Liverpool. Audubon (1999), p. 73; Ford (1987), p. 103; Rathbone (1905), pp. 55–56. Ford and Rhodes refer to him erroneously as William

Rathbone IV. Rhodes (2004), p. 251; Ford (1987), p. 82, note 1.

Ford maintains that William was present on July 25 when Audubon showed his drawings for the first time to the Rathbone clan. Ford (1988), pp. 179–180. Souder and Streshinsky, following Ford's path, make the same assertion. Souder (2004), p. 198; Streshinsky (1993), p. 166. There is absolutely no mention of this in Audubon's journal. His first reference to William Rathbone is on the following day, July 26, when Richard and William called on him, which certainly suggests that this was their initial encounter. Audubon (2011), p. 66; Ford (1987), p. 96.

Moreover, Ford misquotes from her own transcription of the journal in making her case. In her biography, she declares that before Audubon displayed the contents of his portfolio, he overheard William describe him in a whisper to another visitor as "Simple, intelligent." Ford (1988), p. 180. The entry of September 6, 1826, in her edition of the journal says no such thing: "The very first day that I visited 'Green Bank,' thou recollects that I was brought here by Mr. Richard Rathbone and lady, in company with Mr. Pyke. Whilst here and moving from the library or setting-room into the lobby or entry, to examine the collection of stuffed birds there, *I* heard Richard Rathbone say (to some one who I did not see then but whom I now believe was Mr. Reynolds, Sr.) that I was 'simple intelligent.'" Ford (1987), p. 174. Cf. Audubon (2011), p. 141; JJA, Edinburgh to Mrs. William Rathbone IV, Liverpool, 29 Nov. 1826, Audubon (2011), pp. 319–320, Ford (1987), p. 361 (referencing Richard Rathbone as the speaker who described Audubon as "simple intelligent"). Rhodes reads Audubon's journal as I do, maintaining that Audubon did not meet William Rathbone until the following day. Rhodes (2004), p. 252.

16. Streshinsky (1993), p. 167.

17. Audubon (2011), pp. 82–85, 102; Ford (1987), pp. 111–113; 135. The exhibition of Audubon's drawings at the Liverpool Royal Institution took place from July 31 through August 5 and was initially free and open to the public. Audubon (2011), pp. 82, 90–91; Ford (1987), pp. 111–112, 119–121. According to his journal, the exhibition consisted of between 225 (Ford misreads the journal entry as "235")

and 250 of the drawings he brought with him to England, comprising the contents of his Portfolio No. 2, which held his larger compositions. Audubon (2011), pp. 70, 85, 91, 107, 150; Ford (1987), pp. 100, 114, 139, 182; JJA, Liverpool to Nicholas Berthoud, Shippingport, KY, 7 Aug. 1826, Audubon (2011), p. 102, Ford (1987), p. 135. At this point, Audubon was keeping the smaller images in his Portfolio No. 1 "sacred." Audubon (2011), p. 107; Ford (1987), p. 139.

For the first three days of the exhibition, the doors of the Royal Institution opened at noon and closed at 2:00 p.m. But the show proved so popular that Audubon's friends prevailed on him to keep it open for the remainder of the week from 10:00 a.m. to dusk. Audubon (2011), p. 82; Ford (1987), pp. 111–112; JJA, Liverpool to Nicholas Berthoud, Shippingport, KY, 7 Aug. 1826, Audubon (2011), p. 102, Ford (1987), pp. 135–136. On Saturday, August 5, it appears that the exhibition closed at noon, and Audubon packed up his drawings to take them to show Lord Stanley, who had been invited to see them at the home of Adam Hodgson, a Rathbone cousin and former partner of the Rathbone brothers. Audubon (2011), p. 91; Nottingham (1992), p. 36; Ford (1987), p. 121. The exhibition would reopen with an admission fee on August 14. Audubon (2011), p. 107; Ford (1987), p. 139.

Ford and Rhodes erroneously assert that Adam Hodgson was still a partner of William and Richard Rathbone in 1826. Rhodes (2004), pp. 255, 257; Ford (1988), p. 182; Ford (1987), p. 105, note 16. See also, Audubon (2011), p. 75, note 29. In fact, Hodgson was only a partner in the business from 1814 until 1824, when he resigned. Huddleston (2012), p. 283; Nottingham (1992), p. 36.

18. Audubon (2011), pp. 76–77, 81; Ford (1987), pp. 106–107, 111. Audubon finally succeeded in seeing his sister-in-law Ann Bakewell Gordon on Saturday, July 29. In keeping with her husband's coolness, she was initially indifferent, refusing to return his kiss when he greeted her. But their conversation soon turned to old times, and she became more congenial. Audubon recorded in his journal that she seemed "*rather* surprised" that he had been so well received by such luminaries as Richard Rathbone, William Roscoe, and Adam Hodgson. She invited him to dinner the following afternoon. When Audu-

bon arrived at their home on Sunday, July 30, at 3:30 p.m., he was greeted by Alexander Gordon, whose attitude toward him had completely shifted. Gordon now expressed happiness that Audubon was in England and lauded his work. Audubon (2011), p. 81; Ford (1987), p. 111.

Souder asserts that when Audubon saw Ann for the first time, she did not return his kiss "apparently not convinced as to who he was." Souder (2004), p. 199. Not so. Ann clearly knew that Audubon was in Liverpool from his two visits to Alexander Gordon's mercantile house on July 21 and 22 as well as a chance meeting Audubon had with her husband on the street on July 28, the day before the naturalist called upon her. Audubon (2011), pp.53, 55, 71–72; Ford (1987), pp. 81, 84, 102. On the latter occasion, Audubon told Gordon that he had made an earlier attempt to see Ann but had been disappointed she was out and reiterated his strong desire to visit her. Audubon (2011), p. 72; Ford (1987), p. 102. Ann was almost certainly aware of her brother-in-law's intention to pay her a call on July 29. When Audubon made his way to the Gordon's home on that day, it was at an "apointed hour, say 12," suggesting that Gordon had recommended he come by at that time. Moreover, Audubon was met by a "Coarse female" servant and waited downstairs awhile before being admitted to see Ann. Audubon (2011), p. 76. Cf. Ford (1987), p. 106. In such a situation, it would have been customary for Audubon to have given the servant his calling card. He would not have gained admittance to the upstairs parlor without identifying himself. So, while Ann may not have seen him for several years, she had no doubt when he called on her who he was. Her refusal to kiss him was likely due to the poor opinion she and her husband held of him at the time.

19. Audubon (2011), pp. 82, 85; Ford (1987), p. 111–112, 114–115. Dr. Thomas Stewart Traill (1781–1862), the president of the Royal Institution of Liverpool, indicated that "several thousands" visited Audubon's exhibition during the first three days that admission was free. Thomas Stewart Traill, Liverpool to Benjamin A. Heywood, Manchester, Sept. 1826, Audubon (2011), pp. 430–431, Ford (1967), p. 397. Cf. Ford (1987), p. 103, note 13.

Audubon did not record a headcount in his journal during the first two days of the exhibi-

tion. On the opening day, July 31, he merely indicated that when the doors opened at noon, "the Ladies flocked in." Audubon (2011), p. 82; Audubon (1999), p. 167. Cf. Ford (1987), p. 111. The following day, he reported that "the Assemblage was great." Audubon (2011), p. 84. Cf. Ford (1987), p. 114. On August 2, he estimated there were more than one hundred viewers. Audubon (2011), p. 85; Ford (1987), p. 114. On August 3, his journal entry stated that a crowd of 413 people entered the exhibit hall in two hours. Audubon (2011), p. 86; Ford (1987), p. 115. See also, JJA, Liverpool to Nicholas Berthoud, Shippingport, KY, 7 Aug. 1826, Audubon (2011), p. 102, Ford (1997), p. 136. On August 4, he saw "perhaps 200 persons." Audubon (2011), p. 90; Ford (1987), p. 119.

Most of Audubon's modern biographers have misread Audubon's journal in this regard. Ford inexplicably declares that when the exhibition first opened on July 31, "In the first two hours more than 400 visitors passed through." Ford (1988), p. 182. Souder repeats this misstatement. Souder (2004), p. 200. Hart-Davis, apparently relying on the Maria Audubon version of the journal, claims that on the second day, August 1, "413 people came to see the pictures," when this was Audubon's count for August 3. Hart-Davis (2004) p. 59; *AHJ* I, p. 107. Streshinsky similarly errs, attributing this attendance figure to the third day of the exhibition. Streshinsky (1993), p. 169. Only Rhodes accurately summarizes Audubon's journal entries about the numbers of patrons he counted at the exhibition.

20. JJA, Liverpool to Nicholas Berthoud, Shippingport, KY, 7 Aug. 1826, Audubon (2011), p. 102, Ford (1987), p. 135.

21. Audubon (2011), pp. 84–85; Ford (1987), pp. 114–115. Audubon honored Dr. Thomas Stewart Traill by giving his name to an *Empidonax* flycatcher found in eastern and central North America. The bird was known as Traill's Flycatcher until 1973, when the American Ornithologists' Union concluded that it was actually two separate species. They were renamed the Willow Flycatcher and Alder Flycatcher. Sedgwick (2000). Only the Willow Flycatcher now carries the Traill name in its Latin designation, *Empidonax trailli*. Kaufman (1996), p. 381; Mearns (1992), p. 461.

22. Audubon (2011), p. 84; Ford (1987), p. 114.

23. Audubon (2011), pp. 105–106, 110; Ford (1987), pp. 137–139, 141–142.

24. JJA, Manchester to LBA, Bayou Sarah, 17 Sept. 1826, Audubon (2011), p. 171, Ford (1987), p. 206. The paid exhibition of Audubon's drawings ran at the Liverpool Royal Institution from August 14 through September 8. Audubon (2011), pp. 107, 145; Ford (1987), pp. 139, 177. See also, Ford (1988), p. 187.

In the four weeks it was open, the paid exhibition attracted comparatively fewer visitors than when it was free to the public. Thomas Stewart Traill, Liverpool, to B.A. Heywood, Manchester, Sept. 1826, Audubon (2011), p. 431, Ford (1967), p. 397. Certainly, it did not draw the upwards of two thousand visitors Audubon's earnings would suggest. He admitted to his journal that some of his Liverpool friends, including the Swiss entomologist André Melly (1802–1851) and others he did not wish to name, had added "many Pounds Sterling" to the collections "during my Exhibition at the Royal Institution." Audubon (2011), p. 219. Cf. Ford (1987), p. 251.

Ford mistakenly believes that Audubon's friends padded the till during his later exhibition in Manchester. Ford (1988), p. 194. However, that exhibition was held first at the Exchange Building and then at the Manchester Natural History Society, not the Royal Manchester Institution. Significantly, Audubon does not mention the Royal Manchester Institution during any part of his stay in Manchester. Indeed, in 1826 the Royal Manchester Institution was in the process of constructing a building to house its facilities. Slugg (1881), p. 269.

Ford also errs in stating that André Melly was then married to Ellen Greg, the daughter of Samuel Greg of Quarry Bank, outside Manchester, and younger sister of Mrs. William Rathbone V. Ford (1988), p. 190; Ford (1987), p. 98. In fact, Melly married Ellen Greg in July 1828. Audubon (2011), p. 68, note 16; Arkle (1913), p. 74.

As a side note, Melly was at least partially responsible for introducing Audubon to the use of snuff. Audubon (2011), p. 93; Ford (1987) p. 122. Audubon developed a particular taste for what he referred to as No. 37, which would have been Hardham's No. 37, a concoction of Dutch and rappee that originated with 18th century London tobac-

conist John Hardham. Audubon (2011), p. 257, 261; Ford (1987), pp. 296, 298; Lucas (1904), pp. 30, 32; Timbs (1860), p. 144; Hill (1840), p. 29. Audubon assured Lucy that he would not use it much. Audubon (2011), p. 216; Ford (1987), p. 247.

Audubon badly needed the extra income the Liverpool exhibition generated. His financial situation had not been helped by his impulsive decision to purchase expensive gold watches for both himself and Lucy on July 25, shortly after he arrived in Liverpool and before he had any real idea what the future would hold. On the morning after he dined with Richard Rathbone and his family for the first time, Audubon went to Roskell & Son, one of Liverpool's finest watchmakers, and picked out gold watches with chains and seals for himself and Lucy. Audubon (2011), p. 64; Ford (1987), p. 93; JJA, Liverpool to LBA, Bayou Sarah, 26 Dec. 1827 (APS), *Letters* I, p. 54. These watches are now in the collection of the Audubon Museum in Henderson, KY, and are depicted in Harwood & Durant (1985), p. 93.

According to Audubon, this purchase set him back £120, which was more than a third of the £340 he had brought with him from America. JJA, Liverpool to LBA, Bayou Sarah, 26 Dec. 1827 (APS), *Letters* I, p. 54. See also, Rhodes (2004), p. 251; Hart-Davis (2004), p. 14; Arthur (1937), pp. 316–317. Ford avers, mistakenly, that the watches cost him £340, which was in fact the entire sum he carried when he arrived in England. Ford (1988), p. 180. See also, Chapter 1, note 356, *supra*.

Even though Lucy had given him roughly $500 (roughly £102) of the money in his purse so that he could buy her a watch and piano, this was a wildly extravagant purchase at a time when he had limited funds and no assurance that he would be able to supplement them during his stay. Rhodes (2004), p. 238. See also, Chapter 1, note 356, *supra*. Audubon's biographers, with the notable exception of Richard Rhodes, generally consider Audubon to have been a poor businessman, at least prior to undertaking the production of *BOA*. This incident provides additional support for the conventional view by raising legitimate doubts about the soundness of his financial judgment.

25. Hart-Davis (2004), pp. 56–57. Since 1819, Prideaux John Selby (1788–1867) had found a ready

audience for his serial publication of *Illustrations of British Ornithology*, consisting of hand-colored engravings of his mostly life-sized watercolors of British birds. He was also working on a new publication, *Illustrations of Ornithology*, with Scottish baronet Sir William Jardine (1800–1874), whose first wife was the sister of Audubon's engraver, William Home Lizars. Chalmers (2003), pp. 40, 210, 214; Sotheby's (7 Jun. 1989), Lot 197; Jackson (1985), pp. 202, 215.

26. Rhodes (2004), p. 239; Streshinsky (1993), p. 162.

27. Audubon (2011), p. 141; Streshinsky (1993), p. 162; Ford (1987), p. 174. Rhodes takes issue with the comment by Richard Rathbone that Audubon was "*simple Intelligent*," declaring that "Audubon was many things, including mortally shy in the presence of people he feared might be his superiors, but he was never simple." Rhodes (2004), p. 284. It is unclear which definition of "simple" Rhodes is using for his assessment. At that time, as now, the word had a variety of meanings, including: "Plain; artless; unskilled; undesigning; sincere; harmless; uncompounded; unmingled; single; only one; plain; not complicated; silly; not wise; not cunning." Jameson (1826), p. 666.

Certainly, Audubon was not lacking in intelligence, knowledge, experience, or complexity, which is Rhodes's point. But it seems apparent that what Rathbone really meant had more to do with how the naturalist presented himself. Audubon was modest and straightforward in his demeanor. There was no artifice or affectations about him. Essentially, what you saw was what you got.

Indeed, Audubon was routinely described in these terms, including the use of the word "simple," by those he met. Sir Walter Scott was introduced to Audubon in Edinburgh, Scotland, on January 22, 1827, and described him this way: "He is an American by naturalization, a Frenchman by birth, but less of a Frenchman than I have ever seen, — no dash, no glimmer or shine about him, but great simplicity of manners and behaviour; slight in person and plainly dressed; wears long hair which time has not yet tinged; his countenance acute, handsome, and interesting, but simplicity is the predominant characteristic." *AHJ* I, p. 206, note 1.

Martha Pope, the wife of Dr. Nathaniel Pope,

said of him: "His bearing was courteous and refined, simple, and unassuming." Arthur (1937), p. 298. Former New York Mayor Philip Hone noted the same characteristics when he met Audubon in April 1833, depicting him as "an interesting man of about fifty-five years of age, modest in his deportment, possessing general intelligence, an acute mind, and great enthusiasm." Tuckerman (1889) I, p. 73. Benjamin Strobel, M.D., who met Audubon in Key West in 1832, offered a comparable impression, stating that he was "frank, free and amiable in his dispositions, and affable and polite in manners." Hammond (1963), p. 465.

28. Audubon (2011), p. 95; Ford (1987), p. 125. See also, Streshinsky (1993), p. 162. At a dinner at the home of William Roscoe on Sunday, August 6, Audubon entertained the assembled group with the calls of the Wild Turkey, Barred Owl, and Mourning Dove. But they seemed to be surprised he had no tales of facing danger in the wild. As he admitted to his journal, he "never was troubled in the woods by any larger annimals than Ticks and Musquitoes." Audubon (2011), p. 96. Cf. Ford (1987), pp. 125–126.

29. Audubon (2011), p. 82; Ford (1987), p. 111. See also, Streshinsky (1993), pp. 162, 169.

30. Athenaeum (1868), p. 833. See also, Rhodes (2004), p. 253; Herrick (1938) II, p. 200. Rhodes errs in stating that the quoted description of Audubon was written a decade after Audubon arrived in England. In truth, this account of the artist appeared in December 1868 in a review of Robert Buchanan's biography of Audubon in *The Athenæum*, a London literary magazine. Athenaeum (1868), p. 833. See also, Herrick (1838) II, Bibliography No. 152, p. 439. Rhodes refers to the author as "an anonymous observer." Rhodes (2004), p. 253. See also, Harwood & Durant (1985), p. 118. Though the review was unsigned, this vivid depiction of Audubon could only have come from the pen of Henry Fothergill Chorley, the literary critic of *The Athenæum*, who had met Audubon at Greenbank in 1826. Audubon (2011), p. 137; Bledsoe (1998), pp. 23, 27–29, 303; Ford (1987), p. 169. Rhodes (2004), p. 253.

31. Audubon (2011), pp. 74–75, 93–94, 97–98; Ford (1987), pp. 104–105, 123, 130–131. See also, Duff Hart-Davis (2004), pp. 61–62; Ford (1988), p. 182.

32. JJA, Liverpool to LBA, Bayou Sarah, 1 Sept. 1826 (APS), *Letters* I, p. 6.

33. Audubon (2011), pp. 116, 138; Ford (1987), pp. 147, 170.

34. E.g., Audubon (2011), pp. 121–123; Ford (1987), pp. 152–154.

35. Audubon (2011), pp. 98–99, 102; Ford (1987), pp. 131–132, 136; JJA, Liverpool to VGA, Louisville, 1 Sept. 1826 (APS), *Letters* I, p. 3. At the same time that Audubon was planning his tour of England and Scotland, he advised Lucy he was also working on obtaining an appointment to one of the country's Royal Institutions as an artist and ornithologist. JJA, Liverpool to LBA, Bayou Sarah, 1 Sept. 1826 (APS), *Letters* I, p. 6. Audubon was still unclear as to how he could accomplish his goal of publishing his work, and his plans were still very much in flux.

36. Audubon (2011), pp. 149, 151, 153; Ford (1987), pp. 181, 183, 185. Rhodes mistakenly asserts that Audubon traveled to Manchester in the company of the Swiss entomologist André Melly, whom Audubon had gotten to know during his Liverpool stay. Rhodes (2004), p. 263. See also, Audubon (2011), pp. 67, 75, 86, 93, 132–133, 150; Ford (1988), p. 184; Ford (1987), p. 98 and note 7; pp. 105, 115–116, 122, 164–166, 182. Although this was Audubon's original intent, he eventually made the trip with Alexander Munro, the Curator of the Liverpool Royal Institution. Audubon (2011), p. 95 and note 55; pp. 150–153; Ford (1987), p. 125 and note 35; pp. 182–185; JJA, Manchester to LBA, Bayou Sarah, 17 Sept. 1826, Audubon (2011), p. 172, Ford (1987), p. 206; Baines (1824) I, p. 299. See also, Hart-Davis (2004), p. 67. Munro was asked by Dr. Thomas Stewart Traill to accompany the artist and help him set up the exhibition of his drawings in Manchester. Audubon (2011), p. 150; Ford (1987), p. 182; JJA, Manchester to LBA, Bayou Sarah, 17 Sept. 1826, Audubon (2011), p. 172, Ford (1987), p. 206.

37. Audubon (2011), pp. 90–91, 153; Ford (1987), pp. 120–121, 185.

38. Audubon (2011), pp. 154, 184, 192; Ford (1987), pp. 186, 215, 223. On September 11, 1826, the day after he reached Manchester, Audubon paid 3 guineas, the equivalent of 63 shillings or £3.3s, to rent the Exhibition Room at the Exchange Building for a week. Audubon (2011), pp. 154, 156, 180; Ford (1987), pp. 186, 188, 211. In addition, he hired a gentleman named Crookes for 15 shillings per week to collect the entrance fee of a shilling. Audubon (2011), pp. 158, 191; Ford (1987), pp. 189, 222. Two days later, he noted that he had also hired a twelve-year-old lad, John Wilson, to take the tickets for 10 shillings per week. Audubon (2011), p. 163; Ford (1987), p. 194. Thus, his weekly costs ran to 88 shillings.

However, the show did not attract the same attention as it had in Liverpool. On the first day, only "[a]bout 20 persons" came through the door. Audubon (2011), p. 156. Cf. Ford (1987), p. 188. André Melly, one of Audubon's Liverpool friends, examined the receipts from the exhibition when he arrived in Manchester on September 19, and expressed his dissatisfaction with how the show was doing. Audubon (2011), p. 180; Ford (1987), p. 211. Two days later, Audubon complained to Dr. Edward Holme (1770–1847), the president of the Manchester Natural History Society, that the rental fee at the Exchange Building was too high and he was losing money. Audubon (2011), p. 160 and note 9; p. 184; Ford (1987), p. 192 and note 6; p. 215. Holme arranged for a committee of the society to meet on September 23 to discuss granting Audubon free use of a room in the society's building on King Street, which it did unanimously. Audubon (2011), pp. 184–185; Ford (1987), pp. 215–216; Slugg (1881), p. 266. Audubon mistakenly refers to the beneficent institution as the Academy of Natural History. Audubon (2011), pp. 184, 222; Ford (1987), pp. 215, 254. Souder, in error, claims that the free room was given to him by Manchester's Royal Institution. Souder (2004), p. 207.

Patterson and Ford both misread Audubon's journal entry for September 23 as stating the committee's decision would save him "13 shillings per week." Audubon (2011), p. 185; Ford (1987), p. 216. The holograph journal actually reads "63 shillings per week," which is consistent with his earlier statement that the room cost him 3 guineas (63 shillings) weekly. (NHYS Society Misc. Microfilm Reel 29). In any case, if Audubon's stated costs, reflected above, were recorded accurately, it appears that after two weeks the show had drawn fewer than 176 visitors, the number that would have permitted him to break even. This works out to less than fifteen persons a day, a far cry from the substantial crowds that initially swarmed the Liverpool Royal Institution to see Audubon's birds.

39. See note 38, *supra*. The exhibition at the Exchange Building ran through September 25 and was then moved the following day to the Manchester Natural History Society's building on King Street. Audubon (2011), pp. 192–193; Ford (1987), pp. 223–224.

40. JJA, Liverpool to LBA, Bayou Sarah, 1 Oct. 1826, Audubon (2011), p. 206, Ford (1987), p. 237. On the morning of September 29, 1826, the day after he returned to Liverpool, Audubon visited William Roscoe at his home in Lodge Lane and spoke to him about putting together a prospectus to inform potential subscribers about his work. According to Audubon's journal, Roscoe indicated that "nothing could be done in the way of forming a Prospectus for my work without more knowledge of what it could be brought out for." Audubon (2011), p. 201; Ford (1987), p. 232.

41. Audubon (2011), p. 170; Ford (1987), p. 201.

42. Audubon (2011), pp. 199–201; Ford (1987), pp. 229–231.

43. Audubon (2011), p. 202; Ford (1987), pp. 232–233. Henry G. Bohn (1796–1884) was among London's best known and successful booksellers. Audubon (2011), p. 202, note 2; Ford (1987), p. 232, note 3. See also, Rhodes (2004), p. 265. Audubon mistakenly referred to him as John Bohn in an October 1, 1826, letter to Lucy. JJA, Liverpool to LBA, Bayou Sarah, 1 Oct. 1826, Audubon (2011), p. 206, Ford (1967), p. 335. John Bohn (1757–1843) would have been the bookseller father of the "handsome well formed Young Gentleman" Audubon met in Liverpool. Audubon (2011), p. 202, note 2.

44. Audubon (2011), p. 202; Ford (1987), p. 233. See also, Rhodes (2004), p. 266.

45. Audubon (2011), p. 202; Ford (1987), p. 233.

46. Audubon (2011), p. 203; Sotheby's (7 Jun. 1989), Lot 232; Ford (1987), p. 233.

47. Audubon (2011), p. 203. Cf. Ford (1987), pp. 233–234. Souder insists that Audubon never seriously considered Henry Bohn's recommendation that Audubon's drawings be printed at a reduced scale. Souder (2004), p. 208. Streshinsky makes the same claim. Streshinsky (1993), p. 176. Dr. John Chalmers, an eminent Audubon scholar from Edinburgh, Scotland, seemingly concurs, quoting from

Maria Audubon's rewritten version of her grandfather's 1826 journal: "*This I will not do.*" Chalmers (2003), p. 31; *AHJ* I, p. 128. However, this quote appears nowhere in the holographic journal and was entirely fabricated by Maria.

Contrary to these scholars, the line from the original 1826 journal, quoted in the text, as well as Audubon's letter to Lucy written two days later on October 1, clearly indicate that Audubon was persuaded to follow Bohn's advice, at least initially. Audubon (2011), pp. 202–203; Ford (1987), pp. 232–234; JJA, Liverpool to LBA, Bayou Sarah, 1 Oct. 1826, Audubon (2011), pp. 206–208, Ford (1987), pp. 237–239. See also, Rhodes (2004), p. 266. Bohn would change his mind about publishing the drawings life sized once he viewed Audubon's exhibit in Manchester. See text and notes 56–57, *infra*.

It should also be noted that Rhodes misquotes the line from Audubon's journal that appears in the text, substituting "proceed" for "succeed." Cf. Audubon (2011), p. 203; Rhodes (2004), p. 266; Ford (1987), p. 234.

48. Audubon (2011), p. 219, 221; Ford (1987), pp. 251, 253.

49. Audubon (2011), pp. 221, 223; Ford (1987), pp. 253, 255. The Rathbone women were planning to stay with the family of Mrs. Abigail Dockray (1783–1842), who lived with her merchant husband, David, and nine of her ten children in Manchester. Audubon (2011), p. 129, note 81; pp. 223–224; Ford (1987), p. 160, note 57; pp. 255, 257. Mrs. Dockray, a Quaker minister, was the daughter of one of the Queen Bee's cousins, Sarah Benson. Audubon (2011), p. 129, note 81; Ford (1987), p. 160, note 57. Audubon refers to her as the Queen Bee's niece. Audubon (2011), p. 232; Ford (1987), p. 264. Hart-Davis states that "Audubon was keen to meet Mrs Dockray, because she was a Quaker minister and a prison reformer." Hart-Davis (2004), p. 79. In fact, Audubon had met her earlier, on August 17, at the home of William Rathbone V in Liverpool. Audubon (2011), p. 129; Ford (1987), p. 160.

In addition to the Dockrays, the Rathbones were well acquainted with the family of Samuel Greg, a successful Manchester cotton mill owner, who lived outside the city at Quarry Bank. Greg's eldest daughter, Elizabeth, was married to William Rathbone V. Audubon (2011), p. 143, note 96. Audubon was invited to visit the Gregs shortly after his arrival in Manchester and became a frequent guest at their home during his stay. Audubon (2011), pp. 180–184, 193–197, 223–230, 253–255; Ford (1987), pp. 211–214, 224–228, 255–260, 289–291.

In her biography, Ford states, in error, that a group of Rathbone children also made the trip to Manchester in a separate carriage, intending to visit their cousins. Ford (1988), p. 194. There is absolutely no indication of this in Audubon's journal. Ford has evidently misread Audubon's journal entry of October 6, 1826, in which he mentioned the departure of William Rathbone V and his family from Greenbank. Audubon (2011), p. 221; Ford (1987), p. 253. In light of the lack of any subsequent reference by Audubon to any of the passengers in this carriage, it would seem that William Rathbone's family left Greenbank merely to return to their home in Liverpool.

50. In his journal, Audubon repeatedly commented on Hannah Mary Rathbone III's pleasing presence, and it is relatively obvious that he was smitten by her good looks and charm. Audubon (2011), pp. 89, 127–128, 167–168, 231, 255; Ford (1987), pp. 119, 159, 199–200, 262, 291. It is not difficult to understand Audubon's attraction to the captivating and unmarried thirty-five-year-old. She was lovely, with brilliant dark eyes, and Audubon was forever attracted to good-looking women. Audubon (2011), p. 89, 141, 184; Ford (1987), pp. 119, 173, 214–215. Moreover, while Audubon's early weeks in Liverpool had far exceeded his expectations, he was still uncertain and anxious about the future and, consequently, emotionally vulnerable. Lucy remained foremost in his thoughts, but he did not receive any letters from her until mid-September. Rhodes (2004), p. 259, 264. See also, JJA, Manchester to LBA, Bayou Sarah, 17 Sept. 1826, Audubon (2011), p. 171, Ford (1987), p. 205. Hannah Mary filled the void created by Lucy's absence. However, there is no evidence that she shared the depth of Audubon's feelings. It appears that she placed clearly defined boundaries on their relationship. Some evidence of this can be found in comments he added to a picture of a Robin perched on a mossy stone that he drew and presented to her in mid-August. His inscribed sentiments on the back of the drawing probably mean more than they say.

It was my greatest wish to have affixed on the face of this drawing my real thoughts of the amiable Lady for whom I made it in Poetry Divine!—but an injunction from Hannah Rathbone against that wish of my Heart has put an end to it—and now I am forced to think only of her benevolence! of her Filial love! of her Genial affections—her most kind attentions and friendly Civilities to all who come to repose under this hospitable roof—to the Stranger who must now bid her farewell, who will pray for her—her Mother and her Friends and who will be forever her most

> Devoted and Obedient
> Humble
> Servant—
> John J. Audubon

Bland (1977), p. 11. See also, Streshinsky (1993), p. 172 (with minor variations from Bland's transcription). The original drawing was purchased in a 1971 Sotheby's auction by the University of Liverpool and is in the special collections of the University of Liverpool's Victoria Gallery and Museum. Streshinsky (1993), p. 382, note 40; Bland (1977), p. 12.

Audubon's reference to putting his feelings into verse and inscribing them on the face of the drawing is likely a reference to poems that appear on similar drawings he made at about the same time for the wife of William Rathbone V and for the "Queen Bee," Mrs. Hannah Mary Rathbone I, although these did not come from his pen. Audubon (2011), pp. 137, 143; Ford (1987), pp. 169–170, 175. Audubon recorded in an undated journal passage following his entry for August 21 that when he had finished a drawing for the Queen Bee, John Rutter Chorley (1806–1867), a young gentleman who was staying at Greenbank with his brother Henry, "was so kind as to transmit my thoughts into verse in a delightfull manner and I wrote 20 well match[d] Lines under my work." Audubon (2011), p. 137 and note 89. See also, Plamondon (2004); Ford (1987), p. 170. Chorley did the same for the drawing Audubon gave to the wife of William Rathbone V as a birthday gift on August 30. Audubon (2011), p. 143; Ford (1987), p. 175.

As a side note, contrary to what Ford states in her biography, the Chorleys were not orphans, nor were they "permanent guests" at Greenbank. Ford

(1988), pp. 180–181. Their mother, Jane Chorley, was widowed but still very much alive and living with her children in Liverpool with her half-brother, Dr. John Rutter (1762–1838), the founder of the Liverpool Athenaeum. Audubon (2011), pp. 200, 210–211; Ford (1987), pp. 169, note 61; 230, 241. See also, Bledsoe (2004); Bledsoe (1998), pp. 6–9; Greg (1905), p. 6. The Chorleys first spent time at Greenbank in 1819 when Jane Chorley was invited there to care for Dr. Rutter, a cousin of the Rathbone family, who had developed typhus. Bledsoe (1998), pp. 7, 19, note 10; Greg (1905), p. 6.

Audubon's drawing for the Rathbone family matriarch was of two Grey Wagtails with a background showing a building in the garden at Greenbank. *AHJ* I, illus. between pp. 114–115. A transcribed copy of the poem on the back appears in the Deane presentation copy of *AHJ* I, p. 114, at the Newberry Library in Chicago:

To Mrs. Hannah Mary Rathbone

There is a joy, that oft my heart has known,
The secret haunts of Nature to explore,
To hold communion with myself alone,
In Wilds, which man had never trod before—
And well I love, at solitary night,
To hear the wailing Heron's plaintive cry,
My only lamp, the firefly's glorious light;
My only canopy, the fretted sky!—
And in the mighty forest of the West,
Oft have I lov'd, beneath a hoary tree,
Protected by its gloomy shade, to rest—
For Nature's sterner charms have joys for me.
What different scenes have England's shores
    displayed,
Here Nature's wondrous hand no more I find,
In sombre roads and trackless Wilds betrayed,
Yet here I meet her beauties in my mind—
Nor greater joy my soul desires to know,
When, offering up this effort of my art,
To thee, to whom such grateful thanks I owe,
I strive to paint the feelings of my heart.
    John J. Audubon.
    1826.

On the watercolor drawing of a Redbreast that he gave to Mrs. William Rathbone V as a birthday gift, the following inscription appears:

To Mrs. Rathbone.

Kind lady, may a timid guest
Within thy happy dwelling rest?
For me, alas, the barren field
Can now but scanty gleanings yield;
The boor has hous'd his golden sheaves,
And Autumn tints the fading leaves,
And soon the wintry gales will blow,
And shivering trees be clad in snow.
Then let me not in vain aspire
To perch in safety by thy fire!
I'll strive thy bounty to repay,
And hail with song thy natal day!—
Still may that day, through many a year,
Shine bright on all thy heart holds dear,
Still add fresh blessings to the past,
And find thee happier than the last!—
Accept my strain—though rude I sing,
Though sober colors deck my wing,—
My strain's sincere—, though void of art
My wing protects a grateful heart!
    August 30th, 1826.

AHJ I, p. 269 (Ruthven Deane presentation copy, Newberry).

Whether Audubon actually intended to try his hand at a poem for Hannah Mary III is open to question. He admitted to Lucy that "My Poor Brains never measured Time appropriately yet, nor ever will." Audubon (2011), p. 137. Cf. Ford (1987), p. 170. But there are two stanzas on the front end papers of the 1826 journal that sound like the closing of a paean to Hannah Mary. I believe that John Chorley also composed these lines and that Audubon wrote them in his journal to remind himself of her. Since they could be applied just as easily to Lucy, he probably felt he could do so without his wife knowing for whom they were actually written:

hence-forth may her sorrows Cease;
affliction's frown assail her never;
Bless her, Kind heaven, with health and peace,
and Joy attend her steps for ever!
For she is my Supreme Delight;
She can fill my heart with pleasure;
She is most precious to my sight;
She is Nature's choicest treasure!—

Audubon (2011), p. 434. Cf. Ford (1987), p. 435.

It is revealing that Audubon's admitted inadequacies in composing verse did not stop him from taking credit for the lines that graced his pictures for the Rathbone women. William Roscoe and his daughter Jane, who saw the verse on the Queen Bee's drawing, thought that Audubon had composed it, or so the naturalist believed. Roscoe "frequently repeated that the Lines were beautifull," but Audubon apparently did not acknowledge they were written by another because he "wished to have a piece of Mr Roscoe's poetry, and I thought this might tantalize him to set to." Audubon (2011), p. 137. Cf. Ford (1987), p. 170. As in other instances, Audubon was not above shading the truth if he thought he could benefit from it.

On September 8, as he was getting ready to leave Liverpool for Manchester, Audubon sketched a dramatic self-portrait as a parting gift for Hannah Mary III, which he inscribed:

> Audubon at Green Bank
> *Almost*, Happy!! —

Ford (1987), p. 177 and illustration opposite title page. This drawing is now held by the University of Liverpool's Victoria Gallery and Museum. Audubon (2011), p. 145, note 97. On September 9, on the eve of Audubon's departure, Hannah Mary III gave him "a very beautifull Pen Knife and a Piece of Poetry copied by her own hand." Audubon (2011), p. 146. Cf. Ford (1987), p. 178. It was not, as Roberta Olson states, a volume of poems by their mutual friend William Roscoe. Olson (2012), p. 28, Fig. 19 note.

51. Audubon (2011), pp. 141, 145, 222, 231. Cf. Ford (1987), pp. 173, 177, 254, 262.

52. Rhodes (2004), pp. 259–260; Hart-Davis (2004), pp. 19, 66–69; Streshinsky (1993), pp. 171–172; Bland (1977), pp. 10–11.

53. Streshinsky (1993), p. 172. It should be noted that Audubon allowed Hannah Mary III to read his journal from time to time, so she was clearly aware of the admiring comments he made about her. Audubon (2011), pp. 141, 217, 222; Ford (1987), pp. 174, 248, 254. See also *AHJ* I, p. 248.

Hart-Davis asserts that after Audubon left Liverpool to go to Manchester in September 1826, he was "bitterly disappointed" that Hannah Mary III declined to answer his letters. His journal contains copies of two letters to her, dated September 16

and November 24. Audubon (2011), pp. 167–168; 310–311; Ford (1987), pp. 199–201, 349–350. In Harte-Davis's view, she wanted nothing more to do with the naturalist, "whether out of caution or distaste." Hart-Davis (2004), p. 69. At a distance from her married admirer, she may well have concluded it was better not to foster the relationship and evidently did not respond to either letter. JJA, Edinburgh to John Chorley, Liverpool, 21 Dec. 1826, Audubon (2011), p. 373. See also, Audubon (2011), p. 311; Ford (1987), p. 350.

However, to suggest that she was no longer friendly toward Audubon would be untrue. Audubon left Manchester on September 28 and returned the same day to Liverpool, where he stayed a week. He spent most of his evenings and nights at Greenbank, and there is no indication from his journal that there was any tension between him and Hannah Mary. On the first evening he was there, she asked him to help frame the self-portrait that he had given her earlier that month. He also breakfasted with her the following morning. Audubon (2011), pp. 199–201; Ford (1987), pp. 229–232.

He returned to Manchester in the company of the Queen Bee and Hannah Mary III on October 6. Audubon (2011), pp. 219–223; Ford (1987), 251–255. Five days later, he joined them and their cousins, the Dockrays, on a tour of the towns of Bakewell and Matlock in Derbyshire. Audubon (2011), pp. 231–245; Ford (1987), pp. 262–280. In Bakewell, he went shopping with Hannah Mary, and they walked around the church yard, "she leaning on my arm and I supporting her." Audubon (2011), pp. 231–232; Ford (1987), p. 262. It certainly does not appear that she had turned cold toward her admirer.

When Audubon returned to Liverpool in mid-May 1827 on his way to London, he saw Hannah Mary III and the Queen Bee at Woodcroft, the country home of Richard Rathbone where they were staying, and received a warm welcome. "I met my good, kind friends," he told his journal, "the same as ever, full of friendship, benevolence, and candor." He visited with them for "most of the morning" and left his journal for Hannah Mary to read, presumably at her request. *AHJ* I, p. 248. It would seem that the two remained on friendly terms even if she chose not to respond to his letters.

Note that Ford's transcription of Audubon's

journal indicates that Hannah Mary III did write an unsolicited letter to Audubon, which he received on November 19, 1826. Ford (1987), pp. 339-340. However, my review of the original journal reflects that the sender was "Mrs M.H. Rathbone," i.e. Mrs. Richard Rathbone (Hannah Mary II). See also, Audubon (2011), p. 302.

54. Audubon (2011), pp. 223-224. Cf. Ford (1987), pp.254-255.

55. Audubon (2011), p. 223; Ford (1987), p. 255. After terminating Mr. Crookes, the doorkeeper to his exhibition at the Manchester Natural History Society, Audubon relied entirely on young John Wilson, the twelve-year-old ticket taker, to collect the entrance fee. Audubon (2011), pp. 223, 231; Ford (1987), pp. 255, 261.

56. Audubon (2011), p. 230; Ford (1987), p. 261.

57. Audubon (2011), p. 230. Cf. Ford (1987), p. 261; JJA, Edinburgh to Thomas S. Traill, M.D., Liverpool, 28 Oct. 1826, Audubon (2011), p. 282, Ford (1987), p. 317.

58. Audubon (2011), p. 261; Ford (1987), p. 297. Audubon's journal indicates that he departed for the Scottish capital at 5:00 a.m. on October 24. Audubon (2012), p. 261; Ford (1987), p. 297.

59. Audubon's 1826 journal provides no explanation for his decision to go to Edinburgh before heading to London, as Henry Bohn, the London bookseller, had recommended. Ford contends that when Bohn delivered his verdict after seeing Audubon's life-sized drawings in Manchester, he cautioned "against going to London just yet." Ford (1988), p. 194. The journal contains no evidence of such advice. To the contrary, the journal indicates that Bohn "advised me strongly to clear off from Manchester; assured me that in London I would be cherished by the Nobility and could not but succeed with my talent." Audubon (2011), p. 230. Cf. Ford (1987), p. 261.

In his introduction to the first volume of the *OB*, Audubon recalled that when he left Liverpool for Manchester, he was already planning on visiting Edinburgh. He referred to it as "fair Edina, for I longed to see the men and the scenes immortalized by the fervid strains of [Robert] BURNS, and the glowing eloquence of [Walter] SCOTT and [John] WILSON." *OB* I, p. xv. See also, Audubon (2011), pp. 98, 102. Ford (1987), pp. 131, 136. Although Audu-

bon's original plan, developed with the help of his Liverpool friends, had been to travel through the major cities of England and Scotland to help him become known, this had seemingly changed after he met with Bohn at the end of September.

Rhodes believes that Audubon had already formed a plan to have his work published and had jettisoned Bohn's advice to travel to London and Paris to locate the right publisher. Rhodes (2004), p. 267. As support, Rhodes points to a letter Audubon wrote to Charles Bonaparte on October 22 to solicit his name and that of his father, Joseph Bonaparte, as subscribers to his work. In the letter, Audubon brashly predicted that his first Number, consisting of his first several engravings, would be issued within four months. He sent similar letters to DeWitt Clinton, Henry Clay, Gen. Andrew Jackson, and Gen. William Clark. JJA, Manchester to Charles Bonaparte, 22 Oct. 1826, Audubon (2011), pp. 258-259, Ford (1987), p. 294.

However, at that point, Audubon had no immediate prospect of seeing his work published. He had yet to locate an engraver and had turned down Bohn's offer to publish the work if he failed to find someone in London or Paris to do so. Audubon (2011), p. 282; Ford (1987), p. 317. Rhodes misreads Audubon's intent. While Audubon remained optimistic that he would ultimately succeed, his effort to obtain the names of American subscribers was actually part of a clever marketing strategy. He recognized that potential subscribers would be more apt to place their name on a formal subscription list if others, especially ones of note, had already done so. At the same time, few would be willing to allow the use of their name for this form of subtle advertising if there was no promise of publication. So, Audubon had to engage in a bit of hyperbole about the present state of his plans to enhance his likelihood of success.

Streshinsky is probably closer to the truth as to why Audubon decided to head north. She surmises that Audubon's failure to achieve in Manchester the recognition and success he had enjoyed in Liverpool had unsettled him, and "Edinburgh was a logical alternative" before he faced the challenges London would present. Streshinsky (1993), p. 179. It is clear that he did not intend to stay in Edinburgh long, telling Lucy in a letter written on the eve of his departure that he expected to reach London in two weeks. JJA, Manchester to LBA, Bayou Sarah, 22 Oct. 1826, Audubon (2011), p. 260, Ford (1987), p. 294. So, it does not appear that he initially expected Edinburgh to be the gateway to his future.

60. Audubon (2011), p. 261; Audubon (1999), p. 175. Cf. Ford (1987), p. 297.

61. Audubon (2011), p. 246; Ford (1987), p. 282. In his journal entry of October 16, 1826, Audubon indicated that he had called upon virtually everyone he knew in Manchester to request letters of introduction. He did not record who provided him with letters and to whom they were directed. However, we know that Thomas Stewart Traill, M.D., the president of the Liverpool Royal Institution, had given the naturalist letters addressed to some of the leading men of science in Edinburgh, including Prof. Robert Jameson of the University of Edinburgh; Robert Knox, M.D., the well-known anatomist; and Patrick Neill, a local printer as well as secretary of the Wernerian Society. Audubon (2011), pp. 419–420; Ford (1967), pp. 388, 390–391.

62. Audubon (2011), p. 266; Ford (1987), p. 301. The Black Bull Inn and Hotel, located at 1 Catherine Street, had no rooms available when Audubon arrived in Edinburgh on the night of October 25, 1826. Audubon found a room for the night at the Star Hotel, 36 Prince's Street, and moved the following day to rooms in the boardinghouse of Mrs. Dickie, 2 George Street, at a guinea a week. Audubon (2011), pp. 266–268; Ford (1987), pp. 301–303; Chambers (1825), p. 276; Stark (1825) p. 367.

In her biography, Ford insists that Audubon looked for new quarters after his first night at the Star Hotel because of the "laughter, whistling, and coughing that his foreign appearance provoked" at breakfast. Ford (1988), p. 197. Audubon's journal entry for October 26 provides no indication that the noises made by the other guests as he breakfasted were directed at him. Audubon (2011), p. 267. Cf. Ford (1987), p. 303.

63. Audubon (2011), pp. 268–269, 272; Ford (1987), pp. 304, 308 and note 4. See also, Rhodes (2004), p. 269. Audubon carried thirteen letters "of most valuable introduction" from his friends in Liverpool that he delivered when he reached Edinburgh. JJA, Edinburgh to LBA, Bayou Sarah, 10 Dec. 1826, Audubon (2011), p. 338, Ford (1987), p. 380.

On October 26, 1826, his first day in Edinburgh, Audubon managed to meet only two of the men to whom Dr. Thomas Stewart Traill had written on his behalf: Prof. Robert Jameson (1774–1854) and Robert Knox, M.D. (1791–1862). Audubon (2011), pp. 268–269, 419–420; Ford (1987), pp. 304–305. Pressed by other business, Jameson informed the artist that he would not be able to see his birds for several days. Audubon (2011), p. 269; Ford (1987), p. 304. Audubon came to learn that Jameson was involved in the publication of Prideaux John Selby's ornithological drawings of British avifauna, which Audubon felt explained his cool reception. Audubon (2011), pp. 283, 285; Ford (1987), pp. 323, 325; JJA, Edinburgh to Mrs. Richard Rathbone, Woodcroft, 28 Oct. 1826, Audubon (2011), p. 281, Ford (1987), p. 316. Even more disappointing, Jameson told Audubon that Sir Walter Scott, the famous author whom Audubon revered and desperately hoped to meet, was so busy writing a novel along with his biography of Napoleon that it was doubtful Audubon would be able to see him. Audubon (2011), p. 269; Ford (1987), p. 304. Knox was more forthcoming. He told Audubon that he would return the call on Friday, although he did not do so until Sunday, October 29. Audubon (2011), pp. 269, 285; Ford (1987), pp. 305, 325.

Ford contends that Audubon presented Jameson with a letter of introduction from the Manchester banker B.A. Heywood. Ford (1988), p. 198. Audubon does not record in his journal entry which letter or letters Jameson was handed, but in correspondence to Mrs. Richard Rathbone in Liverpool, he indicated that Jameson was given Dr. Traill's letter. JJA, Edinburgh to Mrs. Richard Rathbone, Woodcroft, 28 Oct. 1826, Audubon (2011), p. 281, Ford (1987), p. 316. Ford gives a date of August 7, 1826, to the letter Dr. Traill wrote to Jameson. Ford (1967), p. 388. It was, in fact, dated August 9 as Patterson indicates. Audubon (2011), p. 420.

Streshinsky mistakenly asserts that Audubon found Jameson at his home after a failed attempt to call on him there earlier in the day. Streshinsky (1993), p. 182. In fact, as his journal indicates, Audubon first met Jameson at the University of Edinburgh. Audubon (2011), p. 269; Ford (1987), p. 304.

Audubon called on Patrick Neill, the Scottish

printer and Wernerian Society secretary, on Friday, October 27. According to Audubon's journal, Neill initially mistook the letter Audubon handed him from Dr. Traill as an advertisement for publication. After realizing his error, Neill was very solicitous and promised to return the call. Audubon (2011), p. 272; Ford (1987), p. 308. In her biography, Ford claims, in obvious error, that Neill "turned the artist away at the door of his shop with the advice to return by appointment only." Ford (1988), p. 199.

Ford's biography is also misleading in compressing the first three days of Audubon's visit into what would appear to be one. Cf. Audubon (2011), pp. 267–276, 283–285; Ford (1988), pp. 197–199; Ford (1987), pp. 303–311, 323–325.

64. Audubon (2011), p. 285; Ford (1987), p. 326.

65. Audubon (2011), pp. 285–286; Ford (1987), p. 326. See also, Rhodes (2004), p. 271.

66. Rhodes (2004), p. 271. See also, Audubon (2011), pp. 286, 293; Ford (1987), p. 326, 329.

67. Audubon (2011), pp. 268, 286; Ford (1987), pp. 303, 326; JJA, Edinburgh to William Rathbone, Liverpool, 24 Nov. 1826, Audubon (2011), p. 306; Ford (1987), p. 345.

68. Audubon (2011), p. 286; Ford (1987), p. 326.

69. Audubon (2011), p. 286. Cf. Ford (1987), p. 326.

70. Audubon (2011), p. 286; Ford (1987), p. 327.

71. Audubon (2011), pp. 291–293. Cf. Ford (1987), pp. 327–329.

72. Audubon (2011), p. 296; Ford (1987), pp. 332.

73. Audubon (2011), p. 296. Cf. Ford (1987), pp. 332.

74. Audubon (2011), p. 296. Ford rewrites the quotation from Lizars as "I will engrave and publish this." Ford (1987), p. 332.

75. Audubon (2011), pp. 296–297. Cf. Ford (1987), p. 334.

76. Audubon (2011), p. 301. Cf. Ford (1987), p. 339.

77. Audubon (2011), p. 301, 339. Cf. Ford (1987), pp. 339, 380. While he was in Edinburgh, Audubon painted an oil portrait of a Wild Turkey family, combining his two drawings of the species, with the male followed by the female hen and their young. Although he believed he could have obtained 100 guineas for it, he ultimately donated it to the Royal Institution in appreciation for providing him with a free room to exhibit his drawings to the public. Audubon (2011), p. 378; Ford (1987), p. 415. Souder is mistaken in stating that the portrait was solely of the hen turkey. Souder (2004), p. 215.

Ford also errs in claiming that the finished portrait is at the Harvard Museum of Comparative Zoology. Ford (1987), p. 339, note 28. See also, Fries (1973), p. 9. In fact, it remained at the Royal Institution (now the Royal Scottish Academy) and was discovered in the early 2000s in a damaged state in the attic of the building. See Chalmers in Huyuck Preserve Conference Transcript (2006), p. 23. The painting was restored and, in 2011, the academy announced plans to sell it at auction at Lyon & Turnbull in Edinburgh to raise funds for the academy to pursue the artwork of Scottish artists. Joanna Soden, Ph.D., Collections Curator, The Royal Scottish Academy of Art & Architecture (Personal communication, 22 Mar. 2011). However, Dr. John Chalmers, the author of *Audubon in Edinburgh*, mounted a publicity campaign to block the sale, enlisting even Prince Philip, the Duke of Edinburgh, to his cause. John Chalmers, M.D. (Personal communication, 22 Mar. 2012). The auction never took place, but the academy subsequently negotiated a private sale of the painting to Walmart heiress Alice Walton for £2 million. The painting is now on display at her Crystal Bridges Museum of American Art in Bentonville, AR. "RSA Sells Audubon Treasure for £2m to Walmart Heiress," *The Times* (Saturday, 27 Sept. 2014).

78. Chalmers (2003), p. 45; Ford (1988), p. 203. The reviews of Audubon's exhibition at the Royal Institution were unfailingly positive. Writing in *Blackwood's Magazine* under the pseudonym Christopher North, John Wilson was rapturous:

> Four hundred drawings of about two thousand birds, covered the walls of the Institution-Hall, in the Royal Society Buildings, and the effect was like magic. The spectator imagined himself in the forest — all were of the size of life, from the wren and the humming-bird to the wild turkey and the bird of Washington [the bald eagle]. . . . The colours were all of life too — bright as when borne in beaming beauty through the woods. . . . 'Twas a wild and poetical vision of the heart of

the New World, inhabited as yet almost wholly by the lovely or noble creatures that 'own not man's dominion.'

That all this wonderful creation should have been the unassisted work of one man—in his own country almost unknown, and by his own country wholly unbefriended, was a thought that awoke towards the 'American woodsman' feelings of more than admiration, of the deepest personal interest; and the hearts of all warmed towards Audubon, who were capable of conceiving the difficulties, and dangers, and sacrifices, that must have been encountered, endured, and overcome, before genius had thus embodied these the glory of its innumerable triumphs.

Chalmers (2003), pp. 45–46. The exhibition proved to be a marked success. Audubon grossed £152.18s from the entrance fees and another £20.12s.6d. from 1,101 catalogues, for a total of £173.10s.6d. Audubon indicated that this was equal to $770 (approximately $18,800 in 2016 dollars). Sahr (2015); Audubon (2011), pp. 376–377; Ford (1987), pp. 414–415.

79. Audubon (2011), p. 301; Ford (1987). p. 339. In a letter to Lucy on December 10, 1826, Audubon indicated that Lizars had been at work on the birds for a month. JJA, Edinburgh to LBA, Bayou Sarah, 10 Dec. 1826, Audubon (2011), p. 339, Ford (1987), p. 381.

80. Rhodes (2004), p. 273. The cotton rag paper used in the production of *BOA* was made by one of two English companies—either J. Whatman or J. Whatman/Turkey Mill. Hart-Davis (2004), p. 120. Each individual sheet contains a watermark with the name of the company and the year the paper was produced, easily visible when a full-sized print from *BOA* is backlighted. Steiner (2003), p. 63.

81. JJA, Edinburgh to William Rathbone, Liverpool, 24 Nov. 1826, Audubon (2011), pp. 306, 308. Cf. Ford (1987), pp. 345, 347.

82. JJA, Edinburgh to William Rathbone, Liverpool, 24 Nov. 1826, Audubon (2011), p. 308; Ford (1987), p. 347.

83. Rhodes (2004), p. 273.

84. *OB* I, p. xi. See also, Rhodes (2004), p. 285; Steiner (2003), p. 41.

85. Low (2002), p. 10. Bill Steiner, a scholar on the prints of *BOA*, states that the untrimmed double elephant folio paper that was used by Lizars and later by the Havells measured approximately 27″ or 28″× 39½″. Steiner (2003), p. 90. However, in 2004, Christie's in New York sold the individual prints from the magnificent unbound Sachsen-Meiningen set of the folio. As issued in this state, without the trimming of the sheets that inevitably occurred during the binding process, the double elephant folio paper ranged from 25¾″ to 26⅞″ in width × 38¾″ to 40″ in length. On average, the sheets measured approximately 26½″× 39½″, which is the size given in the text. Christie's (2004), p. 15.

86. Steiner (2003), p. 43.

87. Steiner (2003), p. 43. See also, Blaugrund & Stebbins (1993), p. 56.

88. Rhodes (2004), p. 285. Streshinksy contends, in error, that each Number consisted of one large species "followed by two medium-sized birds, then two small ones." Streshinsky (1993), p. 188. As stated in the text, in addition to a large print, there was only one medium-sized print and three small prints in each Number. This distribution of sizes was announced by Audubon in the earliest extant copy of his prospectus and continued throughout the production of *BOA*. Fries (1973), Appendix F, pp. 385–388.

89. Audubon (2011), p. 303; Ford (1987), p. 342.

90. Audubon (2011), p. 316; Ford (1987), p. 357. Ford contends that Audubon saw "the first finished fragment of *The Birds of America*, a superbly engraved and colored aquatint," on November 20, 1826. Ford (1988), pp. 204–205. Audubon's journal, which must be considered definitive on this point, reflects that the first proof impression of one of his drawings was presented to him on November 28, as stated in the text. Ford also errs in suggesting that Lizars's engravings of Audubon's drawings were aquatinted. Lizars did not use this technique. With aquatinting, an engraver was able to add subtle degrees of shading to the copperplate that would be used to print the image. The engraver first applied powdered rosin to the area on the copperplate to be aquatinted (and varnish to the remainder) and then heated the plate so that the rosin particles hardened. The copperplate was then placed into a bath of nitric acid (*aqua fortis*), which would bite into those

portions of the copperplate that were not covered by either the rosin particles or the varnish. The longer the acid was allowed to work, the darker the shading. Rhodes (2004), p. 300; Goddu (2002), p. 14; Low (2002), p. 12.

In Waldemar Fries's *The Double Elephant Folio*, often called "the bible of Audubon scholars," Fries relies on Maria Audubon's rewritten version of the 1826 journal in his discussion of the early work performed by Lizars's engravers. He claims that Audubon went to Lizars's shop to watch the engravers at work on November 28. He then states that Audubon did not see the first proof impression until "a day or two later." Fries (1973), p. 11. The 1826 journal reflects that these events occurred on November 27 and 28, respectively. Audubon (2011), pp. 314, 316; Ford (1987), pp. 356–357.

91. Audubon (2011), p. 331. Cf. Ford (1987), p. 372. Rhodes states that on Lizars's print of Plate 1, the Great American Cock Male (Wild Turkey), the image was so large that two of the tail feathers extended outside the page margin. Rhodes (2004), p. 281. Not so. When the print was bound as part of Volume I of *BOA*, the tail feathers adjacent to the narrow left hand margin could be lost in the binding. But Plate 1, as it came off the press, showed the complete bird, tail feathers and all, as can be seen in the Christie's catalogue for its March 10, 2000, auction of the Fox-Bute set of the Double Elephant Folio. George Lane Fox's early subscription copy included a first state copy of Plate 1 as it had been engraved by Lizars. Christies (2000), frontispiece and Appendix B, p. 33; Fries (1973), p. 215.

92. JJA, Edinburgh to William Rathbone, Liverpool, 24 Nov. 1826, Audubon (2011), p. 307. Cf. Ford (1987), p. 346.

93. JJA, Edinburgh to LBA, Bayou Sarah, 10 Dec. 1826, Audubon (2011), p. 340, Ford (1987), p. 382; JJA, Edinburgh to William Rathbone at Liverpool, 24 Nov. 1826, Audubon (2011), p. 307, Ford (1987), p. 346. Streshinsky asserts that Lizars had agreed to subsidize the cost of the first Number, agreeing to wait for Audubon to collect subscriber's fees before being paid. Streshinsky (1993), p. 188. Audubon's letter to William Rathbone of November 24, 1826, cited above, does not support this claim. Audubon told Rathbone that "My Plan is to publish *One number* at my own Expense and risk, and travel

with it under my arm & *beg my way*." Audubon (2011), p. 307. Cf. Ford (1987), p. 346. He reiterated this when writing to Lucy on May 16, 1827: "I have been carefull not to have had more copies struck than could possibly be help to try with the least cost the result of the 1*st* number. this consisted of 50 copies only. M*r* Lizars assured me that the filling of that quantity would save and balance the expense of producing them and I felt willing to make the trial at my own expense and risk." JJA, Liverpool to LBA, Bayou Sarah, 16 May 1827 (APS), *Letters* I, p. 23.

On November 28, 1826, Audubon noted in his journal that he had obtained his first subscriber to *BOA*, "D*r* Meikleham of Trinidad." Audubon (2011), p. 316. Cf. Ford (1987), p. 357. Based upon Audubon's subscriber's list, it would appear that this was actually Dr. William McCleham of Mount Stewart, Trinidad. Fries (1973), p. 143. The doctor's subscription was ultimately cancelled, as Audubon later confirmed in a letter on January 22, 1828, to his agent in Edinburgh, Daniel Lizars, the bookseller brother of William Home Lizars. Deane (1908c), p. 413.

The second subscription came in a letter that Audubon received on December 7, 1826, from Prof. Robert Jameson, who asked to have the University of Edinburgh added to the list of subscribers. Audubon (2011), p. 334; Ford (1987), p. 376. The University completed the subscription and retained its copy until 1992, when it sold it at auction to a private collector for $4.1 million. Fries (2006), p. 454; Chalmers in Hyuck (2006), p. 28; Chalmers (2003), p. 55.

Ford maintains that when Audubon went to see Jameson on December 6, the professor had predicted that the University of Edinburgh would subscribe. Ford (1988), p. 207. Audubon described his meeting with Jameson in his 1826 journal and never mentioned that prospect, a likely indication that the conversation described by Ford never occurred. When Audubon received Jameson's note the following day with news of the subscription, he informed his journal that he "was highly pleased with this, [the university] being a powerfull leader." Audubon (2011), p. 334. Cf. Ford (1987), p. 376. Had he gotten wind the day before that the university would probably subscribe, Audubon almost certainly would have referenced it.

94. JJA, Edinburgh to LBA, Bayou Sarah, 9 Dec. 1826 (Princeton, Box 2, Folder 5), Audubon (1999), p. 798. Cf. Audubon (2011), p. 339; Ford (1987), p. 381. Rhodes states that 2 guineas, the price at which Audubon sold each Number, were equivalent to "£2.2." Rhodes (2004), p. 273. However, since a British pound at the time was equal to 20 shillings and a guinea was worth 21 shillings, 2 guineas would be 42 shillings or, if written as a decimal as Rhodes does, £2.1. Blunt (1832), pp. 49–50. The British decimal system was not introduced until 1971. Therefore, to avoid confusion, the proper way to write the value of 2 guineas is "£2.2s," as stated in the text. The conversion of pounds sterling to U.S. dollars is based upon an average exchange rate of $4.50 per pound, and the conversion of 1827 to 2016 dollars relies upon data compiled by Sahr (2015).

95. L. Audubon (1869), pp. 146–147. See also, Fries (1973), Appendix F, pp. 385–386. In addition to the production limitations that effectively prevented the issuance of more than five Numbers each year, Audubon was cognizant of the sizable expense of his publication and did not want the financial burden on his subscribers to be too onerous.

96. Fries (1973), p. 387.

97. JJA, Edinburgh to LBA, Bayou Sarah, 9 Dec. 1826 (Princeton, Box 2, Folder 5), Audubon (1999), p. 797–802. The same letter was copied by Audubon in his journal with a date of December 10. Audubon (2011), pp. 338–344; Ford (1987), pp. 380–386. It also appears in *Letters* under a date of December 21, 1826. *Letters* I, pp. 7–13. Prof. Patterson, in his transcription of Audubon's 1826 journal, expresses "some puzzlement" over the date of this letter given the fact it is dated December 21, 1826 in *Letters*. Audubon (2011), p. 338, note 74. However, it seems that Audubon copied the earlier letter on December 21 to resend it because of the importance of its contents and added an addendum, dated December 22. *Letters* I, p. 13.

98. JJA, Edinburgh to LBA, Bayou Sarah, 9 Dec. 1826 (Princeton, Box 2, Folder 5), Audubon (1999), pp. 799–800. See also, Audubon (2011), p. 341; Ford (1987), pp. 382–383.

99. JJA, Edinburgh to LBA, Bayou Sarah, 9 Dec. 1826 (Princeton, Box 2, Folder 5), Audubon (1999), p. 799. See also, Audubon (2011), p. 341; Ford (1987), p. 383.

100. At the end of 1826, Lucy left Beech Woods and took another teaching position at a nearby plantation owned by William Garrett Johnson known as Beech Grove. Audubon referenced this when he wrote to her on March 12, 1827, and indicated that he had received three of her letters, dated December 31, January 3, and January 8, in which she had disclosed her change of employment. Herrick (1938) I, p. 370.

101. Audubon (2011), p. 341. Cf. Ford (1987), p. 383.

102. JJA, Edinburgh to William Rathbone, Liverpool, 21 Dec. 1826, Audubon (2011), pp. 369–370; Audubon (2011), p. 354; Ford (1987), p. 395. In addition to William Rathbone and Dr. Traill, Samuel Greg, the owner of the Quarry Bank Mills outside Manchester, had doubts that *BOA* would succeed. In a December 14, 1826, letter to his eldest daughter, Elizabeth, the wife of William Rathbone V, he wrote: "What can be done about his *Birds*? It is said they will be more than £210—which will hardly do for individuals, except there could be wheels within wheels and joint stock companies formed." Ford (1988), p. 208 and note 9, p. 444.

According to Ford, Charles-Lucien Bonaparte, who had recently arrived in England, also weighed in about the audacious scope of the project through John Stokoe, one of his Uncle Joseph's agents. Ford (1988), p. 209. Upon landing in Liverpool, Bonaparte was hosted by William Rathbone and spent time at Greenbank, where there was undoubtedly talk of the risky course Audubon was taking. Stroud (2002), p. 84. According to Audubon's 1826 journal, he visited Stokoe on the morning of December 16, shortly before William Rathbone's letter reached him. Stokoe disclosed that the younger Bonaparte "had commissione[d] [him] to mention several particular things to me," but Audubon did not offer the details when he recorded the day's events in his journal. Audubon (2011), p. 354; Ford (1987), p. 395.

However, Audubon was "not in the least disheartened" by the naysayers. Audubon (2011), p. 354; Ford (1987), p. 395. He advised Lucy in his journal on December 16, the same day he received William Rathbone's correspondence and saw John Stokoe, that he would not be deterred: "Since Napoleon became from the Ranks an Emperor, why should not Audubon be able to leave the Woods of America a while and Publish and sell *a Book*? No, No, I will try, by Heavens, untill each and every hair about me will have dropt from my body dead, Grey from old age!!" Audubon (2011), p. 354. Cf. Ford (1987), p. 395.

In a letter to William Rathbone, dated December 21, 1826, Audubon responded to his friend's concern that he would be ruined by the publication of *BOA*: "I am determined to Conquer or Die in the field. It is not my Talents I look to. They are humble, but it is my patience, Industry & perseverance that will enable me to surmount obstacles — I shall have many difficulties, I am quite sure, but I am prepared to meet them & if I do not succeed, as I said I believe before, I shall have tried all in my power and will retire still contented." JJA, Edinburgh to William Rathbone, Liverpool, 21 Dec. 1826, Audubon (2011), pp. 369–370.

103. Audubon (2011), p. 344; Ford (1987), pp. 386–387; JJA, Edinburgh to LBA, Bayou Sarah, 22 Dec. 1826, Audubon (2011), p. 367, Ford (1987), p. 411, *Letters* I, p. 14.

104. JJA, Edinburgh to LBA, Bayou Sarah, 22 Dec. 1826, Audubon (2011), p. 367, Ford (1987), p. 411, *Letters* I, p. 14.

105. JJA, Edinburgh to LBA, Bayou Sarah, 22 Dec. 1826, Ford (1987), p. 411. Cf. Audubon (2011), p. 367 (misreading the long "s" in the word "sound" for an "f" and transcribing the phrase "I wish to sound all well" as "I wish to found all well."); JJA, Edinburgh to LBA, Bayou Sarah, 21–22 Dec. 1826, *Letters* I, pp. 7–17. That Audubon refrained from asking Lucy to join him because of concerns over his ability to support her financially is also clear from his letter to her dated March 24, 1827, where he expressed his hope that his forthcoming trip to London would result in a sufficient number of additional subscribers that he could write and ask her to come. JJA, Edinburgh to LBA, Bayou Sarah, 24 Mar. 1827 (APS), *Letters* I, p. 17.

106. Rhodes (2004), p. 278.

107. Ibid., p. 318. Audubon was well aware of the problems associated with the length of time it took both his and Lucy's correspondence to cross the Atlantic. In a letter in November 1827, he bemoaned the delay and cautioned her to send her correspondence through New Orleans rather than

New York because it would take upwards of a month for the mail to reach New York from Bayou Sarah. JJA, Liverpool to LBA, Bayou Sarah, 25 Nov. 1827 (APS), *Letters* I, p. 53. Of Audubon's many biographers, Rhodes does the best job of exploring Audubon and Lucy's strained relationship as reflected in their correspondence between 1827 and 1829. Rhodes (2004), pp. 302–338.

108. *AHJ* I, p. 225. See also, Rhodes (2004), p. 287; Chalmers (2003), pp. 50–67. Audubon had wanted to leave Edinburgh before April 5, but horrendous winter weather during the month of March had delayed his plans. *AHJ* I, pp. 216, 222, 224. On March 3, he reported in his journal that "more than two feet of snow" had fallen that day. Ibid., p. 215. Five days later, another spate of "dreadful" weather had covered the great roads with as much as six feet of snow. Ibid., p. 216. On March 12, he wrote: "I can scarcely believe that this day, there is in many places six feet of snow." Ibid., p. 218. When he sat down to write Lucy on the same date, he informed her "there [are] in many places 16 feet of snow. [T]he weather has been tremendous." JJA, Edinburgh to LBA, 12 Mar. 1827 Herrick (1938) I, p. 371. The "16 feet of snow" reference in this letter may have been a typographical error since Audubon's journal only mentioned there was six feet of snow. In any case, Rhodes has misread Audubon's letter, suggesting that a blizzard had just "dumped sixteen feet of snow on Edinburgh and the surrounding Scottish countryside." Rhodes (2004), p. 285. What is apparent from the journal is that this was an accumulation of snow over a period of weeks, not the result of a single storm.

Before he left the Scottish capital, Audubon bowed to the urgings of his friends and had his hair cut to a fashionable length in anticipation of his arrival in London. He placed a black border around the page in his journal on which this single entry appeared, dated March 19, 1827: "This day My Hairs were sacrificed and the will of God usurped by the wishes of Man=as the Barber clipped them rapidly it reminded [MS: remainded] me of the horrible times of the French Revolution when the same operation was performed upon all the Victims murdered at the Guillotine — My Heart sank Low." *AHJ* I, facsimile opposite p. 221. This quotation is a transcription of a facsimile of the entry in Audubon's 1827 journal, which was one of those Maria Audubon apparently destroyed after she took what she wanted for *AHJ*. Maria's transcription slightly misquoted her grandfather, who actually wrote: "My Hairs were" rather than "my hair was." Ibid., p. 221. See also, Hart-Davis (2004), p. 112.

With regard to Audubon's reception in Edinburgh, Rhodes repeats a playful quote from Audubon's journal that appeared in Herrick's biography but which originated in Maria's version of the journal entry for December 22, 1826: "It is Mr. Audubon here, and Mr. Audubon there, and I can only hope they will not make a conceited fool of Mr. Audubon at last." Rhodes (2004), p. 282. See also, Herrick (1938) I, p. 362; *AHJ* I, p. 194. However, this quotation did not appear in Audubon's original entry for this date. Maria actually lifted it from a December 21 letter that Audubon wrote from Edinburgh to his young friend John Rutter Chorley of Liverpool: "Here I am truly afloat. Mr Audubon here and Mr Audubon there. I hope they will not make a conceited fool of Mr Audubon at last." JJA, Edinburgh to John Chorley, Liverpool, 21 Dec. 1826, Audubon (2011), p. 373. This is simply one more example of how Maria rewrote her grandfather's journals to suit her own purposes.

Audubon's visit to Edinburgh was successful in a myriad of ways. One of the most important from his personal vantage point was the opportunity to finally meet Sir Walter Scott, the famous Scotch novelist and biographer, whom he idolized. Audubon was introduced to Scott by Capt. Basil Hall on January 22, 1827. *AHJ* I, pp. 206–207. See also, Chalmers (2003), pp. 61–62.

109. Rhodes (2004), p. 287.

110. Rhodes (2004), p. 285–286; Fries (1973), p. 385; *AHJ* I, p. 209, 248. Audubon informed Lucy in a letter dated January 19, 1827, that Lizars planned to print fifty copies of the first five prints the following week. The coloring would be completed about three weeks later. JJA, Edinburgh to LBA, Bayou Sarah, 19 Jan. 1827 (Filson). The naturalist displayed a colored set of the first Number at a meeting of the Royal Society of Edinburgh on February 5, 1827. *AHJ* I, p. 209. Thus, Fries's statement that the copperplates for these prints had not been engraved until March 1827 is in error. Fries (1973), p. 24. But cf. Fries (1973), p. 385 (correctly stating

that "By the end of January 1827 the first number of five plates had been engraved.").

111. JJA, Edinburgh to LBA, Bayou Sarah, 23 Feb. 1827, Christie, Manson & Woods (1993), Lot 4.

112. JJA, Liverpool to LBA, Bayou Sarah, 16 May 1827 (APS), *Letters* I, p. 23. See also, Low (2002), pp. 31–34. Audubon advised Lucy that Lizars had commenced engraving the second Number on May 1, 1827. JJA, London to LBA, Bayou Sarah, 6 Aug. 1827 (APS), Audubon (1999), p. 807, *Letters* I, p. 29.

113. Fries refers to this first issue of Audubon's prospectus, issued in March 1827, as Edition A. Fries (1973), p. 388. A facsimile copy of the prospectus from the collection of the American Philosophical Society in Philadelphia appears in the illustrations between pp. 436–437 of Fries's book and provides the following list of Audubon's distinguished memberships: "Member of the Lyceum of New York; Fellow of the Royal Society of Edinburgh; Member of the Wernerian Natural History Society; Fellow of the Society of Scottish Antiquaries and New Castle Tyne; Member of the Society for Promoting the Useful Arts in Scotland; of the Literary and Philosophical Society of Liverpool, &c. &c."

114. Audubon (2011), pp. 332–333; Ford (1987), p. 374. On December 6, 1826, Audubon visited Prof. Robert Jameson, the president of the Wernerian Natural History Society, and apparently questioned whether it was really necessary for him to present an original paper to the society to gain membership. Jameson assured him that it was "quite necessary, that it would attach me to the Country, and that he would give me all his assistance." Audubon (2011), pp. 332–333. Cf. Ford (1987), p. 374.

115. Souder (2004), pp. 222–224; Chalmers (2003), p. 132, 136–138. Audubon delivered his paper on the rattlesnake to the Wernerian Natural History Society on February 24, 1827. *AHJ* I, p. 213. It appeared in print the same year in the *Edinburgh New Philosophical Journal*, a journal founded by Prof. Jameson. Rhodes (2004), p. 269; Chalmers (2003), p. 144, note 9. In 1828, it was reprinted in Philadelphia in the *The Franklin Journal and American Mechanics' Magazine* and almost immediately gave rise to scathing attacks on the author. Among the preposterous assertions in Audubon's

paper were the claims that rattlesnakes could pursue squirrels through the trees by leaping from branch to branch and would kill their prey by strangulation. He also maintained that he had observed a rattlesnake swallow a killed squirrel tailfirst. Chalmers (2003), pp. 137–138, 144, note 10. In addition, Audubon reported as fact what was no more than a frontier legend involving a series of deaths to the members of a Pennsylvania farming family who, one after another, unknowingly donned a boot in which a rattlesnake's fangs were imbedded. Souder (2004), p. 223.

In Audubon's defense, he may have been thinking of the Black Racer (*Coluber constrictor*), which is swift, agile, and known to climb trees. Herrick points out that this species, when cornered, can also simulate a rattlesnake's rattle by "vibrating the tip of its tail on the ground or leaves." Herrick (1938) II, p. 76. Regardless, there was no excuse for Audubon's mistake, which opened himself up to legitimate attacks by his critics. When his Philadelphia friend Thomas Sully, the eminent portraitist, informed him of the criticism his papers had received in that city, Audubon was "grieved at it" but dismissive:

Those persons in Philadelphia that have felt a desire to contradict my assertions cannot, without lowering themselves very much indeed affect to conceive that the members of the Wernerian Society would have listened to my 'say so' without investigating the subject even if they had not been well versed in the habits of the objects I treated of. Neither can they believe that all my acquaintance and particular friends would permit me to proceed in relating *Tales of Wonder*, which if untrue, would load me with disgrace, ruin my family, nay proved me devoid of all honor! Could I suffer myself to be so blinded at the very moment when I am engaged in the publication of a work of unparalleled magnitude, of which the greatest naturalists and best judges both in America and in Europe have given the fullest praise and firmest support, and from which my very means of pecuniary comfort are to be drawn? . . . I feel assured that the pen that traced them must have been dipped in venom more noxious than that which flows from the jaws of the rattlesnake!"

Herrick (1938) II, pp. 70–71. Audubon may have originally believed, as he composed the papers for the Wernerian Society, that he could get away with offering details he had not actually observed in the wild, naively believing that his words would not be reported across the water where his critics lay in wait. Or perhaps he was simply a babe in the scientific woods, completely unaware of the rigor expected to be followed in drafting a paper for a scientific audience. Regardless, it is worth noting that after this experience, Audubon was much more circumspect about what he wrote for publication. Ford (1988), p. 235.

116. Audubon (1826). See also, Chalmers (2003), pp. 136, 138–139. Audubon's paper on the Turkey Buzzard (Turkey Vulture) was delivered to the Wernerian Natural History Society on December 16, 1826. He asserted, based on a series of experiments he had purportedly conducted in the wild, that Turkey Vultures have a poor olfactory sense and locate food visually. Chalmers (2003), p. 136. Since he was not yet a member, the paper was read by Patrick Neill, the secretary of the society. Audubon followed this up with a demonstration of how he wired his bird specimens to capture them on paper. At the conclusion of this portion of the meeting, Prof. Robert Jameson, the president of the society, moved to dispense with the rules of the society and elect Audubon as an honorary member at the next meeting. Audubon (2011), p. 355; Ford (1987), p. 396.

117. Fries (1973), p. 13; JJA, Liverpool to LBA, Bayou Sara, 16 May 1827 (APS), *Letters* I, pp. 22–23. See also, Souder (2004), p. 226. It is difficult to quantify the precise number of subscribers Audubon had signed up by the time he reached London. The principal problem for scholars is that while Audubon maintained a formal written subscription list, it was subsequently separated from the book in which it was kept and was, in any event, not always kept in chronological order. Fries (1973), pp. 137–138. See also, *AHJ* I, p. 289. Thus, it is difficult to ascertain when various subscribers added their names to the list. Further, it appears that the numbers Audubon offered in early letters back to his family were inflated.

Fries notes that there were "at least" nineteen subscriptions procured during Audubon's stay in Edinburgh. Fries (1973), pp. 13, 142–143. The forty-nine documented names that Audubon obtained on the road to London would increase his subscription list to at least sixty-eight. However, on May 15, 1827, when he wrote to Lucy from Liverpool shortly before departing for London, he announced that he had "nearly 100 subscribers." JJA, Liverpool to LBA, Bayou Sarah, 15 May 1827, Audubon (1999), p. 806. The following day, in a separate letter, he claimed that he had "subscribers enough" to require two printings of fifty copies each of the first Number and proceeded to calculate his projected earnings "now with one hundred Subscribers (who all pay on delivery)." JJA, Liverpool to LBA, Bayou Sara, 16 May 1827 (APS), *Letters* I, pp. 23–24.

On this basis, Audubon biographer Duff Hart-Davis declares that Audubon had collected one hundred subscriptions prior to arriving in London. Hart-Davis (2004), p. 120. This assessment gains further credence from a subsequent letter Audubon wrote Victor from London on August 25, 1827, where he reported that he had "rather more than one hundred Subscribers," although he added that London had provided fewer subscriptions than the eighteen he had signed up in a week in Manchester in the spring. JJA, London to VGA, Louisville, 25 Aug. 1827, *Letters* I, pp. 36, 38. Rhodes claims that the total number of subscribers for Audubon's work as he was preparing to leave Liverpool for London was ninety-four although he does not provide a source citation to justify his assertion. Rhodes (2004), p. 288. Souder is vaguer, pegging the total at "almost a hundred." Souder (2004), p. 228.

The difficulty with these figures is that they do not square with Audubon's later count, which appears to be more accurate and reliable. On November 25, 1827, when Audubon sat down to write Lucy from Liverpool about the results of a canvassing trip he had just made through Manchester, Leeds, York, Edinburgh, and Glasgow, he told her that he then had 114 subscribers. He noted that he had added twenty new subscribers along the way, but we know from his October 31 journal entry that six of his Edinburgh subscribers had cancelled their subscriptions. *AHJ* I, p. 266; JJA, Liverpool to LBA, Bayou Sarah, 25 Nov. 1827, *Letters* I, pp. 45, 48. Thus, his solicitation efforts in the fall of 1827 gave him a net of fourteen new subscribers, which means that when he left London on September 16,

1827, he must have had precisely one hundred. This is consistent with a reference he made in a letter to Lucy on September 20 from Manchester that "With good care and management I have a clear profit of nearly five hundred pounds per annum *on 100 Subscribers*." JJA, Manchester to LBA, Bayou Sarah, 20 Sept. 1827, *Letters* I, p. 40.

Audubon obviously had fewer subscribers when he first arrived in London because we know that he added several during his early months there, although, as reflected in his letter to Victor, the number as of August 25 was under eighteen. Fries (1973), p. 18. Fries names only five: King George IV (1762–1830); the Duchess of Clarence, later Queen Adelaide (1792–1849), wife of King William IV (1765–1837); Lord Stanley (1799–1869); John G. Children (1777–1852) of the British Museum; and Charles-Lucien Bonaparte (1803–1857). Matthew (2004); Fries (1973), p. 19. A look at Audubon's subscriber list would suggest that there were actually as many as twenty-six from his initial visit to London. Combined with the at least sixty-eight documented for the prior period, this would put his list at around ninety-four, within range of the one hundred it appears he actually had when he left London in mid-September. Fries (1973), pp. 141, 144–145. Accordingly, Audubon clearly was exaggerating his success when he told Lucy in mid-May that he had reached the century mark. It seems more likely that he then had around seventy subscribers.

118. *AHJ* I, pp. 251–252. In a letter to Lucy on May 28, 1827, Audubon indicated that he had delivered a total of sixty-three letters of introduction during his first week in London and had about an equal number yet to go, JJA, London to LBA, Bayou Sarah, 28 May 1827, Christie, Manson & Woods (1977), Lot 50. In the *OB*, he stated that he arrived in London with only eighty-two. *OB* II, p. viii.

When Audubon wrote Lucy on August 6, 1827, he informed her that he was living at the home of Mrs. Middlemist. JJA, London to LBA, Bayou Sarah, 6 Aug. 1827 (APS), Audubon (1999), p. 809, *Letters* I, p. 33. It would appear from Audubon's letter that this was the aunt of Jane Middlemist Percy, the woman who owned Beech Woods plantation where Lucy worked up until the end of 1827. Ford (1988), p. 140; JJA, Liverpool to LBA, Bayou Sarah, 16 May 1827 (APS), *Letters* I, pp. 26–28. In the latter half of August 1827, Audubon moved out, explaining to Lucy that "my Painting Room and my Parlour are not sufficiently large and convenient." JJA, London to LBA, Bayou Sarah, 21 Aug. 1827 (APS), *Letters* I, p. 35.

119. Chalmers (2003), p. 207; *AHJ* I, p. 252.

120. *AHJ* I, p. 252.

121. JJA, London to LBA, Bayou Sarah, 28 May 1827, Christie, Manson & Woods (1977), Lot 50. See also, *AHJ* I, p. 252.

122. Souder (2004), p. 227.

123. JJA, London to W.H. Bentley, Manchester, 2 Jun. 1827 (Private collection).

124. *AHJ* I, p. 255; L. Audubon (1869), p. 155. There is a conflict between the two existing, edited versions of Audubon's 1827 journal as to when the naturalist received Lizars's initial letter advising him of the strike by the engraver's colorists. Maria's edition states that the letter arrived on Thursday, June 14. *AHJ* I, p. 255. Lucy's version indicates that this occurred on Monday, June 18. L. Audubon (1869), p. 155. Some biographers have elected to remain neutral, stating merely that the letter arrived in the middle of June 1827. Souder (2004), p. 232; Hart-Davis (2004), p. 123; Herrick (1938) I, p. 380. Others have firmly planted their flag in Maria's camp. Rhodes (2004), p. 292; Fries (1973), p. 23. Chalmers gives June 13 as the date of receipt. Chalmers (2003), p. 122.

Ford takes the position that the first news of the strike came in a letter from Lizars dated Saturday, June 16. Ford (1988), p. 225. However, this letter was clearly a follow-up letter to Lizars's first notice of the strike, as is evident from Lizars's opening sentence where he declared: "I again write you according to promise, but am sorry that I cannot yet say that the colouring of your Work is recommenced." William Lizars, Edinburgh to JJA, London, 16 Jun. 1827 (Yale, Box 5, Folder 231). Lizars explained in that letter that the colorists, who were compensated by the piece, were receiving more to color the work of Prideaux John Selby than Audubon was paying, and this had "poisoned their ideas completely." Ibid. See also, Rhodes (2004), pp. 292–293. Lizars was confident the men would eventually return to work, but he could not be sure when.

While the colorists may have struck in mid-June, they evidently had slowed down the pace of the work much earlier, as is suggested by Audubon's June 2 letter to his Manchester friend W.H. Bentley. JJA, London to W.H. Bentley, Manchester, 2 Jun. 1827 (Private collection). See text and note 123, *supra*.

125. *AHJ* I, pp. 255; L. Audubon (1869), p. 155.

126. Rhodes (2004), p. 293; Williams (1931), p. 28; *AHJ* I, p. 257; L. Audubon (1869), p. 158. Every one of Audubon's biographers takes a slightly different view of his initial meeting with Robert Havell Sr. and Robert Havell Jr., who would go on to replace Lizars in the production of *BOA*. Part of the difficulty stems from the lack of details offered by Audubon in his extant writings. This is compounded by the fact that there are two versions of the original journal entries, as set forth in Lucy's biography and in granddaughter Maria's publication, and they are not entirely consistent. Cf. *AHJ* I, pp. 255–256; L. Audubon (1869), pp. 155–158.

Both versions contain entries for Monday, June 18, 1827, that indicate Audubon was in the process of searching for a colorist to take over that portion of the work, having learned that Lizars's colorists were on strike. Lucy's biography states that Audubon had just received Lizars's letter "this day," which "was quite a shock to my nerves, and for nearly an hour I deliberated whether I should not go at once to Edinburgh, but an engagement at Lord Spencer's where I expected a subscriber, decided me to remain." L. Audubon (1869), p. 155. Audubon showed his drawings at Lord Spencer's and later at the residence of Mr. Ponton, followed by a meeting in his own rooms with Charles-Lucien Bonaparte, who had recently arrived in London. As soon as Bonaparte departed, Audubon's "thoughts returned to the colorers, and I started off at once to find some, but with no success; all the establishments of the kind were closed from want of employment. But happening to pass a print-shop, I inquired if the proprietor knew of any colorers, and he at once gave me the name of one, who offered to work cheaper than I was paying in Edinburgh; and I wrote instantly to Mr. Lizars to send me twenty-five copies; and so I hope all will go on well again." Ibid., p. 156.

Lucy's biography then contains a lengthy account of Audubon's trip to a London slum to meet a prospective colorist. Since this follows the earlier entry of June 18, it would appear to have occurred on June 19. But this is wholly inconsistent with Audubon's statement on the 18th that he had hired a colorist to take over the work of the striking employees in Lizars's shop. In any case, Audubon found the colorist at his cramped apartment, surrounded by his impoverished family, and learned that he was no longer doing this kind of work. However, the man did provide Audubon with the names of three colorists he could recommend. The entry ends with Audubon declaring, "Oh! how sick I am of London." L Audubon (1869), pp. 157–158. There is no mention of Havell.

Maria's entry for Monday, June 18, indicates that the letter from Lizars had arrived the previous Thursday morning, June 14, and that Audubon had been actively searching for a replacement colorist for the past three days. "I have been about the suburbs and dirtier parts of London, and more misery and poverty cannot exist without absolute starvation. By chance I entered a print shop, and the owner gave me the name of a man to whom I went, and who has engaged to color more cheaply than it is done in Edinburgh, and young Kidd has taken a letter from me to Mr. Lizars telling him to send me twenty-five copies." *AHJ* I, p. 256. This entry is very similar to that in Lucy's biography. They both suggest that Audubon had hired Havell as of June 18, although Havell's name is not given.

However, Maria's version of the June 19 entry, which contains no reference to Audubon's visit to the slums, states that he "went five times to see Mr. Havell the colorer, but he was out of town. I am full of anxiety and greatly depressed. Oh! how sick I am of London." Ibid., p. 257. I have to wonder why Audubon would be so intent on seeing Havell Sr. if the two had met the previous day and already struck a deal.

Neither Lucy nor Maria have a journal entry for June 20, but on June 21, Lucy's version states: "Have made an engagement with Mr. Havell for coloring, which I hope will relieve my embarrassment." L. Audubon (1869), p. 158. Maria's version does not reference Havell again until September 30. *AHJ* I, pp. 257–258.

Overall, both accounts make it clear that after Audubon received Lizars's letter about the strike, he began scouring London for a colorist to assume

the work. He was not looking for an engraver. Lizars had not yet decided to abandon that role. Of the two Havells, it was Robert Havell Sr. who was then known as a colorist. Robert Havell Jr. was an engraver.

127. Williams (1916), pp. 234, 236. See also, Williams (1931), p. 28. The tale told in the Havell clan of how Audubon ultimately engaged Robert Havell Sr. and Robert Havell Jr. to produce the remaining plates of *BOA* comes to us from a distant relative, George Alfred Williams (1875–1932), the great-great-grandson of Luke Havell, who was the brother of Robert Havell Sr. Fries (1973), pp. 24–25. Williams wrote two articles about the subject. The first appeared in 1916 in *Print Collector's Quarterly*. Williams (1916). Fifteen years later, he published a second article on the subject in *The Antiquarian*. Williams (1931). In the latter piece, he explained that he was able to clarify what had occurred between the three men because he had known Amelia Jane Havell Lockwood, the eldest daughter of Robert Havell Jr., and had access to family notebooks, correspondence, and the Havell family Bible. Ibid., p. 28. However, both articles suffer from myriad factual errors.

128. Williams (1916), p. 236. See also, Williams (1931), p. 28. The man to whom Robert Havell Sr. supposedly discussed his need for a talented engraver was Paul Colnaghi of Colnaghi & Company, a London publisher. Hart-Davis (2004), p. 125; Williams (1931), p. 28; Williams (1916), p. 236.

129. Williams (1916), p. 236. See also, Williams (1931), p. 28.

130. Williams (1916), p. 230. See also, Williams (1931), p. 27. Robert Havell Jr. was born on November 25, 1793. Matthew (2004); Deane (1908c), p. 406. See also, Havell Obituary Notice found in the papers of Ruthven Deane accompanying his presentation copy of *AHJ* in the Newberry Library, Chicago (VAULT Graff 112). Thus, when Audubon first met him in the summer of 1827, Havell Jr. was only thirty-three, not thirty-four as many biographers have stated or implied. See, e.g., Rhodes (2004), p. 293; Souder (2004), p. 234; Hart-Davis (2004), p. 124; Ford (1988), p. 227; Fries (1973), p. 25; Arthur (1937), p. 354.

131. Williams (1916), p. 230. See also, Williams

(1931), p. 27. Robert Havell Jr. had supposedly left his father's employ in 1825 to paint the landscapes of Monmouthshire. Fries (1973), p. 25.

132. Williams (1916), p. 236.

133. Rhodes (2004), p. 293; Goddu (2002), pp. 17–18; Ford (1988), pp. 226–227; Herrick (1938) I, pp. 382–383.

134. Among the Audubon biographers who share my skepticism about the Havell family lore of timely reconciliation between Robert Havell Sr. and his son are Souder and Hart-Davis. Souder (2004), p. 234; Hart-Davis (2004), p. 125. Ralph Hyde, the author of a concise but informative paper on Robert Havell Jr., concurs. Hyde (1984), p. 91.

135. Goddu (2002), p. 17.

136. Critchett & Woods (1823).

137. Christie's (2002), Lot 89. James Baillie Fraser's *Views of Calcutta and its environs, from drawings Executed by James B. Fraser, Esq. From Sketches made on the Spot* comprised twenty-four aquatint engravings by Robert Havell Jr., Frederick Christian Lewis, and Theodore Fielding. The first three parts consisting of the first nine prints were issued by Rodwell and Martin. Parts 4 through 8 were published by Smith, Elder, and Co. beginning in March 1825. Ibid.

138. Critchett & Woods (1825).

139. Critchett (1828); Critchett (1827); Critchett & Woods (1826).

140. *AHJ* I, p. 257; L. Audubon (1869), p. 158. See also, note 126, *supra*.

141. *AHJ* I, p. 258; L. Audubon (1869), pp. 158, 159–160. See also, JJA, London to LBA, Bayou Sarah, 6 Aug. 1827 (APS), Audubon (1999), p. 807, *Letters* I, p. 30.

142. *AHJ* I, p. 257; L. Audubon (1869), p. 158. It appears that Audubon received at least three letters from Lizars discussing the situation with his colorists. The first and third are mentioned in the 1827 journal. *AHJ* I, pp. 255, 257; L. Audubon (1869), pp. 155, 158. The second letter, which is at Yale, is dated June 16, 1827, and was clearly a follow-up to a previous letter providing first notice of the strike. Audubon wrote crosswise on the first sheet that he had replied to this letter on June 20. William Lizars, Edinburgh to JJA, London, 16 Jun. 1827 (Yale Box 5, Folder 231).

143. Chalmers (2003), p. 123.

144. Hart-Davis (2004), pp. 125–126. Joseph Goddu, in his informative 2002 monograph for the exhibition and sale of a selection of pattern proofs used by the colorists in Havell's shop, reveals that Henry Augustus Havell (1803–1845), another of Robert Havell Sr.'s sons, was also intimately involved in the project. Goddu points out that Henry "would often be called upon to work up the outline etchings, to color the 'pattern prints' to be used as guides for the teams of colorists employed in the project, and to oversee their work." Goddu (2002), p. 17. See also, Schlosser-DeFay Family Tree (April 2008), Ancestry.com (accessed 1 Feb. 2014). While Audubon was in America in 1829, he referenced in several letters having contact with Henry, who was in New York. JJA, Beech Grove to Robert Havell Jr., London, 16 Dec. 1829, Herrick (1938) I, p. 434; JJA, Philadelphia to Robert Havell Jr., London, 27 Oct. 1829 (Harvard (10)), *Letters* I, p. 101; JJA, Philadelphia to Robert Havell Jr., London, 7 Jul. 1829, (Harvard (7)), *Letters* I, p. 87.

145. Williams (1916), p. 242. Many Audubon scholars contend that Robert Havell Sr. retired in June 1828 following the dissolution of the business partnership with his son. Rhodes (2004), p. 309; Hart-Davis (2004), p. 126; Goddu (2002), p. 19. Ford and Souder assert that Audubon fired him in December 1828 and moved the printing and coloring responsibilities to his son. Souder (2004), p. 242; Ford (1988), p. 253. Others maintain that he continued to supervise the printing and coloring of the prints for some period of time before his death in 1832. Chalmers (2003), p. 123; Fries (1973), p. 25; Williams (1916), p. 242.

The record of the duration of Robert Havell Sr.'s involvement in the production of *BOA* is not as clear as one would like. However, by tracking the credit line on the prints that were being issued, we can reach a fairly conclusive answer. The prints in the first Number to come out of the Havells' shop, No. 3 (Plates 11–15), were each inscribed: "Printed & Coloured by R. Havell, Senr. Engraved by R. Havell, Junr." Christie's (2012), p. 29; Low (2002), pp. 35–37; Christie's (2000), pp. 33–34. The same inscription appeared on the three small prints of No. 4 (Plates 18–20), which were likely engraved first. However, the large and medium prints of No. 4 (Plates 16–17) carried the credit line: "Engraved, Printed & Coloured by R. Havell & Son," suggesting that the Havells' formal partnership was established during the course of issuing No. 4 in the autumn of 1827. Christie's (2012), pp. 29–30; Low (2002), pp. 38–40; Christie's (2000), p. 34.

Father and son continued to use this inscription without change from No. 5 (Plates 21–25) through the earliest engraved prints of No. 8 (Plates 36, 38, 39), which were issued in July 1828. Christie's (2012), p. 30; Low (2002), pp. 40–51; Christie's (2000), pp. 34–35; JJA, London to LBA, Bayou Sarah, 8 Aug. 1828 (APS), *Letters* I, pp. 66–67; JJA, London to William Swainson, Tittenhanger Green, Jul. 1828 (Linnean Society). The remaining prints issued with No. 8 (Plates 37, 40) and those issued through the end of 1829, Nos. 9–15 (Plates 41–75), bore the inscription: "Engraved by R. (or "Robt.," see Plate 40) Havell, Junr. Printed & Coloured by R. Havell, Senr." Christie's (2012), pp. 32, 34, 36; Low (2002), pp. 50–73.

Thereafter, No. 16 (Plates 76–80) through No. 20 (Plates 96–100), all of which appeared during the year 1830, carried the inscription: "Engraved, Printed & Coloured by Robert Havell, Junr." Christie's (2012), pp. 36, 38; Low (2002), p. 73; Christie's (2000) pp. 38–41. In 1831, with the beginning of the second volume and the issuance of No. 21 (Prints 101–105) as well as on earlier numbered prints published from that time forward, Robert Havell Jr. abandoned the "Junr" designation (except on Plate 110, see Christie's (2012), p. 41; Christie's (2000), pp. 37, 41), but this was not, as print scholar Susanne Low writes, due to the death that year of his father. Low (2002), p. 73. See also, Christie's (2005), pp. 28–45. Robert Havell Sr. actually died in November 1832. Matthew (2004); Ford (1988), p. 496.

Those scholars who contend that Robert Havell Sr. had retired by 1828 offer no explanation for the inclusion of his name on the prints produced through the following year. We know from a December 1828 letter from Audubon that Robert Havell Sr. was still involved in the project up to the middle of that month. On December 25, 1828, the naturalist wrote to his friend William Swainson to say that he had terminated the senior Havell as of Saturday,

December 20, because of a month's delay in the issuance of No. 10 and that all of the work was now being handled by Robert Havell Jr. "I long since discovered that old Havell was a *daudle* [MS: *doudle*, i.e. "a dawdler"] and have born this untill last Saturday when a little *irritated* at a delay of [MS: ov] nearly one Month in the completion of my N° 10, Je lui ai donné Son Congé pour toujours! ["I gave him his vacation for always!" i.e, "I gave him a permanent vacation."]. Young Havell has now all my business on hand and I feel assured that the colouring will improve under his usual care & promptitude." JJA, London to William Swainson, Tittenhanger Green, 25 Dec. 1828 (Linnean Society). It bears noting that Souder misreads the line in French, asserting that Audubon's decision to end his relationship with the elder Havell was because Havell "took an unannounced vacation." Souder (2004), p. 242. Rather, Audubon was merely saying that he had fired the printer.

Ford similarly errs in claiming that Audubon moved his business at this time "to the son's shop two doors beyond the paternal establishment." Ford (1988), p. 254. Through 1830, Robert Havell Jr. continued to work out of his father's shop at 79 Newman Street, as evidenced by the address Audubon used in sending him letters. See note 147, *infra*.

Notwithstanding the falling out between Audubon and the senior Havell in December 1828, it would appear that the naturalist's relationship with the printer and colorist was subsequently mended. To begin with, all of the prints that were issued over the course of 1829 credited Havell Sr. with the printing and coloring. Moreover, Audubon made a reference in a letter during his 1829 visit to America that certainly implies the elder Havell was still actively engaged in the project. In early October 1829, after months of combing the eastern U.S. for birds to draw, Audubon wrote to Robert Havell Jr. and remarked in reference to the senior Havell, "I will bring over with me Two Years of good Work for Friend Havell." JJA to Robert Havell Jr., London, 4 Oct. 1829 (Harvard (8)), *Letters* I, pp. 95–96. The work Audubon was alluding to was the printing and coloration of prints of the drawings he had just completed.

Based on the evidence, it would appear that Robert Havell Sr. continued to have a role in the production of the prints for *BOA* through 1829 as stated in the text.

146. Steiner (2003), p. 8; Ford (1988), p. 496. Robert Havell Sr. died on November 21, 1832, and is buried in the graveyard at Old St. Pancras Church in London. Matthew (2004).

147. Robert Havell Jr. moved his business from 79 Newman Street to 77 Oxford Street, across from the Pantheon, in early 1831. Audubon had heard of the anticipated move the previous October and, in a letter from Edinburgh on October 31, asked Havell when he would be moving. JJA, Edinburgh to Robert Havell Jr., London, 31 Oct. 1830, (Harvard (28)), *Letters* I, p. 121. When Havell wrote Audubon on December 23, 1830, he was still situated at 79 Newman Street. Robert Havell Jr., London to JJA, n.p., 23 Dec. 1830 (Yale, Box 4, Folder 185). On February 5, 1831, Havell wrote to Audubon to say that the move had been completed and the shop would be opening the following week. Robert Havell Jr., London to JJA, Edinburgh, 5 Feb. 1831 (Yale, Box 4, Folder 185).

148. JJA, London to LBA, Bayou Sarah, 6 Aug. 1827 (APS), Audubon (1999), p. 807, *Letters* I, pp. 29–30. In describing to Lucy in this letter how pleased he was that he had switched the printing work to Robert Havell Sr., Audubon remarked that "the sets colored by him are far Surpassing in beauty those of Mr L." He also broke down the prices he was paying to Havell for each Number of five prints, including the copper engraving and lettering:

	S.^{gs} p.^{cs}
Included is	£42.0.0 —
The Price of Coloring 100 sets @ 8/6	42.10.0 —
Paper for D^o 1 Ream	14.1.0 —
Printing of the 100 sets	11.5.0 —
100 Tin Cases to forward the sets to each person	5.0.0 —
	£114:16:0

JJA, London to LBA, Bayou Sarah, 6 Aug. 1827 (APS), Audubon (1999), p. 807. Cf. *Letters* I, p. 30. See also, JJA, London to VGA, Louisville, 25 Aug. 1827 (APS), *Letters* I, p. 36.

The letter also disclosed that Audubon expected to remain in England another five years, "as Long as I will have Drawings to Keep my Work going on,"

which could not have been welcome news to Lucy. Audubon (1999), p. 808. In a follow-up letter to her on August 21, he extended his estimate to "no less than eight years and perhaps for ever more" if his son John was able to provide the additional drawings needed to complete the work. JJA, London to LBA, Bayou Sarah, 21 Aug. 1827 (APS), *Letters* I, p. 35. However, he did assure her that "I consider myself in a very fair way so much so that if no great Blunder or Mishap takes place between this date and January next, I shall *most undoubtedly* write for thee to come and see thy native land again." Ibid., pp. 34–35.

149. Fries (1973), pp. 18–19; *AHJ* I, pp. 258–259. King George IV's subscription was obtained through the efforts of Sir Jonathan-Wathen Waller (1769–1853), the king's oculist, who was asked by John G. Children to show Audubon's prints to the monarch. *AHJ* I, p. 258; Burke (1838), pp. 997–998; Burke (1826), p. 336. Waller announced the news in an August 26, 1827, letter to Sir Thomas Lawrence (1769–1830), the well-known portrait painter and president of the Royal Academy. Ford (1988), p. 445, note 1. The following day, Waller reported that the Duchess of Clarence also wished to subscribe. JJA, Manchester to LBA, Bayou Sarah, 20 Sept. 1827 (APS), *Letters* I, pp. 39–40. Ford, Fries, and Streshinsky erroneously refer to him as Sir Walthen Waller. Streshinsky (1993), p. 214; Ford (1988), pp. 224, 229, 238, and 445, note 1; Fries (1973), pp. 18–19.

Audubon referred to him in a letter to Lucy as "Sir Mathew Waller." JJA, Manchester to LBA, Bayou Sarah, 20 Sept. 1827 (APS), *Letters* I, p. 40. Ford claims that this was a mistake, but Waller was indeed referenced as "sir Mathew Waller, bart. [baronet] of Pope's Villa, Twickenham, and of Hertford-street, May-fair" in the Annual Register's listing of his daughter's July 1823 wedding. Cf. Ford (1988), p. 445, note 5; *Annual Register* (1824), Appendix to Chronicle, p. 175.

150. Fries (1973), p. 19. Audubon had originally been introduced to Lord Stanley, the fourteenth Earl of Derby, on August 5, 1827, in Liverpool by Adam Hodgson, a former business partner of the Rathbone brothers. Audubon (2011), pp. 91–92; Nottingham (1992), p. 36; Ford (1987), pp. 121–122.

151. JJA, Manchester to LBA, Bayou Sarah, 20

Sept. 1827 (APS), *Letters* I, p. 39. See also, Rhodes (2004), p. 299. Audubon later wrote Lucy and said that he had left London on August 15. JJA, Liverpool to LBA, Bayou Sarah, 25 Nov. 1827 (APS), *Letters* I, p. 43. This was evidently in error, as his earlier letter from Manchester on September 20 had placed his departure from the English capital at "4 days ago." JJA, Manchester to LBA, Bayou Sarah, 20 Sept. 1827 (APS), *Letters* I, p. 39. See note 117, *supra*, for the details of the calculation of the total number of subscribers Audubon had when he left London.

152. *AHJ* I, pp. 258–264. See also, JJA, Liverpool to LBA, Bayou Sarah, 25 Nov. 1827 (APS), *Letters* I, pp. 43–44; JJA, Edinburgh to LBA, Bayou Sarah, 12 Nov. 1827 (APS), *Letters* I, p. 41.

153. JJA, Liverpool to LBA, Bayou Sarah, 25 Nov. 1827 (APS), *Letters* I, p. 48. Audubon augmented his list with nine new subscribers in Manchester, two in York, and a total of eight in Edinburgh. Ibid., pp. 43–44. In his letter of November 25, 1827, Audubon informed Lucy that Manchester had given him ten new subscriptions, but his total count for the trip was only twenty, and that included a subscription from the University of Glasgow. Thus, the number of new Manchester subscribers appears to have only been nine, which is consistent with Audubon's extant subscriber's list. Ibid., pp. 43, 45; Fries (1973), p. 20.

154. *AHJ* I, p. 267; JJA, Liverpool to LBA, Bayou Sarah, 25 Nov. 1827 (APS), *Letters* I, p. 44.

155. *AHJ* I, p. 266.

156. Harwood & Durant (1985), p. 65. In January 1828, Audubon recorded in his journal that he had lost one of his Manchester subscribers and four from Edinburgh. *AHJ* I, pp. 279–280.

157. Harwood & Durant (1985), p. 65.

158. JJA, Liverpool to LBA, Bayou Sarah, 25 Nov. 1827 (APS), *Letters* I, p. 48.

159. *AHJ* I, p. 273.

160. JJA, Liverpool to LBA, Bayou Sarah, 25 Nov. 1827 (APS), *Letters* I, p. 48; JJA, Edinburgh to LBA, Bayou Sarah, 12 Nov. 1827 (APS), *Letters* I, pp. 41–42; JJA, London to LBA, Bayou Sarah, 21 Aug. 1827 (APS), *Letters* I, pp. 34–35.

161. JJA, London to LBA, Bayou Sarah, 26 Dec. 1827 (APS), *Letters* I, pp. 54–55.

162. JJA, London to LBA, Bayou Sarah, 6 Feb. 1828 (APS), *Letters* I, p. 57. Audubon had moved to more spacious accommodations at 95 Great Russell Street in late August 1827. JJA, London to LBA, Bayou Sarah, 21 Aug. 1827 (APS), *Letters* I, p. 35.

163. JJA, London to LBA, Bayou Sarah, 6 Feb. 1828 (APS), *Letters* I, p. 57. Audubon recognized that there were those close to Lucy, including his son Victor and his brother-in-law Nicholas Berthoud, who held a poor opinion of him based on their perception that he was enjoying an extravagant existence abroad while she grew older and carried the financial load of supporting herself and John. Rhodes (2004), p. 295 (transcribing a portion of JJA, London to LBA, Bayou Sarah, 20 Jun. 1827 (Princeton, Box 2, Folder 7)); JJA, Manchester to LBA, Bayou Sarah, 20 Sept. 1827 (APS), *Letters* I, p. 41. Audubon complained to Lucy that his letters to Victor and Nicholas were going unanswered. See, e.g., JJA, London to LBA, Bayou Sarah, 8 Aug. 1828 (APS), *Letters* I, p. 67. He also raised the issue of Nicholas's silence directly with Victor. JJA, London to VGA, Louisville, 22 Dec. 1828 (APS), *Letters* I, p. 74. There is little question that Victor was upset with his father for abandoning his mother, and Nicholas evidently continued to view the artist as a ne'er-do-well. See also, Rhodes (2004), pp. 304, 318.

164. JJA, London to LBA, Bayou Sarah, 6 Feb. 1828 (APS), *Letters* I, p. 58. See also, JJA, London to LBA, Bayou Sarah, 8 Aug. 1828 (APS), *Letters* I, p. 69.

165. JJA, London to LBA, Bayou Sarah, 22 Mar. 1828 (APS), *Letters* I, p. 65.

166. *AHJ* I, p. 292.

167. JJA, London to LBA, Bayou Sarah, 8 Aug. 1828 (APS), *Letters* I, pp. 66–67. Rhodes asserts that No. 8 consisted of Plates 41–45. Rhodes (2004), p. 309. In fact, the eighth Number comprised Plates 36–40. The large plate of the Ruffed Grouse, which Rhodes indicates was the first plate in No. 8, was actually the opening print of No. 9. Low (2002), p. 49–53.

168. JJA, London to LBA, Bayou Sarah, 23 Dec. 1828 (APS), Audubon (2006), p. 224; JJA, London to William Swainson at Tittenhanger Green, 1 Jul. 1828 (Linnean Society), Herrick (1938) I, p. 405.

169. *AHJ* I, pp. 303, 306. Audubon left London for Paris on September 1, 1828, in the company of

William Swainson, his wife Mary, and C.R. Parker, a portrait artist from Natchez who had painted Audubon's portrait in August. *AHJ* I, pp. 300, 303. See also, Rhodes (2004), p. 312. Audubon advised his journal on August 25 that "Mr. Parker has nearly finished my portrait, which he considers a good one, and *so do I*." *AHJ* I, p. 303. This portrait, still in the family's possession, was featured in Harwood & Durant (1985), p. 96.

170. Rhodes (2004), pp. 307–308; Souder (2004), pp. 239–240; Audubon, *Prospectus* (1831), pp. 9–11. Audubon met British naturalist William Swainson (1789–1855) through John C. Loudon (1783–1843), who in the spring of 1828 was about to embark on the publication of the first issue of *The Magazine of Natural History* and asked Audubon to write for it. On April 6, Audubon indicated in his journal that Loudon intended to approach Swainson about reviewing *BOA* for the magazine. *AHJ* I, p. 295. When Loudon subsequently met with Audubon on April 8, he showed the naturalist a copy of a letter Swainson had written in reply. Audubon described the contents in a letter he wrote to Swainson the following day. Swainson had reportedly been extremely complimentary of Audubon and his work, and had agreed to pen the requested review. However, Swainson also wanted Audubon to send him a copy of the fascicles that had been published to date at Audubon's own cost. JJA, London to William Swainson at Tittenhanger Green, 9 Apr. 1828 (Linnean Society), Herrick (1938) I, pp. 400–401. See also, Souder (2004), p. 240. The *quid pro quo* is not explicitly stated, but both Ford and Souder believe that this was clearly Swainson's intent. Souder (2004), p. 240; Ford (1988), p. 235. At a minimum, it would appear that Swainson was looking for additional consideration from Audubon for writing a positive review.

Souder's account could lead one to believe that Swainson had written directly to Audubon and made this proposal. He writes that "Swainson bluntly told Audubon that he would compose a highly favorable notice if Audubon would provide him 'at cost' with a full set of *The Birds of America* as so far completed." Souder (2004), p. 240. He then cites as his source a letter from Swainson to Audubon, dated April 9, 1828, the same date as Audubon's letter, and references the Linnean Society

of London as the holder. Souder (2004), p. 240 and note, p. 335. If there is such a letter, it is not at the Linnean Society. Ben Sherwood, Assistant Librarian, Linnean Society of London (Personal communication, 7 Dec. 2009). Souder has evidently transposed the sender and recipient of the Audubon letter. As indicated above, Swainson did not write Audubon directly but mentioned his desires in a letter to Loudon, presumably knowing that Loudon would relay them to Audubon.

In any event, recognizing the value of good publicity if not the dubious ethics of Swainson's proposal, Audubon readily agreed. But he informed Swainson that if he were to accept the suggested payment terms, Swainson would be burdened by almost twice what Audubon's subscribers were paying. Instead, Audubon declared that he would be content to accept 35 shillings per Number. JJA, London to William Swainson, Tittenhanger Green, 9 Apr. 1828 (Linnean Society), Herrick (1938) I, pp. 400–401. Souder seems to have overlooked this part of Audubon's letter, erroneously asserting that Audubon promised to provide a copy "at a fair price that he would work out." Souder (2004), p. 240. Ford asserts that Audubon substituted some notes on the American Shrike that Swainson needed for a book he was writing in lieu of the prints, but her interpretation of Audubon's letter of April 9 is not borne out by its content. Cf. Ford (1988), p. 235; Herrick (1938) I, p. 401.

Audubon's statement to Swainson that the actual cost of *BOA* was almost twice what the subscribers were paying was an obvious exaggeration. He likely threw this up as a smokescreen because he was unwilling to share the financial details of his production with a man who, at that point, was a complete stranger. He also had no desire to give the prints away at cost. In fact, the 35 shillings that Audubon agreed to charge Swainson for each Number was well above what he paid to have them produced.

According to the accounting that Audubon provided Lucy in his letter of August 6, 1827, it cost him £114.16s to have the Havells produce one hundred sets of each fascicle. JJA, London to LBA, Bayou Sarah, 6 Aug. 1827 (APS), Audubon (1999), p. 807, *Letters* I, p. 30. See also, note 148, *supra*. This means that the cost of a single Number of five prints was 22.96 shillings. The price he quoted to Swainson — 35 shillings — was less than he was charging his subscribers — 42 shillings — but would have still earned him a profit.

Souder evidently reads Audubon's April 9 letter as an indication that he was losing money on the production of *BOA*. "Despite the hopeful calculations he'd been relaying to Lucy," Souder writes, "the truth was that subscriber numbers had not yet reached the breakeven point, and *The Birds of America* was still being produced at a loss." Souder (2004), p. 240. However, by the spring of 1828, that was certainly not the case. Audubon charged 2 guineas or £2.2s per Number, which meant that for one hundred subscribers he grossed £210. Since his costs were only £114.16s, he showed a net profit of £95.4s per one hundred sets of each Number. JJA, London to LBA, Bayou Sarah, 6 Aug. 1827 (APS), Audubon (1999), p. 808; *Letters* I, p. 30. In April 1828, Audubon had approximately 120 subscribers, which netted him just over £114 per Number. JJA, London to LBA, Bayou Sarah, 8 Aug. 1828 (APS), *Letters* I, p. 66–67 (125 subscribers "at present"); Fries (1973), pp. 28–29, 31, 146 (between Audubon's visit to Oxford in late March 1828 and his addition of Lord Milton's subscription in late June, four names appear on his subscription list). With five Numbers being issued each year, Audubon's annual net earnings exceeded £570.

Moreover, since Audubon had been able to front the costs for the first two Numbers produced by Lizars, the publication was now on a self-sustaining basis. JJA, London to VGA, Louisville, 10 Nov. 1828 (APS), *Letters* I, p. 72; JJA, London to LBA, Bayou Sarah, 6 Aug. 1827 (APS), Audubon (1999), p. 808, *Letters* I, p. 30. The payments being made by subscribers as each Number was issued were used to finance the continued production of forthcoming Numbers. As he related to Victor in late 1828, "I owe no money to anybody — I pay my Engravers, colorers & printers as regularly as their work has [MS: as] passed my last inspection. I take regular receipts and keep a Ledger which can prove what is going on." JJA, London to VGA, Louisville, 10 Nov. 1828 (APS), *Letters* I, p. 72.

Of course, Audubon encountered cash flow problems from time to time because he still had to collect on each account, and some of his subscribers were not always forthcoming. For this reason, he had appointed agents throughout England and Scotland, who were responsible for insuring that payments were received with the delivery of each Number. Fries (1973), pp. 19-20. The agents received a percentage of the price of each fascicle they delivered, which reduced Audubon's profits, but there is no reason to believe, as Souder does, that Audubon was losing money on the project.

171. *AHJ* I, p. 298–299. In his journal entry of June 2, 1828, Audubon wrote:

> I was at Mr. Swainson's from May 28 till yesterday, and my visit was of the most agreeable nature. Mr. and Mrs. Swainson have a charming home at Tittenhanger Green, near St. Albans. Mrs. Swainson plays well on the piano, is amiable and kind; Mr. Swainson a superior man indeed; and their children blooming with health and full of spirit. Such talks on birds we have had together. Why, Lucy, thou wouldst think that birds were all that we cared for in this world, but thou knowest this is not so. Whilst there I began a drawing for Mrs. Swainson, and showed Mr. Swainson how to put up birds in my style, which delighted him.

Alice Ford questions the length of Audubon's visit to the Swainson home, noting that Audubon had written Charles-Lucien Bonaparte from London on May 28. Alice Ford (Personal communication). However, Audubon typically awoke before dawn and spent several hours on his correspondence. He very well could have written Bonaparte early that morning and taken a coach to Tittenhanger the same day.

172. Rhodes (2004), pp. 311–312; Souder (2004), p. 241; JJA, London to William Swainson, Tittenhanger Green, Wednesday, [13] Aug. 1828 (Linnean Society), Herrick (1938) I, p. 409. See also, *AHJ* I, p. 300. In the cited letter to Swainson on August 13, 1828, Audubon spoke of his "already despondent spirits," which had not been helped by Lucy's letter delaying indefinitely any plans to join him. He then added that "it may perhaps be well that no Instrument is at hand with which a Woeful Sin might be comitted," an allusion to suicide that Swainson apparently took seriously because he swept into London from his country home the day after receiving it and returned with the ailing naturalist. Rhodes (2004), pp. 311–312; Herrick (1938) I, p. 409.

Audubon experienced occasional mood swings, but it is doubtful he was ever truly suicidal. The reference in his letter to Swainson was more likely hyperbole intended to emphasize how depressed he felt that Lucy was not apt to join him any time soon. What is more interesting and, at the same time, perplexing about Audubon's reaction to Lucy's letter is his inability to recognize that it was his refusal to issue a summons to join him that had left her in Louisiana wondering what he was thinking. See, e.g., LBA, St. Francisville to VGA, Louisville, 15 Jun. 1828, Audubon (2006), p. 217.

173. *AHJ* I, p. 317.

174. Rhodes (2004), p. 316.

175. JJA, London to LBA, Bayou Sarah, 17 Nov. 1828 (APS), Audubon (2006), p. 223; JJA, London to LBA, Bayou Sarah, 2 Nov. 1828 (Princeton, Box 2, Folder 10), Audubon (1999), p. 811. See also, Rhodes (2004), pp. 315–316; Fries (1973), p. 33. Although Audubon informed Lucy in his November 2 letter that he had returned to London from France the day before, it appears that he had actually reached London on October 30 as he stated in a letter to William Swainson on November 1. JJA, London to William Swainson, Tittenhanger Green, 1 Nov. 1828 (Linnean Society). Audubon probably elected to lie to Lucy because he had failed to write her promptly upon his arrival.

176. JJA, London to LBA, Bayou Sarah, 2 Nov. 1828 (Princeton, Box 2, Folder 10), Audubon (1999), p. 811. Audubon still counted 144 subscribers on his list when he drafted a letter to Lucy on December 23, 1828. At that point, he was renting rooms in the home of Robert Havell Jr. JJA, London to LBA, Bayou Sarah, 23 Dec. 1828 (APS), Audubon (2006), p. 224.

177. JJA, London to LBA, Bayou Sarah, 20 Jan. 1829 (APS), *Letters* I, pp. 77–78.

178. Ibid., p. 78. See also, Rhodes (2004), p. 321. In a letter to Victor from Philadelphia on July 18, 1829, Audubon indicated that he wanted to "renew" one hundred drawings. JJA, Philadelphia to VGA, Louisville (APS), 18 Jul. 1829, *Letters* I, p. 91.

179. Rhodes (2004), pp. 319, 321. See also, LBA, Bayou Sarah to VGA, Louisville, 30 Jan. 1829, Audubon (2006), pp. 231–232; LBA, St. Francisville to VGA, Louisville, 19 Jan. 1829, Audubon (2006), p. 228; JJA, London to LBA, Bayou Sarah, 23 Dec.

1828 (APS), Audubon (2006), p. 224. When Audubon reached Louisville in the fall of 1829, he stated that Victor was working with William Bakewell but that he found John at Nicholas Berthoud's establishment. L. Audubon (1869), p. 196.

180. JJA, London to LBA, Bayou Sarah, 20 Jan. 1829 (APS), *Letters* I, pp. 79–80. See also, JJA, London to VGA, Louisville, 2 Feb. 1829 (Yale, Box 1, Folder 4).

181. LBA, Bayou Sarah to VGA, Louisville, 19 Jan. 1829 (Yale, Box 1, Folder 14), Audubon (2006), pp. 226–227. See also, Rhodes (2004), p. 319. Lucy's decision to leave the security of her position in Louisiana and rejoin her husband was precipitated by his "very severe and painful" letter of November 2, 1828, which she received on the night of January 19, 1829. LBA, St. Francisville to VGA, Louisville, 19 Jan. 1829 (Yale, Box 1, Folder 14), Audubon (2006), pp. 226–228; JJA, London to LBA, Bayou Sarah, 2 Nov. 1828 (Princeton, Box 2, Folder 10), Audubon (1999), pp. 811–813. Reading both letters side by side, the degree to which Audubon and Lucy misread each other's feelings, desires, and intentions is brought into stark relief. Audubon believed that Lucy would not come to him until he was truly wealthy. At that point, he was earning "rather more than 600 pound sterling or 2664 Dollars," about $68,400 in 2016 dollars. However, he was convinced she needed him to be "overflowing with cash." JJA, London to LBA, Bayou Sarah, 2 Nov. 1828 (Princeton, Box 2, Folder 10), Audubon (1999), pp. 812–813. See also, Sahr (2015). Meanwhile, Lucy wanted some assurance that he would be able to support her and, just as importantly, that he still wanted her by his side. LBA, St. Francisville to JJA, London, 8 Feb. 1829, Audubon (2006), pp. 234–235; LBA, St. Francisville to VGA, Louisville, 19 Jan. 1829, Audubon (2006), pp. 227–228.

Throughout their separation, Audubon's letters contained glowing accounts of his success and the money he was making, but he invariably failed to include an explicit summons for her to join him. He could not bring himself to do so because he feared she would be disappointed, just as he had disappointed her with his business failure in Henderson and his subsequent inability in Louisville, Cincinnati, and New Orleans to return the family to prosperity. He invited her to make the decision herself,

which would have afforded him cover had she found
the conditions unacceptable when she arrived.
However, when Lucy received Audubon's November 2 letter, in which he reiterated that his publication was going to continue for fourteen years and asserted for the first time that if she did not intend to
join him before it was concluded they should separate and she should remarry, "and I to Spend my
Life most Miserably alone for the remainder of my
days," she made the only decision she could to save
her marriage. JJA, London to LBA, Bayou Sarah,
2 Nov. 1828, Audubon (1999), pp. 812.

182. LBA, St. Francisville to VGA, Louisville, 19
Jan. 1829 (Yale, Box 1, Folder 14), Audubon (2006),
p. 227. See also, Rhodes (2004), p. 320.

183. LBA, St. Francisville to JJA, London,
8 Feb. 1829, Audubon (2006), pp. 234–235.

184. L. Audubon (1869), p. 183. See also, JJA,
London to VGA, Louisville, 29 Mar. 1829 (Yale,
Box 1, Folder 4). When Audubon left England on
April 1, 1828, he apparently was unaware of Lucy's
plans to join him. Rhodes (2004), p. 324. This is evident from his letter to her of May 10, 1829, written
several days after his ship docked in New York, in
which he informed her that he might have to return
as soon as October 1 depending upon the advice
of his English agents, heedless of her stated need
to stay through year's end. JJA, New York to LBA,
Bayou Sarah, 10 May 1829 (APS), Audubon (2006),
p. 241, *Letters* I, p. 81.

Audubon complained of being seasick until the
ship was in sight of America. However, always alert
to marketing opportunities for his work, he did prevail upon a fellow passenger and Member of Parliament, Benjamin Smith, to subscribe. Smith was
making the voyage with his family, eight servants,
and five dogs. Audubon described him as "an excellent and benevolent man." L. Audubon (1869),
p. 183. See also, Fries (1973), p. 168.

185. JJA, New York to LBA, Bayou Sarah, 6 May
1829 (APS), Audubon (2006), p. 240. Audubon had
written to Victor on May 4, when the *Columbia* was
still twenty miles away from New York, to let him
know of his arrival. JJA, off New York 20 Miles to
VGA, Louisville, 4 May 1829 (Yale, Box 1, Folder 10).

186. JJA, New York to LBA, Bayou Sarah, 10
May 1829 (APS), Audubon (2006), pp. 241, 243–

244, *Letters* I, pp. 81, 83–85. In this letter, Audubon advised Lucy that his "immense book has been
laid on the table of the Lyceum," contrary to Ford's
erroneous belief that he hung the individual prints
on the wall. Ford (1988), p. 260. Audubon also mentioned in his letter that Dr. Samuel Latham Mitchell,
who had befriended him during his visit to New
York in August 1824, was "now lost to himself
and to the World" due to drunkenness. Audubon
(2006), p. 244; *Letters* I, pp. 84–85.

187. L. Audubon (1869), p. 184. During Audubon's several week stay in Camden, NJ, he was
assisted by an English taxidermist named Ward,
who was also collecting specimens for William
Swainson. JJA, Camden, NJ to William Swainson, Tittenhanger Green, 14 Sept. 1829 (Linnean
Society). Ford believes that this was Henry Ward,
born Edwin Henry Ward (1812–1878), who was a
member of a well-regarded family of English taxi-
dermists. Ford (1988), p. 256. We know that two
years later, Henry sailed with Audubon from England and joined Audubon on his 1831–1832 collecting expedition to the Floridas. The question is
whether he also crossed the Atlantic with Audubon
in 1829 to serve as the naturalist's assistant, as Ford
asserts.

Christine E. Jackson, who has researched the
Ward family history, has her doubts, as do I. She
points out that Henry was only seventeen years old
in 1829. The Ward who worked with Audubon that
year traveled to New York City in August and reportedly married a woman from London. Henry
evidently did not marry until 1833. Jackson posits
that the Ward mentioned by Audubon may have
been Henry's elder brother, James Frederick Ward
(1807–1863). Christine E. Jackson (personal communication, 5 Mar. 2016).

188. *OB* III, p. 606.

189. JJA, Philadelphia to VGA, Louisville, 18
Jul. 1829 (APS), Audubon (2006), p. 248, *Letters* I,
pp. 90–91. Audubon returned to Philadelphia on
July 4 after spending three weeks at Great Egg Harbor, NJ. JJA, Philadelphia to VGA, Louisville, 5 Jul.
1829, Herrick (1938) I, p. 242. Among the drawings Audubon is believed to have completed during
his visits to Camden and Great Egg Harbor are the
following:

Black Poll Warbler (Blackpoll Warbler)	Inscribed "New Jersey May."	Audubon (1966) I, Plate 197; Havell Plate 133.
Wood Pewee Flycatcher (Eastern Wood Pewee)	Inscribed "New Jersey May."	Audubon (1966) II, Plate 381; Havell Plate 115.
Small Green-crested Flycatcher (Acadian Flycatcher)	Inscribed "New Jersey May."	Audubon (1966) II, Plate 408; Havell Plate 306.
Golden-crowned Thrush (Ovenbird)	Inscribed "New Jersey May."	Audubon (1966) II, Plate 356; Havell Plate 143.
Warbling Flycatcher (Warbling Vireo)	Inscribed "New Jersey May 23"	Audubon (1966) I, Plate 203; Havell Plate 118.
Night-hawk (Common Nighthawk)	Inscribed "June 5"	Audubon (1966) II, Plate 351; Havell Plate 147.
Yellow-breasted Chat (Yellow-breasted Chat)	Inscribed "New Jersey, June 7"	Audubon (1966) II, Plate 243; Havell Plate 137.
Sea Side Finch (Seaside Sparrow)	Inscribed "June 14/ Great Egg Harbour"	Audubon (1966) I, Plate 33; Havell Plate 93).
Marsh Wren (Marsh Wren)	Inscribed "New Jersey June 22[d]"	Audubon (1966) II, Plate 336; Havell Plate 98.
Bay-winged Bunting (Vesper Sparrow)	Inscribed "Great Egg Harbour. June 26."	Audubon (1966) I, Plate 217; Havell Plate 94.
Osprey (Osprey)		Audubon (1966) I, Plate 84; Havell Plate 81.
Laughing Gull (Laughing Gull)		Audubon (1966) II, Plate 366; Havell Plate 314.
Field Sparrow (Field Sparrow)	Inscribed "July 11"	Audubon (1966) II, Plate 289; Havell Plate 139.

See also, Herrick (1938) I, p. 425, note 4.

190. Audubon reached the Great Pine Swamp, which he said was actually a Great Pine Forest, on August 1, 1829. JJA, Great Pine Swamp, Northampton County, PA to VGA, Louisville, 25 Aug. 1829 (APS), *Letters* I, p. 93. According to his Episode "The Great Pine Swamp," he spent a total of six weeks there. *OB* I, p. 56. Herrick asserts that Audubon's stay was actually about ten weeks, running from late July through October 10. Herrick (1938) I, p. 426. However, Audubon told William Swainson that he had returned to Camden, NJ, on September 12, following a six-week excursion to the Great Pine Forest. JJA, Camden, NJ, to William Swainson, Tittenhanger Green, 14 Sept. 1829 (Linnean Society). Moreover, some of his drawings, including of the Connecticut Warbler and Wilson's Warbler, were done in New Jersey in late September. Low (2002), p. 99; Audubon (1966) II, Plates 378, 386.

The October count of Audubon's completed drawings can be found in JJA, Philadelphia to LBA, Bayou Sarah, 11 Oct. 1829 (APS), Audubon (2006), p. 278, *Letters* I, p. 96. Audubon repeated this record of his output in a subsequent letter to Robert Havell Jr. JJA, Philadelphia to Robert Havell Jr., London, 24 Oct. 1829 (Harvard (9)), *Letters* I, p. 99.

191. JJA, Philadelphia to LBA, Bayou Sarah, 11 Oct. 1829 (APS), *Letters* I, p. 97; JJA, Philadelphia to LBA, Bayou Sarah, 15 Jul. 1829 (APS). See also, Rhodes (2004), p. 328.

192. JJA, St. Francisville to Richard Harlan, M.D., Philadelphia, 18 Nov. 1829, Audubon (2006), pp. 282–283, Herrick (1938) I, pp. 427–428; JJA, Philadelphia to Robert Havell Jr., London, 27 Oct. 1829 (Harvard (10)), *Letters* I, p. 101. See also, Rhodes (2004), p. 336, 338; L. Audubon (1869), p. 197.

193. L. Audubon (1869), p. 197. The quotation

in the text is taken from Lucy's biography rather than the overly dramatized and likely invented account appearing in Maria Audubon's biography of her grandfather. *AHJ* I, pp. 62–63. See also, Rhodes (2004), p. 338. Streshinsky points to the obvious similarities between Maria's tale of the 1829 homecoming and Audubon's description of his 1824 reunion with Lucy, following his trip to Philadelphia, to support her view, with which I agree, that the former was largely invented by Maria. Streshinsky (1993), p. xiv; L. Audubon (1869), pp. 115–116.

Streshinsky also questions that Lucy would have been teaching a student at 6:00 a.m. in the morning, when Maria's putative quotation from Audubon's journal indicated he arrived at the plantation of William Garrett Johnson and found her at the piano. Streshinsky (1993), p. xiv. However, on the issue of Lucy's work habits, it appears that she indeed started her days of instruction early. She informed Victor in a letter on January 30, 1829, that she had been "at the piano since five." LBA, St. Francisville to VGA, Louisville, 30 Jan. 1829, Audubon (2006), p. 231.

Audubon wrote to Richard Harlan, M.D., the day after he had arrived at Beech Grove and reported that "I had the happiness of pressing my beloved wife to my breast Yesterday morning." JJA, St. Francisville to Richard Harlan, M.D., Philadelphia, 18 Nov. 1829, Audubon (2006), pp. 282–283, Herrick (1938) I, p. 427.

194. Rhodes (2004), pp. 338–339; L. Audubon (1869), p. 203. During Audubon's three years abroad, Nicholas Berthoud had generally declined to respond to his letters. JJA, London to VGA, Louisville, 22 Dec. 1828 (APS), *Letters* I, p. 74. Whether the time he spent with the Berthouds in Shippingport warmed their frosty relationship cannot be discerned from the limited record of this period. However, within a few years, Berthoud was serving as Audubon's agent for *BOA* in New York. See Chapter 3.

195. L. Audubon (1869), p. 203. See also, Rhodes (2004), p. 339. Before leaving Louisville, Audubon drafted a will with directions to his son Victor as to the manner in which he desired his affairs to be settled in the event either he or both he and Lucy died during their journey. JJA, Louis-

ville to VGA, Louisville, 2 Mar. 1830 (Yale, Box 1, Folder 4), *Letters* I, pp. 103–105.

196. L. Audubon (1869), p. 203; LBA, Washington City to William Bakewell, Louisville, 17 Mar. 1830 (Shaffer Collection, FV2003.08.008). See also, Rhodes (2004), p. 339. Audubon wrote to his sons that the subscription that he procured during his visit to Washington City was that of the U.S. House of Representatives. In fact, it was approved by the Joint Committee of the Library of Congress. He subsequently obtained four more subscriptions, one from a Russian envoy in Washington City and three during a visit to Baltimore while traveling to New York. Fries (1973), p. 40; L. Audubon (1869), p. 203. Audubon left America richer by five subscriptions (six if you count the one placed by Benjamin Smith, MP, while en route to New York), as he relayed to his friend William Swainson upon his return to London. JJA, London to William Swainson, Tittenhanger Green, 5 May 1830 (Linnean Society).

197. Jackson (2013), p. 11; Rhodes (2004), p. 339 and note, p. 470; Herrick (1938) I, p. 437; L. Audubon (1869), p. 203; JJA, At Sea to Robert Havell Jr., London, 27 Apr. 1830 (Harvard (14)); JJA, Louisville to Robert Havell Jr., 29 Jan. 1830 (Harvard (13)), *Letters* I, pp. 102–103. Rhodes asserts that the Audubons sailed from New York on April 2 rather than April 1. This is based upon Audubon's statement in Lucy's biography that their trip across the Atlantic took twenty-five days along with his April 27 letter to Havell indicating that they would dock later that day in Liverpool. However, the New York-Liverpool packets of the Black Ball Line, of which the *Pacific* was a proud member, operated on strict schedules. "Rain or shine, blow high, blow low, one of the Black Ball liners sailed from New York for Liverpool on the first and sixteenth of each month, and for many years these were the European mail days throughout the United States." Clark (1911), pp. 38–40. While it is possible the *Pacific* was delayed a day in leaving New York, Audubon was not always exact when it came to timekeeping. In this instance, I am inclined to believe that his statement of the duration of the voyage was off by a day. In any case, Ford errs in stating that the Audubons arrived in Liverpool on April 2. Ford (1988), p. 271.

198. JJA, Manchester to LBA, Liverpool, 30 Apr. 1830 (APS), *Letters* I, p. 106. According to

Fries, Audubon exhibited his drawings in Manchester between May 1 and the first week of June. Fries (1973), p. 42. See also, JJA, Liverpool to Robert Havell Jr., London, 7 Jun. 1830 (Harvard (17)), *Letters* I, p. 106. Ford's contention that the exhibit was open for only five days appears to be in error. Ford (1988), p. 273.

199. Rhodes (2004), p. 340; Ford (1988), p. 271. Rhodes points out that Ann Bakewell Gordon "suffered from episodic pelvic inflammation," the likely sequella of the delivery of her first and only child, William, in 1828. At that time, physicians were unaware of the role played by bacteria in causing infections and frequently failed to follow aseptic hygiene practices during childbirth. Rhodes (2004), p. 340; Bakewell (1896), pp. 27-28. As a consequence, bacteria could be introduced into the female reproductive tract and lead to puerperal infection, a major cause of maternal death. If not fatal, the sepsis could leave a woman infertile and suffering from chronic pelvic inflammatory disease. Kochhar (1985), pp. 73-75. This is a likely explanation for why Ann Gordon did not bear additional children.

200. L. Audubon (1869), p. 204. Audubon was elected a Fellow of the Royal Society of London on March 18, 1830. Deane (1905), p. 252, note 1.

201. Rhodes (2004), p. 341. Audubon had been elected a member of the Zoological Society of London on February 24, 1828. Deane (1905), p. 249, note 1; *AHJ* I, p. 284. He learned of his newly minted status as a member of the Linnean Society of London on April 1, 1828, after the election had occurred. *AHJ* I, p. 294.

News of Audubon's election to the Royal Society of London was received with disbelief by some of the members of the Academy of Natural Sciences of Philadelphia when it was announced at a regular meeting by Audubon's friend Richard Harlan, M.D. However, as Harlan was quick to say, others rejoiced, including the painter Thomas Sully. Richard Harlan, M.D., Philadelphia to JJA, London, 19 Aug. 1830 (Yale, Box 4, Folder 172). See also, Rhodes (2004), pp. 341-342; Souder (2004), p. 251.

Rhodes errs in asserting that "Benjamin Franklin had been the only other American to be honored up to that time with an F.R.S. [Fellow Royal Society]." Rhodes (2004), p. 341. Actually, a number of Americans besides Franklin were elected

fellows of the Royal Society prior to 1830. For a list of colonial members awarded the distinction up to 1788, see Stearns (1951). Even after American Independence, distinguished scientists from the U.S. continued to be recognized with membership as Fellows in the Royal Society, including James Bowdoin, the second Governor of the Commonwealth of Massachusetts and a founder of the American Academy of Arts and Sciences (on April 3, 1788); David Rittenhouse, a Philadelphia instrument maker, astronomer, and mathematician (on April 16, 1795); and David Hosack, a New York physician (on May 23, 1816). Nathaniel Bowditch, a mathematician and author of *The New American Practical Navigator*, was elected as a Foreign Member (on March 12, 1818) but still referred to himself as a Fellow of the Royal Society. Royal Society (2007); Home (2002), p. 329, note 16; Stearns (1951), pp. 242-244; Bowditch (1826).

202. Fries (1973), p. 42. Audubon instructed Robert Havell Jr. in a letter dated October 27, 1829, to have John G. Children of the British Museum place an advertisement in *The Times* of London to advise his subscribers that he would indeed be returning to England to complete *BOA*, obviously hoping this would prevent additional subscribers from dropping their subscriptions. JJA, Philadelphia to Robert Havell Jr., London, 27 Oct. 1829 (Harvard (10)), *Letters* I, p. 101.

203. JJA, Liverpool to Robert Havell Jr., London, 7 Jun. 1830 (Harvard (17)), *Letters* I, p. 107. See also, Fries (1973), pp. 42-43.

204. JJA, Birmingham to Robert Havell Jr., London, 29 Jun. 1830 (Harvard (18)), *Letters* I, pp. 112-113.

205. JJA, Birmingham to Robert Havell Jr., London, 1 Jul. 1830 (Harvard (19)), *Letters* I, p. 113-114; Robert Havell Jr., London to JJA, Birmingham, 30 Jun. 1830 (Harvard (352)). Rhodes indicates that Havell's June 30 letter is at the APS. Rhodes (2004), p. 342 and note, p. 470. It is actually at Harvard.

206. JJA, New Castle on Tyne to Robert Havell Jr., London, 30 Sept. 1830 (Harvard (26)), *Letters* I, p. 118. See also, Rhodes (2004), p. 345. Rhodes misdates the cited letter as September 20, 1830. Rhodes (2004), p. 345 and note, p. 470. Rhodes also errs in stating that Audubon had seen the proofs of No. 19 when he visited Leeds in mid-

September. Ibid., pp. 344–345. In fact, Audubon first saw them while he was in Newcastle, where he arrived on September 29. JJA, New Castle on Tyne to Robert Havell Jr., London, 30 Sept. 1830 (Harvard (26)), *Letters* I, pp. 117–118. Audubon had been in Leeds on September 8. In a letter to Havell on that date, he noted that he had previously written and directed the engraver to forward the "finished proofs of N° 19. to New Castle." JJA, Leeds to Robert Havell Jr., London, 8 Sept. 1830 (Harvard (23)), *Letters* I, p. 115.

207. Rhodes (2004), p. 343; JJA, Birmingham to Robert Havell Jr., London, 29 Jun. 1830 (Harvard (18)), *Letters* I, p. 113; JJA, Birmingham to Robert Havell Jr., London, 1 Jul. 1830 (Harvard (19)), *Letters* I, pp. 113–114.

208. Jackson (2013), p. 12; Fries (1973), p. 44; L. Audubon (1869), p. 204..

209. L. Audubon (1869), p. 204.

210. Fries (1973), p. 47. Audubon had mentioned his plans to publish a separate letterpress years earlier when he wrote to William Rathbone on November 24, 1826. JJA, Edinburgh to William Rathbone, Liverpool, 24 Nov. 1826, Audubon (2011), p. 308, Ford (1987), p. 347. Note that Maria Audubon lifted substantial portions of this letter and rewrote them as a journal entry for that date. *AHJ* I, pp. 163–164. The original holograph of the 1826 journal in the collection of the Field Museum in Chicago does not contain an entry for November 24. (NYHS Misc. Microfilm Reel 29).

Audubon's decision to keep the text of the *OB* separate from the prints was both a practical and financial one. Under the British Copyright Act of 1709 [1710], also known as the Statute of Anne, an author was required to deposit eleven copies of a printed work at Stationer's Hall for distribution to eleven libraries throughout the United Kingdom. Jackson (1985), p. 204; Fries (1973), p. 47; JJA, Edinburgh to Robert Havell Jr., London, 12 Mar. 1831 (Harvard (37)), *Letters* I, p. 131.

Several Audubon scholars have asserted that only nine copies were mandated. Souder (2004), p. 255; Chalmers (2003), p. 128; Fries (1973), pp. 47, 51. However, in 1801, when Ireland became part of the United Kingdom, two additional copies had to be deposited for Trinity College and King's Inns in Dublin. Copyright Act, London (1801), Commen-

tary, Primary Sources on Copyright (1450–1900), Section VI, p. 210, Bently, L. & M. Kretschmer, eds., www.copyrighthistory.org. See also, van Gompel (2011) p. 77, note 176. The mandate did not apply to purely illustrated works. Fries (1973), p. 51. By keeping his two productions separate, Audubon was saved the significant cost of donating eleven copies of *BOA* to Britain's libraries.

211. JJA, Manchester to William Swainson, Tittenhanger Green, 22 Aug. 1830 (Linnean Society), Herrick (1938) II, pp. 101–102. See also, Chalmers (2003), p. 128.

212. JJA, Edinburgh to Charles-Lucien Bonaparte, 2 Jan. 1831 (APS), Audubon (2006), p. 313. In addition to co-authorship, Swainson also insisted on the standard remuneration he reportedly received from booksellers for similar work, being 12 guineas (approximately $1,500 in 2016 dollars) per sheet of sixteen pages, which would run approximately 6,240 words. In addition, he indicated that he charged extra "to revise and correct the proofs, make alterations etc." based on the time required, which would run between 5 shillings and 7 shillings, 6 pence per sheet. William Swainson, Tittenhanger Green, to JJA, Manchester, 26 Aug. 1830 (Yale, Box 6, Folder 330), Herrick (1938) I, p. 105. According to the original holograph, Audubon answered Swainson's letter on August 29, 1830.

213. Rhodes (2004), pp. 343–344.

214. William Swainson, Tittenhanger Green to JJA, London, 2 Oct. 1830, Herrick (1938) II, pp. 106–108, Coues (1898), pp. 11–13. See also, Rhodes (2004), pp. 343–344. In an irate reply to Audubon's rejection of his proposal, Swainson pointed out that Audubon's refusal to list him as a co-author of the letterpress would deprive him of the credit for his contribution:

You pay me compliments on my scientific knowledge, and wished you possessed a portion; & you liken the acquisition of such a portion to purchasing the sketch of an eminent painter — the simile is good. but allow me to ask you, whether, after procuring the sketch, you would mix it up with your own, and pass it off to your friends as your production? I cannot possibly suppose that such would be your duplicity and I therefore must not suppose that you intended that I should give all the scientific information I have laboured to acquire during twenty years on ornithology—conceal my name,—and transfer my fame to your pages & to your reputation.

Herrick (1938) II, pp. 106-107, Coues (1898), p. 12. Despite the falling out between Swainson and Audubon, they remained cordial if not the close friends they had been earlier. Chalmers (2003), pp. 129-130. In October 1830, while in Edinburgh, Audubon was approached and asked to serve as editor for a new edition of Alexander Wilson's work at a salary of £200. He declined but recommended Swainson in his stead. JJA, Edinburgh to Robert Havell Jr., London, 31 Oct. 1830 (Harvard (28)), *Letters* I, p. 122. The following April, Audubon and Lucy returned to London and found a letter from Swainson, dated April 17. It must have been the first letter Audubon had received from him in quite some time because he remarked in his response that he thought Swainson had dropped him from his list of correspondents. JJA, London to William Swainson at Tittenhanger Green, 28 Apr. 1831 (Linnean Society). Audubon also sent Swainson a copy of the recently published first volume of the *OB*, in which he mentioned Swainson's favorable review of *BOA*. Ibid. Audubon was still very grateful. Ultimately, Swainson named a woodpecker after Audubon, and Audubon gave Swainson's name to a new warbler when he published the second volume of the *OB* in 1834. Chalmers (2003), pp. 129-130; Mearns (1992), pp. 419, 421.

215. Chalmers (2003), pp. 90, 93-94, 146-147; *OB* I, pp. xviii-xix.

216. JJA, Edinburgh to Robert Havell Jr., London, 18 Nov. 1830 (Harvard (29)), *Letters* I, p. 123; L. Audubon (1869), pp. 205-206. When Audubon wrote to Havell on November 18, 1830, he reported that "¼ of the book is nearly ready for press."

217. Fries (1973), p. 50; L. Audubon (1869), pp. 205-206; JJA, Edinburgh to Robert Havell Jr., London, 18 Nov. 1830 (Harvard (29)), *Letters* I, p. 123. Audubon had originally intended to charge his subscribers one guinea (21 shillings) for the volume but later relented and issued it to them free of charge. For non-subscribers, the price was 25 shillings. Fries (1973), p. 50.

While Audubon and MacGillivray were writing

the text, Lucy copied the manuscript for shipment to Philadelphia to insure they secured the copyright in America. L. Audubon (1869), p. 206; JJA, Edinburgh to Robert Havell Jr., London, 18 Nov. 1830 (Harvard (29)), *Letters* I, p. 124. Working with his good friend Richard Harlan, M.D., along with Henry McMurtrie, M.D., Audubon was able to publish the first American edition of the work shortly after the English edition appeared in 1831. JJA, Edinburgh to Henry McMurtry [McMurtrie], M.D., Philadelphia, 21 Feb. 1831 (APS), *Letters* I, pp. 128-129. When the artist wrote to his son Victor on February 21, 1831, he reported that he had instructed Harlan to obtain a copyright for the work in Victor's name, as he was "not very anxious to possess any property in the United States," a reflection of his continuing concern about potential claims by his Kentucky creditors. JJA, Edinburgh to VGA, Louisville (APS), 21 Feb. 1831, *Letters* I, p. 126. See also, Rhodes (2004), p. 348. Ultimately, 500 copies were printed with Harlan's name as the copyright holder. Fries (1973), pp. 50-51; Herrick (1938) II, p. 403. Lucy explained to Victor in a letter on February 26, 1831, that Harlan would obtain the copyright in his own name if he did not find it "practicable" to enter it in Victor's. LBA, Edinburgh to VGA, Louisville, 26 Feb. 1831, Audubon (2006), p. 316.

218. L. Audubon (1869), p. 206. Lucy's biography contains a supposed journal entry by Audubon on March 20, 1831, that references his agreement with Joseph Bartholomew Kidd (1808-1889) to copy in oils the drawings illustrated in the first volume of *BOA*: "Made an arrangement with Mr. J.B. Kidd, a young painter whom I have known for the last four years, to copy some of my drawings in oil, and to put backgrounds to them, so as to make them appear like pictures. It was our intention to send them to the exhibition for sale, and to divide the amount between us. He painted eight, and then I proposed, if he would paint the one hundred engravings which comprise my first volume of the 'Birds of America,' I would pay him one hundred pounds." L. Audubon (1869), pp. 206-207. Herrick indicates that the agreement was reached on March 31, but he offers no source to substantiate this date. Herrick (1938) I, p. 446.

Souder claims that Audubon had hired Kidd in early 1827 as part of "an ambitious partnership" to reproduce each of his watercolor drawings. Souder (2004), p. 226. His assertion is evidently based upon a footnote in Ford's edition of the 1826 journal, where she contends that Audubon hired the young landscape artist "to copy his *Birds* in oil" only "a matter of weeks" after what she believes may have been their first meeting on November 27, 1826. Ford (1988), p. 354, note 36. Their claim is inconsistent with a multitude of other evidence.

The first mention of Kidd by name in any of Audubon's journal entries is on March 1, 1827, when the naturalist indicated he had breakfasted with the nineteen-year-old painter, described as "a promising young artist in landscape." L. Audubon (1869), p. 139. The journal entry continues: "I invited him to come to my rooms daily, and to eat and drink with me, and give me the pleasure of his company and the advantage of his taste in painting. I told him of my ardent desire to improve in the delightful art, and proposed to begin a new picture, in which he should assist with his advice; and proposing to begin it to-morrow, I took down my portfolio, to select a drawing to copy in oil. He had never seen my works before, and appeared astonished as his eyes ranged over the sheets." Ibid., p. 140.

The copy of this entry in Maria Audubon's published European Journals is slightly reworded, although the substance is the same. Maria's version of the journal also includes a mention that Audubon painted with Kidd the following day. *AHJ* I, pp. 214–215. The painting was apparently finished on March 6. L. Audubon (1869), p. 142. On March 22, Audubon wrote that he had "paid young Kidd three guineas for his picture," and the following day's entry relates that they breakfasted together. *AHJ* I, p. 224.

Audubon left Edinburgh for London in early April 1827 and met Kidd there by chance in June. There are three references in his journal to Kidd (June 1, 2, and 18), but nothing anywhere in the published fragments of the 1827 journal to validate Ford's and Souder's claim that Audubon had hired him to copy all or even a portion of the original drawings of *BOA*. *AHJ* I, pp. 254–256.

It would appear that Audubon did not even begin to think about turning his watercolors into oil paintings for an exhibition until sometime in 1828, as he disclosed in a letter to Victor on December 22.

He told his son that "I have a Pupil whom I think will copy all my Original Drawings in oil & *turn them into pictures* with which I intend to have a perpetual exhibition." JJA, London to VGA, Louisville, 22 Dec. 1828 (APS), *Letters* I, p. 75. Clearly, at that time, the project was only a dream for Audubon, not a reality.

In fact, Audubon's idea of creating permanent oil copies of his drawings did not begin to crystallize until late 1830, when he had returned to Edinburgh and evidently encountered Kidd once more. On November 26, Kidd signed a document in which he agreed "to copy in oil one hundred of Mr J.J. Audubon's drawings," being those in the first volume of *BOA*, "for the sum of One hundred Pounds Sterling money," with "Audubon furnishing at his expense the canvasses and mill boards, and myself the colours, varnishes and brushes." Agreement signed by J. B. Kidd (Yale, Box 5, Folder 210). Although this document is not countersigned by Audubon, four days later, on November 30, Audubon wrote to Havell and asked the printer to make arrangements to send him one hundred canvasses sized to fit the three image sizes of the prints. JJA, Edinburgh to Robert Havell Jr., London, 18 Nov. 1830 (Harvard (29)), *Letters* I, pp. 123–124. Thus, it would appear that Audubon and Kidd had struck a deal several months before the naturalist mentioned it in his March 20, 1831, journal entry.

The original agreement called on Kidd to complete the paintings from the first one hundred drawings by May 1, 1831. On April 12, 1831, Kidd acknowledged receipt of £33 in payment for "Thirty-four pictures of our '*mutual agreement*,' Eight of which belong to the *second volume*." Receipt signed by J.B. Kidd (Yale, Box 5, Folder 210). According to Fries, Kidd ultimately produced a total of ninety-four paintings, including several from the second volume, before the arrangement ended in December 1833. Fries (1973), Appendix C, pp. 361–366. For a detailed discussion of the history of Kidd's involvement with *BOA*, see Fries (1973), Appendix C, pp. 360–367.

219. L. Audubon (1869), p. 139–140. See also, *AHJ* I, pp. 214–215. Kidd began serving as Audubon's agent in Edinburgh during the spring of 1828, evidently replacing Daniel Lizars. Joseph B. Kidd, Edinburgh to JJA, London, 8 May 1828 (Yale,

Box 5, Folder 207); Joseph B. Kidd, Edinburgh to JJA, London, 24 Apr. 1828 (Yale, Box 5, Folder 207); Joseph B. Kidd, Edinburgh to JJA, London, 2 Apr. 1828 (Yale, Box 5, Folder 207). The arrangement only lasted about a year. In March 1829, Kidd indicated that he expected to summer in the country doing landscape studies and suggested that Audubon place the work in the hands of a Mr. Hall "at once." Joseph B. Kidd, Edinburgh to JJA, London (Yale, Box 5, Folder 209).

220. Fries (1973), p. 362; JJA, Edinburgh to Robert Havell Jr., London, 18 Nov. 1830, *Letters* I, p. 125.

221. Fries (1973), pp. 53–54; L. Audubon (1869), p. 207.

222. L. Audubon (1869), p. 207; JJA, London to William Swainson, Tittenhanger Green, 28 Apr. 1831 (Linnean Society), Herrick (1938) II, p. 112.

223. JJA, London to William Swainson, Tittenhanger Green, 28 Apr. 1831 (Linnean Society), Herrick (1938) II, p. 112. The Audubons left for Paris on May 6, 1831, and returned on June 4, 1831. Ibid. See also, JJA, London to William Swainson, Tittenhanger Green, 6 Jun. 1831 (Linnean Society). Rhodes is incorrect in placing the Paris trip in the month of July. Rhodes (2004), p. 341.

As early as February 1831, Audubon was anticipating making another trip to America in August of that year, as he told Henry McMurtrie, M.D., saying "recollect that we will sail for New York about the 1st of Aug.t next." JJA, Edinburgh to Henry McMurtry [McMurtrie], M.D., Philadelphia, 21 Feb. 1831 (APS), *Letters* I, p. 129. He had earlier written Charles-Lucien Bonaparte on January 2, 1831, to announce his plans to return to America that year. Rhodes (2004), p. 348.

224. JJA, Portsmouth Harbour to Robert Havell Jr., London, 31 Jul. 1831, *Letters* I, p. 135.

225. Rhodes (2004), pp. 348–349. See also, JJA, Edinburgh to Robert Havell Jr., London, 16 Jan. 1831 (Harvard (34)). Rhodes asserts that after Audubon urged Havell in 1831 to ratchet up the production of the Numbers from five to six per annum, "Havell could and did." Rhodes (2004), p. 348. Actually, Havell issued only five Numbers in 1831 (Nos. 21–25, Plates 101–125) and 1832 (Nos. 26–30, Plates 126–150). Fries (1973), pp. 399–400. It was not until 1833 that Havell exceeded five Numbers

in one year. No. 31 (Plates 151–155), which Fries indicates was engraved in 1832, was not completed and delivered to subscribers until early 1833. VGA, Liverpool to JJA, New York, 15 Jan. 1833 (Yale, Box 15, Folder 693). Havell shipped No. 31 to the American subscribers on March 8. VGA, London to JJA, New York, 29 Mar. 1833 (Yale, Box 15, Folder 693). On June 15, Havell wrote to the naturalist to say that No. 33 (Plates 161–165) was finished and issued to subscribers. Herrick (1938) II, p. 51. Havell would engrave and issue four more Numbers during the course of that year, through No. 37 (Plates 181–185), for a total of seven. VGA, London to JJA, New York, 26 Dec. 1833 (Yale, Box 15, Folder 693).

226. Audubon informed Havell that when he reached New York on September 3, 1831, he "delivered copies of N°s 21, 22 & 23 to Major Lang for Mr Edd Harris," which would indicate that his friend Edward Harris of Moorestown, NJ, had already subscribed. JJA, Philadelphia to Robert Havell Jr., London, 20 Sept. 1831 (Harvard (42)), *Letters* I, p. 136. The two men, who had originally met in Philadelphia in 1824, renewed their acquaintance when Harris visited London in late July, shortly before the Audubons sailed for New York. Herrick (1938) I, p. 448; JJA, London to Edward Harris, London, 27 Jul. 1831 (Harvard (Letters), pf (110), p. 4). This is evidently when Harris added his name as a subscriber. Cf. Fries (1973), pp. 56–57. Their meeting, however, must have been bittersweet. Harris had recently buried his wife, Mary, in Leghorn (Livorno), Italy, where he had taken her in the hope the warm Mediterranean climate would restore her health. Her father, John Lang (c. 1769–1836), was the owner and publisher of the *New-York Gazette & General Advertiser*. Read (1979), p. 7; Stokes (1918), p. 378; Brigham (1917), pp. 426–427.

227. JJA, Philadelphia to Robert Havell Jr., London, 20 Sept. 1831, *Letters* I, pp. 136–137; JJA, New York to Richard Harlan, M.D., Philadelphia, 3 Sept. 1831 (Private collection, sold by Heritage Auctions, Lot 34163, 4 Oct. 2012). Nicholas Berthoud and his family were now living in New York, having left Shippingport evidently as a result of the construction of the Louisville-Portland Canal, which enabled Ohio River traffic to completely bypass the Falls of the Ohio and Shippingport. Rhodes (2004), pp. 337, 349.

228. Fries (1973), p. 56; JJA, Philadelphia to Robert Havell Jr., London, 20 Sept. 1831 (Harvard (42)), *Letters* I, p. 136.

229. JJA, Philadelphia to Robert Havell Jr., London, 20 Sept. 1831 (Harvard (42)), *Letters* I, pp. 136–137.

230. Rhodes (2004), p. 350.

231. Ibid.; Levi Woodbury, Navy Department to Louis McLane, Secretary of the Treasury, 24 Feb. 1832, Herrick (1938) II, pp. 23–24. JJA, St. Augustine to LBA, Louisville, 16 Jan. 1832 (APS), *Letters* I, p. 172.

232. JJA, Richmond to LBA, Louisville, 9 Oct. 1831 (APS), *Letters* I, pp. 137–139.

233. Rhodes (2004), pp. 350–351; JJA, Charleston to LBA, Louisville, 23 Oct. 1831 (APS), *Letters* I, pp. 142–143; JJA, Fayetteville, NC, to LBA, Louisville, 13 Oct. 1831 (APS), *Letters* I, pp. 140–141; JJA, Richmond to LBA, Louisville, 9 Oct. 1831 (APS), *Letters* I, pp. 137–139.

234. Rhodes (2004), pp. 351–352; Shuler (1995), p. 4; Sanders & Ripley (1985), pp. 36–37; JJA, Charleston to LBA, Louisville, 23 Oct. 1831 (APS), *Letters* I, pp. 142–144. John Bachman pronounced his surname "BACK-mun." Stephens (2000), p. 1; LBA, Boston to VGA, London, 30 Oct. 1832 (Yale, Box 1, Folder 5). Cf. Hamel (1995), p. 1 ("BACK-man"). Bachman's blue eyes are evident in John W. Audubon's portrait painted in about 1840, now in the collection of the Charleston Museum.

235. JJA, Charleston to LBA, Louisville, 7 Nov. 1831 (APS), *Letters* I, p. 148.

236. Rhodes (2004), pp. 352–353; JJA, St. Augustine to LBA, Louisville, 23 Nov. 1831, *Letters* I, p. 151.

237. JJA, St. Augustine to LBA, Louisville, 5 Dec. 1831 (APS), *Letters* I, p. 161; JJA, St. Augustine to LBA, Louisville, 29 Nov. 1831, *Letters* I, p. 155. The species that Audubon discovered and believed to be part of a new genus for the U.S. was the Crested Caracara (*Caracara cheriway*), a long legged raptor. Under the Linnean system of classification of living things, developed by the famous Swedish scientist Carl Linnaeus (1707–1778), a "genus" is the larger group into which related species are placed. Multiple genera make up a "family," which along with any related families is placed in an "order." Multiple orders make up the class, in this case that of birds.

238. JJA, St. Augustine to LBA, Louisville, 5 Dec. 1831 (APS), *Letters* I, p. 159.

239. Ibid., p. 161.

240. Rhodes (2004), pp. 358–359. JJA, Gen[l] Hernandez's Plantation, 28 Miles South of S[t] Augustine to LBA, Louisville, 24 Dec. 1831 (Yale, Box 1, Folder 3).

241. JJA, Bulow's Plantation, FL, to LBA, Louisville, 4 Jan. 1832, *Letters* I, p. 171.

242. King (1989), pp. 5, 9–10; JJA, St. Augustine to LBA, Louisville, 16 Jan. 1832 (APS), *Letters* I, p. 172. Treasury Secretary Louis McLane's letter read:

> To the officers commanding Revenue Cutters on the Charleston, Key West and Mobile Station. Treasury Department 23[d] of Dec[r] 1831—
>
> M[r] John J. Audubon a distinguished Naturalist at present engaged in a Scientific excursion in the Territory of the Floridas having requested that the commanding officers of the Revenue Cutters employed on that Coast may be permitted to convey him and those associated with him and their baggage to and from certain points within the Limits of their cruising Stations;— and the Department feeling disposed to lend to the cause of Science every aid which may not be incompatible with a just regard to the public Service, I have to request that you will receive M[r] Audubon and his party with their effects on Board the Cutter under your command at any port where they may present themselves and where you may happen to be; and also that you will convey them to such other point within your cruising limits where the duties appertaining to the Revenue [Cutter] Service may lead you and where they may wish to go.—I am respect.y Sir
> 　　Your Ob[t] Ser[t]
> 　　Louis McLane
> 　　Secretary of the Treasury

The Revenue Cutter Service was the forerunner of what ultimately became the U.S. Coast Guard. King (1989), p. x.

243. JJA, St. John's River off Jacksonville to LBA, Louisville, 9 Feb. 1832, *Letters* I, p. 180; JJA, St. Augustine to LBA, Louisville, 16 Jan. 1832 (APS), *Letters* I, pp. 172–173.

244. Rhodes (2004), pp. 361–362; JJA, 100 miles up the St. John's River, FL, to LBA, Louisville, 17 Feb. 1832, *Letters* I, p. 182; JJA, St. Augustine to LBA, Louisville, 16 Jan. 1832 (APS), *Letters* I, pp. 172–173.

245. Rhodes (2004), p. 362.

246. Rhodes (2004), p. 362; JJA, Charleston to LBA, Louisville, 13 Mar. 1832 (APS), *Letters* I, p. 184. Fries claims, in error, that Audubon's party returned to Charleston aboard the naval schooner *Spark*. Fries (1973), p. 60. As Audubon stated in his March 13 letter to Lucy, they left St. Augustine on March 5 as passengers aboard the packet *Agnes*. Forty miles from port, they were caught in a gale and forced to put in at Savannah, GA, on March 8.

247. JJA, Charleston to LBA, Louisville, 13 Mar. 1832 (APS), *Letters* I, p. 184.

248. Fries (1973), p. 60; JJA, Charleston to LBA, Louisville, 13 Mar. 1832 (APS), *Letters* I, pp. 184–187.

249. JJA, Charleston to LBA, Louisville, 13 Mar. 1832 (APS), *Letters* I, pp. 184–187.

250. JJA, Charleston to LBA, Louisville, 15 Apr. 1832 (APS), *Letters* I, p. 193. See also, Shuler (1995), p. 88.

251. Rhodes (2004), pp. 364–368.

252. Shuler (1995), p. 89.

253. Hammond (1963), pp. 462–463.

254. Rhodes (2004), p. 368; Shuler (1995), p. 91. Audubon was back at the home of John Bachman in Charleston by June 5, 1832. In June 2011, Christie's auctioned a lock of his hair that was evidently cut upon his return from his Florida expedition. The lot included an envelope with the annotation "Given to me by J. James Audubon Es^q at the Revd John Bachman June 5 1832." Christie's (2011), Lot 204. The recipient was evidently Henry Ward. "Audubon's Hair," News from minniesland.com (accessed 15 Sept. 2011).

255. Shuler (1995), p. 93; JJA, Philadelphia to John Bachman, Charleston, 1 Jul. 1832 (Harvard (50)), *Letters* I, p. 195. During the month of June 1832, Audubon drew a new species of sparrow that Bachman had discovered and that Audubon named Bachman's Sparrow. Shuler (1995), p. 92; Audubon (1966) II, Plate 363. Bachman had also discovered a new species of warbler that Audubon subsequently named after William Swainson. However,

this was evidently not illustrated until the winter of 1833–1834, and then by Audubon's son John. Shuler (1995), pp. 91–92; Audubon (1966) I, Plate 153. Havell issued it as Plate 198.

256. LBA, Boston to Euphemia Gifford, Derbyshire, England, 7 Oct. 1832, Audubon (2006), p. 370; JJA, Camden, NJ to Edward Harris, Moorestown, NJ, 9 June [July] 1832 (Harvard (Letters), pf (110), p. 5). See also, Rhodes (2004), pp. 368–369. After arriving in Philadelphia, Audubon initially stayed at the National Hotel but found it too expensive. Consequently, he moved his operations to Camden, NJ, where he boarded at the same boardinghouse operated by Mr. Armstrong on Plum Street as he had on his previous visits. JJA, Camden, NJ, to Edward Harris, Moorestown, NJ, 9 June [July] 1832 (Harvard (Letters), pf (110), p. 5). Referring to this June 9 letter, Rhodes states in an endnote that "Joseph Jeanes's transcription is misdated 9 June, when JJA had not yet left Charleston." Rhodes (2004), p. 473, note 368. Joseph Jeanes (1859–1928) was an early collector of Auduboniana, who donated his collection to Harvard. Audubon (2008), pp. x-xi. In fact, the original holograph letter at the Houghton Library is dated June 9, an error on Audubon's part.

Audubon illustrated three species during his July 1832 stay in Camden: Rough-legged Hawk, King Rail, and Barn Owl. Rhodes (2004), pp. 368–369.

257. JJA, Philadelphia to John Bachman, Charleston, 1 Jul. 1832 (Harvard (50)), *Letters* I, pp. 195–196; Waterton (Apr. 1832). See also, Chalmers (2003), pp. 136.

258. Chalmers (2003), pp. 132, 136; Ford (1988), pp. 299–301.

259. LBA, Boston to Euphemia Gifford, Derbyshire, England, 7 Oct. 1832, Audubon (2006), p. 370. See also, Rhodes (2004), p. 369. According to Lucy's letter to her English cousin, she left Louisville with her sons at the end of June 1832, but low water in the Ohio delayed their arrival in Pittsburgh. They visited her uncle, Benjamin Bakewell, and his family before evidently taking a stage across the mountains to Philadelphia.

In describing the significance of the Audubons reuniting as a family in July 1832, Rhodes asserts that the "family had not lived together since Henderson." Rhodes (2004), p. 370. In fact, as his own biography attests, the Audubons had lived together as a family in multiple locations since leaving Henderson in 1819, including Louisville (1819–1820), Cincinnati (1820), New Orleans (1821–1822), Natchez (1822), and Beech Woods (1823). Audubon and Lucy had also spent time with both boys in Louisville during the early months of 1830 before sailing for England. Ibid., pp. 142–143, 147, 208, 213, 215–217, 338.

260. LBA, Boston to Euphemia Gifford, Derbyshire, England, 7 Oct. 1832, Audubon (2006), p. 370; JJA, New York to Robert Havell Jr., London, 31 Jul. 1832 (Harvard (51)). See also, Rhodes (2004), p. 369; JJA, Boston to Edward Harris, Moorestown, NJ, 14 Aug. 1832 (Harvard (Letters), pf (110), p. 6). The Audubon family arrived in New York on the evening of July 30 and left the following afternoon for Boston.

261. JJA, Boston to Edward Harris, Moorestown, NJ, 14 Aug. 1832 (Harvard (Letters), pf (110), p. 6); JJA, New York to Robert Havell Jr., London, 31 Jul. 1832 (Harvard (51)). See also, Rhodes (2004), p. 369. The fastest route from New York to Boston was ordinarily via steamer to Providence and then by coach to Boston, but the cholera epidemic that had struck New York in the summer of 1832 effectively shut down the steamer lines between the two cities. Dow (1877), p. 12.

262. U.S. Census Bureau, *1830 Fast Facts: 10 Largest Urban Places*, https://www.census.gov/history/www/through_the_decades/fast_facts/1830_fast_facts.html (accessed 1 Aug. 2015); Wied (2008) I, p. 43. In the 1830 U.S. Census, Boston's population was 61,392. Over the next ten years, it would climb by over 50% to 93,383.

263. Weid (2008) I, pp. 44–46.

264. *OB* II, p. xvii.

265. JJA, Boston to Robert Havell Jr., London, 13 Aug. 1832 (Harvard (52)). The seven new Boston subscriptions were identified by Victor in an addendum to his father's August 13 letter to Havell: Thomas H. Perkins; G.W. Pratt (2 copies); J.G. Cushing [John Perkins Cushing]; Samuel Appleton; George C. Shattuck, M.D.; P.J. [T.] Jackson. Ibid. See also, Fries (1973), p. 67. It should be noted that the following day, August 14, Audubon reported to Edward Harris that he had procured nine new patrons, although the naturalist did not provide

the names. JJA, Boston to Edward Harris, Moorestown, NJ, 14 Aug. 1832 (Harvard (Letters), pf (110), p. 6). Rhodes takes Audubon at his word. Rhodes (2004), p. 371. This claim, however, is contradicted by a later letter from Lucy, who informed her English cousin Euphemia Gifford in early October that eight subscriptions had been received in the first two weeks of their stay. LBA, Boston to Euphemia Gifford, Derbyshire, England, 7 Oct. 1832, Audubon (2006), p. 370.

266. JJA, Boston to Edward Harris, Moorestown, NJ, 14 Aug. 1832 (Harvard (Letters), pf (110), p. 6). The three rare birds that Audubon boasted of finding in his letter to Harris were the Nuttall's Lesser Marsh Wren (Sedge Wren)(Havell Plate 175); Olive-sided Flycatcher (Havell Plate 174); and Tawny Thrush (Veery)(Havell Plate 164). Ibid. See also, Low (2002), pp. 108, 113.

267. JJA, Boston to Edward Harris, Moorestown, NJ, 1 Nov. 1832 (Harvard (Letters), pf (110), p. 7); LBA, Boston to Euphemia Gifford, Derbyshire, England, 7 Oct. 1832, Audubon (2006), pp. 370–371; JJA, Portland, ME, to Richard Harlan, M.D., Philadelphia, 2 Oct. 1832 (College of Physicians); JJA, Houlton, ME, to Richard Harlan, M.D., Philadelphia, 23 Sept. 1832 (Harvard (Letters), b (114)); JJA, Boston to Edward Harris, Moorestown, NJ, 14 Aug. 1832 (Harvard (Letters), pf (110), p. 6). Audubon recounted the details of his trip through Maine and New Brunswick in two of the Episodes in the *OB*, which he entitled "Journey in New Brunswick and Maine" and "Force of the Waters." *OB* II, pp. 97–101; 459–463.

268. Coke (1833) II, pp. 99–100.

269. JJA, Boston to Edward Harris, Moorestown, NJ, 1 Nov. 1832 (Harvard (Letters), pf (110), p. 7); LBA, Boston to Euphemia Gifford, Derbyshire, England, 7 Oct. 1832, Audubon (2006), pp. 370–371; JJA, Portland, ME, to Richard Harlan, M.D., Philadelphia, 2 Oct. 1832 (College of Physicians). Victor took passage aboard the packet *South America*, which sailed from New York on October 16, 1832. Streshinsky is mistaken in stating that he left on October 10. Cf. Streshinsky (1993), p. 278; JJA, Boston to Edward Harris, Moorestown, NJ, 1 Nov. 1832 (Harvard (Letters), pf (110), p. 7). See also, VGA holograph account of his trip to England (Yale, Box 15, Folder 717).

270. As late as January 31, 1833, when he wrote his friend Richard Harlan, M.D., Audubon was still weighing whether to travel to California or to Labrador in the coming months. JJA, Boston to Richard Harlan, M.D., Philadelphia, 31 Jan. 1833 (Yale, Box 4, Folder 176). However, it would seem that he favored Labrador because, on January 28, he had written to Victor and said he intended to journey to Labrador during the spring and summer. JJA addendum to LBA, Boston to VGA, London, 28 Jan. 1833 (Yale, Box 1, Folder 5). Apparently, he had earlier sought the counsel of his friend John Bachman, who wrote him on January 23, 1833, and offered these thoughts: "I scarcely know what answer to give to your questions — soliciting advice with regard to your travels in the Spring; but I will say something to convince you that I have thought on the subject. The only reasons why a visit to the coast of Labrador might be advisable, is, that you may be able to complete your dissertations on the habits of the Ducks, Gulls, etc. This would certainly enable you to say more with regard to the habits of our water birds, than has ever been written before; for it cannot be disguised that little, as yet, is known of water birds — and their histories are just as interesting, if properly investigated, as those of the land birds. * * * If your visit to Labrador is indispensable, you had better go in the Spring." Bachman (1888), pp. 131-132. Bachman's letter, which likely reached Boston in early February, must have sealed the deal. When the naturalist wrote his Charleston friend again on February 19, 1833, he had made up his mind and resolved to head for Labrador. JJA, Boston to John Bachman, Charleston, 19 Feb. 1833 (Harvard (53)), *Letters* I, p. 197.

271. *OB* III, p. xi.

272. JJA, Boston to John Bachman, Charleston, 19 Feb. 1833 (Harvard (53)), *Letters* I, p. 197.

273. Julia Webster, Boston to Daniel Webster, Washington City, 3 Mar. 1833, Curtis (1870) I, p. 459; JJA, Boston to James Curtiss, Eastport, 25 Jan. 1833 (Private collection).

274. JJA, Boston to VGA, London, 5 Feb. [Mar.] 1833, Herrick (1938) II, p. 35, Deane (1905), p. 171; JJA, Boston to VGA, London, 24 Feb. 1833 (APS), *Letters* I, p. 200; JJA, Boston to Richard Harlan, M.D., Philadelphia, 31 Jan. 1833 (Yale, Box 4, Folder 176). See also, Rhodes (2004), p. 379. Audubon was still awaiting receipt of copies of *BOA* for his Boston subscribers, which would enable him to collect the subscription price from those who had yet to pay. JJA, Boston to VGA, London, 1 Apr. 1833 (APS), *Letters* I, p. 202; JJA, Boston to Richard Harlan, M.D., Philadelphia, 31 Jan. 1833 (Yale, Box 4, Folder 176). However, the prints were aboard the vessel *Charlotte*, which had yet to reach port.

275. *OB* IV, p. 271; *OB* III, p 336; JJA, Boston to VGA, London, 6 Nov. 1832 (APS); JJA, Boston to James Curtiss, Eastport, 25 Jan. 1833 (Private collection).

276. JJA addendum to LBA, Boston to VGA, London, 28 Jan. 1833 (Yale, Box 1, Folder 5).

277. LBA, Boston to Mrs. Robert Havell Jr., London, 15 Feb. 1833 (Harvard (Letters), b (119)). Ford asserts that U.S. Senator Daniel Webster was among the distinguished Bostonians who came to call on Audubon during his stay in the city. Ford (1988), p. 302–303. Streshinsky repeats the claim. Streshinsky (1993), p. 278. There is, however, no confirmatory evidence of this.

Both biographers evidently rely upon the *OB*, where Audubon wrote that Webster "gave" him specimens of the Red-headed Duck (Redhead) as well as "sent" him a pair of the Pied Duck (Labrador Duck) to illustrate for *BOA*. *OB* IV, pp. 200, 271. In neither case did Audubon say that he had met the senator. Nor did he indicate when any of this occurred. In his 1836 journal, Audubon suggested that the first time he met Webster was on September 29, 1836: "Mr. Isaac P. Davis called to invite me to spend the evening at his house, and to meet Daniel Webster." During their discussion, Webster promised to send Audubon some bird specimens. Whether this was their first meeting or not is unclear. In the same journal entry, Audubon stated that when Webster arrived, "we welcomed each other as friends indeed." L. Audubon (1869), p. 391.

Regardless, based on when Havell issued the prints of these two species, it is plain that Audubon had drawn these ducks before September 1836. Havell published Audubon's drawing of the male and female Redheads in 1836 as Plate 322. Low (2002), p. 167; *OB* IV, p. 198. The Labrador Duck pair appeared later that year as Plate 332. Low (2002), p. 170; *OB* IV, p. 271. Havell had already engraved both images by the time Audubon left London for

America at the end of July. See Chapter 16, note 58, *infra*. See also, Fries (1973), p. 400. Therefore, it seems likely that Audubon received the specimens from Webster in the fall of 1832, when these northern breeding ducks would have returned once again to winter in the coastal waters of Massachusetts and before the senator's congressional duties required him to return to Washington City in December. Curtis (1870) I. p. 434. Dwight and Low seemingly concur. Low (2002), pp. 167, 170; Audubon (1966) I, Plate 221; II, Plate 306. What cannot be said with any conviction is that Webster paid a call on Audubon in Boston in 1832.

278. LBA, Boston to VGA, London, 4 Feb. 1833 (Yale, Box 1, Folder 18). Richard Harlan, M.D., served as Audubon's agent for *BOA* in Philadelphia. The naturalist honored him with the scientific name of the Black Warrior (*Falco harlani*), illustrated in Havell Plate 86. Once considered a separate species known as Harlan's Hawk (*Buteo harlani*), it is recognized today as merely a color phase, or "morph," of the Red-tailed Hawk. Low (2002), p. 78.

The Harlans arrived in Boston on February 4. They left to return to Philadelphia on February 23. JJA, Boston to Richard Harlan, M.D., Philadelphia, 20 Mar. 1833 (Filson), Audubon (2006), p. 373; JJA, Boston to VGA, London, 24–25 Feb. 1833 (APS), *Letters* I, p. 200; LBA, Boston to VGA, London, 4 Feb. 1833 (Yale, Box 1, Folder 18).

279. Rhodes (2004), p. 373; JJA, Boston, to VGA, London, 24–25 Feb. 1833 (APS), *Letters* I, p. 200. See also, Deane (1905), p. 170, note 1; *OB* II, p. 464; Bowen (1833), p. 211. Ethan Allen Greenwood (1779–1856) was an American painter and entrepreneur who opened the New England Museum, located at 76 Court Street in Boston, on July 4, 1818. Bowen (1833), p. 211. In 1833, he was also serving as a member of the Massachusetts House of Representatives from Hubbardston. Loring (1832), p. 26. See also, Barnhill (1993), p. 98.

Rhodes states that Audubon purchased the specimen of the Golden Eagle from Greenwood on February 24, 1833, and refers to him as the proprietor of the Columbian Museum. Rhodes (2004), p. 373. Neither statement is correct.

Audubon actually acquired the raptor on February 25, as is evident from a contemporaneous letter he wrote to Victor. He had begun the letter on February 24, and it is dated as such in the heading. But he continued it on the 25th, explaining that he had held the letter in the hope that he could announce the State of Massachusetts as a new subscriber to *BOA*. He went on to say that "I have had the great gratification of purchasing this day the finest *Golden Eagle* alive which I ever have seen." JJA, Boston to VGA, London, 24–25 Feb. 1833 (APS), *Letters* I, p. 200.

In 1833, Greenwood's establishment was known as the New England Museum. Bowen (1833), p. 211. See also, Ethan Allen Greenwood, Boston to JJA, Boston, 29 Mar. 1833 (MHM)(giving the return address as "New England Museum"). The only source cited by Rhodes for his assertion that Greenwood was the proprietor of the Columbian Museum is Georgia Brady Barnhill's monograph on Greenwood. Rhodes (2004), p. 373 and note, p. 473.

Barnhill is the Andrew W. Mellon Curator of Graphic Arts Emerita at the American Antiquarian Society in Worcester, MA, and is a recognized expert on Greenwood's life and career. She does not, however, support Rhodes on this point. Barnhill writes that "Greenwood opened the New England Museum in Boston on July 4, 1818," and "went on to acquire several other museums and collections," the Columbian Museum being among them. Barnhill (1993), p. 96. Thus, the Columbian Museum was merely one of several collections Greenwood added to the New England Museum after it was opened.

280. Sibley (2003), p. 110; *OB* II, p. 464.

281. *OB* II, p. 464.

282. JJA, Boston to VGA, London, 24–25 Feb. 1833 (APS), *Letters* I, p. 200.

283. *OB* II, p. 465. Of his decision to "take the portrait of the magnificent" Golden Eagle by killing it, Audubon wrote: "I occupied myself a whole day in watching his movements; on the next I came to a determination as to the position in which I might best represent him; and on the third thought of how I could take away his life with the least pain to him." Ibid. Audubon tried to asphyxiate the eagle with carbon monoxide from lighted charcoal placed along with the cage in a small closet, only to find that six hours of exposure had virtually no effect on his captive. JJA, Boston to Richard Harlan, M.D., Philadelphia, 20 Mar. 1833 (Filson), Audubon

(2006), p. 373. Note that Audubon increased the duration of the exposure to ten hours in his *OB* account. *OB* II, p. 465. The next day, he added sulfur to the mix, which similarly failed to affect the bird, although it drove his family from their rooms. JJA, Boston to Richard Harlan, M.D., Philadelphia, 20 Mar. 1833 (Filson), Audubon (2006), p. 373. Finally, he extinguished its life with a "long pointed piece of steel through its heart." *OB* II, p. 465.

284. Deane (1905), p. 171. Deane indicates that Audubon's letter to Victor describing his work on the drawing of the Golden Eagle was dated February 5, 1833, and this date is repeated in a transcription by Herrick. Herrick (1938) II, p. 35. However, Ford correctly deduces that the actual date was March 5, as does Rhodes. Rhodes (2004), p. 375 and note, p. 474; Ford (1988), p. 451. Since Audubon did not acquire the eagle until February 25, the letter obviously could not have been written on February 5. Audubon's exhaustion from the hours spent drawing the eagle perhaps led him to misdate the letter. Although Deane does not indicate to whom the letter was directed, the content indicates it must have been to Victor, who was handling the naturalist's affairs in England. This is clear from his direction to "Push Jos. B. Kidd of Edinburgh if he *can* be pushed to paint copies of our drawings. I look on that series as of great importance to us all." Deane (1905), p. 171.

285. JJA, Boston to Richard Harlan, M.D., Philadelphia, 20 Mar. 1833 (Filson), Audubon (2006), p. 373; Rhodes (2004), p. 375-376; Blaugrund (1993), p. 233. Audubon informed Harlan in his March 20 letter that the drawing of the Golden Eagle had consumed a period of thirteen days, and this figure is used in the text. However, he told the readers of the *OB* that it had taken fourteen days. *OB* II, p. 466. In either case, this would indicate that he continued to work on the drawing for several days after he wrote Victor on March 5, at which point he had already invested sixty hours. JJA, Boston to VGA, London, 5 Feb. [Mar.] 1833, Herrick (1938) II, p. 35; Deane (1905), p. 171. Ford's biography asserts that Audubon's exertions on the drawing amounted to only sixteen hours. Ford (1988), p. 303. This is obviously an error, as the letters of March 5 and 20 attest.

286. Rhodes (2004), p. 376; Audubon (1966) I,

Plate 54. When Havell engraved the drawing of the Golden Eagle, he omitted the buckskin-clad figure believed to be an Audubon self-portrait. Blaugrund (1993), p. 232, note 3.

287. LGA, Boston to VGA, London, 13 Mar. 1833 (Yale, Box 1, Folder 5).

288. JJA, Boston to Richard Harlan, M.D., Philadelphia, 20 Mar. 1833 (Filson), Audubon (2006), p. 372.

CHAPTER 3: NEW YORK AND BOSTON

1. Waterton (Mar. 1833); Waterton (Apr. 1832).

2. Waterton (Jun. 1832).

3. Leahy (2004), pp. 584-585.

4. Waterton (Jun. 1832).

5. Waterton (Nov. 1832); *OB* I, p. 276. Audubon is evidently the only naturalist or ornithologist to have observed the Chuck-Will's Widow removing eggs from its nest after the nest was disturbed. Straight & Cooper (2000), p. 11.

6. Waterton (Mar. 1833); Hunter (January 1833).

7. Waterton (Mar. 1833), pp. 164-166.

8. Ibid., p. 166.

9. Ibid., pp. 166-167.

10. VGA, Edinburgh to Robert Havell Jr., London, 21 Feb. 1833 (Harvard (232)); VGA, New Castle on Tyne to Robert Havell Jr., London, 1 Feb. 1833 (Harvard (228)); VGA, Manchester to Robert Havell Jr., London, 21 Jan. 1833 (Harvard (227)); VGA, Liverpool to Robert Havell Jr., London, 18 Jan. 1833 (Harvard (226)).

11. VGA, Sheffield to Robert Havell Jr., London, 16 Mar. 1833 (Harvard (233)).

12. JJA, Boston to Richard Harlan, M.D., Philadelphia, 20 Mar. 1833 (Filson), Audubon (2006), p. 372

13. *OB* II, pp. 465-466; JJA, Boston to Richard Harlan, M.D., Philadelphia, 20 Mar. 1833 (Filson), Audubon (2006), p. 372; JJA, Boston to VGA, London, 19 Mar. 1833 (APS).

14. VGA, London to LBA, New York, 30 Apr. 1833 (Yale, Box 15, Folder 693).

15. "TIA (Transient Ischemic Attack)," excerpted from "Why Rush?," *Stroke Connection* (January/February 2009) (Science update, Oct. 2012) http://www.strokeassociation.org /STROKEORG/AboutStroke/TypesofStroke

/TIA/TIA-Transient-Ischemic-Attack_UCM
_310942_Article.jsp (accessed 8 Feb. 2014).

16. JJA, Boston to VGA, London, 19 Mar. 1833
(APS).

17. Ibid.

18. JJA, Boston to Richard Harlan, M.D., Philadelphia, 20 Mar. 1833 (Filson), Audubon (2006),
p. 372.

19. Richard Harlan, M.D., Philadelphia to JJA,
New York, 23 Mar. 1833 (Yale, Box 4, Folder 173).

20. Ibid. In his letter to Audubon, Harlan referred to several notable men who had suffered from
paralytic strokes: (1) Lord Liverpool was Robert
Banks Jenkinson (1770–1828), second Earl of Liverpool, who served as British prime minister from
1812 to 1827. He retired in 1827 after suffering a
stroke and died the following year. Gash (2004); (2)
Sir Walter Scott (1771–1832) was the famous Scottish
poet and author of historical novels, including *Ivan-
hoe*. He suffered a series of strokes in 1830 and 1831
before his death the following year. Hewitt (2004);
(3) Dugald Stewart (1753–1828) was a Scottish philosopher who had a stroke in 1821 and required the
assistance of his wife and daughter to continue his
work. He evidently died of a stroke in 1828. Brown
(2004); and (4) Zaccheus Collins (1764–1831) was a
Quaker philanthropist who lived in Philadelphia.
He was a member of the Academy of Natural Sciences of Philadelphia as well as of the American
Philosophical Society and served as a vice president
of the latter organization from 1819 until his death.
Phillips (1889), p. 87; Minutes of the Academy of
Natural Sciences of Philadelphia (1824).

21. LBA postscript to JJA, Boston to Richard
Harlan, M.D., Philadelphia, 20 Mar. 1833 (Filson).

22. JJA, Boston to Richard Harlan, M.D., Philadelphia, 20 Mar. 1833 (Filson), Audubon (2006),
p. 373. Among the five new subscribers in Boston
were: (1) James Brown (1800–1855), a book dealer
with Hilliard, Gray & Co., which would later publish the American edition of the second volume of
the *OB*. Brown would go on to found the publishing
house of Little, Brown and Company; (2) William
Oakes (1799–1848), an Ipswich attorney, zoologist,
and botanist; and (3) James Arnold (1781–1868),
a wealthy New Bedford whaling merchant. JJA,
Boston to VGA, London, 19 Mar. 1833 (APS). See
also, Fries (1973), pp. 155–156, 159–160; McKechnie

(1907), p. 227. The Arnold Arboretum of Harvard
University is named for him.

Three days later, on March 23, 1833, Audubon
collected a sixth name, William Sturgis (1782–1863),
a merchant and partner with Bryant, Sturgis &
Co. at 54 State Street. Fries (1973), p. 288; Stimpson (1833), pp. 98, 311. His completed copy of the
folio was donated in 1921 to the Museum of Fine
Arts in Boston. Fries (1973), p. 288. In a letter to
Victor, written the same day, Audubon counted thirteen subscribers in Boston and single subscribers
in Salem, Ipswich, New Bedford, and Portland,
Maine, for a total of seventeen. JJA, Boston to VGA,
London, 23 Mar. 1833 (Private collection, auctioned
at Heritage Auctions on 11 Feb. 2010). See also,
Fries (1973), p. 156.

23. JJA, Boston to VGA, London, 23 Mar. 1833
(Private collection).

24. GCS, Boston to GCSJr, Bowdoin College,
24 Mar. 1833 (MHS, Box 4, Vol. 11, 14–31 Mar.
1833); JJA, Boston to VGA, London, 23 Mar. 1833
(Private collection). George Cheyne Shattuck Jr.
was born on July 22, 1813. Marshall (2006), p. 5.

25. Quincy (2003), p. 47.

26. GCSJr, Brunswick, ME to GCS, Boston, 27
Mar. 1833 (MHS, Box 4, Vol. 11, 14–31 Mar. 1833).

27. Shuler (1995), p. 73; John Bachman, Charleston to JJA, New York, 27 Mar. 1833 (MHM), Deane
(1929), pp. 182–185. Bachman originally referred
to himself as "Young Jostle" after playfully bestowing the nickname "Old Jostle" on Audubon. Shuler
(1995), p. 73. In addition to the gentle ribbing for
Audubon's complaints about the poor quality of
Southern roads, the nicknames were designed to
highlight the disparity in their ages. Ibid., pp. 1,
73–74. At the time they met in October 1831, Audubon was forty-six, while Bachman was forty-one.
Ibid., pp. 3, 18. However, Bachman soon affectionately extended his nicknames to the other members
of the Audubon clan, referring to Lucy as "Mrs.
Jostle," John as "Young Jostle" or "Jostle No. 1,"
and Victor as "Jostle No. 2." Ibid., pp. 73–74; Bachman (1888), p. 134, note. Bachman then rechristened
himself "Jostle the third." Shuler (1995), p. 74.

28. John Bachman, Charleston to JJA, New
York, 27 Mar. 1833 (MHM), Deane (1929), pp. 182–
185. See also, Shuler (1995), pp. 104–105.

29. Shuler (1995), pp. 96–97; 102. Bachman ap-

parently did not send Audubon the skin of the unknown female warbler he had collected in July 1832
until February 9, 1833, hoping to entice his friend to
return to Charleston to retrieve it along with other
specimens he had procured for the naturalist. Along
with the birdskins, he shipped some botanical drawings that his sister-in-law, Maria Martin, had prepared for whatever use Audubon could put them.
Ibid., pp. 98–102.

30. Shuler (1995), pp. 98, 102, 105; John Bachman, Charleston to JJA, New York, 27 Mar. 1833
(MHM), Deane (1929), pp. 182–183.

31. Shuler (1995), p. 91.

32. Shuler (1995), pp. 105–107. Audubon wrote
in the *OB* that Bachman had discovered the first
specimen of Bachman's Warbler "a few miles from
Charleston, in South Carolina, in July 1833, while
I was rambling over the crags of Labrador." *OB* II,
p. 483. Esteemed Audubon scholar Edward Dwight
repeats this statement and writes that Audubon
painted the pair in the autumn of 1833. Audubon
(1966) II, Plate 419. Susanne Low, another respected expert on the prints, concurs as to the date
of the original painting. Low (2002), p. 116. See
also, Small (2009), p. 174. However, the correspondence between Bachman and Audubon as well as
Audubon's letter to Victor of April 28, 1833, make
it clear this chronology is faulty. As stated in the
text, Bachman discovered the female in the summer
of 1832 and the male the following March. Shuler
(1995), pp. 96–97. Audubon had already completed the illustration on April 28, 1833, when he
was preparing to ship it to Victor in London. JJA,
New York to VGA, London, 28 Apr. 1833, Grinnell
(1916), p. 122. The reference in the *OB* is an example
of the naturalist's less than exacting attention to
some of the factual details he was publishing. It was
clearly not a typographical error because Audubon
related it to his Labrador expedition, which indeed
occurred during the summer of 1833.

33. Sibley (2014), p. xv; Dunn & Alderfer (2011),
p. 546.

34. *New-York Gazette & General Advertiser*, Vol.
45, No. 16,827, p. 2, col. 4 (Saturday, 30 Mar. 1833)
(NYHS). On March 30, the *New-York Gazette*, a
morning newspaper, printed a brief notice of Audubon's arrival that had appeared in the previous evening's edition of the *New-York American*. The family

had evidently arrived on the morning of March 29
by steamship from Providence. Rhodes is mistaken
in placing their trip to New York at the end of April.
Rhodes (2004), p. 379.

It should be noted that Audubon mentioned to
Victor in an April 1, 1833, letter from New York that
he and Lucy had reached the city two days before,
which would place their arrival on March 30. JJA,
New York to VGA, London, 1 Apr. 1833 (APS), *Letters* I, p. 202. The articles in the New York papers
prove otherwise. It may be that he penned the letter
on March 31 but did not date it until the following
day, when he sent it via a packet ship to London.

35. Rhodes (2004), p. 379; New York City Landmarks Preservation Commission (1969), pp. 17–18,
105; Longworth (1833), p. 122; LBA, New York to
John Bachman, Charleston, 7 May 1833 (Harvard
(207)); LBA, Boston to Mrs. Robert Havell Jr., London, 15 Feb. 1833 (Harvard (Letters), b (119)). According to the 1832–33 *New-York Directory*, the Berthouds had previously resided at 45 Bond Street.
Longworth (1832), p. 144.

36. Tuckerman (1889) I, pp. iii–iv. Modestly
born, Philip Hone (1780–1851) earned a fortune in
the auction business and served one term as mayor
of New York from 1826–1827. He is perhaps best
known as a diarist who maintained a daily account
of local and national events, and described the many
interesting and famous people who visited New
York and paid him a visit from 1828 to 1851. Ibid.,
pp. iv, viii–ix. His diaries are now held by the New-
York Historical Society.

37. Tuckerman (1889) I, p. 73.

38. JJA, New York to VGA, London, 1 Apr. 1833
(APS), *Letters* I, pp. 202–204, 206.

39. Ibid, p. 206; Diary of Philip Hone, 1 Apr.
1833 (NYHS). See also, Williams (1835), Appendix, p. 190. There is a conflict in the evidence as to
when Audubon dined with the New York mayor
and his distinguished guests as referenced in the
text. In Audubon's letter to Victor of April 1, he
wrote "I dine tomorrow at the Mayor with Cap*n*
Balk in search of Poor Ross &c." However, Philip
Hone's holographic diary reflects that the dinner to
which the naturalist alluded occurred on April 1.
On April 2, the date Audubon indicated the dinner
was to take place, Hone wrote that he had been invited to two dinner parties that had been cancelled

due to a death in the family of each of the hosts. Thus, there would appear to be no likelihood that Hone misdated his entry regarding the dinner, and I have concluded that his record is more reliable on the subject than Audubon's letter, which appears to have been written on March 31 and post-dated April 1. See also, note 34, *supra*.

40. Shuler (1995), p. 98.

41. "The Birds of America," *New-York Gazette & General Advertiser*, Vol. 45, No. 16,832, p. 2, col. 1 (Friday Morning, 5 Apr. 1833)(NYHS); Diary of Philip Hone, 2 Apr. 1833 (NYHS). The account in the *New-York Gazette* was copied from a story that earlier appeared in the *New-York American*.

42. Lieber (1882), pp. 95–96. Francis Lieber (1798–1872) was a political philosopher, professor, and author of the Lieber Code, the first set of established rules governing the conduct of Union soldiers in occupied territory during the Civil War. These were later adopted internationally as the Law of War. Born in Berlin, Lieber served in the Prussian Army and was wounded at the Battle of Waterloo. While pursuing a doctorate degree at Halle, he was twice jailed as a student radical. He left Prussia in 1827 for Boston, where he founded and served as editor of the *Encyclopædia Americana* and, in 1833, translated Alexis de Tocqueville and Gustave de Beaumont's report on the American prison system. He also served as an informant for de Tocqueville during the writing of his classic, *Democracy in America*. In 1835, Lieber obtained a teaching post at South Carolina College, now the University of South Carolina, and authored a series of important works on representative democracy, including *Political Ethics* (1838) and *Legal and Political Hermeneutics* (1839). His accomplishments led to a pardon by the King of Prussia, and he returned to his native land to serve as a consultant in 1844. He was appointed to teach law at Columbia University in 1858 and, at the time of his death, was considered a giant in the field of international law. Carrington (2009), pp. 335–336.

43. Vrabel (2004), p. 118; Lieber (1882), p. 95. *The Boston Medical Intelligencer*, which was published weekly and was "devoted to the cause of physical education," contained an advertisement for Francis Lieber's swimming school in July 1827: "Dr. L. teaches on the system of M. Pfuel, General in the

Prussian Army, who introduced it in the regiments of Prussia and in many of the first cities of the kingdom, namely, Berlin, Coblentz, Breslau, Koningsberg, &c. . . . Experience shows that a healthy person will usually acquire the art of swimming half an hour uninterruptedly, in about three weeks, taking a lesson every day." *The Boston Medical Intelligencer*, Vol. 5, No. 10, p. 168 (Tuesday, 24 Jul. 1827).

44. Lieber (1882), p. 95.

45. "Audubon's American Ornithology," *New-York Gazette & General Advertiser*, Vol. 45, No. 16,837, p. 2, col. 1 (Thursday Morning, 11 Apr. 1833) (NYHS); "The Birds of America," *New-York Gazette & General Advertiser*, Vol. 45, No. 16,832, p. 2, col. 1 (Friday Morning, 5 Apr. 1833)(NYHS).

46. *New-York Gazette & General Advertiser*, Vol. 45, No. 16,832, p. 2, col. 1 (Friday Morning, 5 Apr. 1833)(NYHS).

47. Ibid.

48. Read (1979). p, 7; LBA, Boston to VGA, London, 13 Mar. 1833 with addendum by JJA (Yale, Box 1, Folder 5).

49. *New-York Gazette & General Advertiser*, Vol. 45, No. 16,832, p. 2, col. 1 (Friday Morning, 5 Apr. 1833)(NYHS). John Lang, the owner and publisher of the *New-York Gazette & General Advertiser*, was the brother-in-law of Edward Harris's father. Read (1979), p. 2.

50. Fries (1973), pp. 72–73; 148; 153–154; *National Gazette and Literary Register*, Vol. XII, No. 1886, p. 1, cols. 1–2 (Philadelphia, Saturday, 4 May 1833). The *National Gazette* article listed only eleven subscriptions from New York. Fries also lists eleven names. However, Lucy informed Victor on May 7 that they had collected a total of thirteen during their stay in New York. LBA, New York to VGA, London, 7 May 1833 (Yale, Box 1, Folder 18). See also, note 59, *infra*. Setting aside the copy ordered by the State of Maryland, that leaves twelve, as stated in the text.

The copy of *BOA* for which the State of New York subscribed was destroyed by a fire at the New York State Library in Albany on March 29, 1911. The Columbia College set is still held by Columbia University in its Rare Book & Manuscript Library. P.J. Stuyvesant completed his subscription to the work, but Waldemar Fries was unable to determine what became of it during his decade-long research into the history of the individual copies of the folio. The Van Rensselaer copy was donated to Princeton University in 1929 by Van Rensselaer's grandson. Fries (1973), pp. 153, 185, 246, 300.

51. Fries (1973), p. 310. The State of Maryland's copy is held in the Special Collections Room of the Maryland State Law Library in Annapolis.

52. LBA, New York to VGA, London, 7 May 1833 (Yale, Box 1, Folder 18); *Boston Daily Advertiser & Patriot*, Vol. XLII, No. 11,058, p. 2, col. 4 (Saturday, 4 May 1833)(AAS); *New-York Gazette & General Advertiser*, Vol. 45, No. 16,855, p. 2, col 1 (Thursday Morning, 2 May 1833)(NYHS).

53. *The Commercial Herald* (Thursday, 18 Apr. 1833), a Philadelphia paper, reprinted in the *New-York Evening Post for the Country* (Monday, 22 April 1833)("Mr. Audubon returned to this city yesterday."). See also, JJA, New York to Robert Havell Jr., London, 20 Apr. 1833 (Harvard (54)), *Letters* I, p. 211; JJA, New York to VGA, London, 15 Apr. 1833 (APS), *Letters* I, p. 210.

54. Sotheby's (1993), Lot 61. Audubon inscribed the copy of the book on North American mammals that Richard Harlan gave him, "Rec^d from my Friend Richd Harlan April 18th 1833. J.J. Audubon F.R.S. &c."

55. JJA, New York to James Curtiss, Eastport, 19 Apr. 1833 (NYHS). The cited letter, which was Audubon's copy, was displayed at the New-York Historical Society's "Audubon's Aviary" exhibition in 2014. However, the society misattributed the recipient of this letter as William Curtiss, an Eastport mariner. There is no question that the letter was directed to the Eastport postmaster, James Curtiss, an Audubon correspondent who was making arrangements for Audubon's accommodations. See Chapter 4, text and notes 25, 26, and 62, *infra*.

56. JJA, Eastport to LBA, New York, 7 May 1833 (Private collection), *Letters* I, p. 218; JJA, Boston to James Curtiss, Eastport, 25 Jan. 1833 (Private collection).

57. *OB* III, p. 336. Audubon wrote in the *OB*: "The specimen from which my figure [of the Large-billed Guillemot] was made was sent to me in ice, along with several other rare birds, from Eastport in Maine. I received it quite fresh and in excellent plumage, on the 18th of February 1833. It had been shot along with several other individuals of the same species while searching for food in the waters of Pasmaquody Bay, which were then covered with broken ice. Its flight was described by Mr CURTIS, who sent it to me, as similar to that of the Foolish Guillemot, with which it associated." James Curtiss was unable to supply Audubon with a specimen of the Northern Hawk Owl. Eventually, the naturalist obtained a specimen from Thomas McCulloch of Pictou, Nova Scotia. *OB* IV, p. 551.

58. JJA, Eastport to LBA, New York, 7 May 1833 (Private collection), *Letters* I, p. 218.

59. JJA, New York to Robert Havell Jr., London, 20 Apr. 1833 (Harvard (54)), *Letters* I, pp. 211–213. Note that Hart-Davis states, incorrectly, that the April 20 letter with Audubon's exhortations about the proper coloration of the prints was written to Victor. Hart-Davis (2004), pp. 198–199.

Audubon's accounting of the number of his American subscribers as of April 20, 1833, which he claimed was fifty-five in his letter of that date to Havell, is at odds with his count just a week later. In his letter to Victor on April 28, he told his son they had only fifty-one subscribers. JJA, New York to VGA, London, 28 Apr. 1833, Grinnell (1916), p. 121. However, he stated that he had not included Dr. Croghan of Kentucky, "from whom not a word has been heard," or Baron Krudener, who had subscribed during Audubon's visit to Washington City in 1830. If these were added, it would make the count fifty-three. As of April 30, he said the number had risen to fifty-four with the addition of the State of New York. Ibid., p. 123. The number of subscribers fluctuated as subscriptions came in and others were cancelled, but the disparity was sometimes attributable to the naturalist, who was not always precise.

On May 4, 1833, the *National Gazette and Literary Register*, a Philadelphia newspaper, provided a breakdown of the subscriptions Audubon had procured in America by city and state, although it listed only a total of fifty-three: "Evidence was recently afforded in Boston and New York, that Americans are not insensible to the value and splendor of Mr. Audubon's labor—the more to be encouraged as they are those of a native countryman. Adequate patronage will not be wanting, we presume, when they shall be more widely known. The ornithologist has been absorbed by his science and the perfection of his drawings, in such wise that he could not look after his work; yet between fifty and sixty subscribers have been obtained in the United States; in Boston 18; New York 11; Philadelphia 4; Baltimore 3; Savannah 7; Louisville 2; New Orleans 3; the Legislatures of Massachusetts, Maryland, New York, South Carolina, and the Congress Library, each a copy." *National Gazette and Literary Register*, Vol. XII, No. 1886, page 1, cols. 1–2 (Philadelphia, Saturday, 4 May 1833).

60. JJA, New York to Robert Havell Jr., London, 20 Apr. 1833 (Harvard (54)), *Letters* I, p. 213.

61. "Mr. Audubon," *The New-York Mirror*, Vol. X, No. 42, p. 335 (20 Apr. 1833).

62. Durant & Harwood (1980), p. 414; LBA, New York to VGA, London, undated addendum to her copy of JJA, New York to VGA, London, 28 April 1833 (Yale, Box 1, Folder 18)(sent by Lucy to accompany a shipment of drawings on 10 May 1833); JJA, New York to VGA, London, 28 Apr. 1833, Grinnell (1916), p. 123.

63. JJA, New York to VGA, London, 28 Apr. 1833, Grinnell (1916), pp. 121–123.

64. Ibid. p. 123.

65. JJA, New York to Charles-Lucien Bonaparte, 1 May 1833, published in facsimile in *The Osprey* (1897). See also, Herrick (1938) II, p. 119. The transcript of this letter in the Ruthven Deane collection at the Missouri History Museum contains a postscript that does not appear in either the facsimile in *The Osprey* or in Herrick's transcription, which states, among other things: "I sail for the coast of Labrador & Hudson Bay *tomorrow*." Audubon would, in fact, leave New York the same day the letter was dated, May 1, suggesting that he likely wrote the contents on April 30 and postdated it.

66. Stroud (2000), p. 118; Mearns (1992), p. 151; *OB* I, p. xi; JJA, New York to Charles-Lucien Bonaparte, 1 May 1833, Herrick (1938) II, p. 119; JJA, New York to VGA, London, 28 Apr. 1833, Grinnell (1916), pp. 122–123. From the cited letter to Victor, we know that Audubon had attended a meeting of the Lyceum of Natural History of New-York on the evening of Monday, April 29. It was there that he must have spoken with William Cooper and learned that Charles-Lucien Bonaparte had taken offense to some of his comments in the Introduction to Volume I of the *OB*. Ford errs in asserting that Bona-

parte was unhappy about where he was listed in Audubon's prospectus. Ford (1988), pp. 305–306.

67. *OB* I, p. xi.

68. Stroud (2000), p. 118.

69. Mearns (1992), p. xvi.

70. JJA, New York to VGA, London, 28 Apr. 1833, Grinnell (1916), pp. 121–122.

71. JJA, New York to Charles-Lucien Bonaparte, 1 May 1833, Herrick (1938) II, p. 119; *OB* I, p. xi.

72. Stroud (2000), p. 118.

73. Ibid., pp. 118–120.

74. *New-York Gazette & General Advertiser*, Vol. 45, No. 16,555, p. 2, col. 1 (Thursday Morning, 2 May 1833)(NYHS). John Woodhouse Audubon was born on November 30, 1812. Rhodes (2004), p. 107; *AHJ* I, p. 32. In the late winter, spring, and summer of 1833, he would have been twenty years of age, not twenty-one as Rhodes has repeatedly asserted. Audubon (2006), p. 374; Rhodes (2004), p. 380.

75. Dow (1877), p. 10.

76. Ibid.

77. JJA, Boston to LBA, New York, 4 May 1833 (Princeton, Box 2, Folder 14), *Letters* I, p. 215; JJA, New York to VGA, London, 28 Apr. 1833, Grinnell (1916), p. 123. See also, Williams (1834), p. 149.

78. *New-York Gazette & General Advertiser*, Vol. 45, No. 16,855, p. 2, col. 1 (Thursday Morning, 2 May 1833)(NYHS).

79. LBA, New York to VGA, London, undated addendum to her copy of a letter from JJA, New York to VGA, London, 28 April 1833 (Yale, Box 1, Folder 18).

80. Ibid.

81. LBA, New York to VGA, London, 23 May 1833 (Yale, Box 1, Folder 18).

82. LBA, New York to VGA, London, 7 May 1833 (Yale, Box 1, Folder 18).

83. Mittlebeeler (1975), pp. 174, 182.

84. See, e.g., LBA, New York to VGA, London, 2 Jul. 1833 (Yale, Box 1, Folder 20); LBA, New York to VGA, London, 8 Jun. 1833 (Yale, Box 1, Folder 19).

85. JJA, New York to VGA, London, 28 Apr. 1833, Grinnell (1916), p. 122;

86. Evenhuis (2003), p. 10; Waterton (May 1833a), pp. 215–216.

87. Waterton (May 1833a), pp. 216–218.

88. *Boston Daily Advertiser & Patriot*, Vol. XLII, No. 11,058, p. 2, col. 4 (Saturday, 4 May 1833) (AAS); JJA, Boston to LBA, New York, 4 May 1833 (Princeton, Box 2, Folder 14). See also, Dow (1877) pp. 10, 12.

89. JJA, Boston to LBA, New York, 4 May 1833 (Princeton, Box 2, Folder 15), *Letters* I, p. 216; JJA, Boston to LBA, New York, 4 May 1833 (Princeton, Box 2, Folder 14), *Letters* I, p. 214. In both of the letters Audubon wrote to Lucy on May 4, 1833, he indicated that he was at "Mrs. Davies'." Audubon customarily used this spelling for the surname "Davis." This was almost certainly a reference to the wife of Joshua Davis, the Boston merchant who resided at Sarah Lekain's Pearl Street boardinghouse. Stimpson (1833), p. 132.

90. JJA, Boston to LBA, New York, 4 May 1833 (Princeton, Box 2, Folder 14), *Letters* I, p. 214. At the time, Audubon's agent in Boston was the broker S.E. Greene, although it is evident from the naturalist's correspondence that he was beginning to rely more and more on Dr. George Parkman, who had become a close friend. In his letter of May 4 to Lucy, Audubon complained that "Greene had done nothing" in connection with the distribution of the copies of the first volume of prints that had reached Boston, so he was compelled to do it himself.

91. Ibid. In his May 4 letter to Lucy, Audubon identified $1,221 that he had collected from the following six subscribers during his visit to Boston: James Arnold; State of Massachusetts; J.P. Cushing, P.T. Jackson, Samuel Appleton, and Frederic Tudor. See also, Fries (1973), pp. 67, 70. He sent $691 of this sum to Nicholas Berthoud via a draft drawn on the Globe Bank in Boston with instructions to his brother-in-law to send £100 Sterling to Victor in London. Audubon told Lucy he was keeping $500 in U.S. notes. He did not address in his letter what happened to the remaining $30.

92. *Daily Evening Transcript*, Vol. III, No. 831, p. 2, col. 3 (Boston, Friday Evening, 3 May 1833) (AAS).

93. GCS, Boston to GCSJr, Brunswick, ME, 4 May 1833 (MHS, Box 5, Vol. 11, 1–13, May 1833). See also, JJA, Boston to LBA, New York, 4 May 1833 (Princeton, Box 2, Folder 14), *Letters* I, p. 216; Stimpson (1833), pp. 32, 294.

94. Smith (1914), 80, 109, 120.

95. Marshall (2006), pp. 2–3; Massachusetts Historical Society (1971); Burrage (1923), pp. 109–110; Harvard (1920), p. 937; Shattuck (1881), p. 164; Shattuck (1808). J.C. Douglas Marshall, the biographer of George C. Shattuck Jr., writes that Shattuck Sr. obtained a medical degree from Harvard in 1807. However, according to Harvard's records, the senior Shattuck was awarded a Master of Arts degree in 1807 under the then custom that enabled recipients of Bachelors' and Masters' degrees from other institutions to apply to Harvard for the same degree. Shattuck had received a Master of Arts degree in 1806 from Dartmouth, which was automatically awarded in course three years after his B.A. degree was bestowed. Harvard (1920), p. 928, note 1; p. 937.

96. Marshall (2006), pp. 3–4; Shattuck (1881), p. 165. Eliza Shattuck's journals of trips taken in New England shortly before she met and married George C. Shattuck Sr. were discovered in 2009 at the Massachusetts Historical Society. Susan Martin, "'. . . it shall be Eliza . . . ;' or, Attributing a Diary," *The Beehive: Official Blog of the Massachusetts Historical Society* (25 Nov. 2009), http://www.masshist .org/blog/192 (accessed 9 Feb. 2014).

97. Marshall (2006), p. 5; Hassam (1882), p. 312.

98. Massachusetts Historical Society (1971); Park (1926) II, pp. 676–677; Burrage (1923), p. 110; Shattuck (1881), pp. 166–169.

99. Marshall (2006), p. 4; Shattuck (1881), pp. 167.

100. GCS, Boston to GCSJr, Brunswick, ME, 4 May 1833 (MHS, Box 5, Vol. 11, 1–13 May 1833). See also, JJA, Boston, to LBA, New York, 4 May 1833 (Princeton, Box 2, Folder 14), *Letters* I, p. 216.

101. According to a letter written by George C. Shattuck Jr. to his father on Sunday, April 28, 1833, the medical lectures for the term at the Medical College of Maine at Bowdoin College were due to be finished at the end of that week. GCSJr, Brunswick, ME to GCS, Boston, 28 Apr. 1833 (MHS, Box 5, Vol. 11, 16–30 April 1833).

102. GCS, Boston to GCSJr, Brunswick, ME, 4 May 1833 (MHS, Box 5, Vol. 11, 1–13 May 1833). An image of this letter can be found in Massachusetts Historical Society (1971).

103. Fries (1973), p. 155; Boston Athenaeum (1907), p. 115; Quincy (1851), pp. 132–133; JJA, Bos-

ton to LBA, New York, 4 May 1833 (Princeton, Box 2, Folder 14), *Letters* I, p. 215.

104. Bowen (1838), p. 291. According to Bowen, beginning on May 1, 1833, "A fair is held at Faneuil Hall, by the ladies of Boston, for the benefit of the blind, which is continued three days. The amount collected was $12,918. Hon. Thomas H. Perkins gave his house in Pearl street [*sic*], valued at $30,000, for an asylum for the blind, and about $38,000 more were contributed."

105. Butler (1835) II, p. 142.

106. Kinney (1989), p. 87; JJA, Boston to LBA, New York, 4 May 1833 (Princeton, Box 2, Folder 14), *Letters* I, p. 214.

107. Kinney (1989), p. 87. The *Edward Preble*, a packet schooner making regular runs between Boston and Eastport, ME, was built at the Eastport shipyard of Robert Huston. Ibid.

108. JJA, Boston to LBA, New York, 4 May 1833 (Princeton, Box 2, Folder 14), *Letters* I, p. 214.

109. Ibid., pp. 214–215.

110. Butler (1835) II, p. 133. The Tremont The-atre at 82 Tremont Street opened on September 24, 1827. Vrabel (2004), p. 118. As described in *Bowen's Picture of Boston*, "This Theatre, from its location and construction, is the most popular in Boston, and receives patronage from the most wealthy and fashionable." Bowen (1838), p. 193.

111. JJA, Boston to LBA, New York, 4 May 1833 (Princeton, Box 2, Folder 14), *Letters* I, p. 215.

112. LBA, New York to VGA, London, 23 May 1833 (Yale, Box 1, Folder 18); JJA, Boston to LBA, New York, 4 May 1833 (Princeton, Box 2, Folder 14), *Letters* I, p. 215.

113. JJA, Boston to LBA, New York, 4 May 1833 (Princeton, Box 2, Folder 14), *Letters* I, p. 215. Anna Quincy, the twenty-year-old daughter of Harvard president and former Boston Mayor Josiah Quincy, had a similar impression of Fanny Kemble when she met the actress at a party following a performance at the Tremont Theater on April 16: "She is not handsome off the stage. She has very fine eyes with very black eyelashes & eyebrows—& fine teeth— her complexion is coarse, & her other features not remarkable—her head is well shaped—& hair dressed like Mrs Cobb's—who, by the way, I think she resembles a little—She appeared like any other

young lady—but had a very intelligent expression when she spoke." Quincy (2003), p. 67.

114. Streshinsky (1993), p. xvi; Ford (1988), p. 306; Harwood & Durant (1985), p. 114; Durant & Harwood (1980), p. 411. Alice Ford originated the notion that Audubon left Fannie Kemble with a glowing impression at their meeting, which the actress supposedly recorded in her daily journal and later published in 1835:

> "[Audubon] called on us Sunday last. He is very enchanting: I wish it had been my good fortune to see him oftener; one of the *great men* of this country, he would have been a first-rate man all the world over; and like all first-rate people, there is a simplicity, and a total want of preten-sion about him that is very delightful. He gave us a description of Niagara, which did what he complained no description of it ever does,— conveyed to us an exact idea of the natural posi-tion and circumstances which render these falls so wonderful; whereas, most describers launch forth into vague and untangible rhapsodies, which, after all, convey no express idea of any-thing of water in the abstract, he gave me, by his few simple words, a more *real* impression of the stupendous cataract, than all that was ever writ or spoken of waterfalls before, not excepting Byron's Terni."

Ford (1988), p. 306, citing Butler (1835) II, pp. 151–152; Ford (1964), p. 301. It is a wonderful vignette that paints an engaging portrait of Audubon as a raconteur. The original diary is no longer extant, but the manuscript for the published journal resides in the Library of Congress. Clinton (2000), p. 11, note 12. However, neither it nor the published journal identifies Audubon by name.

In 1834, Kemble married Pierce Butler of Germantown, PA, the son of James Mease, M.D., of Philadelphia. It was Mease who had introduced Audubon to Charles-Lucien Bonaparte a decade before. Butler changed his surname as a condition for inheriting the property of a relative, who was one of the largest plantation owners in Georgia. Ford (1987), pp. 241–242, note 6. Butler reportedly ob-jected to his wife's plans for bringing the journal to print. David (2007), p. 135. To appease him, Kemble agreed to delete most of the proper names, which was a standard technique at the time. Audubon occasionally followed the same approach in the *OB*.

Many years later, after her marriage to Butler had crumbled and they went through a bitter divorce, Kemble annotated the two-volume set with the missing names as a gift for selected friends. One of these sets, annotated around 1860, is held by the Columbia University Rare Book and Manuscript Library in New York. It reveals that the person Kemble was referring to in the quoted passage, the one who entertained her with such a vibrant and revealing description of Niagara Falls, was not Audubon but Daniel Webster.

Although Kemble's annotation says merely "Webster," there can be little doubt as to whom she was referring. At the time, Daniel Webster (1782–1852) was a powerful and respected U.S Senator from Massachusetts, one of the country's leading lawyers, and an eloquent speaker. Webster was in Boston when this visit to the Kembles occurred. Jenkins (2005), p. 387; Curtis (1870) I, pp. 460–461. Audubon was not.

Kemble stated in her journal entry that the caller came by on "Sunday last." Her journal itself is not clear as to the date of the entry, but it must have been after Thursday, May 2, which is the nearest previously recorded date in the journal. If she was somehow referencing Sunday, April 28, Audubon was in New York on that date. If, instead, she was alluding to Sunday, May 5, which is most likely, Audubon was by then sailing from Boston to Eastport and did not return to Boston until September. Audubon did visit the Kembles, but as stated in the text, this occurred on the morning of Saturday, May 4. It would be nice to believe that Audubon thoroughly enchanted the Kembles during his visit. But the evidence does not support Ford's contention that Fannie mentioned him in her journal.

115. *Boston Daily Advertiser & Patriot*, Vol. XLII, No. 11,058, p. 2, col. 4 (Saturday, 4 May 1833) (AAS). The claim by the Boston paper that Audubon had obtained sixteen subscriptions to the *BOA* in New York could only have originated with the naturalist. However, this appears to have been an exaggeration. Lucy, who presumably knew precisely how many subscriptions had been collected,

informed Victor in a letter on May 7 that they had obtained thirteen. LBA, New York to VGA, London, 7 May 1833 (Yale, Box 1, Folder 18). Audubon no doubt inflated the number to reinforce the popularity of his work. See also, note 50, *supra*.

116. *National Gazette and Literary Register*, Vol. XII, No. 1886, p. 1, cols. 1–2 (Saturday, 4 May 1833).

117. JJA, Boston to LBA, New York, 4 May 1833 (Princeton, Box 2, Folder 15), *Letters* I, p. 216.

118. Bowman is identified as the Master of the *Edward Preble* in the Marine Journal section of Boston's *Daily Evening Transcript*, Vol. III, No. 833, p. 2., col. 4 (Monday Evening, 6 May 1833)(AAS).

119. JJA, Boston to LBA, New York, 4 May 1833 (Princeton, Box 2, Folder 15), *Letters* I, p. 217.

120. Ibid. The Kembles dined with Col. Thomas H. Perkins on Saturday evening, May 4, just as Audubon was getting ready to sail for Eastport. The celebrated actress recorded her impression of the wealthy Perkins in the manuscript of her published journals, now in the Library of Congress:

> Last Saturday week we dined with Colonel _____ one of the richest and most influential men in Boston. 'A royal merchant,' a man worth two millions of dollars, who lives like a nobleman, has six children and grandchildren without limit. Who has given the town of Boston its Athenaeum, or reading room, who moreover has just given the house in which we dined with him, a very large and handsome one, to be an asylum for the Blind — in short, a very fine old gentleman.

Fanny Kemble manuscript (Library of Congress), p. 122. For unknown reasons, this passage was crossed out in the manuscript and did not appear in her published volume.

121. Quincy (2003), pp. 22, 81; JJA, Boston to LBA, New York, 4 May 1833 (Princeton, Box 2, Folder 15), *Letters* I, p. 217. Maria Sophia Quincy (1805–1886), who went by "Sophia," was the third of Josiah Quincy's five daughters. Anna Quincy recorded in her diary for May 4, 1833, that her father and Sophia had left their home in Charleston and gone into town, i.e., Boston. Quincy (2003), pp. 21–22, 81.

122. JJA, Boston to LBA, New York, 4 May 1833

(Princeton, Box 2, Folder 15), *Letters* I, p. 217; JJA, New York to VGA, London, 28 Apr. 1833, Grinnell (1916), p. 123.

123. JWA addendum to JJA, Eastport to LBA, New York, 14 May 1833 (Princeton, Box 2, Folder 16).

124. GCSJr, Brunswick, ME to GCS, Boston, 5 May 1833 (MHS, Box 5, Vol. 11, 1–13 May 1833).

125. Marshall (2006), pp. 5–7, 10–13, 15–17, 19–21, 28, 30–31, 34–36.

126. GCSJr, Brunswick, ME to GCS, Boston, 5 May 1833 (MHS, Box 5, Vol. 11, 1–13 May 1833).

127. Dr. Reuben Dimond Mussey (1780–1866) was born on June 23, 1780, in Pelham, NH. He became a close friend of George C. Shattuck Sr., with whom he attended Dartmouth College, and graduated with an A.B. degree in 1803. Following graduation, Mussey studied medicine with Shattuck under Nathan Smith, M.D., who founded the medical school at Dartmouth, and received A.M. and M.B. degrees from that institution in 1806. He practiced in what is now Essex, MA, before moving to Philadelphia, where he pursued advanced studies in medicine for almost a year and conducted a series of experiments on himself to test prevailing theories of the human skin. He was awarded an M.D. degree from the University of Pennsylvania in 1809 and Dartmouth in 1812. Following his stay in Philadelphia, he relocated to Salem, MA, where he developed a successful medical and surgical practice before being appointed a professor at the Dartmouth College of Medicine. From 1814 to 1820, he was Professor of Theory and Practice of Medicine, and Materia Medica and Therapeutics. From 1814 to 1838, he also served as Professor of Obstetrics. In 1822, he was appointed Professor of Anatomy and Surgery, a position he held until he left Dartmouth in 1838. While still teaching at Dartmouth, he accepted the position of Lecturer on Anatomy and Surgery at the Medical School of Maine at Bowdoin College from 1831 to 1835. In 1838, he was named Professor of Surgery at the Medical College of Ohio in Cincinnati, where he taught until 1852. He then became Professor of Surgery at the Miami Medical College in Cincinnati. He died on June 21, 1866, in Boston. Bowdoin College (1912), p. 38; Dartmouth College (1890), p. 12; Cleaveland (1882), pp. 141–142;

Dr. William Sweetser (1797–1875) was born in Boston on September 8, 1797. He was educated at Harvard, where he received an A.B. degree in 1815 and A.M. and M.D. degrees in 1818. He was Professor of Theory and Practice of Medicine at the University of Vermont from 1825 to 1832. In 1833, he accepted an appointment as a Lecturer on the Theory and Practice of Physic at the Medical School of Maine at Bowdoin College. He returned to Bowdoin in 1842 and thereafter held the positions of Lecturer (1842–1845) and Professor (1845–1850). From 1850 to 1861, he was Professor of the Theory and Practice of Medicine. He also found time to serve as a Professor of Medicine at Hobart College from 1848 to 1855. He died in New York on October 14, 1875. Bowdoin (1912), p. 42.

128. Marshall (2006), p. 27; Dartmouth College (1890), p. 114; Shattuck (1881), p. 164.

129. Marshall (2006), pp. 43–44; Bowdoin College (1912), p. 42.

130. GCSJr, Brunswick, ME to GCS, Boston, 5 May 1833 (MHS, Box 5, Vol. 11, 1–13 May 1833). Dr. Reuben D. Mussey provided another perspective of his meeting with Shattuck Jr. in a May 7 letter to the young man's father: "He asked my advice as to the expediency of joining Mr Audubon. After I had decided in favour of the enterprise, he remarked that although he had a great desire to go, he should not have felt authorized to take the step, had I not concurred." Reuben D. Mussey, M.D., Brunswick, ME to GCS, Boston, 7 May 1833 (MHS, Box 5, Vol. 11, 1–13 May 1833).

131. GCSJr, Brunswick, ME to GCS, Boston, 5 May 1833 (MHS, Box 5, Vol. 11, 1–13 May 1833).

132. Marshall (2006), pp. 38–39.

133. GCSJr, Brunswick, ME to GCS, Boston, 5 May 1833 (MHS, Box 5, Vol. 11, 1–13 May 1833).

134. GCSJr, Brunswick, ME to Benjamin Lincoln, M.D., Burlington, VT, 5 May 1833 (Letters to Benjamin Lincoln, Massachusetts Historical Society (Ms. S-15)).

135. GCSJr, Brunswick, ME to GCS, Boston, 5–6 May 1833 (MHS, Box 5, Vol. 11, 1–13 May 1833). Parker Cleaveland, LL.D. (1780–1858) was Professor of Chemistry, Mineralogy, and Natural Philosophy at Bowdoin College. In 1816, Cleaveland published *An Elementary Treatise on Mineralogy and Geology* (Boston: Cummings and Hilliard, 1816). He has

been called the "father of American mineralogy." Burbank (1988), pp. 145–152; Cleaveland (1882), pp. 126–129. See also, Wilson (2014).

136. GCSJr, Brunswick, ME to GCS, Boston, 5–6 May 1833 (MHS, Box 5, Vol. 11, 1–13 May 1833).

137. Journal of George C. Shattuck Jr., 7 May 1833 (Countway); GCSJr, Brunswick, ME to GCS, Boston, 5–6 May 1833 (MHS, Box 5, Vol. 11, 1–13 May 1833).

138. Journal of George C. Shattuck Jr., 7 May 1833 (Countway).

CHAPTER 4: EASTPORT

1. Kilby (1888), p. 63. The dimensions of Moose Island were measured from the U.S. Geographical Survey map of the Passamaquoddy quadrangle.

2. Ibid., pp. 8, 64, 68. Eastport was incorporated as a city in 1893. Holt (1999), p. 33.

3. Kinney (1989), p. 2; Kilby (1888), pp 76, 78.

4. Zimmerman (1984), p. 17.

5. Ibid., p. 26.

6. Kilby (1888), p. 79.

7. Zimmerman (1984), p. 64.

8. Woodard (2012); Woodard (2004), pp. 152–153.

9. Kilby (1888), p. 68–69.

10. Ibid., pp. 77, 261. The overwhelming majority of the ships docking at Eastport in 1833 were of British registry due to changes in the customs laws, effective October 1830, which permitted the admission of those vessels on the same terms as American ones. Of the 1,820 vessels that landed that year, all but 36, a total of 1,784, were foreign entries. By comparison, the number of foreign vessels entering Boston harbor was only 1,067. New York barely eclipsed the number at Eastport with a total of 1,925 foreign vessels. However, the average tonnage and value of imports going into New York were significantly greater. Ibid., pp. 77–78, 261.

11. Kilby (1888), p. 75.

12. Coke (1833) II, p. 134.

13. Zimmerman (1984), pp. 3, 14–17, 78; Kilby (1888), p. 75.

14. Zimmerman (1984), p. 3. In July 1814, when a small British armada sailed into Passamaquoddy Bay to seize Moose Island and the town of Eastport, the commander of Fort Sullivan, Maj. Putnam, initially refused to accept the terms of surrender presented by a British Army lieutenant on the staff of Sir John Cope Sherbrook. However, several of Eastport's leading citizens, recognizing that the fort would be taken and the town destroyed, prevailed upon Putnam to lower the garrison's U.S. flag and surrender. Kilby (1888), pp. 175–178.

15. Coke (1833) II, p. 134.

16. JJA, Eastport to LBA, New York, 7 May 1833 (Private collection), *Letters* I, pp. 217- 218.

17. Ibid., p. 218.

18. *OB* II, pp. 415–416; JJA, Eastport to LBA, New York, 7 May 1833 (Private collection), *Letters* I, p. 218.

19. JJA, Eastport to LBA, New York, 7 May 1833 (Private collection), *Letters* I, pp. 217–218.

20. *OB* IV, p. 163.

21. *OB* IV, pp. 212–213.

22. *OB* II, pp. 415–416.

23. James Curtiss (1806–1859) was born in Wethersfield, CT, on March 29, 1806. Calnan (2007), p. 39; Morrison (1897), pp. 665–666. He lived in Philadelphia for several years and worked as a printer's apprentice before moving to Portland, ME, where he worked for the *Argus* newspaper. Griffin (1872), p. 148; Obituary (1859). In 1828, he moved to Eastport to serve as the printer of the *Northern Light*, a newly established weekly, pro-Jacksonian paper. Shortly after the paper's inaugural issue, he was named editor and publisher, serving in these capacities until 1832. Griffin (1872), pp. 148–149. On May 18, 1830, he married Mary Kimball, who was born in Newburyport, MA, on June 13, 1809. They welcomed two children during their residence in Eastport: James (b. 3-20 or 3-28-1831) and Mary (b. 12-18-1832). Calnan (2007), p. 39; Morrison (1897), pp. 665–666. In approximately 1830, Curtiss was appointed by President Andrew Jackson to serve as U.S. postmaster in Eastport, a position he held until around 1834, when he was removed from office for reasons that remain unclear. U.S. Senate (1833), pp. 341, 348; U.S. Postmaster (1831), p. 9. The following year, he moved with his family to Chicago. See also, Chapter 5, note 24, *infra*.

24. JJA, Eastport to LBA, New York, 7 May 1833 (Private collection), *Letters* I, p. 218.

25. Ibid. Jonathan D. Weston (1782–1834) was born Jonathan Weston on April 30, 1782, in Reading, MA. He attended Harvard, graduating in

1802, and went on to practice law in Eastport. Kilby (1888), p. 243. In 1805, he changed his name to Jonathan De Lesdernier Weston. Peirce (1885), p. 15. On March 2, 1806, he married Jane Nelson in Reading, MA. He served as Eastport town clerk from 1805 to 1807, and again from 1832 to 1834. He also served as a town selectman and moderator. In 1820, he received an honorary Master of Arts degree from Bowdoin College. He served as the deputy collector of customs in Eastport for many years. He died on October 3, 1834, in his home on Boynton Street. Dodd (2005); Bassett (1921), pp. 310–311; Kilby (1888), pp. 243–244. At the time of the Audubons' visit to Eastport, the Westons had three children: Lucy (1806–1850); Nelson (1808–1838), and Jane (1820–1879). Kelly (2008).

26. LBA, New York to VGA, London, 19 May 1833 (Yale, Box 1, Folder 18); Lucy P. Weston, Eastport to Jane H. Weston, Boston, 15 May 1833 (Rosenberg Library). In her letter to Victor, Lucy wrote that Audubon and John "were very comfortably settled at the house of a Mr Weston, a place provided by Mr Curtis." She clearly was unfamiliar with the Weston name, which would indicate that the families had not met during the summer of 1832. This is contrary to what is stated in the most recently published history of Eastport. Holt (1999), p. 107. The Westons' eldest daughter, Lucy, was born in Eastport on December 3, 1806, and an early daguerreotype reflects that she was a brunette. Shelly Kelly (Personal communication, 28 Apr. 2012).

27. Kilby (1888), p. 244. As of 2016, the Weston house was still standing at 26 Boynton Street in Eastport.

28. Jett Peterson (Personal communication, 25 May 2014); Lucy P. Weston, Eastport to Jane H. Weston, Boston, 15 May 1833 (Rosenberg Library); JJA, Eastport to LBA, New York, 7 May 1833 (Private collection), *Letters* I, p. 218.

29. Ibid. Ichabod Rollins Chadbourne (1787–1855) was born in South Berwick, ME, on January 7, 1787. He graduated from Dartmouth College in 1808 and read for the law, being admitted to the Suffolk, MA, bar in 1812. He opened a practice the same year in South Berwick, where he joined the Berwick Company, 2nd Regiment, 1st Brigade, 6th Division of the Massachusetts Militia. He was

elected to the rank of lieutenant on August 10, 1812. In 1816, he moved to Lubec, ME, where he continued to practice law and served as postmaster. He moved across Passamaquoddy Bay to Eastport shortly before it was returned to the U.S. in 1818 pursuant to the Treaty of Ghent. His first marriage in 1818 ended later that year with the untimely death of his wife, Dolly Dana. In October 1821, he married Hannah Lincoln (1801–1882), eldest daughter of Judge Theodore Lincoln of Dennysville, ME, and the older sister of Tom Lincoln, who accompanied Audubon to Labrador. Chadbourne served as moderator of Eastport in 1821, 1822, 1823, 1825, 1838, 1839, and 1855. He was elected as Eastport's representative to the Maine legislature in 1839 as a Whig and was reelected the following year. He died in Eastport on December 8, 1855, at the age of sixty-eight. Kilby (1888), pp. 261, 269–270, 274, 284; Chapman (1867), p. 137; Book 6B, *1812–1820 Maine Officer Commissions*, pp. 261, 432 (Massachusetts National Guard Archives).

30. Kilby (1888), p. 270.

31. Ichabod Rollins Chadbourne was elected captain of the local volunteer militia, known as the Eastport Light Infantry, on September 16, 1818, and served in this capacity until 1820, at which time he "resigned to accept the position of division inspector on the staff of Major-general Herrick." Kilby (1888), pp. 469–470; Book 6B, *1812–1820 Maine Officer Commissions*, p. 432 (Massachusetts National Guard Archives). This would have been Jedediah Herrick (1780–1847), the commanding general of the 10th Division of the Massachusetts Militia from 1816 to 1820 and then, after Maine became a state in 1820, of the Maine Militia until 1828.

32. Calnan (2007), pp. 30–31; Dennysville (1886), pp. 108–109; *OB* II, p. 437.

33. Hobart (1986), pp. 7–8, 83–84; Draper (1969), pp. 44–45; Davis (1895) II, p. 422; Dennysville (1886), pp. 21, 25, 27, 109; Palmer (1864), p. 1. Theodore Lincoln (1763–1852) was born on December 30, 1763, in Hingham, MA. Cushing (1905), p. 101. He attended Harvard and graduated with an A.M. degree in 1785. Harvard (1930), p. 200. He reportedly studied for the law and was admitted to the bar before his move to Dennysville in 1786. Davis (1895) II, p. 422. On May 6, 1799, he married Hannah Mayhew, who was born in Machias, ME,

on May 10, 1775. They had nine children: Theodore (b. 2-10-1800, d. 4-17-1867); Hannah (b. 5-15-1801, d. 5-25-1882); Benjamin (b. 10-11-1802, d. 2-26-1835); Mary (b. 4-12-1804, d. 6-20-1811); Bela (b. 7-14-1805, d. 4-27-1859); Sarah (b. 6-7-1807, d. 7-26-1886); Edmund (b. 11-12-1809, d. 7-9-1875); Thomas (b. 3-27-1812, d. 3-27-1883); and Mary (b. 2-15-1814, d. 12-6-1843).

34. Dennysville (1886), p. 39.

35. Hobart (1986), p. 85; *OB* II, pp. xviii, 437. Audubon referenced the family of Judge Theodore Lincoln in his account of the Spotted or Canada Grous: "In August 1832, I reached the delightful little village of Dennisville, about eighteen miles distant from Eastport. There I had the good fortune of becoming an inmate of the kind and most hospitable family of Judge LINCOLN, who has resided there for nearly half a century, and who is blessed with a family of sons equal to any with whom I am acquainted, for talents, perseverance and industry. Each of these had his own peculiar avocation, and I naturally attached myself more particularly to one who ever since his childhood has manifested a decided preference for ornithological pursuits. This young gentleman, THOMAS LINCOLN, offered to lead me to those retired woods where the Spruce Partridges were to be found." *OB* II, p. 437.

36. *OB* II, pp. 437–438; Tom Lincoln, Dennysville to JJA, Boston, 8 Jan. 1833 (Yale, Box 5, Folder 228).

37. JJA, Eastport to LBA, New York, 7 May 1833 (Private collection), *Letters* I, p. 218. The quoted portion of this letter in the text is taken from the original holograph, which differs in several ways from that published by Howard Corning in *Letters*. Notably, Corning misread Audubon's reference to Thomas Lincoln as "Thos Gincaler."

38. JJA, Eastport to LBA, New York, 7 May 1833 (Private collection), *Letters* I, p. 218; JJA, Boston to James Curtiss, Eastport, 25 Jan. 1833 (Private collection).

39. JJA, Eastport to LBA, New York, 7 May 1833 (Private collection), *Letters* I, p. 218.

40. *OB* II, p. 486; Force (1833), pp. 333–334.

41. JJA, Eastport to LBA, New York, 7 May 1833 (Private collection), *Letters* I, p. 218.

42. Ibid.

43. Stoughton (2011), p. 146; Cullum (1891) I,

pp. 115–117; Child (1881), p. 677; JJA, Eastport to LBA, New York, 7 May 1833 (Private collection), *Letters* I, p. 218; *Eastern Democrat*, Vol. 1, No. 14, p. 2, cols. 2–3 (Friday Morning, 24 Aug. 1832). Thomas Wells Childs (1796–1853) was born on March 16, 1796, in Pittsfield, MA. He graduated from West Point in 1814 and served as an artillery officer in the War of 1812, initially as a 3rd lieutenant and later 2nd lieutenant with the 1st Artillery before being transferred to the Corps of Artillery. Following the war, he served at various posts, including Fort Niagara, NY (1815–1816); New York Harbor (1816–1818); Ft. Washington, MD (1818–1819); New York Harbor (1819–1820); Commissary duty (1820–1821); and Ft. Washington, MD (1821–1827). He was promoted to 1st lieutenant in the Corps of Artillery in 1818 and was transferred to the 3d Artillery at the same rank in 1821. In 1826, he was elevated to the rank of captain. In 1827, he assumed command of the garrison at Fort Sullivan in Eastport, ME. He served as commandant there through 1836. When the Seminole War broke out in 1836, he was sent to Florida for a year and received a promotion to bvt. major. He returned to Fort Sullivan before being dispatched once more to Florida, where he served in the war against the Seminoles from 1838 to 1842. For his gallant conduct and repeated military successes, he received a further promotion to bvt. lt.-colonel. When the hostilities ended, he was assigned to several posts, including Ft. Johnston, NC (1842–1844); Ft. Moultrie, SC (1844); and Ft. Johnston, NC (1844–1845). He served briefly in the military occupation of Texas from 1845–1846 and subsequently commanded an artillery battalion in the Mexican-American War from 1846 to 1847. He was promoted to bvt. colonel for gallant conduct at the Battle of Palo Alto and the Battle of Resaca de la Palma in May 1846, and was promoted again to major in February of 1847. He served as military governor of Jalapa, Mexico, from April to June 1847 and of the city of Puebla from September to October 1847. For his meritorious conduct in defending Puebla from a siege by Mexican troops, Childs received a promotion to brig.-general. In 1848, he was posted to Ft. McHenry, MD. In 1852, he was sent to East Florida to assume command of military operations. He died of yellow fever at Ft. Brooke, FL, on October 8, 1853. He is buried in Alexandria, VA.

Reporting on his death, a Pittsfield, MA, newspaper stated: "[W]hile all bear testimony to his gallantry as a soldier, his crowning distinction was the moral heroism and singular purity of his character, his faithful and consistent religious life, which, after all the honors of earth have passed away, remain in the hearts of his friends to consecrate his memory, and furnish the brightest and sweetest hope of that better life and more enduring fame which await all the faithful soldiers and servants of God." Cullum (1891) I, pp. 115–117; Nelson Weston, New York to Jane Weston, Eastport, 14 Nov. 1837 (Rosenberg).

44. JJA, Eastport to LBA, New York, 7 May 1833 (Private collection), *Letters* I, p. 219.

45. LBA, New York to John Bachman, Charleston, 7 May 1833 (Harvard (207)).

46. VGA, London to JJA, New York, 30 Aug. 1833 (Yale, Box 2, Folder 38).

47. LBA, New York to John Bachman, Charleston, 7 May 1833 (Harvard (207)).

48. Ibid. See also, Mazÿck (1908), pp. 8–10.

49. JJA, Eastport to LBA, New York, 14 May 1833 (Princeton, Box 2, Folder 16), *Letters* I, p. 219; LBA, New York to John Bachman, Charleston, 7 May 1833 (Harvard (207)). Evidently, the letter to Audubon that Lucy had commenced on May 7 was finished two days later based on Audubon's May 14 response in which he said the letter had the two dates on it. Nicholas Berthoud had written on the outside of her letter that she had received his Boston letters the day she began writing it.

50. LBA, New York to VGA, London, 7 May 1833 (Yale, Box 1, Folder 18).

51. "James Wheelock Ripley, (1786–1835)," *Biographical Directory of the United States Congress*, http://bioguide.congress.gov/scripts/biodisplay .pl?index=R000266 (accessed 16 Feb. 2014); Force (1833), p. 319.

52. JJA, Eastport to LBA, New York, 7 May 1833 (Private collection), *Letters* I, p. 219. When Audubon wrote this letter to Lucy on May 7, he had evidently already made arrangements with Ichabod Rollins Chadbourne to go to Dennysville the following day. There is no documentary confirmation of this trip, but we know that he enlisted Tom Lincoln to join him on the forthcoming voyage to Point Lepreau, NB, which could only have happened if

Audubon had personally paid a visit to the Lincoln homestead on May 8.

53. Washburn (1977), p. 12; Townsend (1924), pp. 237–238. The Georgian architectural design used in the Lincoln home in Dennysville was a popular style in two-story New England homes beginning in the 18th century. It was distinguished by a symmetrical shape with the front door set in the middle of the structure with two windows on either side. On the second story, a window was set immediately above each of the first-story windows, and a fifth window was positioned directly above the door. The roof had a medium pitch with little if any overhang. Craven (2014); Zerbey (1997).

54. Kaufman (1996), p. 412–413; *OB* V, p. 416.

55. Cushing (1905), p. 101. George C. Shattuck Jr. described Judge Lincoln and his wife, Hannah, in his journal: "He is a stout old man, about five feet nine inches high, his hair gray, but his eye undimmed, and his frame unbowed by time. He is in his sixty ninth year, enjoys uniform health, and is as active as a man of thirty. Mrs L is a thin tall woman, to appe[arance] nearly as young as her husband, an excellent housewife, having a cultivated mind." GCSJr, Eastport to Eliza Prentiss and Lucy Shattuck, Boston, 2 Jun. 1833 (MHS, Vol. 11, Jun. 1833).

56. JJA, Eastport to LBA, New York, 14 May 1833 (Princeton, Box 2, Folder 16).

57. GCS, Boston to GCSJr, Eastport, 8 May 1833 (MHS, Box 5, Vol. 11, 1–13 May 1833).

58. Bowdoin (1912), p. 323; GCS, Boston to GCSJr, Eastport, 8 May 1833 (MHS, Box 5, Vol. 11, 1–13 May 1833); Harvard (1826), p. 10.

59. GCS, Boston to JJA, Eastport, 9 May 1833 (Yale, Box 6, Folder 312). To the modern reader, Dr. Shattuck's statement in his note to Audubon— "should your own preparation require addition, I beg you to draw on me at sight, and your draft shall be honored"—may be incomprehensible. At that time, an individual could issue a draft, similar to a check, which would be paid by another individual as opposed to a bank. Shattuck was merely telling Audubon that if he ran short of funds, he should feel free to issue drafts under Shattuck's name, and they would be paid upon presentation to Shattuck in Boston.

60. In the *OB*, Audubon refers to the revenue

cutter tender as both the *Fancy* and the *Nancy*. Cf.
OB IV, p. 213 (*Nancy*); *OB* II, pp. 486, 488, 489
(*Fancy*). The multiple references to the *Fancy* in
his Episode "The Bay of Fundy" as opposed to the
single reference to the *Nancy* in a later species account would suggest that the former was the actual
name of the vessel, while the latter was a typographical error.

61. JJA, Eastport to Edward Harris, New York,
9 May 1833 (Harvard (Letters), pf (110), p. 8).

62. JJA, Eastport to LBA, New York, 14 May
1833 (Princeton, Box 2, Folder 16). In this letter,
Audubon advised Lucy that he and John were accompanied on the trip to Point Lepreau by "W^{am}
Curtiss," not James Curtiss. Although the 1830 U.S.
Census reflects that there was a William Curtiss residing in Eastport who appears to have been in his
thirties and was of an age to have been a suitable
compatriot to Audubon, the evidence convincingly
demonstrates that Audubon was actually referring to
James Curtiss, the Eastport postmaster.

To begin with, it would appear from the May
14th letter that this was someone known to Lucy.
"We had W^{am} Curtiss with us, Thos Lincoln & ourselves," he wrote. The Audubon family had met
James Curtiss during their visit to Eastport during
the summer of 1832, when they traveled through
northern Maine and New Brunswick. Curtiss subsequently corresponded with Audubon in Boston during the winter of 1833 and sent him a specimen of
the Large-billed Guillemot, which Audubon illustrated for *BOA. OB* III, p. 336; JJA, Boston to James
Curtiss, Eastport, 25 Jan. 1833 (Private collection).
Curtiss also made arrangements for Audubon and
his son to stay at the Weston home while they were
visiting Eastport prior to leaving for Labrador. JJA,
Eastport to LBA, New York, 7 May 1833 (Private
collection), *Letters* I, p. 218.

Second, it was James Curtiss who initially recommended that Audubon go to Point Lepreau to
search for birds. JJA, Boston to James Curtiss, Eastport, 25 Jan. 1833 (Private collection). It would be
understandable that Audubon invited him along on
the voyage.

Third, we now know from George C. Shattuck Jr.'s May 1833 journal that James Curtiss was a
member of Audubon's social circle during his stay

in Eastport. GCSJr Journal, 21 May 1833 (Countway). There is absolutely no mention in Shattuck's
journal of William Curtiss. Shattuck also disclosed
that James Curtiss accompanied Audubon on his
voyage to the islands off Grand Manan aboard the
U.S. Revenue Cutter *Swiftsure* between May 23 and
25. Ibid., 23 May 1833. Audubon did not mention
this fact in his Episode "The Bay of Fundy," and it
has not been previously known to Audubon scholars. But it is evident that James Curtiss and Audubon had an established relationship both before and
during the Eastport visit.

Fourth, when Audubon wrote to Tom Lincoln
on November 7, 1833, he asked to be remembered to
"Wm Curtiss" along with Capt. Henry Emery, who
guided Audubon's party to Labrador aboard the
schooner *Ripley*; Capt. Uriah Coolidge of the *Swiftsure*; and Joe Coolidge, the son of Capt. Coolidge
and a member of the Labrador expedition. JJA,
Charleston to Tom Lincoln, Dennysville, 7 Nov.
1833, Townsend (1924), p. 241. Since these latter
three men were among Audubon's closest friends
in Eastport, it is unthinkable that Audubon would
not have included James Curtiss among them. This
appears to have been an example of Audubon just
getting the name wrong. But if he did it in this letter, which is almost certain, it lends support to the
notion that he made the same mistake in his May 14
letter to Lucy about the members of his party.

Fifth, Audubon had a history of making such
mistakes when it came to people's names. Ford
(1987), pp. 304–305, note 5. For example, in a letter
to Audubon in February 1836, Shattuck Jr. wrote
that Dr. George Parkman had shown him a letter in
which Audubon had asked about his "young friend
Wm Shattuck." GCSJr, Boston to JJA, London, 13
Feb. 1836 (Yale, Box 6, Folder 313). Shattuck understood that Audubon had referred to him by the
wrong name and answered the inquiry.

Finally, and most tellingly, Lucy recognized that
Audubon had confused "William" for "James" in
his May 14th letter. In writing to her husband on
May 24, she asked him about this and wondered if
Curtiss's first name was "James or William for you
call him by both names." LBA, New York to JJA,
Eastport, 24 May 1833 (Yale, Box 1, Folder 18). The
evidence convincingly supports the conclusion that

the Eastport postmaster was among Audubon's party when he sailed to Point Lepreau.

63. Holt (1999) pp. 116–117; GCSJr, Eastport to Eliza Prentiss and Lucy Shattuck, Boston, 2 Jun. 1833 (MHS, Box 5, Vol. 11, Jun. 1833).

64. *Eastern Democrat*, Vol. II, No. 19, p. 3, col. 3; p. 4, col. 2 (Tuesday Morning, 1 Oct. 1833); *Eastern Democrat*, Vol. 1, No. 32, p. 3, cols. 4–5; p. 4, col. 4 (Friday Morning, 28 Dec. 1832).

65. GCSJr, Eastport to GCS, Boston, 9 May 1833 (MHS, Box 5, Vol. 11, 1–13 May 1833); GCSJr Journal, 10 May 1833 (Countway). The location of the law office of Ichabod Chadbourne is derived from a notice appearing in the *Eastern Democrat*. *Eastern Democrat*, Vol. II, No. 19, p. 3, col. 5 (Tuesday Morning, 1 Oct. 1833).

66. GCSJr, Eastport to GCS, Boston, 9 May 1833 (MHS, Box 5, Vol. 11, 1–13 May 1833); GCSJr Journal, 10 May 1833 (Countway).

67. George C. Shattuck Jr.'s physical details are taken from his 1836 and 1856 U.S. passport applications. Though a later 1869 application would indicate that he was 5′10″ tall, this is in error. His height of 5′8″ is reflected in the 1836 documents as well as the 1856 application, which is written in his own hand. U.S. Passport Application, 25 Mar. 1856: Age: Not given; Height: 5′8″; Eyes: Blue (physical description in Shattuck's hand). *Passport Applications, 1795–1905*, Collection Number: *ARC Identifier 566612/MLR Number A1 508*; NARA Series: *M1372*; Roll: *54*, Images: *437–438* (Washington, D.C.: National Archives, 25 Mar. 1856); Register of U.S. Passports Granted, 19 Mar. 1836: Age: 22 years; Height: 5′8″; Eyes: Blue, *Registers and Indexes for Passport Applications, 1810–1906*, Collection Number: *ARC Identifier 579314/MLR Number A1 506*; NARA Series: *M1371*; Roll: *1*; Image: *21* (Washington D.C.: National Archives, 19 Mar. 1836); U.S. Passport Application, 18 Mar. 1836: Age: 22 years; Height: 5′8″; Eyes: Blue, *Passport Applications, 1795–1905*, Collection Number: *ARC Identifier 566612/MLR Number A1 508*, NARA Series: *M1372*; Roll: *4*; Image: *120* (Washington D.C.: National Archives, 18 Mar. 1836). See also, JJA, Eastport to LBA, New York, 14 May 1833 (Princeton, Box 2, Folder 16).

68. GCSJr, Eastport to GCS, Boston, 9 May 1833 (MHS, Box 5, Vol. 11, 1–13 May 1833).

69. We know from the content of Audubon's May 9 letter to Edward Harris that he had written to Harris earlier in the day. JJA, Eastport to Edward Harris, New York, 9 May 1833 (Harvard (Letters), pf (110), p. 8). We also know that at least the second letter was posted after he had seen Shattuck Jr. at Ichabod R. Chadbourne's office because the naturalist penned the following line on the outside address flap: "A son of Doc^r Shattuck of Boston has this moment arrived to accompany us—and a young Gentleman in this neighborhood we hope to have to come by all means" Ibid. Since the letter is postmarked May 10, it must have been either mailed by Audubon or given to Chadbourne to do so—likely the latter because Audubon left Eastport on May 9.

70. JJA, Eastport to Edward Harris, New York, 9 May 1833 (Harvard (Letters), pf (110), p. 8).

71. Ibid. See also, Herrick (1938) II, pp. 40–41.

72. GCSJr Journal, 10 May 1833 (Countway); GCSJr, Eastport to GCS, Boston, 9 May 1833 (MHS, Box 5, Vol. 11, 1–13 May 1833). The Chadbourne home is located at 19 Shackford Street in Eastport.

73. Calnan (2007), p. 30; GCSJr, Eastport to Ellen E. Shattuck, Boston, 17 May 1833 (MHS, Box 5, Vol. 11, 14–31 May 1833). When Shattuck Jr. was a guest of the Chadbourne family in May 1833, the family consisted of the following children: (1) Theodore Lincoln (b. 8-1-1822); (2) George Wallingford (b. 1-19-1824); (4) Benjamin Lincoln (b. 4-30-1826); (4) Hannah Lincoln (b. 3-18-1828); (5) Alexander Leaummeu (b. 7-7-1830); and (6) Elizabeth Robbins (b. 7-9-1832). The Chadbournes would ultimately add another three children to their clan. Calnan (2007), pp. 30–31.

74. GCSJr, Eastport to GCS, Boston, 9 May 1833 (MHS, Box 5, Vol. 11, 1–13 May 1833).

75. Kilby (1888), p. 70; GCSJr Journal, 10 May 1833 (Countway).

76. Willey (2003), p. 281; *OB* II, p. 486; Force (1834), p. 253; Force (1833), p. 324; JJA, Eastport to LBA, New York, 14 May 1833 (Princeton, Box 2, Folder 16).

77. *OB* II, p. 486. Alice Ford could not determine the derivation of Audubon's reference to "old wives" as he sailed from Eastport to Head Harbor Bay on Campobello Island. She thought he might be alluding, not to Long-tailed Ducks (formerly Oldsquaws),

but to Mallards. Ford (1969), p. 223. Her confusion is not surprising. In the 19th century, many birds carried local names or nicknames. There were no field guides at the time, and most people did not have access to published works on ornithology.

However, we know that Audubon was referring to the Long-tailed Duck from his account of the species in the *OB*: "Owing to their reiterated cries, these birds are named 'Noisy Ducks;' but they have various appellations, among others those of 'old wives,' and 'old squaws.'" *OB* IV, p. 105. Up until the Forty-second Supplement to the American Ornithologists' Union (AOU) *Check-list of North American Birds*, adopted in 2000, these sea ducks were known as Oldsquaws. The Committee on Classification and Nomenclature of the AOU, which is responsible for updating the official AOU *Check-list*, explained that the name change was made in response to a petition from the U.S. Fish and Wildlife Service in Alaska. The FWS biologists who were responsible for implementing a conservation management plan to arrest an ongoing decline in the species' numbers believed the name Oldsquaw was offensive to the Native Americans, whose assistance was critical in carrying out the plan. The Committee also pointed out that the species is known as the Long-tailed Duck in most of the rest of the world. AOU (2000), pp. 848–849.

78. President Franklin Delano Roosevelt spent his summers on Campobello Island as he was growing up and contracted polio there during a family vacation with his wife, Eleanor, and their children in 1921. Sardone (2014); Gilbert (1988), pp. 33–34.

79. "The History of Head Harbour Lightstation," http://www.campobello.com/lighthouse /litehistory.html (accessed 19 Feb. 2014); "East Quoddy Lighthouse, http://www.campobello.com /east.html (accessed 15 Feb. 2015); Blunt (1833), p. 146.

80. *OB* II, p. 486.

81. GCSJr Journal, 10 May 1833 (Countway).

82. Weiss (2007), pp. 35–36; Weiss (2006); Jacobs (1979), p. 100; Bowdoin College (1912), pp. 70–73, 323; Harvard (1826), p. 10; Ancestry.com, Robert Charles Ashley Family Tree, http://trees .ancestry.com/tree/62316456/person/42211973814 (accessed 2 May 2015).

83. GCSJr Journal, 10 May 1833 (Countway).

84. Van Wyhe (2002), pp. 21–23; Capen (1833), pp. 20, 22, 30–32, 42.

85. Marshall (2006), p. 50; Walsh (1972), p. 191; Colonial Society of Massachusetts (1907), p. 77; Warren (1860) II, p. 12; Spurzheim (1834), p. 111.

86. *OB* II, p. xix. According to a contemporaneous account, Audubon drew an image of Spurzheim after he died. Anon. (1834), p. 130. However, more recent scholarship has been unable to confirm this. Walsh (1972), p. 198, note 49.

87. Weiss (2006); Jacobs (1979), pp. 101–102; Bowdoin (1912), p. 323. See also, U.S. National Library of Medicine, "Isaac Ray (1807–1881)," Diseases of the Mind: Highlights of American Psychiatry through 1900, 19th Century Psychiatrists of Note, http://www.nlm.nih.gov/hmd/diseases/note .html (accessed 18 Feb. 2014). Isaac Ray's landmark book, *A Treatise on the Medical Jurisprudence of Insanity*, was quoted extensively by an English defense attorney in the 1843 trial of Daniel McNaughton, who suffered from delusions about the Tory government and murdered the private secretary of the prime minister after mistaking him for his boss. McNaughton was acquitted by reason of insanity and committed to a mental institution for the remainder of his life. However, public outrage over the verdict led the House of Lords to ask a panel of judges to fashion a standard for determining the insanity of a criminal defendant. Known as the McNaughton Rule, it presumes that a criminal defendant is sane unless the jury clearly finds from expert testimony that the defendant, at the time of the act, "was labouring under such a defect of reason, from disease of the mind, as not to know the nature and quality of the act he was doing, or as not to know that what he was doing was wrong." Asokan (2007); United Kingdom House of Lords Decisions, Daniel M'Naghten's case [1843] UKHL J16 (19 Jun. 1843), http://www.bailii.org/uk/cases/UKHL/1843 /J16.html (accessed 29 Jul. 2015). The McNaughton Rule was widely adopted in the United States in the mid-19th century, but today only twenty-five of the states continue to follow it or a modified version of it. "The Insanity Defense Among the States, Findlaw.com, http://files.findlaw.com/pdf/criminal /criminal.findlaw.com_criminal-procedure_the -insanity-defense-among-the-states.pdf (accessed 29 Jul. 2015).

88. *OB* II, pp. 486–487.

89. Ibid.

90. Ibid., p. 162.

91. Ibid., p. 488; JJA, Eastport to LBA, New York, 14 May 1833 (Princeton, Box 2, Folder 16), *Letters* I, p. 220; GCSJr Journal, 21 May 1833 (Countway).

92. JJA, Eastport to LBA, New York, 14 May 1833 (Princeton, Box 2, Folder 16), *Letters* I, p. 220; *OB* IV, p. 217. Some Audubon scholars believe that, during his Eastport stay, Audubon painted the Buffel-headed Ducks (Buffleheads) that were collected on the excursion to Point Lepreau. Low (2002), p. 168; Audubon (1966) II, Plate 406.

Audubon scholar Edward H. Dwight writes that the Buffleheads were painted by Audubon "in Eastport, Maine, on May 11, 1833." Audubon (1966) II, Plate 406. He apparently bases this conclusion on a reference made by Audubon in the *OB*: "On the 11th of that month [May] in 1833, I shot some of them near Eastport in Maine." *OB* IV, p. 217. However, Audubon certainly did not paint this species in Eastport on that date. As noted in the text, from May 9 to May 14 he was aboard the *Fancy* exploring the area around Point Lepreau, NB.

Moreover, it is questionable that he painted them in Eastport when he returned to port. In a letter to Lucy, dated June 4, 1833, Audubon listed only four species of birds that they had "procured and finished" drawing during their stay in Eastport: Winter Wren, Hyperborean Phalarope (Red-necked Phalarope), Harlequin Duck, and Black Guillemot. JJA, Eastport to LBA, New York, 4 Jun. 1833 (Princeton, Box 2, Folder 22), *Letters* I, p. 236. If he had, indeed, started a composition of the Buffleheads after collecting specimens during his trip to Point Lepreau, there is no explanation why he did not reference it in this letter, unless he was drawing a distinction between drawings that were "finished" and those that he had not yet completed. However, if that was the case, it is curious that he had not finalized the Bufflehead composition when he had started and finished his drawing of the Winter Wrens which he had collected more recently. Further, Audubon advised Lucy in his letter that he was leaving "all our skins, and the finished Drawings" at the home of Jonathan D. Weston, where they were staying. This suggests that the only drawings of birds he had collected in Maine were those that were "finished," and these did not include a composition of the Buffleheads

On December 1, 1833, Lucy wrote from Charleston, SC, on Audubon's behalf to his close friend Edward Harris and asked him to obtain a pair of Buffleheads. LBA, Charleston to Edward Harris, New York, 1 Dec. 1833 (Harvard (Letters), pf (110), f. 68). See also, Fries (1973), p. 81. One can legitimately ask why Audubon was seeking additional specimens of this species if he had already drawn them. The logical inference is that Audubon had not previously illustrated them and did so during his stay in Charleston during the winter of 1833–1834.

93. *OB* II, p. 489; JJA with attached postscript from JWA, Eastport to LBA, New York, 14 May 1833 (Princeton, Box 2, Folder 16), *Letters* I, p. 220 (JJA letter only). In his Episode "The Bay of Fundy," Audubon referred to the capsized craft as a sloop. However, in the cited letter he composed to Lucy upon returning to Eastport on May 14, he described it as a schooner, as did his son John. A sloop is a single-masted vessel, whereas a schooner has two or more masts. Given the sometimes questionable accuracy of statements made by Audubon in the *OB*, it is safer to assume, as I do in the text, that the vessel they passed was a schooner.

John Audubon informed his mother in the cited letter that the *Fancy* would have been out of sight of the smaller vessel when it capsized had they not earlier paused to collect some shells, presumably using what Audubon described in his Episode "The Bay of Fundy" as "a capital dredge." *OB* II, p. 488.

94. *OB* II, p. 489; JJA, Eastport to LBA, New York, 14 May 1833 (Princeton, Box 2, Folder 16), *Letters* I, p. 220. Audubon's letter to Lucy only mentions their son assisting the crew of the *Fancy* on the ropes and sails as they raced to the aid of the capsized schooner. However, it is inconceivable that Tom Lincoln, a down-easter by birth, would have stood by while a Southerner threw himself in to help. Although there is no documentation to support it, I am convinced that Lincoln was just as engaged in the rescue as John. Indeed, the likelihood is that Lincoln jumped in first to assist, and John followed his lead.

95. *OB* II, p. 489; JJA, Eastport to LBA, New

York, 14 May 1833 (Princeton, Box 2, Folder 16), *Letters* I, p. 220. See also, *OB* II, p. 489.

96. JJA with attached postscript from JWA, Eastport to LBA, New York, 14 May 1833 (Princeton, Box 2, Folder 16), *Letters* I, p. 220. Corning's transcription of the quote in the text misreads the word "humane" as "human."

97. JJA, Eastport to LBA at New York, May 14, 1833 (Princeton, Box 2, Folder 16), *Letters* I, p. 219.

98. Ibid., pp. 219–221.

99. Ibid., p. 221. Shattuck Jr. explained Audubon's reasoning in deciding to charter a schooner in a letter that he wrote to his younger sister Lucy and a family friend, Eliza Prentiss, on June 2, 1833. GCSJr, Eastport to Eliza Prentiss and Lucy Shattuck, Boston, 2 Jun. 1833 (MHS, Vol. 11, Jun. 1833).

100. GCSJr, Eastport to Eliza Prentiss and Lucy Shattuck, Boston, 2 Jun. 1833 (MHS, Vol. 11, Jun. 1833).

101. JJA, Eastport to LBA, New York, 14 May 1833 (Princeton, Box 2, Folder 16), *Letters* I, p. 221.

102. LBA, New York to VGA, London, 23 May 1833 (Yale, Box 1, Folder 18).

103. Ibid.

104. JJA, Eastport to Edward Harris, Moorestown, NJ, 14 May 1833 (Harvard (Letters), pf (110), p. 9). See also, Herrick (1938) II, pp. 40–41.

105. JJA, Eastport to Edward Harris, Moorestown, NJ, 14 May 1833 (Harvard (Letters), pf (110), p. 9).

106. GCSJr Journal, 21 May 1833 (Countway). In his journal, Shattuck indicated that Tom Lincoln had returned from Point Lepreau with Audubon, and "we had quite an interesting conversation together on the medical profession; the Indians." It is evident from this and succeeding references that Lincoln was staying with Shattuck at the home of his sister and brother-in-law. Lincoln returned to Dennysville on Thursday, May 16.

107. GCSJr, Eastport to GCS, Boston, 13 May 1833 (MHS, Box 5, Vol. 11, 1–13 May 1833); GCSJr Journal, 21 May 1833 (Countway).

108. GCSJr Journal, 21 May 1833 (Countway).

109. VGA, London to JJA, New York, 6 Jan. 1833 (Yale, Box 2, Folder 37).

110. Kinney (1989), p. 100; GCSJr, Eastport to GCS, Boston, 13 May 1833 (MHS, Box 5, Vol. 11, 1–13 May 1833).

111. GCS, Boston to GCSJr, Eastport, 17 May 1833 (MHS, Box 5, Vol. 11, 14–31 May 1833); GCSJr, Eastport to GCS, Boston, 13 May 1833 (MHS, Box 5, Vol. 11, 1–13 May 1833).

112. Kilby (1888), p. 76; GCSJr Journal, 21 May 1833 (Countway).

113. GCSJr, Eastport to GCS, Boston, 19 May 1833 (MHS, Vol. 11, 14–31 May 1833).

114. Zimmerman (1984), pp. 74, 81.

115. Greene (1903), illus. opp. p. xii; Cullum (1868) I, pp. 240–241. From September 1823 to June 1824, as a 2nd lieutenant of the 3rd Artillery, George S. Greene (1801–1899) held the position of assistant professor of mathematics at the Military Academy at West Point. He spent the next four months at Fort Monroe, VA, as an assistant instructor of mathematics in the Artillery School for Practice before resuming his teaching position at the Military Academy. In August 1826, he was named a principal assistant professor of engineering, a post he held until the following April when his teaching duties ended. Six months of ordinance duty was succeeded by a year assignment at Fort Wolcott, RI. In 1828, he was sent to Fort Sullivan for a year. He was reassigned to the garrison at Fort Independence on Castle Island in Boston Harbor and promoted to 1st lieutenant of the 3rd Artillery in 1829. After a year at this post and a recruiting assignment, he was again posted to Fort Sullivan in 1831, where he had served ever since.

116. GCSJr Journal, 21 May 1833 (Countway).

117. Willey (2003), pp. 121–122; Vinton (1858), p. 285; GCSJr Journal, 21 May 1833 (Countway). See also, Ayer (1910), p. 346. David Zimmerman, the author of a detailed history of Fort Sullivan, claims that the deaths in Lt. Greene's family all occurred "in a one month span in the winter of 1832–33." Zimmerman (1984), p. 92. However, this is in error. Shattuck stated that Greene's entire family had died within a nine month period. This is substantiated by Sarah Connell Ayer, an Eastport resident, whose journal was published in 1910. The birthdates and dates of death of Elizabeth and her children are provided in the genealogy of the Vinton family, from which Elizabeth descended.

118. Ayer (1910), p. 346.

119. GCSJr Journal, 21 May 1833 (Countway).

120. Bowdoin College (1916), p. 522.

121. GCSJr Journal, 21 May 1833 (Countway).

122. VGA, London to JJA, New York, 14 May 1833 (Yale, Box 15, Folder 693).

123. Ibid.

124. LBA, New York to VGA, London, 2 Jul. 1833 (Yale, Box 1, Folder 20); LBA, New York to VGA, London, 15 Jun. 1833 (Yale, Box 1, Folder 19); VGA, London to JJA, New York, 6 May 1833 (Yale Box 15, Folder 693).

125. Rhodes (2004), pp. 299–300; Steiner (2003), pp. 22, 24; JJA, Baltimore to VGA, London, 12 Mar. 1834 (APS), *Letters* II, p. 13; VGA, London to JJA, New York, 29 Mar. 1833 (with March 30 addendum)(Yale, Box 15, Folder 693).

126. VGA, London to JJA, New York, 14 May 1833 (Yale, Box 15, Folder 693); VGA, London to JJA, New York, 29 Mar. 1833 (with March 30 addendum)(Yale, Box 15, Folder 693).

127. VGA, London to JJA, New York, 6 May 1833 (Yale, Box 15, Folder 693). In the cited letter, Victor wrote "No 31" instead of "No. 31" as it appears in the text.

128. LBA, New York to JJA, care of General Ripley, Eastport, 14 July 1833 (Yale, Box 1, Folder 20); VGA, London to LBA, New York, 19 May 1833 (Yale, Box 2, Folder 37); VGA, London to JJA, New York, 14 May 1833 (Yale, Box 15, Folder 693).

129. JJA, Charleston to VGA, London, 4 Nov. 1833, *Letters* I, p. 266; VGA, Liverpool to JJA, New York, 15 Jan. 1833 (Yale, Box 15, Folder 693).

130. VGA, London to JJA, New York, 14 May 1833 (Yale, Box 15, Folder 693); VGA, London to JJA, New York, 6 May 1833 (Yale, Box 15, Folder 693).

131. VGA, London to JJA, New York, 14 May 1833 (Yale, Box 15, Folder 693). In this letter, Victor wrote "No 34" instead of "No. 34" as it appears in the text.

132. LBA, New York to VGA, London, 2 Jul. 1833 (Yale, Box 1, Folder 20); VGA, London to LBA, New York, 19 May 1833 (Yale, Box 2, Folder 37); VGA, London to JJA, New York, 14 May 1833 (Yale, Box 15, Folder 693). The contents of Victor's letter of May 16, 1833, which could not be located, can be deduced from Lucy's July 2, 1833, response.

133. JJA, Eastport to LBA, New York, 14 May 1833 (Princeton, Box 2, Folder 16), *Letters* I, p. 222.

134. Ibid.

135. GCSJr Journal, 21 May 1833 (Countway).

136. Ibid.

137. Emery (1989), p. 97; Dennysville (1886), p. 109; JJA, Eastport to LBA, New York, 19 May 1833 (Princeton, Box 2, Folder 18), *Letters* I, p. 224. In his May 19 letter to Lucy, Audubon erroneously referred to the owners of the *Ripley* as "Messrs Buck & Pinkham." Spencer Tinkham (1797–1872) married Sarah Lincoln (1807–1886) in 1830. Ancestry. com, Brown Tree NEW-2013, http://trees.ancestry .com/tree/55813402/person/34001772881?ssrc= (accessed 10 Feb. 2014); Willey (2003), p. 110. Sarah was the sixth of Judge Lincoln's nine children.

Tinkham's partner, Jonathan Buck (1796–1839), was born in Bucksport, ME, on April 2, 1796. In 1822, he married Ann Octavia Nelson (1797–1878), the sister of Jane Nelson Weston, wife of Jonathan D. Weston. "Jonathan Buck," Find A Grave, http://www.findagrave.com/cgi-bin/fg.cgi ?page=gr&GRid=97074935&ref=acom (accessed 25 Aug. 2015); Mary Grove (Personal communication, 24 Aug. 2015); Calnan (2007), p. 21; Willey (2003), pp. 46, 316.

138. Audubon described the *Ripley* as being 106 tons burden, a reference to the volume of cargo that the vessel could carry. JJA, Eastport to Richard Harlan, M.D., Philadelphia, 26 May 1833 (Princeton, Box 2, Folder 20). Shattuck Jr. made the same statement. GCSJr, Eastport to GCS, Boston, 22 May 1833 (MHS, Vol. 11, 14–31 May 1833). So, too, did Cmdr. Henry Wolsey Bayfield of the British Royal Navy. Bayfield (1984) I, p. 237.

However, Joyce E. Kinney, who conducted exhaustive research of period newspapers and compiled an important volume on the wooden sailing ships constructed in the Passamaquoddy region during the 19th and early 20th centuries, asserts that the vessel was only 98 tons burden. Kinney (1989), p. 97. She states that prior to the Civil War, "Vessel tonnage was figured on a complicated (and sometimes variable) system of cargo-carrying capacity." Ibid., p. 6.

Actually, the calculation of a vessel's tonnage in the 1830's was based upon relatively straightforward mathematical formulas. Separate calculations were made for the carpenter's tonnage, upon which shipwrights were compensated, and for government tonnage, which was used in assessing taxes. Blunt

(1837), pp. 28–32; Blunt (1832), pp. 14–15. To determine the carpenter's tonnage for a single-decked vessel like the *Ripley*, the formula required the multiplication of the vessel's length, breadth at the main beam, and depth of the hold with the product being divided by 95. Blunt (1832), p. 14. The calculation of government tonnage for a single-decked vessel was a bit more involved. It required taking the length of the vessel and subtracting three-fifths of the breadth at the broadest part above the main wales. The remainder would then be multiplied by the breadth of the vessel, and the product thereof multiplied by the depth. The product of that calculation was then divided by 95. Ibid., p. 15. These calculations would result in different tonnage numbers.

Kinney states that the dimensions of the *Ripley* were either 43' (length) x 14' (breadth) x 7' (hold depth) or 71' (length) x 18' (breadth) x 8' (depth). Kinney (1989), p. 97. Although she does not explain the conflict in the data, she presumably obtained it from different sources. However, the former set of dimensions under either calculation would not equate to a vessel of either 98 or 106 tons burden, so they would appear to be erroneous. Using the second set of dimensions gives a carpenter's tonnage of 107.62 tons or a government tonnage of 91.25 tons. The variance in the former calculation and Audubon's statement of the tonnage is probably attributable to approximated dimensions that Kinney found in her research rather than the precise numbers.

139. JJA, Eastport to LBA, New York, 16 May 1833 (Tides Institute),

140. Ibid.; JJA, St. Augustine, East Florida to G.W. Featherstonhaugh, 7 Dec. 1831, Herrick (1938) II, p. 13.

141. JJA, Eastport to LBA, New York, 16 May 1833 (Tides Institute).

142. Ibid.

143. Rhodes (2004), p. 372.

144. LBA, Boston to VGA, London, 5 Nov. 1832 (Audubon Museum). See also, Rhodes (2004), p. 372.

145. JJA, Eastport to LBA, New York, 16 May 1833 (Tides Institute); GCSJr Journal, 21 May 1833 (Countway). The shooting excursion on which John, Shattuck, and Lincoln embarked on the morning of Thursday, May 16, 1833, is not described specifically in Shattuck's journal. Audubon informed Lucy in his letter of the same date that John had gone shooting at 4:30 a.m. Shattuck wrote that "we took a cruise in the woods but saw no birds and returned by twelve oclock." While it is possible the young men undertook these activities separately, Shattuck's journal would suggest that they all dined together when they returned, an indication they were together earlier that day.

146. GCSJr Journal, 21 May 1833 (Countway). Shattuck stated in his journal that Dr. Isaac Ray and Jonathan D. Weston were late for dinner and that the assembled group did not wait for them.

147. Calnan (2007), p. 39; GCSJr Journal, 21 May 1833 (Countway). In recording the events of Thursday, May 16, 1833, Shattuck mentioned that Audubon "never ate meat till his wedding day when he was twenty one years of age." Audubon was actually twenty-two when he married Lucy on April 6, 1808. In his autobiographical essay, *Myself*, Audubon indicated that he subsisted before his marriage "on milk, fruits, and vegetables, with the addition of game and fish at times." Audubon (1999), p. 783; *AHJ* I, p. 27.

148. Ethan Allen Greenwood, Boston to JJA, Mrs. Le Cain's, Pearl Street, Boston, 29 Mar. 1833 (MHM). Audubon wrote on the outside panel of this letter that he answered it on May 17, 1833.

149. Fries (1973), p. 156. According to Fries, Ethan Allen Greenwood completed the subscription to *BOA* and received all eighty-seven Numbers as loose prints, although Audubon apparently experienced difficulty in obtaining the final payment. The New England Museum went out of business in 1839. Its collection was sold to Moses Kimball, who incorporated it in his Boston Museum, which opened two years later. Fries, who mistakenly refers to Greenwood as Nathan A. Greenwood, could not determine from his investigation what happened to the prints from this set.

150. GCSJr Journal, 21 May 1833 (Countway); JJA, Eastport to LBA, New York, 18 May 1833 (Princeton, Box 2, Folder 17), *Letters* I, p. 222.

151. Pesha (2009); Blunt (1833), p. 146; Blunt (1827), p. 24, note.

152. GCSJr Journal, 21 May 1833 (Countway); JJA, Eastport to LBA, New York, 18 May 1833 (Princeton, Box 2, Folder 17), *Letters* I, p. 222.

Napoleon Bonaparte Buford (1807–1883) was born on January 13, 1807, on his family's plantation in Woodford County, KY. Crutcher (2012), p. 214; Buford (1903), pp. 207, 212. He graduated sixth in his class at West Point in 1827 and was promoted to 2nd lieutenant of the 3rd Artillery on July 1, 1827. In 1830 he was posted to Fort Sullivan. Cullum (1868), p. 310; Force (1833), p. 185.

153. JJA, Eastport to LBA, New York, 18 May 1833 (Princeton, Box 2, Folder 17), *Letters* I, p. 222.

154. GCSJr, Eastport to GCS, Boston, 19 May 1833 (MHS, Vol. 11, 14–31 May 1833).

155. Cullum (1868), p. 310.

156. Harvard Law School (1900), pp. 5, 31.

157. GCSJr, Eastport to GCS, Boston, 19 May 1833 (MHS, Vol. 11, 14–31 May 1833).

158. GCSJr Journal, 21 May 1833 (Countway).

159. JJA, Eastport to LBA, New York, 18 May 1833 (Princeton, Box 2, Folder 17), *Letters* I, p. 222.

160. GCSJr Journal, 21 May 1833 (Countway); JJA, Eastport to LBA, New York, 18 May 1833 (Princeton, Box 2, Folder 17), *Letters* I, p. 222.

161. GCSJr Journal, 21 May 1833 (Countway).

162. JJA, Eastport to LBA, New York, 18 May 1833 (Princeton, Box 2, Folder 17), *Letters* I, p. 223. Contrary to Audubon's May 18 letter, where he informed Lucy that the daughter of Capt. Thomas Childs and Ann Eliza Coyton Childs (1800–1875) was born "yesterday morning," Mary Virginia Childs was actually born on May 16, 1833, as reflected on her gravestone. She would go on to marry Dr. William W. Anderson (b. 14 Dec. 1824) in 1855 and give birth to ten children. She died on December 15, 1912, in Montgomery, AL. Ancestry.com, Rogers Family Tree, http://trees.ancestry.com/tree/58709121/person/32105148909?ssrc= (accessed 18 Jun. 2015); "Mary Virginia Childs Anderson," Findagrave.com, http://www.findagrave.com/cgi-bin/fg.cgi?page=pv&GRid=29797092&PIpi=12838213 (accessed 19 Feb. 2014); Stoughton (2011), p. 146; Child (1881), p. 677.

163. Mainardi (2003), p. 187; GCSJr Journal, 21 May 1833 (Countway).

164. GCSJr Journal, 21 May 1833 (Countway). This statement by Audubon completely eviscerates any assertion by his apologists that he may have been justified in claiming David as his master because perhaps one of his drawing tutors studied

under the great Neoclassical painter. Audubon told Shattuck Jr. that he had studied at David's atelier, which was utterly untrue. Audubon lied, plain and simple.

165. Mainardi (2003), pp. 186–188. Of the four well-known French painters who published lithographed images of *Mazeppa*, only Horace Vernet (1789–1863) was of an age that could have placed him at the studio of Jacques-Louis David between 1801 and 1803, when we know little about Audubon's activities. Théodore Géricault (1791–1824) had died nine years before Audubon made the comment in Lt. Buford's room at Fort Sullivan, which would indicate he was not the painter to whom Audubon was referring. Audubon specifically claimed to have studied under David alongside "the man who painted those horses, and who paints horses better than any man now living," an indication that the equine artist was still alive. GCSJr Journal, 21 May 1833 (Countway). Both Eugène Delacroix (1798–1863) and Louis Boulanger (1806–1867) were born too late to have ever been Audubon's classmate.

Other evidence also points to Vernet as the painter to whom Audubon was referring. Vernet was highly regarded for his lively and accurate depiction of horses. A contemporary noted, "His slightest sketches of horses sell for large sums." Knight (1875), p. 266 Moreover, Vernet painted several images from *Mazeppa* and issued lithographs of them that were very popular. His painting *Mazeppa and the Wolves* "became the best known Mazeppa image throughout Europe and America, copied, used in posters, clocks, cameos, vases." Mainardi (2003), pp. 187–188, 198, 200.

166. Horace Vernet was born into a family of well-known French painters. He trained initially with his father, Carle Vernet, and subsequently attended the Ecole des Beaux-Arts of the French Academy in Paris, where he came under the instruction of François-André Vincent (1746–1816). Athanassoglou-Kallmyer (1986), p. 17. He was not a student of Jacques-Louis David.

167. See Prologue, note 41, *supra*. If there was any lingering doubt about the validity of Audubon's claim to having been tutored at the atelier of Jacques-Louis David, it has now been laid to rest by the discovery of Audubon's demonstrably false statement to Shattuck Jr. and Lt. Buford that he

had been a classmate of the man who had painted the lithographed images from *Mazeppa* on Buford's wall. This evidence unequivocally establishes that Audubon did not train under the famous French Neoclassical painter and that he lied about it — to his family and his friends as well as to the public.

168. GCS, Boston to GCSJr, Eastport, 17 May 1833 (MHS, Vol. 11, 14–31 May 1833).

169. Ibid.

170. GCSJr, Eastport to Miss Ellen Shattuck, Boston, 17 May 1833 (MHS, Vol. 11, 14–31 May 1833).

171. JJA, Eastport to LBA, New York, 18 May 1833 (Princeton, Box 2, Folder 17). *Letters* I, pp. 222–223. It is possible to determine that Audubon wrote this letter to Lucy in the morning of Saturday, May 18, 1833, as related in the text, because he spoke of his hope that he would receive a letter from her in the afternoon.

172. Ibid.

173. GCSJr Journal, 21 May 1833 (Countway); JJA, Eastport to LBA, New York, 18 May 1833 (Princeton, Box 2, Folder 17), *Letters* I, pp. 222–223.

174. GCSJr Journal, 21 May 1833 (Countway).

175. *OB* II, p. 511.

176. Dunne (2006), p. 620.

177. *OB* II, p. 511. Theodore Lincoln Chadbourne (1822–1846) was born on August 2, 1822, the oldest child of Ichabod Chadbourne and his wife, Hannah. In the family, he was nicknamed "Linc." He went on to attend West Point, graduating on July 1, 1843. He was fifteenth in his class, eight places ahead of Ulysses S. Grant. Assigned as a second lieutenant to Gen. Zachary Taylor's army in the Mexican-American War, he was killed in Texas on May 9, 1846, at the Battle of Resaca de la Palma. His body was returned to Eastport, and he was buried in the town's Hillside Cemetery. Corder (1993), pp. 4–5, 38, 40, 53, 70. A monument was erected to his memory on which Dr. Isaac Ray composed a tribute that reads: "His last acts/are part of his country's/History./The Memory/of his frank and ingenuous disposition,/of his love of excellence and devotion to duty,/and of his high and generous aims,/is deeply surgraved [sic] on the hearts/of the friends and associates/of his youth, by whom this monument/has been raised." Transcribed by the author during a visit to Lincoln Chadbourne's gravesite (Memorial Day, 26 May 2014). Cf. Corder (1993), pp. 38–39.

178. *OB* II, p. 511.

179. Ibid., p. 341.

180. Shuler (1995), pp. 119–121; JJA, Charleston to VGA, London, 14 Jan. 1834, *Letters* II, p. 6.

181. Shuler (1995), pp. 23, 93.

182. GCSJr Journal, 21 May 1833 (Countway). Shattuck's journal does not reveal how Maj. Chadbourne and Dr. Ray made the trip to Point Pleasant on May 18, but the reasonable deduction is that they went by land, while Audubon's party went by sea. Dr. Ray's presence is not mentioned in the early portion of the entry where Shattuck indicated that Chadbourne had met them there. However, he stated later that Dr. Ray walked home with him, which would indicate that Dr. Ray also made the trip.

183. GCSJr, Eastport to GCS, Boston, 22 May 1833 (MHS, Vol. 11, 14–31 May 1833); GCSJr Journal, 21 May 1833 (Countway).

184. Morton (1988), p. 219; VGA, London to LBA, New York, 19 May 1833 (Yale, Box 2, Folder 37). In the cited letter, Victor referred to "No 33" rather than "No. 33" as used in text.

185. VGA, London to LBA, New York, 19 May 1833 (Yale, Box 2, Folder 37).

186. GCSJr Journal, 21 May 1833 (Countway).

187. Coolidge (1833), 19 May 1833.

188. Able (1999), pp. 17, 19.

189. GCSJr, Eastport to GCS, Boston, 19 May 1833 (MHS, Vol. 11, 14–31 May 1833).

190. GCSJr, Eastport to Miss Ellen E. Shattuck, Boston, 17 May 1833 (MHS, Vol. 11, 14–31 May 1833). Although Shattuck Jr.'s letter to his sister Ellen is clearly dated May 17, 1833, he did not mention writing it on that date in his journal. Indeed, in his account of his daily activities and in a separate list at the back of the journal of all the letters he sent and received during the month of May, he indicated that this letter to Ellen was written on Sunday, May 19. One might be inclined to think then that he simply made an error when he wrote the date. However, we know that when he wrote to his father on May 19, he dated that letter properly. If he wrote the letter to Ellen after completing the letter to his father, which is suggested by his journal description of his activities — "I passed the next day writing a letter of two sheets to father in which I gave an account of my journey from Brunswick, and another

to Ellen"—there would be no excuse for him mis-dating the letter. If, instead, he began writing the letter to Ellen that Sunday before penning the correspondence to his father, then one can fairly ask why he didn't go back and correct the erroneous date when he realized it was May 19? He certainly was not averse to making corrections in his writing when he thought them necessary, as can be seen from his occasional strikethroughs of a misplaced word. However, there is another possibility, which is that he began the letter to Ellen on May 17 and finished it two days later. There is nothing in the content of the letter, apart from the date, that can be used to confirm that he started writing it on May 17. We can confirm that the latter portion of the letter was written on Sunday, May 19, because Shattuck alluded to their planned excursion aboard the revenue cutter "tomorrow," which is consistent with what Audubon wrote Lucy on the same date. Trying to fit all of the facts together, the text adopts this third possibility as the most reasonable interpretation.

191. *OB* II, p. 24.

192. Ibid., p. 54.

193. Harvard Quinquennial Catalogue (1895), pp. 108, 251; Stimpson (1833), pp. 31, 202. Dr. William Ingalls (1769-1851) was born in Newburyport, MA, on May 3, 1769. After graduating from Harvard with a B.A. degree in 1790, he was awarded a Master of Arts degree in 1793 and a Bachelor of Medicine (M.B.) degree in 1794. Harvard Quinquennial Catalogue (1895), pp. 108, 251. Harvard did not award the degree of Doctor of Medicine (M.D.) to the graduates of its medical program until 1811, at which time all of its previous graduates received an M.D. degree. Ibid., p. 252. However, Ingalls had already received an honorary M.D. degree from the university in 1801. Ibid., p. 108. In 1811, he accepted an appointment as the Professor of Anatomy and Surgery in the Medical Department at Brown University in Providence, RI. He resigned from the post in 1816 but continued to offer lectures in Boston, which Brown students could attend and thereby satisfy that portion of their course requirements. Mitchell (1993).

194. Atkinson (1878), p. 329. William Ingalls (1813-1903) was born on January 12, 1813. Ibid. Ruthven Deane's assertion that Ingalls had been born on January 5, 1813 is incorrect. Deane is simi-larly mistaken in stating that Shattuck Jr.'s birthdate was July 23, 1813. Deane (1910), p. 42, notes 5-6. In fact, Shattuck was born on July 22, 1813. Marshall (2006), p. 5.

195. Harvard (1895), p. 143. William Ingalls, the son of William Ingalls, M.D., matriculated at Harvard College in the fall of 1831 as a member of the Class of 1835. Ibid.; Harvard (1831), p. 20. Although six months older than Shattuck Jr., Ingalls was several years behind him in the pursuit of an education. Shattuck entered Harvard in 1829 as a junior and graduated with the Class of 1831. Marshall (2006), pp. 30-31, 36; Harvard (1895), p. 139. When Ingalls began his studies in Cambridge as a freshman in 1831, Shattuck was already in his first year at Harvard Law School. Harvard (1831), pp. 10, 20.

Ingalls did not return to Harvard for his sophomore year in 1832, having apparently decided to study medicine with his father. He was eventually awarded a Bachelor of Arts degree from Harvard in 1878. Harvard (1895), p. 143; Harvard (1832).

196. Deane (1910), p. 44

197. Ibid.

198. GCSJr Journal, 21 May 1833 (Countway).

199. JJA, Eastport to LBA, New York, 19 May 1833 (Princeton, Box 2, Folder 18), *Letters* I, pp. 223-225. We know that Audubon answered this letter in the evening because he closed it, "Good night my Love."

Although Audubon did not identify for Lucy the single bird he had drawn as of May 19, 1833, this can be ascertained by examining his subsequent correspondence. We know that by the end of his stay in Eastport, he had only made four drawings as he acknowledged in a letter to his wife on June 4. He told her that he had done a picture of two Winter Wrens on June 2 and 3. The other three species that he identified as having "procured & finished" were the Black Guillemot, Harlequin Duck, and Hyperborean Phalarope (Red-necked Phalarope). JJA, Eastport to LBA, New York, 4 Jun. 1833 (Princeton, Box 2, Folder 22), *Letters* I, p. 236. Based on a letter he wrote to Lucy a week earlier, on May 28, he had drawn "2 Rare ducks" the previous day, which would have been the Harlequin Ducks he collected during his recent trip to Grand Manan archipelago. JJA, Eastport to LBA, New York, 28 May 1833 (Yale, Box 1, Folder 5); JJA, Eastport to Richard Harlan,

M.D., Philadelphia, 26 May 1833 (Princeton, Box 2, Folder 20). John was at then at work on "a beautifull Drawing of a very rare Phalarope ♂ of which he had the good luck to Shoot Yesterday in the Cutter's boat." JJA, Eastport to LBA, New York, 28 May 1833 (Yale, Box 1, Folder 5). That leaves the Black Guillemot as the sole species he had illustrated during the earlier portion of his stay in Eastport.

200. JJA, Eastport to LBA, New York, 19 May 1833 (Princeton, Box 2, Folder 18), *Letters* I, pp. 223–224.

201. *AHJ* I, p. 359; JJA, Eastport to LBA, New York, 19 May 1833 (Princeton, Box 2, Folder 18), *Letters* I, p. 224.

202. JJA, Eastport to LBA, New York, 19 May 1833 (Princeton, Box 2, Folder 18), *Letters* I, p. 224.

203. Ibid., *Letters* I, p. 225.

204. JJA, Eastport to LBA, New York, 19 May 1833 (Princeton, Box 2, Folder 18).

205. JJA, Eastport to VGA, London, 31 May 1833, *Letters* I, pp. 231–235; JJA, Eastport to LBA, New York, 22 May 1833 (Princeton, Box 2, Folder 19), *Letters* I, p. 228. In his correspondence to Lucy of May 22, Audubon indicated that he had written a lengthy letter to Victor that he intended to forward to her shortly before the expedition left for Labrador. The May 31 letter to Victor is the one to which he was referring. That it was not written on the inscribed date is evident from Audubon's opening sentence stating that they would be sailing for Labrador on June 1. As of May 31, the schooner *Ripley*, which Audubon had chartered for the voyage, had not yet arrived in Eastport. Audubon knew from speaking to the vessel's owners that it would take two days for the schooner to be made ready for the expedition, so it is clear this letter was penned before it was dated. Two other statements in the opening paragraph point to it having been drafted within days of Audubon's May 19 letter to Lucy, where he told he intended to "write a long letter to Victor, before our Departure."

First, he informed Victor that he and John were going to be accompanied on the Labrador expedition by Shattuck Jr. and Tom Lincoln. By May 26, Audubon knew that William Ingalls would also be joining them. JJA, Eastport to LBA, New York, 27 May 1833 (Princeton, Box 2, Folder 21), *Letters* I, p. 229.

Second, Audubon advised his son that his agreement with the owners of the *Ripley* required him to provide the food for his party. That was the original arrangement, but Audubon subsequently concluded it would be wiser to have the owners furnish the provisions. He informed Lucy of the modified terms in his letter to her of May 22. JJA, Eastport to LBA, New York, 22 May 1833 (Princeton, Box 2, Folder 19), *Letters* I, p. 226. Since the May 22 letter was drafted at the crack of dawn and Audubon's earlier letter of May 19, where he disclosed his plan to write Victor, was written at night, it is evident the May 31 letter to Victor was actually drafted on either May 20 or 21.

It is worth noting that Maria Audubon published a completely doctored version of the May 31 in *AHJ*, taking snippets from various letters Audubon had written to Lucy over the preceding days and pretending they were part of the letter to his son. *AHJ* I, pp. 345–347. The original holographic letter to Victor was evidently sold by Goodspeed's Book Shop in Boston in 1950. Dodge (1950), pp. 119–120.

206. JJA, Eastport to VGA, London, 31 May 1833, *Letters* I, pp. 232–233.

207. Ibid., p. 233.

208. GCSJr Journal, 21 May 1833 (Countway).

209. Army and Navy Chronicle (1838), pp. 96, 144; Force (1822), p. 31. Uriah Coolidge (c. 1781–1838) is listed in the U.S. Census records for 1810 and 1820 as a resident of Portland, ME, along with his wife Mary and their children. U.S. Bureau of the Census (1820), Census Place: *Portland, Cumberland County, ME*; Page: *197*; NARA Roll: *M33_33*; Image: *111*; U.S. Bureau of the Census (1810), Census Place: *Portland, Cumberland County, ME*; Roll: *11*; Page: *15*; Image: *0218682*. He was evidently assigned to the Passamaquoddy Customs District by the early 1820s. He was listed as a first mate aboard the district's revenue cutter in 1822 and was noted to be living with his family in Lubec, ME, with his family by August 1824, as reflected in the journal of Sarah Connell Ayer, the wife of Dr. Samuel Ayer of Eastport. Ayer (1910), pp. 242–243; Force (1822), p. 31.

210. Force (1832), p. 285; Force (1822), p. 31.

211. Force (1833), p. 334; Force (1832), p. 285.

212. Ayer (1910), p. 245; Force (1833), p. 334.

Uriah Coolidge Jr. was commissioned a warrant officer in the Revenue Cutter Service on April 16, 1832. Force (1833), p. 334. He is not mentioned in any of the extant letters or journals of Audubon or the members of his party or in a list of the officers serving aboard the nation's revenue cutters as of 1833, suggesting that he had since resigned his commission. Force (1834), pp. 244–246.

213. Calnan (2007), p. 36; "A Californian's Recollection of Naturalist Audubon," *The San Francisco Call*, Vol. LXXX, No. 98, p. 25, cols. 1–7 (Sunday, 6 Sept. 1896)(LOC). Joseph Appleby Coolidge (1815–1901) was born in Portland, ME, on January 15, 1815. Calnan (2007), p. 36; Mortuary Record (1901).

214. Quoddy Maritime Museum (2001); *New-York Gazette & General Advertiser*, Vol. 45, No. 16,892, p. 2, col. 2 (Friday Morning, 14 Jun. 1833) (NYHS). The Coolidge home in Eastport still stands at 49 Washington Street.

215. GCSJr Journal, 21 May 1833 (Countway).

216. Ibid.

217. *New-York Gazette & General Advertiser*, Vol. 45, No. 16,871, p. 2, col. 2 (Tuesday Morning, 21 May 1833)(NYHS).

218. GCSJr Journal, 21 May 1833 (Countway).

219. Ibid.

220. GCSJr, Eastport to GCS, Boston, 2 Jun. 1833 (MHS, Vol. 11, Jun. 1833). Although young Shattuck did not specifically state where he purchased his copy of the first volume of the *OB*, it must have been at H.S. Favor's Bookstore on Water Street. Kilby (1888), p. 273. From all of the evidence, it appears to have been the only bookstore in Eastport. A British officer who stopped in Eastport at around this time, Lt. Edward Coke, commented that he had not seen as good a selection of books in any of the bookstores of Montreal, Quebec, or Halifax, and that it supplied not just the needs of the Eastport community but of much of New Brunswick. Coke (1833) II, p. 134. With Audubon visiting Eastport, it was probably no accident that the store decided to stock a copy of his book.

221. Christie's (2012b), Lot 2, p. 9. On May 18, 2012, Christie's auctioned a portion of the rare book collection of Albert H. Small, a Washington, D.C., collector of Americana and a discerning bibliophile. Among the treasures in this auction was the Shattuck family set of the *OB*. The fact that the first volume in the set came from the most recent 1832 Philadelphia printing by E.L. Carey and A. Hart, and that it contains a personal inscription by Audubon, would indicate that it was the same copy young Shattuck purchased in Eastport. Though it is possible Audubon inscribed the volume to Shattuck Jr., it is more likely the inscription was directed to his father, whose financial resources were used to purchase the book, who was a subscriber to *BOA*, and who then possessed the M.D. title Audubon referenced.

222. JJA, Eastport to LBA, New York, 22 May 1833 (Princeton, Box 2, Folder 19), *Letters*. I, p. 227.

223. Ibid., p. 225. In order for a mariner to reach Eastport via the commercial shipping channel that ran along the western shores of Campobello Island, he would have to sail through the Head Harbor passage and around the northern tip of Campobello Island. When the winds were blowing east or northeast, a sailboat would have to sail directly into the wind. Tacking was not an option given the relatively narrow channel and the proximity of nearby shoals and islands. In addition, the tidal flow through this passage is strong, and if the winds died, the vessel would be "horsed," meaning that it would be carried in a direction the mariner did not wish to go. To safeguard their vessels, passengers, and cargo, mariners would wait for a change in the wind. Colin Windhorst, Dennys River Historical Society (Personal communication, 4 Aug. 2015).

224. Ibid., p. 226.

225. JJA, Eastport to LBA, New York, 22 May 1833 (Princeton, Box 2, Folder 19). Cf. *Letters* I, p. 226.

226. JJA, Eastport to LBA, New York, 22 May 1833 (Princeton, Box 2, Folder 19). Cf. *Letters* I, pp. 227–228.

227. JJA, Eastport to LBA, New York, 22 May 1833 (Princeton, Box 2, Folder 19). Cf. *Letters* I, p. 228.

228. GGSJr, Eastport to GCS, Boston, 22 May 1833 (MHS, Vol. 11, 14–31 May 1833).

229. *OB* II, p. 19. Audubon's account of finding the Canada Warbler nest does not specifically state at what time of the day on May 22 he discovered it. For purposes of the narrative, I have presumed it was during his walk with Shattuck Jr. Since it was

raining, it would not be unusual to find the female sitting on the nest brooding, which is consistent with Audubon's description.

230. GCSJr, Eastport to GCS, Boston, 22 May 1833 (MHS, Vol. 11, 14–31 May 1833).

231. GCSJr Journal, 23 May 1833 (Countway); Coolidge (1833), 22 May 1833.

232. GCSJr Journal, 23–25 May 1833 (Countway). Audubon did not identify the members of his party on the excursion to Grand Manan in his Episode "The Bay of Fundy." *OB* II, pp. 485–489. In correspondence he sent to Lucy after the trip, Audubon mentioned both John and Shattuck. JJA, Eastport to LBA, New York, 26 May 1833 (Yale, Box 1, Folder 5). However, Shattuck's journal reflects that the party also included the Eastport postmaster, James Curtiss. Curtiss's participation has not been previously known by Audubon scholars. Another prospective member of the party was Jonathan D. Weston, who had been hosting the Audubons. However, Weston decided at the last minute not to join the group. See Chapter 5, note 5, *infra*.

As to when Audubon's party boarded the U.S. Revenue Cutter *Swiftsure*, I have relied upon Shattuck's journal. In his entry on the evening of Thursday, May 23, he stated that "We came on board this vessel last evening." He made no mention of other members of the party arriving later, so it seems safe to assume that they all came onboard at the same time. This is consistent with Audubon's statement in his biography of the Herring Gull that his party had been "kindly received" aboard the schooner on May 22, 1833. *OB* III, p. 588.

Capt. Coolidge's entry in his logbook for May 23, which reads in part "Thursday 23,, at 4 AM took on Board Mr Audubon the American Ornithologist Sailed for Grand Mannan," could suggest otherwise. Coolidge (1833), 23 May 1833. However, it would appear the reference to "4 AM" was the time Coolidge was entering the detail in the log as opposed to the time Audubon came aboard.

233. Smith (1989), pp. 36, 39; Smith (1889), p. 383.

234. GCSJr Journal, 23 May 1833 (Countway); U.S. Coast Guard, "Swiftsure/Crawford, 1825," http://www.uscg.mil/history/webcutters/Swiftsure _1825.asp (accessed 11 Feb. 2014).

235. GCSJr Journal, 23 May 1833 (Countway).

236. Ibid.

CHAPTER 5: GRAND MANAN

1. GCSJr Journal, 23 May 1833 (Countway); Force (1833), p. 334.

2. John Gray Whitcomb (1793–1861) was born in North Yarmouth, ME, on November 17, 1793. Whitcomb (1904), p. 69. He was commissioned a 2nd lieutenant in the Revenue Cutter Service on August 23, 1819, the same date Uriah Coolidge became a 1st lieutenant. Force (1832), p. 285; Force (1822), p. 31. He was elevated to 1st lieutenant on December 28, 1832. Force (1834), p. 244. He would be promoted to captain and take over command of the *Alert*, the successor to the *Swiftsure/Crawford*, on December 9, 1839. *Niles National Register*, Vol. LXI, No. 1568, pp. 101–102 (Saturday, 16 Oct. 1841). He was subsequently reassigned to the Boston station, where he took the helm of the revenue cutter *Morris*. In 1854, acting under orders, he returned the fugitive slave Anthony Burns to his Southern owner pursuant to the Fugitive Slave Act. Whitcomb would serve ably in the Revenue Cutter Service for over forty-two years before his death in Boston on December 25, 1861. Whitcomb (1904), p. 88.

3. Thomas Stoddard (1787–1854) was commissioned a warrant officer in the Revenue Cutter Service on March 21, 1831, and was assigned to the Boston revenue cutter *Hamilton* under Capt. Richard Derby. Derby (1861), pp. 283–284; Force (1832), p. 285. On January 5, 1833, he was promoted to 2nd lieutenant and transferred to the *Swiftsure*. Force (1834), p. 244. According to Bigelow's history of Cohasset, MA, "Thomas Stoddard was born in Cohasset, May 14, 1787. His father, Zenas Stoddard, was a Revolutionary soldier and later a seafaring man. Thomas began to learn the carpenter's trade at the age of fifteen, but two years later entered on a seafaring life. He was captain of several Cohasset vessels and made many successful voyages to foreign ports. In 1831 he was appointed to the United States revenue service and was promoted to the rank of first lieutenant. In this position he made many perilous voyages in winter along the coast of New England, giving relief to disabled vessels. He remained in the revenue service until 1847, and died in Cohasset, on North Main Street, in the house

now occupied by Ziba C. Small, March 28, 1854." Bigelow (1898), p. 345.

4. Marshall (2006), p. 4; Smith (1989), p. 39; Smith (1889), p. 383; Derby (1861), pp. 201–204, 283–284; Force (1832), p. 285.

5. GCSJr Journal, 23 May 1833 (Countway). Shattuck wrote his father on May 26, 1833, after returning to Eastport, and reported that the *Swiftsure* had weighed anchor around 3:00 a.m. GCSJr, Eastport to GCS, Boston, 26 May 1833 (MHS, Vol. 11, 14–31 May 1833). However, in his journal, Shattuck indicated that "At three oclock, the officers were called, a boat sent on shore for Mr Weston who declined coming, anchor weighed and we were off." GCSJr Journal, 23 May 1833 (Countway). This would suggest that the vessel did not actually weigh anchor until sometime after 3:00 a.m., presumably when there was sufficient light.

6. "Grand Manan and White Head Islands Geology," http://www.grandmanannb.com/geology.html (accessed 11 Jul. 2015); Sweetser (1875), p. 30; GCSJr, Eastport to GCS, Boston, 26 May 1833 (MHS, Vol. 11, 14–31 May 1833).

7. *OB* II, p. 485.

8. Coolidge (1833), 23 May 1833; GCSJr Journal, 23 May 1833 (Countway); GCSJr, Eastport to GCS, Boston, 26 May 1833 (MHS, Vol. 11, 14–31 May 1833). Capt. Coolidge indicated in the *Swiftsure's* log that the vessel came to in Gull Cove off White Head Island at 9:00 a.m. However, Shattuck recorded in his journal that they anchored around 8:30 a.m. The text relies upon the latter because Coolidge's journal entries all appear to be on the hour, making Shattuck's temporal reference more specific.

9. GCSJr Journal, 23 May 1833 (Countway); GCSJr, Eastport to GCS, Boston, 26 May 1833 (MHS, Vol. 11, 14–31 May 1833).

10. Coolidge (1833), 23 May 1833; GCSJr, Eastport to GCS, Boston, 26 May 1833 (MHS, Vol. 11, 14–31 May 1833). Audubon indicated in his Episode "The Bay of Fundy" that Capt. Coolidge remained onboard the *Swiftsure* while he and his party explored White Head Island. *OB* II, p. 486. We know from Shattuck's journal that the shore party included Capt. Claridge. GCSJr Journal, 23 May 1833 (Countway). Since Coolidge would have likely insisted that one of his staff officers also accompany

the group, either 1st Lt. Whitcomb or 2nd Lt. Stoddard would have rounded out the party along with two crewmen.

11. *OB* III, pp. 588–589; GCSJr, Eastport to GCS, Boston, 26 May 1833 (MHS, Vol. 11, May 14–31 1833). According to Statistics Canada (http://www.statcan.gc.ca), White Head Island comprises an area of 6.17 square kilometers, which would equal 1,524.64 acres. Statistics Canada (2013).

12. William Frankland genealogy, Turner Family Tree, Ancestry.com, http://trees.ancestry.com/tree/37460503/person/20288938284?ssrc= (accessed 21 Feb. 2013); JJA, Eastport to LBA, New York, 26 May 26 1833 (Yale, Box 1, Folder 5); Blunt (1833), p. 148.

13. *OB* III, p. 588; *OB* II, p. 485; GCSJr, Eastport to GCS, Boston, 26 May 1833 (MHS, Vol. 11, 14–31 May 1833); GCSJr Journal, 23 May 1833 (Countway).

14. *OB* III, p. 588; GCSJr, Eastport to GCS, Boston, 26 May 1833 (MHS, Vol. 11, 14–31 May 1833).

15. *OB* III, p. 588.

16. GCSJr, Eastport to GCS, Boston, 26 May 1833 (MHS, Vol. 11, 14–31 May 1833); GCSJr Journal, 23 May 1833 (Countway).

17. JJA, New York to VGA, London, 15 Sept. 1833 (APS), *Letters* I, p. 249; JWA addendum, 6 Jun. 1833, to JJA, Eastport to LBA, New York, 5–6 Jun. 1833 (Princeton, Box 2, Folder 23); William Bakewell, Louisville to JJA, Boston, 15 Nov. 1832 (Yale, Box 2, Folder 64).

18. *OB* III, p. 591; GCSJr, Eastport to GCS, Boston, 26 May 1833 (MHS, Vol. 11, 14–31 May 1833); GCSJr Journal, 23 May 1833 (Countway).

19. GCSJr Journal, 23 May 1833 (Countway). The ship's log of Capt. Coolidge recorded that Audubon's party returned from White Head Island to the *Swiftsure* at 3:00 p.m. Coolidge (1833), 23 May 1833. The text relies instead on Shattuck's journal, where he stated that they "returned at half past three."

20. Bonaparte (1828), pp. 360–361. The asterisked footnote in the quoted text of Bonaparte's description of the Herring Gull states: "Though I have found them constant in all the Italian, English, and North American specimens of both species that I have examined, I cannot give these markings as

sure tests of the two species, which, however, are certainly distinct, and though closely allied, may at once be distinguished by the size." Ibid., p. 361. This was a reference to similarities between the Herring Gull, *Larus argentatus*, and what Bonaparte considered a separate species, *Larus argentatoides*. Ibid., pp. 360–361. Audubon considered them to be the same species, as did later ornithologists who classified them both as *Larus smithsonianus*, now known as the American Herring Gull. Howell (2007), p. 403; Baird (1884) II, p. 235. The taxonomy of the Herring Gull complex continues to be a subject of debate among ornithologists. Howell (2007), p. 401.

21. GCSJr, Eastport to GCS, Boston, 26 May 1833 (MHS, Vol. 11, 14–31 May 1833); GCSJr Journal, 23 May 1833 (Countway).

22. *OB* III, p. 588–589; GCSJr, Eastport to GCS, Boston, 26 May 1833 (MHS, Vol. 11, 14–31 May 1833); GCSJr Journal, 23 May 1833 (Countway).

23. *OB* III, pp. 588–589.

24. GCSJr, Eastport to GCS, Boston, 26 May 1833 (MHS, Vol. 11, 14–31 May 1833); GCSJr Journal, 23 May 1833 (Countway). James Curtiss's decision to move his family to Chicago appears to have been precipitated by his forced removal from office as the Eastport postmaster during the first half of 1834. The reasons for this government action are not entirely clear. I could find no mention of it in the official correspondence of the postmaster general in the National Archives. The Record of Appointment of Postmasters reflects only that Curtiss's successor, Loring F. Wheeler, assumed the position on May 6, 1834. Letters Sent by the Postmaster General, 1789–1836, Record Group 28, M601, Rolls 48–49 (National Archives); Record of Appointment of Postmasters, 1832-September 30, 1971, Record Group 28, M841, Roll 54 (National Archives).

However, on June 23, 1834, U.S. Senator Peleg Sprague (1793–1880), an anti-Jacksonian who served one term as Maine's senator (1829–1835), submitted the following resolution to the Senate: "*Resolved*, That the Postmaster General be directed to communicate to the Senate all the papers in his department relative to the investigation of the conduct of James Curtis, late postmaster at Eastport." Blair & Rives (1834), p. 468. Two days later, on June 25, 1834, the

resolution was "laid on the table"—i.e., tabled or postponed—on the motion of Senator Daniel Webster of Massachusetts. Ibid., p. 471. I could find no evidence that the issue was subsequently addressed.

In 1835, around the time when James Curtiss arrived in Chicago, it was a small but rapidly growing town. The population count that year was 3,265. By March 4, 1837, when Chicago was incorporated as a city, the population had grown to 4,179. Moses (1892) II, p. 940.

Shortly after his arrival, Curtiss was hired as editor of the *Chicago Democrat*, a weekly newspaper owned by John Calhoun. Andreas (1884b) I, pp. 366, 621. The next year, he was appointed town clerk. Andreas (1884b) I, p. 176; Eastman (1911), p. 32. Curtiss had evidently read for the law and been admitted to the bar, although where and when is not clear. From August 1836 to October 1837, he practiced law in partnership with William Stuart. Andreas (1884b) I, p. 428. John M. Palmer wrote of Curtiss's legal career in *The Bench and Bar of Illinois*: "James Curtis came here early, and was a shrewd lawyer and man of ability, but very much inclined to be a demagogue. He was, as the common expression is nowadays, just 'built that way.' He set himself up as the champion of the people and was more inclined to talk politics than practice law. He had many good traits in his character and drew around him many friends and adherents." Palmer (1899) II, p. 626. The description echoes what Shattuck Jr. evidently felt about the man.

The partnership between Curtiss and Stuart was dissolved when Stuart acquired the *Chicago American*, a weekly newspaper. Eastman (1911), p. 32; Moses (1892) II, pp. 945–946; Andreas (1884b) I, p. 372. Curtiss continued practicing from the rear of the *Chicago American* offices, although it appears that he was aiming increasingly toward a career in politics. Andreas (1884b) I., p. 372.

In 1838, Curtiss was elected an alderman of the city's Second Ward. Andreas (1884b) I, p. 184. A year later, he made an unsuccessful bid for mayor as a Democrat in the city's third mayoral election. Eastman (1909), p. 191. In 1842, he was elected city clerk. Andreas (1884b) I, p. 184. From 1841 to 1845, he served as state's attorney for Cook County. Fergus (1896), pp. 6, 48; Andreas (1884a), p. 350; Norris (1844), pp. 31, 67. He served as editor of a weekly newspaper, the *Democratic Advocate and Commercial Advertiser*, from 1844 until the paper closed in 1846. Moses (1892) II, p. 946. In 1845, he was appointed the first clerk of the Cook County Court, a position he held until 1847. Andreas (1884b) I, pp. 446–447.

In 1846, he was elected alderman of the Third Ward. Andreas (1884b) I, p. 184. The following year, he was elected as a Democrat to a one year term as Chicago's eleventh mayor. Eastman (1909), p. 192; Andreas (1884b) I, p. 184. He stood for reelection in 1848 but was defeated by James H. Woodworth. Eastman (1909), p. 192. On March 5, 1850, his mayoral ambitions were again realized when he was elected as the city's thirteenth mayor. Eastman (1909), p. 192.

The U.S. Census in that year listed Curtiss and his wife Mary with eight children: Mary Kimball, 17 (b. 18 Dec. 18 1832); Sarah, 14 (b. 7 Mar. 1836); Lucy Maria, 12 (b. 21 Feb. 1838); Elizabeth, 10 (b. 8 Jan. 1840); Charles Chauncy, 3 (b. 31 Jul. 1847); Laura Minnie, 3 (b. 31 Jul. 1847); and George Warren, 16 months (b. 27 Jan. 1849). U.S. Bureau of the Census (1850), Census Place: *Chicago Ward 6, Cook Co., IL*; Roll: *M432_102*; Page: *331A*; Image: *468*. See also, Marquis (1911), p. 171. Another daughter, Laura Curtiss, had been born on September 8, 1841, but died in 1848 at the age of six. Morrison (1897), p. 666.

Curtiss sought reelection in 1851 and 1852 but lost both times. Eastman (1909), p. 192. In 1855, he became "extensively engaged in farming" in Champaign County, IL. He died in Joliet, IL, on November 2, 1859. Obituary (1859). He was buried in Chicago's City Cemetery, but when the cemetery was moved to create Lincoln Park, his grave and headstone were lost.

Many sources, including his obituary in the *Chicago Press and Tribune*, give Curtiss's birth date as 1803. Holli (1981), p. 88; Obituary (1859). However, the record of his marriage in Eastport clearly states that he was born on March 29, 1806, as do the birth records of Wethersfield, Connecticut. Calnan (2007), p. 39; Wethersfield Town Records, 2:185 (FHC film #1315118). An 1806 birth date is also consistent with the 1850 U.S. Census record, which lists Curtiss as age forty-four in November 1850. While census records are not always reliable, Curtiss's age

as well as that of his wife, Mary, correspond precisely with the birth dates given in the Eastport records. In this instance, the census data appear to be accurate.

25. GCSJr Journal, 23 May 1833 (Countway).

26. JJA, Eastport to LBA, New York, 26 May 1833 (Yale, Box 1, Folder 5); GCSJr Journal, 23 May 1833 (Countway).

27. GCSJr Journal, 23 May 1833 (Countway).

28. GCSJr, Eastport to GCS, Boston, 26 May 1833 (MHS, Vol. 11, 14–31 May 1833); GCSJr Journal, 24 May 1833 (Countway). Shattuck Jr., whose journal provides the most complete extant record of the Grand Manan excursion, did not specifically state when the party returned to the revenue cutter from the home of William Frankland on the night of Thursday, May 23. However, he did inform his father in the cited letter, dated May 26, that he had written in his journal before turning in at 10:30 p.m. Given the length of his journal entry, he probably spent upwards of an hour detailing the events of the day. Thus, I have estimated the time of their return at around 9:00 p.m.

29. GCSJr Journal, 24 May 1833 (Countway); Coolidge (1833), 23 May 1833. According to data provided by the Earth System Research Laboratory of the National Oceanic and Atmospheric Administration, sunrise occurred at the Green Islands, where the *Swiftsure* was anchored west of White Head Island, at 3:50 a.m. EST on May 24, 1833. NOAA Solar Calculator, http://www.esrl.noaa.gov /gmd/grad/solcalc/ (accessed 20 Feb. 2014). However, it is worth noting that in the early 19th century, time was not standardized by time zone as it is today, nor was there such a thing as Daylight Savings Time. Time zones were introduced in the United States in 1883, largely at the behest of the nation's railroads, which had struggled to establish schedules for trains traveling between cities with different local times. Ayers (2008), p. 369. Daylight Savings Time was formally adopted in the U.S. in 1918. "Daylight Saving Bill Signed by President," *The New York Times*, Vol. LXVII, No. 21,970, p. 14, col. 6 (Wednesday, 20 Mar. 1918).

In 1833, people set their clocks to correspond with the mean solar time or "mean time" for the community in which they lived. Mean time, which is based on a 24-hour day, was designed to even out the vagaries in apparent solar time, i.e., the time one would measure using a sundial, caused by the elliptical orbit and tilt of the Earth. The difference between the two, which can be as much as a quarter of an hour depending on the time of year, is called the "equation of time." NOAA, Solar Calculator Glossary, http://www.esrl.noaa.gov/gmd/grad/solcalc /glossary.html (accessed 22 Feb. 2014); Bowditch (1826), p. 154 and Table IV-A, Appendix, p. 69. The equation of time can be measured for any given day and is used to calculate mean time from apparent solar time. Using the NOAA data, the equation of time for May 24, 1833, was a negative 3.50 minutes, which would be subtracted from the time of apparent sunrise to equal mean time. Bowditch (1826), Table IV-A, p. 69. Thus, mean time for the sunrise would have been 3:46:30 a.m. The results are the same for Eastport mean time, which is likely what the watches of Audubon's party would have been set to.

30. GCSJr Journal, 24 May 1833 (Countway). Shattuck wrote in his journal that the members of his party exploring the Three Islands off Grand Manan on Friday, May 24, consisted of "Mr A., Mr C. and Young Frankland." He never specifically identified who "Mr C." was, so it is possible that James Curtiss and not Capt. Joseph Claridge was in the boat that day. I tend to believe, however, that had Curtiss accompanied them, Shattuck would have used Curtiss's surname to identify him as he did elsewhere in the journal. The use of "Mr." signified respect, and Shattuck evidently had little respect for the Eastport postmaster.

31. Leahy (2004), pp. 155, 189; Madge (1988), p. 265; GCSJr Journal, 24 May 1833 (Countway).

32. *OB* III, p. 105; GCSJr Journal, 24 May 1833 (Countway). From Kent Island, "[n]eighboring Hay Island (75 acres/30 ha) and Sheep Island (45 acres/18 ha) can be reached by foot at low tide or by small boat" from Kent Island. "Kent Island," Bowdoin College website, https://www.bowdoin.edu /kent-island/ (accessed 30 May 2015).

In Shattuck's journal, which is the source for the text, he used the colloquial names for the birds they saw—"sea parrots" and "sea pigeons"—as they made their way to Kent Island. Audubon indicated in his species account in the *OB* that the Atlantic Puffin was usually called the "sea parrot."

He did not refer to the Black Guillemot as a "sea pigeon," but Shattuck's description of these birds as having "a white spot on their wings, the rest of their plumage being black, or dark green changeable, and varying as seen in different lights" is diagnostic for this species. Peterson (2008), pp. 216–217; GCSJr, Eastport to GCS, Boston, 26 May 1833 (MHS, Vol. 11, 14–31 May 1833).

33. Wheelwright (2008), p. 28; Graham (1980), p. 12; GCSJr Journal, 24 May 1833 (Countway).

34. GCSJr Journal, 24 May 1833 (Countway).

35. *OB* III, p. 617.

36. *OB* III, p. 118; GCSJr, Eastport to GCS, Boston, 26 May 1833 (MHS, Vol. 11, 14–31 May 1833); GCSJr Journal, 24 May 1833 (Countway). Shattuck indicated in his journal that they had collected a "turnstone" during their excursion to the Three Islands. This would have been a Ruddy Turnstone, the only turnstone found in the eastern U.S. Sibley (2014), p. 176.

37. GCSJr, Eastport to GCS, Boston, 26 May 1833 (MHS, Vol. 11, 14–31 May 1833); GCSJr Journal, 24 May 1833 (Countway). Shattuck told his journal that they returned to the *Swiftsure* after their excursion to the Three Islands at 2:30 p.m. Capt. Coolidge' ship log, on the other hand, recorded that the parties returned at 2:00 p.m. I have favored Shattuck's details in recounting this trip as he appears to have been an accurate historian, and it seems Coolidge's log was not maintained with the same detail.

In the *OB*, Audubon remarked that "On the 31st of May 1833, my son and party killed six Eiders on the island of Grand Manan, off the Bay of Fundy, where the birds were seen in considerable numbers, and were just beginning to breed. A nest containing two eggs, but not a particle of down, was found at a distance of more than fifty yards from the water." *OB* III, p. 343. Audubon was evidently referring to the events of May 24 when John and his party explored the area around the Two Islands off Grand Manan. His date references in the *OB* were often inexact, as demonstrated by this passage.

While Audubon scholar Edward Dwight asserts that Audubon painted a trio of Common Eiders during his stay in Eastport, it would appear that he is in error. Cf. Audubon (1966) I, Plate 185; Chapter 4, note 92, *supra*.

38. GCSJr, Eastport to GCS, Boston, 26 May 1833 (MHS, Vol. 11, 14–31 May 1833).

39. GCSJr, Eastport to GCS, Boston, 26 May 1833 (MHS, Vol. 11, 14–31 May 1833); GCSJr Journal, 24 May 1833 (Countway).

40. *OB* II, p. 486; JJA, Eastport to LBA, New York, 26 May 1833 (Yale, Box 1, Folder 5). In his Episode "The Bay of Fundy," Audubon stated that Frankland and his men had given them "three hearty cheers" on the morning after their first visit to the island. However, the *Swiftsure* was then anchored off the Green Islands, miles away. Rather, this must have occurred when the revenue cutter returned to White Head Island later that day to drop off Frankland's sons.

41. Coolidge (1833), 24 May 1833. Shattuck wrote in his journal entry of May 24 that the *Swiftsure* spent the night at Long Island Harbor, not in Flagg's Cove. GCSJr Journal, 24 May 1833 (Countway). He told his father the same thing in a letter on May 26. GCSJr, Eastport to GCS, Boston, 26 May 1833 (MHS, Vol. 11, 14–31 May 1833). Long Island Bay is situated between Long Island and the Swallowtail, as described in the 1833 edition of Edmund M. Blunt's *American Coast Pilot*, the essential nautical guide used by every mariner sailing a vessel along the coast of the United States. Blunt (1833), pp. 147–148, note. See also, Blunt (1827), p. 23, note. Since Capt. Coolidge was more familiar with the area and indicated that they anchored in Flagg's Cove, this is the geographic location given in the text.

42. GCSJr, Eastport to GCS, Boston, 26 May 1833 (MHS, Vol. 11, 14–31 May 1833); GCSJr Journal, 25 May 1833 (Countway); Coolidge (1833), 25 May 1833.

43. JJA, Eastport to LBA, New York, 26 May 1833 (Yale, Box 1, Folder 5); JJA, Eastport to Richard Harlan, M.D., Philadelphia, 26 May 1833 (Princeton, Box 2, Folder 20); GCSJr, Eastport to GCS, Boston, 26 May 1833 (MHS, Vol. 11, 14–31 May 1833); GCSJr Journal, 25 May 1833 (Countway). There is no evidence that Audubon took one of the young Ravens to Labrador.

Rhodes relies on Audubon's post-excursion letter to Richard Harlan, M.D., for the assertion that the naturalist and his young companions personally descended the cliff face to capture the ravens.

Rhodes (2004), p. 381. That was certainly what Audubon implied, perhaps to reassure Harlan about the state of his health: "Caught Ravens in the way that they are caught in the Orkneys i.e. by going down with Ropes from the top of the precipitous rocks in which they place their nests—in a Word we have had rare sport & plenty of it and I am Audubon again!" JJA, Eastport to Richard Harlan, M.D., Philadelphia, 26 May 1833 (Princeton, Box 2, Folder 20). However, Shattuck's comments in his journal and letter home make it clear that the descent was made by a single sailor from the *Swiftsure*.

44. GCSJr, Eastport to GCS, Boston, 26 May 1833 (MHS, Vol. 11, 14–31 May 1833); Coolidge (1833), 25 May 1833; GCSJr Journal, 25 May 1833 (Countway).

45. JJA, Eastport to LBA, New York, 26 May 1833 (Yale, Box 1, Folder 5).

CHAPTER 6: DEPARTURE

1. JJA, Eastport to LBA at New York, 26 May 1833 (Yale, Box 1, Folder 5). When Audubon awoke at 4:00 a.m. on Sunday, May 26, 1833, it was already light out. Sunrise was at 3:49 a.m. EST according to data provided by NOAA's Earth System Research Laboratory. The equation of time for that date was a negative 3.32 minutes, so mean time at Eastport would have been a little after 3:45 a.m. NOAA Solar Calculator, http://www.esrl.noaa.gov/gmd/grad/solcalc/ (accessed 2 Mar. 2014).

2. LBA, New York to JJA, Eastport, 29 May 1833 (Yale, Box 1, Folder 18); LBA, New York to VGA, London, 19 May 1833 (Yale, Box 1, Folder 18).

3. JJA, Eastport to LBA, New York, 26 May 1833 (Yale, Box 1, Folder 5).

4. Ibid.

5. *OB* III, pp. 118–119; JWA addendum to JJA, Eastport to LBA, New York, 26 May 1833 (Yale, Box 1, Folder 5). "Dash" was also the name of a dog Audubon had in Henderson. He left her with a friend when he moved to Cincinnati in 1820 but retrieved her later that year during his trip by flatboat to New Orleans. Audubon (1999), p. 8; Corning (1929a), pp. 11–12.

6. JJA, Eastport to Richard Harlan, M.D., Philadelphia, 26 May 1833 (Princeton, Box 2, Folder 20).

7. JJA, Eastport to LBA, New York, 27 May 1833 (Princeton, Box 2, Folder 21), *Letters* I, p. 229; LBA,

New York to VGA, London, 23 May 1833 (Yale, Box 1, Folder 18).

8. GCSJr, Eastport to GCS, Boston, 26 May 1833 (MHS, Vol. 11, 14–31 May 1833).

9. GCSJr Journal, 22 [2] Jun. 1833 (Countway); GCSJr, Eastport to GCS, Boston, 29 May 1833 (MHS, Vol. 11, 14–31 May 1833). Pilot bread, also known as ship's biscuit or hardtack, was made from flour and water, and baked into a hard, dry cracker. It was commonly used as a non-perishable foodstuff for sailors while as sea.

10. JJA, Eastport to LBA, New York, 27 May 1833 (Princeton, Box 2, Folder 21), *Letters* I, p. 229.

11. Ibid., p. 228.

12. GCSJr Journal, List of Letters Received and Written, May-June, 1833 (Countway). In the journal Shattuck kept during his stay in Eastport, he recorded a list of the letters he had both received and written. That list reflects that he received letters from his father and from Eliza Prentiss, a family friend, on Sunday, May 26.

13. JJA, Eastport to LBA, New York, 27 May 1833 (Princeton, Box 2, Folder 21), *Letters* I, p. 229. Audubon informed Lucy in his letter of May 27 that they had received word from Dr. Shattuck the previous day that the son of Dr. Ingalls of Boston would be heading for Eastport to join the expedition. Since Shattuck Jr. indicated in his journal that he had received a letter from his father on May 26, it seems relatively clear that this news was conveyed in that letter. However, the Massachusetts Historical Society, which holds the senior Shattuck's papers, does not have this particular letter in its collection, so it has not been possible to verify this.

14. GCSJr Journal, 22 [2] Jun. 1833 (Countway); JJA, Eastport to LBA, New York, 31 May 1833 (Yale, Box 1, Folder 5).

15. GCSJr Journal, 22 [2] Jun. 1833 (Countway); JJA, Eastport to LBA, New York, 27 May 1833 (Princeton, Box 2, Folder 21), *Letters* I, p. 230.

16. JJA, Eastport to LBA, New York, 27 May 1833 (Princeton, Box 2, Folder 21), *Letters* I, pp. 228–230. Audubon told Lucy that "the wind is northeast now—this stops our schooner from coming in." See also, Chapter 4, note 223.

17. Audubon (2006), p. 418; *AHJ* I, p. 405; Knowlton (1875), p. 107; JJA, Eastport to LBA, New York, 27 May 1833 (Princeton, Box 2, Folder 21), *Letters* I, p. 230; JWA addendum, 6 Jun. 1833, to JJA, Eastport to LBA, New York, 5–6 Jun. 1833 (Princeton, Box 2, Folder 23). See also, Kilby (1898), p. 15. Lucy Weston made a positive impression on Audubon. In his May 27 letter to Lucy, Audubon described her as a "fine Daughter."

Sarah Connell Ayer, a deeply religious Eastport resident whose husband, Samuel, was a local physician as well as surveyor for the Passamaquoddy Customs District before his death in 1832, mentioned Lucy Weston in her journal in September 1827: "Lucy Weston has been in this evening. O, how I long to see her, come over to the Lord's side. She is a lovely girl, * * * * She is a most interesting girl." Ayer (1910), pp. 234, 276, 338; Force (1832), p. 189.

Lucy Weston would go on to marry Joshua Clark Shaw, originally from Bath, ME, and, in 1838, move to Galveston, TX. She died there in 1850. Her letters are on loan at the Rosenberg Library in Galveston. Shelly Kelly (Personal communication, 28 Apr. 2012); Kelly (2008).

18. Lucy P. Weston, Eastport to Jane H. Weston, Boston, 15 May 1833 (Rosenberg Library).

19. JJA, Eastport to LBA, New York, 27 May 1833 (Princeton, Box 2, Folder 21), *Letters* I, pp. 230–231.

20. JJA, Eastport to LBA, New York, 28 May 1833 (Yale, Box 1, Folder 5); JJA, Eastport to Richard Harlan, M.D., Philadelphia, 26 May 1833 (Princeton, Box 2, Folder 20).

21. JJA, Eastport to LBA, New York, 28 May 1833 (Yale, Box 1, Folder 5); Coolidge (1833), 27 May 1833. Hobb's Wharf, where the *Swiftsure* had been taken for repairs, was located off Water Street, the main commercial thoroughfare that ran along the Eastport waterfront. Holt (1999), pp. 116–117. The wharf was operated by the commercial firm of G. & I. Hobbs. "Their house was interested in shipping; and their busy wharf was the great grindstone depot, the product of important quarries at the head of the Bay of Fundy passing through their hands." Kilby (1888), p. 269.

22. JJA, Eastport to LBA, New York, 28 May 1833 (Yale, Box 1, Folder 5). In his May 28 letter to Lucy, Audubon did not identify the species of phalarope that John had procured the previous day while out on Passamaquoddy Bay. However, in his

description of the Hyperborean Phalarope (Red-necked Phalarope) in the *OB*, he indicated that his son has shot several of this species during their visit to Eastport. *OB* III, p. 118.

23. Hobart (1986), p. 37; Kilby (1898), pp. 14–15; GCSJr Journal, 22 [2] Jun. 1833 (Countway).

24. Ronald Windhorst, Dennys River Historical Society (Personal communication, 25 May 2014).

25. GCSJr, Eastport to GCS, Boston, 29 May 1833 (MHS, Vol. 11, 14–31 May 1833).

26. GCSJr Journal, 22 [2] Jun. 1833 (Countway); GCSJr, Eastport to GCS, Boston, 29 May 1833 (MHS, Vol. 11, 14–31 May 1833).

27. GCSJr, Eastport to GCS, Boston, 29 May 1833 (MHS, Vol. 11, 14–31 May 1833); Communication with Ronald Windhorst and Melinda Jacques, Dennys River Historical Society (25 May 2014).

28. GCSJr Journal, 22 [2] Jun. 1833 (Countway).

29. GCSJr Journal, 22 [2] Jun. 1833 (Countway); GCSJr, Eastport to GCS, Boston, 29 May 1833 (MHS, Vol. 11, 14–31 May 1833); Communication with Ronald Windhorst, Dennys River Historical Society (25 May 2014).

30. GCSJr Journal, 22 [2] Jun. 1833 (Countway).

31. GCSJr, Eastport to GCS at Boston, 29 May 1833 (MHS, Vol. 11, 14–31 May 1833).

32. GCS, Boston to GCSJr, Eastport, 28 May 1833 (MHS, Vol. 11, May 14–31, 1833).

33. JJA, Eastport to LBA, New York, 28–29 May 1833 (Yale, Box 1, Folder 5).

34. Ibid.

35. JJA, Eastport to LBA, New York, 31 May 1833 (Yale, Box 1, Folder 5); JJA, Eastport to LBA, New York, 28–29 May 1833 (Yale, Box 1, Folder 5).

36. JJA, Eastport to LBA, New York, 28–29 May 1833 (Yale, Box 1, Folder 5).

37. LBA, New York to JJA, Eastport, 29 May 1833 (Yale, Box 1, Folder 18); LBA, New York to Edward Harris, New York, 28 May 1833 (Harvard (208)). In this letter to her husband, Lucy noted that she had written previously on May 8, 13, 19, 22, 24, and 27. Lucy's letter to Edward Harris of May 28 provided him with snippets of Audubon's May 19 correspondence, which appeared in the *New-York Gazette* on May 29. *New-York Gazette & General Advertiser*, Vol. 45, No. 16,878, p. 2, col. 2 (Wednesday, 29 May 1833)(NYHS).

38. Terres (1980), p. 870; *OB* II, p. 334.

39. GCSJr, Eastport to GCS, Boston, 29 May 1833 (MHS, Vol. 11, 14–31 May 1833).

40. "A Californian's Recollection of Naturalist Audubon," *The San Francisco Call*, Vol. LXXX, No. 98, p. 25, cols. 1–7 (Sunday, 6 Sept. 1896)(LOC); *New York Gazette & General Advertiser*, Vol. 45, No. 16,892, p. 2, col. 2 (Friday Morning, 14 Jun. 1833) (NYHS). See also, JJA, Eastport to LBA, New York, 31 May 1833 (Yale, Box 1, Folder 5). The precise date that Audubon dined with the Coolidge family and invited Joe Coolidge to accompany him on the Labrador expedition cannot be determined from the existing records, but it most likely occurred on May 29. In letters to Lucy on May 27 and 28, Audubon mentioned that William Ingalls would be joining the expedition but made no reference to Coolidge. Since the May 28 letter was supplemented by a postscript written by Audubon at dawn on May 29, it is obvious that Coolidge had yet to accept his invitation. However, Audubon wrote to Edward Harris later that day and identified Coolidge as a member of his party. *New York Gazette & General Advertiser*, Vol. 45, No. 16,891, p. 2, col. 2 (Thursday Morning, 13 Jun. 1833). Given the proximity of Audubon's departure for Labrador, it is safe to assume that the Coolidge family would have given him a prompt answer. This strongly suggests that he dined with them on the afternoon of May 29.

41. The Hampton boat was developed around Hampton, NH, in the early 19th century. Widely used by cod fishermen in the Gulf of St. Lawrence, it had a "long, sharp bow and a 'pinky' stern; the boat was two-masted and ketch-rigged, with a shifting bowsprit and jib for light-weather work." Chapelle (1951), pp. 137–138.

Audubon began referring to his young companions as the "Young Gentlemen" in his May 22 letter to Lucy. JJA, Eastport to LBA, New York, 22 May 1833 (Princeton, Box 2, Folder 19).

42. A Californian's Recollection of Naturalist Audubon, "*The San Francisco Call*, Vol. LXXX, No. 98, p. 25, cols. 1–7 (Sunday, 6 Sept. 1896) (LOC).

43. GCSJr Journal, 22 [2] Jun. 1833 (Countway); JJA, Eastport to LBA, New York, 31 May 1833 (Yale, Box 1, Folder 5). According to Capt. Uriah Coolidge's journal for the *Swiftsure*, the steamer *Henrietta* from Saint John, New Brunswick, struck

and became trapped on Clark's Ledge. Coolidge (1833), 30 May 1833.

44. GCSJr Journal, 22 [2] Jun. 1833 (Countway).

45. Audubon (2011), pp. 298 and note 35; 302, 314–315, 361; Ford (1987), pp. 335, 340, 356–357, 399, 402–403. Audubon first met George Combe at a dinner at the home of the printer Patrick Neill on November 3, 1826. He was visited by Combe on November 19 and subsequently dined with Combe and several other members of the Phrenological Society of Edinburgh at Combe's house on November 27. Three weeks later, on December 20, he breakfasted with Combe and his younger brother Andrew, an Edinburgh physician, who was likewise an adherent of phrenology.

46. GCSJr Journal, 22 [2] Jun. 1833 (Countway).

47. Ibid.

48. Ibid. In his discussion with Dr. Isaac Ray on May 30, 1833, Audubon identified France's Baron Cuvier and James Wilson of Scotland as scientists who could determine a bird's singing ability from an examination of its trachea. See generally, Blumenbach (1827), p. 196. Birds are equipped with a unique organ located between the trachea and the two bronchi of the lungs known as the syrinx. Species with elaborate syringeal muscles, such as songbirds, are capable of complex vocalizations or songs, while those without, such as New World vultures, are only able to hiss. Gill (1990), pp. 194–195.

49. JJA, Eastport to LBA, New York, 31 May 1833 (Yale, Box 1, Folder 5).

50. LBA, New York to JJA, Eastport, 24 May 1833 (Yale, Box 1, Folder 18).

51. JJA, Eastport to LBA, New York, May 31, 1833 (Yale, Box 1, Folder 5).

52. Ibid.

53. Ibid.

54. George Parkman, M.D., Boston to JJA, Eastport, 25 May 1833 (Howland), Herrick (1938) II, p. 43. Note that the holograph facsimile published in Herrick is not an exact copy of the original, which states in reference to young William Ingalls: "The son is the father's pupil." The facsimile copy in Herrick's biography instead states: "The son is the father's son." However, Herrick correctly transcribed Parkman's correspondence in his text.

55. JJA, Eastport to LBA, New York, 31 May 1833 (Yale, Box 1, Folder 5).

56. GCSJr Journal, 22 [2] Jun. 1833 (Countway).

57. VGA, London to LBA, Boston, 29 May 1833 (Yale, Box 2, Folder 37); VGA, London to LBA, Boston, 31 May 1833 (Yale, Box 2, Folder 37).

58. VGA, London to LBA, Boston, 31 May 1833 (Yale, Box 2, Folder 37).

59. Robert Bakewell (1767–1843), the well-known British geologist, was a nephew of Lucy's grandfather, Joseph Bakewell. Herrick (1938) I, p. 200; Bakewell (1896), p. 13. See generally, Matthew (2004).

60. Torrens (2014).

61. VGA, London to LBA, Boston, 31 May 1833 (Yale, Box 2, Folder 37).

62. *Mechanics' Magazine* (1833), p. 111.

63. *Mechanics' Magazine* (1832a), p. 405. The original attack by Thomas P. Jones on Audubon's rattlesnake paper appeared in *The Franklin Journal and American Mechanics' Magazine*. Jones (1828). See also, Herrick (1938) II, p. 425.

64. Jones (1828), p. 144, reprinted with slight changes in punctuation in *Mechanics' Magazine* (1832a), p. 405.

65. After the first publication of criticism of Audubon in *Mechanics' Magazine* on March 10, 1832, a running exchange between Audubon's defenders and the editor of the magazine appeared in the following issues: Vol. XVII, No. 453, pp. 23–24 (14 Apr. 1832); Vol. XVII, No. 456, p. 78 (5 May 1832); Vol. XVII, No. 469, pp. 291–294 (4 Aug. 1832); Vol. XVII, No. 476, pp. 406–407 (22 Sept. 1832); Vol. XVIII, No. 478, pp. 11–13 (6 Oct. 1832); Vol. XIX, No. 510, p. 111 (18 May 1833).

66. Abert (1831).

67. *Mechanics' Magazine* (1832b), pp. 291–294.

68. *Mechanics' Magazine*, Vol. XIX, No. 510, p. 111 (18 May 1833).

69. JJA, Eastport to LBA, New York, 4 Jun. 1833 (Princeton, Box 2, Folder 22); GCSJr, Eastport to GCS, Boston (MHS, Vol. 11, Jun. 1833); GCSJr Journal, 22 [2] Jun. 1833 (Countway). The unloading of the *Ripley*, which began on Saturday, June 1, did not resume until the following Monday in recognition of the Sabbath.

70. GCSJr, Eastport to GCS, Boston, 2 Jun. 1833 (MHS, Vol. 11, Jun. 1833).

71. Kinney (1989), p. 97; Townsend (1918), p. 74. See also, Chapter 4, note 138, *supra*. According to

Dr. Charles W. Townsend, who was probably the foremost 20th century scholar of Audubon's Labrador expedition, "[t]he Ripley was what is called a topsail schooner with yard and square top-sails." Townsend (1918), p. 74. However, he was in error in claiming that the *Ripley* was over a hundred feet long. Townsend (1918), p. 74; Townsend (1917), p. 138.

72. Kinney (1989), p. 97; JJA, Eastport to LBA, New York, 4 Jun. 1833 (Princeton, Box 2, Folder 22), *Letters* I, p. 235; GCSJr, Eastport to GCS at Boston, 2 Jun. 1833 (MHS, Vol. 11, June 1833).

73. *OB* III, p. 584; GCSJr, Eastport to GCS, Boston, 2 Jun. 1833 (MHS, Vol. 11, June 1833).

74. Emery (1890), p. 362; JJA, Eastport to LBA, New York, 4 Jun. 1833 (Princeton, Box 2, Folder 22), *Letters* I, p. 235. Henry T. Emery, the master of the *Ripley*, was born on November 10, 1808, in Sanford, ME, the son of Henry Tilton Emery (1783–1865) and his first wife, Elizabeth Morrill. Emery (1890), pp. 361–362.

75. JWA addendum, 6 Jun. 1833, to JJA, Eastport to LBA, New York, 5–6 Jun. 1833 (Princeton, Box 2, Folder 22).

76. GCSJr, Eastport to GCS, Boston, 2 Jun. 1833 (MHS, Vol. 11, Jun. 1833).

77. Emery (1890), p. 362. According to the family genealogy, the Emery family was living in Eastport by 1818.

78. Willey (2003), p. 108. The report of Emery's wedding to Rebecca McKinney, which appeared in the *Eastport Sentinel*, referred to him as Henry T. Emery Jr. Ibid. The charter for the *Ripley* also refers to him as Henry T. Emery. (Yale, Box 16, Folder 719). The family genealogy gives his name as simply Henry Emery. His first child was born in 1840. Emery (1890), pp. 362, 430.

79. Michael Harwood and Mary Durant were the first Audubon scholars to offer any significant details about the life of Henry T. Emery, the master of the *Ripley*, in their delightful 1980 book, *On the Road with John James Audubon*. Durant & Harwood (1980), pp. 416–418. Unfortunately, virtually everything they wrote about him was erroneous. During a visit to Eastport, they met Joyce Emery Kinney, the great-granddaughter of the man who she said had sailed with the naturalist to Labrador. Ms. Kinney told them that her great-grandfather

had been born in 1783 and had been a seaman, town selectman, and state legislator before his death at the age of eighty-one. Better yet, Ms. Kinney had a portrait of her ancestor that she permitted them to publish. A dozen years later, Ms. Kinney repeated the assertion about her ancestor's role in the expedition and republished his portrait in a book she wrote on the sailing vessels of Down-east Maine. Kinney (1992), p. 97–98.

However, Ms. Kinney was mistaken. The contemporary statements of the participants establish, without question, that it was Emery's son and namesake, also known as Henry T. Emery, who captained the *Ripley*. In correspondence to both Lucy and Victor, Audubon described the man who would take the *Ripley* north as a "schoolmate" of twenty-one-year-old Tom Lincoln. JJA, Eastport to VGA, London, 31 May 1833, *Letters* I, p. 231; JJA, Eastport to LBA, New York, 19 May 1833 (Princeton, Box 2, Folder 18), *Letters* I, p. 224. This could not possibly have referred to the elder Emery, who was two years older than Audubon. Additionally, Shattuck Jr. indicated in a letter home on June 2, 1833, the day after the *Ripley* reached Eastport, that the vessel was "commanded by a very enterprising young man, of the name Amory." GCSJr, Eastport to Eliza Prentiss, Boston, 2 Jun. 1833 (MHS, Vol. 11, Jun. 1833). Finally and most tellingly, Tom Lincoln wrote to Audubon on November 17, 1846, and, recalling their Labrador compatriots, reported that "Capt. Emery died in W. Indies of yellowfever [*sic*] six years ago." Grinnell (1924), p. 229. The senior Emery died in 1865. Kilby (1888), p. 277. The men of the Labrador expedition would have known far better than a distant Emery relation who had captained their schooner.

80. JJA, Eastport to LBA, New York, 4 Jun. 1833 (Princeton, Box 2, Folder 22), *Letters* I, p. 235.

81. *OB* III, pp. 584–585; JJA, Eastport to LBA, New York, 5 Jun. 1833 (Princeton, Box 2, Folder 23), *Letters* I, p. 238; JJA, Eastport to LBA, New York, 4 Jun. 1833 (Princeton, Box 2, Folder 22) *Letters* I, p. 235; GCSJr, Eastport to GCS, Boston, 2 Jun. 1833 (MHS, Vol. 11, Jun. 1833).

82. GCSJr, Eastport to GCS, Boston, 2 Jun. 1833 (MHS, Vol. 11, Jun. 1833). See also, Audubon (2006), p. 374; *AHJ* I, p. 349; L. Audubon (1869), p. 296.

83. GCSJr Journal, 22 [2] Jun. 1833 (Countway).

84. GCSJr, Eastport to GCS, Boston, 2 Jun. 1833 (MHS, Vol. 11, Jun. 1833); GCSJr, Eastport to Eliza Prentiss and Lucy Shattuck, Boston, 2 Jun. 1833 (MHS, Vol. 11, June 1833).

85. GCSJr, Eastport to Eliza Prentiss and Lucy Shattuck, Boston, 2 Jun. 1833 (MHS, Vol. 11, Jun. 1833).

86. JJA, Eastport to LBA, New York, 4 Jun. 1833 (Princeton, Box 2, Folder 22). The finished composition of the Winter Wrens shows a male on a short, moss-covered log and an immature bird on a lichen-covered branch above it. Audubon (1966) II, Plate 328. Audubon later cut out and pasted on two additional images: an earlier drawing of a female of this species that he had done during his 1820 Mississippi River trip and a Rock Wren drawn from the skin of a bird collected on the West Coast by Thomas Nuttall and John K. Townsend. Ibid.

87. GCSJr Journal, 11 Jun. 1833 (Countway); Coolidge (1833), 3 Jun. 1833.

88. GCSJr Journal, 11 Jun. 1833 (Countway).

89. JJA, Eastport to LBA, New York, 4 Jun. 1833 (Princeton, Box 2, Folder 22), *Letters* I, p. 236. Citing this letter, Roberta Olson states, in error, that John drew the Black Guillemot, "probably the downy chick" in Audubon's composition. Olson (2012), p. 275. Edward Dwight makes the same mistake. Audubon (1966) I, Plate 47. The letter states quite clearly that John had completed the picture of the three Hyperborean Phalaropes. See also, Chapter 4, note 199, *supra*. Moreover, Audubon would not have been able to collect a specimen of a young Black Guillemot during his Eastport stay. At Kent Island off Grand Manan in the Bay of Fundy, Black Guillemots do not begin to lay eggs until late May or early June. The incubation period varies but is approximately one month. Butler (2002), pp. 15, 18.

90. JJA, Eastport to LBA, New York, 4 Jun. 1833 (Princeton, Box 2, Folder 22), *Letters* I, pp. 235–237.

91. Audubon (2006), p. 374; *AHJ* I, p. 349; L. Audubon (1869), p. 296. Audubon indicated that he went on a ramble in the woods on the morning of June 4, 1833. In the *OB*, he wrote of the Black-throated Blue Warbler: "I am inclined to believe that it breeds in the State of Maine, having seen several individuals of both sexes not far from Eastport,

in the beginning of June 1833, when several other species had nests." *OB* II, p. 310. Although Audubon did not indicate when he observed this species, I have assumed for purposes of the narrative that it took place during his ramble on June 4.

92. See generally, Peterson (2006), pp. 1–9; Peterson & Peterson (1981), Nos. 328–381; Audubon (1966). In addition to the Black-throated Blue Warbler, Audubon misidentified the females or first year birds of several other wood warblers, mistakenly believing them to be separate species. In other cases, he maintained that subspecies were actually unique species and named them after his benefactors. He and other ornithologists of the time, including Alexander Wilson and Thomas Nuttall, were justifiably puzzled by the marked sexual dimorphism prevalent in some species and the confusing first year plumages worn by young birds after fledging. Indeed, the famous 20th century naturalist Roger Tory Peterson described these immature birds as "confusing fall warblers," which every beginning birder will acknowledge. Peterson (1980), pp. 248–251.

The warbler species for which Audubon made multiple identifications, with a breakdown of the names he gave them and their corresponding Havell Plate Nos., include:

(1) Black-throated Blue Warbler (*Setophaga caerulescens*): Black-throated Blue Warbler (adult male), Havell Plate 155; and Pine Swamp Warbler (adult females), Havell Plate 148

(2) Cerulean Warbler (*Setophaga cerulea*): Cerulean Warbler (adult male), Havell Plate 48; and Blue-green Warbler (adult female or first-fall male), Havell Plate 49.

(3) Blackburnian Warbler (*Setophaga fusca*): Blackburnian Warbler (adult male), Havell Plate 135; Blackburnian Warbler (adult female), Havell Plate 399; and Hemlock Warbler (adult female), Havell Plate 134.

(4) Bay-breasted Warbler (*Setophaga castanea*): Bay-breasted Warbler (adult male and female), Havell Plate 69; and Autumnal Warbler (first-fall females), Havell Plate 88.

(5) Pine Warbler (*Setophaga pinus*): Pine-creeping Warbler (adult male and female), Havell Plate 140; and Vigor's Warbler (first-

spring male), Havell Plate 30. Roger Tory Peterson claims that this was an immature bird, but Audubon noted on the original pastel drawing that he drew the bird on April 21, 1812, and stated in the *OB* that it was a male. Thus, it was most likely a first-year male, although the extensive white of the belly is more consistent with that of an adult female. Dunn & Garrett (1997), pp. 80–81, 346–348; Peterson (1980), No. 360; Audubon (1966) I, Plate 23.

(6) Palm Warbler (*Setophaga palmarum*): Palm Warbler (adult male and female), Havell Plate 145; and Yellow Red-poll Warbler (adult male and female), Havell Plate 163.

(7) Yellow Warbler (*Setophaga petechia*): Blue-eyed Yellow Warbler (adult male), Havell Plate 95; Children's Warbler (adult female and first-fall female), Havell Plate 35; and Rathbone Warbler (first-fall females), Havell Plate 65.

(8) Canada Warbler (*Cardellina canadensis*): Canada Warbler (adult male and female), Havell Plate 103; and Bonaparte Flycatcher (first-fall female), Havell Plate 5.

(9) Hooded Warbler (*Setophaga citrina*): Hooded Warbler (adult male and female), Havell Plate 110; and Selby's Flycatcher (juvenile male), Havell Plate 9.

(10) Common Yellow-throat (*Geothlypis trichas*): Maryland Yellow-throat (adult male and female), Havell Plate 23; and Roscoe's Yellow-throat (adult male), Havell Plate 24.

Sibley (2014), pp. 480–497; Peterson & Peterson (1981), Nos. 328–381; Audubon (1966). For illustrations of the varying plumages of these warblers, see Dunn & Garrett (1997); Curson (1994). Audubon also illustrated two warblers that cannot be readily identified today:

(1) Blue Mountain Warbler (Havell Plate 434) This aberrant species was first described by Alexander Wilson, who collected a male from the Blue Ridge Mountains. Audubon prepared his composition from a California specimen that was loaned to him by the Council of the Zoological Society of London. *OB* V, pp. 294–295. Ornithologists

have been unable to determine whether this was a hybrid species or one now lost to science.

(2) Carbonated Warbler (Havell Plate 60) In May 1811, while residing in Henderson, KY, Audubon reportedly collected and drew two males of this species. *OB* I, p. 308. It has never been sighted again, and the American Ornithologists' Union has placed it on a list of hypothetical species lacking convincing documentation. Audubon (1966) II, Plate 348. David Sibley, a master of bird identification and author of the popular *The Sibley Guide to Birds*, posits that Audubon's drawing lacks the detail of many of his other songbird compositions and contains several anatomical errors that suggest he painted the birds from memory. Sibley (2008). If so, Sibley questions the veracity of Audubon's assertion that he actually painted them from freshly killed specimens, which then raises doubt about his entire claim.

Noted Audubon scholar Edward Dwight believes the drawing of the Carbonated Warblers was made around 1825 from an earlier copy. Audubon (1966) II, Plate 348. Given the style of the drawing and Audubon's use of watercolors rather than pastels, Dwight's assessment is undoubtedly true. If so, it is certainly conceivable that in the process of redrawing his earlier work the naturalist made errors or had to supplement what remained of a damaged drawing with his memory. But it is highly doubtful that Audubon deliberately falsified this or any of the other birds he illustrated that are unknown to science, including the Bird of Washington (Havell Plate 11), Cuvier's Regulus (Havell Plate 55), and the Small-headed Flycatcher (Havell Plate 434). His practice of drawing his specimens shortly after they were collected and of taking detailed measurements of anatomical features makes this unlikely. Moreover, there were simply too many legitimate species to record for him to waste his time on fantasy birds. At the same time, he may not have been as exacting in his approach to painting birds in the early years, when he had no plans to publish his drawings, as compared to the drawings he did after 1820, when he had made up his mind to pursue his dream.

Several other possible explanations have been offered by ornithologists trying to make sense of Audubon's illustration of these unknown warblers. Elliot Coues, a late 19th century ornithologist and Audubon scholar, proposed that they were a pair of Cape May x Blackpoll hybrids. Sibley (2008). Kenneth Parkes suggested they were immature male Cape May Warblers in first alternate plumage. Parkes (1985), p. 92. More recently, Paul Hertzel has offered an intriguing possibility based upon a similar appearing, unknown warbler that he and his brother discovered in western Minnesota — that these were Blackpoll Warblers with yellow pigmentation in place of the bird's normally white feathers. Sibley (2008). Since Audubon did not keep the skins of the birds he drew in the early part of his career, we are left with his enigmatic drawing and a series of unanswered questions as to what these birds actually were.

93. Dunn & Garrett (1997), pp. 62-63; 264-265; Audubon (1966) II, Plate 426; *OB* II, p. 310.

94. *OB* II, p. 279.

95. *OB* V, p. 458.

96. Peterson & Peterson (1981), No. 348.

97. Audubon (2006), pp. 374-375; *AHJ* I, p. 349; L. Audubon (1869), p. 296.

98. Leahy (2004), pp. 502-504.

99. Audubon (2006), pp. 374-375; *AHJ* I, p. 349; L. Audubon (1869), p. 296.

100. GCSJr Journal, 11 Jun. 1833 (Countway). On May 27, 2014, I explored Dennysville in the company of Ron Windhorst, Colin Windhorst, and Melinda Jaques of the Dennys River Historical Society. I can attest that the black flies at that time of year, even with the generous use of bug spray, are absolutely dreadful.

101. L. Audubon (1869), p. 296. The reference to Audubon's dinner with Capt. Thomas Childs is absent from the version of his journal edited by his granddaughter Maria.

102. JJA, Eastport to LBA, New York, 5 Jun. 1833 (Princeton, Box 2, Folder 23), *Letters* I, pp. 237-238; LBA, New York to JJA, Eastport, 29 May 1833 (Yale, Box 1, Folder 18).

103. JJA, Eastport to LBA, New York, 5 Jun. 1833 (Princeton, Box 2, Folder 23). Cf. *Letters* I, p. 237 (differing in minor detail from the original holograph).

104. JJA, Eastport to LBA, New York, 5 Jun. 1833 (Princeton, Box 2, Folder 23). Cf. *Letters* I, pp. 237-238 (differing in minor detail from the original holograph). It appears that the man Audubon described as the *Ripley*'s steward, who had worked for many years as a body servant to Vincent Nolte, was serving in a dual capacity aboard the schooner. Audubon did not mention him again either in his journal or in his many references to the expedition in the *OB*.

Based on the record, I believe that the *Ripley* was manned by Capt. Emery, First Mate/Pilot Godwin, the cook, four crewmen, and the two extra sailors and a cabin boy hired by Audubon, which makes ten. GCSJr, Eastport to GCS, Boston, 2 Jun. 1833 (MHS, Vol. 11, Jun. 1833). The six members of Audubon's party would make a total of sixteen. Since Audubon's journal entry of July 18 suggests that the entire complement of the vessel could have been as few as fifteen, there is no place for a separate steward. Audubon (2006), pp. 415, 417; *AHJ* I, pp. 400, 403.

105. GCSJr Journal, 11 Jun. 1833 (Countway); GCSJr addendum, 5 Jun. 1833, to GCSJr, Eastport to GCS, Boston, 2 Jun. 1833 (MHS, Vol. 11, Jun. 1833).

106. "A Californian's Recollection of Naturalist Audubon," *The San Francisco Call*, Vol. LXXX, No. 98, p. 25, cols. 1-7 (Sunday, 6 Sept. 1896)(LOC).

107. Calnan (2007), p. 21; Audubon (2006), p. 375; Willey (2003), p. 46; *AHJ* I, p. 349; Charter-Party of Affreightment, 5 Jun. 1833 (Yale, Box 16, Folder 719). Jonathan Buck's wife, Ann, was the sister of Jonathan D. Weston's wife, Jane. Mary Grove, Great-Great-Granddaughter of Jonathan D. Weston (Personal communication, 24 Aug. 2015). See also, Chapter 4, note 138.

108. JJA, Eastport to VGA, London, 31 May 1833, *Letters* I, p. 231; JJA, Eastport to Richard Harlan, M.D., Philadelphia, 26 May 1833 (Princeton,

Box 2, Folder 20); JJA, Eastport to LBA, New York, 22 May 1833 (Princeton, Box 2, Folder 19); JJA, Eastport to LBA, New York, 16 May 1833 (Tides Institute).

109. L. Audubon (1869), p. 296. Cf. Audubon (2006), p. 374; *AHJ* I, p. 349. The quotation in the text is taken from Lucy's biography. The version appearing in the journal edited by Maria Audubon and republished by Rhodes appears to have been changed in minor but telling ways that suggest her editorial hand:

> Lucy: "The vessel is being prepared for our re-ception and departure; and we have concluded to ship two extra sailors, and a boy, to be a sort of major-domo, to clean our guns, hunt for nests and birds, and assist in skinning them, etc."

> Maria: "Our vessel is being prepared for our re-ception and departure, and we have concluded to hire two extra sailors and a lad; the latter to be a kind of major-domo, to clean our guns, etc., search for nests, and assist in skinning birds."

After hundreds of hours poring over Audubon's original correspondence and journals, one becomes familiar with his voice and manner of expression. I believe he would have used the verb "ship" rather than the pedestrian "hire." His reference to taking along a "boy" along on the voyage was to a cabin boy, not necessarily a youngster. Cabin boys were often young men who shipped out on their first voyage at the age of sixteen, but they could also be adults. Maria, not understanding this and crippled by her Victorian fastidiousness, would have insisted on improving the context by calling him a "lad," although there may have been some truth in this. It should be noted that a similar change was made in editing Audubon's original manuscript for his Episode entitled "Labrador," where the term "boy" was changed to "lad," evidently with Audubon's approval. Cf. "At Labrador," (Missouri History Museum); *OB* II, p. 584. Audubon would have used "etc.," which he wrote as "&c," at the end of the phrase, not in the middle. He also would have pre-ferred the verb "hunt" over Maria's "search." This is admittedly a subjective exercise, and other scholars may well disagree with my conclusions.

In quoting from the two sources for the Labra-dor journal in this book, I have endeavored to make an educated judgment as to which phraseology is closer to the original, sadly believed to have been destroyed by Maria after she completed her whole-sale revisions for publication. I will save the reader an explanation and analysis each time I select one version over the other. However, in each case, I will provide a citation to the quoted source with a cf. ("compare") citation to the other version, as I have done in this endnote. For those with an interest in seeing the discrepancies in the two texts, I will also offer the other variant.

110. Charter-Party of Affreightment, June 5, 1833 (Yale, Box 16, Folder 719).

111. Audubon (2006), p. 375; *AHJ* I, p. 349.

112. JJA, Eastport to LBA, New York, 5–6 Jun. 1833 (Princeton, Box 2, Folder 23), *Letters* I, p. 238; Charter-Party of Affreightment, 5 Jun. 1833 (Yale, Box 16, Folder 719).

113. JWA addendum, 6 Jun. 1833, to JJA, East-port to LBA, New York, 5–6 Jun. 1833 (Princeton, Box 2, Folder 23).

114. Audubon (2006), p. 375; *AHJ* I, p. 349. Audubon described the Hampton boat as having "two oars and lugsails." *OB* II, pp. 522–523.

115. JJA, Eastport to LBA, New York, 5–6 Jun. 1833 (Princeton, Box 2, Folder 23), *Letters* I, p. 238.

116. JWA addendum, 6 Jun. 1833, to JJA, East-port to LBA, New York, 5–6 Jun. 1833 (Princeton, Box 2, Folder 23).

117. JJA, Eastport to LBA, New York, 5–6 Jun. 1833 (Princeton, Box 2, Folder 23), *Letters* I, p. 238.

118. GCSJr Journal, 11 Jun. 1833 (Countway).

119. Benjamin Lincoln, M.D., Burlington, VT to GCS, Boston, 25 Aug. 1833 (MHS, Vol. 11, Aug. 1833).

120. Audubon (2006), p. 375; *AHJ* I, pp. 349–350; L. Audubon (1869), p. 296.

121. L. Audubon (1869), p. 296; Cf. Audubon (2006), p. 375; *AHJ* I, pp. 349–350 ("just as if no schooner the size of the 'Ripley' had ever gone from this mighty port to Labrador").

122. GCSJr, American Harbor, Labrador to GCS, Boston, 22 Jun. 1833 (MHS, Vol. 11, Jun. 1833).

123. Deane (1910), p. 44; *OB* III, p. 584; GCSJr, Eastport to Eliza Prentiss and Lucy Shattuck, Bos-ton, 2 Jun. 1833 (MHS, Vol. 11, Jun. 1833).

124. Audubon (2006), p. 375; *AHJ* I, p. 350; L. Audubon (1869), p. 296; *OB* II, p. xx; GCSJr, American Harbor, Labrador to GCS, Boston, 22 Jun. 1833 (MHS, Vol. 11, Jun. 1833); Coolidge (1833), 6 Jun. 1833. In his Introduction to Volume II of the *OB*, Audubon wrote that the *Swiftsure* was "at anchor" as the *Ripley* passed and received the cutter's four-gun salute. The naturalist used the same reference in an early draft, which is in the collection of the Missouri History Museum. However, the ship's log for the *Swiftsure* makes it clear that the vessel was still tied up at Hobb's Wharf, where the crew was engaged in painting spars.

125. *New-York Gazette & General Advertiser*, Vol. 45, No. 16,892, p. 2, col. 2 (Friday Morning, 14 Jun. 1833)(NYHS). The quoted article from the *New-York Gazette*, about the departure of Audubon's party from Eastport, was evidently copied from one of Eastport's two weekly newspapers—either the *Eastport Sentinel* or the *Eastern Democrat*. The *New-York Gazette* did not indicate the original source of the article, and as far as can be determined, there are no extant copies of either Eastport newspaper for June 1833.

126. Audubon (2006), p. 375; *AHJ* I, p. 350; L. Audubon (1869), p. 296; *OB* II, p. xx; GCSJr, American Harbor, Labrador to GCS, Boston, 22 Jun. 1833 (MHS, Vol. 11, Jun. 1833).

127. Audubon (2006), p. 442; *AHJ* I, p. 435; "A Californian's Recollection of Naturalist Audubon," *The San Francisco Call*, Vol. LXXX, No. 98, p. 25, cols. 1–7 (Sunday, 6 Sept. 1896)(LOC); L. Audubon (1869), p. 364; *OB* IV, pp. 181, 223; GCSJr, Eastport to GCS, Boston, 2 Jun. 1833 (MHS, Vol. 11, Jun. 1833). Though Coolidge claimed that Audubon threw all of the liquor that had been brought onboard the *Ripley* into the waters of the Bay of Fundy, Audubon indicated in the *OB* that there remained an allotment of grog for the crew. *OB* IV, pp. 181–182; 223. However, Audubon recognized that he had a weakness for spirits, grog being a diluted form of rum, and promised Lucy he would steer clear of it during the expedition. Moreover, Shattuck reported in his June 2 letter to his father that there would only be the arsenic-containing drum of rum aboard. Had the *Ripley*, in fact, been carrying grog for the crew, Audubon would have gotten into it during the trip. It seems more likely that his

reference in the *OB* was an example of the naturalist's frequent use of literary license to improve his tale. What is not entirely clear is why Audubon excluded wine from his list of prohibited beverages, as it could be equally potent if imbibed in sufficient quantity. See also, Chapter 13, notes 62, 93.

128. Audubon (2006), p. 375; *AHJ* I, p. 350; L. Audubon (1869), p. 296; *OB* II, p. xx; GCSJr, American Harbor, Labrador to GCS, Boston, 22 Jun. 1833 (MHS, Vol. 11, Jun. 1833).

CHAPTER 7: MAGDALEN ISLANDS AND GANNET ROCKS

1. L. Audubon (1869), p. 297; GCSJr, American Harbor, Labrador to GCS, Boston, 22 Jun. 1833 (MHS, Vol. 11, Jun. 1833). In the 1830 U.S. Census, the village of Cutler, ME, had a population of 454 residents. U.S. Bureau of the Census (1830), Census Place: *Cutler, Washington County, ME*; Pages: *261–263*; NARA Series: *M19*; Roll Number: 47.

2. Audubon (2006), p. 375; *AHJ* I, 350; L. Audubon (1869), p. 297.

3. L. Audubon (1869), p. 297; GCSJr, American Harbor, Labrador to GCS, Boston, 22 Jun. 1833 (MHS, Vol. 11, Jun. 1833). Cf. Audubon (2006), p. 375; *AHJ* I, p. 350 ("the appearance of a breeze brought us back").

4. Audubon (2006), p. 375; *AHJ* I, p. 350; L. Audubon (1869), p. 297.

5. L. Audubon (1869), p. 297. Cf. Audubon (2006), p. 375; *AHJ* I, p. 350 ("in direful apprehensions of ill luck").

6. Audubon (2006), p. 375; *AHJ* I, p. 350; L. Audubon (1869), p. 297.

7. Audubon (2006), pp. 375–376; *AHJ* I, pp. 350–351. Cf. L. Audubon (1869), p. 297 ("all seasick, and crossing that worst of all dreadful bays, the Bay of Fundy").

8. Blunt (1827).

9. Ibid., p. v.

10. Ibid., p. 633.

11. Ibid., pp. 634–635.

12. Audubon (2006), pp. 375–376; *AHJ* I, pp. 350–351; L. Audubon (1869), p. 297; *OB* III, pp. 447, 488, 590; Blunt (1833), p. 136; Blunt (1827), p. 635.

13. Blunt (1833), p. 136.

14. Leahy (2004), p. 529–530; Terres (1980),

p. 618; Baird (1884), pp. 404, 408; *OB* III, p. 434. In *The Audubon Society Encyclopedia of North American Birds*, John K. Terres writes that "Mother Carey" is an Anglicized form of *Mata cara*, "an epithet of the Virgin Mary, who was regarded as a protector of sailors." Terres (1980), p. 618. Christopher Leahy, whose *The Birdwatcher's Companion to North American Birdlife* belongs on every birder's bookshelf, suspects that sailors used the name "to avoid calling an evil spirit by its right name and thus attracting it." Leahy (2004), p. 530.

15. Peterson & Peterson (1981), Commentary to Plates 14-15.

16. GCSJr, American Harbor, Labrador to GCS, Boston, 22 Jun. 1833 (MHS, Vol. 11, Jun. 1833).

17. Audubon (2006), p. 376; *AHJ* I, p. 351.

18. Ibid.

19. *OB* III, pp. 112, 555.

20. Audubon (2006), p. 376; Bayfield (1984) I, p. cvi; *AHJ* I, p. 351; GCSJr, American Harbor, Labrador to GCS, Boston, 22 Jun. 1833 (MHS, Vol. 11, Jun. 1833). Shattuck's letter to his father suggests that the *Ripley* did not meet the *Caledonia* until the night of Sunday, June 9, since he mentioned it after saying they had passed Halifax. However, Audubon's journal entry indicates otherwise, stating: "We came up with the schooner 'Caledonia,' from Boston for Labrador; her captain wished to keep in our company, and we were pretty much together all [Saturday] night and also on Sunday."

21. Audubon (2006), p. 376; *AHJ* I, p. 351; Blunt (1833), p. 116.

22. Blunt (1833), p. 108.

23. Audubon (2006), p. 377; *AHJ* I, p. 352-353.

24. GCS, Boston to GCSJr, Eastport, 28 May 1833 (MHS, Vol. 11, 14-31 May 1833); Haliburton (1829) II, p. 223 footnote. Haliburton wrote in his history of Nova Scotia: "It is said that the derivation of the word Canseau, is from the Spanish 'Ganso,' a goose, a name given to it on account of the immense flocks of wild geese then seen there." Audubon had obviously read this passage because he repeated the assertion in his journal entry of June 11. "After sailing for twenty-one miles, and passing one after another every vessel of the fleet, we entered the Gut of Canseau, so named by the Spanish on account of the innumerable Wild Geese which, in years long

past and forgotten, resorted to this famed passage." Audubon (2006), p. 377; *AHJ* I, p. 352-353.

25. Ganong (1914), pp. 261-263.

26. Audubon (2006), p. 376; *AHJ* I, p. 351; L. Audubon (1869), p. 297.

27. Blunt (1833), p. 108.

28. Audubon (2006), p. 376-377; *AHJ* I, pp. 351-352; GCSJr, American Harbor, Labrador to GCS, Boston, 22 Jun. 1833 (MHS, Vol. 11, Jun. 1833).

29. *AHJ* I, pp. 351-352. See also, Audubon (2006), pp. 376-377. The passage in the text is taken from Maria's version of the Labrador journal. It does not appear in the version that was included in Lucy's biography. Robert Buchanan, the Scottish poet who was hired to edit Lucy's manuscript when it was sent to London for publication, removed many of Audubon's accounts of the natural world. Unfortunately, when Lucy republished the biography under her own name in the United States in 1869, she made relatively few changes to Buchanan's abridged text. These passages were not restored.

30. Audubon (2006), p. 377; *AHJ* I, pp. 352; GCSJr, American Harbor, Labrador to GCS, Boston, 22 Jun. 1833 (MHS, Vol. 11, Jun. 1833).

31. Audubon (2006), p. 377; Deane (1910), p. 44; *AHJ* I, pp. 352.

32. Audubon (2006), p. 377; *AHJ* I, pp. 352. In Lucy's biography, Audubon's journal entry of Tuesday, June 11, is misdated June 12. See Preface, note 18, *supra*. There are notable differences between her version of the journal for this date and that provided by Maria in *AHJ*. I believe Maria's version in this instance is closer to the original because it opens with a discussion of the Great Black-backed Gull, which Lucy's lacks. This is the type of natural history description Audubon was known for and which seldom appears in Lucy's biography. Maria's version also states that Audubon found the *Ripley* under sail when he arrived on deck at 4:00 a.m., which is consistent with what Shattuck wrote his father on June 22. GCSJr, American Harbor, Labrador to GCS, Boston, 22 Jun. 1833 (MHS, Vol. 11, Jun. 1833). Lucy's version suggests a later departure. This is not to say, however, that Maria did not edit her grandfather's prose. She invariably did, sometimes in subtle ways, at other times overtly. For instance,

her version of the journal has Audubon describing the sky on June 11 as being "pure." Lucy quotes him as saying it was "serene." I would wager that Maria changed "serene" to "pure."

33. Audubon (2006), p. 377; *AHJ* I, pp. 352–353; L. Audubon (1869), p. 306.

34. GCSJr, American Harbor, Labrador to GCS, Boston, 22 Jun. 1833 (MHS, Vol. 11, Jun. 1833).

35. L. Audubon (1869), pp. 306–307. Cf. Audubon (2006), pp. 377–378; *AHJ* I, p. 353. ("The land rises on each side in the form of an amphitheatre, and on the Nova Scotia side, to a considerable height. Many *appearances* of dwellings exist, but the country is too poor for comfort; the timber is small, and the land, very stony. Here and there a small patch of ploughed land, planted, or to be planted, with potatoes, was all we could see evincing cultivation. Near one house we saw a few apple-trees, yet without leaves. The general appearance of this passage reminded me of some parts of the Hudson River, and accompanied as we were by thirty smaller vessels, the time passed agreeably. Vegetation about as forward as at Eastport; saw a Chimney Swallow, heard some Blue Jays").

36. Deane (1910), pp. 47–48.

37. Townsend (1924), p. 240. The "Frenchy as thunder" description of Audubon was elicited from Tom Lincoln by his eldest son, Arthur T. Lincoln, M.D., in his youth. According to Dr. Lincoln, he questioned his father about the comment years later "and came to the conclusion that he referred only to that emotional manner that so many of that race have." Ibid., p. 241.

38. "A Californian's Recollection of Naturalist Audubon," *The San Francisco Call*, Vol. LXXX, No. 98, p. 25, cols. 1–7 (6 Sept. 1896)(LOC).

39. JWA addendum to JJA, Eastport to LBA, New York, 14 May 1833 (Princeton, Box 2, Folder 16).

40. Deane (1910), p. 45.

41. GCSJr Journal, 11 Jun. 1833 (Countway).

42. The journal that Shattuck Jr. kept during his stay in Eastport ends with his entry of June 13, 1833, which carries the story through the morning of June 6 when he said goodbye to Dr. Ray before boarding the *Ripley*. GCSJr Journal (Countway). We know from a letter that he wrote to his father on August 5 that he returned home with a written journal of the Labrador expedition. GCSJr, Bradore, Labrador to GCS, Boston, 5 Aug. 1833 (MHS, Vol. 11, 1–8 Aug. 1833). Sadly, what was almost certainly an engaging and richly informative account of the trip was apparently lost at some point because his son Frederick C. Shattuck, M.D., had no knowledge of its existence. Townsend (1918), p. 335, note 1.

43. Audubon (2006), p. 378; *AHJ* I, p. 353; L. Audubon (1869), p. 307; Purdy (1847), p. 150; Blunt (1833), p. 108.

44. L. Audubon (1869), p. 307. Cf. Audubon (2006), p. 378; *AHJ* I, p. 353 ("the large, undulating hills were scattered with many hamlets, and here and there a bit of cultivated land was seen.").

45. Audubon (2006), p. 378; *AHJ* I, p. 353; L. Audubon (1869), p. 307; *OB* IV, p. 81.

46. Stokes & Stokes (1983), p. 46.

47. Audubon (2006), p. 378; *AHJ* I, pp. 353–354.

48. Trudel (2014); Benoît (2012), p. 2.

49. Audubon (2006), p. 378; *AHJ* I, p. 354.

50. Trudel (2014); Blunt (1833), p. 102. The estimated length of the Magdalen Islands was determined using Google Earth, taking points between the southwestern tip of Amherst Island (Île du Havre Aubert) and the northern tip of Bryon Island (Île Brion).

51. Audubon (2006), p. 378; *AHJ* I, p. 354. In Lucy's biography, there is no mention of Audubon coming up on deck at 4:00 a.m. on the morning of June 12, taking a look at the *Ripley*'s position and progress toward the Magdalen Islands, and deciding to return to his berth. L. Audubon (1869), p. 307. As stated in the text, this is very much unlike Audubon, whose hard-charging personality had him going every minute he was awake. Nevertheless, while there is a tendency to question nearly every word in Maria's version of the Labrador journal because of the significant and sometimes inexplicable changes she made to Audubon's extant journals, an evident motivation for her to have added this is lacking. Ironically, the fact that it cuts against the grain of Audubon's typical behavior suggests that it actually happened.

52. Audubon (2006), p. 378; *AHJ* I, p. 354; L. Audubon (1869), p. 307.

53. L. Audubon (1869), pp. 307–308. Cf. Audu-

bon (2006), p. 378; *AHJ* I, p. 354 ("beating their way towards the Atlantic."). Lucy's version of the journal indicates that the ships headed from Miramichi for the Atlantic were carrying "timber," while Maria refers to it as "lumber." In 1833, the province of New Brunswick exported a sizable quantity of both square timber and sawed lumber through its several ports, including Miramichi Bay. The Custom House records reflect total shipments that year from all ports of 208,227 tons of square timber and 30,962,000 feet of deals and boards. Martin (1843), p. 244.

54. L. Audubon (1869), p. 308. According to Lucy's version of her husband's journal, the *Ripley* dropped anchor in Entrée Bay on Wednesday, June 13 "at nine o'clock," without indicating whether it was in the morning or at night. Maria's edited version of the journal states that the schooner reached the Magdalen Islands at 9:00 a.m. on June 12. Audubon (2006), pp. 379; *AHJ* I, pp. 354. It was, as Maria states, June 12, but she is mistaken as to the time. Audubon informed his friend Edward Harris that they arrived at the Magdalen Islands in the evening. JJA, Halifax, Nova Scotia to Edward Harris, New York, 25 Aug. 1833, *New-York Gazette & General Advertiser*, Vol. 45, No. 16,966, p. 2, col. 1 (Tuesday Morning, 10 Sept. 1833)(NYHS). And, indeed, even without the benefit of this letter, that is the only rational conclusion one could reach. Maria would have Audubon and his party remaining aboard ship for an entire day in clear weather before exploring the islands. With Audubon, that never would have happened. The only reason he did not immediately set out in the boats is that the schooner arrived at night.

55. Bayfield (1837), pp. 56–57; Blunt (1833), p. 102.

56. Audubon (2006), pp. 379; *AHJ* I, pp. 354; L. Audubon (1869), p. 308; Bayfield (1837), p. 49.

57. Audubon (2006), pp. 379; *AHJ* I, pp. 354; Bayfield (1837), pp. 56–57; Blunt (1833), p. 102. NOAA Solar Calculator, http://www.esrl.noaa.gov /gmd/grad/solcalc/ (accessed 26 Jun. 2010). According to the NOAA calculator, the apparent sunset at Pleasant Bay (called Entrée Bay by Audubon) on June 12, 1833, was at 8:03 p.m. AST. The equation of time was 0.6 minutes, indicating that mean solar time, or clock time for that location, deviated from

the sun's movements by less than a minute. However, as noted previously, time zones did not exist in 1833, and it is unclear what local time Audubon's watch was set to. Regardless, it appears that twilight would have afforded him an opportunity to see the details of the Magdalen Islands as the schooner approached its anchorage.

58. Audubon (2006), pp. 379; Durant & Harwood (1980), p. 426; *AHJ* I, pp. 355; L. Audubon (1869), p. 308.

59. L. Audubon (1869), p. 308. Cf. Audubon (2006), pp. 379; *AHJ* I, pp. 355 ("about the extreme point of this island.").

60. Audubon (2006), pp. 379; *AHJ* I, pp. 355; L. Audubon (1869), p. 308.

61. GCSJr, Eastport to Eliza Prentiss and Lucy Shattuck, Boston, 2 Jun. 1833 (MHS, Vol. 11, Jun. 1833); JJA, Eastport to LBA, New York, 27 May 1833 (Princeton, Box 2, Folder 21), *Letters* I, p. 230.

62. Audubon (2006), pp. 379; *AHJ* I, pp. 355; L. Audubon (1869), p. 308.

63. Audubon (2006), pp. 379; *AHJ* I, pp. 355.

64. Audubon (2006), pp. 379; *AHJ* I, p. 355; L. Audubon (1869), p. 308; JJA, Eastport to LBA, New York, 18 May 1833 (Princeton, Box 2, Folder 17), *Letters* I, p. 223.

65. L. Audubon (1869), p. 308.

66. Audubon (2006), p. 379; *AHJ* I, p. 355.

67. L. Audubon (1869), p. 308. Cf. Audubon (2006), p. 379; *AHJ* I, p. 355 ("great bluffs").

68. Audubon (2006), p. 380; *AHJ* I, p. 356; *OB* III, p. 366. In the *OB*, cited here, Audubon wrote that upon landing on the Magdalen Islands, "[s]ome of us ascended the more elevated parts of those interesting islands, while others walked along the shores." He implied that he was among those who investigated the sand ridge that extended out toward Entry Island. However, his journal is quite clear that he first visited the island's inhabitants on the higher elevations. As I read his journal and the account in the *OB*, I believe that he explored the shoreline after first visiting the island's residents. It also appears that the shore party divided in two because Audubon referred in his journal to John, Lincoln, and Ingalls "rambling about" and discovering a snake, which Audubon had been informed did not inhabit the island. Audubon (2006), p. 380; *AHJ* I, p. 356. From the context, it is evident that these three were

exploring the island separately. That would leave Shattuck and Coolidge in Audubon's party, which is consistent with Coolidge's later memory of being with the naturalist. "A Californian's Recollection of Naturalist Audubon," *The San Francisco Call*, Vol. LXXX, No. 98, p. 25, cols. 1–7 (6 Sept. 1896) (LOC).

69. Audubon (2006), p. 379; *AHJ* I, p. 355; L. Audubon (1869), p. 308.

70. L. Audubon (1869), p. 308. Cf. Audubon (2006), p. 379; *AHJ* I, p. 355 ("women are always keenest in sight and sympathy, in perseverance and patience, in fortitude, and love, and sorrow, and faith, and for aught I know, much more.").

71. L. Audubon (1869), p. 309. Cf. Audubon (2006), pp. 379–380; *AHJ* I, p. 355 ("a close white cotton cap").

72. L. Audubon (1869), p. 309. Cf. Audubon (2006), p. 380; *AHJ* I, pp. 355–356 ("a wonderful jargon, about one third of which I understood, and abandoned the rest to a better linguist, should one ever come to the island.").

73. Audubon (2006), p. 380; Durant & Harwood (1980), p. 427; Allaire (1910), pp. 87–88; *AHJ* I, p. 356; L. Audubon (1869), p. 309. Père Francois Xavier Brunet (1803–1875) was born on December 6, 1803, in Saint-François-de-Sales parish on Île Jesus just north of Montreal. He pursued his studies in Montreal and was ordained on September 22, 1827. From 1830 to 1833, he served as a Catholic missionary to the Magdalen Islands. Allaire (1910), pp. 87–88; *Montreal Almanack* (1829), p. 128. Durant and Harwood refer to him as J.H. Brunet, which would appear to be erroneous.

74. L. Audubon (1869), p. 309. Cf. Audubon (2006), p. 380; *AHJ* I, p. 356 ("a handsome, youthful, vigorous, black-haired, black-bearded fellow, in a soutane as black as the Raven's wedding-dress, and with a heart as light as a bird on the wing.") ("He is a shrewd-looking fellow, and, if I mistake not, has a dash of the devil in him.").

75. Audubon (2006), pp. 380–381; Durant & Harwood (1980), p. 427; *AHJ* I, pp. 356–357; L. Audubon (1869), pp. 309–310.

76. Audubon (2006), p. 380; *AHJ* I, p. 356; L. Audubon (1869), p. 309.

77. Kaufman (1996), p. 414; *OB* II, p. 416.

78. "A Californian's Recollection of Naturalist Audubon," *The San Francisco Call*, Vol. LXXX, No. 98, p. 25, cols. 1–7 (Sunday, 6 Sept. 1896)(LOC).

79. L. Audubon (1869), p. 310. Cf. Audubon (2006), p. 381; *AHJ* I, p. 358 ("The woods altogether small evergreens, extremely scrubby, almost impenetrable, and swampy beneath.").

80. Audubon (2006), p. 381; *AHJ* I, p. 357; L. Audubon (1869), p. 310; *OB* II, pp. 145, 303.

81. *OB* II, p. 208.

82. Dunn & Garrett (1997), pp. 74, 392–393.

83. *OB* II, p. 208.

84. Dunn & Alderfer (2011), pp. 466–467; Peterson (2010), p. 296; *OB* II, p. 512.

85. Peterson (2010), Map 439; Dunne (2006), pp. 592–593.

86. *OB* III, pp. 366–367.

87. Dunn & Alderfer (2011), pp. 240–241; Audubon (2006), p. 381; *AHJ* I, p. 357; *OB* IV, p. 75.

88. Audubon (2006), p. 381; *AHJ* I, p. 357; *OB* III, p. 367.

89. Dunn & Alderfer (2011), pp. 240–241; Dunne (2006), pp. 283–285; *OB* III, pp. 366–367.

90. *OB* III, pp. 366–367.

91. Ibid., p. 367.

92. Ibid.

93. Blaugrund & Stebbins (1993), p. 7.

94. *OB* III, p. 367.

95. Audubon (2006), p. 381; *AHJ* I, p. 357; *OB* III, p. 154.

96. Dunne (2006), pp. 200–201.

97. Dunn & Alderfer (2011), pp. 168–169; Dunne (2006), p. 200.

98. Audubon (2006), p. 381; *AHJ* I, p. 357.

99. Audubon (2006), p. 381; *AHJ* I, p. 357; L. Audubon (1869), p. 310.

100. Audubon (2006), p. 381; *AHJ* I, p. 358.

101. *OB* III, p. 148.

102. Audubon (2006), p. 381; Durant & Harwood (1980), p. 429; *AHJ* I, pp. 357–358. Audubon stated that the "eastern extremity of these islands," where he had been told he could find nesting waterbirds, was only eighteen miles away from their anchorage. In fact, it was about thirty.

103. L. Audubon (1869), p. 310.

104. Audubon (2006), p. 382; *AHJ* I, p. 359. Note that Lucy's biography gives the date the *Ripley* left the Magdalen Islands as Saturday, June 15. It was, in fact, Friday, June 14, as reflected in both

Maria's version of the journal and Audubon's *OB* account of his visit to the "Great Gannet Rock." *OB* IV, p. 222.

105. Audubon (2006), p. 383; *AHJ* I, p. 359.

106. L. Audubon (1869), p. 310. Cf. Audubon (2006), p. 383; *AHJ* I, p. 359 ("the ultimatum of our desires").

107. Audubon (2006), p. 383, 385; U.S. Hydrographic Office (1908), pp. 76–77; *AHJ* I, pp. 359–360, 362; L. Audubon (1869), p. 310; Sutherland (1862), pp. 18–19. The Gannet Rocks are situated northeast of the Magdalen Islands in the Gulf of St. Lawrence at approximately 47° 50′ 34″ N, 61° 9′ 8″ W. They comprise two rocky islets—then known as Great Bird Rock (now Rocher aux Oiseaux) and North or Little Bird Rock (Rochers aux Margaulx)—composed of "coarse red sandstone, or conglomerate, in strata" approximately 1,400 yards apart. Bayfield (1837), pp. 44–45. Contrary to what is stated in Roberta Olson's *Audubon's Aviary*, the Gannet Rocks are not situated on the Avalon Peninsula of Newfoundland. Cf. Olson (2012), p. 318; *OB* IV (1838), p. 223.

108. Audubon (2006), p. 383; *AHJ* I, p. 359.

109. *AHJ* I, pp. 359–360. Cf. Audubon (2006), p. 383 (missing comma after "times").

110. Audubon (2006), p. 382; *AHJ* I, p. 358.

111. Audubon (2006), pp. 383–385; *AHJ* I, pp. 360–362; *OB* IV, p. 224. In Audubon's day, Brion Island (Île Brion) was known as "Bryon Island." Bayfield (1837), p. 46.

112. Audubon (2006), p. 383; *AHJ* I, p. 360; L. Audubon (1869), p. 310; *OB* IV, p. 222. In his biography of the Common Gannet (Northern Gannet), Audubon quoted the *Ripley*'s pilot as saying that the elevation of Great Bird Rock was about 400 feet. *OB* IV, p. 223. Tom Lincoln indicated in his journal that it was "about 300 feet high." Spiker (1969). However, according to the Royal Navy hydrographic estimates, at the time it was actually "not more than 140 feet high above the sea." Bayfield (1837), p. 45. Today, it is about a hundred feet high. "Bird Rocks Migratory Bird Sanctuary," Environment Canada, http://www.ec.gc.ca/ap-pa /default.asp?lang=en&n=BDB9B5E3-1 (accessed 30 Aug. 2015).

113. Audubon (2006), p. 383; *AHJ* I, p. 360; *OB* IV, p. 222.

114. Audubon (2006), p. 383; *AHJ* I, p. 360; L. Audubon (1869), p. 311; *OB* IV, p. 222.

115. L. Audubon (1869), p. 311. Cf. Audubon (2006), p. 383; *AHJ* I, p. 360 ("They were birds we saw,—a mass of birds of such a size as I never before cast my eyes on.").

116. Audubon (2006), p. 383; *AHJ* I, p. 360; L. Audubon (1869), p. 311.

117. L. Audubon (1869), p. 311. Cf. Audubon (2006), p. 383; *AHJ* I, p. 360 ("The whole of my party stood astounded and amazed, and all came to the conclusion that such a sight was of itself sufficient to invite any one to come across the Gulf to view it at this season.").

118. Audubon (2006), p. 383; Durant & Harwood (1980), p. 429; *AHJ* I, p. 360; L. Audubon (1869), p. 311; Bayfield (1837), p. 44.

119. L. Audubon (1869), p. 311. Cf. Audubon (2006), p. 383; *AHJ* I, p. 360 ("enormous number of these birds, all calmly seated on their eggs or newly hatched brood, their heads all turned to windward, and towards us.").

120. L. Audubon (1869), p. 311. Cf. Audubon (2006), p. 383; *AHJ* I, p. 360 ("The air above for a hundred yards, and for some distance around the whole rock, was filled with Gannets on the wing, which from our position made it appear as if a heavy fall of snow was directly above us.").

121. Audubon (2006), pp. 383–384; *AHJ* I, p. 360; L. Audubon (1869), p. 311; *OB* IV, p. 222. The text relies upon Maria's version of the journal, which states that the whaleboat that attempted a landing on the Gannet Rocks was crewed by Mr. Godwin and two sailors. However, there are other references to the excursion in Audubon's published writings that indicate there were additional members of the shore party. He stated in his biography of the Common Gannet (Northern Gannet) in the *OB* that the boat was "manned by four sturdy 'down-easters'" as well as by John and Lincoln. *OB* IV, pp. 222–223. In his account of the Kittiwake Gull (Black-legged Kittiwake), he reported that Coolidge also joined the outing. *OB* III, p. 186. The lack of a definitive report makes it impossible to know which of these chronicles is true. I have discounted the reliability of the *OB* accounts because Audubon was frequently prone to error in putting them together and often appears not to have con-

sulted his journal notes. I have also concluded that
Coolidge was not aboard the whaleboat because
both Lucy's biography and Maria's edited journal
agree that the only members of Audubon's party to
accompany the crew were John and Lincoln.

122. Audubon (2006), p. 384; *AHJ* I, p. 360;
L. Audubon (1869), p. 311; *OB* IV, p. 223.

123. *OB* III, p. 186.

124. *OB* IV, p. 223.

125. Audubon (2006), p. 384; *AHJ* I, pp. 360–
361; L. Audubon (1869), p. 311.

126. *OB* IV, p. 223; *OB* III, p. 186.

CHAPTER 8: AMERICAN HARBOR, LABRADOR

1. Audubon (2006), p. 386; *AHJ* I, p. 363;
L. Audubon (1869), p. 312. Lucy's biography is in
error in stating that the day following their visit to
the Gannet Rocks was June 17. It was, in fact, Saturday, June 15 as Maria's version of the journal indicates.

2. Audubon (2006), p. 386; *AHJ* I, p. 363;
L. Audubon (1869), p. 312.

3. Audubon (2006), p. 386; *AHJ* I, p. 363;
L. Audubon (1869), p. 312. Lucy's biography is
again mistaken in identifying the date when the
Ripley was becalmed in the Gulf of St. Lawrence as
June 18. It was actually Sunday, June 16, as reflected
in the journal edited by Maria.

4. Audubon (2006), p. 386; *AHJ* I, p. 363.
Audubon stated in the cited journal entry that the
largest cod they caught during their fishing inter-
lude on Sunday, June 16, "measured three feet six
and a half inches."

5. *OB* III, p. 555. There is no mention in Audubon's journal of Wandering Shearwaters and Fulmars (Northern Fulmars) landing on the water
nearby while he and his young friends were fishing in the Gulf of St. Lawrence. However, this is a
reasonable deduction given his account of the Wandering Shearwater in the *OB*. He mentioned there
that he had found them in the Gulf of St. Lawrence
and that "[i]n calm weather, they are fond of alighting on the water, in company with the Fulmars, and
are then easily approached." He then went on to
state that two of the shearwaters were "caught with
hooks," a clear indication that this happened during a fishing excursion. Ibid. Audubon scholars

believe that Audubon illustrated this species during
the Labrador expedition, so he obviously collected
some specimens during the trip. Audubon (1966) I,
Plate 68. The accounts in the journal and that in the
OB square closely enough to believe that this happened on Sunday, June 16.

6. *OB* III, p. 555.

7. Ibid., p. 556.

8. *OB* IV, pp. 161–162.

9. *OB* III, p. 232.

10. *OB* IV, p. 467. In Maria's version of the
Labrador journal, there is a July 13 entry where
Audubon supposedly wrote that, while the *Ripley*
was sailing for the harbor of Little Mecattina,
"About a dozen common Crossbills, and as many
Redpolls (*Fringilla* [*Acanthis*] *linaria*)[Common
Redpolls] came and perched on our top-yards, but
I would not have them shot, and none were caught."
AHJ I, p. 396. This is very similar to what he wrote
on June 16, as referenced in the text, except as to the
species. I question whether this actually occurred
on two separate occasions. During migration, mixed
flocks of passerines are not uncommon. Mid-July,
which is still during the nesting season, would be
somewhat early to see such a flock, especially out
over the water. In addition, Audubon stated in the
OB that he did not see a single Common Crossbill (Red Crossbill) in Labrador or Newfoundland.
In contrast, he indicated that he found the White-
winged Crossbill "tolerably abundant" in both locations. *OB* II, p. 559. Thus, I give little credence to
the entry in Audubon's journal and believe that if
this happened, it occurred on June 16 as Audubon
related in the *OB*.

11. Audubon (2006), p. 386; *AHJ* I, p. 363;
L. Audubon (1869), p. 312. In Lucy's biography,
the journal entry for Monday, June 17, is mistakenly
given a date of June 19.

12. L. Audubon (1869), pp. 312–313. Cf. Audubon (2006), p. 386; *AHJ* I, pp. 363–364 ("The sea
was literally covered with Foolish Guillemots, playing in the very spray of the bow of our vessel, plunging under it, as if in fun, and rising like spirits close
under our rudder.").

13. *OB* III, p. 105.

14. Audubon (2006), p. 386; *AHJ* I, p. 364. Cf.
L. Audubon (1869), p. 313 ("The wind was fair").
Capt. Emery discounted the helmsman's sighting of

land from the topyards saying it did not accord with his "true calculation" of their position.

15. Audubon (2006), p. 387; *AHJ* I, p. 364; L. Audubon (1869), p. 313.

16. *OB* II, p. xx. See also, Audubon (2006), p. 387; *AHJ* I, p. 364; L. Audubon (1869), p. 313.

17. *OB* III, p. 354.

18. Audubon (2006), p. 387; *AHJ* I, p. 364.

19. Audubon (2006), p. 387; *AHJ* I, p. 364-365; Bayfield (1837), p. 148.

20. Audubon (2006), p. 387; *AHJ* I, p. 365. Capt. William Billings was born in Kittery, ME, on February 15, 1794. He married a twenty-year-old Kittery girl, Sarah D. Lampter, on December 10, 1816. They lived for a time in Kittery before moving to Eastport in August 1820. Calnan (2007), pp. 14-15. Billings died in Eastport at the age of sixty-two on November 30, 1856. Willey (2003), p. 152.

Shattuck Jr. told his father that Billings had come to Labrador with five schooners to fish for cod. GCSJr, American Harbor, Labrador to GCS, Boston, 22 Jun. 1833 (MHS, Vol. 11, Jun. 1833). There is a contradictory note in the personal journal of Capt. Henry Wolsey Bayfield of the British Royal Navy, who mentioned in his entry on June 22 that there were six Eastport schooners in the harbor owned by the same person. Bayfield (1984) I, pp. 235-236; Townsend (1919), p. 424. However, I have discounted Bayfield's figure because he wrote this on the day his vessel first arrived at American Harbor, where the *Ripley* and Billings's schooners were anchored, and it is easy to believe he was misinformed. In comparison, Shattuck and his companions had been moored near Billings's vessels for five days. His count, therefore, would appear to be more reliable.

21. Audubon (2006), p. 387; *AHJ* I, p. 365; L. Audubon (1869), p. 313; Bayfield (1837), p. 149.

22. Audubon (2006), p. 387-388; *AHJ* I, p. 365-366. Cf. L. Audubon (1869), p. 313 ("came to anchor in a beautiful bay, wholly secure from any winds."). Bayfield stated that the entrance to American Harbor (Little Natashquan Harbor) "bears N. by E. 4 miles, from the southern entrance of Natashquan River." Bayfield (1837), p. 150. Google Earth indicates that it is over five miles.

23. Bayfield (1837), p. 149. A fathom is a nautical measurement of depth or distance equal to six feet.

24. *OB* II, p. 190.

25. Bastedo (2013); Audubon (2006), p. 387; Durant & Harwood (1980), p. 446; *AHJ* I, p. 365; L. Audubon (1869), pp. 313-314.

26. L. Audubon (1869), p. 314. Cf. Audubon (2006), pp. 387-388; *AHJ* I, p. 365 ("[a] poor, rugged, miserable country; the trees like so many mops of wiry composition, and where the soil is not rocky it is boggy up to a man's waist.").

27. Belvin, p. 10 (2006).

28. Audubon (2006), p. 388; *AHJ* I, pp. 365-366; OB IV, p. 81; *OB* II, p. 303.

29. Dunn & Alderfer (2011), p. 232; Audubon (2006), p. 388; *AHJ* I, p. 365.

30. Dunn & Alderfer (2011), pp. 238-239; *OB* IV, p. 175. Later ornithologists have questioned Audubon's sighting of Least Terns in Labrador. In *The Water Birds of North America*, published in 1884 by three of the preeminent ornithologists of the day—Spencer Fullerton Baird, Thomas M. Brewer, and Robert Ridgway—Audubon's Labrador sighting was noted, but the author of the species account stated that he could "find no corroboration of its presence beyond the Bay of Fundy." Baird (1884) II, p. 310. Charles W. Townsend and Grover M. Allen, who published a monograph on the birds of Labrador in 1907, indicate that Audubon was the only observer to have claimed to have seen Least Terns in Labrador. Townsend & Allen (1907), pp. 318-319. Nevertheless, Audubon was familiar with the species, and it is highly unlikely he was mistaken in his identification. Townsend and Allen concur:

Audubon recorded many birds for southern Labrador that are unknown there today. Some of these are now more northern, others more southern in their distribution. In the case of some of the flycatchers and other poorly marked birds it is probable that he was mistaken in his identification, but we cannot believe that he made an error in the case of other birds such as the Oyster-catcher, Least Tern, or Black-throated Loon. It seems probable that some of these birds were on the frontiers of their breeding grounds in southern Labrador and that as the numbers of birds were diminished by the agency of man, the species as a whole withdrew its outposts and the more favorable central portions of its range were alone utilized. For example the Least Tern which Audubon found breeding in Labrador, also formerly bred on the Massachusetts coast north of Cape Ann but is not found now north of Cape Cod.

Townsend & Allen (1907), pp. 290–291. If the bird once bred along the Labrador coast as Audubon reported, it no longer does so. Dunne (2006), p. 286.

31. "A Californian's Recollection of Naturalist Audubon," *The San Francisco Call*, Vol. LXXX, No. 98, p. 25, cols. 1–7 (Sunday, 6 Sept. 1896)(LOC).

32. *OB* III, p. 585. The quote in the text is taken from Audubon's published Episode entitled "Labrador." His draft manuscript is housed at the Missouri History Museum in St. Louis.

33. Audubon (2006), p. 388; *AHJ* I, p. 366.

34. *OB* III, p. 585. In his Episode entitled "Labrador," cited here, Audubon explained the propensity of Capt. Emery and Coolidge to accompany each other during the daily excursions into the Labrador wilderness: "the Captain and COOLEDGE were fond of each other, the latter having also been an officer." However, this is not what Audubon wrote in his original manuscript, where he stated that "the Captain and Cooledge were fond of each others company the latter having been an officer under his Father." JJA, "At Labrador" (Missouri History Museum Collection).

As far as I have been able to determine, Coolidge never served aboard the *Swiftsure*. However, his older brother, Uriah Coolidge Jr., served briefly as a warrant officer aboard the revenue cutter after receiving his commission on April 16, 1831. Force (1832), p. 334; Force (1832), p. 285. It is conceivable that the naturalist had been told during his stay in Eastport that Capt. Coolidge had a son who had once served as an officer aboard the *Swiftsure* and somehow concluded that this referred to Joe. By the time Audubon sailed to Grand Manan, Uriah Coolidge Jr. was evidently no longer the warrant officer as he was not mentioned in any of the accounts of the excursion. Therefore, it seems quite possible that Audubon could have continued to hold his erroneous view that Joe had previously been an officer under his father, although one has to wonder why this confusion was never cleared up

in the long days that Audubon and Coolidge spent together in Labrador.

35. *OB* III, p. 585. Audubon indicated that the members of the shore parties were equipped with "botanical boxes, and baskets for eggs or minerals." Ibid. That they also were expected to note bird behavior and provide Audubon with their observations is apparent from a review of Audubon's journal. See, e.g., Audubon (2006), pp. 389–390; *AHJ* I, pp. 367–368. See also, Deane (1910), p. 45.

36. Audubon (2006), p. 388; *AHJ* I, p. 366. Audubon advised his journal that he remained aboard the *Ripley* all day on Tuesday, June 18, in order to draw. Lucy's biography erroneously states that this occurred on June 19. L. Audubon (1869), p. 314.

37. Audubon (1999), pp. 754, 761; Audubon (1979), pp. 17, 22; Deane (1910), p. 47.

38. Audubon (1999), p. 754; Audubon (1979), p. 22. During this period in his career, Audubon drew his compositions on the finest English cotton rag paper, which carried either the J. Whatman or a variation of the J. Whatman/Turkey Mill watermark. The former was made by the Balston Mill and the latter by the Hollingsworth Mill. Low (2002), pp. 10–11; Snyder in Blaugrund & Stebbins (1993), p. 55 and note 1, p. 67.

39. Olson (2012), p. 56; Shelley (2012), pp. 111–112.

40. *AHJ* II, p. 40.

41. Audubon (1999), p. 754; Audubon (1979), p. 22.

42. Olson (2012), pp. 56, 112–113, 265, 270, 318; Shelley (2012), p. 112; Audubon (2006), p. 93; Snyder in Blaugrund & Stebbins (1993), p. 56.

43. Audubon (2006), p. 388; *AHJ* I, p. 366.

44. Audubon (1999), p. 754; Audubon (1979), p. 22.

45. JJA, St. Augustine, East Florida to George W. Featherstonhaugh, Philadelphia, 7 Dec. 1831, Herrick (1938) II, p. 13.

46. Audubon (1966) II, Plate 251.

47. Audubon (2006), p. 388; *AHJ* I, p. 366; Townsend (1924), p. 239.

48. Audubon (2006), pp. 388–389, 393; *AHJ* I, pp. 366–367, 373.

49. Audubon (2006), pp. 389; *AHJ* I, pp. 367–368.

50. *AHJ* I, pp. 368. Note that the Labrador journal edited by Richard Rhodes in his 2006 collection of Audubon's writings professes to be "reproduced in full" from the Maria Audubon edition. Audubon (2006), p. 374. However, it omits a portion of Audubon's journal entry for June 18, 1833, where he expressed the view that the Herring Gull was the immature form of the Great Black-backed Gull:

> *AHJ*: "On another rock, not far distant, a number of Gulls of the same size, white, and with the same hoarse note, were to be seen, but they had no nests; these, I am inclined to think (at present) the bird called *Larus argentatus* (Herring Gull), which is simply the immature bird of *Larus marinus*. I am the more led to believe this because, knowing the tyrannical disposition of the *L. marinus*, I am sure they would not suffer a species almost as powerful as themselves in their immediate neighborhood. They fly altogether, but the white ones do not alight on the rocks where the *Marinus* has its nests. John watched their motion and their cry very closely, and gave me this information." *AHJ* I, pp. 367–368 (footnote omitted).

> Rhodes: "On another rock, not far distant, a number of Gulls of the same size, white, and with the same hoarse note, were to be seen, but they had no nests; these, I am inclined to think (at present) the bird called Herring Gull . . . They fly altogether, but the white ones do not alight on the rocks where the Black-backed has its nests. John watched their motion and their cry very closely, and gave me this information." Audubon (2006), p. 389.

As can be seen, Rhodes has also substituted the English names of the birds for the Latin designations that appeared in Maria's journal. As will be seen *infra*, Rhodes's decision to omit the Latin names has resulted in unintended errors in the identification of the named species. See, e.g., note 53, *infra*.

51. Audubon (2006), p. 389; *AHJ* I, p. 368.

52. Cf. *OB* III, pp. 305–316 (Great Black-backed Gull); *OB* III, pp. 588–594 (Herring Gull).

53. Audubon (2006), p. 388; *AHJ* I, p. 366. In connection with Audubon's stated difficulty in iden-

tifying the unknown sandpiper collected by one of his companions on June 18, 1833, Rhodes's edition of the Labrador journal makes a significant mistake in one of the bird names it offers in place of the Latin designation that appears in Maria's edition:

> *AHJ*: "We, however, procured about a dozen of *Alca torda*, *Uria troile*, a female Eider Duck, a male Surf Duck, and a Sandpiper, or *Tringa*— which, I cannot ascertain, although the *least* I ever saw, not the *Pusilla* of Bonaparte's Synopsis." *AHJ* I, p. 366.

> Rhodes: "We, however, procured about a dozen Razor-billed Auks, Foolish Guillemots, a female Eider Duck, a male Surf Duck, and a Sandpiper—which, I cannot ascertain, although the Least Sandpiper I ever saw, not the Least Auklet of Bonaparte's *Synopsis*." Audubon (2006), p. 388.

When Audubon referred to the "*Pusilla* of Bonaparte's Synopsis," he was not alluding to the Least Auklet. Although the Latin name for this species is *Aethia pusilla* (formerly *Uria pusilla*), the Least Auklet is a seabird of the Aleutian Islands and the Bering Sea. Dunn & Alderfer (2011), p. 260; Peterson (2008), p. 222; Baird (1884), p. 507. It has no relationship taxonomically to the Least Sandpiper. It is not even found in Labrador, and Audubon never saw the bird in life. He came to know it from a bird skin he obtained from the Zoological Society of London, evidently in 1837, and presented it in *BOA* as the "Nobbed-billed Auk" (Havell Plate 402). Low (2002), p. 207; Audubon (1966) I, Plate 112; *OB* V, p. 101. Moreover, this species was not even identified in the 1828 edition of Bonaparte's *Synopsis* that Audubon carried with him to Labrador. The Prince would not add it to his listing of American birds until 1838. Cf. Bonaparte (1838), p. 66; Bonaparte (1828), pp. 421–426. Clearly, Audubon was not referring to the Least Auklet.

Rather, Audubon's reference was to *Tringa pusilla*, the Latin name given to the Little Sandpiper (Least Sandpiper), which had been originally described and illustrated by Alexander Wilson. Bonaparte (1828), p. 319. The small size of the collected bird did not seem to match Bonaparte's description of the bird in his *Synopsis*, which led Audubon to initially believe it was not a Least Sandpiper. In essence, what Audubon was trying to say is this: "We, however, procured . . . a Sandpiper, or *Tringa* [the genus name in which the sandpipers were grouped]—which, I cannot ascertain, although [it would be] the [smallest] *least* [sandpiper] I ever saw, [but it is] not the *Pusilla* of Bonaparte's Synopsis." However, later in the same journal entry, he concluded otherwise. "One *Tringa pusilla*, the smallest I ever saw, was procured; these small gentry are puzzles indeed; I do not mean to say in nature, but in Charles's Synopsis." *AHJ* I, p. 368. Cf. Audubon (2006), p. 390.

Audubon believed that Bonaparte had included many purely European species in the *Synopsis*. In his opinion, there were only two species of this genus commonly found in the U.S.: Least Sandpiper (now *Calidris minutilla*), illustrated in Havell Plate 320, and Semipalmated Sandpiper (now *Calidris pusilla*), depicted in Havell Plate 405. In fact, there is a third—the Western Sandpiper (*Calidris mauri*). Peterson (2008), p. 158. Although he did not realize it, Audubon also knew the Western Sandpiper because this species winters in large numbers along the Florida and Gulf coasts, which he visited while working on his publication. However, he mistakenly believed that these birds were Semipalmated Sandpipers. *OB* V, p. 110. Ornithologists today know that Semipalmateds migrate to South America and that the similar appearing Westerns are the ones found along the southern coasts of the United States during the winter. Peterson & Peterson (1981), Plate 177 commentary.

54. Audubon (2006), p. 388; *AHJ* I, p. 368; Bonaparte (1828), pp. 318–319. The sandpipers listed in Bonaparte's *Synopsis* that Audubon considered to be solely of Old World distribution were the Broad-billed Sandpiper, *Tringa platyrhinca* (*Limicola falcinellus*); Little Stint (Temmink's Stint), *T. Temminickii*, Leisler or *T. pusilla*, Bechstein (*Calidris temminckii*); and Pigmy Sandpiper (Little Stint), *T. minuta*, Leisler or *T. minuta*, Temminck (*Calidris minuta*). *OB* IV, p. 180; Nuttall (1834), pp. 114, 117, 119; Bonaparte (1828), pp. 318–319. All are occasionally spotted in North America. Dunn & Alderfer (2011), pp. 194–197.

55. Audubon (2006), p. 390; *AHJ* I, p. 368; *OB* IV, p. 181.

56. Audubon (2006), p. 388, 394; *AHJ* I, pp. 366, 374; L. Audubon (1869), p. 314–316.

57. *OB* III, pp. 82–83.

58. Ibid.

59. Audubon (2006), p. 394; *AHJ* I, p. 374. Cf. L. Audubon (1869), p. 315. Note that Rhodes correctly states that the pertinent entry in Audubon's journal is from June 21, not June 22 as reflected in Maria's version or June 23 as stated in Lucy's biography. Note also that Lucy's account asserts that the eggers collected four hundred thousand eggs the previous season. L. Audubon (1869), pp. 315–316. At twenty-five cents per dozen, the eggers would have made a profit of more than $8,000. Maria's edition states that they made "over $800," and independent evidence would suggest that this was closer to the mark. *AHJ* I, p. 374. Three days after Audubon made this journal entry, he joined Capt. Bayfield and his officers for dinner aboard the *Gulnare* and told them what he had learned so far about the eggers. Bayfield's journal reported that "One vessel of 25 tons is said to have cleared 200 pounds by this 'Egging Business' in a favorable season." Bayfield (1984) I, pp. 236–237. With an exchange rate of around $4.50 to the pound, the £200 would have been worth about $900, closer to the number given in Maria's journal. Fries (1973), p. 387. Thus, it would appear that the eggers had taken only forty thousand eggs in 1832 as stated in the text.

60. L. Audubon (1869), p. 315. Cf. Audubon (2006), p. 394; *AHJ* I, p. 374 ("so some idea may be formed of the birds that are destroyed in this rascally way.").

61. Audubon (2006), p. 394; *AHJ* I, p. 374; L. Audubon (1869), p. 315–316; *OB* III, pp. 82–86.

62. *OB* III, p. 85.

63. JJA, Bulowville, East Florida to George W. Featherstonhaugh, Philadelphia, 31 Dec. 1831, Herrick (1938) II, p. 17.

64. E.g., *OB* III, p. 367.

65. E.g., *OB* III, p. 389.

66. Audubon (2011), pp. 346–348. Cf. Ford (1987), pp. 388–389.

67. Audubon (2006), p. 394; *AHJ* I, p. 374; L. Audubon (1869), p. 315–316; *OB* III, pp. 85–86.

68. *OB* III, pp. 82–86.

69. Graham (1990), pp. 3–6, 9–13, 46; Fox (1981), pp. 152–154.

70. Audubon (2006), pp. 389–390; *AHJ* I, p. 368.

71. *OB* III, p. 507.

72. Townsend (1918), pp. 107–108; *AHJ* I, p. 402, note 2.

73. Dunn & Alderfer (2011), pp. 244–245; Townsend (1917), p. 139.

74. Audubon (2006), p. 390; *AHJ* I, p. 369.

75. Low (2002), p. 152; Audubon (1966) I, Plate 68.

76. Audubon (2006), p. 390–391; *AHJ* I, pp. 369–370.

77. Audubon (2006), p. 391; *AHJ* I, p. 370; *OB* III, p. 308.

78. L. Audubon (1869), p. 314. Cf. Audubon (2006), p. 391; *AHJ* I, p. 370 ("a small river, dark, irony waters, sandy shores, and impenetrable woods along these, except here and there is a small space overgrown with short wiry grass unfit for cattle; a thing of little consequence, as no cattle are to be found here.'). Note that the date given in Lucy's biography for Audubon's afternoon excursion up the Little Natashquan River is incorrect. It was not, as Lucy stated, June 21 but rather June 19 as reflected in Maria's edition of the journal.

79. L. Audubon (1869), p. 326 ("The waters of all the streams we have seen are of a rusty color, probably derived from the decomposing mosses which form the soil on the rocks."). Cf. Audubon (2006), p. 399; *AHJ* I, p. 380 ("The waters of all the streams which we have seen are of a rusty color, probably on account of the decomposed mosses, which appear to be quite of a peaty nature").

80. Audubon (2006), pp. 391–392, 400; *AHJ* I, pp. 370–371, 381,

81. Audubon (2006), p. 392; *AHJ* I, p. 371–372. Note that in his version of the Labrador journal, Rhodes substitutes "Brindled Guillemot" for the Latin designation *Uria troile* that appears in Maria's edition. This is a misspelling of "Bridled Guillemot," which in any case is not a separate species at all but rather a different phase or form of what Audubon knew as the Foolish Guillemot (Common Murre). As the naturalist explained in his biography of this species:

"There is no perceptible difference between the sexes as to colour, but the males are larger than the females. The white line that encircles the eye and extends toward the hind head is common to both sexes, but occurs only in old birds. Thousands of these Guillemots however breed, without having yet acquired it, there merely being indications of it to be seen on parting the feathers on the place, where there is a natural division." *OB* III, p. 145.

Audubon clearly did not understand that the "bridled" form was a plumage phase characteristic of a certain percentage of the colony as opposed to being a feature prevalent in older birds. Based on surveys of breeding colonies conducted between 1978 and 1980, the "bridled" form accounts for between roughly 17% and 25% of Atlantic populations ranging from southern Newfoundland to northern Labrador, although this appears to be a decline from early 20th century numbers. Ainely (2002), p. 3. To be accurate, Rhodes should have substituted "Foolish Guillemot" for Audubon's use of the Latin name to be consistent with Audubon's view of the species as well as Rhodes's previous usage of that former name in the same journal entry.

82. Audubon (2006), pp. 393; *AHJ* I, p. 372; L. Audubon (1869), p. 315.

83. Audubon (2006), pp. 392, 394; *AHJ* I, p. 371, 373. Cf. L. Audubon (1869), p. 315 ("The country a barren rock as far as the eye could reach, and mosses of several species were a foot in depth.").

84. Audubon (2006), pp. 392–393; *AHJ* I, pp. 371–372; *OB* III, p. 435. Audubon's journal, as edited by his granddaughter, states that Capt. Billings's mate "told me of the *Procellarias* breeding in great numbers in and about Mount Desert Island rocks, in the months of June and July." *AHJ* I, p. 372. The species to which Audubon was referring was the Forked-tailed Petrel (Leach's Storm-Petrel), which at the time was considered a member of the genus *Thalassidroma*. *OB* III, pp. 434–435; Bonaparte (1828), pp. 365, 367. However, the *Thalassidroma* had been previously considered a subgenus of the genus *Procellaria*, which explains why Audubon referred to the birds as *Procellarias*. Bonaparte (1828), p. 365, note.

85. Audubon (2006), p. 393; *AHJ* I, p. 372.

86. Audubon (2006), p. 393; *AHJ* I, pp. 372–373.

87. Audubon (2006), pp. 393–394; *AHJ* I, p. 373.

88. Deane (1910), p. 48.

89. Audubon (2006), p. 394; *AHJ* I, pp. 373–374.

90. Audubon (2006), p. 394; *AHJ* I, pp. 373–374.

91. Audubon (2006), p. 395; *AHJ* I, p. 374; Bayfield (1837), p. 150. In his journal, Audubon stated that the Hudson Bay Company settlement along the banks of the Natashquan River was "five miles east." Bayfield's *Sailing Directions for the Gulf and River of St. Lawrence* places it at about four and a half miles south of American Harbor. Bayfield was correct as to the compass point, but Google Earth would suggest that Audubon's mileage estimate was closer to the truth.

92. L. Audubon (1869), p. 323. Cf. Audubon (2006), p. 396; *AHJ* I, p. 376 ("On leaving the harbor this morning we saw a black man-of-war-like looking vessel entering it with the French flag; she anchored near us, and on our return we were told it was the Quebec cutter."). The vessel of which Audubon was speaking was the *Gulnare*, a surveying schooner attached to the British Royal Navy. It flew the British colors as one might expect and, indeed, as Audubon indicated in the version of his journal entry appearing in Lucy's biography cited above. Why Maria's version of the journal indicates otherwise is unknown, but the change has her fingerprints on it. This is just another reminder of the scope of her mischief and the care that must be taken before quoting anything appearing in her edition of the journal.

The time of Audubon's departure for the Hudson Bay Company post on the Natashquan River comes from the personal journal of Capt. Henry W. Bayfield of the *Gulnare*. The *Gulnare* had arrived off the Labrador coast at around 6:00 a.m., but the heavy rain had prevented Bayfield from determining their location. At 7:00 a.m., he recognized that he was at American Harbor and, seeing several schooners anchored there, signaled the need for a pilot with one of his ship's guns. Mr. Phillips, the master of the *Shelburne* of Liverpool, Nova Scotia,

rowed out and, at around 7:30 a.m., came onboard to navigate the British schooner past the rocks at the harbor entrance. Bayfield (1984) I, p. 235. Audubon indicated in his journal that his party saw the vessel coming into the harbor as they were leaving it.

93. Bayfield (1984) I, p. xxxiii; GCSJr, American Harbor, Labrador to GCS, Boston, 22 Jun. 1833 (MHS, Ms. N-909, Vol. 11, Jun. 1833).

94. GCSJr, American Harbor, Labrador to GCS, Boston, 22 Jun. 1833 (MHS, Ms. N-909, Vol. 11, Jun. 1833).

95. Ibid.

96. Audubon (2006), p. 395; *AHJ* I, p. 374; Bayfield (1837), p. 149. Bayfield stated in his *Sailing Directions for the Gulf and River St. Lawrence* that "[t]he sandy beach continues for 3½ miles to the N.N.E. of the entrance [of the Natashquan River], terminating at the mouth of a small stream, called the Little Natashquan, which admits boats only at high water, and which is close to the eastward of the harbour of the same name."

97. Audubon (2006), pp. 395, 399; *AHJ* I, pp. 374–375, 380.

98. Townsend (1913), p. 39; Fortin (1865), p. 10; Bayfield (1837), pp. 148–149; Bayfield Chart, Gulf of St. Lawrence, Sheet III, from Lake Island to Pashasheeboo Point (1832–1834), Archives Canada. Bayfield indicated that the mouth of the Natashquan River was "fully a mile wide." According to Pierre Fortin, who served as a Stipendiary Magistrate for the protection of the fisheries in the Gulf of St. Lawrence in 1864, the river was "a mile and two cable lengths in width at its mouth." With a cable length being about 600 feet, that would make the river mouth just under a mile and a quarter.

99. Audubon (2006), p. 395; *AHJ* I, p. 375; Bayfield (1837), p. 149.

100. Audubon (2006), pp. 395–396; *AHJ* I, pp. 375–376.

101. Audubon (2006), p. 395; *AHJ* I, p. 375.

102. Audubon (2006), p. 396; *AHJ* I, p. 376. See also, Belvin (2006), p. 17.

103. L. Audubon (1869), p. 323. Cf. Audubon (2006), p. 396; *AHJ* I, p. 376 ("The men were stout and good-looking, spoke tolerable French, the skin redder than any Indians I have ever seen, and more *clear*; the women appeared cleaner than usual, their hair braided and hanging down, jet black, but

short."). Note that Lucy's biography incorrectly gives the date Audubon met the party of Montagnais Indians at the Hudson Bay Company post as June 23 when it was actually June 22 as reflected in Maria's published journal.

104. L. Audubon (1869), p. 323. Cf. Audubon (2006), p. 396; *AHJ* I, p. 376 ("coarse moccasins of sealskin").

105. Audubon (2006), pp. 395–396; *AHJ* I, pp. 375–376.

106. Bayfield (1984) I, p. xcix; Audubon (2006), p. 396; *AHJ* I, p. 376; L. Audubon (1869). p. 323; *OB* II, p. xxi.

107. Audubon (2006), p. 396; *AHJ* I, p. 376; Bachman (1888), p. 202.

108. Audubon (2006), p. 396; *AHJ* I, pp. 376–377; Augustus Frederick, the Duke of Sussex, Kensington Palace to The Civil & Military Authorities in British America, 21 Jul. 1831 (Yale, Box 18, p. 94).

109. Bayfield (1984) I, pp. xxxi, 159, 230–231; Audubon (2006), p. 396; *AHJ* I, pp. 376. Although Audubon did not mention it in his journal, it would have been customary for him to have been greeted by the *Gulnare*'s officers. At the time, Bayfield had two officers and assistants aboard the *Gulnare*, both midshipmen—Augustus Bowen and William Barrie. Bayfield (1984) I, pp. xxxi, 159, 230–231. Another officer and long-time assistant, Lt. Philip Collins, had been given charge of a recently constructed 40-ton surveying boat, the *Beaufort*, and with a crew of eight was presently at work surveying the Magdalen Islands. Ibid., pp. xxxi, 226, 234. From a reference Audubon made in a later letter, it would appear that Midshipman Bowen was serving as the *Gulnare*'s 1st lieutenant. JJA, Halifax, Nova Scotia to Edward Harris, New York, 25 [26] Aug. 1833, *New-York Gazette & General Advertiser*, Vol. 45, No. 16,966, p. 2, col. 1 (Tuesday Morning, 10 Sept. 1833)(NYHS).

110. Bayfield (1984) I, pp. xiv-xxi, xxiii-xxv.

111. Ibid., pp. xxv, xxviii-xxix, xxxi-xxxiii, 46, 240. The launch, the longest boat aboard the *Gulnare*, was equipped with "ten double banked Oars" and a sail. Ibid., p. 191, illus. between pp. 274–275.

112. Ibid., p. xxxii.

113. Bayfield (1984) I, p. 236; Audubon (2006), p. 396; *AHJ* I, p. 377.

114. Bayfield (1984) I, p. xxxiii; Audubon (2006), p. 396; *AHJ* I, p. 376.

115. L. Audubon (1869), p. 323. Cf. Audubon (2006), p. 396; *AHJ* I, pp. 376–377 ("I was received politely, and after talking on deck for a while, was invited into the cabin, and was introduced to the doctor, who appeared to be a man of talents, a student of botany and conchology.").

116. L. Audubon (1869), p.324. Cf. Audubon (2006), p. 396; *AHJ* I, p. 377 ("The first lieutenant studies ornithology and collects."). The position of first lieutenant aboard a naval vessel was an appointed position, not a rank. As the senior officer beneath Capt. Bayfield, Midshipman Bowen would have held this position.

Contrary to Audubon's statement that Bowen was interested in birds, George Shattuck wrote his father and indicated that it was Dr. William Kelley, the ship's surgeon, who was the resident ornithologist aboard the *Gulnare*. GCSJr, American Harbor, Labrador to GCS, Boston, 26 Jun. 1833 addendum to letter of 22 Jun. 1833 (MHS, Vol. 11, Jun. 1833). Whether Shattuck was confused or Audubon's reference in his journal was faulty cannot be determined. Bayfield's journal provides no suggestion that either Mr. Bowen or Dr. Kelley focused any attention on birds. However, Bowen did bring Audubon a specimen of a Peregrine Falcon later in the trip, so I have assumed that in this regard Audubon's journal is accurate. Audubon (2006), pp. 407–408; *AHJ* I, p. 391.

117. L. Audubon (1869), pp.324–325. Cf. Audubon (2006), p. 396; *AHJ* I, p. 377 ("Thus men of the same tastes meet everywhere, yet surely I did not expect to meet a naturalist on the Labrador coast.")

118. Audubon (2006), p. 396; *AHJ* I, p. 377; L. Audubon (1869), p. 324.

119. Ford (1988), p. 339.

120. Audubon (2006), pp. 396–397; *AHJ* I, p. 377.

121. Public Archives, p. 118, http://heritage.canadiana.ca/view/oocihm.lac_reel_h9082/1?r=0&s=1 (Image 407). See also Bayfield (1984) I, p. 236, Townsend (1919), pp. 424–425.

122. Public Archives, p. 118, http://heritage.canadiana.ca/view/oocihm.lac_reel_h9082/1?r=0&s=1 (Image 407). See also, Bayfield (1984) I,

p. 236; Townsend (1919), p. 424. Capt. Bayfield's reference to Coolidge as "Mate of the Ripley" is puzzling. There is no other indication of this in the extant records of the expedition. Indeed, Shattuck wrote to his father on June 2, 1833, and stated that the mate of the *Ripley* was also its pilot, an evident allusion to Mr. Godwin of Nova Scotia, who had made the trip to Labrador on several prior occasions. GCSJr, Eastport to GCS, Boston, 2 Jun. 1833 (MHS. Vol. 11, Jun. 1833).

However, Bayfield's other references to the members of Audubon's party were accurate, so one has to believe there was a basis for his statement. If Coolidge was indeed the mate when the *Ripley* arrived in Labrador, how and when did this occur? We know that at the time Audubon signed the charter-party agreement, Coolidge was considered one of the six members of his party. Did Capt. Emery demote Godwin after they sailed from Eastport and replace him with Coolidge? If so, it is significant that neither Audubon nor Coolidge ever mentioned this. Audubon, in particular, grew to dislike Godwin, so if this actually occurred I believe that Audubon would have written about it somewhere. It is also difficult to explain why, toward the tail end of the voyage, Coolidge left the vessel with Audubon and the other members of his party at Pictou, Nova Scotia, to travel overland through the province while the *Ripley* returned to Eastport by sea. Had Coolidge been the mate, he should have remained onboard the schooner for the remainder of the trip. Although the evidence is conflicting, Capt. Bayfield's statement alone does not persuade me that Coolidge was the mate aboard the *Ripley*.

123. Audubon (2006), p. 397; Bayfield (1984) I, p. 236; Townsend (1919), p. 425; *AHJ* I, p. 377; L. Audubon (1869), p. 324. Lucy incorrectly gives the date for these events as June 24 when it was, in truth, June 23. What is not clear is where the *Ripley*'s next planned anchorage was going to be. Audubon indicated that it was located fifty miles to the east of American Harbor, but the *Ripley*'s next stop was Wapitiguan Harbor, almost ninety miles away.

124. Audubon (2006), p. 397; Audubon (1966), Plate 268; *AHJ* I, p. 377.

125. Audubon (2006), p. 397; *AHJ* I, p. 377.

Audubon's journal does not provide any indication as to whether the Guillemots collected on June 23 were Foolish Guillemots (Common Murres) or Black Guillemots.

126. Audubon (2006), p. 397; *AHJ* I, p. 377; *OB* III, p. 308.

127. Audubon (2006), p. 397; Bayfield (1984) I, p. 236; Townsend (1919), p. 425; *AHJ* I, p. 377..

128. Audubon (2006), p. 397; *AHJ* I, pp. 377–378. Cf. L. Audubon (1869), p. 324 ("They came and saluted us soon after we landed, and to my astonishment offered us a glass of rum."). Lucy's version of the journal incorrectly places Audubon's visit to the coastal camp of the Montagnais Indians on June 24 when it was actually June 23.

129. L. Audubon (1869), p. 324 ("The chief of this party is well informed, talks French so as to be understood, is a fine-looking fellow, about forty years old, and has a good-looking wife and baby."). Cf. Audubon (2006), p. 397; *AHJ* I, p. 378 ("The chief of the party proves to be well informed and speaks French so as to be understood. He is a fine-looking fellow of about forty; has a good-looking wife and fine babe.").

130. Audubon (2006), p. 397; *AHJ* I, p. 378. Cf. L. Audubon (1869), p. 324 ("blazing fire").

131. L. Audubon (1869), pp. 324–325. Cf. Audubon (2006), pp. 397–398; *AHJ* I, pp. 378–379:

"The country from here to the first settlement of the Hudson's Bay Co. is as barren and rocky as that about us. Very large lakes of great depth are met with about two hundred miles from this seashore; these lakes abound in very large trout, carp, and white fish, and many mussels, unfit to eat, which they describe as black outside and purple within, and are no doubt unios. Not a bush is to be met with, and the Indians who now and then go across are obligated to carry their tent poles with them, as well as their canoes; they burn moss for fuel. So tedious is the travelling said to be that not more than ten miles on an average per day can be made, and when the journey is made in two months it is considered a good one. Wolves and Black Bear are frequent, no Deer, and not many Caribous; not a bird of any kind except Wild Geese and Brent about the lakes, where they breed in perfect peace. When the journey is undertaken in the winter, which is very seldom the case, it is performed on snow-shoes, and no canoes are taken. Fur animals are scarce, yet some few Beavers and Otters are caught, a few Martens and Sables, and some Foxes and Lynx, but every year diminishes their numbers. The Fur Company may be called the exterminating medium of these wild and almost uninhabitable climes, where cupidity and the love of gold can alone induce man to reside for a while."

132. The "unios" to which Audubon refers in this journal entry are freshwater mussels of the order Unionoida. Those found in North America are classified as members of either the family Margaritiferidae or Unionidae. Watters (2015).

L. Audubon (1869), p. 325. Cf. Audubon (2006), p. 398; *AHJ* I, p. 379 ("Where can I go now, and visit nature undisturbed?").

133. Bayfield (1984) I, p. 236; Townsend (1919), p. 425.

134. Audubon (2006), p. 399; *AHJ* I, p. 379; L. Audubon (1869), p. 325.

135. Audubon (1966) II, Plate 321. Edward Dwight claims that Audubon illustrated the Razor-billed Auks (Razorbills) on June 18, but the naturalist's journal is silent about the date he drew these birds.

136. Audubon (2006), p. 399; *AHJ* I, pp. 379–380.

137. Audubon (2006), p. 399; *AHJ* I, p. 379; L. Audubon (1869), p. 325. See also, Bayfield (1984) I, pp. 236–237; Townsend (1919), pp. 425–426. In his journal entry for June 24 (erroneously identified in Lucy's biography as June 25), Audubon indicated that he dined with "the captain, doctor, and three other officers." L. Audubon (1869), p. 325. Cf. Audubon (2006), p. 399; *AHJ* I, p. 379 ("the captain, surgeon, and three officers"). As far as I have been able to determine from reviewing Bayfield's journal, Midshipmen Bowen and Barrie were the only other naval officers aboard the *Gulnare* at this time. Since Audubon identified three other officers, I presume that he included the master of the *Gulnare*, Mr. Hall. Bayfield (1984) I, p. 224. Hall was

not an officer in the Royal Navy but was employed by the vessel owner. Ibid., xxxii.

138. L. Audubon (1869), p. 325. This reference to the food and wine that Audubon enjoyed aboard the *Gulnare* was omitted by his granddaughter when she published his journal. She also struck the reference to Audubon sampling some snuff. Audubon (2006), p. 399; *AHJ* I, p. 379. She may have wished to conceal the pleasure he derived in both alcohol and snuff, although her thought process is far from clear. It bears noting that later in the journal, she included a reference to him enjoying some snuff offered to him by Prof. Thomas McCulloch during a visit to Truro, Nova Scotia, on August 23. Audubon (2006), p. 444; M. Audubon (1869), p. 438.

139. L. Audubon (1869), p. 325. Cf. Audubon (2006), p. 399; *AHJ* I, p. 379 ("the conversation ranged from botany to politics, from the Established Church of England to the hatching of eggs by steam.").

140. Bayfield (1984) I, pp. 236–237; Townsend (1919), pp. 425–426.

141. Audubon (2006), p. 399; *AHJ* I, pp. 379–380; L. Audubon (1869), p. 325.

142. Audubon (2006), p. 399; *AHJ* I, p. 380; L. Audubon (1869), p. 325.

143. Bayfield (1984) I, p. 237. Audubon mentioned the departure of the fishing schooners in his journal entry of June 26. Audubon (2006), p. 400; *AHJ* I, p. 381. He did not say when this had happened, but I am inclined to accept Capt. Bayfield's journal, where he wrote that this occurred on June 25.

144. Audubon (2006), p. 399; *AHJ* I, p. 380. See Audubon (1966) I, Plate 146. Audubon's final composition of the Arctic Tern was actually a collage, consisting of the image of a single bird in flight that was pasted on a background drawing of the sky. Audubon (1966) I, Plate 146. It appeared in *BOA* as Plate 250.

145. Deane (1910), p. 47. Ingalls's memory was faulty on one point, obviously having been dimmed by the passage of time. The remnants of Audubon's journal do not reflect that he was out shooting the day before he began the drawing of the Arctic Tern. It is more likely that the excursion the young Bostonian recalled had occurred several days earlier.

Audubon (2006), p. 399; *AHJ* I, pp. 379–380;
L. Audubon (1869), p. 325.

146. Audubon (2006), p. 399; *AHJ* I, p. 380.

147. L. Audubon (1869), p. 326. Cf. Audubon
(2006), pp. 399–400; *AHJ* I, p. 380 ("It is to be remarked that so shy of strangers are the agents of the
Fur and Fish Company that they will evade all questions respecting the interior of the country, and indeed will willingly tell you such untruths as at once
disgust and shock you.").

148. L. Audubon (1869), p. 326. Cf. Audubon (2006), p. 400; *AHJ* I, pp. 380–381 ("All this
through the fear that strangers should attempt to
settle here, and divide with them the profits which
they enjoy.").

149. Audubon (2006), p. 400; *AHJ* I, p. 381.

150. Bayfield (1984) I, p. 237.

151. Audubon (2006), p. 400; *AHJ* I, p. 381.

152. Peterson (2008), pp. 374–375.

153. Sibley (2014), p. 534.

154. Audubon (2006), p. 400; *AHJ* I, p. 381.

155. Audubon *OB* (1834) II, pp. 89, 92.

156. Audubon (1966) II, Plate 340; *OB* (1834)
II, pp. 91–92. Audubon's original drawing of two
White-crowned Sparrows was done in Henderson,
KY, on October 13, 1814. It is Havell Plate 114.

157. Audubon (2006), p. 400; *AHJ* I, p. 381.

158. GCSJr, American Harbor, Labrador to
GCS, Boston, 26 Jun. 1833 addendum to letter of 22
Jun. 1833 (MHS, Vol. 11, Jun. 1833).

159. Audubon (2006), p. 400; Bayfield (1984) I,
p. 238; Spiker (1969); *AHJ* I, p. 381.

160. Audubon (2006), p. 400; *AHJ* I, p. 381; *OB*
II, p. 55.

161. *OB* II, p. 55.

162. Audubon (2006), p. 400; *AHJ* I, p. 382; *OB*
II, p. 546.

163. Audubon (2006), p. 401; *AHJ* I, p. 382; *OB*
II, p. 539.

164. *OB* II, p. 539.

165. Audubon (2006), pp. 400–401; *AHJ* I,
p. 382; *OB* II, p. 539. In Audubon's *OB* account of
the Lincoln's Sparrow, he wrote that he returned
to the *Ripley* after his party obtained the first specimen of this bird so that he could begin a drawing
of it. *OB* II, p. 539. However, this conflicts with the
account he gave in his journal, which clearly in-

dicates that he remained with the party and was
present when they returned to the site where the
Ruby-crowned Kinglet had been shot earlier. Audubon also declared in his journal entry that he would
draw the sparrow the next day. Audubon (2006),
p. 400; *AHJ* I, p. 382. The text follows the journal
version of events.

166. Audubon (2006), p. 400; *AHJ* I, p. 382.
Note that in the *OB*, Audubon wrote that his son
found the unidentified "warbler" (determined to
be a Ruby-crowned Kinglet) on June 28, the day
after it was shot, not the same day as the journal asserts. *OB* II, p. 546. I accept the journal account in
this case because both versions of the journal agree
that Audubon began drawing the Lincoln's Finch
on June 28, the day after it was collected. Audubon
(2006), p. 401; *AHJ* I, p. 382; L. Audubon (1869),
pp. 326–327. Audubon would have been entirely
focused on his drawing that day and would not
have had time to go back to shore with his companions to locate the Ruby-crowned Kinglet. Since the
Ripley left American Harbor early that afternoon,
it is clear that the account given in the *OB* is faulty
on this point. This is just one of many examples of
Audubon's erroneous recitation of dates mentioned
in that work.

167. Audubon *OB* (1834), Vol. II, pp. 546–547.
Audubon related in his biography of the Ruby-
crowned Wren (Ruby-crowned Kinglet) that he had
met with this spritely little songbird in Kentucky
and in Louisiana, which would have preceded his
visit to Labrador. Thus, he was familiar with the
bird before his son presented him with the specimen on June 27.

168. Audubon (2006), p. 401; *AHJ* I, p. 382;
L. Audubon (1869), pp. 326–327.

169. Bayfield (1984) I, p. 238; Audubon (2006),
p. 401; *AHJ* I, p. 382; L. Audubon (1869), p. 327.

170. Audubon (2006), p. 401; *AHJ* I, p. 382;
L. Audubon (1869), p. 327. In both versions of the
journal, Audubon described having dinner after the
squall hit around noon on June 28 and then, when
the wind swung around to the southwest, "all was
bustle with us and with the 'Gulnare,' for we both
were preparing our sails and raising our anchors
ere proceeding to sea." Audubon (2006), p. 401;
AHJ I, p. 382. However, the journal of Capt. Bay-

field reflects that the squall brought winds from the west-northwest, which led him to order the crew of the *Gulnare* to make preparations to sail. Bayfield (1984) I, p. 238. It is obvious that the change from the southerly winds, which had been blowing consistently for the past several days and prevented both vessels from sailing out into the gulf, was the precipitating factor in their departure. Audubon's statement that they made ready aboard the *Ripley* once the wind began blowing from the southwest after dinner is erroneous. Almost certainly, Capt. Emery, like Capt. Bayfield, began preparing to depart as soon as the wind shifted with the squall.

171. Bayfield (1984) I, p. 238. See also, Audubon (2006), p. 401; *AHJ* I, p. 382; L. Audubon (1869), p. 327. In his journal, Audubon wrote that the *Ripley* "managed so well that we cleared the outer cape east of our harbor, and went out to sea in good style." Capt. Bayfield, who was a more knowledgeable sailor, recognized that with the shifting wind the American schooner barely made it out of the harbor, and his account provides the basis for the text.

172. Bayfield (1984) I, p. 238.

173. Audubon (2006), p. 401; *AHJ* I, p. 383; L. Audubon (1869), p. 327.

CHAPTER 9: WAPITIGUAN HARBOR, LABRADOR

1. Audubon (2006), p. 401; *AHJ* I, p. 383. Even Edmund Blunt had nothing to offer in the way of guidance to the mariner unfamiliar with the segment of the Labrador shoreline along which the *Ripley* was sailing. There was no discussion at all in the 1827 edition, which Capt. Emery doubtless carried. In Blunt's twelfth edition, published in July 1833, he noted that "there appears to have been no survey yet made of the coast." His only advice was to give the land and the adjacent islands "a wide berth." Blunt (1833), p. 27.

2. Audubon (2006), p. 401; *AHJ* I, p. 383.

3. Deane (1910), p. 45; Bayfield (1837), p. 216.

4. Townsend (1918), p. 121; Townsend (1917), p. 141.

5. Audubon (2006), p. 401; *AHJ* I, p. 383; L. Audubon (1869), p. 327.

6. L. Audubon (1869), p. 327. Cf. Audubon (2006), p. 401; *AHJ* I, p. 383 ("through a heavy surf").

7. Audubon (2006), p. 401; *AHJ* I, p. 383; L. Audubon (1869), p. 327.

8. Audubon (2006), p. 401; *AHJ* I, p. 383; *OB* III, p. 105.

9. *OB* III, pp. 105–106.

10. Audubon (2006), p. 403; *AHJ* I, p. 385.

11. Audubon (2006), p. 402; *AHJ* I, p. 383.

12. OB III, p. 108.

13. Audubon (2006), p. 402; *AHJ* I, p. 384.

14. *OB* III, p. 421.

15. Audubon (2006), p. 402; *AHJ* I, p. 384; *OB* III, pp. 112–113.

16. Deane (1910), p. 45.

17. *OB* III, p. 113.

18. Bayfield (1837), pp. 216–217.

19. *OB* III, p. 113.

20. Audubon (2006), p. 402; *AHJ* I, p. 384.

21. Audubon (2006), pp. 402–403; *AHJ* I, p. 384.

22. Audubon (2006), p. 403; Bayfield (1984) I, pp. 239–240; *AHJ* I, pp. 384–385.

23. L. Audubon (1869), p. 327.

24. Audubon (2006), p. 403; *AHJ* I, p. 385. Edward Dwight, a noted Audubon scholar and art historian, believes that John may have illustrated the Lincoln's Finch (Lincoln's Sparrow) that is illustrated at the bottom of Audubon's drawing of this species. Audubon (1966) I, Plate 167. Audubon's journal, as edited by his granddaughter, indicates otherwise.

25. Audubon (2006), p. 403; *AHJ* I, p. 385.

26. L. Audubon (1869), p. 327. Cf. Audubon (2006), p. 403; *AHJ* I, p. 385 ("The weather was so cold that it was painful for me to draw almost the whole day").

27. Audubon (2006), p. 403; *AHJ* I, p. 385.

28. *OB* III, p. 109.

29. Ibid.

30. Audubon (2006), p. 403; *AHJ* I, pp. 385–386; *OB* V, p. 369. Audubon's journal suggests that he accompanied one of the shore parties on July 1 and was present when they discovered the Pigeon Hawk (Merlin) nest as well as the family of American Ring Plovers (Semipalmated Plovers). I have discounted this because he said in the same entry

that he had worked at his drawing table "almost the whole day."

31. Audubon (2006), p. 403; *AHJ* I, p. 386.

32. Dunn & Alderfer (2011), pp. 168–169; Dunne (2006), p. 199.

33. Leahy (2004), pp. 19, 658, 883–894.

34. Audubon (2006), p. 403; *AHJ* I, p. 386.

35. Audubon (2006), p. 403; Bayfield (1984) I, pp. 240–241; *AHJ* I, p. 386. Bayfield told his journal that when the moon rose on July 1, it was already partially eclipsed. Audubon's journal described "an almost complete eclipse of the moon this evening at half-past seven."

36. V. Audubon (July 1833), p. 369.

37. Bakewell (July 1833), pp. 369–370.

38. Ibid., pp. 370–371.

39. Ibid.

40. Ibid., p. 372.

41. LBA, New York to VGA, London, 2 Jul. 1833 (Yale, Box 1, Folder 20).

42. Ibid.

43. Ibid.

44. Ibid.

45. Ibid.

46. Audubon (2006), p. 403; *AHJ* I, p. 386; L. Audubon (1869), p. 327.

47. Audubon (2006), p. 403; *AHJ* I, p. 386.

48. L. Audubon (1869), pp. 327–328. The portion of the quotation in brackets is taken from the Maria version of Audubon's journal. Audubon (2006), p. 404; *AHJ* I, p. 386. Both versions are similar but differ in telling ways as a comparison will show:

Lucy: The country is so grandly wild and desolate, that I am charmed by its wonderful dreariness. Its mossy grey-clad rocks, heaped and thrown together in huge masses, hanging on smaller ones, as if about to roll down from their insecure resting-places into the sea below them. Bays without end, sprinkled with thousands of rocky inlets of all sizes, shapes, and appearances, and wild birds everywhere, was the scene that presented before me. Besides this there was a peculiar cast of the uncertain sky, butterflies flitting over snow-banks, and probing unfolding dwarf flowerets of many hues pushing out their tender stems through the thick beds of moss which everywhere cover granite rock. Then there is the morass, wherein you plunge up to your knees, or the walking over the stubborn, dwarfish shrubbery, whereby one treads down the forests of Labrador;

Maria: The country, so wild and grand, is of itself enough to interest any one in its wonderful dreariness. Its mossy, gray-clothed rocks, heaped and thrown together as if by chance, in the most fantastical groups imaginable, huge masses hanging on minor ones as if about to roll themselves down from their doubtful-looking situations, into the depths of the sea beneath. Bays without end, sprinkled with rocky islands of all shapes and sizes, where in every fissure a Guillemot, a Cormorant, or some other wild bird retreats to secure its egg, and raise its young, or save itself from the hunter's pursuit. The peculiar cast of the sky, which never seems to be certain, butterflies flitting over snow-banks, probing beautiful dwarf flowerets of many hues pushing their tender stems from the thick bed of moss which everywhere covers the granite rocks. Then the morasses, wherein you plunge up to your knees, or the walking over the stubborn, dwarfish shrubbery, making one think that as he goes he treads down the *forests* of Labrador.

I find the wording of the passage in Lucy's biography to be truer to Audubon's writing style. Audubon loved to use adjectives, and the phrase "grandly wild and desolate" is characteristic of his writing. His reference to the "peculiar cast of the uncertain sky" also strikes me as what he would say as opposed to Maria's clunky, "The peculiar cast of the sky, which never seems to be certain." At the same time, the word "inlets" in Lucy's passage is obviously a typographical error. It probably appeared in the original holograph as "islets." Moreover, Robert Buchanan, who originally edited Lucy's manuscript for publication in England, generally eliminated as many references to specific birds as he could. Lucy made no effort to correct this when she republished the biography under her own name in 1869. I believe that Audubon likely spoke of the guillemots and cormorants nesting among the rocks as stated in Maria's edition of the journal. While it may be unorthodox, I have included this line in the quotation in the text, even though the bulk of that quote comes from Lucy's biography, because I believe it brings it closer to the original.

49. Audubon (2006), p. 404; *AHJ* I, p. 387. The Black-necked Diver (Pacific Loon) no longer breeds along the Labrador coast if it ever did. Townsend & Allen (1907), pp. 290–291. Audubon wrote in the *OB* that he "saw a few pairs courting on wing, much in the manner of the Red-throated Diver; but all our exertions failed to procure any of the nests, which I therefore think must have been placed farther inland than those of the [Common] Loon or Red-throated Diver." *OB* IV, p. 345. Today, the Pacific Loon can be found nesting in the very farthest reaches of the northern Arctic and wintering along the Pacific coast as far south as Baja California. Peterson (2008), p. 66; Dunne (2006), p. 88.

50. Audubon (2006), pp. 404–405; *AHJ* I, p. 387.

51. *OB* IV, p. 257. Contrary to what Audubon wrote in his biography of the American Ring Plovers (Semipalmated Plovers), Maria's version of Audubon's journal states that he and his young companions stayed their hand and refused to collect the family of this species when they encountered it on July 2: "We left them and their young to the Creator. I would not have shot one of the old ones, or taken one of the young for any consideration, and I was glad my young men were as forbearing." Audubon (2006), p. 405; *AHJ* I, p. 387. I suspect that the naturalist's putative forbearance was an editorial change made by Maria, who would have liked her grandfather to have shown some mercy under the circumstances.

52. Audubon (2006), p. 405; Bayfield (1984) I, p. 241; *AHJ* I, p. 387.

53. Audubon (2006), p. 405; *AHJ* I, pp. 387–388.

54. L. Audubon (1869), p. 329. Cf. Audubon (2006), p. 405; *AHJ* I, p. 388 ("We had a regular stiff gale from the eastward the whole day, accompanied with rain and cold weather, and the water so rough that I could not go ashore to get plants to draw.").

55. Audubon (2006), p. 405; *AHJ* I, p. 388; L. Audubon (1869), p. 329.

56. Audubon (2006), p. 405; *AHJ* I, p. 388; *OB* III, pp. 458–459.

57. *OB* III, pp. 458–459. In the *OB*, Audubon wrote that his observation of the nesting family of Common Cormorants (Great Cormorants) on July 3, 1833, took place "about three in the morning." Ibid., p. 459. However, the entry for this date in Maria's version of the journal would suggest that this occurred in the afternoon because bad weather in the morning prevented anyone from leaving the vessel. Audubon (2006), p. 405; *AHJ* I, p. 388. The journal of Capt. Bayfield confirms that the morning weather was marked by rain and fog, lending credence to Maria's account that Audubon's trip to shore that day was in the afternoon. Bayfield (1984) I, p. 241.

58. *OB* III, p. 459.

59. *OB* V, p. 366.

60. Bayfield (1984) I, p. 241.

61. Audubon (2006), p. 405; *AHJ* I, p. 388; *OB* III, pp. 459–460.

62. Small (2009), p. 184; Audubon (1966) I, Plate 167.

63. Audubon (2006), p. 405; *AHJ* I, p. 388.

64. Audubon (2006), pp. 405; *AHJ* I, pp. 388–389; *OB* IV, p. 17.

65. Audubon (2006), pp. 405–406; *AHJ* I, p. 389; *OB* IV, p. 46. In the *OB*, Audubon indicated that Coolidge's party had retrieved the nest of the Great Northern Diver or Loon (Common Loon) on July 5. However, I have found many of the dates given by Audubon in this work to be unreliable and, therefore, I have accepted the July 4 date given in Maria's edition of the journal.

66. Audubon (2006), p. 405; *AHJ* I, p. 388.

67. Audubon (2006), p. 405; *AHJ* I, p. 388–389; "A Californian's Recollection of Naturalist Audubon," *The San Francisco Call*, Vol. LXXX, No. 98, p. 25, cols. 1–7 (Sunday, 6 Sept. 1896)(LOC). Coolidge's account of the July 4 feast, given to a newsman with *The San Francisco Call* sixty-three years later, agrees that the British surveyors sent the Americans a quarter of mutton for their Independence Day dinner. In other particulars, however, Coolidge's memory had faded badly. He believed that they were anchored in American Harbor and recalled, erroneously, that the mutton was given in exchange for two salmon they had caught. Evi-

dently, Coolidge's memory combined the events of Tuesday, June 25, when the "Young Gentlemen" surreptitiously caught three salmon and shared one of the fish with the *Gulnare*'s crew, with those of Capt. Bayfield's Independence Day beneficence.

68. L. Audubon (1869), p. 329. Cf. Audubon (2006), p. 405; *AHJ* I, p. 388–389 ("a rarity, I will venture to say, on this coast even on the Fourth of July.").

69. Audubon (2006), p. 406; Bayfield (1984) I, p. 241; *AHJ* I, p. 389. According to Capt. Bayfield's journal, the rain and fog set in around 2:00 p.m., so Audubon and his son would have had to deal with these weather conditions as they set out to free the Black Guillemot. Audubon's account of this episode in the *OB* also states that it was a "rainy afternoon." *OB* III, p. 151.

70. *OB* III, p. 151. In the cited reference in the *OB* to Audubon's experiment involving the trapped Black Guillemot, he said that there were two birds and that they had been confined for eight days. His journal, however, alludes to a single bird and, given the fact he released the bird on July 4, the most time it could have been trapped was five days since the *Ripley* did not reach Wapitiguan Harbor until the afternoon of June 29. Audubon (2006), p. 406; *AHJ* I, p. 389. I have accepted the journal account of one bird for two reasons. First, I have found the *OB* to frequently differ with other, verifiable facts. Second, only one adult bird at a time would be brooding the two eggs that are ordinarily laid in a clutch. Butler (2002), pp. 1, 11.

71. Audubon (2006), p. 406; *AHJ* I, p. 389; *OB* III, p. 151.

72. *OB* III, p. 151. In the *OB*, Audubon attempted to justify his failure to end the Black Guillemot experiment sooner on bad weather, claiming that "for eight days the wind blew so hard that no boat was safe on the waters without the harbour." This was utter nonsense, as his journal clearly demonstrates. Of the five days the bird was confined, only July 3 had weather conditions that were poor enough to have limited the use of the boats. Even then, the weather cleared up by the afternoon. Evidently, he was concerned that the truth would leave his readers with a poor impression of him, so he lied about it.

73. Bayfield (1984) I, p. 241.

74. Audubon (2006), p. 406; *AHJ* I, p. 389–390; *OB* II, p. 531.

75. Audubon (2006), p. 406; *AHJ* I, p. 390; L. Audubon (1869), p. 329.

76. Audubon (2006), p. 406; *AHJ* I, p. 390; L. Audubon (1869), p. 329; *OB* III, p. 114. Razorbills rarely lay a second egg. Kaufman (1996), p. 271.

77. Audubon (2006), p. 407; *AHJ* I, p. 390.

78. *OB* III, p. 23.

79. L. Audubon (1869), p. 329. Cf. Audubon (2006), p. 406; *AHJ* I, p. 390 ("To tread over the moss of Labrador is a task beyond conception until tried; at every step the foot sinks in a deep, soft cushion which closes over it, and it requires a good deal of exertion to pull it up again. Where this moss happens to be over a marsh, then you sink a couple of feet deep every step you take; to reach a bare rock is delightful, and quite a relief.").

80. Deane (1910), p. 45.

81. Audubon (2006), p. 406; *AHJ* I, p. 389.

82. *AHJ* I, p. 389. Cf. Audubon (2006), p. 406 ("some curious eel").

83. Audubon (2006), p. 406; *AHJ* I, p. 389.

84. *OB* IV, pp. 50–51.

85. Audubon (2006), p. 406; *AHJ* I, p. 389.

86. Audubon (2006), p. 407; *AHJ* I, p. 390.

87. Audubon (2006), p. 407; *AHJ* I, p. 390.

88. Small (2009), p. 194; Audubon (2006), p. 407; Audubon (1966) I, Plate 132; *AHJ* I, p. 390; *OB* III, p. 26.

89. Audubon (1966) I, Plate 132; *OB* III, p. 26. Audubon scholar Edward Dwight asserts that Audubon probably added the winter adult Red-necked Diver (Red-throated Loon) to his composition during the winter of 1833–1834 while residing in Boston. Audubon (1966) I, Plate 132. However, Audubon was not in Boston during that period. Instead, following his return from Labrador, he accepted an invitation from his friend John Bachman to spend the winter with the Bachman family in Charleston, SC. Rhodes (2004), pp. 387–388. Since this drawing was engraved and printed by Robert Havell Jr. as Plate 202 during the first half of 1834, it appears that Audubon must have drawn the young male in its "basic" or winter plumage while in Charleston. The Red-throated Loon winters up and down the Atlantic seaboard, so he would have had very little difficulty obtaining a specimen locally.

Peterson (2008), p. 66; Dunne (2006), p. 86; Fries (1973), p. 400; *OB* III, p. 26.

90. Olson (2012), p. 125; Audubon (2006), p. 407-408; *AHJ* I, pp. 390-391.

91. Audubon (1966) II, Plate 375.

92. Audubon (2006), p. 407; *AHJ* I, p. 390. Cf. L. Audubon (1869), p. 329 ("At noon my fingers were so cold that I could no longer hold my pencil to draw, and I was compelled to go on shore for exercise."). The two versions of Audubon's journal offer completely different accounts as to when Audubon ceased working on July 6. Maria's edition indicates that he had to stop at 5:30 p.m. after painting an adult and recently hatched Red-necked Diver (Red-throated Loon) as well as almost completing a female Willow Grous (Willow Ptarmigan) because his fingers were unable to continue holding a pencil. Lucy's version of the journal states that he had to stop at noon because his fingers were cold. I have elected to accept Maria's account because of the amount of work Audubon reportedly completed that day. Given other descriptions of what he was able to accomplish at his drawing table, I do not believe he could have completed the described work if he had stopped at noon.

93. L. Audubon (1869), p. 330; *OB* V, p. 450. Cf. Audubon (2006), p. 407; *AHJ* I, pp. 390-391 ("go ashore for exercise").

94. Audubon (2006), p. 407; *AHJ* I, p. 391. Cf. L. Audubon (1869), p. 330 ("The fact is I am growing old too fast; alas! I feel it, yet work I will, and may God grant me life to see the last plate of my mammoth work finished.").

95. Peterson (2008), p. 148; Audubon (2006), p. 407; *AHJ* I, p. 391.

96. Audubon (2006), p. 407; *AHJ* I, p. 391.

97. Audubon (2006), pp. 407-408; *AHJ* I, p. 391.

98. Bayfield (1984) I, p. 241.

99. Bayfield (1837), pp. 141-142.

100. Audubon (2006), pp. 407-408; *AHJ* I, p. 391.

101. *OB* III, p. 109.

102. Bayfield (1984) I, p. 242.

103. Audubon (2006), p. 408; *AHJ* I, p. 391; L. Audubon (1869), p. 330.

104. Bayfield (1984) I, p. 242.

105. Audubon (2006), p. 408; *AHJ* I, p. 392.

106. Bayfield (1984) I, p. 242.

107. Audubon (2006), p. 408; *AHJ* I, p. 391.

108. Audubon (2006), p. 408; *AHJ* I, pp. 391-392.

109. *OB* III, pp. 344, 348.

110. Audubon (2006), p. 408; *AHJ* I, p. 392; L. Audubon (1869), p. 330.

111. Audubon (1966) II, Plate 375; Audubon (2006), p. 408; *AHJ* I, p. 392. Audubon's journal entries suggest that he drew eight young Willow Grous (Willow Ptarmigan) as part of his illustration of the species. On July 7, he wrote that he "finished the female Grouse and five young" and the following day, he completed "three more young." Audubon (2006), p. 408; *AHJ* I, pp. 391-392. However, the drawing actually depicts only seven young birds.

112. Audubon (2006), p. 408; *AHJ* I, p. 392.

113. L. Audubon (1869), p. 330. Cf. Audubon (2006), p. 408; *AHJ* I, p. 392 ("The rain falls on my drawing-paper, despite all I can do, and even the fog collects and falls in large drops from the rigging on my table; now and then I am obliged to close my skylight, and then may be said to work almost in darkness.").

114. Audubon (1966) I, p. xxviii; JJA, New York to VGA, London, 20 Sept. 1833 (APS), *Letters* I, p. 254.

115. Audubon (2006), p. 408; *AHJ* I, p. 392.

116. Audubon (2006), p. 408; *AHJ* I, p. 392.

117. Deane (1910), p. 43.

118. Audubon (2006), p. 408; *AHJ* I, p. 392.

119. Peterson (2008), p. 66.

120. Audubon (1966) II, Plate 409.

121. *OB* III, p. 344.

122. L. Audubon (1869), p. 330. Cf. Audubon (2006), p. 408; *AHJ* I, p. 392 ("plants blooming by millions, and at every step you tread on such as would be looked upon with pleasure in more temperate climes.").

123. Audubon (2006), p. 408; *AHJ* I, p. 392.

124. *OB* III, p. 344.

125. Audubon (2006), p. 409; *AHJ* I, p. 393. Cf. L. Audubon (1869), pp. 330-331:

Could I describe one of those dismal gales which blow ever and anon over this dismal country, it would probably be interesting to any one unacquainted with the inclemency of this climate. Nowhere else are the north-east blasts, which sweep over Labrador, felt as they are here. But I cannot describe them. All I can say is, that while we are safe in a land-locked harbor, their effects on our vessel are so strong, that they will not allow me to draw, and sometimes send some of us to our beds. And what the force of these horrid blasts outside the harbor at sea is I can hardly imagine; but it seems as if it would be impossible for any vessel to ride safely before them, and that they will rend these rocky islands asunder. The rain is driven in sheets, and falls with difficulty upon its destination of sea or land. Nay, I cannot call it rain, as it is such a thick cloud of water, that all objects at a distance are lost sight of at intervals of three or four minutes, and the waters around us come up and beat about in our rock-bound harbor, as a newly caught and caged bird beats against the wire walls of his prison cage.

Boreas, referred to by Audubon in the passage from the text, was the Greek god of the north wind. The inclusion of this reference in Maria's edition of the journal lends credence to it being in the original holograph as Audubon frequently used such allusions in his writing.

126. Audubon (2006), p. 410; *AHJ* I, p. 394.

127. Audubon (2006), p. 410; *AHJ* I, p. 394; L. Audubon (1869), p. 331.

128. Audubon (1966) I, Plate 145.

129. *OB* III, p. 458.

130. Audubon (2006), p. 410; *AHJ* I, p. 394.

131. Audubon (2006), p. 410; *AHJ* I, p. 395; L. Audubon (1869), p. 331. See also, Bayfield (1984) I, p. 244.

132. Audubon (2006), p. 410; *AHJ* I, p. 395. In contrast to what appears in Maria's edition of the journal, the July 12 entry in Lucy's biography states that Audubon was unable to complete his drawing of the Common Cormorant (Great Cormorant) family due to the rocking of the schooner. L. Audubon (1869), p. 331. I have elected to trust Maria's journal here because there is no indication in Lucy's biography that Audubon finished the drawing of the Great Cormorant family at another time. Lucy's journal entry for this day is also but a single sentence, and it is evident that a great deal of the original text was omitted.

133. Audubon (2006), p. 411; *AHJ* I, p. 395.

134. Audubon (2006), p. 410; *AHJ* I, p. 395.

135. L. Audubon (1869), p. 331. Cf. Audubon (2006), p. 411; *AHJ* I, p. 395 ("The weather was cloudy and looked bad, as it always does here after a storm.").

136. Audubon (2006), p. 411; *AHJ* I, p. 395. Cf. L. Audubon (1869), p. 331 ("I was anxious to stay on board, and finish the drawing of a grouse I had promised to Dr. Kelly of the Gulnare."). The two versions of Audubon's journal are in direct conflict as to his plans for drawing on July 13. But it seems reasonable to conclude that Maria's is closer to the mark. The naturalist had yet to complete the background of his drawing of the Willow Grous (Willow Ptarmigan), as evidenced by the work he did on this picture on July 15. It seems unlikely that he was working on an image of the same bird to give to Dr. Kelley, which is what Lucy's biography would suggest.

137. Audubon (2006), p. 411; *AHJ* I, pp. 395–396; L. Audubon (1869), p. 331.

138. Audubon (2006), p. 411; *AHJ* I, p. 396; L. Audubon (1869), p. 331.

139. Audubon (2006), p. 411; *AHJ* I, p. 396.

140. Bayfield (1984) I, p. 244.

CHAPTER 10: LITTLE MECATTINA COVE, LABRADOR

1. Audubon (2006), p. 411; Bayfield (1984) I, p. 244; *AHJ* I, p. 396; L. Audubon (1869), p. 332.

2. Audubon (2006), p. 411; *AHJ* I, p. 396; L. Audubon (1869), p. 332; Bayfield (1837), pp. 204–205.

3. Audubon (2006), p. 411; *AHJ* I, p. 396; L. Audubon (1869), p. 331. Townsend has referred to the harbor where Audubon and his party anchored as Hare Harbor (Havre aux Lièvres). Townsend (1918), p. 154; Townsend (1917), p. 142. According to Bayfield, Hare Harbor was actually located farther north of Little Mecattina Cove between the island of Little Mecattina (Île du Petit Mécatina) and a chain of islands to the east. Bayfield (1984) I, pp. 317, 322; Bayfield (1837), pp. 205–206.

4. L. Audubon (1869), p. 332.

5. Audubon (2006), p. 412; *AHJ* I, p. 396.

6. L. Audubon (1869), p. 332.

7. Audubon (2006), p. 412; *AHJ* I, p. 397; L. Audubon (1869), p. 332.

8. *OB* II, p. 200.

9. L. Audubon (1869), p. 332.

10. *OB* II, p. 200.

11. Audubon (2006), p. 412; *AHJ* I, p. 397. Cf. L. Audubon (1869), pp. 332-333. ("to the top of a mountain (for I cannot call it a hill), and there we saw the crest of the island beneath our feet, all rocks, barren, bare rocks, wild as the wildest Apennines").

12. Audubon (2006), p. 412; *AHJ* I, p. 397; L. Audubon (1869), p. 332.

13. Bayfield (1837), p. 204.

14. *OB* II, p. 201.

15. L. Audubon (1869), p. 333. Cf. Audubon (2006), p. 412; *AHJ* I, p. 397 ("the moss only a few inches deep, and the soil or decomposed matter beneath it so moist that, wherever there was an incline, the whole slipped from under our feet like an avalanche, and down we slid for feet or yards.").

16. L. Audubon (1869), p. 333. Cf. Audubon (2006), pp. 412-413; *AHJ* I, p. 397 ("on our return we slid down fifty feet or more into an unknown pit of moss and mire, more or less deep.").

17. Audubon (2006), p. 412; Townsend (1918), p. 159; *AHJ* I, p. 397; L. Audubon (1869), p. 333.

18. Audubon (2006), p. 413; *AHJ* I, p. 397; *OB* II, p. 201.

19. Audubon (2006), p. 413; *AHJ* I, p. 398; L. Audubon (1869), p. 333.

20. Audubon (2006), p. 413; *AHJ* I, p. 398; L. Audubon (1869), p. 333.

21. Audubon (2006), p. 413; *AHJ* I, p. 398; L. Audubon (1869), p. 333

22. Audubon (2006), p. 413; *AHJ* I, p. 398; L. Audubon (1869), p. 333

23. Audubon's extant writings do not reflect that the nest of the White-crowned Bunting (White-crowned Sparrow) collected by Coolidge's party on July 15 was ladened with eggs. However, the fact that Audubon's drawing of the egg of this species was done on that date leads to the conclusion that it was.

24. Fries (1973), p. 386. Audubon illustrated at least five different eggs during the Labrador expedition. In Maria's edition of the journal, he wrote on Wednesday, July 17: "I have drawn five eggs

of landbirds: that of *Falco columbarius, Fringilla leucophyrs, Anthus spinoletta, Sylvia striata*, and *Fringilla savanna*." The original drawing of four of these eggs, now in the collection of the Louisiana State Museum in New Orleans, reveals that they were actually completed over the course of a couple of weeks between early and mid-July. Three of the eggs reference the dates Audubon drew them. He drew the egg of the *Anthus spinoletta* (American Pipit) on July 1. That of the *Sylvia striata* (Blackpoll Warbler) was completed on July 14, and the egg of the *Fringilla leucophyrs* (White-crowned Sparrow) was finished the following day. Audubon (1966) I, p. xxvii, Figure 15. The *Falco columbarius* (Merlin) egg was presumably done around July 1 when his party found a nest of this species. A nest with two eggs of the *Fringilla savanna* (Savannah Sparrow) was located on June 30, so this illustration probably dates from about that time.

25. Davidson in Audubon (1966) I, p. xxvi; Herrick (1938) I, p. 426, note 6.

26. Audubon (2006), pp. 413-414; *AHJ* I, pp. 398-399; *OB* II, p. 6.

27. Small (2009), p. 180; Audubon (2006), p. 414; *AHJ* I, p. 399; L. Audubon (1869), p. 333.

28. Audubon (2006), p. 414; *AHJ* I, p. 399.

29. L. Audubon (1869), p. 333. Cf. Audubon (2006), p. 414; *AHJ* I, p. 399 ("though the fog was as thick as fine rain, these insects attacked me by thousands.").

30. Audubon (2006), p. 414; *AHJ* I, p. 399; L. Audubon (1869), p. 333.

31. Debboun (2007), pp. 4-5. A 2015 study suggests that there may also be a genetic component behind an individual's relative attractiveness to mosquitoes. Fernández-Grandon (2015).

32. Audubon (2006), p. 414; *AHJ* I, p. 399. Capt. Bayfield's journal reflects that on July 17 it was foggy and raining at his location, which was more than halfway between Wapitiguan Harbor and Little Mecattina. Bayfield (1984) I, pp. 245-246. Audubon declared that the winds were from the southwest.

33. Audubon (2006), pp. 414-415; *AHJ* I, pp. 399-400; L. Audubon (1869), p. 333.

34. Audubon (2006), pp. 415, 417; *AHJ* I, pp. 400, 403; L. Audubon (1869), pp. 333-334.

35. OB II, p. 543. Audubon wrote in his jour-

nal entry for July 18: "After breakfast all hands except the cook left the Ripley, in three boats, to visit the main shore, about five miles off." L. Audubon (1869), p. 333. Cf. Audubon (2006), p. 415; *AHJ* I, p. 400 ("We all, with the exception of the cook, left the 'Ripley' in three boats immediately after our early breakfast, and went to the main land, distant some five miles."). Later in the same entry he indicated there were fourteen men with guns who made up the three shore parties that day. Audubon (2006), p. 417; *AHJ* I, p. 403. Since there appears to have been sixteen aboard the vessel, one of the members of the company—possibly the cabin boy—must not have been armed. See Chapter 6, note 104, *supra*.

36. L. Audubon (1869), pp. 333-334. Cf. Audubon (2006), p. 415; *AHJ* I, p. 400 ("As soon as we landed the captain and I went off over a large extent of marsh ground, the first we have yet met with in this country; the earth was wet, our feet sank far in the soil, and walking was extremely irksome.").

37. *OB* IV, p. 162.

38. *OB* II, p. 543. In the *OB*, Audubon referred to the Boreal Chickadee as "The Hudson's Bay Titmouse" in the heading of his species account. However, in the text he called it the "Canada Titmouse." Robert Havell Jr. used one or the other of the two names in the legend printed below the engraved image of the birds in the published print. Low (2002), p. 120.

Audubon wrote that he and Capt. Emery had not found anything of interest while navigating the extensive marsh in which they initially found themselves during their July 18 excursion. This appears to have been a touch of literary license to exaggerate the importance of their discovery of the Canada Titmice. It certainly is belied by his journal description of finding the nest of the Surf Duck (Surf Scoter) in the marsh.

39. Audubon (2006), p. 415; *AHJ* I, pp. 400-401. In his species account of the Boreal Chickadee, Audubon reported that the nest discovered by Capt. Emery "was placed at the height of not more than three feet from the ground," not the "five feet" recorded in Maria's edition of the journal. *OB* II, p. 543.

40. *OB* II, pp. 543-544.

41. Audubon (2006), p. 415; *AHJ* I, p. 400.

42. Audubon (2006), p. 415; *AHJ* I, p. 401.

43. *OB* II, p. 440.

44. Audubon (2006), pp. 415-416; *AHJ* I, p. 401; *OB* II, p. 439.

45. Leahy (2004), p. 516.

46. L. Audubon (1869), p. 334; Cf. Audubon (2006), p. 416; *AHJ* I, p. 401 ("We crossed a savannah of many miles in extent; in many places the soil appeared to wave under us, and we expected at each step to go through the superficial moss carpet up to our middles in the mire; so wet and so spongy was it that I think I never labored harder in a walk of the same extent. In traveling through this quagmire we met with a small grove of good-sized, fine white-birch trees, and a few pines full forty feet high, quite a novelty to us at this juncture.").

47. Audubon (2006), p. 416; *AHJ* I, pp. 401-402.

48. Audubon (2006), p. 416; *AHJ* I, pp 401, 403. Of the two Willow Grous (Willow Ptarmigan) that were killed on this excursion, one was killed by a gun rod.

49. Audubon (2006), p. 416; *AHJ* I, pp. 402-403. In Maria's edition of the journal, cited here, Audubon indicated that the gulls John and his party had found nesting on an island on July 18 were members of the species *Larus canus*. At that time, *Larus canus* was known as the Common or Mew Gull, which is found in Europe and along the western coast of North America. Audubon may have initially identified the Labrador gulls as this species, but he later concluded that they were Common American Gulls, *Larus zonorhynchus* (Ring-billed Gulls). *OB* III, p. 101. See also, *AHJ* I, p. 402, note 1.

50. *OB* II, p. 530.

51. Audubon (2006), p. 417; *AHJ* I, p. 403; L. Audubon (1869), p. 334. See also, note 35, *supra*.

52. L. Audubon (1869), p. 334. Cf. Audubon (2006), p. 416; *AHJ* I, p. 403 ("From the top of a high rock I had fine [*sic*] view of the most extensive and the dreariest wilderness I have ever beheld. It chilled the heart to gaze on these barren lands of Labrador. Indeed I now dread every change of harbor, so horribly rugged and dangerous is the whole coast and country, especially to the inexperienced man either of sea or land.").

53. LBA, New York to VGA, London, 20 Jul.

1833 (Yale, Box 1, Folder 20). Edward Harris was accompanied on his trip to Eastport by a good friend from Moorestown, Dr. John J. Spencer, and by one of his brothers-in-law, evidently John Lang Jr. (c. 1806–1836). Lucy referred to him in her letter only as "young Lang." There were four other Lang sons: Robert U. Lang (c. 1799- 1837), who joined the *New-York Gazette* in 1820 and served as senior editor of the paper upon his father's death in 1836; Charles (c. 1810–1848); William (c. 1813–1850), and Edmund (c. 1815–1856). McDermott (1951), p. 3, note 4; Stokes (1918), p. 378; Brigham (1917), p. 427; Hough (1875), p. 245. However, Harris wrote back to the Lang family on August 22 and mentioned that "Joe" had paddled an Indian canoe "with great skill." Edward Harris, Eastport to John Lang, New York, 22 Aug. 1833, *New-York Gazette & General Advertiser*, Vol. 45, No. 16,961, p. 2, col. 3 (Wednesday Morning, 4 Sept. 1833)(NYHS). I surmise that John Lang Jr. went by the name Joe to distinguish himself from his father.

54. LBA, New York to JJA, care of General Ripley, East Port, 14 Jul. 1833 (Yale, Box 1, Folder 20).

55. Ibid.

56. Audubon (2006), p. 417; *AHJ* I, p. 403. In Lucy's biography, Audubon's journal entry for July 19 states that "there was too much motion of the vessel for drawing," which is at odds with Maria's edition where Audubon indicated that he began the drawing of the Canada Titmice (Boreal Chickadee). L. Audubon (1869), p. 334. We know that Audubon completed the illustration on July 20 because he made a notation of the date and location on the original drawing. Audubon (1966) I, Plate 27. Since his journal for July 20 suggests that he only drew until 10:00 a.m., the likelihood is that he began the composition the previous day as Maria's journal states.

57. Audubon (2006), pp. 417–418; *AHJ* I, pp. 403–405; L. Audubon (1869), pp. 334–335.

58. L. Audubon (1869), pp. 334-335. Cf. Audubon (2006), pp. 417–418; *AHJ* I, pp. 403–405:

We climbed the rocks and followed from one to another, crossing fissures, holding to the moss hand and foot and with difficulty, for about a mile, when suddenly we came upon the de-

serted mansion of a Labrador sealer. It looked snug outside, and we entered it. It was formed of short slabs, all very well greased with seal oil; an oven without a pipe, a salt-box hung on a wooden peg, a three-legged stool, and a wooden box of a bedstead, with a flour-barrel containing some hundreds of seine-floats, and an old Seal seine, completed the list of goods and chattels. Three small windows, with four panes of glass each, were still in pretty good order, and so was the low door, which moved on wooden hinges, for which the maker has received no patent, I'll be bound. This cabin made of hewn logs, brought from the main, was well put together, about twelve feet square, well roofed with bark of birch and spruce, thatched with moss, and every aperture rendered air-tight with oakum. But it was deserted and abandoned; the Seals are all caught, and the sealers have nought to do here now-a-days. We found a pile of good hard wood close to this abode, which we will have removed on board our vessel to-morrow. I discovered that this cabin had been the abode of two French Canadians; first, because their almanac, written with chalk on one of the logs, was in French; and next, the writing was in two very different styles. *AHJ* I, pp. 403–405.

59. Audubon (2006), p. 418; *AHJ* I, p. 404; L. Audubon (1869), p. 335.

60. L. Audubon (1869), p. 335. Cf. Audubon (2006), p. 418; *AHJ* I, p. 404 ("how dreadful they would prove to any one who should be wrecked on so inhospitable a shore.").

61. Audubon (2006), p. 418; *AHJ* I, p. 405.

62. "A Californian's Recollection of Naturalist Audubon," *The San Francisco Call*, Vol. LXXX, No. 98, p. 25, cols. 1–7 (Sunday, 6 Sept. 1896)(LOC).

63. Audubon (2006), p. 418; *AHJ* I, p. 405; L. Audubon (1869), p. 335.

64. L. Audubon (1869), p. 335. Cf. Audubon (2006), p. 418; *AHJ* I, p. 405 ("Labrador deserves credit for *one* fine day!"). Although Lucy's biography, from which the quotation in the text is taken, does not italicize the word "one" as does Maria's edition of the journal, it has been added because Audubon would have unquestionably underlined the word in the original holograph as he invariably

did when he wished to emphasize a point. On that
score, at least, I believe Maria was faithful to her
grandfather's journal.

65. L. Audubon (1869), p. 335. Cf. Audubon
(2006), p. 418; *AHJ* I, p. 405 ("in the Middle States
about the month of May.").

66. Audubon (2006), p. 418; *AHJ* I, p. 405.

67. *OB* IV, pp. 181–182.

68. Ibid., p. 182.

69. Audubon (2006), pp. 409–410, 418; *AHJ* I,
pp. 394, 405; L. Audubon (1869), p. 336.

70. Desormeaux (2010), pp. 42–45, 49–50;
Townsend (1918), p. 154.

71. Small (2009), p. 186; Audubon (2006),
p. 418; *AHJ* I, p. 405.

72. Audubon (1966) I, Plate 27.

73. Audubon (2006), p. 418; *AHJ* I, p. 405.

74. Audubon (2006), pp. 418–419; *AHJ* I, pp.
405–406.

75. Deane (1910), pp. 46–47.

76. Audubon (2006), p. 418; *AHJ* I, p. 405.

77. *OB* II, p. 93.

78. LBA, New York to VGA at London, 20 Jul.
1833 (Yale, Box 1, Folder 20).

79. Ibid.

80. Ibid. In addition to Joshua Davis and his
wife, Lucy would have enjoyed the company of
Eliza Davis and her daughter Maria, who were also
making the trip to Niagara Falls. Lucy referred
to Mrs. Davis in the cited letter as "Bussey," her
maiden name. Eliza Bussey Davis (1783–1841), the
widow of Boston attorney Charles Davis (1777–
1821), lived at 28 Summer Street in Boston. Park
(1926) I, pp. 259–261; Stimpson (1833), p. 131. She
was the daughter of Benjamin Bussey (1757–1842), a
wealthy Boston merchant who had retired to Woodland Hill, his three-hundred-acre estate in West
Roxbury, which is now the Arnold Arboretum. Wilson (2006), p. 20–21. Gilbert Stuart's 1808 paintings
of Charles and Eliza Davis are in collection of the
North Carolina Museum of Art.

CHAPTER 11: PORTAGE BAY, LABRADOR

1. Audubon (2006), p. 419; Bayfield (1984) I,
p. 248; *AHJ* I, p. 406; L. Audubon (1869), p. 336;
Bayfield (1837), p. 200. Capt. Bayfield recorded in
his journal entry for July 22 that it was sixteen miles

from Little Mecattina Cove (Anse du Petit Mécatina) to Grand Mecattina Point (Cape Mecattina
Point). Google Earth places it at closer to seventeen and a half miles on a straight line. Mecattina
Harbor (Havre du Mécatina), to which the *Ripley*
was headed, lies about two and a half miles farther
northeast. Portage Bay (Mutton Bay), where Mr.
Godwin piloted the schooner, lies between Cape
Mecattina Point and Mecattina Harbor. Thus,
Townsend's assertion that it is thirty-three miles
from Little Mecattina Island to Portage Bay is incorrect. Townsend (1917), p. 142.

2. Bayfield (1984) I, p. 247; Townsend (1918),
p. 163; Bayfield (1837), p. 200; Blunt (1833), p. 26;
Blunt (1827), p. 612.

3. Audubon (2006), p. 419; Bayfield (1984) I,
p. 247; *AHJ* I, p. 406; L. Audubon (1869), p. 336.

4. Townsend (1918), p. 163; Blunt (1833), p. 26;
Blunt (1827), p. 612.

5. Audubon (2006), p. 419; *AHJ* I, p. 406;
L. Audubon (1869), p. 336.

6. Audubon (2006), p. 419; *AHJ* I, p. 406;
L. Audubon (1869), p. 336; *OB* V, p. 300.

7. Audubon (2006), p. 419; Bayfield (1984) I, pp.
247–248; *AHJ* I, p. 406.

8. L. Audubon (1869), p. 336. Cf. Audubon
(2006), p. 419; *AHJ* I, p. 406 ("encamped in great
comfort").

9. L. Audubon (1869), p. 336. Cf. Audubon
(2006), pp. 419–420; *AHJ* I, pp. 406–407:

The tea-things were yet arranged on the ironbound bed, the trunks served as seats, and the
sail-cloth clothes-bags as pillows. The moss was
covered with a large tarred cloth, and neither
wind nor damp was admitted. I gazed on the
camp with much pleasure, and it was a great
enjoyment to be with men of education and refined manners, such as are these officers of the
Royal Navy; it was indeed a treat. We talked of
the country where we were, of the beings best
suited to live and prosper here, not only of our
species, but of all species, and also of the enormous destruction of everything here, except the
rocks; the aborigines themselves melting away
before the encroachments of the white man, who
looks without pity upon the decrease of the devoted Indian, from whom he rifles home, food,

clothing, and life. For as the Deer, the Caribou, and all other game is killed for the dollar
its skin brings in, the Indian must search in vain
over the devastated country for that on which
he is accustomed to feed, till, worn out by sorrow, despair, and want, he either goes far from
his early haunts to others, which in time will be
similarly invaded, or he lies on the rocky seashore and dies. We are often told rum kills the
Indian; I think not; it is oftener the want of food,
the loss of hope as he loses sight of all that was
once abundant, before the white man intruded
on his land and killed off the wild quadrupeds
and birds with which he has fed and clothed
himself since his creation. Nature herself seems
perishing. Labrador must shortly be depeopled,
not only of aboriginal man, but of all else having
life, owing to man's cupidity. When no more
fish, no more game, no more birds exist on her
hills, along her coasts, and in her rivers, then she
will be abandoned and deserted like a worn-out
field.

10. Audubon (2006), p. 420; Bayfield (1984) I,
pp. 248–249; *AHJ* I, p. 407; L. Audubon (1869),
p. 337.

11. Audubon (2006), p. 420; *AHJ* I, p. 407;
L. Audubon (1869), p. 337; Bayfield (1837), pp. 200,
202.

12. Audubon (2006), p. 420; Belvin (2006),
pp. 7–8; Bayfield (1984) I, p. 251; *AHJ* I, p. 407;
L. Audubon (1869), p. 337.

13. Belvin (2006), p. 7–8; Lopez (1986), pp. 3–4.
While Right Whales ordinarily floated in death,
there were instances when the carcasses sank. The
New Brunswick whaling crew, which Audubon and
his companions met on July 22, related that three
of the four whales they had struck during their recent hunt had been lost in this fashion, although
this "was a very rare occurrence." Audubon (2006),
p. 420; *AHJ* I, p. 408; L. Audubon (1869), p. 337.

14. Belvin (2006), pp. 7, 27–30.

15. L. Audubon (1869), p. 337. See also, Audubon (2006), p. 420; *AHJ* I, p. 407. Lucy's biography
indicates that the whale blubber was cut into chunks
weighing six to eight pounds. Maria's edition of the
journal asserts that they were six to twenty pounds.

16. L. Audubon (1869), p. 337. Cf. Audubon

(2006), p. 420; *AHJ* I, p. 407 ("a good, sensible
man of that class").

17. Audubon (2006), p. 420; *AHJ* I, pp. 407–
408; L. Audubon (1869), p. 337.

18. Audubon (2006), p. 420; *AHJ* I, p. 408;
L. Audubon (1869), p. 337; *OB* II, pp. 154–155. In
his Episode "The Squatters of Labrador," Audubon
added several elements to the story of his meeting
with Pierre Michaux, the French-Canadian sealer
and trapper, which were not recounted in his extensive journal entry of July 22. He explained to
the readers of the *OB* that he had first seen the
trapper from the *Ripley* as he was scanning the top
of a small island nearby with a telescope. The man
was in prayer, and Audubon's curiosity was sufficiently piqued that he immediately took a boat and
rowed over to the island to speak with him. Later,
at Michaux's cabin, the trapper reportedly went
to retrieve some rum from a hidden store in the
bushes to share with his guests but returned saying it had been stolen by some fishermen or eggers.
Both of these claims appear to have been invented.
To begin with, the harbor where Michaux made his
home was not Portage Bay but Mecattina Harbor
(Havre du Mécatina), a "long mile" away from the
Ripley's anchorage as Bayfield described it. Bayfield
(1837), p. 201. Second, the account would make it
sound like Audubon rowed directly from the *Ripley*
to the island and met Michaux there. Yet this differs notably from the journal entry, where Audubon
described visiting the whaling station at Mecattina
Harbor first. Third, Audubon made no note in his
journal that Michaux had offered them rum during
their visit to his cabin, a glaring oversight for a man
who enjoyed his liquor. Of course, it is possible any
such reference could have been deleted by Maria.
However, her edition of the journal indicates that
the Montagnais Indians served his party rum during
a visit to their camp back on June 23, so any motivation she may have had to excise a reference to rum
here is lacking.

19. Audubon (2006), p. 420; *AHJ* I, p. 408;
L. Audubon (1869), p. 337; *OB* II, pp. 154–155.

20. Audubon (2006), pp. 420–421; *AHJ* I, pp.
408–409; L. Audubon (1869), pp. 337–338; *OB* II,
p. 155.

21. Audubon (2006), pp. 420–421; *AHJ* I, pp.
408–409; L. Audubon (1869), pp. 337–339.

22. Audubon (2006), p. 422; Townsend (1918), p. 166; *AHJ* I, p. 410; L. Audubon (1869), p. 339; Bayfield (1837), p. 202.

23. L. Audubon (1869), p. 339. Cf. Audubon (2006), p. 422; *AHJ* I, p. 410 ("I saw plants with leaves fully a foot in breadth, and grasses three feet high.").

24. Audubon (2006), p. 422; *AHJ* I, p. 410.

25. Audubon (2006), p. 422; Bayfield (1984) I, p. 248; *AHJ* I, p. 410; L. Audubon (1869), pp. 339-340.

26. Marshall (2006), pp. 4-5, 40-41; Audubon (2006), pp. 420-422; *AHJ* I, pp. 407-410.

27. Audubon (2006), p. 422; Bayfield (1984) I, pp. 248, 251; *AHJ* I, p. 410; L. Audubon (1869), p. 340; Bayfield (1837), p. 198. Audubon wrote in his journal that Samuel Robertson's seal and trading station was located at Sparr Point, about six miles (actually closer to seven and a half miles by water according to Google Earth) from Portage Bay. This places it at what is now La Tabatière, Quebec. Tara Nadeau, La Tabatière, Quebec (Personal communication, 29 Jul 2015); Belvin (2006), p. 68 and note 5, p. 174. Charles Townsend, M.D., found Robertson's grandson Samuel Robertson III there on July 20, 1915, while retracing Audubon's route. Townsend (1918), pp. 168-169. However, Bayfield's navigational guide indicated that a "Mr. Robinson" had a seal and trading post located at Fish Harbor (Havre au Poissons), which is near the now-abandoned community of Lac-Salé. It would appear that Bayfield was misinformed.

28. Belvin (2006), pp. 62, 65-66, 68. The Robertson family genealogy reflects that Samuel Robertson was born on April 23, 1793. Ancestry.com, http://records.ancestry.com/Samuel_Robertson_records.ashx?pid=1939522 (accessed 5 Apr. 2014).

29. Belvin (2006), pp. 68, 79; Audubon (2006), pp. 422, 424; Bayfield (1984) I, pp. 309-310; *AHJ* I, pp. 410, 413; L. Audubon (1869), pp. 340-341; Bayfield (1837), p. 188.

30. *OB* II, p. 156.

31. Ibid.

32. Ibid. While Audubon wrote that Samuel Robertson had six children as of 1833, the family genealogy indicates that seven children had been born to Robertson and his wife prior to Audubon's visit: Marie "Anne" (b. c. 1821); Sophia (1823-1861); Samuel John (1826-1886); Christine Adele (1828-1886); John Henry (1829-1853); George (b. 1830); and Stephen (b. 1831). Marie "Anne" is known to have married in 1840, which would suggest that either George or Stephen died at an early age. Ancestry.com, http://records.ancestry.com/Samuel_Robertson_records.ashx?pid=1939522 (accessed 5 Apr. 2014); Ancestry.com, *Quebec, Vital and Church Records (Drouin Collection), 1621-1967* (database on-line)(Provo, UT: Ancestry.com Operations Inc., 2008)(accessed 5 Apr. 2014).

33. *OB* II, p. 156

34. Audubon (2006), pp. 422-423; *AHJ* I, pp. 410-411; L. Audubon (1869), pp. 340-341; *OB* II, p. 156; GCSJr, Bay de Portage to GCS, Boston, 23 Jul. 1833 addendum to letter of 22 and 26 Jun. 1833 (MHS, Vol. 11, June 1833).

35. *OB* II, p. 156.

36. Ibid., p. 157.

37. Audubon (2006), p. 423; *AHJ* I, p. 411; L. Audubon (1869), p. 340.

38. Audubon (2006), pp. 422-423; *AHJ* I, pp. 410-411. See also, L. Audubon (1869), p. 340 ("He told me that his profits last year amounted to three thousand dollars.").

39. *OB* II, p. 157; JJA, Bay de Portage, Labrador to LBA, New York, 23 Jul. 1833 (MHM), Deane (1910), p. 49. See also, Audubon (2006), p. 423; *AHJ* I, p. 411; L. Audubon (1869), p. 340..

40. Audubon (2006), p. 423; *AHJ* I, p. 411; L. Audubon (1869), pp. 340-341; *OB* III, p. 571; *OB* II, pp. 157, 531. In Maria's edition of the journal, Audubon supposedly wrote of Samuel Robertson: "He also told me that during mild winters his little harbor is covered with pure white Gulls (the Silvery), but that all leave at the first appearance of spring." The parenthetical reference is to the White-winged Silvery Gull (Iceland Gull). But the Iceland Gull, while paler than a Herring Gull, is decidedly not a "pure white" gull. Rather, that description (and the description in Lucy's biography of "white gulls") would appear to refer to the Ivory Gull, a smaller, all-white gull of the high Arctic that frequents the Gulf of St. Lawrence during the winter months. Peterson (2008), p. 200; Audubon (1981), Plate 196. And, indeed, Audubon's account of this species in the *OB* makes it relatively clear that this

was the species to which he was alluding in his journal, saying that he had "ascertained that this beautiful species visits the southern coast of Labrador and Newfoundland every winter." *OB* III, p. 571. He made no mention of the appearance of White-winged Silvery Gulls in Labrador during winter. Ibid., p. 553. The parenthetical reference was likely added, in error, by Maria.

41. Audubon (2006), p. 423; *AHJ* I, p. 411; L. Audubon (1869), p. 340

42. JJA, Bay de Portage, Labrador to LBA, New York, 23 Jul. 1833 (MHM), published with minor differences in content, spelling, and punctuation in Deane (1910), pp. 49–52. Quotations from this letter that appear in the text are taken from the original holograph.

43. Ibid.

44. Ibid.

45. Ibid.

46. Ibid. Although Audubon announced in his letter to Lucy of July 23 that he intended to write an Episode for the *OB* entitled "The Sealers," no such narrative by that title appears in his publication. Ruthven Deane, the widely respected Audubon scholar of the first part of the 20th century who transcribed this letter for an article that appeared in *The Auk*, made a note of this and stated that he had also never seen this Episode in "any of Audubon's writings." Deane (1910), p. 51, note 5. What Deane overlooked is that Audubon later decided to combine his account of "The Sealers" with that of "A Labrador Squater" into the single Episode of "The Squatters." However, it should be emphasized that neither Samuel Robertson nor his brother-in-law Capt. William Randall Jones, each of whom operated a major sealing station along the Labrador coast and were a focus of Audubon's tale, were actually squatters. They had purchased the rights to the trading posts following the bankruptcy of the Labrador New Concern in 1820. Belvin (2006), p. 68.

47. JJA, Bay de Portage, Labrador to LBA, New York, 23 Jul. 1833 (MHM).

48. Ibid.

49. Ibid.

50. Audubon (2006), p. 423; *AHJ* I, p. 411. Audubon's journal entry of July 23 indicates that he purchased the skin of a Cross Fox from Samuel Robertson during his visit to Sparr Point. In the

OB, Audubon stated that he made the purchase from Robertson's eldest child. *OB* II, p. 157. Regardless, it was evidently not a fine enough skin to meet Eliza Berthoud's rich taste because he did not mention it to Lucy in his letter of the same date.

51. Audubon (2006), p. 423; Grenfell (1909), pp. 431–433; *AHJ* I, p. 411. Cf. L. Audubon (1869), p. 341 ("the caraboo flies drove our hunters on board to-day, and they looked as bloody as if they had actually had a gouging fight with some rough Kentuckians.").

52. Audubon (2006), p. 423; *AHJ* I, pp. 411–412.

53. GCSJr., Bay de Portage, Labrador to GCS, Boston, 23 Jul. 1833 addendum to letter of 22 and 26 Jun. 1833 (MHS, Vol. 11, Jun. 1833).

54. Audubon (2006), p. 424; *AHJ* I, pp. 412–413.

55. Audubon (2006), p. 424; *AHJ* I, p. 412–413; Bayfield (1837), p. 199; *OB* III, p. 143.

56. *OB* III, p. 143.

57. Ibid., p. 143.

58. Audubon (2006), p. 424; *AHJ* I, p. 412; *OB* IV, p. 228. The text relies principally on Maria's edition of Audubon's journal for the stated facts. Note that Audubon's description of Shattuck and Coolidge's excursion to the Murre Islands in the *OB* contains a number of discrepancies. For example, in his species account of the White-winged Crossbill, he wrote that the excursion took place on July 23, not the 24th as accurately stated in the journal. He also gave credit for collecting the female of this species to Shattuck, not Coolidge. *OB* IV, p. 467.

59. Audubon (2006), p. 424; *AHJ* I, p. 412. Note that Audubon increased the number of eggs supposedly retrieved by the crew from the Murre Rocks when it came time for him to tell the story in the *OB*. There, he claimed they returned to the vessel "with 2500 eggs!" *OB* III, p. 144.

60. *OB* III, p. 144; *OB* II, p. 525.

61. Audubon (2006), p. 424; *AHJ* I, pp. 412–413.

CHAPTER 12 BRAS D'OR, LABRADOR

1. The date of the *Ripley*'s departure from Portage Bay is erroneously given in Lucy's biography as July 26. L. Audubon (1869), p. 341. It was, in fact, July 25, as reflected in Maria's edition of the journal. Audubon (2006), p. 424; *AHJ* I, p. 413. This is confirmed by Shattuck, who informed his father in a

letter dated August 5, 1833, that they had arrived at Bras d'Or, which he anglicized as Bradore, on "Friday July 24." Shattuck confused the calendar date, Friday being actually July 26. However, he mentioned that they had left their previous port the day before. GCSJr to GCS, Boston, 5 Aug. 1833 (MHS, Vol. 11, 1–8 Aug. 1833).

2. Audubon (2006), p. 424; *AHJ* I, p. 413; L. Audubon (1869), p. 341. Audubon told his journal that Chevalier's settlement at St. Paul's River was forty-seven miles up the coast from their anchorage at Portage Bay. In fact, as Google Earth reflects, it is around seventy.

3. Audubon (2006), pp. 424–425; *AHJ* I, p. 413.

4. L. Audubon (1869), p. 341. Cf. Audubon (2006), p. 424; *AHJ* I, p. 413 ("it rain and blew").

5. *OB* III, pp. 142–143.

6. L. Audubon (1869), p. 341. Cf. Audubon (2006), pp. 424–425; *AHJ* I, p. 413 ("The coast we have followed is like that we have hitherto seen, crowded with islands of all sizes and forms, against which the raging waves break in a frightful manner."). In his journal, Audubon indicated that the Ripley arrived at Bonne Espérance, where Chevalier's settlement was situated at Esquimaux River (now St. Paul's River (Rivière-Saint-Paul)), at "eight" without specifying whether it was in the morning or the evening. However, the distance between Portage Bay and Bonne Espérance—about seventy miles according to Google Earth—was far too great for the schooner to have covered it in three or so hours. Clearly, it must have been 8:00 p.m.

7. Audubon (2006), p. 425; *AHJ* I, p. 413; L. Audubon (1869), pp. 341–342; Bayfield (1837), pp. 174–175.

8. OB II, p. 570.

9. Bayfield (1837), p. 173.

10. Audubon (2006), p. 426; *AHJ* I, p. 415.

11. Audubon (2006), p. 425; *AHJ* I, p. 413; L. Audubon (1869), p. 342; *OB* II, p. 570.

12. Audubon (2006), p. 425; *AHJ* I, p. 413. Cf. L. Audubon (1869), p. 342 ("and we found here a flotilla of one hundred and fifty sails, principally fore-and-aft schooners, and mostly from Halifax and the eastern parts of the United States.").

13. Audubon (2006), p. 426; *AHJ* I, p. 415; L. Audubon (1869), p. 344. Audubon indicated that ice had filled the harbor at Bras d'Or two weeks

prior to the *Ripley*'s arrival. See also, Bayfield (1984) I, p. 305.

14. Belvin (2006), p. 82.

15. Audubon (2006), p. 425; *AHJ* I, p. 414; L. Audubon (1869), p. 342; *OB* II, pp. 522–527.

16. Belvin (2006), p. 83; Bayfield (1984) I, p. 236; Bayfield (1837), p. 174.

17. Audubon (2006), p. 425; *AHJ* I, pp. 413–414; L. Audubon (1869), p. 342; OB II, p. 570.

18. L. Audubon (1869), p. 342. "Billingsgate slang" was a coarse form of English commonly heard at Billingsgate, the site of London's fish market on the north side of the River Thames between London Bridge and Tower Bridge.

19. L. Audubon (1869), p. 344; *OB* II, p. 159. In her edition of the journal, Maria omitted any reference to the rotting seal carcasses on shore, which greeted the *Ripley* when it arrived in Bradore Harbor, no doubt disgusted by the very thought.

20. Audubon (2006), pp. 425–426; *AHJ* I, pp. 414–415.

21. Audubon (2006), p. 425; *AHJ* I, p. 414; L. Audubon (1869), p. 342. Lucy's biography indicates that Audubon accompanied the young men to shore after breakfast on the morning they arrived at Bras d'Or. Maria's edition, on the other hand, states that he stayed aboard to draw the images of the female White-winged Crossbills. In this instance, I have opted to accept Maria's version of events given the details she provides of the Young Gentlemen's visit to Capt. Jones's fishing station and of their subsequent excursion inland.

Capt. William Randall Jones was born on January 27, 1790, in Liverpool, Nova Scotia. He married Mary Sophia Chevalier, the daughter of Louis Chevalier of Esquimaux River, and had twelve children. Belvin (2006), p. 79; Ancestry.com, http://records.ancestry.com/William_Randall_Jones_records.ashx?pid=39559210 (accessed 8 Apr. 2014). Audubon scholars Michael Harwood and Mary Durant, who visited Bras d'Or (Bradore) while following in Audubon's footsteps for their book *On the Road with John James Audubon*, spoke with Jones's distant descendants and were informed that the captain was actually born in Wales, not Nova Scotia. Durant & Harwood (1980), p. 452. However, this conflicts with the generally accepted genealogy for the Jones family.

22. Audubon (2006), p. 425; *AHJ* I, p. 414.

23. Audubon (2006), pp. 425–426; *AHJ* I, pp. 414–415.

24. Audubon (2006), p. 426; *AHJ* I, pp. 414–415.

25. Audubon (2006), p. 426; *AHJ* I, p. 415.

26. *OB* I, pp. 58–62; Audubon (July 1828), pp. 115–120. In Audubon's written account of the Bird of Washington, he did not provide the date he succeeded in collecting a specimen of this large, uniformly brown eagle near Henderson, KY. However, he stated that he saw a pair of the species at the Falls of the Ohio the following January. We know that Audubon was living in the Louisville area in January 1820, and it seems likely he made this observation at that time. Consequently, we can approximate the date he collected the specimen as 1819.

27. Buehler (2000), p. 2; Weidensaul (1996), pp. 52–54.

28. Parkes (1985), p. 88. In 1875, three of the finest ornithologists in America, Spencer F. Baird, Thomas Brewer, and Robert Ridgway, wrote of Audubon's Washington Eagle:

The "Bird of Washington" of Audubon was, without the least doubt, a very large immature female, in about the second year: the discrepancies between Audubon's figure and description, and the real characters of the young Bald Eagle, are very probably the result of carelessness and faulty memory; the stretch of wing of "10 feet 2 inches" is, no doubt, an exaggeration; and the peculiar scutellation of the tarsus, as exhibited in his plate, was as certainly caused by this portion of the figure being worked up from memory. The probability is also that the description was made up, or at least very much added to, from this plate, as there is no record of Audubon's specimens having been preserved. It is by no means strange that persons should consider these large grayish Eagles a different species from the smaller white-headed ones, since their proportions are as different as their colors; and throughout the country, unscientific people, and among them experienced hunters, distinguish the three stages described above as the "bald," "big gray," and "black" Eagles. Nothing is more certain, however, than that all are only different stages of one and the same bird.

Baird (1875) III, p. 329. In an accompanying table, the authors showed that the measurements of the wing and tail of the juvenile Bald Eagle generally exceeded those of the adults. Today, ornithologists commonly agree that Audubon's published measurements were faulty and that the Washington Eagle was simply a large, immature northern Bald Eagle. Palmer (1988), p. 193.

29. Peterson & Peterson (1981), Plate 106 commentary; Murphy (1956), p. 336; Mengel (1953), pp. 148–149.

30. Buehler (2000), pp. 2, 28–29.

31. Souder (2004), pp. 159–161; Palmer (1988), pp. 192–193; Stalmaster (1987), p. 15, Table 3.1; Audubon *OB* (1831) I, p. 62; Audubon (July 1828), p. 119. Based upon Audubon's measurements taken of the bird that he collected near Henderson in 1819, it is clear that his male Bird of Washington was significantly larger than even the largest female Bald Eagles, which hail from Alaska:

	Bald Eagle (Juvenile Female)	Bald Eagle (Adult Female)	Bird of Washington (Adult Male)
Weight	9.61–12.69 lbs.	10.20–14.10 lbs.	14.5 lbs.
Length	3′ 1.36″ (avg.)	2′ 11.87″ (avg.)	3′ 7″
Wingspan	7′ 11.50″ (largest)	7′ 3.05″ (avg.)	10′ 2″

In 2003, Audubon biographer William Souder took measurements of Audubon's Washington Eagle from the original Havell print in the Double Elephant Folio held by the James Ford Bell Museum of Natural History in Minneapolis and compared them to the same measurements of Audubon's immature and adult male Bald Eagle from Havell Prints 126 and 31, respectively. Souder (2004), pp. 160–161 and notes, pp. 323–324. Here again, the size disparity between the Bald Eagle and the Washington Eagle is substantial:

	Bald Eagle (Juvenile)	Bald Eagle (Adult Male)	Bird of Washington (Adult Male)
Length	>34″	30¾″	40″
Longest Toe	2¾″	3″	4″
Folded Wing	23⅝″	24″	29½″

32. Maruna (2006); Souder (2004), p. 159.

33. Murphy (1956), p. 346.

34. Souder (2004), p. 159. See also, Maruna (2006).

35. Cf. Buehler (2000), pp. 28–29; *OB* I, p. 62–63; Audubon (July 1828), pp. 119–120.

36. Maruna (2006); Mengel (1953), pp. 148–149.

37. *OB* II, pp. 464–466; *OB* I, pp. 166–167. Audubon illustrated an immature Bald Eagle for *BOA*, which was published as Havell Plate 126. This bird, showing a good degree of white in the tail, would be a two- to three-year-old bird. Peterson & Peterson (1981), Plate 108 commentary. It should be noted that Audubon scholar Edward Dwight erroneously states that the immature bird in Havell Plate 126 would be younger than that of the Washington Eagle in Plate 11. Rather, the all-brown Washington Eagle would be the earliest plumage phase, followed by the young bird in Plate 126. The adult Bald Eagle, illustrated in Plate 31, obtains its distinctive white head and tail in its fourth or fifth year. Sibley (2014), p. 143.

38. Maruna (2006); Souder (2004), p. 158.

39. *OB* I, p. 58; Audubon (1828a), pp. 115–116. In a paper he wrote for John C. Loudon's natural history magazine in 1828 as well as in his species account in the *OB*, Audubon said that he had first observed the Bird of Washington while ascending the upper Mississippi River in February 1814. However, as Audubon scholar John Francis McDermott notes, this date would appear to be in error. Audubon indicated elsewhere that he first saw the species in the vicinity of Grand Tower, a physical landmark located about thirty miles above Cape Girardeau, MO. JJA, Ohio River to My Dearest Beloved Friends, Minnie's Land, 23 Mar. 1843, McDermott (1965), p. 34, note 26. The trip he appears to have been referring to was his trading voyage with Ferdinand Rozier in the winter of 1810–1811. He would have reached Grand Tower in February 1811 (not January 1811 as McDermott asserts), after the ice

on the Mississippi had broken up and his party was able to pole their keelboat up the river past Cape Girardeau. Audubon (1828), pp. 104, 115, 120–121. See also, Chapter 1, note 79, *supra*.

40. *OB* I, pp. 58–60; Audubon (July 1828), pp. 117–118.

41. Audubon (1966) II, Plate 228; Audubon (July 1828), pp. 119–120.

42. *OB* I, p. 61; Audubon (July 1828), p. 119. Though Audubon did not identify the year he collected a Washington Eagle near Henderson, KY, it appears that it was in 1819. See note 26, *supra*.

43. *OB* I, p. 61; Audubon (July 1828), p. 119. In his species account for the Bird of Washington, which was published in 1831, Audubon wrote that his last observation of the bird occurred on November 15, 1821, as he was approaching the mouth of the Ohio River. Souder repeats this claim, which is obviously an error. Souder (2004), p. 158. Audubon was in New Orleans in November 1821. He was clearly referring to the trip he took by flatboat down the Ohio and Mississippi Rivers in the fall of 1820. Audubon (1999), p. 19; Corning (1929a), p. 28.

44. Maruna (2006). It bears noting that in 1837, during an expedition along the Gulf Coast, Audubon reported to his friend John Bachman that "the *Bird of Washington* is found pretty abundant on the Lakes near New Orleans." JJA, Island of Barataria, Grande Terre to John Bachman, Charleston, 6 Apr. 1837, *Letters* II, p. 159. However, this was hearsay from a cousin of former (and future) Louisiana Governor Andre B. Roman.

45. Low (2002), pp. 34–35.

46. Audubon (1966) II, Plate 228. The original painting of the Washington Eagle that Robert Havell Jr. engraved has a notation, "Drawn from Nature by John J. Audubon New Orleans 1822." This was actually a collage. Audubon cut out the image, which was done using a combination of pencil, pastel, watercolor, and ink, and pasted it onto another sheet of paper.

47. Nuttall (1832), pp. 67–69.

48. Ibid., p. 69.

49. Audubon (2006), p. 426; *AHJ* I, p. 415.

50. Buehler (2000), p. 1; *OB* II, p. 162. It is puzzling that none of the people Audubon spoke to at Bras d'Or were familiar with the Bald Eagle. If the Washington Eagle seen by his companions was indeed simply an example of a recently fledged Bald Eagle, one would think that adults with their conspicuous white heads would have been observed from time to time.

51. Audubon (2006), p. 426; *AHJ* I, p. 415; *OB* II, p. 157. See also, Ancestry.com, Stanley/Jones Family Tree, http://records.ancestry.com/William _Randall_Jones_records.ashx?pid=39559210 (accessed 27 Apr. 2014). There is a discrepancy between Maria's edition of the journal and the account of Audubon's first meeting with Capt. Jones laid out in his Episode entitled "Labrador." In the former, the naturalist visited the captain's abode later in the day after his young colleagues had stopped in that morning. In the latter, he was accompanied by his companions for what would appear to have been the first visit to Jones's home. The text adopts Maria's version of events given the frequency with which factual inaccuracies appear in the *OB*.

52. *OB* II, p. 158.

53. L. Audubon (1869), p. 344; *OB* II, pp. 157–158.

54. *OB* II, p. 158.

55. Ibid.

56. Ibid.

57. Audubon (2006), p. 426; *AHJ* I, p. 415; Bayfield (1837), p. 175.

58. Ibid. In Lucy's biography, the events of July 27 are given a date of July 28 and are combined with Maria's description of some of the events of July 28. The text has adopted Maria's chronology in large part because the weather given in her transcription of her grandfather's entries closely tracks that being described by Capt. Henry Bayfield in his journal. On July 28, the *Gulnare* left Wapitiguan Harbor, approximately 135 miles from Bras d'Or. Bayfield (1984) I, p. 250.

59. Audubon (2006), pp. 426–427; *AHJ* I, pp. 415–416.

60. *OB* III, pp. 308–309.

61. Audubon (2006), p. 427; *AHJ* I, p. 416; *OB* II, p. 158.

62. Ibid., pp. 158–159.

63. *OB* IV, p. 483; *OB* II, p. 531.

64. Audubon (2006), pp. 427–428; *AHJ* I, pp. 416–417; L. Audubon (1869), pp. 342–343. Both Lucy's biography and Maria's edition of the journal recount Capt. Jones's description of using Esquimaux dogs under the same date, July 27. However, Lucy's dates are off by one day. See note 58, *supra*. She would have this discussion taking place on the same day the *Ripley* arrived at Bras d'Or Harbor. Maria indicated that it occurred on the following day in connection with Capt. Jones's visit to and dinner aboard the American schooner. The text adopts Maria's version of events.

65. L. Audubon (1869), p. 343. Cf. Audubon (2006), p. 427; *AHJ* I, p. 416 ("The leader is always a well-broken dog, and is placed ahead of the pack with a draught-line of from six to ten fathoms' length, and the rest with gradually shorter ones, to the last, which is about eight feet from the sledge; they are not, however, coupled, as often represented in engravings, but are each attached separately, so that when in motion they are more like a flock of Partridges, all flying loosely and yet in the same course.").

66. Audubon (2006), p. 427; *AHJ* I, pp. 416–417; L. Audubon (1869), p. 343.

67. L. Audubon (1869), pp. 343–344. See also, Audubon (2006), p. 428; *AHJ* I, p. 417. While both Lucy and Maria refer to the tragic tale of Capt. Jones's fourteen-year-old son who died in a snowstorm, note that Lucy's biography asserts that the boy froze to death whereas Maria's edition of the journal states that he died from starvation. Given the weeks required for one to starve to death, it would seem that Maria altered the tale to provide a cause of death that she apparently found more palatable than hypothermia.

68. Genealogical information on the family of Capt. William Randall Jones can be found on Ancestry.com, http://records.ancestry.com/william _randall_jones_records.ashx?pid=39559210 (accessed 27 Apr. 2014); Ancestry.com, Stanley/ Jones Family Tree, http://trees.ancestry.com/tree /36475329/person/18940952341 (accessed 27 Apr.

2014). See also, Local Genealogy Sources, http://
www.rootsweb.ancestry.com/~qclns/family_trees
.html (accessed 27 Apr. 2014).

69. Audubon (2006), pp. 426–427; *AHJ* I, pp.
415–416; L. Audubon (1869), pp. 344–345. I am
convinced that John's excursion to Blanc Sablon
occurred on July 27, as Maria's edition of the journal indicates, not July 28 as Audubon stated in the
OB. The weather described for the day of the excursion — "a tremendous gale" — is consistent with that
recorded by Capt. Bayfield for the 27th. Bayfield
(1984) I, p. 250; *OB* IV, pp. 103, 271. See also, note
75, *infra*.

70. Audubon *OB* (1838), Vol. IV, p. 271. Glen
Chilton, Ph.D., a Canadian ornithologist who is the
world's leading authority on the extinct Labrador
Duck, does not believe that John W. Audubon actually found the nest of this species during his excursion to Blanc Sablon. In his 2009 book, *The Curse of
the Labrador Duck: My Obsessive Quest to the Edge
of Extinction* (New York: Simon & Schuster, 2009),
Chilton asserts that Audubon's account of his son's
discovery was "written many years after the voyage"
and was contradicted by Audubon's own contemporaneous journal entry. Coupled with Audubon's
predilection to shade the truth from time to time,
he writes: "Sadly, I am forced to conclude that
neither Audubon nor his son ever saw a Labrador
Duck nest, and in writing the account to accompany
his painting of the duck, he relied on his memory
rather than his field notes. This is a lot more polite
than saying he made the whole damned thing up."
Chilton (2009), pp. 18–19.

The evidence, however, does not support
Chilton. To begin with, Audubon's species account
of the Labrador Duck, which includes a reference to
John's discovery of the nests near Blanc Sablon, was
written for Volume IV of the *OB*, published in Edinburgh in 1838, only five years after the expedition.
OB IV, p. 271. Audubon customarily used his notes
and journals when authoring these pieces, as he did
in this case. Contrary to Chilton's claim, he was not
relying solely on his memory.

Moreover, I see no conflict whatsoever between
Audubon's species account and his journal entry,
as Chilton does. In Maria's edition of the journal,
Audubon wrote under the date of July 28, 1833:

"The Pied Duck [Labrador Duck] breeds here on
top of the low bushes, but the season is so far advanced we have not found its nest." Chilton reads
this as an explicit admission "that he and his party
did not find Labrador Duck nests in Blanc Sablon."
Chilton (2009), p. 19. I read this sentence entirely
differently.

The first part of Audubon's statement — "The
Pied Duck breeds here on top of the low bushes" —
reports the information John obtained from his informant in Blanc Sablon, namely that these ducks
nested locally on the top of low fir-bushes. This is
fully consistent with the species account in the *OB*,
where Audubon wrote: "Although no birds of this
species occurred to me when I was in Labrador, my
son, John, and the young friends who accompanied
him on the 28th of July to Blanc Sablon, found,
placed on the top of the low tangled fir-bushes, several deserted nests, which from the report of the
English clerk of the fishing establishment there, we
learned to belong to the Pied Duck." *OB* IV, p. 271.

In the next phrase — "but the season is so far advanced we have not found its nest" — Audubon was
saying that they had not found an *active* nest because it was too late in the season. If consistency between Audubon's journal and his species account is
the hallmark of truth, as Chilton evidently believes,
then Audubon's statement that the birds nested in
the vicinity on the tops of low firs is presumably
accurate because it appears in both sources. If so,
then the empty nests could not have been hard to
find. What Audubon's party was unable to do was
locate a nest where a female was still brooding given
the lateness of the season.

If there is a basis to challenge Audubon's statement, it is not for the reasons Chilton gives. Rather,
it is because Audubon's information came solely
from the clerk of the fishing station, and the naturalist offered no foundation for this man's knowledge.
We do not know if he could distinguish a Labrador Duck from any other species. Chilton notes
that other ornithologists have raised doubts about
Audubon's report because of the similarity between
his description of the nests and those of the Common Eider, a species that could be confused with
the Labrador Duck by someone without an intimate
knowledge of birds. Chilton (1997), p. 5. This would

be a legitimate reason for doubting the claim. However, it is a far cry from Chilton's conclusion that Audubon's memory was faulty.

Chilton's description of Audubon's Labrador trip is also fraught with errors, which provides additional grounds to question his scholarship. He states that the party left Eastport on June 4 when in actuality it was June 6. Chilton (2009), p. 11. He indicates that one of Audubon's goals during the voyage was to find Labrador Ducks so that he could paint them for *The Birds of America*. Ibid., p. 10. Audubon was certainly interested in learning more about the biology and behavior of these birds because he would shortly have to begin describing them for science and his subscribers in the pages of his letterpress. However, it is relatively clear that he had, in fact, already illustrated the Labrador Duck from a pair that had been sent to him the prior fall by U.S. Senator Daniel Webster. See Chapter 2, note 277, *supra*. Chilton also asserts that the *Ripley* sailed to Blanc Sablon when Audubon's journal clearly states that his son's company made the trek on foot. Chilton (2009), p. 12. Finally, Chilton mistakenly conflates Audubon's past economic difficulties in Henderson with his financial standing as of 1833 and jokes that the expedition gave the naturalist a three-month respite from his creditors' "past due" notices. Ibid., p. 11. In 1833, Audubon was juggling revenue and expenses as he continued to personally finance his enormous publishing venture. But he was certainly not a deadbeat as Chilton suggests. Although Nicholas Berthoud had recently raised the issue of the old Kentucky debts, Audubon did not sail for Labrador being hounded by creditors.

71. Ford (1988). pp. 302–303; Audubon (1966) II, Plate 305; *OB* IV, p. 271. See Chapter 2, note 277, *supra*.

72. Audubon (1966) II, Plate 305.

73. *OB* IV, p. 271.

74. Chilton (1997), pp. 1, 3, 6–7.

75. L. Audubon (1869), p. 345. Maria's version of the journal is at odds with the text, which is derived from Lucy's biography. Maria's journal recounts that the heavy seas which followed the gale that descended on Bras d'Or on July 27 were present on the morning of July 28. Audubon (2006), p. 428; *AHJ* I, p. 417. Lucy says that the seas were high on the evening of July 28, but her

entry is misdated—it should be July 27. The text adopts Lucy's version with the corrected date because it squares with the journal of Capt. Bayfield, who recorded in his journal on July 27 that it was a "Fine night & Calm, heavy surf on the Rocks outside the harbor." Bayfield (1984) I, p. 250. Although Bayfield was back with the *Gulnare* in Wapitiguan Harbor, his description of the weather during this time period dovetails nicely with that generally given by Audubon, suggesting that, notwithstanding their distance, they were subject to the same weather fronts. It would appear that Maria moved this description of the weather and its impact on the naturalist's stomach to the journal entry of the following day.

76. Bayfield (1984) I, p. 250.

77. Audubon (2006), p. 428; *AHJ* I, p. 417.

78. L. Audubon (1869), p. 345. Cf. Audubon (2006), p. 428; *AHJ* I, p. 417. In Maria's edition of the journal, Audubon entreated Capt. Jones's men to make some "Esquimaux boots and garments" for members of the expedition. Lucy indicated that this petition was made to the chief of the local Native Americans. The rebuff the naturalist received makes more sense if it came from the Native Americans rather than from Capt. Jones's men.

Although Lucy's account would suggest that these natives were Esquimaux, Tom Lincoln wrote in his journal that they did not encounter "a single one" over the course of the expedition. Townsend (1924), p. 240. Therefore, they must have been Montagnais, now known as Innu, which were the predominant Native Americans inhabiting this portion of the Labrador coast. Belvin (2006), p. 19.

79. L. Audubon (1869), p. 345. There is yet another discrepancy between the two versions of the journal as to whom Audubon spoke at Bras d'Or about obtaining a guide to lead a small group of the *Ripley*'s company inland. Whereas Lucy's biography states that the inquiry was made to the chief of the local tribe, Maria's version asserts that it was directed to Capt. Jones, who had a son "of about twenty-three" that might have been willing. Audubon (2006), p. 428; *AHJ* I, p. 417. The text adopts Lucy's account because, according to the Jones family genealogy, Capt. Jones did not have a twenty-three-year-old son. His eldest son, Louis Lloyd Jones, was then only sixteen. Ancestry.com, http://

records.ancestry.com/william_randall_jones
_records.ashx?pid=39559210 (accessed 27 Apr.
2014); Ancestry.com, Stanley/Jones Family Tree,
http://trees.ancestry.com/tree/36475329/person
/18940952341 (accessed 27 Apr. 2014).

80. L. Audubon (1869), p. 345.

81. Audubon (2006), p. 428; *AHJ* I, pp. 417–418;
L. Audubon (1869), p. 345.

82. L. Audubon (1869), p. 345. Cf. Audubon
(2006), p. 428; *AHJ* I, p. 418 ("I am glad that it is in
my power to make a figure of these birds in summer,
winter, and young plumage.").

83. Audubon (2006), p. 428; *AHJ* I, p. 418;
L. Audubon (1869), p. 345.

84. L. Audubon (1869), p. 345. Cf. Audubon
(2006), p. 428; *AHJ* I, p. 418 ("it was placed on the
moss among the grass, close to the water; it contained feathers, but no down as others.").

85. L. Audubon (1869), pp. 345–346. Cf. Audubon (2006), p. 428; *AHJ* I, p. 418 ("but I begged for
its life, and we left it in the care of its mother, and of
its Maker.").

86. *OB* III, pp. 355–356.

87. *OB* IV, pp. 103–104. According to Audubon's
species account for the Long-tailed Duck, he personally collected the young birds during an excursion on Sunday, July 28, 1833, because the "Young
Gentlemen" had left for Blanc Sablon that morning
and John had taken his pointer, Dash, with them.
As indicated in note 69, *supra*, I believe the trip
to Blanc Sablon took place the day before and that
Audubon's companions had returned to the *Ripley*
by that evening.

88. Audubon (1966) II, Plate 229.

89. LBA, New York to JJA, Eastport, 28 Jul.
1833 (Yale, Box 15, Folder 693). See also, LBA, New
York to VGA, London, 31 Jul. 1833 (Yale, Box 1,
Folder 20).

90. Audubon (2006), p. 429; *AHJ* I, p. 418;
L. Audubon (1869), p. 346.

91. L. Audubon (1869), p. 346. Cf. Audubon
(2006), p. 429; *AHJ* I, p. 419 ("When all our party
is present, music, anecdotes, and jokes, journalizing
and comparing notes, make the time pass merrily;").

92. Audubon (2006), p. 429; *AHJ* I, p. 419;
L. Audubon (1869), p. 346.

93. Audubon (2006), p. 429; *AHJ* I, p. 419;
L. Audubon (1869), p. 346; *OB* III, pp. 118–119.

94. *OB* IV, p. 81.

95. Audubon (2006), p. 429; *AHJ* I, p. 419.
In the 2006 edition of Audubon's journal edited
by Richard Rhodes, he mistakenly substitutes the
common name "Brown Phalarope" for the Latin
name *Phalaropus hyperboreus* appearing in Maria's
edition. In fact, *Phalaropus hyperboreus* was the
Hyperborean Phalarope, now known as the Red-
necked Phalarope. There are only three species of
phalarope found in North America: the Red-necked
Phalarope, Wilson's Phalarope, and Red Phalarope.
Peterson (2008), pp. 166–167. Audubon knew them
all, the latter two by the same names they are called
today. *OB* III, pp. 118–121, 400–407. None of the
birds were known as the Brown Phalarope. Audubon (1839), pp. 238–241.

96. Audubon (2006), p. 429; *AHJ* I, p. 419.

97. Audubon (2006), p. 429–430; *AHJ* I, pp.
419–420; Hebert (1849) II, pp. 276–282.

98. Audubon (2006), pp. 429–430; *AHJ* I, pp.
419–420.

99. Audubon (2006), pp. 429–430; *AHJ* I, pp.
419–420; *OB* III, pp. 69–70.

100. L. Audubon (1869), p. 347. Cf. Audubon
(2006), p. 430; *AHJ* I, p. 420 ("such a thing as a
beautiful morning in this mournful country almost
amounts to a phenomenon.").

101. Audubon (2006), p. 430; *AHJ* I, pp. 420–
421.

102. Audubon (2006), p. 430; *AHJ* I, p. 420;
L. Audubon (1869), p. 347.

103. L. Audubon (1869), p. 347; *OB* II, p. 159.

104. Audubon (2006), pp. 430–431; *AHJ* I,
pp. 420–421; Bayfield (1837), pp. 245–246; *OB* III,
p. 396; *OB* II, p.456.

105. Audubon (2006), p. 430; *AHJ* I, pp. 420–
421.

106. Bayfield (1984) I, p. 251.

107. Audubon (2006), p. 431; *AHJ* I, p. 421.

108. Bayfield (1984) I, p. 251; Audubon (2006),
p. 431; *AHJ* I, p. 421; L. Audubon (1869), p. 347.

109. Bayfield (1984) I, pp. 250–252.

110. LBA, New York to VGA, London, 31
Jul.1833 (Yale, Box 1, Folder 20).

111. Ibid. According to Lucy's July 31 letter to
Victor, Alexander and Ann Gordon had arrived at
the Berthouds' the day before, July 30. However, in
her letter to her husband of July 28, she indicated

that they had arrived the previous evening, which would have been July 27. LBA, New York to JJA, Eastport, 28 Jul. 1833 (Yale, Box 15, Folder 693). The only possible explanation for the conflict is that Lucy began writing her letter to Victor on July 28 but did not date it until she finished it on July 31.

112. JJA, Charleston to VGA, London, 4 Nov. 1833, *Letters* I, p. 266; LBA, New York to VGA, London, 31 Jul. 1833 (Yale, Box 1, Folder 20). In her letter to Victor, Lucy stated that Henry Ward had been "discharged from the Philoso. Society of Charleston." She was referring to the museum of the Literary and Philosophical Society of South Carolina, now the Charleston Museum. Mazÿck (1908), pp. 8–10. Lucy also gave the Latin name of the two hawks that Henry Ward had brought with him to New York as "falco Temearies." It was actually "Falco temerarius," the Latin name given to Audubon's "Le Petit Caporal" (Havell Plate 75), which he subsequently determined was actually a Pigeon Hawk (Merlin), a small, dark-plumaged falcon. Audubon (1839), pp. 16–17; *OB* V, p. 368.

113. LBA, New York to VGA, London, 31 Jul. 1833 (Yale, Box 1, Folder 20).

114. Audubon (2006), p. 431; *AHJ* I, p. 421.

115. Peterson (2007), pp. 212–213; Dunne (2006), p.250.

116. Audubon (1966) II, Plate 241.

117. Dunne (2006), pp. 250–251.

118. Audubon (2006), p. 431; *AHJ* I, p. 421; L. Audubon (1869), p. 347; *OB* III, p. 396.

119. Audubon (2006), p. 431; *AHJ* I, p. 421; L. Audubon (1869), pp. 347–348.

120. L. Audubon (1869), pp. 347. Cf. Audubon (2006), p. 431; *AHJ* I, p. 421 ("it looks like a large man-of-war dressed in light green muslin, instead of canvas, and when the sun strikes it, it glitters with intense brilliancy. When these transient monuments of the sea happen to tumble or roll over, the fall is tremendous, and the sound produced resembles that of loud, distant thunder;").

121. Bayfield (1984) I, pp. 251–252.

122. Havell Plate 253.

123. L. Audubon (1869), p. 348. Cf. Audubon (2006), p. 431; *AHJ* I, pp. 421–422 ("a last thorough search").

124. L. Audubon (1869), p. 348. Cf. Audubon (2006), p. 431; *AHJ* I, pp. 422 ("blessed will the day be when I land on those dear shores, where all I long for in the world exists and lives, I hope.").

125. Audubon (2006), p. 431; *AHJ* I, pp. 422.

126. Audubon (2006), p. 431; *AHJ* I, pp. 422; L. Audubon (1869), p. 348.

127. Audubon (2006), p. 431; Willcomb (1902), p. 70; *AHJ* I, pp. 422. In comparison to the *Wizard*, the *Ripley*, at 106 tons burden, was approximately seventy-one feet in length, eighteen in breadth, and eight deep. Kinney (1989), p. 97. See also, Chapter 4, note 138, *supra*, for a discussion of the formula for calculating the tonnage of vessels of that day. If the *Wizard* was 105 tons despite being slightly longer and broader than the *Ripley*, the only feasible explanation is that its hold was not as deep.

128. Willcomb (1902), pp. 66, 70, 77. Capt. William Willcomb (1797–1852) was born on September 7, 1797, in Ipswich, MA. His second son, John Edward Willcomb, died in infancy in January 1832. The house on High Street in Ipswich in which Willcomb lived with his family until his death in 1852 had been acquired by his great-grandfather Joseph Willcomb around 1737. Ibid. p. 37.

129. Fries (1973), p. 159; JJA, Bras d'Or, Labrador to LBA, New York, 5 Aug. 1833 (Princeton, Box 2, Folder 24), *Letters* I, p. 240. According to Audubon's letter to his wife of August 5, Capt. William Willcomb had seen Audubon's Ipswich subscriber, William Oakes, a fortnight before, which would have been on July 22. It appears that Willcomb set sail from Boston on July 24 in light of Audubon's statement that nine days later, on August 2, the *Wizard* arrived at Bras d'Or.

130. Audubon (2006), pp. 431–432; *AHJ* I, pp. 422.

131. Audubon (2006), p. 431; *AHJ* I, pp. 422; L. Audubon (1869), p. 348.

132. L. Audubon (1869), p. 348. Cf. Audubon (2006), p. 431; *AHJ* I, pp. 422 ("we learned with pleasure that our great cities are all healthy").

133. Audubon (2006), p. 431; Bayfield (1984) I, p. 253; *AHJ* I, pp. 422; L. Audubon (1869), p. 348.

134. Audubon (2006), p. 432; *AHJ* I, p. 422. Cf. L. Audubon (1869), p. 348 ("especially of the lesser species").

135. *OB* II, p. 146.

136. *OB* III, p. 345.

137. Audubon (2006), p. 432; *AHJ* I, p. 422. See also L. Audubon (1869), p. 348.

138. Audubon (2006), p. 432; *AHJ* I, p. 422. Capt. Bayfield, whose schooner remained anchored in Forteau Bay on August 3, recorded in his journal that there were "Strong breezes & very heavy squalls and rain, wind between West & SW, [and] a heavy swell setting into the bay." Bayfield (1984) I, p. 253.

139. *OB* III, p. 396.

140. Audubon (2006), p. 432; *AHJ* I, p. 423.

141. Gill (1998), pp. 1, 4–5, 8–9; Gollop (1986) pp. 35–37.

142. Audubon (2006), p. 432; *AHJ* I, p. 423.

143. Audubon (2006), p. 432; *AHJ* I, p. 423. While Audubon recorded a steady rain on Sunday, August 4, Capt. Bayfield, still moored in Forteau Bay, noted "Light breezes from SE to South with Fog at times." Bayfield (1984) I, p, 253.

144. Audubon (2006), p. 432; *AHJ* I, p. 423.

145. Audubon (1966) II, Plate 291.

146. Rough-legged Falcon (Rough-legged Hawk), Audubon (1966) I, Plate 49 (Havell Plate 166); Marsh Hawk (Northern Harrier), Audubon (1966) I; Plate 124 (Havell Plate 356); Great Footed Hawk (Peregrine Falcon), Audubon (1966) II, Plate 315 (Havell Plate 16).

147. Black Backed Gull (Great Black-backed Gull), Audubon (1966), Vol. II, Plate 226 (Havell Plate 241); Golden-Eye Duck (Common Golden-eye), Plate No. 248 (Havell Plate 342).

148. Gill (1998), pp. 1–2, 16–17, 19–21.

149. The Eskimo Curlew was officially listed as endangered in the United States in 1967. Gill (1998), p. 17. It was added to the Canadian list of endangered species in 1980. Gollop (1986), p. 16.

150. Dunn & Alderfer (2011), p. 536.

151. Gollop (1986), pp. 15, 95.

152. Gill (1998), p. 18; Gollop (1986), pp. 30–32. During visits to the historical breeding grounds of the Eskimo Curlew in northern Canada between 1972 and 1986, the Canadian Wildlife Service search team found nesting Whimbrels, a related but larger *Numenius* species that had been uncommon in this area a hundred years earlier. Gollop *et al.* posit that the declining numbers of Eskimo Curlews, which ordinarily nested in densities sufficient to prevent encroachment by Whimbrels, enabled the larger

birds to successfully expand into this habitat. The smaller curlews would have been forced to move to more marginal breeding areas, perhaps contributing further to their population drop.

153. Gill (1998), p. 18.

154. Even today, there remains hope that at least some Eskimo Curlews survive. For a detailed, though unconfirmed, report by an experienced birder of a single bird that sounds intriguingly like an Eskimo Curlew at Peggy's Cove, Nova Scotia, on September 24, 2006, see Hoffman (2007), p. 42.

155. Audubon (2006), pp. 432–433; *AHJ* I, pp. 423–424.

156. Audubon (2006), p. 434; *AHJ* I, pp. 424–425. Rhodes's edition of the Labrador journal substitutes the common name "Rock Sandpiper" in place of the Latin name *Tringa maritima* that appears in Maria's edition. In this Rhodes is mistaken. The *Tringa maritima* of Audubon's day is today the *Calidris maritima* or Purple Sandpiper. Even Audubon knew it by this common name and referred to it as such in the *OB*. *OB* III, p. 558. The Rock Sandpiper (*Calidris ptilocnemis*) is strictly a species of western North America, breeding in Alaska and wintering along the Pacific Coast to Northern California. Sibley (2014), p. 178; Dunne (2006), p. 234.

157. Dunne (2006), p. 228; Peterson (2006), p. 158; *OB* IV, p. 182.

158. *OB* III, p. 558.

159. Dunne (2006), p. 233.

160. Audubon (2006), p. 434; *AHJ* I, pp. 424–425.

161. L. Audubon (1869), p. 349. Cf. Audubon (2006), p. 433; *AHJ* I, p. 424 ("That the Creator should have commanded millions of delicate, diminutive, tender creatures to cross immense spaces of country to all appearance a thousand times more congenial to them than this, to cause them to people, as it were, this desolate land for a time, to enliven it by the songs of the sweet feathered musicians for two months at most, and by the same command induce them to abandon it almost suddenly, is as wonderful as it is beautiful. The fruits are now ripe, yet six weeks ago the whole country was a sheet of snow, the bays locked in ice, the air a constant storm. Now the grass is rich in growth, at every step flowers are met with, insects fill the

air, the snow-banks are melting; now and then an appearance as of summer does exist, but in thirty days all is over; the dark northern clouds will enwrap the mountain summits; the rivulets, the ponds, the rivers, the bays themselves will begin to freeze; heavy snowfalls will cover all these shores, and nature will resume her sleeping state, nay, more wonderful than that, one of desolation and death. Wonderful! Wonderful!").

162. Audubon (2006), p. 434; *AHJ* I, p. 425.

163. Bayfield (1984) I, pp. 251-253.

164. Audubon (2006), p. 434; *AHJ* I, p. 425; L. Audubon (1869), p. 350.

165. GCSJr, Bradore, Labrador to GCS, Boston, 5 Aug. 1833 (MHS, Ms. N-909, Vol. 11, 1-8 Aug. 1833).

166. JJA, Bras d'Or, Labrador to LBA, New York, 5 Aug. 1833 (Princeton, Box 2, Folder 24), *Letters* I, p. 239.

167. Ibid., *Letters* I, pp. 239-240.

168. GCSJr, Bradore, Labrador to GCS, Boston, 5 Aug. 1833 (MHS, Ms. N-909, Vol. 11, 1-8 Aug. 1833).

169. Ibid.

170. Ibid. Unfortunately for Audubon scholars, the journal of the Labrador expedition kept by Shattuck Jr. was lost or destroyed at some point. Charles W. Townsend, M.D., the author of *In Audubon's Labrador*, spoke to Shattuck's son Frederick C. Shattuck, M.D., who was completely unaware of it. Townsend (1918), p. 335, note 1. It is surprising that this particular journal is missing because most of Shattuck's journals survive and are in the collection of the Harvard Medical Library in the Francis A. Countway Library of Medicine in Boston.

171. Townsend (1924), p. 239. Dr. Townsend identifies the river where John, Lincoln, and Coolidge tramped on August 6 as the one flowing into the Gulf of St. Lawrence at Blanc Sablon. However, the Blanc Sablon River is located about eight miles from the *Ripley*'s anchorage rather than the four miles Lincoln estimated. That distance would suggest it was one of two rivers at the head of Bradore Bay. The Bradore West River (now Brador West River) has a magnificent little waterfall and, in its upper reaches, is bordered by high cliffs that would match Audubon's description of it in the *OB*.

The Bradore East River (now Brador East River), on the other hand, has a larger mouth and presumably would have been marked on the charts as the larger of the two rivers. It also has a waterfall upstream. But it does not share the topographical features that Lincoln and Audubon specifically described. Christelle Fortin-Vaillancourt, Brador, Quebec (Personal communications, 23 and 26 Jul. 2012). See also, *OB* II, p. 552.

172. *OB* II, p. 552.

173. Ibid.

174. Audubon (2006), pp. 435-436; *AHJ* I, p. 427.

175. *OB* II, p. 552.

176. Audubon (2006), pp. 435-436; *AHJ* I, p. 427; *OB* II, pp. 553-554.

177. Audubon (2006), p. 436; *AHJ* I, p. 427

178. Audubon (1966) II, Plate 230.

179. *OB* II, p. 554.

180. Dunn & Alderfer (2011), p. 150; Dunne (2006), pp. 177-178; Peterson (2006), p. 122-123;

181. *OB* II, p. 554.

182. Audubon (2006), p. 435; *AHJ* I, p. 426; Bayfield (1837), p. 175; *OB* III, p. 106. Audubon did not provide the date of his visit to Peroquet Island in his journal. In the *OB*, he stated that this ramble occurred on August 12, "the day after my son procured the two Jer-falcons mentioned in the second volume of this work." However, this date is clearly in error as the *Ripley* sailed from Bras d'Or on August 11. Given the parallel reference, it appears that the excursion actually took place on August 7, the day after John collected the Labrador Falcons, as indicated in the text.

183. Bayfield (1837), p. 175; *OB* III, p. 106.

184. Audubon (2006), p. 435; *AHJ* I, pp. 426-427; *OB* III, pp. 106-107. Audubon referred to the sand eels eaten by Atlantic Puffins as lints, his likely phonetic spelling for lances since these fish are also known as sand lances.

185. Audubon (2006), p. 435; *AHJ* I, p. 426; Audubon *OB* (1835), Vol. III, pp. 106-107. In the *OB*, Audubon wrote that he spent a solid hour shooting Puffins on Peroquet Island, "always firing at a single bird on wing." He declined to estimate the number of birds he killed in this time period, but his journal entry, as edited by his granddaughter, states that the total was twenty-seven. If indeed

the birds were as thick as he described and he never had to wait to reload, one would think the number would have been far higher. It is impossible to know if this was an instance where Maria altered the actual total in order to make his conduct sound more reasonable.

186. Audubon (2006), p. 435; *AHJ* I, p. 426.

187. Audubon (2006), p. 435; *AHJ* I, p. 426.

188. Audubon (2006), p. 435; *AHJ* I, p. 427.

189. *OB* II, p. 553.

190. Townsend (1924), p. 239.

191. Audubon (2006), p. 434; *AHJ* I, p. 425; L. Audubon (1869), p. 350. It would appear that Audubon added two new drawings to his portfolio between August 5, when he informed Lucy in a letter that he had done a total of twenty-one, and August 11, when he gave a count of twenty-three to his journal. Audubon (2006), p. 437; *AHJ* I, p. 429; L. Audubon (1869), p. 360; JJA, Bras d'Or, Labrador to LBA, New York, 5 Aug. 1833 (Princeton, Box 2, Folder 24), *Letters* I, p. 239. The first was of the Labrador Falcons. There is no indication in either his journal or the *OB* as to the second subject.

192. Audubon (2006), pp. 434–435; *AHJ* I, pp. 425–426. Cf. L. Audubon (1869), p. 350 ("I now sit down to post up my poor book, while a furious gale is blowing without. I have neglected to make daily records for some days, because I have been so constantly drawing, that when night came I was too weary to wield my pen. Indeed, all my physical powers have been taxed to weariness by this little work of drawing; my neck and shoulders and most of all my fingers have ached from the fatigue; and I have suffered more from this kind of exertion than from walking sixty-five miles in a day, which I once did.").

193. VGA, Franckfort on the Main [Frankfurt] to JJA and LBA, New York, 6 Aug. 1833 (Yale, Box 2, Folder 38); VGA, Carlsrugh [Karlsruhe] to LBA, New York, 21 Jul. 1833 (Yale, Box 2, Folder 37); VGA, Paris to LBA, New York, 8 Jul. 1833 (Yale, Box 2, Folder 37). In July and August 1833, Victor toured parts of Europe seeking subscribers for *BOA*. When he began, he hoped to obtain at least six to eight along the route that was to take him through Strasbourg, Baden-Baden, Karlsruhe, Stuttgart, Heidelberg, Mannheim, Darmstadt, Frankfurt, Mainz (Mayence), Koblenz (Coblenz), and Rotter-

dam before he returned to London. While he received some expressions of interest, he had yet to obtain a single subscription when he wrote his parents on August 6. "I have lost all confidence in my powers of Procuring subscribers," he acknowledged to his father, "for tho' I have made some friends yet not one among them like the friends you so easily find wherever you go."

194. Audubon (2006), pp. 435–436; *AHJ* I, pp. 427–428.

195. *OB* III, p. 108.

196. Audubon (2006), p. 436; *AHJ* I, p. 428.

197. Audubon (2006), pp. 435–436; *AHJ* I, pp. 427–428; *OB* III, p. 70.

198. Audubon (2006), pp. 436–437; *AHJ* I, p. 428.

CHAPTER 13: NEWFOUNDLAND

1. L. Audubon (1869), p. 359. Cf. Audubon (2006), p. 437; *AHJ* I, p. 429 ("high rugged hills partly immersed in masses of the thick fog that usually hovers over them").

2. Audubon (2006), p. 437; *AHJ* I, p. 429; L. Audubon (1869), p. 360.

3. L. Audubon (1869), p. 350. Several of Audubon's biographers rely on Maria's biography of her grandfather in stating that Audubon's party returned from Labrador with only seventy-three birdskins. Rhodes (2004), p. 386; Fries (1973), p. 74; Herrick (1938) II, p. 50; *AHJ* I, p. 68. The cited portion of Lucy's biography, as originally edited by Robert Buchanan, states: "The journal gives a list of the names of one hundred and seventy-three skins of birds, which were obtained on the coast of Labrador by Audubon and his party on this expedition." L. Audubon (1869), p. 350. That this is the true number can be presumed from a statement Audubon made in a letter to Lucy on August 5: "We have not collected I believe 200 Skins of birds." JJA, Bras d'Or, Labrador to LBA, New York, 5 Aug. 1833 (Princeton, Box 2, Folder 24). Maria evidently made a typographical error.

4. Audubon (2006), p. 437; *AHJ* I, pp. 428–429. Cf. L. Audubon (1869), p. 360 ("Seldom in my life have I left a country with as little regret as this.").

5. Townsend (1924), pp. 239–240.

6. Audubon (2006), p. 437; *AHJ* I, p. 429.

7. L. Audubon (1869), p. 360. Cf. Audubon

(2006), p. 437; *AHJ* I, p. 429 ("Whether this voyage will prove a fruitful one remains to be proved.").

8. Audubon (2006), pp. 436–437; *AHJ* I, pp. 428–429; L. Audubon (1869), p. 359.

9. L. Audubon (1869), p. 359. Cf. Audubon (2006), p. 437; *AHJ* I, p. 429 ("The sea is quite smooth; at least I think so, or have become a better seaman through habit.").

10. L. Audubon (1869), p. 360. Cf. Audubon (2006), p. 437; *AHJ* I, p. 429 ("the highest land we have yet seen; in some places the scenery was highly picturesque and agreeable to the eye, though little more vegetation appeared than in Labrador.").

11. Audubon (2006), p. 437; *AHJ* I, p. 429; L. Audubon (1869), p. 360.

12. Audubon (2006), p. 437; Durant & Harwood (1980), p. 472; *AHJ* I, p. 429; L. Audubon (1869), p. 360.

13. Audubon (2006), p. 437; *AHJ* I, p. 429; L. Audubon (1869), p. 360. The distances given in the text were determined using Google Earth.

14. L. Audubon (1869), p. 360. Cf. Audubon (2006), p. 437; *AHJ* I, p. 429–430 ("A more beautiful and ample basin cannot easily be found; not an obstruction is within it. The northeast shores are high and rocky, but the southern ones are sandy, low, and flat.").

15. L. Audubon (1869), pp. 360–361. Cf., Audubon (2006), p. 438; *AHJ* I, p. 430 ("the weather was so mild that it was agreeable on deck").

16. Audubon (2006), p. 438; *AHJ* I, p. 430; L. Audubon (1869), p. 361.

17. Audubon (2006), pp. 437–438; Durant & Harwood (1980), p. 474; *AHJ* I, pp. 429–430; L. Audubon (1869), pp. 360–361. Shuler mistakenly refers to Sandy Point as St. George, Newfoundland. Shuler (1995), p. 117. Audubon indicated in his journal that the population of Sandy Point was "said to contain two hundred inhabitants," a statement that evidently came from one of the residents. Audubon (2006), p. 438; *AHJ* I, pp. 430. However, in 1836, the community census was only 112 residents, suggesting that the number Audubon had been given was likely inflated. Downer (1997), p. 18. The text relies on the count from 1836 along with Audubon's statement that there were about forty homes in the village to conclude the population exceeded one hundred in 1833.

18. L. Audubon (1869), p. 360. Cf. Audubon (2006), p. 438; *AHJ* I, p. 430 ("The village is built on an elongated point of sand, or natural sea-wall").

19. Audubon (2006), p. 438; *AHJ* I, p. 430; L. Audubon (1869), pp. 360–361.

20. Audubon (2006), p. 438; *AHJ* I, p. 430; L. Audubon (1869), p. 361. In his Episode "A Ball in Newfoundland," Audubon reported that when they first arrived at Sandy Point, they "were welcomed and supplied with abundance of fresh provisions." *OB* II, p. 212. His journal indicates otherwise, as reflected in the text. This is yet another example of the naturalist not allowing the facts to interfere with the yarn he preferred to tell his readers.

21. L. Audubon (1869), p. 361. Cf. Audubon (2006), p. 438; *AHJ* I, p. 430 ("Some tell us birds are abundant, others that there are none.").

22. L. Audubon (1869), p. 361. Cf. Audubon (2006), p. 438; *AHJ* I, p. 431 ("All ashore in search of birds, plants, shells, and all the usual *et ceteras* attached to our vocations").

23. L. Audubon (1869), p. 362; *Boston Daily Advertiser & Patriot*, Vol. XLII, No. 11,166, p. 2, cols. 4–5 (Saturday, 7 Sept. 1833)(AAS).

24. L. Audubon (1869), p. 362. Audubon's description of the homes he observed on Sandy Point, some being "miserable hovels" while others appeared to be "habitable houses," was included in Lucy's biography but is completely absent from Maria's edition of the journal.

25. Downer (1997), pp. 9, 18.

26. Ibid., p. 45.

27. L. Audubon (1869), p. 362. Maria dropped any reference in her version of the journal to the evident fear Audubon's shore party instilled in the Sandy Point women they encountered during their excursion on the second day of their visit. It is worth noting that the naturalist described this incident in his Episode "A Ball in Labrador." However, he inexplicably placed it chronologically after the *Ripley* had been anchored in the harbor for several days and the members of the party had been invited to and participated in a community dance. *OB* II, pp. 214–215. In that context, it makes no sense whatsoever.

28. Audubon acknowledged in "A Ball in Labrador" that the presence of his party in the small village of Sandy Point initially caused much consternation among the residents. However, he claimed that

this was soon addressed by Capt. Emery, who had his crew raise the American flag from the *Ripley*'s masthead, alleviating the community's concern. *OB* II, p. 212. This was clearly a factual embellishment for the sake of his readers. His journal, as published by Lucy, indicates there was deep distrust and fear, at least among the women, even the day after the *Ripley* dropped its anchor.

29. L. Audubon (1869), p. 362.

30. Deane (1910), p. 48.

31. Audubon (2006), p. 439; *AHJ* I, p. 431; *OB* IV, p. 483.

32. L. Audubon (1869), p. 361. Cf. Audubon (2006), p. 438; *AHJ* I, p. 431 ("we all were driven on board soon, by a severe storm of wind and rain, showing that Newfoundland has its share of bad weather").

33. L. Audubon (1869), p. 361. Cf. Audubon (2006), p. 438; *AHJ* I, p. 431 ("Whilst on shore we found the country quite rich compared with Labrador, all the vegetable productions being much larger, more abundant, and finer.").

34. *OB* II, p. 416. In Lucy's biography, her transcription of Audubon's journal refers to these birds as "house sparrows, all gay and singing." L. Audubon (1869), p. 361. Maria read the same passage as referring to "House Swallows." *AHJ* I, p. 431. Audubon's own statement in the *OB* that he had observed Barn Swallows in Newfoundland on August 14 would appear to clear up the confusion.

35. Audubon (2006), p. 439; *AHJ* I, p. 431.

36. Audubon (2006), p. 439; *AHJ* I, pp. 431–432; L. Audubon (1869), p. 362.

37. Audubon (2006), p. 439; *AHJ* I, p. 432.

38. Audubon (2006), p. 439; *AHJ* I, p. 432; *OB* IV, p. 175.

39. Audubon (2006), p. 439; *AHJ* I, p. 432; L. Audubon (1869), p. 362; *OB* II, p. 470.

40. Rice (1960), p. 68.

41. L. Audubon (1869), pp. 362–363. Audubon's nod to the "cleverness" of the Mi'kmaq Indians in negotiating a fair price for the fresh game they brought to the *Ripley* on the morning of August 15 is noticeably absent from Maria's edition of the journal. Instead, she simply stated that the deal they negotiated "plainly shows that these Indians know full well the value of the game which they procure." Audubon (2006), p. 439; *AHJ* I, p. 432. Maria evi-

dently preferred to discount the natives' positive character traits, a typical late 19th century attitude among white Americans.

42. Audubon (2006), p. 439; *AHJ* I, p. 432; L. Audubon (1869), p. 362; *OB* II, p. 470.

43. Small (2009), pp. 194–195; Audubon (2006), p. 439; *AHJ* I, p. 432.

44. *OB* III, pp. 20–26.

45. Audubon (2006), pp. 439–440; *AHJ* I, p. 432; L. Audubon (1869), p. 363.

46. Major (2001), pp. 28–29, 49–52; Gatschet (1885), pp. 408.

47. Major (2001), pp. 28, 144–148.

48. Major (2001), p. 145; Downer (1997), pp. 75–78.

49. Downer (1997), pp. 21, 80; Wix (1818), pp. 76–77.

50. Downer (1997), p. 21.

51. Chappell (1818), pp. 74–47, 79.

52. L. Audubon (1869), p. 363. Cf. Audubon (2006), pp. 439–440; *AHJ* I, p. 432 ("We found them, as I expected, all lying down pell-mell in their wigwams. A strong mixture of blood was apparent in their skins, shape, and deportment; some indeed were nearly white, and sorry I am to say that the nearer to our own noble selves, the filthier and lazier they are; the women and children were particularly disgusting.").

53. Small (2009), pp. 184–185; Audubon (2006), p. 440; *AHJ* I, p. 432; L. Audubon (1869), p. 363.

54. Audubon (2006), p. 440; *AHJ* I, pp. 432–433. Cf. L. Audubon (1869), p. 363 ("The Indians cook lobster by roasting them in a pile of brushwood, and eat them without any salt or other condiment.").

55. *OB* II, p. 212.

56. Audubon (2006), p. 440; *AHJ* I, pp. 432–433; L. Audubon (1869), p. 363.

57. Audubon (2006), p. 440; *AHJ* I, p. 432. Cf. L. Audubon (1869), p. 363 ("We bargained with two of the hunters to go with our young men into the interior to hunt for caraboos, hares, and partridges, which they agreed to do for a dollar a day.").

58. L. Audubon (1869), p. 363. Cf. Audubon (2006), p. 440; *AHJ* I, p. 433 ("The flesh here is held in low estimation; it tastes like poor venison.").

59. Audubon (2006), p. 440; *AHJ* I, p. 433; L. Audubon (1869), p. 363.

60. Audubon (2006), p. 440; *AHJ* I, p. 433.

61. Audubon (2006), p. 440; *AHJ* I, p. 433; *OB* II, p. 213. In "A Ball in Newfoundland," the naturalist indicated that the invitation to the dance came in the afternoon, whereas his journal would suggest it was extended later in the evening as he was finishing up his journal entry for the day. On this point, it seems more likely the journal is accurate, but since the discussion appears solely in Maria's edition, it is impossible to know for sure.

Audubon also told the readers of the *OB* that, during the discussion with the visiting group of villagers aboard the *Ripley*, the delegation supposedly mentioned their taste for rum. He claimed that they were invited to sample some of the remaining store of "Old Jamaica" aboard the *Ripley*, which "had lost nothing of its energies by having visited Labrador." *OB* II, p. 213. This was an amusing aside, but it was almost certainly untrue. Audubon knew he had a weakness for alcohol and promised Lucy he would not drink during the expedition. Coolidge recalled that Audubon had all of the liquor collected at the outset of the voyage and tossed it overboard. That would have left only the arsenic salted cask of rum that was placed onboard to preserve some of the specimens they were collecting as well as some bottles of wine that are mentioned elsewhere in the journal. See also, note 92, *infra*; Chapter 6, note 127, *supra*.

62. Chappell (1818), p. 72.

63. Audubon (2006), p. 440; *AHJ* I, p. 433.

64. *OB* II, pp. 212–213.

65. Ibid., pp. 213–214.

66. Ibid., p. 213.

67. "A Californian's Recollection of Naturalist Audubon," *The San Francisco Call*, Vol. LXXX, No. 98, p. 25, cols. 1–7 (Sunday, 6 Sept. 1896)(LOC). The officers of the HMS *Rosamond* who attended a "rustic ball" thrown by the Sandy Pointers in 1813 were similarly amused by the "burlesque finery" worn by the women who attended the dance. Chappell (1818), p. 72.

68. Deane (1910), p. 48.

69. *OB* II, pp. 213–214.

70. Ibid., p. 214.

71. Deane (1910), p. 48.

72. *OB* II, p. 214.

73. Audubon (2006), p. 440; *AHJ* I, p. 433; *OB* II, p. 214. Ford errs in stating that the Young Gentlemen remained at the ball until 7:30 a.m. Ford (1988), p. 309.

74. LBA, New York to VGA, London, 15 Aug. 1833 (Yale, Box 1, Folder 21); VGA, Paris to LBA, New York, 22 Jun. 1833 (Yale, Box 2, Folder 37).

75. LBA, New York to VGA, London, 15 Aug. 1833 (Yale, Box 1, Folder 21).

76. Ibid.

77. VGA, Paris to LBA, New York, 22 Jun. 1833 (Yale, Box 2, Folder 37).

78. LBA, New York to VGA, London, 15 Aug. 1833 (Yale, Box 1, Folder 21).

79. Audubon (2006), p. 440; *AHJ* I, p. 433.

80. Small (2009), pp. 188–189.

81. Audubon (2006), pp. 440–441; *AHJ* I, p. 433. In the *OB*, Audubon indicated that the excursion party that headed inland on August 16 was led by a single "Newfoundland Indian." *OB* IV, p. 415. His journal states that his companions "went off with the Indians," and the text adopts this version of the facts.

82. Audubon (2006), p. 441; *AHJ* I, p. 433; *OB* II, p. 559.

83. *OB* IV, p. 415.

84. Audubon (2006), p. 441; *AHJ* I, pp. 433–434.

85. L. Audubon (1869), pp. 363–364.

86. Audubon (2006), p. 441; *AHJ* I, p. 434; L. Audubon (1869), p. 364.

87. Small (2009), p. 202.

88. Between August 11, when Audubon told his journal as he sailed from Labrador that he had completed twenty-three drawings or nearly so, and September 9, when he wrote Victor after returning to New York that his drawings from the expedition totaled twenty-five, he evidently added two drawings. Cf. Audubon (2006), p. 437; JJA, New York to VGA, London, 9 Sept. 1833 (APS), Grinnell (1916), pp. 125–126, *Letters* I, p. 243; *AHJ* I, p. 429; L. Audubon (1869), p. 360. His journal provides no hint as to which species he might have illustrated over this period, but the Pine Grosbeaks could well have been one of them. However, if so, he only painted the birds. He perched the two adults and immature bird on either a Scrub Pine

(*Pinus virginiana*) or Shortleaf Pine (*Pinus echinata*), neither of which is found farther north than New York State. Dwight believes that the composition was likely painted during the winter of 1833-34 in Charleston, where both species of trees can be found. Audubon (1966) I, Plate 107.

89. L. Audubon (1869), p. 364. In Lucy's biography, Audubon referred to his visitors only as "Mr., Mrs., and Miss Forest." However, I was able to identify them with help from the journal of Archdeacon Edward Wix, a missionary who visited Sandy Point in 1835. Wix mentioned Forrest along with his wife and son and stated that the senior Forrest had recently died. Later, he provided the name of a local Sandy Point merchant as Horatio Henry Forrest, presumably the son. Wix (1836), pp. 165-166; 219. A modern Sandy Point historian, Don Downer, confirms that Horatio Henry Forrest was the son of the elder Forrest. Downer (1997), pp. 220-222. Horatio Forrest's baptismal record on October 9, 1801, reflects that his parents were Henry and Mary Forrest. Ancestry.com, *Quebec, Vital and Church Records (Drouin Collection), 1621-1967* (database on-line) (Provo, UT: Ancestry.com Operations Inc., 2008) (accessed 13 Dec. 2011).

According to genealogies of the Forrest family, available on Ancesty.com, Henry Essex Forrest, was born in Ireland on June 27, 1763, and died in St. George's Bay, Newfoundland, on January 17, 1834. His first wife, Mary, died in 1810. They had one surviving daughter, Ann, and three surviving sons. Ann was born in New York on March 6, 1797, and died on November 3, 1883, having evidently never married. The Drouin Collection records reflect that Henry married Julia Cowan on April 29, 1819. See genealogies of the family of Henry Essex Forrest, available on Ancestry.com (accessed 15 Dec. 2011) and Familytreemaker.genealogy.com (accessed 16 Dec. 2011); Ancestry.com, *Quebec, Vital and Church Records (Drouin Collection), 1621-1967* (database on-line)(Provo, UT: Ancestry.com Operations Inc., 2008)(accessed 13 Dec. 2011); Downer (1997), p. 220-222; Obituary (1877), p. 43.

90. That Henry Essex Forrest was the same individual as the "old European gentleman" Audubon conversed with at the Sandy Point ball is a solid deduction derived from two sets of fact. First, Forrest was born in Ireland and was seventy years of age, which would square with Audubon's description of him. Second, in "A Ball in Newfoundland," Audubon referred to the daughter of this gentleman as a "maiden lady" who "was the only daughter of my talkative companion." *OB* II, p. 214. Forrest's sole surviving daughter, Ann, was unmarried at thirty-six years of age and would have been considered a "maiden lady," a term used in the 19th century to refer to an unmarried older woman or spinster. It also makes sense that after Forrest's pleasant but brief conversation with Audubon at the ball, he would have wanted to visit the naturalist before the *Ripley* sailed from St. George's Harbor.

91. See genealogies of the family of Henry Essex Forrest, available on Ancestry.com (accessed 15 Dec. 2011) and Familytreemaker.genealogy. com (accessed 16 Dec. 2011); Ancestry.com, *Quebec, Vital and Church Records (Drouin Collection), 1621-1967* (database on-line)(Provo, UT:: Ancestry. com Operations Inc., 2008)(accessed 13 Dec. 2011); Downer (1997), pp. 220-222; Obituary (1877), p. 43.

92. L. Audubon (1869), p. 364. It would appear that Audubon's prohibition of liquor on the voyage did not encompass wine. In addition to this reference in Lucy's version of the journal regarding the Forrests' visit to the *Ripley*, there is a second mention of wine being aboard in the August 22 entry in Maria's edition, when the naturalist's party was saying farewell to the captain and crew near Pictou, Nova Scotia. Audubon (2006), p. 442; *AHJ* I, p. 435. See also, Chapter 6, note 127; Chapter 14, note 8. We know from John Bachman that Audubon enjoyed both wine and grog. John Bachman, Charleston to JJA, New York, 27 Mar. 1833 (MHM), Deane (1929), p. 184. What is not clear is why Audubon would have ever allowed wine onboard given his weakness for alcohol.

93. Audubon (2006), p. 441; *AHJ* I, p. 434; L. Audubon (1869), p. 364.

94. Major (2001), pp. 144-148; 210-215; Gatschet (1885), pp. 410, 414.

95. Audubon (2006), p. 441; *AHJ* I, p. 434; L. Audubon (1869), p. 364. See also, Major (2001), pp. 147-148.

96. Major (2001), pp. 144-148.

97. Ibid., pp. 140-145.

98. Audubon (2006), p. 441; *AHJ* I, p. 434; L. Audubon (1869), p. 364.

99. *OB* III, pp. 308–309.

100. Audubon (2006), p. 441; *AHJ* I, p. 434; L. Audubon (1869), p. 364.

101. *OB* II, p. 93.

102. Audubon (2006), p. 418; *AHJ* I, p. 405; *OB* V, pp. 299–300; *OB* II, p. 93.

103. *OB* II, p. 93; Swainson (1831) II, p. 146. Audubon paid $20 for a copy of the *Fauna Boreali Americana* on September 21, 1833, following his return to New York. Academy of Natural Sciences of Philadelphia (1938), Item 84, p. 28.

It is hard to follow Audubon's thought process in concluding that the flycatchers he had observed in Labrador were the same species as the *Tyrannula richardsonii* (Western Wood-Pewee) discovered by Dr. John Richardson in the area around Cumberland House in eastern Saskatchewan. Shortly after returning from the expedition, Audubon described the Labrador bird as smaller than the Wood Pewee (Eastern Wood-Pewee), Traill's Flycatcher (Willow Flycatcher), and the *Muscicapa acadica* (Acadian Flycatcher). *OB* (1834) II, p. 93. See also, Low (2002), pp. 279, 281, 284. According to the *OB*, the Wood Pewee (Eastern Wood-Pewee) measured 6½″; the Traill's Flycatcher (Willow Flycatcher) was 5¾″; and the *Muscicapa acadica* (Acadian Flycatcher) was 5½″. *OB* II, pp. 96, 258; *OB* I, p. 237. By comparison, the *Tyrannula richardsonii* described by William Swainson in *Fauna Boreali-Americana* was decidedly larger than any of these birds, measuring 6⅔″ from the tip of its bill to the end of its tail. Swainson (1831), p. 148. The specimen that Audubon drew for his work was 6¾″. *OB* V, p. 301.

104. Low (2002), p. 230; Swainson (1831) II, p. 146.

105. *OB* V, pp. 299–301. In his species biography, Audubon called his Labrador flycatcher the Short-legged Pewee Flycatcher.

106. *AHJ* I, pp. 405–406, note 2.

107. Peterson & Peterson (1981), Plate 274 commentary; Townsend (1907), pp. 379–380. No less an authority than Roger Tory Peterson, the great 20th century naturalist and painter, identifies Audubon's "Short-legged Pewee Flycatcher" as an Alder Flycatcher (*Empidonax alnorum*).

108. *OB* I, p. 236.

109. Aldrich (1953), pp. 8–11.

110. American Ornithologists' Union (1973), pp. 415–416.

CHAPTER 14: NOVA SCOTIA

1. Audubon (2006), p. 441; *AHJ* I, p. 434; L. Audubon (1869), pp. 364–365; *OB* III, p. 397.

2. Audubon (2006), p. 441; *AHJ* I, p. 434; L. Audubon (1869), pp. 364–365; *OB* III, pp. 309, 397.

3. L. Audubon (1869), p. 365; *Boston Daily Advertiser & Patriot*, Volume XLII, No. 11,166, p. 2, cols. 4–5 (Saturday, 7 Sept. 1833)(AAS). Maria's edition of the journal has no entry for Tuesday, August 20, and, under the date of August 21, states that the storm continued until that day. Audubon (2006), pp. 441–442; *AHJ* I, pp. 434–435. Lucy's version, which includes a description of events occurring on both days, appears the more accurate of the two. Additionally, Audubon told the *Boston Daily Advertiser & Patriot* upon his return that the storm lasted two days and two nights. Maria's account would suggest the storm extended through at least three nights.

4. L. Audubon (1869), p. 365. Cf. Audubon (2006), p. 442; *AHJ* I, p. 435 ("The great desire we all have to see Pictou, Halifax, and the country between them and Eastport, is our inducement.").

5. Audubon (2006), p. 442; *AHJ* I, p. 435; L. Audubon (1869), p. 365.

6. Charter-Party of Affreightment, June 5, 1833 (Yale, Box 16, Folder 719).

7. L. Audubon (1869), p. 365. Cf. Audubon (2006), p. 442; *AHJ* I, p. 435 ("We drank a glass of wine to our wives and our friends, and our excellent little captain took us to the shore, while the vessel stood still, with all sails up, awaiting his return."). As quoted in the text, Lucy's biography refers only to Audubon's party drinking a "parting glass," rather than a "glass of wine." However, since both versions of the journal at different points mention the presence of wine aboard the *Ripley*, it seems likely that there was. See also, Chapter 6, note 127; Chapter 13, note 92.

8. L. Audubon (1869), pp. 365–366. Cf. Audubon (2006), p. 442; *AHJ* I, p. 435 ("we all shook hands most heartily with the captain—to whom we now feel really attached—said farewell to the

crew, and parted, giving three hearty cheers."). Ford errs in stating that the baggage of Audubon's party was transported to Pictou via haycart. Ford (1988), p. 309. As reflected in both versions of the journal, it was taken by boat. Audubon (2006), p. 442; *AHJ* I, pp. 435-436; L. Audubon (1869), pp. 365-366.

9. L. Audubon (1869), p. 366. Cf. Audubon (2006), p. 442; *AHJ* I, pp. 435-436 ("after four days' confinement in our berths, and sick of seasickness, the sea and all its appurtenances, we felt so refreshed that the thought of walking nine miles seemed like nothing more than dancing a quadrille. The air felt deliciously warm, the country, compared with those we have so lately left, appeared perfectly beautiful, and the smell of the new-mown grass was the sweetest that ever existed. Even the music of the crickets was delightful to mine ears, for no such insect does either Labrador or Newfoundland afford. The voice of a Blue Jay was melody to me, and the sight of a Humming-bird quite filled my heart with delight."). This passage offers a good example of Maria Audubon's tendency to delete any of her grandfather's references to matters she considered indelicate, such as his allusion to the "smells and discomforts" of their schooner during the recent storm.

10. Audubon (2006), pp. 442-443; *AHJ* I, pp. 436-437; L. Audubon (1869), pp. 366-367.

11. L. Audubon (1869), p. 366. Cf. Audubon (2006), pp. 442-443; *AHJ* I, p. 436 ("Now and then, as we crossed a hill and looked back over the sea, we saw our beautiful vessel sailing freely before the wind, and as she gradually neared the horizon, she looked like a white speck, or an Eagle high in air. We wished our captain a most safe voyage to Quoddy.").

12. L. Audubon (1869), pp. 366-367; Haliburton (1829) II, p. 53. Cf. Audubon (2006), pp. 442-443; *AHJ* I, pp. 435-436 ("the village, placed at the upper end of a fine bay").

13. Audubon (2006), p. 443; Whitelaw (1985), pp. 13-14; Sherwood (1982), pp. 48-49; Durant & Harwood (1980), pp. 481-483; McCulloch (1920), pp. 22-23, illus. opp. p. 50; *AHJ* I, p. 436; L. Audubon (1869), p. 367.

14. Buggey & Davies (2000); Whitelaw (1985), pp. 4, 7-8; McCulloch (1920), pp. 7-8, 18-20; Patterson (1877), p. 267.

15. Buggey & Davies (2000); Whitelaw (1985), pp. 13-19, 20-22; McCulloch (1920), pp. 20, 42-43, 47-48, 63-64; Haliburton (1829) II, pp. 54-55. There is a conflict among McCulloch scholars as to when Pictou Academy began instruction. Marjory Whitelaw states that classes began in 1817, as does the Reverend George Patterson. Whitelaw (1985), p. 19; Patterson (1877), pp. 328-329. Others, including Susan Buggey, Roland Sherwood, and Gwendolyn Davies, claim that the doors opened in May 1818. Buggey & Davis (2000); Sherwood (1982), pp. 16-17. The text adopts the latter chronology as this is the one reflected in the biography of McCulloch written by his son William. McCulloch (1920), p. 63.

King's College in Windsor was founded in 1789 by the Nova Scotia legislature. In its early years, there were no religious tests placed on admission. In 1802, it received a Royal Charter from King George III, the first granted to any Canadian college. The following year, under the terms of the charter, the Board of Governors adopted Statutes, Rules, and Ordinances modeled after those of Oxford University. Among these was a provision that expressly limited matriculation to Anglican students. This provision was abrogated three years later by the Archbishop of Canterbury, who was the patron of the college. While the board formally acquiesced in this mandate in 1807, the revised statutes still prohibited students from worshiping other than in the Anglican Church and restricted the award of degrees to students of the Anglican faith. Moreover, even these changes, which ostensibly opened up the college to non-Anglicans, were evidently not published for more than a decade. Hind (1890), pp. 21-24, 26-33, 40-42, 46-49. The obvious intention of the board was to limit instruction to students of the Church of England.

16. Whitelaw (1985), pp. 20-21, 25; Sherwood (1982), pp. 48-49; McCulloch (1920), p. 64.

17. Whitelaw (1985), p. 25.

18. McCulloch (1920), pp. 82-85; 145-146.

19. Ibid., p. 146.

20. Haliburton (1829) II, pp. 55-56.

21. McCulloch (1920), pp. 145-147.

22. Audubon (2006), p. 443; McCulloch (1920), p. 9, 146-147; *AHJ* I, p. 436; L. Audubon (1869), p. 367; *OB* II, p. xxi.

23. Audubon (2006), p. 443; Whitelaw (1985), pp. 36–37; McCulloch (1920), p. 11; *AHJ* I, p. 437; L. Audubon (1869), p. 367. Note that Lucy's biography refers to McCulloch's "four sons and daughters" being present at breakfast as compared to Maria's edition of the journal, which indicates there were "four sons and a daughter."

Thomas McCulloch had nine children, eight of whom were living at the time of Audubon's visit to Pictou: Michael (1800–1881); Helen (1801–1875); Elizabeth (1802–1834); David (1805–1891); Isabella (1808–1883); Thomas (1809–1865); William (1811–1895); and James (1813–1835). The youngest son, Robert, born in 1817, died at an early age of scalding. McCulloch Family Tree, Ancestry.com, http://trees.ancestry.com/tree/24100712/person/1472667527 (accessed 10 Feb. 2012); McCulloch (1920).

24. L. Audubon (1869), p. 367. Cf. Audubon (2006), p. 443; *AHJ* I, p. 437 ("I became more pleased with the professor the more he talked.").

25. Audubon (2006), p. 443; *AHJ* I, p. 437; L. Audubon (1869), p. 367.

26. McCulloch (1920), pp. 147–148. The younger Thomas McCulloch (1809–1865) would go on to provide Audubon with specimens of the Pied-billed Dobchick (Pied-billed Grebe)(Havell Plate 248); Bohemian Chatterer (Bohemian Waxwing)(Havell Plate No. 363); and Hawk Owl (Northern Hawk Owl)(Havell Plate 378). *OB* IV, pp. 463–465, 551; *OB* III, pp. 360–361. Audubon scholar Susanne Low is almost certainly mistaken in her assertion that the Hawk Owl specimens were given to the naturalist during his visit to Pictou. Low (2002), p. 192. Audubon indicated in the *OB* that they were given to him "preserved in spirits," and the eyes must have still been intact as the color of the bird's iris was described. *OB* IV, p. 551. The specimens in the natural history museum at Pictou Academy were already prepared and mounted and would have sported glass eyes. It seems more likely that Audubon received the Hawk Owl specimens at a later date.

Thomas also reportedly gave the naturalist a specimen of the Little Night Owl (Little Owl)(Havell Plate 432). However, this is an Old World species and is ordinarily not found in the vicinity of Pictou, where Thomas claimed to have shot it. Peterson (1981), Plate 244 commentary; *OB* V, p. 269.

27. L. Audubon (1869), p. 367. Cf. Audubon (2006), p. 443; *AHJ* I, p. 437 ("we went in a body to the University, once more to examine his fine collection.").

28. *OB* II, pp. 138, 241.

29. *OB* II, p. 208.

30. Audubon (2006), p. 443; *AHJ* I, p. 437; L. Audubon (1869), p. 367.

31. L. Audubon (1869), p. 367. Cf. Audubon (2006), p. 443; *AHJ* I, p. 437 ("he offered them to me with so much apparent good will that I took them.")

32. *OB* III, p. 426.

33. Audubon (1966) I, Plate 31.

34. Audubon (2006), p. 443; *AHJ* I, p. 437; L. Audubon (1869), p. 367; *OB* II, pp. 208, 303–304.

35. Audubon (2006), pp. 443–444; Buggey & Davies (2000); Whitelaw (1985), pp. 24–25; McCulloch (1920), pp. 59, 104; *AHJ* I, p. 437; Patterson (1877), p. 332; L. Audubon (1869), p. 367.

36. Buggey & Davies (2000); Whitelaw (1985), pp. 32, 34; Millman (1983), p. 68; McCulloch (1920), pp. 59, 104–105, 134–138; Patterson (1877), pp. 332–335, 337–338, 341–342, 346–349, 352–358.

37. Audubon (2006), pp. 443–444; *AHJ* I, p. 437; L. Audubon (1869), p. 367. In late 1834, McCulloch's son Thomas traveled to London to sell the Pictou Academy collection of about 400 mounted birdskins, which had almost doubled in size since Audubon's visit. However, by then, the once-robust English market for birdskins had collapsed. JJA, London to John Bachman, 20 Apr. 1835 (Harvard (70)), *Letters* I, pp. 68–69; Thomas McCulloch, Pictou, N.S., to JJA, London, 28 Oct. 1834 (Yale, Box 5, Folder 244).

38. Audubon (2006), p. 444; Beck, "Jotham Blanchard" (2000); Whitelaw (1985), pp. 20, 33–34; McCulloch (1920), pp. 108–111; *AHJ* I, p. 437; L. Audubon (1869), p. 368; Williams (1835), p. 439.

39. Audubon (2006), p. 444; Beck, "Jotham Blanchard" (2000); Sherwood (1982), p. 9; McCulloch (1920), pp. 127–133; *AHJ* I, p. 437; L. Audubon (1869), p. 368; Belcher (1833), p. 76; Belcher (1832), p. 6.

40. Audubon (2006), p. 444; *AHJ*. I, p. 437; L. Audubon (1869), p. 368; Sganzin (1837), pp. 82–83; *Boston Daily Advertiser & Patriot*, Vol. XLII,

No. 11,166, p. 2, cols. 4–5 (Saturday, 7 Sept. 1833) (AAS); Haliburton (1829) II, p. 20.

41. L. Audubon (1869), p. 368. Cf. Audubon (2006), p. 444; *AHJ* I, p. 437 ("We passed through a fine tract of country, well wooded, well cultivated, and a wonderful relief to our eyes after the barren and desolate regions of rocks, snow, tempests, and storms.").

42. Audubon (2006), p. 444; *AHJ* I, pp. 437–438; L. Audubon (1869), pp. 368–369.

43. L. Audubon (1869), p. 369. Cf. Audubon (2006), p. 444; *AHJ* I, p. 438 ("pretty, scattered village").

44. L. Audubon (1869), p. 369. Cf. Audubon (2006), p. 445; *AHJ* I, pp. 438–439 ("It is situated in the middle of a most beautiful valley, of great extent and well cultivated; several brooks water this valley, and empty into the Bay of Fundy, the broad expanse of which we see to the westward. The buildings, though principally of wood, are good-looking, and as cleanly as those in our pretty eastern villages, white, with green shutters. The style of the people, be it loyal or otherwise, is extremely genteel, and I was more than pleased with all those whom I saw."). For a more detailed description of Truro, see Haliburton (1829) II, pp. 37–43.

45. Audubon (2006), p. 444; *AHJ* I, p. 438; L. Audubon (1869), p. 369.

46. Audubon (2006), p. 444; *AHJ* I, p. 438; L. Audubon (1869), p. 369.

47. Audubon (2006), pp. 444–445; Beck, "S.W.G. Archibald" (2000); *AHJ* I, pp. 438–439; L. Audubon (1869), pp. 369–370; Haliburton (1829) II, p. 20.

48. Beck, "S.W.G. Archibald" (2000); Longworth (1881), pp. 2–4, 8–10, 17–20.

49. Lynch (1912), p. 200.

50. Bryson Family Tree, Ancestry.com, http://trees.ancestry.com/tree/24436241/person/124963 21876?ssrc= (accessed 4 May 2014); Audubon (2006), pp. 444–445; Blakely (2000); *AHJ* I, p. 438; L. Audubon (1869), p. 369; Belcher (1833), p. 42; *Boston Daily Advertiser & Patriot*, Vol. XLII, No. 11,166, p. 2, cols. 4–5 (Saturday, 7 Sept. 1833)(AAS).

51. Audubon (2006), p. 445; *AHJ* I, p. 439 ("The coach is at the door, the cover of my trunk is gaping to receive this poor book, and therefore once more, good-night."). Cf. L. Audubon (1869),

p. 369–370 ("The coach is at the door, the corner of my trunk is gasping to swallow this book, and I must put it in and be off.").

52. Audubon (2006), pp. 445–446; *AHJ* I, p. 439–440; L. Audubon (1869), p. 370; American Almanac (1832), p. 40. A good example of Maria Audubon's bollixed editing of her grandfather's journal can be found in the cited references regarding the broken-down mail coach along the Halifax Road. According to Lucy's biography, Audubon wrote: "Looking up the road, the vacillating glimmer of the candle, intended to assist the driver in finding the linch-pin, was all that could be distinguished, and we began to feel what is called 'wolfish.'" Maria, who obviously had never spent time with a group of men in the dead of night throwing wolf howls at the moon, had utterly no idea what her grandfather meant. She altered it completely and, in the process, made that portion of the sentence incomprehensible: "Looking up the road, the vacillating glimmer of the flame intended to assist the coach-man in the recovery of the lost linch-pin was all that could be distinguished, for by this the time was what is called 'wolfy.'"

53. Audubon (2006), p. 446; *AHJ* I, p. 440; L. Audubon (1869), pp. 370–371. The two versions of the journal referenced here conflict as to where the Halifax stage stopped to see if Audubon and his party could get an early breakfast. Lucy's biography describes it as a "wayside tavern" and indicates that the driver inquired about "the prospects of getting some chickens or boiled eggs; but the proprietor said it was impossible for him to furnish breakfast for six persons of our appearance." Maria states that they "drew up at a house where the owner looked us over, and said it would be quite impossible to provide a breakfast for six persons of our appearance." In this context, Maria's account is the more probable of the two. It seems highly unlikely that the proprietor of a roadside tavern catering to the public would have turned away six paying customers for breakfast regardless of their appearance, while this is precisely the reaction one would expect of a random homeowner.

54. L. Audubon (1869), p. 371. Cf. Audubon (2006), p. 446; *AHJ* I, p. 440 ("pleasant summer residence"). Note also that Maria errs in stating that the breakfast tavern was located on "Green

Lake." While there is a Green Lake in Nova Scotia (44°45′54″ N, -62°50′58″ W), it is located about forty miles northeast of Halifax and is nowhere near the roadway Audubon's party took from Truro to Halifax.

55. Audubon (2006), p. 446; *AHJ* I, p. 440; L. Audubon (1869), p. 371; Coke (1833) II, pp. 127–128; Haliburton (1829) II, pp. 26–29.

56. L. Audubon (1869), p. 371. Cf. Audubon (2006), p. 446; *AHJ* I, p. 440 ("The road was now level, but narrow").

57. Audubon (2006), p. 446; *AHJ* I, p. 440; L. Audubon (1869), p. 371.

58. L. Audubon (1869), p. 371; Haliburton (1829) II, p. 26. Cf. Audubon (2006), p. 446; *AHJ* I, p. 440 ("small ferry-boat"). The time given for the party's arrival at the ferry in Dartmouth is an estimate based upon Shattuck's statement in a letter to his father that they reached Halifax around noon. GCSJr, Halifax to GCS, Boston, 25 Aug. 1833 (MHS, Ms. N-909, Vol. 11, 9–31 Aug. 1833).

59. Audubon (2006), p. 446; *AHJ* I, p. 440; L. Audubon (1869), p. 371.

60. Haliburton (1829) II, pp. 14–15.

61. Audubon (2006), p. 446; *AHJ* I, p. 441; L. Audubon (1869), p. 371.

62. Peterson (2008), p. 186; *OB* III, p. 561.

63. GCSJr, Halifax to GCS, Boston, 25 Aug. 1833 (MHS, Ms. N-909, Vol. 11, 9–31 Aug. 1833).

64. Audubon (2006), pp. 446–447; *AHJ* I, p. 441; L. Audubon (1869), p. 371.

65. L. Audubon (1869), pp. 371–372. Cf. Audubon (2006), p. 447; *AHJ* I, p. 441 ("Halifax has not one good hotel for here the attendance is miserable, and the table far from good.").

66. L. Audubon (1869), p. 371. Cf. Audubon (2006), p. 446 ("beggarly-looking Negroes and Negresses"); *AHJ* I, p. 441 ("beggarly-looking negroes and negresses").

67. Akins (1895), p. 163; Coke (1833) II, pp. 128–129; Haliburton (1829) II, pp. 292–293.

68. Audubon (2006), p. 446; *AHJ* I, pp. 440–441; L. Audubon (1869), p. 371.

69. L. Audubon (1869), p. 372. Cf. Audubon (2006), p. 447; *AHJ* I, p. 441 ("the softest, deepest mosses").

70. L. Audubon (1869), p. 372. Maria's edition of the journal omits any reference to the visit

by Audubon's party to the Halifax bathhouse. No doubt the thought of men bathing offended her Victorian sensibilities.

71. Akins (1895), p. 208; L. Audubon (1869), p. 372.

72. Audubon (2006), p. 447; *AHJ* I, p. 441.

73. Dodge (1950), pp. 120, 123. The quotation in the text is taken from the February-March 1950 catalog issued by Goodspeed's Book Shop in Boston. I was not able to locate the original holograph during the course of my research.

74. GCSJr, Halifax to GCS, Boston, 25 Aug. 1833 (MHS, Ms. N-909, Vol. 11, 9–31 Aug. 1833).

75. Audubon (2006), p. 447; *AHJ* I, pp. 441.

76. L. Audubon (1869), p. 372. Cf. Audubon (2006), p. 447; *AHJ* I, pp. 441 ("sentinels at every point").

77. Audubon (2006), p. 447; *AHJ* I, pp. 441.

78. Audubon (2006), p. 447; *AHJ* I, pp. 441; L. Audubon (1869), p. 372. Though Lucy's biography indicates that Audubon and his colleagues attended the Episcopal Church, it is believed that she meant the Anglican Church. Haliburton (1829) II, p. 15.

79. Audubon (2006), p. 447; *AHJ* I, pp. 441; L. Audubon (1869), p. 372.

80. L. Audubon (1869), p. 372. Cf. Audubon (2006), p. 447; *AHJ* I, pp. 441 ("The soldiers walked far apart, with arms reversed; an excellent band executed the most solemn marches and a fine anthem.").

81. Audubon (2006), p. 447; Sutherland (2000); *AHJ* I, pp. 441. Though he served as president of the Halifax Chamber of Commerce at one time, Richard Tremain (1774–1854) was no longer president when he met Audubon in 1833. Belcher (1833), p. 52; Belcher (1832), p. 61.

82. Audubon (2006), p. 447; *AHJ* I, pp. 441.

83. *New-York Gazette & General Advertiser*, Vol. 46, No. 16,966, p, 2, col. 1 (Tuesday, 10 Sept. 1833)(NYHS). Audubon's letter to Edward Harris was dated August 25 and indicated in its first sentence that he and his party had arrived in Pictou "three days ago" and had reached Halifax only the day before. This confirms that he started the letter on August 25, although he did not mention it in his journal until August 26.

84. Ibid.

85. Wheeler (2003), pp. 361–363, 365, 370–372.

86. Peterson & Peterson (1981), commentary to Plates 115–116; *OB* V, p. 368. Audubon's illustration of the adult male Merlin, drawn in 1812 and given the name Le Petit Caporal in *BOA*, was published as Plate 75. The juvenile birds, which were drawn in 1829, are shown in Plate 92. Audubon (1966) I, Plates 30, 156.

87. GCSJr, Halifax to GCS, Boston, 26 Aug. 1833 (MHS, Ms. N-909, Vol. 11, 9–31 Aug. 1833).

88. Audubon (2006), p. 447; *AHJ* I, pp. 441–442.

89. Haliburton (1829) II, p. 20.

90. Audubon (2006), p. 447; *AHJ* I, p. 442; L. Audubon (1869), p. 372.

91. "A Californian's Recollection of Naturalist Audubon," *The San Francisco Call*, Vol. LXXX, No. 98, p. 25, cols. 1–7 (Sunday, 6 Sept. 1896)(LOC).

92. Audubon (2006), p. 447; *AHJ* I, p. 442.

93. William Hewitson (sometimes spelled "Hewetson") was born in 1786 in Kilkenny, Ireland. He married Annette Scholastique Victoire DeManee (b. 1794) and had two children, William (b. 1822) and Adelaide (b. 1827). Rootsweb.com, http://worldconnect.rootsweb.ancestry.com/cgi-bin/igm.cgi?op=GET&db=3363366&id=I1008 (accessed 11 Feb. 2012). Reporting on his death in October 1860, *The Annual Register* said of him: "In early life, as a midshipman on board the *Earl Camden*, Commodore Dance, he was present in the memorable repulse by the China fleet of the French squadron under Admiral Linois. In the commissariat he saw some service at the Cape and in North America. He also served with the army of occupation in France." *Annual Register* (1861), p. 447. According to Belcher's 1834 *Farmer's Almanack*, at the time Hewitson met Audubon's party he was deputy commissary general. Belcher (1833), p. 61.

94. "A Californian's Recollection of Naturalist Audubon," *The San Francisco Call*, Vol. LXXX, No. 98, p. 25, cols. 1–7 (Sunday, 6 Sept. 1896)(LOC).

95. L. Audubon (1869), pp. 372–373 (the text corrects an obviously typographical error in Lucy's biography, "gook-looking"); Belcher (1833), p. 6. Cf. Audubon (2006), pp. 447–448; *AHJ* I, p. 442 ("over hills and through valleys;" "Here and there a country home came in sight."). In Maria's edition of the journal, the entry for Tuesday, August 27,

states that, "though the distance [from Halifax to Windsor] is forty-five miles, we had only one pair of horses, which travelled about six and a half miles an hour." Lucy's version of the journal indicates that they "had but one pair at a time." More than likely, the team was changed when the stage stopped at an inn along the way where the passengers ate.

96. Audubon (2006), p. 448; MacNutt (2000); *AHJ* I, p. 442; L. Audubon (1869), p. 373; Coke (1833) II, p. 126; Haliburton (1829) I, pp. 276–278.

97. L. Audubon (1869), p. 373; Cf. Audubon (2006), p. 448; *AHJ* I, p. 442 ("On leaving the bay, we followed the Salmon River, a small rivulet of swift water, which abounds in salmon, trout, and other fish.").

98. Audubon (2006), p. 448; *AHJ* I, p. 443; Coke (1833) II, pp. 116–117; Haliburton (1829) II, p. 100.

99. Audubon (2006), p. 448; *AHJ* I, p. 442.

100. Audubon (2006), p. 448; Cuthbertson (2000); *AHJ* I, pp. 442–443; L. Audubon (1869), p. 373; Coke (1833) II, p. 117.

101. Audubon (2006), p. 448; Bowsfield (2000); Cuthbertson (2000); *AHJ* I, p. 442; L. Audubon (1869), p. 373; Belcher (1833), p. 42; Belcher (1832), p. 50; Haliburton (1829) II, pp. 312–313. In addition to serving on His Majesty's Council, Thomas Nickleson (sometimes spelled "Nicholson") Jeffery was also the Collector of the Customs for Halifax and the president of the Shubenacadie Canal Company. Cuthbertson (2000); Belcher (1833), pp. 44, 46; Belcher (1832), pp. 58, 81.

102. Audubon (2006), p. 448; *AHJ* I, p. 443; L. Audubon (1869), pp. 373–374; Haliburton (1829) II, pp. 101–102.

103. L. Audubon (1869), p. 373; Haliburton (1829) II, p. 107. Cf. Audubon (2006), p. 448; *AHJ* I, p. 443 ("We saw the college and the common school, built of freestone, both handsome buildings.").

104. Coke (1833) II, pp. 112–113; Haliburton (1829) II, p. 107.

105. L. Audubon (1869), p. 374. Cf. Audubon (2006), p. 448; *AHJ* I, p. 443 ("Our coach stopped at the best *boarding-house* here").

106. L. Audubon (1869), p. 374. Cf. Audubon (2006), p. 448; *AHJ* I, p. 443 ("Windsor is a neat, pretty village").

107. Audubon (2006), p. 448; *AHJ* I, p. 443;
L. Audubon (1869), p. 374; Buckingham (1843),
p. 388; Coke (1833) II, pp. 113–114; Haliburton
(1829) II, pp. 102, 108–109. In his journal, Audubon
mistakenly referred to the Avon River as the "Windsor River."

108. L. Audubon (1869), p. 374. Cf. Audubon
(2006), p. 448; *AHJ* I, p. 443 ("The view was indeed novel").

109. Audubon (2006), pp. 448–449; *AHJ* I,
p. 443; L. Audubon (1869), p. 374.

110. Audubon (2006), p. 448; *AHJ* I, p. 443;
L. Audubon (1869), p. 374.

111. *OB* II, p. 488.

112. Ibid.

113. Audubon (2006), p. 449; *AHJ* I, p. 444.

114. Audubon (2006), p. 449; *AHJ* I, p. 444; *OB*
II, pp. 488–489.

115. Audubon (2006), p. 449; *AHJ* I, p. 444; *OB*
IV, p. 401.

116. Dunn & Alderfer (2011), pp. 132–133; Dunne
(2006), pp. 154–155; Kaufman (1996), pp. 121–122.

117. Audubon (2006), p. 449; *AHJ* I, p. 444.

118. Audubon (2006), p. 449; *AHJ* I, p. 444;
Boston Daily Advertiser & Patriot, Volume XLII,
No. 11,166, p. 2, cols. 4–5 (Saturday, 7 Sept. 1833)
(AAS).

119. Shortt (1913), p. 561; *New Brunswick
Courier* (Saturday, 15 Jun. 1833).

120. *New Brunswick Courier* (Saturday, 6 Jul.
1833).

121. Audubon (2006), p. 449; *AHJ* I, p. 444.

122. L. Audubon (1869), p. 375.

123. Audubon (2006), p. 449; *AHJ* I, p. 444;
L. Audubon (1869), p. 375.

124. Buckingham (1843), p. 397; Haliburton
(1829) II, p. 20.

125. Audubon (2006), p. 449; *AHJ* I, p. 444;
L. Audubon (1869), p. 375; Coke (1833) II, p. 112;
Haliburton (1829) II, p. 4.

126. Audubon (2006), p. 449; *AHJ* I, p. 444;
L. Audubon (1869), p. 375; Murray (1839) II, pp.
228–229; JJA, Eastport to LBA, New York, 31 Aug.
1833 (Howland); Edward Harris, Eastport to John
Lang, New York, 30 Aug. 1833, *New-York Gazette
& General Advertiser*, Vol. 45, No. 16,963, p. 2,
col. 2 (Friday Morning, 6 Sept. 1833)(NYHS); Coke

(1833) II, p. 133; *New Brunswick Courier* (Saturday,
10 Aug. 1833).

127. Edward Harris, Eastport to John Lang,
New York, 22 Aug. 1833, *New-York Gazette & General Advertiser*, Vol. 45, No. 16,961, p. 2, col. 3
(Wednesday Morning, 4 Sept. 1833)(NYHS).

128. Edward Harris, Eastport to John Lang,
New York, 30 Aug. 1833, *New-York Gazette & General Advertiser*, Vol. 45, No. 16,963, p. 2, col. 2 (Friday Morning, 6 Sept. 1833)(NYHS).

129. JJA, Bras d'Or, Labrador to LBA, New
York (Princeton, Box 2, Folder 24). This letter reflects that it was posted from Portsmouth, NH, on
August 31, 1833.

130. Edward Harris, Eastport to John Lang,
New York, 30 Aug. 1833, *New-York Gazette & General Advertiser*, Vol. 45, No. 16,963, p. 2, col. 2 (Friday Morning, 6 Sept. 1833)(NYHS); Edward Harris, Eastport to John Lang, New York, 22 Aug. 1833,
New-York Gazette & General Advertiser, Vol. 45, No.
16,961, p. 2, col. 3 (Wednesday Morning, 4 Sept.
1833)(NYHS).

131. Audubon (2006), p. 449; *AHJ* I, p. 444;
L. Audubon (1869), p. 375; JJA, Eastport to LBA,
New York, 31 Aug. 1833 (Howland); LBA, New York
to JJA, care of General Ripley, East Port, 14 Jul.
1833 (Yale, Box 1, Folder 20).

132. Coke (1833) II, p. 133.

CHAPTER 15: HOME

1. Edward Harris, Eastport to John Lang, New
York, 30 Aug. 1833, *New-York Gazette & General
Advertiser*, Vol. 45, No. 16,963, p. 2, col. 2 (Friday
Morning, 6 Sept. 1833)(NYHS). Note that Audubon
indicated in his journal that he and his party arrived
in Eastport on Friday afternoon, not "forenoon" as
Harris reported in the cited letter. Audubon (2006),
p. 449; AHJ I, p. 444; L. Audubon (1869), p. 375.
The text relies upon Harris's roughly contemporary
statement rather than Audubon's, which was written
the following day.

2. Audubon (2006), pp. 449–450; *AHJ* I, p. 444;
L. Audubon (1869), p. 375; Coke (1833) II, p. 133;
JJA, Eastport to LBA, New York, 31 Aug. 1833
(Howland). There is some conflict in the record as
to when the *Ripley* reached Eastport. Audubon informed Lucy in the cited letter that the schooner

arrived "3 days before" his party, which would have been on Tuesday, August 27. However, Edward Harris wrote to his father-in-law upon landing in Eastport on August 30 and said that the *Ripley* had docked "on Wednesday." Edward Harris, Eastport to John Lang, New York, 30 Aug. 1833, *New-York Gazette & General Advertiser*, Vol. 45, No. 16,963, p. 2, col. 2 (Friday Morning, 6 Sept. 1833)(NYHS). This is also what Audubon subsequently advised Victor. JJA, New York to VGA, London, 9 Sept. 1833 (APS), Grinnell (1916), p. 125, *Letters* I, p. 242. Audubon apparently misspoke in his August 31 letter.

3. U.S. Customs Service (2004)(accessed 23 Apr. 2012). Shattuck Jr.'s biographer, J.C. Douglas Marshall, asserts that Shattuck returned to Boston from Halifax. Marshall (2006), p. 53. The records of the Passamaquoddy Custom House, which list arriving passengers, confirms that he accompanied Audubon's party back to Eastport.

4. JJA, Eastport to LBA, New York, 31 Aug. 1833 (Howland).

5. *OB* II, p. xxii.

6. JJA, New York to VGA, London, 9 Sept. 1833 (APS), Grinnell (1916), p. 125, *Letters* I, p. 243.

7. Audubon (2006), p. 450; *AHJ* I, p. 444

8. JJA, Eastport to LBA at New York, 31 Aug. 1833 (Howland).

9. GCSJr, Boston to Benjamin Lincoln, M.D., Burlington, VT, 26 Sept. 1833 (Letters to Benjamin Lincoln, Massachusetts Historical Society (Ms. S-15)).

10. JJA, Eastport to LBA, New York, 31 Aug. 1833 (Howland). This letter was written by Audubon at the crack of dawn on Saturday, August 31. He noted that everyone in the Weston household was "yet in bed," that John was "sound a Sleep," and that his party had been greeted by their many friends in Eastport "yesterday."

11. JJA, Eastport to LBA at New York, 31 Aug. 1833 (Howland).

12. VGA, London to JJA, New York, 30 Aug. 1833 (Yale Box 2, Folder 38).

13. Ibid.

14. Ibid.

15. Ibid.

16. Ibid.

17. Ibid.

18. LBA, New York to JJA , Eastport, 27Aug. 1833 (Yale, Box 1, Folder 21).

19. Audubon (2006), p. 450; Dodge (1950), pp. 120, 123; *AHJ* I, p. 444; L. Audubon (1869), p. 375; JJA, Eastport to LBA, New York, 31 Aug. 1833 (Howland).

20. *OB* III, p. 309; Edward Harris, Eastport to JJA, New York, 6 Sept. 1833 (Yale, Box 4, Folder 181). Dash, the pointer, must have returned to New York with the Audubons as it subsequently traveled with Audubon and John on their expedition along the Gulf Coast in 1837. L. Audubon (1869), p. 414. See also, JJA, New York to John Bachman, Charleston, 2 Oct. 1836 (Harvard (97)), *Letters* II, p. 134.

21. JJA, Eastport to LBA, New York, 31 Aug. 1833 (Howland).

22. Edward Harris, Eastport to JJA, New York, 6 Sept. 1833 (Yale, Box 4, Folder 181); JJA, Eastport to LBA, New York, 31 Aug. 1833 (Howland).

23. Bonaparte (1828). Audubon's copy of Bonaparte's *Synopsis*, inscribed to Edward Harris and containing Audubon's marginalia, was acquired from Harris's descendants by the Audubon collector Joseph Y. Jeanes. Harwood & Durant (1985), p. 92; Herrick (1938) II, p. 50, note 21. Jeanes donated it to Harvard, where it is now in the collection of the Houghton Library (AC8.Au292.Zz828b). It has been digitally scanned and is accessible through HOLLIS, the Harvard online library catalog.

24. Edward Harris, Eastport to JJA, New York, 6 Sept. 1833 (Yale, Box 4, Folder 181).

25. *OB* III, p. 309; Edward Harris, Eastport to JJA, New York, 6 Sept. 1833 (Yale, Box 4, Folder 181). First Lt. George Sears Greene (1801–1899) would resign his commission and leave the army in 1835, frustrated by the lack of opportunity for advancement in the ranks. He spent the years that followed in a productive career as a civil engineer building railroads in New England, New York, Maryland, and Virginia. He was also responsible for designing and constructing a reservoir in Central Park for the water being delivered to the city through the Croton Aqueduct. In 1852, he joined eleven other engineers in founding the American Society of Civil Engineers and Architects (now the American Society of Civil Engineers).

On the personal side, he married Martha Barrett Dana in 1837, and they went on to have six children, five of whom survived to adulthood. When the Civil War broke out, he volunteered for service on behalf of the Union cause. Even though he was then sixty years old, he received a commission from the governor of New York as a colonel in January 1862 and was promoted to brigadier general in April of that year. He went on to lead troops in the heavy fighting at Cedar Mountain, Manassas, Antietam, and Chancellorsville.

However, he won lasting fame during the second day of fighting at Gettysburg, when his lone brigade of 1,350 men repelled repeated assaults on the Union Army's right flank at Culp's Hill by a Confederate force estimated between fifty-one hundred and over eight thousand troops. If the Confederates had prevailed at Culp's Hill, it may well have changed the course of the entire battle, as Greene's son explained in a memoir written following his father's death in 1899 at the age of ninety-seven: "Had they done so they would have been at Meade's headquarters in a few minutes, would have crushed his right flank, and would have taken in reverse the position at the stone wall—'high-water mark'—where the great fight of the next day occurred; and would have gained possession of the Baltimore turnpike, the only line of retreat for the Union army in case of disaster. There was more than one point where the fate of Gettysburg hung in the balance, and where failure would have resulted in complete disaster in this most critical battle of the war; and Culp's Hill was one of these points and at least the equal of any of them in importance." New York Monuments Commission (1909), pp. 63–91; Greene (1903), pp. x, xii–xvii, xxiii; Hunt (1897), pp. 16–23.

26. Peterson (2008), p. 196; Howell & Dunn (2007), pp. 436–437.

27. *Boston Daily Advertiser & Patriot*, Vol. XLII, No. 11,166, p. 2, cols. 4–5 (Saturday, 7 Sept. 1833) (AAS).

28. L. Audubon (1869), p. 387.

29. *Boston Daily Advertiser & Patriot*, Vol. XLII, No. 11,166, p. 2, cols. 4–5 (Saturday, 7 Sept. 1833) (AAS). This article about the Labrador expedition, based upon a lengthy interview with the naturalist during his brief stop in Boston, was picked up and subsequently reprinted in a number of other papers

around the country. See, e.g., *The National Gazette and Literary Register*, Vol. XIII, No. 3919, p. 2, cols. 4–5 (Tuesday, 10 Sept. 1833); *New-York Gazette & General Advertiser*, Vol. 45, No. 16,965, p. 2, cols. 1–2 (Monday Morning, 9 Sept. 1833)(NYHS).

30. JJA, New York to VGA, London, 9 Sept. 1833 (APS), Grinnell (1916), pp. 125–126, *Letters* I, p. 243.

31. JJA, Eastport to LBA, New York, 27 May 1833 (Princeton, Box 2, Folder 21).

32. JJA, New York to VGA, London, 9 Sept. 1833 (APS), Grinnell (1916), p. 126, *Letters* I, p. 243; GCSJr, Eastport to GCS, Boston, 22 May 1833 (MHS, Vol. 11, 14–31 May 1833).

33. L. Audubon (1869), p. 375. Maria's edition of the journal contains no mention of Audubon's displeasure over the fact he bore the burden of the costs of the expedition.

34. *OB* II, p. xxii.

35. L. Audubon (1869), p. 375. In a letter dated May 9, 1833, Dr. Shattuck had offered to pay any drafts Audubon issued while in Eastport to meet the needs of the expedition. GCS, Boston to JJA, Eastport, 9 May 1833 (Yale, Box 6, Folder 312).

36. Wied (2008), p. 51; Morrison (1903), pp. 265–268; Dow (1877), pp. 9–12; *The Providence Patriot and Columbian Phoenix*, p. 3 (Saturday, 31 Aug. 1833); *American Traveller*, Vol. VIII, No. 88, p. 4, col. 6 (Friday Morning, 3 May 1833). In September 1833, there were two competing steamship lines operating vessels between Providence and New York. The New-York & Boston Steamboat Co. had the *Benjamin Franklin* and the *President* with departures at noon on Mondays, Wednesdays, and Fridays. The Rhode Island & New-York Steamboat Company had the *Boston* and the *Providence* departing from Providence at noon on Tuesdays, Thursdays, and Saturdays. The fare on both lines was $6, and passengers could expect to arrive in New York by the following morning. Under ideal conditions, the *Benjamin Franklin* could make the trip between New York and Providence in as little as fifteen hours, twenty-three minutes. Morrison (1903), pp. 265–268; Dow (1877), pp. 9–12. According to *The Providence Patriot*, which published the schedule for the New York-bound steamers, the *Benjamin Franklin* would have been the steamer leaving Providence on Friday, September 6. Consequently,

this would have been the one Audubon and John took to reach New York on the morning of Saturday, September 7.

37. LBA, New York to VGA, London, 7 Sept. 1833 (Yale, Box 1, Folder 21); *New-York American*, Vol. XIV, No. 4458, p. 1, col. 1 (Thursday Evening, 29 Aug. 1833); JJA, Boston to VGA, London, 23 Mar. 1833 (Private collection). Audubon informed Maria Martin, Bachman's sister-in-law, that he had "crossed the Atlantic 4 times" with Capt. Joseph C. Delano (1796–1886), who was a first cousin, twice removed, of President Franklin Delano Roosevelt. JJA, New York to Maria Martin, Charleston, 6 Apr. 1834, *Letters* II, p. 22; Tacy Family Tree, http://person.ancestry.com/tree/17371763/person/20327118331/facts, Ancestry.com (accessed 27 May 2015). In 1840, Audubon inscribed a copy of his *Synopsis* to Delano "from his Sincere Friend and well wisher." Sotheby's (6 June 1989), Lot 33.

38. American Railroad Journal (21 Sept. 1833), p. 600.

39. LBA, New York to VGA, London, 7 Sept. 1833 (Yale, Box 1, Folder 21). See also, note 36, *supra*. The Liverpool packet was scheduled to leave New York on September 8. The packets to London left New York on the 1st, 10th, and 20th of the month. *New-York American*, Vol. XIV, No. 4458, p. 1, col. 1 (Thursday Evening, 29 Aug. 1833). Lucy evidently used both to communicate with Victor.

40. VGA, London to JJA, New York, 7 Sept. 1833 (Yale, Box 2, Folder 38).

41. Waterton (Sept. 1833a), pp. 464–465.

42. Waterton (Sept. 1833b), pp. 465–467.

43. VGA, London to JJA, New York, 7 Sept. 1833 (Yale, Box 2, Folder 38).

44. Ibid.

45. Audubon (2006), p. 450; *AHJ* I, p. 445; L. Audubon (1869), p. 375; Wied (2008), p. 57. We can safely deduce that by the time Audubon and John reached the Berthoud home on the morning of September 7, Nicholas had already left for his office carrying Lucy's letter. Otherwise, her letter almost certainly would have included a quick postscript announcing their arrival, which it doesn't. LBA, New York to VGA, London, 7 Sept. 1833 (Yale Box 1, Folder 21).

46. *OB* II, p. xxii. There is no record of Lucy's appearance when she greeted Audubon at the Ber-

thoud home on Saturday, September 7. However, she would have known from the steamer schedule that the sole vessel to have left Providence for New York on Friday would be docking early Saturday morning. Since she anticipated her husband's arrival, it is safe to assume, as I have, that after so long a separation she would have tried to look her best.

CHAPTER 16: A MONUMENT TO NATURAL HISTORY

1. JJA, New York to VGA, London, 9 Sept. 1833 (APS), Grinnell (1916), pp. 126, 128, *Letters* I, pp. 244–246.

2. JJA, New York to VGA, London, 15 Sept. 1833 (APS), *Letters* I, p. 249; JJA, New York to VGA, London, 9 Sept. 1833 (APS), Grinnell (1916), pp. 126–127. See also, *Letters* I, p. 244.

3. JJA, New York to VGA, London, 9 Sept. 1833 (APS), Grinnell (1916), p. 129.

4. JJA, New York to VGA, London, 23 Sept. 1833 (APS), *Letters* I, pp.256–258; JJA, New York to VGA, London, 20 Sept. 1833 (APS), *Letters* I, p. 253. See also, JJA, Charleston to VGA, London, 24 Dec. 1833, Herrick (1938) II, p. 60.

5. JJA, New York to VGA, London, 23 Sept. 1833 (APS), *Letters* I, pp. 257–258; JJA, New York to VGA, London, 15 Sept. 1833 (APS), *Letters* I, p. 250; JJA, New York to VGA, London, 9 Sept. 1833 (APS), Grinnell (1916), p. 126, *Letters* I, p. 243. Rhodes claims that John W. Audubon "left for Charleston by boat in late September." Rhodes (2004), p. 387. However, Audubon advised Victor in his correspondence of September 23, cited above, that John would be departing "on the 5th of next month."

6. Low (2002), pp. 118–122; JJA, New York to VGA, London, 23 Sept. 1833 (APS), *Letters* I, p. 258; JJA, New York to VGA, London, 20 Sept. 1833 (APS), *Letters* I, p. 254; JJA, New York to VGA, London, 15 Sept. 1833 (APS), *Letters* I, p. 247.

7. JJA, New York to VGA, London (APS), 23 Sept. 1833, *Letters* I, pp. 258–260; JJA, New York to VGA, London, 20 Sept. 1833 (APS), *Letters* I, p. 252; JJA, New York to VGA, London, 15 Sept. 1833 (APS), *Letters* I, pp. 247–249. Although Audubon informed Victor in a letter on September 23 that the drawings for Nos. 41 to 45 would be shipped

via the *Sovereign*, a London packet that had just reached New York, it appears this did not happen. The first five Numbers for the third volume, showcasing the waterbirds, were evidently not sent until early 1834 from Charleston via New York. JJA, Charleston to VGA, London, 9 Mar. 1834 (APS), *Letters* II, p. 13; JJA, Charleston to Robert Havell Jr., London, 19 Jan. 1834 (Harvard (56))(Lucy's copy), *Letters* II, p. 7; JJA, Charleston to VGA, London, 14, 16 Jan. 1834 (APS), *Letters* II, p. 6. Audubon indicated in correspondence to Victor on February 15 that he had drawn most of them in Labrador and, fearing they might be lost in transit, had them insured for $4,000. JJA, Charleston to VGA, London, 15 Feb. 1834 (APS), *Letters* II, p. 9.

8. John Bachman, Charleston to JJA, New York, 14 Sept. 1833, Bachman (1888), p. 135.

9. Ibid.

10. L. Audubon (1869), pp. 376, 378; *American Railroad Journal*, p. 649 (12 Oct. 1833). Ford errs in stating that John departed for Charleston before his parents left for Philadelphia on September 25. Ford (1988), p. 312. In fact, John was still in New York on September 29 and writing his brother with reports of their parents' doings in Philadelphia. JWA, New York to VGA, London (Yale, Box 1, Folder 12).

11. Mearns (2007), pp. 14, 18–22; JJA, Charleston to Tom Lincoln, Dennysville, 7 Nov. 1833, Townsend (1924), p. 241; JWA, New York to VGA, London, 29 Sept. 1833 (Yale, Box 1, Folder 12). The new bird that Audubon obtained in Philadelphia, given to him by John Kirk Townsend on September 27, 1833, was the Townsend's Finch ('Townsend's Bunting (*Emberiza townsendii*)). Deane (1909), p. 269. The bird has never again been observed. Audubon illustrated the bird when he reached Charleston and then returned it to Townsend. JJA, Charleston to John Kirk Townsend, Philadelphia, 4 Nov. 1833, Christie, Manson & Woods (1993), Lot 6.

While the skin is still extant and is in the collection of the Smithsonian Institution, ornithologists question whether it is a hybrid or a bird with defective pigmentation. Mearns (2007), pp. 19–22. Kenneth Parkes of the Carnegie Museum of Natural History has hypothesized that it was a female Dickcissel (*Spiza americana*) without the normal yellow carotenoid pigment in its feathers. Parkes (1985),

p. 92. However, Townsend's field notes as well as the diary of Ezra Michener, for whom Townsend was collecting when he shot the bird and who donated the mounted specimen to the Smithsonian in 1857, indicate that the specimen was a male. Mearns (2007), pp. 20–22; Deane (1909), p. 271. Townsend also observed it singing at the top of a tree where "it emitted a succession of lively notes somewhat resembling the song of the Indigo Bird (*Fringilla cyanea*)[Indigo Bunting], but louder and more varied," an uncharacteristic display for a female. Mearns (2007), p. 20; Deane (1909), p. 271. Parkes suggests that if it was indeed a male, "[p]erhaps an abnormality resulted in the absence of yellow pigment and, at the same time, prevented the bird from assuming the normal plumage of the adult male." Parkes (1985), p. 92. Another possibility is that it was an abnormally plumaged first year male, as Jeff Holt has suggested in an article in *Cassinia*, the journal of the Delaware Valley Ornithological Club. Holt (2002–2003), p. 24.

12. Shuler (1995), pp. 121–122; L. Audubon (1869), pp. 376, 378; JJA, London to John Bachman, Charleston, 5 May 1835 (Harvard (72)), *Letters* II, pp. 70–71.

13. Howe (2007), pp. 232, 379, 387–388; L. Audubon (1869), pp. 378–379; JJA, Baltimore to VGA, London, 11 Oct. 1833 (APS), *Letters* I, pp. 261–263.

14. Howe (2007), pp. 389, 439–442; L. Audubon (1869), p. 379; JJA, Baltimore to VGA, London, 11 Oct. 1833 (APS), *Letters* I, p. 261. Lucy's biography quotes from a journal Audubon was keeping as he traveled from New York to Charleston. With regard to his meeting with U.S. Treasury Secretary Roger Taney, the naturalist recorded that Taney "at once kindly gave me a letter, granting me the privilege of the revenue cutters along the coast south of Delaware Bay." L. Audubon (1869), p. 379. Audubon made essentially the same statement in letters to Victor from Baltimore on October 11 and to Havell from Charleston on November 4. JJA, Charleston to Robert Havell Jr., London, 4 Nov. 1833 (Dartmouth); JJA, Baltimore to VGA, London, 11 Oct. 1833 (APS), *Letters* I, p. 261. Taney may have made an oral commitment, but based upon the secretary's December correspondence to the naturalist, it seems unlikely that Audubon actually left Washington with

a letter in hand. Roger B. Taney, Washington City to JJA, 16 Dec. 1833 (Yale, Box 6, Folder 338).

Ford suggests that Audubon did not see Treasury Secretary Taney during his visit to Washington City and left it to his friend Washington Irving to do so on his behalf. Ford (1988), p. 312. This is contrary to statements in Lucy's biography and Audubon's correspondence cited above.

15. Shuler (1995), pp. 40, 117–118; L. Audubon (1869), pp. 379–380; Eliza Bachman Audubon, New York to Bachman Family, Charleston, 16 Jun. 1840 (Yale, Box 1, Folder 1).

16. JJA, Charleston to VGA, London, 24 Nov. 1833 (APS), *Letters* I, pp. 269–270. During the Audubons' stay in Charleston during the winter of 1833, John drew a number of birds to develop his skills. One of these, of the Swainson's Warbler, appeared as Havell Plate 198, although John did not receive attribution on the print. Ibid. See also, Audubon (1966) I, Plate 153. A group of ten of John's original watercolors from the collection of David Gage Joyce were sold at Hanzel Galleries Inc. in Chicago on September 23, 1973 (Lot 67) for a price of $19,000. According to the auction catalogue, "Three of the plates appear finished, and are signed: "Bay Wing Bunting", J.W. Audubon, Charleston, S.C. Nov 19, 1833; "Red Eye Flycatcher", J.W. Audubon, Nov. 6, 1833; "Cardinal Grosbeak", J.W. Audubon, Dec. 17, 1833." Hanzel Galleries (1973). A copy of this catalog is at the Newberry Library in Chicago.

17. JJA, Charleston to VGA, London, 7 Dec. 1833 (APS), *Letters* I, p. 271; JJA (LBA as amanuensis), Charleston to Edward Harris, New York, 1 Dec. 1833 (Harvard (Letters), pf (110), f. 68); JJA, Charleston to Robert Havell Jr., London, 24 Nov. 1833 (Harvard (55)), *Letters* I, pp. 267–268; JJA, Charleston to VGA, London, 24 Nov. 1833 (APS), *Letters* I, p. 269.

18. Shuler (1995), pp. 132–133; John Bachman, Charleston to JJA, London, 4 Oct. 1834, Audubon (2006), pp. 479–480; JJA, Charleston to VGA, London, 21 Dec. 1833 (APS), *Letters* I, p. 274.

19. Bachman (1834), pp. 164–175; JJA, Charleston to VGA, London, 21 Dec. 1833 (APS), *Letters* I, pp. 272–273.

20. Bachman (1834), pp. 164–175; JJA, Charleston to VGA, London, 21 Dec. 1833 (APS), *Letters*

I, pp. 272–273. The six independent witnesses to the Turkey Vulture experiments who certified the results were: E.F. Leitner, Lecturer on Botany and Natural History; B.B. Strobel, M.D.; Martin Strobel; Robert Henry, A.M., President, College of South Carolina; John Wagner, M.D., Professor of Surgery, Medical College of the State of South Carolina; and Henry R. Frost, M.D., Professor of Materia Medica, Medical College of the State of South Carolina. Bachman (1834), p. 169.

21. JJA, Charleston to VGA, London, 1 Jan. 1834 (APS), *Letters* I, p. 277; Waterton (Jan. 1834a); Waterton (Jan. 1834b); Waterton (Jan. 1834c). While the experiments conducted by Audubon and Bachman in December 1833 demonstrated that Turkey Vultures use their keen eyesight rather than their olfactory sense to locate food sources, later studies have proven that they actually use both, just as Charles Waterton claimed. Ornithologists have caught these birds in traps using only a scent for bait. Also, a Cuban flower that mimics the smell of carrion has been found to attract them. Palmer (1988), p. 38. In his paper, Bachman made a point of stating that he would not "deny to birds the power of smell altogether; nor would I wish to advance the opinion that the vulture does not possess the faculty of smelling in the slightest degree, although it has not been discovered by our experiments. All that I contend for is, that he is not assisted by this faculty in procuring his food: that he cannot smell better, for instance, than hawks or owls, which, it is known, are indebted to their sight altogether in discovering their prey." Bachman (1834), p. 170.

22. Roger B. Taney, Washington City to JJA, 16 Dec. 1833 (Yale, Box 6, Folder 338).

23. JJA, Baltimore to VGA, London, 12 Mar. 1834 (APS), *Letters* II, p. 13; JJA, Charleston to VGA, London, 14 Jan. 1834 (APS), *Letters* II, p. 3.

24. Howe (2007), pp. 391–392; Shuler (1995), p. 131; Fries (1973), pp. 84–85; L. Audubon (1869), pp. 380–381; JJA, Baltimore to John Bachman, Charleston, 13 Mar. 1834 (Princeton, Box 2, Folder 27); VGA, London to JJA, Charleston, 26 Dec. 1833 (Yale, Box 15, Folder 693).

25. Fries (1973), p. 85.

26. JJA, New York to John Bachman, Charleston, 9 Apr. 1834 (Harvard (59)). In the cited letter, Audubon did not identify which of his Labrador

companions visited him in New York in April 1834. However, he reported that "Two of my Suite from Labrador came from Boston to see John & I," and the only members of his company who lived in Boston were Shattuck and Ingalls. Additionally, when Shattuck wrote to Audubon on February 13, 1836, he noted that "Nearly two years have elapsed since I saw you," which would certainly suggest that they had seen each other in April 1834. GCSJr, Boston to JJA, London, 13 Feb. 1836 (Yale, Box 6, Folder 313).

27. L. Audubon (1869), p. 381; JJA, New York to Maria Martin, Charleston, 6 Apr. 1834 (Harvard (58)), *Letters* II, p. 21.

28. JJA, New York to VGA, London, 15 Apr. 1834 (APS), *Letters* II, p. 26.

29. Fries (1973), p. 86; L. Audubon (1869), p. 381; LBA addendum to JJA, London to John Bachman, Charleston, 25 Aug. 1834 (Harvard (61)); JJA, Liverpool to John Bachman, Charleston, 8 May 1834 (Harvard (60)), *Letters* II, p. 27.

30. Waterton (May 1834a); Waterton (May 1834b); Waterton (May 1834c); Charles Waterton to George Ord, Philadelphia, 4 Mar. 1834, Herrick (1938) II, p. 83.

31. Waterton (May 1834a).

32. Waterton (May 1834b).

33. Waterton (May 1834c).

34. JJA, London to John Bachman, Charleston, 25 Aug. 1834 (Harvard (61)), *Letters* II, p. 28.

35. Goddu (2002), p. 34.

36. Goddu (2002), p. 34; Fries (1973), p. 400; JJA, London to John Bachman, Charleston, 16 Jan. 1835 (Harvard (69)), *Letters* II, p. 62; JJA, Edinburgh to John Bachman, Charleston, 10 Dec. 1834 (Harvard (68)), *Letters* II, p. 58; *OB* II, p. xxvii.

37. Sahr (2015); Fries (1973), p. 93; JJA, Edinburgh to Robert Havell Jr., London, 12 Dec. 1835 (Harvard (87)), *Letters* II, p. 107; JJA, Edinburgh to Robert Havell Jr., London, 1 Nov. 1835 (Harvard (84)), *Letters* II, pp. 100–101; JJA, Edinburgh to John Bachman, Charleston, 15 Sept. 1835 (Harvard (78)), *Letters* II, p. 87.

Audubon informed Bachman in a letter in mid-July 1835 that one Number was then being produced monthly. JJA, Edinburgh to John Bachman, Charleston, 20 Jul. 1835 (Harvard (74)), *Letters* II, p. 79. No. 52 (Plates 256–260) came out at the end of July. JJA, Edinburgh to Robert Havell Jr., Lon-

don, 5 Aug. 1835 (Harvard (75)), *Letters* II, p. 81. No. 53 (Plates 261–265) was shipped on the first of September. JJA, Edinburgh to John Bachman, Charleston, 15 Sept. 1835 (Harvard (78)), *Letters* II, p. 86. No. 54 (Plates 266–270) appeared toward the end of September. Audubon received his copy in Edinburgh on September 26. JJA, Edinburgh to Robert Havell Jr., London, 26 Sept. 1835 (Harvard (81)), *Letters* II, p. 93. No. 55 (Plates 271–275) arrived in Edinburgh on the last day of October, and the naturalist was expecting No. 56 (Plates 276–280) to reach him by the end of November. JJA, Edinburgh to Robert Havell Jr., London, 1 Nov. 1835 (Harvard (84)), *Letters* II, pp. 100–101. At this rate, No. 57 would have appeared in late December. Since the last Number to appear in 1834 was No. 47, this means that Havell issued only ten Numbers in 1835. During the first half of the year, he evidently published a Number at intervals of every month and a half.

38. William MacGillivray, Edinburgh to JJA, London, 18 Jul. 1834, Deane (1901), p. 243; William MacGillivray, Edinburgh to JJA, London, 16 Jun. 1834, Deane (1901), pp. 241–242.

39. JJA, London to John Bachman, Charleston, 25 Aug. 1834 (Harvard (61)), Audubon (1999), pp. 825–826, *Letters* II, pp. 28–29.

40. JJA, London to John Bachman, Charleston, 25 Aug. 1834 (Harvard (61)), Audubon (1999), pp. 827–828, *Letters* II, p. 30.

41. Rhodes (2004), p. 391; Chalmers (2003), p. 162; JJA, Edinburgh to John Bachman, Charleston, 5 Nov. 1834 (Harvard (63)), *Letters* II, p. 49; JJA, Leeds to LBA, London, 22 Sept. 1834 (APS), *Letters* II, pp. 38–47; JJA, Manchester to LBA, London, 5 Sept. 1834 (APS), *Letters* II, pp. 33–38.

42. Ford (1988), p. 329; JJA, Edinburgh to John Bachman, Charleston, 10 Dec. 1834 (Harvard (68)), *Letters* II, pp. 55, 59; *OB* II, title page; JJA, Edinburgh to John Bachman, Charleston, 3 Dec. 1834 (Harvard (66)), *Letters* II, p. 52; JJA, Edinburgh to John Bachman, Charleston, 5 Nov. 1834 (Harvard (63)), *Letters* II, p. 47.

43. JJA, London to John Bachman, Charleston, 16 Jan. 1835 (Harvard (69)), *Letters* II, pp. 60, 62; JJA, Edinburgh to John Bachman, Charleston, 10 Dec. 1834 (Harvard (68)), *Letters* II, p. 59.

44. JJA, London to John Bachman, Charleston,

16 Jan. 1835 (Harvard (69)), *Letters* II, p. 62; JJA, Edinburgh to John Bachman, Charleston, 10 Dec. 1834 (Harvard (68)), *Letters* II, pp. 56–59; JJA, Edinburgh to John Bachman, Charleston, 3 Dec. 1834 (Harvard (66)), *Letters* II, p. 53.

45. JJA, Edinburgh to John Bachman, Charleston, 10 Dec. 1834 (Harvard (68)), *Letters* II, p. 58.

46. JJA, London to John Bachman, Charleston, 16 Jan. 1835 (Harvard (69)), *Letters* II, pp. 60–63; JJA, Edinburgh to John Bachman, Charleston, 10 Dec. 1834 (Harvard (68)), *Letters* II, pp. 56–58. One of the oddest requests Audubon made of Bachman was on behalf of William MacGillivray, who wanted the skulls of Negroes to study. JJA, Edinburgh to John Bachman, Charleston, 20 Jul. 1835 (Harvard (74)), *Letters* II, p. 80; JJA, Edinburgh to John Bachman, Charleston, 4 Oct. 1834 (Harvard (62)). Bachman ignored the request. JJA, Edinburgh to John Bachman, Charleston, 1 Dec. 1835 (Harvard (86)), *Letters* II, p. 106.

47. Ford (1988), p. 332; JJA, London to John Bachman, Charleston, 20 Apr. 1835 (Harvard (70)), *Letters* II, pp. 65–66.

48. Chalmers (2003), pp. 162–163, Appendix 2, p. 218; JJA, London to John Bachman, Charleston, 1 Dec. 1835 (Harvard (86)), *Letters* II, pp. 102, 104–105; JJA, London to John Bachman, Charleston, 5 May 1835 (Harvard (72)), *Letters* II, p. 74.

49. JJA, Edinburgh to John Bachman, Charleston, 1 Dec. 1835 (Harvard (86)), *Letters* II, pp. 104–105; JJA, Edinburgh to John Bachman, Charleston, 15 Sept. 1835 (Harvard (78)), *Letters* II, p. 89; JJA, London to John Bachman, Charleston, 5 May 1835 (Harvard (72)), *Letters* II, p. 74.

50. Ford (1988), pp. 338–339; Herrick (1938) II, p. 144; JJA, Liverpool to John Bachman, Charleston, 27 Dec. 1835 (Harvard (88)), *Letters* II, p. 108; JJA, Edinburgh to Robert Havell Jr. London, 12 Dec. 1835 (Harvard (87)), *Letters* II, p. 107.

51. Waterton (Apr. 1835), pp. 236–238.

52. Waterton (Dec. 1835), pp. 663–664.

53. Herrick (1938) II, p. 80 and facing illus.

54. JJA, London to John Bachman, Charleston, 22 Jan. 1836 (Harvard (90)), *Letters* II, pp. 109–111; JJA, London to John Bachman, Charleston, 20 Apr. 1835 (Harvard (70)), *Letters* II, p. 67.

55. JJA, London to John Bachman, Charleston, 22 Jan. 1836 (Harvard (90)), *Letters* II, pp. 110–111.

56. Chalmers (2003), p. 167; JJA, London to John Bachman, Charleston, 22 Jan. 1836 (Harvard (90)), *Letters* II, pp. 111–112, 114; JJA, Edinburgh to John Bachman, Charleston, 20 Oct. 1836, *Letters* II, pp. 96–99.

57. Rhodes (2004), pp. 392–393; Ford (1988), pp. 337–338; Herrick (1938) II, p. 145; JJA, London to John Bachman, Charleston, 9 Mar. 1836 (Harvard (92)), *Letters* II, p. 117–118; JJA, London to John Bachman, Charleston, 22 Jan. 1836 (Harvard (90)), *Letters* II, p. 113; JJA, Edinburgh to John Bachman, Charleston, 20 Jul. 1835 (Harvard (74)), *Letters* II, p. 80; JJA, Edinburgh to John Bachman, Charleston, 19 Nov. 1834 (Harvard (65)), *Letters* II, p. 51.

58. JJA, London to John Bachman, Charleston, 9 Jul. 1836 (Harvard (95)), *Letters* II, pp. 125–126; JJA, London to John Bachman, Charleston, 12 Jun. 1836 (Harvard (94)), *Letters* II, p. 122; JJA, London to John Bachman, Charleston, 29 May 1836 (Harvard (93)), *Letters* II, p. 120; JJA, London to John Bachman, Charleston, 22 Jan. 1836 (Harvard (90)), *Letters* II, p. 113.

59. Ford (1988), p. 343; L. Audubon (1869), pp. 384–385; JJA, New York to John Bachman, Charleston, 2 Oct. 1836 (Harvard (97)), *Letters* II, p. 134; JJA, New York to John Bachman, Charleston, 10 Sept. 1836 (Harvard (96)), *Letters* II, p. 132; JJA, New York to LBA, London, 7 Sept. 1836 (APS), *Letters* II, pp. 127–128.

60. L. Audubon (1869), pp. 386; John Bachman, Charleston to JJA, New York, 14 Sept. 1836, Bachman (1888), pp. 137–139; JJA, New York to Edward Harris, Moorestown, NJ, 12 Sept. 1836 (Harvard (Letters), pf (110), p. 30), Herrick (1938) II, pp. 147–148; JJA, New York to LBA, London, 7 Sept. 1836 (APS), *Letters* II, pp. 127–128.

61. Mearns (2007), pp. 3, 19, 23, 269; Fries (1973), p. 99; L. Audubon (1869), pp. 386–387; JJA, New York to Edward Harris, Moorestown, NJ, 12 Sept. 1836 (Harvard (Letters), pf (110), p. 30), Herrick (1938) II, pp. 147–148; JJA, New York to John Bachman, Charleston, 10 Sept. 1836 (Harvard (96)), *Letters* II, p. 131. On his voyage back to Boston from San Diego aboard the *Alert,* Thomas Nuttall found one of his former Harvard students, Richard Henry Dana (1815–1882), working on the vessel as a merchant seaman. Dana would go on to pen a memoir of his trip to California, *Two Years Before the*

Mast, that brought him lasting fame. Mearns (1992), p. 343.

62. Fries (1973), p. 97; L. Audubon (1869), pp. 387–388. See also, Epilogue, note 85, *infra*. The statement by Herrick as well as by Barbara and Richard Mearns that Audubon left New York for Boston on September 20 is incorrect. Mearns (2007), pp. 269–270; Herrick (1938) II, pp. 149–150. So too is Fries's assertion that Audubon arrived in Boston on September 20. Fries (1973), p. 99. A close reading of Lucy's biography, which is the source for the details of this trip, reveals that he arrived in Boston on September 19 even though the journal entry in the biography gives the date as September 20. It appears he wrote this in the early morning hours of the 20th. This is followed by a second entry dated September 20, clearly the day after he arrived, where he described meeting with young Roxbury ornithologist Thomas M. Brewer (1814–1880). Since his journal makes it clear that he reached Boston the day after he left New York, it would appear that his steamer sailed from New York on September 18 as stated in the text.

63. Mearns (2007), pp. 269–270; Mearns (1992), pp. 335, 337, 341; Fries (1973), p. 97; Herrick (1938) II, p. 151; L. Audubon (1869), p. 387–388; JJA, New York to John Bachman, Charleston, 2 Oct. 1836 (Harvard (97)), *Letters* II, p. 133. Ford asserts that Audubon traveled to Boston to await the arrival of Thomas Nuttall, who was returning from California. Ford (1988), p. 344. However, Nuttall's vessel had sailed from San Diego in early May 1836, and there is no way Audubon could have known when the naturalist would reach Boston. Graustein (1967), p. 315. In truth, Audubon had other business in Boston and by happenstance was there when Nuttall reached port on September 20. See JJA, New York to John Bachman, Charleston, 10 Sept. 1836 (Harvard (96)), *Letters* II, p. 131.

64. Fries (1973), p. 98; Herrick (1938) II, pp. 151–152; L. Audubon (1869), pp. 389–391. According to Fries, the Boston Society of Natural History sold its subscription copy of *The Birds of America* in 1840 after Col. Thomas H. Perkins, a Boston philanthropist, donated his beautifully colored original-subscriber set. The individuals who had contributed to the purchase of the original copy for the society, including George Parkman and the Shattucks, were named to a committee charged with deciding what to do with that set. They elected to dispose of it to raise funds for the purchase of other natural history volumes. The Perkins set, which the society retained, was sold in 1944 and is now in the Hancock Natural History Collection of the Doheny Memorial Library at the University of Southern California. Fries (1973), pp. 152, 320–321. See also, Hancock Collections and Archives, http://www.usc.edu/libraries/archives/arc/libraries/hancock/archives.html (accessed 11 Jun. 2013).

65. JJA, New York to John Bachman, Charleston, 2 Oct. 1836 (Harvard (97)), *Letters* II, p. 133.

66. Herrick (1938) II, p. 153.

67. L. Audubon (1869), p. 392; JJA, Philadelphia to John Bachman, Charleston, 23 Oct. 1836 (Harvard (101)), *Letters* II, p. 136.

68. L. Audubon (1869), p. 393.

69. *OB* IV, pp. xii, 359; JJA, Philadelphia to John Bachman, Charleston, 23 Oct. 1836 (Harvard (101)), *Letters* II, pp. 135–136.

70. JJA, Philadelphia to John Bachman, Charleston, 23 Oct. 1836 (Harvard (101)), *Letters* II, p. 136.

71. Fries (1973), pp. 101, 277–280; L. Audubon (1869), pp. 393–397; JJA, Baltimore to John Bachman, Charleston, November 6, 1836 (Harvard (103)), *Letters* II, p. 137.

72. L. Audubon (1869), pp. 398–399.

73. L. Audubon (1869), p. 400. Rhodes is in error in stating that the Audubons reached Charleston on November 17, 1836. Rhodes (2004), p. 397. Lucy's biography includes an entry for November 17, in which the naturalist expressly stated that they arrived "last evening." See also, Shuler (1995), p. 143.

74. JJA, Charleston to Robert Havell Jr., London, December 18, 1836 (Princeton, Box 2, Folder 33). Rhodes errs in giving a December 16 date to this letter. Rhodes (2004), p. 476, note at p. 397.

75. Shuler (1995), pp. 143–144; JJA, Charleston to Robert Havell Jr., London, 12 Feb. 1837, Lownes (1935), p. 157.

76. L. Audubon (1869), p. 414; JJA, Mobile, AL to John Bachman, Charleston, 24 Feb. 1837 (Harvard (107)), *Letters* II, pp. 145–147; JJA, Charleston to LBA, London, 13 Feb. 1837 (APS), *Letters* II, p. 140; JJA, New York to John Bachman, Charleston, 2 Oct. 1836 (Harvard (97)), *Letters* II, p. 134.

77. JJA, Charleston to LBA, London, 13 Feb. 1837 (APS), *Letters* II, p. 140.

78. JJA, Mobile, AL to John Bachman, Charleston, 24 Feb. 1837 (Harvard (107)), *Letters* II, pp. 145–146.

79. *OB* IV, p. 226; JJA, Charleston to Thomas M. Brewer, Roxbury, MA, 12 Jun. 1837 (Harvard (113)), Brewer (1880), p. 671.

80. Shuler (1995), pp. 147–148; Fries (1973), p. 103; Herrick (1938) II, p. 157; L. Audubon (1869), pp. 400–401; JJA, Bayou Sallé Bay to John Bachman, Charleston, 18 Apr. 1837 (Harvard (112)), *Letters* II, p. 160; JJA, Côte Blanche to William MacGillivray, Edinburgh, 18 Apr. 1837, Herrick (1938) II, p. 158; JJA, Island of Barataria, Grand Terre to John Bachman, 6 Apr. 1837 (Harvard (111)), *Letters* II, pp. 157–158; JJA, New Orleans to John Bachman, Charleston, 22 Mar. 1837 (Harvard (109)), *Letters* II, p. 152.

81. L. Audubon (1869), pp. 407–413.

82. L. Audubon (1869), p. 414; Joseph T. Crawford, New Orleans to Sir Richard Pakenham, 26 May 1837, Adams (1912), p. 209. Crawford was the British Consul at Tampico, Mexico. After a meeting with President Sam Houston, he joined Audubon's party onboard the *Campbell* for the return trip from Galveston to New Orleans. His May 26 letter to Sir Richard Pakenham, the British Minister at Mexico, referenced their arrival in New Orleans on the evening of May 25. Audubon's letter to Thomas M. Brewer of June 12, where he reported that they had arrived in New Orleans "ten days ago," is obviously in error. JJA, Charleston to Thomas M. Brewer, Roxbury, MA, 12 Jun. 1837 (Harvard (113)), Brewer (1880), p. 671.

83. JJA, Charleston to Thomas M. Brewer, Roxbury, MA, 12 Jun. 1837 (Harvard (113)), Brewer (1880), p. 671. See also, Herrick (1938) II, p. 166.

84. Rhodes (2004), p. 400; L. Audubon (1869), p. 414; JJA, Charleston to Thomas M. Brewer, Roxbury, MA, 12 Jun. 1837 (Harvard (113)), Brewer (1880), p. 671.

85. Herrick (1938) II, p. 165; Arthur (1937), p. 441; L. Audubon (1869), pp. 414–415; JJA, Charleston to Thomas M. Brewer, Roxbury, MA, 12 Jun. 1837 (Harvard (113)), Brewer (1880), p. 671. Cf. Lewis (1991), p. 81. In the portion of Audubon's journal published in Lucy's biography, cited here, the naturalist indicated that their overland trip to Charleston took eight and a half days. This appears to be the basis for Shuler's assertion that the party reached Charleston on June 9. Shuler (1995), p. 150. Fries cites the *OB* for Audubon's statement that their arrival in Charleston occurred on June 5. Fries (1973), p. 104; *OB* IV, p. xix. However, that publication is replete with numerous errors with regard to dates and cannot be trusted as a reliable source. The text relies upon Audubon's letter to Thomas Brewer of June 12, in which he indicated they had arrived back in Charleston "Two days ago."

86. Herrick (1938) II, p. 165; *OB* IV, p. xix.

87. L. Audubon (1869), p. 414; *OB* IV, p. xix. Arthur is mistaken in his assertion that Dash was given to Audubon's nephew, William Bakewell Berthoud. Arthur (1937), p. 441. Audubon indicated in the *OB* that when he returned to New Orleans, he "had the gratification of meeting with my youngest brother-in-law, WILLIAM G. BAKEWELL, Esq. of Louisville, Kentucky, as well as with his amiable wife, neither of whom I had seen for several years." Lucy's biography includes a journal entry for May 31 in which Audubon stated that "We bid adieu to our New Orleans friends, leaving . . . dog Dash for Mr. W. Bakewell."

88. Sanders & Ripley (1986), p. 49. Audubon scholars have generally erred in giving the date for the wedding of John Woodhouse Audubon and Maria Bachman. Souder and Streshinsky place it in May 1837, when Audubon and John were still making their way back to Charleston. Souder (2004), p. 280; Streshinsky (1993), p. 314. Anne Roulhac Coffin, a great-granddaughter of John Bachman, states that it occurred on June 7, but this also would have been before the Audubons' June 10 arrival. Coffin (1965), p. 47. See also, note 85, *supra*. Rhodes asserts that they were married on Saturday, June 24, 1837, although he acknowledges in an accompanying endnote that he could not find a published source and came up with an estimate of the date based on Audubon's surviving correspondence. Otherwise, he indicates that it must have been in the third week of June, which indeed it was. Rhodes (2004), p. 400 and note, p. 476.

89. JJA, New York to LBA, London, 8 Jul. 1837, *Letters* II, p. 166; JJA, Moorestown, NJ to "My Dear Friends" (addressed to Mᵣˢ Bachman, Care of

Revd John Bachman), Charleston, 2 Jul. 1837 (Harvard (114)), *Letters* II, p. 161. Audubon's party had reached Norfolk by June 25 after a thirty-eight-hour trip by steamer from Charleston, suggesting a June 23 departure. *OB* IV, p. xx. From Norfolk they took a steamer to Washington City, where they stayed "nearly 2 days." They then proceeded on to Baltimore and arrived in Philadelphia on June 28 (not June 20 as transcribed in *Letters* II, p. 161).

90. JJA, New York to John Bachman, Charleston, 16 Jul. 1837 (Harvard (117)), *Letters* II, p. 168; JJA, New York to LBA, London, 8 Jul. 1837 (APS), *Letters* II, pp. 165–166. Fries's statement that the *England* sailed from New York on July 16, citing the Introduction to the fourth volume of the *OB*, is mistaken, as Audubon's July 8 and 16 letters to Bachman attest. Fries (1973), p. 105.

91. Ford (1988), pp. 349–350; JJA, Moorestown, NJ to "My Dear Friends" (addressed to Mrs Bachman, Care of Revd John Bachman), Charleston, 2 Jul. 1837 (Harvard (114)), *Letters* II, p. 163.

92. JJA, Moorestown, NJ to "My Dear Friends" (addressed to Mrs Bachman, Care of Revd John Bachman), Charleston, 2 Jul. 1837 (Harvard (114)), *Letters* II, p. 164.

93. JJA, New York to LBA, London, 8 Jul. 1837 (APS), *Letters* II, p. 166.

94. Rhodes (2004), p. 400.

95. Sahr (2015); JJA, New York to John Bachman, Charleston, 16 Jul. 1837 (Harvard (117)), *Letters* II, p. 169.

96. Hart-Davis (2004), p. 247; Chalmers (2003), p. 171; JJA, Packet Ship *England* off Holyhead to LBA, London, 4 Aug. 1837 (APS), *Letters* II, p. 174. Audubon's letter was written on the morning of August 4, at which time the *England* was off the Wales coast at Holyhead. He advised Lucy that he hoped "to be Landed Tomorrow at Liverpool," but at the speed they had made the crossing and the distance between Holyhead and Liverpool, it appears likely they docked the same day. Fries is mistaken in stating that the passage of the *England* between New York and Liverpool took only seventeen days. Audubon expressly stated in his letter to Lucy that, as of August 4, they had been at sea for eighteen. Fries (1973), p. 107.

97. Fries (1973), p. 107; JJA, London to John

Bachman, Charleston, 14 Aug. 1837 (Harvard (119)), *Letters* II, p. 175.

98. JJA, London to John Bachman, Charleston, 14 Aug. 1837 (Harvard (119)), *Letters* II, pp. 175–176.

99. Fries (1973), p. 107; JJA, Charleston to Robert Havell Jr., London, 12 Feb. 1837, Lownes (1935), p. 147.

100. Low (2002), p. 3; JJA, London to John Bachman, Charleston, 14 Apr. 1838 (Harvard (126)), *Letters* II, pp. 201–202.

101. Fries (1973), illus. opp. p. 102; Rhoads (1916), pp. 131–132.

102. JJA, London to John Bachman, Charleston, 14 Apr. 1838 (Harvard (126)), *Letters* II, p. 202.

103. Fries (1973), p. 110; JJA, London to John Bachman, Charleston, 31 Oct. 1837 (Harvard (121)), *Letters* II, p. 189.

104. Rhodes (2004), p. 403, 409; Chalmers (2003), p. 172; Shuler (1995), pp. 157–158; Fries (1973), p. 110; *OB* V, pp. xxiv, 647–651; JJA, Edinburgh to Dr. Samuel Morton, Philadelphia, 25 Jun. 1838 (Samuel George Morton Papers (Mss.B.M843), American Philosophical Society). Audubon stated in the *OB* that *BOA* was completed on June 20, 1838. *OB* IV, p. v. This was also the date he had projected in a May 26, 1838, letter to his Roxbury friend Thomas Brewer. JJA, London to Thomas Brewer, Roxbury, MA, 26 May 1838, Brewer (1880), p. 674. However, given the frequent errors Audubon made in giving dates in the *OB*, I have relied on his more contemporaneous statement in the letter to Dr. Samuel Morton that "The Birds of America were finished on the 16 inst. [i.e., instant]." Note that Hart-Davis mistakenly refers to Morton as "Norton." Hart-Davis (2004), p. 253.

105. *OB* IV, p. v.

106. JJA, Edinburgh to Dr. Samuel Morton, Philadelphia, 25 Jun. 1838 (Samuel George Morton Papers (Mss.B.M843), American Philosophical Society), quoted in Fries (1973), p. 110.

107. Low counted 443 separate species in the Double Elephant Folio at the time of her publication. Low (2002), p. 16. I made an independent tally by updating Peterson (1981) using Sibley (2014), which conforms to the American Ornithologists' Union (AOU) *Check-list of North American Birds* (7th ed., 1998) through the Fifty-fourth Supple-

ment in 2013. Of the 449 species recognized today that Audubon illustrated, eleven are found outside of North America and are not included on the AOU check-list: Great Crested Grebe, Dusky Albatross (Sooty Albatross), Thick-legged Partridge (Crested Bobwhite), Townsend's Oyster-catcher (Blackish Oystercatcher), Trudeau's Tern (Snowy-crowned Tern), Blue-headed Pigeon (Blue-headed Quail-Dove), Little Night Owl (Little Owl), Mangrove Humming Bird (Black-throated Mango), Columbian Jay (Black-throated Magpie-Jay), Black-headed Siskin, and Mexican Goldfinch (Yellow-faced Siskin). Audubon painted these birds from specimens collected by others, erroneously believing that they had been found in North America. Seven of Audubon's birds were at one time counted among North America's avifauna but are known or believed today to be extinct: Labrador Duck, Eskimo Curlew, Great Auk, Passenger Pigeon, Carolina Parakeet, Ivory-billed Woodpecker, and Bachman's Warbler. Sibley (2014), p. xv.

108. Low (2002), p. 16. Audubon's five "mystery birds" are the Small-headed Flycatcher, Blue Mountain Warbler, Cuvier's Kinglet, Carbonated Warbler, and Townsend's Finch (Townsend's Bunting). Parkes (1985). See also, note 11, *supra*.

109. Fries (1973), p. 114. The memorandum with Audubon's calculated costs for the publication of *BOA* is in the collection of the Audubon Museum, Henderson, KY. It runs the numbers through 1839, which would include not only the costs related to the completion of *BOA* in 1838 but also those associated with printing the final volume of the *OB* and the *Synopsis*, both of which appeared in 1839.

110. Fries (1973), p. 114. The biographers who have referenced the roughly $115,000 cost figure for *BOA* include Rhodes (2004), p. 403; Souder (2004), p. 283; Chalmers (2003), p. 172; Tyler (1993), p. 46; Peterson (1981), Introduction. The conversion of this sum to 2016 dollars is calculated using an average of Sahr's annual conversion factors between 1827 and 1839 (0.038). Sahr (2015).

111. Low (2002), p. 15; Fries (1973), p. 198.

112. Fries states that the British pound was worth about $4.50 during the period Audubon was publishing *BOA*. Fries (1973), p. 387. See also, Sahr (2015).

113. Rhodes (2004), pp. 403-404.

114. In contrast to most of Audubon's biographers, Rhodes takes issue with what he calls "the enduring canard that John James Audubon was 'not a good businessman.'" He argues that Audubon's Henderson business failed in 1819 "like nearly every other business in the trans-Appalachian West, in the wake of an economic disaster that was beyond his control." Rhodes (2004), p. 404. Rhodes is correct in stating that the Panic of 1819—the young nation's first true depression—was widespread and catastrophic for many Americans. However, economic downturns occurred fairly frequently in 19th century America. Audubon had seen businesses fail during the Embargo of 1807 and during the years following the embargo that was instituted during the War of 1812. Smart businessmen prepared for them. Those who relied too much on easy credit and speculative investments failed.

The reality is that Audubon exercised very poor judgment in deciding to build a steam-powered gristmill and sawmill that the surrounding area could not support. Moreover, he had borrowed heavily and had not set aside sufficient hard assets to see him through a serious economic downturn. By way of comparison, Tom Bakewell, who moved to Louisville in 1817 and started a successful foundry and steam engine factory, had positioned himself to survive such a panic. Although his earnings dropped dramatically and he had to make it through a few lean years, he remained in business. Sinclair (1966), pp. 236-237.

115. Shuler (1995), pp. 155-156; Ford (1988), p. 359; Happoldt (1960), p. 120.

116. Happoldt (1960), p. 65. Bachman's young traveling companion, Christopher Happoldt, kept a journal of the trip, which was transcribed and published in 1960 by Claude Neuffer, Associate Professor of English at the University of South Carolina.

117. Spady (2007a); Happoldt (1960), pp. 133-134; Bakewell (1896), p. 32; JJA, Edinburgh to LBA, London, 5 Jul. 1838 (Mill Grove, FR1990.03.001). Ford, Streshinsky, and Hart-Davis are in error as to the birth date of John and Maria Audubon's first child, Lucy Green Audubon. Hart-Davis (2004), p. 254 (July 13, 1838); Streshinsky (1993), p. 323 (June 13, 1838); Ford (1988), p. 359 (June 13, 1838).

Both the family genealogy and the 1900 U.S. Census reflect that she was born on June 30, although the census wrongly indicates the year was 1837 instead of 1838. U.S. Bureau of the Census (1900), Census Place: *Greenburgh, Westchester Co., New York*; Roll: *1174*; Page: *1A*; Enumeration District: *0067*; Bakewell (1896), p. 32.

118. Rhodes (2004), p. 405; Streshinsky (1993), p. 324; Happoldt (1960), pp. 134–135; Herrick (1938) II, p. 178. Rhodes and Shuler state that Bachman remained in London for three days before leaving for Edinburgh. Rhodes (2004), p. 405; Shuler (1995), p. 159. However, the journal of Bachman's traveling companion, Christopher Happoldt, reflects that Bachman took the 9:00 p.m. steamer for Edinburgh on the evening of July 7, which was only two days after they arrived at the Audubons. Happoldt (1960), pp. 134–135. Christopher did not accompany Bachman to Edinburgh and remained in London.

119. Streshinsky (1993), p. 324. The printing of the sheets for the fourth volume of the *OB* commenced on July 2. JJA, Edinburgh to LBA, London, 1 Jul. 1838 (Princeton, Box 2, Folder 36), Herrick (1938) II, p. 179, Shufeldt (1894), p. 312.

120. Streshinsky (1993), p. 324; JJA, Edinburgh to JWA, London, 1 Jul. 1838 (Princeton, Box 2, Folder 36), Herrick (1938) II, pp. 179–180, Shufeldt (1894), p. 312.

121. Rhodes (2004), p. 405. Bachman left London on July 7 and returned exactly three weeks later on July 28. Happoldt (1960), pp. 134–135, 141. Subtracting the several days he was in transit, his time in Edinburgh was about two and a half weeks. The suggestion by Shuler and Streshinsky that he remained in Edinburgh for three weeks is incorrect. Shuler (1995), p. 159; Streshinsky (1993), p. 324.

122. *OB* V, p. xi. Audubon wrote to Thomas Brewer on July 19, 1838, and indicated that Bachman would be leaving for London that day. But the pastor's plans must have changed because we know from the Happoldt journal that Bachman did not reach London until July 28, and it certainly would not have taken nine days for Bachman to have traveled south to London via steamer. Cf. Happoldt (1960), p. 141; JJA, Edinburgh to Thomas Brewer, 19 Jul. 1838, Brewer (1880), p. 674.

123. Happoldt (1960), p. 141.

124. JJA, Edinburgh to LBA, London, 1 Aug. 1838 (Princeton, Box 2, Folder 38). See also, Streshinsky (1993), p. 324–325

125. Rhodes (2004), p. 405; Chalmers (2003), p. 172

126. Shuler (1995), pp. 160–164; Happoldt (1960), pp. 151–201; Bachman (1888), p. 174. Ford states that Bachman had received an invitation to the natural history conference in Freyburg and that this was one of the reasons for his trip. Ford (1988), p. 359. It appears, rather, that his attendance at the conference was completely unplanned and that he learned of it only once he was in Germany. Shuler (1995), p. 162; Bachman (1888), p. 172.

127. Happoldt (1960), pp. 207–208; 213–214. Shuler errs in asserting that Bachman reached Charleston on December 27. Shuler (1995), p. 164. The Happoldt journal indicates quite clearly that they landed on the following day.

128. Shuler (1995), pp. 164–165.

129. Chalmers (2003), pp. 173–179; *OB* V, pp. xii–xxi.

130. JJA, Edinburgh to John Bachman, Paris, 29 Sept. 1838 (Harvard (130)), *Letters* II, p. 203.

131. *OB* IV, p. xxiv.

132. JJA, Edinburgh to John Bachman, London, 27 Oct. 1838 (Harvard (132)), *Letters* II, p. 208. In this letter, Audubon informed Bachman that the final sheets of Volume IV were received from the printer on October 26 and that he expected copies of the bound volume would be available in London by November 3.

133. Rhodes (2004), p. 406; *OB* V, p. xxv.

134. Rhodes (2004), p. 407; Audubon (1839), pp. v–vi; JJA, Edinburgh to Robert Havell Jr., Reading, Berks, 30 Jun. 1839 (Harvard (135)), *Letters* II, p. 222; JJA, Edinburgh to John Bachman, Paris, 29 Sept. 1838 (Harvard (130)), *Letters* II, p. 203.

135. Rhodes (2004), pp. 406–408; Ford (1988), pp. 365–366; Fries (1973), pp. 115–116, 122–124. Ford's chronology in her Appendix has the Audubons leaving England in September 1839, an obvious error. Ford (1988), p. 464. Fries points out that when Audubon returned to New York in 1839, his ledger listed fifteen bound sets of *BOA* that Havell had produced for later sale. All were sold between 1839 and 1850. However, the family evidently

also had two other bound sets that Victor sold after Audubon's death. The ledger does not account for these. Fries (1973), pp. 122–124. These may have been original subscriber sets that the family resold for the subscribers. In addition, Havell shipped at least five unbound sets to New York. JJA, Edinburgh to Robert Havell Jr., London, 20 Feb. 1839, Deane (1908c), pp. 408–409. This would suggest that the total number of complete double elephant folio sets was around 180. In the intervening years, numerous sets have been broken up and sold. Others have been destroyed by natural disaster.

As of 2016, only 120 sets are known to exist. Of these, 106 are in institutional collections, and fourteen are privately owned. Sotheby's (2014), p. 18; Christie's (2012a), p. 21; Low (2002), p. 3. See also, "First edition Audubon book sells for $7.9 million," *Reuters* (Friday, 20 Jan. 2012), http://www.reuters.com/article/2012/01/20/us-audubon-idUSTRE80J21420120120; Robert King, "Rare Audubon books fetch $3.77 million," *USA Today* (Tuesday, 1 Apr. 2014) http://www.usatoday.com/story/news/nation/2014/04/01/audubon-books-auction-indiana/7180001/.

136. Shuler (1995), pp. 166–168; Ford (1988), p. 369.

137. Rhodes (2004), p. 407–408; Shuler (1995), p. 170.

138. Rhodes (2004), p. 408.

139. Bledsoe (1998), 27–29, 224–226.

140. Athenaeum (1839), p. 577.

CHAPTER 17: AMERICA'S GREATEST NATURALIST

1. Rhodes (2004), p. 408; Ford (1988), p. 369. See also, U.S. Customs Service (2003). Hart-Davis is mistaken in his assertion that Audubon purchased a house at 84 White Street. Hart-Davis (2004), p. 259. The house was located at 86 White Street, and it was leased. Rhodes (2004), p. 408; Shuler (1995), p. 171; Deane (1906), p. 332, note 1.

2. Rhodes (2004), p. 409; Hart-Davis (2004), p. 259; JJA, New York to Samuel G. Morton, Philadelphia, 9 Sept. 1839 (Samuel George Morton Papers (Mss.B.M843), American Philosophical Society). According to Ron Tyler, whose excellent 1993 book, *Audubon's Great National Work*, provides the definitive account of the production of the small edition of *BOA*, the "royal octavo" edition had dimensions upwards of 7″x 10¾″ untrimmed. Tyler (1993), p. 51. It appears that the size was somewhat variable. In the course of my research, I examined an individual Number in the original paper wrappers, which is how it was distributed to subscribers on the first and fifteenth of each month, that measured an even taller 10⅞″.

3. Tyler (1993), p. 47, 49.

4. Ibid., pp. 51, 76–78.

5. Ibid., pp. 51–52. In 1839, E.G. Dorsey and J.B. Chevalier had been involved in a failed effort by John Kirk Townsend to publish an ornithological work comparable to *The Birds of America*. Without an artist of Audubon's caliber to illustrate it, subscriber interest was slight, and the project folded after the appearance of a single Number. Townsend had approached Audubon in 1838 to see if he would be interested in jointly publishing such a work. Audubon referred Townsend to Victor, who had since returned to America, but the naturalist never really had any intention of partnering with Townsend. Ibid., p. 49.

Audubon considered using Havell to do the illustrations for the octavo *Birds*, but the engraver, now resettled with his family in Brooklyn, was not interested. He had immigrated to America with the idea of starting over as landscape painter. In addition, Audubon had yet to pay him for the extra sets of *BOA* that he had produced before closing his shop, and he likely had reservations about taking on a new project with the naturalist given their sometimes stormy relationship. At the same time, Havell may have recognized that, with the development of less expensive lithography, the days of copperplate engraving were drawing to a close. Rhodes (2004), p. 409; Tyler (2000), p. 135; Tyler (1993), pp. 48, 51–52; JJA, Edinburgh to Robert Havell Jr., London, 15 May 1839 (Harvard (143)), *Letters* II, p. 220.

6. Shuler (1995), pp. 168–169.

7. John Bachman, Charleston to JJA, New York, 24 Dec. 1839 (Charleston Museum). See also, Bachman (1888), p. 179.

8. Shuler (1995), p. 169; John Bachman, Charleston to JJA, New York, 13 Sept. 1839, Bachman (1888), p. 181.

9. Rhodes (2004), p. 410; Shuler (1995), pp. 26, 171–172; JJA, Boston to John Bachman, Charleston, 8 Dec. 1839 (Harvard (148)), *Letters* II, pp. 226–227.

10. Rhodes (2004), p. 410; Shuler (1995), p. 171.

11. Shuler (1995), pp. 171–172; JJA, New York to VGA, Charleston, 24 Nov. 1839 (APS), *Letters* II, p. 224.

12. Rhodes (2004), p. 410; Shuler (1995), p. 172.

13. Shuler (1995), p. 172; JJA, Boston to John Bachman, Charleston, 8 Dec. 1839 (Harvard (148)), *Letters* II, pp. 226

14. Shuler (1995), pp. 172–173. See also, Bachman (1888), pp. 178–179.

15. Audubon (1840) I, p. 251; JJA, New York to John Bachman, Charleston, 2 Jan. 1840 (Harvard (149)), *Letters* II, p. 228, 230. Shuler misreads this letter in stating that Audubon had signed up 160 subscribers during his canvassing trip through New England. Shuler (1995), p. 173.

16. JJA, New York to John Bachman, Charleston, 2 Jan. 1840 (Harvard (149)), *Letters*, II, p. 230.

17. John Bachman, Charleston to JJA, New York, 13 Jan. 1840 (Charleston Museum), quoted with added punctuation in Shuler (1995), p. 174. See also, Bachman (1888), p. 182. Shuler gives this letter a date of January 15, which is in error.

18. Rhodes (2004), p. 412; John Bachman, Charleston to JJA, New York, 13 Jan. 1840 (Charleston Museum), quoted in Shuler (1995), p. 174. See also, Eliza Bachman Audubon, New York to Mary E. Davis, Charleston, 21 Jan. 1840 (Charleston Museum), quoted in Rhodes (2004), p. 411 and Shuler (1995), p. 174. Note that in his source citation to Eliza's January 21 letter, Rhodes indicates that the recipient was her grandmother. Rhodes (2004), p. 477. Actually, Mary E. Davis (Mrs. J.M. Davis) was a Charleston widow and Bachman family friend whom the Bachman children viewed as another grandmother. Shuler (1995), p. 167.

19. John Bachman, Charleston to JJA, New York, 13 Jan. 1840 (Charleston Museum), quoted in Shuler (1995), p. 174. See also, Bachman (1888), p. 182.

20. Rhodes (2004), pp. 411–412; Shuler (1995), pp. 174–175; Bakewell (1896), p. 32; JJA, Baltimore to John Bachman, Charleston, 15 Feb. 1840 (Harvard (150)), *Letters* II, p. 232.

21. JJA, Baltimore to John Bachman, Charles-ton, 15 Feb. 1840 (Harvard (150)), *Letters* II, pp. 231–232.

22. JJA, Baltimore to VGA, New York, 23 Feb. 1840 (APS), *Letters* II, pp. 234–235. See also, Tyler (1993), p. 59.

23. Shuler (1995) p. 175; JJA, Baltimore to VGA, New York, 7 Mar. 1840 (APS), *Letters* II, p. 247; JJA, Baltimore to VGA, New York, 23 Feb. 1840 (APS), *Letters* II, p. 234; JJA, Baltimore to VGA, New York, 21 Feb. 1840, Deane (1908a), p. 168

24. JJA, Baltimore to VGA, New York, 7 Mar. 1840 (APS), *Letters* II, p. 247; JJA, Baltimore to Maria Martin, Charleston, 29 Feb. 1840 (Harvard (151)), *Letters* II, p. 238.

25. JJA, Baltimore to JWA, Charleston, 9 Mar. 1840 (Harvard (152)), *Letters* II, p. 250.

26. Shuler (1995), p. 175; JJA, Baltimore to VGA, New York, 27 Mar. 1840 (APS), *Letters* II, pp. 251–253. Shuler indicates that Audubon sold three hundred copies of the *Birds* in Baltimore. Shuler (1995), p. 175. As reflected in Audubon's March 7 letter to Victor, it was actually 171. JJA, Baltimore to VGA, New York, 7 Mar. 1840 (APS), *Letters* II, p. 247. See also, Tyler (1993), p. 69.

27. JJA, Richmond to JWA, Charleston, 12 Apr. 1840 (Harvard (153)), *Letters* II, p. 254.

28. JJA, Richmond to VGA, New York, 15, 16, 18 April 1840 (APS), *Letters* II, pp. 259–264.

29. Ibid., p. 264; JJA, Richmond to John Bach-man, Charleston, 17 Apr. 1840 (Harvard (154)), *Letters* II, p. 266.

30. Shuler (1995), p. 176; JJA, Charleston to VGA, New York, 4 May 1840 (APS), *Letters* II, p. 268.

31. Shuler (1995), pp. 176–177; John Bachman, Charleston to VGA, New York, 10 May 1840, Bachman (1888), pp. 184–185; JJA, Charleston to VGA, New York, 4 May 1840 (APS), *Letters* II, pp. 267–268.

32. JJA, Charleston to VGA, New York, 7 May 1840 (APS), *Letters* II, p. 269.

33. Shuler (1995), p. 175; John Bachman, Charleston to VGA, New York, 10 May 1840, Bachman (1888), pp. 184–185.

34. Rhodes (2004), pp. 412–413; Shuler (1995), pp. 177–178.

35. Shuler (1995), pp. 180–181.

36. Ibid., p. 181.

37. Rhodes (2004), pp. 413–414; Shuler (1995), pp. 180–182; JJA, New York to Spencer F. Baird, Carlisle, PA, 13 Jun. 1840, Deane (1906), p. 200.

38. JJA, Boston to VGA, New York, 18 Jul. 1840 (APS), *Letters* II, p. 271; Corning (1929b), pp. 160, 164–165.

39. Shuler (1995), p. 182; Corning (1929b), pp. 23–25.

40. Rhodes (2004), p. 414; Corning (1929b), p. 25.

41. Rhodes (2004), pp. 414–415; Shuler (1995), pp. 182–183.

42. Corning (1929b), pp. 154–155.

43. Ibid., p. 46.

44. Ibid., pp. 25–46.

45. Ibid., pp. 46–47.

46. Ibid., pp. 47–64.

47. Tyler (1993), Table One, p. 153.

48. Rhodes (2004), pp. 414–415; Shuler (1995), pp. 118, 182–184; Bachman (1888), p. 194.

49. Ford (1951), p. 49. See also, Rhodes (2004), pp. 415–416; Shuler (1995), p. 184.

50. JJA, New York to W.O. Ayres, Miller's Place, Long Island, 15 Aug. 1841, Herrick (1938) II, p. 229. In a letter to Edward Harris on December 30, 1841, Audubon reported that "I have drawn 61 Species comprising 115 figures." JJA, New York to Edward Harris, Moorestown, NJ, 30 Dec. 1841 (Harvard (Letters), pf (110)). See also, Peck (2000), p. 97. These numbers do not square with those in the cited August 15 letter to W.O. Ayers (36 species comprising about 100 figures).

51. Shuler (1995), pp. 186–187.

52. JJA, New York to W.O. Ayres, Miller's Place, Long Island, 15 Aug. 1841, Herrick (1938) II, p. 229–230.

53. Herrick (1938) II, pp. 218–220; JJA, New York to Spencer Fullerton Baird, Carlisle, PA, 29 Jul. 1841, Herrick (1938) II, p. 226, Deane (1906a), p. 209. Spencer Fullerton Baird was born on February 3, 1823, and would have been seventeen years old when he first wrote to Audubon in June 1840, not fifteen as Herrick states. Cf., Herrick (1938) II, p. 220; Dall (1915), p. 5.

54. JJA, New York to George Parkman, M.D., Boston, 20 Jun. 1841, Herrick (1838) II, p. 228.

55. Shuler (1995), pp. 186–187; John Bachman, Charleston to VGA, New York, 1844, Bachman (1888), pp. 202–203.

56. John Bachman, Charleston to JJA. New York, 22 Nov. 1841, Shuler (1995), p. 186.

57. Shuler (1995), pp. 191–192.

58. Spady (2007b) and (2007c) (maps of 1844 and 1851); Rhodes (2004), p. 416; Ford (1988), p. 388; Ford (1951), p. 27; Herrick (1938) II, pp. 234–235; Corning (1929b), p. 72. When the Audubons acquired Minnie's Land (sometimes written as "Minniesland") on October 1, 1841, the parcel consisted of only fourteen acres as stated in the text, not twenty-three as Shuler states or twenty-four as Ford claims. Spady (2007b), (2007c). Cf. Shuler (1995), p. 187; Ford (1988), p. 388. The family would purchase additional acreage in July 1843 that would bring the total to just under twenty-four acres. Spady (2007b), (2007c).

59. Rhodes (2004), p. 416; Shuler (1995), p. 187; Ford (1988), p. 389; Herrick (1938) II, pp. 234–235.

60. Rhodes (2004), pp. 416–417; *AHJ* I, p. 71; Bachman (1896), p. 32. Caroline Hall was born on December 8, 1811, in Loughborough, Leicestershire, England. She became a naturalized U.S. citizen on May 21, 1858. She died on February 1, 1899 at the age of eighty-seven in Salem, New York. Ancestry.com, http://trees.ancestry.com/tree/18071079/person/1420076163/photo/25a60532-3e3a-46dc-bdce-dc78377ea3f1?src=search (accessed 7 Jun. 2013)(image of Caroline Hall's headstone); *Soundex Index to Petitions for Naturalizations Filed in Federal, State, and Local Courts in New York City, 1792–1906*, Microfilm Serial: *M1674*; Microfilm Roll: 2 (Washington, D.C.: National Archives)(accessed through Ancestry.com, 29 May 2015).

61. Rhodes (2004), p. 419; Ford (1988), p. 396; Bachman (1896), p. 31. Very little seems to be known about the origins of Georgianna Richards Mallory, Victor's second wife. While Maria Audubon noted that she was the second daughter of Daniel Mallory, who had come to know Audubon in Cincinnati in 1820, no Audubon scholar has reported where or when she was born. *AHJ* I, p. 48. Herrick indicates in the first edition of his biography in 1917 that she was an Englishwoman. However, in his 1938 second edition, he states that she was a New Englander. Cf. Herrick (1938) II, p. 294; Herrick (1917) II, p. 294. Based on U.S. Census records, it appears that she was born in the District of Columbia. However, determining her date of birth from these records is an

impossible task. Her stated ages in the 1850, 1860, and 1880 census records would place her birth date anywhere from 1814 to 1820. However, some of the genealogists who have posted family trees on Ancestry.com indicate that she was born on October 16, 1815, in the District of Columbia. We know that she died of pneumonia in New York City on November 13, 1882, at the age of sixty-seven, which would be consistent with this birth date. "DIED. Audubon," *The New-York Times*, Vol. XXXII, No. 9781, p. 5, col. 6 (Tuesday, 14 Nov. 1882).

62. Victor's six children were Mary Eliza (1845–1917); Rosa (1846–1879); Victor Gifford (1847–1915); Delia Talman (1849–1926); Lucy Bakewell (1851–1898); and Annie Gordon (1854–1907). Spady (2007a); Ancestry.com, http://trees.ancestry.com/tree/6772742/person/-1228370542 (accessed 7 Jun. 2013); Bakewell (1896), p. 31.

63. John's seven children with Caroline Hall were John James (1842–1842); Maria Rebecca (1843–1925); John James (1845–1893); William Bakewell (1847–1932); Jane (1849–1853); Florence (1853–1949); and Benjamin Philips (1855–1886). He had two daughters with Maria Rebecca Bachman: Lucy ("Lulu") (1838–1909) and Harriet ("Hattie") (1839–1933). Spady (2007a) and (2007b); Bakewell (1896), p. 32.

64. Spady (2007b); Herrick (1938) II, p. 235; L. Audubon (1869), pp, 436–437.

65. Godwin (1853), pp. 4–5. The quotation in the text is taken from a chapter devoted to Audubon in *Homes of American Authors*, published by G.P. Putnam and Co. in 1853. Lucy's biography also quotes from this volume and states that the writer who visited Minnies Land that day in 1846 was Rufus W. Griswold. L. Audubon (1869), pp. 437–438. So does Rhodes. Rhodes (2004). p. 431. Griswold was the author of *The Prose Writers of America* (Philadelphia: Carey and Hart, 1847), which included a brief biographical sketch of Audubon along with samples of his writing. Griswold was a contributor to *Homes of American Authors*, but Parke Godwin indicated in a later compilation of his writing that he had written this piece. Godwin (1870), p. 110.

66. L. Audubon (1869), p. 439. The quotation in the text, taken from Lucy's biography, is from "another visitor" to Minnies Land, not the person erro-

neously identified in her biography as Rufus Griswold. Rhodes is mistaken in asserting otherwise. Rhodes (2004), p. 431. See also, note 65, *supra*.

67. Tyler (2000), pp. 132, 144, 148; Corning (1929b), p. 65.

68. Corning (1929b), pp. 65–83; Audubon & Bachman (1846), pp. 2–43. Shuler misreads Audubon's journal entries in asserting that, in addition to the prints of the Woodchuck and Florida Rat (or Eastern Wood Rat), Audubon carried the prints of the Bobcat and Red Squirrel during his July 1842 canvassing trip. Cf. Shuler (1995), p. 188; Corning (1929b), pp. 65, 67, 69–72.

69. Corning (1929b), pp. 83–99.

70. Corning (1929b), p. 85; Giles (1851) II, p. 266.

71. Giles (1851) II, p. 266–267.

72. Ibid., p. 267.

73. Ford (1988), p. 393; Durant & Harwood (1980), p. 606; Corning (1929b), pp. 99–100.

74. Corning (1929b), pp. 148–149.

75. Corning (1929b), p. 102. Audubon's trip to Canada took him through St. Johns (now called Saint-Jean-sur-Richelieu), a small community in the province of Quebec that he described as "a miserable village." Ibid., p. 103. Ford has confused this with Saint John, New Brunswick. Ford (1988), p. 393.

76. Fries (1973), p. 347; Corning (1929b), pp. 104–149; 152–153. Herrick is in error in asserting that during Audubon's visit to Canada, "three days were spent at Quebec (September 16–18)." Herrick (1938) II, p. 244. As a careful reading of Audubon's journal reveals, he arrived in Montreal by steamer, not rail as Ford claims, on the morning of September 15, 1842. Ford (1988), p. 393. He left for Quebec that evening, arriving at 8:00 a.m. on September 16. He remained in Quebec until September 27, when he returned to Montreal. On October 1, he left for Kingston and reached that city on the 2nd. He was back in Montreal on October 8 and left Montreal for home on October 12.

77. Corning (1929b), p. 115. As Audubon's journal indicates, he was in Quebec when he overheard Dr. Douglas remark that he would not live to see the completion of the *Quadrupeds*, not Montreal as Shuler asserts. Shuler (1995), p. 189.

78. McDermott (1965), p. 8; Herrick (1938) II,

pp. 242–243; Deane (1908b), pp. 170–173). Rhodes states that John C. Spencer was secretary of the U.S. Treasury Department when Audubon visited Washington City in July 1842. Rhodes (2004), p. 417. In fact, Spencer was secretary of war until March 1843, when he resigned and was appointed treasury secretary. Secretaries of the Treasury, U.S. Department of the Treasury website, http://www.treasury.gov/about/history/Pages/edu_history_secretary_index.aspx; http://www.treasury.gov/about/history/pages/jcspencer.aspx (accessed 20 Jun. 2013); Deane (1908b), p. 172, note 4.

79. Rhodes (2004), p. 420; McDermott (1965), pp. 8–9 and note 16; McDermott (1951), p. 9, note 20; JJA, Washington City to VGA, New York, 17 Jul. 1842 (APS), McDermott (1965), p. 9; The formal name of Pierre Chouteau Jr.'s St. Louis business was Pierre Chouteau Jr. and Company. According to McDermott, it was commonly referred to as the American Fur Company even though that company, founded previously by his father and John Jacob Astor, had ceased to exist in 1842. Rhodes (2004), p. 420; McDermott (1951), p. 9, note 20.

80. JJA, New York to Spencer F. Baird, Carlisle, PA, 29 Nov. 1842, quoted in Deane (1907), p. 53. See also, Herrick (1938) II, p. 248.

81. Peck (2000), p. 76; Shuler (1995), pp. 189–190; Mearns (1992), pp. 67, 403; Harwood (1985b), p. 82; McDermott (1965), pp. 10 and 67, note 8; McDermott (1951), pp. 7–8, 215; Herrick (1938) I, p. 252; Corning (1929b), p. 10; JJA, New York to Spencer F. Baird, Carlisle, PA, 23 Feb. 1843, Dall (1915), p. 92.

82. Tyler (2000), p. 154; Shuler (1995), p. 190.

83. Harwood (1985b), p. 82; Sprague (1843), 11 Mar. 1843.

84. Harwood (1985b), p. 82; *AHJ* I, p. 453; Bell (1843), 11 Mar. 1843.

85. McDermott (1951), p. 44; *AHJ* I, p. 454; JJA, Wheeling, VA to "My Dearest Friends," Minnie's Land, 16 Mar. 1843, McDermott (1965), p. 21. Rhodes errs in stating that Audubon and his companions took a train to Cumberland, KY. Rhodes (2004), p. 419. Their destination was Cumberland, MD, which was en route to their next stop at Wheeling, VA (now Wheeling, WV). Cumberland, KY, would have taken them hundreds of miles out of their way.

86. JJA, Louisville to "My Dearest Friends," Minnie's Land, 19 Mar. 1843, McDermott (1965), pp. 23, 25; McDermott (1951), pp. 11, 44–45.

87. *AHJ* I, p. 454.

88. Rhodes (2004), p. 419; Bakewell (1896), p. 44; JJA, Louisville to "My Dearest Friends," Minnie's Land, 19 Mar. 1843, McDermott (1965), p. 23, note 3; p. 25.

89. Rhodes (2004), p. 419; JJA, Ohio River to "My Dearest Beloved Friends," Minnie's Land, 23 Mar. 1843, McDermott (1965), pp. 28–31; JJA, Louisville to "My Dearest Friends," Minnie's Land, 19 Mar. 1843, McDermott (1965), pp. 23–26.

90. Bakewell (1896), pp. 41–42; JJA, Louisville to "My Dearest Friends," Minnie's Land, 19 Mar. 1843, McDermott (1965), pp. 23–24 and note 5. Nicholas and Eliza Berthoud had seven children: Mary Julia (1816–1907); James (1818–1888); William Bakewell (1820–1880); Augustus Nicholas (c. 1823–1873); Annie Gordon (1826–1904); Elizabeth (1828–1912); and Alexander Gordon (1834–1893). Ancestry.com, Berthoud Family Tapestry, http://trees.ancestry.com/tree/43858/family/familygroup?fpid=-2139305221 (accessed 26 Jun. 2013). Elizabeth Berthoud was born on October 5, 1828, in Shippingport, KY, which would have made her fourteen years of age in March 1843. Ford misreads Audubon's correspondence and mistakenly believes that his in-laws Alexander and Ann Gordon were visiting Louisville when he arrived. In fact, Audubon was referring to Annie and Alexander Berthoud.

91. JJA, St. Louis to "My Dearest Friends," Minnie's Land, 28 Mar. 1843, McDermott (1965), p. 39; JJA, Ohio River to "My Dearest Beloved Friends," Minnie's Land, 23 Mar. 1843, McDermott (1965), p. 31; JJA, Louisville to "My Dearest Friends," Minnie's Land, 19 Mar. 1843, McDermott (1965), p. 24 and note 8. Nicholas Berthoud's St. Louis business was located at 68 Water Street. McDermott, (1965), p. 36, note 2. Eliza Berthoud and her three children, James, Annie, and Gordon, arrived in St. Louis on April 7. Her fourth child, Augustus, was already there with her husband. JJA, St. Louis to "My Dearest Friends," Minnie's Land, 8 Apr. 1843, McDermott (1965), p. 52; JJA, St. Louis to "My Dearest Friends," Minnie's Land, 28 Mar. 1843, McDermott (1965), p. 37 and note 5. Alice Ford's assertion that Nicholas and his son

James had greeted the naturalist upon his arrival in St. Louis is incorrect, as Audubon's letter of March 28 makes clear. Cf. Ford (1988), p. 400; McDermott (1965), pp. 37, 39.

92. *New-Orleans Commercial Bulletin*, "Notices," Vol. XL, No. 125, p. 1, col. 4 (Monday Morning, 17 Apr. 1843)(Notice of partnership of A. Gordon, Wylie & Co., 1 Mar. 1843); JJA, Louisville to "My Dearest Friends," Minnie's Land, 19 Mar. 1843, McDermott (1965), pp. 23–24.

93. Audubon (1841) II, p. 204; Audubon (1840) I, p. 253.

94. McDermott (1951), p. 45; JJA, St. Louis to James Hall, 29 Mar. 1843, *AHJ* I, pp. 450–451; JJA, Ohio River to "My Dearest Beloved Friends." Minnie's Land, 23 Mar. 1843, McDermott (1965), p. 28.

95. McDermott (1951), p. 46; JJA, St. Louis to "My Dearest Friends," Minnie's Land, 28 Mar. 1843, McDermott (1965), pp. 36, 38; JJA, Ohio River to "My Dearest Beloved Friends," Minnie's Land, 23 Mar. 1843, McDermott (1965), pp. 31–34.

96. Rhodes (2004), p. 422; Corbin (2000), Appendix H, p. 208; Durant & Harwood (1980), p. 540; McDermott (1951), p. 6; *AHJ* I, p. 452; JJA, St. Louis to "My Dearest Friends," Minnie's Land, 2 Apr. 1843, McDermott (1965), p. 45; JJA, St. Louis to "My Dearest Friends," Minnie's Land, 31 Mar. 1843, McDermott (1965), p. 40; JJA, St. Louis to "My Dearest Friends," Minnie's Land, 28 Mar. 1843, McDermott (1965), pp. 36–38 and notes 6, 8, 11.

97. JJA, St. Louis to James Hall, 29 Mar. 1843, *AHJ* I, pp. 451–452.

98. McDermott (1951), p. 47; JJA, St. Louis to "My Dearest Friends," Minnie's Land, 17 Apr. 1843, McDermott (1965), pp. 55–56; JJA, St. Louis to "My Dearest Friends," Minnie's Land, 8 Apr. 1843, McDermott (1965), p. 52; JJA, St. Louis to James Hall, 29 Mar. 1843, *AHJ* I, p. 452; JJA, St. Louis to "My Dearest Friends," Minnie's Land, 28 Mar. 1843, McDermott (1965), p. 37 and note 7.

99. Rhodes (2004), pp. 421–422; JJA, St. Louis to "My Dearest Friends," Minnie's Land, 20 Apr. 1843, McDermott (1965), p. 60; JJA, St. Louis to "My Dearest Friends," Minnie's Land, 17 Apr. 1843, McDermott (1965), p. 58; JJA, St. Louis to "My Dearest Friends," Minnie's Land, 8 Apr. 1843, McDermott (1965), p. 52; JJA, St. Louis to "My

Dearest Friends," Minnie's Land, 28 Mar. 1843, McDermott (1965), p. 37.

100. McDermott (1965), p. 14.

101. Sage (1917), p. 239.

102. Peck (2000), p. 80; JJA, St. Louis to "My Dearest Friends," Minnie's Land, 23 Apr. 1843, McDermott (1965), p. 65.

103. JJA, Boonville, MO to "My Dearest Friends," Minnie's Land, 29 Apr. 1843, McDermott (1965), p. 77; JJA, St. Louis to LBA, Minnie's Land, 23 Apr. 1843, McDermott (1965), pp. 62–66; JJA, St. Louis to "My Dearest Friends," Minnie's Land, 20 Apr. 1843, McDermott (1965), p. 60; *AHJ* II, p. 188. The Capt. William Clark manuscript journal, covering the period September 11 to December 31, 1805, was given to Audubon on April 19, not April 23 as Rhodes suggests. Rhodes (2004), p. 422. The journal is in the collection of the Missouri History Museum in St. Louis (referred to as Voorhis Journal No. 6 (Elfskin-bound Journal)) and contains the following inscription: "Presented to J.J. Audubon at Sᵗ Louis April 19ᵗʰ 1843 — by D.D. Mitchell, Supt. — Indian Affairs." Tyler (2000), p. 189, note 63; Lewis (1983) II, Appendix C, p. 557; McDermott (1965), p. 64, note 4.

104. *AHJ* I, p. 455. There is some mild disagreement as to the time the *Omega* left St. Louis on April 25. McDermott's transcription of a letter Audubon wrote to his family on the day of their departure has them leaving the wharf at 10:30 a.m. JJA, St. Charles, Missouri River to "My Dearest Friends," Minnie's Land, 25 Apr. 1843, McDermott (1965), p. 72. However, in his journal, Audubon stated that they departed at 11:30 a.m. *AHJ* I, p. 455. Isaac Sprague and John G. Bell recorded the same thing in their own journals. Bell (1843), 25 Apr. 1843; Sprague (1843), 25 Apr. 1843. However, Edward Harris asserted that "it was about noon before we got under way." McDermott (1951), p. 54.

105. Harwood (1985b), pp. 85–86; *AHJ* I, pp. 455–456; JJA, St. Charles, Missouri River to "My Dearest Friends," Minnie's Land, 25 Apr. 1843, McDermott (1965), p. 72; JJA, St. Louis to LBA, Minnie's Land, 23 Apr. 1843, McDermott (1965), p. 63; JJA, St. Louis to "My Dearest Friends," Minnie's Land, 2 Apr. 1843, McDermott (1965), p. 45.

106. Harwood (1985b), p, 91; JJA, St. Charles, Missouri River to "My Dearest Friends," Minnie's

Land, 25 Apr. 1843, McDermott (1965), pp. 73; JJA, St. Louis to LBA, Minnie's Land, 23 Apr. 1843, McDermott (1965), p. 63.

107. Harwood (1985b), pp. 91-92; JJA, Independence, MO to "My Dearest Friends," Minnie's Land, 2 May 1843, McDermott (1965), pp. 79-80; JJA, Boonville, MO to "My Dearest Friends," Minnie's Land, 29 Apr. 1843, McDermott (1965), pp. 75-76.

108. Harwood (1985b), p. 92; *AHJ* I, p. 492.

109. Peterson (2008); p, 374; Mearns (1992), pp. 67-68, 221; Harwood (1985b), pp. 92-94; JJA, Black Snake Hills, Missouri New Purchase to "My Dearest Friends," Minnie's Land, 5 May 1843, McDermott (1965), p. 83; *AHJ* I, p. 470-473; Audubon (1844) VII, pp. 331-334, 338-340.

110. Harwood (1985b), p. 102; JJA, Vermillion River to "My Dearest Friends," Minnie's Land, 17 May 1843, McDermott (1965), p. 92; JJA, Council Bluffs [Bellevue], Missouri Territory to "My Dearest Friends," Minnie's Land, 8 May 1843, McDermott (1965), p. 87.

111. JJA, Black Snake Hills, Missouri New Purchase to "My Dearest Friends," Minnie's Land, 5 May 1843, McDermott (1965), p. 83.

112. JJA, Council Bluffs [Bellevue], Missouri Territory to "My Dearest Friends," Minnie's Land, 8 May 1843, McDermott (1965), p. 87. Audubon misdated this letter May 8. The *Omega* actually reached Bellevue on May 9. McDermott (1965), p. 85, note 1; *AHJ* I, p. 477.

113. JJA, Fort Pierre to "My Dearest Friends," Minnie's Land, 1 Jun. 1843, McDermott (1965), p. 105.

114. Rhodes (2004), p. 425; Harwood (1985b), pp. 95, 98.

115. JJA, Council Bluffs [Bellevue], Missouri Territory to "My Dearest Friends," Minnie's Land, 8 May 1843, McDermott (1965), p. 89.

116. *AHJ* I, p. 477.

117. McDermott (1951), p. 69; *AHJ* I, p. 507.

118. *AHJ* I, p. 518.

119. *AHJ* II, pp. 11, 14.

120. Harwood (1985b), p. 95.

121. Arader (1988), pp. 91-92.

122. Rhodes (2004), p. 425; McDermott (1951), pp. 108-109.

123. *AHJ* II, pp. 47-48, note 1.

124. JJA, Fort Pierre to "My Dearest Friends," Minnie's Land, 1 Jun. 1843, McDermott (1965), pp. 95, 98.

125. *AHJ* I, pp. 497-498.

126. McDermott (1951), p. 139.

127. Boehme (2000), p. 60; Harwood (1985b), p. 101; *AHJ* II pp. 28-29, 180. Edwin T. Denig, the chief clerk at Fort Union, wrote up a description of the fort for Audubon on July 30, 1843, which indicated that it was situated on the northern banks of the Missouri River "about six and a half miles above the mouth of the Yellowstone River." McDermott (1951), p. 27; *AHJ* II, p. 180. Audubon stated that the fort was only about three miles from the confluence of the two rivers. McDermott (1951), p. 97, note 25; JJA, Fort Union to "My Dearest Friends," Minnie's Land, 13 Jun. 1843, McDermott (1965), p. 115 and note 4; *AHJ* II, p. 28. Denig's estimate was evidently based on river miles, whereas Audubon was describing the straight-line distance. The channels of the two rivers have shifted in that vicinity since 1843, but Google Earth allows a visualization of the large oxbow that once existed between the Yellowstone and Fort Union that accounted for the significantly greater distance by water. Fred MacVaugh, Museum Curator, Fort Union Trading Post National Historic Site (Personal communication, 28 Aug. 2015). Alice Ford's assertion that the fort was situated six miles below the Yellowstone River is flatly incorrect. Ford (1988), p. 405.

128. Peck (2000), p. 52; Durant & Harwood, (1980), p. 540; Petersen (1971), p. 582; McDermott (1965), p. 106, note 15; Ford (1951), p. 43; McDermott (1951), p. 97; Taft (1946), p. 149; JJA, Fort Union to "My Dearest Friends," Minnie's Land, 13 Jun. 1843, McDermott (1965), p. 115; JJA, Vermillion River to "My Dearest Friends," Minnie's Land, 17 May 1843, McDermott (1965), p. 92; *AHJ* II, pp. 28-29. Audubon indicated that the *Omega* had made the trek upriver to Fort Union "upward of 20 days" faster than any previous vessel. Harris said it was "by about 15 days." Petersen notes that the distance between Fort Union and St. Louis was 1,757 miles, a figure taken from engineering surveys of the Missouri River performed between 1889 and 1893 by the Missouri River Commission. Though distances along a meandering river like the Missouri can change over time, Ford's statement that the dis-

tance was only 1,400 miles would appear to be a substantial error. Ford (1988), p. 405.

129. McDermott (1965), p. 114, note 2; *AHJ* II, pp. 29, 182. Ford asserts that after the *Omega* landed, Audubon and Harris were "promptly treated to a fast, rough wagon ride over the prairie." Ford (1988), p. 405. Audubon's journal indicates that this happened the day after their arrival. *AHJ* II, p. 29. Ford has evidently combined the events of two days (June 12 and 13) into one. See also, McDermott (1951), pp. 97–98. To the extent Ford implies that Audubon was transported to the fort by wagon, she is in error. Fort Union was situated only about twenty five feet from the banks of the Missouri River. *AHJ* II, p. 180. From the landing to the front entrance it was about seventy-five yards. Harwood (1985b), p. 101. Audubon indicated in his journal that he walked up to the fort. *AHJ* II, p. 29.

130. *AHJ* II, pp. 29–30. After arriving at Fort Union, Audubon and his companions slept aboard the *Omega* for two nights, not one as Ford claims. Cf. Ford (1988), p. 405; McDermott (1951), pp. 98–99; *AHJ* II, pp. 29–30. Ford and McDermott both err in suggesting the *Omega* left for its return voyage the day after it reached Fort Union. McDermott (1965), p. 17; Ford (1988), p. 405.

131. *AHJ* II, pp. 29, 34. Ford describes the room that Audubon's party was initially assigned at Fort Union — the one used a decade before by Prince Maximilian — as a "big chamber," completely ignoring the naturalist's journal entries cited here where he complained about its small size. Ford (1988), p. 407.

132. *AHJ* II, pp. 34–35.

133. McDermott (1951), p. 98.

134. Harwood (1985b), pp. 101–102; *AHJ* II, pp. 181–187.

135. Harwood (1985b), p. 106.

136. Rhodes (2004), p. 421; Harwood (1985b), p. 103; McDermott (1965), p. 46, note 5; McDermott (1951), p. 98, note 28.

137. Harwood (1985b), p. 103; McDermott (1951), pp. 113, note 58; 124; JJA, Fort Union to "My Dearest Friends," Minnie's Land, 13 Jun. 1843, McDermott (1965), p. 115 and note 4.

138. McDermott (1951), pp. 67, 88–89; *AHJ* I, p. 501.

139. McDermott (1951), pp. 135–136, 145–150, 154–160, 165–168, 173–176.

140. Ibid., pp. 99–100; 102; 104–106, 116, 131, 134–135.

141. Ibid., pp. 103–104; 118–119, 124, 171.

142. Harwood (1985b), p. 110.

143. Tyler (2000), p. 155; McDermott (1951), p. 146. It bears noting that Maria Audubon lifted a portion of Edward Harris's journal entry for July 16, 1843, in which he described a Buffalo hunt during an excursion up the Yellowstone River, and incorporated it virtually wholesale into her edition of Audubon's journal, substituting her grandfather for Harris. Cf. McDermott (1951), pp. 138–139; *AHJ* II, pp. 93–94. Audubon was actually off fishing at the time. Edward Harris, New Orleans to John J. Spencer, M.D., Moorestown, NJ, 1 Dec. 1842, McDermott (1951), p. 31. Maria obviously wanted to place Audubon at the center of a more exciting and dramatic tale than his own journal entry afforded.

144. Harwood (1985b), p. 110; *AHJ* I, pp. 508–509.

145. McDermott (1951), p. 149.

146. Harwood (1985b), p. 107; McDermott (1951), pp. 106–107, 130, 132, 169; *AHJ* II, pp. 49–50.

147. McDermott (1951), p. 105; *AHJ* II, p. 41; Audubon (1844) VII, p. 334.

148. McDermott (1951), pp. 105–106; Audubon (1844) VII, pp. 345–346, 359.

149. Eastman (2000), p. 235; Audubon (1844) VII, p. 347.

150. Peterson (2008), p. 258; Harwood (1985b), p. 106; McDermott (1951), pp. 105, 111, 119–123; *AHJ* II, p. 41.

151. Harwood (1985b), p. 110; McDermott (1951), p. 176; *AHJ* II, p. 154; JJA, Fort Union to "My Dearest Friends," Minnie's Land, 13 Jun. 1843, McDermott (1965), p. 114. Rhodes errs in stating that Audubon's party left Fort Union on September 14, 1843. Rhodes (2004), p. 429. Their departure, as stated in the text, took place on August 16. Rhodes has confused Fort Union with Fort Pierre, which the party visited during their downstream voyage and left on September 14. McDermott (1951), p. 178; *AHJ* II, pp. 164–165.

152. *AHJ* II, pp. 139–140. Rhodes is mistaken

in his assertion that Audubon's party substituted a larger boat at Fort Union after it was determined that the forty-foot mackinaw boat built for them, the *Union*, was too small. This actually occurred downstream at Fort Pierre, as did their visit to a farm situated below that fort to stock up on food stores. Cf. Rhodes (2004), pp. 428–429; *AHJ* II, pp. 164–165.

153. Gifford (1975), p. 9; McDermott (1951), pp. 154, note 30; 176, note 11; Audubon (1844) VII, p. 350.

154. Tyler (2000), p. 157–158; Boehme (2000), p. 58; Ford (1988), p. 410; Harwood (1985b), pp. 110–112, 114; Ford (1951), p. 48; *AHJ* II, pp. 11–12, 166–168; Webber (1851), p. 95.

155. Harwood (1985b), p. 111; *AHJ* II, p. 163; *OB* V, p. 335.

156. *OB* V, p. 335.

157. Audubon (1844) VII, p. 350–51. The Nuttall's Whip-poor-will appears as Plate 495 in the octavo edition of *BOA*. Audubon's species account in that edition would suggest that the specimen was procured on September 8. However, both Audubon and Harris indicated in their journals that it was on September 7 as stated in the text. McDermott (1951), p. 178; *AHJ* II, p. 163.

158. Harwood (1985b), p. 111.

159. *AHJ* II, p. 164.

160. *AHJ* II, pp. 74, 76–79, 82, 84–85. The portraits painted by Audubon and Isaac Sprague of Alexander Culbertson and of his wife Natawista and their son are illustrated in Harwood (1985b), p. 99.

161. Christie, Manson & Woods (1993), Lot 16. The lithographed proof plate given by Audubon to Alexander Culbertson on August 11, 1843, depicted the American Cross Fox, Plate VI, and was signed by the naturalist in pencil: "Presented to Alex^r Culbertson Es^qr by John J. Audubon the 11th of August 1843." The plate survived Culbertson's career on the frontier and eventually made it into the Auduboniana collection of the 20th century bibliophile Dr. Evan Morton Evans (1870–1955). It was auctioned at Christie's in 1993.

162. *AHJ* II, p. 164.

163. Tyler (2000), p. 162; Shuler (1995), pp. 200–201; Harwood (1985b), p. 115; Audubon & Bachman (folio text)(1851) II, pp. 298–299.

164. U.S. Fish and Wildlife Service, "Black-footed Ferret, Mustela nigripes," http://www.fws.gov/mountain-prairie/factsheets/Black-Footed-Ferret.pdf (accessed 19 Jul. 2015); U.S. Fish and Wildlife Service, "Endangerd Species: Black-footed Ferret, http://www.fws.gov/mountain-prairie/species/mammals/blackfootedferret/ (accessed 6 Nov. 2013); Black Footed Ferret: Recovery Program, http://www.blackfootedferret.org/reintroduction (accessed 6 Nov. 2013); Belant, J., P. Gober & D. Biggins, *Mustela nigripes* in *The IUCN Red List of Threatened Species*, Version 2015.2 (2008), http://www.iucnredlist.org (accessed 19 Jul. 2015); Shuler (1995), p. 201.

165. Harwood (1985b), p. 111; *AHJ* II, p. 165.

166. *AHJ* II, p. 175.

167. McDermott (1951), p. 184, note 10.

168. Ibid., Appendix IV, pp. 207–211.

169. Tyler (2000), p. 164; Harwood (1985b), pp. 114–166. The canal boat that Audubon took through the Allegheny Mountains was part of the Pennsylvania Canal, not the Erie Canal as Ford states. The Erie Canal crossed upstate New York from Lake Erie at Buffalo to the Hudson River at Albany. Cf. Ford (1988), p. 410; Durant & Harwood (1980), p. 599.

170. Webber (1851), pp. 93, 95–96. Ford erroneously refers to Charles W. Webber (1819–1856) as a boy. Ford (1988), p. 410.

171. McDermott (1951), pp. 185–187.

172. *AHJ* II, pp. 175–176, note 1. Shuler mistakenly gives the date of Audubon's return as November 5. Shuler (1995), p. 193.

173. Tyler (2000), p. 158; Shuler (1995), pp. 193–194; JJA, Minnie's Land to John Bachman, Charleston, 12 Nov. 1843 (Harvard (160)), Audubon (1999), pp. 856–857; John Bachman, Charleston to JJA, Minnie's Land, 1 Nov. 1843 (Charleston Museum).

174. Peck (2000), pp. 84, 86; Tyler (2000), pp. 158, 161; JJA, Minnie's Land to John Bachman, Charleston, 12 Nov. 1843 (Harvard (160)), Audubon (1999), p. 857; Shuler (1995), p. 194; Herrick (1938) II, p. 270.

175. JJA, Minnie's Land to John Bachman, Charleston, 12 Nov. 1843 (Harvard (160)), Audubon (1999), p. 857. Shuler's reading of Audubon's November 12 letter as saying "14 New Skins of Birds" is in error. Shuler (1995), p. 194. As indicated

in the text, the letter refers to "14 New Species of Birds."

176. Tyler (1993), p. 107; Table One, p. 155.

177. Sahr (2015); Rhodes (2004), p. 430; Tyler (1993), p. 104. To calculate Audubon's profit from the octavo *Birds* in 2016 dollars, the inflation conversion figures from Sahr were averaged for the years 1840 (.037), 1841 (.037), 1842 (.035), 1843 (.031), and 1844 (.032).

178. Rhodes (2004), p. 430.

179. Blaugrund (2000), p. 26; Peck (2000), pp. 97, 101, 110; Shuler (1995), pp. 185–186; Tyler (1993), p. 107; Ford (1988), p. 417; JJA, Minnie's Land to John Bachman, Charleston, 8 Jan. 1845, Herrick (1938) II, pp. 265–266. Audubon prepared written accounts for many of the fifty species of quadrupeds illustrated in the first volume. His manuscripts for twenty-four of them—Nos. 1–7, 10, 13–17, 19, 25, 28, 31, 32, 34, 36, 38, 40, 41, and 45—are in the John James Audubon Collection at Princeton University.

180. GCS, Boston to JJA, Minnie's Land, 21 Nov. 1843 (transcript)(MHM).

181. Durant & Harwood (1980), p. 606.

182. Peck (2000), pp. 89–90; Tyler (2000), p. 166.

183. Ford (1988), p. 414.

184. Tyler (2000), p. 170.

185. Tyler (2000), p. 166 (five Numbers per year); John Bachman, Charleston to Edward Harris, 24 Dec. 1845, Herrick (1938) II, p. 270 (six Numbers per year).

186. Tyler (2000), p. 168.

187. Shuler (1995), pp. 194–195; Fries (1973), p. 126; Herrick (1938) II, p. 268; Bachman (1888), p. 205; John Bachman, Charleston to Edward Harris, 24 Dec. 1845, Herrick (1938) II, p. 270; John Bachman, Charleston to VGA, Minnie's Land, 1844, Bachman (1888), pp. 202–203.

188. John Bachman, Charleston to Edward Harris, 24 Dec. 1845, Herrick (1938) II, p. 269.

189. Tyler (2000), p. 171.

190. John Bachman, Charleston to Edward Harris, 24 Dec. 1845, Herrick (1938) II, p. 270.

191. Blaugrund (2000), p. 26; Ford (1988), p. 418–419; Herrick (1938) II, pp. 272–273, 280; J.W. Audubon (1906), p. 30.

192. JJA and VGA, New York to John Bachman, Charleston, 27 Dec. 1845 (Harvard (255)) (transcribed copy). Two pages of the holograph were missing from the file at the Houghton Library when I examined it on April 14, 2014, but there is a transcription of the letter that includes Audubon's description of the ranges of the species in the first volume of the *Quadrupeds*.

193. Shuler (1995), pp. 199–201; Ford (1988), p. 418; Herrick (1938) II, pp. 270–274.

194. John Bachman, Charleston to JJA, Minnie's Land, 6 Mar. 1846 (Charleston Museum).

195. JJA, New York to John Bachman, Charleston, 12 Mar. 1846 (Harvard (168)).

196. Tyler (2000), p. 170; Shuler (1995), pp. 197, 200.

197. Tyler (2000), p. 170; Shuler (1995), p. 200–203; Herrick (1938) II, pp. 274–275.

198. Tyler (2000), p. 174; Shuler (1995), pp. 202–206; Herrick (1938) II, p. 274.

199. Rhodes (2004), p. 432; Ford (1988), p. 419; *AHJ* I, p. 76. Souder hypothesizes that Audubon's dementia may have been caused by his chronic exposure to arsenic and mercury compounds, which were used in preserving birdskins, and to the toxic compounds in some oil paints. Souder (2004), pp. 288–289.

200. Peck (2000), p. 101. Audubon scholars do not agree on how many of the prints for the imperial folio can be attributed to Audubon's brush. Ron Tyler asserts that Audubon completed seventy-seven of the 150 folio-sized drawings that were lithographed by John Bowen with the remaining seventy-three by John. Tyler (1993), p. 108. Herrick and Ford give Audubon credit for seventy-eight of the prints. Ford (1951), pp. 79–189; Herrick (1938) II, p. 406.

It should be noted that the folio prints credited Audubon with ten illustrations that were subsequently attributed to John when they were published in the subsequent octavo edition. Ford (1951), p. 58. In my personal review of a set of the octavo *Quadrupeds*, I found that Audubon was identified as the illustrator on seventy-seven of the prints, all of them in the first two volumes. The Hare Squirrel (Western Gray Squirrel), Plate 43, in this set omitted the attribution, although Ford states that this was done by Audubon. If so, then he was responsible for drawing seventy-eight of the compositions.

John illustrated the remaining seventy-two images and later added another six octavo-sized drawings, which were included as a supplement to the third volume of the letterpress. Tyler (1993), pp. 107–108; Christie, Manson & Woods (1993), Lot 17. See also, Epilogue, note 11.

201. Herrick (1938) II, pp. 279, 288; Dall (1915), pp. 160–161. Audubon was still writing cogent letters to his friends and correspondents as late as April 1847. JJA, Minnie's Land to C.A. Clinton, New York, 6 Apr. 1847, R&R Enterprises Autograph Auctions, Catalog 317, Lot 544 (17 Jan. 2007).

202. Ford (1988), p. 428.

203. Tyler (2000), p. 174.

204. John Bachman, New York to Maria Martin, Charleston, 11 May 1848 (Charleston Museum). See also, Rhodes (2004), p. 433. The portion of this letter quoted in the text has appeared in numerous Audubon biographies but is often inaccurately transcribed. See, e.g., Adams (1966), p. 467; Arthur (1937), p. 461; Bachman (1888), p. 255. The transcription provided by Rhodes in Audubon (2006), pp. 602–603, is taken not from the original holograph in the Charleston Museum, which Rhodes relied upon and quoted in his 2004 biography, but from the 1888 Bachman biography, which is faulty in multiple respects.

205. National Academy of Design (2013); Blaugrund (2000), p. 26; Reynolds (1982), p. 63, note 87.

206. VGA, Minnie's Land to William Bakewell, Louisville, 2 Feb. 1846, Ford (1988), p. 420.

207. Bonham's (2011), Lot 198; Flynn (2008); Tyler (2000), pp. 174; Shuler (1995), pp. 209–210; Henderson (1977), p. 44; Herrick (1938) II, p. 405. Contrary to what is stated by Ford and Herrick, the first volume of the octavo *Quadrupeds* appeared in 1849. Ford (1988), p. 495; Herrick (1938) II, p. 406. There are subsequent printing dates for this first volume corresponding with the first and later printings of the second and third octavo volumes, which have led to considerable confusion among Audubon scholars. Flynn (2008).

208. J.W. Audubon (1906), pp. 31–32, 42.

209. Ibid., pp. 45, 47, 75, and 241, note 1.

210. Shuler (1995), p. 196; J.W. Audubon (1906), pp. 35, 46, 48.

211. Bakewell (1896), p. 27.

212. Herrick (1938) II, p. 290, J.W. Audubon (1906), pp. 15, 48–50.

213. Van Nostrand (1942), pp. 291–293; J.W. Audubon (1906), pp. 15, 58–81.

214. Ford (1988), pp. 427–428; J.W. Audubon (1906), pp. 16–17; 32–33, 80–190, and 241, note 1. Ford's account of John Audubon's western journey contains two factual errors. First, the company never traveled from northern Mexico to Colorado as she states. The references in John's journal are to the Colorado River. Second, Jacob Henry Bachman, a nephew of John Bachman, was not among those who turned back. He remained with Audubon's company and reached San Francisco. After the company dissolved, he lived the remainder of his life as a prospector in Calaveras County, CA. Van Nostrand (1943), pp. 67–83; Van Nostrand (1942), pp. 289–304.

John's journal, consisting of several small notebooks, and thirty-four sketches that he had prepared between July 4, 1849, and May 30, 1850, were the only record of the expedition that returned to New York. He had a much larger portfolio of some two hundred drawings, along with a collection of specimens, which were stored in San Francisco for several years by a friend and member of the company, Robert Simson. When another member of the company, John Stevens, decided to return to New York in 1857, Simpson asked him to take along John's things. All was lost when Stevens's vessel, the *Central America*, sank in a storm off Cape Hatteras on September 12. The sketches that survived were donated by John's daughters to the Southwest Museum in Los Angeles in 1912 and later published by the Book Club of California. Finding Aid to the Documents Relating to John Woodhouse Audubon Drawings at the Southwest Museum MS.625 (2012); J.W. Audubon (1957). The drawings are now held by the Libraries and Archives at the Autry Resources Center in Burbank.

215. Ford (1988), p. 428.

216. Rhodes (2004), p. 434; L. Audubon (1869), p. 442.

217. VGA, New York to Edward Harris, Moorestown, NJ, 4 Feb. 1851 (Harris Papers, Box 2, Folder 7); VGA, Minnie's Land to Samuel Morton, M.D., Philadelphia, 3 Feb. 1851 (Library Company of Philadelphia). See also, Rhodes (2004), p. 434.

218. L. Audubon (1869), p. 442; VGA, Minnie's Land to Samuel Morton, M.D., Philadelphia, 3 Feb. 1851 (Library Company of Philadelphia).

219. Ford (1988), p. 429. See also, Rhodes (2004), p. 434; Streshinsky (1993), p. 363; Arthur (1937), p. 461. Rhodes places William Bakewell's visit to Minnie's Land during Christmas of 1850. Streshinsky and Arthur say it took place that fall.

220. VGA, New York to Edward Harris, Moorestown, NJ, 4 Feb. 1851 (Harris Papers, Box 2, Folder 7); VGA, Minnie's Land to Samuel Morton, M.D., Philadelphia, 3 Feb. 1851 (Library Company of Philadelphia). The two cited letters from Victor, written within days of his father's death, are the only reliable sources detailing Audubon's last days. Both Lucy and Maria gave different times for his death in their published accounts, neither of which was close to being accurate. Lucy's biography asserted that Audubon died shortly after 5:00 a.m. on "Thursday," January 27, although January 27, 1851, was a Monday. L. Audubon (1869), p. 442. Maria provided an entirely contrived, overly romanticized ending to his life, writing that his death came in the late afternoon "just as sunset was flooding the pure, snow-covered landscape with golden light, at five o'clock on Monday, January 27, 1851." *AHJ* I, p. 77. As Victor informed Edward Harris, Audubon's last breath came at around 10:15 a.m.

Ford relies upon Victor's letter to Samuel Morton for her statement that Audubon died at 10:15 p.m. Ford (1988), p. 429. However, that correspondence, while stating the time, does not indicate whether the naturalist's death came in the morning or the evening. Victor's letter to Harris does.

EPILOGUE

1. LBA, New York to Mrs. Samuel Cumings, 14 Feb. 1851 (Shaffer Collection, FV 2003.08.053).

2. Spady (2007b); "The Burial of Audubon," *New-York Daily Tribune*, Vol. X, No. 3054, p. 5, col. 2 (Thursday, 30 Jan. 1851)(LOC). Ford's statement that the funeral was held at Trinity Church is incorrect. Ford (1988), p. 429. As reflected in the January 30 issue of the *New-York Daily Tribune*, the service was held at the Church of the Intercession, an Episcopal church situated at West 154th Street and Tenth Avenue (now Amsterdam Avenue). Vetter, Janet, "A Short History of the Church of the

Intercession," http://www.intercessionnyc.org /history/ (accessed 1 Dec. 2013). Trinity Church, which was (and still is) located in lower Manhattan near the corner of Broadway and Wall Street, had opened a cemetery directly south of Minnie's Land as it outgrew its existing cemetery downtown, and it was here that Audubon was laid to rest. The funeral service was presided over by the rector of the Church of the Intercession, the Reverend Richard M. Abercrombie. *New-York Daily Tribune*, *supra*; Pretyman (1851), p. 235. The *New-York Daily Tribune* reported that the naturalist's casket "bore a plain silver plate with the following inscription: JOHN JAMES AUDUBON: Died January 27, 1851. Aged 76 years." The reference to Audubon's age was a continuation of the family's efforts to obscure Audubon's origins. Based upon a daguerreotype taken in 1850, his final image, he certainly looked to be in his early to midseventies before he died. *AHJ* II, illus. opp. p. 74. In truth, however, he was only sixty-five.

3. Obituary, "John James Audubon," *New-York Daily Tribune*, Vol. X, No. 3053, p. 5, col. 1 (Wednesday, 29 Jan. 1851)(LOC).

4. Ford (1988), p. 420; Fries (1973), pp. 127–129.

5. Obituary, "John James Audubon," *Boston Daily Atlas* (Monday Morning, 3 Feb. 1851), Fries (1973), pp. 127–128.

6. Obituary (1851).

7. Ford (1988), pp. 415–416.

8. Charles Waterton, Walton Hall to George Ord, Philadelphia, 27 Jul. 1849, Ford (1988), p. 427.

9. Ford (1988), pp. 415–416.

10. George Ord, Philadelphia to Charles Waterton, Walton Hall, 22 Jun. 1845 (George Ord Collection, American Philosophical Society), Tyler (1993), p. 110.

11. Shuler (1995), p. 196; Francis H. Herrick, Cleveland to Henry R. Howland, Buffalo, 9 May 1915 (Private collection).

12. Bonham's (2011), Lot 198; Flynn (2008); Peck (2000), p. 115; Tyler (2000), p. 175, 177; Bannon & Clark (1998), pp. 74, 76; Shuler (1995), pp. 209–210; Tyler (1993), pp. 107–108; Christie, Manson & Woods (1993), Lot 17; Ford (1988), pp. 494–495; Henderson (1977), p. 44; Herrick (1938) II, p. 291, note 1; p. 391, Author's Note; p. 406; Audubon &

Bachman (1854) III (folio); John Bachman, Charleston to Edward Harris, 13 Mar. 1852, Herrick (1938) II, pp. 291–292, Bachman (1888), pp. 276–277;

The octavo *Quadrupeds* consists of thirty-one parts with No. 31 containing five of the six new octavo images that the Audubons published as a supplement to the imperial folio edition. The sixth image—of the Mountain Brook Mink—was substituted for folio Plate 124, which was combined with Plate 109 to become a composite plate showing an adult and young of the Mexican Marmot Squirrel. All of the new prints were lithographed from drawings by John. Tyler (1993), p. 108; Audubon & Bachman (1854) III (octavo), pp. 42, 104–107. As a consequence, John was ultimately responsible for seventy-eight, exactly half, of the images that made up the work.

13. Tyler (2000), p. 175, 177; Peck (2000), p. 115; Tyler (1993), pp. 107–108.

14. Sotheby's (2010), Lot 780; J.W. Audubon (1915), Editors Preface and Preface; "Illustrated Notes of an Expedition through Mexico and California," *New-York Daily Tribune*, Vol. XII, No. 3,450, p. 8, col. 5 (Saturday, 8 May 1852)(LOC).

15. Spady (2007b).

16. Spady (2007b); Herrick (1938) II, illus. opp. p. 295; "For Sale (Residence of the Late V.G. Audubon)," *New-York Daily Tribune*, Vol. XX, No. 6,053, p. 2, col. 2 (Tuesday, 18 Sept. 1860)(LOC).

17. Spady (2007b).

18. Spady (2007b); Herrick (1938) II, p. 300.

19. Tyler (1993), pp. 113–114. Bannon & Clark indicate that the second edition of the octavo *Quadrupeds* is dated 1852–1854–1854. Bannon & Clark (1998), p. 76. We know that as Volumes II and III were being printed in 1851 and 1854, respectively, Victor reissued the prior volume(s) to enable new subscribers to complete the set. Thus, there are copies of Volume I with dates of 1851 and 1854 and copies of Volume II with an 1854 date. However, there is much confusion regarding the publishing history of this work because it seems that Victor continually reprinted the title pages with the current date whenever they were needed. As a consequence, sets of the octavo *Quadrupeds* frequently have multiple dates that do not fit neatly into the identified editions. Flynn (2013); Tyler (1993), p. 185, note 20. How one categorizes these volumes is entirely

unclear and perhaps not that important except to bibliophiles since the text and prints remained the same throughout.

20. Flynn (2013); Clark & Bannon (1998), p. 76; Tyler (1993), pp. 113–114.

21. Rhodes (2004), p. 436; Souder (2004), p. 290; Herrick (1938) II, p. 295 and note 5. The precise date Victor suffered his back injury is not known. Herrick vaguely indicates that it occurred "[a]t about" the time the 1856 second edition of the octavo *Birds* was being published. Souder relies solely upon Herrick but is more definitive in asserting that Victor sustained the fall in 1856. Rhodes is of the view that the accident occurred in 1857, but he cites no sources to corroborate that assertion.

22. VGA to John Bachman, Charleston, 12 May 1852 (Harvard (294)).

23. Herrick (1938) II, p. 295, note 5; Francis H. Herrick, Cleveland to Henry R. Howland, Buffalo, 9 May 1915 (Private collection).

24. J.W. Audubon (1906), p. 36; U.S. Bureau of the Census (1860), Census Place: *New York Ward 12, District 3, New York, New York*; Roll: *M653_802*; Page: *1052*; Image: *641*.

25. Victor Gifford Audubon Collection, GEN MSS 343 (Box 1, Folder 13, Beinecke Rare Book and Manuscript Library, Yale University).

26. Spady (2007b); J.W. Audubon (1906), p. 37.

27. Spady (2007b); Tyler (1993), pp. 125–127; Marzio (1976); J.W. Audubon (1906), p. 37.

28. Low (2002), p. 327; Blaugrund (1993), p. 41; Tyler (1993), p. 125–127; Marzio (1976); Herrick (1938) II, pp. 389–390; "Audubon's Original Work," *New-York Daily Tribune*, Vol. XVIII, No. 5547, p. 1, col. 3 (Monday, 31 Jan. 1859)(LOC). The advertisement for the Bien edition that appeared in the *New-York Daily Tribune* between January 31 and February 2, 1859, stated that each Number would cost $10, not $11 as stated by Annette Blaugrund. Blaugrund (1993), p. 41. See also, "Great National Work," *New-York Daily Tribune*, Vol. XIX, No. 5,635, p. 1, col. 3 (Friday, 13 May 1859).

29. "The Counterfeit of Presentments," *The New-York Times*, Vol. X, No 2930, p. 2, col. 3 (Monday, 11 Feb. 1861); JWA, New York to Edward Harris, 3 May 1859 (Harris Papers, Box 2, Folder 7).

30. Steiner (2003), pp. 73–75; Low (2002), pp. 323, 327; Tyler (1993), p. 127; Fries (1973), p. 356;

Herrick (1938) II, pp. 407–408; Zimmer (1926) I, pp. 24–25.

31. Tyler (1993), pp. 109–112; 114–115. Cassin went on to self-publish the first volume of his work with a scientific text and fifty hand-colored prints of inconsistent artistic quality, using Bowen for the later printing work, but the publication received inadequate support and was discontinued.

32. Ibid., pp. 114–116, 125.

33. Clark & Bannon (1998), p. 50; Tyler (1993), p. 164; Herrick (1938) II, pp. 407–408. Note that Herrick fails to identify either the 1859 (3rd ed.) or 1860 (4th ed.) editions of the octavo *Birds*, both of which are listed by Zimmer in his bibliography of the Edward E. Ayer ornithological library at Chicago's Field Museum. Zimmer (1926) I, pp. 22–24. Cornell University and the Brooklyn Museum have copies of the 1861 (5th ed.) edition of the octavo *Birds* with the plates. Tyler (1993), p. 127 and note 32, p. 186.

34. J.W. Audubon (1906), p. 36; L. Audubon (1869), p. 443; "Died (Victor G. Audubon)," *The New-York Times*, Vol. IX, No. 2780, p. 5, col. 4 (Saturday, 18 Aug. 1860); U.S. Bureau of the Census (1860), Census Place: *New York Ward 12, District 3, New York, New York*; Roll: *M653_802*; Page: *1052*; Image: *641*; JWA, New York to Edward Harris, 3 May 1859 (Harris Papers, Box 2, Folder 7). Souder and Herrick both err in stating that Victor died on August 18. Souder (2004), p. 290; Herrick (1938) II, p. 295.

35. J.W. Audubon (1906), p. 37.

36. Steiner (2003), pp. 71, 74; Tyler (1993), pp. 127–128; Harwood & Durant (1985), p. 81; Fries (1973), p. 356; Herrick (1938) II, pp. 296–297.

37. Steiner (2003), pp. 138–140; Tyler (1993), pp. 129, 164–165. There is a single bibliographic reference by Elliott Coues to an edition of the octavo *Birds* being published in 1863. Tyler refers to this as a "[g]host edition" as no one has ever located a copy. See also, Bannon & Clark (1998), pp, 50–51.

38. Olson (2012), pp. 34–35; Blaugrund & Stebbins (1993), p. vii, 41, 65; Harwood & Durant (1985), p. 81. See also, note 45, *infra*.

39. Holt & Filemyr (2008), pp. 3–6, 69–72; Fries (1973), pp. 306–307. Although the Audubon family set of the Double Elephant Folio changed hands several times, it is now in the collection of the Nelda C. and H.J. Lutcher Stark Foundation and is housed at the Stark Museum of Art in Orange, TX. Fries (1973), p. 307.

Two of the other sets that included the thirteen composite plates were owned by Edward Harris and by Dr. Benjamin Phillips, the Audubons' London physician. VGA, Edinburgh to Robert Havell Jr., London, 26 Sept. 1838 (Harvard (245)). It is believed the Harris set was broken up and dispersed. The Phillips set is at the Field Museum in Chicago. Note that in the first edition of his book, Fries incorrectly identified the original owner of the Field Museum set as Lucy's English cousin Euphemia Gifford. Holt & Filemyr (2008), p. 4; Fries (2004), p. 455; Steiner (2003), pp. 61–62; Low (2002), pp. 20–21. Cf. Fries (1973), pp. 257–259.

Composite plates have also been found in the *BOA* sets currently held by the John James Audubon Center at Mill Grove (8 prints); Library of Parliament in Ottawa (7 prints); Bowdoin College (4 prints); Lehigh University (2 prints); and Yale University (1 print). Holt & Filemyr (2008), p. 4, note 6.

40. J.W. Audubon (1906), p. 37.

41. Rhodes (2004), p. 436; Ann Gordon, New Orleans to LBA, New York, 12 Jun. 1862 (Shaffer Collection, FV2003.08.080). Roberta Olson's statement that both of Lucy's sons had died "by 1860" is obviously incorrect. Olson (2012), p. 34.

42. "Died (John W. Audubon)," *The New-York Times*, Vol. XI, No. 3251, p. 5, col. 6 (Sunday, February 23, 1862).

43. J.W. Audubon (1906), p. 37.

44. Spady (2007b).

45. Olson (2012), p. 35; Spady (2007b); Blaugrund & Stebbins (1993), p. vii-viii. The 470 drawings acquired by the New-York Historical Society comprised 434 of the compositions used by Havell in preparing the prints for *BOA*. The drawings for Plates 84 (Blue Grey Flycatcher), 155 (Black-Throated Blue Warbler), and 426 (California Vulture) were not included. In addition, there were 36 other studies included in the sale. The society subsequently received donations of three more Audubon drawings in 1962 and, in 1966, the illustration of the California Vulture (California Condor) used for Havell Plate 426. Olson (2012), p. 8; Blaugrund & Stebbins (1993), pp. viii, 367–377.

Several Audubon scholars, including Rhodes, Durant & Harwood, and Adams, have asserted that Lucy sold the original watercolor drawings for only $2,000. Rhodes (2004), pp. 436, 438; Durant & Harwood (1980), p. 615; Adams (1966), p. 470. Not so. The New-York Historical Society has a secretarial copy of Lucy's directive to the society, dated May 25, 1863, to pay the sum of $4,000 for the drawings to Burgess & Seaver, a firm run by her friend George Burgess, together with Burgess & Seaver's receipt for the check in that sum, dated June 6, 1863. (NHYS).

46. Fries (1973), pp. 390–398. See also, Tyler (1993), p. 128.

47. Spady (2007b); LBA, Washington Heights to Martha Cumings, 11 Jul. 1865, Herrick (1938) II, p. 301. By order of a referee for the New York Supreme Court, which is the trial court in that state, John W. Audubon's home in Audubon Park was to be sold at auction on March 10, 1864. "Supreme Court Sale of Audubon Park Property," *The New-York Times*, Vol. XIII, No. 3883, p. 6, col. 4 (Friday, 4 Mar. 1864).

48. LBA, Washington Heights to Martha Cumings, 11 Jul. 1865, Herrick (1938) II, p. 301; Alice Ford (Personal communication).

49. Harwood & Durant (1985), p. 78; Herrick (1938) I, p. 18. As of 1866, biographies of Audubon had been published by Mrs. Horace St. John (*Audubon, the Naturalist of the New World*, Philadelphia: J.B. Lippincott, 1856); Henry T. Tuckerman ("The Ornithologist, John James Audubon," in *Essays, Biographical and Critical; or, Studies of Character*, Boston: Phillips, Sampson and Company, 1857); Samuel Smiles (*Brief Biographies*, Boston: Ticknor & Fields, 1861); and B.K. Pierce (*Life in the Woods; or The Adventures of Audubon*, New York: Carlton & Lanahan, 1863). Mrs. St. John, whose biography went through multiple printings, was the grand-daughter of William Roscoe, who counseled Audubon during the early months of his visit to Liverpool in 1826. Fries (1973), p. xxi.

50. Harwood & Durant (1985), p. 78; Herrick (1938) I, pp. 18–19; L. Audubon (1869), p. iii; Alice Ford (Personal communication).

51. Harwood & Durant (1985), p. 78; Herrick (1938) I, pp. 19–20; Buchanan (1868), pp. v, vii.

52. Buchanan (1868), pp. vi-vii.

53. Harwood & Durant (1985), pp. 78, 80; L. Audubon (1869), p. iii. In an otherwise favorable review of Buchanan's edition of Audubon's biography, *The New-York Times* thought it "unpardonable" that Buchanan would criticize the naturalist for his vanity, especially in the face of Lucy's objections. "Audubon the Naturalist," *The New-York Times*, Vol. XVIII, No. 5,367, p. 2, cols. 1–4 (Sunday, 6 Dec. 1868).

54. "Personal and Literary," *The New-York Times*, Vol. XVIII, No. 5308, p. 7, col. 2 (Monday, 28 Sept. 1868).

55. Spady (2007b); Rhodes (2004), p. 438; Souder (2004), p. 291; Durant & Harwood (1980), p. 616; Herrick (1938) II, pp. 302–303; Maria Bakewell, Shelbyville, KY to Mrs. B.D. Kennedy, Contra Costa Co., CA, 20 Jun. 1874 (Shaffer Collection, FV2003.08.140); LBA, New York to "My dear Sister," 10 Jun. 1869 (Shaffer Collection, FV2003.08.128); LBA, New York to William Bakewell, 17 May 1869 (Shaffer Collection, FV2003.08.127). Rhodes, Durant & Harwood, and Herrick inexplicably state that Lucy died at the age of eighty-six. She was born on January 18, 1787, as the family genealogy confirms, so she would have celebrated her eighty-seventh birthday precisely five months before she died.

Several of the New York papers misreported details of Lucy's death. *The New-York Times* indicated that Lucy had died in Kellyville, KY, at the age of eighty-eight. "Obituary: Mrs. Audubon," *The New-York Times*, Vol. XXIII, No. 7101, p. 4, col. 6 (Saturday, 20 Jun. 1874). The *New-York Daily Tribune* also claimed that she was eighty-eight. "Funeral of Mrs. Audubon," *New-York Daily Tribune*, Vol. XXXIV, No. 10,367, p. 2, col. 2 (Wednesday, 24 Jun. 1874) (LOC). *The Sun* reported that she died on Wednesday, June 17. *The Sun*, Vol. XLI, No. 254, p. 3, col. 4 (Wednesday, 24 Jun. 1874)(LOC). Correspondence from Lucy's sister-in-law Maria Bakewell confirms that she died in Shelbyville on Thursday, June 18, at around 8:00 p.m. Maria Bakewell, Shelbyville, KY to Mrs. B.D. Kennedy, Contra Costa Co., CA, 20 Jun. 1874 (Shaffer Collection, FV2003.08.140).

56. Maria Bakewell, New York to Alicia Bakewell, Shelbyville, KY, 22 Jun. 1874 (Shaffer Collection, FV2003.08.141). Rhodes's assertion that Lucy's body was accompanied to New York by two

of her granddaughters is mistaken, as the cited letter indicates. Rhodes (2004), p. 438. He has evidently confused Maria Bakewell (Mrs. William Bakewell) for Lucy's granddaughter Maria Rebecca Audubon.

57. Spady (2007b); Rhodes (2004), p. 438; Durant & Harwood (1980), p. 608; "Funeral of Mrs. Audubon, *New-York Tribune*, Vol. XXXIV, No. 10,367, p. 2, col. 2 (Wednesday, 24 Jun. 1874) (LOC); "Audubon's Widow's Funeral," *The Sun*, Vol. XLI, No. 254, p. 3, col. 4 (Wednesday, 24 Jun. 1874)(LOC).

Herrick's statement that Charles A. Stoddard, the pastor of the Washington Heights Presbyterian Church, officiated at Lucy's funeral is in error. Herrick (1938) II, p. 303, note 17. As stated in the text and as reported by both the *New-York Tribune* and *The Sun*, that duty was handled by the Reverend Dr. Thomas McClure Peters and the Reverend Dr. Richard M. Abercrombie, both Episcopal priests. The reason for Herrick's confusion is that Stoddard delivered a memorial sermon in Lucy's memory during his service on the following Sunday, June 28, which was subsequently reported in the papers and printed in pamphlet form. Stoddard (1874); "The Late Mme. Audubon," *The New-York Times*, Vol. XXIII, No. 7108, p. 8, col. 2 (Monday, 29 Jun. 1874). This was not the eulogy delivered at Lucy's funeral service, as Souder suggests. Also, Souder is incorrect in stating that Lucy's ashes were interred at Trinity Church Cemetery. Souder (2004), p. 291 and note, p. 348; Stoddard (1874), p. 3. Maria Bakewell makes it quite clear that they returned her body to New York for burial. Maria Bakewell, New York to Alicia Bakewell, Shelbyville, KY, 22 Jun. 1874 (Shaffer Collection, FV2003.08.141).

58. Mearns (1992), p. 294; Hobart (1986), pp. 42, 85; Little (1909) I, p. 402.

59. Mearns (1992), p. 294; Hobart (1986), pp. 42, 86; Little (1909) I, p. 403; Vose (1886), p. 109; Ancestry.com, BROWNN~2 Family Tree, http://trees.ancestry.com/tree/37997259/person/19167827474?ssrc= (accessed 2 May 2015).

60. Little (1909) I, p. 402.

61. Ibid., pp. 402–403.

62. Hobart (1986), p. 85.

63. Little (1909) I, p. 402.

64. Ibid., p. 403.

65. Townsend (1924), p. 241; *OB* II, p. 544.

66. *OB* II, p. 341; JJA, Charleston to Tom Lincoln, Dennysville, 7 Nov. 1833, Townsend (1924), p. 241.

67. JWA, London to Tom Lincoln, Dennysville, 24 Aug. 1834, Audubon (2006), pp. 472–473.

68. JWA, Minnie's Land to Tom Lincoln, Dennysville, 11 Mar. 1845 (Yale, Box 5, Folder 229), Audubon (2006), p. 600.

69. Ibid.

70. JWA, New York to VGA, London, 29 Sept. 1833 (Yale, Box 1, Folder 12).

71. Grinnell (1924), p. 224.

72. Ibid., pp. 224–230.

73. Mearns (1992), p. 294; Spiker (1969); Townsend (1924), p.239; Tom Lincoln, Dennysville to Spencer F. Baird, 3 Aug. 1872, U.S. Commission of Fish and Fisheries (1874), pp. 369–370.

74. Little (1909) I, p. 402.

75. Marshall (2006), p. 53; Harvard University (1833), pp. 11, 31; GCSJr to Benjamin Lincoln, M.D., Burlington, VT, 26 Sept. 1833 (Letters to Benjamin Lincoln, Massachusetts Historical Society (Ms. S-15)). This account of the life of George C. Shattuck Jr. relies heavily on the superb biography by J.C. Douglas Marshall. Note that Marshall states that Eleanor (Ellen) Shattuck was thirteen when her brother George returned from Labrador. Given her January 27, 1819, birthdate, she was actually fourteen. Hassam (1882), p. 312.

76. McCullough (2011), p. 104–108; Marshall (2006), pp. 53–54

77. Marshall (2006), p. 54; Bowdoin (1912), p. 70. Dr. Isaac Ray wrote a glowing obituary of Dr. Benjamin Lincoln that appeared in *The New-England Magazine* in August 1835. Ray (1835). See also, Cleaveland (1882), pp. 272–273. Ray obviously cared deeply about Lincoln. He would name his only son, born in 1836, Benjamin Lincoln Ray. Ancestry.com, Robert Charles Ashley Family Tree, http://trees.ancestry.com/tree/62316456/person/42211973814 (accessed 2 May 2015).

78. Marshall (2006), pp. 54–56.

79. Marshall (2006), pp. 56–62; GCSJr, Boston to JJA, London, 13 Feb. 1836 (Yale, Box 6, Folder 313).

80. Marshall (2006), pp. 62–66; GCSJr, Boston to JJA, London, 13 Feb. 1836 (Yale, Box 6, Folder 313).

81. Marshall (2006), pp. 66–69; GCSJr, Boston to JJA, London, 13 Feb. 1836 (Yale, Box 6, Folder 313).

82. Marshall (2006), p. 73; Bowen (1834), pp. 262–263; Harvard (1834), pp. 31–32.

83. Marshall (2006), pp. 72–76.

84. GCSJr, Boston to JJA, London, 13 Feb. 13, 1836 (Yale, Box 6, Folder 313).

85. Marshall (2006), pp. 76–79; Ford (1988), p. 341. Note that in the text of her biography, Ford places Audubon's receipt of news of the destruction of the Boston edition of Volume II of the *OB* during George Shattuck's visit to London in 1836. However, in her chronology in the Appendix, she states that this occurred in 1835. Ford (1988), p. 463. If the news was delivered by Shattuck, it would have been the former.

86. Marshall (2006), pp. 79–81, 83.

87. Ibid., pp. 84–88.

88. Ibid., pp. 46, 98–104.

89. Christie's (2012b), Lot 2, p. 9; Marshall (2006), pp. 104–106; George C. Shattuck Jr. (1840a); George C. Shattuck Jr. (1840b). The Shattuck family's personal set of the *OB* was auctioned by Christie's in 2012. Volume I, which Shattuck Jr. purchased in Eastport, is the second American edition published in 1832 in Philadelphia and was inscribed by Audubon to Shattuck's father. Volume II is the exceedingly rare first American edition published in Boston in 1835, one year after the first Edinburgh edition. Most of the copies of the American edition were destroyed in a Boston fire. Ford (1988), p. 341. Beginning with Volume III in 1835, Audubon discontinued the publication of an American edition of the text and had it printed only in Edinburgh. Copies that were distributed in America can be distinguished by the presence of a U.S. copyright notice glued on the half title page. The Shattuck copy of Volume III is such a copy. Volumes IV and V appeared in Edinburgh in November 1838 and May 1839, respectively. Audubon understood that it was unnecessary to include the copyright notice in the final two volumes because he had already secured the U.S. copyright. Thus, those supplied to the American market are indistinguishable from those sold in England and Scotland. Lownes (1935), pp. 103–104. The fact that the Shattuck copy of Volume IV is the only one of the set with his hand-

written surname points to it having been acquired during his 1839 visit to London. For a description of the various editions of the *OB*, see Herrick (1938) II, pp. 402–403 and Braislin (1918), pp. 360–362.

90. Marshall (2006), pp. 106–108; Beggs-Humphreys (2006), p. 47; Williams (1840), p. 85. The *Great Western* steamer carrying Shattuck Jr. reached New York on April 14, 1839, twenty one and a half days after it left Bristol, England. As a consequence, Shattuck could not have returned to Boston until mid-April, not early April as Shattuck's biographer, J.C. Douglas Marshall, states. Marshall is also in error in asserting that the vessel docked in Boston.

91. Marshall (2006), pp. 59, 108–111 and notes, p. 236.

92. Marshall (2006), pp. 110, 112–115 and notes, p. 236; Corning (1929b), p. 23; Farlow (1925), p. 165.

93. Marshall (2006), pp. 116–118.

94. Ibid., pp. 118–120.

95. Ibid., pp. 125–133.

96. Marshall (2006), pp. 123, 132, 139; Editorial, "George Brune Shattuck–1845–1923," *The Boston Medical and Surgical Journal*, Vol. 188, No. 20, p. 777 (17 May 1923).

97. Marshall (2006), pp. 121–122, 132, 135.

98. Ibid., pp. 135–140.

99. Ibid., pp.140–150.

100. Ibid., pp. 151–152.

101. Ibid., pp. 155–157.

102. Ibid., pp. 157–158; 160–161.

103. Harrington (1905) II, pp. 811–812.

104. Marshall (2006), pp. 171–172.

105. Ibid., Marshall (2006), pp. 167–170, 173–174, 204.

106. Ibid., pp. 174, 177–178, 189–190, 192–193.

107. Ibid., 179–181, 186–188.

108. Ibid., pp. 205–207.

109. *Members of the American Academy of Arts & Sciences: 1780–2013*, p. 501 (database on-line), https://www.amacad.org/multimedia/pdfs /publications/bookofmembers/ChapterS.pdf (accessed 5 Jun. 2014); Marshall (2006), pp. 194–195, 204, 216; Harrington (1905), p. 1466.

110. Marshall (2006), pp. 215–216, 221.

111. Obituary (1893), p. 355.

112. Calnan (2007), p. 36. According to Calnan, Clara Goold was born on December 7, 1819, on

Indian Island, New Brunswick. Mary Vose Coolidge was born on April 4, 1846, in Eastport. She died on November 28, 1846. Coolidge's middle name, Appleby, is found in the 1867 Great Register of Voters for San Francisco. General List (1867).

113. *Washington County Court Indexes, 1839–1845* (database on-line) http://files.usgwarchives.net /me/washington/court/index/wccourtc.txt (accessed 14 Mar. 2015).

114. Grinnell (1924), p. 229.

115. "A Californian's Recollection of Naturalist Audubon," *The San Francisco Call*, Vol. LXXX, No. 98, p. 25, cols. 1–7 (Sunday, 6 Sept. 1896)(LOC). John left New York for San Francisco with Col. H.L. Webb's California Company on February 8, 1849. We know that Coolidge did not reach San Francisco until sometime after Thanksgiving 1849, so Coolidge's conversation at the Audubon home in New York appears to have been with Victor. Hodder (1906), p. 42. See also, note 116, *infra*.

116. "In the Days of the Rival Ship Exchanges," *The San Francisco Call*, Vol. LXXIX, No. 127, p. 17, cols. 5–6 (Sunday, 5 Apr. 1896)(LOC); Barry (1873), p. 24. Since Coolidge's first Thanksgiving in San Francisco was in 1850, he could not have reached the city until sometime after the prior year's Thanksgiving. "The First Thanksgiving Day Celebration in California," *The San Francisco Call*, Vol. LXXX, No. 175, p. 17 (Sunday, 22 Nov. 1896)(LOC).

117. U.S. Bureau of the Census (1850), Census Place: *Eastport, Washington Co., ME*; Roll: *M432_273*; Page: *230A*; Image: *438*.

118. "The First Thanksgiving Day Celebration in California," *The San Francisco Call*, Vol. LXXX, No. 175, p. 17 (Sunday, 22 Nov. 1896)(LOC).

119. San Francisco Directory for the Year 1852–53, p. 45 (San Francisco: Monson, Haswell & Co., Printers, 1852); A.W. Morgan & Co. (1852).

120. This information is available through the Maritime Heritage Project, accessible on line at http://www.maritimeheritage.org/PassLists /gg021456.html (accessed 1 Jul. 2007).

121. Schellens Collection, Vol. 134, p. 125 (San Mateo County Genealogical Society).

122. San Francisco Almanac (1859), p. 115.

123. U.S. Bureau of the Census (1860), Census Place: *San Francisco District 9, San Francisco Co., CA*; Roll: *M653_68*; Page: *1012*; Image: *205*. The census enumerator who conducted the census of Coolidge's household on June 15, 1860, erroneously gives Coolidge's age as forty-four. He was actually forty-five on that date. Clara is said to have been thirty-eight and born in Maine. She actually was forty years old and had been born on Indian Island, New Brunswick, just over the Canadian border and less than a mile from Eastport. Ada was accurately identified as a fifteen-year-old who had been born in Maine.

124. San Francisco Directory (1863), p. 424.

125. Langley (1864), pp. 483, 546; Langley (1863), pp. 487, 497.

126. "The History of the Marine Exchange," Marine Exchange of the San Francisco Bay Region, http://www.sfmx.org/aboutus/mxhistory.php (accessed 12 Jun. 2015); Camp (1947), p. 199; "In the Days of the Rival Ship Exchanges," *The San Francisco Call*, Vol. LXXIX, No. 127, p. 17, cols. 5–6 (Sunday, 5 Apr. 1896)(LOC).

127. Ada Coolidge married Lt. Charles Evans Kilbourne, a 2nd lieutenant with the U.S. Army 2nd Artillery, in April 1868. Their third son, Charles E. Jr. (b. 12-23-1873), was "the first person in American history to hold simultaneously the nation's three highest military awards: The Medal of Honor, the Distinguished Service Cross, and the Distinguished Service Medal." Virginia Military Institute, Historical Rosters Database, http:// archivesweb.vmi.edu/rosters/record.php?ID=4077 (accessed 26 Jul. 2015).

128. Coolidge and his wife Clara were actually counted twice in the 1870 U.S. Census. On July 11, 1870, they were counted in the 2nd Precinct, 8th Ward of San Francisco, at which time they were living in a boardinghouse. U.S. Bureau of the Census (1870), Census Place: *San Francisco Ward 8, San Francisco Co., CA*; Roll: *M593_82*; Page: *437*; Image: *301*. On August 11, 1870, the Coolidges, Ada, and her infant son Lincoln were counted in the 1st Precinct, 12th Ward. Given the fact that their data entries almost immediately follow those for the U.S. Army troops stationed at the Presidio, it can be surmised that the family was living near the base, where Ada's husband, 1st Lt. Charles Evans Kilbourne, was stationed. The enumerator accurately recorded Coolidge's age and place of birth but misspelled his surname "Coolage," and incorrectly stated

that Clara was fifty-one. U.S. Bureau of the Census (1870), Census Place: *San Francisco Ward 12, San Francisco Co., CA*: Roll: *M593_85*; Page: *759A*; Image: *95*.

129. *The Nation* (1886), p. 273; United States (1877), pp. 489–496.

130. California Legislature (1881), pp. 18, 39.

131. The date of Clara Coolidge's death is recorded on the grave marker at Roselawn Memorial Park. It is also recorded in the cemetery's records, http://www.l-ags.org/cem_liv/rl16.html (accessed 14 Feb. 2013). Clara Coolidge's older brother, Gardner Goold (1818–1880), was buried in an adjacent plot, which explains why this site was selected for her resting place. Prior to his death, Gardner was a farmer in a community in Contra Costa County known as Sycamore, CA. Calnan (2007), p.48; U.S. Bureau of the Census (*1880*), Census Place: *Sycamore, Contra Costa Co., CA*; Roll: *64*; Page: *611A*; Enumeration District: *046*; Image: *0467*.

132. "A Californian's Recollection of Naturalist Audubon," *The San Francisco Call*, Vol. LXXX, No. 98, p. 25, cols. 1–7 (Sunday, 6 Sept. 1896)(LOC).

133. Maria R. Audubon's Scrapbook No. 2 (Private collection).

134. John W. Audubon painted several different images of his father, so it is unclear which of these Maria Audubon sent to Coolidge. In 1839 in Edinburgh, he painted a sitting portrait of his father dressed in a suit. *AHJ* II, illus. opp. p. 234. In about 1841, Audubon sat for a full-size portrait in oils, 44"× 60", in which he is pictured seated in front of a landscape background with a rifle resting in the crook of his left arm, a Springer spaniel lying at his left side, and a chestnut horse to his right. This painting is now in the collection of the American Museum of Natural History in New York City. In addition, the AMNH owns a half-length portrait of Audubon painted in oils about the same time by John and Victor. Finally, John painted the naturalist upon his return from the Missouri River expedition in November 1843. In that portrait, which is also at the AMNH, Audubon is pictured with white hair hanging down to his shoulders and a thick white beard. See generally, Herrick (1938) II, pp. 396–397.

135. Maria R. Audubon's Scrapbook No. 2 (Private collection).

136. Deane (1910), p. 43.

137. The cause of Coolidge's death is given in the Mortuary Record of the City and County of San Francisco, Book P., as recorded on July 31, 1901. The complete record is written in a fine hand horizontally in columns across two facing pages as follows: | No.: *812* | Date: *July 31* | Name: *Joseph A. Coolidge* | Sex: *M* | Age: Years: *86* | Mos.: *6* | Days: *10* | Race: *W* | Occupation: *Retired* | Place of Birth: *Maine* | Social Conditions: *W* [Widower] | Place of Death: *1303 Leavenworth* | Date of Death: *July 30* | Causes of Death - Chief and Determining: *Asthma*; Contributing: *Old age* | Place of Burial: *Livermore Cal* | Physician: *J.S. Ballard* | Undertakers: *Halsted & Co.* Mortuary Record (1901).

The brief obituary in *The San Francisco Call* states: "COOLIDGE-In this city. July 30, 1901, Joseph A. Coolidge, father of Mrs. Charles E. Kilbourne, aged 86 years. Services private." "Died," *The San Francisco Call*, Vol. XC, No. 61, p. 11, col. 6 (Wednesday, 31 Jul. 1901)(LOC).

138. Harvard University (1930), pp. 235, 857; Obituary (1903), p. 661; Atkinson (1878), p. 329; Harvard (1833), p. 11.

139. Obituary (1903), p. 661; Davis (1884), pp. 99–101, 250; Atkinson (1878), p. 329. Julia Ann Matilda Davis was born on October 8, 1815, in Cambridge, MA. She died in Boston on October 28, 1906, at the age of ninety-one. Davis (1884), p. 100; Ancestry.com, *Massachusetts, Death Records, 1841–1915; Return of a Death-1906: Boston*, Register No.: 9378 (database on-line)(Provo, UT: Ancestry.com Operations, Inc., 2013)(accessed 24 Sept. 2015).

140. Obituary (1903), p. 661.

141. Davis (1884), p. 250.

142. Harrington (1905) III, p. 1467; Obituary (1903), p. 661; Adams (1848), pp. 163, 328.

143. Davis (1884), p. 250. Mary Elizabeth Ingalls died on August 17, 1900, at the age of forty-eight. Ancestry.com, *Massachusetts, Death Records, 1841–1915* (database on-line)(Provo, UT: Ancestry.com Operations, Inc., 2013)(accessed 24 Sept. 2015).

144. Davis (1884), p. 250. See also, Knight, Ellen, "Historic Buildings in the News," *Daily Times Chronicle*, http://www.winchestermass.org/hist_build.html (accessed 26 Jul. 2015).

145. Historical Data Systems (1999); Adjutant General (1931) I, p. 301.

146. Adjutant General (1931) I, p. 300; Roe

(1911), pp. 119, 128–129, 133–134, 164–183; Harrington (1905) III, p. 1467.

147. Sons of the American Revolution (1907), 147–148.

148. Historical Data Systems (1999); Adjutant General (1931) V, pp. 48–50; Harrington (1905) III, p. 1467; Headley (1866), 467–469.

149. Obituary (1903), pp. 661–662. The mine explosion during the siege of Petersburg, VA, occurred on July 30, 1864, and led to what is commonly known as the Battle of the Crater.

150. Ibid., p. 661.

151. Ibid.

152. Harrington (1905) III, p. 1467; Atkinson (1878), p. 329; Sampson, Davenport, & Co. (1873), pp. 407, 898; Sampson, Davenport, & Co. (1868). pp. 322, 704.

153. Retureta (1998).

154. Cheever (1906), p. 206.

155. Ibid. Dr. David Cheever took this description of Ingalls from a memorial tribute that he and two colleagues, J.G. Blake, M.D., and F.S. Watson, M.D., submitted on behalf of the staff of Boston City Hospital as part of the obituary published in the January 28, 1904, issue of *The Boston Medical and Surgical Journal*. Shattuck (1904), p. 106.

156. Obituary (1903), p. 662.

157. Obituary (1904), p. 106; Obituary (1903), p. 662; Ingalls (1877).

158. Obituary (1903), p. 662.

159. Ingalls (1896).

160. Deane (1910), pp. 42–48.

161. Obituary (1903), pp. 661–662. See also, *Fortieth Annual Report of the Trustees of The Boston City Hospital* (1904), pp. 30–31. William Ingalls is buried with his wife and children in the family plot at Mt. Auburn Cemetery in Cambridge, MA. "William W. Ingalls," Findagrave.com, http://www .findagrave.com/cgi-bin/fg.cgi?page=gr&GSln =Ingalls&GSfn=william&GSby=1813&GSbyrel =in&GSdy=1903&GSdyrel=in&GScntry=4&GSob =n&GRid=111055624&df=all& (accessed 22 Sept. 2015).

162. Obituary (1904), p. 106.

BIBLIOGRAPHY

MANUSCRIPT COLLECTIONS

Alabama Department of Archives and History, Montgomery, Alabama.

American Antiquarian Society, Worcester, Massachusetts.

American Philosophical Society, Philadelphia, Pennsylvania.

Boston Athenaeum, Boston, Massachusetts.

Bowdoin College, George J. Mitchell Department of Special Collections & Archives, Brunswick, Maine.

Buffalo Museum of Science Research Library, Buffalo, New York.

Case Western Reserve University Library, Cleveland, Ohio.

Center for the History of Medicine in the Francis A. Countway Library of Medicine, Boston, Massachusetts.

The College of Physicians of Philadelphia, Philadelphia, Pennsylvania.

Columbia University, Rare Book & Manuscript Library, New York, New York.

Dartmouth College, Rauner Special Collections Library, Hanover, New Hampshire.

Filson Club Historical Society, Louisville, Kentucky.

Harvard University, Houghton Library, Cambridge, Massachusetts.

John James Audubon Center at Mill Grove, Audubon, Pennsylvania.

Library of Congress, Washington, D.C.

Linnean Society of London, London, England.

Massachusetts Historical Society, Boston, Massachusetts.

Massachusetts National Guard Museum and Archives, Worcester, Massachusetts.

Missouri History Museum, St. Louis, Missouri.

National Archives, Washington, D.C., Waltham, Massachusetts, and San Bruno, California.

Newberry Library, Chicago, Illinois.

New-York Historical Society, New York, New York.

Princeton University, Department of Rare Books & Special Collections, Firestone Library, Princeton, New Jersey.

Rhode Island Historical Society, Providence, Rhode Island.

San Mateo County Genealogical Society, Redwood City, California.

Yale School of Medicine, Harvey Cushing/John Hay Whitney Medical Library, New Haven, Connecticut.

Yale University, Beinecke Rare Book and Manuscript Library, New Haven, Connecticut.

BOOKS, NEWSPAPERS, AND PERIODICALS

Abert, Col. John. "Habits of Climbing of the Rattle-Snake." *The Monthly American Journal of Geology and Natural Science*. Vol. I, No. 5, pp. 221–223 (November 1831).

Able Kenneth P., ed. *Gatherings of Angels: Migrating Birds and Their Ecology*. Ithaca, NY and London: Comstock Books, 1999.

Academy of Natural Sciences of Philadelphia. *Minutes and Correspondence of the Academy of Natural Sciences of Philadelphia: 1812–1924*. Microfilm, Roll 2. Minutes, 1824–1827.

Academy of Natural Sciences of Philadelphia. *John J. Audubon: A National Exhibition*. Philadelphia: The Academy of Natural Sciences of Philadelphia, 1938.

Adams, Alexander. *John James Audubon: A Biography*. New York: G. P. Putnam's Sons, 1966.

Adams, Ephraim Douglas. "Correspondence from the British Archives Concerning Texas, 1837–1846." *The Quarterly of the Texas State Historical Association*. Vol. 15, No. 3, pp. 201–265 (January 1912). http://texashistory.unt.edu/ark:/67531/metapth101056/ (accessed 31 May 2014).

Adams, Frank P., Sr. "Notes on the Maritime History of Lubec, Maine." Reprinted from *The American Neptune*. Vol. XXIV, No. 1 (January 1964).

Adams, George. *The Boston Directory: 1848–9*. Boston: James French and Charles Stimpson, 1848.

———. *The Massachusetts Register: A State Record for the Year 1852*. Boston: Damrell and Moore, 1852.

———. *The Massachusetts Register for the Year 1853*. Boston: Damrell and Moore, 1853.

Adjutant General. *Massachusetts Soldiers, Sailors and Marines in the Civil War*. Vols. I, V. Norwood, MA: Norwood Press, 1931–1932.

Ainley, David G., David N. Nettleship, Harry R. Carter, and Anne E. Storey. "Common Murre (*Uria aalge*)." In *The Birds of North America*." No. 666. Edited by Alan Poole and Frank Gill. Philadelphia: The Birds of North America, Inc., 2002.

Akins, Dr. Thomas B. *History of Halifax City*. Halifax, NS: Nova Scotia Historical Society, 1895.

Aldrich, John W. "Habits and Habitat Differences in Two Races of Traill's Flycatcher." *The Wilson Bulletin*. Vol. 65, No. 1, pp. 8–11 (March 1953).

Allaire, J.-B.-A. *Dictionnaire Biographique du Clergé Canadien-Français*. Montreal: Imprimerie de l'École Catholique des Sourds-Muets, 1910.

Allen, Michael. *Western Rivermen, 1763–1861: Ohio and Mississippi Boatmen and the Myth of the Alligator Horse*. Baton Rouge: Louisiana State University Press, 1994.

Allen, Nathan, M.D., ed. "The Edinburgh Phrenological Journal." *The Phrenological Journal and Miscellany*. Vol. III, No. 11, pp. 523–526 (August 1, 1841).

———. "Biography of Dr. Spurzheim." *The Phrenological Journal and Miscellany*. Vol. III, No. 1, pp. 1–13 (October 1, 1841).

American Almanac and Repository of Useful Knowledge for the Year 1833. Boston: Gray and Bowen, 1832.

American Ornithologists' Union. "Forty-second Supplement to the American Ornithologists' Union *Check-list of North American Birds*." *The Auk*. Vol. 117, No. 3, pp. 847–858 (July 2000).

———. "Thirty-second Supplement to the American Ornithologists' Union *Check-list of North American Birds*." *The Auk*. Vol. 90, No. 2, pp. 411–419 (April 1973).

American Railroad Journal. "Meteorological Record, Kept in the City of New York, From the 27th of August to the 16th Day of September, 1833, Inclusive." Vol. II, No 38, p. 600 (Saturday, September 21, 1833).

Andreas, A. T. *History of Cook County Illinois: From the Earliest Period to the Present Time*. Chicago: A. T. Andreas, 1884.

———. *History of Chicago*. 3 vols. Chicago: A. T. Andreas, 1884–1886. Reprint, New York: Arno Press, 1975.

The Annual Register, or a View of the History, Politics, and Literature, of the Year 1823. London: Baldwin, Cradock, and Joy, 1824.

The Annual Register: Or a View of the History and Politics of the Year 1860. London: J. & F.H. Rivington, 1861.

Arader, W. Graham, III, and Wendy J. Shadwell. *Native Grace: Prints of the New World, 1590–1876*. Charlottesville, VA: Thomasson-Grant, 1988.

Arkle, T. H. "Andrew or George Melly." *Notes and Queries: A Medium of Intercommunication for Literary Men, General Readers, Etc*. Eleventh Series. Vol. VIII, p. 74 London: John C. Francis and J. Edward Francis, July 26, 1913.

Army and Navy Chronicle. "Death: Commander Uriah Coolidge." Vol. VII, No. 6, p. 96 (August 9, 1838).

———. "Navy, Revenue Cutter Service, Deaths." Vol. VII, No. 9, p. 144 (August 30, 1838).

Arnold, Howard Payson. *Memoir of John Collins Warren, M.D.* Cambridge, MA: John Wilson and Son, 1882.

Arthur, Stanley Clisby. *Audubon: An Intimate Life of the American Woodsman*. New Orleans: Harmanson, 1937.

Arthur, Stanley Clisby, George Campbell Huchet de Kernion, and Charles Patton Dimitry. *Old Families of Louisiana*. New Orleans: Harmanson, 1931.

Asokan, T. V. "Daniel McNaughton (1813-1865)." *Indian J. Psychiatry*. Vol. 49, No. 3, pp. 223-224 (July-September 2007).

Athanassoglou-Kallmyer, Nina Marie. "Horace Vernet's *Academic Study of an Adolescent Boy* and the Artist's Student Years." *Record of the Art Museum, Princeton University*. Vol. 45, No. 2, pp. 16-24 (1986).

Atkinson, W. B., M.D., ed. *The Physicians and Surgeons of the United States*. Philadelphia: Charles Robson, 1878.

Audubon, John James. *Manuscript Journal: October 12, 1820 to December 31, 1831*. Museum of Comparative Zoology, Special Collections. MCZF117. Harvard University.

———. "Note on the Hirundo fulva." *Annals of The Lyceum of Natural History of New-York*. Vol. I, Part the First, pp. 163-166. New-York: J. Seymour, 1824a.

———. "Facts and Observations on the Permanent Residence of the Swallow in the United States. *Annals of The Lyceum of Natural History of New-York*. Vol. I, Part the First, pp. 166-168. New-York: J. Seymour, 1824b.

———. "Account of the Habits of the Turkey Buzzard (Vultur aura)." *Edinburgh New Philosophical Journal*. Vol. 2, pp. 172-184 (1826).

———. "Notes on the Rattlesnake (*Crotalus horridus*)." *Edinburgh New Philosophical Journal*. Vol. 3, pp. 21-30 (1827).

———. *The Birds of America*. 4 vols. Edinburgh and London: Published by the Author, 1827-1838.

———. "Notes on the Rattlesnake." *Journal of the Franklin Institute and American Mechanics' Magazine*. Vol. VI, No. 1, pp. 32-37 (July 1828).

———. "Notes on the Bird of Washington (*Fálco Washingtoniana*), or Great American Sea Eagle." *The Magazine of Natural History*. Vol. I, No. 2, pp. 115-120 (July 1828).

———. "Journey Up the Mississippi." *The Winter's Wreath for MDCCCXXIX*. pp. 104-127. London: George B. Whittaker, 1828.

———. "*Prospectus for* The Birds of America. Edinburgh: Neill & Co. Printers, 1831.

———. *Ornithological Biography, or An Account of the Habits of the Birds of the United States of America; Accompanied by Descriptions of the Objects Represented in the Work Entitled* The Birds of America, *and Interspersed with Delineations of Scenery and Manners*. 5 vols. Edinburgh: Adam Black, 1831; Edinburgh: Adam & Charles Black, 1834, 1835, 1838, 1849 [1839].

———. *A Synopsis of the Birds of North America*. Edinburgh: Adam and Charles Black, 1839.

———. *The Birds of America from Drawings Made in the United States and its Territories*. 7 vols. New York: J. J. Audubon and Philadelphia: J. B. Chevalier, 1840, 1841, 1841, 1842, 1842; New York: J. J. Audubon, 1843, 1844.

———. *Delineations of American Scenery and Character*. Introduction by Francis Hobart Herrick. New York: G. A. Baker, 1926.

———. *Audubon in the West*. Compiled, edited, and with an introduction by John Francis McDermott. Norman, OK: University of Oklahoma Press, 1965.

———. *The Original Water-Color Paintings by John James Audubon for* The Birds of America. Introduction by Marshall B. Davidson. New York: American Heritage Publishing Co., Inc., 1966.

———. *My Style of Drawing Birds*. Introduction by Michael Zinman. Ardsley, NY: The Overland Press, 1979.

———. *Writings and Drawings*. Edited by Christoph Irmscher. New York: The Library of America, 1999.

———. *The Audubon Reader*. Edited by Richard Rhodes. New York: Alfred A. Knopf, 2006.

———. *Audubon: Early Drawings*. Forward by Leslie A. Morris, Introduction by Richard Rhodes, and Scientific Commentary by Scott V. Edwards. Cambridge, MA: The Belknap Press of Harvard University Press, 2008.

————. *John James Audubon's Journal of 1826: The Voyage to* The Birds of America. Edited by Daniel Patterson and Patricio J. Serrano. Lincoln, NE: University of Nebraska Press, 2011.

————. *The Birds of America: The Bien Chromolithographic Edition*. Edited by Joel Oppenheimer and Laura Oppenheimer. New York: W.W. Norton & Company. 2013.

Audubon, John James and John Bachman. *The Viviaparous Quadrupeds of North America*. 3 vols. New York: J.J. Audubon, 1846; New York: V. G. Audubon, 1851 and 1854.

————. *The Quadrupeds of North America*. 3 vols. New York: V. G. Audubon, 1849, 1851, and 1854.

Audubon, John Woodhouse. *Illustrated Notes of an Expedition through Mexico and California*. New York: J. W. Audubon, 1852. Reprint, Tarrytown: William Abbatt, 1915.

————. *Audubon's Western Journal: 1849–1850: Being the Record of a Trip from New York to Texas, and an Overland Journey Through Mexico and Arizona and the Gold Fields of California*. Edited by Maria R. Audubon and Frank Heywood Hodder. Cleveland: The Arthur H. Clark Co., 1906.

————. *The Drawings of John Woodhouse Audubon: Illustrating his Adventures through Mexico and California, 1849–1850: With an Introduction and Notes on the Drawings*. San Francisco: Book Club of California, 1957.

Audubon, Lucy, ed., *The Life of John James Audubon, the Naturalist*. Introduction by James Grant Wilson. New York: G. P. Putnam & Son, 1869.

Audubon, Maria R. "Reminiscences of Audubon." *Scribner's Monthly*. Vol. XII, No. 1, pp. 334-336. New York: Scribner & Co., 1876.

————. "Audubon's Story of His Youth." *Scribner's Magazine*. Vol. XIII, No. 3, pp. 267-289. New York: Charles Scribner's Sons, 1893.

Audubon, Maria R., and Elliott Coues, eds. *Audubon and His Journals*. 2 vols. New York: Charles Scribner's Sons, 1897.

Audubon, Victor G. "Mr. Audubon, Jun., in Reply to Mr. Waterton's Remarks on Audubon's Biography of Birds." *The Magazine of Natural History*, Vol. VI, No. 34, p. 369 (July 1833).

————. "Mr. Audubon and his Work, the 'Biography of Birds:' Mr. Audubon, jun., in Reply to Mr. Waterton." *The Magazine of Natural History*. Vol. VI, No. 36, pp. 550-553 (November 1833).

Ayer, Sarah Connell. *Diary of Sarah Connell Ayer*. Edited by M.H. Jewell. Portland, ME: Lefavor-Tower Company, 1910.

Ayers, Edward L., Lewis L. Gould, David M. Oshinsky, and Jean R. Soderlund. *American Passages: A History of the United States*. Brief 4th ed. Boston: Wadsworth Cengage Learning, 2012.

Bachman, Catherine. *John Bachman*. Charleston, SC: Walker, Evans & Cogswell, 1888.

Bachman, John. "Remarks in Defence of Mr. Audubon the Author of the 'Biography of the Birds of America.'" *The Magazine of Natural History*. Vol. VII, No. 38, pp. 164-175 (March 1834).

Baicich, Paul J., and Colin J.O. Harrison. *Nests, Eggs, and Nestlings of North American Birds*. 2nd ed. Princeton, NJ and Oxford: Princeton University Press, 2005.

Baines, Edward and W. Parson. *History, Directory, and Gazetteer of the County Palatine of Lancaster; With a Variety of Commercial & Statistical Information*. 2 vols. Liverpool: Wm. Wales & Co., 1824.

Baird, Spencer F., Thomas M. Brewer, and Robert Ridgway. *The Water Birds of North America*. 2 vols. Boston: Little, Brown, and Company, 1884.

Bakewell, B.G., comp. *The Family Book of Bakewell*Page*Campbell: Being Some Account of the Descendants of John Bakewell, of Castle Donington, Leicestershire, England, Born in 1638. Benjamin Page, Born in 1765, at Norwich, England. William Campbell, Born July 1, 1766, at Mauchline, Ayrshire, Scotland. John Harding, of Leicester*. Pittsburgh, PA: Wm. G. Johnston & Co., 1896.

Bakewell, Alexander Gordon. "Reminiscences of Audubon." *Publications of the Louisiana Historical Society*. Vol. V-1911, pp. 31-41. New Orleans: The Louisiana Historical Society, 1911.

Bakewell, Robert. "Observations on Mr. Waterton's Attacks on Mr. Audubon." *The Magazine of Natural History*. Vol. VI, No. 34, pp. 369-372 (July 1833).

Bakewell, Thomas W. "Audubon & Bakewell Partners: Sketch of the Life of Thomas Woodhouse Bakewell, Written by Himself." *The Cardinal*. Vol. IV, No. 2, pp. 34–42. Sewickley, PA: Audubon Society of the Sewickley Valley, 1935.

Barnhill, Georgia Brady. "Extracts from the Journals of Ethan A. Greenwood: Portrait Painter and Museum Proprietor." *Proceedings of the American Antiquarian Society*. Vol. 103, Part 1, pp. 91–178 (April 1993).

Barry, T. A., and B. A. Patten. *Men and Memories of San Francisco in the Spring of '50*. San Francisco: A. L. Bancroft & Company, 1873.

Bassett, Norman L. ed. *Report of the Maine State Bar Association for 1920 and 1921*. Vol. 22, pp. 310–311. Augusta, ME: Charles E. Nash & Son, 1921.

Bastedo, Jamie. "Shield." *The Canadian Encyclopedia* (database online). 2013. http://www.thecanadian encyclopedia.com/en/article/shield/ (accessed 15 Mar. 2014).

Bates, William C. "Mr. Samuel Appleton." In *Memorial Biographies of The New England Historic Genealogical Society: 1853–1855*. Vol. II, pp. 62–68. Boston: Published by the Society, 1881.

Bayfield, Henry Wolsey, Captain Royal Navy, F.R.A.S. *Sailing Directions for the Gulf and River of St. Lawrence*. London: Printed for the Hydrographic Office, 1837.

———, Rear-Admiral, F.R.A.S. *The St. Lawrence Pilot: Comprising Sailing Directions for the Gulf and River*. 4th ed. 2 vols. London: Printed for the Hydrographic Office, Admiralty, 1860.

———, *The St. Lawrence Survey Journals of Captain Henry Wolsey Bayfield: 1829–1853*. Edited and with an introduction by Ruth McKenzie. 2 vols. Toronto: The Champlain Society, 1984.

Beck, J. Murray. "Archibald, Samuel George William." *Dictionary of Canadian Biography*. Vol. 7. University of Toronto/Université Laval, 2003–. http://www.biographi.ca/en/bio/archibald_samuel_george _william_7E.html (accessed 23 Jan. 2012).

———. "Blanchard, Jotham." *Dictionary of Canadian Biography*. Vol. 7. University of Toronto/Université Laval, 2003–. http://www.biographi.ca/en/bio/blanchard_jotham_7E.html (accessed 23 Jan. 2012).

Beggs-Humphreys, Mary, Hugh Gregor, and Darlow Humphreys. *The Industrial Revolution*. Abingdon, England: Routledge, 2006.

Belcher, C. H. *Belcher's Farmer's Almanack for the Year of our Lord 1833*. Halifax, NS: n.d. [1832].

———. *Belcher's Farmer's Almanack for the Year of our Lord 1834*. Halifax, NS: n.d. [1833].

Bell, John G. *Diaries of an Expedition with John James Audubon, March 11-December 31, 1843*. 3 Vols. Beinecke Rare Book & Manuscript Library, Yale University (WA MSS S-1752).

Belvin, Cleophas. *The Forgotten Labrador: Kegashka to Blanc-Sablon*. Montreal & Kingston: McGill-Queen's University Press, 2006.

Benoît, Hugues P., Jacques A. Gagné, Claude Savenkoff, Patrick Ouellet, and Marie—Noëlle Bourassa, eds. "State of the Ocean Report for the Gulf of St. Lawrence Integrated Management (GOSLIM) Area." *Canadian Manuscript Report of Fisheries and Aquatic Sciences 2986*. 2012.

Bigelow, E. Victor. *A Narrative History of the Town of Cohasset, Massachusetts*. Boston: The Committee on Town History, 1898.

D. M. Bishop & Co., comp. *The New City Annual Directory of San Francisco*. San Francisco: D. M. Bishop & Co. Printers, 1875.

Blair, Francis P. and John C. Rives, eds. *The Congressional Globe: Sketches of the Debates and Proceedings of the Twenty-Third Congress*. City of Washington: The Congressional Globe, 1834.

Blakely, Phyllis R. "Halliburton, Sir Brenton." *Dictionary of Canadian Biography*. Vol. 8. University of Toronto/Université Laval, 2003–. http://www.biographi.ca/en/bio/halliburton_brenton_8E.html (accessed 6 Feb. 2012).

Bland, D. S., *John James Audubon in Liverpool: 1826–27*. Liverpool: The Author, 1977.

Blaugrund, Annette. "The Artist as Entrepreneur." In Annette Blaugrund and Theodore E. Stebbins Jr., eds. *John James Audubon: The Watercolors for* "The Birds of America." pp. 27–42. New York: Villard Books and The New-York Historical Society, 1993.

———. *The Essential John James Audubon*. New York: Henry N. Abrams, Inc., 1999.

———. "'My Style of Drawing:' Audubon and His Artistic Milieu." In Sarah E. Boehme. *John James Audubon in the West: The Last Expedition*, pp. 11–33. New York: Harry N. Abrams, Inc. in association with the Buffalo Bill Historical Center, 2000.

Blaugrund, Annette, and Theodore E. Stebbins Jr., eds. *John James Audubon: The Watercolors for* "The Birds of America." New York: Villard Books and The New-York Historical Society, 1993.

Bledsoe, Robert Terrell. *Henry Fothergill Chorley: Victorian Journalist*. Brookfield, VT: Ashgate Publishing Company, 1998.

———. "Chorley, Henry Fothergill (1808–1872)." *Oxford Dictionary of National Biography* (online). London: Oxford University Press, 2004. http://www.oxforddnb.com/view/article/5350 (accessed 11 Jan. 2014).

Blockstein, David E. "Passenger Pigeon (*Ectopistes migratorius*)." In *The Birds of North America*. No. 611. Edited by Alan Poole and Frank Gill. Philadelphia: The Birds of North America, Inc., 2002.

Blumenbach, Johann Friedrich. *A Manual of Comparative Anatomy*. 2nd ed. London: W. Simpkin and R. Marshall, 1827.

Blunt, Edmund M. *The American Coast Pilot*. 11th ed. New York: Edmund and George W. Blunt, 1827.

———. *The American Coast Pilot*. 12th ed. New York: Edmund and George W. Blunt, 1833.

Blunt, Joseph. *The Merchant's and Shipmaster's Assistant; Containing Information Useful to the American Merchants, Shipowners, and Masters of Ships*. New York: Edmund M. Blunt, 1822.

———. *The Merchant's and Shipmaster's Assistant; Containing Information Useful to the American Merchants, Shipowners, and Masters of Ships*. New York: E & G.W. Blunt, 1832.

———. *The Shipmaster's Assistant, and Commercial Digest: Containing Information Useful to Merchants, Owners, and Masters of Ships*. New York: E & G.W. Blunt, 1837.

Boehme, Sarah E. *John James Audubon in the West: The Last Expedition*. New York: Harry N. Abrams, Inc. in association with the Buffalo Bill Historical Center, 2000.

Brannan, Peter A. *Edward Harris: Friend of Audubon*. New York: Newcomen Society of England, American Branch, 1947.

Bonaparte, Charles Lucian. *The Genera of North American Birds, and a Synopsis of the Species Found within the Territory of the United States*. New York: J. Seymour, 1828.

———. *A Geographical and Comparative List of the Birds of Europe and North America*. London: John Van Voorst, 1838.

Bonhams. *The Robert H. and Donna L. Jackson Collection, Part I: 19th Century Literature*. Auction 19545. October 18, 2011. New York: Bonhams, 2011.

Book, J. David. "Audubon in Louisville, 1807–1810." *The Filson Club History Quarterly*. Vol. 45, No. 2, pp. 186–198 (April 1971).

Boston Athenaeum. *The Influence and History of the Boston Athenaeum: from 1807 to 1907*. Boston: Boston Athenaeum, 1907.

Bowditch, Nathaniel. *The New American Practical Navigator*. 6th ed. New York: Edmund M. Blunt, 1826.

Bowdoin College. *General Catalogue of Bowdoin College and the Medical School of Maine, 1794–1912*. Brunswick, ME: Bowdoin College, 1912.

———. *General Catalogue of the Non-Graduates of Bowdoin College, 1794–1915*. Brunswick, ME: Bowdoin College, 1916.

Bowen, Abel. *Bowen's Picture of Boston, or The Citizen's and Stranger's Guide to the Metropolis of Massachusetts, and Its Environs. To Which Is Prefixed the Annals of Boston*. 2nd ed. Boston: Published by Lilly Wait & Co. and Lorenzo H. Bowen, 1833.

———. *Bowen's Picture of Boston, or the Citizen's and Stranger's Guide to the Metropolis of Massachusetts, and Its Environs. To Which Is Affixed the Annals of Boston*. 3rd ed. Boston: Otis, Broaders and Company, 1838.

Bowen, Charles. *The American Almanac and Repository of Useful Information for the Year 1835*. Boston: Charles Bowen, 1834.

Bowsfield, Hartwell. "Maitland, Sir Peregrine." *Dictionary of Canadian Biography*. Vol. 8. University of Toronto/Université Laval, 2003-. http://www.biographi.ca/en/bio/maitland_peregrine_8E.html (accessed 18 Feb. 2012).

Braislin, William C., M.D. "An American Edition of Audubon's *Ornithological Biography*." *The Auk*. Vol. XXXV, No. 3, pp. 360-362 (July 1918).

Brewer, Thomas M. "Reminiscences of John James Audubon." *Harper's New Monthly Magazine*. Vol. LXI, No. CCCLXV, pp. 665-675 (October 1880).

Brigham, Clarence S. "Bibliography of American Newspapers, 1690-1820, Part VIII: New York City." *Proceedings of the American Antiquarian Society*. New Series. Vol. 27, pp. 375-513. Worcester, MA: Published by the Society, 1917.

Brown, C. Donald. *Eastport: A Maritime History*. Eastport, ME: Down East Associates, 1968. Reprinted from *The American Neptune*. Vol. XXVIII, No. 2 (1968).

Brown, Michael P. "Stewart, Dugald (1753-1828)." *Oxford Dictionary of National Biography* (online). Oxford: Oxford University Press, 2004. http://www.oxforddnb.com/view/article/26471 (accessed 8 Feb. 2014).

Buchanan, Robert, ed. *The Life and Adventures of John James Audubon, the Naturalist*. London: Sampson Low, Son, & Marston, 1868.

Buckingham, James S. *Canada, Nova Scotia, New Brunswick, and the other British Provinces in North America*. London: Fisher, Son, & Co., 1843.

Buehler, David A. "Bald Eagle (*Haliaeetus leucocephalus*)." In *The Birds of North America*. No. 506. Edited by Alan Poole and Frank Gill. Philadelphia: The Birds of North America, Inc., 2000.

Buford, Marcus Bainbridge. *A Genealogy of the Buford Family in America*. San Francisco: Privately Printed, 1903.

Buggey, Susan and Gwendolyn Davies. "McCulloch, Thomas." *Dictionary of Canadian Biography*. Vol. 7. University of Toronto/Université Laval, 2003-. http://www.biographi.ca/en/bio/mcculloch_thomas_7E.html (accessed 23 Jan. 2012).

Burant, Jim. "The Military Artist and the Documentary Art Record." *Archivaria*. Vol. 26, pp. 33-51 (Summer 1988).

Burbank, B.B. "James Bowdoin and Parker Cleaveland." *Mineralogical Record*. Vol. 19, No. 3, pp. 145-152 (May/June 1988).

Burke, Sir Bernard. *A Genealogic and Heraldic Dictionary of the Landed Gentry of Great Britain & Ireland*. 4th ed. 2 vols. London: Harrison, Pall Mall, 1863.

Burke, John. *A General and Heraldic Dictionary of the Peerage and Baronetage of the United Kingdom*. London: Henry Colburn, 1826.

———. *A General and Heraldic Dictionary of the Peerage and Baronetage of the British Empire*. 5th ed. London: Henry Colburn, Publisher, 1838.

Burke, John and John Bernard Burke. *A Genealogic and Heraldic Dictionary of the Landed Gentry of Great Britain & Ireland*. 2 vols. London: Henry Colburn, Publisher, 1847.

Burrage, Walter L, M.D. *A History of the Massachusetts Medical Society*. Norwood, MA: Privately Printed, 1923.

Burroughs, John. *John James Audubon*. Boston: Small, Maynard, 1902.

Burroughs, Franklin. *Passion or Conquest*. Haverford, PA: Green Shade, 2001.

Burtt, Edward H., Jr., and William E. Davis Jr.. *Alexander Wilson: The Scot Who Founded American Ornithology*. Cambridge, MA and London: The Belknap Press of Harvard University Press, 2013.

Butler, Frances Anne. *Journal of Frances Anne Butler*. 2 vols. Philadelphia: Carey, Lea & Blanchard, 1835.

Butler, Ronald G. and Daniel E. Buckley. "Black Guillemot (*Cepphus grylle*)." In *The Birds of North America*. No. 675. Edited by Alan Poole and Frank Gill. Philadelphia: The Birds of North America, Inc., 2002.

California Legislature. *The Journal of the Senate during the Twenty-Fourth Session of the Legislature of the State of California: 1881*. Sacramento: State Office, 1881.

Callary, Edward. *Place Names of Illinois*. Urbana, IL: University of Illinois Press, 2009.

Calnan, Maureen. *Eastport, Maine Early Recorded Families: 1700s-1800s*. N.P: Privately Printed, 2007.

Camp, William Martin. *San Francisco: Port of Gold*. Garden City, NY: Doubleday & Company, Inc., 1947.

Capen, Nahum. "A Biography of the Author (J.G. Spurzheim)." In J.G. Spurzheim, *Phrenology in Connection With the Study of Physiognomy*. Boston: Marsh, Capen & Lyon, 1833.

———. *Massachusetts State Record and Yearbook of General Information: 1847*. Boston: James French, 1847.

Carrington, Paul D. "Francis Lieber (1798-1872)." In Roger K. Newman, ed., *The Yale Biographical Dictionary of American Law*, pp. 335-336. New Haven, CT: Yale University Press, 2009.

Cates, William L. R., ed. *A Dictionary of General Biography*. London: Longmans, Green, and Co., 1867.

Casseday, Ben. *The History of Louisville: From Its Earliest Settlement Till the Year 1852*. Louisville, KY: Hull and Brother, 1852.

Chalmers, John, M.D. *Audubon in Edinburgh*. Edinburgh: NMS Publishing, 2003.

Chambers, Robert. *Walks in Edinburgh*. Edinburgh: William Hunter, 1825.

Chancellor, John. *Audubon*. New York: The Viking Press, 1978.

Chapman, George T., D.D. *Sketches of the Alumni of Dartmouth College*. Cambridge, MA: Riverside Press, 1867.

Chappell, Lieut. Edward, R.N. *Voyage of His Majesty's Ship Rosamond to Newfoundland and the Southern Coast of Labrador*. London: J. Mawman, 1818.

Chapelle, Howard Irving. *American Small Sailing Craft, Their Design, Development, and Construction*. New York: W.W. Norton and Company, Inc., 1951.

Cheever, David W., ed., *A History of the Boston City Hospital from Its Foundation Until 1904*. Boston: Municipal Printing Office, 1906.

Cheyne, John, M.D. *An Essay on Hydrocephalus Acutus or Dropsy in the Brain*. Edinburgh: Mundell, Doig, & Stevenson, 1808.

Child, Elias. *Genealogy of the Child, Childs and Childe Families*. Utica, NY: Curtiss and Childs, 1881.

Chilton, Glen. "Labrador Duck (*Camptorhynchus labradorius*)." In *The Birds of North America*. No. 307. Edited by Alan Poole and Frank Gill. Philadelphia: The Academy of Natural Sciences and Washington, D.C.: The American Ornithologists' Union, 1997.

———. *The Curse of the Labrador Duck: My Obsessive Quest to the Edge of Extinction*. New York: Simon & Schuster, 2009.

Christie, Manson & Woods International Inc. *Highly Important Natural History Books and Autographs Including Audubon's* Birds of America *and an Extensive Collection of His Manuscripts*. May 26, 1977. New York: Christie, Manson & Woods International Inc., 1977.

———. *John James Audubon and His Circle*. October 29, 1993. New York: Christie, Manson & Woods International Inc., 1993.

Christie's. *John James Audubon's* The Birds of America: *The Early Subscriber's Set of George Lane Fox*. Sale No. 9326. March 10, 2000. New York: Christie's, 2000.

———. *Printed Books and Manuscripts from Longleat*. Sale No. 6681. June 13, 2002. London: Christie's, 2002.

———. *The Magnificent Sachsen-Meiningen Set of Audubon's* The Birds of America. Sale No. 1395. June 25, 2004. New York: Christie's, 2004.

———. *Fine Printed Books and Manuscripts*. Sale No. 6332. June 13, 2011. South Kensington, England: Christie's, 2011.

————. *John James Audubon's* The Birds of America: *The Duke of Portland Set*. Sale No. 2526. January 20, 2012. New York: Christie's, 2012a.

————. *Important Printed Books and Americana from the Albert H. Small Collection*. Sale No. 2655. May 18, 2012. New York: Christie's, 2012b.

Christy, Bayard H. "Four Audubon Letters." *The Cardinal*. Vol. IV, No. 7, pp. 167–174. Sewickley, PA: Audubon Society of the Sewickley Valley, 1938.

————. "Audubon's Autobiography." *The Auk*. Vol. 59, No. 3, pp. 450–451 (July 1942).

Clark, Arthur H. *The Clipper Ship Era: An Epitome of Famous American and British Clipper Ships, Their Owners, Builders, Commanders, and Crews, 1843–1869*. New York and London: G. P. Putnam's Sons, 1911.

Clark, Taylor and Lois Elmer Bannon. *Handbook of Audubon Prints*. 4th ed. Gretna, LA: Pelican Publishing Company, 1998.

Cleaveland, Nehemiah and Alpheus Spring Packard. *History of Bowdoin College with Biographical Sketches of its Graduates*. Boston: James Ripley Osgood & Company, 1882.

Clinton, Catherine. *Fanny Kemble's Civil Wars*. New York: Simon & Schuster, 2000.

————, ed. *Fanny Kemble's Journals*. Cambridge, MA and London: Harvard University Press, 2000.

Coffin, Annie Roulhac. "Audubon's Friend — Maria Martin." *The New-York Historical Society Quarterly*. Vol. XLIX, No. 1, pp. 29–51 (January 1965).

Coffin, John G., ed. "Advertisements, Swimming School." *The Boston Medical Intelligencer*. Vol. 5, No. 10, p. 168 (Tuesday, July 24, 1827).

Coke, E. T. *A Subaltern's Furlough*. 2 vols. New York: J. and J. Harper, 1833.

Colonial Society of Massachusetts. *Publications of The Colonial Society of Massachusetts*. Vol. X, Transactions 1904–1906. Boston: Published by The Society, 1907.

Connelley, William Elsey and E. M. Coulter. *History of Kentucky*. 5 vols. (Chicago and New York: The American Historical Society, 1922.

Coolidge, Uriah, Capt., "Transcript of the U.S. Revenue Cutter *Swiftsure's* Journal." May-June 1833. *Journals of Revenue Cutters, Treasury Department, 1833*. National Archives, Washington, D.C.

Corbin, Annalies. *The Material Culture of Steamboat Passengers: Archeological Evidence from the Missouri River*. New York: Kluwer Academic/Plenum Publishers, 2000.

Corder, Jim W. *Hunting Lieutenant Chadbourne*. Athens, GA: University of Georgia Press, 1993.

Corning, Howard, ed. *Journal of John James Audubon Made During His Trip to New Orleans in 1820–1821*. Cambridge, MA: Club of Odd Volumes, 1929a.

————, ed. *Journal of John James Audubon Made While Obtaining Subscriptions to His "Birds of America" 1840–1843*. Cambridge, MA: Club of Odd Volumes, 1929b.

————, ed. *Letters of John James Audubon, 1826–1840*. 2 vols. Cambridge, MA: Club of Odd Volumes, 1930.

Craven, Jackie. "1690s – 1830s: Georgian Colonial House Style: A British Style Takes Root in the New World." About.com. http://architecture.about.com/od/periodsstyles/ig/House-Styles/Georgian.htm (accessed 19 Feb. 2014).

Crawford, Mary Caroline. *Romantic Days in Old Boston: The Story of the City and of Its People During the 19th Century*. Boston: Little, Brown, and Company, 1910.

Creed, Percy R., ed. *The Boston Society of Natural History: 1830–1930*. Boston: Printed for the Society, 1930.

Critchett, B. *The Post-Office London Directory for 1828*. London: n.d. [1827].

————. *The Post-Office London Directory for 1829*. (London: n.d. [1828].

Critchett and Woods. *The Post-Office London Directory for 1824*. London: n.d. [1823].

————. *The Post-Office London Directory for 1826*. London: n.d. [1825].

————. *The Post-Office London Directory for 1827*. London: n.d. [1826].

Crutcher, Lawrence M. *George Keats of Kentucky: A Life*. Lexington, KY: The University Press of Kentucky, 2012.

Cullum, Bvt. Major-General George W. *Biographical Register of the Officers and Graduates of the U.S. Military Academy at West Point, N.Y., from its Establishment in 1802, to the Army Re-Organization of 1866–67*. 2nd ed. 2 vols. New York: D. Van Nostrand, 1868.

———. *Biographical Register of the Officers and Graduates of the U.S. Military Academy at West Point, N.Y., from its Establishment in 1802, to 1890: With the Early History of the United States Military Academy*. 3rd ed. 3 vols. Boston: Houghton, Mifflin and Company, 1891.

Curson, Jon, David Quinn, and David Beadle. *Warblers of the Americas: An Identification Guide*. Boston: Houghton Mifflin Company, 1994.

Curtis, George Ticknor. *Life of Daniel Webster*. 2 vols. New York: D. Appleton and Company, 1870.

Cushing, James Stevenson. *The Genealogy of the Cushing Family*. Montreal: The Perrault Printing Co., 1905.

Cuthbertson, B. C. "Jeffery, Thomas Nickleson." *Dictionary of Canadian Biography*. Vol. 7. University of Toronto/Université Laval, 2003–. http://www.biographi.ca/en/bio/jeffery_thomas_nickleson_7E.html (accessed 8 Feb. 2012).

Dall, William Healey. *Spencer Fullerton Baird: A Biography*. New York & London: J.B. Lippincott Company, 1915.

Dallett, Francis James. "Citizen Audubon: A Document Discovery." *Princeton University Library Chronicle*. Vol. XXI, Nos. 1 & 2, pp. 89–93 (1960).

Daly, Reginald A. "The Geology of the Northeast Coast of Labrador." *Bulletin of the Museum of Comparative Zoology at Harvard University*. Vol. XXXVIII, Geological Series, Vol. V, No. 5. Cambridge, MA: Museum of Comparative Zoology, 1902.

Dartmouth College. *General Catalogue of Dartmouth College and the Associated Institutions*. Hanover, NH: Dartmouth College, 1890.

David, Dierdre. *Fanny Kemble: A Performed Life*. Philadelphia: University of Pennsylvania Press, 2007.

Davis, George L., comp. *Samuel Davis, of Oxford, Mass., and Joseph Davis, of Dudley Mass., and Their Descendants*. North Andover, MA: George L. Davis, 1884.

Davis, William Thomas. *Bench and Bar of the Commonwealth of Massachusetts*. 2 vols. Boston: The Boston History Company, 1895.

Deane, Ruthven. "Unpublished Letters of John James Audubon and Spencer F. Baird." *The Auk*. Vol. XXI, No. 2, pp. 255–259 (April 1904).

———. "Extracts from an Unpublished Journal of John James Audubon." *The Auk*. Vol. XXI, No. 3, pp. 334–338 (July 1904).

———. "A Hitherto Unpublished Letter of John James Audubon." *The Auk*. Vol. XXII, No. 2, pp. 170–172 (April 1905).

———. "Unpublished Letters of John James Audubon and Spencer F. Baird." Part I. *The Auk*. Vol. XXIII, No. 2, pp. 194–209 (April 1906).

———. "Unpublished Letters of John James Audubon and Spencer F. Baird." Part II. *The Auk*. Vol. XXIII, No. 3, pp. 318–334 (July 1906).

———. "Unpublished Letters of John James Audubon and Spencer F. Baird." Part III. *The Auk*. Vol. XXIV, No. 1, pp. 53–70 (January 1907).

———. "An Unpublished Letter of John James Audubon to his Family." *The Auk*. Vol. XXV, No. 2, pp. 166–169 (April 1908a).

———. "Unpublished Letters of Introduction Carried by John James Audubon on His Missouri River Expedition." *The Auk*. Vol. XXV, No. 2, pp. 170–173 (April 1908b).

———. "The Copper-Plates of the Folio Edition of Audubon's *Birds of America*, With a Brief Sketch of the Engravers." *The Auk*, Vol. XXV, No. 4, pp. 401–413 (October 1908c).

———. "Audubon's Labrador Trip of 1833." *The Auk*. Vol. XXVII, No. 1, pp. 42–52 (January 1910).

———. "Some Letters of Bachman to Audubon." *The Auk*. Vol. XLVI, No. 2, pp. 177–185 (April 1929).

"Death of Dr. Spurzheim." *The Phrenological Journal and Miscellany*. Vol VIII, p. 130 (June 1834).

Debboun, Mustapha, Stephen P. Frances, and Daniel Strickman, eds. *Insect Repellents: Principles, Methods, and Uses*. Boca Raton, FL: CRC Press, 2007.

Delatte, Carolyn E. *Lucy Audubon: A Biography*. Baton Rouge: Louisiana State University Press, 1982.

Dennysville, Maine. *Memorial of the 100th Anniversary of the Settlement of Dennysville, Maine, 1886*. Portland, ME: B. Thurston & Company, Printers, 1886.

Derby, Perley, comp. "Genealogy of the Derby Family." *Historical Collections of the Essex Institute*. Vol. III, No. 5, pp. 201–207 (October 1861).

———. "Genealogy of the Derby Family. *Historical Collections of the Essex Institute*. Vol. III, No. 6, pp. 283–289 (December 1861).

Desormeaux, Vincent, and Raymonde Pomerleau. *Parc National de la Région de Harrington Harbour Project: Status Report*. Québec: Service des Parcs, 2010.

Dodd, J., Liahona Research, comp. *Massachusetts Marriages, 1633–1850*. Accessed through Ancestry.com (database on-line). Provo, UT: The Generations Network, Inc., 2005.

Dodge, Norman L. ed. *The Month at Goodspeed's*. Vol. 21, Nos. 5–6. Boston: Goodspeed's Book Shop, February-March 1950.

Dormon, James H., ed. *Audubon: A Retrospective*. Lafayette, LA: University of Southwestern Louisiana, 1990.

Dow, Charles H., and David S. Babcock. *History of Steam Navigation between New York and Providence: From 1792–1877*. New York: Wm. Turner & Co., Printers, 1877.

Downer, Don. *Turbulent Tides: A Social History of Sandy Point*. Portugal Cove, NL: ESP Press Limited, 1997.

Drake, Samuel Adams. *Old Landmarks and Historic Personages of Boston*. Boston: James R. Osgood and Company, 1873.

Draper, Ruth L. W. "Through the Stereoscope." *Down East*. Vol. XV, No. 9, pp. 44–47 (June 1969).

Dunlap, William. *A History of the Rise and Progress of the Arts of Design in the United States*. 2 vols. New York: George P. Scott and Co. Printers, 1834.

———. *Diary of William Dunlap (1766–1839): The Memoirs of a Dramatist, Theatrical Manager, Painter, Critic, Novelist, and Historian*. 3 vols. New York: New-York Historical Society, 1930.

Dunn, Jon L. and Kimball L. Garrett. *A Field Guide to Warblers of North America*. Boston and New York: Houghton Mifflin Company, 1997.

Dunn, Jon L. and Jonathan Alderfer, eds. *National Geographic Field Guide to the Birds of North America*. 6th ed. Washington, D.C.: National Geographic Society, 2011.

Dunne, Pete. *Pete Dunne's Essential Field Guide Companion*. Boston and New York: Houghton Mifflin Company, 2006.

Durant, Mary and Michael Harwood. *On the Road with John James Audubon*. New York: Dodd, Mead, 1980.

Dwight, Edward H. "The Autobiographical Writings of John James Audubon." *The Bulletin*. Vol. XIX, No. 1, pp. 26–35. St. Louis: Missouri Historical Society, 1962.

———. *Audubon: Watercolors and Drawings*. Utica, NY: Munson-Williams-Proctor Institute and Pierpont Morgan Library, 1965.

Eastman, Francis A. *Chicago City Manual 1909*. Chicago: Bureau of Statistics and Municipal Library, 1909.

———. *Chicago City Manual 1911*. Chicago: Bureau of Statistics and Municipal Library, 1911.

Eastman, John. *Birds of Field and Shore: Grassland and Shoreline Birds of Eastern North America*. Mechanicsburg, PA: Stackpole Books, 2000.

Ehrlich, Paul R., David S. Dobkin, and Darryl Wheye. *Birds in Jeopardy: The Imperiled and Extinct Birds of the United States and Canada Including Hawaii and Puerto Rico*. Stanford, CA: Stanford University Press, 1992.

Eitner, Lorenz E. A. *Géricault: His Life and Work*. London: Orbis Publishing, 1983.

———. "Introduction." *Theodore Géricault (1791–1824): An Exhibition*. New York: Salander-O'Reilly Galleries, Inc., 1987.

Elliot, Jonathan. *The Funding System of the United States and of Great Britain*. Washington, D.C.: Blair and Rives, Printers, 1845.

Elphick, Chris, John B. Dunning Jr., and David Allen Sibley, eds. *The Sibley Guide to Bird Life & Behavior*. New York: Alfred A. Knopf, 2001.

Emery, Rufus, comp. *Genealogical Records of the Descendants of John and Anthony Emery, of Newbury, Mass: 1590–1890*. Salem, MA: Emery Cleaves, 1890.

Evans, Howard Ensign. *The Natural History of the Long Expedition to the Rocky Mountains: 1819–1820*. New York: Oxford University Press, 1997.

Evenhuis, Neal L. "Publication and Dating of the Journals Forming the *Annals and Magazine of Natural History* and the *Journal of Natural History*." *Zootaxa*. No. 385, pp. 1–68 (2003).

Farlow, John W., M.D. "The Staniford Street Dispensary." *Boston Medical & Surgical Journal*. Vol. 192, No. 4, pp. 165–171 (January 22, 1925).

Fergus, Robert. *Directory of the City of Chicago, Illinois, for 1843*. Chicago: Fergus Printing Company, 1896.

Fernández-Grandon, G. Mandella, Salvador A. Gezan, John A. L. Armour, John A. Pickett, and James G. Logan. "Heritability of Attractiveness to Mosquitoes." *PLoS ONE*. 10(4): e0122716. doi: 10.1371/journal.pone.0122716 (April 22, 2015).

Flynn, Ron. "Do You Really Own a 1st Edition Octavo Quad Print?" (2008). http://www.auduboninfo.net/articles/really%201st%20edition%20quad.htm (accessed 27 Nov. 2013).

Force, Peter. *The National Calendar, and Annals of the United States; for MDCCCXXII*. Vol. III. Washington City: Davis & Force, 1822.

———. *The National Calendar, and Annals of the United States; for MDCCCXXXII*. Vol. X. Washington City: Peter Force, 1832.

———. *The National Calendar, and Annals of the United States; for MDCCCXXXIII*. Vol. XI. Washington City: Peter Force, 1833.

———. *The National Calendar, and Annals of the United States; for MDCCCXXXIV*. Vol. XII. Washington City: Pishey Thompson and Franck Taylor, 1834.

Ford, Alice, ed. *Audubon's Animals: The Quadrupeds of North America*. New York: Studio Publications, 1951.

———, ed. *Audubon's Butterflies, Moths and Other Studies*. New York: Studio Publications, 1952.

———, ed. *The Bird Biographies of John James Audubon*. New York: Macmillan, 1957.

———. *John James Audubon*. Norman, OK: University of Oklahoma Press, 1964.

———, ed. *The 1826 Journal of John James Audubon*. Norman, OK: University of Oklahoma Press, 1967.

———, ed. *Audubon, By Himself*. Garden City, NY: Natural History Press, 1969.

———, ed. *The 1826 Journal of John James Audubon*. 2nd ed. New York: Abbeville Press, 1987.

———. *John James Audubon: A Biography*. 2nd ed. New York: Abbeville Press, 1988.

Forkner, Ben, ed. *John James Audubon: Selected Journals and Other Writings*. New York: Penguin Books, 1996.

Fortin, Pierre. *Annual Report of Pierre Fortin, Esq., Stipendiary Magistrate, Commander of the Expedition for the Protection of the Fisheries in the Gulf of St. Lawrence, on Board 'La Canadienne,' During the Season of 1864*. Quebec: Hunter, Rose & Co., 1865.

Foshay, Ella M. *John James Audubon*. New York: Henry N. Abrams, 1997.

Fox, Stephen. *John Muir and His Legacy: The American Conservation Movement*. Boston and Toronto: Little, Brown and Company, 1981.

Frederic C. Detwiller Consulting Services Group and Society for the Preservation of New England Antiquities. *One Post Office Square: The Best of the Old and the New*. Boston: Beacon Companies, 1980.

Fries, Waldemar H. "John James Audubon: Some Remarks on His Writings." *Princeton University Library Chronicle*. Vol. XXI, Nos. 1 & 2, pp. 1–7 (1960).

———. *The Double Elephant Folio: The Story of Audubon's Birds of America*. Chicago: American Library Association, 1973.

Fries, Waldemar H., and Susanne M. Low. *The Double Elephant Folio: The Story of Audubon's Birds of America*. 2nd ed. Amherst, MA: Zenaida Publishing, Inc., 2006.

Ganong, W. F. *An Organization of the Scientific Investigation of the Indian Place-Nomenclature of the Maritime Provinces of Canada*. Ottawa: The Royal Society of Canada, 1914.

Gash, Norman. "Jenkinson, Robert Banks, second earl of Liverpool (1770–1828)." *Oxford Dictionary of National Biography* (online). Oxford: Oxford University Press, 2004. http://www.oxforddnb.com/view/article/14740 (accessed 8 Feb. 2014).

Gatschet, Albert S. "The Beothuk Indians." *Proceedings of the American Philosophical Society*. Vol. 22, No. 120, Part IV, pp. 408–424 (October 1885).

General List of Citizens of the United States, Resident in the City and County of San Francisco: And Registered in the Great Register of Said City and County, July 1867. San Francisco: Towne and Bacon, 1867.

Gibson, Campbell. *Population of the 100 Largest Cities and Other Urban Places in the United States: 1790 to 1990*. Washington, D.C.: U.S. Bureau of the Census, 1998. http://www.census.gov/population/www/documentation/twps0027/twps0027.html (accessed 14 Mar. 2009).

Gifford, G. Edmund, M.D. "Isaac Sprague: Audubon's Massachusetts Artist." *Massachusetts Audubon Newsletter*. pp. 7–10 (January 1975).

Gigante, Denise. *The Keats Brothers: The Life of John and George*. Cambridge, MA and London: The Belknap Press of Harvard University Press, 2011.

Gilbert, Robert E. "Disability, Illness, and the Presidency: The Case of Franklin D. Roosevelt." *Politics and the Life Sciences*. Vol. 7, No. 1, pp. 33–49 (August 1988).

Giles, Henry. *Lectures and Essays*. 2 vols. Boston: Ticknor, Reed, and Fields, 1851.

Gill, Frank B. *Ornithology*. New York: W. H. Freeman and Company, 1990.

Gill, Robert E., Jr., Pablo Canevari, and Eve H. Iversen. "Eskimo Curlew (*Numenius borealis*)." In *The Birds of North America*. No. 347. Edited by Alan Poole and Frank Gill. Philadelphia: The Birds of North America, Inc., 1998.

Goddu, Joseph. *Artist's Proofs for* The Birds of America. New York: Hirschl & Adler Galleries, 2002.

Godwin, Parke. "John James Audubon." In *Homes of American Authors: Comprising Anecdotical, Personal, and Descriptive Sketches, by Various Writers*. pp. 3–17. New-York: G. P. Putnam and Co., 1853.

———. *Out of the Past: Critical and Literary Papers*. New York: G. P. Putnam & Sons, 1870.

Gollop, J. B., T. W. Barry, and E. H. Iverson. *Eskimo Curlew: A Vanishing Species?* Regina, SK: Saskatchewan Natural History Society, 1986.

Govier, Katherine. *Creation: A Novel*. New York: The Overlook Press, 2002.

Graham, Frank, Jr. "To Kill an Albatross." *Audubon*. Vol. 82, No. 5, pp. 8, 12 (September 1980).

———. *The Audubon Ark: A History of the National Audubon Society*. New York: Alfred A. Knopf, Inc., 1990.

Graustein, Jeannette E. *Thomas Nuttall, Naturalist: Explorations in America 1808–1841*. Cambridge, MA: Harvard University Press, 1967.

Greg, Emily R., ed. *Reynolds-Rathbone Diaries and Letters: 1753–1839*. Edinburgh: Printed for Private Circulation, 1905.

Greene, George Sears., *The Greenes of Rhode Island: With Historical Records of English Ancestry, 1534–1902*. New York: The Knickerbocker Press, 1903.

Grenfell, Wilfred T. *Labrador: The Country and the People*. New York: The Macmillan Company, 1909.

Griffin, Joseph. *History of the Press of Maine.* Brunswick, ME: Brunswick Press, 1872.

Grinnell, George Bird. "Some Audubon Letters." *The Auk.* Vol. XXXIII, No. 2, pp. 119–130 (April 1916).

———. "A Letter to Audubon," *Journal of Mammalogy,* Vol. 5, No. 4, pp. 223–230 (November 1924).

Haliburton, Thomas C. *An Historical and Statistical Account of Nova-Scotia.* 2 vols. Halifax, NS: Joseph Howe, 1829.

Hamel, Paul B. "Bachman's Warbler (*Vermivora bachmanii*)." In *The Birds of North America.* No. 150. Edited by Alan Poole and Frank Gill. Philadelphia and Washington, D.C.: The Academy of Natural Sciences and The American Ornithologists' Union, 1995.

Hammond, E. A. "Dr. Strobel's Account of John J. Audubon." *The Auk.* Vol. 80, No. 4, pp. 462–466 (October 1963).

Hanzel Galleries Inc. *Public Auction: Literary and Historical Manuscripts, Autographs, Books, Original Audubon Watercolor Drawings; The Collection Formed By The Late David Gage Joyce.* Chicago: Hanzel Galleries Inc., 1973.

Happoldt, Christopher. *The Christopher Happoldt Journal: His European Tour with the Rev. John Bachman (June-December, 1838).* Edited by Claude Henry Neuffer. Charleston, SC: The Charleston Museum, 1960.

Harrington, Thomas Francis, M.D., and James Gregory Mumford, M.D., eds. *The Harvard Medical School: A History, Narrative and Documentary.* 3 vols. New York and Chicago: Lewis Publishing Company, 1905.

Hart-Davis, Duff. *Audubon's Elephant: America's Greatest Naturalist and the Making of* The Birds of America. New York: Henry Holt and Company, 2004.

Harvard Law School. *Quinquennial Catalogue of the Law School of Harvard University: 1817–1899.* Cambridge, MA: Harvard Law School, 1900.

Harvard University. *A Catalogue of the Officers and Students of the University in Cambridge, Massachusetts: September, 1826.* Cambridge, MA: University Press—Hilliard, Metcalf, & Co., 1826.

———. *A Catalogue of the Officers and Students of Harvard University for the Academical Year 1831-2.* Cambridge, MA: Hilliard and Brown, 1831.

———. *A Catalogue of the Officers and Students of Harvard University for the Academical Year 1832-3.* Cambridge, MA: Brown, Shattuck, and Company, 1832.

———. *A Catalogue of the Officers and Students of Harvard University for the Academical Year 1833-4.* Cambridge, MA: Brown, Shattuck, and Company, 1833.

———. *A Catalogue of the Officers and Students of Harvard University for the Academical Year 1834-5.* Cambridge, MA: Charles Folsom, 1834.

———. *Annual Reports of the President and Treasurer of Harvard College: 1869-1870.* Cambridge, MA: University Press, 1871.

———. *Quinquennial Catalogue of the Officers and Graduates of Harvard University: 1636-1895.* Cambridge, MA: Published by the University, 1895.

———. *Quinquennial Catalogue of the Officers and Graduates: 1636-1920.* Cambridge, MA: The University Press, 1920.

———. *Quinquennial Catalogue of the Officers and Graduates: 1636-1930.* Cambridge, MA: The University, 1930.

Harwood, Michael. *Audubon Demythologized.* New York: National Audubon Society, n.d. [1985a].

———. "Mr. Audubon's Last Hurrah." *Audubon.* Vol. 87, No. 6, pp. 80–117 (November 1985b).

Harwood, Michael and Mary Durant. "In Search of the Real Mr. Audubon." *Audubon.* Vol. 87, No. 3, pp. 58–119 (May 1985).

Hassam, John T. "Bartholomew and Richard Cheever and Some of Their Descendants." *The New-England Historical and Genealogical Record.* Vol. XXXVI, pp. 305–313 (July 1882).

Hasty-Pudding Club. *A Catalogue of the Members and Library of the Hasty-Pudding Club in Harvard University*. Cambridge, MA: Cambridge Press: Metcalf, Torry, and Ballou, 1841.

Haven, Nathaniel Appleton. *The Remains of Nathaniel Appleton Haven, with a Memoir of his Life*. Cambridge, MA: Hilliard, Metcalf & Company, 1827.

Headley, P. C. *Massachusetts in the Rebellion: A Record of the Historical Position of the Commonwealth and the Services of the Leading Statesmen, the Military, the Colleges, and the People in the Civil War of 1861– 1865*. Boston: Walker, Fuller, and Company, 1866.

Healy, George P.A. *Reminiscences of a Portrait Painter*. Chicago: A. C. McClurg and Company, 1894.

Hebert, Luke. *The Engineer's and Mechanic's Encyclopaedia*. 2 vols. London: Thomas Kelly, 1849.

Henderson, Robert William, comp. *Early American Sport: A Checklist of Books by American and Foreign Authors Published in America Prior to 1860, Including Sporting Songs*. 3rd ed. Cranbury, N.J.: Associated University Presses, Inc., 1977.

Herrick, Francis Hobart. *Audubon the Naturalist: A History of His Life and Times*. 2 vols. New York: D. Appleton Company, 1917.

———. *Audubon the Naturalist: A History of His Life and Times*. 2nd ed. New York: D. Appleton-Century Company, 1938.

Herrick, William Francis, and Octavian Hoogs. *San Francisco Almanac for the Year 1859*. San Francisco: W. F. Herrick and Octavian Hoogs, 1858.

Hewitt, David. "Scott, Sir Walter (1771–1832)." *Oxford Dictionary of National Biography* (online). Oxford: Oxford University Press, 2004. http://www.oxforddnb.com/view/article/24928 (accessed 8 Feb. 2014).

Hill, Benson Earle, writing as Dean Snift. *A Pinch — of Snuff*. London: Robert Tyas, 1840.

Hind, Henry Youle. *The University of King's College, Windsor, Nova Scotia: 1790–1890*. New York: The Church Review Company, 1890.

Historical Data Systems, comp. *American Civil War Soldiers*. Accessed through Ancestry.com (database online). Provo, Utah: The Generations Network, Inc., 1999.

Hobart, Rebecca W. *Dennysville 1786–1986 . . . and Edmunds, Too!* Ellsworth, ME: The Dennysville Bicentennial Commission, 1986.

Hoffman, Randy. "Another Grail Bird." *Birder's World*. Vol. 21, No. 5, pp. 42–45, 72 (October 2007).

Holli, Melvin G. and Peter d' A. Jones. *Biographical Dictionary of American Mayors, 1820–1980*. Westport, CT: Greenwood Press, 1981.

Holmes, Jack D.L. "The Value of the Arpent in Spanish Louisiana and West Florida." *Louisiana History: The Journal of the Louisiana Historical Association*. Vol. 24, No. 3, pp. 314–320 (Summer 1983).

Holt, Jeff. "Notes on Audubon's 'Mystery' Birds." *Cassinia*. Vol. 70, pp. 22–24 (2002–2003).

Holt, Jeff, and Albert Filemyr. *The Composite Plates of Audubon's* "Birds of America." Philadelphia: Delaware Valley Ornithological Club, 2008.

Holt, John "Terry." *The Island City: A History of Eastport, Moose Island, Maine. From Its Founding to Present Times*. Eastport, ME: Eastport 2000 Committee, 1999.

Home, R. W. "The Royal Society and the Empire: The Colonial and Commonwealth Fellowship, Part 1. 1731–1847." *Notes and Records of the Royal Society of London*. Vol. 56, No. 3, pp. 307–332 (September 2002).

Hone, Philip. *Diaries: 1826–1851*. 28 vols. New-York Historical Society, Mss Collection (BV Hone, Philip, Non-circulating).

Hough, Franklin B. *American Biographical Notes*. Albany, NY: Joel Munsell, 1875.

Howe, Daniel Walker. *What Hath God Wrought: The Transformation of America, 1815–1848*. New York: Oxford University Press, 2007.

Howell, Steve N. G. and Jon Dunn. *A Reference Guide to Gulls of the Americas*. Boston and New York: Houghton Mifflin Company, 2007.

Huddleston, Jonathan. *And the Children's Teeth are Set on Edge: Adam Hodgson and the Razing of Caton Chapel*. http://www.tioli.co.uk/ATCTv04.pdf (Ebook, 2010–2011).

Hunt, Charles Warren. *Historical Sketch of the American Society of Civil Engineers*. New York: Press of the Evening Post Job Printing Office, 1897.

Hunter, Clark. *The Life and Letters of Alexander Wilson*. Philadelphia: American Philosophical Society, 1983.

Hunter, Perceval. "Retrospective Criticism re the Means by which the Vulture (*Vúltur Aúra* L.) Traces its Food." *The Magazine of Natural History*. Vol. VI, No. 31, pp. 83–88 (January 1833).

Hyde, Ralph. "Robert Havell Junior, Artist and Aquatinter." In Robin Myers and Michael Harris, eds. *Maps and Prints: Aspects of the English Book Trade*. pp. 81–108. Oxford, England: Oxford Polytechnic Press, 1984.

Ingalls, William, M.D. "A Synopsis of Private Obstetrical Practice for Forty-Two Years Previous to January 1, 1876." *The Boston Medical and Surgical Journal*. Vol. XCVI, No. 17, pp. 485–498 (April 26, 1877).

———. "How to Live Long and be Happy." *The Boston Sunday Globe*. Vol. L, No. 12, p. 20, col. 5 (Sunday, July 12, 1896).

Irmscher, Christoph. "Audubon and the Veiled Lady." *The American Scholar*. Vol. 68, No. 3, pp. 65–76 (Summer 1999).

Jackson, Christine E. *Bird Etchings: The Illustrators and Their Books, 1655–1855*. Ithaca, NY: Cornell University Press, 1985.

———. *John James Laforest Audubon: An English Perspective*. Withersfield, Suffolk, England: Published privately by Christine E. Jackson, 2013.

Jacobs, Fred. "Isaac Ray and the Profession of Psychiatry." *Rhode Island History*. Vol. 38, No. 4, pp. 99–111 (November 1979).

Jameson, Robert. *The Edinburgh New Philosophical Journal: October 1834–April 1835*. Vol. XVIII. Edinburgh: Adams & Charles Black, 1835.

Jameson, Robert S. *A Dictionary of the English Language: by Samuel Johnson, LL.D. and John Walker*. 2nd ed. London: William Pickering, 1828.

Jenkins, Rebecca. *Fanny Kemble: A Reluctant Celebrity*. London: Simon & Schuster, 2005.

Johnson, Dorothy. *Jacques-Louis David: Art in Metamorphosis*. Princeton, NJ: Princeton University Press, 1993.

Johnson, John Q. A. "Recipients of Honorary Degrees." *The Harvard Register*. Vol. III, No. 7, pp. 410–425 (July 1881).

Jones, C. H., comp. *Recent Art and Society as Described in the Autobiography and Memoirs of Henry Fothergill Chorley*. New York: Henry Holt and Company, 1874.

Jones, R. R. *The Ohio River: Charts, Drawings, and Description of Features Affecting Navigation*. Washington, D.C.: Government Printing Office, 1920.

Jones, Thomas P., M.D., ed. "The Romance of the Rattlesnake," *The Franklin Journal and American Mechanics' Magazine*, Vol. II, p. 144 (August 1828).

Journal of the Academy of Natural Sciences of Philadelphia. Vol. IV, Part I. Philadelphia: J. Harding, 1824.

Kaufman, Kenn. *Lives of North American Birds*. Boston: Houghton Mifflin, 1996.

Kelly, Shelly. "My Dear Mother: The Letters of Lucy Shaw, 1838–1850." Presentation to Texas State Historical Association. 2008.

Kendall, John. *History of New Orleans*. Chicago and New York: The Lewis Publishing Company, 1922.

Kinney, Joyce E. *The Vessels of Way Down East*. Bangor, ME: Furbush-Roberts Printing Co., 1989.

Kilby, Cyrus H. "Incidents in the Settlement of Dennysville and Edmunds in Washington County." *Maine Historical and Genealogical Recorder*. Vol. IX, No. 1, pp. 11–18 (January 1898).

Kilby, William H., ed. *Eastport and Passamaquoddy: A Collection of Historical and Biographical Sketches*. Eastport, ME: Edward E. Shead & Company, 1888.

King, Irving H. *The Coast Guard Under Sail: The U.S. Revenue Cutter Service 1789–1865*. Annapolis, MD: Naval Institute Press, 1989.

Kirk, David A., and Michael J. Mossman. "Turkey Vulture (*Cathartes aura*)." In *The Birds of North America*. No. 339. Edited by Alan Poole and Frank Gill. Philadelphia: The Birds of North America, Inc., 1998.

Kitts, Katherine Wallace. *Henry Pawling and Some of His Descendants*. Sharon Hill, PA: n.p., 1903.

Kleber, John E., ed. *The Kentucky Encyclopedia*. Lexington, KY: University Press of Kentucky, 1992.

Knight, Cornelia, and Thomas Raikes. *Personal Reminiscences*. Edited by Richard Henry Stoddard. New York: Scribner, Armstrong, and Company, 1875.

Knight, Ora Willis. *Birds of Maine*. Bangor, ME: Privately Printed, 1908.

Knowlton, I. C. *Annals of Calais, Maine, and St. Stephen, New Brunswick: Including the Village of Milltown, Me., and the Present Town of Milltown, N.B.* Calais, ME: J. A. Sears, printer, 1875.

Kochhar, M. "Puerperal Infection with Special Reference to India." In Louis G. Keith, M.D., Gary S. Berger, M.D., and David A. Edelman, Ph.D., eds. *Uncommon Infections and Special Topics*. Lancaster, England: MTP Press Limited, 1985.

Langley, Henry G., comp. *The San Francisco Directory, for the Year Commencing October, 1863*. San Francisco: Excelsior Steam Presses, 1863.

———. *The San Francisco Directory, for the Year Commencing October, 1864*. San Francisco: Excelsior Steam Presses, 1864.

———. *The San Francisco Directory for the Year Commencing April, 1876*. San Francisco: Henry G. Langley, Publisher, 1876.

———. *The San Francisco Directory for the Year Commencing March, 1877*. San Francisco: Henry G. Langley, Publisher, 1877.

Langtry, J. *History of the Church in Eastern Canada and Newfoundland*. London: Society for Promoting Christian Knowledge, 1892.

Lank, David M. *Audubon's Wilderness Palette*. Toronto: Key Porter Books, 1998.

Leach, Josiah Granville. *Some Account of the Pawling Family of New York and Pennsylvania*. Lancaster, PA: Wickersham Press, 1918.

Leahy, Christopher W. *The Birdwatcher's Companion to North American Birdlife*. 2nd ed. Princeton, NJ and Oxford: Princeton University Press, 2004.

Lewis, Douglas. "John James Audubon (1785–1851): Annotated Chronology of Activity in the Deep South, 1819–1837." *The Southerly Quarterly*. Vol 29, No. 4, pp. 63–82 (Summer 1991).

Lewis, Meriwether, and William Clark. *The Journals of the Lewis and Clark Expedition*. Edited by Gary E. Moulton and Thomas W. Dunlay. 13 vols. Lincoln, NE: University of Nebraska Press, 1983–2001.

Lieber, Francis. *The Life and Letters of Francis Lieber*. Edited by Thomas Sergeant Perry. Boston: James R. Osgood and Company, 1882.

Lindsey, Alton A., ed. *The Bicentennial of John James Audubon*. Bloomington, IN: Indiana University Press, 1985.

Little, George Thomas, ed. *Genealogical and Family of the State of Maine*. 4 vols. New York: Lewis Historical Publishing Company, 1909.

Longworth, Israel. *Life of S.G.W. Archibald*. Halifax, N.S.: Printed by S. F. Huestis, 1881.

Longworth, Thomas. *Longworth's American Almanac, New-York Register and City Directory for the Fifty-Seventh Year of American Independence*. New York: Thomas Longworth, 1832.

———. *Longworth's American Almanac, New-York Register and City Directory for the Fifty-Eighth Year of American Independence*. New York: Thomas Longworth, 1833.

Lopez, Barry. *Arctic Dreams*. New York: Charles Scribner's Sons, 1986.

Loring, James, comp. *The Massachusetts Register and United States Calendar for 1833*. Boston: James Loring, n.d. [1832].

Low, Susanne M. *A Guide to Audubon's Birds of America*. New Haven, CT: William Reese Company & Donald A. Heald, 2002.

Lownes, Albert E. "Notes on Audubon's Ornithological Biography." *The Auk*. Vol. LII, No. 1, pp. 103–104 (January 1935).

————. "Ten Audubon Letters," *The Auk*, Vol. LII, No. 2, pp. 154–168 (April 1935).

Lucas, E.V. *Highways and Byways in Sussex*. London: Macmillan and Co., Limited, 1904.

Lynch, Peter. "Early Reminiscences of Halifax—Men Who Have Passed From Us." *Collections of the Nova Scotia Historical Society*. Vol. XVI, pp. 171–204. Halifax, NS: Wm. Macnab & Son, 1912.

Madge, Steve, and Hilary Burn. *Waterfowl: An Identification Guide to the Ducks, Geese and Swans of the World*. Boston: Houghton Mifflin, 1988.

MacNutt, W.S. "Edward Augustus, Duke of Kent and Strathearn." *Dictionary of Canadian Biography*. Vol. 5. University of Toronto/Université Laval, 2003-. http://www.biographi.ca/en/bio/edward_augustus_5E.html (accessed 11 Feb. 2012).

Marquis, Albert Nelson, ed. *The Book of Chicagoans: A Biographical Dictionary of Leading Living Men of the City of Chicago*. Chicago: A. N. Marquis & Company, 1911.

Marshall, J. C. Douglas. *Things Temporal and Things Eternal: The Life of George Cheyne Shattuck, Jr*. Chevy Chase, MD: Posterity Press, 2006.

Martin, Robert Montgomery. *History of the Colonies of the British Empire*. London: Wm. H. Allen and Co. and George Routledge, 1843.

Maruna, Scott. "Substantiating Audubon's Washington Eagle," http://biofort.blogspot.com/2006/10/substantiating-audubons-washington.html (posted October 14, 2006).

Marzio, Peter C. "Mr. Audubon and Mr. Bien: An Early Phase in the History of American Chromolithography." Exhibition Catalog. Frankfort, KY: The Old State Capitol, (December 1976-January 1977).

Massachusetts Historical Society. *Pro Bono Publico: The Shattucks of Boston*. Forward by Henry Lee. Boston: Massachusetts Historical Society, 1971.

Matthew, H. C. G. and Brian Harrison, eds. *Oxford Dictionary of National Biography*. 60 vols. Oxford: Oxford University Press, 2004.

Mazÿck, William G. *The Charleston Museum: Its Genesis and Development*. Charleston, S.C.: Walker, Evans & Cogswell Co., 1908.

McKechnie, F. B. "Notes on the Ornithological Works of John James Audubon." *The Auk*. Vol. XXIV, No. 2, pp. 226–227 (April 1907).

McCulloch, William, D.D. *Life of Thomas McCulloch, D.D., Pictou*. Edited by Isabella Walker McCulloch and Jean Wallace McCulloch. N.p.: n.d. [1920]. ((

McCullough, David. *The Greater Journey: Americans in Paris*. New York: Simon & Schuster, 2011.

McDermott, John Francis, ed. *Up the Missouri with Audubon: The Journal of Edward Harris*. Norman, OK: University of Oklahoma Press, 1951.

————. "Audubon's Earliest Oil Portraits." *Antiques*. Vol. LXXIV, No. 5, pp. 434–435 (November, 1958).

————, ed. *Audubon in the West*. Norman, OK: University of Oklahoma Press, 1965.

Mearns, Barbara and Richard Mearns. *Audubon to Xantus: The Lives of Those Commemorated in North American Bird Names*. San Diego: Academic Press, 1992.

————. *John Kirk Townsend: Collector of Audubon's Western Birds and Mammals*. Dumfries, Scotland: Barbara and Richard Mearns, 2007.

Mechanics' Magazine. "The Arcana of Science for 1832." Vol. XVI, No. 448, pp. 403–405 (March 10, 1832a).

————. "Mr. Audubon and the Rattlesnakes." Vol. XVII, No. 469, pp. 291–294 (August 4, 1832b).

————. "Mr. Audubon." Vol. XIX, No. 510, p. 111 (May 18, 1833).

Mengel, Robert M. "On the Name of the Northern Bald Eagle and the Identity of Audubon's Gigantic 'Bird of Washington.'" *The Wilson Bulletin*. Vol. 65, No. 3, pp. 145–151 (September 1953).

Melish, John. *Travels through the United States of America in 1806 & 1807, and 1809, 1810, & 1811*. London: George Cowie and Co., 1818.

Melville, George W. *An Illustrated Chapter of Representative Men Who Have Occupied the Executive Chair of the Most Wonderful of All American Cities*. Chicago: G. Melville, 1887.

Millman, Thomas R., and A.R. Kelley. *Atlantic Canada to 1900: A History of the Anglican Church*. Toronto: Anglican Book Centre, 1983.

Mitchell, Martha. *Encyclopedia Brunoniana*. Providence, RI: Brown University Library, 1993.

Mittlebeeler, Emmet V. "The Decline of Imprisonment for Debt in Kentucky." *The Filson Club History Quarterly*. Vol. 49, No. 2, pp. 169–189 (April 1975).

The Montreal Almanack, or Lower Canada Register, for 1830: Being Second After Leap Year. Montreal: Robert Armour, 1829.

A.W. Morgan & Co. *A.W. Morgan & Co.'s San Francisco City Directory: September 1852*. San Francisco: F.A. Bonnard, 1852.

Morrison, John H. *History of American Steam Navigation*. New York: W.F. Sametz & Co., Inc., 1903.

Morrison, Leonard Allison and Stephen Paschall Sharples. *History of the Kimball Family in America, from 1634 to 1897: And of Its Ancestors the Kemballs or Kemboldes of England: with an Account of the Kembles of Boston, Massachusetts*. Boston: Damrell & Upham, 1897.

Morton, Brian N. *Americans in London: An Anecdotal Street Guide to the Homes and Haunts of Americans from John Adams to Fred Astaire*. London: Macdonald, 1988.

Mortuary Record of the City and County of San Francisco. Book P. (July 31, 1901).

Moses, John. *Illinois: Historical and Statistical: Comprising the Essential Facts of Its Planting and Growth As a Province, County, Territory, and State. Derived from the Most Authentic Sources, Including Original Documents and Papers. Together with Carefully Prepared Statistical Tables*. 2 vols. Chicago: Fergus Printing Company, 1889–1892.

Murphy, Robert Cushman. "John James Audubon (1785–1851): An Evaluation of the Man and His Work." *New-York Historical Society Quarterly*, pp. 315–350 (New York: National Audubon Society reprint, 1956).

Murray, Hugh. *An Historical and Descriptive Account of British America*. 3 vols. 2nd ed. Edinburgh: Oliver & Boyd, 1839.

Muschamp, Edward. *Audacious Audubon: The Story of a Great Pioneer, Artist, Naturalist and Man*. New York: Brentano, 1929.

Muzzey, A.B. *Reminiscences and Memorials of Men of the Revolution and their Families*. Boston: Estes and Lauriat, 1883.

The Nation. "The Other Side of the Chinese Question." Vol. XLII, No. 1083, pp. 272–273 (April 1, 1886).

National Academy of Design. *National Academicians*. http://www.nationalacademy.org/academy/national-academicians/?na=A (accessed 13 Nov. 2013).

Newman, Roger K., ed. *The Yale Biographical Dictionary of American Law*. New Haven, CT: Yale University Press, 2009.

New York City Landmarks Preservation Commission. *Greenwich Village Historic District Designation Report*. Vol. 1. New York: Landmarks Preservation Commission, 1969.

New York Monuments Commission. *In Memoriam, George Sears Greene: Brevet Major-General, United States Volunteers, 1801–1899*. Albany, NY: New York Monuments Commission, 1909.

Nolte, Vincent. *Fifty Years in Both Hemispheres, or, Reminiscences of the Life of a Former Merchant*. New York: Redfield, 1854.

Norris, J.W. *General Directory and Business Advertiser of the City of Chicago for the Year 1844*. Chicago: Ellis & Fergus, 1844.

The North American Review. Vol. LXI. Boston: Charles Bowen, 1835.

North, Christopher (John Wilson). "Audubon's Ornithological Biography: Introduction." *Blackwood's Edinburgh Magazine.* Vol. XXX, No. CLXXXII, pp. 1–16 (July 1831).

Nottingham, Lucie. *Rathbone Brothers: From Merchant to Banker 1742–1992.* London: Rathbone Brothers plc, 1992.

Nuttall, Thomas. *A Manual of the Ornithology of the United States and of Canada: The Land Birds.* Cambridge, MA: Hilliard and Brown, 1832.

———. *A Manual of the Ornithology of the United States and of Canada: The Water Birds.* Boston: Hilliard, Gray, and Company, 1834.

"Obituary.— George C. Shattuck, M.D." *The Boston Medical and Surgical Journal.* Vol. CXXVIII, No. 14, pp. 354–355 (April 6, 1893).

Obituary. "Hon. James Curtiss." *Chicago Press and Tribune.* (Friday, November 4, 1859).

Obituary. "In Memoriam—William Ingalls, M.D." *The Boston Medical and Surgical Journal.* Vol. CL, No 4, p. 106 (January 28, 1904).

Obituary. "John James Audubon." *Harpers New Monthly Magazine.* Vol. II, No. X, pp. 561–563 (March 1851).

Obituary. "Dr. [William] Forrest, of St. Claire, Q.[uebec]." *The Canada Medical Record.* Vol. VI, No. 2, pp. 43–44 (November 1877).

"Obituary: William Ingalls, M.D." *The Boston Medical and Surgical Journal.* Vol. CXLIX, No. 24, pp. 661–662 (December 10, 1903).

Officer, Lawrence H. *Information on Dollar-Pound Exchange Rate.* MeasuringWorth.com (2007) http://www.measuringworth.com/exchangepound/poundsource.html (accessed 28 Jan. 2014).

———. *Dollar-Pound Exchange Rate From 1791.* MeasuringWorth (2014), http://www.measuringworth.com/datasets/exchangepound/result.php (accessed 28 Jan. 2014).

Olson, Robert J.M. *Audubon's Aviary: The Original Watercolors for* The Birds of America. New York: New-York Historical Society and Skira Rizzoli, 2012.

Osgood, Wilfred H. "In Memoriam: Ruthven Deane 1851–1934." *The Auk.* Vol. LII, No. 1, pp. 1–14 (January 1935).

The Osprey. "Facsimile Letter from Audubon to Bonaparte in 1833." Vol 2, No. 3, Frontpiece (November 1897).

Palmer, Arlene. *Artistry and Innovation in Pittsburgh Glass, 1808–1882: From Bakewell & Ensell to Bakewell, Pears & Co.* Pittsburgh, PA: Frick Art & Historical Center, 2004.

Palmer, David W. *The Forgotten Hero of Gettysburg.* N.p.: Xlibris Corporation, 2004.

Palmer, John M., ed. *The Bench and Bar of Illinois: Historical and Reminiscent.* 2 vols. Chicago: The Lewis Publishing Company, 1899.

Palmer, Joseph. *Necrology of Alumni of Harvard College: 1851–52 to 1862–63.* Boston: John Wilson and Son, 1864.

Palmer, Ralph S. *Handbook of North American Birds: Diurnal Raptors* (Part 1). Vol. 4. New Haven, CT and London: Yale University Press, 1988.

Park, Lawrence, John Hill Morgan, and Royal Cortissoz. *Gilbert Stuart: An Illustrated Descriptive List of His Works.* 4 vols. New York: W.E. Rudge, 1926.

Parkes, Kenneth C. "Audubon's Mystery Birds." *Natural History.* Vol. 94, No. 4, pp. 88–93 (April 1985).

Partridge, Linda Dugan. "By the Book: Audubon and the Tradition of Ornithological Illustration." *The Huntington Library Quarterly.* Vol. 59, No. 2/3, pp. 269–301 (1996).

Patterson, George. *A History of the County of Pictou, Nova Scotia.* Montreal: Dawson Brothers, 1877.

Patton, Anthony S. "Murder Most Harvard." *Harvard Medical Alumni Bulletin.* pp. 40–47 (Spring 2000).

Pawling, Albert Schoch. *Pawling Genealogy.* Lewisburg, PA, 1905.

Peattie, Donald Culross, ed. *Audubon's America: The Narratives and Experiences of John James Audubon.* Boston: Houghton Mifflin, 1940.

Peck, Robert McCracken. "Audubon and Bachman: A Collaboration in Science." In Sarah E. Boehme. *John James Audubon in the West: The Last Expedition*, pp. 71-115. New York: Harry N. Abrams, Inc. in association with the Buffalo Bill Historical Center, 2000.

Pedersen, Susan. *Eleanor Rathbone and the Politics of Conscience.* New Haven, CT and London: Yale University Press, 2004.

Peirce, Henry B. *List of Persons Whose Names Have Been Changed in Massachusetts, 1780–1883.* Boston: Wright & Potter Printing Company, 1885.

Perkins Institution and Massachusetts School for the Blind. *Sixty-Ninth Annual Report of the Trustees of the Perkins Institution and Massachusetts School for the Blind for the Year Ending August 31, 1900.* Boston: George H. Ellis, 1901.

Pesha, Ronald. "The Lighthouse at West Quoddy Head." *Maine Memory Network: Lubec, Maine.* http://lubec.mainememory.net/page/797/display.html (accessed 5 Nov. 2009).

Peter, Robert, M.D. *The History of the Medical Department of Transylvania University.* Louisville, KY: John P. Morton & Company, 1905.

Petersen, William, J., ed. "Audubon on the Missouri in 1843." *The Palimpset.* Vol. LII, No. 11, pp. 545-584 (Iowa City: The State Historical Society of Iowa, November 1971).

Peterson, Roger Tory. *A Field Guide to the Birds.* 4th ed. Boston: Houghton Mifflin Company, 1980.

———. *All Things Reconsidered: My Birding Adventures.* Edited by Bill Thompson III. Boston and New York: Houghton Mifflin Company, 2006.

———. *Peterson Field Guide to Birds of North America.* 5th ed. Boston and New York: Houghton Mifflin Company, 2008.

———. *Peterson Field Guide to Birds of Eastern and Central North America.* 6th ed. Boston and New York: Houghton Mifflin Company, 2010.

Peterson, Roger Tory, and Virginia Marie Peterson. *Audubon's Birds of America* (The Audubon Society Baby Elephant Folio). New York: Abbeville Press, 1981.

Phillips, Henry, Jr., comp. "A List of the Officers and Councilors of the American Philosophical Society from 1769 to 1890." *Proceedings of the American Philosophical Society.* Vol. XXVII, No. 131, p. 87 (Philadelphia: Printed for the Society by MacCalla & Company, 1889).

Phillips, Maurice E. "The Academy of Natural Sciences of Philadelphia." *Transactions of the American Philosophical Society.* New Series, Vol. 43, No. 1, pp. 266-274 (1953).

Phillips, Venia T. and Maurice E. Phillips, eds. *Guide to the Microfilm Publication of the Minutes and Correspondence of the Academy of Natural Sciences of Philadelphia 1812–1924.* Philadelphia: Academy of Natural Sciences of Philadelphia, 1967.

Pick, Nancy and Mark Sloan. "Audubon's Untruth." *The Rarest of the Rare: Stories Behind the Treasures at the Harvard Museum of Natural History.* pp. 144-145. New York: Harper Collins, 2004.

Plamondon, Marc R. "Chorley, John Rutter (1806-1867)." *Oxford Dictionary of National Biography* (online). London: Oxford University Press, 2004. http://www.oxforddnb.com/view/article/5351 (accessed 11 Jan. 2014).

Pretyman, George. *Journal of the Proceedings of the Bishops, Clergy, and Laity of the Protestant Episcopal Church in the United States of America, in a General Convention, Held in Christ Church, in the City of Cincinnati, from October 2d to October 16th, Inclusive, in the Year of Our Lord 1850; with an Appendix, Containing the Constitution and Canons, a List of the Clergy, &c.* Philadelphia: King & Baird, Printers, 1851.

Public Archives of Canada. *Henry Wolsey Bayfield Papers.* MG24, F28. Vol. 4 (on microfilm reel H-982). http://heritage.canadiana.ca/view/oocihm.lac_reel_h982/1?r=0&s=1.

Purdy, John and Alexander G. Findlay. *The British American Navigator.* 2nd ed. London: R.H. Laurie, 1847.

Quincy, Anna Cabot Lowell, *A Woman's Wit & Whimsy: The 1833 Diary of Anna Cabot Lowell Quincy.* Edited by Beverly Wilson Palmer. Boston: Massachusetts Historical Society and Northeastern University Press, 2003.

Quincy, Josiah. *The History of the Boston Anthenaeum.* Cambridge, MA: Metcalf and Company, 1851.

Ralph, Robert. *William MacGillivray.* London: HMSO, 1993.

Rathbone, Eleanor F. *William Rathbone: A Memoir.* London: Macmillan and Co., Limited, 1905.

Ray, Isaac, M.D. "Obituary: Benjamin Lincoln, M.D." *The New-England Magazine.* Vol. IX, No. 8, pp. 145-151 (Boston: E. R. Broaders, August 1835).

Read, Irraine. *Edward Harris: A Footnote in Time.* Moorestown, NJ: Historical Society of Moorestown, 1979.

Retureta, Abelardo A., M.D., et al. "The Children's Hospital, Boston." *International Pediatrics.* Vol. 13, No. 4 (December 1998).

Reynolds, Gary. *John James Audubon and His Sons.* New York: Grey Art Gallery and Study Center, 1982.

Rhoads, Samuel N. "More Light on Audubon's Folio 'Birds of America.'" *The Auk*, Vol. XXXIII, No. 2 (April 1916).

Rhodes, Richard. *John James Audubon: The Making of an American.* New York: Alfred A. Knopf, 2004.

Rice, Howard C., Jr., comp. "The World of John James Audubon: Catalogue of an Exhibition in the Princeton University Library, 15 May-30 September 1959." *Princeton University Library Chronicle.* Vol. XXI, Nos. 1 & 2 (1960).

Richards, Irving T. "Audubon, Joseph R. Mason, and John Neal." *American Literature.* Vol. 6, No. 2, pp. 122-140 (May 1934).

Roe, Alfred S. *The Fifth Regiment Massachusetts Volunteer Infantry.* Boston: Fifth Regiment Veteran Association, 1911.

Rosen, Peter S. "Boulder Barricades." In Maurice L. Schwartz, ed. *Encyclopedia of Coastal Science.* pp. 204-206. Dordrecht, Netherlands: Springer, 2005.

Rothbard, Murray N. *The Panic of 1819: Reactions and Policies.* Auburn, AL: Ludwig von Mises Institute, 2007.

The Royal Society, Library and Information Services. "List of Fellows of The Royal Society: 1660-2007." London: The Royal Society, 2007.

Ruutz-Rees, J. *Horace Vernet.* London: Sampson Low, Marston, Searle, & Rivington, 1880.

Sage, John H. "Description of Audubon." *The Auk.* Vol. XXXIV, No. 2, pp. 239-240 (April 1917).

Sahr, Robert C. *Consumer Price Index (CPI) Conversion Factors for Years 1774 to Estimated 2025 to Convert to Dollars of 2014.* Revised February 5, 2015. http://liberalarts.oregonstate.edu/sites/liberalarts.oregonstate.edu/files/polisci/faculty-research/sahr/inflation-conversion/pdf/cv2014.pdf (accessed 12 Apr. 2015).

Sampson, Davenport & Co. *The Boston Directory for the Year Commencing July 1, 1868.* Boston: Sampson, Davenport, & Co., 1868.

———. *The Boston Directory for the Year Commencing July 1, 1873.* No. LXIX. Boston: Sampson, Davenport, & Co., 1873.

Sanders, Albert E., and Warren Ripley, eds. *Audubon: The Charleston Connection.* Charleston, SC: Charleston Museum, 1986.

San Francisco Directory for the Year 1852-53. San Francisco: James M. Parker, 1852.

San Francisco Directory for the Year Commencing October, 1863. San Francisco: Excelsior Steam Presses: Towne & Bacon, 1863.

Sardone, Susan Breslow. "Campobello." *About.com.* http://honeymoons.about.com/od/maine/ss/campobello.htm (accessed 19 Feb. 2014).

Schama, Simon. "Death of a Harvard Man." *Granta*. No. 34, pp. 13–76 (Autumn 1990).

Sedgwick, James A. "Willow Flycatcher (*Empidonax traillii*)." In *The Birds of North America*. No. 533. Edited by Alan Poole and Frank Gill. Philadelphia: The Birds of North America, Inc., 2000.

Sganzin, M.I. *An Elementary Course of Civil Engineering*. 3rd ed. Boston: Hilliard, Gray, and Company, 1837.

Sharp, Mary Rozier and Louis J. Sharp III. *Between the Gabouri: A History of Ferdinand Rozier and "Nearly" All His Descendants*. Ste. Genevieve, MO: Histoire de Rozier, 1981.

Shattuck, George B., M.D., and E. W. Taylor, M.D. "Obituary: In Memoriam—William Ingalls, M.D." *The Boston Medical and Surgical Journal*. Vol. CL, No. 4, p. 106 (January 28, 1904).

Shattuck, George Cheyne, M.D. *Three Dissertations on Boylston Prize Questions for the Years 1806 and 1807*. Boston: Farrand, Mallory, & Co. and Hastings, Etheridge, & Bliss, 1808.

Shattuck, George C., Jr., M.D. "On the Continued Fevers of Great Britain." Part I. *Medical Examiner*. Vol. III, No. 9, pp. 133–138 (Saturday, February 29, 1840a).

————. "On the Continued Fevers of Great Britain." Part II. *Medical Examiner*. Vol. III, No. 10, pp. 149–153 (Saturday, March 7, 1840b).

————. "George Cheyne Shattuck." In *Memorial Biographies of The New England Historic Genealogical Society: 1853–1855*. Vol. II, pp. 164–171. Boston: Published by the Society, 1881.

Shaw, Francis George. "Hon. Robert Gould Shaw." In *Memorial Biographies of The New England Historic Genealogical Society: 1853–1855*. Vol. II, pp. 38–61. Boston: Published by the Society, 1881.

Sheehan, Jacquelyn L. "A Pair of Unrecorded Audubon Portraits." *The American Art Journal*. Vol. 11, No. 1, pp. 87–88 (January 1979).

Shelley, Marjorie. "Drawing Birds: Audubon's Artistic Practices." In Roberta J.M. Olson, *Audubon's Aviary: The Original Watercolors for* "The Birds of America. New York: New-York Historical Society and Skira Rizzoli Publications, Inc., 2012.

Sherwood, Roland H. *Jotham Blanchard: The Forgotten Patriot of Pictou*. Hantsport, NS: Lancelot Press, 1982.

Shortt, Adam and Arthur G. Doughty, eds. *Canada and its Provinces*. Vol. X. Toronto: Edinburgh University Press, 1913.

Shufeldt, R. W., M.D., and Maria R. Audubon. "The Last Portrait of Audubon, Together with a Letter to His Son. *The Auk*. Vol. XI, No. 4, pp. 309–313 (October 1894).

Shuler, Jay. *Had I the Wings: The Friendship of Bachman and Audubon*. Athens, GA: University of Georgia Press, 1995.

Sibley, David Allen. *The Sibley Field Guide to Birds of Eastern North America*. New York: Alfred A. Knopf, 2003.

————. *Audubon's Mysteries: Carbonated Swamp Warbler* (commentary and reader comments on Sibley Guides internet blog. http://www.sibleyguides.com/2008/03/audubons-mysteries-carbonated-swamp -warbler/ (accessed 29 May 2010).

————. *The Sibley Guide to Birds*. 2nd ed. New York: Alfred A. Knopf, 2014.

Sinclair, Bruce. "Thomas Woodhouse Bakewell's Autobiographical Sketch." *The Filson Club History Quarterly*. Vol. 40, No. 3, pp. 235–248 (July 1966).

Slugg, J. T. *Reminiscences of Manchester Fifty Years Ago*. Manchester, England: J. E. Cornish, 1881.

Small, Ernest, Paul M. Catling, Jacques Cayouette, and Brenda Brookes. *Audubon: Beyond Birds*. Ottawa: NRC Research Press, 2009.

Smith, Emily A. *The Life and Letters of Nathan Smith, M.B., M.D.* New Haven, CT: Yale University Press, 1914.

Smith, Horatio D. "Old Uniforms of the United States Service." *United Service*. Vol. II, No. 4, pp. 375–388 (October 1889).

Smith, Horatio D. *Early History of the United States Marine Service or (United States Revenue Cutter*

Service): 1789–1849. Edited by Elliot Snow. Washington, D.C.: Coast Guard Bicentennial Publication, 1989.

Sons of the American Revolution and Grand Army of the Republic. *Watertown's Military History*. Boston: David Clapp & Son, 1907.

Sotheby's. *The Library of H. Bradley Martin: John James Audubon — Magnificent Books and Manuscripts*. June 6, 1989. New York: Sotheby's, 1989.

———. *The Library of H. Bradley Martin: Magnificent Color-Plate Ornithology*. June 7, 1989. New York: Sotheby's, 1989.

———. *Fine Books and Manuscripts*. June 14 and 15, 1993. New York: Sotheby's, 1993.

———. *Magnificent Ornithology from the Collection of Brooks McCormick: Sold for the Benefit of the International Crane Foundation*. October 5, 2007. New York: Sotheby's, 2007.

———. *The James S. Copley Library: Magnificent American, Historical Documents: Second Selection*. Sale No. 780. October 10, 2010. New York: Sotheby's, 2010.

———. *John James Audubon:* The Birds of America, The Viviparous Quadrupeds of North America. Sale No. N09133. April 1, 2014. New York: Sotheby's 2014.

Souder, William. *Under a Wild Sky*. New York: North Point Press, 2004.

Spady, Matthew. *The Audubons of Minniesland*. (2007a). http://www.audubonparkny.com/audubonfamily .html (accessed 7 Jun. 2013).

———. *Audubon Park: A Brief History*. (2007b). http://www.audubonparkny.com/AudubonParkBrief History.html#anchor_138 (accessed 7 Jun. 2013).

———. *Audubon Park: City Map Register 1844*. (2007c). http://www.audubonparkny.com/AudubonPark MinnieslandMap1844.html (accessed 9 Jun. 2013).

Spiker, La Rue. "Maine's Lincoln." *Maine Sunday Telegram* (Sunday, May 4, 1969).

Sprague, Isaac. *Diary, 1843*. Boston Athenaeum (Mss.S68).

Stalmaster, Mark. *The Bald Eagle*. New York: Universe Books, 1987.

Stark, James. *Picture of Edinburgh: Containing a Description of the City and its Environs*. 4th ed. Edinburgh: John Fairbain, 1825.

Statistics Canada. *Population and Dwelling Counts for Canada and Designated Places: 2011 and 2006 Censuses*. http://www12.statcan.gc.ca/census-recensement/2011/dp-pd/hlt-fst/pd-pl/Table-Tableau.cfm? LANG=Eng&T=1301&SR=526&S=72&O=A&RPP=25&PR=0&CMA=0 (accessed 21 Feb. 2013).

Stearns, Raymond Phineas. "Colonial Fellows of the Royal Society of London, 1661-1788." *Notes and Records of the Royal Society of London*. Vol. 8, No. 2, pp. 178-246 (April 1951).

Steiner, Bill. *Audubon Art Prints: A Collector's Guide to Every Edition*. Columbia, SC: University of South Carolina Press, 2003.

Stephens, Lester D. *Science, Race, and Religion in the American South: John Bachman and the Charleston Circle of Naturalists, 1815–1895*. Chapel Hill and London: The University of North Carolina Press, 2000.

Stimpson, Charles Jr. *Stimpson's Boston Directory: Containing the Names of the Inhabitants, Their Occupations, Places of Business, and Dwelling Houses, and the City Register, with Lists of the Streets, Lanes and Wharves, the City Officers, Public Offices and Banks, and Other Useful Information*. Boston: Charles Stimpson Jr., 1833.

Stoddard, Charles A. *A Noble Woman's Life: A Memorial Sermon to the late Madame Audubon*. New York: Anson D. F. Randolph & Co., 1874.

Stokes, Donald W. and Lillian Q. Stokes. *A Guide to Bird Behavior*. Vol. II. Boston: Little, Brown and Company, 1983.

Stokes, Samuel E. "Tombstone Inscriptions: Lane Burying Ground, Westchester Co., New York." *The New York Genealogical and Biographical Record*. Vol. XLIX, No. 4, pp. 377-379 (October 1918).

Stone, Witmer. "A Bibliography and Nomenclator of the Ornithological Works of John James Audubon." *The Auk*. Vol. XXIII, No. 3, pp. 298-312 (July 1906).

Storm, Colton, comp. *A Catalogue of the Everett D. Graff Collection of Western Americana*. Chicago: The University of Chicago Press, 1968.

Stoughton, Ralph M. *Genealogies of Gill, Massachusetts*. Vols. III and IV of *The History of Gill, Massachusetts: 1793–1943*. Ralph M. Stoughton, 1950. Accessed through Ancestry.com, *Massachusetts, Town and Vital Records, 1620–1988* (database on-line)(Provo, UT: Ancestry.com Operations, Inc., 2011).

Straight, Carrie A. and Robert J. Cooper. "Chuck-will's-widow (*Caprimulgus carolinensis*)." In *The Birds of North America*. No. 499. Edited by Alan Poole and Frank Gill. Philadelphia: The Birds of North America, Inc., 2000.

Streshinsky, Shirley. *Audubon: Life and Art in the American Wilderness*. New York: Villard Books, 1993.

Stroud, Patricia Tyson. *The Emperor of Nature: Charles-Lucien Bonaparte and His World*. Philadelphia: University of Pennsylvania Press, 2000.

Sutherland, David A. "Tremain, Richard." *Dictionary of Canadian Biography*. Vol. 8. University of Toronto/Université Laval, 2003-. http://www.biographi.ca/en/bio/tremain_richard_8E.html (accessed 8 Feb. 2012).

Sutherland, George. *The Magdalen Islands: Their Topograpy, Natural History, Social Condition and Commercial Importance*. Charlottetown, PE: George T. Haszard, 1862.

Sutton, George Miksch. *Birds of Pennsylvania*. Harrisburg, PA: J. Horace McFarland Company, 1928.

Swainson, William. "Mr. Audubon and his Work, the 'Biography of Birds:' Mr. Swainson in Reply to Mr. Waterson." *The Magazine of Natural History*. Vol. VI, No. 36, p. 550 (November 1833).

Swainson, William, and John Richardson, M.D. *Fauna Boreali-Americana; or the Zoology of the Northern Parts of British America, Part Second: The Birds*. London: John Murray, 1831.

Sweetser, M. F. *The Maritime Provinces: A Handbook for Travellers*. Boston: J. R. Osgood and Company, 1875.

Taft, Robert. "The Pictorial Record of the Old West: Part II, W. J. Hays." *Kansas Historical Quarterly*. Vol. 14, No. 2, pp. 145–165 (May 1946).

Terres, John K. *The Audubon Society Encyclopedia of North American Birds*. New York: Alfred A. Knopf, 1980.

Thomas, Robert B. The *(Old) Farmer's Almanack, Calculated on a New and Improved Plan. for the Year of Our Lord 1833*. Boston: Carter, Hendee and Co., 1832.

Thomas, Samuel W., and Eugene H. Conner. "Henry McMurtrie, M.D. (1793–1865): First Historian and Promoter of Louisville." *The Filson Club History Quarterly*. Vol. 43, No. 4, pp. 311–324 (October 1969).

Timbs, John. *Anecdote Biography*. London: Richard Bentley, 1860.

Tocque, Philip. *Newfoundland: As It Was, and As It Is in 1877*. Toronto: John B. Magurn, 1878.

Torrens, H.S. "Robert Bakewell (1767–1843), geologist." *Oxford Dictionary of National Biography* (online). Oxford: Oxford University Press, 2004. http://www.oxforddnb.com.ezproxy.sfpl.org/view/article/1147?docPos=2 (accessed 9 Jun. 2014).

Townsend, Charles Wendell, M.D. *Along the Labrador Coast*. Boston: Dana Estes & Company, 1907.

———. "A Short Trip into the Labrador Peninsula by Way of the Natashquan River." *The Bulletin of the Geographical Society of Philadelphia*. Vol. XI, pp. 170–182 (January-October 1913).

———. "In Audubon's Labrador." *The Auk*. Vol. XXXIV, No. 2, pp. 133–146 (April 1917).

———. *In Audubon's Labrador*. Boston and New York: Houghton Mifflin Company, 1918.

———. "Note on Audubon's Labrador Trip." *The Auk*. Vol. XXXVI, No. 3, pp. 424–426 (July 1919).

———. "A Visit to Tom Lincoln's House with Some Auduboniana." *The Auk*. Vol. XLI, No. 2, pp. 237–242 (April 1924).

Townsend, Charles Wendell, M.D., and Glover M. Allen. "Birds of Labrador." *Proceedings of the Boston Society of Natural History*. Vol. 33, No. 7, pp. 277–428. Boston: Printed for the Society, July 1907.

Truax, Rhoda. *The Doctors Warren of Boston*. Boston: Houghton Mifflin, 1968.

Marcel Trudel. "Cartier, Jacques (1491–1557)." *Dictionary of Canadian Biography*. Vol. 1. University of

Toronto/Université Laval, 2003–. http://www.biographi.ca/en/bio/cartier_jacques_1491_1557_1E.html (accessed 13 Mar. 2014).

Tuckerman, Bayard, ed. *The Diary of Philip Hone: 1828–1851*. 2 vols. New York: Dodd, Mead and Company, 1889.

Tyler, Ron. *Nature's Classics: John James Audubon's Birds and Animals*. Orange, TX: The Stark Museum of Art, 1992.

———. *Audubon's Great National Work: The Royal Octavo Edition of* The Birds of America. Austin: University of Texas Press, 1993.

———. "The Publication of *The Viviparous Quadrupeds of North America*." In Sarah E. Boehme. *John James Audubon in the West: The Last Expedition*, pp. 119–182. New York: Harry N. Abrams, Inc. in association with the Buffalo Bill Historical Center, 2000.

United States. *Report of the Joint Special Committee to Investigate Chinese Immigration: February 27, 1877*. Washington, D.C.: Government Printing Office, 1877.

U.S. Bureau of the Census. *Third Census of the United States, 1810*. Record Group 29. NARA Microfilm Publication M252. 71 rolls. Washington, D.C.: National Archives. Accessed through Ancestry.com. *1810 United States Federal Census* (database on-line). Provo, UT: Ancestry.com Operations, Inc., 2010.

———. *Fourth Census of the United States, 1820*. Record Group 29. NARA Microfilm Publication M33. 142 rolls. Washington, D.C.: National Archives. Accessed through Ancestry.com. *1820 United States Federal Census* (database on-line). Provo, UT: Ancestry.com Operations, Inc., 2010.

———. *Fifth Census of the United States, 1830*. Record Group 29. NARA Microfilm Publication M19. 201 rolls. Washington, D.C.: National Archives. Accessed through Ancestry.com. *1830 United States Federal Census* (database on-line). Provo, UT: Ancestry.com Operations, Inc., 2010).

———. *Seventh Census of the United States, 1850*. Record Group 29. NARA Microfilm Publication M432. 1009 rolls. Washington, D.C.: National Archives. Accessed through Ancestry.com. *1850 United States Federal Census* (database on-line). Provo, UT: Ancestry.com Operations, Inc., 2009.

———. *Eighth Census of the United States, 1860*. Record Group 29. NARA Microfilm Publication M653. 1,438 rolls. Washington, D.C.: National Archives. Accessed through Ancestry.com. *1860 United States Federal Census* (database on-line). Provo, UT: Ancestry.com Operations, Inc., 2009.

———. *Ninth Census of the United States, 1870*. Record Group 29. NARA Microfilm Publication M593. 1,761 rolls. Washington, D.C.: National Archives. Accessed through Ancestry.com. *1870 United States Federal Census* (database on-line). Provo, UT: Ancestry.com Operations, Inc., 2009.

———. *Tenth Census of the United States, 1880*. Record Group 29. NARA Microfilm Publication T9. 1,454 rolls. Washington, D.C.: National Archives. Accessed through Ancestry.com. *1880 United States Federal Census* (database on-line). Provo, UT: Ancestry.com Operations, Inc., 2010.

———. *Twelfth Census of the United States, 1900*. Record Group 29. NARA Microfilm Publication T623. 1854 rolls. Washington, D.C.: National Archives. Accessed through Ancestry.com. *1880 United States Federal Census* (database on-line). Provo, UT: Ancestry.com Operations, Inc., 2004.

U.S. Commission of Fish and Fisheries. *Report of the Commissioner for 1872 and 1873*. Washington: Government Printing Office, 1874.

U.S. Customs Service. *Registers of Vessels Arriving at the Port of New York from Foreign Ports, 1789–1919*. NARA Microfilm Publication M237. Roll 39. List No.: *630*. Washington, D.C.: National Archives. Accessed through Ancestry.com. *New York, Passenger and Immigration Lists, 1820–1850* (database on-line). Provo, UT: Ancestry.com Operations Inc., 2003.

———. *Copies of Lists of Passengers Arriving at Miscellaneous Ports on the Atlantic and Gulf Coasts and at Ports on the Great Lakes, 1820–1873*. Record Group 036. NARA Microfilm Publication M575. Roll 7. Washington, D.C.: National Archives. Accessed through Ancestry.com. *Atlantic Ports, Gulf Coasts, and Great Lakes Passenger Lists, Roll 7: 1820–1835* (database on-line). Provo, UT: Ancestry.com Operations Inc., 2004.

U.S. Department of Commerce. *Distances Between United States Ports*. 12th ed. Washington: National Oceanic and Atmospheric Administration and National Ocean Service, 2012.

U.S. Hydrographic Office. *The Gulf and River St. Lawrence*. 3rd ed. Washington, D.C.: Government Printing Office, 1908.

U.S. Postmaster. *Table of the Post Offices in the United States*. Washington: Duff Green, 1831.

U.S. Senate. *Journal of the Senate of the United States of America: Being the First Session of the Twenty-Third Congress, Begun and Held at the City of Washington, December 2, 1833*. Washington: Duff Green, 1833.

van Gompel, Stef. *Formalities in Copyright Law: An Analysis of Their History, Rationales and Possible Future*. Alphen aan den Rijn, Netherlands: Kluwer Law International, 2011.

Van Nostrand, Jeanne Skinner, and Jacob Henry Bachman. "Audubon's Ill-Fated Western Journey: Recalled by the Diary of J. H. Bachman." *California Historical Society Quarterly*. Vol. 21, No. 4, pp. 289–310 (December 1942).

———. "The Diary of a 'Used-up' Miner: Jacob Henry Bachman." *California Historical Society Quarterly*. Vol. 22, No. 1, pp. 67–83 (March 1943).

Van Wyhe, John. "The Authority of Human Nature: The 'Schädellehre' of Franz Joseph Gall." *The British Journal for the History of Science*. Vol. 35, No. 1, pp. 17–42 (March 2002).

Vinton, John Adams. *The Vinton Memorial, Comprising a Genealogy of the Descendants of John Vinton of Lynn*. Boston: S.K. Whipple and Company, 1858.

Vrabel, Jim. *When in Boston: A Time Line and Almanac*. Boston: Northeastern University Press, 2004.

Vose, Peter E. "Genealogies of Some of the Older Families in Dennysville." In *Memorial of the 100th Anniversary of the Settlement of Dennysville, Maine: 1886*. Portland, ME: B. Thurston & Company, Printers, 1886.

Walsh, Anthony A. "The American Tour of Dr. Spurzheim." *Journal of the History of Medicine and Allied Sciences*. Vol. XXVII, No. 2, pp. 187–205 (April 1972).

Warren, Edward, M.D. *The Life of John Collins Warren, M.D.* 2 vols. Boston: Ticknor & Fields, 1860.

Washburn, Karlene. "Dennysville Lincoln House Restored as Inn." *Bangor Daily News*. p. 12 (Monday, January 24, 1977).

Waterton, Charles. "On the Faculty of Scent in the Vulture." *The Magazine of Natural History*. Vol. V, No. 25, pp. 233–241 (April 1832).

———. "On Birds using Oil from Glands, for the Purpose of Lubricating the Surface of their Plumage." *The Magazine of Natural History*. Vol. V, No. 27, pp. 412–415 (June 1832).

———. "Answer to the Question at p. 603 on the Nightjar's Transporting its Eggs, as Suggested by Audubon's Declaration of the Carolina Goatsucker's so Doing." *The Magazine of Natural History*. Vol. V, No. 30, pp. 726–727 (November 1832).

———. "Remarks on Mr. Audubon's 'Account of the Habits of the Turkey Buzzard (Vúltur Aúra), Particularly with the View of Exploding the Opinion Generally Entertained of Its Extraordinary Powers of Smelling.'" *The Magazine of Natural History*. Vol. VI, No. 32, pp. 163–171 (March 1833).

———. "On the 'Biography of Birds' of J. J. Audubon." *The Magazine of Natural History*. Vol. VI, No. 33, pp. 215–218 (May 1833a).

———. "The Gland on the Rump of Birds." *The Magazine of Natural History*. Vol. VI, No. 33, pp. 274–277 (May 1833b).

———. "Mr. Audubon." *The Magazine of Natural History*. Vol. VI, No. 35, pp. 464–465 (September 1833a).

———. "Mr. Audubon Again." *The Magazine of Natural History*. Vol. VI, No. 35, pp. 465–468 (September 1833b).

———. "Mr. Audubon and his Work, the Biography of Birds." *The Magazine of Natural History*. Vol. VII, No. 37, pp. 66–67 (January 1834a).

———. "Mr. Audubon, jun." *The Magazine of Natural History*. Vol. VII, No. 37, pp. 67–69 (January 1834b).

———. "Aerial Encounter of the Eagle and the Vulture." *The Magazine of Natural History*. Vol. VII, No. 37, pp. 69–71 (January 1834c).

———. "The Vulture's Nose." *The Magazine of Natural History*. Vol. VII, No. 39, pp. 276–278 (May 1834a).

———. "Audubon's Claim to the Authorship of the Biography of Birds." *The Magazine of Natural History*. Vol. VII, No. 39, pp. 278–279 (May 1834b).

———. "Audubon and his Ornithology." *The Magazine of Natural History*. Vol. VII, No. 39, pp. 279–283 (May 1834c).

———. "Audubon's Plates of *The Birds of America*." *The Magazine of Natural History*. Vol. VIII, No. 48, pp. 236–238 (April 1835).

———. "On Snakes, Their Fangs, and Their Mode of Procuring Food." *The Magazine of Natural History*. Vol. VIII, No. 56, pp. 663–667 (December 1835).

Watters, Thomas G. "American Freshwater Mussels." Conchologists of America, Inc., http://www.conchologistsofamerica.org/theshells/amfrmussels.asp (accessed 27 Jun. 2015).

Webber, Charles W. *The Hunter-Naturalist*. Philadelphia: J. W. Bradley, 1851.

Webster, Noah. *An American Dictionary of the English Language: Exhibiting the Origin, Orthography, Pronunciation, and Definitions of Words*. 3rd ed. New York: S. Converse, 1830.

Weidensaul, Scott. *Raptors: The Birds of Prey*. New York: Lyons & Burford, 1996.

Weiss, Kenneth J. "Isaac Ray's Affair with Phrenology." *Journal of Psychiatry & Law*. Vol. 34, pp. 455–494 (2006).

———. "Isaac Ray's Advice to Medical Witnesses: Still Relevant?" *American Journal of Forensic Psychiatry*." Vol. 28, No. 2, pp. 35–49 (2007).

Wheeler, Brian K. *Raptors of Eastern North America*. Princeton, NJ: Princeton University Press, 2003.

Wheelwright, Nathaniel T. "First, There Was an Albatross." *Bowdoin Magazine*. Vol. 79, No. 2, pp. 26–33 (Winter 2008).

Whitcomb, Charlotte. *The Whitcomb Family in America: A Biographical Genealogy*. Minneapolis: Privately Printed, 1904.

Whitelaw, Marjory. *Thomas McCulloch: His Life and Times*. Halifax, NS: Nova Scotia Museum, 1985.

Wied, Maximilian. *The North American Journals of Prince Maximilian of Wied*. Edited by Stephen S. Witte, Marsha V. Gallagher, and William J. Orr. 3 vols. Norman, OK:
University of Oklahoma Press, 2008, 2010, 2012.

Willcomb, Oliver Clifton. *Genealogy of the Willcomb Family of New England (1665–1902)*. Lynn, MA: Privately Printed, 1902.

Willey, Kenneth, L., ed. *Vital Records from the* Eastport Sentinel *of Eastport, Maine: 1818–1900*. Camden, ME: Picton Press, 2003.

Williams, David H., comp. *The American Almanac and Repository of Useful Information for the Year 1841*. Boston: David H. Williams, 1840.

Williams, Edwin, ed. *New-York As It Is, in 1834: Containing, a General Description of the City and Environs, List of Officers, Public Institutions, and Other Useful Information; for the Convenience of Citizens, as a Book of Reference, and a Guide to Strangers; With a Correct Map of the City*. New York: J. Disturnell, 1834.

———, comp. *Narrative of the Recent Voyage of Captain Ross to the Arctic Regions, in the Years 1829–30–31–32–33: And a Notice of Captain Back's Expedition; With a Preliminary Sketch of Polar Discoveries, from the Earliest Period to the Year 1827*. New York: Wiley & Long, 1835.

———. *The New-York Annual Register for the Year of Our Lord 1835*. New York: Edwin Williams, 1835.

Williams, George Alfred. "Robert Havell, Junior, Engraver of Audubon's *The Birds of America*." *Print-Collector's Quarterly*. Vol. 6, No. 3, pp. 226–257 (October 1916).

————. "An English Engraver of American Nature: Havell." *The Antiquarian*. Vol. XVII, No. 1, pp. 27–30, 62, 64 (July 1931).

Willis, N.P. *American Scenery; or Land, Lake, and River Illustrations of Transatlantic Nature*. 2 vols. London: George Virtue, 1840.

Wilson, Mary Jane McClintock. *Master of Woodland Hill*. Boston: Arnold Arboretum of Harvard University, 2006.

Wilson, Wendell E. "Parker Cleaveland." *Mineralogical Record: Biographical Archive* (2014). http://www.mineralogicalrecord.com (accessed 9 Feb. 2014).

Winsor, Justin, ed. *The Memorial History of Boston: Including Suffolk County, Massachusetts. 1630–1880*. 4 vols. Boston: Ticknor and Company, 1886.

Wix, Edward. *Six Months of a Newfoundland Missionary's Journal, from February to August 1835*. London: Smith, Elder and Co., 1836.

Woodard, Colin. *The Lobster Coast*. New York: Viking/Penguin, 2004.

————. "The War that made Maine a State." *Maine Sunday Telegram* (Sunday, June 24, 2012). http://www.pressherald.com/opinion/200-years-ago_2012-06-24.html?pagenum=full (accessed 15 Feb. 2014).

Work Projects Administration in the State of Kentucky. *Henderson: A Guide to Audubon's Home Town in Kentucky*. Northport, NY: Bacon, Percy & Daggett, 1941.

Younger, Andrew. "The History of the Shubenacadie Canal." http://www.shubenacadiecanal.ca/history-shubenacadie-canal#.U2ZS8bnn_4h (accessed 4 May 2014).

Zerbey, Nancy. "Name that House!" *Yankee*. (June 1997). http://www.yankeemagazine.com/article/diy-home-3/house-styles (accessed 19 Feb. 2014).

Zimmer, John Todd. "Catalogue of the Edward E. Ayer Ornithological Library." *Field Museum of Natural History*. Publication 239. Vol. XVI. 2 vols. Chicago: Field Museum of Natural History, 1926.

Zimmerman, David. *Coastal Fort: A History of Fort Sullivan, Eastport, Maine*. Eastport, ME: Research Committee, Border Historical Society, 1984.

ACKNOWLEDGEMENTS

This book could never have been written or completed without the inspiration, assistance, and support of a wide circle of people.

My infatuation with John James Audubon began long before I ever dreamed of telling this story. William Logan, my elder brother and life-long trail guide, triggered my interest in birds and Audubon as we were growing up in the late 1950s in Westport Point, Massachusetts. I also owe him my heartfelt thanks for taking his time while in England to comb through early 19th century London business directories at the Cambridge University Library as part of my effort to trace the history of the London engraving and printing firm of Robert Havell & Son. In addition, he paid a visit to the Linnean Society in London and made arrangements for them to provide me with digital copies of their important Audubon correspondence to William Swainson.

Alice Ford, who assumed the mantle of Audubon's principal biographer in the second half of the 20th century, offered me her friendship and generously shared some of her vast knowledge about Audubon before her death in 1997. She is very much missed.

My research took me to some of the finest academic institutions, museums, and libraries in America and England, and the archivists, curators, and librarians who assisted me along the way deserve recognition and my sincere thanks: Charles B. Greifenstein, Associate Librarian, and Hannah Sisk, Curatorial Assistant, at the American Philosophical Society in Philadelphia; Joan R. McKenzie, Technical Services Librarian, and Sofie Sereda, Public Services and Library Administrative Assistant, at The College of Physicians in Philadelphia; Margaret Sherry Rich, Reference Librarian/Archivist and Don C. Skemer, Curator of Manuscripts, at the Rare Books & Special Collections Department of the Princeton University Library; Natalia Sciarini, Lead, Stacks Management, June Can, Public Services, and Adrienne Leigh Sharpe, Access Services Assistant, at the Beinecke Rare Book and Manuscript Library at Yale University; James J. Holmberg, Curator of Special Collections, The Filson Historical Society in Louisville, KY; Rachel Borchard, Librarian, and Kacey Page, Collections Manager, at the Buffalo Museum of Science Research Library; Daniel Hope, Special Collections & Archives Assistant at the George J. Mitchell Department of Special Collections & Archives, Bowdoin College in Brunswick, ME; Jennifer B. Lee at the Rare Book & Manuscript Library at Columbia University; Chris Killillay at the National Archives in Washington, D.C. and Nathaniel Wiltzen at the National Archives in Waltham, MA; Jill Tatem and Helen Conger, University Archivists, at Case Western Reserve University in Cleveland; Dennis Northcott, Associate Archivist for Reference, at the Missouri History Museum in St. Louis; Leslie A. Morris, Curator of Modern Books and Manuscripts, along with the wonderful reading room staff at the Houghton Library at Harvard University; Col. Leonid Kondratiuk, Director, National Guard Museum and Archives, Commonwealth of Massachusetts in Worcester, MA; Elizabeth Watts Pope and George R. Laurie, Reference Librarians, at the American Antiquarian Society in Worcester, MA; Elaine Grublin, Reference Librarian, and Jeremy Dibbell, Assistant Reference Librarian, at the Massachusetts Historical Society in Boston; Andi Bartelstein of the Rauner Special Collections Library, Dartmouth College; the able and helpful staff at the Newberry Library, Chicago; Jack Eckert, Public Services Librarian, Jessica Murphy, Reference Archivist, and Lucretia McClure, Special Assistant to the Library Director, at the Center for the History of Medicine in the Francis A. Countway Library of Medicine, Harvard University in Boston; Robert Young, Special Collections Librarian, and Dana Fisher, Special Collections Assistant, at the Ernst Mayr Library at the Museum of Comparative Zoology at Harvard University; Joanna Soden, Ph.D., Collections Curator, The Royal Scottish Academy of Art & Architecture, Edinburgh, Scotland; Ben Sherwood, Assistant Librarian, at the Linnean Society of London; Joe Festa, Manuscript Department, and Robert Delap, Assistant, Department of Rights & Reproductions, at the New-York Historical Society; Carol Mowrey, Research Librarian, at the G.W. Blunt White Library, Mystic Seaport; Florence Gillich, Historical Medical Library Assistant, at the Harvey Cushing/John Hay Whitney Medical Library at the Yale School of Medicine; Carolle Morini at the Boston Athenaeum; Nicole Joniec, Print Department Assistant & Digital Collections Manager, The Library Company of Philadelphia; Jennifer McCormick, Assistant Curator, Archives, The Charleston Museum, Charleston, SC; Susan Pavlik, Curator, John James Audubon Center at Mill Grove, Audubon, PA; Lisa Parrott Rolfe, Registrar, The Speed Art Museum, Louisville, KY; Colin Smith, Library Assistant, Special Collections and

[695]

Archives, University of Liverpool Library, Liverpool, England; Peggy Dillard, Head of Special Collections, Rosenberg Library, Galveston, TX; Stephen Jensen, Imaging Specialist, at the Chicago History Museum; Anna Gospodinovich, Assistant Registrar, Rights & Reproductions, Louisiana State Museum; Violetta Wolf, Assistant Curator of Collections, Museum of Science, Boston; Douglas R. Atkins, Library Technician, History of Medicine Division, National Library of Medicine; Lacy Schutz, Chief Administrative Officer, Exhibitions & Collections, at the Museum of the City of New York; Diana Chaccour, Rights and Images Department, National Portrait Gallery, London; Sarah Jeffcott, Librarian and Research Assistant, Scottish National Portrait Gallery; Wes Johnston and Dianne Landry at Dalhousie University, Halifax, NS; Thomas Lisanti, Manager, Permissions & Reproduction Services, The New York Public Library; Meredith McDonough, Archivist, and Sarah McQueen, Cultural Resources Assistant, Alabama Department of Archives and History, Montgomery, AL; Kathleen Fahey, Wellesley Historical Society, Wellesley, MA; Cédric Lafontaine, Rights and Licensing Specialist, Library and Archives Canada; Don Boarman, John James Audubon Museum, Henderson, KY; Jill MacMicken, Provincial Archivist, Public Archives and Records Office, Prince Edward Island; and Shilpa Patel, American Museum of Natural History.

I also am indebted to the many genealogists whose tireless research provided me with essential background information regarding the individuals whom Audubon met during his travels and thereby provided an essential part of their personal stories. Special recognition is due Kenneth L. Willey and Maureen Calnan, who teased important details about the early residents of Eastport, ME, from the *Eastport Sentinel* and the town's records, respectively.

Tara Nadeau in La Tabatière, Quebec, and Christelle Fortin-Vaillancourt in Brador, Quebec, helped immeasurably in answering my questions about the local topography, and I thank them for sharing their knowledge. Mary Grove, Margaret Hillenbrand, Alice Murphy, and Dr. William Richardson also went out of their way to support my efforts.

Richard Rubenstein, M.D., a board certified neurologist and good friend, assisted me in describing the symptomatology of Audubon's "spasmodic affection," which opens the book. He made sure I got the details right, for which I am most appreciative.

My dear friends Chris and Kathi Glynn generously hosted me during an early trip to Boston to work in the collections at Harvard University and the Massachusetts Historical Society. I also wish to thank my sister and brother-in-law, Wendy and Andy Thompson, who repeatedly opened their beautiful Long Island home to me whenever I made trips to the East Coast to conduct research. My brother and sister-in-law, Jim and Pat Logan, were similarly obliging during my visit to Maine.

I was fortunate to have been invited to join a writing group in the early days of preparing the text of this book. My colleagues, Hon. M. Lynn Duryee and Larry Townsend, gifted authors in their own right, dutifully read and provided constructive criticism as the manuscript went through its initial draft. Their encouragement was wholehearted and, I daresay, very much appreciated.

During a visit to Edinburgh, I followed Audubon's footsteps with John Chalmers, M.D., the author of *Audubon in Edinburgh*. Other than Mill Grove, there is no place in the world where the naturalist's lingering presence can be felt so strongly because the city remains much as it was when Audubon walked its streets in the 19th century. And certainly there is no better guide to Audubon's "fair Edina" than John. I am grateful beyond words for John's willingness to share it with me and for his and his lovely wife Gwyneth's warm hospitality. John also read an advance copy of the book and provided me with his sage counsel as to how it could be improved.

Several other noted Audubon scholars graciously agreed to review the manuscript before it was published. I wish to thank Christine E. Jackson, Ron Tyler, Christoph Irmscher, and Robert McCracken Peck for doing so. They are, however, in no way responsible for any errors that may remain in the text or the notes.

Every writer needs an editor, and I was fortunate to have a superb one in Anne Ross. I also wish to thank Ted Weinstein, Peter Beren, Lorna Garano, and Joel Friedlander for their assistance in navigating the challenging terrain of the publishing world.

Rich Hendel created the masterful design of this book, and I thank him for that and for much else. There is no better (and patient) book designer working today.

In Dennysville, ME, I was delighted to meet long-time residents who were equally passionate about Audubon. My sincere thanks go to Ronald A. Windhorst and Colin Windhorst of the Dennys River Historical

Society, who generously shared the history of the family of Judge Theodore Lincoln and the surrounding community. The current owners of the Lincoln home, Melinda and Jonathan Jaques, kindly showed me the house, and what I thought would be a short afternoon visit lasted well into the evening as we discussed Audubon's storied life.

In Eastport, I met Jett and John Peterson, the friendly owners of the former home of Jonathan D. Weston, where Audubon and his son John stayed during their 1833 visit. Operated for many years as a bed and breakfast, the house has changed very little since Audubon's day. From the windows of the spacious second-floor bedroom where I slept and where it is believed the Audubons roomed, I could look out over Passamaquoddy Bay and see the same view Audubon saw as he looked anxiously for the sails of the schooner *Ripley* that would take him and his companions on their voyage to Labrador. I also wish to thank Hugh French, the director of the Tides Institute in Eastport and a respected local historian, who could not have been more helpful.

I always knew that this story would not be complete without a series of maps to help guide the reader through each step of Audubon's journey. The only cartographer I wanted to work with was Jeffrey L. Ward, whose maps are truly works of art. I was thrilled when Jeff agreed to take on this project, and I thank him profusely.

During the time I was working on this book, I was blessed to have a companion who forced me out of bed every morning before 6:00 a.m., helped get my creative juices flowing with a mile walk, and then was only too happy to stretch out on the couch in my study to keep me company while I wrote. My beloved yellow Labrador retriever, Jessie, slept through much of the daily toil, but her quiet presence made the solitary act of writing much less lonely.

My children provided invaluable help and encouragement, for which I am eternally grateful. Christopher Logan gently nudged the book along with his regular requests for updates and, after graduating from Williams College, assisted me with some late-stage research from his perch in Boston, along with some early editing. Andrew Logan performed some essential research for me at the beautiful Knight Library at the University of Oregon. Caroline Logan located an important newspaper article about Tom Lincoln in the collection of the Hawthorne-Longfellow Library at Bowdoin College. Pierce Freeman was my in-house computer expert, handling all my computer-related issues, fine-tuning some of the illustrations despite a heavy course load at Stanford, and making sure my laptop computer was backed up to an external hard drive.

Finally, and most importantly, I wish to thank my wife, Deborah Freeman, who has inspired me in all things and served as my sounding board, muse, and dearest friend. She saw the makings of a book in this tale before I did and displayed a remarkable patience and understanding over the many years it took me to bring it to life. To her and to my beloved children, this book is warmly dedicated.

ILLUSTRATION CREDITS

I. Photo of Mill Grove, by the author

II. Portrait of Alexander Wilson, by Rembrandt Peale
    Oil on wood, 24¼ × 22″, 1809–1813
    Gift of Dr. Nathaniel Chapman, 1822
    Courtesy American Philosophical Society

III. Portrait of George Ord, by Henry T. Smith
    Oil on canvas, 41 × 36¼″, 1894
    Gift of the members, 1894
    Courtesy American Philosophical Society

IV. Portrait of Hannah Mary Rathbone I
    Watercolor
    Courtesy The University of Liverpool Library
    (RP XXV.8.30)

V. Portrait of Charles Waterton, by Charles Willson Peale
    Oil on canvas, 24⅛ × 20¼″, 1824
    Courtesy National Portrait Gallery, London

VI. Portrait of Rev. John Bachman, by John W. Audubon
    Oil on canvas, 30 × 25″, 1837
    Courtesy The Charleston Museum

VII. View of the City of Boston from Dorchester Heights, by Robert Havell Jr.
    Aquatint engraving, 15⅛ × 20¾″, 1841
    Courtesy Library of Congress (LC-DIG-pga-03789)

VIII. Portrait of George C. Shattuck Sr., M.D., by Gilbert Stuart
    Oil on canvas, 29⅝ × 24½″, 1827
    Private collection

IX. Eastport from Passamaquoddy Bay, by Victor de Grailly
    Oil on canvas, 17¼ × 23½″
    Courtesy Tides Institute & Museum of Art, Eastport, ME

X. Portrait of John James Audubon, by Nicola Marschall, after Henry Inman
    Courtesy John James Audubon Museum, Henderson, KY

XI. Golden Eagle (*Aquila chrysaetos*), by John J. Audubon
    Watercolor, pastel, graphite, and selective glazing, 38 × 25½″, Feb.-Mar. 1833
    Courtesy New-York Historical Society (1863.17.181)
    Digital image by Oppenheimer Editions

XII. Black Guillemot (*Cepphus grylle*), by John J. Audubon
    Watercolor, graphite, black ink, and pastel with touches of gouache and glazing, with mat, 23 × 29″, 1833
    Courtesy New-York Historical Society (1863.17.219)
    Digital image by Oppenheimer Editions

XIII. Harlequin Duck (*Histrionicus histrionicus*), by John J. Audubon
    Watercolor, collage, graphite on paper, with mat, 31 × 41″, May 1833
    Courtesy New-York Historical Society (1863.17.297)
    Digital image by Oppenheimer Editions

XIV. Red-necked Phalarope (*Phalaropus lobatus*), by John J. Audubon and John W. Audubon
    Watercolor, graphite, pastel, gouache, and black ink with selective glazing on paper, with mat, 23 × 29″, May-Jun. 1833
    Courtesy New-York Historical Society (1863.17.215)
    Digital image by Oppenheimer Editions

XV. Winter Wren (*Troglodytes hiemalis*) and Rock Wren (*Salpinctes obsoletus*), by John J. Audubon
    Watercolor, gouache, pastel, and graphite on paper, 20¾ × 13¹⁵⁄₁₆″, 2-3 Jun. 1833, 1836
    Courtesy New-York Historical Society (1863.17.360)
    Digital image by Oppenheimer Editions

XVI. Arctic Tern (*Sterna paradisaea*), by John J. Audubon
    Watercolor, collage, graphite, gouache, pastel, black chalk, and black ink on paper, laid on card, with mat, 29 × 23″, 25 Jun. 1833
    Courtesy New-York Historical Society (1863.17.250)
    Digital image by Oppenheimer Editions

XVII. Piping Plover (*Chradrius melodus*), by John J. Audubon
    Watercolor and graphite on paper, with mat, 23 × 29″, Jun. 1833
    Courtesy New-York Historical Society (1863.17.220)
    Digital image by Oppenheimer Editions

XVIII. Northern Gannet (*Morus bassanus*), by John J. Audubon
    Watercolor, graphite, pastel, black chalk, black ink, collage, and gouache with scratching out and scraping on paper, laid on card, 24¾ × 37⅝″, Jun. 1833
    Courtesy New-York Historical Society (1863.17.326)
    Digital image by Oppenheimer Editions

XIX. Greater Shearwater (*Puffinus gravis*), by John J. Audubon
    Watercolor and graphite on paper, with mat, 23 × 29″, 1833
    Courtesy New-York Historical Society (1863.17.283)
    Digital image by Oppenheimer Editions

XX. Common Murre (*Uria aalge*), by John J. Audubon
    Watercolor, graphite, black ink, and pastel with scraping and touches of glazing on paper, with mat, 23 × 29″, 20 Jun. 1833
    Courtesy New-York Historical Society (1863.17.218)
    Digital image by Oppenheimer Editions

XXI. Razorbill (*Alca torda*), by John J. Audubon

Watercolor and graphite on paper, with mat,
23 × 29″, Jun. 1833
Courtesy New-York Historical Society (1863.17.214)
Digital image by Oppenheimer Editions

XXII. Surf Scoter (*Melanitta perspicillata*), by John J.
Audubon
Watercolor, graphite, pastel, black chalk, and black
ink with touches of gouache on paper, with mat,
31 × 41″, 1833
Courtesy New-York Historical Society (1863.17.317)
Digital image by Oppenheimer Editions

XXIII. Lincoln's Sparrow (*Melospiza lincolnii*), by
John J. Audubon
Watercolor and graphite on paper, with mat,
23 × 29″, Jun.-Jul. 1833
Courtesy New-York Historical Society (1863.17.193)
Digital image by Oppenheimer Editions

XXIV. Ruby-crowned Kinglet (*Regulus calendula*), by
John J. Audubon
Watercolor, collage, and graphite on paper, with
mat, 23 × 29″, Summer 1833
Courtesy New-York Historical Society (1863.17.195)
Digital image by Oppenheimer Editions

XXV. White-winged Crossbill (*Loxia leucoptera*), by John
J. Audubon
Watercolor and graphite on paper, with mat,
23 × 29″, Summer 1833
Courtesy New-York Historical Society (1863.17.364)
Digital image by Oppenheimer Editions

XXVI. Double-crested Cormorant (*Phalacrocorax
auritus*), by John J. Audubon
Watercolor and graphite on paper, with mat,
40 × 30″, Jun. 1833
Courtesy New-York Historical Society (1863.17.257)
Digital image by Oppenheimer Editions

XXVII. Atlantic Puffin (*Fratercula arctica*), by John J.
Audubon
Watercolor, gouache, and graphite on paper, with
mat, 22 × 28″, Jul. 1833
Courtesy New-York Historical Society (1863.17.213)
Digital image by Oppenheimer Editions

XXVIII. Red-throated Loon (*Gavia stellata*), by John J.
Audubon
Watercolor, pastel, graphite, gouache, white lead
pigment, and black ink with scratching out and
touches of glazing on paper, with mat, 30 × 40″,
Jul. 1833
Courtesy New-York Historical Society (1863.17.202)
Digital image by Oppenheimer Editions

XXIX. Willow Ptarmigan (*Lagopus lagopus*), by John J.
Audubon
Watercolor and graphite on paper, with mat,
39 × 53″, Jul. 1833
Courtesy New-York Historical Society (1863.17.191)
Digital image by Oppenheimer Editions

XXX. Common Loon (*Gavia immer*), by John James
Audubon

Watercolor, graphite, pastel, black chalk, black
ink, and gouache with scratching out and selective
glazing on paper, 25⁷⁄₁₆ × 37⅛″, 1833
Courtesy New-York Historical Society (1863.17.306)
Digital image by Oppenheimer Editions

XXXI. Great Cormorant (*Phalacrocorax carbo*), by
John J. Audubon
Watercolor, gouache, and graphite on paper, with
mat, 38 × 52″, Jul 1833, Mar. 1834
Courtesy New-York Historical Society (1863.17.297)
Digital image by Oppenheimer Editions

XXXII. Drawing of Bird Eggs, by John J. Audubon
Watercolor on paper, Jun-Jul. 1833
Courtesy Collections of the Louisiana State Museum
(T0600.1967.82)

XXXIII. Boreal Chickadee (*Parus hudsonicus*), by
John J. Audubon
Watercolor, graphite, pastel, black ink, and black
chalk with touches of gouache on paper, with mat,
23 × 29″, Jul. 19–20, 1833
Courtesy New-York Historical Society (1863.17.194)
Digital image by Oppenheimer Editions

XXXIV. Bald Eagle (Bird of Washington) (*Haliaeetus
leucocephalus*), by John J. Audubon
Watercolor, collage, black ink, graphite, pastel, and
white lead pigment with selective glazing on paper,
38⁵⁄₁₆ × 23⅝″, 1822
Courtesy New-York Historical Society (1863.17.011)
Digital image by Oppenheimer Editions

XXXV. Common Redpoll (*Carduelis flammea*), by
John J. Audubon
Watercolor, graphite, and pastel with touches of
gouache and black ink on paper, with mat, 29 × 23″,
Jul. 1833
Courtesy New-York Historical Society (1863.17.375)
Digital image by Oppenheimer Editions

XXXVI. Horned Lark (*Eromephila alpestris*), by John J.
Audubon
Watercolor and graphite on paper, with mat,
22 × 28″, 1833
Courtesy New-York Historical Society (1863.17.200)
Digital image by Oppenheimer Editions

XXXVII. Pomarine Jaeger (*Stercorarius pomarinus*), by
John J. Audubon
Watercolor, graphite, pastel, black chalk, black ink,
and gouache with touches of glazing on paper, with
mat, 23 × 29″, Aug. 1833
Courtesy New-York Historical Society (1863.17.253)
Digital image by Oppenheimer Editions

XXXVIII. Eskimo Curlew (*Numenius borealis*), by John J.
Audubon
Watercolor, graphite, pastel, gouache, and black ink
with scratching out and selective glazing on paper,
with mat, 23 × 29″, Aug. 1833
Courtesy New-York Historical Society (1863.17.208)
Digital image by Oppenheimer Editions

XXXIX. Gyrfalcon (*Falco rusticolus*), by John J. Audubon

Watercolor, graphite, pastel, and black ink with
touches of gouache and selective glazing on paper,
with mat, 39 × 53″, Aug. 1833
Courtesy New-York Historical Society (1863.17.196)
Digital image by Oppenheimer Editions

XL. Pine Grosbeak (*Pinicola enucleator*), by John J.
Audubon and John W. Audubon
Watercolor and graphite on paper, 20¹⁄₁₆ × 14⁷⁄₁₆″,
1833–34
Courtesy New-York Historical Society (1863.17.358)
Digital image by Oppenheimer Editions

XLI. Short-legged Pewit (*Tyrannula richardsonii*), by
William Swainson
Plate 46 to *Fauna Boreali-Americana*, Vol. II
Western Wood-Peewee (*Contopus sordidulus*), by
John J. Audubon (detail)
Aquatint engraving by Robert Havell Jr., Plate No.
434, 1838
Courtesy National Audubon Society

XLII. Portrait of Jonathan D. Weston
Private collection

XLIII. Portrait of Capt. Joseph H. Claridge
Private collection

XLIV. Portrait of Capt. Henry Wolsey Bayfield
c. 1840
Courtesy Public Archives and Records Office of
Prince Edward Island (Acc4156/1)

XLV. Portrait of Rev. Dr. Thomas McCulloch Sr. (first
President of Dalhousie University, 1838–1843),
by Daniel Munro
Pastel on paper
Gift of Isabell McCulloch, 1939
Collection of Dalhousie University

XLVI. Portrait of John James Audubon, by George P. A.
Healy
Oil on canvas, 50¾ × 40½″, 1838
Courtesy Museum of Science, Boston

XLVII. Residence of J. J. Audubon, Esq., by William
Rickarby Miller
1857
Courtesy Museum of the City of New York
(34.100.41)

XLVIII. Self-portrait, by Isaac Sprague
Courtesy Wellesley Historical Society, Wellesley,
MA

XLIX. View of Fort Union, Upper Missouri, by Isaac
Sprague
Watercolor, black ink, graphite, and touches of
gouache with scratching out on paper, 11⅛ × 15¼″,
Jul. 1843
© Collection of the New-York Historical Society,
USA/Bridgeman

L. Portrait of John J. Audubon, by John W. Audubon
Oil on canvas, 35 × 27½″, 1843
Courtesy American Museum of Natural History
(1498)

LI. Portrait of George C. Shattuck Jr., by E. T. Billings

1889
Courtesy Center for the History of Medicine,
Francis A. Countway Library of Medicine, Harvard
University

1. Portrait of Nicholas Augustus Berthoud, by John J.
Audubon
Black chalk on paper, 10 × 8″, c. 1819
Museum Purchase, 1935.35.3
Collection of the Speed Art Museum, Louisville, KY

2. Portrait of Thomas W. Bakewell, by John J. Audubon
Graphite on paper, 1820
Courtesy of Mill Grove, County of Montgomery,
Audubon, PA

3. Portrait of Richard Harlan, M.D., by Michele Pekenino,
after a painting by Jacob Eichholtz
Stipple engraving, 2¾ × 2⁹⁄₁₆″, c. 1821–1822
Courtesy U.S. National Library of Medicine

4. Portrait of William Rathbone V
From E.F. Rathbone, *William Rathbone: A Memoir*,
1905

5. Portrait of Richard Rathbone, from a miniature by
Hargreaves
From E. Greg, *Reynolds-Rathbone Diaries & Letters*,
1905

6. Drawing of Greenbank, by Hannah Mary Rathbone
1816
From E. Greg, *Reynolds-Rathbone Diaries & Letters*,
1905

7. Portrait of Henry F. Chorley, by Alfred, Count D'Orsay
Pencil and chalk, 6⅜ × 4¾″, 1841
Purchased, 1957
Courtesy National Portrait Gallery, London
(NPG 4026(13))

8. Self-portrait, by John J. Audubon
Pencil on paper, 14 × 11 cm., 1826
© University of Liverpool Art Gallery &
Collections, UK/Bridgeman Images

9. Self-portrait, by William Home Lizars
Chalk on paper, 43 × 35.70 cm.
Gift of R. K. Sanderson, 1970
Courtesy Scottish National Portrait Gallery
(PG 2175)

10. Portrait of Robert Havell Jr., by Amelia Jane Havell
Watercolor, 5¾ × 4⅛″, 1845
From *The Print-Collectors Quarterly*, 1917

11. Portrait of Lucy Audubon, from a miniature by
Frederick Cruickshank
c. 1831
From M. R. Audubon, *Audubon and His Journals*,
1897

12. Portrait of Victor G. Audubon, from a miniature by
Frederick Cruickshank
1836
From M. R. Audubon, *Audubon and His Journals*,
1897

13. Portrait of John W. Audubon, from a miniature by
Frederick Cruickshank

1836
From M. R. Audubon, *Audubon and His Journals*,
1897

14. Portrait of Prof. Parker Cleaveland, Bowdoin College
Engraving from N. Cleaveland & A. S. Packard,
History of Bowdoin College, 1882

15. Photograph of Water Street, Eastport, Maine
c. 1870s
Courtesy Tides Institute & Museum of Art,
Eastport, ME

16. Photograph of James Curtiss (detail of Photographs
of former Chicago mayors John P. Chapin, James
Curtiss, and James H. Woodworth)
Glass negative
Courtesy Chicago History Museum (DN-0063413)

17. Photograph of Judge Theodore Lincoln
Courtesy Dennys River Historical Society

18. Photograph of Tom Lincoln
Courtesy Dennys River Historical Society

19. Photograph of Lincoln House, Dennysville, Maine
From early 20th century postcard
Private collection

20. Photograph of George C. Shattuck Jr., M.D.
1846
Courtesy Center for the History of Medicine,
Francis A. Countway Library of Medicine, Harvard
University

21. Photograph of Isaac Ray, M.D.
Between 1865 and 1880
Courtesy Library of Congress (LC-DIG-cwpbh-
05189

22. Portrait of George S. Greene
1836
From G. S. Greene, *The Greenes of Rhode Island:
With Historical Records of English Ancestry, 1534–
1902*, 1903

23. Photograph of Union Gen. Napoleon B. Buford
c. 1862–1865
Courtesy National Archives and Records
Administration

24. Photograph of Union Surgeon William Ingalls, M.D.
c. 1862–1865
Private collection

25. Photograph of Joseph A. Coolidge
From C. W. Townsend, *In Audubon's Labrador*,
1918

26. Portrait of Capt. William Willcomb
1835
From O. C. Willcomb, *Genealogy of the Willcomb
Family of New England (1665–1902)*, 1902

27. Portrait of the *Wizard*
1833
From O. C. Willcomb, *Genealogy of the Willcomb
Family of New England (1665–1902)*, 1902

28. Photograph of Edward Harris
Courtesy Alabama Department of Archives and
History, Montgomery, AL

29. Portrait of John James Audubon, by Isaac Sprague
1843
From M. R. Audubon, *Audubon and His Journals*,
1897

30. Photograph of Victor G. Audubon
1853
From M. R. Audubon, *Audubon and His Journals*,
1897

31. Photograph of John W. Audubon
1853
From M. R. Audubon, *Audubon and His Journals*,
1897

32. Photograph of Lucy Bakewell Audubon
1854
From M. R. Audubon, *Audubon and His Journals*,
1897

33. Photograph of Thomas Lincoln
Courtesy Dennys River Historical Society

34. Photograph of William Ingalls at Boston City Hospital
(detail of Photograph of Visiting Surgeons)
1882
Courtesy Center for the History of Medicine,
Francis A. Countway Library of Medicine, Harvard
University (00159.089)

INDEX

This book is set in Monotype Bulmer

by Tseng Information Systems in Durham, North Carolina.

The original design for Bulmer was made by William Martin in 1792.

It is named for the printer William Bulmer at The Shakespeare Press,

for whom Martin supplied the font.

The modern design of Bulmer was created for the Nonesuch Press in the 1930s.

The book was manufactured by Thomson-Shore in Dexter, Michigan.

Book and jacket design by Richard Hendel, Chapel Hill, North Carolina.

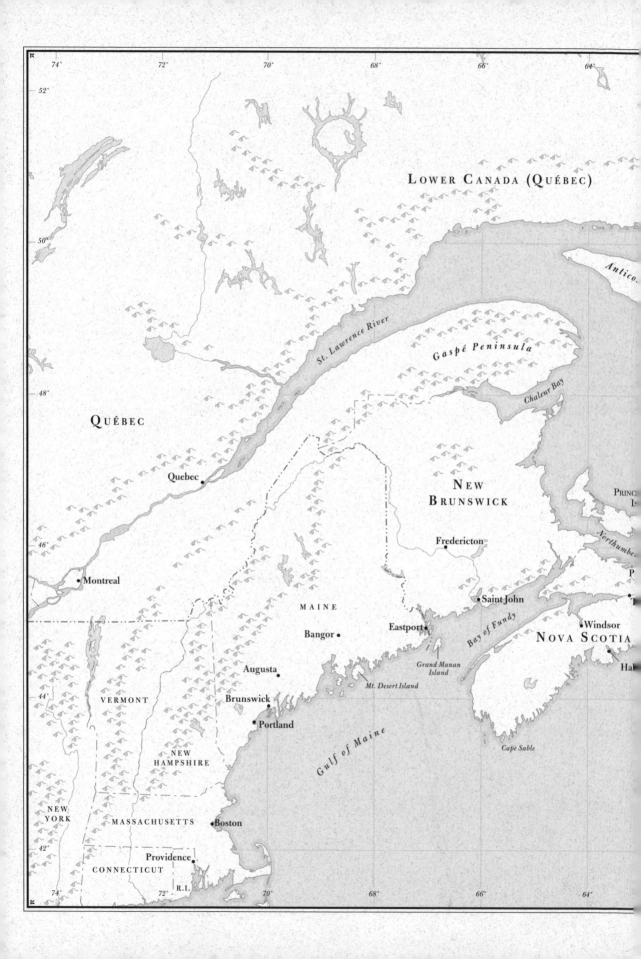